AN INTRODUCTION TO LITERATURE

AN INTRODUCTION TO
LITERATURE

Fiction | Poetry | Drama

Eighth Edition

Edited by

Sylvan Barnet, *Tufts University*

Morton Berman, *Boston University*

William Burto, *University of Lowell*

LITTLE, BROWN AND COMPANY
Boston   Toronto

Library of Congress Cataloging in Publication Data
Main entry under title:

An Introduction to literature.

      Includes index.
      1. Literature — Collections. I. Barnet, Sylvan.
II. Berman, Morton. III. Burto, William.
PN6014.I57 1984   808'.8   84-21780
ISBN 0-316-08227-9

Library of Congress Catalog Card No. 84-21780

ISBN 0-316-08227-9

9 8 7 6 5 4

MV

Published simultaneously in Canada
by Little, Brown & Company (Canada) Limited

Printed in the United States of America

Acknowledgments

Brace Jovanovich, Inc.; copyright © 1963, 1964 by T. S. Eliot. Reprinted by permission of the publisher and Faber & Faber, Ltd.

William Faulkner. "The Bear." Copyright 1942 and renewed 1970 by Estelle Faulkner and Jill Faulkner Summers. An expanded version of this story appears in *Go Down, Moses* by William Faulkner. "A Rose for Emily." Copyright 1930 and renewed 1958 by William Faulkner. Reprinted from *Collected Stories of William Faulkner.* "Barn Burning." Copyright 1939 and renewed 1967 by Estelle Faulkner and Jill Faulkner Summers. Reprinted from *Collected Stories of William Faulkner.* Reprinted by permission of Random House, Inc.

Letter written by William Faulkner in *The New York Times,* December 26, 1954. Copyright © 1954 by The New York Times Company. Reprinted by permission.

Lawrence Ferlinghetti. "Constantly risking absurdity and death," from *A Coney Island of the Mind* by Lawrence Ferlinghetti. Copyright © 1958 by Lawrence Ferlinghetti. Reprinted by permission of New Directions.

Robert Francis. "The Pitcher," from *The Orb Weaver.* Copyright © 1960 by Robert Francis. Reprinted by permission of Wesleyan University Press.

Robert Frost. "Stopping by Woods on a Snowy Evening," "Mending Wall," "The Pasture," "Design," "Acquainted with the Night," and "The Road Not Taken," from *The Poetry of Robert Frost* edited by Edward Connery Lathem. Copyright 1916, 1923, 1928, 1930, 1939, © 1967, 1969 by Holt, Rinehart and Winston. Copyright © 1964, 1967 by Lesley Frost Ballantine. Reprinted by permissioin of Holt, Rinehart and Winston.

Allen Ginsberg. "A Supermarket in California" from *Howl and Other Poems* by Allen Ginsberg. Copyright © 1956, 1959 by Allen Ginsberg. Reprinted by permission of City Lights Books.

Nikki Giovanni. "Master Charge Blues" from *Re:Creation* by Nikki Giovanni. Copyright © 1970 by Nikki Giovanni; Broadside/Crummell Press, Detroit, Michigan. Reprinted by permission of the publisher.

Susan Glaspell. "Trifles" from *Plays* by Susan Glaspell. Copyright 1920 by Dodd, Mead & Company. Copyright renewed 1948 by Susan Glaspell. Reprinted by permission of Dodd, Mead & Company.

Robert Hayden. "Those Winter Sundays" from *Angle of Ascent, New and Selected Poems,* by Robert Hayden. Copyright © 1975, 1972, 1970, 1966 by Robert Hayden. Reprinted by permission of Liveright Publishing Corporation.

Seamus Heaney. "The Skunk" from *Field Work* by Seamus Heaney. Copyright © 1976, 1979 by Seamus Heaney. Reprinted by permission of Farrar, Straus and Giroux, Inc. and Faber & Faber Ltd.

Anthony Hecht. "The Dover Bitch" from *The Hard Hours* by Anthony Hecht. Copyright © 1960 by Anthony Hecht. Appeared originally in *Transatlantic Review.* Reprinted by permission of Atheneum Publishers.

Ernest Hemingway. "The Short Happy Life of Francis Macomber," from *The Short Stories of Ernest Hemingway.* Reprinted by permission of Charles Scribner's Sons.

Gerard Manley Hopkins. "Spring and Fall: To a Young Child," "God's Grandeur," "Pied Beauty," and "The Windhover" from *The Poems of Gerard Manley Hopkins,* 4th Edition, edited by W. H. Gardner and N. H. Mackenzie, published by arrangement with the Society of Jesus.

A. E. Housman. "Eight O'Clock" and "Shropshire Lad #27: To An Athlete Dying Young" from *Collected Poems.* Reprinted by permission of the Society of Authors as the literary representative of the Estate of A. E. Housman, and Jonathan Cape Ltd., publishers. "Is My Team Ploughing" and "Terence, This Is Stupid Stuff," from "A Shropshire Lad" — Authorised Edition — from *The Collected Poems of A. E. Housman.* Copyright 1939, 1940, © 1965 by Holt, Rinehart

Dylan Thomas. "Do not go gentle into that good night" and "Fern Hill" from *Collected Poems.* Copyright 1946 by New Directions Publishing Corporation: 1952 by Dylan Thomas. Reprinted by permission of New Directions and David Higham Associates Limited.

James Thurber. "The Secret Life of Walter Mitty," from *My World — And Welcome to It,* published by Harcourt Brace Jovanovich, Inc. Copyright © 1942 by James Thurber. Copyright 1970 by Helen Thurber. Originally appeared in *The New Yorker.* Reprinted by permission of Mrs. James Thurber.

John Updike. "A & P." Copyright © 1962 by John Updike. Reprinted from *Pigeon Feathers and Other Stories,* by John Updike. Originally appeared in *The New Yorker.* "Youth's Progress" from *The Carpentered Hen and Other Tame Creatures* by John Updike. Copyright © 1955 by John Updike. Reprinted by permission of Alfred A. Knopf, Inc.

Alice Walker. "Everyday Use" from *In Love & Trouble* by Alice Walker. Copyright © 1973 by Alice Walker. Reprinted by permission of Harcourt Brace Jovanovich, Inc.

Eudora Welty. "Livvie" from *The Wide Net and Other Stories* by Eudora Welty. Copyright 1942, 1970 by Eudora Welty. Reprinted by permission of Harcourt Brace Jovanovich, Inc.

Richard Wilbur. "Love Calls Us to the Things of This World" from *Things of This World* by Richard Wilbur. Copyright © 1956 by Richard Wilbur. Reprinted by permission of Harcourt Brace Jovanovich, Inc.

Tennessee Williams. "The Glass Menagerie" by Tennessee Williams. Copyright 1945 by Tennessee Williams and Edwina D. Williams and renewed 1973 by Tennessee Williams. Reprinted by permission of Random House, Inc.

William Carlos Williams. "The Use of Force," from *The Farmer's Daughters* by William Carlos Williams. Copyright 1938 by William Carlos Williams. Reprinted by permission of New Directions Publishing Corporation.

William Carlos Williams. "The Red Wheelbarrow," "Spring and All," from *Collected Earlier Poems* by William Carlos Williams. Copyright 1938 by New Directions Publishing Corporation. "The Dance" and "A Sort of Song" from *Collected Later Poems.* Copyright 1944 by William Carlos Williams. Reprinted by permission of New Directions.

William Butler Yeats. "For Anne Gregory." Copyright 1933 by Macmillan Publishing Co., Inc., renewed 1961 by Bertha Georgie Yeats. "An Irish Airman Foresees His Death," and "Memory." Copyright 1919 by Macmillan Publishing Co., Inc., renewed 1947 by Bertha Georgie Yeats. "The Second Coming." Copyright 1924 by Macmillan Publishing Co., Inc., renewed 1952 by Bertha Georgie Yeats. "Leda and the Swan" and "Sailing to Byzantium." Copyright 1928 by Macmillan Publishing Co., Inc., renewed 1956 by Georgie Yeats. All poems from *Collected Poems* by William Butler Yeats. Reprinted by permission of Macmillan Publishing Company and A. P. Watt Ltd.

Preface

"A big book," said Callimachus, "is a big misfortune." He might have added that a big book is heavy. Aware that many instructors have found needlessly bulky most of the textbooks designed for introductory courses in literature, the editors and publisher of *An Introduction to Literature* have produced a book that is smaller than most books intended for such courses. They have kept in mind Dr. Johnson's maxim: "Books that you may . . . hold readily in your hand are the most useful after all."

The relative brevity of this volume has been achieved partly by assuming that much of what is included here will please the instructor and therefore need not be reinforced by numerous alternative selections, and partly by refusing to allow the editorial apparatus to usurp the province of the classroom. Both of these points deserve further comment.

We have offered much material that can be called "classical," both to keep the bulk down and because we believe that students ought for the most part to read first-rate material. There is something wrong with a book that includes a dozen stories of the last year or two and nothing by Hawthorne. We include some very recent work, and about half of the selections are from the twentieth century, but we have tried not to neglect such classic writers as Shakespeare, Dickinson, Hawthorne, and Whitman. Classic works, of course, are not the same things as chestnuts. The former, Maurice Beebe has explained, "are in a sense the freshest of stories simply because they obviously may be seen in many different lights and even yet have not given up all their secrets. The chestnuts are those stories that — like 'Haircut,' 'The Necklace,' and 'The Furnished Room' — give up all their secrets on an initial reading and hence require as little classroom discussion as they have evoked published criticism. I see no objection to a text made up primarily of classics."

The editorial material is brief and yet fairly complete. The paradox is easily explained: this book does not try to do what only the teacher can do. The proper place for a detailed discussion of the multiple meanings in a word or line is, we believe, the classroom. Textbook analyses that for pages drag the student through a short poem or story rarely accomplish much. The object of an anthology of literature is to allow students to read and to think and perhaps to write down their responses, but it is doubtful if a long exegesis stimulates a student. We have tried in our editorial apparatus to give succinct definitions of the terms commonly used in talking about literature, and to *begin* (but by no means to finish) a critical reading of literature. About half of the selections in the book are briefly discussed or have questions appended; the other half are unsullied. We have kept in mind Frost's remark: "You don't chew a poem — macerate a poem — for an evening's pleasure, for a Roman holiday. You touch it. You are aware that a good deal of it is missed."

USING THE BOOK

Probably most instructors teach fiction, then poetry, and then drama — the order followed here. But the three sections can be taught in any sequence, because each is relatively independent: for example, symbolism is discussed in each of the three sections, and although the three discussions have a cumulative effect, any of the three can be used first. This flexibility runs throughout the book; we hope that instructors will not feel that the first chapter must be taught first. Indeed, the first chapter — a survey of some theories of literature — can be used effectively midway or even at the end. There is a similar flexibility within the three chief sections of the book: one can teach everything straight through a section, or skip one's way through a section, or bring in wherever one wishes the stories and poems that conclude the sections.

Although comparatively brief, *An Introduction to Literature* contains ample material for a one-semester course; supplemented by a few paperback books, it can provide a core volume for a full-year course. We have not tried to predict what paperback novels might be added, but we have included "Observations on the Novel," an attempt to distinguish the novel from other prose fiction. We have tried to make our apparatus sufficiently broad so that it can serve as an aid to whatever additional books are read. The introduction to tragedy is not an introduction to *Antigone* or to *Hamlet* but an introduction to *tragedy;* because it examines definitions of tragedy by a Jacobean dramatist, a Soviet critic, and an American dramatist, and discusses such terms as *hamartia, hybris,* and *catharsis,* it will be helpful in thinking about all tragedies, from

Greek to contemporary American. We have also included "Some Observations on Film," in which we discuss the relation of film to literature.

An appendix, "Writing about Literature," is drawn from Sylvan Barnet's *A Short Guide to Writing about Literature,* Fifth Edition (1985). It includes not only information about manuscript form, a sample explication, and two sample analyses, but also detailed suggestions that may help students to choose a topic and get their responses down on paper.

If this new edition has been strengthened and enhanced, it is primarily because of the encouraging comments from users of the earlier editions. Among the new selections are stories by Frank O'Connor, D. H. Lawrence, Tillie Olsen, Alice Adams, and Ursula K. LeGuin, and poems by Lawrence, W. B. Yeats, A. E. Housman, Elizabeth Bishop, and Adrienne Rich. The drama section in particular has been enlarged and now includes two short plays (John Millington Synge's *Riders to the Sea* and Susan Glaspell's *Trifles*) as well as eight full-length plays: *Oedipus Rex, Antigonê, Hamlet, A Doll's House, The Importance of Being Earnest, The Glass Menagerie, Death of a Salesman,* and Marsha Norman's recent Pulitzer Prize play, *'night, Mother.*

Finally, after this elaborate explanation of what has been done, we wish to thank people who helped us do it: Jane Aaron, Linda Bamber, David Cavitch, Charles Christensen, Robert Cyr, Doris Holmes Eyges, Joan Feinberg, Arthur Friedman, David Giele, Nancy Grayson, Margaret Guindon, X. J. Kennedy, Martha Lappen, Judy Maas, Bernard McCabe, Patricia Meier, Ronald E. Pepin, Carolyn Potts, Virginia Pye, William Roberts, Clair Seng-Niemoeller, Virginia Shine, Warren R. Stone, Marcia Stubbs, Jeff Titon, Helen Vendler, Charles L. Walker, and Ann Chalmers Watts.

Our thanks also to the following users of the earlier editions who gave us advice on how and where to make improvements: Joseph D. Adams, Ginger Allsopp, Bruce Anawalt, Elizabeth Andersen, David Anderson, Donald F. Andrews, Abraham Avni, Pam Baker, Rance Baker, William Barker, Tom Barthel, Ben Bennani, Linda Ben-Zvi, Norman J. Betz, Anthony J. Bialas, Robert F. Birt, Michael Boardman, J. M. Braffett, Jack Branscomb, Harry Brent, Michael C. Broome, Jon C. Burton, David Carroll, Edward H. Cohen, Mary Louise Collier, Daniel P. Deneau, Emanuel DiPasquale, Sallie R. Duhling, Russell T. Fowler, David O. Frantz, Ann Garbett, Norma Gaskey, Barbara Gitenstein, Alan J. Glossner, Anne Greco, C. M. Grieco, R. P. Griffin, Kathryn Harris, Styron Harris, John Henderson, David E. Hoffman, B. Jean Holleman,

Elizabeth House, Margaret Hoyle, H. H. Hughey, Edward Ifkovic, Muriel B. Ingham, Kathryn Jenson, Mark A. Johnson, Robert C. Jones, Steven Knight, Joy Labishak, Patricia Lawhon, Bruce Leggat, Nancy Lippert, M. Doring Loomis, Brent MacLeod, Kathleen McCoy, Paul Marx, Richard Maxwell, Marilyn Miller, Frank Moon, Jean S. Moore, Nan Morrison, Don Nemanich, James Obertino, Ruth Olmsted, Lawrence Parker, Frank M. Patterson, William Pell, Otto Lewis Pfeiff, Roy E. Pipher, Elmer Pry, Bernard Rechtschaffen, John R. Reuter, Nancy Rich, Chester F. Riegle, Anna T. Robinson, Glenn Ruihley, Donald H. Sanborn, Robert G. Schwartz, Jr., George J. Searles, Ruth E. Shore, David L. Smith, Nancy Sommers, David Stout, Tom Sullivan, Gordon P. Symonds, Larry G. Thompson, Celia Urion, Isaac Walker, James Watt, Dennis L. Williams, John Wills, Linda Wyman, Alfred Youn, Kenneth J. Zahorski, Joseph Zaitchik, and James E. Zemek.

S. B.

M. B.

W. B.

Contents

5. Style   64

A Note on Tone.

Eudora Welty, Livvie   67

6. A Collection of Short Fiction   81

7. Observations on the Novel   425

Poetry

Drama

AN INTRODUCTION TO LITERATURE

1
Some Theories of Literature

WHAT IS LITERATURE?

Literature is sometimes defined as anything written, but this definition is both too broad and too narrow. Although it is true that anyone can ask the Department of Agriculture for "literature" about canning artichokes, surely we can distinguish between literature in the sense of any writing and literature in the sense of verbal works of art. On the other hand, to say that literature must be written or printed is too narrow, because it excludes such oral literature as ballads that are sung and stories that are recited.

We can begin by saying that literature is (to quote Robert Frost) a "performance in words." It has in it an element of entertaining display, and surely we expect literature to afford pleasure. That literature is an adult game, a sort of make-believe, is suggested in some of the words we apply to pieces of literature — "fiction," "story," "tale," "play."

Now, what makes literature pleasant? Without attempting a complete answer, perhaps we can say that a literary work seizes our interest and more or less — at least for a moment — makes the rest of the world fade or vanish. If the writer has done the job well, our attention is focused on the work, and we are at least partially detached from our usual surroundings. Consider, as an analogy, our reaction when we suddenly get a whiff of new-mown hay. We are walking along a road, either fretting about a dozen things or engaged in a pleasant vague reverie, when suddenly we smell the hay. At once we are caught up, keenly interested in this experience, intensely aware of this one thing, a thing that seems complete and satisfying in itself. For the moment we forget about the time of day, the dust of the road, the heat of the sun, and we find in this thing which is complete, whole, independent, something that catches us up and delights us. A work of art has this power to catch us up momentarily, and to delight us.

But it may well be objected that *Hamlet* is surely more than a load of hay. Art, it is commonly said, offers truth as well as pleasure. Such a view is at least superficially plausible, but when we begin to think about it, we encounter problems. What "truth" is there in *Hamlet*? The characters in the play are fictional, so we cannot say that Shakespeare is giving us a true picture of Danish history. There is a ghost in the play, but many people today have serious doubts about the existence of ghosts. Perhaps we will seize on certain lines, such as "Neither a borrower nor a lender be," but even this much-quoted line can hardly be defended as an unquestioned truth: there are surely times when it is good to borrow or to lend. Let us leave *Hamlet* (though not with the implication that the concept of truth is irrelevant to it) and glance at an amusing short poem, "Tender-handed touch a nettle," written more than two hundred years ago by Aaron Hill. (A nettle is, in the words of a dictionary, a plant whose leaves are covered with "hairs that secrete a stinging fluid that affects the skin on contact.")

> Tender-handed touch a nettle,
>   And it stings you for your pains,
> Grasp it like a man of mettle,
>   And it soft as silk remains.
> So it is with human natures,
>   Treat them gently, they rebel,
> But be as rough as nutmeg graters,
>   And the rogues obey you well.

It is true that if "tender-handed" you touch a nettle it will sting, and that if you seize it firmly you will not feel the sting, but is it true that if you treat people roughly they will "obey you well"? Some people, perhaps. But isn't it apparent that whatever value Hill's poem has (and many children have enjoyed it during its two centuries) is not in its botany or in its psychology, but in its engaging impudence, in its *playful* assertion that all people are "rogues" who need to be knocked about. The meter, the rhyme, the pun on mettle/metal, and the comparison to a nutmeg grater hardly allow us to take the piece very seriously. We value it more for the pleasure that it offers than for the truth it claims to offer.

What literature is, and what sort of truth (if any) it offers, are big problems, and they have not yet been solved to general satisfaction. There is a diversity of theories, and nothing is gained by pretending that everyone knows or agrees what literature is or does. But most theories of literature can, without much distortion, be put into one of three pigeonholes — which can be called "imitative," "expressive," and "affective" — and these are what we want to talk about first. Good literature deserves to be talked about as well as read and enjoyed, and such discussion may help sharpen a reader's perceptions.

THE IMITATIVE THEORY

The imitative theory holds that art is an imitation of something. In his *Poetics,* Aristotle (384–322 B.C.) says that a tragedy is an imitation of an action that is serious and complete. Because imitation now has pejorative associations, it is well to think of Aristotle's *mimesis* as not only "imitation" but also "re-creation" or "re-presentation." In an artistic imitation, Aristotle holds, a form is re-created or re-presented in a substance not natural to it. Thus, Michelangelo imitated Moses in stone; van Gogh imitated sunflowers in pigment on canvas; Shakespeare imitated Caesar in an actor's words and gestures. Music, too, Aristotle holds, is imitative; Tchaikovsky imitates Napoleon's defeat in Russia in the "1812 Overture." Aristotle would have approved of Thomas De Quincey's remark that although no one whistled at Waterloo, one might whistle Waterloo. The imitative instinct, of course, is not the artist's private possession. A child says to another, "You be the cop and I'll be the robber and you say 'Halt' and I'll run away." This natural tendency to imitate is combined, Aristotle says, with a tendency toward rhythm or pattern, and the result can be a work of art.

In its simplest form the imitative theory appeals to the naive: "How lifelike that wax apple is!" "How like a Frenchman that actor looks!" But more sophisticated people may ask: "What is so pleasing about a wax apple? There are plenty of real apples for us to look at." Aristotle's theory includes such a close copy of nature as a wax apple, but by coupling imitation with harmony, Aristotle goes further. He says that art is superior to history because although history must stick to the facts, art refines nature, showing, one might say, not what happened but what should have happened in a world free from accident. The artist is a sort of greenhouse keeper, producing not the rose that grows wild, cankered, and stunted, but the rose that has fulfilled all its potential, the rose that is more a rose than any wild rose. The artist, in short, does not imitate servilely; the artist re-creates reality and presents it to us in a fashion in which we see its essence more clearly.

It is only half-true, then, to say that Aristotle's imitator is a maker of an imitation. (This idea of the artist as a maker, by the way, survives dimly in the word "playwright" — "wright" being a maker, as in "shipwright," and having nothing to do with "write.") Because the artist's imitation is more than a copy of what is apparent to every eye, the imitation is in some measure a creation. It is imaginative and interpretive; it reflects a special view of reality.

The imitative theory often includes the notion that art gives us not only pleasure but also knowledge, insight into the nature of reality. If you say that we enjoy wax apples simply because we enjoy seeing exhibitions of man's skill at imitation, you are not introducing the criterion of knowledge. If, however, you say that by looking at the imitation we come to know something about reality, you are saying that art furnishes knowledge, and that its value depends partly on its truth. This problem of truth does not arise in all the arts: no one asks the Taj Mahal to be true. But many people want their literature to be true — to be an illuminating reflection of reality. The danger, of course, is that the reader may turn literature into a message: hunting for detachable tags ("Frailty, thy name is woman," "To thine own self be true"), the reader reduces the whole work to a neat moral and gives A's to those works whose messages seem right. But what does anyone really learn from a work of literature? Do we learn from *Julius Caesar* not to be a tyrant? Or not to assassinate a tyrant? Or the difficulty of assassinating a tyrant and getting away with it? Surely we knew all this before.

Perhaps the answer to the question "Does literature give knowledge?" is that we do not learn from literature how to act in a particular situation (we'll never get the chance to be Roman tyrants), but we do learn something about life in general. After seeing a play, we feel that we have achieved at least a momentary understanding of some of the facts of life. The happenings in the book or on the stage not only resemble things in real life, but also clarify real life, making us say: "Yes, people are like that, but I hadn't noticed it before." James Baldwin has said that in *Julius Caesar* he discovered the tension between idealism and blind passion, or, to put it another way, the guilt that is part of a hero's "desperate singlemindedness." When we read a piece of literature, we may have known intellectually that this or that is so, but what earlier had been a lifeless platitude now becomes a vital part of our being. James Joyce expressed the view that literature imitates life and influences behavior when he complained to a publisher who refused to issue his book of short stories, *Dubliners*:

> It is not my fault that the odor of ashpits and old weeds and offal hangs round my stories. I seriously believe that you will retard the course of civilization in Ireland by preventing the Irish people from having one good look at themselves in my nicely polished looking-glass.

THE EXPRESSIVE THEORY

The second theory, usually called the expressive theory, can be treated more briefly. It holds that the artist is not essentially an imitator but one who expresses his feelings. D. H. Lawrence said, "One sheds one's sicknesses in books, repeats and presents again one's emotions to be master of them." Here is a powerful expression of feeling, thinly disguised as a statement about the ancient Israelites:

> When Israel was in Egypt's land,
>   Let my people go!
> Oppressed so hard they could not stand,
>   Let my people go!
>
> (*Chorus*)
> Go down, Moses,
> 'Way down in Egypt's land;
> Tell old Pharaoh,
> Let my people go!

One understands easily enough what Frederick Douglass, a fugitive slave, meant when he said that songs can relieve an aching heart, and that he often sang to drown his sorrow. Two quotations from William Wordsworth may be useful. "Poetry," he said, "is the spontaneous overflow of powerful feelings"; the poet's job is "to treat of things not as they *are* . . . but as they *seem* to exist to the *senses, and the passions.*" (This is by no means a complete summary of Wordsworth's theories, but it is enough to illustrate the gist of expressive theories.) The artist's vision, the theory holds, is more inward than outward; the work of art is not an imitation of the external world but an expression of the internal world, the embodiment of an emotion. This theory sometimes holds that "truth" has nothing to do with literature. Art expresses an artist's feelings, and his feelings cannot be true or false. They simply exist. Sometimes, however, an expressive theory insists that a work is true if it is sincere. We do not ordinarily say that laughter or tears are true or false, but if we discover that the laughter or tears are hypocritical rather than sincere, we call them false. Since, however, the reader of a piece of literature cannot know if the author was sincere, the criterion of sincerity is valueless. We cannot say that *Julius Caesar* is sincere; perhaps Shakespeare wrote it merely to make money. We cannot even say that his sonnets reflect his true feelings; though Wordsworth said that in them Shakespeare "unlocked his heart," how can we be sure? Furthermore, writing that is indubitably sincere is not necessarily good writing. Aldous Huxley is surely correct in his observation that "a bad book is as much labor to write as a good one; it comes as sincerely from the author's soul."

Moreover, what value does expressive writing have? One can reply it is valuable for the writer: "If I don't write to empty my mind," Byron said, "I go mad." Yeats, at the end of his career, put it less heroically: "I have sometimes wondered if I did not write poetry to find a cure for my own ailment, as constipated cats do when they eat valerian." But if this relief from pressure is its only value, the written piece might just as well be left lying on the writer's desk. Most expressions of emotions, after all, are valueless to everyone but the person expressing them. Our laughter, mumblings, and cries of despair are all very expressive and afford us a relief, but who would call them works of art that are of value to other people?

Advocates of the expressive theory argue that by showing us how he sees and feels something, the writer may pluck the blinders from our eyes and melt the ice around our heart. He may jolt us out of our usual rut, and widen the area of our sensibilities. Wordsworth's view of daffodils may force upon us the awareness that our own views are narrow. An awareness of how other people feel is, after all, a way of expanding and enriching one's own personality.

THE AFFECTIVE THEORY

Finally, there is the affective theory of art, which holds that a work of art ought to arouse a particular emotion, or affect (to use the psychologist's term), in the perceiver. This theory is often closely related to the expressive theory: the artist allegedly expresses his emotion, embodying it in a work of art, and this work evokes in the perceiver a similar or identical emotion. Presumably by describing certain things in a certain way the writer can evoke the proper response. The most famous presentation of this theory is Tolstoi's *What Is Art?*, a sentence of which is here quoted:

> Art is a human activity consisting in this, that one man consciously, by means of certain external signs, hands on to others feelings he has lived through, and that others are infected by these feelings, and also experience them.

In Alexander Pope's words, the artist

> gives my breast a thousand pains,
> Can make me feel each passion that he feigns;
> Enrage, compose, with more than magic art,
> With pity and with terror tear my heart;
> And snatch me o'er the earth or through the air,
> To Thebes, to Athens, when he will, and where.

Affective theories hold that the stimulation of certain emotions is, for some reason, good: we need an occasional release (a good cry), or we need to have our emotions organized into a pleasant pattern (as the fretful child needs his mother's smile, to induce in him good spirits). That some readers seek emotional stimulus from books is beyond doubt; they want to identify themselves with the central character, experiencing bursts of love, sorrow, and so forth. But a good work of art neither invites this identification nor triggers stereotyped emotions. How many people have felt totally at one with Hamlet, Macbeth, Brutus?

Usually the affective theory insists that the aim is not to induce a temporary emotional state, but to induce an emotional state that will lead to action. Such a theory might hold that the artist should stimulate in people an awareness of the horror of war so that they will go out and do something about stopping wars. Tolstoi, who held such a view, regarded the evocation of emotion not as an end but as a means:

> The task of art is enormous. Through the influence of real art, aided by science, guided by religion, that peaceful co-operation of man which is now maintained by external means — by our lawcourts, police, charitable institutions, factory inspection, and so forth — should be obtained by man's free and joyous activity. Art should cause violence to be set aside.

Jean Pierre Gorin, close associate of film director Jean-Luc Godard, put the matter quite simply when asked, "What is the function of cinema?" "Cinema is part of the ideological struggle. And a revolutionary film is on the side of revolution." Ezekiel Mphahlele, an exiled South African black writer, has said that the best poetry is a "memorable" expression of "revolutionary passion and ideas," and Imamu Amiri Baraka (LeRoi Jones) has said that revolutionary writing must "transform reality." But against the view that a good work of art prompts us to action, one can put Robert Frost's deceptively simple question: "How soon?"

SOME TENTATIVE CONCLUSIONS

This chapter opened with the query, "What is literature?" and it has not yet given a satisfactory answer. Nor will it. No one has come up with a satisfactory answer so far. Textbooks and theoretical treatises are filled with neat definitions, but no definition has yet withstood all criticism. It would be nice to say that literature evokes emotion, but so does a good deal of nonliterature (for example, a documentary account of the bombing of Hiroshima), and perhaps much literature evokes "attention" rather than "emotion." It would be nice to say that literature is essentially fictional, but is a poem on, say, the power of God fictional? Is such a poem fictional to the believer who composes it or to the believer who reads it? Moreover, it can be argued that although works of art are superficially fictional, they are essentially true. It would be nice to say that in literature there is complexity and unity, but these are characteristics of a telephone book as well as of *Hamlet*. And so it goes, definition after definition failing when applied to specific works that we know are works of art.

The brief sketch of critical theories in the preceding pages, however, may help a reader toward a tentative definition. Surely we can agree that a piece of literature is a performance in words; it strongly holds our attention, seeming complete in itself; it is not primarily regarded as a source of factual information; it offers a unique delight or satisfaction. To these, most people would add that literature offers some sort of truth, though not the sort of truth found in factual propositions such as $E = mc^2$. Finally, most people would say that it has a beneficial effect on the perceiver. Tolstoi may be claiming too much for the arts, but is it absurd to believe that they can play a role in civilizing man? Music has beneficial effects on animals: cows are said to give more milk when music is played in barns, race horses are soothed by music at the starting gate at Aqueduct, and wolves reduce their howling when they hear classical music. Is there nothing in the following lines from *The Merchant of Venice*?

Jessica. I am never merry when I hear sweet music.
Lorenzo. The reason is your spirits are attentive;
   For do but note a wild and wanton herd,
   Or race of youthful and unhandled colts,
   Fetching mad bounds, bellowing and neighing loud,
   Which is the hot condition of their blood —
   If they but hear perchance a trumpet sound,
   Or any air of music touch their ears,
   You shall perceive them make a mutual stand,
   Their savage eyes turned to a modest gaze
   By the sweet power of music. Therefore the poet
   Did feign that Orpheus drew trees, stones, and floods,
   Since nought so stockish, hard, and full of rage,
   But music for the time doth change his nature.
   The man that hath no music in himself,
   Nor is not moved with concord of sweet sounds,
   Is fit for treasons, stratagems, and spoils.

Is it not possible that works of art give us an insight into reality (as the imitative theory usually holds), that they broaden our awareness of the possibilities of experience (as the expressive theory usually holds), and that they valuably affect our nervous system (as the affective theory usually holds)? This is not to say that every work of art does all these things, but only that all of these theories may have something to contribute to a deeper and more conscious awareness of what is valuable in the works we read. If we look back into our experiences, can we not find moments that seem to verify aspects of each theory? This book will offer further experiences; as you encounter them, you are invited to test these theories.

Fiction

2
Stories and
Meanings

People tell stories for many reasons, including the sheer egotistical delight of talking, but probably most of the best storytelling proceeds from one of two more commendable desires: a desire to entertain or a desire to instruct. Among the most famous of the stories designed to instruct are the parables that Jesus told. (*Parable* comes from the Greek word meaning "to throw beside," that is, "to compare," and we are to compare these little stories with our own behavior.) Here is one of them, addressed to a man who asked Jesus, "Who is my neighbor?" in the command to love one's neighbor as one's self.

Luke 10:30–37

Parable of the Good Samaritan

And Jesus answering said, "A certain man went down from Jerusalem to Jericho, and fell among thieves, which stripped him of his raiment, and wounded him, and departed, leaving him half dead. And by chance there came down a certain priest that way: and when he saw him, he passed by on the other side. And likewise a Levite, when he was at the place, came and looked on him, and passed by on the other side. But a certain Samaritan, as he journeyed, came where he was: and when he saw him, he had compassion on him, and went to him, and bound up his wounds, pouring in oil and wine, and set him on his own beast, and brought him to an inn, and took care of him. And on the morrow when he departed, he took out two pence, and gave them to the host, and said unto him, 'Take care of him; and whatsoever thou spendest more, when I come again, I will repay thee.' Which now of these three, thinkest thou, was neighbor unto him that fell among the thieves?''

And he said, "He that shewed mercy on him."

Then said Jesus unto him, "Go, and do thou likewise."

The narrative proper concludes before the question at the end of the first paragraph, and then the theme, or point, or message — for the story is about something more than an imagined encounter between a wounded man and three passers-by — is made explicit in a few additional lines. We say that the story is told for the sake of the point; we can also say that it is told for our sake, because we are implicitly invited to see ourselves in the story, and to live our lives in accordance with it. This simple but powerful story, with its memorable characters — though nameless and briefly sketched — makes us feel the point in our hearts.

Even older than Jesus' parables are the fables attributed to Aesop, some of which go back to the seventh century before Christ. These stories also teach lessons by telling brief incidents from which homely morals may easily be drawn, even though the stories are utterly fanciful. Among famous examples are the stories of the hare and the tortoise, the boy who cried "Wolf," the ant and the grasshopper, and a good many others that stick in the mind because of the sharply contrasted characters in sharply imagined situations. The fables just mentioned take only four or five sentences apiece, but, brief as they are, Aesop told some briefer ones. Here is the briefest of all:

> A vixen sneered at a lioness because she never bore more
> than one cub. "Only one," the lioness replied, "but a lion."

Just that: a situation with a conflict (the mere confrontation of a fox and a lion brings together the ignoble and the noble) and a resolution (*something* must come out of such a confrontation). There is no setting (we are not told that "one day in June a vixen, walking down a road, met a lioness"), but none is needed here. What there is — however briefly set forth — is characterization. The fox's baseness is effectively communicated through the verb "sneered" and through her taunt, and the lioness's nobility is even more effectively communicated through the brevity and the decisiveness of her reply. This reply at first seems to agree with the fox ("Only one") and then, after a suspenseful delay provided by the words "the lioness replied," the reply is tersely and powerfully completed ("but a lion"), placing the matter firmly in a new light. Granted that the story is not much of a story, still, it is finely told, and more potent — more memorable, more lively, we might even say more real, despite its talking animals — than the mere moral, "Small-minded people confuse quantity with quality."

Here is a much later short tale, from nineteenth-century Japan. It is said to be true, but whether it really occurred or not is scarcely of any importance. It is the story, not the history, that counts.

> Tanzan and Ekido were once traveling together down a muddy road. A heavy rain was still falling.
>
> Coming around a bend, they met a lovely girl in a silk kimono and sash, unable to cross the intersection.
>
> "Come on, girl," said Tanzan at once. Lifting her in his arms, he carried her over the mud.
>
> Ekido did not speak again until that night when they reached a lodging temple. Then he no longer could restrain himself. "We monks don't go near females," he told Tanzan, "especially not young and lovely ones. It is dangerous. Why did you do that?"
>
> "I left the girl there," said Tanzan. "Are you still carrying her?"

A superb story. The opening paragraph, though simple and matter-of-fact, holds our attention: we sense that something interesting is going to happen during this journey along a muddy road on a rainy day. Perhaps we even sense, somehow, by virtue of the references to the mud and the rain, that the journey itself rather than the travelers' destination will be the heart of the story: getting there will be more than half the fun. And then, after the introduction of the two characters and the setting, we quickly get the complicating factor, the encounter with the girl. Still there is apparently no conflict, though in "Ekido did not speak again until that night" we sense an unspoken conflict, an action (or, in this case, an inaction) that must be explained, an imbalance that must be righted before we are finished. At last Ekido, no longer able to contain his thoughts, lets his indignation burst out: "We monks don't go near females . . . , especially not young and lovely ones. It is dangerous. Why did you do that?" His statement and his question reveal not only his moral principles but also his insecurity and the anger that grows from it. And now, when the conflict is out in the open, comes the brief reply that reveals Tanzan's very different character as clearly as the outburst revealed Ekido's. This reply — though we could not have predicted it — strikes us as exactly right, bringing the story to a perfect end, i.e., to a point (like the ends of Christ's parable and Aesop's fable) at which there is no more to be said.

Let us look at another short piece, though this one, from the *Satyricon,* a witty, cynical book attributed to Petronius, director-in-chief of Nero's entertainments, is considerably longer than the stories we have just read, and it is aimed more at entertaining than at teaching.

Petronius (1st Century A.D.)

The Widow of Ephesus

Translated by William Arrowsmith

Once upon a time there was a certain married woman in the city of Ephesus whose fidelity to her husband was so famous that the women from all the neighboring towns and villages used to troop into Ephesus merely to stare at this prodigy. It happened, however, that her husband one day died. Finding the normal custom of following the cortege with hair unbound and beating her breast in public quite inadequate to express her grief, the lady insisted on following the corpse right into the tomb, an underground vault of the Greek type, and there set herself to guard the body, weeping and wailing night and day. Although in her extremes of grief she was clearly courting death from starvation, her parents were utterly unable to persuade her to leave, and even the magistrates, after one last supreme attempt, were rebuffed and driven away. In short, all Ephesus had gone into mourning for this extraordinary woman, all the more since the lady was now passing her fifth consecutive day without once tasting food. Beside the failing woman sat her devoted maid, sharing her mistress's grief and relighting the lamp whenever it flickered out. The whole city could speak, in fact, of nothing else: here at last, all classes alike agreed, was the one true example of conjugal fidelity and love.

In the meantime, however, the governor of the province gave orders that several thieves should be crucified in a spot close by the vault where the lady was mourning her dead husband's corpse. So, on the following night, the soldier who had been assigned to keep watch on the crosses so that nobody could remove the thieves' bodies for burial suddenly noticed a light blazing among the tombs and heard the sounds of groaning. And prompted by a natural human curiosity to know who or what was making those sounds, he descended into the vault.

But at the sight of a strikingly beautiful woman, he stopped short in terror, thinking he must be seeing some ghostly apparition out of hell. Then, observing the corpse and seeing the tears on the lady's face and the scratches her fingernails had gashed in her cheeks, he realized what it was: a widow, in inconsolable grief. Promptly fetching his little supper back down to the tomb, he implored the lady not to persist in her sorrow or break her heart with useless mourning. All men alike, he reminded her, have the same end; the same resting place awaits us all. He used, in short, all those platitudes we use to comfort the suffering and bring them back to life. His consolations, being unwelcome, only exasperated the widow more; more violently than ever she beat her breast, and tearing out her hair by the roots, scattered it over the dead man's body. Undismayed, the soldier repeated his arguments and pressed her to take some food, until the little maid, quite overcome by the smell of the wine, succumbed and stretched out her hand to her tempter. Then, restored by the food and wine, she began herself to assail her mistress's obstinate refusal.

"How will it help you," she asked the lady, "if you faint from hunger? Why should you bury yourself alive, and go down to death before the Fates have called you? What does Vergil say? —

> *Do you suppose the shades and ashes of the dead are by such sorrow touched?*

No, begin your life afresh. Shake off these woman's scruples; enjoy the light while you can. Look at that corpse of your poor husband: doesn't it tell you more eloquently than any words that you should live?"

None of us, of course, really dislikes being told that we must eat, that life is to be lived. And the lady was no exception. Weakened by her long days of fasting, her resistance crumbled at last, and she ate the food the soldier offered her as hungrily as the little maid had eaten earlier.

Well, you know what temptations are normally aroused in a man on a full stomach. So the soldier, mustering all those blandishments by means of which he had persuaded the lady to live, now laid determined siege to her virtue. And chaste though she was, the lady found him singularly attractive and his arguments persuasive. As for the maid, she did all she could to help the soldier's cause, repeating like a refrain the appropriate line of Vergil:

If love is pleasing, lady, yield yourself to love.

To make the matter short, the lady's body soon gave up the struggle; she yielded and our happy warrior enjoyed a total triumph on both counts. That very night their marriage was consummated, and they slept together the second and the third night too, carefully shutting the door of the tomb so that any passing friends or strangers would have thought the lady of famous chastity had at last expired over her dead husband's body.

As you can perhaps imagine, our soldier was a very happy man, utterly delighted with his lady's ample beauty and that special charm that a secret love confers. Every night, as soon as the sun had set, he bought what few provisions his slender pay permitted and smuggled them down to the tomb. One night, however, the parents of one of the crucified thieves, noticing that the watch was being badly kept, took advantage of our hero's absence to remove their son's body and bury it. The next morning, of course, the soldier was horror-struck to discover one of the bodies missing from its cross, and ran to tell his mistress of the horrible punishment which awaited him for neglecting his duty. In the circumstances, he told her, he would not wait to be tried and sentenced, but would punish himself then and there with his own sword. All he asked of her was that she make room for another corpse and allow the same gloomy tomb to enclose husband and lover together.

Our lady's heart, however, was no less tender than pure. "God forbid," she cried, "that I should have to see at one and the same time the dead bodies of the only two men I have ever loved. No, better far, I say, to hang the dead than kill the living." With these words, she gave orders that her husband's body should be taken from its bier and strung up on the empty cross. The soldier followed this good advice, and the next morning the whole city wondered by what miracle the dead man had climbed up on the cross.

Petronius tells us that the sailors who heard this tale greeted it "with great guffaws," surely the appropriate response. It is an amusing story, largely because it is well-told. Let us look at it as a piece of craftsmanship. The happenings, as they are selected and arranged by the author, are the **plot;** the participants are the **characters;** the meaning or point is the **theme.**

The traditional plot has this structure:

1. **Exposition** (setting forth of the beginning)
2. **Conflict** (a complication that moves to a climax)
3. **Dénouement** (literally, "unknotting," the outcome of the conflict; the resolution)

Petronius's exposition is in the opening paragraph, which sets forth a situation that seems to be stable (the lady is resolved to die). We do not ask why she was so virtuous or of what her husband died; we simply accept the exposition, and wait for something to disturb the situation it describes. The second paragraph begins the conflict by introducing a complication (a soldier goes to the tomb). It is important that the conflict is not so much the lady against the soldier as it is the lady against her own ideals. This conflict or complication (literally, folding or weaving together) is momentarily resolved when the lady exchanges widowhood for a new marriage, but the resolution gives rise to another complication, the disappearance of the thief's body. At this point the conflict is at its height, for the soldier's life is at stake. (Although at the start the widow's life was in danger, the tension was slight because she was doing what she wished; now that the lovers wish to live, the tension is greatest.) This moment of greatest tension is called the **climax;** it is here dissipated by an action of the lady, whose love for the soldier is as great as was her grief for her husband. Her suggestion to substitute her husband's corpse for the missing one unties the knot or the weaving begun with the complication. The soldier's acceptance of her suggestion, and the townsmen's bewilderment, constitute the dénouement. We have moved, then, from a situation that seemed static (the widow's grief), through a complication that became acute, into a new situation that is stable. The lady may later leave the soldier for another man, but such happenings do not concern us; we feel that we have seen a unified action — something with a beginning, a middle, and an end.*

The things that happen are in large measure caused by the characters, who act believably. Although in Petronius's tale it is a coincidence that a thief has been crucified near the tomb containing the grieving wife, all the subsequent happenings arise from **character** (the personality of each of the figures): the soldier visits the tomb "prompted by a natural human curiosity," and, after he has consoled the widow and has eaten, he undergoes the

---

* Though we have defined "plot" as the author's selection and arrangement of happenings, some critics define "plot" as the happenings in their chronological order. The term is further discussed on pages 601–03.

temptations [that] are normally aroused in a man on a full
stomach. So the soldier, mustering all those blandishments
by means of which he had persuaded the lady to live, now
laid determined siege to her virtue. And chaste though she
was, the lady found him singularly attractive and his arguments
persuasive.

Similarly, there is **motivation** (a basis in personality) for the
disappearance of the thief's corpse; the fact that the soldier had
been stationed to guard it gives us clear indication that the thief's
family will bury it if given the chance. The soldier's fear and
despair are similarly plausible, and, finally, so too is the lady's
ingenious suggestion that saves the soldier, for her love for him
is now as deep as it had been for her husband. The crucifixion of
her husband's corpse, then, like the soldier's visit and the lady's
change of heart, is motivated; we feel it is plausible in the light
of the characters involved. And our interest in the tale is not only
an interest in occurrences, but also an interest in the people who
engender the occurrences.

In some stories, of course, we are chiefly interested in plot
(the arrangement of happenings or doings), in others we are chiefly
interested in character (the personalities of the doers), but on the
whole the two are so intertwined that interest in one involves
interest in the other. Happenings occur (people cross paths), and
personalities respond to them, engendering further happenings. As
Henry James rhetorically asked, "What is character but the determination of incident? What is incident but the illustration of
character?" Commonly, as a good story proceeds and we become
increasingly familiar with the characters, we get intimations of
what they may do in the future. We may not know precisely how
they will act, but we have a fairly good idea, and when in fact
we see their subsequent actions, we usually recognize the appro-
priateness. Sometimes there are hints of what is to come, and
because of this **foreshadowing** we are not shocked by what happens,
but rather we experience suspense as we wait for the expected to
come about. Coleridge had Shakespeare's use of foreshadowing
in mind when he praised him for giving us not surprise but expectation and then the satisfaction of perfect knowledge. E. M.
Forster, in *Aspects of the Novel,* has a shrewd comment on the
importance of both fulfilling expectation and offering a slight surprise:
"Shock, followed by the feeling, 'Oh, that's all right,' is a sign
that all is well with the plot: characters, to be real, ought to run
smoothly, but a plot ought to cause surprise."

Finally, a few words about **theme.** Usually, a story is about
something, it has a meaning, a point — a theme. The narrator of
"The Widow of Ephesus" prefaced the tale by declaring that "no

woman was so chaste or faithful that she couldn't be seduced," and his story was told in order to make this statement meaningful. A vulgar fellow, he interprets his story rather cheaply, even indecently. But the reader can more accurately restate the theme, giving it greater significance and making it more acceptable: life and love are too strong to be buried alive. A word of caution, however, is needed here: a story is not simply an illustration of a theme. A story has a variety of details that modify any abstract statement; in Petronius's story the lady was "weakened by her long days of fasting," and the soldier was "singularly attractive." Such details, not present in the narrator's own statement of his "theme," are important modifications of the theme. To state the theme either as the narrator stated it or as we have restated it is to falsify the story, for Petronius's story is about a particular widow's encounter with a particular soldier, under particular circumstances. And what lives in our memory is not an abstract statement — and certainly not a thesis, i.e., a proposition offered and argued. What lives is an image that by every word in the story has convinced us that it is a representation, if not of "reality," at least of an aspect of reality. Still, the artist was guided by a theme in his choice of details; of many possible details he chose to present only a few. The musical sense of the word "theme" can help us to understand what a theme in literature is: "a melody constituting the basis of variation, development, or the like." The variations and the development cannot be random but must have a basis. What is it, Robert Frost asks, that prevents the writer from kicking himself "from one chance suggestion to another in all directions as of a hot afternoon in the life of a grasshopper?" Frost's answer: "Theme alone can steady us down."

We can, then, talk about the theme — what the story adds up to — as long as we do not think a statement of the theme is equivalent to or a substitute for the whole story. As Flannery O'Connor says, "Some people have the notion that you can read the story and then climb out of it into the meaning, but for the fiction writer himself the whole story is the meaning." A theme, Miss O'Connor says, is not like a string tying a sack of chicken feed, to be pulled out so that the feed can be got at. "A story is a way to say something that can't be said any other way." (On theme, see also pages 617–18.)

QUESTIONS

1. Most of the story is narrated, rather than dramatized through dialogue. Is the use of dialogue haphazard or is it in the right place?

2. What does the presence of the maid contribute to the story?
3. We are told that the lady decides to surrender the corpse because she is "no less tender than pure." Does the narrator mean exactly what he says? Explain.
4. The lady's virtue is set forth at some length; the desecration of the corpse is set forth very briefly. Why is this disparity effective?
5. The last sentence of the story is characteristic of the prevailing tone in which the story is told. How would you describe that tone, and how does it affect the theme?

Below are two additional short pieces: the first is another of Jesus' parables; the second is an American story written in the late nineteenth century.

Luke 15

Parable of the Prodigal Son

And he said, "A certain man had two sons: and the younger of them said to his father, 'Father, give me the portion of goods that falleth to me.' And he divided unto them his living. And not many days after, the younger son gathered all together, and took his journey into a far country, and there wasted his substance with riotous living. And when he had spent all, there arose a mighty famine in that land, and he began to be in want. And he went and joined himself to a citizen of that country, and he sent him into his fields to feed swine. And he would fain have filled his belly with the husks that the swine did eat: and no man gave unto him. And when he came to himself he said, 'How many hired servants of my father's have bread enough and to spare, and I perish with hunger? I will arise and go to my father, and will say unto him, "Father, I have sinned against heaven, and before thee. And am no more worthy to be called thy son: make me as one of thy hired servants."' And he arose, and came to his father. But when he was yet a great way off, his father saw him, and had compassion, and ran, and fell on his neck, and kissed him. And the son said unto him, 'Father, I have sinned against heaven, and in thy sight, and am no more worthy to be called thy son.' But the father said to his servants, 'Bring forth the best robe, and put it on him, and put a ring on his hand, and shoes on his feet. And bring hither the fatted calf and kill it, and let us eat, and be merry. For this my son was dead, and is alive again; he was lost, and is found.' And they began to be merry. Now his elder son was in the field, and as he came and drew nigh to the house, he heard music and dancing. And he called one of the servants, and asked what these things meant. And he said unto him, 'Thy brother is come, and thy father hath killed the fatted calf, because he hath received him safe and sound.' And he was angry, and would not go in: therefore came his father out, and entreated him. And he answering said to his father, 'Lo, these many years do I serve thee, neither transgressed I at any time thy commandment, and yet thou never gavest me a kid, that I might make merry with my friends: but as soon as this thy son was come, which hath devoured thy living with harlots, thou hast killed for him the fatted calf.' And he said unto him, 'Son, thou art ever with me, and all that I have is thine. It was meet that we should make merry, and be glad: for this thy brother was dead, and is alive again: and was lost, and is found.' "

Kate Chopin (1851–1904)

The Story of an Hour

Knowing that Mrs. Mallard was afflicted with a heart trouble, great care was taken to break to her as gently as possible the news of her husband's death.

It was her sister Josephine who told her, in broken sentences, veiled hints that revealed in half concealing. Her husband's friend Richards was there, too, near her. It was he who had been in the newspaper office when intelligence of the railroad disaster was received, with Brently Mallard's name leading the list of "killed." He had only taken the time to assure himself of its truth by a second telegram, and had hastened to forestall any less careful, less tender friend in bearing the sad message.

She did not hear the story as many women have heard the same, with a paralyzed inability to accept its significance. She wept at once, with sudden, wild abandonment, in her sister's arms. When the storm of grief had spent itself she went away to her room alone. She would have no one follow her.

There stood, facing the open window, a comfortable, roomy armchair. Into this she sank, pressed down by a physical exhaustion that haunted her body and seemed to reach into her soul.

She could see in the open square before her house the tops of trees that were all aquiver with the new spring life. The delicious breath of rain was in the air. In the street below a peddler was crying his wares. The notes of a distant song which some one was singing reached her faintly, and countless sparrows were twittering in the eaves.

There were patches of blue sky showing here and there through the clouds that had met and piled above the other in the west facing her window.

She sat with her head thrown back upon the cushion of the chair quite motionless, except when a sob came up into her throat and shook her, as a child who has cried itself to sleep continues to sob in its dreams.

She was young, with a fair, calm face, whose lines bespoke repression and even a certain strength. But now there was a dull stare in her eyes, whose gaze was fixed away off yonder on one of those patches of blue sky. It was not a glance of reflection, but rather indicated a suspension of intelligent thought.

There was something coming to her and she was waiting for it, fearfully. What was it? She did not know; it was too subtle and elusive to name. But she felt it, creeping out of the sky, reaching toward her through the sounds, the scents, the color that filled the air.

Now her bosom rose and fell tumultuously. She was beginning to recognize this thing that was approaching to possess her, and she was striving to beat it back with her will — as powerless as her two white slender hands would have been.

When she abandoned herself a little whispered word escaped her slightly parted lips. She said it over and over under her breath: "Free, free, free!" The vacant stare and the look of terror that had followed it went from her eyes. They stayed keen and bright. Her pulses beat fast, and the coursing blood warmed and relaxed every inch of her body.

She did not stop to ask if it were not a monstrous joy that held her. A clear and exalted perception enabled her to dismiss the suggestion as trivial.

She knew that she would weep again when she saw the kind, tender hands folded in death; the face that had never looked save with love upon her, fixed and gray and dead. But she saw beyond that bitter moment a long procession of years to come that would belong to her absolutely. And she opened and spread her arms out to them in welcome.

There would be no one to live for during those coming years; she would live for herself. There would be no powerful will bending her in that blind persistence with which men and women believe they have a right to impose a private will upon a fellow creature. A kind intention or a cruel intention made the act seem no less a crime as she looked upon it in that brief moment of illumination.

And yet she had loved him — sometimes. Often she had not. What did it matter! What could love, the unsolved mystery, count for in face of this possession of self-assertion which she suddenly recognized as the strongest impulse of her being.

"Free! Body and soul free!" she kept whispering.

Josephine was kneeling before the closed door with her lips to the keyhole, imploring for admission. "Louise, open the door! I beg; open the door — you will make yourself ill. What are you doing, Louise? For heaven's sake open the door."

"Go away. I am not making myself ill." No; she was drinking in a very elixir of life through that open window.

Her fancy was running riot along those days ahead of her. Spring days, and summer days, and all sorts of days that would be her own. She breathed a quick prayer that life might be long. It was only yesterday she had thought with a shudder that life might be long.

She arose at length and opened the door to her sister's importunities. There was a feverish triumph in her eyes, and she carried herself unwittingly like a goddess of Victory. She clasped her sister's waist, and together they descended the stairs. Richards stood waiting for them at the bottom.

Some one was opening the front door with a latchkey. It was Brently Mallard who entered, a little travel-stained, composedly carrying his grip-sack and umbrella. He had been far from the scene of accident, and did not even know there had been one. He stood amazed at Josephine's piercing cry; at Richards' quick motion to screen him from the view of his wife.

But Richards was too late.

When the doctors came they said she had died of heart disease — of joy that kills.

QUESTIONS

1. Is Mrs. Mallard's grief sincere?
2. In the first half of the story, how does Chopin help to prepare for Mrs. Mallard's words, "Free, free, free"?
3. How accurate is the doctors' final diagnosis?

3
Narrative Point of View

Every story is told by someone. Mark Twain wrote *The Adventures of Huckleberry Finn,* but he does not tell the story; the story is told by Huck, and it begins thus:

> You don't know about me without you have read a book by the name of *The Adventures of Tom Sawyer* but that ain't no matter. That book was made by Mr. Mark Twain, and he told the truth, mainly. There was things which he stretched, but mainly he told the truth.

Similarly, Petronius wrote "The Widow of Ephesus," but this story is told by one Eumolpus, who makes no claim to have witnessed the happening. It might, however, have been told by the widow herself, or by an outraged moralist. An author must choose a point of view (or several points of view) from which to narrate the story. This choice is perhaps analogous to the poet's choice of free verse, blank verse, or rhyme, and the choice will contribute to the total effect that the story will have. Eumolpus, the teller of "The Widow of Ephesus," recounts the tale with very little intrusion of himself, but just before the end he analyzes the lady's feelings: "Our lady's heart, however, was no less tender than pure." Now, this wry, inexact, seemingly ingenuous appraisal of her character is largely what gives the story its effect; if the story had been told by a moralist or by the lady herself or by the soldier, it would have been a different story.

Narrative points of view can be divided into two sorts: **participant** (or **first person**) and **nonparticipant** (or **third person**). Each of these two divisions can be subdivided:

I. Participant (first person)
   A. Narrator as a major character
   B. Narrator as a minor character
II. Nonparticipant (third person)
   A. Omniscient
   B. Selective omniscient
   C. Objective

PARTICIPANT POINTS OF VIEW

In the story by Frank O'Connor at the end of this chapter the narrator is, like Huckleberry Finn, a major character. He, and not O'Connor, tells the story, and the story is chiefly about him; hence one can say that O'Connor uses a first-person (or participant) point of view. O'Connor has invented an Irishman who has fought against the English, and this narrator tells of the impact a happening had on him: "And anything that happened to me afterwards, I never felt the same about again."

But sometimes a first-person narrator tells a story that focuses on some other character; the narrator is a minor character, a peripheral witness, for example, to a story about Jones, and we get the story of Jones filtered through, say, the eyes of Jones's friend or brother or cat. One special kind of first-person narrator (whether major or minor) is the **innocent eye:** the narrator is naive (usually a child, an idiot, or a not-too-bright adult), telling what he or she sees and feels; the contrast between what the narrator perceives and what the reader understands produces an ironic effect. Such a story, in which the reader understands more than the teller himself does, is Ring Lardner's "Haircut," a story told by a garrulous barber who does not perceive that the "accident" he is describing is in fact a murder.

NONPARTICIPANT POINTS OF VIEW

In a nonparticipant (third-person) point of view, the teller of the tale is not a character in the tale. The narrator has receded from the story. If the point of view is **omniscient,** the narrator relates what he wishes about the thoughts as well as the deeds of his characters. The omniscient teller can at any time enter the mind of any or all of his characters; whereas the first-person narrator can only say, "I was angry," or "Jones seemed angry to me," the omniscient narrator can say, "Jones was inwardly angry but gave no sign; Smith continued chatting, but he sensed Jones's anger." Furthermore, a distinction can be made between **neutral omniscience** (the narrator recounts deeds and thoughts, but does not judge) and **editorial omniscience** (the narrator not only recounts but also judges). The narrator in Hawthorne's "Young Goodman Brown" knows what goes on in the mind of Brown, and he comments approvingly or disapprovingly: "With this excellent resolve for the future, Goodman Brown felt himself justified in making more haste on his present evil purpose."

Because a short story can scarcely hope to develop effectively a picture of several minds, an author may prefer to limit his or her omniscience to the minds of only a few of the characters, or even to that of one of the characters; that is, the author may use **selective omniscience** as the point of view. Selective omniscience provides a focus, especially if it is limited to a single character. When thus limited, the author hovers over the shoulder of one character, seeing him or her from outside and from inside and seeing other characters only from the outside and from the impact they make upon the mind of this selected receptor. In "Young Goodman Brown" the reader sees things mostly as they make their impact upon the protagonist's mind:

> He could have well-nigh sworn that the shape of his own dead father beckoned him to advance, looking downward from a smoke wreath, while a woman, with dim features of despair, threw out her hand to warn him back. Was it his mother? But he had no power to retreat one step, nor to resist, even in thought, when the minister and good old Deacon Gookin seized his arms and led him to the blazing rock.

When selective omniscience attempts to record mental activity ranging from consciousness to the unconscious, from clear perceptions to confused longings, it is sometimes labeled the **stream-of-consciousness** point of view. The following example is from Katherine Anne Porter's "The Jilting of Granny Weatherall":

> Her eyelids wavered and let in streamers of blue-gray light like tissue paper over her eyes. She must get up and pull the shades down or she'd never sleep. She was in bed again and the shades were not down. How could that happen? Better turn over, hide from the light, sleeping in the light gave you nightmares. "Mother, how do you feel now?" and a stinging wetness on her forehead. But I don't like having my face washed in cold water!

In an effort to reproduce the unending activity of the mind, some authors who use the stream-of-consciousness point of view dispense with conventional syntax, punctuation, and logical transitions. The last forty-six pages in James Joyce's *Ulysses* are an unpunctuated flow of one character's thoughts.

Finally, sometimes a third-person narrator does not enter even a single mind, but records only what crosses a dispassionate eye and ear. Such a point of view is **objective** (sometimes called **the camera** or **fly-on-the-wall**). The absence of editorializing and of dissection of the mind often produces the effect of a play; we see and hear the characters in action. Much of Hemingway's "A Clean, Well-Lighted Place" is objective, consisting of bits of dialogue that make the story look like a play:

> "The guard will pick him up," one waiter said.
> "What does it matter if he gets what he's after?"
> "He had better get off the street now. The guard will get him. They went by five minutes ago."
> The old man sitting in the shadow rapped on his saucer with his glass. The younger waiter went over to him.

But the word "objective" is almost a misnomer, for to describe happenings is — by one's choice of words — to comment on them too, however unobtrusively. How objective is the point of view if a man is described as "fat" instead of "stout" or "stout" instead of "heavy" or "heavy" instead of "two hundred and fifty pounds in weight"? The objective point of view, even though it expressly enters no mind, often is a camouflaged version of the selective omniscient point of view.

THE POINT OF A POINT OF VIEW

Generalizations about the effect of a point of view are risky, but two have already been made: that the innocent eye can achieve an ironic effect otherwise unattainable, and that an objective point of view is dramatic. Three other generalizations are often made: (1) that a first-person point of view lends a sense of immediacy or reality, (2) that an omniscient point of view suggests human littleness, and (3) that the point of view must be consistent.

To take the first of these: it is true that when Poe begins a story "The thousand injuries of Fortunato I had borne as I best could, but when he ventured upon insult, I vowed revenge," we feel that the author has gripped us by the lapels; but, on the other hand, we know that we are only reading a piece of fiction, and we do not really believe in the existence of the "I" or of Fortunato; and furthermore, when we pick up a story that begins with *any* point of view we agree (by picking up the book) to pretend to believe the fictions we are being told. That is, all fiction — whether in the first person or not — is known to be literally false but is read with the pretense that it is true. The writer must hold our attention, and make us feel that the fiction is meaningful, but the use of the first-person pronoun does not of itself confer reality. The second generalization, that an omniscient point of view can make puppets of its characters, is equally misleading; this point of view can also reveal in them a depth and complexity quite foreign to the idea of human littleness. The third generalization, that the narrator's point of view must be consistent lest the illusion of reality be shattered, has been much preached by the followers of Henry James. But E. M. Forster has suggested, in *Aspects of the Novel,* that what is important is not consistency but "the power of the writer to bounce the reader into accepting what he says." Forster notes that in *Bleak House* Dickens uses in Chapter I an omniscient point of view, in Chapter II a selective omniscient point of view, and in Chapter III a first-person point of view. "Logically," Forster says, "*Bleak House* is all to pieces, but Dickens bounces us, so that we do not mind the shiftings of the viewpoint."

Perhaps the only sound generalizations possible are that (1) because point of view is one of the things that give form to a story, a good author chooses the point (or points) of view that he or she feels best for the particular story, and (2) the use of any other point of view would turn the story into a different story.

Frank O'Connor (1903–1966)

Guests of the Nation

I

At dusk the big Englishman, Belcher, would shift his long legs out of the ashes and say "Well, chums, what about it?" and Noble or me would say "All right, chum" (for we had picked up some of their curious expressions), and the little Englishman, Hawkins, would light the lamp and bring out the cards. Sometimes

Jeremiah Donovan would come up and supervise the game and get excited over Hawkins's cards, which he always played badly, and shout at him as if he was one of our own "Ah, you divil, you, why didn't you play the tray?"

But ordinarily Jeremiah was a sober and contented poor devil like the big Englishman, Belcher, and was looked up to only because he was a fair hand at documents, though he was slow enough even with them. He wore a small cloth hat and big gaiters over his long pants, and you seldom saw him with his hands out of his pockets. He reddened when you talked to him, tilting from toe to heel and back, and looking down all the time at his big farmer's feet. Noble and me used to make fun of his broad accent, because we were from the town.

I couldn't at the time see the point of me and Noble guarding Belcher and Hawkins at all, for it was my belief that you could have planted that pair down anywhere from this to Claregalway and they'd have taken root there like a native weed. I never in my short experience seen two men to take to the country as they did.

They were handed on to us by the Second Battalion when the search for them became too hot, and Noble and myself, being young, took over with a natural feeling of responsibility, but Hawkins made us look like fools when he showed that he knew the country better than we did.

"You're the bloke they calls Bonaparte," he says to me. "Mary Brigid O'Connell told me to ask you what you done with the pair of her brother's socks you borrowed."

For it seemed, as they explained it, that the Second used to have little evenings, and some of the girls of the neighborhood turned in, and, seeing they were such decent chaps, our fellows couldn't leave the two Englishmen out of them. Hawkins learned to dance "The Walls of Limerick," "The Siege of Ennis," and "The Waves of Tory" as well as any of them, though, naturally, we couldn't return the compliment, because our lads at that time did not dance foreign dances on principle.

So whatever privileges Belcher and Hawkins had with the Second they just naturally took with us, and after the first day or two we gave up all pretense of keeping a close eye on them. Not that they could have got far, for they had accents you could cut with a knife and wore khaki tunics and overcoats with civilian boots. But it's my belief that they never had any idea of escaping and were quite content to be where they were.

It was a treat to see how Belcher got off with the old woman of the house where we were staying. She was a great warrant to

scold, and cranky even with us, but before ever she had a chance
of giving our guests, as I may call them, a lick of her tongue,
Belcher had made her his friend for life. She was breaking sticks,
and Belcher, who hadn't been more than ten minutes in the house,
jumped up from his seat and went over to her.

"Allow me, madam," he says, smiling his queer little smile,
"please allow me"; and he takes the bloody hatchet. She was struck
too paralytic to speak, and after that, Belcher would be at her
heels, carrying a bucket, a basket, or a load of turf as the case
might be. As Noble said, he got into looking before she leapt,
and hot water, or any little thing she wanted, Belcher would have
it ready for her. For such a huge man (and though I am five foot
ten myself I had to look up at him) he had an uncommon shortness
— or should I say lack? — of speech. It took us some time to get
used to him, walking in and out, like a ghost, without a word.
Especially because Hawkins talked enough for a platoon, it was
strange to hear big Belcher with his toes in the ashes come out
with a solitary "Excuse me, chum," or "That's right, chum." His
one and only passion was cards, and I will say for him that he
was a good cardplayer. He could have fleeced myself and Noble,
but whatever we lost to him Hawkins lost to us, and Hawkins
played with the money Belcher gave him.

Hawkins lost to us because he had too much old gab, and
we probably lost to Belcher for the same reason. Hawkins and
Noble would spit at one another about religion into the early
hours of the morning, and Hawkins worried the soul out of Noble,
whose brother was a priest, with a string of questions that would
puzzle a cardinal. To make it worse, even in treating of holy
subjects, Hawkins had a deplorable tongue. I never in all my career
met a man who could mix such a variety of cursing and bad
language into an argument. He was a terrible man, and a fright
to argue. He never did a stroke of work, and when he had no
one else to talk to, he got stuck in the old woman.

He met his match in her, for one day when he tried to get
her to complain profanely of the drought, she gave him a great
come-down by blaming it entirely on Jupiter Pluvius (a deity
neither Hawkins nor I had ever heard of, though Noble said that
among the pagans it was believed that he had something to do
with the rain). Another day he was swearing at the capitalists for
starting the German war when the old lady laid down her iron,
puckered up her little crab's mouth, and said: "Mr. Hawkins, you
can say what you like about the war, and think you'll deceive me
because I'm only a simple poor countrywoman, but I know what

started the war. It was the Italian Count that stole the heathen
divinity out of the temple in Japan. Believe me, Mr. Hawkins,
nothing but sorrow and want can follow the people that disturb
the hidden powers."

A queer old girl, all right.

II

We had our tea one evening, and Hawkins lit the lamp and
we all sat into cards. Jeremiah Donovan came in too, and sat down
and watched us for a while, and it suddenly struck me that he
had no great love for the two Englishmen. It came as a great
surprise to me, because I hadn't noticed anything about him before.

Late in the evening a really terrible argument blew up between
Hawkins and Noble, about capitalists and priests and love of your
country.

"The capitalists," says Hawkins with an angry gulp, "pays
the priests to tell you about the next world so as you won't notice
what the bastards are up to in this."

"Nonsense, man!" says Noble, losing his temper. "Before
ever a capitalist was thought of, people believed in the next world."

Hawkins stood up as though he was preaching a sermon.
"Oh, they did, did they?" he says with a sneer. "They believed
all the things you believe, isn't that what you mean? And you
believe that God created Adam, and Adam created Shem, and
Shem created Jehoshaphat. You believe all that silly old fairytale
about Eve and Eden and the apple. Well, listen to me, chum. If
you're entitled to hold a silly belief like that, I'm entitled to hold
my silly belief — which is that the first thing your God created
was a bleeding capitalist, with morality and Rolls-Royce complete.
Am I right, chum?" he says to Belcher.

"You're right, chum," says Belcher with his amused smile,
and got up from the table to stretch his long legs into the fire and
stroke his moustache. So, seeing that Jeremiah Donovan was going,
and that there was no knowing when the argument about religion
would be over, I went out with him. We strolled down to the
village together, and then he stopped and started blushing and
mumbling and saying I ought to be behind, keeping guard on the
prisoners. I didn't like the tone he took with me, and anyway I
was bored with life in the cottage, so I replied by asking him what
the hell we wanted guarding them at all for. I told him I'd talked
it over with Noble, and that we'd both rather be out with a fighting
column.

"What use are those fellows to us?" says I.

He looked at me in surprise and said: "I thought you knew we were keeping them as hostages."

"Hostages?" I said.

"The enemy have prisoners belonging to us," he says, "and now they're talking of shooting them. If they shoot our prisoners, we'll shoot theirs."

"Shoot them?" I said.

"What else did you think we were keeping them for?" he says.

"Wasn't it very unforeseen of you not to warn Noble and myself of that in the beginning?" I said.

"How was it?" says he. "You might have known it."

"We couldn't know it, Jeremiah Donovan," says I. "How could we when they were on our hands so long?"

"The enemy have our prisoners as long and longer," says he.

"That's not the same thing at all," says I.

"What difference is there?" says he.

I couldn't tell him, because I knew he wouldn't understand. If it was only an old dog that was going to the vet's, you'd try and not get too fond of him, but Jeremiah Donovan wasn't a man that would ever be in danger of that.

"And when is this thing going to be decided?" says I.

"We might hear tonight," he says. "Or tomorrow or the next day at latest. So if it's only hanging round here that's a trouble to you, you'll be free soon enough."

It wasn't the hanging round that was a trouble to me at all by this time. I had worse things to worry about. When I got back to the cottage the argument was still on. Hawkins was holding forth in his best style, maintaining that there was no next world, and Noble was maintaining that there was; but I could see that Hawkins had had the best of it.

"Do you know what, chum?" he was saying with a saucy smile. "I think you're just as big a bleeding unbeliever as I am. You say you believe in the next world, and you know just as much about the next world as I do, which is sweet damn-all. What's heaven? You don't know. Where's heaven? You don't know. You know sweet damn-all! I ask you again, do they wear wings?"

"Very well, then," says Noble, "they do. Is that enough for you? They do wear wings."

"Where do they get them, then? Who makes them? Have

they a factory for wings? Have they a sort of store where you hands in your chit and takes your bleeding wings?"

"You're an impossible man to argue with," says Noble. "Now, listen to me —" And they were off again.

It was long after midnight when we locked up and went to bed. As I blew out the candle I told Noble what Jeremiah Donovan was after telling me. Noble took it very quietly. When we'd been in bed about an hour he asked me did I think we ought to tell the Englishmen. I didn't think we should, because it was more than likely that the English wouldn't shoot our men, and even if they did, the brigade officers, who were always up and down with the Second Battalion and knew the Englishmen well, wouldn't be likely to want them plugged. "I think so too," says Noble. "It would be great cruelty to put the wind up them now."

"It was very unforeseen of Jeremiah Donovan anyhow," says I.

It was next morning that we found it so hard to face Belcher and Hawkins. We went about the house all day scarcely saying a word. Belcher didn't seem to notice; he was stretched into the ashes as usual, with his usual look of waiting in quietness for something unforeseen to happen, but Hawkins noticed and put it down to Noble's being beaten in the argument of the night before.

"Why can't you take a discussion in the proper spirit?" he says severely. "You and your Adam and Eve! I'm a Communist, that's what I am. Communist or anarchist, it all comes to much the same thing." And for hours he went round the house, muttering when the fit took him. "Adam and Eve! Adam and Eve! Nothing better to do with their time than picking bleeding apples!"

III

I don't know how we got through that day, but I was very glad when it was over, the tea things were cleared away, and Belcher said in his peaceable way: "Well, chums, what about it?" We sat round the table and Hawkins took out the cards, and just then I heard Jeremiah Donovan's footstep on the path and a dark presentiment crossed my mind. I rose from the table and caught him before he reached the door.

"What do you want?" I asked.

"I want those two soldier friends of yours," he says, getting red.

"Is that the way, Jeremiah Donovan?" I asked.

"That's the way. There were four of our lads shot this morning, one of them a boy of sixteen."

"That's bad," I said.

At that moment Noble followed me out, and the three of us walked down the path together, talking in whispers. Feeney, the local intelligence officer, was standing by the gate.

"What are you going to do about it?" I asked Jeremiah Donovan.

"I want you and Noble to get them out; tell them they're being shifted again; that'll be the quietest way."

"Leave me out of that," says Noble under his breath.

Jeremiah Donovan looks at him hard.

"All right," he says. "You and Feeney get a few tools from the shed and dig a hole by the far end of the bog. Bonaparte and myself will be after you. Don't let anyone see you with the tools. I wouldn't like it to go beyond ourselves."

We saw Feeney and Noble go round to the shed and went in ourselves. I left Jeremiah Donovan to do the explanations. He told them that he had orders to send them back to the Second Battalion. Hawkins let out a mouthful of curses, and you could see that though Belcher didn't say anything, he was a bit upset too. The old woman was for having them stay in spite of us, and she didn't stop advising them until Jeremiah Donovan lost his temper and turned on her. He had a nasty temper, I noticed. It was pitch-dark in the cottage by this time, but no one thought of lighting the lamp, and in the darkness the two Englishmen fetched their topcoats and said good-bye to the old woman.

"Just as a man makes a home of a bleeding place, some bastard at headquarters thinks you're too cushy and shunts you off," says Hawkins, shaking her hand.

"A thousand thanks, madam," says Belcher. "A thousand thanks for everything" — as though he'd made it up.

We went round to the back of the house and down towards the bog, it was only then that Jeremiah Donovan told them. He was shaking with excitement.

"There were four of our fellows shot in Cork this morning and now you're to be shot as a reprisal."

"What are you talking about?" snaps Hawkins. "It's bad enough being mucked about as we are without having to put up with your funny jokes."

"It isn't a joke," says Donovan. "I'm sorry, Hawkins, but it's true," and begins on the usual rigmarole about duty and how unpleasant it is.

I never noticed that people who talk a lot about duty find it much of a trouble to them.

"Oh, cut it out!" says Hawkins.

"Ask Bonaparte," says Donovan, seeing that Hawkins isn't taking him seriously. "Isn't it true, Bonaparte?"

"It is," I say, and Hawkins stops.

"Ah, for Christ's sake, chum."

"I mean it, chum," I say.

"You don't sound as if you meant it."

"If he doesn't mean it, I do," says Donovan, working himself up.

"What have you against me, Jeremiah Donovan?"

"I never said I had anything against you. But why did your people take out four of our prisoners and shoot them in cold blood?"

He took Hawkins by the arm and dragged him on, but it was impossible to make him understand that we were in earnest. I had the Smith and Wesson in my pocket and I kept fingering it and wondering what I'd do if they put up a fight for it or ran, and wishing to God they'd do one or the other. I knew if they did run for it, that I'd never fire on them. Hawkins wanted to know was Noble in it, and when we said yes, he asked us why Noble wanted to plug him. Why did any of us want to plug him? What had he done to us? Weren't we all chums? Didn't we understand him and didn't he understand us? Did we imagine for an instant that he'd shoot us for all the so-and-so officers in the so-and-so British Army?

By this time we'd reached the bog, and I was so sick I couldn't even answer him. We walked along the edge of it in the darkness, and every now and then Hawkins would call a halt and begin all over again, as if he was wound up, about our being chums, and I knew that nothing but the sight of the grave would convince him that we had to do it. And all the time I was hoping that something would happen; that they'd run for it or that Noble would take over the responsibility from me. I had the feeling that it was worse on Noble than on me.

IV

At last we saw the lantern in the distance and made towards it. Noble was carrying it, and Feeney was standing somewhere in the darkness behind him, and the picture of them so still and silent in the bogland brought it home to me that we were in earnest, and banished the last bit of hope I had.

Belcher, on recognizing Noble, said: "Hallo, chum," in his quiet way, but Hawkins flew at him at once, and the argument began all over again, only this time Noble had nothing to say for

himself and stood with his head down, holding the lantern between
his legs.

It was Jeremiah Donovan who did the answering. For the
twentieth time, as though it was haunting his mind, Hawkins
asked if anybody thought he'd shoot Noble.

"Yes, you would," says Jeremiah Donovan.

"No, I wouldn't, damn you!"

"You would, because you'd know you'd be shot for not
doing it."

"I wouldn't, not if I was to be shot twenty times over. I
wouldn't shoot a pal. And Belcher wouldn't — isn't that right,
Belcher?"

"That's right, chum," Belcher said, but more by way of
answering the question than of joining in the argument. Belcher
sounded as though whatever unforeseen thing he'd always been
waiting for had come at last.

"Anyway, who says Noble would be shot if I wasn't? What
do you think I'd do if I was in his place, out in the middle of a
blasted bog?"

"What would you do?" asks Donovan.

"I'd go with him wherever he was going, of course. Share
my last bob with him and stick by him through thick and thin.
No one can ever say of me that I let down a pal."

"We had enough of this," says Jeremiah Donovan, cocking
his revolver. "Is there any message you want to send?"

"No, there isn't."

"Do you want to say your prayers?"

Hawkins came out with a cold-blooded remark that even
shocked me and turned on Noble again.

"Listen to me, Noble," he says. "You and me are chums.
You can't come over to my side, so I'll come over to your side.
That show you I mean what I say? Give me a rifle and I'll go
along with you and the other lads."

Nobody answered him. We knew that was no way out.

"Hear what I'm saying?" he says. "I'm through with it. I'm
a deserter or anything else you like. I don't believe in your stuff,
but it's no worse than mine. That satisfy you?"

Noble raised his head, but Donovan began to speak and he
lowered it again without replying.

"For the last time, have you any messages to send?" says
Donovan in a cold, excited sort of voice.

"Shut up, Donovan! You don't understand me, but these
lads do. They're not the sort to make a pal and kill a pal. They're
not the tools of any capitalist."

I alone of the crowd saw Donovan raise his Webley to the back of Hawkins's neck, and as he did so I shut my eyes and tried to pray. Hawkins had begun to say something else when Donovan fired, and as I opened my eyes at the bang, I saw Hawkins stagger at the knees and lie out flat at Noble's feet, slowly and as quiet as a kid falling asleep, with the lantern-light on his lean legs and bright farmer's boots. We all stood very still, watching him settle out in the last agony.

Then Belcher took out a handkerchief and began to tie it about his own eyes (in our excitement we'd forgotten to do the same for Hawkins), and, seeing it wasn't big enough, turned and asked for the loan of mine. I gave it to him and he knotted the two together and pointed with his foot at Hawkins.

"He's not quite dead," he says. "Better give him another." Sure enough, Hawkins's left knee is beginning to rise. I bend down and put my gun to his head; then, recollecting myself, I get up again. Belcher understands what's in my mind.

"Give him his first," he says. "I don't mind. Poor bastard, we don't know what's happening to him now."

I knelt and fired. By this time I didn't seem to know what I was doing. Belcher, who was fumbling a bit awkwardly with the handkerchiefs, came out with a laugh as he heard the shot. It was the first time I heard him laugh and it sent a shudder down my back; it sounded so unnatural.

"Poor bugger!" he said quietly. "And last night he was so curious about it all. It's very queer, chums, I always think. Now he knows as much about it as they'll ever let him know, and last night he was all in the dark."

Donovan helped him to tie the handkerchiefs about his eyes. "Thanks, chum," he said. Donovan asked if there were any messages he wanted sent.

"No, chum," he says. "Not for me. If any of you would like to write to Hawkins's mother, you'll find a letter from her in his pocket. He and his mother were great chums. But my missus left me eight years ago. Went away with another fellow and took the kid with her. I like the feeling of a home, as you may have noticed, but I couldn't start again after that."

It was an extraordinary thing, but in those few minutes Belcher said more than in all the weeks before. It was just as if the sound of the shot had started a flood of talk in him and he could go on the whole night like that, quite happily, talking about himself. We stood round like fools now that he couldn't see us any longer. Donovan looked at Noble, and Noble shook his head. Then Donovan raised his Webley, and at that moment Belcher

gives his queer laugh again. He may have thought we were talking
about him, or perhaps he noticed the same thing I'd noticed and
couldn't understand it.

"Excuse me, chums," he says. "I feel I'm talking the hell
of a lot, and so silly, about my being so handy about a house and
things like that. But this thing came on me suddenly. You'll
forgive me, I'm sure."

"You don't want to say a prayer?" asked Donovan.

"No, chum," he says. "I don't think it would help. I'm
ready, and you boys want to get it over."

"You understand that we're only doing our duty?" says
Donovan.

Belcher's head was raised like a blind man's, so that you
could only see his chin and the tip of his nose in the lantern-light.

"I never could make out what duty was myself," he said.
"I think you're all good lads, if that's what you mean. I'm not complaining."

Noble, just as if he couldn't bear any more of it, raised his
fist at Donovan, and in a flash Donovan raised his gun and fired.
The big man went over like a sack of meal, and this time there
was no need of a second shot.

I don't remember much about the burying, but that it was
worse than all the rest because we had to carry them to the grave.
It was all mad lonely with nothing but a patch of lantern-light
between ourselves and the dark, and birds hooting and screeching
all round, disturbed by the guns. Noble went through Hawkins's
belongings to find the letter from his mother, and then joined his
hands together. He did the same with Belcher. Then, when we'd
filled in the grave, we separated from Jeremiah Donovan and
Feeney and took our tools back to the shed. All the way we didn't
speak a word. The kitchen was dark and cold as we'd left it, and
the old woman was sitting over the hearth, saying her beads. We
walked past her into the room, and Noble struck a match to light
the lamp. She rose quietly and came to the doorway with all her
cantankerousness gone.

"What did ye do with them?" she asked in a whisper, and
Noble started so that the match went out in his hand.

"What's that?" he asked without turning round.

"I heard ye," she said.

"What did you hear?" asked Noble.

"I heard ye. Do ye think I didn't hear ye, putting the spade
back in the houseen?"

Noble struck another match and this time the lamp lit for
him.

"Was that what ye did to them?" she asked.

Then, by God, in the very doorway, she fell on her knees and began praying, and after looking at her for a minute or two Noble did the same by the fireplace. I pushed my way out past her and left them at it. I stood at the door, watching the stars and listening to the shrieking of the birds dying out over the bogs. It is so strange what you feel at times like that you can't describe it. Noble says he saw everything ten times the size, as though there were nothing in the whole world but that little patch of bog with the two Englishmen stiffening into it, but with me it was as if the patch of bog where the Englishmen were was a million miles away, and even Noble and the old woman, mumbling behind me, and the birds and the bloody stars were all far away, and I was somehow very small and very lost and lonely like a child astray in the snow. And anything that happened to me afterwards, I never felt the same about again.

QUESTIONS

1. Although the narrator, Noble, and Donovan are all patriotic Irishmen, Donovan's attitude toward the English prisoners is quite different from that of the other two. How does that difference in attitude help point up the story's theme?
2. How does the constant bickering between Noble and Hawkins help to prepare us for the conclusion of the story? How does it contribute to the theme?
3. When he hears he is about to be shot, Hawkins, to save his life, volunteers to join the Irish cause. Is his turnabout simply evidence of his cowardice and hypocrisy? Explain.
4. Throughout most of the story Belcher is shy and speaks little; just before his execution, however, he suddenly becomes loquacious. Is he trying to stall for time? Would it have been more in character for Belcher to have remained stoically taciturn to the end, or do the narrator's remarks about Belcher's change make it plausible?
5. Does the old woman's presence in the story merely furnish local color or picturesqueness? If so, is it necessary or desirable? Or does her presence further contribute to the story's meaning? If so, how?
6. The following is the last paragraph of an earlier version:

> So then, by God, she fell on her two knees by the door, and began telling her beads, and after a minute or two Noble went on his knees by the fireplace, so I pushed my way past her, and stood at the door, watching the stars and listening to the damned shrieking of the birds.

It is so strange what you feel at such moments, and not to be written afterwards. Noble says he felt he seen everything ten times as big, perceiving nothing around him but the little patch of black bog with the two Englishmen stiffening into it; but with me it was the other way, as though the patch of bog where the two Englishmen were was a thousand miles away from me, and even Noble mumbling just behind me and the old woman and the birds and the bloody stars were all far away, and I was somehow very small and very lonely. And nothing that ever happened to me after I never felt the same about again.

Which is the more effective conclusion? Why?

7. How does the point of view help to emphasize the narrator's development from innocence to awareness? If the story had been told in the third person, how would it have affected the story's impact?

4
Allegory and Symbolism

In Chapter 2 we looked at some fables and parables, short fictions that were evidently meant to teach us: the characters clearly stood for principles of behavior, and the fictions as a whole evidently taught us lessons. Closely related to these forms is the **allegory,** which presents items that are understood to have equivalents: Bunyan's allegory, *The Pilgrim's Progress,* tells of a man named Christian, who, on the road to the Celestial City, encounters, among others, Giant Despair, Mr. Worldly Wiseman, and Faithful. What these are equivalent to is clear from their names, and it is clear that Christian's journey stands for the trials of a soul in this world.

Modern short stories rarely have either the parable's explicit moral or the allegory's clear system of equivalents, but they nevertheless can be said to be about something. As Robert Frost once said, "There is no story written that has any value at all, however straightforward it looks and free from doubleness, double entendre, and duplicity and double play, that you'd value at all if it didn't have intimations of something more than itself." Such a detailed, realistic story as "Guests of the Nation" (in the preceding chapter) may be a very good picture of Irish military life, but it also implies or suggests things not limited to that subject. This is not to say that after reading the story we discard the richly detailed narrative in favor of some abstraction that it implies — we do not throw away the narrative and cling to the implication. Frost went on to say, "The anecdote, the parable, the surface meaning has got to be good and got to be sufficient in itself." We feel that the narrative is meaningful. "Guests of the Nation" presents abundant precise details, and these details somehow add up to give the stories a generality or universality. The numerous details are so interrelated that they are a revelation of what is otherwise inexpressible.

In "Guests of the Nation" the narrative forces into the edges of our minds thoughts of the inhumanity of officialdom, the power of hatred, the average man's impotence, the power of friendship, and the enormous aftereffect a deed can have. These thoughts are sharply controlled by the details of the story, and they do not separate themselves from the details. But the thoughts are there, though we scarcely think of them; in the story they are just under the surface. Quite properly we take small notice of the substratum and concentrate on the surface details. But in other stories — such as parables and allegories — the details are so presented that we are forced to look from them to their implied equivalents.

Between these two extremes, writing that is almost all surface and writing that is almost all implication, are stories in which we strongly feel both the surface happenings and their implication. In *Place in Fiction,* Eudora Welty uses an image of a china lamp that unlit showed London and lit showed the Great Fire of London to explain literature that presents an interesting surface texture filled with rich significance. Though she is talking about the novel, her words apply equally to the short story, as a reading of her story, "Livvie" (page 67) will show. Like a painted porcelain lamp which, when illuminated, reveals an inner picture shining through the outer, the physical details in a work are illuminated from within by the author's imaginative vision. The outer painting, the literal details, presents "a continuous, shapely, pleasing, and finished surface to the eye," but this surface is not the whole: "The lamp alight is the combination of internal and external, glowing at the imagination as one; and so is the good novel. . . . The good novel should be steadily alight, revealing."

The unified picture, the details and what they suggest by virtue of the inner illumination with which the artist endows them, constitutes the symbolic level of a piece of literature. Here is Ishmael, in *Moby Dick,* perceiving the symbolic meaning of Father Mapple's ascent into the pulpit:

> I was not prepared to see Father Mapple after gaining the height, slowly turn round, and stooping over the pulpit, deliberately drag up the ladder step by step, till the whole was deposited within, leaving him impregnable in his little Quebec.
>
> I pondered some time without fully comprehending the reason for this. Father Mapple enjoyed such a wide reputation for sincerity and sanctity, that I could not suspect him of

courting notoriety by any mere tricks of the stage. No, thought I, there must be some sober reason for this thing; furthermore, it must symbolize something unseen. Can it be, then, that by that act of physical isolation, he signifies his spiritual withdrawal from the time, from all outward worldly ties and connections? Yes, for replenished with the meat and wine of the world, to the faithful man of God, this pulpit, I see, is a self-containing stronghold — a lofty Ehrenbreitstein, with a perennial well of water within the walls.

Ishmael's interpretation strikes the reader as well-stated and convincing, but many symbolic interpretations of literature (especially of *Moby Dick*) are neither. An ingenious reader may overcomplicate or overemphasize the symbolism of a work, or he may distort it by omitting some of the details and by unduly focusing on others. In many works the details glow, but the glow is so gentle and subtle that even to talk about them is to overstate them and to understate other equally important aspects of the work.

Yet if it is false to overstate the significance of a detail, it is also false to understate a significant detail. For example, the let's-have-no-nonsense literal reader who holds that Faulkner's "The Bear" (which appears later in this chapter) is only an adventure story about a bear hunt impoverishes the story by neglecting the rich symbolic meaning just as much as the symbol-hunter impoverishes O'Connor's "Guests of the Nation" by slighting the literal meaning. Faulkner's insistence on the bear's magnificence (the beast is compared to King Priam, to a locomotive, to an immortal creature) compels the reader to attend to its symbolic meaning, as does his insistence that not until "the three lifeless mechanicals" (the watch, the compass, and the stick) are surrendered can the bear be fully seen. Near the end of the story Faulkner underlines the symbolic quality by having the boy's father explain that Keats's "Ode on a Grecian Urn" is not (as the son says) only "about a girl"; the talk about a girl, the father goes on, is a vehicle by which Keats communicates an insight about truth. "He had to talk about something. . . . He was talking about truth." Faulkner, too, had to talk about something in order to communicate his insight, so he chose as a meaningful vehicle a bear hunt.

There has been a tendency, for about a century and a half now, to call **allegoric** those works whose images have precise equivalents that can be paraphrased with some accuracy, and to call **symbolic** those works whose images cast long shadows, give off multiple suggestions that do not allow for easy substitutions. This view might turn Father Mapple's gesture into an allegory and *Moby Dick* (which Melville called an allegory) into a symbolic work. D. H. Lawrence's pronouncement can serve as an example of modern usage:

> You can't give a great symbol a "meaning," any more than you can give a cat a "meaning." Symbols are organic units of consciousness with a life of their own, and you can never explain them away, because their value is dynamic, emotional, belonging to the sense-consciousness of the body and soul, and not simply mental. An allegorical image has a *meaning*. Mr. Facing-both-ways has a meaning. But I defy you to lay your finger on the full meaning of Janus, who is a symbol.

Whether or not we like the modern distinction between allegory and symbol (much that today is called symbolic was in the Middle Ages called allegorical), the distinction seems here to stay. But we should recall that every piece of art — including allegory as well as writing that might be called "realistic" — is, in Robert Frost's words, "a symbol small or great of the way the will has to pitch into commitments deeper and deeper to a rounded conclusion."

A NOTE ON SETTING

The **setting** of a story — not only the physical locale but also the time of day or year or century — may or may not be symbolic. Sometimes the setting is lightly sketched, presented only because the story had to take place somewhere and at some time. Often, however, the setting is more important, giving us the feel of the people who move through it. But if scenery is drawn in detail, yet adds up to nothing, we share the impatience Robert Louis Stevenson expressed in a letter: "'Roland approached the house; it had green doors and window blinds; and there was a scraper on the upper step.' To hell with Roland and the scraper." Yes, of course; but if the green doors and the scraper were to tell us something about the tenant, they could be important. And it might even be that the green doors and the scraper were so important that the story would be more or less about them. As the novelist Elizabeth Bowen has said, "Nothing can happen nowhere. The locale of the happening always colors the happening, and often, to a degree, shapes it." A rocky New England farm may be an analogue to the farmer who cultivates it, and the story may be as much about the farm as about the farmer. In Steinbeck's "Chrysanthemums" (page 294), Elisa's sense of isolation is partly established by the setting: a fog "closed off the Salinas Valley from the sky and from all the rest of the world." Another obvious example is the setting in Thomas Hardy's *The Return of the Native.* Oppressive Egdon Heath is so much a part of the novel that it almost takes on the role of a major character (Henry James neatly said that in fiction "landscape is character") and, in large part, it is made responsible for the tragic fate of the novel's characters.

Though the wilderness in "The Bear" is described in little detail, it is not mere background but an important part of what the story is about. Take, for example, the following passage:

> On the second day he even found the gutted log where he had first seen the crooked print. It was almost completely crumbled now, healing with unbelievable speed, a passionate and almost visible relinquishment, back into the earth from which the tree had grown.

This is not just local color: it is also one of the ways by which Faulkner talks about the importance of contact with nature; it helps us understand what is involved when (a page or two later) the boy

> . . . stood for a moment, alien and small in the green and topless solitude. . . . He hung the watch and compass carefully on a bush and leaned the stick beside them and relinquished completely to it.

It is no accident that "relinquish" appears in both passages; like the gutted log, the boy derives his vitality by merging himself with the wilderness. What the wilderness stands for is something that can be grasped only by reading the story.

William Faulkner (1897–1962)

The Bear

He was ten. But it had already begun, long before that day when at last he wrote his age in two figures and he saw for the first time the camp where his father and Major de Spain and old General Compson and the others spent two weeks each November and two weeks again each June. He had already inherited then, without ever having seen it, the tremendous bear with one trap-ruined foot which, in an area almost a hundred miles deep, had earned itself a name, a definite designation like a living man.

He had listened to it for years: the long legend of corncribs rifled, of shotes and grown pigs and even calves carried bodily into the woods and devoured, of traps and deadfalls overthrown and dogs mangled and slain, and shotgun and even rifle charges delivered at point-blank range and with no more effect than so many peas blown through a tube by a boy — a corridor of wreckage and destruction beginning back before he was born, through which sped, not fast but rather with the ruthless and irresistible deliberation of a locomotive, the shaggy tremendous shape.

It ran in his knowledge before he ever saw it. It loomed and towered in his dreams before he even saw the unaxed woods where it left its crooked print, shaggy, huge, red-eyed, not malevolent but just big — too big for the dogs which tried to bay it, for the horses which tried to ride it down, for the men and the bullets they fired into it, too big for the very country which was its constricting scope. He seemed to see it entire with a child's complete divination before he ever laid eyes on either — the doomed wilderness whose edges were being constantly and punily gnawed at by men with axes and plows who feared it because it was wilderness, men myriad and nameless even to one another in the land where the old bear had earned a name, through which ran not even a mortal animal but an anachronism, indomitable and invincible, out of an old dead time, a phantom, epitome and apotheosis of the old wild life at which the puny humans swarmed and hacked in a fury of abhorrence and fear, like pygmies about the ankles of a drowsing elephant: the old bear solitary, indomitable and alone, widowered, childless, and absolved of mortality — old Priam reft of his old wife and having outlived all his sons.

Until he was ten, each November he would watch the wagon containing the dogs and the bedding and food and guns and his father and Tennie's Jim, the Negro, and Sam Fathers, the Indian, son of a slave woman and a Chickasaw chief, depart on the road to town, to Jefferson, where Major de Spain and the others would join them. To the boy, at seven, eight, and nine, they were not going into the Big Bottom to hunt bear and deer, but to keep yearly rendezvous with the bear which they did not even intend to kill. Two weeks later they would return, with no trophy, no head and skin. He had not expected it. He had not even been afraid it would be in the wagon. He believed that even after he was ten and his father would let him go too, for those two weeks in November, he would merely make another one, along with his father and Major de Spain and General Compson and the others, the dogs which feared to bay at it and the rifles and shotguns which failed even to bleed it, in the yearly pageant of the old bear's furious immortality.

Then he heard the dogs. It was in the second week of his first time in the camp. He stood with Sam Fathers against a big oak beside the faint crossing where they had stood each dawn for nine days now, hearing the dogs. He had heard them once before, one morning last week — a murmur, sourceless, echoing through the wet woods, swelling presently into separate voices which he could recognize and call by name. He had raised and cocked the gun as Sam told him and stood motionless again while the uproar, the invisible course, swept up and past and faded; it seemed to him that he could actually see the deer, the buck, blond, smoke-colored, elongated with speed, fleeing, vanishing, the woods, the gray solitude, still ringing even when the cries of the dogs had died away.

"Now let the hammers down," Sam said.

"You knew they were not coming here too," he said.

"Yes," Sam said. "I want you to learn how to do when you didn't shoot. It's after the chance for the bear or the deer has done already come and gone that men and dogs get killed."

"Anyway," he said, "it was just a deer."

Then on the tenth morning he heard the dogs again. And he readied the too-long, too-heavy gun as Sam had taught him, before Sam even spoke. But this time it was no deer, no ringing chorus of dogs running strong on a free scent, but a moiling yapping an octave too high, with something more than indecision and even abjectness in it, not even moving very fast, taking a long time to pass completely out of hearing, leaving then somewhere in the air that echo, thin, slightly hysterical, abject, almost grieving, with no sense of a fleeting, unseen, smoke-colored, grass-eating shape ahead of it, and Sam, who had taught him first of all to cock the gun and take position where he could see everywhere and then never move again, had himself moved up beside him; he could hear Sam breathing at his shoulder, and he could see the arched curve of the old man's inhaling nostrils.

"Hah," Sam said. "Not even running. Walking."

"Old Ben!" the boy said. "But up here!" he cried. "Way up here!"

"He do it every year," Sam said. "Once. Maybe to see who in camp this time, if he can shoot or not. Whether we got the dog yet that can bay and hold him. He'll take them to the river, then he'll send them back home. We may as well go back too; see how they look when they come back to camp."

When they reached the camp the hounds were already there, ten of them crouching back under the kitchen, the boy and Sam squatting to peer back into the obscurity where they had huddled, quiet, the eyes luminous, glowing at them and vanishing, and no sound, only that effluvium of something more than dog, stronger than dog and not just animal, just beast, because still there had been nothing in front of that abject and almost painful yapping save the solitude, the wilderness, so that when the eleventh hound came in at noon and with all the others watching — even old Uncle Ash, who called himself first a cook — Sam daubed the tattered ear and the raked shoulder with turpentine and axle grease, to the boy it was still no living creature, but the wilderness which, leaning for the moment down, had patted lightly once the hound's temerity.

"Just like a man," Sam said. "Just like folks. Put off as long as she could having to be brave, knowing all the time that sooner or later she would have to be brave to keep on living with herself, and knowing all the time beforehand what was going to happen to her when she done it."

That afternoon, himself on the one-eyed wagon mule which did not mind the smell of blood nor, as they told him, of bear, and with Sam on the other one, they rode for more than three hours through the rapid, shortening winter day. They followed no path, no trail even that he could see; almost at once they were in a country which he had never seen before. Then he knew why Sam had made him ride the mule which would not spook. The sound one stopped short and tried to whirl and bolt even as Sam got down, blowing its breath, jerking and wrenching at the rein, while Sam held it, coaxing it forward with his voice, since he could not risk tying it, drawing it forward while the boy got down from the marred one.

Then, standing beside Sam in the gloom of the dying afternoon, he looked down at the rotted over-turned log, gutted and scored with claw marks and, in the wet earth beside it, the print of the enormous warped two-toed foot. He knew now what he had smelled when he peered under the kitchen where the dogs huddled. He realized for the first time that the bear which had run in his listening and loomed in his dreams since before he could remember to the contrary, and which, therefore, must have existed in the listening and dreams of his father and Major de Spain and even old General Compson, too, before they began to remember in their turn, was a mortal animal, and that if they had departed for the camp each November without any actual hope of bringing its trophy back, it was not because it could not be slain, but because so far they had had no actual hope to.

"Tomorrow," he said.

"We'll try tomorrow," Sam said. "We ain't got the dog yet."

"We've got eleven. They ran him this morning."

"It won't need but one," Sam said. "He ain't here. Maybe he ain't nowhere. The only other way will be for him to run by accident over somebody that has a gun."

"That wouldn't be me," the boy said. "It will be Walter or Major or ———"

"It might," Sam said. "You watch close in the morning. Because he's smart. That's how come he has lived this long. If he gets hemmed up and has to pick out somebody to run over, he will pick out you."

"How?" the boy said. "How will he know — " He ceased. "You mean he already knows me, that I ain't never been here before, ain't had time to find out yet whether I — " He ceased again, looking at Sam, the old man whose face revealed nothing until it smiled. He said humbly, not even amazed, "It was me he was watching. I don't reckon he did need to come but once."

The next morning they left the camp three hours before daylight. They rode this time because it was too far to walk, even the dogs in the wagon; again the first gray light found him in a place which he had never seen before, where Sam had placed him and told him to stay and then departed. With the gun which was too big for him, which did not even belong to him, but to Major de Spain, and which he had fired only once — at a stump on the first day, to learn the recoil and how to reload it — he stood against a gum tree beside a little bayou whose black still water crept without movement out of a canebrake and crossed a small clearing and into cane again, where, invisible, a bird — the big woodpecker called Lord-to-God by Negroes — clattered at a dead limb.

It was a stand like any other, dissimilar only in incidentals to the one where he had stood each morning for ten days; a territory new to him, yet no less familiar than that other one which, after almost two weeks, he had come to believe he knew a little — the same solitude, the same loneliness through which human beings had merely passed without altering it, leaving no mark, no scar, which looked exactly as it must have looked when the first ancestor of Sam Fathers' Chickasaw predecessors crept into it and looked about, club or stone ax or bone arrow drawn and poised; different only because, squatting at the edge of the kitchen, he smelled the hounds huddled and cringing beneath it and saw the raked ear and shoulder of the one who, Sam said, had had to be brave once in order to live with herself, and saw yesterday in the earth beside the gutted log the print of the living foot.

He heard no dogs at all. He never did hear them. He only heard the drumming of the woodpecker stop short off and knew that the bear was looking at him. He never saw it. He did not know whether it was in front of him or behind him. He did not move, holding the useless gun, which he had not even had warning to cock and which even now he did not cock, tasting in his saliva that taint as of brass which he knew now because he had smelled it when he peered under the kitchen at the huddled dogs.

Then it was gone. As abruptly as it had ceased, the wood-pecker's dry, monotonous clatter set up again, and after a while he even believed he could hear the dogs — a murmur, scarce a sound even, which he had probably been hearing for some time before he even remarked it, drifting into hearing and then out again, dying away. They came nowhere near him. If it was a bear they ran, it was another bear. It was Sam himself who came out of the cane and crossed the bayou, followed by the injured bitch of yesterday. She was almost at heel, like a bird dog, making no sound. She came and crouched against his leg, trembling, staring off into the cane.

"I didn't see him," he said. "I didn't, Sam!"

"I know it," Sam said. "He done the looking. You didn't hear him neither, did you?"

"No," the boy said. "I ——"

"He's smart," Sam said. "Too smart." He looked down at the hound, trembling faintly and steadily against the boy's knee. From the raked shoulder a few drops of fresh blood oozed and clung. "Too big. We ain't got the dog yet. But maybe someday. Maybe not next time. But someday."

So I must see him, he thought. *I must look at him.* Otherwise, it seemed to him that it would go on like this forever, as it had gone on with his father and Major de Spain, who was older than his father, and even with old General Compson, who had been old enough to be a brigade commander in 1865. Otherwise, it would go on so forever, next time and next time, after and after and after. It seemed to him that he could never see the two of them, himself and the bear, shadowy in the limbo from which time emerged, becoming time; the old bear absolved of mortality and himself partaking, sharing a little of it, enough of it. And he knew now what he had smelled in the huddled dogs and tasted in his saliva. He recognized fear. *So I will have to see him,* he thought, without dread or even hope. *I will have to look at him.*

It was in June of the next year. He was eleven. They were in camp again, celebrating Major de Spain's and General Compson's birthdays. Although the one had been born in September and the other in the depth of winter and in another decade, they had met for two weeks to fish and shoot squirrels and turkey and run coons and wildcats with the dogs at night. That is, he and Boon Hoggenbeck and the Negroes fished and shot squirrels and ran the coons and cats, because the proved hunters, not only Major de Spain and old General Compson, who spent those two weeks sitting in a rocking chair before a tremendous iron pot of Brunswick stew, stirring and tasting, with old Ash to quarrel with about how he was making it and Tennie's Jim to pour whiskey from the demijohn into the tin dipper from which he drank it, but even the boy's father and Walter Ewell, who were still young enough, scorned such, other than shooting the wild gobblers with pistols for wagers on their marksmanship.

Or, that is, his father and the others believed he was hunting squirrels. Until the third day, he thought that Sam Fathers believed that too. Each morning he would leave the camp right after breakfast. He had his own gun now, a Christmas present. He went back to the tree beside the bayou where he had stood that morning. Using the compass which old General Compson had given him, he ranged from that point; he was teaching himself to be a better-than-fair woodsman without knowing he was doing it. On the second day he even found the gutted log where he had first seen the crooked print. It was almost completely crumbled now, healing with unbelievable speed, a passionate and almost visible relinquishment, back into the earth from which the tree had grown.

He ranged the summer woods now, green with gloom; if anything, actually dimmer than in November's gray dissolution, where, even at noon, the sun fell only in intermittent dappling upon the earth, which never completely dried out and which crawled with snakes — moccasins and water snakes and rattlers, themselves the color of the dappling gloom, so that he would not always see them until they moved, returning later and later, first day, second day, passing in the twilight of the third evening the little log pen enclosing the log stable where Sam was putting up the horses for the night.

"You ain't looked right yet," Sam said.

He stopped. For a moment he didn't answer. Then he said peacefully, in a peaceful rushing burst as when a boy's miniature dam in a little brook gives way, "All right. But how? I went to the bayou. I even found that log again. I ——"

"I reckon that was all right. Likely he's been watching you. You never saw his foot?"

"I," the boy said — "I didn't — I never thought ——"

"It's the gun," Sam said. He stood beside the fence motionless

— the old man, the Indian, in the battered faded overalls and the five-cent straw hat which in the Negro's race had been the badge of his enslavement and was now the regalia of his freedom. The camp — the clearing, the house, the barn and its tiny lot with which Major de Spain in his turn had scratched punily and evanescently at the wilderness — faded in the dusk, back into the immemorial darkness of the woods. *The gun,* the boy thought. *The gun.*

"Be scared," Sam said. "You can't help that. But don't be afraid. Ain't nothing in the woods going to hurt you unless you corner it, or it smells that you are afraid. A bear or a deer, too, has got to be scared of a coward the same as a brave man has got to be."

The gun, the boy thought.

"You will have to choose," Sam said.

He left the camp before daylight, long before Uncle Ash would wake in his quilts on the kitchen floor and start the fire for breakfast. He had only the compass and a stick for snakes. He could go almost a mile before he would begin to need the compass. He sat on a log, the invisible compass in his invisible hand, while the secret night sounds, fallen still at his movements, scurried again and then ceased for good, and the owls ceased and gave over to the waking of day birds, and he could see the compass. Then he went fast yet still quietly; he was becoming better and better as a woodsman, still without having yet realized it.

He jumped a doe and a fawn at sunrise, walked them out of the bed, close enough to see them — the crash of undergrowth, the white scut, the fawn scudding behind her faster than he had believed it could run. He was hunting right, upwind, as Sam had taught him; not that it mattered now. He had left the gun; of his own will and relinquishment he had accepted not a gambit, not a choice, but a condition in which not only the bear's heretofore inviolable anonymity but all the old rules and balances of hunter and hunted had been abrogated. He would not even be afraid, not even in the moment when the fear would take him completely — blood, skin, bowels, bones, memory from the long time before it became his memory — all save that thin, clear, immortal lucidity which alone differed him from this bear and from all the other bear and deer he would ever kill in the humility and pride of his skill and endurance, to which Sam had spoken when he leaned in the twilight on the lot fence yesterday.

By noon he was far beyond the little bayou, farther into the new and alien country than he had ever been. He was traveling now not only by the compass but by the old, heavy, biscuit-thick silver watch which had belonged to his grandfather. When he stopped at last, it was for the first time since he had risen from the log at dawn when he could see the compass. It was far enough. He had left the camp nine hours ago; nine hours from now, dark would have already been an hour old. But he didn't think that. He thought, *All right. Yes. But what?* and stood for a moment, alien and small in the green and topless solitude, answering his own question before it had formed and ceased. It was the watch, the compass, the stick — the three lifeless mechanicals with which for nine hours he had fended the wilderness off; he hung the watch and compass carefully on a bush and leaned the stick beside them and relinquished completely to it.

He had not been going very fast for the last two or three hours. He went no faster now, since distance would not matter even if he could have gone fast. And he was trying to keep a bearing on the tree where he had left the compass, trying to complete a circle which would bring him back to it or at least intersect itself, since direction would not matter now either. But the tree was not here, and he did as Sam had schooled him — made the next circle in the opposite direction, so that the two patterns would bisect somewhere, but crossing no print of his own feet, finding the tree at last, but in the wrong place — no bush, no compass, no watch — and the tree not even the tree, because there was a down log beside it and he did what Sam Fathers had told him was the next thing and the last.

As he sat down on the log he saw the crooked print — the warped, tremendous, two-toed indentation which, even as he watched it, filled with water. As he looked up, the wilderness coalesced, solidified — the glade, the tree he sought, the bush, the watch and the compass glinting where the ray of sunshine touched them. Then he saw the bear. It did not emerge, appear; it was just there, immobile, solid, fixed in the hot dappling of the green and windless noon, not as big as he had dreamed it, but as big as he had expected it, bigger, dimensionless, against the dappled obscurity, looking at him where he sat quietly on the log and looked back at it.

Then it moved. It made no sound. It did not hurry. It crossed the glade, walking for an instant into the full glare of the sun; when it reached the other side it stopped again and looked back at him across one shoulder while his quiet breathing inhaled and exhaled three times.

Then it was gone. It didn't walk into the woods, the undergrowth. It faded, sank back into the wilderness as he had watched a fish, a huge old bass, sink and vanish into the dark depths of its pool without even any movement of its fins.

He thought, *It will be next fall.* But it was not next fall, nor the next nor the next. He was fourteen then. He had killed his buck, and Sam Fathers had marked his face with the hot blood, and in the next year he killed a bear. But even before that accolade he had become as competent in the woods as many grown men with the same experience; by his fourteenth year he was a better woodsman than most grown men with more. There was no territory within thirty miles of the camp that he did not know — bayou, ridge, brake, landmark, tree and path. He could have led anyone to any point in it without deviation, and brought them out again. He knew the game trails that even Sam Fathers did not know; in his thirteenth year he found a buck's bedding place, and unbeknown to his father he borrowed Walter Ewell's rifle and lay in wait at dawn and killed the buck when it walked back to the bed, as Sam had told him how the old Chickasaw fathers did.

But not the old bear, although by now he knew its footprints better than he did his own, and not only the crooked one. He could see any one of three sound ones and distinguish it from any other, and not only by its size. There were other bears within these thirty miles which left tracks almost as large, but this was more than that. If Sam Fathers had been his mentor and the back-yard rabbits and squirrels at home his kindergarten, then the wilderness the old bear ran was his college, the old male bear itself, so long unwifed and childless as to have become its own ungendered progenitor, was his alma mater. But he never saw it.

He could find the crooked print now almost whenever he liked, fifteen or ten or five miles, or sometimes nearer the camp than that. Twice while on stand during the three years he heard the dogs strike its trail by accident; on the second time they jumped it seemingly, the voices high, abject, almost human in hysteria, as on that first morning two years ago. But not the bear itself. He would remember that noon three years ago, the glade, himself and the bear fixed during that moment in the windless and dappled blaze, and it would seem to him that it had never happened, that he had dreamed that too. But it had happened. They had looked at each other, they had emerged from the wilderness old as earth, synchronized to the instant by something more than the blood that moved the flesh and bones which bore them, and touched, pledged something, affirmed, something more lasting than the frail web of bones and flesh which any accident could obliterate.

Then he saw it again. Because of the very fact that he thought of nothing else, he had forgotten to look for it. He was still hunting with Walter Ewell's rifle. He saw it cross the end of a long blow-down, a corridor where a tornado had swept, rushing through rather than over the tangle of trunks and branches as a locomotive would have, faster than he had ever believed it could move, almost as fast as a deer even, because a deer would have spent most of that time in the air, faster than he could bring the rifle sights up with it. And now he knew what had been wrong during all the three years. He sat on a log, shaking and trembling as if he had never seen the woods before nor anything that ran them, wondering with incredulous amazement how he could have forgotten the very thing which Sam Fathers had told him and which the bear itself had proved the next day and had now returned after three years to reaffirm.

And now he knew what Sam Fathers had meant about the right dog, a dog in which size would mean less than nothing. So when he returned alone in April — school was out then, so that the sons of farmers could help with the land's planting, and at last his father had granted him permission, on his promise to be back in four days — he had the dog. It was his own, a mongrel of the sort called by Negroes a fyce, a ratter, itself not much bigger than a rat and possessing that bravery which had long since stopped being courage and had become foolhardiness.

It did not take four days. Alone again, he found the trail on the first morning. It was not a stalk; it was an ambush. He timed the meeting almost as if it were an appointment with a human being. Himself holding the fyce muffled in a feed sack and Sam Fathers with two of the hounds on a piece of a plowline rope, they lay down wind of the trail at dawn of the second morning. They were so close that the bear turned without even running, as if in surprised amazement at the shrill and frantic uproar of the released fyce, turning at bay against the trunk of a tree, on its hind feet; it seemed to the boy that it would never stop rising, taller and taller, and even the two hounds seemed to take a desperate and despairing courage from the fyce, following it as it went in.

Then he realized that the fyce was actually not going to stop. He flung, threw the gun away, and ran; when he overtook and grasped the frantically pin-wheeling little dog, it seemed to him that he was directly under the bear.

He could smell it, strong and hot and rank. Sprawling, he looked up to where it loomed and towered over him like a cloudburst and colored like a thunderclap, quite familiar, peacefully and even lucidly familiar, until he remembered: This was the way he had used to dream about it. Then it was gone. He didn't see it go. He knelt, holding the frantic fyce with both hands, hearing the abashed wailing of the hounds drawing farther and farther away, until Sam came up. He carried the gun. He laid it down quietly beside the boy and stood looking down at him.

"You've done seed him twice now with a gun in your hands," he said. "This time you couldn't have missed him."

The boy rose. He still held the fyce. Even in his arms and clear of the ground, it yapped frantically, straining and surging after the fading uproar of the two hounds like a tangle of wire springs. He was panting a little but he was neither shaking nor trembling now.

"Neither could you!" he said. "You had the gun! Neither did you!"

"And you didn't shoot," his father said. "How close were you?"

"I don't know, sir," he said. "There was a big wood tick inside his right hind leg. I saw that. But I didn't have the gun then."

"But you didn't shoot when you had the gun," his father said. "Why?"

But he didn't answer, and his father didn't wait for him to, rising and crossing the room, across the pelt of the bear which the boy had killed two years ago and the larger one which his father had killed before he was born, to the bookcase beneath the mounted head of the boy's first buck. It was the room which his father called the office, from which all the plantation business was transacted; in it for the fourteen years of his life he had heard the best of all talking. Major de Spain would be there and sometimes old General Compson, and Walter Ewell and Boon Hoggenbeck and Sam Fathers and Tennie's Jim, too, were hunters, knew the woods and what ran them.

He would hear it, not talking himself but listening — the wilderness, the big woods, bigger and older than any recorded document of white man fatuous enough to believe he had bought any fragment of it or Indian ruthless enough to pretend that any fragment of it had been his to convey. It was of the men, not white nor black nor red, but men, hunters with the will and hardihood to endure and the humility and skill to survive, and the dogs and the bear and deer juxtaposed and reliefed against it, ordered and compelled by and within the wilderness in the ancient and unremitting contest by the ancient and immitigable rules which voided all regrets and brooked no quarter, the voices quiet and weighty and deliberate for retrospection and recollection and exact remembering, while he squatted in the blazing firelight as Tennie's Jim squatted, who stirred only to put more wood on the fire and to pass the bottle from one glass to another. Because the bottle was always present, so that after a while it seemed to him that those fierce instants of heart and brain and courage and wiliness and speed were concentrated and distilled into that brown liquor which not women, not boys and children, but only hunters drank, drinking not of the blood they had spilled but some condensation of the wild immortal spirit, drinking it moderately, humbly even, not with the pagan's base hope of acquiring the virtues of cunning and strength and speed, but in salute to them.

His father returned with the book and sat down again and opened it. "Listen," he said. He read the five stanzas aloud, his voice quiet and deliberate in the room where there was no fire now because it was already spring. Then he looked up. The boy watched him. "All right," his father said. "Listen." He read again, but only the second stanza this time, to the end of it, the last two lines, and closed the book and put it on the table beside him. "She cannot fade, though thou hast not thy bliss, forever wilt thou love, and she be fair," he said.

"He's talking about a girl," the boy said.

"He had to talk about something," his father said. Then he said, "He was talking about truth. Truth doesn't change. Truth is one thing. It covers all things which touch the heart — honor and pride and pity and justice and courage and love. Do you see now?"

He didn't know. Somehow it was simpler than that. There was an old bear, fierce and ruthless, not merely just to stay alive, but with the fierce pride of liberty and freedom, proud enough of the liberty and freedom to see it threatened without fear or even alarm; nay, who at times even seemed deliberately to put that freedom and liberty in jeopardy in order to savor them, to remind his old strong bones and flesh to keep supple and quick to defend and preserve them. There was an old man, son of a Negro slave and an Indian king, inheritor on the one side of the long chronicle of a people who had learned humility through suffering, and pride through the endurance which survived the suffering and injustice, and on the other side, the chronicle of a people even longer in the land than the first, yet who no longer existed in the land at all save in the solitary brotherhood of an old Negro's alien blood and the wild and invincible spirit of an old bear. There was a boy who wished to learn humility and pride in order to become skillful and worthy in the woods, who suddenly found himself becoming so skillful so rapidly that he feared he would never become worthy because he had not learned humility and pride, although he had tried to, until one day and as suddenly he discovered that an old man who could not have defined either had led him, as though by the hand, to that point where an old bear and a little mongrel of a dog showed him that, by possessing one thing other, he would possess them both.

And a little dog, nameless and mongrel and many-fathered, grown, yet weighing less than six pounds, saying as if to itself, "I can't be dangerous, because there's nothing much smaller than I am; I can't be fierce, because they would call it just a noise; I can't be humble, because I'm already too close to the ground to genuflect; I can't be proud, because I wouldn't be near enough to it for anyone to know who was casting the shadow, and I don't even know that I'm not going to heaven, because they have already decided that I don't possess an immortal soul. So all I can be is brave. But it's all right. I can be that, even if they still call it just noise."

That was all. It was simple, much simpler than somebody talking in a book about youth and a girl he would never need to grieve over, because he could never approach any nearer her and would never have to get any farther away. He had heard about a bear, and finally got big enough to trail it, and he trailed it four years and at last met it with a gun in his hands and he didn't shoot. Because a little dog — But he could have shot long before the little dog covered the twenty yards to where the bear waited, and Sam Fathers could have shot at any time during that interminable minute while Old Ben stood on his hind feet over them. He stopped. His father was watching him gravely across the spring-rife twilight of the room; when he spoke, his words were as quiet as the twilight, too, not loud, because they did not need to be because they would last. "Courage, and honor, and pride," his father said, "and pity, and love of justice and of liberty. They all touch the heart, and what the heart holds to becomes truth, as far as we know the truth. Do you see now?"

Sam, and Old Ben, and Nip, he thought. And himself too. He had been all right too. His father had said so. "Yes, sir," he said.

Several of Faulkner's comments on "The Bear," made during interviews at the University of Virginia (printed in *Faulkner in the University,* ed. F. L. Gwynn and J. W. Blotner, 1959), though not necessarily definitive, are suggestive:

One symbol was the bear represented the vanishing wilderness. The little dog that wasn't scared of the bear represented the indomitable spirit of man. I'll have to dig back and get up some more of those symbols, because I have learned around an even dozen that I put into that story without knowing it. But there are two pretty good ones that you can hold to.

Asked the significance of the fyce, Faulkner said that it is

. . . the antithesis of the bear. The bear represented the obsolete primitive. The fyce represents the creature who has coped with environment and is still on top of it, you might say. That he has — instead of sticking to his breeding and becoming a decadent degenerate creature, he has mixed himself up with the good stock where he picked and chose. And he's quite smart, he's quite brave. All's against him is his size. But I never knew a fyce yet that realized that he wasn't big as anything else he ever saw, even a bear.

Asked to explain what the "one thing" was that would enable the boy to learn "humility and pride," Faulkner replied: "Courage, it was. A little dog that never saw a bear bigger than he was."

QUESTIONS

1. In the opening three paragraphs of the story, the pronoun "it" usually refers to Old Ben. But does "it" always have the same referent in this opening section of the story? How might the "it" be said to function ambiguously and thus prepare the reader for the symbolism in the story? How does the fact that the boy is nameless throughout the story add to the symbolic meaning?

2. Compare the characterizations of the bear in the second and third paragraphs. How do they affect our attitude toward the bear? Does the fact that it is given a name and does the name itself affect our attitude toward Old Ben?

3. What is the distinction Sam Fathers makes between being "scared" and being "afraid"? Aren't the words synonymous, or is there, in the context, some crucial difference? If so, what might it be?

4. The boy relinquishes the three lifeless mechanicals before he is permitted to see the bear. Why? Is Faulkner making some social comment about modern man that goes beyond the limits of a bear hunt? How is the following letter, written by Faulkner to *The New York Times* (December 26, 1954), relevant to "The Bear"?

This is about the Italian airliner which undershot the runway and crashed at Idlewild after failing three times to hold the instrument glide-path which would have brought it down to the runway.

It is written on the idea (postulate, if you like) that the instrument or instruments — altimeter-cum-drift-indicator — failed or had failed, was already out of order or incorrect before the moment when the pilot committed irrevocably the aircraft to it.

It is written in grief. Not just for the sorrow of the bereaved ones of those who died in the crash, and for the airline, the public carrier which, in selling the tickets, promised or anyway implied security for the trip, but for the crew, the pilot himself, who will be blamed for the crash and whose record and memory will be tarnished by it; who, along with his unaware passengers, was victim not even of the failed instruments but victim of that mystical, unquestioning, almost religious awe and veneration in which our culture has trained us to hold gadgets — any gadget, if it is only complex enough and cryptic enough and costs enough.

I imagine that even after the first failure to hold the glide-path, certainly after the second one, his instinct — the seat of his pants, call it what you will — after that many hours in the air, told him that something was wrong. And his seniority as a four-engine over-water captain probably told him where the trouble was. But he dared not accept that knowledge and (this presumes that even after the second failure he still had enough fuel left to reach a field which he could see) act on it.

Possibly at some time during the four attempts to land, very likely at some one of the final rapid seconds before he had irrevocably committed the aircraft — that compounding of mass and weight by velocity — to the ground, his co-pilot (or flight engineer or whoever else might have been in the cockpit at the time) probably said to him: "Look. We're wrong. Get the flaps and gear up and let's get to hell out of here." But he dared not. He dared not so flout and affront, even with his own life too at stake, our cultural postulate of the infallibility of machines, instruments, gadgets — a Power more ruthless even than the old Hebrew concept of its God, since ours is not even jealous and vengeful, caring nothing about individuals.

He dared not commit that sacrilege. If he had, nothing would have remained to him save to open the cockpit hatch and (a Roman) cast himself onto the turning blades of one of the inboard air-screws. I grieve for him, for that moment's victims. We all had better grieve for all people beneath a culture which holds any mechanical superior to any man simply because the one, being mechanical, is infallible, while the other, being nothing but man, is not just subject to failure but doomed to it.

5. On page 59 the hunters pass around a bottle. What is symbolized by this action?
6. Why doesn't the boy kill the bear?
7. A careful reading of Keats's "Ode on a Grecian Urn" (pages 459–460) may illuminate the father's comments to his son. What is the particular relevance of the second stanza?

5
Style

"Style" comes from the Latin word *stilus*, a pointed instrument used to engrave or write. The meaning has been transferred from the instrument to the product, so we talk of the style of a piece of writing, or, more generally, of an author's style, or, for that matter, of anyone's style — way of hitting a tennis ball, of dancing, of dealing with people, or whatever.

What style shall a writer use?

Put this way, it is clear that there is no simple answer; anything can be right or wrong, depending on what effect is sought. James Joyce, in *A Portrait of the Artist as a Young Man,* uses a variety of styles, and each of them is right. Here are three passages from the novel — the opening sentence, a sentence from the middle, and the closing sentence:

> Once upon a time and a very good time it was there was a moocow coming down along the road and this moocow that was down along the road met a nicens little boy named baby tuckoo. . . .

> Only at times, in the pauses of his desire, when the luxury that was wasting him gave room to a softer languor, the image of Mercedes traversed the background of his memory.

> April 27. Old father, old artificer, stand me now and ever in good stead.

The first of these, in a childlike style, describes the protagonist's infancy. The second, in a luxurious style, describes the fantasies of his adolescence. And the third, in a spare style, describes his preparation for self-exile.

Or consider the opening of D. H. Lawrence's "The Rocking-Horse Winner" (page 218):

> There was a woman who was beautiful, who started with all the advantages, yet she had no luck.

The fairy-tale tone, perhaps only faintly heard here, is continued at the beginning of the second paragraph:

> There were a boy and two little girls. They lived in a pleasant house, with a garden, and they had discrete servants, and felt themselves superior to anyone in the neighbourhood.

A responsive reader, hearing this special voice of a narrator, will be properly prepared for the strange, magical happenings that are related, and will recognize that the story, for all its magic, is a kind of fable about real life.

The following are the first two sentences in the opening paragraph of Eudora Welty's "Livvie":

> Solomon carried Livvie twenty-one miles away from her home when he married her. He carried her away up on the Old Natchez Trace into the deep country to live in his house.

These sentences can easily be transposed and combined into:

> When Solomon married Livvie, he carried her away up on the Old Natchez Trace into the deep country to live in his house, twenty-one miles away.

The words are the same, but everything is changed. By failing to repeat the structure of subject-verb ("Solomon carried," "He carried"), the suggestion of Livvie's own voice is lost. Though the lines, as Miss Welty wrote them, are not spoken by Livvie, they carry within them a suggestion of her simplicity. Take the first two sentences of the second paragraph:

> It was a nice house, inside and outside both. In the first place, it had three rooms.

These can be combined into:

> The three-room house was nice, inside and out.

Again, the innocence of Livvie's voice is missing. In these lines, Miss Welty is not communicating information only about Livvie's house; she is also giving us an image of Livvie's mind, and the paraphrase does not.

A more subtle example may be useful. When Miss Welty first published "Livvie," the third sentence of the opening paragraph was simply:

> She was sixteen then.

But in the revision, printed in this book, the sentence runs:

> She was sixteen — an only girl, then.

Of course the revision has an additional piece of information, but what is important for our present purpose is the difference in style. "She was sixteen then" is a quite ordinary sentence, such as any of us might write. But "She was sixteen — an only girl, then" presents us with a special mind. It almost seems to suggest that Livvie is no longer an only girl, yet this point is never made. What the revision adds is a hint of Livvie's slightly wistful, disjointed view of the past. Ordinarily the sentence might run, "She was sixteen then, an only girl'; by being placed at the end of the sentence, after some material that it does not logically follow, "then" is somewhat unexpected, rather like the last step down to the cellar. The slight jolt we feel in "then" both reveals Livvie's special way of thinking and gives the past an emphasis lacking in the original "She was sixteen then" and lacking in "She was sixteen then, an only girl."

These comments do not come near to revealing the special power of Miss Welty's sentences, but perhaps they have made clear that in good writing words cannot be rearranged without change in meaning. "I began to speak of style," Isaac Babel writes in one of his stories, "of the army of words, of the army in which all kinds of weapons may come into play. No iron can stab the heart with such force as a period put just at the right place."

A NOTE ON TONE

A speaker's tone of voice conveys part of the meaning: "Good Lord" can be a pious invocation; it can also be a blasphemous expletive, and the tone, quite as well as the context, can tell us which it is. **Tone** in a story is commonly defined as the author's voice (in distinction from the voices of the characters); it is, let us say, the author's attitude as the reader infers it. The characters may speak angrily, but the reader may rightly detect that the author's tone is gentle and compassionate. The characters may speak gaily and wittily, but the reader may rightly detect that the author's tone is scornful. When we talk about the author's sympathies and antipathies, his or her cynicism or solemnity or flippancy, we are talking about the author's tone. And it is through a pervasive style that the author's tone is heard.*

---

* Although Chapter 10, "The Speaking Tone of Voice," draws its illustrative material from poems, the points it makes are relevant here. The reader may find it useful to consult the first half-dozen pages of that chapter now.

Eudora Welty (b. 1909)

Livvie

Solomon carried Livvie twenty-one miles away from her home
when he married her. He carried her away up on the Old Natchez
Trace into the deep country to live in his house. She was sixteen
— an only girl, then. Once people said he thought nobody would
ever come along there. He told her himself that it had been a long
time, and a day she did not know about, since that road was a
traveled road with *people* coming and going. He was good to her,
but he kept her in the house. She had not thought that she could
not get back. Where she came from, people said an old man did
not want anybody in the world to ever find his wife, for fear they
would steal her back from him. Solomon asked her before he took
her, "Would she be happy?" — very dignified, for he was a colored
man that owned his land and had it written down in the courthouse;
and she said, "Yes, sir," since he was an old man and she was
young and just listened and answered. He asked her, if she was
choosing winter, would she pine for spring, and she said, "No
indeed." Whatever she said, always, was because he was an old
man . . . while nine years went by. All the time, he got old, and
he got so old he gave out. At least he slept the whole day in bed,
and she was young still.

It was a nice house, inside and outside both. In the first
place, it had three rooms. The front room was papered in holly
paper, with green palmettos from the swamp spaced at careful
intervals over the walls. There was fresh newspaper cut with fancy
borders on the mantelshelf, on which were propped photographs
of old or very young men printed in faint yellow — Solomon's
people. Solomon had a houseful of furniture. There was a double
settee, a tall scrolled rocker and an organ in the front room, all
around a three-legged table with a pink marble top, on which was
set a lamp with three gold feet, beside a jelly glass with pretty hen
feathers in it. Behind the front room, the other room had the
bright iron bed with the polished knobs like a throne, in which
Solomon slept all day. There were snow-white curtains of wiry
lace at the window, and a lace bedspread belonged on the bed.
But what old Solomon slept sound under was a big feather-stitched
piece-quilt in the pattern "Trip Around the World," which had
twenty-one different colors, four hundred and forty pieces, and a
thousand yards of thread, and that was what Solomon's mother
made in her life and old age. There was a table holding the Bible,

and a trunk with a key. On the wall were two calendars, and a diploma from somewhere in Solomon's family, and under that Livvie's one possession was nailed, a picture of the little white baby of the family she worked for, back in Natchez before she was married. Going through that room and on to the kitchen, there was a big wood stove and a big round table always with a wet top and with the knives and forks in one jelly glass and the spoons in another, and a cut-glass vinegar bottle between, and going out from those, many shallow dishes of pickled peaches, fig preserves, watermelon pickles and blackberry jam always sitting there. The churn sat in the sun, the doors of the safe were always both shut, and there were four baited mouse-traps in the kitchen, one in every corner.

The outside of Solomon's house looked nice. It was not painted, but across the porch was an even balance. On each side there was one easy chair with high springs, looking out, and a fern basket hanging over it from the ceiling, and a dishpan of zinnia seedlings growing at its foot on the floor. By the door was a plow-wheel, just a pretty iron circle, nailed up on one wall and a square mirror on the other, a turquoise-blue comb stuck up in the frame, with the wash stand beneath it. On the door was a wooden knob with a pearl in the end, and Solomon's black hat hung on that, if he was in the house.

Out front was a clean dirt yard with every vestige of grass patiently uprooted and the ground scarred in deep whorls from the strike of Livvie's broom. Rose bushes with tiny blood-red roses blooming every month grew in threes on either side of the steps. On one side was a peach tree, on the other a pomegranate. Then coming around up the path from the deep cut of the Natchez Trace below was a line of bare crape-myrtle trees with every branch of them ending in a colored bottle, green or blue. There was no word that fell from Solomon's lips to say what they were for, but Livvie knew that there could be a spell put in trees, and she was familiar from the time she was born with the way bottle trees kept evil spirits from coming into the house — by luring them inside the colored bottles, where they cannot get out again. Solomon had made the bottle trees with his own hands over the nine years, in labor amounting to about a tree a year, and without a sign that he had any uneasiness in his heart, for he took as much pride in his precautions against spirits coming in the house as he took in the house, and sometimes in the sun the bottle trees looked prettier than the house did.

It was a nice house. It was in a place where the days would go by and surprise anyone that they were over. The lamplight and the firelight would shine out the door after dark, over the still and breathing country, lighting the roses and the bottle trees, and all was quiet there.

But there was nobody, nobody at all, not even a white person. And if there had been anybody, Solomon would not have let Livvie look at them, just as he would not let her look at a field hand, or a field hand look at her. There was no house near, except for the cabins of the tenants that were forbidden to her, and there was no house as far as she had been, stealing away down the still, deep Trace. She felt as if she waded a river when she went, for the dead leaves on the ground reached as high as her knees, and when she was all scratched and bleeding she said it was not like a road that went anywhere. One day, climbing up the high bank, she had found a graveyard without a church; with ribbon-grass growing about the foot of an angel (she had climbed up because she thought she saw angel wings), and in the sun, trees shining like burning flames through the great caterpillar nets which enclosed them. Scarey thistles stood looking like the prophets in the Bible in Solomon's house. Indian paint brushes grew over her head, and the mourning dove made the only sound in the world. Oh for a stirring of the leaves, and a breaking of the nets! But not by a ghost, prayed Livvie, jumping down the bank. After Solomon took to his bed, she never went out, except one more time.

Livvie knew she made a nice girl to wait on anybody. She fixed things to eat on a tray like a surprise. She could keep from singing when she ironed, and to sit by a bed and fan away the flies, she could be so still she could not hear herself breathe. She could clean up the house and never drop a thing, and wash the dishes without a sound, and she would step outside to churn, for churning sounded too sad to her, like sobbing, and if it made her home-sick and not Solomon, she did not think of that.

But Solomon scarcely opened his eyes to see her, and scarcely tasted his food. He was not sick or paralyzed or in any pain that he mentioned, but he was surely wearing out in the body, and no matter what nice hot thing Livvie would bring him to taste, he would only look at it now, as if he was past seeing how he could add anything more to himself. Before she could beg him, he would go fast asleep. She could not surprise him any more, if he would not taste, and she was afraid that he was never in the world going to taste another thing she brought him — and so how could he last?

But one morning it was breakfast time and she cooked his eggs and grits, carried them in on a tray, and called his name. He was sound asleep. He lay in a dignified way with his watch beside

him, on his back in the middle of the bed. One hand drew the
quilt up high, though it was the first day of spring. Through the
white lace curtains a little puffy wind was blowing as if it came
from round cheeks. All night the frogs had sung out in the swamp,
like a commotion in the room, and he had not stirred, though
she lay wide awake and saying, "Shh, frogs!" for fear he would
mind them.

He looked as if he would like to sleep a little longer, and
so she put back the tray and waited a little. When she tiptoed and
stayed so quiet, she surrounded herself with a little reverie, and
sometimes it seemed to her when she was so stealthy that the
quiet she kept was for a sleeping baby, and that she had a baby
and was its mother. When she stood at Solomon's bed and looked
down at him, she would be thinking, "He sleeps so well," and
she would hate to wake him up. And in some other way, too,
she was afraid to wake him up because even in his sleep he seemed
to be such a strict man.

Of course, nailed to the wall over the bed — only she would
forget who it was — there was a picture of him when he was
young. Then he had a fan of hair over his forehead like a king's
crown. Now his hair lay down on his head, the spring had gone
out of it. Solomon had a lightish face, with eyebrows scattered
but rugged, the way privet grows, strong eyes, with second sight,
a strict mouth, and a little gold smile. This was the way he looked
in his clothes, but in bed in the daytime he looked like a different
and smaller man, even when he was wide awake, and holding the
Bible. He looked like somebody kin to himself. And then sometimes
when he lay in sleep and she stood fanning the flies away, and
the light came in, his face was like new, so smooth and clear that
it was like a glass of jelly held to the window, and she could
almost look through his forehead and see what he thought.

She fanned him and at length he opened his eyes and spoke
her name, but he would not taste the nice eggs she had kept warm
under a pan.

Back in the kitchen she ate heartily, his breakfast and hers,
and looked out the open door at what went on. The whole day,
and the whole night before, she had felt the stir of spring close
to her. It was as present in the house as a young man would be.
The moon was in the last quarter and outside they were turning
the sod and planting peas and beans. Up and down the red fields,
over which smoke from the brush-burning hung showing like a
little skirt of sky, a white horse and a white mule pulled the plow.
At intervals hoarse shouts came through the air and roused her as
if she dozed neglectfully in the shade, and they were telling her,

"Jump up!" She could see how over each ribbon of field were moving men and girls, on foot and mounted on mules, with hats set on their heads and bright with tall hoes and forks as if they carried streamers on them and were going to some place on a journey — and how as if at a signal now and then they would all start at once shouting, hollering, cajoling, calling and answering back, running, being leaped on and breaking away, flinging to earth with a shout and lying motionless in the trance of twelve o'clock. The old women came out of the cabins and brought them food they had ready for them, and then all worked together, spread evenly out. The little children came too, like a bouncing stream overflowing the fields, and set upon the men, the women, the dogs, the rushing birds, and the wave-like rows of earth, their little voices almost too high to be heard. In the middle distance like some white-and-gold towers were the haystacks, with black cows coming around to eat their edges. High above everything, the wheel of fields, house, and cabins, and the deep road surrounding like a moat to keep them in, was the turning sky, blue with long, far-flung white mare's tail clouds, serene and still as high flames. And sound asleep while all this went around him that was his, Solomon was like a little still spot in the middle.

Even in the house the earth was sweet to breathe. Solomon had never let Livvie go any farther than the chicken house and the well. But what if she would walk now into the heart of the fields and take a hoe and work until she fell stretched out and drenched with her efforts, like other girls, and laid her cheek against the laid-open earth, and shamed the old man with her humbleness and delight? To shame him! A cruel wish would come in uninvited and so fast while she looked out the back door. She washed the dishes and scrubbed the table. She could hear the cries of the little lambs. Her mother, that she had not seen since her wedding day, had said one time, "I rather a man be anything, than a woman be mean."

So all morning she kept tasting the chicken broth on the stove, and when it was right she poured off a nice cupful. She carried it in to Solomon, and there he lay having a dream. Now what did he dream about? For she saw him sigh gently as if not to disturb some whole thing he held round in his mind, like a fresh egg. So even an old man dreamed about something pretty. Did he dream of her, while his eyes were shut and sunken, and his small hand with the wedding ring curled close in sleep around the quilt? He might be dreaming of what time it was, for even through his sleep he kept track of it like a clock, and knew how much of it went by, and waked up knowing where the hands were even before he consulted the silver watch that he never let go. He would sleep with the watch in his palm, and even holding it to his cheek like a child that loves a plaything. Or he might dream of journeys and travels on a steamboat to Natchez. Yet she thought he dreamed of her; but even while she scrutinized him, the rods of the foot of the bed seemed to rise up like a rail fence between them, and she could see that people never could be sure of anything as long as one of them was asleep and the other awake. To look at him dreaming of her when he might be going to die frightened her a little, as if he might carry her with him that way, and she wanted to run out of the room. She took hold of the bed and held on, and Solomon opened his eyes and called her name, but he did not want anything. He would not taste the good broth.

Just a little after that, as she was taking up the ashes in the front room for the last time in the year, she heard a sound. It was somebody coming. She pulled the curtains together and looked through the slit.

Coming up the path under the bottle trees was a white lady. At first she looked young, but then she looked old. Marvelous to see, a little car stood steaming like a kettle out in the field-track — it had come without a road.

Livvie stood listening to the long, repeated knockings at the door, and after a while she opened it just a little. The lady came in through the crack, though she was more than middle-sized and wore a big hat.

"My name is Miss Baby Marie," she said.

Livvie gazed respectfully at the lady and at the little suitcase she was holding close to her by the handle until the proper moment. The lady's eyes were running over the room, from palmetto to palmetto, but she was saying, "I live at home . . . out from Natchez . . . and get out and show these pretty cosmetic things to the white people and the colored people both . . . all around . . . years and years. . . . Both shades of powder and rouge. . . . It's the kind of work a girl can do and not go clear 'way from home. . . ." And the harder she looked, the more she talked. Suddenly she turned up her nose and said, "It's not Christian or sanitary to put feathers in a vase," and then she took a gold key out of the front of her dress and began unlocking the locks on her suitcase. Her face drew the light, the way it was covered with intense white and red, with a little patty-cake of white between the wrinkles by her upper lip. Little red tassels of hair bobbed under the rusty wires of her picture-hat, as with an air of triumph and secrecy she now drew open her little suitcase and brought out bottle after bottle and jar after jar, which she put down on the table, the mantlepiece, the settee, and the organ.

"Did you ever see so many cosmetics in your life?" cried Miss Baby Marie.

"No'm," Livvie tried to say, but the cat had her tongue.

"Have you ever applied cosmetics?" asked Miss Baby Marie next.

"No'm," Livvie tried to say.

"Then look!" she said, and pulling out the last thing of all, "Try this!" she said. And in her hand was unclenched a golden lipstick which popped open like magic. A fragrance came out of it like incense, and Livvie cried out suddenly, "Chinaberry flowers!"

Her hand took the lipstick, and in an instant she was carried away in the air through the spring, and looking down with a half-drowsy smile from a purple cloud she saw from above a chinaberry tree, dark and smooth and neatly leaved, neat as a guinea hen in the dooryard, and there was her home that she had left. On one side of the tree was her mama holding up her heavy apron, and she could see it was loaded with ripe figs, and on the other side was her papa holding a fish-pole over the pond, and she could see it transparently, the little clear fishes swimming up to the brim.

"Oh, no, not chinaberry flowers — secret ingredients," said Miss Baby Marie. "My cosmetics have secret ingredients — not chinaberry flowers."

"It's purple," Livvie breathed, and Miss Baby Marie said, "Use it freely. Rub it on."

Livvie tiptoed out to the wash stand on the front porch and before the mirror put the paint on her mouth. In the wavery surface her face danced before her like a flame. Miss Baby Marie followed her out, took a look at what she had done, and said, "That's it."

Livvie tried to say "Thank you" without moving her parted lips where the paint lay so new.

By now Miss Baby Marie stood behind Livvie and looked in the mirror over her shoulder, twisting up the tassels of her hair. "The lipstick I can let you have for only two dollars," she said, close to her neck.

"Lady, but I don't have no money, never did have," said Livvie.

"Oh, but you don't pay the first time. I make another trip, that's the way I do. I come back again — later."

"Oh," said Livvie, pretending she understood everything so as to please the lady.

"But if you don't take it now, this may be the last time I'll call at your house," said Miss Baby Marie sharply. "It's far away from anywhere, I'll tell you that. You don't live close to anywhere."

"Yes'm. My husband, he keep the *money*," said Livvie, trembling. "He is strict as he can be. He don't know *you* walk in here — Miss Baby Marie!"

"Where is he?"

"Right now, he in yonder sound asleep, an old man. I wouldn't ever ask him for anything."

Miss Baby Marie took back the lipstick and packed it up. She gathered up the jars for both black and white and got them all inside the suitcase, with the same little fuss of triumph with which she had brought them out. She started away.

"Goodbye," she said, making herself look grand from the back, but at the last minute she turned around in the door. Her old hat wobbled as she whispered, "Let me see your husband."

Livvie obediently went on tiptoe and opened the door to the other room. Miss Baby Marie came behind her and rose on her toes and looked in.

"My, what a little tiny old, old man!" she whispered, clasping her hands and shaking her head over them. "What a beautiful quilt! What a tiny old, old man!"

"He can sleep like that all day," whispered Livvie proudly.

They looked at him awhile so fast asleep, and then all at once they looked at each other. Somehow that was as if they had a secret, for he had never stirred. Livvie then politely, but all at once, closed the door.

"Well! I'd certainly like to leave you with a lipstick!" said Miss Baby Marie vivaciously. She smiled in the door.

"Lady, but I told you I don't have no money, and never did have."

"And never will?" In the air and all around, like a bright halo around the white lady's nodding head, it was a true spring day.

"Would you take eggs, lady?" asked Livvie softly.

"No, I have plenty of eggs — plenty," said Miss Baby Marie.

"I still don't have no money," said Livvie, and Miss Baby Marie took her suitcase and went on somewhere else.

Livvie stood watching her go, and all the time she felt her heart beating in her left side. She touched the place with her hand. It seemed as if her heart beat and her whole face flamed from the pulsing color of her lips. She went to sit by Solomon and when he opened his eyes he could not see a change in her. "He's fixin' to die," she said inside. That was the secret. That was when she went out of the house for a little breath of air.

She went down the path and down the Natchez Trace a way, and she did not know how far she had gone, but it was not far, when she saw a sight. It was a man, looking like a vision — she standing on one side of the Old Natchez Trace and he standing on the other.

As soon as this man caught sight of her, he began to look himself over. Starting at the bottom with his pointed shoes, he began to look up, lifting his peg-top pants the higher to see fully his bright socks. His coat long and wide and leaf-green he opened like doors to see his high-up tawny pants and his pants he smoothed downward from the points of his collar, and he wore a luminous baby-pink satin shirt. At the end, he reached gently above his wide platter-shaped round hat, the color of a plum, and one finger touched at the feather, emerald green, blowing in the spring winds.

No matter how she looked, she could never look so fine as he did, and she was not sorry for that, she was pleased.

He took three jumps, one down and two up, and was by her side.

"My name is Cash," he said.

He had a guinea pig in his pocket. They began to walk along. She stared on and on at him, as if he were doing some daring spectacular thing, instead of just walking beside her. It was not simply the city way he was dressed that made her look at him and see hope in its insolence looking back. It was not only the way he moved along kicking the flowers as if he could break through everything in the way and destroy anything in the world, that made her eyes grow bright. It might be, if he had not appeared the way he did appear that day she would never have looked so closely at him, but the time people come makes a difference.

They walked through the still leaves of the Natchez Trace, the light and the shade falling through trees about them, the white irises shining like candles on the banks and the new ferns shining like green stars up in the oak branches. They came out at Solomon's house, bottle trees and all. Livvie stopped and hung her head.

Cash began whistling a little tune. She did not know what it was, but she had heard it before from a distance, and she had a revelation. Cash was a field hand. He was a transformed field hand. Cash belonged to Solomon. But he had stepped out of his overalls into this. There in front of Solomon's house he laughed. He had a round head, a round face, all of him was young, and he flung his head up, rolled it against the mare's-tail sky in his round hat, and he could laugh just to see Solomon's house sitting there. Livvie looked at it, and there was Solomon's black hat hanging on the peg on the front door, the blackest thing in the world.

"I been to Natchez," Cash said, wagging his head around the sky. "*I* taken a trip, *I* ready for Easter!"

How was it possible to look so fine before the harvest? Cash must have stolen the money, stolen it from Solomon. He stood in the path and lifted his spread hand high and brought it down again and again in his laughter. He kicked up his heels. A little chill went through her. It was as if Cash was bringing that strong hand down to beat a drum or to rain blows upon a man, such an abandon and menace were in his laugh. Frowning, she went closer to him and his swinging arm drew her in at once and the fright was crushed from her body, as a little match-flame might be smothered out by what it lighted. She gathered the folds of his coat behind him and fastened her red lips to his mouth, and she was dazzled by herself then, the way he had been dazzled with himself to begin with.

In that instant she felt something that could not be told — that Solomon's death was at hand, that he was the same to her as if he were dead now. She cried out, and uttering little cries turned and ran for the house.

At once Cash was coming, following after, he was running behind her. He came close, and half-way up the path he laughed and passed her. He even picked up a stone and sailed it into the bottle trees. She put her hands over her head, and sounds clattered through the bottle trees like cries of outrage. Cash stamped and plunged zigzag up the front steps and in at the door.

When she got there, he had stuck his hands in his pockets and was turning slowly about in the front room. The little guinea pig peeped out. Around Cash, the pinned-up palmettos looked as if a lazy green monkey had walked up and down and around the walls leaving green prints of his hands and feet.

She got through the room and his hands were still in his pockets, and she fell upon the closed door to the other room and pushed it open. She ran to Solomon's bed, calling "Solomon! Solomon!" The little shape of the old man never moved at all, wrapped under the quilt as if it were winter still.

"Solomon!" She pulled the quilt away, but there was another one under that, and she fell on her knees beside him. He made no sound except a sigh, and then she could hear in the silence the light springy steps of Cash walking and walking in the front room, and the ticking of Solomon's silver watch, which came from the bed. Old Solomon was far away in his sleep, his face looked small, relentless, and devout, as if he were walking somewhere where she could imagine the snow falling.

Then there was a noise like a hoof pawing the floor, and the door gave a creak, and Cash appeared beside her. When she looked up, Cash's face was so black it was bright, and so bright and bare of pity that it looked sweet to her. She stood up and held up her head. Cash was so powerful that his presence gave her strength even when she did not need any.

Under their eyes Solomon slept. People's faces tell of things and places not known to the one who looks at them while they sleep, and while Solomon slept under the eyes of Livvie and Cash his face told them like a mythical story that all his life he had built, little scrap by little scrap, respect. A beetle could not have been more laborious or more ingenious in the task of its destiny. When Solomon was young, as he was in his picture overhead, it was the infinite thing with him, and he could see no end to the respect he would contrive and keep in a house. He had built a lonely house, the way he would make a cage, but it grew to be the same with him as a great monumental pyramid and sometimes in his absorption of getting it erected he was like the builder-slaves of Egypt who forgot or never knew the origin and meaning of the thing to which they gave all their strength of their bodies and used up all their days. Livvie and Cash could see that as a man might rest from a life-labor he lay in his bed, and they could hear how, wrapped in his quilt, he sighed to himself comfortably in sleep, while in his dreams he might have been an ant, a beetle, a bird, an Egyptian, assembling and carrying on his back and building with his hands, or he might have been an old man of India or a swaddled baby, about to smile and brush all away.

Then without warning old Solomon's eyes flew wide open under the hedgelike brows. He was wide awake.

And instantly Cash raised his quick arm. A radiant sweat stood on his temples. But he did not bring his arm down — it stayed in the air, as if something might have taken hold.

It was not Livvie — she did not move. As if something said "Wait," she stood waiting. Even while her eyes burned under motionless lids, her lips parted in a stiff grimace, and with her arms stiff at her sides she stood above the prone old man and the panting young one, erect and apart.

Movement when it came came in Solomon's face. It was an old and strict face, a frail face, but behind it, like a covered light, came an animation that could play hide and seek, that would dart and escape, had always escaped. The mystery flickered in him, and invited from his eyes. It was that very mystery that Cash with his quick arm would have to strike, and that Livvie could not weep for. But Cash only stood holding his arm in the air, when the gentlest flick of his great strength, almost a puff of his breath, would have been enough, if he had known how to give it, to send the old man over the obstruction that kept him away from death.

If it could not be that the tiny illumination in the fragile and ancient face caused a crisis, a mystery in the room that would not permit a blow to fall, at least it was certain that Cash, throbbing in his Easter clothes, felt a pang of shame that the vigor of a man would come to such an end that he could not be struck without warning. He took down his hand and stepped back behind Livvie, like a round-eyed schoolboy on whose unsuspecting head the dunce cap has been set.

"Young ones can't wait," said Solomon.

Livvie shuddered violently, and then in a gush of tears she stooped for a glass of water and handed it to him, but he did not see her.

"So here come the young man Livvie wait for. Was no prevention. No prevention. Now I lay eyes on young man and it come to be somebody I know all the time, and been knowing since he were born in a cotton patch, and watched grow up year to year, Cash McCord, growed to size, growed up to come in my house in the end — ragged and barefoot."

Solomon gave a cough of distaste. Then he shut his eyes vigorously, and his lips began to move like a chanter's.

"When Livvie married, her husband were already somebody. He had paid great cost for his land. He spread sycamore leaves over the ground from wagon to door, day he brought her home, so her foot would not have to touch ground. He carried her through his door. Then he growed old and could not lift her, and she were still young."

Livvie's sobs followed his words like a soft melody repeating each thing as he stated it. His lips moved for a little without sound, or she cried too fervently, and unheard he might have been telling his whole life, and then he said, "God forgive Solomon for sins great and small. God forgive Solomon for carrying away too young girl for wife and keeping her away from her people and from all the young people would clamor for her back."

Then he lifted up his right hand toward Livvie where she stood by the bed and offered her his silver watch. He dangled it before her eyes, and she hushed crying; her tears stopped. For a moment the watch could be heard ticking as it always did, precisely in his proud hand. She lifted it away. Then he took hold of the quilt; then he was dead.

Livvie left Solomon dead and went out of the room. Stealthily, nearly without noise, Cash went beside her. He was like a shadow, but his shiny shoes moved over the floor in spangles, and the green downy feather shone like a light in his hat. As they reached the front room, he seized her deftly as a long black cat and dragged her hanging by the waist round and round him, while he turned in a circle, his face bent down to hers. The first moment, she kept one arm and its hand stiff and still, the one that held Solomon's watch. Then the fingers softly let go, all of her was limp, and the watch fell somewhere on the floor. It ticked away in the still room, and all at once there began outside the full song of a bird.

They moved around and around the room and into the brightness of the open door, then he stopped and shook her once. She rested in silence in his trembling arms, unprotesting as a bird on a nest. Outside the redbirds were flying and criss-crossing, the sun was in all the bottles on the prisoned trees, and the young peach was shining in the middle of them with the bursting light of spring.

QUESTIONS

1. Of another of her stories, Eudora Welty wrote:

   > Above all I had no wish to sound mystical, but did expect to sound mysterious now and then, if I could: this was a circumstantial realistic story in which the reality *was* mystery.

   "Livvie," too, can be described as a "realistic story in which the reality *was* mystery." Which details in the story serve to make it both "realistic" and mysterious? Why does the story take place shortly before Easter? Why are Cash's clothes "luminous" and green and brown, and why is he described as "looking like a vision" (page 75)?

2. To a large extent the story is one of contrast, both explicit and implicit. What are some of the contrasting elements, and how do they reflect or illuminate the story's theme? Compare and contrast the four characters. Are any of their names significant? How?

3. Does Miss Welty say explicitly that Livvie is confined? Does Livvie feel confined? Do we feel that Livvie is confined? Explain.

4. Though there is a basic conflict between young Livvie and

old Solomon, how does Miss Welty avoid a simple "good-bad" dichotomy?

5. Is the appearance of Miss Baby Marie an intrusion? Is she introduced merely for comic relief? Explain.

6. How are the bottle trees and Solomon's watch significant?

7. Compare the tone of "Livvie" with the tone of another story with a somewhat similar theme, "The Widow of Ephesus." How would you characterize the tone of each of the stories? How does it, in each case, help to illuminate the theme?

8. In the last two paragraphs of the story, which sentences most reflect Livvie's thought? Which sentences least reflect Livvie's thought? Explain.

6

A Collection of Short Fiction

The stories of Ruth, Samson, and Joseph in the Old Testament and the parables of Jesus in the New Testament are sufficient evidence that brief narratives existed in ancient times. The short tales in Boccaccio's *Decameron* and Chaucer's *Canterbury Tales* (the latter an amazing variety of narrative poems ranging from bawdy stories to legends of saints) are medieval examples of the ancient form. But, speaking generally, short narratives before the nineteenth century were either didactic pieces, with the narrative existing for the sake of a moral point, or they were "curious and striking" tales (to use Maugham's words for his favorite kind of story) recounted in order to entertain. The contemporary short story is rather different from both of these genres, which can be called the **parable** and the **anecdote.** Like the parable, the contemporary short story has a point, a meaning; but unlike the parable, it has a richness of surface as well as depth, so that it is interesting whether or not the reader goes on to ponder "the meaning." The short story, like the anecdote, relates a happening, but whereas the happening in the anecdote is curious and is the center of interest, the happening in the contemporary story often is less interesting in itself than as a manifestation of a character's state of mind. A good short story usually has a psychological interest that an anecdote lacks.

The anecdotal story is what "story" means for most readers. It is an interesting happening or series of happenings, usually with a somewhat surprising ending. The anecdotal story, however, is quite different from most of the contemporary short stories in this book. The anecdote is good entertainment, and good entertainment should not be lightly dismissed. But it has two elements within it that prevent it (unless it is something in addition to an anecdote) from taking a high place among the world's literature. First, it cannot be reread with increasing or even continued pleasure. Even when it is well told, once we know the happening we may lose patience with the telling. Second, effective anecdotes are often highly implausible. Now, implausible anecdotes alleged to be true have a special impact by virtue of their alleged truth: they make us say to ourselves, "Truth is stranger than fiction." But the invented anecdote lacks this power; its unlikely coincidence, its unconvincing ironic situation, its surprise ending, are both untrue and unbelievable. It is entertaining but it is usually not especially meaningful.

The modern short story is not an anecdote and is not an abbreviated novel. If it were the latter, *Reader's Digest* condensations of novels would be short stories. But they aren't; they are only eviscerated novels. The novelist usually covers a long period of time, presenting not only a few individuals but also something of a society. He often tells of the development of several many-sided figures. In contrast, the short-story writer, having only a few pages, usually focuses on a single figure in a single episode, revealing his character rather than recording his development. Whereas the novel is narrative, the contemporary short story often seems less narrative than lyric or dramatic: in the short story we have a sense of a present mood or personality revealed, rather than the sense of a history reported. The revelation in a story is presented through incidents, of course, but the interest commonly resides in the character revealed through the incidents, rather than in the incidents themselves. Little "happens," in the sense that there is little rushing from place to place. What does "happen" is usually a mental reaction to an experience, and the mental reaction, rather than the external experience, is the heart of the story. In older narratives the plot usually involves a conflict that is resolved, bringing about a change in the protagonist's condition; in contemporary stories the plot usually is designed to reveal a protagonist's state of mind. This de-emphasis of overt actions results in an affinity with the lyric and the drama.

The de-emphasis on narrative in the contemporary short story is not an invention of the twentieth-century mind. It goes back at least to three important American writers of the early nineteenth century — Washington Irving, Nathaniel Hawthorne, and Edgar Allan Poe. In 1824 Irving wrote:

> I fancy much of what I value myself upon in writing, escapes
> the observation of the great mass of my readers: who are

intent more upon the story than the way in which it is told. For my part I consider a story merely as a frame on which to stretch my materials. It is the play of thought, and sentiments and language; the weaving in of characters, lightly yet expressively delineated; the familiar and faithful exhibition of scenes in common life; and the half-concealed vein of humor that is often playing through the whole — these are among what I aim at, and upon which I felicitate myself in proportion as I think I succeed.

Hawthorne and Poe may seem stranger than Irving as forebears of the contemporary short story: both are known for their fantastic narratives (and, in addition, Poe is known as the inventor of the detective story, a genre in which there is strong interest in curious happenings). But because Hawthorne's fantastic narratives are, as he said, highly allegorical, the reader's interest is pushed beyond the narrative to the moral significance. Poe's "arabesques," as he called his fanciful tales (in distinction from his detective tales of "ratiocination"), are aimed at revealing and arousing unusual mental states. The weird happenings and personages are symbolic representations of the mind or soul. In "The Fall of the House of Usher" the twins Roderick and Madeline probably represent complementary parts of a single personality, just as the house described in the poem within this story represents a person: the "banners yellow" are hair, the "two luminous windows" are eyes, the "fair palace door" of "pearl and ruby" is a mouth, and so on. But, it must be noted, in both Hawthorne and Poe we usually get what is commonly called the **tale** rather than the **short story:** we get short prose fiction dealing with the strange rather than the usual. (This distinction between the wondrous and the ordinary is discussed at some length in "Observations on the Novel," page 425.)

A paragraph from Poe's review (1842) of Hawthorne's *Twice Told Tales,* though more useful in revealing Poe's theory of fiction than Hawthorne's, illuminates something of the kinship between the contemporary short story and the best short fictions of the earlier nineteenth century. In the review Poe has been explaining that because "unity of effect or impression" is essential, a tale (Poe doubtless uses "tale" to mean short fiction in general, rather than the special type just discussed) that can be read at a single sitting has an advantage over the novel.

> A skillful artist has constructed a tale. He has not fashioned his thoughts to accommodate his incidents, but having deliberately conceived a certain single effect to be wrought, he then invents such incidents, he then combines such events, and discusses them in such tone as may best serve him in establishing this preconceived effect. If his very first sentence

tends not to the outbringing of this effect, then in his very first step has he committed a blunder. In the whole composition there should be no word written of which the tendency, direct or indirect, is not to the one pre-established design. And by such means, with such care and skill a picture is at length painted which leaves in the mind of him who contemplates it with a kindred art, a sense of the fullest satisfaction. The idea of the tale, its thesis, has been presented unblemished, because undisturbed — an end absolutely demanded, yet, in the novel, altogether unattainable.

Nothing that has been said here should be construed as suggesting that contemporary short stories are necessarily better than older short narratives. The object of these comments has not been to evaluate, but to call attention to the characteristics dominating most good contemporary brief fiction. Furthermore, it should not be thought that contemporary fiction is all of a piece; the preceding stories have already demonstrated its variety. The following are also varied; if the reader does not like one he need not despair; he need only (in Chaucer's words) "turne over the leef and chese another tale."

Nathaniel Hawthorne (1804–1864)

Young Goodman Brown

Young Goodman Brown came forth at sunset into the street at Salem village; but put his head back, after crossing the threshold, to exchange a parting kiss with his young wife. And Faith, as the wife was aptly named, thrust her own pretty head into the street, letting the wind play with the pink ribbons of her cap while she called to Goodman Brown.

"Dearest heart," whispered she, softly and rather sadly, when her lips were close to his ear, "prithee put off your journey until sunrise and sleep in your own bed to-night. A lone woman is troubled with such dreams and such thoughts that she's afeared of herself sometimes. Pray tarry with me this night, dear husband, of all nights in the year."

"My love and my Faith," replied young Goodman Brown, "of all nights in the year, this one night must I tarry away from thee. My journey, as thou callest it, forth and back again, must needs be done 'twixt now and sunrise. What, my sweet, pretty wife, dost thou doubt me already, and we but three months married?"

"Then God bless you!" said Faith, with the pink ribbons; "and may you find all well when you come back."

"Amen!" cried Goodman Brown. "Say thy prayers, dear Faith, and go to bed at dusk, and no harm will come to thee."

So they parted; and the young man pursued his way until, being about to turn the corner by the meeting-house, he looked back and saw the head of Faith still peeping after him with a melancholy air, in spite of her pink ribbons.

"Poor little Faith!" thought he, for his heart smote him. "What a wretch am I to leave her on such an errand! She talks of dreams, too. Methought as she spoke there was trouble in her face, as if a dream had warned her what work is to be done to-night. But no, no; 'twould kill her to think it. Well, she's a blessed angel on earth; and after this one night I'll cling to her skirts and follow her to heaven."

With this excellent resolve for the future, Goodman Brown felt himself justified in making more haste on his present evil purpose. He had taken a dreary road, darkened by all the gloomiest trees of the forest, which barely stood aside to let the narrow path creep through, and closed immediately behind. It was all as lonely as could be; and there is this peculiarity in such a solitude, that the traveller knows not who may be concealed by the innumerable trunks and the thick boughs overhead; so that with lonely footsteps he may yet be passing through an unseen multitude.

"There may be a devilish Indian behind every tree," said Goodman Brown to himself and he glanced fearfully behind him as he added, "What if the devil himself should be at my very elbow!"

His head being turned back, he passed a crook of the road, and, looking forward again, beheld the figure of a man, in grave and decent attire, seated at the foot of an old tree. He arose at Goodman Brown's approach and walked onward side by side with him.

"You are late, Goodman Brown," said he. "The clock of the Old South was striking as I came through Boston, and that is full fifteen minutes agone."

"Faith kept me back a while," replied the young man, with a tremor in his voice, caused by the sudden appearance of his companion, though not wholly unexpected.

It was now deep dusk in the forest, and deepest in that part of it where these two were journeying. As nearly as could be discerned, the second traveller was about fifty years old, apparently in the same rank of life as Goodman Brown, and bearing a considerable resemblance to him, though perhaps more in expression than features. Still they might have been taken for father and son. And yet, though the elder person was as simply clad as the younger, and as simple in manner too, he had an indescribable air of one who knew the world, and who would not have felt abashed at the governor's dinner table or in King William's court, were it possible that his affairs should call him thither. But the only thing about him that could be fixed upon as remarkable was his staff, which bore the likeness of a great black snake, so curiously wrought that it might almost be seen to twist and wriggle itself like a living serpent. This, of course, must have been an ocular deception, assisted by the uncertain light.

"Come, Goodman Brown," cried his fellow-traveller, "this is a dull pace for the beginning of a journey. Take my staff, if you are so soon weary."

"Friend," said the other, exchanging his slow pace for a full stop, "having kept covenant by meeting thee here, it is my purpose now to return whence I came. I have scruples touching the matter thou wot'st of."

"Sayest thou so?" replied he of the serpent, smiling apart. "Let us walk on, nevertheless, reasoning as we go; and if I convince thee not thou shalt turn back. We are but a little way in the forest yet."

"Too far! too far!" exclaimed the goodman, unconsciously resuming his walk. "My father never went into the woods on such an errand, nor his father before him. We have been a race of honest men and good Christians since the days of the martyrs; and shall I be the first of the name of Brown that ever took this path and kept —"

"Such company, thou wouldst say," observed the elder person, interpreting his pause. "Well said, Goodman Brown! I have been as well acquainted with your family as with ever a one among the Puritans; and that's no trifle to say. I helped your grandfather, the constable, when he lashed the Quaker woman so smartly through the streets of Salem; and it was I that brought your father a pitch-pine knot, kindled at my own hearth, to set fire to an Indian village, in King Philip's war. They were my good friends, both; and many a pleasant walk have we had along this path, and returned merrily after midnight. I would fain be friends with you for their sake."

"If it be as thou sayest," replied Goodman Brown, "I marvel they never spoke of these matters; or, verily, I marvel not, seeing that the least rumor of the sort would have driven them from New England. We are a people of prayer, and good works to boot, and abide no such wickedness."

"Wickedness or not," said the traveller with the twisted staff, "I have a very general acquaintance here in New England. The deacons of many a church have drunk the communion wine with me; the selectmen of divers towns make me their chairman; and a majority of the Great and General Court are firm supporters of my interest. The governor and I, too — But these are state secrets."

"Can this be so?" cried Goodman Brown, with a stare of amazement at his undisturbed companion. "Howbeit, I have nothing to do with the governor and council; they have their own ways, and are no rule for a simple husbandman like me. But, were I to go on with thee, how should I meet the eye of that good old man, or minister, at Salem village? Oh, his voice would make me tremble both Sabbath day and lecture day."

Thus far the elder traveller had listened with due gravity; but now burst into a fit of irrepressible mirth, shaking himself so violently that his snake-like staff actually seemed to wriggle in sympathy.

"Ha! ha! ha!" shouted he again and again; then composing himself, "Well, go on, Goodman Brown, go on; but, prithee, don't kill me with laughing."

"Well, then, to end the matter at once," said Goodman Brown, considerably nettled, "there is my wife, Faith. It would break her dear little heart; and I'd rather break my own."

"Nay, if that be the case," answered the other, "e'en go thy ways, Goodman Brown. I would not for twenty old women like the one hobbling before us that Faith should come to any harm."

As he spoke he pointed his staff at a female figure on the path, in whom Goodman Brown recognized a very pious and exemplary dame, who had taught him his catechism in youth, and was still his moral and spiritual adviser, jointly with the minister and Deacon Gookin.

"A marvel, truly, that Goody Cloyse should be so far in the wilderness at nightfall," said he. "But with your leave, friend, I shall take a cut through the woods until we have left this Christian woman behind. Being a stranger to you, she might ask whom I was consorting with and whither I was going."

"Be it so," said his fellow-traveller. "Betake you the woods, and let me keep the path."

Accordingly the young man turned aside, but took care to watch his companion, who advanced softly along the road until he had come within a staff's length of the old dame. She, meanwhile, was making the best of her way, with singular speed for so aged a woman, and mumbling some indistinct words — a prayer, doubtless — as she went. The traveller put forth his staff and touched her withered neck with what seemed the serpent's tail.

"The devil!" screamed the pious old lady.

"Then Goody Cloyse knows her old friend?" observed the traveller, confronting her and leaning on his writhing stick.

"Ah, forsooth, and is it your worship indeed?" cried the good dame. "Yea, truly is it, and in the very image of my old gossip, Goodman Brown, the grandfather of the silly fellow that now is. But — would your worship believe it? — my broomstick hath strangely disappeared, stolen, as I suspect, by that unhanged witch, Goody Cory, and that, too, when I was all anointed with the juice of smallage, and cinquefoil, and wolf's bane —"

"Mingled with fine wheat and the fat of a new-born babe," said the shape of old Goodman Brown.

"Ah, your worship knows the recipe," cried the old lady, cackling aloud. "So, as I was saying, being all ready for the meeting, and no horse to ride on, I made up my mind to foot it; for they tell me there is a nice young man to be taken into communion tonight. But now your good worship will lend me your arm, and we shall be there in a twinkling."

"That can hardly be," answered her friend. "I may not spare you my arm, Goody Cloyse; but here is my staff, if you will."

So saying, he threw it down at her feet, where, perhaps, it assumed life, being one of the rods which its owner had formerly lent to the Egyptian magi. Of this fact, however, Goodman Brown could not take cognizance. He had cast up his eyes in astonishment, and, looking down again, beheld neither Goody Cloyse nor the serpentine staff but his fellow-traveller alone, who waited for him as calmly as if nothing had happened.

"That old woman taught me my catechism," said the young man; and there was a world of meaning in this simple comment.

They continued to walk onward, while the elder traveller exhorted his companion to make good speed and persevere in the path, discoursing so aptly that his arguments seemed rather to spring up in the bosom of his auditor than to be suggested by himself. As they went, he plucked a branch of maple to serve for a walking stick, and began to strip it of the twigs and little boughs, which were wet with evening dew. The moment his fingers touched them they became strangly withered and dried up as with a week's sunshine. Thus the pair proceeded, at a good free pace, until suddenly, in a gloomy hollow of the road, Goodman Brown sat himself down on the stump of a tree and refused to go any farther.

"Friend," said he, stubbornly, "my mind is made up. Not

another step will I budge on this errand. What if a wretched old woman do choose to go to the devil when I thought she was going to heaven: is that any reason why I should quit my dear Faith and go after her?"

"You will think better of this by and by," said his acquaintance, composedly. "Sit here and rest yourself a while; and when you feel like moving again, there is my staff to help you along."

Without more words, he threw his companion the maple stick, and was as speedily out of sight as if he had vanished into the deepening gloom. The young man sat a few moments by the roadside, applauding himself greatly, and thinking with how clear a conscience he should meet the minister in his morning walk, nor shrink from the eye of good old Deacon Gookin. And what calm sleep would be his that very night, which was to have been spent so wickedly, but so purely and sweetly now, in the arms of Faith! Amidst these pleasant and praiseworthy meditations, Goodman Brown heard the tramp of horses along the road, and deemed it advisable to conceal himself within the verge of the forest, conscious of the guilty purpose that had brought him thither, though now so happily turned from it.

On came the hoof tramps and the voices of the riders, two grave old voices, conversing soberly as they drew near. These mingled sounds appeared to pass along the road, within a few yards of the young man's hiding-place; but, owing doubtless to the depth of the gloom at that particular spot, neither the travellers nor their steeds were visible. Though their figures brushed the small boughs by the wayside, it could not be seen that they intercepted, even for a moment, the faint gleam from the strip of bright sky athwart which they must have passed. Goodman Brown alternately crouched and stood on tiptoe, pulling aside the branches and thrusting forth his head as far as he durst without discerning so much as a shadow. It vexed him the more, because he could have sworn, were such a thing possible, that he recognized the voices of the minister and Deacon Gookin, jogging along quietly, as they were wont to do, when bound to some ordination or ecclesiastical council. While yet within hearing, one of the riders stopped to pluck a switch.

"Of the two, reverend sir," said the voice like the deacon's, "I had rather miss an ordination dinner than to-night's meeting. They tell me that some of our community are to be here from Falmouth and beyond, and others from Connecticut and Rhode Island, besides several of the Indian powwows, who, after their fashion, know almost as much deviltry as the best of us. Moreover, there is a goodly young woman to be taken into communion."

"Mighty well, Deacon Gookin!" replied the solemn old tones

of the minister. "Spur up, or we shall be late. Nothing can be done, you know, until I get on the ground."

The hoofs clattered again; and the voices, talking so strangely in the empty air, passed on through the forest, where no church had ever been gathered or solitary Christian prayed. Whither, then, could these holy men be journeying so deep into the heathen wilderness? Young Goodman Brown caught hold of a tree for support, being ready to sink down on the ground, faint and over-burdened with the heavy sickness of his heart. He looked up to the sky, doubting whether there really was a heaven above him. Yet there was the blue arch, and the stars brightening in it.

"With heaven above and Faith below, I will yet stand firm against the devil!" cried Goodman Brown.

While he still gazed upward into the deep arch of the firmament and had lifted his hands to pray, a cloud, though no wind was stirring, hurried across the zenith and hid the brightening stars. The blue sky was still visible, except directly overhead, where this black mass of cloud was sweeping swiftly northward. Aloft in the air, as if from the depths of the cloud, came a confused and doubtful sound of voices. Once the listener fancied that he could distinguish the accents of townspeople of his own, men and women, both pious and ungodly, many of whom he had met at the communion table, and had seen others rioting at the tavern. The next moment, so indistinct were the sounds, he doubted whether he had heard aught but the murmur of the old forest, whispering without a wind. Then came a stronger swell of those familiar tones, heard daily in the sunshine at Salem village, but never until now from a cloud of night. There was one voice, of a young woman, uttering lamentations, yet with an uncertain sorrow, and entreating for some favor, which, perhaps, it would grieve her to obtain; and all the unseen multitude, both saints and sinners, seemed to encourage her onward.

"Faith!" shouted Goodman Brown, in a voice of agony and desperation; and the echoes of the forest mocked him, crying, "Faith! Faith!" as if bewildered wretches were seeking her all through the wilderness.

The cry of grief, rage, and terror was yet piercing the night, when the unhappy husband held his breath for a response. There was a scream, drowned immediately in a louder murmur of voices, fading into far-off laughter, as the dark cloud swept away, leaving the clear and silent sky above Goodman Brown. But something fluttered lightly down through the air and caught on the branch of a tree. The young man seized it, and beheld a pink ribbon.

"My Faith is gone!" cried he, after one stupefied moment.

"There is no good on earth; and sin is but a name. Come, devil; for to thee is this world given."

And, maddened with despair, so that he laughed loud and long, did Goodman Brown grasp his staff and set forth again, at such a rate that he seemed to fly along the forest path rather than to walk or run. The road grew wilder and drearier and more faintly traced, and vanished at length, leaving him in the heart of the dark wilderness, still rushing onward with the instinct that guides mortal man to evil. The whole forest was peopled with frightful sounds — the creaking of the trees, the howling of wild beasts, and the yell of Indians; while sometimes the wind tolled like a distant church bell, and sometimes gave a broad roar around the traveller, as if all Nature were laughing him to scorn. But he was himself the chief horror of the scene, and shrank not from its other horrors.

"Ha! ha! ha!" roared Goodman Brown when the wind laughed at him. "Let us hear which will laugh loudest. Think not to frighten me with your deviltry. Come witch, come wizard, come Indian powwow, come devil himself, and here comes Goodman Brown. You may as well fear him as he fear you."

In truth, all through the haunted forest there could be nothing more frightful than the figure of Goodman Brown. On he flew among the black pines, brandishing his staff with frenzied gestures, now giving vent to an inspiration of horrid blasphemy, and now shouting forth such laughter as set all the echoes of the forest laughing like demons around him. The fiend in his own shape is less hideous than when he rages in the breast of man. Thus sped the demoniac on his course, until, quivering among the trees, he saw a red light before him, as when the felled trunks and branches of a clearing have been set on fire, and throw up their lurid blaze against the sky, at the hour of midnight. He paused, in a lull of the tempest that had driven him onward, and heard the swell of what seemed a hymn, rolling solemnly from a distance with the weight of many voices. He knew the tune; it was a familiar one in the choir of the village meeting-house. The verse died heavily away, and was lengthened by a chorus, not of human voices, but of all the sounds of the benighted wilderness pealing in awful harmony together. Goodman Brown cried out, and his cry was lost to his own ear by its unison with the cry of the desert.

In the interval of silence he stole forward until the light glared full upon his eyes. At one extremity of an open space, hemmed in by the dark wall of the forest, arose a rock, bearing some rude, natural resemblance either to an altar or a pulpit, and surrounded by four blazing pines, their tops aflame, their stems untouched, like candles at an evening meeting. The mass of foliage that had overgrown the summit of the rock was all on fire, blazing high into the night and fitfully illuminating the whole field. Each pendent twig and leafy festoon was in a blaze. As the red light arose and fell, a numerous congregation alternately shone forth, then disappeared in shadow, and again grew, as it were, out of the darkness, peopling the heart of the solitary woods at once.

"A grave and dark-clad company," quoth Goodman Brown.

In truth they were such. Among them, quivering to and fro between gloom and splendor, appeared faces that would be seen next day at the council board of the province, and others which, Sabbath after Sabbath, looked devoutly heavenward, and benignantly over the crowded pews, from the holiest pulpits in the land. Some affirm that the lady of the governor was there. At least there were high dames well known to her, and wives of honored husbands, and widows, a great multitude, and ancient maidens, all of excellent repute, and fair young girls, who trembled lest their mothers should espy them. Either the sudden gleams of light flashing over the obscure field bedazzled Goodman Brown, or he recognized a score of the church members of Salem village famous for their especial sanctity. Good old Deacon Gookin had arrived, and waited at the skirts of that venerable saint, his revered pastor. But, irreverently consorting with these grave, reputable, and pious people, these elders of the church, these chaste dames and dewy virgins, there were men of dissolute lives and women of spotted fame, wretches given over to all mean and filthy vice, and suspected even of horrid crimes. It was strange to see that the good shrank not from the wicked, nor were the sinners abashed by the saints. Scattered also among their pale-faced enemies were the Indian priests, or powwows, who had often scared their native forest with more hideous incantations than any known to English witchcraft.

"But where is Faith?" thought Goodman Brown; and, as hope came into his heart, he trembled.

Another verse of the hymn arose, a slow and mournful strain, such as the pious love, but joined to words which expressed all that our nature can conceive of sin, and darkly hinted at far more. Unfathomable to mere mortals is the lore of fiends. Verse after verse was sung; and still the chorus of the desert swelled between like the deepest tone of a mighty organ; and with the final peal of that dreadful anthem there came a sound, as if the roaring wind, the rushing streams, the howling beasts, and every other voice of the unconcerted wilderness were mingling and according with the voice of guilty man in homage to the prince of all. The four blazing pines threw up a loftier flame, and obscurely discovered shapes and visages of horror on the smoke wreaths above the impious assembly. At the same moment the fire on the rock shot redly forth and formed a glowing arch above its base, where now appeared a figure. With reverence be it spoken, the figure bore no slight similitude, both in garb and manner, to some grave divine of the New England churches.

"Bring forth the converts!" cried a voice that echoed through the field and rolled into the forest.

At the word, Goodman Brown stepped forth from the shadow of the trees and approached the congregation, with whom he felt a loathful brotherhood by the sympathy of all that was wicked in his heart. He could have well-nigh sworn that the shape of his own dead father beckoned him to advance, looking downward from a smoke wreath, while a woman, with dim features of despair, threw out her hand to warn him back. Was it his mother? But he had no power to retreat one step, nor to resist, even in thought, when the minister and good old Deacon Gookin seized his arms and led him to the blazing rock. Thither came also the slender form of a veiled female, led between Goody Cloyse, that pious teacher of the catechism, and Martha Carrier, who had received the devil's promise to be queen of hell. A rampant hag was she. And there stood the proselytes beneath the canopy of fire.

"Welcome, my children," said the dark figure, "to the communion of your race. Ye have found thus young your nature and your destiny. My children, look behind you!"

They turned; and flashing forth, as it were, in a sheet of flame, the fiend worshippers were seen; the smile of welcome gleamed darkly on every visage.

"There," resumed the sable form, "are all whom ye have reverenced from youth. Ye deemed them holier than yourselves, and shrank from your own sin, contrasting it with their lives of righteousness and prayerful aspirations heavenward. Yet here are they all in my worshipping assembly. This night it shall be granted you to know their secret deeds: how hoary-bearded elders of the church have whispered wanton words to the young maids of their households; how many a woman, eager for widows' weeds, has given her husband a drink at bedtime and let him sleep his last sleep in her bosom; how beardless youths have made haste to inherit their fathers' wealth; and how fair damsels — blush not, sweet ones — have dug little graves in the garden, and bidden me, the sole guest, to an infant's funeral. By the sympathy of your human hearts for sin ye shall scent out all the places — whether in church, bed-chamber, street, field, or forest — where crime has been committed, and shall exult to behold the whole earth one stain of guilt, one mighty blood spot. Far more than this. It shall be yours to penetrate, in every bosom, the deep mystery of sin, the fountain of all wicked arts, and which inexhaustibly supplies more evil impulses than human power — than my power at its utmost — can make manifest in deeds. And now, my children, look upon each other."

They did so; and, by the blaze of the hell-kindled torches, the wretched man beheld his Faith, and the wife her husband, trembling before that unhallowed altar.

"Lo, there ye stand, my children," said the figure, in a deep and solemn tone, almost sad with its despairing awfulness, as if his once angelic nature could yet mourn for our miserable race. "Depending upon one another's hearts, ye had still hoped that virtue were not all a dream. Now are ye undeceived. Evil is the nature of mankind. Evil must be your only happiness. Welcome again, my children, to the communion of your race."

"Welcome," repeated the fiend worshippers, in one cry of despair and triumph.

And there they stood, the only pair, as it seemed, who were yet hesitating on the verge of wickedness in this dark world. A basin was hollowed, naturally, in the rock. Did it contain water, reddened by the lurid light! or was it blood? or, perchance, a liquid flame? Herein did the shape of evil dip his hand and prepare to lay the mark of baptism upon their foreheads, that they might be partakers of the mystery of sin, more conscious of the secret guilt of others, both in deed and thought, than they could now be of their own. The husband cast one look at his pale wife, and Faith at him. What polluted wretches would the next glance show them to each other, shuddering alike at what they disclosed and what they saw!

"Faith! Faith!" cried the husband, "look up to heaven, and resist the wicked one."

Whether Faith obeyed he knew not. Hardly had he spoken when he found himself amid calm night and solitude, listening to a roar of the wind which died heavily away through the forest. He staggered against the rock, and felt it chill and damp; while a hanging twig, that had been all on fire, besprinkled his cheek with the coldest dew.

The next morning young Goodman Brown came slowly into the street of Salem village, staring around him like a bewildered man. The good old minister was taking a walk along the graveyard to get an appetite for breakfast and meditate his sermon, and bestowed a blessing, as he passed, on Goodman Brown. He shrank from the venerable saint as if to avoid an anathema. Old Deacon Gookin was at domestic worship, and the holy words of his prayer were heard through the open window. "What God doth the wizard pray to?" quoth Goodman Brown. Goody Cloyse, that excellent old Christian, stood in the early sunshine at her own lattice, catechizing a little girl who had brought her a pint of morning's milk. Goodman Brown snatched away the child as from the grasp of the fiend himself. Turning the corner by the meeting-house, he spied the head of Faith, with the pink ribbons, gazing anxiously forth, and bursting into such joy at sight of him that she skipped along the street and almost kissed her husband before the whole village. But Goodman Brown looked sternly and sadly into her face, and passed on without a greeting.

Had Goodman Brown fallen asleep in the forest and only dreamed a wild dream of a witch-meeting?

Be it so if you will; but, alas! it was a dream of evil omen for young Goodman Brown. A stern, a sad, a darkly meditative, a distrustful, if not a desperate man did he become from the night of that fearful dream. On the Sabbath day, when the congregation were singing a holy psalm, he could not listen because an anthem of sin rushed loudly upon his ear and drowned all the blessed strain. When the minister spoke from the pulpit with power and fervid eloquence, and, with his hand on the open Bible, of the sacred truths of our religion, and of saint-like lives and triumphant deaths, and of future bliss or misery unutterable, then did Goodman Brown turn pale, dreading lest the roof should thunder down upon the gray blasphemer and his hearers. Often, awaking suddenly at midnight, he shrank from the bosom of Faith; and at morning or eventide, when the family knelt down at prayer, he scowled and muttered to himself, and gazed sternly at his wife, and turned away. And when he had lived long, and was borne to his grave a hoary corpse, followed by Faith, an aged woman, and children and grandchildren, a goodly procession, besides neighbors not a few, they carved no hopeful verse upon his tombstone, for his dying hour was gloom.

Edgar Allan Poe (1809–1849)

The Cask of Amontillado

The thousand injuries of Fortunato I had borne as I best could, but when he ventured upon insult, I vowed revenge. You, who so well know the nature of my soul, will not suppose, however, that I gave utterance to a threat. *At length* I would be avenged; this was a point definitely settled — but the very definitiveness with which it was resolved precluded the idea of risk. I must not only punish, but punish with impunity. A wrong is unredressed when retribution overtakes its redresser. It is equally unredressed when the avenger fails to make himself felt as such to him who has done the wrong.

It must be understood that neither by word nor deed had I given Fortunato cause to doubt my good will. I continued, as was my wont, to smile in his face, and he did not perceive that my smile *now* was at the thought of his immolation.

He had a weak point — this Fortunato — although in other regards he was a man to be respected and even feared. He prided himself on his connoisseurship in wine. Few Italians have the true virtuoso spirit. For the most part their enthusiasm is adopted to suit the time and opportunity to practice imposture upon the British and Austrian *millionaires*. In painting and gemmary Fortunato, like his countrymen, was a quack, but in the matter of old wines he was sincere. In this respect I did not differ from him materially; — I was skillful in the Italian vintages myself, and bought largely whenever I could.

It was about dusk, one evening during the supreme madness of the carnival season, that I encountered my friend. He accosted me with excessive warmth, for he had been drinking much. The man wore motley. He had on a tight-fitting parti-striped dress, and his head was surmounted by the conical cap and bells. I was so pleased to see him, that I thought I should never have done wringing his hand.

I said to him — "My dear Fortunato, you are luckily met. How remarkably well you are looking to-day! But I have received a pipe° of what passes for Amontillado, and I have my doubts."

"How?" said he, "Amontillado? A pipe? Impossible! And in the middle of the carnival?"

"I have my doubts," I replied; "and I was silly enough to

pipe   wine cask

pay the full Amontillado price without consulting you in the matter. You were not to be found, and I was fearful of losing a bargain."

"Amontillado!"

"I have my doubts."

"Amontillado!"

"And I must satisfy them."

"Amontillado!"

"As you are engaged, I am on my way to Luchesi. If any one has a critical turn, it is he. He will tell me —"

"Luchesi cannot tell Amontillado from Sherry."

"And yet some fools will have it that his taste is a match for your own."

"Come, let us go."

"Whither?"

"To your vaults."

"My friend, no; I will not impose upon your good nature. I perceive you have an engagement. Luchesi —"

"I have no engagement; come."

"My friend, no. It is not the engagement, but the severe cold with which I perceive you are afflicted. The vaults are insufferably damp. They are encrusted with nitre."

"Let us go, nevertheless. The cold is merely nothing. Amontillado! You have been imposed upon; and as for Luchesi, he cannot distinguish Sherry from Amontillado."

Thus speaking, Fortunato possessed himself of my arm. Putting on a mask of black silk, and drawing a *roquelaure*° closely about my person, I suffered him to hurry me to my palazzo.

There were no attendants at home; they had absconded to make merry in honor of the time. I had told them that I should not return until the morning, and had given them explicit orders not to stir from the house. These orders were sufficient, I well knew, to insure their immediate disappearance, one and all, as soon as my back was turned.

I took from their sconces two flambeaux, and giving one to Fortunato, bowed him through several suites of rooms to the archway that led into the vaults. I passed down a long and winding staircase, requesting him to be cautious as he followed. We came at length to the foot of the descent, and stood together on the damp ground of the catacombs of the Montresors.

The gait of my friend was unsteady, and the bells upon his cap jingled as he strode.

"The pipe," said he.

roquelaure   short cloak

"It is farther on," said I; "but observe the white web-work which gleams from these cavern walls."

He turned towards me, and looked into my eyes with two filmy orbs that distilled the rheum of intoxication.

"Nitre?" he asked, at length.

"Nitre," I replied. "How long have you had that cough?"

"Ugh! ugh! ugh! — ugh! ugh! ugh! — ugh! ugh! ugh! — ugh! ugh! ugh! — ugh! ugh! ugh!"

My poor friend found it impossible to reply for many minutes.

"It is nothing," he said, at last.

"Come," I said, with decision, "we will go back; your health is precious. You are rich, respected, admired, beloved; you are happy, as once I was. You are a man to be missed. For me it is no matter. We will go back; you will be ill, and I cannot be responsible. Besides, there is Luchesi —"

"Enough," he said; "the cough is a mere nothing: it will not kill me. I shall not die of a cough."

"True — true," I replied; "and, indeed, I had no intention of alarming you unnecessarily — but you should use all proper caution. A draught of this Medoc will defend us from the damps."

Here I knocked off the neck of a bottle which I drew from a long row of its fellows that lay upon the mould.

"Drink," I said, presenting him the wine.

He raised it to his lips with a leer. He paused and nodded to me familiarly, while his bells jingled.

"I drink," he said, "to the buried that repose around us."

"And I to your long life."

He again took my arm, and we proceeded.

"These vaults," he said, "are extensive."

"The Montresors," I replied, "were a great and numerous family."

"I forget your arms."

"A huge human foot d'or, in a field azure; the foot crushes a serpent rampant whose fangs are imbedded in the heel."

"And the motto?"

"Nemo me impune lacessit."°

"Good!" he said.

The wine sparkled in his eyes and the bells jingled. My own fancy grew warm with the Medoc. We had passed through walls of piled bones, with casks and puncheons intermingling, into the

---

Nemo me impune lacessit. No one dare attack me with impunity (the motto of Scotland)

inmost recesses of the catacombs. I paused again, and this time I made bold to seize Fortunato by an arm above the elbow.

"The nitre!" I said; "see, it increases. It hangs like moss upon the vaults. We are below the river's bed. The drops of moisture trickle among the bones. Come, we will go back ere it is too late. Your cough —"

"It is nothing," he said; "let us go on. But first, another draught of the Medoc."

I broke and reached him a flagon of De Grâve. He emptied it at a breath. His eyes flashed with a fierce light. He laughed and threw the bottle upwards with a gesticulation I did not understand.

I looked at him in surprise. He repeated the movement — a grotesque one.

"You do not comprehend?" he said.

"Not I," I replied.

"Then you are not of the brotherhood."

"How?"

"You are not of the masons."

"Yes, yes," I said, "yes, yes."

"You? Impossible! A mason?"

"A mason," I replied.

"A sign," he said.

"It is this," I answered, producing a trowel from beneath the folds of my *roquelaure.*

"You jest," he exclaimed, recoiling a few paces. "But let us proceed to the Amontillado."

"Be it so," I said, replacing the tool beneath the cloak, and again offering him my arm. He leaned upon it heavily. We continued our route in search of the Amontillado. We passed through a range of low arches, descended, passed on, and descending again, arrived at a deep crypt, in which the foulness of the air caused our flambeaux rather to glow than flame.

At the most remote end of the crypt there appeared another less spacious. Its walls had been lined with human remains piled to the vault overhead, in the fashion of the great catacombs of Paris. Three sides of this interior crypt were still ornamented in this manner. From the fourth the bones had been thrown down, and lay promiscuously upon the earth, forming at one point a mound of some size. Within the wall thus exposed by the displacing of the bones, we perceived a still interior recess, in depth about four feet, in width three, in height six or seven. It seemed to have been constructed for no especial use within itself, but formed merely the interval between two of the colossal supports of the roof of the catacombs, and was backed by one of their circumscribing walls of solid granite.

It was in vain that Fortunato, uplifting his dull torch, endeavored to pry into the depths of the recess. Its termination the feeble light did not enable us to see.

"Proceed," I said; "herein is the Amontillado. As for Luchesi —"

"He is an ignoramus," interrupted my friend, as he stepped unsteadily forward, while I followed immediately at his heels. In an instant he had reached the extremity of the niche, and finding his progress arrested by the rock, stood stupidly bewildered. A moment more and I had fettered him to the granite. In its surface were two iron staples, distant from each other about two feet, horizontally. From one of these depended a short chain, from the other a padlock. Throwing the links about his waist, it was but the work of a few seconds to secure it. He was too much astounded to resist. Withdrawing the key I stepped back from the recess.

"Pass your hand," I said, "over the wall; you cannot help feeling the nitre. Indeed it is *very* damp. Once more let me *implore* you to return. No? Then I must positively leave you. But I must first render you all the little attentions in my power."

"The Amontillado!" ejaculated my friend, not yet recovered from his astonishment.

"True," I replied; "the Amontillado."

As I said these words I busied myself among the pile of bones of which I have before spoken. Throwing them aside, I soon uncovered a quantity of building-stone and mortar. With these materials and with the aid of my trowel, I began vigorously to wall up the entrance of the niche.

I had scarcely laid the first tier of masonry when I discovered that the intoxication of Fortunato had in a great measure worn off. The earliest indication I had of this was a low moaning cry from the depth of the recess. It was *not* the cry of a drunken man. There was then a long and obstinate silence. I laid the second tier, and the third, and the fourth; and then I heard the furious vibrations of the chain. The noise lasted for several minutes, during which, that I might hearken to it with the more satisfaction, I ceased my labors and sat down upon the bones. When at last the clanking subsided, I resumed the trowel, and finished without interruption the fifth, the sixth, and the seventh tier. The wall was now nearly upon a level with my breast. I again paused, and holding the flambeaux over the masonwork, threw a few feeble rays upon the figure within.

A succession of loud and shrill screams, bursting suddenly

from the throat of the chained form, seemed to thrust me violently back. For a brief moment I hesitated — I trembled. Unsheathing my rapier, I began to grope with it about the recess; but the thought of an instant reassured me. I placed my hand upon the solid fabric of the catacombs, and felt satisfied. I reapproached the wall. I replied to the yells of him who clamored. I re-echoed — I aided — I surpassed them in volume and in strength. I did this, and the clamorer grew still.

It was now midnight, and my task was drawing to a close. I had completed the eighth, the ninth, and the tenth tier. I had finished a portion of the last and the eleventh; there remained but a single stone to be fitted and plastered in. I struggled with its weight; I placed it partially in its destined position. But now there came from out the niche a low laugh that erected the hairs upon my head. It was succeeded by a sad voice, which I had difficulty in recognizing as that of the noble Fortunato. The voice said —

"Ha! ha! ha! — he! he! he! — a very good joke indeed — an excellent jest. We will have many a rich laugh about it at the palazzo — he! he! he! — over our wine — he! he! he!"

"The Amontillado!" I said.

"He! he! he! — he! he! he! — yes, the Amontillado. But is it not getting late? Will not they be awaiting us at the palazzo, the Lady Fortunato and the rest? Let us be gone."

"Yes," I said, "let us be gone."

"For the love of God, Montresor!"

"Yes," I said, "for the love of God!"

But to these words I hearkened in vain for a reply. I grew impatient. I called aloud;

"Fortunato!"

No answer. I called again;

"Fortunato!"

No answer still, I thrust a torch through the remaining aperture and let it fall within. There came forth in return only a jingling of the bells. My heart grew sick — on account of the dampness of the catacombs. I hastened to make an end of my labor. I forced the last stone into its position; I plastered it up. Against the new masonry I reerected the old rampart of bones. For the half of a century no mortal had disturbed them. *In pace requiescat!°*

In pace requiescat! May he rest in peace!

Charlotte Perkins Gilman (1860–1935)

The Yellow Wallpaper

It is very seldom that mere ordinary people like John and myself secure ancestral halls for the summer.

A colonial mansion, a hereditary estate, I would say a haunted house, and reach the height of romantic felicity — but that would be asking too much of fate!

Still I will proudly declare that there is something queer about it.

Else, why should it be let so cheaply? And why have stood so long untenanted?

John laughs at me, of course, but one expects that in marriage.

John is practical in the extreme. He has no patience with faith, an intense horror of superstition, and he scoffs openly at any talk of things not to be felt and seen and put down in figures.

John is a physician, and *perhaps* — (I would not say it to a living soul, of course, but this is dead paper and a great relief to my mind) — *perhaps* that is one reason I do not get well faster.

You see he does not believe I am sick!

And what can one do?

If a physician of high standing, and one's own husband, assures friends and relatives that there is really nothing the matter with one but temporary nervous depression — a slight hysterical tendency — what is one to do?

My brother is also a physician, and also of high standing, and he says the same thing.

So I take phosphates or phosphites — whichever it is, and tonics, and journeys, and air, and exercise, and am absolutely forbidden to "work" until I am well again.

Personally, I disagree with their ideas.

Personally, I believe that congenial work, with excitement and change, would do me good.

But what is one to do?

I did write for a while in spite of them; but it *does* exhaust me a good deal — having to be so sly about it, or else meet with heavy opposition.

I sometimes fancy that in my condition if I had less opposition and more society and stimulus — but John says the very worst thing I can do is to think about my condition, and I confess it always makes me feel bad.

So I will let it alone and talk about the house.

The most beautiful place! It is quite alone, standing well back from the road, quite three miles from the village. It makes me think of English places that you read about, for there are hedges and walls and gates that lock, and lots of separate little houses for the gardeners and people.

There is a *delicious* garden! I never saw such a garden — large and shady, full of box-bordered paths, and lined with long grapecovered arbors with seats under them.

There were greenhouses, too, but they are all broken now. There was some legal trouble, I believe, something about the heirs and coheirs; anyhow, the place has been empty for years.

That spoils my ghostliness, I am afraid, but I don't care — there is something strange about the house — I can feel it.

I even said so to John one moonlight evening, but he said what I felt was a *draught,* and shut the window.

I get unreasonably angry with John sometimes. I'm sure I never used to be so sensitive. I think it is due to this nervous condition.

But John says if I feel so, I shall neglect proper self-control; so I take pains to control myself — before him, at least, and that makes me very tired.

I don't like our room a bit. I wanted one downstairs that opened on the piazza and had roses all over the window, and such pretty old-fashioned chintz hangings! but John would not hear of it.

He said there was only one window and not room for two beds, and no near room for him if he took another.

He is very careful and loving, and hardly lets me stir without special direction.

I have a schedule prescription for each hour in the day; he takes all care from me, and so I feel basely ungrateful not to value it more.

He said we came here solely on my account, that I was to have perfect rest and all the air I could get. "Your exercise depends on your strength, my dear," said he, "and your food somewhat on your appetite; but air you can absorb all the time." So we took the nursery at the top of the house.

It is a big, airy room, the whole floor nearly, with windows that look all ways, and air and sunshine galore. It was nursery first and then playroom and gymnasium, I should judge; for the windows are barred for little children, and there are rings and things in the walls.

The paint and paper look as if a boys' school had used it. It is stripped off — the paper — in great patches all around the head of my bed, about as far as I can reach, and in a great place on the other side of the room low down. I never saw a worse paper in my life.

One of those sprawling flamboyant patterns committing every artistic sin.

It is dull enough to confuse the eye in following, pronounced enough to constantly irritate and provoke study, and when you follow the lame uncertain curves for a little distance they suddenly commit suicide — plunge off at outrageous angles, destroy themselves in unheard of contradictions.

The color is repellent, almost revolting; a smouldering unclean yellow, strangely faded by the slow-turning sunlight.

It is a dull yet lurid orange in some places, a sickly sulphur tint in others.

No wonder the children hated it! I should hate it myself if I had to live in this room long.

There comes John, and I must put this away, — he hates to have me write a word.

We have been here two weeks, and I haven't felt like writing before, since that first day.

I am sitting by the window now, up in this atrocious nursery, and there is nothing to hinder my writing as much as I please, save lack of strength.

John is away all day, and even some nights when his cases are serious.

I am glad my case is not serious!

But these nervous troubles are dreadfully depressing.

John does not know how much I really suffer. He knows there is no *reason* to suffer, and that satisfies him.

Of course it is only nervousness. It does weigh on me so not to do my duty in any way!

I meant to be such a help to John, such a real rest and comfort, and here I am a comparative burden already!

Nobody would believe what an effort it is to do what little I am able, — to dress and entertain, and order things.

It is fortunate Mary is so good with the baby. Such a dear baby!

And yet I *cannot* be with him, it makes me so nervous.

I suppose John never was nervous in his life. He laughs at me so about this wallpaper!

At first he meant to repaper the room, but afterwards he said that I was letting it get the better of me, and that nothing was worse for a nervous patient than to give way to such fancies.

He said that after the wallpaper was changed it would be the heavy bedstead, and then the barred windows, and then that gate at the head of the stairs, and so on.

"You know the place is doing you good," he said, "and really, dear, I don't care to renovate the house just for a three months' rental."

"Then do let us go downstairs," I said, "there are such pretty rooms there."

Then he took me in his arms and called me a blessed little goose, and said he would go down to the cellar, if I wished, and have it whitewashed into the bargain.

But he is right enough about the beds and windows and things.

It is an airy and comfortable room as any one need wish, and, of course, I would not be so silly as to make him uncomfortable just for a whim.

I'm really getting quite fond of the big room, all but that horrid paper.

Out of one window I can see the garden, those mysterious deepshaded arbors, the riotous old-fashioned flowers, and bushes and gnarly trees.

Out of another I get a lovely view of the bay and a little private wharf belonging to the estate. There is a beautiful shaded lane that runs down there from the house. I always fancy I see people walking in these numerous paths and arbors, but John has cautioned me not to give way to fancy in the least. He says that with my imaginative power and habit of story-making, a nervous weakness like mine is sure to lead to all manner of excited fancies, and that I ought to use my will and good sense to check the tendency. So I try.

I think sometimes that if I were only well enough to write a little it would relieve the press of ideas and rest me.

But I find I get pretty tired when I try.

It is so discouraging not to have any advice and companionship about my work. When I get really well, John says we will ask Cousin Henry and Julia down for a long visit; but he says he would as soon put fireworks in my pillow-case as to let me have those stimulating people about now.

I wish I could get well faster.

But I must not think about that. This paper looks to me as if it *knew* what a vicious influence it had!

There is a recurrent spot where the pattern lolls like a broken neck and two bulbous eyes stare at you upside down.

I get positively angry with the impertinence of it and the

everlastingness. Up and down and sideways they crawl, and those absurd, unblinking eyes are everywhere. There is one place where two breadths didn't match, and the eyes go all up and down the line, one a little higher than the other.

I never saw so much expression in an inanimate thing before, and we all know how much expression they have! I used to lie awake as a child and get more entertainment and terror out of blank walls and plain furniture than most children could find in a toystore.

I remember what a kindly wink the knobs of our big, old bureau used to have, and there was one chair that always seemed like a strong friend.

I used to feel that if any of the other things looked too fierce I could always hop into that chair and be safe.

The furniture in this room is no worse than inharmonious, however, for we had to bring it all from downstairs. I suppose when this was used as a playroom they had to take the nursery things out, and no wonder! I never saw such ravages as the children have made here.

The wallpaper, as I said before, is torn off in spots, and it sticketh closer than a brother — they must have had perseverance as well as hatred.

Then the floor is scratched and gouged and splintered, the plaster itself is dug out here and there, and this great heavy bed which is all we found in the room, looks as if it had been through the wars.

But I don't mind it a bit — only the paper.

There comes John's sister. Such a dear girl as she is, and so careful of me! I must not let her find me writing.

She is a perfect and enthusiastic housekeeper, and hopes for no better profession. I verily believe she thinks it is the writing which made me sick!

But I can write when she is out, and see her a long way off from these windows.

There is one that commands the road, a lovely shaded winding road, and one that just looks off over the country. A lovely country, too, full of great elms and velvet meadows.

This wallpaper has a kind of sub-pattern in a different shade, a particularly irritating one, for you can only see it in certain lights, and not clearly then.

But in the places where it isn't faded and where the sun is just so — I can see a strange, provoking, formless sort of figure, that seems to skulk about behind that silly and conspicuous front design.

There's sister on the stairs!

Well, the Fourth of July is over! The people are all gone and I am tired out. John thought it might do me good to see a little company, so we just had mother and Nellie and the children down for a week.

Of course I didn't do a thing. Jennie sees to everything now. But it tired me all the same.

John says if I don't pick up faster he shall send me to Weir Mitchell in the fall.

But I don't want to go there at all. I had a friend who was in his hands once, and she says he is just like John and my brother, only more so!

Besides, it is such an undertaking to go so far.

I don't feel as if it was worth while to turn my hand over for anything, and I'm getting dreadfully fretful and querulous.

I cry at nothing, and cry most of the time.

Of course I don't when John is here, or anybody else, but when I am alone.

And I am alone a good deal just now. John is kept in town very often by serious cases, and Jennie is good and lets me alone when I want her to.

So I walk a little in the garden or down that lovely lane, sit on the porch under the roses, and lie down up here a good deal.

I'm getting really fond of the room in spite of the wallpaper. Perhaps *because* of the wallpaper.

It dwells in my mind so!

I lie here on this great immovable bed — it is nailed down, I believe — and follow that pattern about by the hour. It is as good as gymnastics, I assure you. I start, we'll say, at the bottom, down in the corner over there where it has not been touched, and I determine for the thousandth time that I *will* follow that pointless pattern to some sort of a conclusion.

I know a little of the principle of design, and I know this thing was not arranged on any laws of radiation, or alternation, or repetition, or symmetry, or anything else that I ever heard of.

It is repeated, of course, by the breadths, but not otherwise.

Looked at in one way each breadth stands alone, the bloated curves and flourishes — a kind of "debased Romanesque" with *delirium tremens* — go waddling up and down in isolated columns of fatuity.

But, on the other hand, they connect diagonally, and the sprawling outlines run off in great slanting waves of optic horror, like a lot of wallowing seaweeds in full chase.

The whole thing goes horizontally, too, at least it seems so, and I exhaust myself in trying to distinguish the order of its going in that direction.

They have used a horizontal breadth for a frieze, and that adds wonderfully to the confusion.

There is one end of the room where it is almost intact, and there, when the crosslights fade and the low sun shines directly upon it, I can almost fancy radiation after all, — the interminable grotesques seem to form around a common center and rush off in headlong plunges of equal distraction.

It makes me tired to follow it. I will take a nap I guess.

I don't know why I should write this.

I don't want to.

I don't feel able.

And I know John would think it absurd. But I *must* say what I feel and think in some way — it is such a relief

But the effort is getting to be greater than the relief!

Half the time now I am awfully lazy, and lie down ever so much.

John says I mustn't lose my strength, and has me take cod liver oil and lots of tonics and things, to say nothing of ale and wine and rare meat.

Dear John! He loves me very dearly, and hates to have me sick. I tried to have a real earnest reasonable talk with him the other day, and tell him how I wish he would let me go and make a visit to Cousin Henry and Julia.

But he said I wasn't able to go, nor able to stand it after I got there; and I did not make out a very good case for myself, for I was crying before I had finished.

It is getting to be a great effort for me to think straight. Just this nervous weakness I suppose.

And dear John gathered me up in his arms, and just carried me upstairs and laid me on the bed, and sat by me and read to me till it tired my head.

He said I was his darling and his comfort and all he had, and that I must take care of myself for his sake, and keep well.

He says no one but myself can help me out of it, that I must use my will and self-control and not let any silly fancies run away with me.

There's one comfort, the baby is well and happy, and does not have to occupy this nursery with the horrid wallpaper.

If we had not used it, that blessed child would have! What a fortunate escape! Why, I wouldn't have a child of mine, an impressionable little thing, live in such a room for worlds.

I never thought of it before, but it is lucky that John kept me here after all, I can stand it so much easier than a baby, you see.

Of course I never mention it to them any more — I am too wise, — but I keep watch of it all the same.

There are things in that paper that nobody knows but me, or ever will.

Behind that outside pattern the dim shapes get clearer every day.

It is always the same shape, only very numerous.

And it is like a woman stooping down and creeping about behind that pattern. I don't like it a bit. I wonder — I begin to think — I wish John would take me away from here!

It is so hard to talk with John about my case, because he is so wise, and because he loves me so.

But I tried it last night.

It was moonlight. The moon shines in all around just as the sun does.

I hate to see it sometimes, it creeps so slowly, and always comes in by one window or another.

John was asleep and I hated to waken him, so I kept still and watched the moonlight on that undulating wallpaper till I felt creepy.

The faint figure behind seemed to shake the pattern, just as if she wanted to get out.

I got up softly and went to feel and see if the paper *did* move, and when I came back John was awake.

"What is it, little girl?" he said. "Don't go walking about like that — you'll get cold."

I thought it was a good time to talk, so I told him that I really was not gaining here, and that I wished he would take me away.

"Why darling!" said he, "our lease will be up in three weeks, and I can't see how to leave before.

"The repairs are not done at home, and I cannot possibly leave town just now. Of course if you were in any danger, I could and would, but you really are better, dear, whether you can see it or not. I am a doctor, dear, and I know. You are gaining flesh and color, your appetite is better, I feel really much easier about you."

"I don't weigh a bit more," said I, "nor as much; and my appetite may be better in the evening when you are here, but it is worse in the morning when you are away!"

"Bless her little heart!" said he with a big hug, "she shall be as sick as she pleases! But now let's improve the shining hours by going to sleep, and talk about it in the morning!"

"And you won't go away?" I asked gloomily.

"Why, how can I, dear? It is only three weeks more and then we will take a nice little trip of a few days while Jennie is getting the house ready. Really dear you are better!"

"Better in body perhaps — " I began, and stopped short, for he sat up straight and looked at me with such a stern, reproachful look that I could not say another word.

"My darling," said he, "I beg of you, for my sake and for our child's sake, as well as for your own, that you will never for one instant let that idea enter your mind! There is nothing so dangerous, so fascinating, to a temperament like yours. It is a false and foolish fancy. Can you not trust me as a physician when I tell you so?"

So of course I said no more on that score, and we went to sleep before long. He thought I was asleep first, but I wasn't, and lay there for hours trying to decide whether that front pattern and the back pattern really did move together or separately.

On a pattern like this, by daylight, there is a lack of sequence, a defiance of law, that is a constant irritant to a normal mind.

The color is hideous enough, and unreliable enough, and infuriating enough, but the pattern is torturing.

You think you have mastered it, but just as you get well underway in following, it turns a back-somersault and there you are. It slaps you in the face, knocks you down, and tramples upon you. It is like a bad dream.

The outside pattern is a florid arabesque, reminding one of a fungus. If you can imagine a toadstool in joints, an interminable string of toadstools, budding and sprouting in endless convolutions — why, that is something like it.

That is, sometimes!

There is one marked peculiarity about this paper, a thing nobody seems to notice but myself, and that is that it changes as the light changes.

When the sun shoots in through the east window — I always watch for that first long, straight ray — it changes so quickly that I never can quite believe it.

That is why I watch it always.

By moonlight — the moon shines in all night when there is a moon — I wouldn't know it was the same paper.

At night in any kind of light, in twilight, candle light, lamp-light, and worst of all by moonlight, it becomes bars! The outside pattern I mean, and the woman behind it is as plain as can be.

I didn't realize for a long time what the thing was that

showed behind, that dim sub-pattern, but now I am quite sure it is a woman.

By daylight she is subdued, quiet. I fancy it is the pattern that keeps her so still. It is so puzzling. It keeps me quiet by the hour.

I lie down ever so much now. John says it is good for me, and to sleep all I can.

Indeed he started the habit by making me lie down for an hour after each meal.

It is a very bad habit I am convinced, for you see I don't sleep.

And that cultivates deceit, for I don't tell them I'm awake — O no!

The fact is I am getting a little afraid of John.

He seems very queer sometimes, and even Jennie has an inexplicable look.

It strikes me occasionally, just as a scientific hypothesis, — that perhaps it is the paper!

I have watched John when he did not know I was looking, and come into the room suddenly on the most innocent excuses, and I've caught him several times *looking at the paper!* And Jennie too. I caught Jennie with her hand on it once.

She didn't know I was in the room, and when I asked her in a quiet, a very quiet voice, with the most restrained manner possible, what she was doing with the paper — she turned around as if she had been caught stealing, and looked quite angry — asked me why I should frighten her so!

Then she said that the paper stained everything it touched, that she had found yellow smooches on all my clothes and John's, and she wished we would be more careful!

Did not that sound innocent? But I know she was studying that pattern, and I am determined that nobody shall find it out but myself!

Life is very much more exciting now than it used to be. You see I have something more to expect, to look forward to, to watch. I really do eat better, and am more quiet than I was.

John is so pleased to see me improve! He laughed a little the other day, and said I seemed to be flourishing in spite of my wallpaper.

I turned it off with a laugh. I had no intention of telling him it was *because* of the wallpaper — he would make fun of me. He might even want to take me away.

I don't want to leave now until I have found it out. There is a week more, and I think that will be enough.

I'm feeling ever so much better! I don't sleep much at night, for it is so interesting to watch developments; but I sleep a good deal in the daytime.

In the daytime it is tiresome and perplexing.

There are always new shoots on the fungus, and new shades of yellow all over it. I cannot keep count of them, though I have tried conscientiously.

It is the strangest yellow, that wallpaper! It makes me think of all the yellow things I ever saw — not beautiful ones like buttercups, but old foul, bad yellow things.

But there is something else about that paper — the smell! I noticed it the moment we came into the room, but with so much air and sun it was not bad. Now we have had a week of fog and rain, and whether the windows are open or not, the smell is here.

It creeps all over the house.

I find it hovering in the dining-room, skulking in the parlor, hiding in the hall, lying in wait for me on the stairs.

It gets into my hair.

Even when I go to ride, if I turn my head suddenly and surprise it — there is that smell!

Such a peculiar odor, too! I have spent hours in trying to analyze it, to find what it smelled like.

It is not bad — at first, and very gentle, but quite the subtlest, most enduring odor I ever met.

In this damp weather it is awful, I wake up in the night and find it hanging over me.

It used to disturb me at first. I thought seriously of burning the house — to reach the smell.

But now I am used to it. The only thing I can think of that it is like is the *color* of the paper! A yellow smell.

There is a very funny mark on this wall, low down, near the mopboard. A streak that runs round the room. It goes behind every piece of furniture, except the bed, a long, straight, even *smooch,* as if it had been rubbed over and over.

I wonder how it was done and who did it, and what they did it for. Round and round and round — round and round and round — it makes me dizzy!

I really have discovered something at last.

Through watching so much at night, when it changes so, I have finally found out.

The front pattern *does* move — and no wonder! The woman behind shakes it!

Sometimes I think there are a great many women behind, and sometimes only one, and she crawls around fast, and her crawling shakes it all over.

Then in the very bright spots she keeps still, and in the very shady spots she just takes hold of the bars and shakes them hard.

And she is all the time trying to climb through. But nobody could climb through that pattern — it strangles so; I think that is why it has so many heads.

They get through, and then the pattern strangles them off and turns them upside down, and makes their eyes white!

If those heads were covered or taken off it would not be half so bad.

I think that woman gets out in the daytime!

And I'll tell you why — privately — I've seen her!

I can see her out of every one of my windows!

It is the same woman, I know, for she is always creeping, and most women do not creep by daylight.

I see her on that long road under the trees, creeping along, and when a carriage comes she hides under the blackberry vines.

I don't blame her a bit. It must be very humiliating to be caught creeping by daylight!

I always lock the door when I creep by daylight. I can't do it at night, for I know John would suspect something at once.

And John is so queer now, that I don't want to irritate him. I wish he would take another room! Besides, I don't want anybody to get that woman out at night but myself.

I often wonder if I could see her out of all the windows at once.

But, turn as fast as I can, I can only see out of one at one time. And though I always see her, she *may* be able to creep faster than I can turn!

I have watched her sometimes away off in the open country, creeping as fast as a cloud shadow in a high wind.

If only that top pattern could be gotten off from the under one! I mean to try it, little by little.

I have found out another funny thing, but I shan't tell it this time! It does not do to trust people too much.

There are only two more days to get this paper off, and I believe John is beginning to notice. I don't like the look in his eyes.

And I heard him ask Jennie a lot of professional questions about me. She had a very good report to give.

She said I slept a good deal in the daytime.

John knows I don't sleep very well at night, for all I'm so quiet!

He asked me all sorts of questions, too, and pretended to be very loving and kind.

As if I couldn't see through him!

Still, I don't wonder he acts so, sleeping under this paper for three months.

It only interests me, but I feel sure John and Jennie are secretly affected by it.

Hurrah! This is the last day, but it is enough. John to stay in town over night, and won't be out until this evening.

Jennie wanted to sleep with me — the sly thing! But I told her I should undoubtedly rest better for a night all alone.

That was clever, for really I wasn't alone a bit! As soon as it was moonlight and that poor thing began to crawl and shake the pattern, I got up and ran to help her.

I pulled and she shook, I shook and she pulled, and before morning we had peeled off yards of that paper.

A strip about as high as my head and half around the room. And then when the sun came and that awful pattern began to laugh at me, I declared I would finish it to-day!

We go away to-morrow, and they are moving all my furniture down again to leave things as they were before.

Jennie looked at the wall in amazement, but I told her merrily that I did it out of pure spite at the vicious thing.

She laughed and said she wouldn't mind doing it herself, but I must not get tired.

How she betrayed herself that time!

But I am here, and no person touches this paper but me — not *alive!*

She tried to get me out of the room — it was too patent! But I said it was so quiet and empty and clean now that I believed I would lie down again and sleep all I could; and not to wake me even for dinner — I would call when I woke.

So now she is gone, and the servants are gone, and the things are gone, and there is nothing left but that great bedstead nailed down, with the canvas mattress we found on it.

We shall sleep downstairs to-night, and take the boat home to-morrow.

I quite enjoy the room, now it is bare again.

How those children did tear about here!

This bedstead is fairly gnawed!

But I must get to work.

I have locked the door and thrown the key down into the front path.

I don't want to go out, and I don't want to have anybody come in, till John comes.

I want to astonish him.

I've got a rope up here that even Jennie did not find. If that woman does get out, and tries to get away, I can tie her!

But I forgot I could not reach far without anything to stand on! This bed will *not* move!

I tried to lift and push it until I was lame, and then I got so angry I bit off a little piece at one corner — but it hurt my teeth.

Then I peeled off all the paper I could reach standing on the floor. It sticks horribly and the pattern just enjoys it! All those strangled heads and bulbous eyes and waddling fungus growths just shriek with derision!

I am getting angry enough to do something desperate. To jump out of the window would be admirable exercise, but the bars are too strong even to try.

Besides I wouldn't do it. Of course not. I know well enough that a step like that is improper and might be misconstrued.

I don't like to *look* out of the windows even — there are so many of those creeping women, and they creep so fast.

I wonder if they all come out of that wallpaper as I did?

But I am securely fastened now by my well-hidden rope — you don't get *me* out in the road there!

I suppose I shall have to get back behind the pattern when it comes night, and that is hard!

It is so pleasant to be out in this great room and creep around as I please!

I don't want to go outside. I won't, even if Jennie asks me to.

For outside you have to creep on the ground, and everything is green instead of yellow.

But here I can creep smoothly on the floor, and my shoulder just fits in that long smooch around the wall, so I cannot lose my way.

Why there's John at the door!

It is no use, young man, you can't open it!

How he does call and pound!

Now he's crying for an axe.

It would be a shame to break down that beautiful door!

"John dear!" said I in the gentlest voice, "the key is down by the front steps, under a plantain leaf!"

That silenced him for a few moments.

Then he said — very quietly indeed, "Open the door, my darling!"

"I can't," said I. "The key is down by the front door under a plantain leaf!"

And then I said it again, several times, very gently and slowly, and said it so often that he had to go and see, and he got it of course, and came in. He stopped short by the door.

"What is the matter?" he cried. "For God's sake, what are you doing!"

I kept on creeping just the same, but I looked at him over my shoulder.

"I've got out at last," said I, "in spite of you and Jane. And I've pulled off most of the paper, so you can't put me back!"

Now why should that man have fainted? But he did, and right across my path by the wall, so that I had to creep over him every time!

James Joyce (1882–1941)

Araby

North Richmond Street, being blind, was a quiet street except at the hour when the Christian Brothers' School set the boys free. An uninhabited house of two storeys stood at the blind end, detached from its neighbours in a square ground. The other houses of the street, conscious of decent lives within them, gazed at one another with brown imperturbable faces.

The former tenant of our house, a priest, had died in the back drawing-room. Air, musty from having been long enclosed, hung in all the rooms, and the waste room behind the kitchen was littered with old useless papers. Among these I found a few papercovered books, the pages of which were curled and damp: *The Abbot,* by Walter Scott, *The Devout Communicant* and *The Memoirs of Vidocq.* I liked the last best because its leaves were yellow. The wild garden behind the house contained a central apple-tree and a few straggling bushes under one of which I found the late tenant's rusty bicycle-pump. He had been a very charitable priest; in his will he had left all his money to institutions and the furniture of his house to his sister.

When the short days of winter came dusk fell before we had well eaten our dinners. When we met in the street the houses had grown sombre. The space of sky above us was the colour of everchanging violet and towards it the lamps of the street lifted their feeble lanterns. The cold air stung us and we played till our bodies glowed. Our shouts echoed in the silent street. The career of our play brought us through the dark muddy lanes behind the houses where we ran the gantlet of the rough tribes from the cottages, to the back doors of the dark dripping gardens where odours arose from the ashpits, to the dark odorous stables where a coachman smoothed and combed the horse or shook music from the buckled harness. When we returned to the street light from the kitchen windows had filled the areas. If my uncle was seen turning the corner we hid in the shadow until we had seen him safely housed. Or if Mangan's sister came out on the doorstep to call her brother in to his tea we watched her from our shadow peer up and down the street. We waited to see whether she would remain or go in and, if she remained, we left our shadow and walked up to Mangan's steps resignedly. She was waiting for us, her figure defined by the light from the half-opened door. Her brother always teased her before he obeyed and I stood by the railings looking at her. Her dress swung as she moved her body and the soft rope of her hair tossed from side to side.

Every morning I lay on the floor in the front parlour watching her door. The blind was pulled down to within an inch of the sash so that I could not be seen. When she came out on the doorstep my heart leaped. I ran to the hall, seized my books and followed her. I kept her brown figure always in my eye and, when we came near the point at which our ways diverged, I quickened my pace and passed her. This happened morning after morning. I had never spoken to her, except for a few casual words, and yet her name was like a summons to all my foolish blood.

Her image accompanied me even in places the most hostile to romance. On Saturday evenings when my aunt went marketing I had to go to carry some of the parcels. We walked through the flaring streets, jostled by drunken men and bargaining women, amid the curses of labourers, the shrill litanies of shop-boys who stood on guard by the barrels of pigs' cheeks, the nasal chanting of street-singers, who sang a *come-all-you* about O'Donovan Rossa, or a ballad about the troubles in our native land. These noises converged in a single sensation of life for me: I imagined that I bore my chalice safely through a throng of foes. Her name sprang to my lips at moments in strange prayers and praises which I myself did not understand. My eyes were often full of tears (I could not tell why) and at times a flood from my heart seemed to pour itself out into my bosom. I thought little of the future. I did not know whether I would ever speak to her or not or, if I spoke to her, how I could tell her of my confused adoration. But my body was like a harp and her words and gestures were like fingers running upon the wires.

One evening I went into the back drawing-room in which the priest had died. It was a dark rainy evening and there was no sound in the house. Through one of the broken panes I heard the rain impinge upon the earth, the fine incessant needles of water playing in the sodden beds. Some distant lamp or lighted window gleamed below me. I was thankful that I could see so little. All my senses seemed to desire to veil themselves and, feeling that I was about to slip from them, I pressed the palms of my hands together until they trembled, murmuring: *O love! O love!* many times.

At last she spoke to me. When she addressed the first words to me I was so confused that I did not know what to answer. She asked me was I going to Araby. I forget whether I answered yes or no. It would be a splendid bazaar, she said; she would love to go.

— And why can't you? I asked.

While she spoke she turned a silver bracelet round and round her wrist. She could not go, she said, because there would be a retreat that week in her convent. Her brother and two other boys were fighting for their caps and I was alone at the railings. She held one of the spikes, bowing her head towards me. The light from the lamp opposite our door caught the white curve of her neck, lit up her hair that rested there and, falling, lit up the hand upon the railing. It fell over one side of her dress and caught the white border of a petticoat, just visible as she stood at ease.

— It's well for you, she said.

— If I go, I said, I will bring you something.

What innumerable follies laid waste my waking and sleeping thoughts after that evening! I wished to annihilate the tedious intervening days. I chafed against the work of school. At night in my bedroom and by day in the classroom her image came between me and the page I strove to read. The syllables of the word *Araby* were called to me through the silence in which my soul luxuriated and cast an Eastern enchantment over me. I asked for leave to go to the bazaar on Saturday night. My aunt was surprised and hoped it was not some Freemason affair. I answered few questions in class, I watched my master's face pass from amiability to sternness; he hoped I was not beginning to idle. I could not call my wandering thoughts together. I had hardly any patience with the serious work of life which, now that it stood between me and my desire, seemed to me child's play, ugly monotonous child's play.

On Saturday morning I reminded my uncle that I wished to go to the bazaar in the evening. He was fussing at the hallstand, looking for the hat-brush, and answered me curtly:

— Yes, boy, I know.

As he was in the hall I could not go into the front parlour and lie at the window. I left the house in bad humour and walked slowly towards the school. The air was pitilessly raw and already my heart misgave me.

When I came home to dinner my uncle had not yet been home. Still it was early. I sat staring at the clock for some time and, when its ticking began to irritate me, I left the room. I mounted the staircase and gained the upper part of the house. The high cold empty gloomy rooms liberated me and I went from room to room singing. From the front window I saw my companions playing below in the street. Their cries reached me weakened and indistinct and, leaning my forehead against the cool glass, I looked over at the dark house where she lived. I may have stood there for an hour, seeing nothing but the brown-clad figure cast by my imagination, touched discreetly by the lamplight at the curved neck, at the hand upon the railings and at the border below the dress.

When I came downstairs again I found Mrs Mercer sitting at the fire. She was an old garrulous woman, a pawnbroker's widow, who collected used stamps for some pious purpose. I had to endure the gossip of the tea-table. The meal was prolonged beyond an hour and still my uncle did not come. Mrs Mercer stood up to go: she was sorry she couldn't wait any longer, but it was after eight o'clock and she did not like to be out late, as the night air was bad for her. When she had gone I began to walk up and down the room, clenching my fists. My aunt said:

— I'm afraid you may put off your bazaar for this night of Our Lord.

At nine o'clock I heard my uncle's latchkey in the halldoor. I heard him talking to himself and heard the hallstand rocking when it had received the weight of his overcoat. I could interpret these signs. When he was midway through his dinner I asked him to ~ive me the money to go to the bazaar. He had forgotten.

— The people are in bed and after their first sleep now, he said.

I did not smile. My aunt said to him energetically:

— Can't you give him the money and let him go? You've kept him late enough as it is.

My uncle said he was very sorry he had forgotten. He said he believed in the old saying: *All work and no play makes Jack a dull boy.* He asked me where I was going and, when I had told him a second time he asked me did I know *The Arab's Farewell to his Steed.* When I left the kitchen he was about to recite the opening lines of the piece to my aunt.

I held a florin tightly in my hand as I strode down Buckingham Street towards the station. The sight of the streets thronged with buyers and glaring with gas recalled to me the purpose of my journey. I took my seat in a third-class carriage of a deserted train. After an intolerable delay the train moved out of the station slowly. It crept onward among ruinous houses and over the twinkling river. At Westland Row Station a crowd of people pressed to the carriage doors; but the porters moved them back, saying that it was a special train for the bazaar. I remained alone in the bare carriage. In a few minutes the train drew up beside an improvised wooden platform. I passed out on to the road and saw by the lighted dial of a clock that it was ten minutes to ten. In front of me was a large building which displayed the magical name.

I could not find any sixpenny entrance and, fearing that the bazaar would be closed, I passed in quickly through a turnstile, handing a shilling to a weary-looking man. I found myself in a big hall girdled at half its height by a gallery. Nearly all the stalls were closed and the greater part of the hall was in darkness. I recognised a silence like that which pervades a church after a service. I walked into the centre of the bazaar timidly. A few people were gathered about the stalls which were still open. Before a curtain, over which the words *Café Chantant* were written in coloured lamps, two men were counting money on a salver. I listened to the fall of the coins.

Remembering with difficulty why I had come I went over to one of the stalls and examined porcelain vases and flowered teasets. At the door of the stall a young lady was talking and laughing with two young gentlemen. I remarked their English accents and listened vaguely to their conversation.

— O, I never said such a thing!

— O, but you did!

— O, but I didn't!

— Didn't she say that?

— Yes! I heard her.

— O, there's a . . . fib!

Observing me the young lady came over and asked me did I wish to buy anything. The tone of her voice was not encouraging; she seemed to have spoken to me out of a sense of duty. I looked humbly at the great jars that stood like eastern guards at either side of the dark entrance to the stall and murmured:

— No, thank you.

The young lady changed the position of one of the vases and went back to the two young men. They began to talk of the same subject. Once or twice the young lady glared at me over her shoulder.

I lingered before her stall, though I knew my stay was useless, to make my interest in her wares seem the more real. Then I turned away slowly and walked down the middle of the bazaar. I allowed the two pennies to fall against the sixpence in my pocket. I heard a voice call from one end of the gallery that the light was out. The upper part of the hall was now completely dark.

Gazing up into darkness I saw myself as a creature driven and derided by vanity; and my eyes burned with anguish and anger.

James Joyce (1882–1941)

The Dead

Lily, the caretaker's daughter, was literally run off her feet. Hardly had she brought one gentleman into the little pantry behind the office on the ground floor and helped him off with his overcoat than the wheezy hall-door bell clanged again and she had to scamper along the bare hallway to let in another guest. It was well for her she had not to attend to the ladies also. But Miss Kate and Miss Julia had thought of that and had converted the bathroom upstairs into a ladies' dressing-room. Miss Kate and Miss Julia were there, gossiping and laughing and fussing, walking after each other to the head of the stairs, peering down over the banisters and calling down to Lily to ask her who had come.

It was always a great affair, the Misses Morkan's annual dance. Everybody who knew them came to it, members of the family, old friends of the family, the members of Julia's choir, any of Kate's pupils that were grown up enough, and even some of Mary Jane's pupils too. Never once had it fallen flat. For years and years it had gone off in splendid style, as long as anyone could remember; ever since Kate and Julia, after the death of their brother Pat, had left the house in Stoney Batter and taken Mary Jane, their only niece, to live with them in the dark, gaunt house on Usher's Island, the upper part of which they had rented from Mr. Fulham, the corn-factor on the ground floor. That was a good thirty years ago if it was a day. Mary Jane, who was then a little girl in short clothes, was now the main prop of the household, for she had the organ in Haddington Road. She had been through the Academy and gave a pupils' concert every year in the upper room of the Antient Concert Rooms. Many of her pupils belonged to the better-class families on the Kingstown and Dalkey line. Old as they were, her aunts also did their share. Julia, though she was quite grey, was still the leading soprano in Adam and Eve's, and Kate, being too feeble to go about much, gave music lessons to beginners on the old square piano in the back room. Lily, the caretaker's daughter, did housemaid's work for them. Though their life was modest, they believed in eating well; the best of everything: diamond-bone sirloins, three-shilling tea and the best bottled stout. But Lily seldom made a mistake in the orders, so that she got on well with her three mistresses. They were fussy, that was all. But the only thing they would not stand was back answers.

Of course, they had good reason to be fussy on such a night. And then it was long after ten o'clock and yet there was no sign of Gabriel and his wife. Besides they were dreadfully afraid that Freddy Malins might turn up screwed. They would not wish for worlds that any of Mary Jane's pupils should see him under the influence; and when he was like that it was sometimes very hard to manage him. Freddy Malins always came later, but they wondered what could be keeping Gabriel: and that was what brought them every two minutes to the banisters to ask Lily had Gabriel or Freddy come.

"O, Mr. Conroy," said Lily to Gabriel when she opened the door for him, "Miss Kate and Miss Julia thought you were never coming. Good-night, Mrs. Conroy."

"I'll engage they did," said Gabriel, "but they forget that my wife here takes three mortal hours to dress herself."

He stood on the mat scraping the snow from his goloshes, while Lily led his wife to the foot of the stairs and called out:

"Miss Kate, here's Mrs. Conroy."

Kate and Julia came toddling down the dark stairs at once. Both of them kissed Gabriel's wife, said she must be perished alive, and asked was Gabriel with her.

"Here I am as right as the mail, Aunt Kate! Go on up. I'll follow," called out Gabriel from the dark.

He continued scraping his feet vigorously while the three women went upstairs, laughing, to the ladies' dressing-room. A light fringe of snow lay like a cape on the shoulders of his overcoat and like toecaps on the toes of his goloshes; and, as the buttons of his overcoat slipped with a squeaking noise through the snow-stiffened freeze, a cold, fragrant air from out-of-doors escaped from crevices and folds.

"Is it snowing again, Mr. Conroy?" asked Lily.

She had preceded him into the pantry to help him off with his overcoat. Gabriel smiled at the three syllables she had given his surname and glanced at her. She was a slim, growing girl, pale in complexion and with hay-coloured hair. The gas in the pantry made her look still paler. Gabriel had known her when she was a child and used to sit on the lowest step nursing a rag doll.

"Yes, Lily," he answered, "and I think we're in for a night of it."

He looked up at the pantry ceiling, which was shaking with the stamping and shuffling of feet on the floor above, listened for a moment to the piano and then glanced at the girl, who was folding his overcoat carefully at the end of a shelf.

"Tell me, Lily," he said in a friendly tone, "do you still go to school?"

"O no, sir," she answered. "I'm done schooling this year and more."

"O, then," said Gabriel gaily, "I suppose we'll be going to your wedding one of these fine days with your young man, eh?"

The girl glanced back at him over her shoulder and said with great bitterness:

"The men that is now is only all palaver and what they can get out of you."

Gabriel coloured, as if he felt he had made a mistake and, without looking at her, kicked off his goloshes and flicked actively with his muffler at his patent-leather shoes.

He was a stout, tallish young man. The high colour of his cheeks pushed upwards even to his forehead, where it scattered itself in a few formless patches of pale red; and on his hairless face there scintillated restlessly the polished lenses and the bright gilt rims of the glasses which screened his delicate and restless eyes. His glossy black hair was parted in the middle and brushed in a long curve behind his ears where it curled slightly beneath the groove left by his hat.

When he had flicked lustre into his shoes he stood up and pulled his waistcoat down more tightly on his plump body. Then he took a coin rapidly from his pocket.

"O Lily," he said, thrusting it into her hands, "it's Christmastime, isn't it? Just . . . here's a little. . . ."

He walked rapidly towards the door.

"O no, sir!" cried the girl, following him. "Really, sir, I wouldn't take it."

"Christmas-time! Christmas-time!" said Gabriel, almost trotting to the stairs and waving his hand to her in deprecation.

The girl, seeing that he had gained the stairs, called out after him:

"Well, thank you, sir."

He waited outside the drawing-room door until the waltz should finish, listening to the skirts that swept against it and to the shuffling of feet. He was still discomposed by the girl's bitter and sudden retort. It had cast a gloom over him which he tried to dispel by arranging his cuffs and the bows of his tie. He then took from his waistcoat pocket a little paper and glanced at the headings he had made for his speech. He was undecided about the lines from Robert Browning, for he feared they would be above the heads of his hearers. Some quotation that they would recognise from Shakespeare or from the Melodies would be better. The indelicate clacking of the men's heels and the shuffling of their soles reminded him that their grade of culture differed from his. He would only make himself ridiculous by quoting poetry to them which they could not understand. They would think that he was airing his superior education. He would fail with them just as he had failed with the girl in the pantry. He had taken up a wrong tone. His whole speech was a mistake from first to last, an utter failure.

Just then his aunts and his wife came out of the ladies' dressing-room. His aunts were two small, plainly dressed old women. Aunt Julia was an inch or so the taller. Her hair, drawn low over the tops of her ears, was grey; and grey also, with darker shadows, was her large flaccid face. Though she was stout in build and stood erect, her slow eyes and parted lips gave her the appearance of a woman who did not know where she was or where she was going.

Aunt Kate was more vivacious. Her face, healthier than her sister's, was all puckers and creases, like a shrivelled red apple, and her hair, braided in the same old-fashioned way, had not lost its ripe nut colour.

They both kissed Gabriel frankly. He was their favourite nephew, the son of their dead elder sister, Ellen, who had married T. J. Conroy of the Port and Docks.

"Gretta tells me you're not going to take a cab back to Monkstown tonight, Gabriel," said Aunt Kate.

"No," said Gabriel, turning to his wife, "we had quite enough of that last year, hadn't we? Don't you remember, Aunt Kate, what a cold Gretta got out of it? Cab windows rattling all the way, and the east wind blowing in after we passed Merrion. Very jolly it was. Gretta caught a dreadful cold."

Aunt Kate frowned severely and nodded her head at every word.

"Quite right, Gabriel, quite right," she said. "You can't be too careful."

"But as for Gretta there," said Gabriel, "she'd walk home in the snow if she were let."

Mrs. Conroy laughed.

"Don't mind him, Aunt Kate," she said. "He's really an awful bother, what with green shades for Tom's eyes at night and making him do the dumb-bells, and forcing Eva to eat the stirabout. The poor child! And she simply hates the sight of it! . . . O, but you'll never guess what he makes me wear now!"

She broke out into a peal of laughter and glanced at her husband, whose admiring and happy eyes had been wandering from her dress to her face and hair. The two aunts laughed heartily, too, for Gabriel's solicitude was a standing joke with them.

"Goloshes!" said Mrs. Conroy. "That's the latest. Whenever it's wet underfoot I must put on my goloshes. Tonight even, he wanted me to put them on, but I wouldn't. The next thing he'll buy me will be a diving suit."

Gabriel laughed nervously and patted his tie reassuringly, while Aunt Kate nearly doubled herself, so heartily did she enjoy the joke. The smile soon faded from Aunt Julia's face and her mirthless eyes were directed towards her nephew's face. After a pause she asked:

"And what are goloshes, Gabriel?"

"Goloshes, Julia!" exclaimed her sister. "Goodness me, don't you know what goloshes are? You wear them over your . . . over your boots, Gretta, isn't it?"

"Yes," said Mrs. Conroy. "Guttapercha things. We both

have a pair now. Gabriel says everyone wears them on the Continent."

"O, on the Continent," murmured Aunt Julia, nodding her head slowly.

Gabriel knitted his brows and said, as if he were slightly angered:

"It's nothing very wonderful, but Gretta thinks it very funny because she says the word reminds her of Christy Minstrels."

"But tell me, Gabriel," said Aunt Kate, with brisk tact. "Of course, you've seen about the room. Gretta was saying . . ."

"O, the room is all right," replied Gabriel. "I've taken one in the Gresham."

"To be sure," said Aunt Kate, "by far the best thing to do. And the children, Gretta, you're not anxious about them?"

"O, for one night," said Mrs. Conroy. "Besides, Bessie will look after them."

"To be sure," said Aunt Kate again. "What a comfort it is to have a girl like that, one you can depend on! There's that Lily, I'm sure I don't know what has come over her lately. She's not the girl she was at all."

Gabriel was about to ask his aunt some questions on this point, but she broke off suddenly to gaze after her sister, who had wandered down the stairs and was craning her neck over the banisters.

"Now, I ask you," she said almost testily, "where is Julia going? Julia! Julia! Where are you going?"

Julia, who had gone half way down one flight, came back and announced blandly: "Here's Freddy."

At the same moment a clapping of hands and a final flourish of the pianist told that the waltz had ended. The drawing-room door was opened from within and some couples came out. Aunt Kate drew Gabriel aside hurriedly and whispered into his ear:

"Slip down, Gabriel, like a good fellow and see if he's all right, and don't let him up if he's screwed. I'm sure he's screwed. I'm sure he is."

Gabriel went to the stairs and listened over the banisters. He could hear two persons talking in the pantry. Then he recognised Freddy Malins' laugh. He went down the stairs noisily.

"It's such a relief," said Aunt Kate to Mrs. Conroy, "that Gabriel is here. I always feel easier in my mind when he's here. . . . Julia, there's Miss Daly and Miss Power will take some re-freshment. Thanks for your beautiful waltz, Miss Daly. It made lovely time."

A tall wizen-faced man, with a stiff grizzled moustache and swarthy skin, who was passing out with his partner, said:

"And may we have some refreshment, too, Miss Morkan?"

"Julia," said Aunt Kate summarily, "and here's Mr. Browne and Miss Furlong. Take them in, Julia, with Miss Daly and Miss Power."

"I'm the man for the ladies," said Mr. Browne, pursing his lips until his moustache bristled and smiling in all his wrinkles. "You know, Miss Morkan, the reason they are so fond of me is —"

He did not finish his sentence, but, seeing that Aunt Kate was out of earshot, at once led the three young ladies into the back room. The middle of the room was occupied by two square tables placed end to end, and on these Aunt Julia and the caretaker were straightening and smoothing a large cloth. On the sideboard were arrayed dishes and plates, and glasses and bundles of knives and forks and spoons. The top of the closed square piano served also as a sideboard for viands and sweets. At a smaller sideboard in one corner two young men were standing, drinking hop-bitters.

Mr. Browne led his charges thither and invited them all, in jest, to some ladies' punch, hot, strong and sweet. As they said they never took anything strong, he opened three bottles of lemonade for them. Then he asked one of the young men to move aside, and, taking hold of the decanter, filled out for himself a goodly measure of whisky. The young men eyed him respectfully while he took a trial sip.

"God help me," he said, smiling, "it's the doctors orders."

His wizened face broke into a broader smile, and the three young ladies laughed in musical echo to his pleasantry, swaying their bodies to and fro, with nervous jerks of their shoulders. The boldest said:

"O, now Mr. Browne, I'm sure the doctor never ordered anything of the kind."

Mr. Browne took another sip of his whisky and said, with sidling mimicry:

"Well, you see, I'm like the famous Mrs. Cassidy, who is reported to have said: 'Now, Mary Grimes, if I don't take it, make me take it, for I feel I want it.'"

His hot face had leaned forward a little too confidentially and he had assumed a very low Dublin accent so that the young ladies, with one instinct, received his speech in silence. Miss Furlong, who was one of Mary Jane's pupils, asked Miss Daly what was the name of the pretty waltz she had played; and Mr. Browne, seeing that he was ignored, turned promptly to the two young men who were more appreciative.

A red-faced young woman, dressed in pansy, came into the room, excitedly clapping her hands and crying:

"Quadrilles! Quadrilles!"

Close on her heels came Aunt Kate, crying:

"Two gentlemen and three ladies, Mary Jane!"

"O, here's Mr. Bergin and Mr. Kerrigan," said Mary Jane. "Mr. Kerrigan, will you take Miss Power? Miss Furlong, may I get you a partner, Mr. Bergin. O, that'll just do now."

"Three ladies, Mary Jane," said Aunt Kate.

The two young gentlemen asked the ladies if they might have the pleasure, and Mary Jane turned to Miss Daly.

"O, Miss Daly, you're really awfully good, after playing for the last two dances, but really we're so short of ladies tonight."

"I don't mind in the least, Miss Morkan."

"But I've a nice partner for you, Mr. Bartell D'Arcy, the tenor. I'll get him to sing later on. All Dublin is raving about him."

"Lovely voice, lovely voice!" said Aunt Kate.

As the piano had twice begun the prelude to the first figure Mary Jane led her recruits quickly from the room. They had hardly gone when Aunt Julia wandered slowly into the room, looking behind her at something.

"What is the matter, Julia?" asked Aunt Kate anxiously. "Who is it?"

Julia, who was carrying in a column of table-napkins, turned to her sister and said, simply, as if the question had surprised her:

"It's only Freddy, Kate, and Gabriel with him."

In fact right behind her Gabriel could be seen piloting Freddy Malins across the landing. The latter, a young man of about forty, was of Gabriel's size and build, with very round shoulders. His face was fleshy and pallid, touched with colour only at the thick hanging lobes of his ears and at the wide wings of his nose. He had coarse features, a blunt nose, a convex and receding brow, tumid and protruded lips. His heavy-lidded eyes and the disorder of his scanty hair made him look sleepy. He was laughing heartily in a high key at a story which he had been telling Gabriel on the stairs and at the same time rubbing the knuckles of his left fist backwards and forwards into his left eye.

"Good evening, Freddy," said Aunt Julia.

Freddy Malins bade the Misses Morkan good-evening in what seemed an offhand fashion by reason of the habitual catch in his voice and then, seeing that Mr. Browne was grinning at him from the sideboard, crossed the room on rather shaky legs and began to repeat in an undertone the story he had just told to Gabriel.

"He's not so bad, is he?" said Aunt Kate to Gabriel.

Gabriel's brows were dark but he raised them quickly and answered:

"O, no, hardly noticeable."

"Now, isn't he a terrible fellow!" she said. "And his poor mother made him take the pledge on New Year's Eve. But come on, Gabriel, into the drawing-room."

Before leaving the room with Gabriel she signalled to Mr. Browne by frowning and shaking her forefinger in warning to and fro. Mr. Browne nodded in answer and, when she had gone, said to Freddy Malins:

"Now, then, Teddy, I'm going to fill you out a good glass of lemonade just to buck you up."

Freddy Malins, who was nearing the climax of his story, waved the offer aside impatiently but Mr. Browne, having first called Freddy Malins' attention to a disarray in his dress, filled out and handed him a full glass of lemonade. Freddy Malins' left hand accepted the glass mechanically, his right hand being engaged in the mechanical readjustment of his dress. Mr. Browne, whose face was once more wrinkling with mirth, poured out for himself a glass of whisky while Freddy Malins exploded, before he had well reached the climax of his story, in a kink of high-pitched bronchitic laughter and, setting down his untasted and overflowing glass, began to rub the knuckles of his left fist backwards and forwards into his left eye, repeating words of his last phrase as well as his fit of laughter would allow him.

Gabriel could not listen while Mary Jane was playing her Academy piece, full of runs and difficult passages, to the hushed drawing-room. He liked music but the piece she was playing had no melody for him and he doubted whether it had any melody for the other listeners, though they had begged Mary Jane to play something. Four young men, who had come from the refreshment-room to stand in the doorway at the sound of the piano, had gone away quietly in couples after a few minutes. The only persons who seemed to follow the music were Mary Jane herself, her hands racing along the key-board or lifted from it at the pauses like those of a priestess in momentary imprecation, and Aunt Kate standing at her elbow to turn the page.

Gabriel's eyes, irritated by the floor, which glittered with beeswax under the heavy chandelier, wandered to the wall above the piano. A picture of the balcony scene in *Romeo and Juliet* hung there and beside it was a picture of the two murdered princes in the Tower which Aunt Julia had worked in red, blue and brown wools when she was a girl. Probably in the school they had gone to as girls that kind of work had been taught for one year. His mother had worked for him as a birthday present a waistcoat of purple tabinet, with little foxes' heads upon it, lined with brown satin and having round mulberry buttons. It was strange that his mother had had no musical talent though Aunt Kate used to call her the brains carrier of the Morkan family. Both she and Julia had always seemed a little proud of their serious and matronly sister. Her photograph stood before the pierglass. She held an open book on her knees and was pointing out something in it to Constantine who, dressed in a man-o'-war suit, lay at her feet. It was she who had chosen the names of her sons for she was very sensible of the dignity of family life. Thanks to her, Constantine was now senior curate in Balbriggan and, thanks to her, Gabriel himself had taken his degree in the Royal University. A shadow passed over his face as he remembered her sullen opposition to his marriage. Some slighting phrases she had used still rankled in his memory; she had once spoken of Gretta as being country cute and that was not true of Gretta at all. It was Gretta who had nursed her during all her last long illness in their house at Monkstown.

He knew that Mary Jane must be near the end of her piece for she was playing again the opening melody with runs of scales after every bar and while he waited for the end the resentment died down in his heart. The piece ended with a trill of octaves in the trebles and a final deep octave in the bass. Great applause greeted Mary Jane as, blushing and rolling up her music nervously, she escaped from the room. The most vigorous clapping came from the four young men in the doorway who had gone away to the refreshment-room at the beginning of the piece but had come back when the piano had stopped.

Lancers were arranged. Gabriel found himself partnered with Miss Ivors. She was a frank-mannered talkative young lady, with a freckled face and prominent brown eyes. She did not wear a low-cut bodice and the large brooch which was fixed in the front of her collar bore on it an Irish device and motto.

When they had taken their places she said abruptly:

"I have a crow to pluck with you."

"With me?" said Gabriel.

She nodded her head gravely.

"What is it?" asked Gabriel, smiling at her solemn manner.

"Who is G. C.?" answered Miss Ivors, turning her eyes upon him.

Gabriel coloured and was about to knit his brows, as if he did not understand, when she said bluntly:

"O, innocent Amy! I have found out that you write for *The Daily Express*. Now, aren't you ashamed of yourself?"

"Why should I be ashamed of myself?" asked Gabriel, blinking his eyes and trying to smile.

"Well, I'm ashamed of you," said Miss Ivors frankly. "To say you'd write for a paper like that. I didn't think you were a West Briton."

A look of perplexity appeared on Gabriel's face. It was true that he wrote a literary column every Wednesday in *The Daily Express* for which he was paid fifteen shillings. But that did not make him a West Briton surely. The books he received for review were almost more welcome than the paltry cheque. He loved to feel the covers and turn over the pages of newly printed books. Nearly every day when his teaching in the college was ended he used to wander down the quays to the second-hand booksellers, to Hickey's on Bachelor's Walk, to Webb's or Massey's on Aston's Quay, or to O'Clohissey's in the by-street. He did not know how to meet her charge. He wanted to say that literature was above politics. But they were friends of many years' standing and their careers had been parallel, first at the University and then as teachers: he could not risk a grandiose phrase with her. He continued blinking his eyes and trying to smile and murmured lamely that he saw nothing political in writing reviews of books.

When their turn to cross had come he was still perplexed and inattentive. Miss Ivors promptly took his hand in a warm grasp and said in a soft friendly tone:

"Of course, I was only joking. Come, we cross now."

When they were together again she spoke of the University question and Gabriel felt more at ease. A friend of hers had shown her his review of Browning's poems. That was how she had found out the secret: but she liked the review immensely. Then she said suddenly:

"O, Mr. Conroy, will you come for an excursion to the Aran Isles this summer? We're going to stay there a whole month. It will be splendid out on the Atlantic. You ought to come. Mr. Clancy is coming, and Mr. Kilkelly and Kathleen Kearney. It would be splendid for Gretta too if she'd come. She's from Connacht, isn't she?"

"Her people are," said Gabriel shortly.

"But you will come, won't you?" said Miss Ivors, laying her warm hand eagerly on his arm.

"The fact is," said Gabriel, "I have just arranged to go —"

"Go where?" asked Miss Ivors.

"Well, you know, every year I go for a cycling tour with some fellows and so —"

"But where?" asked Miss Ivors.

"Well, we usually go to France or Belgium or perhaps Germany," said Gabriel awkwardly.

"And why do you go to France and Belgium," said Miss Ivors, "instead of visiting your own land?"

"Well," said Gabriel, "it's partly to keep in touch with the languages and partly for a change."

"And haven't you your own language to keep in touch with —Irish?" asked Miss Ivors.

"Well," said Gabriel, "if it comes to that, you know, Irish is not my language."

Their neighbours had turned to listen to the cross-examination. Gabriel glanced right and left nervously and tried to keep his good humour under the ordeal which was making a blush invade his forehead.

"And haven't you your own land to visit," continued Miss Ivors, "that you know nothing of, your own people, and your own country?"

"O, to tell you the truth," retorted Gabriel suddenly, "I'm sick of my own country, sick of it!"

"Why?" asked Miss Ivors.

Gabriel did not answer for his retort had heated him.

"Why?" repeated Miss Ivors.

They had to go visiting together and, as he had not answered her, Miss Ivors said warmly:

"Of course, you've no answer."

Gabriel tried to cover his agitation by taking part in the dance with great energy. He avoided her eyes for he had seen a sour expression on her face. But when they met in the long chain he was surprised to feel his hand firmly pressed. She looked at him from under her brows for a moment quizzically until he smiled. Then, just as the chain was about to start again, she stood on tiptoe and whispered into his ear:

"West Briton!"

When the lancers were over Gabriel went away to a remote corner of the room where Freddy Malins' mother was sitting. She was a stout feeble old woman with white hair. Her voice had a catch in it like her son's and she stuttered slightly. She had been told that Freddy had come and that he was nearly all right. Gabriel asked her whether she had had a good crossing. She lived with her married daughter in Glasgow and came to Dublin on a visit once a year. She answered placidly that she had had a beautiful crossing and that the captain had been most attentive to her. She spoke also of the beautiful house her daughter kept in Glasgow, and of all the friends they had there. While her tongue rambled on Gabriel tried to banish from his mind all memory of the unpleasant incident with Miss Ivors. Of course the girl or woman, or whatever she was, was an enthusiast but there was a time for all things. Perhaps he ought not to have answered her like that. But she had no right to call him a West Briton before people, even in joke. She had tried to make him ridiculous before people, heckling him and staring at him with her rabbit's eyes.

He saw his wife making her way towards him through the waltzing couples. When she reached him she said into his ear:

"Gabriel, Aunt Kate wants to know won't you carve the goose as usual. Miss Daly will carve the ham and I'll do the pudding."

"All right," said Gabriel.

"She's sending in the younger ones first as soon as this waltz is over so that we'll have the table to ourselves."

"Were you dancing?" asked Gabriel.

"Of course I was. Didn't you see me? What row had you with Molly Ivors?"

"No row. Why? Did she say so?"

"Something like that. I'm trying to get that Mr. D'Arcy to sing. He's full of conceit, I think."

"There was no row," said Gabriel moodily, "only she wanted me to go for a trip to the west of Ireland and I said I wouldn't."

His wife clasped her hands excitedly and gave a little jump.

"O, do go, Gabriel," she cried. "I'd love to see Galway again."

"You can go if you like," said Gabriel coldly.

She looked at him for a moment, then turned to Mrs. Malins and said:

"There's a nice husband for you, Mrs. Malins."

While she was threading her way back across the room Mrs. Malins, without adverting to the interruption, went on to tell Gabriel what beautiful places there were in Scotland and beautiful scenery. Her son-in-law brought them every year to the lakes and they used to go fishing. Her son-in-law was a splendid fisher. One day he caught a beautiful big fish and the man in the hotel cooked it for their dinner.

Gabriel hardly heard what she said. Now that supper was coming near he began to think again about his speech and about the quotation. When he saw Freddy Malins coming across the room to visit his mother Gabriel left the chair free for him and retired into the embrasure of the window. The room had already cleared and from the back room came the clatter of plates and knives. Those who still remained in the drawing-room seemed tired of dancing and were conversing quietly in little groups. Gabriel's warm trembling fingers tapped the cold pane of the window. How cool it must be outside! How pleasant it would be to walk out alone, first along by the river and then through the park! The snow would be lying on the branches of the trees and forming a bright cap on the top of the Wellington Monument. How much more pleasant it would be there than at the supper-table!

He ran over the headings of his speech: Irish hospitality, sad memories, the Three Graces, Paris, the quotation from Browning. He repeated to himself a phrase he had written in his review: "One feels that one is listening to a thought-tormented music." Miss Ivors had praised the review. Was she sincere? Had she really any life of her own behind all her propagandism? There had never been any ill-feeling between them until that night. It unnerved him to think that she would be at the supper-table, looking up at him while he spoke with her critical quizzing eyes. Perhaps she would not be sorry to see him fail in his speech. An idea came into his mind and gave him courage. He would say, alluding to Aunt Kate and Aunt Julia: "Ladies and Gentlemen, the generation which is now on the wane among us may have had its faults but for my part I think it had certain qualities of hospitality, of humour, of humanity, which the new and very serious and hypereducated generation that is growing up around us seems to me to lack." Very good: that was one for Miss Ivors. What did he care that his aunts were only two ignorant old women?

A murmur in the room attracted his attention. Mr. Browne was advancing from the door, gallantly escorting Aunt Julia, who leaned upon his arm, smiling and hanging her head. An irregular musketry of applause escorted her also as far as the piano and then, as Mary Jane seated herself on the stool, and Aunt Julia, no longer smiling, half turned so as to pitch her voice fairly into the room, gradually ceased. Gabriel recognised the prelude. It was that of an old song of Aunt Julia's —*Arrayed for the Bridal*. Her voice, strong and clear in tone, attacked with great spirit the runs which embellish the air and though she sang very rapidly she did not miss even the smallest of the grace notes. To follow the voice, without looking at the singer's face, was to feel and share the excitement of swift and secure flight. Gabriel applauded loudly with all the others at the close of the song and loud applause was borne in from the invisible supper-table. It sounded so genuine that a little colour struggled into Aunt Julia's face as she bent to replace in the music-stand the old leather-bound song-book that had her initials on the cover. Freddy Malins, who had listened with his head perched sideways to hear her better, was still applauding when everyone else had ceased and talking animatedly to his mother who nodded her head gravely and slowly in acquiescence. At last, when he could clap no more, he stood up suddenly and hurried across the room to Aunt Julia whose hand he seized and held in both his hands, shaking it when words failed him or the catch in his voice proved too much for him.

"I was just telling my mother," he said, "I never heard you sing so well, never. No, I never heard your voice so good as it is tonight. Now! Would you believe that now? That's the truth. Upon my word and honour that's the truth. I never heard your voice sound so fresh and so . . . so clear and fresh, never."

Aunt Julia smiled broadly and murmured something about compliments as she released her hand from his grasp. Mr. Browne extended his open hand towards her and said to those who were near him in the manner of a show-man introducing a prodigy to an audience:

"Miss Julia Morkan, my latest discovery!"

He was laughing very heartily at this himself when Freddy Malins turned to him and said:

"Well, Browne, if you're serious you might make a worse discovery. All I can say is I never heard her sing half so well as long as I am coming here. And that's the honest truth."

"Neither did I," said Mr. Browne. "I think her voice has greatly improved."

Aunt Julia shrugged her shoulders and said with meek pride:

"Thirty years ago I hadn't a bad voice as voices go."

"I often told Julia," said Aunt Kate emphatically, "that she was simply thrown away in that choir. But she never would be said by me."

She turned as if to appeal to the good sense of the others against a refractory child while Aunt Julia gazed in front of her, a vague smile of reminiscence playing on her face.

"No," continued Aunt Kate, "she wouldn't be said or led by anyone, slaving there in that choir night and day, night and day. Six o'clock on Christmas morning! And all for what?"

"Well, isn't it for the honour of God, Aunt Kate?" asked Mary Jane, twisting round on the piano-stool and smiling.

Aunt Kate turned fiercely on her niece and said:

"I know all about the honour of God, Mary Jane, but I think it's not at all honourable for the pope to turn out the women out of the choirs that have slaved there all their lives and put little whipper-snappers of boys over their heads. I suppose it is for the good of the Church if the pope does it. But it's not just, Mary Jane, and it's not right."

She had worked herself into a passion and would have continued in defence of her sister for it was a sore subject with her but Mary Jane, seeing that all the dancers had come back, intervened pacifically:

"Now, Aunt Kate, you're giving scandal to Mr. Browne who is of the other persuasion."

Aunt Kate turned to Mr. Browne, who was grinning at this allusion to his religion, and said hastily:

"O, I don't question the pope's being right. I'm only a stupid old woman and I wouldn't presume to do such a thing. But there's such a thing as common everyday politeness and gratitude. And if I were in Julia's place I'd tell that Father Healey straight up to his face . . ."

"And besides, Aunt Kate," said Mary Jane, "we really are all hungry and when we are hungry we are all very quarrelsome."

"And when we are thirsty we are also quarrelsome," added Mr. Browne.

"So that we had better go to supper," said Mary Jane, "and finish the discussion afterwards."

On the landing outside the drawing-room Gabriel found his wife and Mary Jane trying to persuade Miss Ivors to stay for supper. But Miss Ivors, who had put on her hat and was buttoning her cloak, would not stay. She did not feel in the least hungry and she had already overstayed her time.

"But only for ten minutes, Molly," said Mrs. Conroy. "That won't delay you."

"To take a pick itself," said Mary Jane, "after all your dancing."

"I really couldn't," said Miss Ivors.

"I am afraid you didn't enjoy yourself at all," said Mary Jane hopelessly.

"Ever so much, I assure you," said Miss Ivors, "but you really must let me run off now."

"But how can you get home?" asked Mrs. Conroy.

"O, it's only two steps up the quay."

Gabriel hesitated a moment and said:

"If you will allow me, Miss Ivors, I'll see you home if you are really obliged to go."

But Miss Ivors broke away from them.

"I won't hear of it," she cried. "For goodness' sake go in to your suppers and don't mind me. I'm quite well able to take care of myself."

"Well, you're the comical girl, Molly," said Mrs. Conroy frankly.

"*Beannacht libh,*" cried Miss Ivors, with a laugh, as she ran down the staircase.

Mary Jane gazed after her, a moody puzzled expression on her face, while Mrs. Conroy leaned over the banisters to listen for the hall-door. Gabriel asked himself was he the cause of her abrupt departure. But she did not seem to be in ill humor: she had gone away laughing. He stared blankly down the staircase.

At the moment Aunt Kate came toddling out of the supper-room, almost wringing her hands in despair.

"Where is Gabriel?" she cried. "Where on earth is Gabriel? There's everyone waiting in there, stage to let, and nobody to carve the goose!"

"Here I am, Aunt Kate!" cried Gabriel, with sudden animation, "ready to carve a flock of geese, if necessary."

A fat brown goose lay at one end of the table and at the other end, on a bed of creased paper strewn with sprigs of parsley, lay a great ham, stripped of its outer skin and peppered over with crust crumbs, a neat paper frill round its shin and beside this was a round of spiced beef. Between these rival ends ran parallel lines of side-dishes: two little minsters of jelly, red and yellow; a shallow dish full of blocks of blancmange and red jam, a large green leaf-shaped dish with a stalk-shaped handle, on which lay bunches of purple raisins and peeled almonds, a companion dish on which lay a solid rectangle of Smyrna figs, a dish of custard topped with grated nutmeg, a small bowl full of chocolates and sweets wrapped in gold and silver papers and a glass vase in which stood some tall celery stalks. In the centre of the table there stood, as sentries to a fruit-stand which upheld a pyramid of oranges and American apples, two squat old-fashioned decanters of cut glass, one containing port and the other dark sherry. On the closed square piano a pudding in a huge yellow dish lay in waiting and behind it were three squads of bottles of stout and ale and minerals, drawn up according to the colours of their uniforms, the first two black, with brown and red labels, the third and smallest squad white, with transverse green sashes.

Gabriel took his seat boldly at the head of the table and, having looked to the edge of the carver, plunged his fork firmly into the goose. He felt quite at ease now for he was an expert carver and liked nothing better than to find himself at the head of a well-laden table.

"Miss Furlong, what shall I send you?" he asked. "A wing or a slice of the breast?"

"Just a small slice of the breast."

"Miss Higgins, what for you?"

"O, anything at all, Mr. Conroy."

While Gabriel and Miss Daly exchanged plates of goose and plates of ham and spiced beef Lily went from guest to guest with a dish of hot floury potatoes wrapped in a white napkin. This was Mary Jane's idea and she had also suggested apple sauce for the goose but Aunt Kate had said that plain roast goose without any apple sauce had always been good enough for her and she hoped she might never eat worse. Mary Jane waited on her pupils and saw that they got the best slices and Aunt Kate and Aunt Julia opened and carried across from the piano bottles of stout and ale for the gentlemen and bottles of minerals for the ladies. There was a great deal of confusion and laughter and noise, the noise of orders and counter-orders, of knives and forks, of corks and glass-stoppers. Gabriel began to carve second helpings as soon as he had finished the first round without serving himself. Everyone protested loudly so that he compromised by taking a long draught of stout for he had found the carving hot work. Mary Jane settled down quietly to her supper but Aunt Kate and Aunt Julia were still toddling round the table, walking on each other's heels, getting in each other's way and giving each other unheeded orders. Mr. Browne begged of them to sit down and eat their suppers and so did Gabriel but they said there was time enough, so that, at last, Freddy Malins stood up and, capturing Aunt Kate, plumped her down on her chair amid general laughter.

When everyone had been well served Gabriel said, smiling:

"Now, if anyone wants a little more of what vulgar people call stuffing let him or her speak."

A chorus of voices invited him to begin his own supper and Lily came forward with three potatoes which she had reserved for him.

"Very well," said Gabriel amiably, as he took another preparatory draught, "kindly forget my existence, ladies and gentlemen, for a few minutes."

He set to his supper and took no part in the conversation with which the table covered Lily's removal of the plates. The subject of talk was the opera company which was then at the Theatre Royal. Mr. Bartell D'Arcy, the tenor, a dark-complexioned young man with a smart moustache, praised very highly the leading contralto of the company but Miss Furlong thought she had a rather vulgar style of production. Freddy Malins said there was a Negro chieftain singing in the second part of the Gaiety pantomime who had one of the finest tenor voices he had ever heard.

"Have you heard him?" he asked Mr. Bartell D'Arcy across the table.

"No," answered Mr. Bartell D'Arcy carelessly.

"Because," Freddy Malins explained, "now I'd be curious to hear your opinion of him. I think he has a grand voice."

"It takes Teddy to find out the really good things," said Mr. Browne familiarly to the table.

"And why couldn't he have a voice too?" asked Freddy Malins sharply. "Is it because he's only a black?"

Nobody answered this question and Mary Jane led the table back to the legitimate opera. One of her pupils had given her a pass for *Mignon*. Of course it was very fine, she said, but it made her think of poor Georgina Burns. Mr. Browne could go back farther still, to the old Italian companies that used to come to Dublin — Tietjens, Ilma de Murzka, Campanini, the great Trebelli, Giuglini, Ravelli, Aramburo. Those were the days, he said, when there was something like singing to be heard in Dublin. He told too of how the top gallery of the old Royal used to be packed night after night, of how one night an Italian tenor had sung five encores to *Let me like a Soldier fall,* introducing a high C every time, and of how the gallery boys would sometimes in their enthusiasm unyoke the horses from the carriage of some great *prima donna* and pull her themselves through the streets to her hotel. Why did they never play the grand old operas now, he asked, *Dinorah, Lucrezia Borgia?* Because they could not get the voices to sing them: that was why.

"O, well," said Mr. Bartell D'Arcy, "I presume there are as good singers today as there were then."

"Where are they?" asked Mr. Browne defiantly.

"In London, Paris, Milan," said Mr. Bartell D'Arcy warmly. "I suppose Caruso, for example, is quite as good, if not better than any of the men you have mentioned."

"Maybe so," said Mr. Browne. "But I may tell you I doubt it strongly."

"O, I'd give anything to hear Caruso sing," said Mary Jane.

"For me," said Aunt Kate, who had been picking a bone, "there was only one tenor. To please me, I mean. But I suppose none of you ever heard of him."

"Who was he, Miss Morkan?" asked Mr. Bartell D'Arcy politely.

"His name," said Aunt Kate, "was Parkinson. I heard him when he was in his prime and I think he had then the purest tenor voice that was ever put into a man's throat."

"Strange," said Mr. Bartell D'Arcy. "I never even heard of him."

"Yes, yes, Miss Morkan is right," said Mr. Browne. "I remember hearing of old Parkinson but he's too far back for me."

"A beautiful, pure, sweet, mellow English tenor," said Aunt Kate with enthusiasm.

Gabriel having finished, the huge pudding was transferred to the table. The clatter of forks and spoons began again. Gabriel's wife served out spoonfuls of the pudding and passed the plates down the table. Midway down they were held up by Mary Jane, who replenished them with raspberry or orange jelly or with blancmange and jam. The pudding was of Aunt Julia's making and she received praises for it from all quarters. She herself said that it was not quite brown enough.

"Well, I hope, Miss Morkan," said Mr. Browne, "that I'm brown enough for you because, you know, I'm all brown."

All the gentlemen, except Gabriel, ate some of the pudding out of compliment to Aunt Julia. As Gabriel never ate sweets the celery had been left for him. Freddy Malins also took a stalk of celery and ate it with his pudding. He had been told that celery was a capital thing for the blood and he was just then under doctor's care. Mrs. Malins, who had been silent all through the supper, said that her son was going down to Mount Melleray in a week or so. The table then spoke of Mount Melleray, how bracing the air was down there, how hospitable the monks were and how they never asked for a penny-piece from their guests.

"And do you mean to say," asked Mr. Browne incredulously, "that a chap can go down there and put up there as if it were a hotel and live on the fat of the land and then come away without paying anything?"

"O, most people give some donation to the monastery when they leave," said Mary Jane.

"I wish we had an institution like that in our Church," said Mr. Browne candidly.

He was astonished to hear that the monks never spoke, got up at two in the morning and slept in their coffins. He asked what they did it for.

"That's the rule of the order," said Aunt Kate firmly.

"Yes, but why?" asked Mr. Browne.

Aunt Kate repeated that it was the rule, that was all. Mr. Browne still seemed not to understand. Freddy Malins explained to him, as best he could, that the monks were trying to make up for the sins committed by all the sinners in the outside world. The explanation was not very clear for Mr. Browne grinned and said:

"I like that idea very much but wouldn't a comfortable spring bed do them as well as a coffin?"

"The coffin," said Mary Jane, "is to remind them of their last end."

As the subject had grown lugubrious it was buried in a silence of the table during which Mrs. Malins could be heard saying to her neighbour in an indistinct undertone:

"They are very good men, the monks, very pious men."

The raisins and almonds and figs and apples and oranges and chocolates and sweets were now passed about the table and Aunt Julia invited all the guests to have either port or sherry. At first Mr. Bartell D'Arcy refused to take either but one of his neighbours nudged him and whispered something to him upon which he allowed his glass to be filled. Gradually as the last glasses were being filled the conversation ceased. A pause followed, broken only by the noise of the wine and by unsettlings of chairs. The Misses Morkan, all three, looked down at the tablecloth. Someone coughed once or twice and then a few gentlemen patted the table gently as a signal for silence. The silence came and Gabriel pushed back his chair and stood up.

The patting at once grew louder in encouragement and then ceased altogether. Gabriel leaned his ten trembling fingers on the tablecloth and smiled nervously at the company. Meeting a row of upturned faces he raised his eyes to the chandelier. The piano was playing a waltz tune and he could hear the skirts sweeping against the drawing-room door. People, perhaps, were standing in the snow on the quay outside, gazing up at the lighted windows and listening to the waltz music. The air was pure there. In the distance lay the park where the trees were weighted with snow. The Wellington Monument wore a gleaming cap of snow that flashed over the white field of Fifteen Acres.

He began:

"Ladies and Gentlemen,

"It has fallen to my lot this evening, as in years past, to perform a very pleasing task but a task for which I am afraid my poor powers as a speaker are all too inadequate."

"No, no!" said Mr. Browne.

"But, however that may be, I can only ask you tonight to take the will for the deed and to lend me your attention for a few moments while I endeavour to express to you in words what my feelings are on this occasion.

"Ladies and Gentlemen, it is not the first time that we have gathered together under this hospitable roof, around this hospitable board. It is not the first time that we have been the recipients — or perhaps, I had better say, the victims — of the hospitality of certain good ladies."

He made a circle in the air with his arm and paused. Everyone laughed or smiled at Aunt Kate and Aunt Julia and Mary Jane who all turned crimson with pleasure. Gabriel went on more boldly:

"I feel more strongly with every recurring year that our country has no tradition which does it so much honour and which it should guard so jealously as that of its hospitality. It is a tradition that is unique as far as my experience goes (and I have visited not a few places abroad) among the modern nations. Some would say, perhaps, that with us it is rather a failing than anything to be boasted of. But granted even that, it is, to my mind, a princely failing, and one that I trust will long be cultivated among us. Of one thing, at least, I am sure. As long as this one roof shelters the good ladies aforesaid — and I wish from my heart it may do so for many and many a long year to come — the tradition of genuine warm-hearted courteous Irish hospitality, which our fore-fathers have handed down to us and which we in turn must hand down to our descendants, is still alive among us."

A hearty murmur of assent ran round the table. It shot through Gabriel's mind that Miss Ivors was not there and that she had gone away discourteously: and he said with confidence in himself:

"Ladies and Gentlemen,

"A new generation is growing up in our midst, a generation actuated by new ideas and new principles. It is serious and enthusiastic for these new ideas and its enthusiasm, even when it is misdirected, is, I believe, in the main sincere. But we are living in a sceptical and, if I may use the phrase, a thought-tormented age: and sometimes I fear that this new generation, educated or hypereducated as it is, will lack those qualities of humanity, of hospitality, of kindly humour which belonged to an older day. Listening tonight to the names of all those great singers of the past it seemed to me, I must confess, that we were living in a less spacious age. Those days might, without exaggeration, be called spacious days: and if they are gone beyond recall let us hope, at least, that in gatherings such as this we shall still speak of them with pride and affection, still cherish in our hearts the memory of those dead and gone great ones whose fame the world will not willingly let die."

"Hear, hear!" said Mr. Browne loudly.

"But yet," continued Gabriel, his voice falling into a softer inflection, "there are always in gatherings such as this sadder thoughts that will recur to our minds: thoughts of the past, of youth, of changes, of absent faces that we miss here tonight. Our path through life is strewn with many such sad memories: and were we to brood upon them always we could not find the heart to go on bravely with our work among the living. We have all of us living duties and living affections which claim, and rightly claim, our strenuous endeavours.

"Therefore, I will not linger on the past. I will not let any gloomy moralising intrude upon us here tonight. Here we are gathered together for a brief moment from the bustle and rush of our everyday routine. We are met here as friends, in the spirit of good-fellowship, as colleagues, also to a certain extent, in the true spirit of *camaraderie,* and as the guests of — what shall I call them? — the Three Graces of the Dublin musical world."

The table burst into applause and laughter at this allusion. Aunt Julia vainly asked each of her neighbours in turn to tell her what Gabriel had said.

"He says we are the Three Graces, Aunt Julia," said Mary Jane.

Aunt Julia did not understand but she looked up, smiling, at Gabriel, who continued in the same vein:

"Ladies and Gentlemen,

"I will not attempt to play tonight the part that Paris played on another occasion. I will not attempt to choose between them. The task would be an invidious one and one beyond my poor powers. For when I view them in turn, whether it be our chief hostess herself, whose good heart, whose too good heart, has become a byword with all who know her, or her sister, who seems to be gifted with perennial youth and whose singing must have been a surprise and a revelation to us all tonight, or, last but not least, when I consider our youngest hostess, talented, cheerful, hard-working and the best of nieces, I confess, Ladies and Gentlemen, that I do not know to which of them I should award the prize."

Gabriel glanced down at his aunts and, seeing the large smile on Aunt Julia's face and the tears which had risen to Aunt Kate's eyes, hastened to his close. He raised his glass of port gallantly, while evey member of the company fingered a glass expectantly, and said loudly:

"Let us toast them all three together. Let us drink to their health, wealth, long life, happiness and prosperity and may they long continue to hold the proud and self-won position which they hold in their profession and the position of honour and affection which they hold in our hearts."

All the guests stood up, glass in hand, and turning towards the three seated ladies, sang in unison, with Mr. Browne as leader:

> For they are jolly gay fellows,
> For they are jolly gay fellows,
> For they are jolly gay fellows,
> Which nobody can deny.

Aunt Kate was making frank use of her handkerchief and even Aunt Julia seemed moved. Freddy Malins beat time with his pudding-fork and the singers turned towards one another, as if in melodious conference, while they sang with emphasis:

> Unless he tells a lie,
> Unless he tells a lie,

Then, turning once more towards their hostesses, they sang:

> For they are jolly gay fellows,
> For they are jolly gay fellows,
> For they are jolly gay fellows,
> Which nobody can deny.

The acclamation which followed was taken up beyond the door of the supper-room by many of the other guests and renewed time after time, Freddy Malins acting as officer with his fork on high.

The piercing morning air came into the hall where they were standing so that Aunt Kate said:

"Close the door, somebody. Mrs. Malins will get her death of cold."

"Browne is out there, Aunt Kate," said Mary Jane.

"Browne is everywhere," said Aunt Kate, lowering her voice.

Mary Jane laughed at her tone.

"Really," she said archly, "he is very attentive."

"He has been laid on here like the gas," said Aunt Kate in the same tone, "all during the Christmas."

She laughed herself this time good-humouredly and then added quickly:

"But tell him to come in, Mary Jane, and close the door. I hope to goodness he didn't hear me."

At that moment the hall-door was opened and Mr. Browne came in from the doorstep, laughing as if his heart would break. He was dressed in a long green overcoat with mock astrakhan cuffs and collar and wore on his head an oval fur cap. He pointed down the snow-covered quay from where the sound of shrill prolonged whistling was borne in.

"Teddy will have all the cabs in Dublin out," he said.

Gabriel advanced from the little pantry behind the office, struggling into his overcoat and, looking round the hall, said:

"Gretta not down yet?"

"She's getting on her things, Gabriel," sad Aunt Kate.

"Who's playing up there?" asked Gabriel.

"Nobody. They're all gone."

"O no, Aunt Kate," said Mary Jane. "Bartell D'Arcy and Miss O'Callaghan aren't gone yet."

"Someone is fooling at the piano anyhow," said Gabriel.

Mary Jane glanced at Gabriel and Mr. Browne and said with a shiver:

"It makes me feel cold to look at you two gentlemen muffled up like that. I wouldn't like to face your journey home at this hour."

"I'd like nothing better this minute," said Mr. Browne stoutly, "than a rattling fine walk in the country or a fast drive with a good spanking goer between the shafts."

"We used to have a very good horse and trap at home," said Aunt Julia sadly.

"The never-to-be-forgotten Johnny," said Mary Jane, laughing.

Aunt Kate and Gabriel laughed too.

"Why, what was wonderful about Johnny?" asked Mr. Browne.

"The late lamented Patrick Morkan, our grandfather, that is," explained Gabriel, "commonly known in his later years as the old gentleman, was a glue-boiler."

"O, now, Gabriel," said Aunt Kate, laughing, "he had a starch mill."

"Well, glue or starch," said Gabriel, "the old gentleman had a horse by the name of Johnny. And Johnny used to work in the old gentleman's mill, walking round and round in order to drive the mill. That was all very well; but now comes the tragic part about Johnny. One fine day the old gentleman thought he'd like to drive out with the quality to a military review in the park."

"The Lord have mercy on his soul," said Aunt Kate compassionately.

"Amen," said Gabriel. "So the old gentleman, as I said, harnessed Johnny and put on his very best tall hat and his very best stock collar and drove out in grand style from his ancestral mansion somewhere near Back Lane, I think."

Everyone laughed, even Mrs. Malins, at Gabriel's manner and Aunt Kate said:

"O, now, Gabriel, he didn't live in Back Lane, really. Only the mill was there."

"Out from the mansion of his forefathers," continued Gabriel, "he drove with Johnny. And everything went on beautifully until Johnny came in sight of King Billy's statue; and whether he fell in love with the horse King Billy sits on or whether he thought he was back again in the mill, anyhow he began to walk round the statue."

Gabriel paced in a circle round the hall in his goloshes amid the laughter of the others.

"Round and round he went," said Gabriel, "and the old gentleman, who was a very pompous old gentleman, was highly indignant. 'Go on, sir! What do you mean, sir? Johnny! Johnny! Most extraordinary conduct! Can't understand the horse!'"

The peal of laughter which followed Gabriel's imitation of the incident was interrupted by a resounding knock at the hall door. Mary Jane ran to open it and let in Freddy Malins. Freddy Malins, with his hat well back on his head and his shoulders humped with cold, was puffing and steaming after his exertions.

"I could only get one cab," he said.

"O, we'll find another along the quay," said Gabriel.

"Yes," said Aunt Kate. "Better not keep Mrs. Malins standing in the draught."

Mrs. Malins was helped down the front steps by her son and Mr. Browne and, after many maneuvres, hoisted into the cab. Freddy Malins clambered in after her and spent a long time settling her on the seat, Mr. Browne helping him with advice. At last she was settled comfortably and Freddy Malins invited Mr. Browne into the cab. There was a good deal of confused talk, and then Mr. Browne got into the cab. The cabman settled his rug over his knees, and bent down for the address. The confusion grew greater and the cabman was directed differently by Freddy Malins and Mr. Browne, each of whom had his head out through a window of the cab. The difficulty was to know where to drop Mr. Browne along the route, and Aunt Kate, Aunt Julia and Mary Jane helped the discussion from the doorstep with cross-directions and contradictions and abundance of laughter. As for Freddy Malins he was speechless with laughter. He popped his head in and out of the window every moment to the great danger of his hat, and told his mother how the discussion was progressing, till at last Mr. Browne shouted to the bewildered cabman above the din of everybody's laughter:

"Do you know Trinity College?"

"Yes, sir," said the cabman.

"Well, drive bang up against Trinity College gates," said Mr. Browne, "and then we'll tell you where to go. You understand now?"

"Yes, sir," said the cabman.

"Make like a bird for Trinity College."

"Right, sir," said the cabman.

The horse was whipped up and the cab rattled off along the quay amid a chorus of laughter and adieus.

Gabriel had not gone to the door with the others. He was in a dark part of the hall gazing up the staircase. A woman was standing near the top of the first flight, in the shadow also. He could not see her face but he could see the terra-cotta and salmon-pink panels of her skirt which the shadow made appear black and white. It was his wife. She was leaning on the banisters, listening to something. Gabriel was surprised at her stillness and strained his ear to listen also. But he could hear little save the noise of laughter and dispute on the front steps, a few chords struck on the piano and a few notes of a man's voice singing.

He stood still in the gloom of the hall, trying to catch the air that the voice was singing and gazing up at his wife. There was grace and mystery in her attitude as if she were a symbol of something. He asked himself what is a woman standing on the stairs in the shadow, listening to distant music, a symbol of. If he were a painter he would paint her in that attitude. Her blue felt hat would show off the bronze of her hair against the darkness and the dark panels of her skirt would show off the light ones. *Distant Music* he would call the picture if he were a painter.

The hall-door was closed; and Aunt Kate, Aunt Julia and Mary Jane came down the hall, still laughing.

"Well, isn't Freddy terrible?" said Mary Jane. "He's really terrible."

Gabriel said nothing but pointed up the stairs towards where his wife was standing. Now that the hall-door was closed the voice and the piano could be heard more clearly. Gabriel held up his hand for them to be silent. The song seemed to be in the old Irish tonality and the singer seemed uncertain both of his words and of his voice. The voice, made plaintive by distance and by the singer's hoarseness, faintly illuminated the cadence of the air with words expressing grief:

> O, the rain falls on my heavy locks
> And the dew wets my skin,
> My babe lies cold . . .

"Oh," exclaimed Mary Jane. "It's Bartell D'Arcy singing and he wouldn't sing all the night. O, I'll get him to sing a song before he goes."

"O, do Mary Jane," said Aunt Kate.

Mary Jane brushed past the others and ran to the staircase, but before she reached it the singing stopped and the piano was closed abruptly.

"O, what a pity!" she cried. "Is he coming down, Gretta?"

Gabriel heard his wife answer yes and saw her come down towards them. A few steps behind her were Mr. Bartell D'Arcy and Miss O'Callaghan.

"O, Mr. D'Arcy," cried Mary Jane, "it's downright mean of you to break off like that when we were all in raptures listening to you."

"I have been at him all the evening," said Miss O'Callaghan, "and Mrs. Conroy, too, and he told us he had a dreadful cold and couldn't sing."

"O, Mr. D'Arcy," said Aunt Kate, "now that was a great fib to tell."

"Can't you see that I'm as hoarse as a crow?" said Mr. D'Arcy roughly.

He went into the pantry hastily and put on his overcoat. The others, taken aback by his rude speech, could find nothing to say. Aunt Kate wrinkled her brows and made signs to the others to drop the subject. Mr. D'Arcy stood swathing his neck carefully and frowning.

"It's the weather," said Aunt Julia, after a pause.

"Yes, everybody has colds," said Aunt Kate readily, "everybody."

"They say," said Mary Jane, "we haven't had snow like it for thirty years; and I read this morning in the newspapers that the snow is general all over Ireland."

"I love the look of snow," said Aunt Julia sadly.

"So do I," said Miss O'Callaghan. "I think Christmas is never really Christmas unless we have snow on the ground."

"But poor Mr. D'Arcy doesn't like the snow," said Aunt Kate, smiling.

Mr. D'Arcy came from the pantry, fully swathed and buttoned, and in a repentant tone told them the history of his cold. Everyone gave him advice and said it was a great pity and urged him to be very careful of his throat in the night air. Gabriel watched his wife, who did not join in the conversation. She was standing right under the dusty fanlight and the flame of the gas lit up the rich bronze of her hair, which he had seen her drying at the fire a few days before. She was in the same attitude and seemed unaware of the talk about her. At last she turned towards them and Gabriel saw that there was colour on her cheeks and that her eyes were shining. A sudden tide of joy went leaping out of his heart.

"Mr. D'Arcy," she said, "what is the name of that song you were singing?"

"It's called *The Lass of Aughrim*," said Mr. D'Arcy, "but I couldn't remember it properly. Why? Do you know it?"

"*The Lass of Aughrim*," she repeated. "I couldn't think of the name."

"It's a very nice air," said Mary Jane. "I'm sorry you were not in voice tonight."

"Now, Mary Jane," said Aunt Kate, "don't annoy Mr. D'Arcy. I won't have him annoyed."

Seeing that all were ready to start she shepherded them to the door, where good-night was said:

"Well, good-night, Aunt Kate, and thanks for the pleasant evening."

"Good-night, Gabriel. Good-night, Gretta!"

"Good-night, Aunt Kate, and thanks ever so much. Good-night, Aunt Julia."

"O, good-night, Gretta. I didn't see you."

"Good-night, Mr. D'Arcy. Good-night, Miss O'Callaghan."

"Good-night, Miss Morkan."

"Good-night, again."

"Good-night, all. Safe home."

"Good-night. Good night."

The morning was still dark. A dull, yellow light brooded over the houses and the river; and the sky seemed to be descending. It was slushy underfoot; and only streaks and patches of snow lay on the roofs, on the parapets of the quay and on the area railings. The lamps were still burning redly in the murky air and, across the river, the palace of the Four Courts stood out menacingly against the heavy sky.

She was walking on before him with Mr. Bartell D'Arcy, her shoes in a brown parcel tucked under one arm and her hands holding her skirt up from the slush. She had no longer any grace of attitude, but Gabriel's eyes were still bright with happiness. The blood went bounding along his veins; and the thoughts went rioting through his brain, proud, joyful, tender, valorous.

She was walking on before him so lightly and so erect that he longed to run after her noiselessly, catch her by the shoulders and say something foolish and affectionate into her ear. She seemed to him so frail that he longed to defend her against something and then to be alone with her. Moments of their secret life together burst like stars upon his memory. A heliotrope envelope was lying beside his breakfast cup and he was caressing it with his hand. Birds were twittering in the ivy and the sunny web of the curtain was shimmering along the floor: he could not eat for happiness. They were standing on the crowded platform and he was placing a ticket inside the warm palm of her glove. He was standing with her in the cold, looking in through a grated window at a man making bottles in a roaring furnace. It was very cold. Her face, fragrant in the cold air, was quite close to his; and suddenly he called out to the man at the furnace:

"Is the fire hot, sir?"

But the man could not hear with the noise of the furnace. It was just as well. He might have answered rudely.

A wave of yet more tender joy escaped from his heart and went coursing in warm flood along his arteries. Like the tender fire of stars moments of their life together, that no one knew of or would ever know of, broke upon and illumined his memory. He longed to recall to her those moments, to make her forget the years of their dull existence together and remember only their moments of ecstasy. For the years, he felt, had not quenched his soul or hers. Their children, his writing, her household cares had not quenched all their souls' tender fire. In one letter that he had written to her then he had said: "Why is it that words like these seem to me so dull and cold? Is it because there is no word tender enough to be your name?"

Like distant music these words that he had written years before were borne towards him from the past. He longed to be alone with her. When the others had gone away, when he and she were in the room in the hotel, then they would be alone together. He would call her softly:

"Gretta!"

Perhaps she would not hear at once: she would be undressing. Then something in his voice would strike her. She would turn and look at him. . . .

At the corner of Winetavern Street they met a cab. He was glad of its rattling noise as it saved him from conversation. She was looking out of the window and seemed tired. The others spoke only a few words, pointing out some building or street. The horse galloped along wearily under the murky morning sky, dragging his old rattling box after his heels, and Gabriel was again in a cab with her, galloping to catch the boat, galloping to their honeymoon.

As the cab drove across O'Connell Bridge Miss O'Callaghan said:

"They say you never cross O'Connell Bridge without seeing a white horse."

"I see a white man this time," said Gabriel.

"Where?" asked Mr. Bartell D'Arcy.

Gabriel pointed to the statue, on which lay patches of snow. Then he nodded familiarly to it and waved his hand.

"Good-night, Dan," he said gaily.

When the cab drew up before the hotel, Gabriel jumped out and, in spite of Mr. Bartell D'Arcy's protest, paid the driver. He gave the man a shilling over his fare. The man saluted and said:

"A prosperous New Year to you, sir."

"The same to you," said Gabriel cordially.

She leaned for a moment on his arm in getting out of the cab and while standing at the curbstone, bidding the others good-night. She leaned lightly on his arm, as lightly as when she had danced with him a few hours before. He had felt proud and happy then, happy that she was his, proud of her grace and wifely carriage. But now, after the kindling again of so many memories, the first touch of her body, musical and strange and perfumed, sent through him a keen pang of lust. Under cover of her silence he pressed her arm closely to his side; and, as they stood at the hotel door, he felt that they had escaped from their lives and duties, escaped from home and friends and run away together with wild and radiant hearts to a new adventure.

An old man was dozing in a great hooded chair in the hall. He lit a candle in the office and went before them to the stairs. They followed him in silence, their feet falling in soft thuds on the thickly carpeted stairs. She mounted the stairs behind the porter, her head bowed in the ascent, her frail shoulders curved as with a burden, her skirt girt tightly about her. He could have flung his arms about her hips and held her still, for his arms were trembling with desire to seize her and only the stress of his nails against the palms of his hands held the wild impulse of his body in check. The porter halted on the stairs to settle his guttering candle. They halted, too, on the steps below him. In the silence Gabriel could hear the falling of the molten wax into the tray and the thumping of his own heart against his ribs.

The porter led them along a corridor and opened a door.

Then he set his unstable candle down on a toilet-table and asked at what hour they were to be called in the morning.

"Eight," said Gabriel.

The porter pointed to the tap of the electric-light and began a muttered apology, but Gabriel cut him short.

"We don't want any light. We have light enough from the street. And I say," he added, pointing to the candle, "you might remove that handsome article, like a good man."

The porter took up his candle again, but slowly, for he was surprised by such a novel idea. Then he mumbled good-night and went out. Gabriel shot the lock to.

A ghastly light from the street lamp lay in a long shaft from one window to the door. Gabriel threw his overcoat and hat on a couch and crossed the room towards the window. He looked down into the street in order that his emotion might calm a little. Then he turned and leaned against a chest of drawers with his back to the light. She had taken off her hat and cloak and was standing before a large swinging mirror, unhooking her waist. Gabriel paused for a few moments, watching her and then said:

"Gretta!"

She turned away from the mirror slowly and walked along the shaft of light towards him. Her face looked so serious and weary that the words would not pass Gabriel's lips. No, it was not the moment yet.

"You look tired," he said.

"I am a little," she answered.

"You don't feel ill or weak?"

"No, tired: that's all."

She went on to the window and stood there, looking out. Gabriel waited again and then, fearing that diffidence was about to conquer him, he said abruptly:

"By the way, Gretta!"

"What is it?"

"You know that poor fellow Malins?" he said quickly.

"Yes. What about him?"

"Well, poor fellow, he's a decent sort of chap, after all," continued Gabriel in a false voice. "He gave me back that sovereign I lent him, and I didn't expect it, really. It's a pity he wouldn't keep away from that Browne, because he's not a bad fellow, really."

He was trembling now with annoyance. Why did she seem so abstracted? He did not know how he could begin. Was she annoyed, too, about something? If she would only turn to him or come to him of her own accord! To take her as she was would be brutal. No, he must see some ardour in her eyes first. He longed to be master of her strange mood.

"When did you lend him the pound?" she asked, after a pause.

Gabriel strove to restrain himself from breaking out into brutal language about the sottish Malins and his pound. He longed to cry to her from his soul, to crush her body against his, to overmaster her. But he said:

"O, at Christmas, when he opened that little Christmas-card shop in Henry Street."

He was in such a fever of rage and desire that he did not hear her come from the window. She stood before him for an instant, looking at him strangely. Then, suddenly raising herself on tiptoe and resting her hands lightly on his shoulders, she kissed him.

"You are a very generous person, Gabriel," she said.

Gabriel, trembling with delight at her sudden kiss and at the quaintness of her phrase, put his hands on her hair and began smoothing it back, scarcely touching it with his fingers. The washing had made it fine and brilliant. His heart was brimming over with happiness. Just when he was wishing for it she had come to him of her own accord. Perhaps her thoughts had been running with his. Perhaps she had felt the impetuous desire that was in him, and then the yielding mood had come upon her. Now that she had fallen to him so easily, he wondered why he had been so diffident.

He stood, holding her head between his hands. Then, slipping one arm swiftly about her body and drawing her towards him, he said softly:

"Gretta, dear, what are you thinking about?"

She did not answer nor yield wholly to his arm. He said again, softly:

"Tell me what it is, Gretta. I think I know what is the matter. Do I know?"

She did not answer at once. Then she said in an outburst of tears:

"O, I am thinking about that song, *The Lass of Aughrim*."

She broke loose from him and ran to the bed and, throwing her arms across the bed-rail, hid her face. Gabriel stood stock-still for a moment in astonishment and then followed her. As he passed in the way of the chevalglass he caught sight of himself in full length, his broad, well-filled shirt-front, the face whose expression always puzzled him when he saw it in a mirror, and his glimmering gilt-rimmed eyeglasses. He halted a few paces from her and said:

"What about the song? Why does that make you cry?"

She raised her head from her arms and dried her eyes with the back of her hand like a child. A kinder note than he had intended went into his voice.

"Why, Gretta?" he asked.

"I am thinking about a person long ago who used to sing that song."

"And who was the person long ago?" asked Gabriel, smiling.

"It was a person I used to know in Galway when I was living with my grandmother," she said.

The smile passed away from Gabriel's face. A dull anger began to gather again at the back of his mind and the dull fires of his lust began to glow angrily in his veins.

"Someone you were in love with?" he asked ironically.

"It was a young boy I used to know," she answered, "named Michael Furey. He used to sing that song, *The Lass of Aughrim*. He was very delicate."

Gabriel was silent. He did not wish her to think that he was interested in this delicate boy.

"I can see him so plainly," she said, after a moment. "Such eyes as he had: big, dark eyes! And such an expression in them — an expression!"

"O then, you are in love with him?" said Gabriel.

"I used to go out walking with him," she said "when I was in Galway."

A thought flew across Gabriel's mind.

"Perhaps that was why you wanted to go to Galway with that Ivors girl?" he said coldly.

She looked at him and asked in surprise:

"What for?"

Her eyes made Gabriel feel awkward. He shugged his shoulders and said:

"How do I know? To see him, perhaps."

She looked away from him along the shaft of light towards the window in silence.

"He is dead," she said at length. "He died when he was only seventeen. Isn't it a terrible thing to die so young as that?"

"What was he?" asked Gabriel, still ironically.

"He was in the gasworks," she said.

Gabriel felt humiliated by the failure of his irony and by the evocation of this figure from the dead, a boy in the gasworks. While he had been full of memories of their secret life together, full of tenderness and joy and desire, she had been comparing him in her mind with another. A shameful consciousness of his own person assailed him. He saw himself as a ludicrous figure, acting as a pennyboy for his aunts, a nervous, well-meaning sentimentalist, orating to vulgarians and idealising his own clownish lusts, the pitiable fatuous fellow he had caught a glimpse of in the mirror. Instinctively he turned his back more to the light lest she might see the shame that burned upon his forehead.

He tried to keep up his tone of cold interrogation, but his voice when he spoke was humble and indifferent.

"I suppose you were in love with this Michael Furey, Gretta," he said.

"I was great with him at that time," she said.

Her voice was veiled and sad. Gabriel, feeling now how vain it would be to try to lead her whither he had purposed, caressed one of her hands and said, also sadly:

"And what did he die of so young, Gretta? Consumption, was it?"

"I think he died for me," she answered.

A vague terror seized Gabriel at this answer, as if, at that hour when he had hoped to triumph, some impalpable and vindictive being was coming against him, gathering forces against him in its vague world. But he shook himself free of it with an effort of reason and continued to caress her hand. He did not question her again, for he felt that she would tell him of herself. Her hand was warm and moist: it did not respond to his touch, but he continued to caress it just as he had caressed her first letter to him that spring morning.

"It was in the winter," she said, "about the beginning of the winter when I was going to leave my grandmother's and come up here to the convent. And he was ill at the time in his lodgings in Galway and wouldn't be let out, and his people in Oughterard were written to. He was in decline, they said, or something like that. I never knew rightly."

She paused for a moment and sighed.

"Poor fellow," she said. "He was very fond of me and he was such a gentle boy. We used to go out together, walking, you know, Gabriel, like the way they do in the country. He was going to study singing only for his health. He had a very good voice, poor Michael Furey."

"Well; and then?" asked Gabriel.

"And then when it came to the time for me to leave Galway and come up to the convent he was much worse and I wouldn't be let see him so I wrote him a letter saying I was going up to Dublin and would be back in the summer, and hoping he would be better then."

She paused for a moment to get her voice under control, and then went on:

"Then the night before I left, I was in my grandmother's house in Nuns' Island, packing up, and I heard gravel thrown up against the window. The window was so wet I couldn't see, so I ran downstairs as I was and slipped out the back into the garden and there was the poor fellow at the end of the garden, shivering."

"And did you not tell him to go back?" asked Gabriel.

"I implored of him to go home at once and told him he would get his death in the rain. But he said he did not want to live. I can see his eyes as well as well! He was standing at the end of the wall where there was a tree."

"And did he go home?' asked Gabriel.

"Yes, he went home. And when I was only a week in the convent he died and he was buried in Oughterard, where his people come from. O, the day I heard that, that he was dead!"

She stopped, choking with sobs, and, overcome by emotion, flung herself face downward on the bed, sobbing in the quilt. Gabriel held her hand for a moment longer, irresolutely, and then, shy of intruding on her grief, let it fall gently and walked quietly to the window.

She was fast asleep.

Gabriel, leaning on his elbow, looked for a few moments unresentfully on her tangled hair and half-open mouth, listening to her deep-drawn breath. So she had had that romance in her life: a man had died for her sake. It hardly pained him now to think how poor a part he, her husband, had played in her life. He watched her while she slept, as though he and she had never lived together as man and wife. His curious eyes rested long upon her face and on her hair: and, as he thought of what she must have been then, in that time of her first girlish beauty, a strange, friendly pity for her entered his soul. He did not like to say even to himself that her face was no longer beautiful, but he knew that it was no longer the face for which Michael Furey had braved death.

Perhaps she had not told him all the story. His eyes moved to the chair over which she had thrown some of her clothes. A petticoat string dangled to the floor. One boot stood upright, its limp upper fallen down: the fellow of it lay upon its side. He wondered at his riot of emotions of an hour before. From what had it proceeded? From his aunt's supper, from his own foolish speech, from the wine and dancing, the merry-making when saying good-night in the hall, the pleasure of the walk along the river in the snow. Poor Aunt Julia! She, too, would soon be a shade with the shade of Patrick Morkan and his horse. He had caught that haggard look upon her face for a moment when she was singing *Arrayed for the Bridal*. Soon, perhaps, he would be sitting in that same drawing-room, dressed in black, his silk hat on his knees. The blinds would be drawn down and Aunt Kate would be sitting beside him crying, and blowing her nose and telling him how Julia had died. He would cast about in his mind for some words that might console her, and would find only lame and useless ones. Yes, yes: that would happen very soon.

The air of the room chilled his shoulders. He stretched himself cautiously along under the sheets and lay down beside his wife. One by one, they were all becoming shades. Better pass boldly into that other world, in the full glory of some passion, than fade and wither dismally with age. He thought of how she who lay beside him had locked in her heart for so many years that image of her lover's eyes when he had told her that he did not wish to live.

Generous tears filled Gabriel's eyes. He had never felt like that himself towards any woman, but he knew that such a feeling must be love. The tears gathered more thickly in his eyes and in the partial darkness he imagined he saw the form of a young man standing under a dripping tree. Other forms were near. His soul had approached that region where dwell the vast hosts of the dead. He was conscious of, but could not apprehend, their wayward and flickering existence. His own identity was fading out into a grey impalpable world: the solid world itself, which these dead had one time reared and lived in, was dissolving and dwindling.

A few light taps upon the pane made him turn to the window. It had begun to snow again. He watched sleepily the flakes, silver and dark, falling obliquely against the lamplight. The time had come for him to set out on his journey westward. Yes, the newspapers were right: snow was general all over Ireland. It was falling on every part of the dark central plain, on the treeless hills, falling softly upon the Bog of Allen and, farther westward, softly falling into the dark mutinous Shannon wave. It was falling, too, upon every part of the lonely churchyard on the hill where Michael Furey lay buried. It lay thickly drifted on the crooked crosses and headstones, on the spears of the little gate, on the barren thorns. His soul swooned slowly as he heard the snow falling faintly through the universe and faintly falling, like the descent of their last end, upon all the living and the dead.

Franz Kafka (1883–1924)

The Metamorphosis

Translated by Willa and Edwin Muir

I

As Gregor Samsa awoke one morning from uneasy dreams he found himself transformed in his bed into a gigantic insect. He was lying on his hard, as it were armor-plated, back and when he lifted his head a little he could see his dome-like brown belly divided into stiff arched segments on top of which the bed quilt could hardly keep in position and was about to slide off completely. His numerous legs, which were pitifully thin compared to the rest of his bulk, waved helplessly before his eyes.

What has happened to me? he thought. It was no dream. His room, a regular human bedroom, only rather too small, lay quiet between the four familiar walls. Above the table on which a collection of cloth samples was unpacked and spread out — Samsa was a commercial traveler — hung the picture which he had recently cut out of an illustrated magazine and put into a pretty gilt frame. It showed a lady, with a fur cap on and a fur stole, sitting upright and holding out to the spectator a huge fur muff into which the whole of her forearm had vanished!

Gregor's eyes turned next to the window, and the overcast sky — one could hear rain drops beating on the window gutter — made him quite melancholy. What about sleeping a little longer and forgetting all this nonsense, he thought, but it could not be done, for he was accustomed to sleep on his right side and in his present condition he could not turn himself over. However violently he forced himself towards his right side he always rolled on to his back again. He tried it at least a hundred times, shutting his eyes to keep from seeing his struggling legs, and only desisted when he began to feel in his side a faint dull ache he had never experienced before.

Oh God, he thought, what an exhausting job I've picked on! Traveling about day in, day out. It's much more irritating work than doing the actual business in the office, and on top of that there's the trouble of constant traveling, of worrying about train connections, the bed and irregular meals, casual acquaintances that are always new and never become intimate friends. The devil take it all! He felt a slight itching up on his belly; slowly pushed himself on his back nearer to the top of the bed so that he could lift his head more easily; identified the itching place which was surrounded by many small white spots the nature of which he could not understand and made to touch it with a leg, but drew the leg back immediately, for the contact made a cold shiver run through him.

He slid down again into his former position. This getting up early, he thought, makes one quite stupid. A man needs his sleep. Other commercials live like harem women. For instance, when I come back to the hotel of a morning to write up the orders I've got, these others are only sitting down to breakfast. Let me just try that with my chief; I'd be sacked on the spot. Anyhow, that might be quite a good thing for me, who can tell? If I didn't have to hold my hand because of my parents I'd have given notice long ago, I'd have gone to the chief and told him exactly what I think of him. That would knock him endways from his desk! It's a queer way of doing, too, this sitting on high at a desk and talking down to employees, especially when they have to come quite near because the chief is hard of hearing. Well, there's still hope; once I've saved enough money to pay back my parents' debts to him — that should take another five or six years — I'll do it without fail. I'll cut myself completely loose then. For the moment, though, I'd better get up, since my train goes at five.

He looked at the alarm clock ticking on the chest. Heavenly Father! he thought. It was half-past six o'clock and the hands were quietly moving on, it was even past the half-hour, it was getting on toward a quarter to seven. Had the alarm clock not gone off? From the bed one could see that it had been properly set for four o'clock; of course it must have gone off. Yes, but was it possible to sleep quietly through that ear-splitting noise? Well, he had not slept quietly, yet apparently all the more soundly for that. But what was he to do now? The next train went at seven o'clock; to catch that he would need to hurry like mad and his samples weren't even packed up, and he himself wasn't feeling particularly fresh and active. And even if he did catch the train he wouldn't avoid a row with the chief, since the firm's porter would have been waiting for the five o'clock train and would have long since reported his failure to turn up. The porter was a creature of the chief's, spineless and stupid. Well, supposing he were to say he was sick? But that would be most unpleasant and would look suspicious, since during his five years' employment he had not been ill once. The chief himself would be sure to come with the sick-insurance doctor, would reproach his parents with their son's laziness and would cut all excuses short by referring to the insurance doctor, who of course regarded all mankind as perfectly healthy malingerers.

And would he be so far wrong on this occasion? Gregor really felt quite well, apart from a drowsiness that was utterly superfluous after such a long sleep, and he was even unusually hungry.

As all this was running through his mind at top speed without his being able to decide to leave his bed — the alarm clock had just struck a quarter to seven — there came a cautious tap at the door behind the head of his bed. "Gregor," said a voice — it was his mother's — "it's a quarter to seven. Hadn't you a train to catch?" That gentle voice! Gregor had a shock as he heard his own voice answering hers, unmistakably his own voice, it was true, but with a persistent horrible twittering squeak behind it like an undertone, that left the words in their clear shape only for the first moment and then rose up reverberating round them to destroy their sense, so that one could not be sure one had heard them rightly. Gregor wanted to answer at length and explain everything, but in the circumstances he confined himself to saying: "Yes, yes, thank you, Mother, I'm getting up now." The wooden door between them must have kept the change in his voice from being noticeable outside, for his mother contented herself with this statement and shuffled away. Yet this brief exchange of words had made the other members of the family aware that Gregor was still in the house, as they had not expected, and at one of the side doors his father was already knocking, gently, yet with his fist. "Gregor, Gregor," he called, "what's the matter with you?" And after a little while he called again in a deeper voice: "Gregor! Gregor!" At the other side door his sister was saying in a low, plaintive tone: "Gregor? Aren't you well? Are you needing anything?" He answered them both at once: "I'm just ready," and did his best to make his voice sound as normal as possible by enunciating the words very clearly and leaving long pauses between them. So his father went back to his breakfast, but his sister whispered: "Gregor, open the door, do." However, he was not thinking of opening the door, and felt thankful for the prudent habit he had acquired in traveling of locking all doors during the night, even at home.

His immediate intention was to get up quietly without being disturbed, to put on his clothes and above all eat his breakfast, and only then to consider what else was to be done, since in bed, he was well aware, his meditations would come to no sensible conclusion. He remembered that often enough in bed he had felt small aches and pains, probably caused by awkward postures, which had proved purely imaginary once he got up, and he looked forward eagerly to seeing this morning's delusions gradually fall away. That the change in his voice was nothing but the precursor of a severe chill, a standing ailment of commercial travelers, he had not the least possible doubt.

To get rid of the quilt was quite easy; he had only to inflate himself a little and it fell off by itself. But the next move was difficult, especially because he was so uncommonly broad. He would have needed arms and hands to hoist himself up; instead he had only the numerous little legs which never stopped waving in all directions and which he could not control in the least. When he tried to bend one of them it was the first to stretch itself straight; and did he succeed at last in making it do what he wanted, all the other legs meanwhile waved the more wildly in a high degree of unpleasant agitation. "But what's the use of lying idle in bed," said Gregor to himself.

He thought that he might get out of bed with the lower part of his body first, but this lower part, which he had not yet seen and of which he could form no clear conception, proved too difficult to move; it shifted so slowly; and when finally, almost wild with annoyance, he gathered his forces together and thrust out recklessly, he had miscalculated the direction and bumped heavily against the lower end of the bed, and the stinging pain he felt informed him that precisely this lower part of his body was at the moment probably the most sensitive.

So he tried to get the top part of himself out first, and cautiously moved his head towards the edge of the bed. That proved easy enough, and despite its breadth and mass the bulk of his body at last slowly followed the movement of his head. Still, when he finally got his head free over the edge of the bed he felt too scared to go on advancing, for after all if he let himself fall in this way it would take a miracle to keep his head from being injured. And at all costs he must not lose consciousness now, precisely now; he would rather stay in bed.

But when after a repetition of the same efforts he lay in his former position again, sighing, and watched his little legs struggling against each other more wildly than ever, if that were possible, and saw no way of bringing any order into this arbitrary confusion, he told himself again that it was impossible to stay in bed and that the most sensible course was to risk everything for the smallest hope of getting away from it. At the same time he did not forget meanwhile to remind himself that cool reflection, the coolest possible, was much better than desperate resolves. In such moments he focused his eyes as sharply as possible on the window, but, unfortunately, the prospect of the morning fog, which muffled even the other side of the narrow street, brought him little encouragement and comfort. "Seven o'clock already," he said to himself when the alarm clock chimed again, "seven o'clock already and still such a thick fog." And for a little while he lay quiet, breathing lightly, as if perhaps expecting such complete repose to restore all things to their real and normal condition.

But then he said to himself: "Before it strikes a quarter past seven I must be quite out of this bed, without fail. Anyhow, by that time someone will have come from the office to ask for me, since it opens before seven." And he set himself to rocking his whole body at once in a regular rhythm, with the idea of swinging it out of the bed. If he tipped himself out in that way he could keep his head from injury by lifting it at an acute angle when he fell. His back seemed to be hard and was not likely to suffer from a fall on the carpet. His biggest worry was the loud crash he would not be able to help making, which would probably cause anxiety, if not terror, behind all the doors. Still, he must take the risk.

When he was already half out of the bed — the new method was more a game than an effort, for he needed only to hitch himself across by rocking to and fro — it struck him how simple it would be if he could get help. Two strong people — he thought of his father and the servant girl — would be amply sufficient; they would only have to thrust their arms under his convex back, lever him out of the bed, bend down with their burden and then be patient enough to let him turn himself right over on to the floor, where it was to be hoped his legs would then find their proper function. Well, ignoring the fact that the doors were all locked, ought he really to call for help? In spite of his misery he could not suppress a smile at the very idea of it.

He had got so far that he could barely keep his equilibrium when he rocked himself strongly, and he would have to nerve himself very soon for the final decision since in five minutes' time it would be a quarter past seven — when the front doorbell rang. "That's someone from the office," he said to himself, and grew almost rigid, while his little legs only jigged about all the faster. For a moment everything stayed quiet. "They're not going to open the door," said Gregor to himself, catching at some kind of irrational hope. But then of course the servant girl went as usual to the door with her heavy tread and opened it. Gregor needed only to hear the first good morning of the visitor to know immediately who it was — the chief clerk himself. What a fate, to be condemned to work for a firm where the smallest omission at once gave rise to the gravest suspicion! Were all employees in a body nothing but scoundrels, was there not among them one single loyal devoted man who, had he wasted only an hour or so of the firm's time in a morning, was so tormented by conscience as to be driven out of his mind and actually incapable of leaving his bed? Wouldn't it really have been sufficient to send an apprentice to inquire — if any inquiry were necessary at all — did the chief clerk himself have to come and thus indicate to the entire family, an innocent family, that this suspicious circumstance could be investigated by no one less versed in affairs than himself? And more through the agitation caused by these reflections than through any act of will Gregor swung himself out of bed with all his strength. There was a loud thump, but it was not really a crash. His fall was broken to some extent by the carpet, his back, too, was less stiff than he thought, and so there was merely a dull thud, not so very startling. Only he had not lifted his head carefully enough and had hit it; he turned it and rubbed it on the carpet in pain and irritation.

"That was something falling down in there," said the chief clerk in the next room to the left. Gregor tried to suppose to himself that something like what had happened to him today might some day happen to the chief clerk; one really could not deny that it was possible. But as if in brusque reply to this supposition the chief clerk took a couple of firm steps in the next-door room and his patent leather boots creaked. From the right-hand room his sister was whispering to inform him of the situation: "Gregor, the chief clerk's here." "I know," muttered Gregor to himself; but he didn't dare to make his voice loud enough for his sister to hear it.

"Gregor," said his father now from the left-hand room, "the chief clerk has come and wants to know why you didn't catch the early train. We don't know what to say to him. Besides, he wants to talk to you in person. So open the door, please. He will be good enough to excuse the untidiness of your room." "Good morning, Mr. Samsa," the chief clerk was calling amiably meanwhile. "He's not well," said his mother to the visitor, while his father was still speaking through the door, "he's not well, sir, believe me. What else would make him miss a train! The boy thinks about nothing but his work. It makes me almost cross the way he never goes out in the evenings; he's been here the last eight days and has stayed at home every single evening. He just sits there quietly at the table reading a newspaper or looking through railway timetables. The only amusement he gets is doing fretwork. For instance, he spent two or three evenings cutting out a little picture frame; you would be surprised to see how pretty it is; it's hanging in his room; you'll see it in a minute when Gregor opens the door. I must say I'm glad you've come, sir; we should never have got him to unlock the door by ourselves; he's so obstinate; and I'm sure he's unwell, though he wouldn't have it to be so this morning." "I'm just coming," said Gregor slowly and carefully, not moving an inch for fear of losing one word of the conversation. "I can't think of any other explanation, madam," said the chief clerk, "I hope it's nothing serious. Although on the other hand I must say that we men of business — fortunately or unfortunately — very often simply have to ignore any slight indisposition, since business must be attended to." "Well, can the chief clerk come in now?" asked Gregor's father impatiently, again knocking on the door. "No," said Gregor. In the left-hand room a painful silence followed this refusal, in the right-hand room his sister began to sob.

Why didn't his sister join the others? She was probably newly out of bed and hadn't even begun to put on her clothes yet. Well, why was she crying? Because he wouldn't get up and let the chief clerk in, because he was in danger of losing his job, and because the chief would begin dunning his parents again for the old debts? Surely these were things one didn't need to worry about for the present. Gregor was still at home and not in the least thinking of deserting the family. At the moment, true, he was lying on the carpet and no one who knew the condition he was in could seriously expect him to admit the chief clerk. But for such a small discourtesy, which could plausibly be explained away somehow later on, Gregor could hardly be dismissed on the spot. And it seemed to Gregor that it would be much more sensible to leave him in peace for the present than to trouble him with tears and entreaties. Still, of course, their uncertainty bewildered them all and excused their behavior.

"Mr. Samsa," the chief clerk called now in a louder voice, "what's the matter with you? Here you are, barricading yourself in your room, giving only 'yes' and 'no' for answers, causing your parents a lot of unnecessary trouble and neglecting — I mention this only in passing — neglecting your business duties in an incredible fashion. I am speaking here in the name of your parents and of your chief, and I beg you quite seriously to give me an immediate and precise explanation. You amaze me, you amaze me. I thought you were a quiet, dependable person, and now all at once you seem bent on making a disgraceful exhibition of yourself. The chief did hint to me early this morning a possible explanation for your disappearance — with reference to the cash payments that were entrusted to you recently — but I almost pledged my solemn word of honor that this could not be so. But now that I see how incredibly obstinate you are, I no longer have the slightest desire to take your part at all. And your position in the firm is not so unassailable. I came with the intention of telling you all this in private, but since you are wasting my time so needlessly I don't see why your parents shouldn't hear it too. For some time past your work has been most unsatisfactory; this is not the season of the year for a business boom, of course, we admit that, but a season of the year for doing no business at all, that does not exist, Mr. Samsa, must not exist."

"But, sir," cried Gregor, beside himself and in his agitation forgetting everything else, "I'm just going to open the door this very minute. A slight illness, an attack of giddiness, has kept me from getting up. I'm still lying in bed. But I feel all right again. I'm getting out of bed now. Just give me a moment or two longer! I'm not quite so well as I thought. But I'm all right, really. How a thing like that can suddenly strike one down! Only last night I was quite well, my parents can tell you, or rather I did have a slight presentiment. I must have showed some sign of it. Why didn't I report it at the office! But one always thinks that an indisposition can be got over without staying in the house. Oh sir, do spare my parents! All that you're reproaching me with now has no foundation; no one has ever said a word to me about it. Perhaps you haven't looked at the last orders I sent in. Anyhow, I can still catch the eight o'clock train, I'm much the better for my few hours' rest. Don't let me detain you here, sir; I'll be attending to business very soon, and do be good enough to tell the chief so and to make my excuses to him!"

And while all this was tumbling out pell-mell and Gregor hardly knew what he was saying, he had reached the chest quite easily, perhaps because of the practice he had had in bed, and was now trying to lever himself upright by means of it. He meant actually to open the door, actually to show himself and speak to the chief clerk; he was eager to find out what the others, after all their insistence, would say at the sight of him. If they were horrified then the responsibility was no longer his and he could stay quiet. But if they took it calmly, then he had no reason either to be upset, and could really get to the station for the eight o'clock train if he hurried. At first he slipped down a few times from the polished surface of the chest, but at length with a last heave he stood upright; he paid no more attention to the pains in the lower part of his body, however they smarted. Then he let himself fall against the back of a nearby chair, and clung with his little legs to the edges of it. That brought him into control of himself again and he stopped speaking, for now he could listen to what the chief clerk was saying.

"Did you understand a word of it?" the chief clerk was asking; "surely he can't be trying to make fools of us?" "Oh dear," cried his mother, in tears, "perhaps he's terribly ill and we're tormenting him. Grete! Grete!" she called out then. "Yes Mother?" called his sister from the other side. They were calling to each other across Gregor's room. "You must go this minute for the doctor. Gregor is ill. Go for the doctor, quick. Did you hear how he was speaking?" "That was no human voice," said the chief clerk in a voice noticeably low beside the shrillness of the mother's. "Anna! Anna!" his father was calling through the hall to the kitchen, clapping his hands, "get a locksmith at once!" And the two girls were already running through the hall with a swish of skirts — how could his sister have got dressed so quickly? — and were tearing the front door open. There was no sound of its closing again; they had evidently left it open as one does in houses where some great misfortune has happened.

But Gregor was now much calmer. The words he uttered were no longer understandable, apparently, although they seemed clear enough to him, even clearer than before, perhaps because his ear had grown accustomed to the sound of them. Yet at any rate people now believed that something was wrong with him, and were ready to help him. The positive certainty with which these first measures had been taken comforted him. He felt himself drawn once more into the human circle and hoped for great and remarkable results from both the doctor and the locksmith, without really distinguishing precisely between them. To make his voice as clear as possible for the decisive conversation that was now imminent he coughed a little, as quietly as he could, of course, since this noise too might not sound like a human cough for all he was able to judge. In the next room meanwhile there was complete silence. Perhaps his parents were sitting at the table with the chief clerk, whispering, perhaps they were all leaning against the door and listening.

Slowly Gregor pushed the chair towards the door, then let go of it, caught hold of the door for support — the soles at the end of his little legs were somewhat sticky — and rested against it for a moment after his efforts. Then he set himself to turning the key in the lock with his mouth. It seemed, unhappily, that he hadn't really any teeth — what could he grip the key with? — but on the other hand his jaws were certainly very strong; with their help he did manage to set the key in motion, heedless of the fact that he was undoubtedly damaging them somewhere, since a brown fluid issued from his mouth, flowed over the key and dripped on the floor. "Just listen to that," said the chief clerk next door; "he's turning the key." That was a great encouragement to Gregor; but they should all have shouted encouragement to him, his father and mother too: "Go on, Gregor," they should have called out, "keep going, hold on to that key!" And in the belief that they were all following his efforts intently, he clenched his jaws recklessly on the key with all the force at his command. As the turning of the key progressed he circled round the lock, holding on now only with his mouth, pushing on the key, as required, or pulling it down again with all the weight of his body. The louder click of the finally yielding lock literally quickened Gregor. With a deep breath of relief he said to himself. "So I didn't need the locksmith," and laid his head on the handle to open the door wide.

Since he had to pull the door towards him, he was still invisible when it was really wide open. He had to edge himself very slowly round the near half of the double door, and to do it very carefully if he was not to fall plump upon his back just on the threshold. He was still carrying out this difficult manoeuvre, with no time to observe anything else, when he heard the chief clerk utter a loud "Oh!" — it sounded like a gust of wind — and now he could see the man, standing as he was nearest to the door, clapping one hand before his open mouth and slowly backing away as if driven by some invisible steady pressure. His mother — in spite of the chief clerk's being there her hair was still undone and sticking up in all directions — first clasped her hands and looked at his father, then took two steps towards Gregor and fell on the floor among her outspread skirts, her face quite hidden on her breast. His father knotted his fist with a fierce expression on his face as if he meant to knock Gregor back into his room, then looked uncertainly round the living room, covered his eyes with his hands and wept till his great chest heaved.

Gregor did not go now into the living room, but leaned against the inside of the firmly shut wing of the door, so that only half his body was visible and his head above it bending sideways to look at the others. The light had meanwhile strengthened; on the other side of the street one could see clearly a section of the endlessly long, dark gray building opposite — it was a hospital — abruptly punctuated by its row of regular windows; the rain was still falling, but only in large singly discernible and literally singly splashing drops. The breakfast dishes were set out on the table lavishly, for breakfast was the most important meal of the day to Gregor's father, who lingered it out for hours over various newspapers. Right opposite Gregor on the wall hung a photograph of himself on military service, as a lieutenant, hand on sword, a carefree smile on his face, inviting one to respect his uniform and military bearing. The door leading to the hall was open, and one could see that the front door stood open too, showing the landing beyond and the beginning of the stairs going down.

"Well," said Gregor, knowing perfectly that he was the only

one who had retained any composure, "I'll put my clothes on at once, pack up my samples and start off. Will you only let me go? You see, sir, I'm not obstinate, and I'm willing to work; traveling is a hard life, but I couldn't live without it. Where are you going, sir? To the office? Yes? Will you give a true account of all this? One can be temporarily incapacitated, but that's just the moment for remembering former services and bearing in mind that later on, when the incapacity has been got over, one will certainly work with all the more industry and concentration. I'm loyally bound to serve the chief, you know that very well. Besides, I have to provide for my parents and my sister. I'm in great difficulties, but I'll get out of them again. Don't make things any worse for me than they are. Stand up for me in the firm. Travelers are not popular there, I know. People think they earn sacks of money and just have a good time. A prejudice there's no particular reason for revising. But you, sir, have a more comprehensive view of affairs than the rest of the staff, yes, let me tell you in confidence, a more comprehensive view than the chief himself, who, being the owner, lets his judgment easily be swayed against one of his employees. And you know very well that the traveler, who is never seen in the office almost the whole year round, can so easily fall a victim to gossip and ill luck and unfounded complaints, which he mostly knows nothing about, except when he comes back exhausted from his rounds, and only then suffers in person from their evil consequences, which he can no longer trace back to the original causes. Sir, sir, don't go away without a word to me to show that you think me in the right at least to some extent!"

But at Gregor's very first words the chief clerk had already backed away and only stared at him with parted lips over one twitching shoulder. And while Gregor was speaking he did not stand still one moment but stole away towards the door, without taking his eyes off Gregor, yet only an inch at a time, as if obeying some secret injunction to leave the room. He was already at the hall, and the suddenness with which he took his last step out of the living room would have made one believe he had burned the sole of his foot. Once in the hall he stretched his right arm before him towards the staircase, as if some supernatural power were waiting there to deliver him.

Gregor perceived that the chief clerk must on no account be allowed to go away in this frame of mind if his position in the firm were not to be endangered to the utmost. His parents did not understand this so well; they had convinced themselves in the course of years that Gregor was settled for life in this firm, and besides they were so occupied with their immediate troubles that all foresight had forsaken them. Yet Gregor had this foresight. The chief clerk must be detained, soothed, persuaded and finally won over; the whole future of Gregor and his family depended on it! If only his sister had been there! She was intelligent; she had begun to cry while Gregor was still lying quietly on his back. And no doubt the chief clerk, so partial to ladies, would have been guided by her; she would have shut the door of the flat and in the hall talked him out of his horror. But she was not there, and Gregor would have to handle the situation himself. And without remembering that he was still unaware what powers of movement he possessed, without even remembering that his words in all possibility, indeed in all likelihood, would again be unintelligible, he let go the wing of the door, pushed himself through the opening, started to walk towards the chief clerk, who was already ridiculously clinging with both hands to the railing on the landing; but immediately, as he was feeling for a support, he fell down with a little cry upon all his numerous legs. Hardly was he down when he experienced for the first time this morning a sense of physical comfort; his legs had firm ground under them; they were completely obedient, as he noted with joy; they even strove to carry him forward in whatever direction he chose; and he was inclined to believe that a final relief from all his sufferings was at hand. But in the same moment as he found himself on the floor, rocking with suppressed eagerness to move, not far from his mother, indeed just in front of her, she, who had seemed so completely crushed, sprang all at once to her feet, her arms and fingers outspread, cried: "Help, for God's sake, help!" bent her head down as if to see Gregor better, yet on the contrary kept backing senselessly away; had quite forgotten that the laden table stood behind her; sat upon it hastily, as if in absence of mind, when she bumped into it; and seemed altogether unaware that the big coffee pot beside her was upset and pouring coffee in a flood over the carpet.

"Mother, Mother," said Gregor in a low voice, and looked up at her. The chief clerk, for the moment, had quite slipped from his mind; instead he could not resist snapping his jaws together at the sight of the streaming coffee. That made his mother scream again, she fled from the table and fell into the arms of his father, who hastened to catch her. But Gregor had now no time to spare for his parents; the chief clerk was already on the stairs; with his chin on the banisters he was taking one last backward look. Gregor made a spring, to be as sure as possible of overtaking him; the chief clerk must have divined his intention, for he leaped down several steps and vanished; he was still yelling "Ugh!" and it echoed through the whole staircase.

Unfortunately, the flight of the chief clerk seemed completely to upset Gregor's father, who had remained relatively calm until now, for instead of running after the man himself, or at least not hindering Gregor in his pursuit, he seized in his right hand the walking stick which the chief clerk had left behind on a chair, together with a hat and greatcoat, snatched in his left hand a large newspaper from the table and began stamping his feet and flourishing the stick and the newspaper to drive Gregor back into his room. No entreaty of Gregor's availed, indeed no entreaty was even understood; however humbly he bent his head his father only stamped on the floor the more loudly. Behind his father his mother had torn open a window, despite the cold weather, and was leaning far out of it with her face in her hands. A strong draught set in from the street to the staircase, the window curtain blew in, the newspapers on the table fluttered, stray pages whisked over the floor. Pitilessly Gregor's father drove him back, hissing and crying "Shoo!" like a savage. But Gregor was quite unpracticed in walking backwards, it really was a slow business. If he only had a chance to turn round he could get back to his room at once, but he was afraid of exasperating his father by the slowness of such a rotation and at any moment the stick in his father's hand might hit him a fatal blow on the back or on the head. In the end, however, nothing else was left for him to do since to his horror he observed that in moving backwards he could not even control the direction he took; and so, keeping an anxious eye on his father all the time over his shoulder, he began to turn round as quickly as he could, which was in reality very slowly. Perhaps his father noted his good intentions, for he did not interfere except every now and then to help him in the manoeuvre from a distance with the point of the stick. If only he would have stopped making that unbearable hissing noise! It made Gregor quite lose his head. He had turned almost completely round when the hissing noise so distracted him that he even turned a little the wrong way again. But when at last his head was fortunately right in front of the doorway, it appeared that his body was too broad simply to get through the opening. His father, of course, in his present mood was far from thinking of such a thing as opening the other half of the door, to let Gregor have enough space. He had merely the fixed idea of driving Gregor back into his room as quickly as possible. He would have never suffered Gregor to make the circumstantial preparations for standing up on end and perhaps slipping his way through the door. Maybe he was now making more noise than ever to urge Gregor forward, as if no obstacle impeded him; to Gregor, anyhow, the noise in his rear sounded no longer like the voice of one single father; this was really no joke, and Gregor thrust himself — come what might — into the doorway. One side of his body rose up, he was tilted at an angle in the doorway, his flank was quite bruised, horrid blotches stained the white door, soon he was stuck fast and, left to himself, could not have moved at all, his legs on one side fluttered trembling in the air, those on the other were crushed painfully to the floor — when from behind his father gave him a strong push which was literally a deliverance and he flew far into the room, bleeding freely. The door was slammed behind him with the stick, and then at last there was silence.

II

Not until it was twilight did Gregor awake out of a deep sleep, more like a swoon than a sleep. He would certainly have waked up of his own accord not much later, for he felt himself sufficiently rested and well-slept, but it seemed to him as if a fleeting step and a cautious shutting of the door leading into the hall had aroused him. The electric lights in the street cast a pale sheen here and there on the ceiling and the upper surfaces of the furniture, but down below, where he lay, it was dark. Slowly, awkwardly trying out his feelers, which he now first learned to appreciate, he pushed his way to the door to see what had been happening there. His left side felt like one single long, unpleasantly tense scar, and he had actually to limp on his two rows of legs. One little leg, moreover, had been severely damaged in the course of that morning's events — it was almost a miracle that only one had been damaged — and trailed uselessly behind him.

He had reached the door before he discovered what had really drawn him to it: the smell of food. For there stood a basin filled with fresh milk in which floated little sops of white bread. He could almost have laughed with joy, since he was now still hungrier than in the morning, and dipped his head almost over the eyes straight into the milk. But soon in disappointment he withdrew it again; not only did he find it difficult to feed because of his tender left side — and he could only feed with the palpitating collaboration of his whole body — he did not like the milk either, although milk had been his favorite drink and that was certainly why his sister had set it there for him, indeed it was almost with repulsion that he turned away from the basin and crawled back to the middle of the room.

He could see through the crack of the door that the gas was turned on in the living room, but while usually at this time his father made a habit of reading the afternoon newspaper in a loud voice to his mother and occasionally to his sister as well, not a sound was now to be heard. Well, perhaps his father had recently given up this habit of reading aloud, which his sister had mentioned so often in conversation and in her letters. But there was the same silence all around, although the flat was certainly not empty of occupants. "What a quiet life our family has been leading," said Gregor to himself, and as he sat there motionless staring into the darkness he felt great pride in the fact that he had been able to provide such a life for his parents and sister in such a fine flat. But what if all the quiet, the comfort, the contentment were now to end in horror? To keep himself from being lost in such thoughts Gregor took refuge in movement and crawled up and down the room.

Once during the long evening one of the side doors was opened a little and quickly shut again, later the other side door too; someone had apparently wanted to come in and then thought better of it. Gregor now stationed himself immediately before the living room door, determined to persuade any hesitating visitor to come in or at least to discover who it might be; but the door was not opened again and he waited in vain. In the early morning, when the doors were locked, they had all wanted to come in, now that he had opened one door and the other had apparently been opened during the day, no one came in and even the keys were on the other side of the doors.

It was late at night before the gas went out in the living room, and Gregor could easily tell that his parents and his sister had all stayed awake until then, for he could clearly hear the three of them stealing away on tiptoe. No one was likely to visit him, not until the morning, that was certain; so he had plenty of time to meditate at his leisure on how he was to arrange his life afresh. But the lofty, empty room in which he had to lie flat on the floor filled him with an apprehension he could not account for, since it had been his very own room for the past five years — and with a half-unconscious action, not without a slight feeling of shame, he scuttled under the sofa, where he felt comfortable at once, although his back was a little cramped and he could not lift his head up, and his only regret was that his body was too broad to get the whole of it under the sofa.

He stayed there all night, spending the time partly in a light slumber, from which his hunger kept waking him up with a start, and partly in worrying and sketching vague hopes, which all led to the same conclusion, that he must lie low for the present and, by exercising patience and the utmost consideration, help the family to bear the inconvenience he was bound to cause them in his present condition.

Very early in the morning, it was still almost night, Gregor had the chance to test the strength of his new resolutions, for his sister, nearly fully dressed, opened the door from the hall and peered in. She did not see him at once, yet when she caught sight of him under the sofa — well, he had to be somewhere, he couldn't have flown away, could he? — she was so startled that without being able to help it she slammed the door shut again. But as if regretting her behavior she opened the door again immediately and came in on tiptoe, as if she were visiting an invalid or even a stranger. Gregor had pushed his head forward to the very edge of the sofa and watched her. Would she notice that he had left the milk standing, and not for lack of hunger, and would she bring in some other kind of food more to his taste? If she did not do it of her own accord, he would rather starve than draw her attention to the fact, although he felt a wild impulse to dart out from under the sofa, throw himself at her feet and beg her for something to eat. But his sister at once noticed, with surprise, that the basin was still full, except for a little milk that had been spilt all around it, she lifted it immediately, not with her bare hands, true, but with a cloth and carried it away. Gregor was wildly curious to know what she would bring instead, and made various speculations about it. Yet what she actually did next, in the goodness of her heart, he could never have guessed at. To find out what he liked she brought him a whole selection of food, all set out on an old newspaper. There were old, half-decayed vegetables, bones from last night's supper covered with a white sauce that had thickened; some raisins and almonds; a piece of cheese that Gregor would have called uneatable two days ago; a dry roll of bread, a buttered roll, and a roll both buttered and salted. Besides all that, she set down again the same basin, into which she had poured some water, and which was apparently to be reserved for his exclusive use. And with fine tact, knowing that Gregor would not eat in her presence, she withdrew quickly and even turned the key, to let him understand that he could take his ease as much as he liked. Gregor's legs all whizzed towards the food. His wounds must have healed completely, moreover, for he felt no disability, which amazed him and made him reflect how more than a month ago he had cut one finger a little with a knife and had still suffered pain from the wound only the day before yesterday. Am I less sensitive now? he thought, and sucked greedily at the cheese, which above all the other edibles attracted him at once and strongly. One after another and with tears of satisfaction in his eyes he quickly devoured the cheese, the vegetables and the sauce; the fresh food, on the other hand, had no charms for him, he could not even stand the smell of it and actually dragged away to some little distance the things he could eat. He had long finished his meal and was only lying lazily on the same spot when his sister turned the key slowly as a sign for him to retreat. That roused him at once, although he was nearly asleep, and he hurried under the sofa again. But it took considerable self-control for him to stay under the sofa, even for the short time his sister was in the room, since the large meal had swollen his body somewhat and he was so cramped he could hardly breathe. Slight attacks of breathlessness afflicted him and his eyes were starting a little out of his head as he watched his unsuspecting sister sweeping together with a broom not only the remains of what he had eaten but even the things he had not touched, as if these were now of no use to anyone, and hastily shoveling it all into a bucket, which she covered with a wooden lid and carried away. Hardly had she turned her back when Gregor came from under the sofa and stretched and puffed himself out.

In this manner Gregor was fed, once in the early morning while his parents and the servant girl were still asleep, and a second time after they had all had their midday dinner, for then his parents took a short nap and the servant girl could be sent out on some errand or other by his sister. Not that they would have wanted him to starve, of course, but perhaps they could not have borne to know more about his feeding than from hearsay, perhaps too his sister wanted to spare them such little anxieties wherever possible, since they had quite enough to bear as it was.

Under what pretext the doctor and the locksmith had been got rid of on that first morning Gregor could not discover, for since what he said was not understood by the others it never struck any of them, not even his sister, that he could understand what they said, and so whenever his sister came into his room he had to content himself with hearing her utter only a sigh now and then and an occasional appeal to the saints. Later on, when she had got a little used to the situation — of course she could never get completely used to it — she sometimes threw out a remark which was kindly meant or could be so interpreted. "Well, he liked his dinner today," she would say when Gregor had made a good clearance of his food; and when he had not eaten, which gradually happened more and more often, she would say almost sadly: "Everything's been left standing again."

But although Gregor could get no news directly, he overheard a lot from the neighboring rooms, and as soon as voices were audible, he would run to the door of the room concerned and press his whole body against it. In the first few days especially there was no conversation that did not refer to him somehow, even if only indirectly. For two whole days there were family consultations at every mealtime about what should be done; but also between meals the same subject was discussed, for there were always at least two members of the family at home, since no one wanted to be alone in the flat and to leave it quite empty was unthinkable. And on the very first of these days the household cook — it was not quite clear what and how much she knew of the situation — went down on her knees to his mother and begged leave to go, and when she departed, a quarter of an hour later, gave thanks for her dismissal with tears in her eyes as if for the greatest benefit that could have been conferred on her, and without any prompting swore a solemn oath that she would never say a single word to anyone about what had happened.

Now Gregor's sister had to cook too, helping her mother; true, the cooking did not amount to much, for they ate scarcely anything. Gregor was always hearing one of the family vainly urging another to eat and getting no answer but: "Thanks, I've had all I want," or something similar. Perhaps they drank nothing either. Time and again his sister kept asking his father if he wouldn't like some beer and offered kindly to go and fetch it herself, and when he made no answer suggested that she could ask the concierge to fetch it, so that he need feel no sense of obligation, but then a round "No" came from his father and no more was said about it.

In the course of that very first day Gregor's father explained the family's financial position and prospects to both his mother and his sister. Now and then he rose from the table to get some voucher or memorandum out of the small safe he had rescued from the collapse of his business five years earlier. One could hear him opening the complicated lock and rustling papers out and shutting it again. This statement made by his father was the first cheerful information Gregor had heard since his imprisonment. He had been of the opinion that nothing at all was left over from his father's business, at least his father had never said anything to the contrary, and of course he had not asked him directly. At that time Gregor's sole desire was to do his utmost to help the family to forget as soon as possible the catastrophe which had overwhelmed the business and thrown them all into a state of complete despair. And so he had set to work with unusual ardor and almost overnight had become a commercial traveler instead of a little clerk, with of course much greater chances of earning money, and his success was immediately translated into good round coin which he could lay on the table for his amazed and happy family. These had been fine times, and they had never recurred, at least not with the same sense of glory, although later on Gregor had earned so much money that he was able to meet the expenses of the whole household and did so. They had simply got used to it, both the family and Gregor; the money was gratefully accepted and gladly given, but there was no special uprush of warm feeling. With his sister alone had he remained intimate, and it was a secret plan of his that she, who loved music, unlike himself, and could play movingly on the violin, should be sent next year to study at the Conservatorium, despite the great expense that would entail, which must be made up in some other way. During his brief visits home the Conservatorium was often mentioned in the talks he had with his sister, but always merely as a beautiful dream which could never come true, and his parents discouraged even these innocent references to it; yet Gregor had made up his mind firmly about it and meant to announce the fact with due solemnity on Christmas Day.

Such were the thoughts, completely futile in his present condition, that went through his head as he stood clinging upright to the door and listening. Sometimes out of sheer weariness he had to give up listening and let his head fall negligently against the door, but he always had to pull himself together again at once, for even the slight sound his head made was audible next door and brought all conversation to a stop. "What can he be doing now?" his father would say after a while, obviously turning towards the door, and only then would the interrupted conversation gradually be set going again.

Gregor was now informed as amply as he could wish — for his father tended to repeat himself in his explanations, partly because it was a long time since he had handled such matters and partly because his mother could not always grasp things at once — that a certain amount of investments, a very small amount it was true, had survived the wreck of their fortunes and had even increased a little because the dividends had not been touched meanwhile. And besides that, the money Gregor brought home every month — he had kept only a few dollars for himself — had never been quite used up and now amounted to a small capital sum. Behind the door Gregor nodded his head eagerly, rejoiced at this evidence of unexpected thrift and foresight. True, he could really have paid off some more of his father's debts to the chief with this extra money, and so brought much nearer the day on which he could quit his job, but doubtless it was better the way his father had arranged it.

Yet this capital was by no means sufficient to let the family live on the interest of it; for one year, perhaps, or at the most two, they could live on the principal, that was all. It was simply a sum that ought not to be touched and should be kept for a rainy day; money for living expenses would have to be earned. Now his father was still hale enough but an old man, and he had done no work for the past five years and could not be expected to do much; during these five years, the first years of leisure in his laborious though unsuccessful life, he had grown rather fat and become sluggish. And Gregor's old mother, how was she to earn a living with her asthma, which troubled her even when she walked through the flat and kept her lying on a sofa every other day panting for breath beside an open window? And was his sister to earn her bread, she who was still a child of seventeen and whose life hitherto had been so pleasant, consisting as it did in dressing herself nicely, sleeping long, helping in the housekeeping, going out to a few modest entertainments and above all playing the violin? At first whenever the need for earning money was mentioned Gregor let go his hold on the door and threw himself down on the cool leather sofa beside it, he felt so hot with shame and grief.

Often he just lay there the long nights through without sleeping at all, scrabbling for hours on the leather. Or he nerved himself to the great effort of pushing an armchair to the window, then crawled up over the window sill and, braced against the chair, leaned against the window panes, obviously in some recollection of the sense of freedom that looking out of a window always used to give him. For in reality day by day things that were even a little way off were growing dimmer to his sight; the hospital across the street, which he used to execrate for being all too often before his eyes, was not quite beyond his range of vision, and if he had not known that he lived in Charlotte Street, a quiet street but still a city street, he might have believed that his window gave on a desert waste where gray sky and gray land blended indistinguishably into each other. His quick-witted sister only needed to observe twice that the armchair stood by the window; after that whenever she had tidied the room she always pushed the chair back to the same place at the window and even left the inner casements open.

If he could have spoken to her and thanked her for all she had to do for him, he could have borne her ministrations better; as it was, they oppressed him. She certainly tried to make as light as possible of whatever was disagreeable in her task, and as time went on she succeeded, of course, more and more, but time brought more enlightenment to Gregor too. The very way she came in distressed him. Hardly was she in the room when she rushed to the window, without even taking time to shut the door, careful as she was usually to shield the sight of Gregor's room from the others, and as if she were almost suffocating tore the casements open with hasty fingers, standing then in the open draught for a while even in the bitterest cold and drawing deep breaths. This noisy scurry of hers upset Gregor twice a day; he would crouch trembling under the sofa all the time, knowing quite well that she would certainly have spared him such a disturbance had she found it at all possible to stay in his presence without opening the window.

On one occasion, about a month after Gregor's metamorphosis, when there was surely no reason for her to be still startled at his appearance, she came a little earlier than usual and found him gazing out of the window, quite motionless, and thus well placed to look like a bogey. Gregor would not have been surprised had she not come in at all, for she could not immediately open the window while he was there, but not only did she retreat, she jumped back as if in alarm and banged the door shut; a stranger might well have thought that he had been lying in wait for her there meaning to bite her. Of course he hid himself under the sofa at once, but he had to wait until midday before she came again, and she seemed more ill at ease than usual. This made him realize how repulsive the sight of him still was to her, and that it was bound to go on being repulsive, and what an effort it must cost her not to run away even from the sight of the small portion of his body that stuck out from under the sofa. In order to spare her that, therefore, one day he carried a sheet on his back to the sofa — it cost him four hours' labor — and arranged it there in such a way as to hide him completely, so that even if she were to bend down she could not see him. Had she considered the sheet unnecessary, she would certainly have stripped it off the sofa again, for it was clear enough that this curtaining and confining of himself was not likely to conduce Gregor's comfort, but she left it where it was, and Gregor even fancied that he caught a thankful glance from her eye when he lifted the sheet carefully a very little with his head to see how she was taking the new arrangement.

For the first fortnight his parents could not bring themselves to the point of entering his room, and he often heard them expressing their appreciation of his sister's activities, whereas formerly they had frequently scolded her for being as they thought a somewhat useless daughter. But now, both of them often waited outside the door, his father and his mother, while his sister tidied his room, and as soon as she came out she had to tell them exactly how things were in the room, what Gregor had eaten, how he had conducted himself this time and whether there was not perhaps some slight improvement in his condition. His mother, moreover, began relatively soon to want to visit him, but his father and sister dissuaded her at first with arguments which Gregor listened to very attentively and altogether approved. Later, however, she had to be held back by main force, and when she cried out: "Do let me in to Gregor, he is my unfortunate son! Can't you understand that I must go to him?" Gregor thought that it might be well to have her come in, not every day, of course, but perhaps once a week; she understood things, after all, much better than his sister, who was only a child despite the efforts she was making and had perhaps taken on so difficult a task merely out of childish thoughtlessness.

Gregor's desire to see his mother was soon fulfilled. During the daytime he did not want to show himself at the window, out of consideration for his parents, but he could not crawl very far around the few square yards of floor space he had, nor could he bear lying quietly at rest all during the night, while he was fast losing any interest he had ever taken in food, so that for mere recreation he had formed the habit of crawling crisscross over the walls and ceiling. He especially enjoyed hanging suspended from the ceiling; it was much better than lying on the floor. One could breathe more freely; one's body swung and rocked lightly; and in the almost blissful absorption induced by this suspension it could happen to his own surprise that he let go and fell plump on the floor. Yet he now had his body much better under control than formerly, and even such a big fall did him no harm. His sister at once remarked the new distraction Gregor had found for himself — he left traces behind him of the sticky stuff on his soles wherever he crawled — and she got the idea in her head of giving him as wide a field as possible to crawl in and of removing the pieces of furniture that hindered him, above all the chest of drawers and the writing desk. But that was more than she could manage all by herself, she did not dare ask her father to help her; and as for the servant girl, a young creature of sixteen who had had the courage to stay on after the cook's departure, she could not be asked to help, for she had begged as an especial favor that she might keep the kitchen door locked and open it only on a definite summons; so there was nothing left but to apply to her mother at an hour when her father was out. And the old lady did come, with exclamations of joyful eagerness, which, however, died away at the door of Gregor's room. Gregor's sister, of course, went in first, to see that everything was in order before letting his mother enter. In great haste Gregor pulled the sheet lower and tucked it more in folds so that it really looked as if it had been thrown accidentally over the sofa. And this time he did not peer out from under it; he renounced the pleasure of seeing his mother on this occasion and was only glad that she had come at all. "Come in, he's out of sight," said his sister, obviously leading her mother by the hand. Gregor could now hear the two women struggling to shift the heavy old chest from its place, and his sister claiming the greater part of the labor for herself, without listening to the admonitions of her mother who feared she might overstrain herself. It took a long time. After at least a quarter of an hour's tugging his mother objected that the chest had better be left where it was, for in the first place it was too heavy and could never be got out before his father came home, and standing in the middle of the room like that it would only hamper Gregor's movements, while in the second place it was not at all certain that removing the furniture would be doing a service to Gregor. She was inclined to think to the contrary; the sight of the naked walls made her own heart heavy, and why shouldn't Gregor have the same feeling, considering that he had been used to his furniture for so long and might feel forlorn without it. "And doesn't it look," she concluded in a low voice — in fact she had been almost whispering all the time as if to avoid letting Gregor, whose exact whereabouts she did not know, hear even the tones of her voice, for she was convinced that he could not understand her words — "doesn't it look as if we were showing him, by taking away his furniture, that we have given up hope of his ever getting better and are just leaving him coldly to himself? I think it would be best to keep his room exactly as it has always been, so that when he comes back to us he will find everything unchanged and be able all the more easily to forget what has happened in between."

On hearing these words from his mother Gregor realized that the lack of all direct human speech for the past two months together with the monotony of family life must have confused his mind, otherwise he could not account for the fact that he had quite earnestly looked forward to having his room emptied of furnishing. Did he really want his warm room, so comfortably fitted with old family furniture, to be turned into a naked den in which he would certainly be able to crawl unhampered in all directions but at the price of shedding simultaneously all recollection of his human background? He had indeed been so near the brink of forgetfulness that only the voice of his mother, which he had not heard for so long, had drawn him back from it. Nothing should be taken out of his room; everything must stay as it was; he could not dispense with the good influence of the furniture on his state of mind; and even if the furniture did hamper him in his senseless crawling round and round, that was no drawback but a great advantage.

Unfortunately his sister was of the contrary opinion; she had grown accustomed, and not without reason, to consider herself an expert in Gregor's affairs as against her parents, and so her mother's advice was now enough to make her determined on the removal not only of the chest and the writing desk, which had been her first intention, but of all the furniture except the indispensable sofa. This determination was not, of course, merely the outcome of childish recalcitrance and of the self-confidence she had recently developed so unexpectedly and at such cost; she had in fact perceived that Gregor needed a lot of space to crawl about in, while on the other hand he never used the furniture at all, so far as could be seen. Another factor might have been also the enthusiastic temperament of an adolescent girl, which seeks to indulge itself on every opportunity and which now tempted Grete to exaggerate the horror of her brother's circumstances in order that she might do all the more for him. In a room where Gregor lorded it all alone over empty walls no one save herself was likely ever to set foot.

And so she was not to be moved from her resolve by her mother who seemed moreover to be ill at ease in Gregor's room and therefore unsure of herself, was soon reduced to silence and helped her daughter as best she could to push the chest outside. Now, Gregor could do without the chest, if need be, but the writing desk he must retain. As soon as the two women had got the chest out of his room, groaning as they pushed it, Gregor stuck his head out from under the sofa to see how he might intervene as kindly and cautiously as possible. But as bad luck would have it, his mother was the first to return, leaving Grete clasping the chest in the room next door where she was trying to shift it all by herself, without of course moving it from the spot. His mother however was not accustomed to the sight of him, it might sicken her and so in alarm Gregor backed quickly to the other end of the sofa, yet could not prevent the sheet from swaying a little in front. That was enough to put her on the alert. She paused, stood still for a moment and then went back to Grete.

Although Gregor kept reassuring himself that nothing out of the way was happening, but only a few bits of furniture were being changed round, he soon had to admit that all this trotting to and fro of the two women, their little ejaculations and the scraping of furniture along the floor affected him like a vast disturbance coming from all sides at once, and however much he tucked in his head and legs and cowered to the very floor he was bound to confess that he would not be able to stand it for long. They were clearing his room out; taking away everything he loved;

the chest in which he kept his fret saw and other tools was already dragged off, they were now loosening the writing desk which had almost sunk into the floor, the desk at which he had done all his homework when he was at the commercial academy, at the grammar school before that, and, yes, even at the primary school — he had no more time to waste in weighing the good intentions of the two women, whose existence he had by now almost forgotten, for they were so exhausted that they were laboring in silence and nothing could be heard but the heavy scuffling of their feet.

And so he rushed out — the women were just leaning against the writing desk in the next room to give themselves a breather — and four times changed his direction, since he really did not know what to rescue first, then on the wall opposite, which was already otherwise cleared, he was struck by the picture of the lady muffled in so much fur and quickly crawled up to it and pressed himself to the glass, which was a good surface to hold on to and comforted his hot belly. This picture at least, which was entirely hidden beneath him, was going to be removed by nobody. He turned his head towards the door of the living room so as to observe the women when they came back.

They had not allowed themselves much of a rest and were already coming; Grete had twined her arm round her mother and was almost supporting her. "Well, what shall we take now?" said Grete, looking round. Her eyes met Gregor's from the wall. She kept her composure, presumably because of her mother, bent her head down to her mother, to keep her from looking up, and said, although in a fluttering, unpremeditated voice: "Come, hadn't we better go back to the living room for a moment?" Her intentions were clear enough to Gregor, she wanted to bestow her mother in safety and then chase him down from the wall. Well, just let her try it! He clung to his picture and would not give it up. He would rather fly in Grete's face.

But Grete's words had succeeded in disquieting her mother, who took a step to one side, caught sight of the huge brown mass on the flowered wallpaper, and before she was really conscious that what she saw was Gregor screamed in a loud, hoarse voice: "Oh God, oh God!" fell with outspread arms over the sofa as if giving up and did not move. "Gregor!" cried his sister, shaking her fist and glaring at him. This was the first time she had directly addressed him since his metamorphosis. She ran into the next room for some aromatic essence with which to rouse her mother from her fainting fit. Gregor wanted to help too — there was still time to rescue the picture — but he was stuck fast to the glass and had to tear himself loose; he then ran after his sister into the next room as if he could advise her, as he used to do; but then had to stand helplessly behind her; she meanwhile searched among various small bottles and when she turned round started in alarm at the sight of him; one bottle fell on the floor and broke; a splinter of glass cut Gregor's face and some kind of corrosive medicine splashed him; without pausing a moment longer Grete gathered up all the bottles she could carry and ran to her mother with them; she banged the door shut with her foot. Gregor was now cut off from his mother, who was perhaps nearly dying because of him; he dared not open the door for fear of frightening away his sister, who had to stay with her mother; there was nothing he could do but wait; and harassed by self-reproach and worry he began now to crawl to and fro, over everything, walls, furniture and ceiling, and finally in his despair, when the whole room seemed to be reeling round him, fell down on to the middle of the big table.

A little while elapsed, Gregor was still lying there feebly and all around was quiet, perhaps that was a good omen. Then the doorbell rang. The servant girl was of course locked in her kitchen, and Grete would have to open the door. It was his father. "What's been happening?" were his first words; Grete's face must have told him everything. Grete answered in a muffled voice, apparently hiding her head on his breast: "Mother has been fainting, but she's better now. Gregor's broken loose." "Just what I expected," said his father, "just what I've been telling you, but you women would never listen." It was clear to Gregor that his father had taken the worst interpretation of Grete's all too brief statement and was assuming that Gregor had been guilty of some violent act. Therefore Gregor must now try to propitiate his father, since he had neither time nor means for an explanation. And so he fled to the door of his own room and crouched against it, to let his father see as soon as he came in from the hall that his son had the good intention of getting back into his room immediately and that it was not necessary to drive him there, but that if only the door were opened he would disappear at once.

Yet his father was not in the mood to perceive such fine distinctions. "Ah!" he cried as soon as he appeared, in a tone which sounded at once angry and exultant. Gregor drew his head back from the door and lifted it to look at his father. Truly, this was not the father he had imagined to himself, admittedly he had been too absorbed of late in his new recreation of crawling over the ceiling to take the same interest as before in what was happening elsewhere in the flat, and he ought really to be prepared for some changes. And yet, and yet, could that be his father? The man who used to lie wearily sunk in bed whenever Gregor set out on a business journey; who welcomed him back of an evening lying in a long chair in a dressing gown; who could not really rise to his feet but only lifted his arms in greeting, and on the rare occasions when he did go out with his family, on one or two Sundays a year and on high holidays, walked between Gregor and his mother, who were slow walkers anyhow, even more slowly than they did, muffled in his old greatcoat, shuffling laboriously forward with the help of his crook-handled stick which he set down most cautiously at every step and, whenever he wanted to say anything, nearly always came to a full stop and gathered his escort around him? Now he was standing there in fine shape; dressed in a smart blue uniform with gold buttons, such as bank messengers wear; his strong double chin bulged over the stiff high collar of his jacket; from under his bushy eyebrows his black eyes darted fresh and penetrating glances; his one-time tangled white hair had been combed flat on either side of a shining and carefully exact parting. He pitched his cap, which bore a gold monogram, probably the badge of some bank, in a wide sweep across the whole room on to a sofa and with the tail-ends of his jacket thrown back, his hands in his trouser pockets, advanced with a grim visage towards Gregor. Likely enough he did not himself know what he meant to do; at any rate he lifted his feet uncommonly high, and Gregor was dumbfounded at the enormous size of his shoe soles. But Gregor could not risk standing up to him, aware as he had been from the very first day of his new life that his father believed only the severest measures suitable for dealing with him. And so he ran before his father, stopping when he stopped and scuttling forward again when his father made any kind of move. In this way they circled the room several times without anything decisive happening, indeed the whole operation did not even look like a pursuit because it was carried out so slowly. And so Gregor did not leave the floor, for he feared that his father might take as a piece of peculiar wickedness any excursion of his over the walls or the ceiling. All the same, he could not stay this course much longer, for while his father took one step he had to carry out a whole series of movements. He was already beginning to feel breathless, just as in his former life his lungs had not been very dependable. As he was staggering along, trying to concentrate his energy on running, hardly keeping his eyes open; in his dazed state never even thinking of any other escape than simply going forward; and having almost forgotten that the walls were free to him, which in this room were well provided with finely carved pieces of furniture full of knobs and crevices — suddenly something lightly flung landed close behind him and rolled before him. It was an apple; a second apple followed immediately; Gregor came to a stop in alarm; there was no point in running on, for his father was determined to bombard him. He had filled his pockets with fruit from the dish on the sideboard and was now shying apple after apple, without taking particularly good aim for the moment. The small red apples rolled about the floor as if magnetized and cannoned into each other. An apple thrown without much force grazed Gregor's back and glanced off harmlessly. But another following immediately landed right on his back and sank in; Gregor wanted to drag himself forward, as if this startling, incredible pain could be left behind him; but he felt as if nailed to the spot and flattened himself out in a complete derangement of all his senses. With his last conscious look he saw the door of his room being torn open and his mother rushing out ahead of his screaming sister, in her underbodice, for her daughter had loosened her clothing to let her breathe more freely and recover from her swoon, he saw his mother rushing towards his father, leaving one after another behind her on the floor her loosened petticoats, stumbling over her petticoats straight to his father and embracing him, in complete union with him — but here Gregor's sight began to fail — with her hands clasped round his father's neck as she begged for her son's life.

III

The serious injury done to Gregor, which disabled him for more than a month — the apple went on sticking in his body as a visible reminder, since no one ventured to remove it — seemed to have made even his father recollect that Gregor was a member of the family, despite his present unfortunate and repulsive shape, and ought not to be treated as an enemy, that, on the contrary, family duty required the suppression of disgust and the exercise of patience, nothing but patience.

And although his injury had impaired, probably for ever, his power of movement, and for the time being it took him long, long minutes to creep across his room like an old invalid — there was no question now of crawling up the wall — yet in his own opinion he was sufficiently compensated for this worsening of his condition by the fact that towards evening the living-room door, which he used to watch intently for an hour or two beforehand, was always thrown open, so that lying in the darkness of his room, invisible to the family, he could see them all at the lamp-lit table and listen to their talk, by general consent as it were, very different from his earlier eavesdropping.

True, their intercourse lacked the lively character of former times, which he had always called to mind with a certain wistfulness in the small hotel bedrooms where he had been wont to throw himself down, tired out, on damp bedding. They were now mostly very silent. Soon after supper his father would fall asleep in his armchair; his mother and sister would admonish each other to be silent; his mother, bending low over the lamp, stitched at fine sewing for an underwear firm; his sister, who had taken a job as a salesgirl, was learning shorthand and French in the evenings on the chance of bettering herself. Sometimes his father woke up, and as if quite unaware that he had been sleeping said to his mother: "What a lot of sewing you're doing today!" and at once fell asleep again, while the two women exchanged a tired smile.

With a kind of mulishness his father persisted in keeping his uniform on even in the house; his dressing gown hung uselessly on its peg and he slept fully dressed where he sat, as if he were ready for service at any moment and even here only at the beck and call of his superior. As a result, his uniform, which was not brand-new to start with, began to look dirty, despite all the loving care of the mother and sister to keep it clean, and Gregor often spent whole evenings gazing at the many greasy spots on the garment, gleaming with gold buttons always in a high state of polish, in which the old man sat sleeping in extreme discomfort and yet quite peacefully.

As soon as the clock struck ten his mother tried to rouse his father with gentle words and to persuade him after that to get into bed, for sitting there he could not have a proper sleep and that was what he needed most, since he had to go to duty at six. But with the mulishness that had obsessed him since he became a bank messenger he always insisted on staying longer at the table, although he regularly fell asleep again and in the end only with the greatest trouble could be got out of his armchair and into his bed. However insistently Gregor's mother and sister kept urging him with gentle reminders, he would go on slowly shaking his head for a quarter of an hour, keeping his eyes shut, and refuse to get to his feet. The mother plucked at his sleeve, whispering endearments in his ear, the sister left her lessons to come to her mother's help, but Gregor's father was not to be caught. He would only sink down deeper in his chair. Not until the two women hoisted him up by the armpits did he open his eyes and look at them both, one after the other, usually with the remark: "This is a life. This is the peace and quiet of my old age." And leaning on the two of them he would heave himself up, with difficulty, as if he were a great burden to himself, suffer them to lead him as far as the door and then wave them off and go on alone, while the mother abandoned her needlework and the sister her pen in order to run after him and help him farther.

Who could find time, in this overworked and tired-out family, to bother about Gregor more than was absolutely needful? The household was reduced more and more; the servant girl was turned off; a gigantic bony charwoman with white hair flying round her head came in morning and evening to do the rough work; everything else was done by Gregor's mother, as well as great piles of sewing. Even various family ornaments, which his mother and sister used to wear with pride at parties and celebrations, had to be sold, as Gregor discovered of an evening from hearing them all discuss the prices obtained. But what they lamented most was the fact that they could not leave the flat which was much too big for their present circumstances, because they could not think of any way to shift Gregor. Yet Gregor saw well enough that consideration for him was not the main difficulty preventing the removal, for they could have easily shifted him in some suitable box with a few air holes in it; what really kept them from moving into another flat was rather their own complete hopelessness and the belief that they had been singled out for a misfortune such as had never happened to any of their relations or acquaintances. They fulfilled to the uttermost all that the world demands of poor people, the father fetched breakfast for the small clerks in the bank, the mother devoted her energy to making underwear for strangers, the sister trotted to and fro behind the counter at the behest of customers, but more than this they had not the strength to do. And the wound in Gregor's back began to nag at him afresh when his mother and sister, after getting his father into bed, came back again, left their work lying, drew close to each other and sat cheek by cheek; when his mother, pointing towards his room, said: "Shut that door now, Grete," and he was left again in darkness, while next door the women mingled their tears or perhaps sat dry-eyed staring at the table.

Gregor hardly slept at all by night or by day. He was often haunted by the idea that next time the door opened he would take the family's affairs in hand again just as he used to do; once more, after this long interval, there appeared in his thoughts the figures of the chief and the chief clerk, the commercial travelers and the apprentices, the porter who was so dull-witted, two or three friends in other firms, a chambermaid in one of the rural hotels, a sweet and fleeting memory, a cashier in a milliner's shop, whom he had wooed earnestly but too slowly — they all appeared, together with strangers or people he had quite forgotten, but instead of helping him and his family they were one and all unapproachable and he was glad when they vanished. At other times he would not be in the mood to bother about his family, he was only filled with rage at the way they were neglecting him, and although he had no clear idea of what he might care to eat he would make plans for getting into the larder to take the food that was after all his due, even if he were not hungry. His sister no longer took thought to bring him what might especially please him, but in the morning and at noon before she went to business hurriedly pushed into his room with her foot any food that was available, and in the evening cleared it out again with one sweep of the broom, heedless of whether it had been merely tasted, or — as most frequently happened — left untouched. The cleaning of his room, which she now did always in the evenings, could not have been more hastily done. Streaks of dirt stretched along the walls, here and there lay balls of dust and filth. At first Gregor used to station himself in some particularly filthy corner when his sister arrived, in order to reproach her with it, so to speak. But he could have sat there for weeks without getting her to make any improvements; she could see the dirt as well as he did, but she had simply made up her mind to leave it alone. And yet, with a touchiness that was new to her, which seemed anyhow to have infected the whole family, she jealously guarded her claim to be the sole caretaker of Gregor's room. His mother once subjected his room to a thorough cleaning, which was achieved only by means of several buckets of water — all this dampness of course upset Gregor too and he lay wide-spread, sulky and motionless on the sofa — but she was well punished for it. Hardly had his sister noticed the changed aspect of his room that evening than she rushed in high dudgeon into the living room and, despite the imploringly raised hands of her mother, burst into a storm of weeping, while her parents — her father had of course been startled out of his chair — looked on at first in helpless amazement; then they too began to go into action; the father reproached the mother on his right for not having left the cleaning of Gregor's room to his sister; shrieked at the sister on his left that never again was she to be allowed to clean Gregor's room; while the mother tried to pull the father into his bedroom, since he was beyond himself with agitation; the sister, shaken with sobs, then beat upon the table with her small fists; and Gregor hissed loudly with rage because not one of them thought of shutting the door to spare him such a spectacle and so much noise.

Still, even if the sister, exhausted by her daily work, had grown tired of looking after Gregor as she did formerly, there was no need for his mother's intervention or for Gregor's being neglected at all. The charwoman was there. This old widow, whose strong bony frame had enabled her to survive the worst a long life could offer, by no means recoiled from Gregor. Without being in the least curious she had once by chance opened the door of his room and at the sight of Gregor, who, taken by surprise, began to rush to and fro although no one was chasing him, merely stood there with her arms folded. From that time she never failed to open his door a little for a moment, morning and evening, to have a look at him. At first she even used to call him to her, with words which apparently she took to be friendly; such as: "Come along, then, you old dung beetle!" or "Look at the old dung beetle, then!" To such allocutions Gregor made no answer, but stayed motionless where he was, as if the door had never been opened. Instead of being allowed to disturb him so senselessly whenever the whim took her, she should rather have been ordered to clean out his room daily, that charwoman! Once, early in the morning — heavy rain was lashing on the windowpanes, perhaps a sign that spring was on the way — Gregor was so exasperated when she began addressing him again that he ran for her, as if to attack her, although slowly and feebly enough. But the charwoman instead of showing fright merely lifted high a chair that happened to be beside the door, and as she stood there with her mouth wide open it was clear that she meant to shut it only when she brought the chair down on Gregor's back. "So you're not coming any nearer?" she asked, as Gregor turned away again, and quietly put the chair back into the corner.

Gregor was now eating hardly anything. Only when he happened to pass the food laid out for him did he take a bit of something in his mouth as a pastime, kept it there for an hour at a time and usually spat it out again. At first he thought it was chagrin over the state of his room that prevented him from eating, yet he soon got used to the various changes in his room. It had become a habit in the family to push into his room things there was no room for elsewhere, and there were plenty of these now, since one of the rooms had been let to three lodgers. These serious gentlemen — all three of them with full beards, as Gregor once observed through a crack in the door — had a passion for order, not only in their own room but, since they were now members of the household, in all its arrangements, especially in the kitchen. Superfluous, not to say dirty, objects they could not bear. Besides, they had brought with them most of the furnishings they needed. For this reason many things could be dispensed with that it was no use trying to sell but that should not be thrown away either. All of them found their way into Gregor's room. The ash can likewise and the kitchen garbage can. Anything that was not needed for the moment was simply flung into Gregor's room by the charwoman, who did everything in a hurry; fortunately Gregor usually saw only the object, whatever it was, and the hand that held it. Perhaps she intended to take the things away again as time and opportunity offered, or to collect them until she could throw them all out in a heap, but in fact they just lay wherever she happened to throw them, except when Gregor pushed his way through the junk heap and shifted it somewhat, at first out of necessity, because he had not room enough to crawl, but later with increasing enjoyment, although after such excursions, being sad and weary to death, he would lie motionless for hours. And since the lodgers often ate their supper at home in the common living room, the living-room door stayed shut many an evening, yet Gregor reconciled himself quite easily to the shutting of the door, for often enough on evenings when it was opened he had disregarded it entirely and lain in the darkest corner of his room, quite unnoticed by the family. But on one occasion the charwoman left the door open a little and it stayed ajar even when the lodgers came in for supper and the lamp was lit. They set themselves at the top end of the table where formerly Gregor and his father and mother had eaten their meals, unfolded their napkins and took knife and fork in hand. At once his mother appeared in the doorway with a dish of meat and close behind her his sister with a dish of potatoes piled high. The food steamed with a thick vapor. The lodgers bent over the food set before them as if to scrutinize it before eating, in fact the man in the middle, who seemed to pass for an authority with the other two, cut a piece of meat as it lay on the dish, obviously to discover if it were tender or should be sent back to the kitchen. He showed satisfaction, and Gregor's mother and sister, who had been watching anxiously, breathed freely and began to smile.

The family itself took its meals in the kitchen. None the less, Gregor's father came into the living room before going into the kitchen and with one prolonged bow, cap in hand, made a round of the table. The lodgers all stood up and murmured something in their beards. When they were alone again they ate their food in almost complete silence. It seemed remarkable to Gregor that among the various noises coming from the table he could always distinguish the sound of their masticating teeth, as if this were a sign to Gregor that one needed teeth in order to eat, and that with toothless jaws even of the finest make one could do nothing. "I'm hungry enough," said Gregor sadly to himself, "but not for that kind of food. How these lodgers are stuffing themselves, and here am I dying of starvation!"

On that very evening — during the whole of his time there Gregor could not remember ever having heard the violin — the sound of violin-playing came from the kitchen. The lodgers had already finished their supper, the one in the middle had brought out a newspaper and given the other two a page apiece, and now they were leaning back at ease reading and smoking. When the violin began to play they pricked up their ears, got to their feet, and went on tiptoe to the hall door where they stood huddled together. Their movements must have been heard in the kitchen, for Gregor's father called out: "Is the violin-playing disturbing you gentlemen? It can be stopped at once." "On the contrary," said the middle lodger, "could not Fräulein Samsa come and play in this room, beside us, where it is much more convenient and comfortable?" "Oh certainly," cried Gregor's father, as if he were the violin player. The lodgers came back into the living room and waited. Presently Gregor's father arrived with the music stand, his mother carrying the music and his sister with the violin. His sister quietly made everything ready to start playing; his parents, who had never let rooms before and so had an exaggerated idea of the courtesy due to lodgers, did not venture to sit down on their own chairs; his father leaned against the door, the right hand thrust between two buttons of his livery coat, which was formally buttoned up; but his mother was offered a chair by one of the lodgers and, since she left the chair just where he had happened to put it, sat down in a corner to one side.

Gregor's sister began to play; the father and mother, from either side, intently watched the movements of her hands. Gregor, attracted by the playing, ventured to move forward a little until his head was actually inside the living room. He felt hardly any surprise at his growing lack of consideration for the others; there had been a time when he prided himself on being considerate. And yet just on this occasion he had more reason than ever to hide himself, since owing to the amount of dust which lay thick in his room and rose into the air at the slightest movement, he too was covered with dust; fluff and hair and remnants of food trailed with him, caught on his back and along his sides; his indifference to everything was much too great for him to turn on his back and scrape himself clean on the carpet, as once he had done several times a day. And in spite of his condition, no shame deterred him from advancing a little over the spotless floor of the living room.

To be sure, no one was aware of him. The family was entirely absorbed in the violin-playing; the lodgers, however, who first of all had stationed themselves, hands in pockets, much too close behind the music stand so that they could all have read the music, which must have bothered his sister, had soon retreated to the window, half-whispering with downbent heads, and stayed there while his father turned an anxious eye on them. Indeed, they were making it more than obvious that they had been disappointed in their expectation of hearing good or enjoyable violin-playing, that they had had more than enough of the performance and only out of courtesy suffered a continued disturbance of their peace. From the way they all kept blowing the smoke of their cigars high in the air through nose and mouth one could divine their irritation. And yet Gregor's sister was playing so beautifully. Her face leaned sideways, intently and sadly her eyes followed the notes of music. Gregor crawled a little farther forward and lowered his head to the ground so that it might be possible for his eyes to meet hers. Was he an animal, that music had such an effect upon him? He felt as if the way were opening before him to the unknown nourishment he craved. He was determined to push forward till he reached his sister, to pull at her skirt and so let her know that she was to come into his room with her violin, for no one here appreciated her playing as he would appreciate it. He would never let her out of his room, at least, not so long as he lived; his frightful appearance would become, for the first time, useful to him; he would watch all the doors of his room at once and spit at intruders; but his sister should need no constraint, she should stay with him of her own free will; she should sit beside him on the sofa, bend down her ear to him and hear him confide that he had had the firm intention of sending her to the Conservatorium, and that, but for his mishap, last Christmas — surely Christmas was long past? — he would have announced it to everybody without allowing a single objection. After this confession his sister would be so touched that she would burst into tears, and Gregor would then raise himself to her shoulder and kiss her on the neck, which, now that she went to business, she kept free of any ribbon or collar.

"Mr. Samsa!" cried the middle lodger, to Gregor's father, and pointed, without wasting any more words, at Gregor, now working himself slowly forwards. The violin fell silent, the middle lodger first smiled to his friends with a shake of the head and then looked at Gregor again. Instead of driving Gregor out, his father seemed to think it more needful to begin by soothing down the lodgers, although they were not at all agitated and apparently found Gregor more entertaining than the violin-playing. He hurried towards them and, spreading out his arms, tried to urge them back into their own room and at the same time to block their view of Gregor. They now began to be really a little angry, one could not tell whether because of the old man's behavior or because it just dawned on them that all unwittingly they had such a neighbor as Gregor next door. They demanded explanations of his father, they waved their arms like him, tugged uneasily at their beards, and only with reluctance backed towards their room. Meanwhile Gregor's sister, who stood there as if lost when her playing was so abruptly broken off, came to life again, pulled herself together all at once after standing for a while holding violin and bow in nervelessly hanging hands and staring at her music, pushed her violin into the lap of her mother, who was still sitting in her chair fighting asthmatically for breath, and ran into the lodgers' room to which they were now being shepherded by her father rather more quickly than before. One could see the pillows and blankets on the beds flying under her accustomed fingers and being laid in order. Before the lodgers had actually reached their room she had finished making the beds and slipped out.

The old man seemed once more to be so possessed by his mulish self-assertiveness that he was forgetting all the respect he should show to his lodgers. He kept driving them on and driving them on until in the very door of the bedroom the middle lodger stamped his foot loudly on the floor and so brought him to a halt. "I beg to announce," said the lodger, lifting one hand and looking also at Gregor's mother and sister, "that because of the disgusting conditions prevailing in this household and family" — here he spat on the floor with emphatic brevity — "I give you notice on the spot. Naturally I won't pay you a penny for the days I have lived here, on the contrary I shall consider bringing an action for damages against you, based on claims — believe me — that will be easily susceptible of proof." He ceased and stared straight in front of him, as if he expected something. In fact his two friends at once rushed into the breach with these words: "And we too give notice on the spot." On that he seized the door-handle and shut the door with a slam.

Gregor's father, groping with his hands, staggered forward and fell into his chair; it looked as if he were stretching himself there for his ordinary evening nap, but the marked jerkings of his head, which was as if uncontrollable, showed that he was far from asleep. Gregor had simply stayed quietly all the time on the spot where the lodgers had espied him. Disappointment at the failure of his plan, perhaps also the weakness arising from extreme hunger, made it impossible for him to move. He feared, with a fair degree of certainty, that at any moment the general tension would discharge itself in a combined attack upon him, and he lay waiting. He did not react even to the noise made by the violin as it fell off his mother's lap from under her trembling fingers and gave out a resonant note.

"My dear parents," said his sister, slapping her hand on the table by way of introduction, "things can't go on like this. Perhaps you don't realize that, but I do. I won't utter my brother's name in the presence of this creature, and so all I say is: we must try to get rid of it. We've tried to look after it and to put up with it as far as is humanly possible, and I don't think anyone could reproach us in the slightest."

"She is more than right," said Gregor's father to himself. His mother, who was still choking for lack of breath, began to cough hollowly into her hand with a wild look in her eyes.

His sister rushed over to her and held her forehead. His father's thoughts seemed to have lost their vagueness at Grete's words, he sat more upright, fingering his service cap that lay among the plates still lying on the table from the lodgers' supper, and from time to time looked at the still form of Gregor.

"We must try to get rid of it," his sister now said explicitly to her father, since her mother was coughing too much to hear a word, "it will be the death of both of you, I can see that coming. When one has to work as hard as we do, all of us, one can't stand this continual torment at home on top of it. At least I can't stand it any longer." And she burst into such a passion of sobbing that her tears dropped on her mother's face, where she wiped them off mechanically.

"My dear," said the old man sympathetically, and with evident understanding, "but what can we do?"

Gregor's sister merely shrugged her shoulders to indicate the feeling of helplessness that had now overmastered her during her weeping fit, in contrast to her former confidence.

"If he could understand us," said her father, half questioningly; Grete, still sobbing, vehemently waved a hand to show how unthinkable that was.

"If he could understand us," repeated the old man, shutting his eyes to consider his daughter's conviction that understanding was impossible, "then perhaps we might come to some agreement with him. But as it is —"

"He must go," cried Gregor's sister, "that's the only solution, Father. You must just try to get rid of the idea that this is Gregor. The fact that we've believed it for so long is the root of all our trouble. But how can it be Gregor? If this were Gregor, he would have realized long ago that human beings can't live with such a creature, and he'd have gone away on his own accord. Then we wouldn't have any brother, but we'd be able to go on living and keep his memory in honor. As it is, this creature persecutes us, drives away our lodgers, obviously wants the whole apartment to himself and would have us all sleep in the gutter. Just look, Father," she shrieked all at once, "he's at it again!" And in an access of panic that was quite incomprehensible to Gregor she even quitted her mother, literally thrusting the chair from her as if she would rather sacrifice her mother than stay so near to Gregor, and rushed behind her father, who also rose up, being simply upset by her agitation, and half-spread his arms out as if to protect her.

Yet Gregor had not the slightest intention of frightening anyone, far less his sister. He had only begun to turn round in order to crawl back to his room, but it was certainly a startling operation to watch, since because of his disabled condition he could not execute the difficult turning movements except by lifting his head and then bracing it against the floor over and over again. He paused and looked round. His good intentions seemed to have been recognized; the alarm had only been momentary. Now they were all watching him in melancholy silence. His mother lay in her chair, her legs stiffly outstretched and pressed together, her eyes almost closing for sheer weariness; his father and his sister were sitting beside each other, his sister's arm around the old man's neck.

Perhaps I can go on turning round now, thought Gregor, and began his labors again. He could not stop himself from panting with the effort, and had to pause now and then to take breath. Nor did anyone harass him, he was left entirely to himself. When he had completed the turn-round he began at once to crawl straight back. He was amazed at the distance separating him from his room and could not understand how in his weak state he had managed to accomplish the same journey so recently, almost without remarking it. Intent on crawling as fast as possible, he barely noticed that not a single word, not an ejaculation from his family, interfered with his progress. Only when he was already in the doorway did he turn his head round, not completely, for his neck muscles were getting stiff, but enough to see that nothing had changed behind him except that his sister had risen to her feet. His last glance fell on his mother, who was not quite overcome by sleep.

Hardly was he well inside his room when the door was hastily pushed shut, bolted and locked. The sudden noise in his rear startled him so much that his little legs gave beneath him. It was his sister who had shown such haste. She had been standing ready waiting and had made a light spring forward. Gregor had not even heard her coming, and she cried "At last!" to her parents as she turned the key in the lock.

"And what now?" said Gregor to himself, looking round in the darkness. Soon he made the discovery that he was now unable to stir a limb. This did not surprise him, rather it seemed unnatural that he should ever actually have been able to move on these feeble little legs. Otherwise he felt relatively comfortable. True, his whole body was aching, but it seemed that the pain was gradually growing less and would finally pass away. The rotting apple in his back and the inflamed area around it, all covered with soft dust, already hardly troubled him. He thought of his family with tenderness and love. The decision that he must disappear was one that he held to even more strongly than his sister, if that were possible. In this state of vacant and peaceful meditation he remained until the tower clock struck three in the morning. The first broadening of light in the world outside the window entered his consciousness once more. Then his head sank to the floor of its own accord and from his nostrils came the last faint flicker of his breath.

When the charwoman arrived early in the morning — what between her strength and her impatience she slammed all the doors so loudly, never mind how often she had been begged not to do so, that no one in the whole apartment could enjoy any quiet sleep after her arrival — she noticed nothing unusual as she took her customary peep into Gregor's room. She thought he was lying motionless on purpose, pretending to be in the sulks; she credited him with every kind of intelligence. Since she happened to have the longhandled broom in her hand she tried to tickle him up with it from the doorway. When that too produced no reaction she felt provoked and poked at him a little harder, and only when she had pushed him along the floor without meeting any resistance was her attention aroused. It did not take her long to establish the truth of the matter, and her eyes widened, she let out a whistle, yet did not waste much time over it but tore open the door of the Samsas' bedroom and yelled into the darkness at the top of her voice: "Just look at this, it's dead; it's lying here dead and done for!"

Mr. and Mrs. Samsa started up in their double bed and before they realized the nature of the charwoman's announcement had some difficulty in overcoming the shock of it. But then they got out of bed quickly, one on either side, Mr. Samsa throwing a blanket over his shoulders, Mrs. Samsa in nothing but her nightgown; in this array they entered Gregor's room. Meanwhile the door of the living room opened, too, where Grete had been sleeping since the advent of the lodgers; she was completely dressed as if she had not been to bed, which seemed to be confirmed also by the paleness of her face. "Dead?" said Mrs. Samsa, looking questioningly at the charwoman, although she could have investigated for herself, and the fact was obvious enough without investigation. "I should say so," said the charwoman, proving her words by pushing Gregor's corpse a long way to one side with her broomstick. Mrs. Samsa made a movement as if to stop her, but checked it. "Well," said Mr. Samsa, "now thanks be to God." He crossed himself, and the three women followed his example. Grete, whose eyes never left the corpse, said: "Just see how thin he was. It's such a long time since he's eaten anything. The food came out again just as it went in." Indeed, Gregor's body was completely flat and dry, as could only now be seen when it was no longer supported by the legs and nothing prevented one from looking closely at it.

"Come in beside us, Grete, for a little while," said Mrs. Samsa with a tremulous smile, and Grete, not without looking back at the corpse, followed her parents into their bedroom. The charwoman shut the door and opened the window wide. Although it was so early in the morning a certain softness was perceptible in the fresh air. After all, it was already the end of March.

The three lodgers emerged from their room and were surprised to see no breakfast; they had been forgotten. "Where's our breakfast?" said the middle lodger peevishly to the charwoman. But she put her finger to her lips and hastily, without a word, indicated by gestures that they should go into Gregor's room. They did so and stood, their hands in the pockets of their somewhat shabby coats, around Gregor's corpse in the room where it was now fully light.

At that the door of the Samsas' bedroom opened and Mr. Samsa appeared in his uniform, his wife on one arm, his daughter on the other. They all looked a little as if they had been crying; from time to time Grete hid her face on her father's arm.

"Leave my house at once!" said Mr. Samsa, and pointed to the door without disengaging himself from the women. "What do you mean by that?" said the middle lodger, taken somewhat aback, with a feeble smile. The two others put their hands behind them and kept rubbing them together, as if in gleeful expectation of a fine set-to in which they were bound to come off the winners. "I mean just what I say," answered Mr. Samsa, and advanced in a straight line with his two companions towards the lodger. He stood his ground at first quietly, looking at the floor as if his thoughts were taking a new pattern in his head. "Then let us go, by all means," he said and looked up at Mr. Samsa as if in a sudden access of humility he were expecting some renewed sanction for this decision. Mr. Samsa merely nodded briefly once or twice with meaning eyes. Upon that the lodger really did go with long strides into the hall, his two friends had been listening and had quite stopped rubbing their hands for some moments and now went scuttling after him as if afraid that Mr. Samsa might get into the hall before them and cut them off from their leader. In the hall they all three took their hats from the rack, their sticks from the umbrella stand, bowed in silence and quitted the apartment. With a suspiciousness which proved quite unfounded Mr. Samsa and the two women followed them out to the landing; leaning over the banister they watched the three figures slowly but surely going down the long stairs, vanishing from sight at a certain turn of the staircase on every floor and coming into view again after a moment or so; the more they dwindled, the more the Samsa family's interest in them dwindled, and when a butcher's boy met them and passed them on the stairs coming up proudly with a tray on his head, Mr. Samsa and the two women soon left the landing and as if a burden had been lifted from them went back into their apartment.

They decided to spend this day in resting and going for a stroll; they had not only deserved such a respite from work, but absolutely needed it. And so they sat down at the table and wrote three notes of excuse, Mr. Samsa to his board of management, Mrs. Samsa to her employer and Grete to the head of her firm. While they were writing, the charwoman came in to say that she was going now, since her morning's work was finished. At first they only nodded without looking up, but as she kept hovering there they eyed her irritably. "Well?" said Mr. Samsa. The charwoman stood grinning in the doorway as if she had good news to impart to the family but meant not to say a word unless properly questioned. The small ostrich feather standing upright on her hat, which had annoyed Mr. Samsa ever since she was engaged, was waving gaily in all directions. "Well, what is it then?" asked Mrs. Samsa, who obtained more respect from the charwoman than the others. "Oh," said the charwoman, giggling so amiably that she could not at once continue, "just this, you don't need to bother about how to get rid of the thing next door. It's been seen to already." Mrs. Samsa and Grete bent over their letters again, as if preoccupied; Mr. Samsa, who perceived that she was eager to begin describing it all in detail, stopped her with a decisive hand. But since she was not allowed to tell her story, she remembered the great hurry she was in, being obviously deeply huffed: "Bye, everybody," she said, whirling off violently, and departed with a frightful slamming of doors.

"She'll be given notice tonight," said Mr. Samsa, but neither from his wife nor his daughter did he get any answer, for the charwoman seemed to have shattered again the composure they had barely achieved. They rose, went to the window and stayed there, clasping each other tight. Mr. Samsa turned in his chair to look at them and quietly observed them for a little. Then he called out: "Come along, now, do. Let bygones be bygones. And you might have some consideration for me." The two of them complied at once, hastened to him, caressed him and quickly finished their letters.

Then they all three left the apartment together, which was more than they had done for months, and went by tram into the open country outside the town. The tram, in which they were the only passengers, was filled with warm sunshine. Leaning comfortably back in their seats they canvassed their prospects for the future, and it appeared on closer inspection that these were not at all bad, for the jobs they had got, which so far they had never really discussed with each other, were all three admirable and likely to lead to better things later on. The greatest immediate improvement in their condition would of course arise from moving to another house; they wanted to take a smaller and cheaper but also better situated and more easily run apartment than the one they had, which Gregor had selected. While they were thus conversing, it struck both Mr. and Mrs. Samsa, almost at the same moment, as they became aware of their daughter's increasing vivacity, that in spite of all the sorrow of recent times, which had made her cheeks pale, she had bloomed into a pretty girl with a good figure. They grew quieter and half unconsciously exchanged glances of complete agreement, having come to the conclusion that it would soon be time to find a good husband for her. And it was like a confirmation of their new dreams and excellent intentions that at the end of their journey their daughter sprang to her feet first and stretched her young body.

William Carlos Williams (*1883–1963*)

The Use of Force

They were new patients to me, all I had was the name, Olson. Please come down as soon as you can, my daughter is very sick.

When I arrived I was met by the mother, a big startled looking woman, very clean and apologetic who merely said, Is this the doctor? and let me in. In the back, she added. You must excuse us, doctor, we have her in the kitchen where it is warm. It is very damp here sometimes.

The child was fully dressed and sitting on her father's lap near the kitchen table. He tried to get up, but I motioned for him not to bother, took off my overcoat and started to look things over. I could see that they were all very nervous, eyeing me up and down distrustfully. As often, in such cases, they weren't telling me more than they had to, it was up to me to tell them; that's why they were spending three dollars on me.

The child was fairly eating me up with her cold, steady eyes, and no expression to her face whatever. She did not move and seemed, inwardly, quiet; an unusually attractive little thing, and as strong as a heifer in appearance. But her face was flushed, she was breathing rapidly, and I realized that she had a high fever. She had magnificent blonde hair, in profusion. One of those picture children often reproduced in advertising leaflets and the photogravure sections of the Sunday papers.

She'd had a fever for three days, began the father and we don't know what it comes from. My wife has given her things, you know, like people do, but it don't do no good. And there's been a lot of sickness around. So we tho't you'd better look her over and tell us what is the matter.

As doctors often do I took a trial shot at it as a point of departure. Has she had a sore throat?

Both parents answered me together, No . . . No, she says her throat don't hurt her.

Does your throat hurt you? added the mother to the child. But the little girl's expression didn't change nor did she move her eyes from my face.

Have you looked?

I tried to, said the mother, but I couldn't see.

As it happens we had been having a number of cases of diphtheria in the school to which this child went during that month and we were all, quite apparently, thinking of that, though no one had as yet spoken of the thing.

Well, I said, suppose we take a look at the throat first. I smiled in my best professional manner and for asking the child's first name I said, come on, Mathilda, open your mouth and let's take a look at your throat.

Nothing doing.

Aw, come on, I coaxed, just open your mouth wide and let me take a look. Look, I said opening both hands wide, I haven't anything in my hands. Just open up and let me see.

Such a nice man, put in the mother. Look how kind he is to you. Come on, do what he tells you to. He won't hurt you.

At that I ground my teeth in disgust. If only they wouldn't use the word "hurt" I might be able to get somewhere. But I did not allow myself to be hurried or disturbed but speaking quietly and slowly I approached the child again.

As I moved my chair a little nearer suddenly with one catlike movement both her hands clawed instinctively for my eyes and she almost reached them too. In fact she knocked my glasses flying and they fell, though unbroken, several feet away from me on the kitchen floor.

Both the mother and father almost turned themselves inside out in embarrassment and apology. You bad girl, said the mother, taking her and shaking her by one arm. Look what you've done. The nice man . . .

For heaven's sake, I broke in. Don't call me a nice man to her. I'm here to look at her throat on the chance that she might have diphtheria and possibly die of it. But that's nothing to her. Look here, I said to the child, we're going to look at your throat. You're old enough to understand what I'm saying. Will you open it now by yourself or shall we have to open it for you?

Not a move. Even her expression hadn't changed. Her breaths however were coming faster and faster. Then the battle began. I had to do it. I had to have a throat culture for her own protection. But first I told the parents that it was entirely up to them. I explained the danger but said that I would not insist on a throat examination so long as they would take the responsibility.

If you don't do what the doctor says you'll have to go to the hospital, the mother admonished her severely.

Oh yeah? I had to smile to myself. After all, I had already fallen in love with the savage brat, the parents were contemptible to me. In the ensuing struggle they grew more and more abject, crushed, exhausted while she surely rose to magnificent heights of insane fury of effort bred of her terror of me.

The father tried his best, and he was a big man but the fact that she was his daughter, his shame at her behavior and his dread of hurting her made him release her just at the critical times when I had almost achieved success, till I wanted to kill him. But his dread also that she might have diphtheria made him tell me to go on, go on though he himself was almost fainting, while the mother moved back and forth behind us raising and lowering her hands in an agony of apprehension.

Put her in front of you on your lap, I ordered, and hold both her wrists.

But as soon as he did the child let out a scream. Don't, you're hurting me. Let go of my hands. Let them go I tell you. Then she shrieked terrifyingly, hysterically. Stop it! Stop it! You're killing me!

Do you think she can stand it, doctor! said the mother.

You get out, said the husband to his wife. Do you want her to die of diphtheria?

Come on now, hold her, I said.

Then I grasped the child's head with my left hand and tried to get the wooden tongue depressor between her teeth. She fought, with clenched teeth, desperately! But now I also had grown furious — at a child. I tried to hold myself down but I couldn't. I know how to expose a throat for inspection. And I did my best. When finally I got the wooden spatula behind the last teeth and just the point of it into the mouth cavity, she opened up for an instant but before I could see anything she came down again and gripping the wooden blade between her molars she reduced it to splinters before I could get it out again.

Aren't you ashamed, the mother yelled at her. Aren't you ashamed to act like that in front of the doctor?

Get me a smooth-handled spoon of some sort, I told the mother. We're going through with this. The child's mouth was already bleeding. Her tongue was cut and she was screaming in wild hysterical shrieks. Perhaps I should have desisted and come back in an hour or more. No doubt it would have been better. But I have seen at least two children lying dead in bed of neglect in such cases, and feeling that I must get a diagnosis now or never I went at it again. But the worst of it was that I too had got beyond reason. I could have torn the child apart in my own fury and enjoyed it. It was pleasure to attack her. My face was burning with it.

The damned little brat must be protected against her own idiocy, one says to one's self at such times. Others must be protected against her. It is a social necessity. And all these things are true. But a blind fury, a feeling of adult shame, bred of a longing for muscular release are the operatives. One goes on to the end.

In a final unreasoning assault I overpowered the child's neck and jaws. I forced the heavy silver spoon back of her teeth and down her throat till she gagged. And there it was — both tonsils covered with membrane. She had fought valiantly to keep me from knowing her secret. She had been hiding that sore throat for three days at least and lying to her parents in order to escape just such an outcome as this.

Now truly she was furious. She had been on the defensive before but now she attacked. Tried to get off her father's lap and fly at me while tears of defeat blinded her eyes.

D. H. Lawrence (1885–1930)

The Horse Dealer's Daughter

"Well, Mabel, and what are you going to do with yourself?" asked Joe, with foolish flippancy. He felt quite safe himself. Without listening for an answer, he turned aside, worked a grain of tobacco to the tip of his tongue and spat it out. He did not care about anything, since he felt safe himself.

The three brothers and the sister sat round the desolate breakfast table, attempting some sort of desultory consultation. The morning's post had given the final tap to the family fortune, and all was over. The dreary dining room itself, with its heavy mahogany furniture, looked as if it were waiting to be done away with.

But the consultation amounted to nothing. There was a strange air of ineffectuality about the three men, as they sprawled at table, smoking and reflecting vaguely on their own condition. The girl was alone, a rather short, sullen-looking young woman of twenty-seven. She did not share the same life as her brothers. She would have been good-looking, save for the impassive fixity of her face, "bull-dog," as her brothers called it.

There was a confused tramping of horses' feet outside. The three men all sprawled round in their chairs to watch. Beyond the dark holly bushes that separated the strip of lawn from the highroad, they could see a cavalcade of shire horses swinging out of their own yard, being taken for exercise. This was the last time. These were the last horses that would go through their hands. The young men watched with critical, callous looks. They were all frightened at the collapse of their lives, and the sense of disaster in which they were involved left them no inner freedom.

Yet they were three fine, well-set fellows enough. Joe, the eldest, was a man of thirty-three, broad and handsome in a hot, flushed way. His face was red, he twisted his black moustache over a thick finger, his eyes were shallow and restless. He had a sensual way of uncovering his teeth when he laughed, and his bearing was stupid. Now he watched the horses with a glazed look of helplessness in his eyes, a certain stupor of downfall.

The great draught-horses swung past. They were tied head to tail, four of them, and they heaved along to where a lane branched off from the highroad, planting their great hoofs floutingly in the fine black mud, swinging their great rounded haunches sumptuously, and trotting a few sudden steps as they were led into the lane, round the corner. Every movement showed a massive, slumbrous strength, and a stupidity which held them in subjection. The groom at the head looked back, jerking the leading rope. And the cavalcade moved out of sight up the lane, the tail of the last horse, bobbed up tight and stiff, held out taut from the swinging great haunches as they rocked behind the hedges in a motion-like sleep.

Joe watched with glazed hopeless eyes. The horses were almost like his own body to him. He felt he was done for now. Luckily he was engaged to a woman as old as himself, and therefore her father, who was steward of a neighboring estate, would provide him with a job. He would marry and go into harness. His life was over, he would be a subject animal now.

He turned uneasily aside, the retreating steps of the horses echoing in his ears. Then, with foolish restlessness, he reached for the scraps of bacon rind from the plates, and making a faint whistling sound, flung them to the terrier that lay against the fender. He watched the dog swallow them, and waited till the creature looked into his eyes. Then a faint grin came on his face, and in a high, foolish voice he said:

"You won't get much more bacon, shall you, you little bitch?"

The dog faintly and dismally wagged its tail, then lowered its haunches, circled round, and lay down again.

There was another helpless silence at the table. Joe sprawled uneasily in his seat, not willing to go till the family conclave was dissolved. Fred Henry, the second brother, was erect, cleanlimbed, alert. He had watched the passing of the horses with more sangfroid. If he was an animal, like Joe, he was an animal which controls, not one which is controlled. He was master of any horse, and he carried himself with a well-tempered air of mastery. But he was not master of the situations of life. He pushed his coarse brown moustache upwards, off his lip, and glanced irritably at his sister, who sat impassive and inscrutable.

"You'll go and stop with Lucy for a bit, shan't you?" he asked. The girl did not answer.

"I don't see what else you can do," persisted Fred Henry.

"Go as a skivvy," Joe interpolated laconically.

The girl did not move a muscle.

"If I was her, I should go in for training for a nurse," said Malcolm, the youngest of them all. He was the baby of the family, a young man of twenty-two, with a fresh, jaunty *museau*.°

But Mabel did not take any notice of him. They had talked at her and round her for so many years, that she hardly heard them at all.

The marble clock on the mantelpiece softly chimed the half-hour, the dog rose uneasily from the hearthrug and looked at the party at the breakfast table. But still they sat on in effectual conclave.

"Oh, all right," said Joe suddenly, apropos of nothing. "I'll get a move on."

He pushed back his chair, straddled his knees with a downward jerk, to get them free, in horsey fashion, and went to the fire. Still he did not go out of the room; he was curious to know what the others would do or say. He began to charge his pipe, looking down at the dog and saying, in a high, affected voice:

"Going wi' me? Going wi' me are ter? Tha'rt goin' further tha that counts on just now, dost hear?"

The dog faintly wagged its tail, the man stuck out his jaw and covered his pipe with his hands, and puffed intently, losing himself in the tobacco, looking down all the while at the dog with an absent brown eye. The dog looked at him in mournful distrust. Joe stood with his knees stuck out, in real horsey fashion.

"Have you had a letter from Lucy?" Fred Henry asked of his sister.

"Last week," came the neutral reply.

"And what does she say?"

There was no answer.

"Does she *ask* you to go and stop there?" persisted Fred Henry.

"She says I can if I like."

"Well, then, you'd better. Tell her you'll come on Monday." This was received in silence.

"That's what you'll do then, is it?" said Fred Henry, in some exasperation.

But she made no answer. There was a silence of futility and irritation in the room. Malcolm grinned fatuously.

"You'll have to make up your mind between now and next Wednesday," said Joe loudly, "or else find yourself lodgings on the curbstone."

museau   jaw (literally muzzle or snout of a beast)

The face of the young woman darkened, but she sat on immutable.

"Here's Jack Fergusson!" exclaimed Malcolm, who was looking aimlessly out of the window.

"Where?" exclaimed Joe, loudly.

"Just gone past."

"Coming in?"

Malcolm craned his neck to see the gate.

"Yes," he said.

There was a silence. Mabel sat on like one condemned, at the head of the table. Then a whistle was heard from the kitchen. The dog got up and barked sharply. Joe opened the door and shouted:

"Come on."

After a moment a young man entered. He was muffled up in overcoat and a purple woolen scarf, and his tweed cap, which he did not remove, was pulled down on his head. He was of medium height, his face was rather long and pale, his eyes looked tired.

"Hello, Jack! Well, Jack!" exclaimed Malcolm and Joe. Fred Henry merely said, "Jack."

"What's doing?" asked the newcomer, evidently addressing Fred Henry.

"Same. We've got to be out by Wednesday. Got a cold?"

"I have — got it bad, too."

"Why don't you stop in?"

"*Me* stop in? When I can't stand on my legs, perhaps I shall have a chance." The young man spoke huskily. He had a slight Scotch accent.

"It's a knock-out, isn't it," said Joe, boisterously, "if a doctor goes round croaking with a cold. Looks bad for the patients, doesn't it?"

The young doctor looked at him slowly.

"Anything the matter with *you,* then?" he asked sarcastically.

"Not as I know of. Damn your eyes, I hope not. Why?"

"I thought you were very concerned about the patients, wondered if you might be one yourself."

"Damn it, no, I've never been patient to no flaming doctor, and hope I never shall be," returned Joe.

At this point Mabel rose from the table, and they all seemed to become aware of her existence. She began putting the dishes together. The young doctor looked at her, but did not address her. He had not greeted her. She went out of the room with the tray, her face impassive and unchanged.

"When are you off then, all of you?" asked the doctor.

"I'm catching the eleven-forty," replied Malcolm. "Are you goin' down wi' th' trap, Joe?"

"Yes, I've told you I'm going down wi' th' trap, haven't I?"

"We'd better be getting her in then. So long, Jack, if I don't see you before I go," said Malcolm, shaking hands.

He went out, followed by Joe, who seemed to have his tail between his legs.

"Well, this is the devil's own," exclaimed the doctor, when he was left alone with Fred Henry. "Going before Wednesday, are you?"

"That's the orders," replied the other.

"Where, to Northampton?"

"That's it."

"The devil!" exclaimed Fergusson, with quiet chagrin.

And there was silence between the two.

"All settled up, are you?" asked Fergusson.

"About."

There was another pause.

"Well, I shall miss yer, Freddy, boy," said the young doctor.

"And I shall miss thee, Jack," returned the other.

"Miss you like hell," mused the doctor.

Fred Henry turned aside. There was nothing to say. Mabel came in again, to finish clearing the table.

"What are *you* going to do, then, Miss Pervin?" asked Fergusson. "Going to your sister's, are you?"

Mabel looked at him with her steady, dangerous eyes, that always made him uncomfortable, unsettling his superficial ease.

"No," she said.

"Well, what in the name of fortune *are* you going to do? Say what you mean to do," cried Fred Henry, with futile intensity.

But she only averted her head, and continued her work. She folded the white table-cloth, and put on the chenille cloth.

"The sulkiest bitch that ever trod!" muttered her brother.

But she finished her task with perfectly impassive face, the young doctor watching her interestedly all the while. Then she went out.

Fred Henry stared after her, clenching his lips, his blue eyes fixing in sharp antagonism, as he made a grimace of sour exasperation.

"You could bray her into bits, and that's all you'd get out of her," he said in a small, narrowed tone.

The doctor smiled faintly.

"What's she *going* to do, then?" he asked.

"Strike me if *I* know!" returned the other.

There was a pause. Then the doctor stirred.

"I'll be seeing you to-night, shall I?" he said to his friend.

"Ay — where's it to be? Are we going over to Jessdale?"

"I don't know. I've got such a cold on me. I'll come round to the Moon and Stars, anyway."

"Let Lizzie and May miss their night for once, eh?"

"That's it — if I feel as I do now."

"All's one —"

The two young men went through the passage and down to the back door together. The house was large, but it was servantless now, and desolate. At the back was a small bricked house-yard, and beyond that a big square, graveled fine and red, and having stables on two sides. Sloping, dank, winter-dark fields stretched away on the open sides.

But the stables were empty. Joseph Pervin, the father of the family, had been a man of no education, who had become a fairly large horse dealer. The stables had been full of horses, there was a great turmoil and come-and-go of horses and of dealers and grooms. Then the kitchen was full of servants. But of late things had declined. The old man had married a second time, to retrieve his fortunes. Now he was dead and everything was gone to the dogs, there was nothing but debt and threatening.

For months, Mabel had been servantless in the big house, keeping the home together in penury for her ineffectual brothers. She had kept house for ten years. But previously it was with unstinted means. Then, however brutal and coarse everything was, the sense of money had kept her proud, confident. The men might be foul-mouthed, the women in the kitchen might have bad reputations, her brothers might have illegitimate children. But so long as there was money, the girl felt herself established, and brutally proud, reserved.

No company came to the house, save dealers and coarse men. Mabel had no associates of her own sex, after her sister went away. But she did not mind. She went regularly to church, she attended to her father. And she lived in the memory of her mother, who had died when she was fourteen, and whom she had loved. She had loved her father, too, in a different way, depending upon him, and feeling secure in him, until at the age of fifty-four he married again. And then she had set hard against him. Now he had died and left them all hopelessly in debt.

She had suffered badly during the period of poverty. Nothing, however, could shake the curious sullen, animal pride that dominated each member of the family. Now, for Mabel, the end had come.

Still she would not cast about her. She would follow her own way just the same. She would always hold the keys of her own situation. Mindless and persistent, she endured from day to day. Why should she think? Why should she answer anybody? It was enough that this was the end, and there was no way out. She need not pass any more darkly along the main street of the small town, avoiding every eye. She need not demean herself any more, going into the shops and buying the cheapest food. This was at an end. She thought of nobody, not even of herself. Mindless and persistent, she seemed in a sort of ecstasy to be coming nearer to her fulfillment, her own glorification, approaching her dead mother, who was glorified.

In the afternoon she took a little bag, with shears and sponge and a small scrubbing brush, and went out. It was a gray, wintry day, with saddened, dark green fields and an atmosphere blackened by the smoke of foundries not far off. She went quickly, darkly along the causeway, heeding nobody, through the town to the churchyard.

There she always felt secure, as if no one could see her, although as a matter of fact she was exposed to the stare of every one who passed along under the churchyard wall. Nevertheless, once under the shadow of the great looming church, among the graves, she felt immune from the world, reserved within the thick churchyard wall as in another country.

Carefully she clipped the grass from the grave, and arranged the pinky white, small chrysanthemums in the tin cross. When this was done, she took an empty jar from a neighboring grave, brought water, and carefully, most scrupulously sponged the marble headstone and the coping-stone. It gave her sincere satisfaction to do this. She felt in immediate contact with the world of her mother. She took minute pains, went through the park in a state bordering on pure happiness, as if in performing this task she came into a subtle, intimate connection with her mother. For the life she followed here in the world was far less real than the world of death she inherited from her mother.

The doctor's house was just by the church. Fergusson, being a mere hired assistant, was slave to the countryside. As he hurried now to attend to the outpatients in the surgery, glancing across the graveyard with his quick eyes, he saw the girl at her task at the grave. She seemed so intent and remote, it was like looking into another world. Some mystical element was touched in him. He slowed down as he walked, watching her as if spellbound.

She lifted her eyes, feeling him looking. Their eyes met. And each looked away again at once, each feeling, in some way, found out by the other. He lifted his cap and passed on down the road. There remained distinct in his consciousness, like a vision, the memory of her face, lifted from the tombstone in the churchyard, and looking at him with slow, large, portentous eyes. It *was* portentous, her face. It seemed to mesmerize him. There was a heavy power in her eyes which laid hold of his whole being, as if he had drunk some powerful drug. He had been feeling weak and done before. Now the life came back into him, he felt delivered from his own fretted, daily self.

He finished his duties at the surgery as quickly as might be, hastily filling up the bottles of the waiting people with cheap drugs. Then, in perpetual haste, he set off again to visit several cases in another part of his round, before teatime. At all times he preferred to walk if he could, but particularly when he was not well. He fancied the motion restored him.

The afternoon was falling. It was gray, deadened, and wintry, with a slow, moist, heavy coldness sinking in and deadening all the faculties. But why should he think or notice? He hastily climbed the hill and turned across the dark green fields, following the black cindertrack. In the distance, across a shallow dip in the country, the small town was clustered like smouldering ash, a tower, a spire, a heap of low, raw, extinct houses. And on the nearest fringe of the town, sloping into the dip, was Oldmeadow, the Pervins's house. He could see the stables and the outbuildings distinctly, as they lay towards him on the slope. Well, he would not go there many more times! Another resource would be lost to him, another place gone: the only company he cared for in the alien, ugly little town he was losing. Nothing but work, drudgery, constant hastening from dwelling to dwelling among the colliers and the iron-workers. It wore him out, but at the same time he had a craving for it. It was a stimulant to him to be in the homes of the working people, moving as it were through the innermost body of their life. His nerves were excited and gratified. He could come so near, into the very lives of the rough, inarticulate, powerfully emotional men and women. He grumbled, he said he hated the hellish hole. But as a matter of fact it excited him, the contact with the rough, strongly-feeling people was a stimulant applied direct to his nerves.

Below Oldmeadow, in the green, shallow, soddened hollow of fields, lay a square, deep pond. Roving across the landscape, the doctor's quick eye detected a figure in black passing through the gate of the field, down towards the pond. He looked again. It would be Mabel Pervin. His mind suddenly became alive and attentive.

Why was she going down there? He pulled up on the path

on the slope above, and stood staring. He could just make sure of the small black figure moving in the hollow of the failing day. He seemed to see her in the midst of such obscurity, that he was like a clairvoyant, seeing rather with the mind's eye than with ordinary sight. Yet he could see her positively enough, while he kept his eye attentive. He felt, if he looked away from her, in the thick, ugly falling dusk, he would lose her altogether.

He followed her minutely as she moved, direct and intent, like something transmitted rather than stirring in voluntary activity, straight down the field towards the pond. There she stood on the bank for a moment. She never raised her head. Then she waded slowly into the water.

He stood motionless as the small black figure walked slowly and deliberately towards the center of the pond, very slowly, gradually moving deeper into the motionless water, and still moving forward as the water got up to her breast. Then he could see her no more in the dusk of the dead afternoon.

"There!" he exclaimed. "Would you believe it?"

And he hastened straight down, running over the wet, soddened fields, pushing through the hedges, down into the depression of callous wintry obscurity. It took him several minutes to come to the pond. He stood on the bank, breathing heavily. He could see nothing. His eyes seemed to penetrate the dead water. Yes, perhaps that was the dark shadow of her black clothing beneath the surface of the water.

He slowly ventured into the pond. The bottom was deep, soft clay, he sank in, and the water clasped dead cold round his legs. As he stirred he could smell the cold, rotten clay that fouled up into the water. It was objectionable in his lungs. Still, repelled and yet not heeding, he moved deeper into the pond. The cold water rose over his thighs, over his loins, upon his abdomen. The lower part of his body was all sunk in the hideous cold element. And the bottom was so deeply soft and uncertain he was afraid of pitching with his mouth underneath. He could not swim, and was afraid.

He crouched a little, spreading his hands under the water and moving them round, trying to feel for her. The dead cold pond swayed upon his chest. He moved again, a little deeper, and again, with his hands underneath, he felt all around under the water. And he touched her clothing. But it evaded his fingers. He made a desperate effort to grasp it.

And so doing he lost his balance and went under, horribly, suffocating in the foul earthy water, struggling madly for a few moments. At last, after what seemed an eternity, he got his footing, rose again into the air and looked around. He gasped, and knew he was in the world. Then he looked at the water. She had risen near him. He grasped her clothing, and drawing her nearer, turned to take his way to land again.

He went very slowly, carefully, absorbed in the slow progress. He rose higher, climbing out of the pond. The water was now only about his legs; he was thankful, full of relief to be out of the clutches of the pond. He lifted her and staggered on to the bank, out of the horror of wet, gray clay.

He laid her down on the bank. She was quite unconscious and running with water. He made the water come from her mouth, he worked to restore her. He did not have to work very long before he could feel the breathing begin again in her; she was breathing naturally. He worked a little longer. He could feel her live beneath his hands; she was coming back. He wiped her face, wrapped her in his overcoat, looked round into the dim, dark gray world, then lifted her and staggered down the bank and across the fields.

It seemed an unthinkably long way, and his burden so heavy he felt he would never get to the house. But at last he was in the stableyard, and then in the house-yard. He opened the door and went into the house. In the kitchen he laid her down on the hearth-rug, and called. The house was empty. But the fire was burning in the grate.

Then again he kneeled to attend to her. She was breathing regularly, her eyes were wide open and as if conscious, but there seemed something missing in her look. She was conscious in herself, but unconscious of her surroundings.

He ran upstairs, took blankets from a bed, and put them before the fire to warm. Then he removed her saturated, earthy-smelling clothing, rubbed her dry with a towel, and wrapped her naked in the blankets. Then he went into the dining-room, to look for spirits. There was a little whisky. He drank a gulp himself, and put some into her mouth.

The effect was instantaneous. She looked full into his face, as if she had been seeing him for some time, and yet had only just become conscious of him.

"Dr. Fergusson?" she said.

"What?" he answered.

He was divesting himself of his coat, intending to find some dry clothing upstairs. He could not bear the smell of the dead, clayey water, and he was mortally afraid of his own health.

"What did I do?" she asked.

"Walked into the pond," he replied. He had begun to shudder

like one sick, and could hardly attend to her. Her eyes remained full on him, he seemed to be going dark in his mind, looking back at her helplessly. The shuddering became quieter in him, his life came back in him, dark and unknowing, but strong again.

"Was I out of my mind?" she asked, while her eyes were fixed on him all the time.

"Maybe, for the moment," he replied. He felt quiet, because his strength came back. The strange fretful strain had left him.

"Am I out of my mind now?" she asked.

"Are you?" he reflected a moment. "No," he answered truthfully, "I don't see that you are." He turned his face aside. He was afraid now, because he felt dazed, and felt dimly that her power was stronger than his, in this issue. And she continued to look at him fixedly all the time. "Can you tell me where I shall find some dry things to put on?" he asked.

"Did you dive into the pond for me?" she asked.

"No," he answered. "I walked in. But I went in overhead as well."

There was silence for a moment. He hesitated. He very much wanted to go upstairs to get into dry clothing. But there was another desire in him. And she seemed to hold him. His will seemed to have gone to sleep, and left him, standing there slack before her. But he felt warm inside himself. He did not shudder at all, though his clothes were sodden on him.

"Why did you?" she asked.

"Because I didn't want you to do such a foolish thing," he said.

"It wasn't foolish," she said, still gazing at him as she lay on the floor, with a sofa cushion under her head. "It was the right thing to do. *I* knew best, then."

"I'll go and shift these wet things," he said. But still he had not the power to move out of her presence, until she sent him. It was as if she had the life of his body in her hands, and he could not extricate himself. Or perhaps he did not want to.

Suddenly she sat up. Then she became aware of her own immediate condition. She felt the blankets about her, she knew her own limbs. For a moment it seemed as if her reason were going. She looked round, with wild eye, as if seeking something. He stood still with fear. She saw her clothing lying scattered.

"Who undressed me?" she asked, her eyes resting full and inevitable on his face.

"I did," he replied, "to bring you round."

For some moments she sat and gazed at him awfully, her lips parted.

"Do you love me, then?" she asked.

He only stood and stared at her, fascinated. His soul seemed to melt.

She shuffled forward on her knees, and put her arms round him, round his legs, as he stood there, pressing her breasts against his knees and thighs, clutching him with strange, convulsive certainty, pressing his thighs against her, drawing him to her face, her throat, as she looked up at him with flaring, humble eyes of transfiguration, triumphant in first possession.

"You love me," she murmured, in strange transport, yearning and triumphant and confident. "You love me. I know you love me, I know."

And she was passionately kissing his knees, through the wet clothing, passionately and indiscriminately kissing his knees, his legs, as if unaware of everything.

He looked down at the tangled wet hair, the wild, bare, animal shoulders. He was amazed, bewildered, and afraid. He had never thought of loving her. He had never wanted to love her. When he rescued her and restored her, he was a doctor, and she was a patient. He had had no single personal thought of her. Nay, this introduction of the personal element was very distasteful to him, a violation of his professional honor. It was horrible to have her there embracing his knees. It was horrible. He revolted from it, violently. And yet — and yet — he had not the power to break away.

She looked at him again, with the same supplication of powerful love, and that same transcendent, frightening light of triumph. In view of the delicate flame which seemed to come from her face like a light, he was powerless. And yet he had never intended to love her. He had never intended. And something stubborn in him could not give way.

"You love me," she repeated, in a murmur of deep, rhapsodic assurance. "You love me."

Her hands were drawing him, drawing him down to her. He was afraid, even a little horrified. For he had, really, no intention of loving her. Yet her hands were drawing him towards her. He put out his hand quickly to steady himself, and grasped her bare shoulder. A flame seemed to burn the hand that grasped her soft shoulder. He had no intention of loving her: his whole will was against his yielding. It was horrible. And yet wonderful was the touch of her shoulders, beautiful the shining of her face. Was she perhaps mad? He had a horror of yielding to her. Yet something in him ached also.

He had been staring away at the door, away from her. But

his hand remained on her shoulder. She had gone suddenly very still. He looked down at her. Her eyes were now wide with fear, with doubt, the light was dying from her face, a shadow of terrible grayness was returning. He could not bear the touch of her eyes' question upon him, and the look of death behind the question.

With an inward groan he gave way, and let his heart yield towards her. A sudden gentle smile came on his face. And her eyes, which never left his face, slowly, slowly filled with tears. He watched the strange water rise in her eyes, like some slow fountain coming up. And his heart seemed to burn and melt away in his breast.

He could not bear to look at her any more. He dropped on his knees and caught her head with his arms and pressed her face against his throat. She was very still. His heart, which seemed to have broken, was burning with a kind of agony in his breast. And he felt her slow, hot tears wetting his throat. But he could not move.

He felt the hot tears wet his neck and the hollows of his neck, and he remained motionless, suspended through one of man's eternities. Only now it had become indispensable to him to have her face pressed close to him; he could never let her go again. He could never let her head go away from the close clutch of his arm. He wanted to remain like that for ever, with his heart hurting him in a pain that was also life to him. Without knowing, he was looking down on her damp, soft brown hair.

Then, as it were suddenly, he smelt the horrid stagnant smell of that water. And at the same moment she drew away from him and looked at him. Her eyes were wistful and unfathomable. He was afraid of them, and he fell to kissing her, not knowing what he was doing. He wanted her eyes not to have that terrible, wistful, unfathomable look.

When she turned her face to him again, a faint delicate flush was glowing, and there was again dawning that terrible shining of joy in her eyes, which really terrified him, and yet which he now wanted to see, because he feared the look of doubt still more.

"You love me?" she said, rather faltering.

"Yes." The word cost him a painful effort. Not because it wasn't true. But because it was too newly true, the *saying* seemed to tear open again his newly torn heart. And he hardly wanted it to be true, even now.

She lifted her face to him, and he bent forward and kissed her on the mouth, gently, with the one kiss that is an eternal pledge. And as he kissed her his heart strained again in his breast. He never intended to love her. But now it was over. He had crossed over the gulf to her, and all that he had left behind had shriveled and become void.

After the kiss, her eyes again slowly filled with tears. She sat still, away from him, with her face drooped aside, and her hands folded in her lap. The tears fell very slowly. There was complete silence. He too sat there motionless and silent on the hearthrug. The strange pain of his heart that was broken seemed to consume him. That he should love her? That this was love! That he should be ripped open in this way! Him, a doctor! How they would all jeer if they knew! It was agony to him to think they might know.

In the curious naked pain of the thought he looked again to her. She was sitting there drooped into a muse. He saw a tear fall, and his heart flared hot. He saw for the first time that one of her shoulders was quite uncovered, one arm bare, he could see one of her small breasts; dimly, because it had become almost dark in the room.

"Why are you crying?" he asked, in an altered voice.

She looked up at him, and behind her tears the consciousness of her situation for the first time brought a dark look of shame to her eyes.

"I'm not crying, really," she said, watching him half frightened.

He reached his hand, and softly closed it on her bare arm.

"I love you! I love you!" he said in a soft, low vibrating voice, unlike himself.

She shrank, and dropped her head. The soft, penetrating grip of his hand on her arm distressed her. She looked up at him.

"I want to go," she said. "I want to go and get you some dry things."

"Why?" he said. "I'm all right."

"But I want to go," she said. "And I want you to change your things."

He released her arm, and she wrapped herself in the blanket, looking at him rather frightened. And still she did not rise.

"Kiss me," she said wistfully.

He kissed her, but briefly, half in anger.

Then, after a second, she rose nervously, all mixed up in the blanket. He watched her in her confusion, as she tried to extricate herself and wrap herself up so that she could walk. He watched her relentlessly, as she knew. And as she went, the blanket trailing, and as he saw a glimpse of her feet and her white leg, he tried to remember her as she was when he had wrapped her in the blanket. But then he didn't want to remember, because she had been nothing to him then, and his nature revolted from re-membering her as she was when she was nothing to him.

A tumbling, muffled noise from within the dark house startled him. Then he heard her voice: — "There are clothes." He rose and went to the foot of the stairs, and gathered up the garments she had thrown down. Then he came back to the fire, to rub himself down and dress. He grinned at his own appearance when he had finished.

The fire was sinking, so he put on coal. The house was now quite dark, save for the light of a street-lamp that shone in faintly from beyond the holly trees. He lit the gas with matches he found on the mantelpiece. Then he emptied the pockets of his own clothes, and threw all his wet things in a heap into the scullery. After which he gathered up her sodden clothes, gently, and put them in a separate heap on the copper-top in the scullery.

It was six o'clock on the clock. His own watch had stopped. He ought to go back to the surgery. He waited, and still she did not come down. So he went to the foot of the stairs and called:

"I shall have to go."

Almost immediately he heard her coming down. She had on her best dress of black voile, and her hair was tidy, but still damp. She looked at him — and in spite of herself, smiled.

"I don't like you in those clothes," she said.

"Do I look a sight?" he answered.

They were shy of one another.

"I'll make you some tea," she said.

"No, I must go."

"Must you?" And she looked at him again with the wide, strained, doubtful eyes. And again, from the pain of his breast, he knew how he loved her. He went and bent to kiss her, gently, passionately, with his heart's painful kiss.

"And my hair smells so horrible," she murmured in distraction. "And I'm so awful, I'm so awful! Oh, no, I'm too awful." And she broke into bitter, heart-broken sobbing. "You can't want to love me, I'm horrible."

"Don't be silly, don't be silly," he said, trying to comfort her, kissing her, holding her in his arms. "I want you, I want to marry you, we're going to be married, quickly, quickly — tomor-row if I can."

But she only sobbed terribly, and cried:

"I feel awful. I feel awful. I feel I'm horrible to you."

"No, I want you, I want you," was all he answered, blindly, with that terrible intonation which frightened her almost more than her horror lest he should *not* want her.

D. H. Lawrence *(1885–1930)*

The Rocking-Horse Winner

There was a woman who was beautiful, who started with all the advantages, yet she had no luck. She married for love, and the love turned to dust. She had bonny children, yet she felt they had been thrust upon her, and she could not love them. They looked at her coldly, as if they were finding fault with her. And hurriedly she felt she must cover up some fault in herself. Yet what it was that she must cover up she never knew. Nevertheless, when her children were present, she always felt the centre of her heart go hard. This troubled her, and in her manner she was all the more gentle and anxious for her children, as if she loved them very much. Only she herself knew that at the centre of her heart was a hard little place that could not feel love, no, not for anybody. Everybody else said of her: "She is such a good mother. She adores her children." Only she herself, and her children themselves, knew it was not so. They read it in each other's eyes.

There were a boy and two little girls. They lived in a pleasant house, with a garden, and they had discreet servants, and felt themselves superior to anyone in the neighbourhood.

Although they lived in style, they felt always an anxiety in the house. There was never enough money. The mother had a small income, and the father had a small income, but not nearly enough for the social position which they had to keep up. The father went into town to some office. But though he had good prospects, these prospects never materialised. There was always the grinding sense of the shortage of money, though the style was always kept up.

At last the mother said: "I will see if *I* can't make something." But she did not know where to begin. She racked her brains, and tried this thing and the other, but could not find anything successful. The failure made deep lines come into her face. Her children were growing up, they would have to go to school. There must be more money, there must be more money. The father, who was always very handsome and expensive in his tastes, seemed as if he never *would* be able to do anything worth doing. And the mother, who had a great belief in herself, did not succeed any better, and her tastes were just as expensive.

And so the house came to be haunted by the unspoken phrase: *There must be more money! There must be more money!* The children could hear it all the time, though nobody said it aloud. They heard it at Christmas, when the expensive and splendid toys filled the nursery. Behind the shining modern rocking-horse, behind the smart doll's house, a voice would start whispering: "There *must* be more money! There *must* be more money!" And the children would stop playing, to listen for a moment. They would look into each other's eyes, to see if they had all heard. And each one saw in the eyes of the other two that they too had heard. "There *must* be more money! There *must* be more money!"

It came whispering from the springs of the still-swaying rocking-horse, and even the horse, bending his wooden, champing head, heard it. The big doll, sitting so pink and smirking in her new pram, could hear it quite plainly, and seemed to be smirking all the more self-consciously because of it. The foolish puppy, too, that took the place of the teddy-bear, he was looking so extraordinarily foolish for no other reason but that he heard the secret whisper all over the house: "There *must* be more money!"

Yet nobody ever said it aloud. The whisper was everywhere, and therefore no one spoke it. Just as no one ever says: "We are breathing!" in spite of the fact that breath is coming and going all the time.

"Mother," said the boy Paul one day, "why don't we keep a car of our own? Why do we always use uncle's, or else a taxi?"

"Because we're the poor members of the family," said the mother.

"But why *are* we, mother?"

"Well — I suppose," she said slowly and bitterly, "it's because your father has no luck."

The boy was silent for some time.

"Is luck money, mother?" he asked, rather timidly.

"No, Paul. Not quite. It's what causes you to have money."

"Oh!" said Paul vaguely. "I thought when Uncle Oscar said *filthy lucker,* it meant money."

"*Filthy lucre* does mean money," said the mother. "But it's lucre, not luck."

"Oh!" said the boy. "Then what *is* luck, mother?"

"It's what causes you to have money. If you're lucky you have money. That's why it's better to be born lucky than rich. If you're rich, you may lose your money. But if you're lucky, you will always get more money."

"Oh! Will you? And is father not lucky?"

"Very unlucky, I should say," she said bitterly.

The boy watched her with unsure eyes.

"Why?" he asked.

"I don't know. Nobody ever knows why one person is lucky and another unlucky."

"Don't they? Nobody at all? Does *nobody* know?"

"Perhaps God. But He never tells."

"He ought to, then. And aren't you lucky either, mother?"

"I can't be, if I married an unlucky husband."

"But by yourself, aren't you?"

"I use to think I was, before I married. Now I think I am very unlucky indeed."

"Why?"

"Well — never mind! Perhaps I'm not really," she said.

The child looked at her to see if she meant it. But he saw, by the lines of her mouth, that she was only trying to hide something from him.

"Well, anyhow," he said stoutly, "I'm a lucky person."

"Why?" said his mother, with a sudden laugh.

He stared at her. He didn't even know why he had said it.

"God told me," he asserted, brazening it out.

"I hope He did, dear!" she said, again with a laugh, but rather bitter.

"He did, mother!"

"Excellent!" said the mother, using one of her husband's exclamations.

The boy saw she did not believe him; or rather, that she paid no attention to his assertion. This angered him somewhere, and made him want to compel her attention.

He went off by himself, vaguely, in a childish way, seeking for the clue to "luck." Absorbed, taking no heed of other people, he went about with a sort of stealth, seeking inwardly for luck. He wanted luck, he wanted it, he wanted it. When the two girls were playing dolls in the nursery, he would sit on his big rocking-horse, charging madly into space, with a frenzy that made the little girls peer at him uneasily. Wildly the horse careered, the waving dark hair of the boy tossed, his eyes had a strange glare in them. The little girls dared not speak to him.

When he had ridden to the end of his mad little journey, he climbed down and stood in front of his rocking-horse, staring fixedly into its lowered face. Its red mouth was slightly open, its big eye was wide and glassy-bright.

"Now!" he would silently command the snorting steed. "Now, take me to where there is luck! Now take me!"

And he would slash the horse on the neck with the little whip he had asked Uncle Oscar for. He *knew* the horse could take him to where there was luck, if only he forced it. So he would mount again and start on his furious ride, hoping at last to get there. He knew he could get there.

"You'll break your horse, Paul!" said the nurse.

"He's always riding like that! I wish he'd leave off!" said his elder sister Joan.

But he only glared down on them in silence. Nurse gave him up. She could make nothing of him. Anyhow, he was growing beyond her.

One day his mother and his Uncle Oscar came in when he was on one of his furious rides. He did not speak to them.

"Hallo, you young jockey! Riding a winner?" said his uncle.

"Aren't you growing too big for a rocking-horse? You're not a very little boy any longer, you know," said his mother.

But Paul only gave a blue glare from his big, rather close-set eyes. He would speak to nobody when he was in full tilt. His mother watched him with an anxious expression on her face.

At last he suddenly stopped forcing his horse into the mechanical gallop and slid down.

"Well, I got there!" he announced fiercely, his blue eyes still flaring, and his sturdy long legs straddling apart.

"Where did you get to?" asked his mother.

"Where I wanted to go," he flared back at her.

"That's right, son!" said Uncle Oscar. "Don't you stop till you get there. What's the horse's name?"

"He doesn't have a name," said the boy.

"Gets on without all right?" asked the uncle.

"Well, he has different names. He was called Sansovino last week."

"Sansovino, eh? Won the Ascot. How did you know this name?"

"He always talks about horse-races with Bassett," said Joan.

The uncle was delighted to find that his small nephew was posted with all the racing news. Bassett, the young gardener, who had been wounded in the left foot in the war and had got his present job through Oscar Cresswell, whose batman he had been, was a perfect blade of the "turf." He lived in the racing events, and the small boy lived with him.

Oscar Cresswell got it all from Bassett.

"Master Paul comes and asks me, so I can't do more than tell him, sir," said Bassett, his face terribly serious, as if he were speaking of religious matters.

"And does he ever put anything on a horse he fancies?"

"Well — I don't want to give him away — he's a young sport, a fine sport, sir. Would you mind asking him himself? He sort of takes a pleasure in it, and perhaps he'd feel I was giving him away, sir, if you don't mind."

Bassett was serious as a church.

The uncle went back to his nephew and took him off for a ride in the car.

"Say, Paul, old man, do you ever put anything on a horse?" the uncle asked.

The boy watched the handsome man closely.

"Why, do you think I oughtn't to?" he parried.

"Not a bit of it! I thought perhaps you might give me a tip for the Lincoln."

The car sped on into the country, going down to Uncle Oscar's place in Hampshire.

"Honour bright?" said the nephew.

"Honour bright, son!" said the uncle.

"Well, then, Daffodil."

"Daffodil! I doubt it, sonny. What about Mirza?"

"I only know the winner," said the boy. "That's Daffodil."

"Daffodil, eh?"

There was a pause. Daffodil was an obscure horse comparatively.

"Uncle!"

"Yes, son?"

"You won't let it go any further, will you? I promised Bassett."

"Bassett be damned, old man! What's he got to do with it?"

"We're partners. We've been partners from the first. Uncle, he lent me my first five shillings, which I lost. I promised him, honour bright, it was only between me and him; only you gave me that ten-shilling note I started winning with, so I thought you were lucky. You won't let it go any further, will you?"

The boy gazed at his uncle from those big, hot, blue eyes, set rather close together. The uncle stirred and laughed uneasily.

"Right you are, son! I'll keep your tip private. Daffodil, eh? How much are you putting on him?"

"All except twenty pounds," said the boy. "I keep that in reserve."

The uncle thought it a good joke.

"You keep twenty pounds in reserve, do you, you young romancer? What are you betting, then?"

"I'm betting three hundred," said the boy gravely. "But it's between you and me, Uncle Oscar! Honour bright?"

The uncle burst into a roar of laughter.

"It's between you and me all right, you young Nat Gould," he said, laughing. "But where's your three hundred?"

"Bassett keeps it for me. We're partners."

"You are, are you! And what is Bassett putting on Daffodil?"

"He won't go quite as high as I do, I expect. Perhaps he'll go a hundred and fifty."

"What, pennies?" laughed the uncle.

"Pounds," said the child, with a surprised look at his uncle. "Bassett keeps a bigger reserve than I do."

Between wonder and amusement Uncle Oscar was silent. He pursued the matter no further, but he determined to take his nephew with him to the Lincoln races.

"Now, son," he said, "I'm putting twenty on Mirza, and I'll put five on for you on any horse you fancy. What's your pick?"

"Daffodil, uncle."

"No, not the fiver on Daffodil!"

"I should if it was my own fiver," said the child.

"Good! Good! Right you are! A fiver for me and a fiver for you on Daffodil."

The child had never been to a race-meeting before, and his eyes were blue fire. He pursed his mouth tight and watched. A Frenchman just in front had put his money on Lancelot. Wild with excitement, he flayed his arms up and down, yelling "*Lancelot! Lancelot!*" in his French accent.

Daffodil came in first, Lancelot second, Mirza third. The child, flushed and with eyes blazing, was curiously serene. His uncle brought him four five-pound notes, four to one.

"What am I to do with these?" he cried, waving them before the boy's eyes.

"I suppose we'll talk to Bassett," said the boy. "I expect I have fifteen hundred now; and twenty in reserve; and this twenty."

His uncle studied him for some moments.

"Look here, son!" he said. "You're not serious about Bassett and that fifteen hundred, are you?"

"Yes, I am. But it's between you and me, uncle. Honour bright?"

"Honour bright all right, son! But I must talk to Bassett."

"If you'd like to be a partner, uncle, with Bassett and me, we could all be partners. Only, you'd have to promise, honour bright, uncle, not to let it go beyond us three. Bassett and I are lucky, and you must be lucky, because it was your ten shillings I started winning with. . . ."

Uncle Oscar took both Bassett and Paul into Richmond Park for an afternoon, and there they talked.

"It's like this, you see, sir," Bassett said. "Master Paul would get me talking about racing events, spinning yarns, you know, sir. And he was always keen on knowing if I'd made or if I'd lost. It's about a year since, now, that I put five shillings on Blush of Dawn for him: and we lost. Then the luck turned, with that ten shillings he had from you: that we put on Singhalese. And since that time, it's been pretty steady, all things considering. What do you say, Master Paul?"

"We're all right when we're sure," said Paul. "It's when we're not quite sure that we go down."

"Oh, but we're careful then," said Bassett.

"But when are you *sure?*" smiled Uncle Oscar.

"It's Master Paul, sir," said Bassett in a secret, religious voice. "It's as if he had it from heaven. Like Daffodil, now, for the Lincoln. That was as sure as eggs."

"Did you put anything on Daffodil?" asked Oscar Cresswell.

"Yes, sir. I made my bit."

"And my nephew?"

Bassett was obstinately silent, looking at Paul.

"I made twelve hundred, didn't I, Bassett? I told uncle I was putting three hundred on Daffodil."

"That's right," said Bassett, nodding.

"But where's the money?" asked the uncle.

"I keep it safe locked up, sir. Master Paul he can have it any minute he likes to ask for it."

"What, fifteen hundred pounds?"

"And twenty! And *forty,* that is, with the twenty he made on the course."

"It's amazing!" said the uncle.

"If Master Paul offers you to be partners, sir, I would, if I were you: if you'll excuse me," said Bassett.

Oscar Cresswell thought about it.

"I'll see the money," he said.

They drove home again, and, sure enough, Bassett came round to the garden-house with fifteen hundred pounds in notes. The twenty pounds reserve was left with Joe Glee, in the Turf Commission deposit.

"You see, it's all right, uncle, when I'm *sure!* Then we go strong, for all we're worth. Don't we, Bassett?"

"We do that, Master Paul."

"And when are you sure?" said the uncle, laughing.

"Oh, well, sometimes I'm *absolutely* sure, like about Daffodil," said the boy; "and sometimes I have an idea; and sometimes I haven't even an idea, have I, Bassett? Then we're careful, because we mostly go down."

"You do, do you! And when you're sure, like about Daffodil, what makes you sure, sonny?"

"Oh, well, I don't know," said the boy uneasily. "I'm sure, you know, uncle; that's all."

"It's as if he had it from heaven, sir," Bassett reiterated.

"I should say so!" said the uncle.

But he became a partner. And when the Leger was coming on Paul was "sure" about Lively Spark, which was a quite inconsiderable horse. The boy insisted on putting a thousand on the horse, Bassett was for five hundred, and Oscar Cresswell two hundred. Lively Spark came in first, and the betting had been ten to one against him. Paul had made ten thousand.

"You see," he said, "I was absolutely sure of him."

Even Oscar Cresswell had cleared two thousand.

"Look here, son," he said, "this sort of thing makes me nervous."

"It needn't, uncle! Perhaps I shan't be sure again for a long time."

"But what are you going to do with your money?" asked the uncle.

"Of course," said the boy, "I started it for mother. She said she had no luck, because father is unlucky, so I thought if *I* was lucky, it might stop whispering."

"What might stop whispering?"

"Our house. I *hate* our house for whispering."

"What does it whisper?"

"Why — why" — the boy fidgeted — "why, I don't know. But it's always short of money, you know, uncle."

"I know it, son, I know it."

"You know people send mother writs, don't you, uncle?"

"I'm afraid I do," said the uncle.

"And then the house whispers, like people laughing at you behind your back. It's awful, that is! I thought if I was lucky—"

"You might stop it," added the uncle.

The boy watched him with big blue eyes, that had an uncanny cold fire in them, and he said never a word.

"Well, then!" said the uncle "What are we doing?"

"I shouldn't like mother to know I was lucky," said the boy.

"Why not, son?"

"She'd stop me."

"I don't think she would."

"Oh!" — and the boy writhed in an odd way — "I *don't* want her to know, uncle."

"All right, son! We'll manage it without her knowing."

They managed it very easily. Paul, at the other's suggestion, handed over five thousand pounds to his uncle, who deposited it with the family lawyer, who was then to inform Paul's mother that a relative had put five thousand pounds into his hands, which sum was to be paid out a thousand pounds at a time, on the mother's birthday, for the next five years.

"So she'll have a birthday present of a thousand pounds for five successive years," said Uncle Oscar. "I hope it won't make it all the harder for her later."

Paul's mother had her birthday in November. The house had been "whispering" worse than ever lately, and, even in spite of his luck, Paul could not bear up against it. He was very anxious to see the effect of the birthday letter, telling his mother about the thousand pounds.

When there were no visitors, Paul now took his meals with his parents, as he was beyond the nursery control. His mother went into town nearly every day. She had discovered that she had an odd knack of sketching furs and dress materials, so she worked secretly in the studio of a friend who was the chief "artist" for the leading drapers. She drew the figures of ladies in furs and ladies in silk and sequins for the newspaper advertisements. This young woman artist earned several thousands pounds a year, but Paul's mother only made several hundreds, and she was again dissatisfied. She so wanted to be first in something, and she did not succeed, even in making sketches for drapery advertisements.

She was down to breakfast on the morning of her birthday. Paul watched her face as she read her letters. He knew the lawyer's letter. As his mother read it, her face hardened and became more expressionless. Then a cold, determined look came on her mouth. She hid the letter under the pile of others, and said not a word about it.

"Didn't you have anything nice in the post for your birthday, mother?" said Paul.

"Quite moderately nice," she said, her voice cold and absent.

She went away to town without saying more.

But in the afternoon Uncle Oscar appeared. He said Paul's mother had had a long interview with the lawyer, asking if the whole five thousand could not be advanced at once, as she was in debt.

"What do you think, uncle?" said the boy.

"I leave it to you, son."

"Oh, let her have it, then! We can get some more with the other," said the boy.

"A bird in the hand is worth two in the bush, laddie!" said Uncle Oscar.

"But I'm sure to *know* for the Grand National; or the Lincolnshire; or else the Derby. I'm sure to know for *one* of them," said Paul.

So Uncle Oscar signed the agreement, and Paul's mother touched the whole five thousand. Then something very curious happened. The voices in the house suddenly went mad, like a chorus of frogs on a spring evening. There were certain new furnishings, and Paul had a tutor. He was *really* going to Eton, his father's school, in the following autumn. There were flowers in the winter, and a blossoming of the luxury Paul's mother had been used to. And yet the voices in the house, behind the sprays of mimosa and almondblossom, and from under the piles of iridescent cushions, simply trilled and screamed in a sort of ecstasy: "There *must* be more money! Oh-h-h; there *must* be more money. Oh, now, now-w! Now-w-w — there *must* be more money! — more than ever! More than ever!"

It frightened Paul terribly. He studied away at his Latin and Greek with his tutor. But his intense hours were spent with Bassett. The Grand National had gone by: he had not "known," and had lost a hundred pounds. Summer was at hand. He was in agony for the Lincoln. But even for the Lincoln he didn't "know," and he lost fifty pounds. He became wild-eyed and strange, as if something were going to explode in him.

"Let it alone, son! Don't you bother about it!" urged Uncle Oscar. But it was as if the boy couldn't really hear what his uncle was saying.

"I've got to know for the Derby! I've got to know for the Derby!" the child reiterated, his big blue eyes blazing with a sort of madness.

His mother noticed how overwrought he was.

"You'd better go to the seaside. Wouldn't you like to go now to the seaside, instead of waiting? I think you'd better," she said, looking down at him anxiously, her heart curiously heavy because of him.

But the child lifted his uncanny blue eyes.

"I couldn't possibly go before the Derby, mother!" he said. "I couldn't possibly!"

"Why not?" she said, her voice becoming heavy when she was opposed. "Why not? You can still go from the seaside to see the Derby with your Uncle Oscar, if that's what you wish. No need for you to wait here. Besides, I think you care too much about these races. It's a bad sign. My family has been a gambling family, and you won't know till you grow up how much damage it has done. But it has done damage. I shall have to send Bassett away, and ask Uncle Oscar not to talk racing to you, unless you promise to be reasonable about it: go away to the seaside and forget it. You're all nerves!"

"I'll do what you like, mother, so long as you don't send me away till after the Derby," the boy said.

"Send you away from where? Just from this house?"

"Yes," he said, gazing at her.

"Why, you curious child, what makes you care about this house so much, suddenly? I never knew you loved it."

He gazed at her without speaking. He had a secret within a secret, something he had not divulged, even to Bassett or to his Uncle Oscar.

But his mother, after standing undecided and a little bit sullen for some moments, said:

"Very well, then! Don't go to the seaside till after the Derby, if you don't wish it. But promise me you won't let your nerves go to pieces. Promise you won't think so much about horse-racing and *events,* as you call them!"

"Oh no," said the boy casually. "I won't think much about them, mother. You needn't worry. I wouldn't worry, mother, if I were you."

"If you were me and I were you," said his mother, "I wonder what we *should* do!"

"But you know you needn't worry, mother, don't you?" the boy repeated.

"I should be awfully glad to know it," she said wearily.

"Oh, well, you *can,* you know. I mean, you *ought* to know you needn't worry," he insisted.

"Ought I? Then I'll see about it," she said.

Paul's secret of secrets was his wooden horse, that which had no name. Since he was emancipated from a nurse and a nursery-governess, he had had his rocking-horse removed to his own bedroom at the top of the house.

"Surely you're too big for a rocking-horse!" his mother had remonstrated.

"Well, you see, mother, till I can have a *real* horse, I like to have *some* sort of animal about," had been his quaint answer.

"Do you feel he keeps you company?" she laughed.

"Oh yes! He's very good, he always keeps me company, when I'm there," said Paul.

So the horse, rather shabby, stood in an arrested prance in the boy's bedroom.

The Derby was drawing near, and the boy grew more and more tense. He hardly heard what was spoken to him, he was very frail, and his eyes were really uncanny. His mother had sudden strange seizures of uneasiness about him. Sometimes, for half an hour, she would feel a sudden anxiety about him that was almost anguish. She wanted to rush to him at once, and know he was safe.

Two nights before the Derby, she was at a big party in town, when one of her rushes of anxiety about her boy, her first-born, gripped her heart till she could hardly speak. She fought with the feeling, might and main, for she believed in common sense. But it was too strong. She had to leave the dance and go downstairs to telephone to the country. The children's nursery-governess was terribly surprised and startled at being rung up in the night.

"Are the children all right, Miss Wilmot?"

"Oh yes, they are quite all right."

"Master Paul? Is he all right?"

"He went to bed as right as a trivet. Shall I run up and look at him?"

"No," said Paul's mother reluctantly. "No! Don't trouble. It's all right. Don't sit up. We shall be home fairly soon." She did not want her son's privacy intruded upon.

"Very good," said the governess.

It was about one o'clock when Paul's mother and father drove up to their house. All was still. Paul's mother went to her room and slipped off her white fur cloak. She had told her maid not to wait up for her. She heard her husband downstairs, mixing a whisky and soda.

And then, because of the strange anxiety at her heart, she stole upstairs to her son's room. Noiselessly she went along the upper corridor. Was there a faint noise? What was it?

She stood, with arrested muscles, outside his door, listening. There was a strange, heavy, and yet not loud noise. Her heart stood still. It was a soundless noise, yet rushing and powerful. Something huge, in violent, hushed motion. What was it? What in God's name was it? She ought to know. She felt that she knew the noise. She knew what it was.

Yet she could not place it. She couldn't say what it was. And on and on it went, like a madness.

Softly, frozen with anxiety and fear, she turned the doorhandle.

The room was dark. Yet in the space near the window, she heard and saw something plunging to and fro. She gazed in fear and amazement.

Then suddenly she switched on the light, and saw her son, in his green pyjamas, madly surging on the rocking-horse. The blaze of light suddenly lit him up, as he urged the wooden horse, and lit her up, as she stood, blonde, in her dress of pale green and crystal, in the doorway.

"Paul!" she cried. "Whatever are you doing?"

"It's Malabar!" he screamed in a powerful, strange voice. "It's Malabar!"

His eyes blazed at her for one strange and senseless second, as he ceased urging his wooden horse. Then he fell with a crash to the ground, and she, all her tormented motherhood flooding upon her, rushed to gather him up.

But he was unconscious, and unconscious he remained, with some brain-fever. He talked and tossed, and his mother sat stonily by his side.

"Malabar! It's Malabar! Bassett, Bassett, I *know!* It's Malabar!"

So the child cried, trying to get up and urge the rocking-horse that gave him his inspiration.

"What does he mean by Malabar?" asked the heart-frozen mother.

"I don't know," said the father stonily.

"What does he mean by Malabar?" she asked her brother Oscar.

"It's one of the horses running for the Derby," was the answer.

And, in spite of himself, Oscar Cresswell spoke to Bassett, and himself put a thousand on Malabar: at fourteen to one.

The third day of the illness was critical: they were waiting for a change. The boy, with his rather long, curly hair, was tossing ceaselessly on the pillow. He neither slept nor regained consciousness, and his eyes were like blue stones. His mother sat, feeling her heart had gone, turned actually into a stone.

In the evening, Oscar Cresswell did not come, but Bassett sent a message, saying could he come up for one moment, just one moment? Paul's mother was very angry at the intrusion, but on second thoughts she agreed. The boy was the same. Perhaps Bassett might bring him to consciousness.

The gardener, a shortish fellow with a little brown moustache and sharp little brown eyes, tiptoed into the room, touched his imaginary cap to Paul's mother, and stole to the bedside, staring with glittering, smallish eyes at the tossing, dying child.

"Master Paul!" he whispered. "Master Paul! Malabar came in first all right, a clean win. I did as you told me. You've made over seventy thousand pounds, you have; you've got over eighty thousand. Malabar came in all right, Master Paul."

"Malabar! Malabar! Did I say Malabar, mother? Did I say Malabar? Do you think I'm lucky, mother? I knew Malabar, didn't I? Over eighty thousand pounds! I call that lucky, don't you, mother? Over eighty thousand pounds! I knew, didn't I know I knew? Malabar came in all right. If I ride my horse till I'm sure, then I tell you, Bassett, you can go as high as you like. Did you go for all you were worth, Bassett?"

"I went a thousand on it, Master Paul."

"I never told you, mother, that if I can ride my horse, and *get there,* then I'm absolutely sure — oh, absolutely! Mother, did I ever tell you? I *am* lucky!"

"No, you never did," said his mother.

But the boy died in the night.

And even as he lay dead, his mother heard her brother's voice saying to her: "My God, Hester, you're eighty-odd thousand to the good and a poor devil of a son to the bad. But, poor devil, poor devil, he's best gone out of a life where he rides his rocking-horse to find a winner."

Katherine Anne Porter *(1890–1980)*

The Jilting of Granny Weatherall

She flicked her wrist neatly out of Doctor Harry's pudgy careful fingers and pulled the sheet up to her chin. The brat ought to be in knee breeches. Doctoring around the country with spectacles on his nose! "Get along now, take your schoolbooks and go. There's nothing wrong with me."

Doctor Harry spread a warm paw like a cushion on her forehead where the forked green vein danced and made her eyelids twitch. "Now, now, be a good girl, and we'll have you up in no time."

"That's no way to speak to a woman nearly eighty years old just because she's down. I'd have you respect your elders, young man."

"Well, Missy, excuse me." Doctor Harry patted her cheek. "But I've got to warn you, haven't I? You're a marvel, but you must be careful or you're going to be good and sorry."

"Don't tell me what I'm going to be. I'm on my feet now, morally speaking. It's Cornelia. I had to go to bed to get rid of her."

Her bones felt loose, and floated around in her skin, and Doctor Harry floated like a balloon around the foot of the bed.

He floated and pulled down his waistcoat and swung his glasses on a cord. "Well, stay where you are, it certainly can't hurt you."

"Get along and doctor your sick," said Granny Weatherall. "Leave a well woman alone. I'll call for you when I want you. . . . Where were you forty years ago when I pulled through milk-leg and double pneumonia? You weren't even born. Don't let Cornelia lead you on," she shouted, because Doctor Harry appeared to float up to the ceiling and out. "I pay my own bills, and I don't throw my money away on nonsense!"

She meant to wave good-by, but it was too much trouble. Her eyes closed of themselves, it was like a dark curtain drawn around the bed. The pillow rose and floated under her, pleasant as a hammock in a light wind. She listened to the leaves rustling outside the window. No, somebody was swishing newspapers: no, Cornelia and Doctor Harry were whispering together. She leaped broad awake, thinking they whispered in her ear.

"She was never like this, *never* like this!" "Well, what can we expect?" "Yes, eighty years old. . . ."

Well, and what if she was? She still had ears. It was like Cornelia to whisper around doors. She always kept things secret in such a public way. She was always being tactful and kind. Cornelia was dutiful; that was the trouble with her. Dutiful and good: "So good and dutiful," said Granny, "and I'd like to spank her." She saw herself spanking Cornelia and making a fine job of it.

"What'd you say, Mother?"

Granny felt her face tying up in hard knots.

"Can't a body think, I'd like to know?"

"I thought you might want something."

"I do. I want a lot of things. First off, go away and don't whisper."

She lay and drowsed, hoping in her sleep that the children would keep out and let her rest a minute. It had been a long day. Not that she was tired. It was always pleasant to snatch a minute now and then. There was always so much to be done, let me see: tomorrow.

Tomorrow was far away and there was nothing to trouble about. Things were finished somehow when the time came; thank God there was always a little margin over for peace: then a person could spread out the plan of life and tuck in the edges orderly. It was good to have everything clean and folded away, with the hair brushes and tonic bottles sitting straight on the white embroidered linen: the day started without fuss and the pantry shelves laid out with rows of jelly glasses and brown jugs and white stone-china jars with blue whirligigs and words painted on them: coffee, tea, sugar, ginger, cinnamon, allspice: and the bronze clock with the lion on top nicely dusted off. The dust that lion could collect in twenty-four hours! The box in the attic with all those letters tied up, well, she'd have to go through that tomorrow. All those letters — George's letters and John's letters and her letters to them both — lying around for the children to find afterwards made her uneasy. Yes, that would be tomorrow's business. No use to let them know how silly she had been once.

While she was rummaging around she found death in her mind and it felt clammy and unfamiliar. She had spent so much time preparing for death there was no need for bringing it up again. Let it take care of itself now. When she was sixty she had felt very old, finished, and went around making farewell trips to see her children and grandchildren, with a secret in her mind: This is the very last of your mother, children! Then she made her will and came down with a long fever. That was all just a notion like a lot of other things, but it was lucky too, for she had once for all got over the idea of dying for a long time. Now she couldn't be worried. She hoped she had better sense now. Her father had lived to be one hundred and two years old and had drunk a noggin of strong hot toddy on his last birthday. He told the reporters it was his daily habit, and he owed his long life to that. He had made quite a scandal and was very pleased about it. She believed she'd just plague Cornelia a little.

"Cornelia! Cornelia!" No footsteps, but a sudden hand on her cheek. "Bless you, where have you been?"

"Here, Mother."

"Well, Cornelia, I want a noggin of hot toddy."

"Are you cold, darling?"

"I'm chilly, Cornelia. Lying in bed stops the circulation. I must have told you that a thousand times."

Well, she could just hear Cornelia telling her husband that Mother was getting a little childish and they'd have to humor her. The thing that most annoyed her was that Cornelia thought she was deaf, dumb, and blind. Little hasty glances and tiny gestures tossed around her and over her head saying, "Don't cross her, let her have her way, she's eighty years old," and she sitting there as if she lived in a thin glass cage. Sometimes Granny almost made up her mind to pack up and move back to her own house where nobody could remind her every minute that she was old. Wait, wait, Cornelia, till your own children whisper behind your back!

In her day she had kept a better house and had got more work done. She wasn't too old yet for Lydia to be driving eighty miles for advice when one of the children jumped the track, and Jimmy still dropped in and talked things over: "Now, Mammy, you've a good business head, I want to know what you think of this? . . ." Old. Cornelia couldn't change the furniture around without asking. Little things, little things! They had been so sweet when they were little. Granny wished the old days were back again with the children young and everything to be done over. It had been a hard pull, but not too much for her. When she thought of all the food she had cooked, and all the clothes she had cut and sewed, and all the gardens she had made — well, the children showed it. There they were, made out of her, and they couldn't get away from that. Sometimes she wanted to see John again and point to them and say, Well, I didn't do so badly, did I? But that would have to wait. That was for tomorrow. She used to think of him as a man, but now all the children were older than their father, and he would be a child beside her if she saw him now. It seemed strange and there was something wrong in the idea. Why, he couldn't possibly recognize her. She had fenced in a hundred acres once, digging the post holes herself and clamping the wires with just a negro boy to help. That changed a woman. John would be looking for a young woman with the peaked Spanish comb in her hair and the painted fan. Digging post holes changed a woman. Riding country roads in the winter when women had their babies was another thing: sitting up nights with sick horses and sick negroes and sick children and hardly ever losing one. John, I hardly ever lost one of them! John would see that in a minute, that would be something he could understand, she wouldn't have to explain anything!

It made her feel like rolling up her sleeves and putting the whole place to rights again. No matter if Cornelia was determined to be everywhere at once, there were a great many things left undone on this place. She would start tomorrow and do them. It was good to be strong enough for everything, even if all you made melted and changed and slipped under your hands, so that by the time you finished you almost forgot what you were working for. What was it I set out to do? she asked herself intently, but she could not remember. A fog rose over the valley, she saw it marching across the creek swallowing the trees and moving up the hill like an army of ghosts. Soon it would be at the near edge of the orchard, and then it was time to go in and light the lamps. Come in, children, don't stay out in the night air.

Lighting the lamps had been beautiful. The children huddled up to her and breathed like little calves waiting at the bars in the twilight. Their eyes followed the match and watched the flame rise and settle in a blue curve, then they moved away from her.

The lamp was lit, they didn't have to be scared and hang on to mother any more. Never, never, never more. God, for all my life I thank Thee. Without Thee, my God, I could never have done it. Hail, Mary, full of grace.

I want you to pick all the fruit this year and see that nothing is wasted. There's always someone who can use it. Don't let good things rot for want of using. You waste life when you waste good food. Don't let things get lost. It's bitter to lose things. Now, don't let me get to thinking, not when I am tired and taking a little nap before supper. . . .

The pillow rose about her shoulders and pressed against her heart and the memory was being squeezed out of it: oh, push down the pillow, somebody: it would smother her if she tried to hold it. Such a fresh breeze blowing and such a green day with no threats in it. But he had not come, just the same. What does a woman do when she has put on the white veil and set out the white cake for a man and he doesn't come? She tried to remember. No, I swear he never harmed me but in that. He never harmed me but in that . . . and what if he did? There was the day, the day, but a whirl of dark smoke rose and covered it, crept up and over into the bright field where everything was planted so carefully in orderly rows. That was hell, she knew hell when she saw it. For sixty years she had prayed against remembering him and against losing her soul in the deep pit of hell, and now the two things were mingled in one and the thought of him was a smoky cloud from hell that moved and crept in her head when she had just got rid of Doctor Harry and was trying to rest a minute. Wounded vanity, Ellen, said a sharp voice in the top of her mind. Don't let your wounded vanity get the upper hand of you. Plenty of girls get jilted. You were jilted, weren't you? Then stand up to it. Her eyelids wavered and let in streamers of blue-gray light like tissue paper over her eyes. She must get up and pull the shades down or she'd never sleep. She was in bed again and the shades were not down. How could that happen? Better turn over, hide from the light, sleeping in the light gave you nightmares. "Mother, how do you feel now?" and a stinging wetness on her forehead. But I don't like having my face washed in cold water!

Hapsy? George? Lydia? Jimmy? No, Cornelia, and her features were swollen and full of little puddles. "They're coming, darling, they'll all be here soon." Go wash your face, child, you look funny.

Instead of obeying, Cornelia knelt down and put her head on the pillow. She seemed to be talking but there was no sound. "Well, are you tongue-tied? Whose birthday is it? Are you going to give a party?"

Cornelia's mouth moved urgently in strange shapes. "Don't do that, you bother me, daughter."

"Oh, no, Mother. Oh, no. . . ."

Nonsense. It was strange about children. They disputed your every word. "No what, Cornelia?"

"Here's Doctor Harry."

"I won't see that boy again. He just left five minutes ago."

"That was this morning, Mother. It's night now. Here's the nurse."

"This is Doctor Harry, Mrs. Weatherall. I never saw you look so young and happy!"

"Ah, I'll never be young again — but I'd be happy if they'd let me lie in peace and get rested."

She thought she spoke up loudly, but no one answered. A warm weight on her forehead, a warm bracelet on her wrist, and a breeze went on whispering, trying to tell her something. A shuffle of leaves in the everlasting hand of God. He blew on them and they danced and rattled. "Mother, don't mind, we're going to give you a little hypodermic." "Look here, daughter, how do ants get in this bed? I saw sugar ants yesterday." Did you send for Hapsy too?

It was Hapsy she really wanted. She had to go a long way back through a great many rooms to find Hapsy standing with a baby on her arm. She seemed to herself to be Hapsy also, and the baby on Hapsy's arm was Hapsy and himself and herself, all at once, and there was no surprise in the meeting. Then Hapsy melted from within and turned flimsy as gray gauze and the baby was a gauzy shadow, and Hapsy came up close and said, "I thought you'd never come," and looked at her very searchingly and said, "You haven't changed a bit!" They leaned forward to kiss, when Cornelia began whispering from a long way off, "Oh, is there anything you want to tell me? Is there anything I can do for you?"

Yes, she had changed her mind after sixty years and she would like to see George. I want you to find George. Find him and be sure to tell him I forgot him. I want him to know I had my husband just the same and my children and my house like any other woman. A good house too and a good husband that I loved and fine children out of him. Better than I hoped for even. Tell him I was given back everything he took away and more. Oh, no, oh, God, no, there was something else besides the house and the man and the children. Oh, surely they were not all? What was it? Something not given back. . . . Her breath crowded down under her ribs and grew into a monstrous frightening shape with cutting edges; it bored up into her head, and the agony was unbelievable: Yes, John, get the doctor now, no more talk, my time has come.

When this one was born it should be the last. The last. It should have been born first, for it was the one she had truly wanted. Everything came in good time. Nothing left out, left over. She was strong, in three days she would be as well as ever. Better. A woman needed milk in her to have her full health.

"Mother, do you hear me?"

"I've been telling you —"

"Mother, Father Connolly's here."

"I went to Holy Communion only last week. Tell him I'm not so sinful as all that."

"Father just wants to speak to you."

He could speak as much as he pleased. It was like him to drop in and inquire about her soul as if it were a teething baby, and then stay on for a cup of tea and a round of cards and gossip. He always had a funny story of some sort, usually about an Irishman who made his little mistakes and confessed them, and the point lay in some absurd thing he would blurt out in the confessional showing his struggles between native piety and original sin. Granny felt easy about her soul. Cornelia, where are your manners? Give Father Connolly a chair. She had her secret comfortable understanding with a few favorite saints who cleared a straight road to God for her. All as surely signed and sealed as the papers for the new Forty Acres. Forever . . . heirs and assigns forever. Since the day the wedding cake was not cut, but thrown out and wasted. The whole bottom dropped out of the world, and there she was blind and sweating with nothing under her feet and the walls falling away.

His hand had caught her under the breast, she had not fallen, there was the freshly polished floor with the green rug on it, just as before. He had cursed like a sailor's parrot and said, "I'll kill him for you." Don't lay a hand on him, for my sake leave something to God. "Now, Ellen, you must believe what I tell you. . . ."

So there was nothing, nothing to worry about any more, except sometimes in the night one of the children screamed in a nightmare, and they both hustled out shaking and hunting for the matches and calling, "There, wait a minute, here we are!" John, get the doctor now, Hapsy's time has come. But there was Hapsy standing by the bed in a white cap. "Cornelia, tell Hapsy to take off her cap. I can't see her plain."

Her eyes opened very wide and the room stood out like a picture she had seen somewhere. Dark colors with the shadows rising towards the ceiling in long angles. The tall black dresser gleamed with nothing on it but John's picture, enlarged from a little one, with John's eyes very black when they should have been blue. You never saw him, so how do you know how he looked?

But the man insisted the copy was perfect, it was very rich and handsome. For a picture, yes, but it's not my husband. The table by the bed had a linen cover and a candle and a crucifix. The light was blue from Cornelia's silk lampshades. No sort of light at all, just frippery. You had to live forty years with kerosene lamps to appreciate honest electricity. She felt very strong and she saw Doctor Harry with a rosy nimbus around him.

"You look like a saint, Doctor Harry, and I vow that's as near as you'll ever come to it."

"She's saying something."

"I heard you, Cornelia. What's all this carrying on?"

"Father Connolly's saying —"

Cornelia's voice staggered and bumped like a cart in a bad road. It rounded corners and turned back again and arrived nowhere. Granny stepped up in the cart very lightly and reached for the reins, but a man sat beside her and she knew him by his hands, driving the cart. She did not look in his face, for she knew without seeing, but looked instead down the road where the trees leaned over and bowed to each other and a thousand birds were singing a Mass. She felt like singing too, but she put her hand in the bosom of her dress and pulled out a rosary, and Father Connolly murmured Latin in a very solemn voice and tickled her feet. My God, will you stop that nonsense? I'm a married woman. What if he did run away and leave me to face the priest by myself? I found another a whole world better. I wouldn't have exchanged my husband for anybody except St. Michael himself, and you may tell him that for me with a thank you in the bargain.

Light flashed on her closed eyelids, and a deep roaring shook her. Cornelia, is that lightning? I hear thunder. There's going to be a storm. Close all the windows. Call the children in. . . . "Mother, here we are, all of us." "Is that you, Hapsy?" "Oh, no, I'm Lydia. We drove as fast as we could." Their faces drifted above her, drifted away. The rosary fell out of her hands and Lydia put it back. Jimmy tried to help, their hands fumbled together, and Granny closed two fingers around Jimmy's thumb. Beads wouldn't do, it must be something alive. She was so amazed her thoughts ran round and round. So, my dear Lord, this is my death and I wasn't even thinking about it. My children have come to see me die. But I can't, it's not time. Oh, I always hated surprises. I wanted to give Cornelia the amethyst set — Cornelia, you're to have the amethyst set, but Hapsy's to wear it when she wants, and, Doctor Harry, do shut up. Nobody sent for you. Oh, my dear Lord, do wait a minute. I meant to do something about the Forty Acres, Jimmy doesn't need it and Lydia will later on, with that worthless husband of hers. I meant to finish the altar cloth and send six bottles of wine to Sister Borgia for her dyspepsia. I want to send six bottles of wine to Sister Borgia, Father Connolly, now don't let me forget.

Cornelia's voice made short turns and tilted over and crashed. "Oh, Mother, oh, Mother, oh, Mother. . . ."

"I'm not going, Cornelia. I'm taken by surprise. I can't go."

You'll see Hapsy again. What about her? "I thought you'd never come." Granny made a long journey outward, looking for Hapsy. What if I don't find her? What then? Her heart sank down and down, there was no bottom to death, she couldn't come to the end of it. The blue light from Cornelia's lampshade drew into a tiny point in the center of her brain, it flickered and winked like an eye, quietly it fluttered and dwindled. Granny lay curled down within herself, amazed and watchful, staring at the point of light that was herself, her body was now only a deeper mass of shadow in an endless darkness and this darkness would curl around the light and swallow it up. God, give a sign!

For the second time there was no sign. Again no bridegroom and the priest in the house. She could not remember any other sorrow because this grief wiped them all away. Oh, no, there's nothing more cruel than this — I'll never forgive it. She stretched herself with a deep breath and blew out the light.

James Thurber (1894–1961)

The Secret Life of Walter Mitty

"We're going through!" The Commander's voice was like thin ice breaking. He wore his full-dress uniform, with the heavily braided white cap pulled down rakishly over one cold gray eye. "We can't make it, sir. It's spoiling for a hurricane, if you ask me." "I'm not asking you, Lieutenant Berg," said the Commander. "Throw on the power lights! Rev her up to 8500! We're going through!" The pounding of the cylinders increased; ta-pocketa-pocketa-pocketa-*pocketa-pocketa*. The Commander stared at the ice forming on the pilot window. He walked over and twisted a row of complicated dials. "Switch on No. 8 auxiliary!" he shouted. "Switch on No. 8 auxiliary!" repeated Lieutenant Berg. "Full strength in No. 3 turret!" shouted the Commander. "Full strength in No. 3 turret!" The crew, bending to their various tasks in the huge, hurtling eight-engined Navy hydroplane, looked at each other and grinned. "The Old Man'll get us through," they said to one another. "The Old Man ain't afraid of Hell!". . .

"Not so fast! You're driving too fast!" said Mrs. Mitty. "What are you driving so fast for?"

"Hmm?" said Walter Mitty. He looked at his wife, in the seat beside him, with shocked astonishment. She seemed grossly unfamiliar, like a strange woman who had yelled at him in a crowd. "You were up to fifty-five," she said. "You know I don't like to go more than forty. You were up to fifty-five." Walter Mitty drove on toward Waterbury in silence, the roaring of the SN202 through the worst storm in twenty years of Navy flying fading in the remote, intimate airways of his mind. "You're tensed up again," said Mrs. Mitty. "It's one of your days. I wish you'd let Dr. Renshaw look you over."

Walter Mitty stopped the car in front of the building where his wife went to have her hair done. "Remember to get those overshoes while I'm having my hair done," she said. "I don't need overshoes," said Mitty. She put her mirror back into her bag. "We've been all through that," she said, getting out of the car. "You're not a young man any longer." He raced the engine a little. "Why don't you wear your gloves? Have you lost your gloves?" Walter Mitty reached in a pocket and brought out the gloves. He put them on, but after she had turned and gone into the building and he had driven on to a red light, he took them off again. "Pick it up, brother," snapped a cop as the light changed, and Mitty hastily pulled on his gloves and lurched ahead. He drove around the streets aimlessly for a time, and then he drove past the hospital on his way to the parking lot.

. . . "It's the millionaire banker, Wellington McMillan," said the pretty nurse. "Yes?" said Walter Mitty, removing his gloves slowly. "Who has the case?" "Dr. Renshaw and Dr. Benbow, but there are two specialists here, Dr. Remington from New York and Dr. Pritchard-Mitford from London. He flew over." A door opened down a long, cool corridor and Dr. Renshaw came out. He looked distraught and haggard. "Hello, Mitty," he said. "We're having the devil's own time with McMillan, the millionaire banker and close personal friend of Roosevelt. Obstreosis of the ductal tract. Tertiary. Wish you'd take a look at him." "Glad to," said Mitty.

In the operating room there were whispered introductions: "Dr. Remington, Dr. Mitty, Dr. Pritchard-Mitford, Dr. Mitty." "I've read your book on streptothricosis," said Pritchard-Mitford, shaking hands. "A brilliant performance, sir." "Thank you," said Walter Mitty. "Didn't know you were in the States, Mitty," grumbled Remington. "Coals to Newcastle, bringing Mitford and me up here for a tertiary." "You are very kind," said Mitty. A huge, complicated machine, connected to the operating table, with many tubes and wires, began at this moment to go pocketa-pocketa-pocketa. "The new anaesthetizer is giving away!" shouted an intern. "There is no one in the East who knows how to fix it!" "Quiet, man!" said Mitty, in a low, cool voice. He sprang to the machine, which was now going pocketa-pocketa-queep-pocketa-queep. He began fingering delicately a row of glistening dials. "Give me a fountain pen!" he snapped. Someone handed him a fountain pen. He pulled a faulty piston out of the machine and inserted the pen in its place. "That will hold for ten minutes," he said. "Get on with the operation." A nurse hurried over and whispered to Renshaw, and Mitty saw the man turn pale. "Coreopsis has set in," said Renshaw nervously. "If you would take over, Mitty?" Mitty looked at him and at the craven figure of Benbow, who drank, and at the grave, uncertain faces of the two great specialists. "If you wish," he said. They slipped a white gown on him; he adjusted a mask and drew on thin gloves; nurses handed him shining . . .

"Back it up, Mac! Look out for that Buick!" Walter Mitty jammed on the brakes. "Wrong lane, Mac," said the parking-lot attendant, looking at Mitty closely. "Gee. Yeh," muttered Mitty. He began cautiously to back out of the lane marked Exit Only. "Leave her sit there," said the attendant. "I'll put her away." Mitty got out of the car. "Hey, better leave the key." "Oh," said Mitty, handing the man the ignition key. The attendant vaulted into the car, backed it up with insolent skill, and put it where it belonged.

They're so damn cocky, thought Walter Mitty, walking along Main Street; they think they know everything. Once he had tried to take his chains off, outside New Milford, and he had got them wound around the axles. A man had had to come out in a wrecking car and unwind them, a young, grinning garage man. Since then Mrs. Mitty always made him drive to a garage to have the chains taken off. The next time, he thought, I'll wear my right arm in a sling; they won't grin at me then. I'll have my right arm in a sling and they'll see I couldn't possibly take the chains off myself. He kicked at the slush on the sidewalk. "Overshoes," he said to himself, and he began looking for a shoe store.

When he came out into the street again, with the overshoes in a box under his arm, Walter Mitty began to wonder what the other thing was his wife had told him to get. She had told him, twice before they set out from their house for Waterbury. In a way he hated these weekly trips to town — he was always getting something wrong. Kleenex, he thought, Squibb's, razor blades? No. Toothpaste, toothbrush, bicarbonate, carborundum, initiative and referendum? He gave it up. But she would remember it. "Where's the what's-its-name?" she would ask. "Don't tell me you forgot the what's-its-name." A newsboy went by shouting something about the Waterbury trial.

. . . "Perhaps this will refresh your memory." The District Attorney suddenly thrust a heavy automatic at the quiet figure on the witness stand. "Have you ever seen this before?" Walter Mitty took the gun and examined it expertly. "This is my Webley-Vickers 50.80," he said calmly. An excited buzz ran around the courtroom. The judge rapped for order. "You are a crack shot with any sort of firearms, I believe?" said the District Attorney, insinuatingly. "Objection!" shouted Mitty's attorney. "We have shown that the defendant could not have fired the shot. We have shown that he wore his right arm in a sling on the night of the fourteenth of July." Walter Mitty raised his hand briefly and the bickering attorneys were stilled. "With any known make of gun," he said evenly, "I could have killed Gregory Fitzhurst at three hundred feet *with my left hand.*" Pandemonium broke loose in the courtroom. A woman's scream rose above the bedlam and suddenly a lovely, dark-haired girl was in Walter Mitty's arms. The District Attorney struck at her savagely. Without rising from his chair, Mitty let the man have it on the point of the chin. "You miserable cur!" . . .

"Puppy biscuit," said Walter Mitty. He stopped walking and the buildings of Waterbury rose up out of the misty courtroom and surrounded him again. A woman who was passing laughed. "He said 'Puppy biscuit,' " she said to her companion. "That man said 'Puppy biscuit' to himself." Walter Mitty hurried on. He went into an A. & P., not the first one he came to but a smaller one farther up the street. "I want some biscuit for small, young dogs," he said to the clerk. "Any special brand, sir?" The greatest pistol shot in the world thought a moment. "It says 'Puppies Bark for It' on the box," said Walter Mitty.

His wife would be through at the hairdresser's in fifteen minutes, Mitty saw in looking at his watch, unless they had trouble drying it; sometimes they had trouble drying it. She didn't like to get to the hotel first; she would want him to be there waiting for her as usual. He found a big leather chair in the lobby, facing a window, and he put the overshoes and the puppy biscuit on the floor beside it. He picked up an old copy of *Liberty* and sank down into the chair. "Can Germany Conquer the World through the

Air?" Walter Mitty looked at the pictures of bombing planes and of ruined streets.

. . . "The cannonading has got the wind up in young Raleigh, sir," said the sergeant. Captain Mitty looked up at him through tousled hair. "Get him to bed," he said wearily, "with the others. I'll fly alone." "But you can't, sir," said the sergeant anxiously. "It takes two men to handle that bomber and the Archies are pounding hell out of the air. Von Richtman's circus is between here and Saulier." "Somebody's got to get that ammunition dump," said Mitty. "I'm going over. Spot of brandy?" He poured a drink for the sergeant and one for himself. War thundered and whined around the dugout and battered at the door. There was a rending of wood and splinters flew through the room. "A bit of a near thing," said Captain Mitty carelessly. "The box barrage is closing in," said the sergeant. "We only live once, sergeant," said Mitty, with his faint, fleeting smile. "Or do we?" He poured another brandy and tossed it off. "I never see a man could hold his brandy like you, sir," said the sergeant. "Begging your pardon, sir." Captain Mitty stood up and strapped on his huge Webley-Vickers automatic. "It's forty kilometers through hell, sir," said the sergeant. Mitty finished one last brandy. "After all," he said softly, "what isn't?" The pounding of the cannon increased; there was the rat-tat-tatting of machine guns, and from somewhere came the menacing pocketa-pocketa-pocketa of the new flame-throwers. Walter Mitty walked to the door of the dugout humming "*Auprès de Ma Blonde.*" He turned and waved to the sergeant. "Cheerio!" he said. . . .

Something struck his shoulder. "I've been looking all over this hotel for you," said Mrs. Mitty. "Why do you have to hide in this old chair? How did you expect me to find you?" "Things close in," said Walter Mitty vaguely. "What?" Mrs. Mitty said. "Did you get the what's-its-name? The puppy biscuit? What's in that box?" "Overshoes," said Mitty. "Couldn't you have put them on in the store?" "I was thinking," said Walter Mitty. "Does it ever occur to you that I am sometimes thinking?" She looked at him. "I'm going to take your temperature when I get you home," she said.

They went out through the revolving doors that made a faintly derisive whistling sound when you pushed them. It was two blocks to the parking lot. At the drugstore on the corner she said, "Wait here for me. I forgot something. I won't be a minute." She was more than a minute. Walter Mitty lighted a cigarette. It began to rain, rain with sleet in it. He stood up against the wall of the drugstore, smoking. . . . He put his shoulders back and his heels together. "To hell with the handkerchief," said Walter Mitty scornfully. He took one last drag on his cigarette and snapped it away. Then, with that faint, fleeting smile playing about his lips, he faced the firing squad; erect and motionless, proud and disdainful, Walter Mitty the Undefeated, inscrutable to the last.

William Faulkner (1897–1962)

A Rose for Emily

I

When Miss Emily Grierson died, our whole town went to her funeral: the men through a sort of respectful affection for a fallen monument, the women mostly out of curiosity to see the inside of her house, which no one save an old manservant — a combined gardener and cook — had seen in at least ten years.

It was a big, squarish frame house that had once been white, decorated with cupolas and spires and scrolled balconies in the heavily lightsome style of the seventies, set on what had once been our most select street. But garages and cotton gins had encroached and obliterated even the august names of that neighborhood; only Miss Emily's house was left, lifting its stubborn and coquettish decay above the cotton wagons and the gasoline pumps — an eyesore among eyesores. And now Miss Emily had gone to join the representatives of those august names where they lay in the cedar-bemused cemetery among the ranked and anonymous graves of Union and Confederate soldiers who fell at the battle of Jefferson.

Alive, Miss Emily had been a tradition, a duty, and a care; a sort of hereditary obligation upon the town, dating from that day in 1894 when Colonel Sartoris, the mayor — he who fathered the edict that no Negro woman should appear on the streets without an apron — remitted her taxes, the dispensation dating from the death of her father on into perpetuity. Not that Miss Emily would have accepted charity. Colonel Sartoris invented an involved tale to the effect that Miss Emily's father had loaned money to the town, which the town, as a matter of business, preferred this way of repaying. Only a man of Colonel Sartoris' generation and thought could have invented it, and only a woman could have believed it.

When the next generation, with its more modern ideas, became mayors and aldermen, this arrangement created some little dissatisfaction. On the first of the year they mailed her a tax notice. February came, and there was no reply. They wrote her a formal letter, asking her to call at the sheriff's office at her convenience. A week later the mayor wrote her himself, offering to call or to send his car for her, and received in reply a note on paper of an archaic shape, in a thin, flowing calligraphy in faded ink, to the effect that she no longer went out at all. The tax notice was also enclosed, without comment.

They called a special meeting of the Board of Aldermen. A deputation waited upon her, knocked at the door through which no visitor had passed since she ceased giving china-painting lessons eight or ten years earlier. They were admitted by the old Negro into a dim hall from which a staircase mounted into still more shadow. It smelled of dust and disuse — a close, dank smell. The Negro led them into the parlor. It was furnished in heavy, leather-covered furniture. When the Negro opened the blinds of one window, a faint dust rose sluggishly about their thighs, spinning with slow notes in the single sunray. On a tarnished gilt easel before the fireplace stood a crayon portrait of Miss Emily's father.

They rose when she entered — a small, fat woman in black, with a thin gold chain descending to her waist and vanishing into her belt, leaning on an ebony cane with a tarnished gold head. Her skeleton was small and spare; perhaps that was why what would have been merely plumpness in another was obesity in her. She looked bloated, like a body long submerged in motionless water, and of that pallid hue. Her eyes, lost in the fatty ridges of her face, looked like two small pieces of coal pressed into a lump of dough as they moved from one face to another while the visitors stated their errand.

She did not ask them to sit. She just stood in the door and listened quietly until the spokesman came to a stumbling halt. Then they could hear the invisible watch ticking at the end of the gold chain.

Her voice was dry and cold. "I have no taxes in Jefferson. Colonel Sartoris explained it to me. Perhaps one of you can gain access to the city records and satisfy yourselves."

"But we have. We are the city authorities, Miss Emily. Didn't you get a notice from the sheriff, signed by him?"

"I received a paper, yes," Miss Emily said. "Perhaps he considers himself the sheriff. . . . I have no taxes in Jefferson."

"But there is nothing on the books to show that, you see. We must go by the —"

"See Colonel Sartoris. I have no taxes in Jefferson."

"But, Miss Emily —"

"See Colonel Sartoris." (Colonel Sartoris had been dead almost ten years.) "I have no taxes in Jefferson. Tobe!" The Negro appeared. "Show these gentlemen out."

II

So she vanquished them, horse and foot, just as she had vanquished their fathers thirty years before about the smell. That was two years after her father's death and a short time after her sweetheart — the one we believed would marry her — had deserted her. After her father's death she went out very little; after her sweetheart went away, people hardly saw her at all. A few of the ladies had the temerity to call, but were not received, and the only sign of life about the place was the Negro man — a young man then — going in and out with a market basket.

"Just as if a man — any man — could keep a kitchen properly," the ladies said; so they were not surprised when the smell developed. It was another link between the gross, teeming world and the high and mighty Griersons.

A neighbor, a woman, complained to the mayor, Judge Stevens, eighty years old.

"But what will you have me do about it, madam?" he said.

"Why, send her word to stop it," the woman said. "Isn't there a law?"

"I'm sure that won't be necessary," Judge Stevens said. "It's probably just a snake or a rat that nigger of hers killed in the yard. I'll speak to him about it."

The next day he received two more complaints, one from a man who came in diffident deprecation. "We really must do something about it, Judge. I'd be the last one in the world to bother Miss Emily, but we've got to do something." That night the Board of Aldermen met — three gray-beards and one younger man, a member of the rising generation.

"It's simple enough," he said. "Send her word to have her place cleaned up. Give her a certain time to do it in, and if she don't . . ."

"Dammit, sir," Judge Stevens said, "will you accuse a lady to her face of smelling bad?"

So the next night, after midnight, four men crossed Miss Emily's lawn and slunk about the house like burglars, sniffing along the base of the brickwork and at the cellar openings while one of them performed a regular sowing motion with his hand out of a sack slung from his shoulder. They broke open the cellar door and sprinkled lime there, and in all the out-buildings. As they recrossed the lawn, a window that had been dark was lighted and Miss Emily sat in it, the light behind her, and her upright torso motionless as that of an idol. They crept quietly across the lawn and into the shadow of the locusts that lined the street. After a week or two the smell went away.

That was when people had begun to feel really sorry for her. People in our town remembering how old lady Wyatt, her great-aunt, had gone completely crazy at last, believed that the Griersons held themselves a little too high for what they really were. None of the young men were quite good enough for Miss Emily and such. We had long thought of them as a tableau; Miss Emily a slender figure in white in the background, her father a spraddled silhouette in the foreground, his back to her and clutching a horsewhip, the two of them framed by the back-flung front door. So when she got to be thirty and was still single, we were not pleased exactly, but vindicated; even with insanity in the family she wouldn't have turned down all of her chances if they had really materialized.

When her father died, it got about that the house was all that was left to her; and in a way, people were glad. At last they could pity Miss Emily. Being left alone, and a pauper, she had become humanized. Now she too would know the old thrill and the old despair of a penny more or less.

The day after his death all the ladies prepared to call at the house and offer condolence and aid, as is our custom. Miss Emily met them at the door, dressed as usual and with no trace of grief on her face. She told them that her father was not dead. She did that for three days, with the ministers calling on her, and the doctors, trying to persuade her to let them dispose of the body. Just as they were about to resort to law and force, she broke down, and they buried her father quickly.

We did not say she was crazy then. We believed she had to do that. We remembered all the young men her father had driven away, and we knew that with nothing left, she would have to cling to that which had robbed her, as people will.

III

She was sick for a long time. When we saw her again, her hair was cut short, making her look like a girl, with a vague resemblance to those angels in colored church windows — sort of tragic and serene.

The town had just let the contracts for paving the sidewalks, and in the summer after her father's death they began to work. The construction company came with niggers and mules and ma-chinery, and a foreman named Homer Barron, a Yankee — a big, dark, ready man, with a big voice and eyes lighter than his face. The little boys would follow in groups to hear him cuss the niggers, and the niggers singing in time to the rise and fall of picks. Pretty soon he knew everybody in town. Whenever you heard a lot of laughing anywhere about the square, Homer Barron would be in the center of the group. Presently we began to see him and Miss Emily on Sunday afternoons driving in the yellow-wheeled buggy and the matched team of bays from the livery stable.

At first we were glad that Miss Emily would have an interest, because the ladies all said, "Of course a Grierson would not think seriously of a Northerner, a day laborer." But there were still others, older people, who said that even grief could not cause a real lady to forget *noblesse oblige* — without calling it *noblesse oblige.* They just said, "Poor Emily. Her kinsfolk should come to her." She had some kin in Alabama; but years ago her father had fallen out with them over the estate of old lady Wyatt, the crazy woman, and there was no communication between the two families. They had not even been represented at the funeral.

And as soon as the old people said, "Poor Emily," the whispering began. "Do you suppose it's really so?" they said to one another. "Of course it is. What else could . . ." This behind their hands; rustling of craned silk and satin behind jalousies closed upon the sun of Sunday afternoon as the thin, swift clop-clop-clop of the matched team passed: "Poor Emily."

She carried her head high enough — even when we believed that she was fallen. It was as if she demanded more than ever the recognition of her dignity as the last Grierson; as if it had wanted that touch of earthiness to reaffirm her imperviousness. Like when she bought the rat poison, the arsenic. That was over a year after they had begun to say "Poor Emily," and while the two female cousins were visiting her.

"I want some poison," she said to the druggist. She was over thirty then, still a slight woman, though thinner than usual, with cold, haughty black eyes in a face the flesh of which was strained across the temples and about the eyesockets as you imagine a lighthousekeeper's face ought to look. "I want some poison," she said.

"Yes, Miss Emily. What kind? For rats and such? I'd recom —"

"I want the best you have. I don't care what kind."

The druggist named several. "They'll kill anything up to an elephant. But what you want is —"

"Arsenic," Miss Emily said. "Is that a good one?"

"Is . . . arsenic? Yes ma'am. But what you want —"

"I want arsenic."

The druggist looked down at her. She looked back at him, erect, her face like a strained flag. "Why, of course," the druggist said. "If that's what you want. But the law requires you to tell what you are going to use it for."

Miss Emily just stared at him, her head tilted back in order to look him eye for eye, until he looked away and went and got the arsenic and wrapped it up. The Negro delivery boy brought her the package; the druggist didn't come back. When she opened the package at home there was written on the box, under the skull and bones: "For rats."

IV

So the next day we all said, "She will kill herself"; and we said it would be the best thing. When she had first begun to be seen with Homer Barron, we had said, "She will marry him." Then we said, "She will persuade him yet," because Homer himself had remarked — he liked men, and it was known that he drank with the younger men in the Elk's Club — that he was not a marrying man. Later we said, "Poor Emily," behind the jalousies as they passed on Sunday afternoon in the glittering buggy, Miss Emily with her head high and Homer Barron with his hat cocked and a cigar in his teeth, reins and whip in a yellow glove.

Then some of the ladies began to say that it was a disgrace to the town and a bad example to the young people. The men did not want to interfere, but at last the ladies forced the Baptist minister — Miss Emily's people were Episcopal — to call upon her. He would never divulge what happened during that interview, but he refused to go back again. The next Sunday they again drove about the streets, and the following day the minister's wife wrote to Miss Emily's relations in Alabama.

So she had blood-kin under her roof again and we sat back to watch developments. At first nothing happened. Then we were sure that they were to be married. We learned that Miss Emily had been to the jeweler's and ordered a man's toilet set in silver, with the letters H.B. on each piece. Two days later we learned that she had bought a complete outfit of men's clothing, including a nightshirt, and we said, "They are married." We were really glad. We were glad because the two female cousins were even more Grierson than Miss Emily had ever been.

So we were surprised when Homer Barron — the streets had been finished some time since — was gone. We were a little disappointed that there was not a public blowing-off, but we believed that he had gone on to prepare for Miss Emily's coming, or to give a chance to get rid of the cousins. (By that time it was a cabal, and we were all Miss Emily's allies to help circumvent the cousins.) Sure enough, after another week they departed. And, as we had expected all along, within three days Homer Barron was back in town. A neighbor saw the Negro man admit him at the kitchen door at dusk one evening.

And that was the last we saw of Homer Barron. And of Miss Emily for some time. The Negro man went in and out with the market basket, but the front door remained closed. Now and then we would see her at a window for a moment, as the men did that night when they sprinkled the lime, but for almost six months she did not appear on the streets. Then we knew that this was to be expected too; as if that quality of her father which had thwarted her woman's life so many times had been too virulent and too furious to die.

When we next saw Miss Emily, she had grown fat and her hair was turning gray. During the next few years it grew grayer and grayer until it attained an even pepper-and-salt iron-gray, when it ceased turning. Up to the day of her death at seventy-four it was still that vigorous iron-gray, like the hair of an active man.

From that time on her front door remained closed, save for a period of six or seven years, when she was about forty, during which she gave lessons in china-painting. She fitted up a studio in one of the downstairs rooms, where the daughters and grand-daughters of Colonel Sartoris' contemporaries were sent to her with the same regularity and in the same spirit that they were sent on Sundays with a twenty-five cent piece for the collection plate. Meanwhile her taxes had been remitted.

Then the newer generation became the backbone and the spirit of the town, and the painting pupils grew up and fell away and did not send their children to her with boxes of color and tedious brushes and pictures cut from the ladies' magazines. The front door closed upon the last one and remained closed for good. When the town got free postal delivery Miss Emily alone refused to let them fasten the metal numbers above her door and attach a mailbox to it. She would not listen to them.

Daily, monthly, yearly we watched the Negro grow grayer and more stooped, going in and out with the market basket. Each December we sent her a tax notice, which would be returned by the post office a week later, unclaimed. Now and then we would see her in one of the downstairs windows — she had evidently shut up the top floor of the house — like the carven torso of an idol in a niche, looking or not looking at us, we could never tell which. Thus she passed from generation to generation — dear, inescapable, impervious, tranquil, and perverse.

And so she died. Fell ill in the house filled with dust and shadows, with only a doddering Negro man to wait on her. We did not even know she was sick; we had long since given up trying to get any information from the Negro. He talked to no one, probably not even to her, for his voice had grown harsh and rusty, as if from disuse.

She died in one of the downstairs rooms, in a heavy walnut bed with a curtain, her gray head propped on a pillow yellow and moldy with age and lack of sunlight.

V

The Negro met the first of the ladies at the front door and let them in, with their hushed, sibilant voices and their quick, curious glances, and then he disappeared. He walked right through the house and out the back and was not seen again.

The two female cousins came at once. They held the funeral on the second day, with the town coming to look at Miss Emily beneath a mass of bought flowers, with the crayon face of her father musing profoundly above the bier and the ladies sibilant and macabre; and the very old men — some in their brushed Confederate uniforms — on the porch and the lawn, talking of Miss Emily as if she had been a contemporary of theirs, believing that they had danced with her and courted her perhaps, confusing time with its mathematical progression, as the old do, to whom all the past is not a diminishing road, but, instead, a huge meadow which no winter ever quite touches, divided from them now by the narrow bottleneck of the most recent decade of years.

Already we knew that there was one room in that region above stairs which no one had seen in forty years, and which would have to be forced. They waited until Miss Emily was decently in the ground before they opened it.

The violence of breaking down the door seemed to fill this room with pervading dust. A thin, acrid pall as of the tomb seemed to lie everywhere upon this room decked and furnished as for a bridal: upon the valance curtains of faded rose color, upon the rose-shaded lights, upon the dressing table, upon the delicate array of crystal and the man's toilet things backed with tarnished silver, silver so tarnished that the monogram was obscured. Among them lay a collar and tie, as if they had just been removed, which, lifted, left upon the surface a pale crescent in the dust. Upon a chair hung the suit, carefully folded; beneath it the two mute shoes and the discarded socks.

The man himself lay in the bed.

For a long while we just stood there, looking down at the profound and fleshless grin. The body had apparently once lain in the attitude of an embrace, but now the long sleep that outlasts love, that conquers even the grimace of love, had cuckolded him. What was left of him, rotted beneath what was left of the nightshirt,

had become inextricable from the bed in which he lay; and upon
him and upon the pillow beside him lay that even coating of the
patient and biding dust.

Then we noticed that in the second pillow was the indentation
of a head. One of us lifted something from it, and leaning forward,
that faint and invisible dust dry and acrid in the nostrils, we saw
a long strand of iron-gray hair.

William Faulkner (*1897–1962*)

Barn Burning

The store in which the Justice of the Peace's court was sitting
smelled of cheese. The boy, crouched on his nail keg at the back
of the crowded room, knew he smelled cheese, and more: from
where he sat he could see the ranked shelves close-packed with
the solid, squat, dynamic shapes of tin cans whose labels his stomach
read, not from the lettering which meant nothing to his mind but
from the scarlet devils and the silver curve of fish — this, the
cheese which he knew he smelled and the hermetic meat which
his intestines believed he smelled coming in intermittent gusts
momentary and brief between the other constant one, the smell
and sense just a little of fear because mostly of despair and grief,
the old fierce pull of blood. He could not see the table where the
Justice sat and before which his father and his father's enemy (*our
enemy* he thought in that despair; *ourn! mine and hisn both! He's my
father!*) stood, but he could hear them, the two of them that is,
because his father had said no word yet:

"But what proof have you, Mr. Harris?"

"I told you. The hog got into my corn. I caught it up and
sent it back to him. He had no fence that would hold it. I told
him so, warned him. The next time I put the hog in my pen.
When he came to get it I gave him enough wire to patch up his
pen. The next time I put the hog up and kept it. I rode down to
his house and saw the wire I gave him still rolled on to the spool
in his yard. I told him he could have the hog when he paid me
a dollar pound fee. That evening a nigger came with the dollar
and got the hog. He was a strange nigger. He said, 'He say to
tell you wood and hay kin burn.' I said, 'What?' 'That whut he
say to tell you,' the nigger said. 'Wood and hay kin burn.' That
night my barn burned. I got the stock out but I lost the barn."

"Where is the nigger? Have you got him?"

"He was a strange nigger, I tell you. I don't know what became of him."

"But that's not proof. Don't you see that's not proof?"

"Get that boy up here. He knows." For a moment the boy thought too that the man meant his older brother until Harris said, "Not him. The little one. The boy," and, crouching, small for his age, small and wiry like his father, in patched and faded jeans even too small for him, with straight, uncombed, brown hair and eyes gray and wild as storm scud, he saw the men between himself and the table part and become a lane of grim faces, at the end of which he saw the Justice, a shabby, collarless, graying man in spectacles, beckoning him. He felt no floor under his bare feet; he seemed to walk beneath the palpable weight of the grim turning faces. His father, stiff in his black Sunday coat donned not for the trial but for the moving, did not even look at him. *He aims for me to lie,* he thought, again with that frantic grief and despair. *And I will have to do hit.*

"What's your name, boy?" the Justice said.

"Colonel Sartoris Snopes," the boy whispered.

"Hey?" the Justice said. "Talk louder. Colonel Sartoris? I reckon anybody named for Colonel Sartoris in this country can't help but tell the truth, can they?" The boy said nothing. *Enemy! Enemy!* he thought; for a moment he could not even see, could not see that the Justice's face was kindly nor discern that his voice was troubled when he spoke to the man named Harris: "Do you want me to question this boy?" But he could hear, and during those subsequent long seconds while there was absolutely no sound in the crowded little room save that of quiet and intent breathing it was as if he had swung outward at the end of a grape vine, over a ravine, and at the top of the swing had been caught in a prolonged instant of mesmerized gravity, weightless in time.

"No!" Harris said violently, explosively. "Damnation! Send him out of here!" Now time, the fluid world, rushed beneath him again, the voices coming to him again through the smell of cheese and sealed meat, the fear and despair and the old grief of blood:

"This case is closed. I can't find against you, Snopes, but I can give you advice. Leave this country and don't come back to it."

His father spoke for the first time, his voice cold and harsh, level, without emphasis: "I aim to. I don't figure to stay in a country among people who . . ." he said something unprintable and vile, addressed to no one.

"That'll do," the Justice said. "Take your wagon and get out of this country before dark. Case dismissed."

His father turned, and he followed the stiff black coat, the wiry figure walking a little stiffly from where a Confederate provost's man's musket ball had taken him in the heel on a stolen horse thirty years ago, followed the two backs now, since his older brother had appeared from somewhere in the crowd, no taller than the father but thicker, chewing tobacco steadily, between the two lines of grim-faced men and out of the store and across the worn gallery and down the sagging steps and among the dogs and half-grown boys in the mild May dust, where as he passed a voice hissed:

"Barn burner!"

Again he could not see, whirling; there was a face in a red haze, moonlike, bigger than the full moon, the owner of it half again his size, he leaping in the red haze toward the face, feeling no blow, feeling no shock when his head struck the earth, scrabbling up and leaping again, feeling no blow this time either and tasting no blood, scrabbling up to see the other boy in full flight and himself already leaping into pursuit as his father's hand jerked him back, the harsh, cold voice speaking above him: "Go get in the wagon."

It stood in a grove of locusts and mulberries across the road. His two hulking sisters in their Sunday dresses and his mother and her sister in calico and sunbonnets were already in it, sitting on and among the sorry residue of the dozen and more movings which even the boy could remember — the battered stove, the broken beds and chairs, the clock inlaid with mother-of-pearl, which would not run, stopped at some fourteen minutes past two o'clock of a dead and forgotten day and time, which had been his mother's dowry. She was crying, though when she saw him she drew her sleeve across her face and began to descend from the wagon. "Get back," the father said.

"He's hurt. I got to get some water and wash his . . ."

"Get back in the wagon," his father said. He got in too, over the tail-gate. His father mounted to the seat where the older brother already sat and struck the gaunt mules two savage blows with the peeled willow, but without heat. It was not even sadistic; it was exactly that same quality which in later years would cause his descendants to over-run the engine before putting a motor car into motion, striking and reining back in the same movement. The wagon went on, the store with its quiet crowd of grimly watching men dropped behind; a curve in the road hid it. *Forever* he thought. *Maybe he's done satisfied now, now that he has . . .* stopping himself, not to say it aloud even to himself. His mother's hand touched his shoulder.

"Does hit hurt?" she said.

"Naw," he said. "Hit don't hurt. Lemme be."

"Can't you wipe some of the blood off before hit dries?"

"I'll wash to-night," he said. "Lemme be, I tell you."

The wagon went on. He did not know where they were going. None of them ever did or ever asked, because it was always somewhere, always a house of sorts waiting for them a day or two days or even three days away. Likely his father had already arranged to make a crop on another farm before he . . . Again he had to stop himself. He (the father) always did. There was something about his wolflike independence and even courage when the advantage was at least neutral which impressed strangers, as if they got from his latent ravening ferocity not so much a sense of dependability as a feeling that his ferocious conviction in the rightness of his own actions would be of advantage to all whose interest lay with his.

That night they camped, in a grove of oaks and beeches where a spring ran. The nights were still cool and they had a fire against it, of a rail lifted from a nearby fence and cut into lengths — a small fire, neat, niggard almost, a shrewd fire; such fires were his father's habit and custom always, even in freezing weather. Older, the boy might have remarked this and wondered why not a big one; why should not a man who had not only seen the waste and extravagance of war, but who had in his blood an inherent voracious prodigality with material not his own, have burned everything in sight? Then he might have gone a step farther and thought that that was the reason: that niggard blaze was the living fruit of nights passed during those four years in the woods hiding from all men, blue or gray, with his strings of horses (captured horses, he called them). And older still, he might have divined the true reason: that the element of fire spoke to some deep mainspring of his father's being, as the element of steel or of powder spoke to other men, as the one weapon for the preservation of integrity, else breath were not worth the breathing, and hence to be regarded with respect and used with discretion.

But he did not think this now and he had seen those same niggard blazes all his life. He merely ate his supper beside it and was already half asleep over his iron plate when his father called him, and once more he followed the stiff back, the stiff and ruthless limp, up the slope and on to the starlit road where, turning, he could see his father against the stars but without face or depth — a shape black, flat, and bloodless as though cut from tin in the iron folds of the frockcoat which had not been made for him, the voice harsh like tin and without heat like tin:

"You were fixing to tell them. You would have told him."
He didn't answer. His father struck him with the flat of his hand
on the side of the head, hard but without heat, exactly as he had
struck the two mules at the store, exactly as he would strike either
of them with any stick in order to kill a horse fly, his voice still
without heat or anger: "You're getting to be a man. You got to
learn. You got to learn to stick to your own blood or you ain't
going to have any blood to stick to you. Do you think either of
them, any man there this morning, would? Don't you know all
they wanted was a chance to get at me because they knew I had
them beat? Eh?" Later, twenty years later, he was to tell himself,
"If I had said they wanted only truth, justice, he would have hit
me again." But now he said nothing. He was not crying. He just
stood there. "Answer me," his father said.

"Yes," he whispered. His father turned.

"Get on to bed. We'll be there to-morrow."

To-morrow they were there. In the early afternoon the wagon
stopped before a paintless two-room house identical almost with
the dozen others it had stopped before even in the boy's ten years,
and again, as on the other dozen occasions, his mother and aunt
got down and began to unload the wagon, although his two sisters
and his father and brother had not moved.

"Likely hit ain't fitten for hawgs," one of the sisters said.

"Nevertheless, fit it will and you'll hog it and like it," his
father said. "Get out of them chairs and help your Ma unload."

The two sisters got down, big, bovine, in a flutter of cheap
ribbons; one of them drew from the jumbled wagon bed a battered
lantern, the other a worn broom. His father handed the reins to
the older son and began to climb stiffly over the wheel. "When
they get unloaded, take the team to the barn and feed them."
Then he said, and at first the boy thought he was still speaking
to his brother: "Come with me."

"Me?" he said.

"Yes," his father said. "You."

"Abner," his mother said. His father paused and looked back
— the harsh level stare beneath the shaggy, graying, irascible
brows.

"I reckon I'll have a word with the man that aims to begin
to-morrow owning me body and soul for the next eight months."

They went back up the road. A week ago — or before last
night, that is — he would have asked where they were going, but
not now. His father had struck him before last night but never
before had he paused afterward to explain why; it was as if the
blow and the following calm, outrageous voice still rang, reper-

cussed, divulging nothing to him save the terrible handicap of being young, the light weight of his few years, just heavy enough to prevent his soaring free of the world as it seemed to be ordered but not heavy enough to keep him footed solid in it, to resist it and try to change the course of its events.

Presently he could see the grove of oaks and cedars and the other flowering trees and shrubs where the house would be, though not the house yet. They walked beside a fence massed with honey-suckle and Cherokee roses and came to a gate swinging open between two brick pillars, and now, beyond a sweep of drive, he saw the house for the first time and at that instant he forgot his father and the terror and despair both, and even when he remembered his father again (who had not stopped) the terror and despair did not return. Because, for all the twelve movings, they had sojourned until now in a poor country, a land of small farms and fields and houses, and he had never seen a house like this before. *Hit's big as a courthouse* he thought quietly, with a surge of peace and joy whose reason he could not have thought into words, being too young for that: *They are safe from him. People whose lives are a part of this peace and dignity are beyond his touch, he no more to them than a buzzing wasp: capable of stinging for a little moment but that's all; the spell of this peace and dignity rendering even the barns and stable and cribs which belong to it impervious to the puny flames he might contrive* . . . this, the peace and joy, ebbing for an instant as he looked again at the stiff black back, the stiff and implacable limp of the figure which was not dwarfed by the house, for the reason that it had never looked big anywhere and which now, against the serene columned backdrop, had more than ever that impervious quality of something cut ruthlessly from tin, depthless, as though, sidewise to the sun, it would cast no shadow. Watching him, the boy remarked the absolutely undeviating course which his father held and saw the stiff foot come squarely down in a pile of fresh droppings where a horse had stood in the drive and which his father could have avoided by a simple change of stride. But it ebbed only for a moment, though he could not have thought this into words either, walking on in the spell of the house, which he could even want but without envy, without sorrow, certainly never with that ravening and jealous rage which unknown to him walked in the ironlike black coat before him: *Maybe he will feel it too. Maybe it will even change him now from what maybe he couldn't help but be.*

They crossed the portico. Now he could hear his father's stiff foot as it came down on the boards with clocklike finality, a sound out of all proportion to the displacement of the body it bore and which was not dwarfed either by the white door before it, as though it had attained to a sort of vicious and ravening minimum not to be dwarfed by anything — the flat, wide, black hat, the formal coat of broadcloth which had once been black but which had now that friction-glazed greenish cast of the bodies of old house flies, the lifted sleeve which was too large, the lifted hand like a curled claw. The door opened so promptly that the boy knew the Negro must have been watching them all the time, an old man with neat grizzled hair, in a linen jacket, who stood barring the door with his body, saying, "Wipe yo foots, white man, fo you come in here. Major ain't home nohow."

"Get out of my way, nigger," his father said, without heat too, flinging the door back and the Negro also and entering, his hat still on his head. And now the boy saw the prints of the stiff foot on the doorjamb and saw them appear on the pale rug behind the machinelike deliberation of the foot which seemed to bear (or transmit) twice the weight which the body compassed. The Negro was shouting "Miss Lula! Miss Lula!" somewhere behind them, then the boy, deluged as though by a warm wave by a suave turn of carpeted stair and a pendant glitter of chandeliers and a mute gleam of gold frames, heard the swift feet and saw her too, a lady — perhaps he had never seen her like before either — in a gray, smooth gown with lace at the throat and an apron tied at the waist and the sleeves turned back, wiping cake or biscuit dough from her hands with a towel as she came up the hall, looking not at his father at all but at the tracks on the blond rug with an expression of incredulous amazement.

"I tried," the Negro cried. "I tole him to . . ."

"Will you please go away?" she said in a shaking voice. "Major de Spain is not at home. Will you please go away?"

His father had not spoken again. He did not speak again. He did not even look at her. He just stood stiff in the center of the rug, in his hat, the shaggy iron-gray brows twitching slightly above the pebble-colored eyes as he appeared to examine the house with brief deliberation. Then with the same deliberation he turned; the boy watched him pivot on the good leg and saw the stiff foot drag round the arc of the turning, leaving a final long and fading smear. His father never looked at it, he never once looked down at the rug. The Negro held the door. It closed behind them, upon the hysteric and indistinguishable woman-wail. His father stopped at the top of the steps and scraped his boot clean on the edge of it. At the gate he stopped again. He stood for a moment, planted stiffly on the stiff foot, looking back at the house. "Pretty and white, ain't it?" he said. "That's sweat. Nigger sweat. Maybe it ain't white enough yet to suit him. Maybe he wants to mix some white sweat with it."

Two hours later the boy was chopping wood behind the house within which his mother and aunt and the two sisters (the mother and aunt, not the two girls, he knew that; even at this distance and muffled by walls the flat loud voices of the two girls emanated an incorrigible idle inertia) were setting up the stove to prepare a meal, when he heard the hooves and saw the linen-clad man on a fine sorrel mare, whom he recognized even before he saw the rolled rug in front of the Negro youth following on a fat bay carriage horse — a suffused, angry face vanishing, still at full gallop, beyond the corner of the house where his father and brother were sitting in the two tilted chairs; and a moment later, almost before he could have put the axe down, he heard the hooves again and watched the sorrel mare go back out of the yard, already galloping again. Then his father began to shout one of the sisters' names, who presently emerged backward from the kitchen door dragging the rolled rug along the ground by one end while the other sister walked behind it.

"If you ain't going to tote, go on and set up the wash pot," the first said.

"You, Sarty!" the second shouted. "Set up the wash pot!" His father appeared at the door, framed against that shabbiness, as he had been against that other bland perfection, impervious to either, the mother's anxious face at his shoulder.

"Go on," the father said. "Pick it up." The two sisters stooped, broad, lethargic; stooping, they presented an incredible expanse of pale cloth and a flutter of tawdry ribbons.

"If I thought enough of a rug to have to git hit all the way from France I wouldn't keep hit where folks coming in would have to tromp on hit," the first said. They raised the rug.

"Abner," the mother said. "Let me do it."

"You go back and git dinner," his father said. "I'll tend to this."

From the woodpile through the rest of the afternoon the boy watched them, the rug spread flat in the dust beside the bubbling wash-pot, the two sisters stooping over it with that profound and lethargic reluctance, while the father stood over them in turn, implacable and grim, driving them though never raising his voice again. He could smell the harsh homemade lye they were using; he saw his mother come to the door once and look toward them with an expression not anxious now but very like despair; he saw his father turn, and he fell to with the axe and saw from the corner of his eye his father raise from the ground a flattish fragment of field stone and examine it and return to the pot, and this time his mother actually spoke: "Abner. Abner. Please don't. Please, Abner."

Then he was done too. It was dusk; the whippoorwills had already begun. He could smell coffee from the room where they would presently eat the cold food remaining from the midafternoon meal, though when he entered the house he realized they were having coffee again probably because there was a fire on the hearth, before which the rug now lay spread over the backs of the two chairs. The tracks of his father's foot were gone. Where they had been were now long, water-cloudy scoriations resembling the sporadic course of a lilliputian mowing machine.

It still hung there while they ate the cold food and then went to bed, scattered without order or claim up and down the two rooms, his mother in one bed, where his father would later lie, the older brother in the other, himself, the aunt, and the two sisters on pallets on the floor. But his father was not in bed yet. The last thing the boy remembered was the depthless, harsh silhouette of the hat and coat bending over the rug and it seemed to him that he had not even closed his eyes when the silhouette was standing over him, the fire almost dead behind it, the stiff foot prodding him awake. "Catch up the mule," his father said.

When he returned with the mule his father was standing in the black door, the rolled rug over his shoulder. "Ain't you going to ride?" he said.

"No. Give me your foot."

He bent his knee into his father's hand, the wiry, surprising power flowed smoothly, rising, he rising with it, on to the mule's bare back (they had owned a saddle once; the boy could remember it though not when or where) and with the same effortlessness his father swung the rug up in front of him. Now in the starlight they retraced the afternoon's path, up the dusty road rife with honeysuckle, through the gate and up the black tunnel of the drive to the lightless house, where he sat on the mule and felt the rough warp of the rug drag across his thighs and vanish.

"Don't you want me to help?" he whispered. His father did not answer and now he heard again that stiff foot striking the hollow portico with that wooden and clocklike deliberation, that outrageous overstatement of the weight it carried. The rug, hunched, not flung (the boy could tell that even in the darkness) from his father's shoulder struck the angle of wall and floor with a sound unbelievably loud, thunderous, then the foot again, unhurried and enormous; a light came on in the house and the boy sat, tense, breathing steadily and quietly and just a little fast, though the foot itself did not increase its beat at all, descending the steps now; now the boy could see him.

"Don't you want to ride now?" he whispered. "We kin both ride now," the light within the house altering now, flaring up and sinking. *He's coming down the stairs now,* he thought. He had already ridden the mule up beside the horse block; presently his father was up behind him and he doubled the reins over and slashed the mule across the neck, but before the animal could begin to trot the hard, thin arm came round him, the hard, knotted hand jerking the mule back to a walk.

In the first red rays of the sun they were in the lot, putting plow gear on the mules. This time the sorrel mare was in the lot before he heard it at all, the rider collarless and even bareheaded, trembling, speaking in a shaking voice as the woman in the house had done. His father merely looking up once before stooping again to the hame he was buckling, so that the man on the mare spoke to his stooping back:

"You must realize you have ruined that rug. Wasn't there anybody here, any of your women . . ." he ceased, shaking, the boy watching him, the older brother leaning now in the stable door, chewing, blinking slowly and steadily at nothing apparently. "It cost a hundred dollars. But you never had a hundred dollars. You never will. So I'm going to charge you twenty bushels of corn against your crop. I'll add it in your contract and when you come to the commissary you can sign it. That won't keep Mrs. de Spain quiet but maybe it will teach you to wipe your feet off before you enter her house again."

Then he was gone. The boy looked at his father, who still had not spoken or even looked up again, who was now adjusting the loggerhead in the hame.

"Pap," he said. His father looked at him — the inscrutable face, the shaggy brows beneath which the gray eyes glinted coldly. Suddenly the boy went toward him, fast, stopping as suddenly. "You done the best you could!" he cried. "If he wanted hit done different why didn't he wait and tell you how? He won't git no twenty bushels! He won't git none! We'll gether hit and hide hit! I kin watch . . ."

"Did you put the cutter back in that straight stock like I told you?"

"No, sir," he said.

"Then go do it."

That was Wednesday. During the rest of that week he worked steadily, at what was within his scope and some which was beyond it, with an industry that did not need to be driven nor even commanded twice; he had this from his mother, with the difference that some at least of what he did he liked to do, such as splitting wood with the half-size axe which his mother and aunt had earned, or saved money somehow, to present him with at Christmas. In company with the two older women (and on one afternoon, even one of the sisters), he built pens for the shoat and the cow which were a part of his father's contract with the landlord, and one afternoon, his father being absent, gone somewhere on one of the mules, he went to the field.

They were running a middle buster now, his brother holding the plow straight while he handled the reins, and walking beside the straining mule, the rich black soil shearing cool and damp against his bare ankles, he thought *Maybe this is the end of it. Maybe even that twenty bushels that seems hard to have to pay for just a rug will be a cheap price for him to stop forever and always from being what he used to be;* thinking, dreaming now, so that his brother had to speak sharply to him to mind the mule: *Maybe he even won't collect the twenty bushels. Maybe it will all add up and balance and vanish — corn, rug, fire; the terror and grief, the being pulled two ways like between two teams of horses — gone, done with for ever and ever.*

Then it was Saturday; he looked up from beneath the mule he was harnessing and saw his father in the black coat and hat. "Not that," his father said. "The wagon gear." And then, two hours later, sitting in the wagon bed behind his father and brother on the seat, the wagon accomplished a final curve, and he saw the weathered paintless store with its tattered tobacco- and patent-medicine posters and the tethered wagons and saddle animals below the gallery. He mounted the gnawed steps behind his father and brother, and there again was the lane of quiet, watching faces for the three of them to walk through. He saw the man in spectacles sitting at the plank table and he did not need to be told this was a Justice of the Peace; he sent one glare of fierce, exultant, partisan defiance at the man in collar and cravat now, whom he had seen but twice before in his life, and that on a galloping horse, who now wore on his face an expression not of rage but of amazed unbelief which the boy could not have known was at the incredible circumstance of being sued by one of his own tenants, and came and stood against his father and cried at the Justice: "He ain't done it! He ain't burnt . . ."

"Go back to the wagon," his father said.

"Burnt?" the Justice said. "Do I understand this rug was burned too?"

"Does anybody here claim it was?" his father said. "Go back to the wagon." But he did not, he merely retreated to the rear of the room, crowded as that other had been, but not to sit down this time, instead, to stand pressing among the motionless bodies, listening to the voices:

"And you claim twenty bushels of corn is too high for the damage you did to the rug?"

"He brought the rug to me and said he wanted the tracks washed out of it. I washed the tracks out and took the rug back to him."

"But you didn't carry the rug back to him in the same condition it was in before you made the tracks on it."

His father did not answer, and now for perhaps half a minute there was no sound at all save that of breathing, the faint, steady suspiration of complete and intent listening.

"You decline to answer that, Mr. Snopes?" Again his father did not answer. "I'm going to find against you, Mr. Snopes. I'm going to find that you were responsible for the injury to Major de Spain's rug and hold you liable for it. But twenty bushels of corn seems a little high for a man in your circumstances to have to pay. Major de Spain claims it cost a hundred dollars. October corn will be worth about fifty cents. I figure that if Major de Spain can stand a ninety-five-dollar loss on something he paid cash for, you can stand a five-dollar loss you haven't earned yet. I hold you in damages to Major de Spain to the amount of ten bushels of corn over and above your contract with him, to be paid to him out of your crop at gathering time. Court adjourned."

It had taken no time hardly, the morning was but half begun. He thought they would return home and perhaps back to the field, since they were late, far behind all other farmers. But instead his father passed on behind the wagon, merely indicating with his hand for the older brother to follow with it, and crossed the road toward the blacksmith shop opposite, pressing on after his father, overtaking him, speaking, whispering up at the harsh, calm face beneath the weathered hat: "He won't git no ten bushels neither. He won't git one. We'll . . ." until his father glanced for an instant down at him, the face absolutely calm, the grizzled eyebrows tangled above the cold eyes, the voice almost pleasant, almost gentle:

"You think so? Well, we'll wait till October anyway."

The matter of the wagon — the setting of a spoke or two and the tightening of the tires — did not take long either, the business of the tires accomplished by driving the wagon into the spring branch behind the shop and letting it stand there, the mules nuzzling into the water from time to time, and the boy on the seat with the idle reins, looking up the slope and through the sooty tunnel of the shed where the slow hammer rang and where his father sat on an upended cypress bolt, easily, either talking or listening, still sitting there when the boy brought the dripping wagon up out of the branch and halted it before the door.

"Take them on to the shade and hitch," his father said. He did so and returned. His father and the smith and a third man squatting on his heels inside the door were talking, about crops and animals; the boy, squatting too in the ammoniac dust and hoof-parings and scales of rust, heard his father tell a long and unhurried story out of the time before the birth of the older brother even when he had been a professional horsetrader. And then his father came up beside him where he stood before a tattered last year's circus poster on the other side of the store, gazing rapt and quiet at the scarlet horses, the incredible poisings and convolutions of tulle and tights and the painted leers of comedians, and said, "It's time to eat."

But not at home. Squatting beside his brother against the front wall, he watched his father emerge from the store and produce from a paper sack a segment of cheese and divide it carefully and deliberately into three with his pocket knife and produce crackers from the same sack. They all three squatted on the gallery and ate, slowly, without talking; then in the store again, they drank from a tin dipper tepid water smelling of the cedar bucket and of living beech trees. And still they did not go home. It was a horse lot this time, a tall rail fence upon and along which men stood and sat and out of which one by one horses were led, to be walked and trotted and then cantered back and forth along the road while the slow swapping and buying went on and the sun began to slant westward, they — the three of them — watching and listening, the older brother with his muddy eyes and his steady, inevitable tobacco, the father commenting now and then on certain of the animals, to no one in particular.

It was after sundown when they reached home. They ate supper by lamplight, then, sitting on the doorstep, the boy watched the night fully accomplish, listening to the whippoorwills and the frogs, when he heard his mother's voice: "Abner! No! No! Oh, God. Oh, God. Abner!" and he rose, whirled, and saw the altered light through the door where a candle stub now burned in a bottle neck on the table and his father, still in the hat and coat, at once formal and burlesque as though dressed carefully for some shabby and ceremonial violence, emptying the reservoir of the lamp back into the five-gallon kerosene can from which it had been filled, while the mother tugged at his arm until he shifted the lamp to the other hand and flung her back, not savagely or viciously, just hard, into the wall, her hands flung out against the wall for balance, her mouth open and in her face the same quality of hopeless despair as had been in her voice. Then his father saw him standing in the door.

"Go to the barn and get that can of oil we were oiling the wagon with," he said. The boy did not move. Then he could speak.

"What . . ." he cried. "What are you . . ."

"Go get that oil," his father said. "Go."

Then he was moving, running, outside the house, toward the stable: this the old habit, the old blood which he had not been permitted to choose for himself, which had been bequeathed him willy nilly and which had run for so long (and who knew where, battening on what of outrage and savagery and lust) before it came to him. *I could keep on,* he thought. *I could run on and on and never look back, never need to see his face again. Only I can't. I can't,* the rusted can in his hand now, the liquid sploshing in it as he ran back to the house and into it, into the sound of his mother's weeping in the next room, and handed the can to his father.

"Ain't you going to even send a nigger?" he cried. "At least you sent a nigger before!"

This time his father didn't strike him. The hand came even faster than the blow had, the same hand which had set the can on the table with almost excruciating care flashing from the can to ward him too quick for him to follow it, gripping him by the back of his shirt and on to tiptoe before he had seen it quit the can, the face stooping at him in breathless and frozen ferocity, the cold, dead voice speaking over him to the older brother who leaned against the table, chewing with that steady, curious, sidewise motion of cows:

"Empty the can into the big one and go on. I'll catch up with you."

"Better tie him up to the bedpost," the brother said.

"Do like I told you," the father said. Then the boy was moving, his bunched shirt and the hard, bony hand between his shoulderblades, his toes just touching the floor, across the room and into the other one, past the sisters sitting with spread heavy thighs in the two chairs over the cold hearth, and to where his mother and aunt sat side by side on the bed, the aunt's arms about his mother's shoulders.

"Hold him," the father said. The aunt made a startled movement. "Not you," the father said. "Lennie. Take hold of him. I want to see you do it." His mother took him by the wrist. "You'll hold him better than that. If he gets loose don't you know what he is going to do? He will go up yonder." He jerked his head toward the road. "Maybe I'd better tie him."

"I'll hold him," his mother whispered.

"See you do then." Then his father was gone, the stiff foot heavy and measured upon the boards, ceasing at last.

Then he began to struggle. His mother caught him in both arms, he jerking and wrenching at them. He would be stronger in the end, he knew that. But he had no time to wait for it. "Lemme go!" he cried. "I don't want to have to hit you!"

"Let him go!" the aunt said. "If he don't go, before God, I am going up there myself!"

"Don't you see I can't?" his mother cried. "Sarty! Sarty! No! No! Help me, Lizzie!"

Then he was free. His aunt grasped at him but it was too late. He whirled, running, his mother stumbled forward on to her knees behind him, crying to the nearer sister: "Catch him, Net! Catch him!" But that was too late too, the sister (the sisters were twins, born at the same time, yet either of them now gave the impression of being, encompassing as much living meat and volume and weight as any other two of the family) not yet having begun to rise from the chair, her head, face, alone merely turned, presenting to him in the flying instant an astonishing expanse of young female features untroubled by any surprise even, wearing only an expression of bovine interest. Then he was out of the room, out of the house, in the mild dust of the starlit road and the heavy rifeness of honeysuckle, the pale ribbon unspooling with terrific slowness under his running feet, reaching the gate at last and turning in, running, his heart and lungs drumming, on up the drive toward the lighted house, the lighted door. He did not knock, he burst in, sobbing for breath, incapable for the moment of speech; he saw the astonished face of the Negro in the linen jacket without knowing when the Negro had appeared.

"De Spain!" he cried, panted. "Where's . . ." then he saw the white man too emerging from a white door down the hall. "Barn!" he cried. "Barn!"

"What?" the white man said. "Barn?"

"Yes!" the boy cried. "Barn!"

"Catch him!" the white man shouted.

But it was too late this time too. The Negro grasped his shirt, but the entire sleeve, rotten with washing, carried away, and he was out that door too and in the drive again, and had actually never ceased to run even while he was screaming into the white man's face.

Behind him the white man was shouting, "My horse! Fetch my horse!" and he thought for an instant of cutting across the park and climbing the fence into the road, but he did not know the park nor how high the vine-massed fence might be and he dared not risk it. So he ran on down the drive, blood and breath roaring; presently he was in the road again though he could not see it. He could not hear either: the galloping mare was almost upon him before he heard her, and even then he held his course, as if the very urgency of his wild grief and need must in a moment more find him wings, waiting until the ultimate instant to hurl himself aside and into the weed-choked roadside ditch as the horse thundered past and on, for an instant in furious silhouette against the stars, the tranquil early summer night sky which, even before the shape of the horse and rider vanished, stained abruptly and violently upward: a long, swirling roar incredible and soundless, blotting the stars, and he springing up and into the road again, running again, knowing it was too late yet still running even after he heard the shot and, an instant later, two shots, pausing now without knowing he had ceased to run, crying "Pap! Pap!", running again before he knew he had begun to run, stumbling, tripping over something and scrabbling up again without ceasing to run, looking backward over his shoulder at the glares as he got up, running on among the invisible trees, panting, sobbing, "Father! Father!"

At midnight he was sitting on the crest of a hill. He did not know it was midnight and he did not know how far he had come. But there was no glare behind him now and he sat now, his back toward what he had called home for four days anyhow, his face toward the dark woods which he would enter when breath was strong again, small, shaking steadily in the chill darkness, hugging himself into the remainder of his thin, rotten shirt, the grief and despair now no longer terror and fear but just grief and despair. *Father. My father,* he thought. "He was brave!" He cried suddenly, aloud but not loud, no more than a whisper: "He was! He was in the war! He was in Colonel Sartoris' cav'ry!" not knowing that his father had gone to that war a private in the fine old European sense, wearing no uniform, admitting the authority of and giving fidelity to no man or army or flag, going to war as Malbrouck himself did: for booty — it meant nothing and less than nothing to him if it were enemy booty or his own.

The slow constellations wheeled on. It would be dawn and then sun-up after a while and he would be hungry. But that would be to-morrow and now he was only cold, and walking would cure that. His breathing was easier now and he decided to get up and go on, and then he found that he had been asleep because he knew it was almost dawn, the night almost over. He could tell that from the whippoorwills. They were everywhere now among the dark trees below him, constant and inflectioned and ceaseless, so that, as the instant for giving over to the day birds drew nearer and nearer, there was no interval at all between them. He got up. He was a little stiff, but walking would cure that too as it would the cold, and soon there would be the sun. He went on down the hill, toward the dark woods within which the liquid silver voices of the birds called unceasing — the rapid and urgent beating of the urgent and quiring heart of the late spring night. He did not look back.

Ernest Hemingway (1899–1961)

The Short Happy Life of Francis Macomber

It was now lunch time and they were all sitting under the double green fly of the dining tent pretending that nothing had happened.

"Will you have lime juice or lemon squash?" Macomber asked.

"I'll have a gimlet," Robert Wilson told him.

"I'll have a gimlet too. I need something." Macomber's wife said.

"I suppose it's the thing to do," Macomber agreed. "Tell him to make three gimlets."

The mess boy had started them already, lifting the bottles out of the canvas cooling bags that sweated wet in the wind that blew through the trees that shaded the tents.

"What had I ought to give them?" Macomber asked.

"A quid would be plenty," Wilson told him. "You don't want to spoil them."

"Will the headman distribute it?"

"Absolutely."

Francis Macomber had, half an hour before, been carried to his tent from the edge of the camp in triumph on the arms and shoulders of the cook, the personal boys, the skinner and the porters. The gun-bearers had taken no part in the demonstration. When the native boys put him down at the door of his tent, he had shaken all their hands, received their congratulations, and then gone into the tent and sat on the bed until his wife came in. She did not speak to him when she came in and he left the tent at once to wash his face and hands in the portable wash basin outside and go over to the dining tent to sit in a comfortable canvas chair in the breeze and the shade.

"You've got your lion," Robert Wilson said to him, "and a damned fine one too."

Mrs. Macomber looked at Wilson quickly. She was an extremely handsome and well-kept woman of the beauty and social position which had, five years before, commanded five thousand dollars as the price of endorsing, with photographs, a beauty product which she had never used. She had been married to Francis Macomber for eleven years.

"He is a good lion, isn't he?" Macomber said. His wife looked at him now. She looked at both these men as though she had never seen them before.

One, Wilson, the white hunter, she knew she had never truly seen before. He was about middle height with sandy hair, a stubby mustache, a very red face and extremely cold blue eyes with faint white wrinkles at the corners that grooved merrily when he smiled. He smiled at her now and she looked away from his face at the way his shoulders sloped in the loose tunic he wore with the four big cartridges held in loops where the left breast procket should have been, at his big brown hands, his old slacks, his very dirty boots and back to his red face again. She noticed where the baked red of his face stopped in a white line that marked the circle left by his Stetson hat that hung now from one of the pegs of the tent pole.

"Well, here's to the lion," Robert Wilson said. He smiled at her again and, not smiling, she looked curiously at her husband.

Francis Macomber was very tall, very well built if you did not mind that length of bone, dark, his hair cropped like an oarsman, rather thin-lipped, and was considered handsome. He was dressed in the same sort of safari clothes that Wilson wore except that his were new, he was thirty-five years old, kept himself very fit, was good at court games, had a number of big-game fishing records, and had just shown himself, very publicly, to be a coward.

"Here's to the lion," he said. "I can't ever thank you for what you did."

Margaret, his wife, looked away from him and back to Wilson.

"Let's not talk about the lion," she said.

Wilson looked over at her without smiling and now she smiled at him.

"It's been a very strange day," she said. "Hadn't you ought to put your hat on even under the canvas at noon? You told me that, you know."

"Might put it on," said Wilson.

"You know you have a very red face, Mr. Wilson," she told him and smiled again.

"Drink," said Wilson.

"I don't think so," she said. "Francis drinks a great deal, but his face is never red."

"It's red today," Macomber tried a joke.

"No," said Margaret. "It's mine that's red today. But Mr. Wilson's is always red."

"Must be racial," said Wilson. "I say, you wouldn't like to drop my beauty as a topic, would you?"

"I've just started on it."

"Let's chuck it," said Wilson.

"Conversation is going to be so difficult," Margaret said.

"Don't be silly, Margot," her husband said.

"No difficulty," Wilson said. "Got a damn fine lion."

Margot looked at them both and they both saw that she was going to cry. Wilson had seen it coming for a long time and he dreaded it. Macomber was past dreading it.

"I wish it hadn't happened. Oh, I wish it hadn't happened," she said and started for her tent. She made no noise of crying but they could see that her shoulders were shaking under the rose-colored, sun-proofed shirt she wore.

"Women upset," said Wilson to the tall man. "Amounts to nothing. Strain on the nerves and one thing'n another."

"No," said Macomber. "I suppose that I rate that for the rest of my life now."

"Nonsense. Let's have a spot of the giant killer," said Wilson. "Forget the whole thing. Nothing to it anyway."

"We might try," said Macomber. "I won't forget what you did for me though."

"Nothing," said Wilson. "All nonsense."

So they sat there in the shade where the camp was pitched under some wide-topped acacia trees with a boulder-strewn cliff behind them, and a stretch of grass that ran to the bank of a boulder-filled stream in front with forest beyond it, and drank their just-cool lime drinks and avoided one another's eyes while the boys set the table for lunch. Wilson could tell that the boys all knew about it now and when he saw Macomber's personal boy looking curiously at his master while he was putting dishes on the table he snapped at him in Swahili. The boy turned away with his face blank.

"What were you telling him?" Macomber asked.

"Nothing. Told him to look alive or I'd see he got about fifteen of the best."

"What's that? Lashes?"

"It's quite illegal," Wilson said. "You're supposed to fine them."

"Do you still have them whipped?"

"Oh, yes. They could raise a row if they chose to complain. But they don't. They prefer it to the fines."

"How strange!" said Macomber.

"Not strange, really," Wilson said. "Which would you rather do? Take a good birching or lose your pay?"

Then he felt embarrassed at asking it and before Macomber could answer he went on, "We all take a beating every day, you know, one way or another."

This was no better. "Good God," he thought. "I am a diplomat, aren't I?"

"Yes, we take a beating," said Macomber, still not looking at him. "I'm awfully sorry about that lion business. It doesn't have to go any further, does it? I mean no one will hear about it, will they?"

"You mean will I tell it at the Mathaiga Club?" Wilson looked at him now coldly. He had not expected this. So he's a bloody four-letter man as well as a bloody coward, he thought. I rather liked him too until today. But how is one to know about an American?

"No," said Wilson. "I'm a professional hunter. We never talk about our clients. You can be quite easy on that. It's supposed to be bad form to ask us not to talk though."

He had decided now that to break would be much easier. He would eat, then, by himself and could read a book with his meals. They would eat by themselves. He would see them through the safari on a very formal basis — what was it the French called it? Distinguished consideration — and it would be a damn sight easier than having to go through this emotional trash. He'd insult him and make a good clean break. Then he could read a book with his meals and he'd still be drinking their whisky. That was the phrase for it when a safari went bad. You ran into another white hunter and you asked, "How is everything going?" and he answered, "Oh, I'm still drinking their whisky," and you knew everything had gone to pot.

"I'm sorry," Macomber said and looked at him with his American face that would stay adolescent until it became middle-aged, and Wilson noted his crew-cropped hair, fine eyes only faintly shifty, good nose, thin lips and handsome jaw. "I'm sorry I didn't realize that. There are lots of things I don't know."

So what could he do, Wilson thought. He was all ready to break it off quickly and neatly and here the beggar was apologizing after he had just insulted him. He made one more attempt. "Don't worry about me talking," he said. "I have a living to make. You know in Africa no woman ever misses her lion and no white man ever bolts."

"I bolted like a rabbit," Macomber said.

Now what in hell were you going to do about a man who talked like that, Wilson wondered.

Wilson looked at Macomber with his flat, blue, machine-gunner's eyes and the other smiled back at him. He had a pleasant smile if you did not notice how his eyes showed when he was hurt.

"Maybe I can fix it up on buffalo," he said. "We're after them next, aren't we?"

"In the morning if you like," Wilson told him. Perhaps he had been wrong. This was certainly the way to take it. You most certainly could not tell a damned thing about an American. He was all for Macomber again. If you could forget the morning. But, of course, you couldn't. The morning had been about as bad as they come.

"Here comes the Memsahib," he said. She was walking over from her tent looking refreshed and cheerful and quite lovely. She had a very perfect oval face, so perfect that you expected her to be stupid. But she wasn't stupid, Wilson thought, no, not stupid.

"How is the beautiful red-faced Mr. Wilson? Are you feeling better, Francis, my pearl?"

"Oh, much," said Macomber.

"I've dropped the whole thing," she said, sitting down at the table. "What importance is there to whether Francis is any good at killing lions? That's not his trade. That's Mr. Wilson's trade. Mr. Wilson is really very impressive killing anything. You do kill anything, don't you?"

"Oh, anything," said Wilson. "Simply anything." They are, he thought, the hardest in the world; the hardest, the cruelest, the most predatory and the most attractive and their men have softened or gone to pieces nervously as they have hardened. Or is it that they pick men they can handle? They can't know that much at the age they marry, he thought. He was grateful that he had gone through his education on American women before now because this was a very attractive one.

"We're going after buff in the morning," he told her.

"I'm coming," she said.

"No, you're not."

"Oh, yes, I am. Mayn't I, Francis?"

"Why not stay in camp?"

"Not for anything," she said. "I wouldn't miss something like today for anything."

When she left, Wilson was thinking, when she went off to cry, she seemed a hell of a fine woman. She seemed to understand, to realize, to be hurt for him and for herself and to know how things really stood. She is away for twenty minutes and now she is back, simply enamelled in that American female cruelty. They are the damnedest women. Really the damnedest.

"We'll put on another show for you tomorrow," Francis Macomber said.

"You're not coming," Wilson said.

"You're very mistaken," she told him. "And I want *so* to see you perform again. You were lovely this morning. That is if blowing things' heads off is lovely."

"Here's the lunch," said Wilson. "You're very merry, aren't you?"

"Why not? I didn't come out here to be dull."

"Well, it hasn't been dull," Wilson said. He could see the boulders in the river and the high bank beyond with the trees and he remembered the morning.

"Oh, no," she said. "It's been charming. And tomorrow. You don't know how I look forward to tomorrow."

"That's eland he's offering you," Wilson said.

"They're the big cowy things that jump like hares, aren't they?"

"I suppose that describes them," Wilson said.

"It's very good meat," Macomber said.

"Did you shoot it, Francis?" she asked.

"Yes."

"They're not dangerous, are they?"

"Only if they fall on you," Wilson told her.

"I'm so glad."

"Why not let up on the bitchery just a little, Margot," Macomber said, cutting the eland steak and putting some mashed potato, gravy and carrot on the down-turned fork that tined through the piece of meat.

"I suppose I could," she said, "since you put it so prettily."

"Tonight we'll have champagne for the lion," Wilson said. "It's a bit too hot at noon."

"Oh, the lion," Margot said. "I'd forgotten the lion!"

So, Robert Wilson thought to himself, she *is* giving him a ride, isn't she? Or do you suppose that's her idea of putting up a good show? How should a woman act when she discovers her husband is a bloody coward? She's damn cruel but they're all cruel. They govern, of course, and to govern one has to be cruel sometimes. Still, I've seen enough of their damn terrorism.

"Have some more eland," he said to her politely.

That afternoon, late, Wilson and Macomber went out in the motor car with the native driver and the two gun-bearers. Mrs. Macomber stayed in the camp. It was too hot to go out, she said, and she was going with them in the early morning. As they drove off Wilson saw her standing under the big tree, looking pretty rather than beautiful in her faintly rosy khaki, her dark hair drawn back off her forehead and gathered in a knot low on her neck, her face as fresh, he thought, as though she were in England. She waved to them as the car went off through the swale of high grass and curved around through the trees into the small hills of orchard bush.

In the orchard bush they found a herd of impala, and leaving the car they stalked one old ram with long, wide-spread horns and Macomber killed it with a very creditable shot that knocked the buck down at a good two hundred yards and sent the herd off bounding wildly and leaping over one another's backs in long, leg-drawn-up leaps as unbelievable and as floating as those one makes sometimes in dreams.

"That was a good shot," Wilson said. "They're a small target."

"Is it a worth-while head?" Macomber asked.

"It's excellent," Wilson told him. "You shoot like that and you'll have no trouble."

"Do you think we'll find buffalo tomorrow?"

"There's a good chance of it. They feed out early in the morning and with luck we may catch them in the open."

"I'd like to clear away that lion business," Macomber said. "It's not very pleasant to have your wife see you do something like that."

I should think it would be even more unpleasant to do it, Wilson thought, wife or no wife, or to talk about it having done it. But he said, "I wouldn't think about that any more. Any one could be upset by his first lion. That's all over."

But that night after dinner and a whisky and soda by the fire before going to bed, as Francis Macomber lay on his cot with the mosquito bar over him and listened to the night noises it was not all over. It was neither all over nor was it beginning. It was there exactly as it happened with some parts of it indelibly emphasized and he was miserably ashamed at it. But more than shame he felt cold, hollow fear in him. The fear was still there like a cold slimy hollow in all the emptiness where once his confidence had been and it made him feel sick. It was still there with him now.

It had started the night before when he had wakened and heard the lion roaring somewhere up along the river. It was a deep sound and at the end there were sort of coughing grunts that made him seem just outside the tent, and when Francis Macomber woke in the night to hear it he was afraid. He could hear his wife breathing quietly, asleep. There was no one to tell he was afraid, nor to be afraid with him, and, lying alone, he did not know the Somali proverb that says a brave man is always frightened three times by a lion; when he first sees his track, when he first hears him roar and when he first confronts him. Then while they were eating breakfast by lantern light out in the dining tent, before the sun was up, the lion roared again and Francis thought he was just at the edge of camp.

"Sounds like an old-timer," Robert Wilson said, looking up from his kippers and coffee. "Listen to him cough."

"Is he very close?"

"A mile or so up the stream."

"Will we see him?"

"We'll have a look."

"Does his roaring carry that far? It sounds as though he were right in camp."

"Carries a hell of a long way," said Robert Wilson. "It's strange the way it carries. Hope he's a shootable cat. The boys said there was a very big one about here."

"If I get a shot, where should I hit him," Macomber asked, "to stop him?"

"In the shoulders," Wilson said. "In the neck if you can make it. Shoot for bone. Break him down."

"I hope I can place it properly," Macomber said.

"You shoot very well," Wilson told him. "Take your time. Make sure of him. The first one in is the one that counts."

"What range will it be?"

"Can't tell. Lion has something to say about that. Don't shoot unless it's close enough so you can make sure."

"At under a hundred yards?" Macomber asked.

Wilson looked at him quickly.

"Hundred's about right. Might have to take him a bit under. Shouldn't chance a shot at much over that. A hundred's a decent range. You can hit him wherever you want at that. Here comes the Memsahib."

"Good morning," she said. "Are we going after that lion?"

"As soon as you deal with your breakfast," Wilson said. "How are you feeling?"

"Marvellous," she said. "I'm very excited."

"I'll just go and see that everything is ready." Wilson went off. As he left the lion roared again.

"Noisy beggar," Wilson said. "We'll put a stop to that."

"What's the matter, Francis?" his wife asked him.

"Nothing," Macomber said.

"Yes, there is," she said. "What are you upset about?"

"Nothing," he said.

"Tell me," she looked at him. "Don't you feel well?"

"It's that damned roaring," he said. "It's been going on all night, you know."

"Why didn't you wake me," she said. "I'd love to have heard it."

"I've got to kill the damned thing," Macomber said, miserably.

"Well, that's what you're out here for, isn't it?"

"Yes. But I'm nervous. Hearing the thing roar gets on my nerves."

"Well then, as Wilson said, kill him and stop his roaring."

"Yes, darling," said Francis Macomber. "It sounds easy, doesn't it?"

"You're not afraid, are you?"

"Of course not. But I'm nervous from hearing him roar all night."

"You'll kill him marvellously," she said. "I know you will. I'm awfully anxious to see it."

"Finish your breakfast and we'll be starting."

"It's not light yet," she said. "This is a ridiculous hour."

Just then the lion roared in a deep-chested moaning, suddenly guttural, ascending vibration that seemed to shake the air and ended in a sigh and a heavy, deep-chested grunt.

"He sounds almost here," Macomber's wife said.

"My God," said Macomber. "I hate that damned noise."

"It's very impressive."

"Impressive. It's frightful."

Robert Wilson came up then carrying his short, ugly, shockingly big-bored .505 Gibbs and grinning.

"Come on," he said. "Your gun-bearer has your Springfield and the big gun. Everything's in the car. Have you solids?"

"Yes."

"I'm ready," Mrs. Macomber said.

"Must make him stop that racket," Wilson said. "You get in front. The Memsahib can sit back here with me."

They climbed into the motor car and, in the gray first daylight, moved off up the river through the trees. Macomber opened the breech of his rifle and saw he had metal-cased bullets, shut the bolt and put the rifle on safety. He saw his hand was trembling. He felt in his pocket for more cartridges and moved his fingers over the cartridges in the loops of his tunic front. He turned back to where Wilson sat in the rear seat of the doorless, box-bodied motor car beside his wife, them both grinning, with excitement, and Wilson leaned forward and whispered,

"See the birds dropping. Means the old boy has left his kill."

On the far bank of the stream Macomber could see, above the trees, vultures circling and plummeting down.

"Chances are he'll come to drink along here," Wilson whispered. "Before he goes to lay up. Keep an eye out."

They were driving slowly along the high bank of the stream which here cut deeply to its boulder-filled bed, and they wound in and out through big trees as they drove. Macomber was watching the opposite bank when he felt Wilson take hold of his arm. The car stopped.

"There he is," he heard the whisper. "Ahead and to the right. Get out and take him. He's a marvellous lion."

Macomber saw the lion now. He was standing almost broadside, his great head up and turned toward them. The early morning breeze that blew toward them was just stirring his dark mane, and the lion looked huge, silhouetted on the rise of bank in the gray morning light, his shoulders heavy, his barrel of a body bulking smoothly.

"How far is he?" asked Macomber, raising his rifle.

"About seventy-five. Get out and take him."

"Why not shoot from where I am?"

"You don't shoot them from cars," he heard Wilson saying in his ear. "Get out. He's not going to stay there all day."

Macomber stepped out of the curved opening at the side of the front seat, onto the step and down onto the ground. The lion still stood looking majestically and coolly toward this object that his eyes only showed in silhouette, bulking like some super-rhino. There was no man smell carried toward him and he watched the object, moving his great head a little from side to side. Then watching the object, not afraid, but hesitating before going down the bank to drink with such a thing opposite him, he saw a man figure detach itself from it and he turned his heavy head and swung away toward the cover of the trees as he heard a cracking crash and felt the slam of a .30–06 220-grain solid bullet that bit his flank and ripped in sudden hot scalding nausea through his stomach. He trotted, heavy, big-footed, swinging wounded full-bellied, through the trees toward the tall grass and cover, and the crash came again to go past him ripping the air apart. Then it crashed again and he felt the blow as it hit his lower ribs and ripped on through, blood sudden hot and frothy in his mouth, and he galloped toward the high grass where he could crouch and not be seen and make them bring the crashing thing close enough so he could make a rush and get the man that held it.

Macomber had not thought how the lion felt as he got out of the car. He only knew his hands were shaking and as he walked away from the car it was almost impossible for him to make his legs move. They were stiff in the thighs, but he could feel the muscles fluttering. He raised the rifle, sighted on the junction of the lion's head and shoulders and pulled the trigger. Nothing happened though he pulled until he thought his finger would break. Then he knew he had the safety on and as he lowered the rifle to move the safety over he moved another frozen pace forward, and the lion seeing his silhouette now clear of the silhouette of the car, turned and started off at a trot, and, as Macomber fired, he heard a whunk that meant that the bullet was home; but the lion kept on going. Macomber shot again and every one saw the bullet throw a spout of dirt beyond the trotting lion. He shot again, remembering to lower his aim, and they all heard the bullet hit, and the lion went into a gallop and was in the tall grass before he had the bolt pushed forward.

Macomber stood there feeling sick at his stomach, his hands that held the Springfield still cocked, shaking, and his wife and Robert Wilson were standing by him. Beside him too were the two gun-bearers chattering in Wakamba.

"I hit him," Macomber said. "I hit him twice."

"You gut-shot him and you hit him somewhere forward," Wilson said without enthusiasm. The gun-bearers looked very grave. They were silent now.

"You may have killed him," Wilson went on. "We'll have to wait a while before we go in to find out."

"What do you mean?"

"Let him get sick before we follow him up."

"Oh," said Macomber.

"He's a hell of a fine lion," Wilson said cheerfully. "He's gotten into a bad place though."

"Why is it bad?"

"Can't see him until you're on him."

"Oh," said Macomber.

"Come on," said Wilson. "The Memsahib can stay here in the car. We'll go to have a look at the blood spoor."

"Stay here, Margot," Macomber said to his wife. His mouth was very dry and it was hard for him to talk.

"Why?" she asked.

"Wilson says to."

"We're going to have a look," Wilson said. "You stay here. You can see even better from here."

"All right."

Wilson spoke in Swahili to the driver. He nodded and said, "Yes, Bwana."

Then they went down the steep bank and across the stream, climbing over and around the boulders and up the other bank, pulling up by some projecting roots, and along it until they found where the lion had been trotting when Macomber first shot. There was dark blood on the short grass that the gun-bearers pointed out with grass stems, and that ran away behind the river bank trees.

"What do we do?" asked Macomber.

"Not much choice," said Wilson. "We can't bring the car over. Bank's too steep. We'll let him stiffen up a bit and then you and I'll go in and have a look for him."

"Can't we set the grass on fire?" Macomber asked.

"Too green."

"Can't we send beaters?"

Wilson looked at him appraisingly. "Of course we can," he said. "But it's just a touch murderous. You see we know the lion's wounded. You can drive an unwounded lion — he'll move on ahead of a noise — but a wounded lion's going to charge. You can't see him until you're right on him. He'll make himself perfectly flat in cover you wouldn't think would hide a hare. You can't very well send boys in there to that sort of a show. Somebody is bound to get mauled."

"What about the gun-bearers?"

"Oh, they'll go with us. It's their *shauri*. You see, they signed on for it. They don't look too happy though, do they?"

"I don't want to go in there," said Macomber. It was out before he knew he'd said it.

"Neither do I," said Wilson very cheerily. "Really no choice though." Then, as an afterthought, he glanced at Macomber and saw suddenly how he was trembling and the pitiful look on his face.

"You don't have to go in, of course," he said. "That's what I'm hired for, you know. That's why I'm so expensive."

"You mean you'd go in by yourself? Why not leave him there?"

Robert Wilson, whose entire occupation had been with the lion and the problem he presented, and who had not been thinking about Macomber except to note that he was rather windy, suddenly felt as though he had opened the wrong door in a hotel and seen something shameful.

"What do you mean?"

"Why not just leave him?"

"You mean pretend to ourselves he hasn't been hit?"

"No. Just drop it."

"It isn't done."

"Why not?"

"For one thing, he's certain to be suffering. For another, some one else might run onto him."

"I see."

"But you don't have to have anything to do with it."

"I'd like to," Macomber said. "I'm just scared, you know."

"I'll go ahead when we go in," Wilson said, "with Kongoni tracking. You keep behind me and a little to one side. Chances are we'll hear him growl. If we see him we'll both shoot. Don't worry about anything. I'll keep you backed up. As a matter of fact, you know, perhaps you'd better not go. It might be much better. Why don't you go over and join the Memsahib while I just get it over with?"

"No, I want to go."

"All right," said Wilson. "But don't go in if you don't want to. This is my *shauri* now, you know."

"I want to go," said Macomber.

They sat under a tree and smoked.

"Want to go back and speak to the Memsahib while we're waiting?" Wilson asked.

"No."

"I'll just step back and tell her to be patient."

"Good," said Macomber. He sat there, sweating under his arms, his mouth dry, his stomach hollow feeling, wanting to find courage to tell Wilson to go on and finish off the lion without him. He could not know that Wilson was furious because he had not noticed the state he was in earlier and sent him back to his wife. While he sat there Wilson came up. "I have your big gun," he said. "Take it. We've given him time, I think. Come on."

Macomber took the big gun and Wilson said:

"Keep behind me and about five yards to the right and do exactly as I tell you." Then he spoke in Swahili to the two gun-bearers who looked the picture of gloom.

"Let's go," he said.

"Could I have a drink of water?" Macomber asked. Wilson spoke to the older gun-bearer, who wore a canteen on his belt, and the man unbuckled it, unscrewed the top and handed it to Macomber, who took it noticing how heavy it seemed and how hairy and shoddy the felt covering was in his hand. He raised it to drink and looked ahead at the high grass with the flat-topped trees behind it. A breeze was blowing toward them and the grass rippled gently in the wind. He looked at the gun-bearer and he could see the gun-bearer was suffering too with fear.

Thirty-five yards into the grass the big lion lay flattened out along the ground. His ears were back and his only movement was a slight twitching up and down of his long, black-tufted tail. He had turned at bay as soon as he had reached this cover and he was sick with the wound through his full belly, and weakening with the wound through his lungs that brought a thin foamy red to his mouth each time he breathed. His flanks were wet and hot and flies were on the little openings the solid bullets had made in his tawny hide, and his big yellow eyes, narrowed with hate, looked straight ahead, only blinking when the pain came as he breathed, and his claws dug in the soft baked earth. All of him, pain, sickness, hatred and all of his remaining strength, was tightening into an absolute concentration for a rush. He could hear the men talking and he waited, gathering all of himself into this preparation for a charge as soon as the men would come into the grass. As he heard their voices his tail stiffened to twitch up and down, and, as they came into the edge of the grass, he made a coughing grunt and charged.

Kongoni, the old gun-bearer, in the lead watching the blood spoor, Wilson watching the grass for any movement, his big gun ready, the second gun-bearer looking ahead and listening, Macomber close to Wilson, his rifle cocked, they had just moved into the grass when Macomber heard the blood-choked coughing grunt, and saw the swishing rush in the grass. The next thing he knew he was running; running wildly, in panic in the open, running toward the stream.

He heard the *ca-ra-wong!* of Wilson's big rifle, and again in a second crashing *carawong!* and turning saw the lion, horrible-looking now, with half his head seeming to be gone, crawling toward Wilson in the edge of the tall grass while the red-faced man worked the bolt on the short ugly rifle and aimed carefully as another blasting *carawong!* came from the muzzle, and the crawling, heavy, yellow bulk of the lion stiffened and the huge, mutilated head slid forward and Macomber, standing by himself in the clearing where he had run, holding a loaded rifle, while two black men and a white man looked back at him in contempt, knew the lion was dead. He came toward Wilson, his tallness all seeming a naked reproach, and Wilson looked at him and said:

"Want to take pictures?"

"No," he said.

That was all any one had said until they reached the motor car. Then Wilson had said:

"Hell of a fine lion. Boys will skin him out. We might as well stay here in the shade."

Macomber's wife had not looked at him nor he at her and he had sat by her in the back seat with Wilson sitting in the front seat. Once he had reached over and taken his wife's hand without looking at her and she had removed her hand from his. Looking across the stream to where the gun-bearers were skinning out the lion he could see that she had been able to see the whole thing. While they sat there his wife had reached forward and put her hand on Wilson's shoulder. He turned and she had leaned forward over the low seat and kissed him on the mouth.

"Oh, I say," said Wilson, going redder than his natural baked color.

"Mr. Robert Wilson," she said. "The beautiful red-faced Mr. Robert Wilson."

Then she sat down beside Macomber again and looked away across the stream to where the lion lay, with uplifted, white-muscled, tendon-marked naked forearms, and white bloating belly, as the black men fleshed away the skin. Finally the gun-bearers brought the skin over, wet and heavy, and climbed in behind with it, rolling it up before they got in, and the motor car started. No one had said anything more until they were back in camp.

That was the story of the lion. Macomber did not know how the lion had felt before he started his rush, nor during it when the unbelievable smash of the .505 with a muzzle velocity of two tons had hit him in the mouth, nor what kept him coming after that, when the second ripping crash had smashed his hind quarters and he had come crawling on toward the crashing, blasting thing that had destroyed him. Wilson knew something about it and only expressed it by saying, "Damned fine lion," but Macomber did not know how Wilson felt about things either. He did not know how his wife felt except that she was through with him.

His wife had been through with him before but it never lasted. He was very wealthy, and would be much wealthier, and he knew she would not leave him ever now. That was one of the few things that he really knew. He knew about that, about motor cycles — that was earliest — about motor cars, about duck-shooting, about fishing, trout, salmon and big-sea, about sex in books, many books, too many books, about all court games, about dogs, not much about horses, about hanging on to his money, about most of the other things his world dealt in, and about his wife not leaving him. His wife had been a great beauty and she was still a great beauty in Africa, but she was not a great enough beauty any more at home to be able to leave him and better herself and she knew it and he knew it. She had missed the chance to leave him and he knew it. If he had been better with women she would probably have started to worry about him getting another new beautiful wife; but she knew too much about him to worry about him either. Also, he had always had a great tolerance which seemed the nicest thing about him if it were not the most sinister.

All in all they were known as a comparatively happily married couple, one of those whose disruption is often rumored but never occurs, and as the society columnist put it, they were adding more than a spice of *adventure* to their much envied and ever-enduring *Romance* by a *Safari* in what was known as *Darkest Africa* until the Martin Johnsons lighted it on so many silver screens where they were pursuing *Old Simba* the lion, the buffalo, *Tembo* the elephant and as well collecting specimens for the Museum of Natural History. This same columnist had reported them *on the verge* at least three times in the past and they had been. But they always made it up. They had a sound basis of union. Margot was too beautiful for Macomber to divorce her and Macomber had too much money for Margot ever to leave him.

It was now about three o'clock in the morning and Francis Macomber, who had been asleep a little while after he had stopped thinking about the lion, wakened and then slept again, woke suddenly, frightened in a dream of the blood-headed lion standing over him, and listening while his heart pounded, he realized that his wife was not in the other cot in the tent. He lay awake with that knowledge for two hours.

At the end of that time his wife came into the tent, lifted her mosquito bar and crawled cozily into bed.

"Where have you been?" Macomber asked in the darkness.

"Hello," she said. "Are you awake?"

"Where have you been?"

"I just went out to get a breath of air."

"You did, like hell."

"What do you want me to say, darling?"

"Where have you been?"

"Out to get a breath of air."

"That's a new name for it. You *are* a bitch."

"Well, you're a coward."

"All right," he said. "What of it?"

"Nothing as far as I'm concerned. But please let's not talk, darling, because I'm very sleepy."

"You think that I'll take anything."

"I know you will, sweet."

"Well, I won't."

"Please, darling, let's not talk. I'm so very sleepy."

"There wasn't going to be any of that. You promised there wouldn't be."

"Well, there is now," she said sweetly.

"You said if we made this trip that there would be none of that. You promised."

"Yes, darling. That's the way I meant it to be. But the trip was spoiled yesterday. We don't have to talk about it, do we?"

"You don't wait long when you have an advantage, do you?"

"Please let's not talk. I'm so sleepy, darling."

"I'm going to talk."

"Don't mind me then, because I'm going to sleep." And she did.

At breakfast they were all three at the table before daylight and Francis Macomber found that, of all the many men that he had hated, he hated Robert Wilson the most.

"Sleep well?" Wilson asked in his throaty voice, filling a pipe.

"Did you?"

"Topping," the white hunter told him.

You bastard, thought Macomber, you insolent bastard.

So she woke him when she came in, Wilson thought, looking at them both with his flat, cold eyes. Well, why doesn't he keep his wife where she belongs? What does he think I am, a bloody plaster saint? Let him keep her where she belongs. It's his own fault.

"Do you think we'll find buffalo?" Margot asked, pushing away a dish of apricots.

"Chance of it," Wilson said and smiled at her. "Why don't you stay in camp?"

"Not for anything," she told him.

"Why not order her to stay in camp?" Wilson said to Macomber.

"You order her," said Macomber coldly.

"Let's not have any ordering, nor," turning to Macomber, "any silliness, Francis," Margot said quite pleasantly.

"Are you ready to start?" Macomber asked.

"Any time," Wilson told him. "Do you want the Memsahib to go?"

"Does it make any difference whether I do or not?"

The hell with it, thought Robert Wilson. The utter complete hell with it. So this is what it's going to be like. Well, this is what it's going to be like, then.

"Makes no difference," he said.

"You're sure you wouldn't like to stay in camp with her yourself and let me go out and hunt the buffalo?" Macomber asked.

"Can't do that," said Wilson. "Wouldn't talk rot if I were you."

"I'm not talking rot. I'm disgusted."

"Bad word, disgusted."

"Francis, will you please try to speak sensibly?" his wife said.

"I speak too damned sensibly," Macomber said. "Did you ever eat such filthy food?"

"Something wrong with the food?" asked Wilson quietly.

"No more than with everything else."

"I'd pull yourself together, laddybuck," Wilson said very quietly. "There's a boy waits at table that understands a little English."

"The hell with him."

Wilson stood up and puffing on his pipe strolled away, speaking a few words in Swahili to one of the gun-bearers who was standing waiting for him. Macomber and his wife sat on at the table. He was staring at his coffee cup.

"If you make a scene I'll leave you, darling," Margot said quietly.

"No, you won't."

"You can try it and see."

"You won't leave me."

"No," she said. "I won't leave you and you'll behave yourself."

"Behave myself? That's a way to talk. Behave myself."

"Yes. Behave yourself."

"Why don't *you* try behaving?"

"I've tried it so long. So very long."

"I hate that red-faced swine," Macomber said. "I loathe the sight of him."

"He's really *very* nice."

"Oh, *shut up*," Macomber almost shouted. Just then the car came up and stopped in front of the dining tent and the driver and the two gun-bearers got out. Wilson walked over and looked at the husband and wife sitting there at the table.

"Going shooting?" he asked.

"Yes," said Macomber, standing up. "Yes."

"Better bring a woolly. It will be cool in the car," Wilson said.

"I'll get my leather jacket," Margot said.

"The boy has it," Wilson told her. He climbed into the front with the driver and Francis Macomber and his wife sat, not speaking, in the back seat.

Hope the silly beggar doesn't take a notion to blow the back of my head off, Wilson thought to himself. Women *are* a nuisance on safari.

The car was grinding down to cross the river at a pebbly ford in the gray daylight and then climbed, angling up the steep bank, where Wilson had ordered a way shovelled out the day before so they could reach the parklike wooded rolling country on the far side.

It was a good morning, Wilson thought. There was a heavy dew and as the wheels went through the grass and low bushes he could smell the odor of the crushed fronds. It was an odor like verbena and he liked this early morning smell of the dew, the crushed bracken and the look of the tree trunks showing black through the early morning mist, as the car made its way through the untracked, parklike country. He had put the two in the back seat out of his mind now and was thinking about buffalo. The buffalo that he was after stayed in the daytime in a thick swamp where it was impossible to get a shot, but in the night they fed out into an open stretch of country and if he could come between them and their swamp with the car, Macomber would have a good chance at them in the open. He did not want to hunt buff with Macomber in thick cover. He did not want to hunt buff or anything else with Macomber at all, but he was a professional hunter and he had hunted with some rare ones in his time. If they got buff today there would only be rhino to come and the poor man would have gone through his dangerous game and things might pick up. He'd have nothing more to do with the woman and Macomber would get over that too. He must have gone through plenty of that before by the look of things. Poor beggar. He must have a way of getting over it. Well, it was the poor sod's own bloody fault.

He, Robert Wilson, carried a double size cot on safari to accommodate any windfalls he might receive. He had hunted for a certain clientele, the international, fast, sporting set, where the women did not feel they were getting their money's worth unless they had shared that cot with the white hunter. He despised them when he was away from them although he liked some of them well enough at the time, but he made his living by them; and their standards were his standards as long as they were hiring him.

They were his standards in all except the shooting. He had his own standards about the killing and they could live up to them or get some one else to hunt them. He knew, too, that they all respected him for this. This Macomber was an odd one though. Damned if he wasn't. Now the wife. Well, the wife. Yes, the wife. Hm, the wife. Well he'd dropped all that. He looked around at them. Macomber sat grim and furious. Margot smiled at him. She looked younger today, more innocent and fresher and not so professionally beautiful. What's in her heart God knows, Wilson thought. She hadn't talked much last night. At that it was a pleasure to see her.

The motor car climbed up a slight rise and went on through the trees and then out into a grassy prairie-like opening and kept in the shelter of the trees along the edge, the driver going slowly and Wilson looking carefully out across the prairie and all along its far side. He stopped the car and studied the opening with his field glasses. Then he motioned to the driver to go on and the car moved slowly along, the driver avoiding wart-hog holes and driving around the mud castles ants had built. Then, looking across the opening, Wilson suddenly turned and said,

"By God, there they are!"

And looking where he pointed, while the car jumped forward and Wilson spoke in rapid Swahili to the driver, Macomber saw three huge, black animals looking almost cylindrical in their long heaviness, like big black tank cars, moving at a gallop across the far edge of the open prairie. They moved at a stiff-necked, stiff bodied gallop and he could see the upswept wide black horns on their heads as they galloped heads out; the heads not moving.

"They're three old bulls," Wilson said. "We'll cut them off before they get to the swamp."

The car was going a wild forty-five miles an hour across the open and as Macomber watched, the buffalo got bigger and bigger until he could see the gray, hairless, scabby look of one huge bull and how his neck was a part of his shoulders and the shiny black of his horns as he galloped a little behind the others that were strung out in that steady plunging gait; and then, the car swaying as though it had just jumped a road, they drew up close and he could see the plunging hugeness of the bull, and the dust in his sparsely haired hide, the wide boss of horn and his outstretched, wide-nostrilled muzzle, and he was raising his rifle when Wilson shouted, "Not from the car, you fool!" and he had no fear, only hatred of Wilson, while the brakes clamped on and the car skidded, plowing sideways to an almost stop and Wilson was out on one side and he on the other, stumbling as his feet hit the still speeding-by of the earth, and then he was shooting at the bull as he moved away, hearing the bullets wunk into him, emptying his rifle at him as he moved steadily away, finally remembering to get his shots forward into the shoulder, and as he fumbled to re-load, he saw the bull was down. Down on his knees, his big head tossing, and seeing the other two still galloping he shot at the leader and hit him. He shot again and missed and he heard the *carawonging* roar as Wilson shot and saw the leading bull slide forward onto his nose.

"Get that other," Wilson said. "Now you're shooting!"

But the other bull was moving steadily at the same gallop and he missed, throwing a spout of dirt, and Wilson missed and the dust rose in a cloud and Wilson shouted, "Come on. He's too far!" and grabbed his arm and they were in the car again, Macomber and Wilson hanging on the sides and rocketing swayingly over the uneven ground, drawing up on the steady, plunging, heavy-necked, straight-moving gallop of the bull.

They were behind him and Macomber was filling his rifle, dropping shells onto the ground, jamming it, clearing the jam, then they were almost up with the bull when Wilson yelled "Stop," and the car skidded so that it almost swung over and Macomber fell forward onto his feet, slammed his bolt forward and fired as far forward as he could aim into the galloping, rounded black back, aimed and shot again, then again, then again, and the bullets, all of them hitting, had no effect on the buffalo that he could see. Then Wilson shot, the roar deafening him, and he could see the bull stagger. Macomber shot again, aiming carefully, and down he came, onto his knees.

"All right," Wilson said. "Nice work. That's the three."

Macomber felt a drunken elation.

"How many times did you shoot?" he asked.

"Just three," Wilson said. "You killed the first bull. The biggest one. I helped you finish the other two. Afraid they might have got into cover. You had them killed. I was just mopping up a little. You shot damn well."

"Let's go to the car," said Macomber. "I want a drink."

"Got to finish off that buff first," Wilson told him. The buffalo was on his knees and he jerked his head furiously and bellowed in pig-eyed, roaring rage as they came toward him.

"Watch he doesn't get up," Wilson said. Then, "Get a little broadside and take him in the neck just behind the ear."

Macomber aimed carefully at the center of the huge, jerking, rage-driven neck and shot. At the shot the head dropped forward.

"That does it," said Wilson. "Got the spine. They're a hell of a looking thing, aren't they?"

"Let's get the drink," said Macomber. In his life he had never felt so good.

In the car Macomber's wife sat very white faced. "You were marvellous, darling," she said to Macomber. "What a ride."

"Was it rough?" Wilson asked.

"It was frightful. I've never been more frightened in my life."

"Let's all have a drink," Macomber said.

"By all means," said Wilson. "Give it to the Memsahib." She drank the neat whisky from the flask and shuddered a little when she swallowed. She handed the flask to Macomber who handed it to Wilson.

"It was frightfully exciting," she said. "It's given me a dreadful headache. I didn't know you were allowed to shoot them from cars though."

"No one shot from cars," said Wilson coldly.

"I mean chase them from cars."

"Wouldn't ordinarily," Wilson said. "Seemed sporting enough to me though while we were doing it. Taking more chance driving that way across the plain full of holes and one thing and another than hunting on foot. Buffalo could have charged us each time we shot if he liked. Gave him every chance. Wouldn't mention it to any one though. It's illegal if that's what you mean."

"It seemed very unfair to me," Margot said, "chasing those big helpless things in a motor car."

"Did it?" said Wilson.

"What would happen if they heard about in Nairobi?"

"I'd lose my license for one thing. Other unpleasantnesses," Wilson said, taking a drink from the flask. "I'd be out of business."

"Really?"

"Yes, really."

"Well," said Macomber, and he smiled for the first time all day. "Now she has something on you."

"You have such a pretty way of putting things, Francis," Margot Macomber said. Wilson looked at them both. If a four-letter man marries a five-letter woman, he was thinking, what number of letters would their children be? What he said was, "We lost a gun-bearer. Did you notice it?"

"My God, no," Macomber said.

"Here he comes," Wilson said. "He's all right. He must have fallen off when we left the first bull."

Approaching them was the middle-aged gun-bearer, limping along in his knitted cap, khaki tunic, shorts and rubber sandals, gloomy-faced and disgusted looking. As he came up he called out to Wilson in Swahili and they all saw the change in the white hunter's face.

"What does he say?" asked Margot.

"He says the first bull got up and went into the bush," Wilson said with no expression in his voice.

"Oh," said Macomber blankly.

"Then it's going to be just like the lion," said Margot, full of anticipation.

"It's not going to be a damned bit like the lion," Wilson told her. "Did you want another drink, Macomber?"

"Thanks, yes," Macomber said. He expected the feeling he had had about the lion to come back but it did not. For the first time in his life he really felt wholly without fear. Instead of fear he had a feeling of definite elation.

"We'll go and have a look at the second bull," Wilson said. "I'll tell the driver to put the car in the shade."

"What are you going to do?" asked Margaret Macomber.

"Take a look at the buff," Wilson said.

"I'll come."

"Come along."

The three of them walked over to where the second buffalo bulked blackly in the open, head forward on the grass, the massive horns swung wide.

"He's a very good head," Wilson said. "That's close to a fifty-inch spread."

Macomber was looking at him with delight.

"He's hateful looking," said Margot. "Can't we go into the shade?"

"Of course," Wilson said. "Look," he said to Macomber, and pointed. "See that patch of bush?"

"Yes."

"That's where the first bull went in. The gun-bearer said when he fell off the bull was down. He was watching us helling along and the other two buff galloping. When he looked up there was the bull up and looking at him. Gun-bearer ran like hell and the bull went off slowly into that bush."

"Can we go in after him now?" asked Macomber eagerly.

Wilson looked at him appraisingly. Damned if this isn't a

strange one, he thought. Yesterday he's scared sick and today he's a ruddy fire eater.

"No, we'll give him a while."

"Let's please go into the shade," Margot said. Her face was white and she looked ill.

They made their way to the car where it stood under a single, wide-spreading tree and all climbed in.

"Chances are he's dead in there," Wilson remarked. "After a little we'll have a look."

Macomber felt a wild unreasonable happiness that he had never known before.

"By God, that was a chase," he said. "I've never felt any such feeling. Wasn't it marvellous, Margot?"

"I hated it."

"Why?"

"I hated it," she said bitterly. "I loathed it."

"You know I don't think I'd ever be afraid of anything again," Macomber said to Wilson. "Something happened in me after we first saw the buff and started after him. Like a dam bursting. It was pure excitement."

"Cleans out your liver," said Wilson. "Damn funny things happen to people."

Macomber's face was shining. "You know something did happen to me," he said. "I feel absolutely different."

His wife said nothing and eyed him strangely. She was sitting far back in the seat and Macomber was sitting forward talking to Wilson who turned sideways talking over the back of the front seat.

"You know, I'd like to try another lion," Macomber said. "I'm really not afraid of them now. After all, what can they do to you?"

"That's it," said Wilson. "Worst one can do is kill you. How does it go? Shakespeare. Damned good. See if I can remember. Oh, damned good. Used to quote it to myself at one time. Let's see. 'By my troth, I care not; a man can die but once; we owe God a death and let it go which way it will, he that dies this year is quit for the next.' Damned fine, eh?"

He was very embarrassed, having brought out this thing he had lived by, but he had seen men come of age before and it always moved him. It was not a matter of their twenty-first birthday.

It had taken a strange chance of hunting, a sudden precipitation into action without opportunity for worrying beforehand, to bring this about with Macomber, but regardless of how it had happened it had most certainly happened. Look at the beggar now, Wilson thought. It's that some of them stay little boys so long, Wilson thought. Sometimes all their lives. Their figures stay boyish when they're fifty. The great American boy-men. Damned strange people. But he liked this Macomber now. Damned strange fellow. Probably meant the end of cuckoldry too. Well, that would be a damned good thing. Damned good thing. Beggar had probably been afraid all his life. Don't know what started it. But over now. Hadn't had time to be afraid with the buff. That and being angry too. Motor car too. Motor cars made it familiar. Be a damn fire eater now. He'd seen it in the war work the same way. More of a change than any loss of virginity. Fear gone like an operation. Something else grew in its place. Main thing a man had. Made him into a man. Women knew it too. No bloody fear.

From the far corner of the seat Margaret Macomber looked at the two of them. There was no change in Wilson. She saw Wilson as she had seen him the day before when she had first realized what a great talent was. But she saw the change in Francis Macomber now.

"Do you have that feeling of happiness about what's going to happen?" Macomber asked, still exploring his new wealth.

"You're not supposed to mention it," Wilson said, looking in the other's face. "Much more fashionable to say you're scared. Mind you, you'll be scared too, plenty of times."

"But you *have* a feeling of happiness about action to come?"

"Yes," said Wilson. "There's that. Doesn't do to talk too much about all this. Talk the whole thing away. No pleasure in anything if you mouth it up too much."

"You're both talking rot," said Margot. "Just because you've chased some helpless animals in a motor car you talk like heroes."

"Sorry," said Wilson. "I have been gassing too much." She's worried about it already, he thought.

"If you don't know what we're talking about why not keep out of it?" Macomber asked his wife.

"You've gotten awfully brave, awfully suddenly," his wife said contemptuously, but her contempt was not secure. She was very afraid of something.

Macomber laughed, a very natural hearty laugh. "You know I *have,*" he said. "I really have."

"Isn't it sort of late?" Margot said bitterly. Because she had done the best she could for many years back and the way they were together now was no one person's fault.

"Not for me," said Macomber.

Margot said nothing but sat back in the corner of the seat.

"Do you think we've given him time enough?" Macomber asked Wilson cheerfully.

"We might have a look," Wilson said. "Have you any solids left?"

"The gun-bearer has some."

Wilson called in Swahili and the older gun-bearer, who was skinning out one of the heads, straightened up, pulled a box of solids out of his pocket and brought them over to Macomber, who filled his magazine and put the remaining shells in his pocket.

"You might as well shoot the Springfield," Wilson said. "You're used to it. We'll leave the Mannlicher in the car with the Memsahib. Your gun-bearer can carry your heavy gun. I've this damned cannon. Now let me tell you about them." He had saved this until the last because he did not want to worry Macomber. "When a buff comes he comes with his head high and thrust straight out. The boss of the horns covers any sort of a brain shot. The only shot is straight into the nose. The only other shot is into his chest or, if you're to one side, into the neck or the shoulders. After they've been hit once they take a hell of a lot of killing. Don't try anything fancy. Take the easiest shot there is. They've finished skinning out that head now. Should we get started?"

He called to the gun-bearers, who came up wiping their hands, and the older one got into the back.

"I'll only take Kongoni," Wilson said. "The other can watch to keep the birds away."

As the car moved slowly across the open space toward the island of brushy trees that ran in a tongue of foliage along a dry water course that cut the open swale, Macomber felt his heart pounding and his mouth was dry again, but it was excitement, not fear.

"Here's where he went in," Wilson said. Then to the gun-bearer in Swahili, "Take the blood spoor."

The car was parallel to the patch of bush. Macomber, Wilson and the gun-bearer got down. Macomber, looking back, saw his wife, with the rifle by her side, looking at him. He waved to her and she did not wave back.

The brush was very thick ahead and the ground was dry. The middle-aged gun-bearer was sweating heavily and Wilson had his hat down over his eyes and his red neck showed just ahead of Macomber. Suddenly the gun-bearer said something in Swahili to Wilson and ran forward.

"He's dead in there," Wilson said. "Good work," and he turned to grip Macomber's hand and as they shook hands, grinning at each other, the gun-bearer shouted wildly and they saw him coming out of the bush sideways, fast as a crab, and the bull coming, nose out, mouth tight closed, blood dripping, massive head straight out, coming in a charge, his little pig eyes blood-shot as he looked at them. Wilson, who was ahead, was kneeling shooting, and Macomber, as he fired, unhearing his shot in the roaring of Wilson's gun, saw fragments like slate burst from the huge boss of the horns, and the head jerked, he shot again at the wide nostrils and saw the horns jolt again and fragments fly, and he did not see Wilson now and, aiming carefully, shot again with the buffalo's huge bulk almost on him and his rifle almost level with the on-coming head, nose out, and he could see the little wicked eyes and the head started to lower and he felt a sudden white-hot, blinding flash explode inside his head and that was all he ever felt.

Wilson had ducked to one side to get in a shoulder shot. Macomber had stood solid and shot for the nose, shooting a touch high each time and hitting the heavy horns, splintering and chipping them like hitting a slate roof, and Mrs. Macomber, in the car, had shot at the buffalo with the 6.5 Mannlicher as it seemed about to gore Macomber and had hit her husband about two inches up and a little to one side of the base of his skull.

Francis Macomber lay now, face down, not two yards from where the buffalo lay on his side and his wife knelt over him with Wilson beside her.

"I wouldn't turn him over," Wilson said.

The woman was crying hysterically.

"I'd get back in the car," Wilson said. "Where's the rifle?"

She shook her head, her face contorted. The gun-bearer picked up the rifle.

"Leave it as it is," said Wilson. Then, "Go get Abdulla so that he may witness the manner of the accident."

He knelt down, took a handkerchief from his pocket, and spread it over Francis Macomber's crew-cropped head where it lay. The blood sank into the dry, loose earth.

Wilson stood up and saw the buffalo on his side, his legs out, his thinly-haired belly crawling with ticks. "Hell of a good bull," his brain registered automatically. "A good fifty inches, or better. Better." He called to the driver and told him to spread a blanket over the body and stay by it. Then he walked over to the motor car where the woman sat crying in the corner.

"That was a pretty thing to do," he said in a toneless voice. "He *would* have left you too."

"Stop it," she said.

"Of course it's an accident," he said. "I know that."

"Stop it," she said.

"Don't worry," he said. "There will be a certain amount of unpleasantness but I will have some photographs taken that will be very useful at the inquest. There's the testimony of the gun-bearers and the driver too. You're perfectly all right."

"Stop it," she said.

"There's a hell of a lot to be done," he said. "And I'll have to send a truck off to the lake to wireless for a plane to take the three of us into Nairobi. Why didn't you poison him? That's what they do in England."

"Stop it. Stop it. Stop it," the woman cried.

Wilson looked at her with his flat blue eyes.

"I'm through now," he said. "I was a little angry. I'd begun to like your husband."

"Oh, please stop it," she said. "Please, please stop it."

"That's better," Wilson said. "Please is much better. Now I'll stop."

John Steinbeck (1902–1968)

The Chrysanthemums

The high grey-flannel fog of winter closed off the Salinas Valley from the sky and from all the rest of the world. On every side it sat like a lid on the mountains and made of the great valley a closed pot. On the broad, level land floor the gang plows bit deep and left the black earth shining like metal where the shares had cut. On the foothill ranches across the Salinas River, the yellow stubble fields seemed to be bathed in pale cold sunshine, but there was no sunshine in the valley now in December. The thick willow scrub along the river flamed with sharp and positive yellow leaves.

It was a time of quiet and of waiting. The air was cold and tender. A light wind blew up from the southwest so that the farmers were mildly hopeful of a good rain before long; but fog and rain do not go together.

Across the river, on Henry Allen's foothill ranch there was little work to be done, for the hay was cut and stored and the orchards were plowed up to receive the rain deeply when it should come. The cattle on the higher slopes were becoming shaggy and rough-coated.

Elisa Allen, working in her flower garden, looked down across the yard and saw Henry, her husband, talking to two men in business suits. The three of them stood by the tractor shed, each man with one foot on the side of the little Fordson. They smoked cigarettes and studied the machine as they talked.

Elisa watched them for a moment and then went back to her work. She was thirty-five. Her face was lean and strong and her eyes were as clear as water. Her figure looked blocked and heavy in her gardening costume, a man's black hat pulled low down over her eyes, clod-hopper shoes, a figured print dress almost completely covered by a big corduroy apron with four big pockets to hold the snips, the trowel and scratcher, the seeds and the knife she worked with. She wore heavy leather gloves to protect her hands while she worked.

She was cutting down the old year's chrysanthemum stalks with a pair of short and powerful scissors. She looked down toward the men by the tractor shed now and then. Her face was eager and mature and handsome; even her work with the scissors was over-eager, over-powerful. The chrysanthemum stems seemed too small and easy for her energy.

She brushed a cloud of hair out of her eyes with the back of her glove, and left a smudge of earth on her cheek in doing it. Behind her stood the neat white farm house with red geraniums close-banked around it as high as the windows. It was a hard-swept looking little house with hard-polished windows, and a clean mud-mat on the front steps.

Elisa cast another glance toward the tractor shed. The strangers were getting into their Ford coupe. She took off a glove and put her strong fingers down into the forest of new green chrysanthemum sprouts that were growing around the old roots. She spread the leaves and looked down among the close-growing stems. No aphids were there, no sowbugs or snails or cutworms. Her terrier fingers destroyed such pests before they could get started.

Elisa started at the sound of her husband's voice. He had come near quietly, and he leaned over the wire fence that protected her flower garden from cattle and dogs and chickens.

"At it again," he said. "You've got a strong new crop coming."

Elisa straightened her back and pulled on the gardening glove again. "Yes. They'll be strong this coming year." In her tone and on her face there was a little smugness.

"You've got a gift with things," Henry observed. "Some of those yellow chrysanthemums you had this year were ten inches across. I wish you'd work out in the orchard and raise some apples that big."

Her eyes sharpened. "Maybe I could do it, too. I've a gift with things, all right. My mother had it. She could stick anything in the ground and make it grow. She said it was having planters' hands that knew how to do it."

"Well, it sure works with flowers," he said.

"Henry, who were those men you were talking to?"

"Why, sure, that's what I came to tell you. They were from the Western Meat Company. I sold those thirty head of three-year-old steers. Got nearly my own price, too."

"Good," she said. "Good for you."

"And I thought," he continued, "I thought how it's Saturday afternoon, and we might go into Salinas for dinner at a restaurant, and then to a picture show — to celebrate, you see."

"Good," she repeated. "Oh, yes. That will be good."

Henry put on his joking tone. "There's fights tonight. How'd you like to go to the fights?"

"Oh, no," she said breathlessly. "No, I wouldn't like fights."

"Just fooling, Elisa. We'll go to a movie. Let's see. It's two now. I'm going to take Scotty and bring down those steers from the hill. It'll take us maybe two hours. We'll go in town about five and have dinner at the Cominos Hotel. Like that?"

"Of course I'll like it. It's good to eat away from home."

"All right, then. I'll go get up a couple of horses."

She said, "I'll have plenty of time to transplant some of these sets, I guess."

She heard her husband calling Scotty down by the barn. And a little later she saw the two men ride up the pale yellow hillside in search of the steers.

There was a little square sandy bed kept for rooting the chrysanthemums. With her trowel she turned the soil over and over, and smoothed it and patted it firm. Then she dug ten parallel trenches to receive the sets. Back at the chrysanthemum bed she pulled out the little crisp shoots, trimmed off the leaves of each one with her scissors and laid it on a small orderly pile.

A squeak of wheels and plod of hoofs came from the road. Elisa looked up. The country road ran along the dense bank of willows and cottonwoods that bordered the river, and up this road came a curious vehicle, curiously drawn. It was an old spring-wagon, with a round canvas top on it like the cover of a prairie schooner. It was drawn by an old bay horse and a little grey-and-white burro. A big stubble-bearded man sat between the cover flaps and drove the crawling team. Underneath the wagon, between the hind wheels, a lean and rangy mongrel dog walked sedately. Words were painted on the canvas, in clumsy, crooked letters. "Pots, pans, knives, sisors, lawn mores, Fixed." Two rows of articles, and the triumphantly definitive "Fixed" below. The black paint had run down in little sharp points beneath each letter.

Elisa, squatting on the ground, watched to see the crazy, loose-jointed wagon pass by. But it didn't pass. It turned into the farm road in front of her house, crooked old wheels skirling and squeaking. The rangy dog darted from between the wheels and ran ahead. Instantly the two ranch shepherds flew out at him. Then all three stopped, and with stiff and quivering tails, with taut straight legs, with ambassadorial dignity, they slowly circled, sniffing daintily. The caravan pulled up to Elisa's wire fence and stopped. Now the newcomer dog, feeling out-numbered, lowered his tail and retired under the wagon with raised hackles and bared teeth.

The man on the wagon seat called out, "That's a bad dog in a fight when he gets started."

Elisa laughed. "I see he is. How soon does he generally get started?"

The man caught up her laughter and echoed it heartily. "Sometimes not for weeks and weeks," he said. He climbed stiffly down, over the wheel. The horse and the donkey drooped like unwatered flowers.

Elisa saw that he was a very big man. Although his hair and beard were greying, he did not look old. His worn black suit was wrinkled and spotted with grease. The laughter had disappeared from his face and eyes the moment his laughing voice ceased. His eyes were dark, and they were full of the brooding that gets in the eyes of teamsters and of sailors. The calloused hands he rested on the wire fence were cracked, and every crack was a black line. He took off his battered hat.

"I'm off my general road, ma'am," he said. "Does this dirt road cut over across the river to the Los Angeles highway?"

Elisa stood up and shoved the thick scissors in her apron pocket. "Well, yes, it does, but it winds around and then fords the river. I don't think your team could pull through the sand."

He replied with some asperity, "It might surprise you what them beasts can pull through."

"When they get started?" she asked.

He smiled for a second. "Yes. When they get started."

"Well," said Elisa, "I think you'll save time if you go back to the Salinas road and pick up the highway there."

He drew a big finger down the chicken wire and made it sing. "I ain't in any hurry, ma'am. I go from Seattle to San Diego and back every year. Takes all my time. About six months each way. I aim to follow nice weather."

Elisa took off her gloves and stuffed them in the apron pocket with the scissors. She touched the under edge of her man's hat, searching for fugitive hairs. "That sounds like a nice kind of a way to live," she said.

He leaned confidentially over the fence. "Maybe you noticed the writing on my wagon. I mend pots and sharpen knives and scissors. You got any of them things to do?"

"Oh, no," she said quickly. "Nothing like that." Her eyes hardened with resistance.

"Scissors is the worst thing," he explained. "Most people just ruin scissors trying to sharpen 'em, but I know how. I got a special tool. It's a little bobbit kind of thing, and patented. But it sure does the trick."

"No. My scissors are all sharp."

"All right, then. Take a pot," he continued earnestly, "a bent pot, or a pot with a hole. I can make it like new so you don't have to buy no new ones. That's a saving for you."

"No," she said shortly. "I tell you I have nothing like that for you to do."

His face fell to an exaggerated sadness. His voice took on a whining undertone. "I ain't had a thing to do today. Maybe I won't have no supper tonight. You see I'm off my regular road. I know folks on the highway clear from Seattle to San Diego. They save their things for me to sharpen up because they know I do it so good and save them money."

"I'm sorry," Elisa said irritably. "I haven't anything for you to do."

His eyes left her face and fell to searching the ground. They roamed about until they came to the chrysanthemum bed where she had been working. "What's them plants, ma'am?"

The irritation and resistance melted from Elisa's face. "Oh, those are chrysanthemums, giant whites and yellows. I raise them every year, bigger than anybody around here."

"Kind of a long-stemmed flower? Looks like a quick puff of colored smoke?" he asked.

"That's it. What a nice way to describe them."

"They smell kind of nasty till you get used to them," he said.

"It's a good bitter smell," she retorted, "not nasty at all."

He changed his tone quickly. "I like the smell myself."

"I had ten-inch blooms this year," she said.

The man leaned farther over the fence. "Look. I know a lady down the road a piece, has got the nicest garden you ever seen. Got nearly every kind of flower but no chrysantheums. Last time I was mending a copper-bottom wash-tub for her (that's a hard job but I do it good), she said to me, 'If you ever run acrost some nice chrysantheums I wish you'd try to get me a few seeds.' That's what she told me."

Elisa's eyes grew alert and eager. "She couldn't have known much about chrysanthemums. You *can* raise them from seed, but it's much easier to root the little sprouts you see there."

"Oh," he said. "I s'pose I can't take none to her, then."

"Why yes you can," Elisa cried. "I can put some in damp sand, and you can carry them right along with you. They'll take root in the pot if you keep them damp. And then she can transplant them."

"She'd sure like to have some, ma'am. You say they're nice ones?"

"Beautiful," she said. "Oh, beautiful." Her eyes shone. She tore off the battered hat and shook out her dark pretty hair. "I'll put them in a flower pot, and you can take them right with you. Come into the yard."

While the man came through the picket gate Elisa ran excitedly along the geranium-bordered path to the back of the house. And she returned carrying a big red flower pot. The gloves were forgotten now. She kneeled on the ground by the starting bed and dug up the sandy soil with her fingers and scooped it into the bright new flower pot. Then she picked up the little pile of shoots she had prepared. With her strong fingers she pressed them into the sand and tamped around them with her knuckles. The man stood over her. "I'll tell you what to do," she said. "You remember so you can tell the lady."

"Yes, I'll try to remember."

"Well, look. These will take root in about a month. Then she must set them out, about a foot apart in good rich earth like this, see?" She lifted a handful of dark soil for him to look at. "They'll grow fast and tall. Now remember this: In July tell her to cut them down, about eight inches from the ground."

"Before they bloom?" he asked.

"Yes, before they bloom." Her face was tight with eagerness. "They'll grow right up again. About the last of September the buds will start."

She stopped and seemed perplexed. "It's the budding that takes the most care," she said hesitantly. "I don't know how to tell you." She looked deep into his eyes, searchingly. Her mouth opened a little, and she seemed to be listening. "I'll try to tell you," she said. "Did you ever hear of planting hands?"

"Can't say I have, ma'am."

"Well, I can only tell you what it feels like. It's when you're picking off the buds you don't want. Everything goes right down into your fingertips. You watch your fingers work. They do it themselves. You can feel how it is. They pick and pick the buds. They never make a mistake. They're with the plant. Do you see? Your fingers and the plant. You can feel that, right up your arm. They know. They never make a mistake. You can feel it. When you're like that you can't do anything wrong. Do you see that? Can you understand that?"

She was kneeling on the ground looking up at him. Her breast swelled passionately.

The man's eyes narrowed. He looked away self-consciously. "Maybe I know," he said. "Sometimes in the night in the wagon there —"

Elisa's voice grew husky. She broke in on him, "I've never lived as you do, but I know what you mean. When the night is dark — why, the stars are sharp-pointed, and there's quiet. Why, you rise up and up! Every pointed star gets driven into your body. It's like that. Hot and sharp and — lovely."

Kneeling there, her hand went out toward his legs in the

greasy black trousers. Her hesitant fingers almost touched the cloth. Then her hand dropped to the ground. She crouched low like a fawning dog.

He said, "It's nice, just like you say. Only when you don't have no dinner, it ain't."

She stood up then, very straight, and her face was ashamed. She held the flower pot out to him and placed it gently in his arms. "Here. Put it in your wagon, on the seat, where you can watch it. Maybe I can find something for you to do."

At the back of the house she dug in the can pile and found two old and battered aluminum saucepans. She carried them back and gave them to him. "Here, maybe you can fix these."

His manner changed. He became professional. "Good as new I can fix them." At the back of his wagon he set a little anvil, and out of an oily tool box dug a small machine hammer. Elisa came through the gate to watch him while he pounded out the dents in the kettles. His mouth grew sure and knowing. At a difficult part of the work he sucked his under-lip.

"You sleep right in the wagon?" Elisa asked.

"Right in the wagon, ma'am. Rain or shine I'm dry as a cow in there."

"It must be nice," she said. "It must be very nice. I wish women could do such things."

"It ain't the right kind of life for a woman."

Her upper lip raised a little, showing her teeth. "How do you know? How can you tell?" she said.

"I don't know, ma'am," he protested. "Of course I don't know. Now here's your kettles, done. You don't have to buy no new ones."

"How much?"

"Oh, fifty cents'll do. I keep my prices down and my work good. That's why I have all them satisfied customers up and down the highway."

Elisa brought him a fifty-cent piece from the house and dropped it in his hand. "You might be surprised to have a rival some time. I can sharpen scissors, too. And I can beat the dents out of little pots. I could show you what a woman might do."

He put his hammer back in the oily box and shoved the little anvil out of sight. "It would be a lonely life for a woman, ma'am, and a scarey life, too, with animals creeping under the wagon all night." He climbed over the singletree, steadying himself with a hand on the burro's white rump. He settled himself in the seat, picked up the lines. "Thank you kindly, ma'am," he said. "I'll do like you told me; I'll go back and catch the Salinas road."

"Mind," she called, "if you're long in getting there, keep the sand damp."

"Sand, ma'am? . . . Sand? Oh, sure. You mean around the chrysantheums. Sure I will." He clucked his tongue. The beasts leaned luxuriously into their collars. The mongrel dog took his place between the back wheels. The wagon turned and crawled out the entrance road and back the way it had come, along the river.

Elisa stood in front of her wire fence watching the slow progress of the caravan. Her shoulders were straight, her head thrown back, her eyes half-closed, so that the scene came vaguely into them. Her lips moved silently, forming the words "Good-bye — good-bye." Then she whispered, "That's a bright direction. There's a glowing there." The sound of her whisper startled her. She shook herself free and looked about to see whether anyone had been listening. Only the dogs had heard. They lifted their heads toward her from their sleeping in the dust, and then stretched out their chins and settled asleep again. Elisa turned and ran hurriedly into the house.

In the kitchen she reached behind the stove and felt the water tank. It was full of hot water from the noonday cooking. In the bathroom she tore off her soiled clothes and flung them into the corner. And then she scrubbed herself with a little block of pumice, legs and thighs, loins and chest and arms, until her skin was scratched and red. When she had dried herself she stood in front of a mirror in her bedroom and looked at her body. She tightened her stomach and threw out her chest. She turned and looked over her shoulder at her back.

After a while she began to dress, slowly. She put on her newest underclothing and her nicest stockings and the dress which was the symbol of her prettiness. She worked carefully on her hair, penciled her eyebrows and rouged her lips.

Before she was finished she heard the little thunder hoofs and the shouts of Henry and his helper as they drove the red steers into the corral. She heard the gate bang shut and set herself for Henry's arrival.

His step sounded on the porch. He entered the house calling, "Elisa, where are you?"

"In my room, dressing. I'm not ready. There's hot water for your bath. Hurry up. It's getting late."

When she heard him splashing in the tub, Elisa laid his dark suit on the bed, and shirt and socks and tie beside it. She stood his polished shoes on the floor beside the bed. Then she went to the porch and sat primly and stiffly down. She looked toward the river road where the willow-line was still yellow with frosted leaves so that under the high grey fog they seemed a thin band of sunshine. This was the only color in the grey afternoon. She sat unmoving for a long time. Her eyes blinked rarely.

Henry came banging out of the door shoving his tie inside his vest as he came. Elisa stiffened and her face grew tight. Henry stopped short and looked at her. "Why — why, Elisa. You look so nice!"

"Nice? You think I look nice? What do you mean by 'nice'?"

Henry blundered on. "I don't know. I mean you look different, strong and happy."

"I am strong? Yes, strong. What do you mean 'strong'?"

He looked bewildered. "You're playing some kind of a game," he said helplessly. "It's a kind of a play. You look strong enough to break a calf over your knee, happy enough to eat it like a watermelon."

For a second she lost her rigidity. "Henry! Don't talk like that. You didn't know what you said." She grew complete again. "I'm strong," she boasted. "I never knew before how strong."

Henry looked down toward the tractor shed, and when he brought his eyes back to her, they were his own again. "I'll get out the car. You can put on your coat while I'm starting."

Elisa went into the house. She heard him drive to the gate and idle down his motor, and then she took a long time to put on her hat. She pulled it here and pressed it there. When Henry turned the motor off she slipped into her coat and went out.

The little roadster bounced along on the dirt road by the river, raising the birds and driving the rabbits into the brush. Two cranes flapped heavily over the willow-line and dropped into the river-bed.

Far ahead on the road Elisa saw a dark speck. She knew.

She tried not to look as they passed it, but her eyes would not obey. She whispered to herself sadly, "He might have thrown them off the road. That wouldn't have been much trouble, not very much. But he kept the pot," she explained. "He had to keep the pot. That's why he couldn't get them off the road."

The roadster turned a bend and she saw the caravan ahead. She swung full around toward her husband so she could not see the little covered wagon and the mismatched team as the car passed them.

In a moment it was over. The thing was done. She did not look back.

She said loudly, to be heard above the motor, "It will be good, tonight, a good dinner."

"Now you're changed again," Henry complained. He took one hand from the wheel and patted her knee. "I ought to take you in to dinner oftener. It would be good for both of us. We get so heavy out on the ranch."

"Henry," she asked, "could we have wine at dinner?"

"Sure we could. Say! That will be fine."

She was silent for a while; then she said, "Henry, at those prize fights, do the men hurt each other very much?"

"Sometimes a little, not often. Why?"

"Well, I've read how they break noses, and blood runs down their chests. I've read how the fighting gloves get heavy and soggy with blood."

He looked around at her. "What's the matter, Elisa? I didn't know you read things like that." He brought the car to a stop, then turned to the right over the Salinas River bridge.

"Do any women ever go to the fights?" she asked.

"Oh, sure, some. What's the matter, Elisa? Do you want to go? I don't think you'd like it, but I'll take you if you really want to go."

She relaxed limply in the seat. "Oh, no. No. I don't want to go. I'm sure I don't." Her face was turned away from him. "It will be enough if we can have wine. It will be plenty." She turned up her coat collar so he could not see that she was crying weakly — like an old woman.

Frank O'Connor (*1903–1966*)

My Oedipus Complex

Father was in the army all through the war — the first war, I mean — so, up to the age of five, I never saw much of him, and what I saw did not worry me. Sometimes I woke and there was a big figure in khaki peering down at me in the candlelight. Sometimes in the early morning I heard the slamming of the front door and the clatter of nailed boots down the cobbles of the lane. These were Father's entrances and exits. Like Santa Claus he came and went mysteriously.

In fact, I rather liked his visits, though it was an uncomfortable squeeze between Mother and him when I got into the big bed in the early morning. He smoked, which gave him a pleasant musty smell, and shaved, an operation of astounding interest. Each time he left a trail of souvenirs — model tanks and Gurkha knives with handles made of bullet cases, and German helmets and cap badges and button-sticks, and all sorts of military equipment — carefully stowed away in a long box on top of the wardrobe, in case they ever came in handy. There was a bit of the magpie about Father; he expected everything to come in handy. When his back was turned, Mother let me get a chair and rummage through his treasures. She didn't seem to think so highly of them as he did.

The war was the most peaceful period of my life. The window

of my attic faced southeast. My mother had curtained it, but that
had small effect. I always woke with the first light and, with all
the responsibilities of the previous day melted, feeling myself rather
like the sun, ready to illumine and rejoice. Life never seemed so
simple and clear and full of responsibilities as then. I put my feet
out from under the clothes — I called them Mrs. Left and Mrs.
Right — and invented dramatic situations for them in which they
discussed the problems of the day. At least Mrs. Right did; she
was very demonstrative, but I hadn't the same control of Mrs.
Left, so she mostly contented herself with nodding agreement.

They discussed what Mother and I should do during the
day, what Santa Claus should give a fellow for Christmas, and
what steps should be taken to brighten the home. There was that
little matter of the baby, for instance. Mother and I could never
agree about that. Ours was the only house in the terrace without
a new baby, and Mother said we couldn't afford one till Father
came back from the war because they cost seventeen and six. That
showed how simple she was. The Geneys up the road had a baby,
and everyone knew they couldn't afford seventeen and six. It was
probably a cheap baby, and Mother wanted something really good,
but I felt she was too exclusive. The Geneys' baby would have
done us fine.

Having settled my plans for the day, I got up, put a chair
under the attic window, and lifted the frame high enough to stick
out my head. The window overlooked the front gardens of the
terrace behind ours, and beyond these it looked over a deep valley
to the tall, red-brick houses terraced up the opposite hillside, which
were all still in shadow, while those at our side of the valley were
all lit up, though with long strange shadows that made them seem
unfamiliar; rigid and painted.

After that I went into Mother's room and climbed into the
big bed. She woke and I began to tell her of my schemes. By this
time, though I never seem to have noticed it, I was petrified in
my nightshirt, and I thawed as I talked until, the last frost melted,
I fell asleep beside her and woke again only when I heard her
below in the kitchen, making the breakfast.

After breakfast we went into town; heard Mass at St. Au-
gustine's and said a prayer for Father, and did the shopping. If
the afternoon was fine we either went for a walk in the country
or a visit to Mother's great friend in the convent, Mother St.
Dominic. Mother had them all praying for Father, and every night,
going to bed, I asked God to send him back safe from the war
to us. Little, indeed, did I know what I was praying for!

One morning, I got into the big bed, and there, sure enough,
was Father in his usual Santa Claus manner, but later, instead of
uniform, he put on his best blue suit, and Mother was as pleased

as anything. I saw nothing to be pleased about, because, out of uniform, Father was altogether less interesting, but she only beamed, and explained that our prayers had been answered, and off we went to Mass to thank God for having brought Father safely home.

The irony of it! That very day when he came in to dinner he took off his boots and put on his slippers, donned the dirty old cap he wore about the house to save him from colds, crossed his legs, and began to talk gravely to Mother, who looked anxious. Naturally, I disliked her looking anxious, because it destroyed her good looks, so I interrupted him.

"Just a moment, Larry!" she said gently.

This was only what she said when we had boring visitors, so I attached no importance to it and went on talking.

"Do be quiet, Larry!" she said impatiently. "Don't you hear me talking to Daddy?"

This was the first time I had heard those ominous words, "talking to Daddy," and I couldn't help feeling that if this was how God answered prayers, he couldn't listen to them very attentively.

"Why are you talking to Daddy?" I asked with as great a show of indifference as I could muster.

"Because Daddy and I have business to discuss. Now, don't interrupt again!"

In the afternoon, at Mother's request, Father took me for a walk. This time we went into town instead of out to the country, and I thought at first, in my usual optimistic way, that it might be an improvement. It was nothing of the sort. Father and I had quite different notions of a walk in town. He had no proper interest in trams, ships, and horses, and the only thing that seemed to divert him was talking to fellows as old as himself. When I wanted to stop he simply went on, dragging me behind him by the hand; when he wanted to stop I had no alternative but to do the same. I noticed that it seemed to be a sign that he wanted to stop for a long time whenever he leaned against a wall. The second time I saw him do it I got wild. He seemed to be settling himself forever. I pulled him by the coat and trousers, but, unlike Mother who, if you were too persistent, got into a wax and said: "Larry, if you don't behave yourself, I'll give you a good slap," Father had an extraordinary capacity for amiable inattention. I sized him up and wondered would I cry, but he seemed to be too remote to be annoyed even by that. Really, it was like going for a walk with a mountain! He either ignored the wrenching and pummeling entirely, or else glanced down with a grin of amusement from his peak. I had never met anyone so absorbed in himself as he seemed.

At teatime, "talking to Daddy" began again, complicated this time by the fact that he had an evening paper, and every few minutes he put it down and told Mother something new out of it. I felt this was foul play. Man for man, I was prepared to compete with him any time for Mother's attention, but when he had it all made up for him by other people it left me no chance. Several times I tried to change the subject without success.

"You must be quiet while Daddy is reading, Larry," Mother said impatiently.

It was clear that she either genuinely liked talking to Father better than talking to me, or else that he had some terrible hold on her which made her afraid to admit the truth.

"Mummy," I said that night when she was tucking me up, "do you think if I prayed hard God would send Daddy back to the war?"

She seemed to think about that for a moment.

"No, dear," she said with a smile. "I don't think he would."

"Why wouldn't he, Mummy?"

"Because there isn't a war any longer, dear."

"But, Mummy, couldn't God make another war, if he liked?"

"He wouldn't like to, dear. It's not God who makes wars, but bad people."

"Oh!" I said.

I was disappointed about that. I began to think that God wasn't quite what he was cracked up to be.

Next morning I woke at my usual hour, feeling like a bottle of champagne. I put out my feet and invented a long conversation in which Mrs. Right talked of the trouble she had with her own father till she put him in the Home. I didn't quite know what the Home was but it sounded the right place for Father. Then I got my chair and stuck my head out of the attic window. Dawn was just breaking, with a guilty air that made me feel I had caught it in the act. My head bursting with stories and schemes, I stumbled in next door, and in the half-darkness scrambled into the big bed. There was no room at Mother's side so I had to get between her and Father. For the time being I had forgotten about him, and for several minutes I sat bolt upright, racking my brains to know what I could do with him. He was taking up more than his fair share of the bed, and I couldn't get comfortable, so I gave him several kicks that made him grunt and stretch. He made room all right, though. Mother waked and felt for me. I settled back comfortably in the warmth of the bed with my thumb in my mouth.

"Mummy!" I hummed, loudly and contentedly.

"Sssh! dear," she whispered. "Don't wake Daddy!"

This was a new development, which threatened to be even more serious than "talking to Daddy." Life without my early-morning conferences was unthinkable.

"Why?" I asked severely.

"Because poor Daddy is tired."

This seemed to me a quite inadequate reason, and I was sickened by the sentimentality of her "poor Daddy." I never liked that sort of gush; it always struck me as insincere.

"Oh!" I said lightly. Then in my most winning tone: "Do you know where I want to go with you today, Mummy?"

"No, dear," she sighed.

"I want to go down the Glen and fish for thornybacks with my new net, and then I want to go out to the Fox and Hounds, and —"

"Don't-wake-Daddy!" she hissed angrily, clapping her hand across my mouth.

But it was too late. He was awake, or nearly so. He grunted and reached for the matches. Then he stared incredulously at his watch.

"Like a cup of tea, dear?" asked Mother in a meek, hushed voice I had never heard her use before. It sounded almost as though she were afraid.

"Tea?" he exclaimed indignantly. "Do you know what the time is?"

"And after that I want to go up the Rathcooney Road," I said loudly, afraid I'd forget something in all those interruptions.

"Go to sleep at once, Larry!" she said sharply.

I began to snivel. I couldn't concentrate, the way that pair went on, and smothering my early-morning schemes was like burying a family from the cradle.

Father said nothing, but lit his pipe and sucked it, looking out into the shadows without minding Mother or me. I knew he was mad. Every time I make a remark Mother hushed me irritably. I was mortified. I felt it wasn't fair; there was even something sinister in it. Every time I had pointed out to her the waste of making two beds when we could both sleep in one, she had told me it was healthier like that, and now here was this man, this stranger, sleeping with her without the least regard for her health!

He got up early and made tea, but though he brought Mother a cup he brought none for me.

"Mummy," I shouted, "I want a cup of tea, too."

"Yes, dear," she said patiently. "You can drink from Mummy's saucer."

That settled it. Either Father or I would have to leave the house. I didn't want to drink from Mother's saucer; I wanted to be treated as an equal in my own home, so, just to spite her, I drank it all and left none for her. She took that quietly, too.

But that night when she was putting me to bed she said gently:

"Larry, I want you to promise me something."

"What is it?" I asked.

"Not to come in and disturb poor Daddy in the morning. Promise?"

"Poor Daddy" again! I was becoming suspicious of everything involving that quite impossible man.

"Why?" I asked.

"Because poor Daddy is worried and tired and he doesn't sleep well."

"Why doesn't he, Mummy?"

"Well, you know, don't you, that while he was at the war Mummy got the pennies from the Post Office?"

"From Miss MacCarthy?"

"That's right. But now, you see, Miss MacCarthy hasn't any more pennies, so Daddy must go out and find us some. You know what would happen if he couldn't?"

"No," I said, "tell us."

"Well, I think we might have to go out and beg for them like the poor old woman on Fridays. We wouldn't like that, would we?"

"No," I agreed. "We wouldn't."

"So you'll promise not to come in and wake him?"

"Promise."

Mind you, I meant that. I knew pennies were a serious matter, and I was all against having to go out and beg like the old woman on Fridays. Mother laid out all my toys in a complete ring round the bed so that, whatever way I got out, I was bound to fall over one of them.

When I woke I remembered my promise all right. I got up and sat on the floor and played — for hours, it seemed to me. Then I got my chair and looked out the attic window for more hours. I wished it was time for Father to wake; I wished someone would make me a cup of tea. I didn't feel in the least like the sun; instead, I was bored and so very, very cold! I simply longed for the warmth and depth of the big featherbed.

At last I could stand it no longer. I went into the next room. As there was still no room at Mother's side I climbed over her and she woke with a start.

"Larry," she whispered, gripping my arm very tightly, "what did you promise?"

"But I did, Mummy," I wailed, caught in the very act. "I was quiet for ever so long."

"Oh, dear, and you're perished!" she said sadly, feeling me all over. "Now, if I let you stay will you promise not to talk?"

"But I want to talk, Mummy," I wailed.

"That has nothing to do with it," she said with a firmness

that was new to me. "Daddy wants to sleep. Now, do you understand that?"

I understood it only too well. I wanted to talk, he wanted to sleep — whose house was it, anyway?

"Mummy," I said with equal firmness, "I think it would be healthier for Daddy to sleep in his own bed."

That seemed to stagger her, because she said nothing for a while.

"Now, once for all," she went on, "you're to be perfectly quiet or go back to your own bed. Which is it to be?"

The injustice of it got me down. I had convicted her out of her own mouth of inconsistency and unreasonableness, and she hadn't even attempted to reply. Full of spite, I gave Father a kick, which she didn't notice but which made him grunt and open his eyes in alarm.

"What time is it?" he asked in a panic-stricken voice, not looking at Mother but the door, as if he saw someone there.

"It's early yet," she replied soothingly. "It's only the child. Go to sleep again. . . . Now, Larry," she added, getting out of bed, "you've wakened Daddy and you must go back."

This time, for all her quiet air, I knew she meant it, and knew that my principal rights and privileges were as good as lost unless I asserted them at once. As she lifted me, I gave a screech, enough to wake the dead, not to mind Father. He groaned.

"That damn child! Doesn't he ever sleep?"

"It's only a habit, dear," she said quietly, though I could see she was vexed.

"Well, it's time he got out of it," shouted Father, beginning to heave in the bed. He suddenly gathered all the bedclothes about him, turned to the wall, and then looked back over his shoulder with nothing showing only two small, spiteful, dark eyes. The man looked very wicked.

To open the bedroom door, Mother had to let me down, and I broke free and dashed for the farthest corner, screeching. Father sat bolt upright in bed.

"Shut up, you little puppy!" he said in a choking voice.

I was so astonished that I stopped screeching. Never, never had anyone spoken to me in that tone before. I looked at him incredulously and saw his face convulsed with rage. It was only then that I fully realized how God had codded me, listening to my prayers for the safe return of this monster.

"Shut up, you!" I bawled, beside myself.

"What's that you said?" shouted Father, making a wild leap out of bed.

"Mick, Mick!" cried Mother. "Don't you see the child isn't used to you?"

"I see he's better fed than taught," snarled Father, waving his arms wildly. "He wants his bottom smacked."

All his previous shouting was as nothing to these obscene words referring to my person. They really made my blood boil.

"Smack your own!" I screamed hysterically. "Smack your own! Shut up! Shut up!"

At this he lost his patience and let fly at me. He did it with the lack of conviction you'd expect of a man under Mother's horrified eyes, and it ended up as a mere tap, but the sheer indignity of being struck at all by a stranger, a total stranger who had cajoled his way back from the war into our big bed as a result of my innocent intercession, made me completely dotty. I shrieked and shrieked, and danced in my bare feet, and Father, looking awkward and hairy in nothing but a short grey army shirt, glared down at me like a mountain out for murder. I think it must have been then that I realized he was jealous too. And there stood Mother in her nightdress, looking as if her heart was broken between us. I hoped she felt as she looked. It seemed to me that she deserved it all.

From that morning out my life was a hell. Father and I were enemies, open and avowed. We conducted a series of skirmishes against one another, he trying to steal my time with Mother and I his. When she was sitting on my bed, telling me a story, he took to looking for some pair of old boots which he alleged he had left behind him at the beginning of the war. While he talked to Mother I played loudly with my toys to show my total lack of concern. He created a terrible scene one evening when he came in from work and found me at his box, playing with his regimental badges, Gurkha knives and buttonsticks. Mother got up and took the box from me.

"You mustn't play with Daddy's toys unless he lets you, Larry," she said severely. "Daddy doesn't play with yours."

For some reason Father looked at her as if she had struck him and then turned away with a scowl.

"Those are not toys," he growled, taking down the box again to see had I lifted anything. "Some of those curios are very rare and valuable."

But as time went on I saw more and more how he managed to alienate Mother and me. What made it worse was that I couldn't grasp his method or see what attraction he had for Mother. In every possible way he was less winning than I. He had a common accent and made noises at his tea. I thought for a while that it might be the newspapers she was interested in, so I made up bits of news of my own to read to her. Then I thought it might be the smoking, which I personally thought attractive, and took his pipes and went round the house dribbling into them till he caught me. I even made noises at my tea, but Mother only told me I was disgusting. It all seemed to hinge round that unhealthy habit of sleeping together, so I made a point of dropping into their bedroom and nosing round, talking to myself, so that they wouldn't know I was watching them, but they were never up to anything that I could see. In the end it beat me. It seemed to depend on being grown-up and giving people rings, and I realized I'd have to wait.

But at the same time I wanted him to see that I was only waiting, not giving up the fight. One evening when he was being particularly obnoxious, chattering away well above my head, I let him have it.

"Mummy," I said, "do you know what I'm going to do when I grow up?"

"No, dear," she replied. "What?"

"I'm going to marry you," I said quietly.

Father gave a great guffaw out of him, but he didn't take me in. I knew it must only be pretense. And Mother, in spite of everything, was pleased. I felt she was probably relieved to know that one day Father's hold on her would be broken.

"Won't that be nice?" she said with a smile.

"It'll be very nice," I said confidently. "Because we're going to have lots and lots of babies."

"That's right, dear," she said placidly. "I think we'll have one soon, and then you'll have plenty of company."

I was no end pleased about that because it showed that in spite of the way she gave in to Father she still considered my wishes. Besides, it would put the Geneys in their place.

It didn't turn out like that, though. To begin with, she was very preoccupied — I supposed about where she would get the seventeen and six — and though Father took to staying out late in the evenings it did me no particular good. She stopped taking me for walks, became as touchy as blazes, and smacked me for nothing at all. Sometimes I wished I'd never mentioned the confounded baby — I seemed to have a genius for bringing calamity on myself.

And calamity it was! Sonny arrived in the most appalling hullabaloo — even that much he couldn't do without a fuss — and from the first moment I disliked him. He was a difficult child — so far as I was concerned he was always difficult — and demanded far too much attention. Mother was simply silly about him, and couldn't see when he was only showing off. As company he was worse than useless. He slept all day, and I had to go round the house on tiptoe to avoid waking him. It wasn't any longer a question of not waking Father. The slogan now was "Don't-wake-Sonny!" I couldn't understand why the child wouldn't sleep at the proper time, so whenever Mother's back was turned I woke him.

Sometimes to keep him awake I pinched him as well. Mother caught me at it one day and gave me a most unmerciful flaking.

One evening, when Father was coming in from work, I was playing trains in the front garden. I let on not to notice him; instead, I pretended to be talking to myself, and said in a loud voice: "If another bloody baby comes into this house, I'm going out."

Father stopped dead and looked at me over his shoulder.

"What's that you said?" he asked sternly.

"I was only talking to myself," I replied, trying to conceal my panic. "It's private."

He turned and went in without a word. Mind you, I intended it as a solemn warning, but its effect was quite different. Father started being quite nice to me. I could understand that, of course. Mother was quite sickening about Sonny. Even at mealtimes she'd get up and gawk at him in the cradle with an idiotic smile, and tell Father to do the same. He was always polite about it, but he looked so puzzled you could see he didn't know what she was talking about. He complained of the way Sonny cried at night, but she only got cross and said that Sonny never cried except when there was something up with him — which was a flaming lie, because Sonny never had anything up with him, and only cried for attention. It was really painful to see how simple-minded she was. Father wasn't attractive, but he had a fine intelligence. He saw through Sonny, and now he knew that I saw through him as well.

One night I woke with a start. There was someone beside me in the bed. For one wild moment I felt sure it must be Mother, having come to her senses and left Father for good, but then I heard Sonny in convulsions in the next room, and Mother saying: "There! There! There!" and I knew it wasn't she. It was Father. He was lying beside me, wide awake, breathing hard and apparently as mad as hell.

After a while it came to me what he was mad about. It was his turn now. After turning me out of the big bed, he had been turned out himself. Mother had no consideration for anyone but that poisonous pup, Sonny. I couldn't help feeling sorry for Father. I had been through it all myself, and even at that age I was magnanimous. I began to stroke him down and say: "There! There!" He wasn't exactly responsive.

"Aren't you asleep either?" he snarled.

"Ah, come on and put your arm around us, can't you?" I said, and he did, in a sort of way. Gingerly, I suppose, is how you'd describe it. He was very bony but better than nothing.

At Christmas he went out of his way to buy me a really nice model railway.

Tillie Olsen (*b. 1912*)

I Stand Here Ironing

I stand here ironing, and what you asked me moves tormented back and forth with the iron.

"I wish you would manage the time to come in and talk with me about your daughter. I'm sure you can help me understand her. She's a youngster who needs help and whom I'm deeply interested in helping."

"Who needs help." . . . Even if I came, what good would it do? You think because I am her mother I have a key, or that in some way you could use me as a key? She has lived for nineteen years. There is all that life that has happened outside of me, beyond me.

And when is there time to remember, to sift, to weigh, to estimate, to total? I will start and there will be an interruption and I will have to gather it all together again. Or I will become engulfed with all I did or did not do, with what should have been and what cannot be helped.

She was a beautiful baby. The first and only one of our five that was beautiful at birth. You do not guess how new and uneasy her tenancy in her now-loveliness. You did not know her all those years she was thought homely, or see her poring over her baby pictures, making me tell her over and over how beautiful she had been — and would be, I would tell her — and was now, to the seeing eye. But the seeing eyes were few or non-existent. Including mine.

I nursed her. They feel that's important nowadays. I nursed all the children, but with her, with all the fierce rigidity of first mothcrhood, I did like the books then said. Though her cries battered me to trembling and my breasts ached with swollenness, I waited till the clock decreed.

Why do I put that first? I do not even know if it matters, or if it explains anything.

She was a beautiful baby. She blew shining bubbles of sound. She loved motion, loved light, loved color and music and textures. She would lie on the floor in her blue overalls patting the surface so hard in ecstasy her hands and feet would blur. She was a miracle to me, but when she was eight months old I had to leave her daytimes with the woman downstairs to whom she was no miracle at all, for I worked or looked for work and for Emily's father, who "could no longer endure" (he wrote in his good-bye note) "sharing want with us."

I was nineteen. It was the pre-relief, pre-WPA world of the depression. I would start running as soon as I got off the streetcar, running up the stairs, the place smelling sour, and awake or asleep to startle awake, when she saw me she would break into a clogged weeping that could not be comforted, a weeping I can hear yet.

After a while I found a job hashing at night so I could be with her days, and it was better. But it came to where I had to bring her to his family and leave her.

It took a long time to raise the money for her fare back. Then she got chicken pox and I had to wait longer. When she finally came, I hardly knew her, walking quick and nervous like her father, looking like her father, thin, and dressed in a shoddy red that yellowed her skin and glared at the pockmarks. All the baby loveliness gone.

She was two. Old enough for nursery school they said, and I did not know then what I know now — the fatigue of the long day, and the lacerations of group life in the kinds of nurseries that are only parking places for children.

Except that it would have made no difference if I had known. It was the only place there was. It was the only way we could be together, the only way I could hold a job.

And even without knowing, I knew. I knew the teacher that was evil because all these years it has curdled into my memory, the little boy hunched in the corner, her rasp, "why aren't you outside, because Alvin hits you? that's no reason, go out, scaredy." I knew Emily hated it even if she did not clutch and implore "don't go Mommy" like the other children, mornings.

She always had a reason why we should stay home. Momma, you look sick. Momma, I feel sick. Momma, the teachers aren't there today, they're sick. Momma, we can't go, there was a fire there last night. Momma, it's a holiday today no school, they told me.

But never a direct protest, never rebellion. I think of our others in their three-, four-year-oldness — the explosions, the tempers, the denunciations, the demands — and I feel suddenly ill. I put the iron down. What in me demanded that goodness in her? And what was the cost, the cost to her of such goodness?

The old man living in the back once said in his gentle way: "You should smile at Emily more when you look at her." What *was* in my face when I looked at her? I loved her. There were all the acts of love.

It was only with the others I remembered what he said, and it was the face of joy, and not of care or tightness or worry I turned to them — too late for Emily. She does not smile easily, let alone almost always as her brothers and sisters do. Her face is closed and sombre, but when she wants, how fluid. You must have seen it in her pantomimes, you spoke of her rare gift for comedy on the stage that rouses a laughter out of the audience so dear they applaud and applaud and do not want to let her go.

Where does it come from, that comedy? There was none of it in her when she came back to me that second time, after I had had to send her away again. She had a new daddy now to learn to love, and I think perhaps it was a better time.

Except when we left her alone nights, telling ourselves she was old enough.

"Can't you go some other time, Mommy, like tomorrow?" she would ask. "Will it be just a little while you'll be gone? Do you promise?"

The time we came back, the front door open, the clock on the floor in the hall. She rigid awake. "It wasn't just a little while. I didn't cry. Three times I called you, just three times, and then I ran downstairs to open the door so you could come faster. The clock talked loud. I threw it away, it scared me what it talked."

She said the clock talked loud again that night I went to the hospital to have Susan. She was delirious with the fever that comes before red measles, but she was fully conscious all the week I was gone and the week after we were home when she could not come near the new baby or me.

She did not get well. She stayed skeleton thin, not wanting to eat, and night after night she had nightmares. She would call for me, and I would rouse from exhaustion to sleepily call back: "You're all right, darling, go to sleep, it's just a dream," and if she still called, in a sterner voice, "now go to sleep, Emily, there's nothing to hurt you." Twice, only twice, when I had to get up for Susan anyhow, I went in to sit with her.

Now when it is too late (as if she would let me hold and comfort her like I do the others) I get up and go to her at once at her moan or restless stirring. "Are you awake, Emily? Can I get you something?" And the answer is always the same: "No, I'm all right, go back to sleep, Mother."

They persuaded me at the clinic to send her away to a convalescent home in the country where "she can have the kind of food and care you can't manage for her, and you'll be free to concentrate on the new baby." They still send children to that place. I see pictures on the society page of sleek young women planning affairs to raise money for it, or dancing at the affairs, or decorating Easter eggs or filling Christmas stockings for the children.

They never have a picture of the children so I do not know if the girls still wear those gigantic red bows and the ravaged looks on the every other Sunday when parents can come to visit "unless otherwise notified" — as we were notified the first six weeks.

Oh it is a handsome place, green lawns and tall trees and fluted flower beds. High up on the balconies of each cottage the children stand, the girls in their red bows and white dresses, the boys in white suits and giant red ties. The parents stand below shrieking up to be heard and the children shriek down to be heard, and between them the invisible wall "Not To Be Contaminated by Parental Germs or Physical Affection."

There was a tiny girl who always stood hand in hand with Emily. Her parents never came. One visit she was gone. "They moved her to Rose Cottage" Emily shouted in explanation. "They don't like you to love anybody here."

She wrote once a week, the labored writing of a seven-year-old. "I am fine. How is the baby. If I write my leter nicly I will have a star. Love." There never was a star. We wrote every other day, letters she could never hold or keep but only hear read — once. "We simply do not have room for children to keep any personal possessions," they patiently explained when we pieced one Sunday's shrieking together to plead how much it would mean to Emily, who loved so to keep things, to be allowed to keep her letters and cards.

Each visit she looked frailer. "She isn't eating" they told us.

(They had runny eggs for breakfast or mush with lumps, Emily said later, I'd hold it in my mouth and not swallow. Nothing ever tasted good, just when they had chicken.)

It took us eight months to get her released home, and only the fact that she gained back so little of her seven lost pounds convinced the social worker.

I used to try to hold and love her after she came back, but her body would stay stiff, and after a while she'd push away. She ate little. Food sickened her, and I think much of life too. Oh she had physical lightness and brightness, twinkling by on skates, bouncing like a ball up and down up and down over the jump rope, skimming over the hill; but these were momentary.

She fretted about her appearance, thin and dark and foreign-looking at a time when every little girl was supposed to look or thought she should look a chubby blonde replica of Shirley Temple. The doorbell sometimes rang for her, but no one seemed to come and play in the house or be a best friend. Maybe because we moved so much.

There was a boy she loved painfully through two school semesters. Months later she told me how she had taken pennies from my purse to buy him candy. "Licorice was his favorite and I brought him some every day, but he still liked Jennifer better'n me. Why, Mommy?" The kind of question for which there is no answer.

School was a worry to her. She was not glib or quick in a world where glibness and quickness were easily confused with ability to learn. To her overworked and exasperated teachers she was an overconscientious "slow learner" who kept trying to catch up and was absent entirely too often.

I let her be absent, though sometimes the illness was imaginary. How different from my now-strictness about attendance with the others. I wasn't working. We had a new baby, I was home anyhow. Sometimes, after Susan grew old enough, I would keep her home from school, too, to have them all together.

Mostly Emily had asthma, and her breathing, harsh and labored, would fill the house with a curiously tranquil sound. I would bring the two old dresser mirrors and her boxes of collections to her bed. She would select beads and single earrings, bottle tops and shells, dried flowers and pebbles, old postcards and scraps, all sorts of oddments; then she and Susan would play Kingdom, setting up landscapes and furniture, peopling them with action.

Those were the only times of peaceful companionship between her and Susan. I have edged away from it, that poisonous feeling between them, that terrible balancing of hurts and needs I had to do between the two, and did so badly, those earlier years.

Oh there are conflicts between the others too, each one human, needing, demanding, hurting, taking — but only between Emily and Susan, no, Emily toward Susan that corroding resentment. It seems so obvious on the surface, yet it is not obvious. Susan, the second child, Susan, golden- and curly-haired and chubby, quick and articulate and assured, everything in appearance and manner Emily was not; Susan, not able to resist Emily's precious things, losing or sometimes clumsily breaking them; Susan telling jokes and riddles to company for applause while Emily sat silent (to say to me later: that was *my* riddle, Mother, I told it to Susan); Susan, who for all the five years' difference in age was just a year behind Emily in developing physically.

I am glad for that slow physical development that widened the difference between her and her contemporaries, though she suffered over it. She was too vulnerable for that terrible world of youthful competition, of preening and parading, of constant measuring of yourself against every other, of envy, "If I had that copper hair," "If I had that skin. . . ." She tormented herself enough about not looking like the others, there was enough of the unsureness, the having to be conscious of words before you speak, the constant caring — what are they thinking of me? without having it all magnified by the merciless physical drives.

Ronnie is calling. He is wet and I change him. It is rare there is such a cry now. That time of motherhood is almost behind me when the ear is not one's own but must always be racked and listening for the child cry, the child call. We sit for a while and

I hold him, looking out over the city spread in charcoal with its soft aisles of light. *"Shoogily,"* he breathes and curls closer. I carry him back to bed, asleep. *Shoogily.* A funny word, a family word, inherited from Emily, invented by her to say: *comfort.*

In this and other ways she leaves her seal, I say aloud. And startle at my saying it. What do I mean? What did I start to gather together, to try and make coherent? I was at the terrible, growing years. War years. I do not remember them well. I was working, there were four smaller ones now, there was not time for her. She had to help be a mother, and housekeeper, and shopper. She had to set her seal. Mornings of crisis and near hysteria trying to get lunches packed, hair combed, coats and shoes found, everyone to school or Child Care on time, the baby ready for transportation. And always the paper scribbled on by a smaller one, the book looked at by Susan then mislaid, the homework not done. Running out to that huge school where she was one, she was lost, she was a drop; suffering over the unpreparedness, stammering and unsure in her classes.

There was so little time left at night after the kids were bedded down. She would struggle over books, always eating (it was in those years she developed her enormous appetite that is legendary in our family) and I would be ironing, or preparing food for the next day, or writing V-mail to Bill, or tending the baby. Sometimes, to make me laugh, or out of her despair, she would imitate happenings or types at school.

I think I said once: "Why don't you do something like this in the school amateur show?" One morning she phoned me at work, hardly understandable through the weeping: "Mother, I did it. I won, I won; they gave me first prize; they clapped and clapped and wouldn't let me go."

Now suddenly she was Somebody, and as imprisoned in her difference as she had been in anonymity.

She began to be asked to perform at other high schools, even in colleges, then at city and statewide affairs. The first one we went to, I only recognized her that first moment when thin, shy, she almost drowned herself into the curtains. Then: Was this Emily? The control, the command, the convulsing and deadly clowning, the spell, then the roaring, stamping audience, unwilling to let this rare and precious laughter out of their lives.

Afterwards: You ought to do something about her with a gift like that — but without money or knowing how, what does one do? We have left it all to her, and the gift has as often eddied inside, clogged and clotted, as been used and growing.

She is coming. She runs up the stairs two at a time with her light graceful step, and I know she is happy tonight. Whatever it was that occasioned your call did not happen today.

"Aren't you ever going to finish the ironing, Mother? Whistler painted his mother in a rocker. I'd have to paint mine standing over an ironing board." This is one of her communicative nights and she tells me everything and nothing as she fixes herself a plate of food out of the icebox.

She is so lovely. Why did you want me to come in at all? Why were you concerned? She will find her way.

She starts up the stairs to bed. "Don't get me up with the rest in the morning." "But I thought you were having midterms." "Oh, those," she comes back in, kisses me, and says quite lightly, "in a couple of years when we'll all be atom-dead they won't matter a bit."

She has said it before. She *believes* it. But because I have been dredging the past, and all that compounds a human being is so heavy and meaningful in me, I cannot endure it tonight.

I will never total it all. I will never come in to say: She was a child seldom smiled at. Her father left me before she was a year old. I had to work her first six years when there was work, or I sent her home and to his relatives. There were years she had care she hated. She was dark and thin and foreign-looking in a world where the prestige went to blondeness and curly hair and dimples, she was slow where glibness was prized. She was a child of anxious, not proud, love. We were poor and could not afford for her the soil of easy growth. I was a young mother, I was a distracted mother. There were the other children pushing up, demanding. Her younger sister seemed all that she was not. There were years she did not want me to touch her. She kept too much in herself, her life was such she had to keep too much in herself. My wisdom came too late. She has much to her and probably little will come of it. She is a child of her age, of depression, of war, of fear.

Let her be. So all that is in her will not bloom — but in how many does it? There is still enough left to live by. Only help her to know — help make it so there is cause for her to know — that she is more than this dress on the ironing board, helpless before the iron. 1953–1954

Bernard Malamud *(b. 1914)*

The Magic Barrel

Not long ago there lived in uptown New York, in a small, almost meager room, though crowded with books, Leo Finkle, a rabbinical student in the Yeshivah University. Finkle, after six years of study, was to be ordained in June and had been advised by an acquaintance that he might find it easier to win himself a congregation if he were married. Since he had no present prospects of marriage, after two tormented days of turning it over in his mind, he called in Pinye Salzman, a marriage broker whose two-line advertisement he had read in the *Forward*.°

The matchmaker appeared one night out of the dark fourth-floor hallway of the graystone rooming house where Finkle lived, grasping a black, strapped portfolio that had been worn thin with use. Salzman, who had been long in the business, was of slight but dignified build, wearing an old hat, and an overcoat too short and tight for him. He smelled frankly of fish, which he loved to eat, and although he was missing a few teeth, his presence was not displeasing, because of an amiable manner curiously contrasted with mournful eyes. His voice, his lips, his wisp of beard, his bony fingers were animated, but give him a moment of repose and his mild blue eyes revealed a depth of sadness, a characteristic that put Leo a little at ease although the situation, for him, was inherently tense.

He at once informed Salzman why he had asked him to come, explaining that his home was in Cleveland, and that but for his parents, who had married comparatively late in life, he was alone in the world. He had for six years devoted himself almost entirely to his studies, as a result of which, understandably, he had found himself without time for a social life and the company of young women. Therefore he thought it the better part of trial and error — of embarrassing fumbling — to call in an experienced person to advise him on these matters. He remarked in passing that the function of the marriage broker was ancient and honorable, highly approved in the Jewish community, because it made practical the necessary without hindering joy. Moreover, his own parents had been brought together by a matchmaker. They had made, if not a financially profitable marriage — since neither had possessed any worldly goods to speak of — at least a successful one in the sense of their everlasting devotion to each other. Salzman listened in embarrassed surprise, sensing a sort of apology. Later, however, he experienced a glow of pride in his work, an emotion that had left him years ago, and he heartily approved of Finkle.

The two went to their business. Leo had led Salzman to the only clear place in the room, a table near a window that overlooked the lamp-lit city. He seated himself at the matchmaker's side but facing him, attempting by an act of will to suppress the unpleasant tickle in his throat. Salzman eagerly unstrapped his portfolio and

° Yiddish newspaper published in New York. (Editors' note)

removed a loose rubber band from a thin packet of much-handled cards. As he flipped through them, a gesture and sound that physically hurt Leo, the student pretended not to see and gazed steadfastly out the window. Although it was still February, winter was on its last legs, signs of which he had for the first time in years begun to notice. He now observed the round white moon, moving high in the sky through a cloud menagerie, and watched with half-open mouth as it penetrated a huge hen, and dropped out of her like an egg laying itself. Salzman, though pretending through eyeglasses he had just slipped on, to be engaged in scanning the writing on the cards, stole occasional glances at the young man's distinguished face, noting with pleasure the long, severe scholar's nose, brown eyes heavy with learning, sensitive yet ascetic lips, and a certain, almost hollow quality of the dark cheeks. He gazed around at shelves upon shelves of books and let out a soft, contented sigh.

When Leo's eyes fell upon the cards, he counted six spread out in Salzman's hand.

"So few?" he asked in disappointment.

"You wouldn't believe me how much cards I got in my office," Salzman replied. "The drawers are already filled to the top, so I keep them now in a barrel, but is every girl good for a new rabbi?"

Leo blushed at this, regretting all he had revealed of himself in a curriculum vitae he had sent to Salzman. He had thought it best to acquaint him with his strict standards and specifications, but in having done so, felt he had told the marriage broker more than was absolutely necessary.

He hesitantly inquired, "Do you keep photographs of your clients on file?"

"First comes family, amount of dowry, also what kind promises," Salzman replied, unbuttoning his tight coat and settling himself in the chair. "After comes pictures, rabbi."

"Call me Mr. Finkle. I'm not yet a rabbi."

Salzman said he would, but instead called him doctor, which he changed to rabbi when Leo was not listening too attentively.

Salzman adjusted his horn-rimmed spectacles, gently cleared his throat and read in an eager voice the contents of the top card:

"Sophie P. Twenty-four years. Widow one year. No children. Educated high school and two years college. Father promises eight thousand dollars. Has wonderful wholesale business. Also real estate. On the mother's side comes teachers, also one actor. Well known on Second Avenue."

Leo gazed up in surprise. "Did you say a widow?"

"A widow don't mean spoiled, rabbi. She lived with her husband maybe four months. He was a sick boy she made a mistake to marry him."

"Marrying a widow has never entered my mind."

"This is because you have no experience. A widow, especially if she is young and healthy like this girl, is a wonderful person to marry. She will be thankful to you the rest of her life. Believe me, if I was looking now for a bride, I would marry a widow."

Leo reflected, then shook his head.

Salzman hunched his shoulders in an almost imperceptible gesture of disappointment. He placed the card down on the wooden table and began to read another:

"Lily H. High school teacher. Regular. Not a substitute. Has savings and new Dodge car. Lived in Paris one year. Father is successful dentist thirty-five years. Interested in professional man. Well Americanized family. Wonderful opportunity."

"I knew her personally," said Salzman. "I wish you could see this girl. She is a doll. Also very intelligent. All day you could talk to her about books and theater and what not. She also knows current events."

"I don't believe you mentioned her age?"

"Her age?" Salzman said, raising his brows. "Her age is thirty-two years."

Leo said after a while, "I'm afraid that seems a little too old."

Salzman let out a laugh. "So how old are you, rabbi?"

"Twenty-seven."

"So what is the difference, tell me, between twenty-seven and thirty-two? My own wife is seven years older than me. So what did I suffer? — Nothing. If Rothschild's daughter wants to marry you, would you say on account her age, no?"

"Yes," Leo said dryly.

Salzman shook off the no in the yes. "Five years don't mean a thing. I give you my word that when you will live with her for one week you will forget her age. What does it means five years — that she lived more and knows more than somebody who is younger? On this girl, God bless her, years are not wasted. Each one that it comes makes better the bargain."

"What subject does she teach in high school?"

"Languages. If you heard the way she speaks French, you will think it is music. I am in the business twenty-five years, and I recommend her with my whole heart. Believe me, I know what I'm talking, rabbi."

"What's on the next card?" Leo said abruptly.

Salzman reluctantly turned up the third card:

"Ruth K. Nineteen years. Honor student. Father offers thirteen thousand cash to the right bridegroom. He is a medical doctor. Stomach specialist with marvelous practice. Brother-in-law owns own garment business. Particular people."

Salzman looked as if he had read his trump card.

"Did you say nineteen?" Leo asked with interest.

"On the dot."

"Is she attractive?" He blushed. "Pretty?"

Salzman kissed his finger tips. "A little doll. On this I give you my word. Let me call the father tonight and you will see what means pretty."

But Leo was troubled. "You're sure she's that young?"

"This I am positive. The father will show you the birth certificate."

"Are you positive there isn't something wrong with her?" Leo insisted.

"Who says there is wrong?"

"I don't understand why an American girl her age should go to a marriage broker."

A smile spread over Salzman's face.

"So for the same reason you went, she comes."

Leo flushed. "I am pressed for time."

Salzman, realizing he had been tactless, quickly explained. "The father came, not her. He wants she should have the best, so he looks around himself. When we will locate the right boy he will introduce him and encourage. This makes a better marriage than if a young girl without experience takes for herself. I don't have to tell you this."

"But don't you think this young girl believes in love?" Leo spoke uneasily.

Salzman was about to guffaw but caught himself and said soberly, "Love comes with the right person, not before."

Leo parted dry lips but did not speak. Noticing that Salzman had snatched a glance at the next card, he cleverly asked, "How is her health?"

"Perfect," Salzman said, breathing with difficulty. "Of course, she is a little lame on her right foot from an auto accident that it happened to her when she was twelve years, but nobody notices on account she is so brilliant and also beautiful."

Leo got up heavily and went to the window. He felt curiously bitter and upbraided himself for having called in the marriage broker. Finally, he shook his head.

"Why not?" Salzman persisted, the pitch of his voice rising.

"Because I detest stomach specialists."

"So what do you care what is his business? After you marry her do you need him? Who says he must come every Friday night in your house?"

Ashamed of the way the talk was going, Leo dismissed Salzman, who went home with heavy, melancholy eyes.

Though he had felt only relief at the marriage broker's departure, Leo was in low spirits the next day. He explained it as arising from Salzman's failure to produce a suitable bride for him. He did not care for his type of clientele. But when Leo found himself hesitating whether to seek out another matchmaker, one more polished than Pinye, he wondered if it could be — his protestations to the contrary, and although he honored his father and mother — that he did not, in essence, care for the match-making institution? This thought he quickly put out of mind yet found himself still upset. All day he ran around in the woods — missed an important appointment, forgot to give out his laundry, walked out of a Broadway cafeteria without paying and had to run back with the ticket in his hand; had even not recognized his landlady in the street when she passed with a friend and courteously called out, "A good evening to you, Doctor Finkle." By nightfall, however, he had regained sufficient calm to sink his nose into a book and there found peace from his thoughts.

Almost at once there came a knock on the door. Before Leo could say enter, Salzman, commercial cupid, was standing in the room. His face was gray and meager, his expression hungry, and he looked as if he would expire on his feet. Yet the marriage broker managed, by some trick of the muscles, to display a broad smile.

"So good evening. I am invited?"

Leo nodded, disturbed to see him again, yet unwilling to ask the man to leave.

Beaming still, Salzman laid his portfolio on the table. "Rabbi, I got for you tonight good news."

"I've asked you not to call me rabbi. I'm still a student."

"Your worries are finished. I have for you a first-class bride."

"Leave me in peace concerning this subect." Leo pretended lack of interest.

"The world will dance at your wedding."

"Please, Mr. Salzman, no more."

"But first must come back my strength," Salzman said weakly. He fumbled with the portfolio straps and took out of the leather case an oily paper bag, from which he extracted a hard, seeded roll and a small, smoked white fish. With a quick motion of his hand he stripped the fish out of its skin and began ravenously to chew. "All day in a rush," he muttered.

Leo watched him eat.

"A sliced tomato you have maybe?" Salzman hesitantly inquired.

"No."

The marriage broker shut his eyes and ate. When he had finished he carefully cleaned up the crumbs and rolled up the remains of the fish, in the paper bag. His spectacled eyes roamed the room until he discovered, amid some piles of books, a one-burner gas stove. Lifting his hat he humbly asked, "A glass of tea you got, rabbi?"

Conscience-stricken, Leo rose and brewed the tea. He served it with a chuck of lemon and two cubes of lump sugar, delighting Salzman.

After he had drunk his tea, Salzman's strength and good spirits were restored.

"So tell me, rabbi," he said amiably, "you considered some more the three clients I mentioned yesterday?"

"There was no need to consider."

"Why not?"

"None of them suits me."

"What then suits you?"

Leo let it pass because he could give only a confused answer.

Without waiting for a reply, Salzman asked, "You remember this girl I talked to you — the high school teacher?"

"Age thirty-two?"

But, surprisingly, Salzman's face lit in a smile. "Age twenty-nine."

Leo shot him a look. "Reduced from thirty-two?"

"A mistake," Salzman avowed. "I talked today with the dentist. He took me to his safety deposit box and showed me the birth certificate. She was twenty-nine years last August. They made her a party in the mountains where she went for her vacation. When her father spoke to me the first time I forgot to write the age and I told you thirty-two, but now I remember this was a different client, a widow."

"The same one you told me about? I thought she was twenty-four?"

"A different. Am I responsible that the world is filled with widows?"

"No, but I'm not interested in them, nor for that matter, in school teachers."

Salzman pulled his clasped hands to his breast. Looking at

the ceiling he devoutly exclaimed, "Yiddishe kinder, what can I say to somebody that he is not interested in high school teachers? So what then you are interested?"

Leo flushed but controlled himself.

"In what else will you be interested," Salzman went on, "if you not interested in this fine girl that she speaks four languages and has personally in the bank ten thousand dollars? Also her father guarantees further twelve thousand. Also she has a new car, wonderful clothes, talks on all subjects, and she will give you a first-class home and children. How near do we come in our life to paradise?"

"If she's so wonderful, why wasn't she married ten years ago?"

"Why?" said Salzman with a heavy laugh. " — Why? Because she is *partikiler*. This is why. She wants the *best*."

Leo was silent, amused at how he had entangled himself. But Salzman had aroused his interest in Lily H., and he began seriously to consider calling on her. When the marriage broker observed how intently Leo's mind was at work on the facts he had supplied, he felt certain they would soon come to an agreement.

Late Saturday afternoon, conscious of Salzman, Leo Finkle walked with Lily Hirschorn along Riverside Drive. He walked briskly and erectly, wearing with distinction the black fedora he had that morning taken with trepidation out of the dusty hat box on his closet shelf, and the heavy black Saturday coat he had thoroughly whisked clean. Leo also owned a walking stick, a present from a distant relative, but quickly put temptation aside and did not use it. Lily, petite and not unpretty, had on something signifying the approach of spring. She was au courant, animatedly, with all sorts of subjects, and he weighed her words and found her surprisingly sound — score another for Salzman, whom he uneasily sensed to be somewhat around, hiding perhaps high in a tree along the street, flashing the lady signals with a pocket mirror; or perhaps a cloven-hoofed Pan, piping nuptial ditties as he danced his invisible way before them, strewing wild buds on the walk and purple grapes in their path, symbolizing fruit of a union, though there was of course still none.

Lily startled Leo by remarking, "I was thinking of Mr. Salzman, a curious figure, wouldn't you say?"

Not certain what to answer, he nodded.

She bravely went on, blushing, "I for one am grateful for his introducing us. Aren't you?"

He courteously replied, "I am."

"I mean," she said with a little laugh — and it was all in

good taste, or at least gave the effect of being not in bad — "do you mind that we came together so?"

He was not displeased with her honesty, recognizing that she meant to set the relationship aright, and understanding that it took a certain amount of experience in life, and courage, to want to do it quite that way. One had to have some sort of past to make that kind of beginning.

He said that he did not mind. Salzman's function was traditional and honorable — valuable for what it might achieve, which, he pointed out, was frequently nothing.

Lily agreed with a sigh. They walked on for a while and she said after a long silence, again with a nervous laugh, "Would you mind if I asked you something a little bit personal? Frankly, I find the subject fascinating." Although Leo shrugged, she went on half embarrassedly, "How was it that you came to your calling? I mean was it a sudden passionate inspiration?"

Leo, after a time, slowly replied, "I was always interested in the Law."

"You saw revealed in it the presence of the Highest?"

He nodded and changed the subject. "I understand that you spent a little time in Paris, Miss Hirschorn?"

"Oh, did Mr. Salzman tell you, Rabbi Finkle?" Leo winced but she went on, "It was ages ago and almost forgotten. I remember I had to return for my sister's wedding."

And Lily would not be put off. "When," she asked in a trembly voice, "did you become enamored of God?"

He stared at her. Then it came to him that she was talking not about Leo Finkle, but of a total stranger, some mystical figure, perhaps even passionate prophet that Salzman had dreamed up for her — no relation to the living or dead. Leo trembled with rage and weakness. The trickster had obviously sold her a bill of goods, just as he had him, who'd expected to become acquainted with a young lady of twenty-nine, only to behold, the moment he laid eyes upon her strained and anxious face, a woman past thirty-five and aging rapidly. Only his self-control had kept him this long in her presence.

"I am not," he said gravely, "a talented religious person," and in seeking words to go on, found himself possessed by shame and fear. "I think," he said in a strained manner, "that I came to God not because I loved Him, but because I did not."

This confession he spoke harshly because its unexpectedness shook him.

Lily wilted. Leo saw a profusion of loaves of bread go flying like ducks high over his head, not unlike the winged loaves by which he had counted himself to sleep last night. Mercifully, then, it snowed, which he would not put past Salzman's machinations.

He was infuriated with the marriage broker and swore he would throw him out of the room the minute he reappeared. But Salzman did not come that night, and when Leo's anger had subsided, an unaccountable despair grew in its place. At first he thought this was caused by his disappointment in Lily, but before long it became evident that he had involved himself with Salzman without a true knowledge of his own intent. He gradually realized — with an emptiness that seized him with six hands — that he had called in the broker to find him a bride because he was incapable of doing it himself. This terrifying insight he had derived as a result of his meeting and conversation with Lily Hirschorn. Her probing questions had somehow irritated him into revealing — to himself more than her — the true nature of his relationship to God, and from that it had come upon him, with shocking force, that apart from his parents, he had never loved anyone. Or perhaps it went the other way, that he did not love God so well as he might, because he had not loved man. It seemed to Leo that his whole life stood starkly revealed and he saw himself for the first time as he truly was — unloved and loveless. This bitter but somehow not fully unexpected revelation brought him to a point of panic, controlled only by extraordinary effort. He covered his face with his hands and cried.

The week that followed was the worst of his life. He did not eat and lost weight. His beard darkened and grew ragged. He stopped attending seminars and almost never opened a book. He seriously considered leaving the Yeshivah, although he was deeply troubled at the thought of the loss of all his years of study — saw them like pages torn from a book, strewn over the city — and at the devastating effect of this decision upon his parents. But he had lived without knowledge of himself, and never in the Five Books and all the Commentaries — mea culpa — had the truth been revealed to him. He did not know where to turn, and in all this desolating loneliness there was no *to whom,* although he often thought of Lily but not once could bring himself to go downstairs and make the call. He became touchy and irritable, especially with his landlady, who asked him all manner of personal questions; on the other hand, sensing his own disagreeableness, he waylaid her on the stairs and apologized abjectly, until mortified, she ran from him. Out of this, however, he drew the consolation that he was a Jew and that a Jew suffered. But gradually, as the long and terrible week drew to a close, he regained his composure and some idea of purpose in life: to go on as planned. Although he was imperfect, the idea was not. As for his quest of a bride, the thought of continuing afflicted him with anxiety and heartburn, yet perhaps with this new knowledge of himself he would be more successful than in the past. Perhaps love would now come to him and a bride to that love. And for this sanctified seeking who needed a Salzman?

The marriage broker, a skeleton with haunted eyes, returned that very night. He looked, withal, the picture of frustrated expectancy — as if he had steadfastly waited the week at Miss Lily Hirschorn's side for a telephone call that never came.

Casually coughing, Salzman came immediately to the point: "So how did you like her?"

Leo's anger rose and he could not refrain from chiding the matchmaker: "Why did you lie to me, Salzman?"

Salzman's pale face went dead white, the world had snowed on him.

"Did you not state that she was twenty-nine?" Leo insisted.

"I give you my word —"

"She was thirty-five, if a day. At *least* thirty-five."

"Of this don't be too sure. Her father told me —"

"Never mind. The worst of it was that you lied to her."

"How did I lie to her, tell me?"

"You told her things about me that weren't true. You made me out to be more, consequently less, than I am. She had in mind a totally different person, a sort of semi-mystical Wonder Rabbi."

"All I said, you was a religious man."

"I can imagine."

Salzman sighed. "This is my weakness that I have," he confessed. "My wife says to me I shouldn't be a salesman, but when I have two fine people that they would be wonderful to be married, I am so happy that I talk too much." He smiled wanly. "This is why Salzman is a poor man."

Leo's anger left him. "Well, Salzman, I'm afraid that's all."

The marriage broker fastened hungry eyes on him.

"You don't want any more a bride?"

"I do," said Leo, "but I have decided to seek her in a different way. I am no longer interested in an arranged marriage. To be frank, I now admit the necessity of premarital love. That is, I want to be in love with the one I marry."

"Love?" said Salzman, astounded. After a moment he remarked, "For us, our love is our life, not for the ladies. In the ghetto they —"

"I know, I know," said Leo. "I've thought of it often. Love, I have said to myself, should be a by-product of living and worship rather than its own end. Yet for myself I find it necessary to establish the level of my need and fulfill it."

Salzman shrugged but answered, "Listen, rabbi, if you want love, this I can find for you also. I have such beautiful clients that you will love them the minute your eyes will see them."

Leo smiled unhappily. "I'm afraid you don't understand."

But Salzman hastily unstrapped his portfolio and withdrew a manila packet from it.

"Pictures," he said, quickly laying the envelope on the table.

Leo called after him to take the pictures away, but as if on the wings of the wind, Salzman had disappeared.

March came. Leo had returned to his regular routine. Although he felt not quite himself yet — lacked energy — he was making plans for a more active social life. Of course it would cost something, but he was an expert in cutting corners; and when there were no corners left he would make circles rounder. All the while Salzman's pictures had lain on the table, gathering dust. Occasionally as Leo sat studying, or enjoying a cup of tea, his eyes fell on the manila envelope, but he never opened it.

The days went by and no social life to speak of developed with a member of the opposite sex — it was difficult, given the circumstances of his situation. One morning Leo toiled up the stairs to his room and stared out the window at the city. Although the day was bright his view of it was dark. For some time he watched the people in the street below hurrying along and then turned with a heavy heart to his little room. On the table was the packet. With a sudden relentless gesture he tore it open. For a half-hour he stood by the table in a state of excitement, examining the photographs of the ladies Salzman had included. Finally, with a deep sigh he put them down. There were six, of varying degrees of attractiveness, but look at them long enough and they all became Lily Hirschorn: all past their prime, all starved behind bright smiles, not a true personality in the lot. Life, despite their frantic yoohooings, had passed them by; they were pictures in a briefcase that stank of fish. After a while, however, as Leo attempted to return the photographs into the envelope, he found in it another, a snapshot of the type taken by a machine for a quarter. He gazed at it a moment and let out a cry.

Her face deeply moved him. Why, he could at first not say. It gave him the impression of youth — spring flowers, yet age — a sense of having been used to the bone, wasted; this came from the eyes, which were hauntingly familiar, yet absolutely strange. He had a vivid impression that he had met her before, but try as he might he could not place her although he could almost recall her name, as if he had read it in her own handwriting. No, this couldn't be; he would have remembered her. It was not, he affirmed, that she had an extraordinary beauty — no, though her face was attractive enough; it was that *something* about her moved him. Feature for feature, even some of the ladies of the photographs could do better; but she leaped forth to his heart — had *lived,* or wanted to — more than just wanted, perhaps regretted how she had lived — had somehow deeply suffered: it could be seen in the depths of those reluctant eyes, from the way the light enclosed and shone from her, and within her, opening realms of possibility: this was her own. Her he desired. His head ached and eyes narrowed with the intensity of his gazing, then, as if an obscure fog had blown up in the mind, he experienced fear of her and was aware that he had received an impression, somehow, of evil. He shuddered, saying softly, it is thus with us all. Leo brewed some tea in a small pot and sat sipping it without sugar, to calm himself. But before he had finished drinking, again with excitement he examined the face and found it good: good for Leo Finkle. Only such a one could understand him and help him seek whatever he was seeking. She might, perhaps, love him. How she had happened to be among the discards in Salzman's barrel he could never guess, but he knew he must urgently go find her.

Leo rushed downstairs, grabbed up the Bronx telephone book, and searched for Salzman's home address. He was not listed, nor was his office. Neither was he in the Manhattan book. But Leo remembered having written down the address on a slip of paper after he had read Salzman's advertisement in the "personals" column of the *Forward.* He ran up to his room and tore through his papers, without luck. It was exasperating. Just when he needed the matchmaker he was nowhere to be found. Fortunately Leo remembered to look in his wallet. There on a card he found his name written and a Bronx address. No phone number was listed, the reason — Leo now recalled — he had originally communicated with Salzman by letter. He got on his coat, put a hat on over his skull cap and hurried to the subway station. All the way to the far end of the Bronx he sat on the edge of his seat. He was more than once tempted to take out the picture and see if the girl's face was as he remembered it, but he refrained, allowing the snapshot to remain in his inside coat pocket, content to have her so close. When the train pulled into the station he was waiting at the door and bolted out. He quickly located the street Salzman had advertised.

The building he sought was less than a block from the subway, but it was not an office building, nor even a loft, nor a store in which one could rent office space. It was a very old tenement house. Leo found Salzman's name in pencil on a soiled tag under the bell and climbed three dark flights to his apartment. When he knocked, the door was opened by a thin, asthmatic, gray-haired woman, in felt slippers.

"Yes?" she said, expecting nothing. She listened without listening. He could have sworn he had seen her, too, before but knew it was an illusion.

"Salzman — does he live here? Pinye Salzman," he said, "the matchmaker?"

She stared at him a long minute. "Of course."

He felt embarrassed. "Is he in?"

"No." Her mouth, though left open, offered nothing more.

"The matter is urgent. Can you tell me where his office is?"

"In the air." She pointed upward.

"You mean he has no office?" Leo asked.

"In his socks."

He peered into the apartment. It was sunless and dingy, one large room divided by a half-open curtain, beyond which he could see a sagging metal bed. The near side of the room was crowded with rickety chairs, old bureaus, a three-legged table, racks of cooking utensils, and all the apparatus of a kitchen. But there was no sign of Salzman or his magic barrel, probably also a figment of the imagination. An odor of frying fish made Leo weak to the knees.

"Where is he?" he insisted. "I've got to see your husband."

At length she answered, "So who knows where he is? Every time he thinks a new thought he runs to a different place. Go home, he will find you."

"Tell him Leo Finkle."

She gave no sign she had heard.

He walked downstairs, depressed.

But Salzman, breathless, stood waiting at his door.

Leo was astounded and overjoyed. "How did you get here before me?"

"I rushed."

"Come inside."

They entered. Leo fixed tea, and a sardine sandwich for Salzman. As they were drinking he reached behind him for the packet of pictures and handed them to the marriage broker.

Salzman put down his glass and said expectantly, "You found somebody you like?"

"Not among these."

The marriage broker turned away.

"Here is the one I want." Leo held forth the snapshot.

Salzman slipped on his glasses and took the picture into his trembling hand. He turned ghastly and let out a groan.

"What's the matter?" cried Leo.

"Excuse me. Was an accident this picture. She isn't for you."

Salzman frantically shoved the manila packet into his portfolio. He thrust the snapshot into his pocket and fled down the stairs.

Leo, after momentary paralysis, gave chase and cornered the marriage broker in the vestibule. The landlady made hysterical outcries but neither of them listened.

"Give me back the picture, Salzman."

"No." The pain in his eyes was terrible.

"Tell me who she is then."

"This I can't tell you. Excuse me."

He made to depart, but Leo, forgetting himself, seized the matchmaker by his tight coat and shook him frenziedly.

"Please," sighed Salzman. "*Please.*"

Leo ashamedly let him go. "Tell me who she is," he begged. "It's very important for me to know."

"She is not for you. She is a wild one — wild, without shame. This is not a bride for a rabbi."

"What do you mean wild?"

"Like an animal. Like a dog. For her to be poor was a sin. This is why to me she is dead now."

"In God's name, what do you mean?"

"Her I can't introduce to you," Salzman cried.

"Why are you so excited?"

"Why, he asks," Salzman said, bursting into tears. "This is my baby, my Stella, she should burn in hell."

Leo hurried up to bed and hid under the covers. Under the covers he thought his life through. Although he soon fell asleep he could not sleep her out of his mind. He woke, beating his breast. Though he prayed to be rid of her, his prayers went unanswered. Through days of torment he endlessly struggled not to love her; fearing success, he escaped it. He then concluded to convert her to goodness, himself to God. The idea alternately nauseated and exalted him.

He perhaps did not know that he had come to a final decision until he encountered Salzman in a Broadway cafeteria. He was sitting alone at a rear table, sucking the bony remains of a fish. The marriage broker appeared haggard, and transparent to the point of vanishing.

Salzman looked up at first without recognizing him. Leo had grown a pointed beard and his eyes were weighted with wisdom.

"Salzman," he said, "love has at last come to my heart."

"Who can love from a picture?" mocked the marriage broker.

"It is not impossible."

"If you can love her, then you can love anybody. Let me show you some new clients that they just sent me their photographs. One is a little doll."

"Just her I want," Leo murmured.

"Don't be a fool, doctor. Don't bother with her."

"Put me in touch with her, Salzman," Leo said humbly. "Perhaps I can be of service."

Salzman had stopped eating and Leo understood with emotion that it was now arranged.

Leaving the cafeteria he was, however, afflicted by a tormenting suspicion that Salzman had planned it all to happen this way.

Leo was informed by letter that she would meet him on a certain corner, and she was there one spring night, waiting under a street lamp. He appeared, carrying a small bouquet of violets and rosebuds. Stella stood by the lamp post, smoking. She wore white with red shoes, which fitted his expectations, although in a troubled moment he had imagined the dress red, and only the shoes white. She waited uneasily and shyly. From afar he saw that her eyes — clearly her father's — were filled with desperate innocence. He pictured, in her, his own redemption. Violins and lit candles revolved in the sky. Leo ran forward with flowers outthrust.

Around the corner, Salzman, leaning against a wall, chanted prayers for the dead.

Shirley Jackson (1919–1965)

The Lottery

The morning of June 27th was clear and sunny, with the fresh warmth of a full-summer day; the flowers were blossoming profusely and the grass was richly green. The people of the village began to gather in the square, between the post office and the bank, around ten o'clock; in some towns there were so many people that the lottery took two days and had to be started on June 26th, but in this village, where there were only about three hundred people, the whole lottery took less than two hours, so it could begin at ten o'clock in the morning and still be through in time to allow the villagers to get home for noon dinner.

The children assembled first, of course. School was recently over for the summer, and the feeling of liberty sat uneasily on most of them; they tended to gather together quietly for a while before they broke into boisterous play, and their talk was still of the classroom and the teacher, of books and reprimands. Bobby Martin had already stuffed his pockets full of stones, and the other boys soon followed his example, selecting the smoothest and roundest stones; Bobby and Harry Jones and Dickie Delacroix — the villagers pronounced this name "Dellacroy" — eventually made a great pile of stones in one corner of the square and guarded it against the raids of the other boys. The girls stood aside, talking among themselves, looking over their shoulders at the boys, and the very small children rolled in the dust or clung to the hands of their older brothers or sisters.

Soon the men began to gather, surveying their own children, speaking of planting and rain, tractors and taxes. They stood together, away from the pile of stones in the corner, and their jokes were quiet and they smiled rather than laughed. The women, wearing faded house dresses and sweaters, came shortly after their menfolk. They greeted one another and exchanged bits of gossip as they went to join their husbands. Soon the women, standing by their husbands, began to call to their children, and the children came reluctantly, having to be called four or five times. Bobby Martin ducked under his mother's grasping hand and ran, laughing, back to the pile of stones. His father spoke up sharply, and Bobby came quickly and took his place between his father and his oldest brother.

The lottery was conducted — as were the square dances, the teenage club, the Halloween program — by Mr. Summers, who had time and energy to devote to civic activities. He was a round-faced, jovial man and he ran the coal business, and people were sorry for him, because he had no children and his wife was a scold. When he arrived in the square, carrying the black wooden box, there was a murmur of conversation among the villagers and he waved and called, "Little late today, folks." The postmaster, Mr. Graves, followed him, carrying a three-legged stool, and the stool was put in the center of the square and Mr. Summers set the black box down on it. The villagers kept their distance, leaving a space between themselves and the stool, and when Mr. Summers said, "Some of you fellows want to give me a hand?" there was a hesitation before two men, Mr. Martin and his oldest son, Baxter, came forward to hold the box steady on the stool while Mr. Summers stirred up the papers inside it.

The original paraphernalia for the lottery had been lost long ago, and the black box now resting on the stool had been put into use even before Old Man Warner, the oldest man in town, was born. Mr. Summers spoke frequently to the villagers about making a new box, but no one liked to upset even as much tradition as was represented by the black box. There was a story that the present box had been made with some pieces of the box that had preceded it, the one that had been constructed when the first people settled down to make a village here. Every year, after the lottery, Mr. Summers began talking again about a new box, but every year the subject was allowed to fade off without anything's being done. The black box grew shabbier each year; by now it was no longer completely black but splintered badly along one side to show the original wood color, and in some places faded or stained.

Mr. Martin and his oldest son, Baxter, held the black box securely on the stool until Mr. Summers had stirred the papers thoroughly with his hand. Because so much of the ritual had been forgotten or discarded, Mr. Summers had been successful in having slips of paper substituted for the chips of wood that had been used for generations. Chips of wood, Mr. Summers had argued, had been all very well when the village was tiny, but now that the population was more than three hundred and likely to keep on growing, it was necessary to use something that would fit more easily into the black box. The night before the lottery, Mr. Summers and Mr. Graves made up the slips of paper and put them in the box, and it was then taken to the safe of Mr. Summers's coal company and locked up until Mr. Summers was ready to take it to the square next morning. The rest of the year, the box was put away, sometimes one place, sometimes another; it had spent one year in Mr. Graves's barn and another year underfoot in the post office, and sometimes it was set on a shelf in the Martin grocery and left there.

There was a great deal of fussing to be done before Mr. Summers declared the lottery open. There were lists to make up — of heads of families, heads of households in each family, members of each household in each family. There was the proper swearing-in of Mr. Summers by the postmaster, as the official of the lottery; at one time, some people remembered, there had been a recital of some sort, performed by the official of the lottery, a perfunctory, tuneless chant that had been rattled off duly each year; some people believed that the official of the lottery used to stand just so when he said or sang it, others believed that he was supposed to walk among the people, but years and years ago this part of the ritual had been allowed to lapse. There had been, also, a ritual salute, which the official of the lottery had had to use in addressing each person who came up to draw from the box, but this also had changed with time, until now it was felt necessary only for the official to speak to each person approaching. Mr. Summers was very good at all this; in his clean white shirt and blue jeans, with one hand resting carelessly on the black box, he seemed very proper and important as he talked interminably to Mr. Graves and the Martins.

Just as Mr. Summers finally left off talking and turned to the assembled villagers, Mrs. Hutchinson came hurriedly along the path to the square, her sweater thrown over her shoulders, and slid into place in the back of the crowd. "Clean forgot what day it was," she said to Mrs. Delacroix, who stood next to her, and they both laughed softly. "Thought my old man was out back stacking wood," Mrs. Hutchinson went on, "and then I looked out the window and the kids were gone, and then I re-membered it was the twenty-seventh and came a-running." She dried her hands on her apron, and Mrs. Delacroix said, "You're in time, though. They're still talking away up there."

Mrs. Hutchinson craned her neck to see through the crowd and found her husband and children standing near the front. She tapped Mrs. Delacroix on the arm as a farewell and began to make her way through the crowd. The people separated goodhumoredly to let her through; two or three people said, in voices just loud enough to be heard across the crowd, "Here comes your Missus, Hutchinson," and "Bill, she made it after all." Mrs. Hutchinson reached her husband, and Mr. Summers, who had been waiting, said cheerfully, "Thought we were going to have to get on without you, Tessie." Mrs. Hutchinson said, grinning, "Wouldn't have me leave m'dishes in the sink, now would you, Joe?," and soft laughter ran through the crowd as the people stirred back into position after Mrs. Hutchinson's arrival.

"Well, now," Mr. Summers said soberly, "guess we better get started, get this over with, so's we can go back to work. Anybody ain't here?"

"Dunbar," several people said. "Dunbar, Dunbar."

Mr. Summers consulted his list. "Clyde Dunbar," he said. "That's right. He's broke his leg, hasn't he? Who's drawing for him?"

"Me, I guess," a woman said, and Mr. Summers turned to

look at her. "Wife draws for her husband," Mr. Summers said. "Don't you have a grown boy to do it for you, Janey?" Although Mr. Summers and everyone else in the village knew the answer perfectly well, it was the business of the official of the lottery to ask such questions formally. Mr. Summers waited with an expression of polite interest while Mrs. Dunbar answered.

"Horace's not but sixteen yet," Mrs. Dunbar said regretfully. "Guess I gotta fill in for the old man this year."

"Right," Mr. Summers said. He made a note on the list he was holding. Then he asked, "Watson boy drawing this year?"

A tall boy in the crowd raised his hand. "Here," he said. "I'm drawing for m'mother and me." He blinked his eyes nervously and ducked his head as several voices in the crowd said things like "Good fellow, Jack," and "Glad to see your mother's got a man to do it."

"Well," Mr. Summers said, "guess that's everyone. Old Man Warner make it?"

"Here," a voice said, and Mr. Summers nodded.

A sudden hush fell on the crowd as Mr. Summers cleared his throat and looked at the list. "All ready?" he called. "Now, I'll read the names — heads of families first — and the men come up and take a paper out of the box. Keep the paper folded in your hand without looking at it until everyone has had a turn. Everything clear?"

The people had done it so many times that they only half listened to the directions, most of them were quiet, wetting their lips, not looking around. Then Mr. Summers raised one hand high and said, "Adams." A man disengaged himself from the crowd and came forward. "Hi, Steve," Mr. Summers said, and Mr. Adams said, "Hi, Joe." They grinned at one another humorlessly and nervously. Then Mr. Adams reached into the black box and took out a folded paper. He held it firmly by one corner as he turned and went hastily back to his place in the crowd, where he stood a little apart from his family, not looking down at his hand.

"Allen," Mr. Summers said. "Anderson. . . . Bentham."

"Seems like there's no time at all between lotteries any more," Mrs. Delacroix said to Mrs. Graves in the back row. "Seems like we got through with the last one only last week."

"Time sure goes fast," Mrs. Graves said.

"Clark. . . . Delacroix."

"There goes my old man," Mrs. Delacroix said. She held her breath while her husband went forward.

"Dunbar," Mr. Summers said, and Mrs. Dunbar went steadily to the box while one of the women said, "Go on, Janey," and another said, "There she goes."

"We're next," Mrs. Graves said. She watched while Mr. Graves came around from the side of the box, greeted Mr. Summers gravely, and selected a slip of paper from the box. By now, all through the crowd there were men holding the small folded papers in their large hands, turning them over and over nervously. Mrs. Dunbar and her two sons stood together, Mrs. Dunbar holding the slip of paper.

"Harburt. . . . Hutchinson."

"Get up there, Bill," Mrs. Hutchinson said, and the people near her laughed.

"Jones."

"They do say," Mr. Adams said to Old Man Warner, who stood next to him, "that over in the north village they're talking of giving up the lottery."

Old Man Warner snorted, "Pack of crazy fools," he said. "Listening to the young folks, nothing's good enough for *them*. Next thing you know, they'll be wanting to go back to living in caves, nobody work any more, live *that* way for a while. Used to be a saying about 'Lottery in June, corn be heavy soon.' First thing you know, we'd all be eating stewed chickweed and acorns. There's *always* been a lottery," he added petulantly. "Bad enough to see young Joe Summers up there joking with everybody."

"Some places have already quit lotteries," Mrs. Adams said.

"Nothing but trouble in *that*," Old Man Warner said stoutly. "Pack of young fools."

"Martin." And Bobby Martin watched his father go forward. "Overdyke. . . . Percy."

"I wish they'd hurry," Mrs. Dunbar said to her older son. "I wish they'd hurry."

"They're almost through," her son said.

"You get ready to run tell Dad," Mrs. Dunbar said.

Mr. Summers called his own name and then stepped forward precisely and selected a slip from the box. Then he called, "Warner."

"Seventy-seventh year I been in the lottery," Old Man Warner said as he went through the crowd. "Seventy-seventh time."

"Watson." The tall boy came awkwardly through the crowd. Someone said, "Don't be nervous, Jack," and Mr. Summers said, "Take your time, son."

"Zanini."

After that, there was a long pause, a breathless pause, until Mr. Summers, holding his slip of paper in the air, said, "All right, fellows." For a minute, no one moved, and then all the slips of paper were opened. Suddenly, all women began to speak at once, saying, "Who is it?," "Who's got it?," "Is it the Dunbars?," "Is it the Watsons?" Then the voices began to say, "It's Hutchinson. It's Bill." "Bill Hutchinson's got it."

"Go tell your father," Mrs. Dunbar said to her older son.

People began to look around to see the Hutchinsons. Bill Hutchinson was standing quiet, staring down at the paper in his hand. Suddenly, Tessie Hutchinson shouted to Mr. Summers, "You didn't give him time enough to take any paper he wanted. I saw you. It wasn't fair!"

"Be a good sport, Tessie," Mrs. Delacroix called, and Mrs. Graves said, "All of us took the same chance."

"Shut up, Tessie," Bill Hutchinson said.

"Well, everyone," Mr. Summers said, "that was done pretty fast, and now we've got to be hurrying a little more to get done in time." He consulted his next list. "Bill," he said, "you draw for the Hutchinson family. You got any other households in the Hutchinsons?"

"There's Don and Eva," Mrs. Hutchinson yelled. "Make *them* take their chance!"

"Daughters draw with their husbands' families, Tessie," Mr. Summers said gently. "You know that as well as anyone else."

"It wasn't fair," Tessie said.

"I guess not, Joe," Bill Hutchinson said regretfully. "My daughter draws with her husband's family, that's only fair. And I've got no other family except the kids."

"Then, as far as drawing for families is concerned, it's you," Mr. Summers said in explanation, "and as far as drawing for households is concerned, that's you, too. Right?"

"Right," Bill Hutchinson said.

"How many kids, Bill?" Mr. Summers asked formally.

"Three," Bill Hutchinson said. "There's Bill, Jr., and Nancy, and little Dave. And Tessie and me."

"All right, then," Mr. Summers said. "Harry, you got their tickets back?"

Mr. Graves nodded and held up the slips of paper. "Put them in the box, then," Mr. Summers directed. "Take Bill's and put it in."

"I think we ought to start over," Mrs. Hutchinson said, as quietly as she could. "I tell you it wasn't *fair*. You didn't give him time enough to choose. *Every*body saw that."

Mr. Graves had selected the five slips and put them in the box, and he dropped all the papers but those onto the ground, where the breeze caught them and lifted them off.

"Listen, everybody," Mrs. Hutchinson was saying to the people around her.

"Ready, Bill?" Mr. Summers asked, and Bill Hutchinson, with one quick glance around at his wife and children, nodded.

"Remember," Mr. Summers said, "take the slips and keep them folded until each person has taken one. Harry, you help little Dave." Mr. Graves took the hand of the little boy, who came willingly with him up to the box. "Take a paper out of the box, Davy," Mr. Summers said. Davy put his hand into the box and laughed. "Take just *one* paper," Mr. Summers said. "Harry, you hold it for him." Mr. Graves took the child's hand and removed the folded paper from the tight fist and held it while little Dave stood next to him and looked up at him wonderingly.

"Nancy next," Mr. Summers said. Nancy was twelve, and her school friends breathed heavily as she went forward, switching her skirt, and took a slip daintily from the box. "Bill, Jr.," Mr. Summers said, and Billy, his face red and his feet over-large, nearly knocked the box over as he got a paper out. "Tessie," Mr. Summers said. She hesitated for a minute, looking around defiantly, and then set her lips and went up to the box. She snatched a paper out and held it behind her.

"Bill," Mr. Summers said, and Bill Hutchinson reached into the box and felt around, bringing his hand out at last with the slip of paper in it.

The crowd was quiet. A girl whispered, "I hope it's not Nancy," and the sound of the whisper reached the edges of the crowd.

"It's not the way it used to be," Old Man Warner said clearly. "People ain't the way they used to be."

"All right," Mr. Summers said. "Open the papers. Harry, you open little Dave's."

Mr. Graves opened the slip of paper and there was a general sigh through the crowd as he held it up and everyone could see that it was blank. Nancy and Bill, Jr., opened theirs at the same time, and both beamed and laughed, turning around to the crowd and holding their slips of paper above their heads.

"Tessie," Mr. Summers said. There was a pause, and then Mr. Summers looked at Bill Hutchinson, and Bill unfolded his paper and showed it. It was blank.

"It's Tessie," Mr. Summers said, and his voice was hushed. "Show us her paper, Bill."

Bill Hutchinson went over to his wife and forced the slip of paper out of her hand. It had a black spot on it, the black spot Mr. Summers had made the night before with the heavy pencil in the coal-company office. Bill Hutchinson held it up, and there was a stir in the crowd.

"All right, folks," Mr. Summers said, "let's finish quickly."

Although the villagers had forgotten the ritual and lost the original black box, they still remembered to use stones. The pile of stones the boys had made earlier was ready; there were stones on the ground with the blowing scraps of paper that had come out of the box. Mrs. Delacroix selected a stone so large she had to pick it up with both hands and turned to Mrs. Dunbar. "Come on," she said. "Hurry up."

Mrs. Dunbar had small stones in both hands, and she said, gasping for breath, "I can't run at all. You'll have to go ahead and I'll catch up with you."

The children had stones already, and someone gave little Davy Hutchinson a few pebbles.

Tessie Hutchinson was in the center of a cleared space by now, and she held her hands out desperately as the villagers moved in on her. "It isn't fair," she said. A stone hit her on the side of the head.

Old Man Warner was saying, "Come on, come on, everyone." Steve Adams was in the front of the crowd of villagers, with Mrs. Graves beside him.

"It isn't fair, it isn't right," Mrs. Hutchinson screamed, and then they were upon her.

Flannery O'Connor (1925–1964)

A Good Man Is Hard to Find

The grandmother didn't want to go to Florida. She wanted to visit some of her connections in east Tennessee and she was seizing at every chance to change Bailey's mind. Bailey was the son she lived with, her only boy. He was sitting on the edge of his chair at the table, bent over the orange sports section of the *Journal*. "Now look here, Bailey," she said, "see here, read this," and she stood with one hand on her thin hip and the other rattling the newspaper at his bald head. "Here this fellow that calls himself The Misfit is aloose from the Federal Pen and headed toward Florida and you read here what it says he did to these people. Just you read it. I wouldn't take my children in any direction with a criminal like that aloose in it. I couldn't answer to my conscience if I did."

Bailey didn't look up from his reading so she wheeled around then and faced the children's mother, a young woman in slacks, whose face was as broad and innocent as a cabbage and was tied round with a green head-kerchief that had two points on the top like rabbit's ears. She was sitting on the sofa, feeding the baby his apricots out of a jar. "The children have been to Florida before," the old lady said. "You all ought to take them somewhere else for a change so they would see different parts of the world and be broad. They never have been to east Tennessee."

The children's mother didn't seem to hear her but the eight-year-old boy, John Wesley, a stocky child with glasses, said, "If you don't want to go to Florida, why dontcha stay at home?" He and the little girl, June Star, were reading the funny papers on the floor.

"She wouldn't stay at home to be queen for a day," June Star said without raising her yellow head.

"Yes and what would you do if this fellow, The Misfit, caught you?" the grandmother asked.

"I'd smack his face," John Wesley said.

"She wouldn't stay at home for a million bucks," June Star said. "Afraid she'd miss something. She has to go everywhere we go."

"All right, Miss," the grandmother said. "Just remember that the next time you want me to curl your hair."

June Star said her hair was naturally curly.

The next morning the grandmother was the first one in the car, ready to go. She had her big black valise that looked like the head of a hippopotamus in one corner, and underneath it she was hiding a basket with Pitty Sing, the cat, in it. She didn't intend for the cat to be left alone in the house for three days because he would miss her too much and she was afraid he might brush against one of the gas burners and accidentally asphyxiate himself. Her son, Bailey, didn't like to arrive at a motel with a cat.

She sat in the middle of the back seat with John Wesley and June Star on either side of her. Bailey and the children's mother and the baby sat in the front and they left Atlanta at eight forty-five with the mileage on the car at 55890. The grandmother wrote this down because she thought it would be interesting to say how many miles they had been when they got back. It took them twenty minutes to reach the outskirts of the city.

The old lady settled herself comfortably, removing her white cotton gloves and putting them up with her purse on the shelf in front of the back window. The children's mother still had on slacks and still had her head tied up in a green kerchief, but the grandmother had on a navy blue straw sailor hat with a bunch of white violets on the brim and a navy blue dress with a small white dot in the print. Her collar and cuffs were white organdy trimmed with lace and at her neckline she had pinned a purple spray of cloth violets containing a sachet. In case of an accident, anyone seeing her dead on the highway would know at once that she was a lady.

She said she thought it was going to be a good day for driving, neither too hot nor too cold, and she cautioned Bailey that the speed limit was fifty-five miles an hour and that the patrolmen hid themselves behind billboards and small clumps of trees and sped out after you before you had a chance to slow down. She pointed out interesting details of the scenery: Stone Mountain; the blue granite that in some places came up to both sides of the highway; the brilliant red clay banks slightly streaked with purple; and the various crops that made rows of green lace-work on the ground. The trees were full of silver-white sunlight and the meanest of them sparkled. The children were reading comic magazines and their mother had gone back to sleep.

"Let's go through Georgia fast so we won't have to look at it much," John Wesley said.

"If I were a little boy," said the grandmother, "I wouldn't talk about my native state that way. Tennessee has the mountains and Georgia has the hills."

"Tennessee is just a hillbilly dumping ground," John Wesley said, "and Georgia is a lousy state too."

"You said it," June Star said.

"In my time," said the grandmother, folding her thin veined fingers, "children were more respectful of their native states and their parents and everything else. People did right then. Oh look at the cute little pickaninny!" she said and pointed to a Negro child standing in the door of a shack. "Wouldn't that make a picture, now?" she asked and they all turned and looked at the little Negro out of the back window. He waved.

"He didn't have any britches on," June Star said.

"He probably didn't have any," the grandmother explained. "Little niggers in the country don't have things like we do. If I could paint, I'd paint that picture," she said.

The children exchanged comic books.

The grandmother offered to hold the baby and the children's mother passed him over the front seat to her. She set him on her knee and bounced him and told him about the things they were passing. She rolled her eyes and screwed up her mouth and stuck her leathery thin face into his smooth bland one. Occasionally he gave her a faraway smile. They passed a large cotton field with five or six graves fenced in the middle of it, like a small island. "Look at the graveyard!" the grandmother said, pointing it out. "That was the old family burying ground. That belonged to the plantation."

"Where's the plantation?" John Wesley asked.

"Gone With the Wind," said the grandmother. "Ha. Ha."

When the children finished all the comic books they had brought, they opened the lunch and ate it. The grandmother ate a peanut butter sandwich and an olive and would not let the children throw the box and the paper napkins out the window. When there was nothing else to do they played a game by choosing a cloud and making the other two guess what shape it suggested. John Wesley took one the shape of a cow and June Star guessed a cow and John Wesley said, no, an automobile, and June Star said he didn't play fair, and they began to slap each other over the grandmother.

The grandmother said she would tell them a story if they would keep quiet. When she told a story, she rolled her eyes and waved her head and was very dramatic. She said once when she was a maiden lady she had been courted by a Mr. Edgar Atkins Teagarden from Jasper, Georgia. She said he was a very good-looking man and a gentleman and that he brought her a watermelon every Saturday afternoon with his initials cut in it, E. A. T. Well, one Saturday, she said, Mr. Teagarden brought the watermelon and there was nobody at home and he left it on the front porch and returned in his buggy to Jasper, but she never got the watermelon, she said, because a nigger boy ate it when he saw the initials, E. A. T.! This story tickled John Wesley's funny bone and he giggled and giggled but June Star didn't think it was any good. She said she wouldn't marry a man that just brought her a watermelon on Saturday. The grandmother said she would have done well to marry Mr. Teagarden because he was a gentleman and had bought Coca-Cola stock when it first came out and that he had died only a few years ago, a very wealthy man.

They stopped at The Tower for barbecued sandwiches. The Tower was a part stucco and part wood filling station and dance hall set in a clearing outside of Timothy. A fat man named Red Sammy Butts ran it and there were signs stuck here and there on the building and for miles up and down the highway saying, TRY RED SAMMY'S FAMOUS BARBECUE. NONE LIKE FAMOUS RED SAMMY'S! RED SAM! THE FAT BOY WITH THE HAPPY LAUGH. A VETERAN! RED SAMMY'S YOUR MAN!

Red Sammy was lying on the bare ground outside The Tower

with his head under a truck while a gray monkey about a foot high, chained to a small chinaberry tree, chattered nearby. The monkey sprang back into the tree and got on the highest limb as soon as he saw the children jump out of the car and run toward him.

Inside, The Tower was a long dark room with a counter at one end and tables at the other and dancing space in the middle. They all sat down at a broad table next to the nickelodeon and Red Sam's wife, a tall burnt-brown woman with hair and eyes lighter than her skin, came and took their order. The children's mother put a dime in the machine and played "The Tennessee Waltz," and the grandmother said that tune always made her want to dance. She asked Bailey if he would like to dance but he only glared at her. He didn't have a naturally sunny disposition like she did and trips made him nervous. The grandmother's brown eyes were very bright. She swayed her head from side to side and pretended she was dancing in her chair. June Star said play something she could tap to so the children's mother put in another dime and played a fast number and June Star stepped out onto the dance floor and did her tap routine.

"Ain't she cute?" Red Sam's wife said, leaning over the counter. "Would you like to come be my little girl?"

"No I certainly wouldn't," June Star said. "I wouldn't live in a broken-down place like this for a million bucks!" and she ran back to the table.

"Ain't she cute?" the woman repeated, stretching her mouth politely.

"Aren't you ashamed?" hissed the grandmother.

Red Sam came in and told his wife to quit lounging on the counter and hurry with these people's order. His khaki trousers reached just to his hip bones and his stomach hung over them like a sack of meal swaying under his shirt. He came over and sat down at a table nearby and let out a combination sigh and yodel. "You can't win," he said. "You can't win," and he wiped his sweating red face off with a gray handkerchief. "These days you don't know who to trust," he said. "Ain't that the truth?"

"People are certainly not nice like they used to be," said the grandmother.

"Two fellers come in here last week," Red Sammy said, "driving a Chrysler. It was a old beat-up car but it was a good one and these boys looked all right to me. Said they worked at the mill and you know I let them fellers charge the gas they bought? Now why did I do that?"

"Because you're a good man!" the grandmother said at once.

"Yes'm, I suppose so," Red Sam said as if he were struck with the answer.

His wife brought the orders, carrying the five plates all at once without a tray, two in each hand and one balanced on her arm. "It isn't a soul in this green world of God's that you can trust," she said. "And I don't count anybody out of that, not nobody," she repeated, looking at Red Sammy.

"Did you read about that criminal, The Misfit, that's escaped?" asked the grandmother.

"I wouldn't be a bit surprised if he didn't attack this place right here," said the woman. "If he hears about it being here, I wouldn't be none surprised to see him. If he hears it's two cent in the cash register, I wouldn't be a tall surprised if he . . ."

"That'll do," Red Sam said. "Go bring these people their Co'Colas," and the woman went off to get the rest of the order.

"A good man is hard to find," Red Sammy said. "Everything is getting terrible. I remember the day you could go off and leave your screen door unlatched. Not no more."

He and the grandmother discussed better times. The old lady said that in her opinion Europe was entirely to blame for the way things were now. She said the way Europe acted you would think we were made of money and Red Sam said it was no use talking about it, she was exactly right. The children ran outside into the white sunlight and looked at the monkey in the lacy chinaberry tree. He was busy catching fleas on himself and biting each one carefully between his teeth as if it were a delicacy.

They drove off again into the hot afternoon. The grandmother took cat naps and woke up every few minutes with her own snoring. Outside of Toombsboro she woke up and recalled an old plantation that she had visited in this neighborhood once when she was a young lady. She said the house had six white columns across the front and that there was an avenue of oaks leading up to it and two little wooden trellis arbors on either side in front where you sat down with your suitor after a stroll in the garden. She recalled exactly which road to turn off to get to it. She knew that Bailey would not be willing to lose any time looking at an old house, but the more she talked about it, the more she wanted to see it once again and find out if the little twin arbors were still standing. "There was a secret panel in this house," she said craftily, not telling the truth but wishing that she were, "and the story went that all the family silver was hidden in it when Sherman came through but it was never found . . ."

"Hey!" John Wesley said. "Let's go see it! We'll find it! We'll poke all the woodwork and find it! Who lives there? Where do you turn off at? Hey Pop, can't we turn off there?"

"We never have seen a house with a secret panel!" June Star shrieked. "Let's go to the house with the secret panel! Hey, Pop, can't we go see the house with the secret panel!"

"It's not far from here, I know," the grandmother said. "It wouldn't take over twenty minutes."

Bailey was looking straight ahead. His jaw was as rigid as a horseshoe. "No," he said.

The children began to yell and scream that they wanted to see the house with the secret panel. John Wesley kicked the back of the front seat and June Star hung over her mother's shoulder and whined desperately into her ear that they never had any fun even on their vacation, and that they could never do what THEY wanted to do. The baby began to scream and John Wesley kicked the back of the seat so hard that his father could feel the blows in his kidney.

"All right!" he shouted, and drew the car to a stop at the side of the road. "Will you all shut up? Will you all just shut up for one second? If you don't shut up, we won't go anywhere."

"It would be very educational for them," the grandmother murmured.

"All right," Bailey said, "but get this: this is the only time we're going to stop for anything like this. This is the one and only time."

"The dirt road that you have to turn down is about a mile back," the grandmother directed. "I marked it when we passed."

"A dirt road," Bailey groaned.

After they had turned around and were headed toward the dirt road, the grandmother recalled other points about the house, the beautiful glass over the front doorway and the candle-lamp in the hall. John Wesley said that the secret panel was probably in the fireplace.

"You can't go inside this house," Bailey said. "You don't know who lives there."

"While you all talk to the people in front, I'll run around behind and get in a window," John Wesley suggested.

"We'll all stay in the car," his mother said.

They turned onto the dirt road and the car raced roughly along in a swirl of pink dust. The grandmother recalled the times when there were no paved roads and thirty miles was a day's journey. The dirt road was hilly and there were sudden washes in it and sharp curves on dangerous embankments. All at once they would be on a hill, looking down over the blue tops of trees for miles around, then the next minute, they would be in a red depression with the dust-coated trees looking down on them.

"This place had better turn up in a minute," Bailey said, "or I'm going to turn around."

The road looked as if no one had traveled on it in months.

"It's not much farther," the grandmother said and just as she said it, a horrible thought came to her. The thought was so embarrassing that she turned red in the face and her eyes dilated and her feet jumped up, upsetting her valise in the corner. The instant the valise moved, the newspaper top she had over the basket under it rose with a snarl and Pitty Sing, the cat, sprang onto Bailey's shoulder.

The children were thrown to the floor and their mother, clutching the baby, was thrown out of the door onto the ground, the old lady was thrown into the front seat. The car turned over once and landed rightside up in a gulch on the side of the road. Bailey remained in the driver's seat with the cat — gray-striped with a broad white face and an orange nose — clinging to his neck like a caterpillar.

As soon as the children saw they could move their arms and legs, they scrambled out of the car, shouting, "We've had an ACCIDENT!" The grandmother was curled up under the dashboard, hoping she was injured so that Bailey's wrath would not come down on her all at once. The horrible thought she had had before the accident was that the house she had remembered so vividly was not in Georgia but in Tennessee.

Bailey removed the cat from his neck with both hands and flung it out the window against the side of a pine tree. Then he got out of the car and started looking for the children's mother. She was sitting against the side of the red gutted ditch, holding the screaming baby, but she only had a cut down her face and a broken shoulder. "We've had an ACCIDENT!" the children screamed in a frenzy of delight.

"But nobody's killed," June Star said with disappointment as the grandmother limped out of the car, her hat still pinned to her head but the broken front brim standing up at a jaunty angle and the violet spray hanging off the side. They all sat down in the ditch, except the children, to recover from the shock. They were all shaking.

"Maybe a car will come along," said the children's mother hoarsely.

"I believe I have injured an organ," said the grandmother, pressing her side, but no one answered her. Bailey's teeth were clattering. He had on a yellow sport shirt with bright blue parrots designed in it and his face was as yellow as the shirt. The grandmother decided that she would not mention that the house was in Tennessee.

The road was about ten feet above and they could see only the tops of the trees on the other side of it. Behind the ditch they were sitting in there were more woods, tall and dark and deep. In a few minutes they saw a car some distance away on top of a hill, coming slowly as if the occupants were watching them. The grandmother stood up and waved both arms dramatically to attract their attention. The car continued to come on slowly, disappeared around a bend and appeared again, moving even slower, on top of the hill they had gone over. It was a big black battered hearselike automobile. There were three men in it.

It came to a stop just over them and for some minutes, the driver looked down with a steady expressionless gaze to where they were sitting, and didn't speak. Then he turned his head and muttered something to the other two and they got out. One was a fat boy in black trousers and a red sweat shirt with a silver stallion embossed on the front of it. He moved around on the right side of them and stood staring, his mouth partly open in a kind of loose grin. The other had on khaki pants and a blue striped coat and a gray hat pulled down very low, hiding most of his face. He came around slowly on the left side. Neither spoke.

The driver got out of the car and stood by the side of it, looking down at them. He was an older man than the other two. His hair was just beginning to gray and he wore silver-rimmed spectacles that gave him a scholarly look. He had a long creased face and didn't have on any shirt or undershirt. He had on blue jeans that were too tight for him and was holding a black hat and a gun. The two boys also had guns.

"We've had an ACCIDENT!" the children screamed.

The grandmother had the peculiar feeling that the bespectacled man was someone she knew. His face was as familiar to her as if she had known him all her life, but she could not recall who he was. He moved away from the car and began to come down the embankment, placing his feet carefully so that he wouldn't slip. He had on tan and white shoes and no socks, and his ankles were red and thin. "Good afternoon," he said. "I see you all had you a little spill."

"We turned over twice!" said the grandmother.

"Oncet," he corrected. "We seen it happen. Try their car and see will it run, Hiram," he said quietly to the boy with the gray hat.

"What you got that gun for?" John Wesley asked. "Watcha gonna do with that gun?"

"Lady," the man said to the children's mother, "would you mind calling them children to set down by you? Children make me nervous. I want all you all to sit down right together there where you're at."

"What are you telling us what to do for?" June Star asked.

Behind them the line of woods gaped like a dark open mouth. "Come here," said their mother.

"Look here now," Bailey began suddenly, "we're in a predicament! We're in . . ."

The grandmother shrieked. She scrambled to her feet and stood staring. "You're The Misfit!" she said. "I recognized you at once."

"Yes'm," the man said, smiling slightly as if he were pleased in spite of himself to be known, "but it would have been better for all of you, lady, if you hadn't of recognized me."

Bailey turned his head sharply and said something to his mother that shocked even the children. The old lady began to cry and The Misfit reddened.

"Lady," he said, "don't you get upset. Sometimes a man says things he don't mean. I don't reckon he meant to talk to you thataway."

"You wouldn't shoot a lady, would you?" the grandmother said and removed a clean handkerchief from her cuff and began to slap at her eyes with it.

The Misfit pointed the toe of his shoe into the ground and made a little hole and then covered it up again. "I would hate to have to," he said.

"Listen," the grandmother almost screamed, "I know you're a good man. You don't look a bit like you have common blood. I know you must come from nice people!"

"Yes ma'm," he said, "finest people in the world." When he smiled he showed a row of strong white teeth. "God never made a finer woman than my mother and my daddy's heart was pure gold," he said. The boy with the red sweat shirt had come around behind them and was standing with his gun at his hip. The Misfit squatted down on the ground. "Watch them children, Bobby Lee," he said. "You know they make me nervous." He looked at the six of them huddled together in front of him and he seemed to be embarrassed as if he couldn't think of anything to say. "Ain't a cloud in the sky," he remarked, looking up at it. "Don't see no sun but don't see no cloud neither."

"Yes, it's a beautiful day," said the grandmother. "Listen," she said, "you shouldn't call yourself The Misfit because I know you're a good man at heart. I can just look at you and tell."

"Hush!" Bailey yelled. "Hush! Everybody shut up and let me handle this!" He was squatting in the position of a runner about to sprint forward but he didn't move.

"I pre-chate that, lady," The Misfit said and drew a little circle in the ground with the butt of his gun.

"It'll take a half a hour to fix this here car," Hiram called, looking over the raised hood of it.

"Well, first you and Bobby Lee get him and that little boy to step over yonder with you," The Misfit said, pointing to Bailey and John Wesley. "The boys want to ask you something," he said to Bailey. "Would you mind stepping back in them woods there with them?"

"Listen," Bailey began, "we're in a terrible predicament. Nobody realizes what this is," and his voice cracked. His eyes were as blue and intense as the parrots in his shirt and he remained perfectly still.

The grandmother reached up to adjust her hat brim as if she were going to the woods with him but it came off in her hand. She stood staring at it and after a second she let it fall on the ground. Hiram pulled Bailey up by the arm as if he were assisting an old man. John Wesley caught hold of his father's hand and Bobby Lee followed. They went off toward the woods and just as they reached the dark edge, Bailey turned and supporting himself against a gray naked pine trunk, he shouted, "I'll be back in a minute, Mamma, wait on me!"

"Come back this instant!" his mother shrilled but they all disappeared into the woods.

"Bailey Boy!" the grandmother called in a tragic voice but she found she was looking at The Misfit squatting on the ground in front of her. "I just know you're a good man," she said desperately. "You're not a bit common!"

"Nome, I ain't a good man," The Misfit said after a second as if he had considered her statement carefully, "but I ain't the worst in the world neither. My daddy said I was a different breed of dog from my brothers and sisters. 'You know,' Daddy said, 'it's some that can live their whole life out without asking about it and it's others has to know why it is, and this boy is one of the latters. He's going to be into everything!'" He put on his black hat and looked up suddenly and then away deep into the woods as if he were embarrassed again. "I'm sorry I don't have on a shirt before you ladies," he said, hunching his shoulders slightly. "We buried our clothes that we had on when we escaped and we're just making do until we can get better. We borrowed these from some folks we met," he explained.

"That's perfectly all right," the grandmother said. "Maybe Bailey has an extra shirt in his suitcase."

"I'll look and see terrectly," The Misfit said.

"Where are they taking him?" the children's mother screamed.

"Daddy was a card himself," The Misfit said. "You couldn't put anything over on him. He never got in trouble with the Authorities though. Just had the knack of handling them."

"You could be honest too if you'd only try," said the grandmother. "Think how wonderful it would be to settle down and live a comfortable life and not have to think about somebody chasing you all the time."

The Misfit kept scratching in the ground with the butt of his gun as if he were thinking about it. "Yes'm, somebody is always after you," he murmured.

The grandmother noticed how thin his shoulder blades were just behind his hat because she was standing up looking down on him. "Do you ever pray?" she asked.

He shook his head. All she saw was the black hat wiggle between shoulder blades. "Nome," he said.

There was a pistol shot from the woods, followed closely by another. Then silence. The old lady's head jerked around. She could hear the wind move through the tree tops like a long satisfied insuck of breath. "Bailey Boy!" she called.

"I was a gospel singer for a while," The Misfit said. "I been most everything. Been in the arm service, both land and sea, at home and abroad, been twict married, been an undertaker, been with the railroads, plowed Mother Earth, been in a tornado, seen a man burnt alive oncet," and he looked up at the children's mother and the little girl who were sitting close together, their faces white and their eyes glassy; "I even seen a woman flogged," he said.

"Pray, pray," the grandmother began, "pray, pray . . ."

"I never was a bad boy that I remember of," The Misfit said in an almost dreamy voice, "but somewheres along the line I done something wrong and got sent to the penitentiary. I was buried alive," and he looked up and held her attention to him by a steady stare.

"That's when you should have started to pray," she said. "What did you do to get sent to the penitentiary that first time?"

"Turn to the right, it was a wall," The Misfit said, looking up again at the cloudless sky. "Turn to the left, it was a wall. Look up it was a ceiling, look down it was a floor. I forget what

I done, lady. I set there and set there, trying to remember what it was I done and I ain't recalled it to this day. Oncet in a while, I would think it was coming to me, but it never come."

"Maybe they put you in by mistake," the old lady said vaguely.

"Nome," he said. "It wasn't no mistake. They had the papers on me."

"You must have stolen something," she said.

The Misfit sneered slightly. "Nobody had nothing I wanted," he said. "It was a head-doctor at the penitentiary said what I had done was kill my daddy but I know that for a lie. My daddy died in nineteen ought nineteen of the epidemic flu and I never had a thing to do with it. He was buried in the Mount Hopewell Baptist churchyard and you can go there and see for yourself."

"If you would pray," the old lady said, "Jesus would help you."

"That's right," The Misfit said.

"Well then, why don't you pray?" she asked trembling with delight suddenly.

"I don't want no hep," he said. "I'm doing all right by myself."

Bobby Lee and Hiram came ambling back from the woods. Bobby Lee was dragging a yellow shirt with bright blue parrots in it.

"Throw me that shirt, Bobby Lee," The Misfit said. The shirt came flying at him and landed on his shoulder and he put it on. The grandmother couldn't name what the shirt reminded her of. "No, lady," The Misfit said while he was buttoning it up. "I found out the crime don't matter. You can do one thing or you can do another, kill a man or take a tire off his car, because sooner or later you're going to forget what it was you done and just be punished for it."

The children's mother had begun to make heaving noises as if she couldn't get her breath. "Lady," he asked, "would you and that little girl like to step off yonder with Bobby Lee and Hiram and join your husband?"

"Yes, thank you," the mother said faintly. Her left arm dangled helplessly and she was holding the baby, who had gone to sleep, in the other. "Hep that lady up, Hiram," The Misfit said as she struggled to climb out of the ditch, "and Bobby Lee, you hold onto that little girl's hand."

"I don't want to hold hands with him," June Star said. "He reminds me of a pig."

The fat boy blushed and laughed and caught her by the arm and pulled her off into the woods after Hiram and her mother.

Alone with The Misfit, the grandmother found that she had lost her voice. There was not a cloud in the sky nor any sun. There was nothing around her but woods. She wanted to tell him that he must pray. She opened and closed her mouth several times before anything came out. Finally she found herself saying, "Jesus, Jesus," meaning Jesus will help you, but the way she was saying it, it sounded as if she might be cursing.

"Yes'm," The Misfit said as if he agreed. "Jesus thown everything off balance. It was the same case with Him as with me except He hadn't committed any crime and they could prove I had committed one because they had the papers on me. Of course," he said, "they never shown me my papers. That's why I sign myself now. I said long ago, you get you a signature and sign everything you do and keep a copy of it. Then you'll know what you done and you can hold up the crime to the punishment and see do they match and in the end you'll have something to prove you ain't been treated right. I call myself The Misfit," he said, "because I can't make what all I done wrong fit what all I gone through in punishment."

There was a piercing scream from the woods, followed closely by a pistol report. "Does it seem right to you, lady, that one is punished a heap and another ain't punished at all?"

"Jesus!" the old lady cried. "You've got good blood! I know you wouldn't shoot a lady! I know you come from nice people! Pray! Jesus, you ought not to shoot a lady. I'll give you all the money I've got!"

"Lady," The Misfit said, looking beyond her far into the woods, "there never was a body that give the undertaker a tip."

There were two more pistol reports and the grandmother raised her head like a parched old turkey hen crying for water and called, "Bailey Boy, Bailey Boy!" as if her heart would break.

"Jesus was the only One that ever raised the dead." The Misfit continued, "and He shouldn't have done it. He thown everything off balance. If He did what He said, then it's nothing for you to do but thow away everything and follow Him, and if He didn't, then it's nothing for you to do but enjoy the few minutes you got left the best way you can — by killing somebody or burning down his house or doing some other meanness to him. No pleasure but meanness," he said and his voice had become almost a snarl.

"Maybe He didn't raise the dead," the old lady mumbled, not knowing what she was saying and feeling so dizzy that she sank down in the ditch with her legs twisted under her.

"I wasn't there so I can't say He didn't," The Misfit said. "I wisht I had of been there," he said, hitting the ground with his fist. "It ain't right I wasn't there because if I had of been there I would of known. Listen lady," he said in a high voice, "if I had of been there I would of known and I wouldn't be like I am now." His voice seemed about to crack and the grandmother's head cleared for an instant. She saw the man's face twisted close to her own as if he were going to cry and she murmured, "Why you're one of my babies. You're one of my own children!" She reached out and touched him on the shoulder. The Misfit sprang back as if a snake had bitten him and shot her three times through the chest. Then he put his gun down on the ground and took off his glasses and began to clean them.

Hiram and Bobby Lee returned from the woods and stood over the ditch, looking down at the grandmother who half sat and half lay in a puddle of blood with her legs crossed under her like a child's and her face smiling up at the cloudless sky.

Without his glasses, The Misfit's eyes were red-rimmed and pale and defenseless-looking. "Take her off and thow her where you thown the others," he said, picking up the cat that was rubbing itself against his leg.

"She was a talker, wasn't she?" Bobby Lee said, sliding down the ditch with a yodel.

"She would of been a good woman," The Misfit said, "if it had been somebody there to shoot her every minute of her life."

"Some fun!" Bobby Lee said.

"Shut up, Bobby Lee," The Misfit said. "It's no real pleasure in life."

Flannery O'Connor (1925–1964)

Revelation

The doctor's waiting room, which was very small, was almost full when the Turpins entered and Mrs. Turpin, who was very large, made it look even smaller by her presence. She stood looming at the head of the magazine table set in the center of it, a living demonstration that the room was inadequate and ridiculous. Her little bright black eyes took in all the patients as she sized up the seating situation. There was one vacant chair and a place on the sofa occupied by a blond child in a dirty blue romper who should have been told to move over and make room for the lady. He was five or six, but Mrs. Turpin saw at once that no one was going to tell him to move over. He was slumped down in the seat, his arms idle at his sides and his eyes idle in his head; his nose ran unchecked.

Mrs. Turpin put a firm hand on Claud's shoulder and said in a voice that included everyone that wanted to listen, "Claud, you sit in that chair there," and gave him a push down into the vacant one. Claud was florid and bald and sturdy, somewhat shorter than Mrs. Turpin, but he sat down as if he were accustomed to doing what she told him to.

Mrs. Turpin remained standing. The only man in the room besides Claud was a lean stringy old fellow with a rusty hand spread out on each knee, whose eyes were closed as if he were asleep or dead or pretending to be so as not to get up and offer her his seat. Her gaze settled agreeably on a well-dressed gray-haired lady whose eyes met hers and whose expression said: If that child belonged to me, he would have some manners and move over — there's plenty of room there for you and him too.

Claud looked up with a sigh and made as if to rise.

"Sit down," Mrs. Turpin said. "You know you're not supposed to stand on that leg. He has an ulcer on his leg," she explained.

Claud lifted his foot onto the magazine table and rolled his trouser leg up to reveal a purple swelling on a plump marble-white calf.

"My!" the pleasant lady said. "How did you do that?"

"A cow kicked him," Mrs. Turpin said.

"Goodness!" said the lady.

Claud rolled his trouser leg down.

"Maybe the little boy would move over," the lady suggested, but the child did not stir.

"Somebody will be leaving in a minute," Mrs. Turpin said. She could not understand why a doctor — with as much money as they made charging five dollars a day just to stick their head in the hospital door and look at you — couldn't afford a decent-sized waiting room. This one was hardly bigger than a garage. The table was cluttered with limp-looking magazines and at one end of it there was a big green glass ash tray full of cigaret butts and cotton wads with little blood spots on them. If she had had anything to do with the running of the place, that would have been emptied every so often. There were no chairs against the wall at the head of the room. It had a rectangular-shaped panel in it that permitted a view of the office where the nurse came and went and the secretary listened to the radio. A plastic fern in a gold pot sat in the opening and trailed its fronds down almost to the floor. The radio was softly playing gospel music.

Just then the inner door opened and a nurse with the highest stack of yellow hair Mrs. Turpin had ever seen put her face in the crack and called for the next patient. The woman sitting beside Claud grasped the two arms of her chair and hoisted herself up; she pulled her dress free from her legs and lumbered through the door where the nurse had disappeared.

Mrs. Turpin eased into the vacant chair, which held her tight as a corset. "I wish I could reduce," she said, and rolled her eyes and gave a comic sigh.

"Oh, *you* aren't fat," the stylish lady said.

"Ooooo I am too," Mrs. Turpin said. "Claud he eats all he wants to and never weighs over one hundred and seventy-five pounds, but me I just look at something good to eat and I gain some weight," and her stomach and shoulders shook with laughter. "You can eat all you want to, can't you, Claud?" she asked turning to him.

Claud only grinned.

"Well, as long as you have such a good disposition," the stylish lady said, "I don't think it makes a bit of difference what size you are. You just can't beat a good disposition."

Next to her was a fat girl of eighteen or nineteen, scowling into a thick blue book which Mrs. Turpin saw was entitled *Human Development*. The girl raised her head and directed her scowl at Mrs. Turpin as if she did not like her looks. She appeared annoyed that anyone should speak while she tried to read. The poor girl's face was blue with acne and Mrs. Turpin thought how pitiful it was to have a face like that at that age. She gave the girl a friendly smile but the girl only scowled the harder. Mrs. Turpin herself was fat but she had always had good skin, and, though she was forty-seven years old, there was not a wrinkle in her face except around her eyes from laughing too much.

Next to the ugly girl was the child, still in exactly the same position, and next to him was a thin leathery old woman in a cotton print dress. She and Claud had three sacks of chicken feed in their pump house that was in the same print. She had seen from the first that the child belonged with the old woman. She could tell by the way they sat — kind of vacant and white-trashy, as if they would sit there until Doomsday if nobody called and told them to get up. And at right angles but next to the well-dressed pleasant lady was a lank-faced woman who was certainly the child's mother. She had on a yellow sweat shirt and wine-colored slacks, both gritty-looking, and the rims of her lips were stained with snuff. Her dirty yellow hair was tied behind with a little piece of red paper ribbon. Worse than niggers any day, Mrs. Turpin thought.

The gospel hymn playing was, "When I looked up and He looked down," and Mrs. Turpin, who knew it, supplied the last line mentally, "And wona these days I know I'll we-eara crown."

Without appearing to, Mrs. Turpin always noticed people's feet. The well-dressed lady had on red and gray suede shoes to match her dress. Mrs. Turpin had on her good black patent leather pumps. The ugly girl had on Girl Scout shoes and heavy socks. The old woman had on tennis shoes and the white-trashy mother had on what appeared to be bedroom slippers, black straw with gold braid threaded through them — exactly what you would have expected her to have on.

Sometimes at night when she couldn't go to sleep, Mrs. Turpin would occupy herself with the question of who she would have chosen to be if she couldn't have been herself. If Jesus had said to her before he made her, "There's only two places available for you. You can either be a nigger or white-trash," what would she have said? "Please, Jesus, please," she would have said, "just let me wait until there's another place available," and he would have said, "No, you have to go right now and I have only those two places so make up your mind." She would have wiggled and squirmed and begged and pleaded but it would have been no use and finally she would have said, "All right, make me a nigger then — but that don't mean a trashy one." And he would have made her a neat clean respectable Negro woman, herself but black.

Next to the child's mother was a red-headed youngish woman, reading one of the magazines and working a piece of chewing gum, hell for leather, as Claud would say. Mrs. Turpin could not see the woman's feet. She was not white-trash, just common. Sometimes Mrs. Turpin occupied herself at night naming the classes of people. On the bottom of the heap were most colored people, not the kind she would have been if she had been one, but most of them; then next to them — not above, just away from — were the white-trash; then above them were the homeowners, and above them the home-and-land owners, to which she and Claud belonged. Above she and Claud were people with a lot of money and much bigger houses and much more land. But here the complexity of it would begin to bear in on her, for some of the people with a lot of money were common and ought to be below she and Claud and some of the people who had good blood had lost their money and had to rent and then there were colored people who owned their homes and land as well. There was a colored dentist in town who had two red Lincolns and a swimming pool and a farm with registered white-face cattle on it. Usually by the time she had fallen asleep all the classes of people were moiling and roiling around in her head, and she would dream they were all crammed in together in a box car, being ridden off to be put in a gas oven.

"That's a beautiful clock," she said and nodded to her right. It was a big wall clock, the face encased in a brass sunburst.

"Yes, it's very pretty," the stylish lady said agreeably. "And right on the dot too," she added, glancing at her watch.

The ugly girl beside her cast an eye upward at the clock, smirked, then looked directly at Mrs. Turpin and smirked again. Then she returned her eyes to her book. She was obviously the lady's daughter because, although they didn't look anything alike as to disposition, they both had the same shape of face and the same blue eyes. On the lady they sparkled pleasantly but in the girl's seared face they appeared alternately to smolder and to blaze.

What if Jesus had said, "All right, you can be white-trash or a nigger or ugly"!

Mrs. Turpin felt an awful pity for the girl, though she thought it was one thing to be ugly and another to act ugly.

The woman with the snuff-stained lips turned around in her chair and looked up at the clock. Then she turned back and appeared to look a little to the side of Mrs. Turpin. There was a cast in one of her eyes. "You want to know wher you can get one of themther clocks?" she asked in a loud voice.

"No, I already have a nice clock," Mrs. Turpin said. Once somebody like her got a leg in the conversation, she would be all over it.

"You can get you one with green stamps," the woman said. "That's most likely wher he got hisn. Save you up enough, you can get you most anythang. I got me some joo'ry."

Ought to have got you a wash rag and some soap, Mrs. Turpin thought.

"I get contour sheets with mine," the pleasant lady said.

The daughter slammed her book shut. She looked straight in front of her, directly through Mrs. Turpin and on through the yellow curtain and the plate glass window which made the wall behind her. The girl's eyes seemed lit all of a sudden with a peculiar light, an unnatural light like night road signs give. Mrs. Turpin turned her head to see if there was anything going on outside that she should see, but she could not see anything. Figures passing cast only a pale shadow through the curtain. There was no reason the girl should single her out for her ugly looks.

"Miss Finley," the nurse said, cracking the door. The gum-chewing woman got up and passed in front of her and Claud and went into the office. She had on red high-heeled shoes.

Directly across the table, the ugly girl's eyes were fixed on Mrs. Turpin as if she had some very special reason for disliking her.

"This is wonderful weather, isn't it?" the girl's mother said.

"It's good weather for cotton if you can get the niggers to pick it," Mrs. Turpin said, "but niggers don't want to pick cotton any more. You can't get the white folks to pick it and now you can't get the niggers — because they got to be right up there with the white folks."

"They gonna *try* anyways," the white-trash woman said, leaning forward.

"Do you have one of those cotton-picking machines?" the pleasant lady asked.

"No," Mrs. Turpin said, "they leave half the cotton in the field. We don't have much cotton anyway. If you want to make it farming now, you have to have a little of everything. We got a couple of acres of cotton and a few hogs and chickens and just enough white-face that Claud can look after them himself."

"One thang I don't want," the white-trash woman said, wiping her mouth with the back of her hand. "Hogs. Nasty stinking things, a-gruntin and a-rootin all over the place."

Mrs. Turpin gave her the merest edge of her attention. "Our hogs are not dirty and they don't stink," she said. "They're cleaner than some children I've seen. Their feet never touch the ground. We have a pig-parlor — that's where you raise them on concrete," she explained to the pleasant lady, "and Claud scoots them down with the hose every afternoon and washes off the floor." Cleaner by far than that child right there, she thought. Poor nasty little thing. He had not moved except to put the thumb of his dirty hand into his mouth.

The woman turned her face away from Mrs. Turpin. "I know I wouldn't scoot down no hog with no hose," she said to the wall.

You wouldn't have no hog to scoot down, Mrs. Turpin said to herself.

"A-gruntin and a-rootin and a-groanin," the woman muttered.

"We got a little of everything," Mrs. Turpin said to the pleasant lady. "It's no use in having more than you can handle yourself with help like it is. We found enough niggers to pick our cotton this year but Claud he has to go after them and take them home again in the evening. They can't walk that half a mile. No they can't. I tell you," she said and laughed merrily, "I sure am tired of buttering up niggers, but you got to love em if you want em to work for you. When they come in the morning, I run out and I say, 'Hi yawl this morning?' and when Claud drives them off to the field I just wave to beat the band and they just wave back." And she waved her hand rapidly to illustrate.

"Like you read out of the same book," the lady said, showing she understood perfectly.

"Child, yes," Mrs. Turpin said. "And when they come in from the field, I run out with a bucket of icewater. That's the way it's going to be from now on," she said. "You may as well face it."

"One thang I know," the white-trash woman said. "Two thangs I ain't going to do: love no niggers or scoot down no hog with no hose." And she let out a bark of contempt.

The look that Mrs. Turpin and the pleasant lady exchanged indicated they both understood that you had to *have* certain things before you could *know* certain things. But every time Mrs. Turpin exchanged a look with the lady, she was aware that the ugly girl's peculiar eyes were still on her, and she had trouble bringing her attention back to the conversation.

"When you got something," she said, "you got to look after it." And when you ain't got a thing but breath and britches, she added to herself, you can afford to come to town every morning and just sit on the Court House coping and spit.

A grotesque revolving shadow passed across the curtain behind her and was thrown palely on the opposite wall. Then a bicycle clattered down against the outside of the building. The door opened and a colored boy glided in with a tray from the drug store. It had two large red and white paper cups on it with tops on them. He was a tall, very black boy in discolored white pants and a green nylon shirt. He was chewing gum slowly, as if to music. He set the tray down in the office opening next to the fern and stuck his head through to look for the secretary. She was not in there. He rested his arms on the ledge and waited, his narrow bottom stuck out, swaying slowly to the left and right. He raised a hand over his head and scratched the base of his skull.

"You see that button there, boy?" Mrs. Turpin said. "You can punch that and she'll come. She's probably in the back somewhere."

"Is thas right?" the boy said agreeably, as if he had never seen the button before. He leaned to the right and put his finger on it. "She sometime out," he said and twisted around to face his audience, his elbows behind him on the counter. The nurse appeared and he twisted back again. She handed him a dollar and he rooted in his pocket and made the change and counted it out to her. She gave him fifteen cents for a tip and he went out with the empty tray. The heavy door swung to slowly and closed at length with the sound of suction. For a moment no one spoke.

"They ought to send all them niggers back to Africa," the white-trash woman said. "That's wher they come from in the first place."

"Oh, I couldn't do without my good colored friends," the pleasant lady said.

"There's a heap of things worse than a nigger," Mrs. Turpin agreed. "It's all kinds of them just like it's all kinds of us."

"Yes, and it takes all kinds to make the world go round," the lady said in her musical voice.

As she said it, the raw-complexioned girl snapped her teeth together. Her lower lip turned downwards and inside out, revealing the pale pink inside of her mouth. After a second it rolled back up. It was the ugliest face Mrs. Turpin had ever seen anyone make and for a moment she was certain that the girl had made it at her. She was looking at her as if she had known and disliked her all her life — all of Mrs. Turpin's life, it seemed too, not just all the girl's life. Why, girl, I don't even know you, Mrs. Turpin said silently.

She forced her attention back to the discussion. "It wouldn't be practical to send them back to Africa," she said. "They wouldn't want to go. They got it too good here."

"Wouldn't be what they wanted — if I had anythang to do with it," the woman said.

"It wouldn't be a way in the world you could get all the niggers back over there," Mrs. Turpin said. "They'd be hiding out and lying down and turning sick on you and wailing and hollering and raring and pitching. It wouldn't be a way in the world to get them over there."

"They got over here," the trashy woman said. "Get back like they got over."

"It wasn't so many of them then," Mrs. Turpin explained.

The woman looked at Mrs. Turpin as if here was an idiot indeed but Mrs. Turpin was not bothered by the look, considering where it came from.

"Nooo," she said, "they're going to stay here where they can go to New York and marry white folks and improve their color. That's what they all want to do, every one of them, improve their color."

"You know what comes of that, don't you?" Claude asked.

"No, Claud, what?" Mrs. Turpin said.

Claud's eyes twinkled. "White-faced niggers," he said with never a smile.

Everybody in the office laughed except the white-trash and the ugly girl. The girl gripped the book in her lap with white fingers. The trashy woman looked around her from face to face as if she thought they were all idiots. The old woman in the feed sack dress continued to gaze expressionless across the floor at the high-top shoes of the man opposite her, the one who had been pretending to be asleep when the Turpins came in. He was laughing heartily, his hands still spread out on his knees. The child had fallen to the side and was lying now almost face down in the old woman's lap.

While they recovered from their laughter, the nasal chorus on the radio kept the room from silence.

> You go to blank blank
> And I'll go to mine
> But we'll all blank along
> To-geth-ther
> And all along the blank
> We'll hep each other out
> Smile-ling in any kind of
> Weath-ther!

Mrs. Turpin didn't catch every word but she caught enough to agree with the spirit of the song and it turned her thoughts sober. To help anybody out that needed it was her philosophy of life. She never spared herself when she found somebody in need, whether they were white or black, trash or decent. And of all she had to be thankful for, she was most thankful that this was so. If Jesus had said, "You can be high society and have all the money you want and be thin and svelte-like, but you can't be a good woman with it," she would have had to say, "Well don't make me that then. Make me a good woman and it don't matter what else, how fat or how ugly or how poor!" Her heart rose. He had not made her a nigger or white-trash or ugly! He had made her herself and given her a little of everything. Jesus, thank you! she said. Thank you thank you thank you! Whenever she counted her blessings she felt as buoyant as if she weighed one hundred and twenty-five pounds instead of one hundred and eighty.

"What's wrong with your little boy?" the pleasant lady asked the white-trashy woman.

"He has a ulcer," the woman said proudly. "He ain't give me a minute's peace since he was born. Him and her are just alike," she said, nodding at the old woman, who was running her leathery fingers through the child's pale hair. "Look like I can't get nothing down them two but Co'Cola and candy."

That's all you try to get down em, Mrs. Turpin said to herself. Too lazy to light the fire. There was nothing you could tell her about people like them that she didn't know already. And it was not just that they didn't have anything. Because if you gave them everything, in two weeks it would all be broken or filthy or they would have chopped it up for lightwood. She knew all this from her own experience. Help them you must, but help them you couldn't.

All at once the ugly girl turned her lips inside out again. Her eyes were fixed like two drills on Mrs. Turpin. This time there was no mistaking that there was something urgent behind them.

Girl, Mrs. Turpin exclaimed silently, I haven't done a thing to you! The girl might be confusing her with somebody else. There was no need to sit by and let herself be intimidated. "You must be in college," she said boldly, looking directly at the girl. "I see you reading a book there."

The girl continued to stare and pointedly did not answer.

Her mother blushed at this rudeness. "The lady asked you a question, Mary Grace," she said under her breath.

"I have ears," Mary Grace said.

The poor mother blushed again. "Mary Grace goes to Wellesley College," she explained. She twisted one of the buttons on her dress. "In Massachusetts," she added with a grimace. "And in the summer she just keeps right on studying. Just reads all the time, a real book worm. She's done real well at Wellesley; she's taking English and Math and History and Psychology and Social Studies," she rattled on, "and I think it's too much. I think she ought to get out and have fun."

The girl looked as if she would like to hurl them all through the plate glass window.

"Way up north," Mrs. Turpin murmured and thought, well, it hasn't done much for her manners.

"I'd almost rather to have him sick," the white-trash woman said, wrenching the attention back to herself. "He's so mean when he ain't. Look like some children just take natural to meanness. It's some gets bad when they get sick but he was the opposite. Took sick and turned good. He don't give me no trouble now. It's me waitin to see the doctor," she said.

If I was going to send anybody back to Africa, Mrs. Turpin thought, it would be your kind, woman. "Yes, indeed," she said aloud, but looking up at the ceiling, "it's a heap of things worse than a nigger." And dirtier than a hog, she added to herself.

"I think people with bad dispositions are more to be pitied than anyone on earth," the pleasant lady said in a voice that was decidedly thin.

"I thank the Lord he has blessed me with a good one," Mrs. Turpin said. "The day has never dawned that I couldn't find something to laugh at."

"Not since she married me anyways," Claud said with a comical straight face.

Everybody laughed except the girl and the white-trash.

Mrs. Turpin's stomach shook. "He's such a caution," she said, "that I can't help but laugh at him."

The girl made a loud ugly noise through her teeth.

Her mother's mouth grew thin and tight. "I think the worst thing in the world," she said, "is an ungrateful person. To have everything and not appreciate it. I know a girl," she said, "who has parents who would give her anything, a little brother who loves her dearly, who is getting a good education, who wears the best clothes, but who can never say a kind word to anyone, who never smiles, who just criticizes and complains all day long."

"Is she too old to paddle?" Claud asked.

The girl's face was almost purple.

"Yes," the lady said, "I'm afraid there's nothing to do but leave her to her folly. Some day she'll wake up and it'll be too late."

"It never hurt anyone to smile," Mrs. Turpin said. "It just makes you feel better all over."

"Of course," the lady said sadly, "but there are just some people you can't tell anything to. They can't take criticism."

"If it's one thing I am," Mrs. Turpin said with feeling, "it's grateful. When I think who all I could have been besides myself and what all I got, a little of everything, and a good disposition besides, I just feel like shouting, 'Thank you, Jesus, for making everything the way it is!' It could have been different!" For one thing, somebody else could have got Claud. At the thought of this, she was flooded with gratitude and a terrible pang of joy ran through her. "Oh thank you, Jesus, Jesus, thank you!" she cried aloud.

The book struck her directly over her left eye. It struck almost at the same instant that she realized the girl was about to hurl it. Before she could utter a sound, the raw face came crashing across the table toward her, howling. The girl's fingers sank like clamps into the soft flesh of her neck. She heard the mother cry

out and Claud shout, "Whoa!" There was an instant when she
was certain that she was about to be in an earthquake.

All at once her vision narrowed and she saw everything as
if it were happening in a small room far away, or as if she were
looking at it through the wrong end of a telescope. Claud's face
crumpled and fell out of sight. The nurse ran in, then out, then
in again. Then the gangling figure of the doctor rushed out of the
inner door. Magazines flew this way and that as the table turned
over. The girl fell with a thud and Mrs. Turpin's vision suddenly
reversed itself and she saw everything large instead of small. The
eyes of the white-trashy woman were staring hugely at the floor.
There the girl, held down on one side by the nurse and on the
other by her mother, was wrenching and turning in their grasp.
The doctor was kneeling astride her, trying to hold her arm down.
He managed after a second to sink a long needle into it.

Mrs. Turpin felt entirely hollow except for her heart which
swung from side to side as if it were agitated in a great empty
drum of flesh.

"Somebody that's not busy call for the ambulance," the
doctor said in the off-hand voice young doctors adopt for terrible
occasions.

Mrs. Turpin could not have moved a finger. The old man
who had been sitting next to her skipped nimbly into the office
and made the call, for the secretary still seemed to be gone.

"Claud!" Mrs. Turpin called.

He was not in his chair. She knew she must jump up and
find him but she felt like some one trying to catch a train in a
dream, when everything moves in slow motion and the faster you
try to run the slower you go.

"Here I am," a suffocated voice, very unlike Claud's, said.

He was doubled up in the corner on the floor, pale as paper,
holding his leg. She wanted to get up and go to him but she could
not move. Instead, her gaze was drawn slowly downward to the
churning face on the floor, which she could see over the doctor's
shoulder.

The girl's eyes stopped rolling and focused on her. They
seemed a much lighter blue than before, as if a door that had been
tightly closed behind them was now open to admit light and air.

Mrs. Turpin's head cleared and her power of motion returned.
She leaned forward until she was looking directly into the fierce
brilliant eyes. There was no doubt in her mind that the girl did
know her, knew her in some intense and personal way, beyond
time and place and condition. "What you got to say to me?" she
asked hoarsely and held her breath, waiting, as for a revelation.

The girl raised her head. Her gaze locked with Mrs. Turpin's. "Go back to hell where you came from, you old wart hog," she whispered. Her voice was low but clear. Her eyes burned for a moment as if she saw with pleasure that her message had struck its target.

Mrs. Turpin sank back in her chair.

After a moment the girl's eyes closed and she turned her head wearily to the side.

The doctor rose and handed the nurse the empty syringe. He leaned over and put both hands for a moment on the mother's shoulders, which were shaking. She was sitting on the floor, her lips pressed together, holding Mary Grace's hand in her lap. The girl's fingers were gripped like a baby's around her thumb. "Go on to the hospital," he said. "I'll call and make the arrangements."

"Now let's see that neck," he said in a jovial voice to Mrs. Turpin. He began to inspect her neck with his first two fingers. Two little moon-shaped lines like pink fish bones were indented over her windpipe. There was the beginning of an angry red swelling above her eye. His fingers passed over this also.

"Lea' me be," she said thickly and shook him off. "See about Claud. She kicked him."

"I'll see about him in a minute," he said and felt her pulse. He was a thin gray-haired man, given to pleasantries. "Go home and have yourself a vacation the rest of the day," he said and patted her on the shoulder.

Quit your pattin me, Mrs. Turpin growled to herself.

"And put an ice pack over that eye," he said. Then he went and squatted down beside Claud and looked at his leg. After a moment he pulled him up and Claud limped after him into the office.

Until the ambulance came, the only sounds in the room were the tremulous moans of the girl's mother, who continued to sit on the floor. The white-trash woman did not take her eyes off the girl. Mrs. Turpin looked straight ahead at nothing. Presently the ambulance drew up, a long dark shadow, behind the curtain. The attendants came in and set the stretcher down beside the girl and lifted her expertly onto it and carried her out. The nurse helped the mother gather up her things. The shadow of the ambulance moved silently away and the nurse came back in the office.

"That ther girl is going to be a lunatic, ain't she?" the white-trash woman asked the nurse, but the nurse kept on to the back and never answered her.

"Yes, she's going to be a lunatic," the white-trash woman said to the rest of them.

"Po' critter," the old woman murmured. The child's face was still in her lap. His eyes looked idly out over her knees. He had not moved during the disturbance except to draw one leg up under him.

"I thank Gawd," the white-trash woman said fervently, "I ain't a lunatic."

Claud came limping out and the Turpins went home.

As their pick-up truck turned into their own dirt road and made the crest of the hill, Mrs. Turpin gripped the window ledge and looked out suspiciously. The land sloped gracefully down through a field dotted with lavender weeds and at the start of the rise their small yellow frame house, with its little flower beds spread out around it like a fancy apron, sat primly in its accustomed place between two giant hickory trees. She would not have been startled to see a burnt wound between two blackened chimneys.

Neither of them felt like eating so they put on their house clothes and lowered the shade in the bedroom and lay down, Claud with his leg on a pillow and herself with a damp washcloth over her eye. The instant she was flat on her back, the image of a razorbacked hog with warts on its face and horns coming out behind its ears snorted into her head. She moaned, a low quiet moan.

"I am not," she said tearfully, "a wart hog. From hell." But the denial had no force. The girl's eyes and her words, even the tone of her voice, low but clear, directed only to her, brooked no repudiation. She had been singled out for the message, though there was trash in the room to whom it might justly have been applied. The full force of this fact struck her only now. There was a woman there who was neglecting her own child but she had been overlooked. The message had been given to Ruby Turpin, a respectable, hard-working, church-going woman. The tears dried. Her eyes began to burn instead with wrath.

She rose on her elbow and the washcloth fell into her hand. Claud was lying on his back, snoring. She wanted to tell him what the girl had said. At the same time, she did not wish to put the image of herself as a wart hog from hell into his mind.

"Hey, Claud," she muttered and pushed his shoulder.

Claud opened one pale baby blue eye.

She looked into it warily. He did not think about anything. He just went his way.

"Wha, whasit?" he said and closed the eye again.

"Nothing," she said. "Does your leg pain you?"

"Hurts like hell," Claud said.

"It'll quit terreckly," she said and lay back down. In a

moment Claud was snoring again. For the rest of the afternoon they lay there. Claud slept. She scowled at the ceiling. Occasionally she raised her fist and made a small stabbing motion over her chest as if she was defending her innocence to invisible guests who were like the comforters of Job, reasonable-seeming but wrong.

About five-thirty Claud stirred. "Got to go after those niggers," he sighed, not moving.

She was looking straight up as if there were unintelligible handwriting on the ceiling. The protuberance over her eye had turned a greenish-blue. "Listen here," she said.

"What?"

"Kiss me."

Claud leaned over and kissed her loudly on the mouth. He pinched her side and their hands interlocked. Her expression of ferocious concentration did not change. Claud got up, groaning and growling, and limped off. She continued to study the ceiling.

She did not get up until she heard the pick-up truck coming back with the Negroes. Then she rose and thrust her feet in her brown oxfords, which she did not bother to lace, and stumped out onto the back porch and got her red plastic bucket. She emptied a tray of ice cubes into it and filled it half full of water and went out into the back yard. Every afternoon after Claud brought the hands in, one of the boys helped him put out hay and the rest waited in the back of the truck until he was ready to take them home. The truck was parked in the shade under one of the hickory trees.

"Hi yawl this evening?" Mrs. Turpin asked grimly, appearing with the bucket and the dipper. There were three women and a boy in the truck.

"Us doin nicely," the oldest woman said. "Hi you doin?" and her gaze stuck immediately on the dark lump on Mrs. Turpin's forehead. "You done fell down, ain't you?" she asked in a solicitous voice. The old woman was dark and almost toothless. She had on an old felt hat of Claud's set back on her head. The other two women were younger and lighter and they both had new bright green sun hats. One of them had hers on her head; the other had taken hers off and the boy was grinning beneath it.

Mrs. Turpin set the bucket down on the floor of the truck. "Yawl hep yourselves," she said. She looked around to make sure Claud had gone. "No. I didn't fall down," she said, folding her arms. "It was something worse than that."

"Ain't nothing bad happen to you!" the old woman said. She said it as if they all knew that Mrs. Turpin was protected in some special way by Divine Providence. "You just had you a little fall."

"We were in town at the doctor's office for where the cow kicked Mr. Turpin," Mrs. Turpin said in a flat tone that indicated they could leave off their foolishness. "And there was this girl there. A big fat girl with her face all broke out. I could look at that girl and tell she was peculiar but I couldn't tell how. And me and her mama were just talking and going along and all of a sudden WHAM! She throws this big book she was reading at me and . . ."

"Naw!" the old woman cried out.

"And then she jumps over the table and commences to choke me."

"Naw!" they all exclaimed, "naw!"

"Hi come she do that?" the old woman asked. "What ail her?"

Mrs. Turpin only glared in front of her.

"Somethin ail her," the old woman said.

"They carried her off in an ambulance," Mrs. Turpin continued, "but before she went she was rolling on the floor and they were trying to hold her down to give her a shot and she said something to me." She paused. "You know what she said to me?"

"What she say?" they asked.

"She said," Mrs. Turpin began, and stopped, her face very dark and heavy. The sun was getting whiter and whiter, blanching the sky overhead so that the leaves of the hickory tree were black in the face of it. She could not bring forth the words. "Something real ugly," she muttered.

"She sho shouldn't said nothing ugly to you," the old woman said. "You so sweet. You the sweetest lady I know."

"She pretty too," the one with the hat on said.

"And stout," the other one said. "I never knowed no sweeter white lady."

"That's the truth befo' Jesus," the old woman said. "Amen! You des as sweet and pretty as you can be."

Mrs. Turpin knew just exactly how much Negro flattery was worth and it added to her rage. "She said," she began again and finished this time with a fierce rush of breath, "that I was an old wart hog from hell."

There was an astounded silence.

"Where she at?" the youngest woman cried in a piercing voice.

"Lemme see her. I'll kill her!"

"I'll kill her with you!" the other one cried.

"She b'long in the sylum," the old woman said emphatically. "You the sweetest white lady I know."

"She pretty too," the other two said. "Stout as she can be and sweet. Jesus satisfied with her!"

"Deed he is," the old woman declared.

Idiots! Mrs. Turpin growled to herself. You could never say anything intelligent to a nigger. You could talk at them but not with them. "Yawl ain't drunk your water," she said shortly. "Leave the bucket in the truck when you're finished with it. I got more to do than just stand around and pass the time of day," and she moved off and into the house.

She stood for a moment in the middle of the kitchen. The dark protuberance over her eye looked like a miniature tornado cloud which might any moment sweep across the horizon of her brow. Her lower lip protruded dangerously. She squared her massive shoulders. Then she marched into the front of the house and out the side door and started down the road to the pig parlor. She had the look of a woman going single-handed, weaponless, into battle.

The sun was a deep yellow now like a harvest moon and was riding westward very fast over the far tree line as if it meant to reach the hogs before she did. The road was rutted and she kicked several good-sized stones out of her path as she strode along. The pig parlor was on a little knoll at the end of a lane that ran off from the side of the barn. It was a square of concrete as large as a small room, with a board fence about four feet high around it. The concrete floor sloped slightly so that the hog wash could drain off into a trench where it was carried to the field for fertilizer. Claud was standing on the outside, on the edge of the concrete, hanging onto the top board, hosing down the floor inside. The hose was connected to the faucet of a water trough nearby.

Mrs. Turpin climbed up beside him and glowered down at the hogs inside. There were seven long-snouted bristly shoats in it — tan with liver-colored spots — and an old sow a few weeks off from farrowing. She was lying on her side grunting. The shoats were running about shaking themselves like idiot children, their little slit pig eyes searching the floor for anything left. She had read that pigs were the most intelligent animal. She doubted it. They were supposed to be smarter than dogs. There had even been a pig astronaut. He had performed his assignment perfectly but died of a heart attack afterwards because they left him in his electric suit, sitting upright throughout his examination when naturally a hog should be on all fours.

A-gruntin and a-rootin and a-groanin.

"Gimme that hose," she said, yanking it away from Claud. "Go on and carry them niggers home and then get off that leg."

"You look like you might have swallowed a mad dog," Claud observed, but he got down and limped off. He paid no attention to her humors.

Until he was out of earshot, Mrs. Turpin stood on the side of the pen, holding the hose and pointing the stream of water at the hind quarter of any shoat that looked as if it might try to lie down. When he had had time to get over the hill, she turned her head slightly and her wrathful eyes scanned the path. He was nowhere in sight. She turned back again and seemed to gather herself up. Her shoulders rose and she drew in her breath.

"What do you send me a message like that for?" she said in a low fierce voice, barely above a whisper but with the force of a shout in its concentrated fury. "How am I a hog and me both? How am I saved and from hell too?" Her free fist was knotted and with the other she gripped the hose, blindly pointing the stream of water in and out of the eye of the old sow whose outraged squeal she did not hear.

The pig parlor commanded a view of the back pasture where their twenty beef cows were gathered around the hay-bales Claud and the boy had put out. The freshly cut pasture sloped down to the highway. Across it was their cotton field and beyond that a dark green dusty wood which they owned as well. The sun was behind the wood, very red, looking over the paling of trees like a farmer inspecting his own hogs.

"Why me?" she rumbled. "It's no trash around here, black or white, that I haven't given to. And break my back to the bone every day working. And do for the church."

She appeared to be the right size woman to command the arena before her. "How am I a hog?" she demanded. "Exactly how am I like them?" and she jabbed the stream of water at the shoats. "There was plenty of trash there. It didn't have to be me."

"If you like trash better, go get yourself some trash then," she railed. "You could have made me trash. Or a nigger. If trash is what you wanted why didn't you make me trash?" She shook her fist with the hose in it and a watery snake appeared momentarily in the air. "I could quit working and take it easy and be filthy," she growled. "Lounge about the sidewalks all day drinking root beer. Dip snuff and spit in every puddle and have it all over my face. I could be nasty."

"Or you could have made me a nigger. It's too late for me to be a nigger," she said with deep sarcasm, "but I could act like one. Lay down in the middle of the road and stop traffic. Roll on the ground."

In the deepening light everything was taking on a mysterious hue. The pasture was growing a peculiar glassy green and the streak of highway had turned lavender. She braced herself for a final assault and this time her voice rolled out over the pasture. "Go on," she yelled, "call me a hog! Call me a hog again. From hell. Call me a wart hog from hell. Put that bottom rail on top. There'll still be a top and bottom!"

A garbled echo returned to her.

A final surge of fury shook her and she roared, "Who do you think you are?"

The color of everything, field and crimson sky, burned for a moment with a transparent intensity. The question carried over the pasture and across the highway and the cotton field and returned to her clearly like an answer from beyond the wood.

She opened her mouth but no sound came out of it.

A tiny truck, Claud's, appeared on the highway, heading rapidly out of sight. Its gears scraped thinly. It looked like a child's toy. At any moment a bigger truck might smash into it and scatter Claud's and the niggers' brains all over the road.

Mrs. Turpin stood there, her gaze fixed on the highway, all her muscles rigid, until in five or six minutes the truck reappeared, returning. She waited until it had had time to turn into their own road. Then like a monumental statue coming to life, she bent her head slowly and gazed, as if through the very heart of the mystery, down into the pig parlor at the hogs. They had settled all in one corner around the old sow who was grunting softly. A red glow suffused them. They appeared to pant with a secret life.

Until the sun slipped finally behind the tree line, Mrs. Turpin remained there with her gaze bent to them as if she were absorbing some abysmal life-giving knowledge. At last she lifted her head. There was only a purple streak in the sky, cutting through a field of crimson and leading, like an extension of the highway, into the descending dusk. She raised her hands from the side of the pen in a gesture hieratic and profound. A visionary light settled in her eyes. She saw the streak as a vast swinging bridge extending upward from the earth through a field of living fire. Upon it a vast horde of souls were rumbling toward heaven. There were whole companies of white-trash, clean for the first time in their lives, and bands of black niggers in white robes, and battalions of freaks and lunatics shouting and clapping and leaping like frogs.

And bringing up the end of the procession was a tribe of people whom she recognized at once as those who, like herself and Claud, had always had a little of everything and the God-given wit to use it right. She leaned forward to observe them closer. They were marching behind the others with great dignity, accountable as they had always been for good order and common sense and respectable behavior. They alone were on key. Yet she could see by their shocked and altered faces that even their virtues were being burned away. She lowered her hands and gripped the rail of the hog pen, her eyes small but fixed unblinkingly on what lay ahead. In a moment the vision faded but she remained where she was, immobile.

At length she got down and turned off the faucet and made her slow way on the darkening path to the house. In the woods around her the invisible cricket choruses had struck up, but what she heard were the voices of the souls climbing upward into the starry field and shouting hallelujah.

Alice Adams (b. 1926)

Gift of Grass

"But what's so great about money — or marriages and houses, for that matter?" Strengthened perhaps by two recent cups of tea (rose hips, brewed with honey and a few grass seeds), Cathy had raised herself on one elbow and turned to face the doctor. "Couldn't there be other ways to live?" she asked, consciously childish and pleading.

"Have you thought of one?" Oppressed by weariness and annoyance, Dr. Fredericks was unaware that both those emotions sounded in his soft, controlled voice. Once, in a burst of confidence, Cathy had said to him accusingly, "You speak so softly just to make me listen." Now she said nothing. Believing himself to be in command, Dr. Fredericks also believed his patient to be overcome by what he saw as her transference. She saw her feelings toward him as simple dislike and a more complicated distrust.

She lay back down, giving up, and reconsidered the large space that served as both the doctor's office and his living room. It was coolly blue and green — olive walls and ceiling, royal-blue carpet, navy silk chair and sofa, pale-blue linen lampshades on green pottery lamps. Only the couch on which Cathy lay was neither green nor blue; it was upholstered with a worn Oriental

rug, as though that might disguise its function. Like most children
— she was sixteen — Cathy knew more than her elders thought
she did. She knew that at one time her mother had been a patient
of Dr. Fredericks's, and she recognized her mother's touch in that
room. Her mother, who was an interior decorator, had evidently
"done" it. As payment for her hours of lying there? It would have
been an expensive job; Cathy saw that, too. God knows how
many hours it would have taken to pay for all that silk.

All her mother had ever said, in a tearful voice that was
supposed to extract similar sincerity from Cathy, was "At one
time in my life when I was very troubled, a psychiatrist really
helped me a great deal. In fact, you might say that he saved our
marriage, Bill's and mine." Not wanting Cathy to sense a conspiracy,
she had not told Cathy that she was sending her to her own
psychiatrist. This was in August, when Cathy had said that she
was not going back to school in the fall, and her mother and Bill
— her stepfather for the past ten years — had told her that in that
case she must go to see Dr. Fredericks.

"But I'm not troubled," Cathy had lied. Then she had giggled
in her unrelated, unnerving way. "Or married. I just don't want
to go to school for a while," she had said.

"But I hope you will be married," her mother had said. She
had sighed, frowned and then smiled, attempting reassurance. "Dr.
James helped me a great deal," she said. "He's one of the best
doctors in San Francisco." She used the first name of Dr. Fredericks
— Dr. James Fredericks — which Cathy did not think was a very
smart disguise.

While the long pause after his question lasted, Dr. Fredericks
struggled with his counter-transference. He stared down at Cathy's
rather squat, short body in its jeans and black turtleneck sweater,
at the long, limp brown hair that fell from the edge of the couch
and the perfectly round brown eyes in a pale, round face. He had
to admit it — he couldn't stand the little girl. Injecting kindliness
into his voice, he said, "Isn't there anything on your mind that
you'd like to tell me about?"

At this, Cathy burst into tears. A quick, noisy storm of sobs
shook her shoulders and her chest, then stopped, and she said,
"You dumb fink."

He leaned back comfortably in his raw-silk chair that did
not creak. Seductively he said, "I suppose by your standards I am
in some ways rather dumb." He did not say, Such as they are.

"Such as they are," she said. "I'm not interested in standards,
or school or earning money or getting married."

"I wish I knew what you were interested in," he said.

This seemed to Cathy his most heartfelt and least contrived remark of the hour, and she answered him. "Clouds," she said. "And foghorns. I wonder where they all are."

"If you really wonder, you could go to the library and get a book."

"I'd rather wonder." She giggled.

"The 'trip' is more important than the destination, is that what you mean?" Despite himself, he had underlined "trip."

"I don't drop acid, I've told you that," she said, dead-pan.

"Well," he said, warming to his task, "that's a reasonable enough fear. But perhaps you have some other less reasonable fears."

"Deer-hunters. God, they have the worst faces I ever saw," she suddenly brought out, forgetting him and remembering the weekend just past. She and her mother and Bill had driven up to Lake Tahoe — a jaunt intended to prove that they were not really angry with Cathy, that they loved her nevertheless. By an unfortunate coincidence, this was also the first weekend of the deer season. On the other side of Sacramento, winding up past Auburn through beautiful mountain rocks and trees, Highway 80 had been lined with white camper trucks bearing hunters. The men wore ugly red caps and red plaid shirts. They had looked remarkably alike, at least to Cathy — as alike as their campers. Fathers and sons and friends, their faces had been coarse and unintelligent, excited, jovial and greedy. "God, I hope they all shoot each other," she said to Dr. Fredericks.

"Well," he said hopefully. "Let's see if we can find out what deer-hunters mean to you. I doubt somehow that it's sheer dislike of killing. For instance, you don't seem to be upset about the war in Vietnam."

"That's so bad I can't think about it at all," said Cathy, with total candor.

"Well, let's see." Dr. Fredericks, almost alone among his colleagues, was more opposed to protesters than to the war, but bringing up Vietnam had been a ploy. He now thrust his real point home. "I do seem to remember that your stepfather is something of a hunter," he said.

Cathy heard the light note of triumph in his voice, to which she reacted with rage and despair and a prolonged silence. Why bother to tell him that Bill only hunted ducks — and only with his father, before that awful old man had died? During the silence, she listened to the leisurely sounds of outlying San Francisco traffic and the faint, distant foghorns from the Bay. Concentrating on these, she was able to stop the echo of Dr. Fredericks's voice in her mind. Their voices were what she could stand least about adults: Dr. Fredericks's bored hostility; her teachers' voices, loud and smug; the alternately anxious and preening, knowing voice of her mother. The only thing that she could remember about her natural father, who had divorced her mother when Cathy was two, was his voice. It was high-pitched, almost a whine — nothing much to miss. Actually, Bill had a nice warm deep voice, until he drank too much and it blurred.

A heavy truck went by, creaking and lumbering as though weighted with old furniture or barrels of china and glass. Brakes screeched several blocks away. Then the traffic sounds continued as before. For a few minutes there were no foghorns, and then there they were again, discordant, with no rhythm.

Both Cathy and Dr. Fredericks glanced over at the clock on his desk. Five minutes to go. He sighed softly and pleasurably. He had recently stopped smoking and he enjoyed the air in his expanded lungs. Although he was nearing sixty, he was well pre-served. Squash and swimming at his club had kept him in shape; he felt a certain snobbery toward many of his colleagues who were running to fat. He and his wife, who owned and ran an extremely successful chain of gift shops, spent vacations at health spas, playing tennis and dieting together. A blue-eyed Southerner, from West Virginia, Dr. Fredericks liked to view himself as a maverick among psychoanalysts — another breed, one might say.

Cathy swung her short legs off the couch and sat up. She clutched her knees and faced him. "Look," she said. "It's hopeless. You and Mother think it's important to get married and save marriages and get money and save that, and I don't."

"We're trying to find out what you do think is important," he said. He did not bother to conceal his impatience.

Neither did she. "So am I."

"Next week?" They both stood up.

Out of context (he felt), she giggled.

Cathy's parents lived about ten blocks from Dr. Fredericks in the same expensive and fog-ridden San Francisco neighborhood, but instead of going home Cathy walked to the park she often went to, along the broad streets and down the hill leading toward the Bay. Here the sun was shining. She pulled a small box of raisins from her pocket and began to eat them as she walked.

The park was surrounded by rolling woods of pine and fir, cypress and eucalyptus, through which on clear days one could catch blue views of the Bay, red glimpses of the Golden Gate Bridge. Cathy walked past creaking swings and a slide crowded with small children. Out on a playing field, lounging about on the beaten grass, there were some kids her own age whom she thought she knew, so she hurried on toward the woods.

Off the path, she came to a place where there was a large sloping patch of sand. She sat down and reached into the back pocket of her jeans, where there was a very mashed joint, which she lit. She lay back, her left arm protecting her hair from the sand. She sucked in and waited for the melting of her despair.

The air smelled of the sea, of lemon-scented eucalyptus, of pine and of the dank, dark earth. It was nearly a clear day, but the foghorns sounded more strongly to her from the water. Soon the fog would come in, gigantically billowing through the Golden Gate. Now, in the visible sky above the dark thatched cypresses, there were only a few large clouds; they were as heavy and slow and lumbering as bulls, a slow-motion lumbering of bulls across the sky. Cathy concentrated on their changes, their slow and formal shifts in shape and pattern. Then, in the peace, in the warm silence, she fell asleep.

Bill, Cathy's stepfather, had at moments a few of the reactions to Cathy that she evoked in Dr. Fredericks. At worst, he despaired of ever reaching her. But he was exceptionally sensitive to the feelings of women. He could often feel what Cathy felt, and could bear it no better than she. It was his sensitivity, in fact, that had kept him from leaving Cathy's mother, Barbara, who was his second wife. The extent of Barbara's anxiety and despair when they first spoke of separation had got through to him. They had seen Dr. Fredericks, together and separately, for more than a year. But before their meetings with him began Bill had already decided not, after all, to leave Barbara for Ruth, his girl friend. (Ruth had been unhappy, too, but she was younger and more resilient; her despair hit Bill with lesser force.)

Perhaps to avoid a discussion of Ruth, Bill had talked about his inheritance from his father, and Dr. Fredericks had given Bill good advice about investing it. Bill gave him credit for that. Actually investments were Fredericks's real but unacknowledged field of expertise. Bill was a commercial artist, and not a terribly successful one. The investment had brought his income well within range of his wife's, so it may have been Dr. Fredericks, after all, who saved the marriage.

It was nearly dinnertime when Cathy came home from the park, and Bill and her mother were sitting in the living room having drinks. Barbara had done their living room, like Dr. Fredericks's, in cool blues and greens, except for the brown leather sofa — a kind of tribute to Bill's masculine presence; ordinarily, she did not use leather. Bill almost never sat on it. He would sit instead, as he did now, on a small Victorian dark-blue silk chair that must have been intended for Cathy. Fortunately, he was light — a very thin, narrowly built man with delicate bones and sparse blondish hair. Barbara, wearing a smart gray wool dress, was sitting on the leather sofa, and Cathy joined her there. During the cocktail hour, they would sit that way, at opposite ends of the sofa, facing Bill rather than each other.

Mother and daughter appeared to Bill remarkably alike. Barbara's eyes, too, were round and often opaque; her body tended to be squat. Its shape was childlike, which at times Bill found quite touching. At other times, it turned him off, and on to voluptuous Ruth. In Cathy, naturally enough, the sexlessness was more marked. Bill sometimes wondered how he would have felt with a voluptuous daughter, a swinging chick. Would it have made him more uncomfortable?

"I told Dr. Fredericks how much I hated deer-hunters," proffered Cathy. Since Barbara, on principle, would never ask what went on during "her hour," Cathy would throw out indecipherable and tantalizing tidbits.

Feeling his second drink, Bill said, "God, I hate them too. They all remind me of my father." Bill's father had been a mighty hunter, out of the great Northwest, with rather Bunyanesque notions of manhood, so that Bill had trouble from time to time believing in himself as a man, feeling that if those coarse, red-faced, hunting cretins were men he was not one. Indeed, he had been told by several women, including Barbara, that he played around only in order to prove his manhood to himself. At times, he thought that might be true. At other times, he thought it was simply because he very much liked women, lots of them.

But he was not supposed to voice as strong an emotion as hatred in the presence of Cathy, and he sensed reproof in Barbara's slightly stiffened posture. She was an extremely nice woman who wanted things to be perfect — her house, her husband, her daughter and especially herself. Now, instead of reproving Bill, she smiled at him, sighed and said, "God, I'm tired. I really did have a day."

"You didn't like your father?" Cathy asked in a neutral voice that bore, for Bill, an unnerving resemblance to Dr. Fredericks's therapeutic blandness. But it was almost the first personal question that he could remember Cathy's ever asking him, and he found that his chest warmed and expanded with pleasure. "To tell you the truth," he said, "I was very much afraid of him. The way I find hunters frightening."

"Oh," said Cathy, and then for no reason she giggled.

"We're having a really wicked dinner," Barbara said. "Prawns with that sour-cream sauce. I absolutely couldn't resist them in the Grant Market, so big and perfect. And, of course, rice."

"You *are* wicked," Bill responded, since this was how they talked to each other, but he was hearing them both with Cathy's ears, and he wondered how she could bear their middle-aged fatuity. She was staring at a small porcelain vase of tiny blue strawflowers as though she had never seen it before. Bill asked Barbara if she wanted another drink.

He made them strong, and by the end of dinner, during which he and Barbara drank wine and told Cathy illuminating vignettes from their own histories, stressing education and travel and friendship, reminding her that they had once been young — by the time all that was over, Bill was almost drunk and Barbara had a headache. But he was still aware of the troubled depths of tenderness in Barbara's round brown eyes as she said good night to them both — quite out of character, she had decided to give in to her headache and go to bed.

"Cathy and I will clear up," said Bill decisively.

The truth was that he liked to wash dishes, which his father had seen to it that he was not allowed to do. He liked all that warm, foamy water around his hands and the essential and marvelous simplicity of the task. He handed each hot, clean dish to Cathy, who dried it with a sparklingly clean white towel, in the blue-and-white-tiled, Philippine-mahogany room.

For no real reason, a picture of Cathy the first time he had ever seen her came to Bill's mind — a small, square girl with chocolate cake and frosting all over her face and hands. It was during what he and Barbara ironically referred to as their courtship, a protracted and difficult period during which they had both been concerned with Bill's shedding his wife — and with the difficulty of seeing each other privately, what with Barbara's child and his wife. Barbara's first husband had moved to Dallas and had not seen Cathy since the divorce, but Barbara had felt that Bill and her daughter should not meet until Bill was actually free. So it was quite a while before Barbara could invite Bill for dinner. And on that occasion Cathy found the perfect, beautiful chocolate cake that Barbara had made and plunged her hands into its dark, moist depths, then smeared her face. Barbara had chosen to laugh rather than to scold, and Bill had liked her for that. Now the remembered sight of small, smeared Cathy moved him. He wanted to tell her about it, but he knew she would not understand; nor could she know that simply watching someone grow can make you care for them. So instead of any of that he said, "As a matter of fact I think James Fredericks is a jackass," and handed her a wet wineglass.

Carefully polishing, as she had been taught by her mother, Cathy asked, "Is he? I don't know."

"God, yes. All he can talk about is what he likes to call 'finances.' He can't say 'money.' Besides, you don't see his name on any anti-war petitions of doctors, do you? He probably owns stock in Dow Chemical."

Plunging his hands back into the sink, Bill realized that he had been wanting to say this for a long time. He had forgotten that Cathy was not supposed to know that he and Barbara had gone to Fredericks, and he wanted to reassure her, to tell her that if she didn't dig Fredericks it was certainly O.K. with him. But then he felt her mind float off to some clouded private distance of her own, and suddenly he couldn't stand it, and he turned furiously to confront her. "Listen," he said loudly, "you think you're confused, and that the world is difficult. Christ, what do you think it's like to be forty-one? Christ, talk about confused and difficult. Do you think I like getting outside myself and seeing a fatuous drunk whose scalp is beginning to show through? Christ! And believe me, being married is a hell of a lot more difficult than not being married, let me tell you. Your mother has to diet or she'd be fat, and she can't stand fat. And it's very hard to live without a lot of money and booze. You give it a little thought — just try."

Cathy's round eyes did not blink and she went on polishing the second wineglass. Then she glanced quickly at Bill and said, "O.K." Then she said, "I think I'll go to bed now," and Bill was left alone to clean the sink and wipe off the unvarnished wooden chopping table.

After he had finished that, he went into the small room off the living room that was known as his study; his books were there, and some portfolios of old drawings, and a collection of dirty pipes that he would have smoked only in that room. Now as he entered he found placed squarely in the middle of his desk a white sheet of paper, and on it were what he recognized as two joints.

He sat down in the comfortable green wool upholstered chair that Barbara had provided him, presumably for meditation, and he meditated, seeking a variety of explanations for Cathy's present, or gesture — whatever it was. However, nothing rational came to his mind. Or, rather, reasonable explanations approached but then as quickly dissolved, like clouds or shadows. Instead, salty and unmasculine tears stung at his eyes, and then he fell asleep in his chair, having just decided not to think at all.

Ursula K. Le Guin (b. 1929)

The Ones Who Walk Away from Omelas

With a clamor of bells that set the swallows soaring, the Festival of Summer came to the city Omelas, bright-towered by the sea. The rigging of the boats in harbor sparkled with flags. In the streets between houses with red roofs and painted walls, between old moss-grown gardens and under avenues of trees, past great parks and public buildings, processions moved. Some were decorous: old people in long stiff robes of mauve and gray, grave master workmen, quiet, merry women carrying their babies and chatting as they walked. In other streets the music beat faster, a shimmering of gong and tambourine, and the people went dancing, the procession was a dance. Children dodged in and out, their high calls rising like the swallows' crossing flights over the music and the singing. All the processions wound towards the north side of the city, where on the great water-meadow called the Green Fields boys and girls, naked in the bright air, with mudstained feet and ankles and long, lithe arms, exercised their restive horses before the race. The horses wore no gear at all but a halter without bit. Their manes were braided with streamers of silver, gold, and green. They flared their nostrils and pranced and boasted to one another; they were vastly excited, the horse being the only animal who has adopted our ceremonies as his own. Far off to the north and west the mountains stood up half encircling Omelas on her bay. The air of morning was so clear that the snow still crowning the Eighteen Peaks burned with white-gold fire across the miles of sunlit air, under the dark blue of the sky. There was just enough wind to make the banners that marked the racecourse snap and flutter now and then. In the silence of the broad green meadows one could hear the music winding through the city streets, farther and nearer and ever approaching, a cheerful faint sweetness of the air that from time to time trembled and gathered together and broke out into the great joyous clanging of the bells.

Joyous! How is one to tell about joy? How describe the citizens of Omelas?

They were not simple folk, you see, though they were happy.
But we do not say the words of cheer much any more. All smiles
have become archaic. Given a description such as this one tends
to make certain assumptions. Given a description such as this one
tends to look next for the King, mounted on a splendid stallion
and surrounded by his noble knights, or perhaps in a golden litter
borne by great-muscled slaves. But there was no king. They did
not use swords, or keep slaves. They were not barbarians. I do
not know the rules and laws of their society, but I suspect that
they were singularly few. As they did without monarchy and
slavery, so they also go on without the stock exchange, the advertisement, the secret police, and the bomb. Yet I repeat that
these were not simple folk, not dulcet shepherds, noble savages,
bland utopians. They were not less complex than us. The trouble
is that we have a bad habit, encouraged by pedants and sophisticates,
of considering happiness as something rather stupid. Only pain is
intellectual, only evil interesting. This is the treason of the artist:
a refusal to admit the banality of evil and the terrible boredom of
pain. If you can't lick 'em, join 'em. If it hurts, repeat it. But to
praise despair is to condemn delight, to embrace violence is to
lose hold of everything else. We have almost lost hold, we can
no longer describe a happy man, nor make any celebration of joy.
How can I tell you about the people of Omelas? They were not
naïve and happy children — though their children were, in fact,
happy. They were mature, intelligent, passionate adults whose
lives were not wretched. O miracle! but I wish I could describe
it better. I wish I could convince you. Omelas sounds in my words
like a city in a fairy tale, long ago and far away, once upon a
time. Perhaps it would be best if you imagined it as your own
fancy bids, assuming it will rise to the occasion, for certainly I
cannot suit you all. For instance, how about technology? I think
that there would be no cars or helicopters in and above the streets;
this follows from the fact that the people of Omelas are happy
people. Happiness is based on a just discrimination of what is
necessary, what is neither necessary nor destructive, and what is
destructive. In the middle category, however — that of the unnecessary but undestructive, that of comfort, luxury, exuberance,
etc. — they could perfectly well have central heating, subway
trains, washing machines, and all kinds of marvelous devices not
yet invented here, floating light-sources, fuelless power, a cure for
the common cold. Or they could have none of that: it doesn't
matter. As you like it. I incline to think that people from towns
up and down the coast have been coming in to Omelas during

the last days before the Festival on very fast little trains and double-decked trams, and that the train station of Omelas is actually the handsomest building in town, though plainer than the magnificent Farmers' Market. But even granted trains, I fear that Omelas so far strikes some of you as goody-goody. Smiles, bells, parades, horses, bleh. If so, please add an orgy. If an orgy would help, don't hesitate. Let us not, however, have temples from which issue beautiful nude priests and priestesses already half in ecstasy and ready to copulate with any man or woman, lover or stranger, who desires union with the deep godhead of the blood, although that was my first idea. But really it would be better not to have any temples in Omelas — at least, not manned temples. Religion yes, clergy no. Surely the beautiful nudes can just wander about, offering themselves like divine soufflés to the hunger of the needy and the rapture of the flesh. Let them join the processions. Let tambourines be struck above the copulations, and the glory of desire be proclaimed upon the gongs, and (a not unimportant point) let the offspring of these delightful rituals be beloved and looked after by all. One thing I know there is none of in Omelas is guilt. But what else should there be? I thought that first there were no drugs, but that is puritanical. For those who like it, the faint insistent sweetness of *drooz* may perfume the ways of the city, *drooz* which first brings a great lightness and brilliance to the mind and limbs, and then after some hours a dreamy languor, and wonderful visions at last of the very arcana and inmost secrets of the Universe, as well as exciting the pleasure of sex beyond all belief; and it is not habit-forming. For more modest tastes I think there ought to be beer. What else, what else belongs in the joyous city? The sense of victory, surely, the celebration of courage. But as we did without clergy, let us do without soldiers. The joy built upon successful slaughter is not the right kind of joy; it will not do; it is fearful and it is trivial. A boundless and generous contentment, a magnanimous triumph felt not against some outer enemy but in communion with the finest and fairest in the souls of all men everywhere and the splendor of the world's summer: this is what swells the hearts of the people of Omelas, and the victory they celebrate is that of life. I really don't think many of them need to take *drooz*.

Most of the processions have reached the Green Fields by now. A marvelous smell of cooking goes forth from the red and blue tents of the provisioners. The faces of small children are amiably sticky; in the benign grey beard of a man a couple of crumbs of rich pastry are entangled. The youths and girls have mounted their horses and are beginning to group around the starting line of the course. An old woman, small, fat, and laughing, is passing out flowers from a basket, and tall young men wear her flowers in their shining hair. A child of nine or ten sits at the edge of the crowd, alone, playing on a wooden flute. People pause to listen, and they smile, but they do not speak to him, for he never ceases playing and never sees them, his dark eyes wholly rapt in the sweet, thin magic of the tune.

He finishes, and slowly lowers his hands holding the wooden flute.

As if that little private silence were the signal, all at once a trumpet sounds from the pavilion near the starting line: imperious, melancholy, piercing. The horses rear on their slender legs, and some of them neigh in answer. Sober-faced, the young riders stroke the horses' necks and soothe them, whispering, "Quiet, quiet, there my beauty, my hope. . . ." They begin to form in rank along the starting line. The crowds along the racecourse are like a field of grass and flowers in the wind. The Festival of Summer has begun.

Do you believe? Do you accept the festival, the city, the joy? No? Then let me describe one more thing.

In a basement under one of the beautiful public buildings of Omelas, or perhaps in the cellar of one of its spacious private homes, there is a room. It has one locked door, and no window. A little light seeps in dustily between cracks in the boards, secondhand from a cobwebbed window somewhere across the cellar. In one corner of the little room a couple of mops, with stiff, clotted, foul-smelling heads, stand near a rusty bucket. The floor is dirt, a little damp to the touch, as cellar dirt usually is. The room is about three paces long and two wide: a mere broom closet or disused tool room. In the room a child is sitting. It could be a boy or a girl. It looks about six, but actually is nearly ten. It is feeble-minded. Perhaps it was born defective, or perhaps it has become imbecile through fear, malnutrition, and neglect. It picks its nose and occasionally fumbles vaguely with its toes or genitals, as it sits hunched in the corner farthest from the bucket and the two mops. It is afraid of the mops. It finds them horrible. It shuts its eyes, but it knows the mops are still standing there; and the door is locked; and nobody will come. The door is always locked; and nobody ever comes, except that sometimes — the child has no understanding of time or interval — sometimes the door rattles terribly and opens, and a person, or several people, are there. One of them may come in and kick the child to make it stand up. The others never come close, but peer in at it with frightened, disgusted eyes. The food bowl and the water jug are hastily filled, the door is locked, the eyes disappear. The people at the door never say anything, but the child, who has not always lived in the tool room, and can remember sunlight and its mother's voice, sometimes speaks. "I will be good," it says. "Please let me out. I will be good!" They never answer. The child used to scream for help at night, and cry a good deal, but now it only makes a kind of whining, "eh-haa, eh-haa," and it speaks less and less often. It is so thin there are no calves to its legs; its belly protrudes; it lives on a half-bowl of corn meal and grease a day. It is naked. Its buttocks and thighs are a mass of festered sores, as it sits in its own excrement continually.

They all know it is there, all the people of Omelas. Some of them have come to see it, others are content merely to know it is there. They all know that it has to be there. Some of them understand why, and some do not, but they all understand that their happiness, the beauty of their city, the tenderness of their friendships, the health of their children, the wisdom of their scholars, the skill of their makers, even the abundance of their harvest and the kindly weathers of their skies, depend wholly on this child's abominable misery.

This is usually explained to children when they are between eight and twelve, whenever they seem capable of understanding; and most of those who come to see the child are young people, though often enough an adult comes, or comes back, to see the child. No matter how well the matter has been explained to them, these young spectators are always shocked and sickened at the sight. They feel disgust, which they had thought themselves superior to. They feel anger, outrage, impotence, despite all the explanations. They would like to do something for the child. But there is nothing they can do. If the child were brought up into the sunlight out of that vile place, if it were cleaned and fed and comforted, that would be a good thing, indeed; but if it were done, in that day and hour all the prosperity and beauty and delight of Omelas would wither and be destroyed. Those are the terms. To exchange all the goodness and grace of every life in Omelas for that single, small improvement: to throw away the happiness of thousands for the chance of the happiness of one: that would be to let guilt within the walls indeed.

The terms are strict and absolute; there may not even be a kind word spoken to the child.

Often the young people go home in tears, or in a tearless

rage, when they have seen the child and faced this terrible paradox. They may brood over it for weeks or years. But as times goes on they begin to realize that even if the child could be released, it would not get much good of its freedom: a little vague pleasure of warmth and food, no doubt, but little more. It is too degraded and imbecile to know any real joy. It has been afraid too long ever to be free of fear. Its habits are too uncouth for it to respond to humane treatment. Indeed, after so long it would probably be wretched without walls about it to protect it, and darkness for its eyes, and its own excrement to sit in. Their tears at the bitter injustice dry when they begin to perceive the terrible justice of reality, and to accept it. Yet it is their tears and anger, the trying of their generosity and the acceptance of their helplessness, which are perhaps the true source of the splendor of their lives. Theirs is no vapid, irresponsible happiness. They know that they, like the child, are not free. They know compassion. It is the existence of the child, and their knowledge of its existence, that makes possible the nobility of their architecture, the poignancy of their music, the profundity of their science. It is because of the child that they are so gentle with children. They know that if the wretched one were not there snivelling in the dark, the other one, the flute-player, could make no joyful music as the young riders line up in their beauty for the race in the sunlight of the first morning of summer.

Now do you believe in them? Are they not more credible? But there is one more thing to tell, and this is quite incredible.

At times one of the adolescent girls or boys who go to see the child does not go home to weep or rage, does not, in fact, go home at all. Sometimes also a man or woman much older falls silent for a day or two, and then leaves home. These people go out into the street, and walk down the street alone. They keep walking, and walk straight out of the city of Omelas, through the beautiful gates. They keep walking across the farmlands of Omelas. Each one goes alone, youth or girl, man or woman. Night falls; the traveler must pass down village streets, between the houses with yellow-lit windows, and on out into the darkness of the fields. Each alone, they go west or north, towards the mountains. They go on. They leave Omelas, they walk ahead into the darkness, and they do not come back. The place they go towards is a place even less imaginable to most of us than the city of happiness. I cannot describe it at all. It is possible that it does not exist. But they seem to know where they are going, the ones who walk away from Omelas.

John Updike (b. 1932)

A & P

In walks these three girls in nothing but bathing suits. I'm in the
third checkout slot, with my back to the door, so I don't see them
until they're over by the bread. The one that caught my eye first
was the one in the plaid green two-piece. She was a chunky kid,
with a good tan and a sweet broad soft-looking can with those
two crescents of white just under it, where the sun never seems
to hit, at the top of the backs of her legs. I stood there with my
hand on a box of HiHo crackers trying to remember if I rang it
up or not. I ring it up again and the customer starts giving me
hell. She's one of these cash-register-watchers, a witch about fifty
with rouge on her cheekbones and no eyebrows, and I know it
made her day to trip me up. She'd been watching cash registers
for fifty years and probably never seen a mistake before.

By the time I got her feathers smoothed and her goodies
into a bag — she gives me a little snort in passing, if she'd been
born at the right time they would have burned her over in Salem
— by the time I get her on her way the girls had circled around
the bread and were coming back, without a pushcart, back my
way along the counters, in the aisle between the checkouts and
the Special bins. They didn't even have shoes on. There was this
chunky one, with the two-piece — it was bright green and the
seams on the bra were still sharp and her belly was still pretty
pale so I guessed she just got it (the suit) — there was this one,
with one of those chubby berry-faces, the lips all bunched together
under her nose, this one, and a tall one, with black hair that hadn't
quite frizzed right, and one of these sunburns right across under
the eyes, and a chin that was too long — you know, the kind of
girl other girls think is very "striking" and "attractive" but never
quite makes it, as they very well know, which is why they like
her so much — and then the third one, that wasn't quite so tall.
She was the queen. She kind of led them, the other two peeking
around and making their shoulders round. She didn't look around,
not this queen, she just walked straight on slowly, on these long
white prima-donna legs. She came down a little hard on her heels,
as if she didn't walk in her bare feet that much, putting down her
heels and then letting the weight move along to her toes as if she
was testing the floor with every step, putting a little deliberate
extra action into it. You never know for sure how girls' minds
work (do you really think it's a mind in there or just a little buzz

like a bee in a glass jar?) but you got the idea she had talked the
other two into coming in here with her, and now she was showing
them how to do it, walk slow and hold yourself straight.

She had on a kind of dirty-pink — beige maybe, I don't
know — bathing suit with a little nubble all over it and, what
got me, the straps were down. They were off her shoulders looped
loose around the cool tops of her arms, and I guess as a result the
suit had slipped a little on her, so all around the top of the cloth
there was this shining rim. If it hadn't been there you wouldn't
have known there could have been anything whiter than those
shoulders. With the straps pushed off, there was nothing between
the top of the suit and the top of her head except just *her,* this
clean bare plane of the top of her chest down from the shoulder
bones like a dented sheet of metal tilted in the light. I mean, it
was more than pretty.

She had sort of oaky hair that the sun and salt had bleached,
done up in a bun that was unravelling, and a kind of prim face.
Walking into the A & P with your straps down, I suppose it's
the only kind of face you *can* have. She held her head so high her
neck, coming up out of those white shoulders, looked kind of
stretched, but I didn't mind. The longer her neck was, the more
of her there was.

She must have felt in the corner of her eye me and over my
shoulder Stokesie in the second slot watching, but she didn't tip.
Not this queen. She kept her eyes moving across the racks, and
stopped, and turned so slow it made my stomach rub the inside
of my apron, and buzzed to the other two, who kind of huddled
against her for relief, and then they all three of them went up the
cat and dog food-breakfast cereal-macaroni-rice-raisins-seasonings-
spreads-spaghetti-soft drinks-crackers-and-cookies aisle. From the
third slot I look straight up this aisle to the meat counter, and I
watched them all the way. The fat one with the tan sort of fumbled
with the cookies, but on second thought she put the package back.
The sheep pushing their carts down the aisle — the girls were
walking against the usual traffic (not that we have one-way signs
or anything) — were pretty hilarious. You could see them, when
Queenie's white shoulders dawned on them, kind of jerk, or hop,
or hiccup, but their eyes snapped back to their own baskets and
on they pushed. I bet you could set off dynamite in an A & P
and the people would by and large keep reaching and checking
oatmeal off their lists and muttering "Let me see, there was a third
thing, began with A, asparagus, no, ah, yes, applesauce!" or whatever
it is they do mutter. But there was no doubt, this jiggled them.
A few house slaves in pin curlers even look around after pushing
their carts past to make sure what they had seen was correct.

You know, it's one thing to have a girl in a bathing suit down on the beach, where what with the glare nobody can look at each other much anyway, and another thing in the cool of the A & P, under the fluorescent lights, against all those stacked packages, with her feet paddling along naked over our checker-board green-and-cream rubber-tile floor.

"Oh, Daddy," Stokesie said beside me. "I feel so faint."

"Darling," I said. "Hold me tight." Stokesie's married, with two babies chalked up on his fuselage already, but as far as I can tell that's the only difference. He's twenty-two, and I was nineteen this April.

"Is it done?" he asks, the responsible married man finding his voice. I forgot to say he thinks he's going to be manager some sunny day, maybe in 1990 when it's called the Great Alexandrov and Petrooshki Tea Company or something.

What he meant was, our town is five miles from a beach, with a big summer colony out on the Point, but we're right in the middle of town, and the women generally put on a shirt or shorts or something before they get out of the car into the street. And anyway these are usually women with six children and varicose veins mapping their legs and nobody, including them, could care less. As I say, we're right in the middle of town, and if you stand at our front doors you can see two banks and the Congregational church and the newspaper store and three real estate offices and about twenty-seven old freeloaders tearing up Central Street because the sewer broke again. It's not as if we're on the Cape; we're north of Boston and there's people in this town haven't seen the ocean for twenty years.

The girls had reached the meat counter and were asking McMahon something. He pointed, they pointed, and they shuffled out of sight behind a pyramid of Diet Delight peaches. All that was left for us to see was old McMahon patting his mouth and looking after them sizing up their joints. Poor kids, I began to feel sorry for them, they couldn't help it.

Now here comes the sad part of the story, at least my family says it's sad, but I don't think it's so sad myself. The store's pretty empty, it being Thursday afternoon, so there was nothing much to do except lean on the register and wait for the girls to show up again. The whole store was like a pinball machine and I didn't know which tunnel they'd come out of. After a while they come around out of the far aisle, around the light bulbs, records at discount of the Caribbean Six or Tony Martin Sings or some such gunk you wonder they waste the wax on, sixpacks of candy bars, and plastic toys done up in cellophane that fall apart when a kid looks at them anyway. Around they come, Queenie still leading the way, and holding a little gray jar in her hand. Slots Three through Seven are unmanned and I could see her wondering between Stokes and me, but Stokesie with his usual luck draws an old party in baggy gray pants who stumbles up with four giant cans of pineapple juice (what do these bums *do* with all that pineapple juice? I've often asked myself) so the girls come to me. Queenie puts down the jar and I take it into my fingers icy cold. Kingfish Fancy Herring Snacks in Pure Sour Cream: 49¢. Now her hands are empty, not a ring or a bracelet, bare as God made them, and I wonder where the money's coming from. Still with that prim look she lifts a folded dollar bill out of the hollow at the center of her nubbled pink top. The jar went heavy in my hand. Really, I thought that was so cute.

Then everybody's luck begins to run out. Lengel comes in from haggling with a truck full of cabbages on the lot and is about to scuttle into the door marked MANAGER behind which he hides all day when the girls touch his eye. Lengel's pretty dreary, teaches Sunday school and the rest, but he doesn't miss that much. He comes over and says, "Girls, this isn't the beach."

Queenie blushes, though maybe it's just a brush of sunburn I was noticing for the first time, now that she was so close. "My mother asked me to pick up a jar of herring snacks." Her voice kind of startled me, the way voices do when you see the people first, coming out so flat and dumb yet kind of tony, too, the way it ticked over "pick up" and "snacks." All of a sudden I slid right down her voice into her living room. Her father and the other men were standing around in ice-cream coats and bow ties and the women were in sandals picking up herring snacks on toothpicks off a big glass plate and they were all holding drinks the color of water with olives and sprigs of mint in them. When my parents have somebody over they get lemonade and if it's a real racy affair Schlitz in tall glasses with "They'll Do It Every Time" cartoons stencilled on.

"That's all right," Lengel said. "But this isn't the beach." His repeating this struck me as funny, as if it had just occurred to him, and he had been thinking all these years the A & P was a great big dune and he was the head lifeguard. He didn't like my smiling — as I say he doesn't miss much — but he concentrates on giving the girls that sad Sunday-school-superintendent stare.

Queenie's blush is no sunburn now, and the plump one in plaid, that I liked better from the back — a really sweet can — pipes up, "We weren't doing any shopping. We just came in for the one thing."

"That makes no difference," Lengel tells her, and I could

see from the way his eyes went that he hadn't noticed she was wearing a two-piece before. "We want you decently dressed when you come in here."

"We *are* decent," Queenie says suddenly, her lower lip pushing, getting sore now that she remembers her place, a place from which the crowd that runs the A & P must look pretty crummy. Fancy Herring Snacks flashed in her very blue eyes.

"Girls, I don't want to argue with you. After this come in here with your shoulders covered. It's our policy." He turns his back. That's policy for you. Policy is what the kingpins want. What the others want is juvenile delinquency.

All this while, the customers had been showing up with their carts but, you know, sheep, seeing a scene, they had all bunched up on Stokesie, who shook open a paper bag as gently as peeling a peach, not wanting to miss a word. I could feel in the silence everybody getting nervous, most of all Lengel, who asks me, "Sammy, have you rung up this purchase?"

I thought and said "No" but it wasn't about that I was thinking. I go through the punches, 4, 9, GROC, TOT — it's more complicated than you think and after you do it often enough, it begins to make a little song, that you hear words to, in my case "Hello (*bing*) there, you (*gung*) hap-py *peepul* (*splat*)!" — the *splat* being the drawer flying out. I uncrease the bill, tenderly as you may imagine, it just having come from between the two smoothest scoops of vanilla I had ever known were there, and pass a half and a penny into her narrow pink palm, and nestle the herrings in a bag and twist its neck and hand it over, all the time thinking.

The girls, and who'd blame them, are in a hurry to get out, so I say "I quit" to Lengel quick enough for them to hear, hoping they'll stop and watch me, their unsuspected hero. They keep right on going, into the electric eye; the door flies open and they flicker across the lot to their car, Queenie and Plaid and Big Tall Goony-Goony (not that as raw material she was so bad), leaving me with Lengel and a kink in his eyebrow.

"Did you say something, Sammy?"

"I said I quit."

"I thought you did."

"You didn't have to embarrass them."

"It was they who were embarrassing us."

I started to say something that came out "Fiddle-de-doo." It's a saying of my grandmother's, and I know she would have been pleased.

"I don't think you know what you're saying," Lengel said.

"I know you don't," I said. "But I do." I pull the bow at

the back of my apron and start shrugging it off my shoulders. A couple customers that had been heading for my slot begin to knock against each other, like scared pigs in a chute.

Lengel sighs and begins to look very patient and old and gray. He's been a friend of my parents for years. "Sammy, you don't want to do this to your Mom and Dad," he tells me. It's true, I don't. But it seems to me that once you begin a gesture it's fatal not to go through with it. I fold the apron, "Sammy" stitched in red on the pocket, and put it on the counter, and drop the bow tie on top of it. The bow tie is theirs, if you've ever wondered. "You'll feel this for the rest of your life," Lengel says, and I know that's true, too, but remembering how he made that pretty girl blush makes me so scrunchy inside I punch the No Sale tab and the machine whirs "pee-pul" and the drawer splats out. One advantage to this scene taking place in summer, I can follow this up with a clean exit, there's no fumbling around getting your coat and galoshes, I just saunter into the electric eye in my white shirt that my mother ironed the night before, and the door heaves itself open, and outside the sunshine is skating around on the asphalt.

I look around for my girls, but they're gone, of course. There wasn't anybody but some young married screaming with her children about some candy they didn't get by the door of a powder-blue Falcon station wagon. Looking back in the big windows, over the bags of peat moss and aluminum lawn furniture stacked on the pavement, I could see Lengel in my place in the slot, checking the sheep through. His face was dark gray and his back stiff, as if he'd just had an injection of iron, and my stomach kind of fell as I felt how hard the world was going to be to me hereafter.

Joyce Carol Oates (b. 1938)

Where Are You Going, Where Have You Been?

To Bob Dylan

Her name was Connie. She was fifteen and she had a quick nervous giggling habit of craning her neck to glance into mirrors or checking other people's faces to make sure her own was all right. Her mother, who noticed everything and knew everything and who hadn't much reason any longer to look at her own face, always scolded Connie about it. "Stop gawking at yourself, who are you? You think you're so pretty?" she would say. Connie would raise her eyebrows at these familiar complaints and look right through her mother, into a shadowy vision of herself as she was right at that moment: she knew she was pretty and that was everything. Her mother had been pretty once too, if you could believe those old snapshots in the album, but now her looks were gone and that was why she was always after Connie.

"Why don't you keep your room clean like your sister? How've you got your hair fixed — what the hell stinks? Hair spray? You don't see your sister using that junk."

Her sister June was twenty-four and still lived at home. She was a secretary in the high school Connie attended, and if that wasn't bad enough — with her in the same building — she was so plain and chunky and steady that Connie had to hear her praised all the time by her mother and her mother's sisters. June did this, June did that, she saved money and helped clean the house and cooked and Connie couldn't do a thing, her mind was all filled with trashy daydreams. Their father was away at work most of the time and when he came home he wanted supper and he read the newspaper at supper and after supper he went to bed. He didn't bother talking much to them, but around his bent head Connie's mother kept picking at her until Connie wished her mother were dead and she herself were dead and it were all over. "She makes me want to throw up sometimes," she complained to her friends. She had a high, breathless, amused voice which made everything she said sound a little forced, whether it was sincere or not.

There was one good thing: June went places with girlfriends of hers, girls who were just as plain and steady as she, and so when Connie wanted to do that her mother had no objections. The father of Connie's best girlfriend drove the girls the three miles to town and left them off at a shopping plaza, so that they could walk through the stores or go to a movie, and when he came to pick them up again at eleven he never bothered to ask what they had done.

They must have been familiar sights, walking around that shopping plaza in their shorts and flat ballerina slippers that always scuffed the sidewalk, with charm bracelets jingling on their thin wrists; they would lean together to whisper and laugh secretly if someone passed by who amused or interested them. Connie had long dark blond hair that drew anyone's eye to it, and she wore part of it pulled up on her head and puffed out and the rest of it she let fall down her back. She wore a pullover jersey blouse that looked one way when she was at home and another way when she was away from home. Everything about her had two sides to it, one for home and one for anywhere that was not home: her walk that could be childlike and bobbing, or languid enough to make anyone think she was hearing music in her head, her mouth which was pale and smirking most of the time, but bright and pink on these evenings out, her laugh which was cynical and drawling at home — "Ha, ha, very funny" — but high-pitched and nervous anywhere else, like the jingling of the charms on her bracelet.

Sometimes they did go shopping or to a movie, but sometimes they went across the highway, ducking fast across the busy road, to a drive-in restaurant where older kids hung out. The restaurant was shaped like a big bottle, though squatter than a real bottle, and on its cap was a revolving figure of a grinning boy who held a hamburger aloft. One night in midsummer they ran across, breathless with daring, and right away someone leaned out a car window and invited them over, but it was just a boy from high school they didn't like. It made them feel good to be able to ignore him. They went up through the maze of parked and cruising cars to the bright-lit, fly-infested restaurant, their faces pleased and expectant as if they were entering a sacred building that loomed out of the night to give them what haven and what blessing they yearned for. They sat at the counter and crossed their legs at the ankles, their thin shoulders rigid with excitement, and listened to the music that made everything so good: the music was always in the background like music at a church service, it was something to depend upon.

A boy named Eddie came in to talk with them. He sat backward on his stool, turning himself jerkily around in semicircles and then stopping and turning again, and after a while he asked Connie if she would like something to eat. She said she did and so she tapped her friend's arm on her way out — her friend pulled her face up into a brave droll look — and Connie said she would meet her at eleven, across the way. "I just hate to leave her like that," Connie said earnestly, but the boy said that she wouldn't be alone for long. So they went out to his car and on the way Connie couldn't help but let her eyes wander over the windshields and faces all around her, her face gleaming with a joy that had nothing to do with Eddie or even this place; it might have been the music. She drew her shoulders up and sucked in her breath with the pure pleasure of being alive, and just at that moment she happened to glance at a face just a few feet from hers. It was a boy with shaggy black hair, in a convertible jalopy painted gold. He stared at her and then his lips widened into a grin. Connie slit her eyes at him and turned away, but she couldn't help glancing back and there he was still watching her. He wagged a finger and laughed and said, "Gonna get you, baby," and Connie turned away again without Eddie noticing anything.

She spent three hours with him, at the restaurant where they ate hamburgers and drank Cokes in wax cups that were always sweating, and then down an alley a mile or so away, and when he left her off at five to eleven only the movie house was still open at the plaza. Her girlfriend was there, talking with a boy. When Connie came up the two girls smiled at each other and Connie said, "How was the movie?" and the girl said, "*You* should know." They rode off with the girl's father, sleepy and pleased, and Connie couldn't help but look at the darkened shopping plaza with its big empty parking lot and its signs that were faded and ghostly now, and over at the drive-in restaurant where cars were still circling tirelessly. She couldn't hear the music at this distance.

Next morning June asked her how the movie was and Connie said, "So-so."

She and that girl and occasionally another girl went out several times a week that way, and the rest of the time Connie spent around the house — it was summer vacation — getting in her mother's way and thinking, dreaming, about the boys she met. But all the boys fell back and dissolved into a single face that was not even a face, but an idea, a feeling, mixed up with the urgent insistent pounding of the music and the humid night air of July. Connie's mother kept dragging her back to the daylight by finding things for her to do or saying, suddenly, "What's this about the Pettinger girl?"

And Connie would say nervously, "Oh, her. That dope." She always drew thick clear lines between herself and such girls, and her mother was simple and kindly enough to believe her. Her mother was so simple, Connie thought, that it was maybe cruel to fool her so much. Her mother went scuffling around the house in old bedroom slippers and complained over the telephone to one sister about the other, then the other called up and the two of them complained about the third one. If June's name was mentioned her mother's tone was approving, and if Connie's name was mentioned it was disapproving. This did not really mean she disliked Connie and actually Connie thought that her mother preferred her to June because she was prettier, but the two of them kept up a pretense of exasperation, a sense that they were tugging and struggling over something of little value to either of them. Sometimes, over coffee, they were almost friends, but something would come up — some vexation that was like a fly buzzing suddenly around their heads — and their faces went hard with contempt.

One Sunday Connie got up at eleven — none of them bothered with church — and washed her hair so that it could dry all day long, in the sun. Her parents and sisters were going to a barbecue at an aunt's house and Connie said no, she wasn't interested, rolling her eyes to let her mother know just what she thought of it. "Stay home alone then," her mother said sharply. Connie sat out back in a lawn chair and watched them drive away, her father quiet and bald, hunched around so that he could back the car out, her mother with a look that was still angry and not at all softened through the windshield, and in the back seat poor old June all dressed up as if she didn't know what a barbecue was, with all the running yelling kids and the flies. Connie sat with her eyes closed in the sun, dreaming and dazed with the warmth about her as if this were a kind of love, the caresses of love, and her mind slipped over onto thoughts of the boy she had been with the night before and how nice he had been, how sweet it always was, not the way someone like June would suppose but sweet, gentle, the way it was in movies and promised in songs; and when she opened her eyes she hardly knew where she was, the back yard ran off into weeds and a fence line of trees and behind it the sky was perfectly blue and still. The asbestos "ranch house" that was now three years old startled her — it looked small. She shook her head as if to get awake.

It was too hot. She went inside the house and turned on the radio to drown out the quiet. She sat on the edge of her bed, barefoot, and listened for an hour and a half to a program called XYZ Sunday Jamboree, record after record of hard, fast, shrieking songs she sang along with, interspersed by exclamations from "Bobby King": "An' look here you girls at Napoleon's — Son and Charley want you to pay real close attention to this song coming up!"

And Connie paid close attention herself, bathed in a glow of slow-pulsed joy that seemed to rise mysteriously out of the music itself and lay languidly about the airless little room, breathed in and breathed out with each gentle rise and fall of her chest.

After a while she heard a car coming up the drive. She sat up at once, startled, because it couldn't be her father so soon. The gravel kept crunching all the way in from the road — the driveway was long — and Connie ran to the window. It was a car she didn't know. It was an open jalopy, painted a bright gold that caught the sunlight opaquely. Her heart began to pound and her fingers snatched at her hair, checking it, and she whispered "Christ, Christ," wondering how bad she looked. The car came to a stop at the side door and the horn sounded four short taps as if this were a signal Connie knew.

She went into the kitchen and approached the door slowly, then hung out the screen door, her bare toes curling down off the step. There were two boys in the car and now she recognized the driver: he had shaggy, shabby black hair that looked crazy as a wig and he was grinning at her.

"I ain't late, am I?" he said.

"Who the hell do you think you are?" Connie said.

"Toldja I'd be out, didn't I?"

"I don't even know who you are."

She spoke sullenly, careful to show no interest or pleasure, and he spoke in a fast bright monotone. Connie looked past him to the other boy, taking her time. He had fair brown hair, with a lock that fell onto his forehead. His sideburns gave him a fierce, embarrassed look, but so far he hadn't even bothered to glance at her. Both boys wore sunglasses. The driver's glasses were metallic and mirrored everything in miniature.

"You wanta come for a ride?" he said.

Connie smirked and let her hair fall loose over one shoulder.

"Don'tcha like my car? New paint job," he said. "Hey."

"What?"

"You're cute."

She pretended to fidget, chasing flies away from the door.

"Don'tcha believe me, or what?" he said.

"Look, I don't even know who you are," Connie said in disgust.

"Hey, Ellie's got a radio, see. Mine's broke down." He lifted his friend's arm and showed her the little transistor the boy was holding, and now Connie began to hear the music. It was the same program that was playing inside the house.

"Bobby King?" she said.

"I listen to him all the time. I think he's great."

"He's kind of great," Connie said reluctantly.

"Listen, that guy's *great*. He knows where the action is."

Connie blushed a little, because the glasses made it impossible for her to see just what this boy was looking at. She couldn't decide if she liked him or if he was just a jerk, and so she dawdled in the doorway and wouldn't come down or go back inside. She said, "What's all that stuff painted on your car?"

"Can'tcha read it?" He opened the door very carefully, as

if he was afraid it might fall off. He slid out just as carefully, planting his feet firmly on the ground, the tiny metallic world in his glasses slowing down like gelatine hardening and in the midst of it Connie's bright green blouse. "This here is my name, to begin with," he said. ARNOLD FRIEND was written in tarlike black letters on the side, with a drawing of a round grinning face that reminded Connie of a pumpkin, except it wore sunglasses. "I wanta introduce myself, I'm Arnold Friend and that's my real name and I'm gonna be your friend, honey, and inside the car's Ellie Oscar, he's kinda shy." Ellie brought his transistor radio up to his shoulder and balanced it there. "Now these numbers are a secret code, honey," Arnold Friend explained. He read off the numbers 33, 19, 17 and raised his eyebrows at her to see what she thought of that, but she didn't think much of it. The left rear fender had been smashed and around it was written, on the gleaming gold background: DONE BY CRAZY WOMAN DRIVER. Connie had to laugh at that. Arnold Friend was pleased at her laughter and looked up at her. "Around the other side's a lot more — you wanta come and see them?"

"No."

"Why not?"

"Why should I?"

"Don'tcha wanta see what's on the car? Don'tcha wanta go for a ride?"

"I don't know."

"Why not?"

"I got things to do."

"Like what?"

"Things."

He laughed as if she had said something funny. He slapped his thighs. He was standing in a strange way, leaning back against the car as if he were balancing himself. He wasn't tall, only an inch or so taller than she would be if she came down to him. Connie liked the way he was dressed, which was the way all of them dressed: tight faded jeans stuffed into black, scuffed boots, a belt that pulled his waist in and showed how lean he was, and a white pullover shirt that was a little soiled and showed the hard small muscles of his arms and shoulders. He looked as if he probably did hard work, lifting and carrying things. Even his neck looked muscular. And his face was a familiar face, somehow: the jaw and chin and cheeks slightly darkened, because he hadn't shaved for a day or two, and the nose long and hawklike, sniffing as if she were a treat he was going to gobble up and it was all a joke.

"Connie, you ain't telling the truth. This is your day set aside for a ride with me and you know it," he said, still laughing.

The way he straightened and recovered from his fit of laughing showed that it had been all fake.

"How do you know what my name is?" she said suspiciously.

"It's Connie."

"Maybe and maybe not."

"I know my Connie," he said, wagging his finger. Now she remembered him even better, back at the restaurant, and her cheeks warmed at the thought of how she sucked in her breath just at the moment she passed him — how she must have looked at him. And he had remembered her. "Ellie and I come out here especially for you," he said. "Ellie can sit in back. How about it?"

"Where?"

"Where what?"

"Where're we going?"

He looked at her. He took off the sunglasses and she saw how pale the skin around his eyes was, like holes that were not in shadow but instead in light. His eyes were like chips of broken glass that catch the light in an amiable way. He smiled. It was as if the idea of going for a ride somewhere, to some place, was a new idea to him.

"Just for a ride, Connie sweetheart."

"I never said my name was Connie," she said.

"But I know what it is. I know your name and all about you, lots of things," Arnold Friend said. He had not moved yet but stood still leaning back against the side of his jalopy. "I took a special interest in you, such a pretty girl, and found out all about you like I know your parents and sister are gone somewheres and I know where and how long they're going to be gone, and I know who you were with last night, and your best girlfriend's name is Betty. Right?"

He spoke in a simple lilting voice, exactly as if he were reciting the words to a song. His smile assured her that everything was fine. In the car Ellie turned up the volume on his radio and did not bother to look around at them.

"Ellie can sit in the back seat," Arnold Friend said. He indicated his friend with a casual jerk of his chin, as if Ellie did not count and she should not bother with him.

"How'd you find out all that stuff?" Connie said.

"Listen: Betty Schultz and Tony Fitch and Jimmy Pettinger and Nancy Pettinger," he said, in a chant. "Raymond Stanley and Bob Hutter — "

"Do you know all those kids?"

"I know everybody."

"Look, you're kidding. You're not from around here."

"Sure."

"But — how come we never saw you before?"

"Sure you saw me before," he said. He looked down at his boots, as if he were a little offended. "You just don't remember."

"I guess I'd remember you," Connie said.

"Yeah?" He looked up at this, beaming. He was pleased. He began to mark time with the music from Ellie's radio, tapping his fists lightly together. Connie looked away from his smile to the car, which was painted so bright it almost hurt her eyes to look at it. She looked at that name. ARNOLD FRIEND. And up at the front fender was an expression that was familiar — MAN THE FLYING SAUCERS. It was an expression kids had used the year before, but didn't use this year. She looked at it for a while as if the words meant something to her that she did not yet know.

"What're you thinking about? Huh?" Arnold Friend demanded. "Not worried about your hair blowing around in the car, are you?"

"No."

"Think I maybe can't drive good?"

"How do I know?"

"You're a hard girl to handle. How come?" he said. "Don't you know I'm your friend? Didn't you see me put my sign in the air when you walked by?"

"What sign?"

"My sign." And he drew an X in the air, leaning out toward her. They were maybe ten feet apart. After his hand fell back to his side the X was still in the air, almost visible. Connie let the screen door close and stood perfectly still inside it, listening to the music from her radio and the boy's blend together. She stared at Arnold Friend. He stood there so stiffly relaxed, pretending to be relaxed, with one hand idly on the door handle as if he were keeping himself up that way and had no intention of ever moving again. She recognized most things about him, the tight jeans that showed his thighs and buttocks and the greasy leather boots and the tight shirt, and even that slippery friendly smile of his, that sleepy dreamy smile that all the boys used to get across ideas they didn't want to put into words. She recognized all this and also the singsong way he talked, slightly mocking, kidding, but serious and a little melancholy, and she recognized the way he tapped one fist against the other in homage of the perpetual music behind him. But all these things did not come together.

She said suddenly, "Hey, how old are you?"

His smile faded. She could see then that he wasn't a kid, he was much older — thirty, maybe more. At this knowledge her heart began to pound faster.

"That's a crazy thing to ask. Can'tcha see I'm your own age?"

"Like hell you are."

"Or maybe a coupla years older, I'm eighteen."

"Eighteen?" she said doubtfully.

He grinned to reassure her and lines appeared at the corners of his mouth. His teeth were big and white. He grinned so broadly his eyes became slits and she saw how thick the lashes were, thick and black as if painted with a black tarlike material. Then he seemed to become embarrassed, abruptly, and looked over his shoulder at Ellie. "*Him,* he's crazy," he said. "Ain't he a riot, he's a nut, a real character." Ellie was still listening to the music. His sunglasses told nothing about what he was thinking. He wore a bright orange shirt unbuttoned halfway to show his chest, which was a pale, bluish chest and not muscular like Arnold Friend's. His shirt collar was turned up all around and the very tips of the collar pointed out past his chin as if they were protecting him. He was pressing the transistor radio up against his ear and sat there in a kind of daze, right in the sun.

"He's kinda strange," Connie said.

"Hey, she says you're kinda strange! Kinda strange!" Arnold Friend cried. He pounded on the car to get Ellie's attention. Ellie turned for the first time and Connie saw with shock that he wasn't a kid either — he had a fair, hairless face, cheeks reddened slightly as if the veins grew too close to the surface of his skin, the face of a forty-year-old baby. Connie felt a wave of dizziness rise in her at this sight and she stared at him as if waiting for something to change the shock of the moment, make it all right again. Ellie's lips kept shaping words, mumbling along with the words blasting in his ear.

"Maybe you two better go away," Connie said faintly.

"What? How come?" Arnold Friend cried. "We come out here to take you for a ride. It's Sunday." He had the voice of the man on the radio now. It was the same voice, Connie thought. "Don'tcha know it's Sunday all day and honey, no matter who you were with last night today you're with Arnold Friend and don't you forget it! — Maybe you better step out here," he said, and this last was in a different voice. It was a little flatter, as if the heat was finally getting to him.

"No. I got things to do."

"Hey."

"You two better leave."

"We ain't leaving until you come with us."

"Like hell I am —"

"Connie, don't fool around with me. I mean, I mean, don't

fool *around*," he said, shaking his head. He laughed incredulously.
He placed his sunglasses on top of his head, carefully, as if he
were indeed wearing a wig, and brought the stems down behind
his ears. Connie stared at him, another wave of dizziness and fear
rising in her so that for a moment he wasn't even in focus but
was just a blur, standing there against his gold car, and she had
the idea that he had driven up the driveway all right but had come
from nowhere before that and belonged nowhere and that everything
about him and even about the music that was so familiar to her
was only half real.

"If my father comes and sees you —"

"He ain't coming. He's at a barbecue."

"How do you know that?"

"Aunt Tillie's. Right now they're — uh — they're drinking.
Sitting around," he said vaguely, squinting as if he were staring
all the way to town and over to Aunt Tillie's back yard. Then
the vision seemed to get clear and he nodded energetically. "Yeah.
Sitting around. There's your sister in a blue dress, huh? And high
heels, the poor sad bitch — nothing like you, sweetheart! And
your mother's helping some fat woman with the corn, they're
cleaning the corn — husking the corn —"

"What fat woman?" Connie cried.

"How do I know what fat woman, I don't know every
goddam fat woman in the world!" Arnold laughed.

"Oh, that's Mrs. Hornby . . . Who invited her?" Connie
said. She felt a little light-headed. Her breath was coming quickly.

"She's too fat. I don't like them fat. I like them the way
you are, honey," he said, smiling sleepily at her. They stared at
each other for a while, through the screen door. He said softly,
"Now what you're going to do is this: you're going to come out
that door. You're going to sit up front with me and Ellie's going
to sit in the back, the hell with Ellie, right? This isn't Ellie's date.
You're my date. I'm your lover, honey."

"What? You're crazy —"

"Yes, I'm your lover. You don't know what that is, but
you will," he said. "I know that too. I know all about you. But
look: it's real nice and you couldn't ask for nobody better than
me, or more polite. I always keep my word. I'll tell you how it
is, I'm always nice at first, the first time. I'll hold you so tight
you won't think you have to try to get away or pretend anything
because you'll know you can't. And I'll come inside you where
it's all secret and you'll give in to me and you'll love me —"

"Shut up! You're crazy!" Connie said. She backed away from
the door. She put her hands against her ears as if she'd heard

something terrible, something not meant for her. "People don't talk like that, you're crazy," she muttered. Her heart was almost too big now for her chest and its pumping made sweat break out all over her. She looked out to see Arnold Friend pause and then take a step toward the porch lurching. He almost fell. But, like a clever drunken man, he managed to catch his balance. He wobbled in his high boots and grabbed hold of one of the porch posts.

"Honey?" he said. "You still listening?"

"Get the hell out of here!"

"Be nice, honey. Listen."

"I'm going to call the police —"

He wobbled again and out of the side of his mouth came a fast spat curse, an aside not meant for her to hear. But even this "Christ!" sounded forced. Then he began to smile again. She watched this smile come, awkward as if he were smiling from inside a mask. His whole face was a mask, she thought wildly, tanned down onto his throat but then running out as if he had plastered makeup on his face but had forgotten about his throat.

"Honey — ? Listen, here's how it is. I always tell the truth and I promise you this: I ain't coming in that house after you."

"You better not! I'm going to call the police if you — if you don't —"

"Honey," he said, talking right through her voice, "honey, I'm not coming in there but you are coming out here. You know why?"

She was panting. The kitchen looked like a place she had never seen before, some room she had run inside but which wasn't good enough, wasn't going to help her. The kitchen window had never had a curtain, after three years, and there were dishes in the sink for her to do — probably — and if you ran your hand across the table you'd probably feel something sticky there.

"You listening, honey? Hey?"

" — going to call the police — "

"Soon as you touch the phone I don't need to keep my promise and can come inside. You won't want that."

She rushed forward and tried to lock the door. Her fingers were shaking. "But why lock it," Arnold Friend said gently, talking right into her face. "It's just a screen door. It's just nothing." One of his boots was at a strange angle, as if his foot wasn't in it. It pointed out to the left, bent at the ankle. "I mean, anybody can break through a screen door and glass and wood and iron or anything else if he needs to, anybody at all and specially Arnold Friend. If the place got lit up with a fire honey you'd come runnin' out into my arms, right into my arms an' safe at home — like you knew I was your lover and'd stopped fooling around. I don't mind a nice shy girl but I don't like no fooling around." Part of those words were spoken with a slight rhythmic lilt, and Connie somehow recognized them — the echo of a song from last year, about a girl rushing into her boyfriend's arms and coming home again —

Connie stood barefoot on the linoleum floor, staring at him. "What do you want?" she whispered.

"I want you," he said.

"What?"

"Seen you that night and thought, that's the one, yes sir. I never needed to look any more."

"But my father's coming back. He's coming to get me. I had to wash my hair first —" She spoke in a dry, rapid voice, hardly raising it for him to hear.

"No, your Daddy is not coming and yes, you had to wash your hair and you washed it for me. It's nice and shining and all for me, I thank you, sweetheart," he said, with a mock bow, but again he almost lost his balance. He had to bend and adjust his boots. Evidently his feet did not go all the way down; the boots must have been stuffed with something so that he would seem taller. Connie stared out at him and behind him Ellie in the car, who seemed to be looking off toward Connie's right into nothing. This Ellie said, pulling the words out of the air one after another as if he were just discovering them, "You want me to pull out the phone?"

"Shut your mouth and keep it shut," Arnold Friend said, his face red from bending over or maybe from embarrassment because Connie had seen his boots. "This ain't none of your business."

"What — what are you doing? What do you want?" Connie said. "If I call the police they'll get you, they'll arrest you —"

"Promise was not to come in unless you touch that phone, and I'll keep that promise," he said. He resumed his erect position and tried to force his shoulders back. He sounded like a hero in a movie, declaring something important. He spoke too loudly and it was as if he were speaking to someone behind Connie. "I ain't made plans for coming in that house where I don't belong but just for you to come out to me, the way you should. Don't you know who I am?"

"You're crazy," she whispered. She backed away from the door but did not want to go into another part of the house, as if this would give him permission to come through the door. "What do you . . . You're crazy, you . . ."

"Huh? What're you saying, honey?"

Her eyes darted everywhere in the kitchen. She could not remember what it was, this room.

"This is how it is, honey: you come out and we'll drive away, have a nice ride. But if you don't come out we're gonna wait till your people come home and then they're all going to get it."

"You want that telephone pulled out?" Ellie said. He held the radio away from his ear and grimaced, as if without the radio the air was too much for him.

"I toldja shut up, Ellie," Arnold Friend said, "you're deaf, get a hearing aid, right? Fix yourself up. This little girl's no trouble and's gonna be nice to me, so Ellie keep to yourself, this ain't your date — right? Don't hem in on me. Don't hog. Don't crush. Don't bird dog. Don't trail me," he said in a rapid meaningless voice, as if he were running through all the expressions he'd learned but was no longer sure which one of them was in style, then rushing on to new ones, making them up with his eyes closed, "Don't crawl under my fence, don't squeeze in my chipmunk hole, don't sniff my glue, suck my popsicle, keep your own greasy fingers on yourself!" He shaded his eyes and peered in at Connie, who was backed against the kitchen table. "Don't mind him honey he's just a creep. He's a dope. Right? I'm the boy for you and like I said you come out here nice like a lady and give me your hand, and nobody else gets hurt, I mean, your nice old bald-headed daddy and your mummy and your sister in her high heels. Because listen: why bring them in this?"

"Leave me alone," Connie whispered.

"Hey, you know that old woman down the road, the one with the chickens and stuff — you know her?"

"She's dead!"

"Dead? What? You know her?" Arnold Friend said.

"She's dead —"

"Don't you like her?"

"She's dead — she's — she isn't here any more —"

"But don't you like her, I mean, you got something against her? Some grudge or something?" Then his voice dipped as if he were conscious of a rudeness. He touched the sunglasses perched on top of his head as if to make sure they were still there. "Now you be a good girl."

"What are you going to do?"

"Just two things, or maybe three," Arnold Friend said. "But I promise it won't last long and you'll like me the way you get to like people you're close to. You will. It's all over for you here, so come on out. You don't want your people in any trouble, do you?"

She turned and bumped against a chair or something, hurting her leg, but she ran into the back room and picked up the telephone. Something roared in her ear, a tiny roaring, and she was so sick with fear that she could do nothing but listen to it — the telephone was clammy and very heavy and her fingers groped down to the dial but were too weak to touch it. She began to scream into the phone, into the roaring. She cried out, she cried for her mother, she felt her breath start jerking back and forth in her lungs as if it were something Arnold Friend were stabbing her with again and again with no tenderness. A noisy sorrowful wailing rose all about her and she was locked inside it the way she was locked inside this house.

After a while she could hear again. She was sitting on the floor with her wet back against the wall.

Arnold Friend was saying from the door, "That's a good girl. Put the phone back."

She kicked the phone away from her.

"No, honey. Pick it up. Put it back right."

She picked it up and put it back. The dial tone stopped.

"That's a good girl. Now you come outside."

She was hollow with what had been fear, but what was now just an emptiness. All that screaming had blasted it out of her. She sat, one leg cramped under her, and deep inside her brain was something like a pinpoint of light that kept going and would not let her relax. She thought, I'm not going to see my mother again. She thought, I'm not going to sleep in my bed again. Her bright green blouse was all wet.

Arnold Friend said, in a gentle-loud voice that was like a stage voice. "The place where you came from ain't there any more, and where you had in mind to go is canceled out. This place you are now — inside your daddy's house — is nothing but a cardboard box I can knock down any time. You know that and always did know it. You hear me?"

She thought, I have got to think. I have to know what to do.

"We'll go out to a nice field, out in the country here where it smells so nice and it's sunny," Arnold Friend said. "I'll have my arms tight around you so you won't need to try to get away and I'll show you what love is like, what it does. The hell with this house! It looks solid all right," he said. He ran a fingernail down the screen and the noise did not make Connie shiver, as it would have the day before. "Now put your hand on your heart, honey. Feel that? That feels solid too, but we know better, be nice to me, be sweet like you can because what else is there for a girl like you but to be sweet and pretty and give in? — and get away before her people come back?"

She felt her pounding heart. Her hand seemed to enclose it. She thought for the first time in her life that it was nothing that was hers, that belonged to her, but just a pounding, living thing inside this body that wasn't really hers either.

"You don't want them to get hurt," Arnold Friend went on. "Now get up, honey. Get up all by yourself."

She stood.

"Now turn this way. That's right. Come over here to me — Ellie, put that away, didn't I tell you? You dope. You miserable creepy dope," Arnold Friend said. His words were not angry but only part of an incantation. The incantation was kindly. "Now come out through the kitchen to me honey, and let's see a smile, try it, you're a brave sweet little girl and now they're eating corn and hot dogs cooked to bursting over an outdoor fire, and they don't know one thing about you and never did and honey you're better than them because not a one of them would have done this for you."

Connie felt the linoleum under her feet; it was cool. She brushed her hair back out of her eyes. Arnold Friend let go of the post tentatively and opened his arms for her, his elbows pointing in toward each other and his wrists limp, to show that this was an embarrassed embrace and a little mocking, he didn't want to make her self-conscious.

She put out her hand against the screen. She watched herself push the door slowly open as if she were safe back somewhere in the other doorway, watching this body and this head of long hair moving out into the sunlight where Arnold Friend waited.

"My sweet little blue-eyed girl," he said, in a half-sung sigh that had nothing to do with her brown eyes but was taken up just the same by the vast sunlit reaches of the land behind him and on all sides of him, so much land that Connie had never seen before and did not recognize except to know that she was going to it.

Toni Cade Bambara (b. 1939)

The Lesson

Back in the days when everyone was old and stupid or young and foolish and me and Sugar were the only ones just right, this lady moved on our block with nappy hair and proper speech and no makeup. And quite naturally we laughed at her, laughed the way we did at the junk man who went about his business like he was some big-time president and his sorry-ass horse his secretary. And we kinda hated her too, hated the way we did the winos who cluttered up our parks and pissed on our handball walls and stank up our hallways and stairs so you couldn't halfway play hide-and-seek without a goddamn gas mask. Miss Moore was her name. The only woman on the block with no first name. And she was black as hell, cept for her feet, which were fish-white and spooky. And she was always planning these boring-ass things for us to do, us being my cousin, mostly, who lived on the block cause we all moved North the same time and to the same apartment then spread out gradual to breathe. And our parents would yank our heads into some kinda shape and crisp up our clothes so we'd be presentable for travel with Miss Moore, who always looked like she was going to church, though she never did. Which is just one of the things the grownups talked about when they talked behind her back like a dog. But when she came calling with some sachet she'd sewed up or some gingerbread she'd made or some book, why then they'd all be too embarrassed to turn her down and we'd get handed over all spruced up. She'd been to college and said it was only right that she should take responsibility for the young ones' education, and she not even related by marriage or blood. So they'd go for it. Specially Aunt Gretchen. She was the main gofer in the family. You got some ole dumb shit foolishness you want somebody to go for, you send for Aunt Gretchen. She been screwed into the go-along for so long, it's a blood-deep natural thing with her. Which is how she got saddled with me and Sugar and Junior in the first place while our mothers were in a la-de-da apartment up the block having a good ole time.

So this one day Miss Moore rounds us all up at the mailbox and it's puredee hot and she's knockin herself out about arithmetic. And school suppose to let up in summer I heard, but she don't never let up. And the starch in my pinafore scratching the shit outta me and I'm really hating this nappy-head bitch and her goddamn college degree. I'd much rather go to the pool or to the show where it's cool. So me and Sugar leaning on the mailbox being surly, which is a Miss Moore word. And Flyboy checking out what everybody brought for lunch. And Fat Butt already wasting his peanut-butter-and-jelly sandwich like the pig he is. And Junebug punchin on Q.T.'s arm for potato chips. And Rosie Giraffe shifting from one hip to the other waiting for somebody to step on her foot or ask her if she from Georgia so she can kick ass, preferably Mercedes'. And Miss Moore asking us do we know what money is, like we a bunch of retards. I mean real money, she say, like it's only poker chips or monopoly papers we lay on the grocer. So right away I'm tired of this and say so. And would much rather snatch Sugar and go to the Sunset and terrorize the West Indian kids and take their hair ribbons and their money too. And Miss Moore files that remark away for next week's lesson on brotherhood, I can tell. And finally I say we oughta get to the subway cause it's cooler and besides we might meet some cute boys. Sugar done swiped her mama's lipstick, so we ready.

So we heading down the street and she's boring us silly about what things cost and what our parents make and how much goes for rent and how money ain't divided up right in this country. And then she gets to the part about we all poor and live in the slums, which I don't feature. And I'm ready to speak on that, but she steps out in the street and hails two cabs just like that. Then she hustles half the crew in with her and hands me a five-dollar bill and tells me to calculate 10 percent tip for the driver. And we're off. Me and Sugar and Junebug and Flyboy hangin out the window and hollering to everybody, putting lipstick on each other cause Flyboy a faggot anyway, and making farts with our sweaty armpits. But I'm mostly trying to figure how to spend this money. But they all fascinated with the meter ticking and Junebug starts laying bets as to how much it'll read when Flyboy can't hold his breath no more. Then Sugar lays bets as to how much it'll be when we get there. So I'm stuck. Don't nobody want to go for my plan, which is to jump out at the next light and run off to the first bar-b-que we can find. Then the driver tells us to get the hell out cause we there already. And the meter reads eighty-five cents. And I'm stalling to figure out the tip and Sugar say give him a dime. And I decide he don't need it bad as I do, so later for him. But then he tries to take off with Junebug foot still in the door so we talk about his mama something ferocious. Then we check out that we on Fifth Avenue and everybody dressed up in stockings. One lady in a fur coat, hot as it is. White folks crazy.

"This is the place," Miss Moore say, presenting it to us in the voice she uses at the museum. "Let's look in the windows before we go in."

"Can we steal?" Sugar asks very serious like she's getting the ground rules squared away before she plays. "I beg your pardon," say Miss Moore, and we fall out. So she leads us around the windows of the toy store and me and Sugar screamin, "This is mine, that's mine, I gotta have that, that was made for me, I was born for that," till Big Butt drowns us out.

"Hey, I'm goin to buy that there."

"That there? You don't even know what it is, stupid."

"I do so," he say punchin on Rosie Giraffe. "It's a microscope."

"Whatcha gonna do with a microscope, fool?"

"Look at things."

"Like what, Ronald?" ask Miss Moore. And Big Butt ain't got the first notion. So here go Miss Moore gabbing about the thousands of bacteria in a drop of water and the somethinorother in a speck of blood and the million and one living things in the air around us is invisible to the naked eye. And what she say that for? Junebug go to town on that "naked" and we rolling. Then Miss Moore ask what it cost. So we all jam into the window smudgin it up and the price tag say $300. So then she ask how long'd take for Big Butt and Junebug to save up their allowances. "Too long," I say. "Yeh," adds Sugar, "outgrown it by that time." And Miss Moore say no, you never outgrow learning instruments. "Why, even medical students and interns and," blah, blah, blah. And we ready to choke Big Butt for bringing it up in the first damn place.

"This here costs four hundred eighty dollars," say Rosie Giraffe. So we pile up all over her to see what she pointin out. My eyes tell me it's a chunk of glass cracked with something heavy, and different-color inks dripped into the splits, then the whole thing put into a oven or something. But for $480 it don't make sense.

"That's a paperweight made of semi-precious stones fused together under tremendous pressure," she explains slowly, with her hands doing the mining and all the factory work.

"So what's a paperweight?" asks Rosie Giraffe.

"To weigh paper with, dumbbell," say Flyboy, the wise man from the East.

"Not exactly," say Miss Moore, which is what she say when you warm or way off too. "It's to weigh paper down so it won't scatter and make your desk untidy." So right away me and Sugar curtsy to each other and then to Mercedes who is more the tidy type.

"We don't keep paper on top of the desk in my class," say Junebug, figuring Miss Moore crazy or lyin one.

"At home, then," she say. "Don't you have a calendar and a pencil case and a blotter and a letter-opener on your desk at home where you do your homework?" And she know damn well what our homes look like cause she nosys around in them every chance she gets.

"I don't even have a desk," say Junebug. "Do we?"

"No. And I don't get no homework neither," says Big Butt.

"And I don't even have a home," say Flyboy like he do at school to keep the white folks off his back and sorry for him. Send this poor kid to camp posters, is his specialty.

"I do," says Mercedes. "I have a box of stationery on my desk and a picture of my cat. My godmother bought the stationery and the desk. There's a big rose on each sheet and the envelopes smell like roses."

"Who wants to know about your smelly-ass stationery," say Rosie Giraffe fore I can get my two cents in.

"It's important to have a work area all your own so that . . ."

"Will you look at this sailboat, please," say Flyboy, cuttin her off and pointin to the thing like it was his. So once again we tumble all over each other to gaze at this magnificent thing in the toy store which is just big enough to maybe sail two kittens across the pond if you strap them to the posts tight. We all start reciting the price tag like we in assembly. "Handcrafted sailboat of fiberglass at one thousand one hundred ninety-five dollars."

"Unbelievable," I hear myself say and am really stunned. I read it again for myself just in case the group recitation put me in a trance. Same thing. For some reason this pisses me off. We look at Miss Moore and she lookin at us, waiting for I dunno what.

"Who'd pay all that when you can buy a sailboat set for a quarter at Pop's, a tube of glue for a dime, and a ball of string for eight cents? It must have a motor and a whole lot else besides," I say. "My sailboat cost me about fifty cents."

"But will it take water?" say Mercedes with her smart ass.

"Took mine to Alley Pond Park once," say Flyboy. "String broke. Lost it. Pity."

"Sailed mine in Central Park and it keeled over and sank. Had to ask my father for another dollar."

"And you got the strap," laugh Big Butt. "The jerk didn't even have a string on it. My old man wailed on his behind."

Little Q.T. was staring hard at the sailboat and you could see he wanted it bad. But he too little and somebody'd just take it from him. So what the hell. "This boat for kids, Miss Moore?"

"Parents silly to buy something like that just to get all broke up," say Rosie Giraffe.

"That much money it should last forever," I figure.

"My father'd buy it for me if I wanted it."

"Your father, my ass," say Rosie Giraffe getting a chance to finally push Mercedes.

"Must be rich people shop here," say Q.T.

"You are a very bright boy," say Flyboy. "What was your first clue?" And he rap him on the head with the back of his knuckles, since Q.T. the only one he could get away with. Though Q.T. liable to come up behind you years later and get his licks in when you half expect it.

"What I want to know is," I says to Miss Moore though I never talk to her, I wouldn't give the bitch that satisfaction, "is how much a real boat costs? I figure a thousand'd get you a yacht any day."

"Why don't you check that out," she says, "and report back to the group?" Which really pains my ass. If you gonna mess up a perfectly good swim day least you could do is have some answers. "Let's go in," she say like she got something up her sleeve. Only she don't lead the way. So me and Sugar turn the corner to where the entrance is, but when we get there I kinda hang back. Not that I'm scared, what's there to be afraid of, just a toy store. But I feel funny, shame. But what I got to be shamed about? Got as much right to go in as anybody. But somehow I can't seem to get hold of the door, so I step away for Sugar to lead. But she hangs back too. And I look at her and she looks at me and this is ridiculous. I mean, damn, I have never ever been shy about doing nothing or going nowhere. But then Mercedes steps up and then Rosie Giraffe and Big Butt crowd in behind and shove, and next thing we all stuffed into the doorway with only Mercedes squeezing past us, smoothing out her jumper and walking right down the aisle. Then the rest of us tumble in like a glued-together jigsaw done all wrong. And people lookin at us. And it's like the time me and Sugar crashed into the Catholic church on a dare. But once we got in there and everything so hushed and holy and the candles and the bowin and the handkerchiefs on all the drooping heads, I just couldn't go through with the plan. Which was for me to run up to the altar and do a tap dance while Sugar played the nose flute and messed around in the holy water. And Sugar kept givin me the elbow. Then later teased me so bad I tied her up in the shower and turned it on and locked her in. And she'd be there till this day if Aunt Gretchen hadn't finally figured I was lyin about the boarder takin a shower.

Same thing in the store. We all walkin on tiptoe and hardly touchin the games and puzzles and things. And I watched Miss Moore who is steady watchin us like she waitin for a sign. Like Mama Drewery watches the sky and sniffs the air and takes note of just how much slant is in the bird formation. Then me and Sugar bump smack into each other, so busy gazing at the toys, 'specially the sailboat. But we don't laugh and go into our fat-lady bump-stomach routine. We just stare at that price tag. Then Sugar run a finger over the whole boat. And I'm jealous and want to hit her. Maybe not her, but I sure want to punch somebody in the mouth.

"Watcha bring us here for, Miss Moore?"

"You sound angry, Sylvia. Are you mad about something?" Givin me one of them grins like she tellin a grown-up joke that never turns out to be funny. And she's lookin very closely at me like maybe she plannin to do my portrait from memory. I'm mad, but I won't give her that satisfaction. So I slouch around the store bein very bored and say, "Let's go."

Me and Sugar at the back of the train watchin the tracks whizzin by large then small then gettin gobbled up in the dark. I'm thinkin about this tricky toy I saw in the store. A clown that somersaults on a bar then does chin-ups just cause you yank lightly at his leg. Cost $35. I could see me askin my mother for a $35 birthday clown. "You wanna who that costs what?" she'd say, cocking her head to the side to get a better view of the hole in my head. Thirty-five dollars could buy new bunk beds for Junior and Gretchen's boy. Thirty-five dollars and the whole household could go visit Granddaddy Nelson in the country. Thirty-five dollars would pay for the rent and the piano bill too. Who are these people that spend that much for performing clowns and $1000 for toy sailboats? What kinda work they do and how they live and how come we ain't in on it? Where we are is who we are, Miss Moore always pointin out. But it don't necessarily have to be that way, she always adds then waits for somebody to say that poor people have to wake up and demand their share of the pie and don't none of us know what kind of pie she talkin about in the first damn place. But she ain't so smart cause I still got her four dollars from the taxi and she sure ain't gettin it. Messin up my day with this shit. Sugar nudges me in my pocket and winks.

Miss Moore lines us up in front of the mailbox where we started from, seem like years ago, and I got a headache for thinkin so hard. And we lean all over each other so we can hold up under the draggy-ass lecture she always finishes us off with at the end before we thank her for borin us to tears. But she just looks at us like she readin tea leaves. Finally she say, "Well, what did you think of F. A. O. Schwarz?"

Rosie Giraffe mumbles, "White folks crazy."

"I'd like to go there again when I get my birthday money," says Mercedes, and we shove her out the pack so she has to lean on the mailbox by herself.

"I'd like a shower. Tiring day," say Flyboy.

Then Sugar surprises me by sayin, "You know, Miss Moore, I don't think all of us here put together eat in a year what that sailboat costs." And Miss Moore lights up like somebody goosed her. "And?" she say, urging Sugar on. Only I'm standin on her foot so she don't continue.

"Imagine for a minute what kind of society it is in which some people can spend on a toy what it would cost to feed a family of six or seven. What do you think?"

"I think," say Sugar pushing me off her feet like she never done before, cause I whip her ass in a minute, "that this is not much of a democracy if you ask me. Equal chance to pursue happiness means an equal crack at the dough, don't it?" Miss Moore is besides herself and I am disgusted with Sugar's treachery. So I stand on her foot one more time to see if she'll shove me. She shuts up, and Miss Moore looks at me, sorrowfully I'm thinkin. And somethin weird is goin on, I can feel it in my chest.

"Anybody else learn anything today?" lookin dead at me. I walk away and Sugar has to run to catch up and don't even seem to notice when I shrug her arm off my shoulder.

"Well, we got four dollars anyway," she says.

"Uh hunh."

"We could go to Hascombs and get half a chocolate layer and then go to the Sunset and still have plenty money for potato chips and ice cream sodas."

"Uh hunh."

"Race you to Hascombs," she say.

We start down the block and she gets ahead which is O.K. by me cause I'm going to the West End and then over to the Drive to think this day through. She can run if she want to and even run faster. But ain't nobody gonna beat me at nuthin.

Alice Walker (b. 1944)

Everyday Use

For your grandmama

I will wait for her in the yard that Maggie and I made so clean and wavy yesterday afternoon. A yard like this is more comfortable than most people know. It is not just a yard. It is like an extended living room. When the hard clay is swept clean as a floor and the fine sand around the edges lined with tiny, irregular grooves anyone can come and sit and look up into the elm tree and wait for the breezes that never come inside the house.

Maggie will be nervous until after her sister goes: she will stand hopelessly in corners homely and ashamed of the burn scars down her arms and legs, eyeing her sister with a mixture of envy and awe. She thinks her sister has held life always in the palm of one hand, that "no" is a word the world never learned to say to her.

You've no doubt seen those TV shows where the child who has "made it" is confronted, as a surprise, by her own mother and father, tottering in weakly from backstage. (A pleasant surprise, of course: What would they do if parent and child came on the show only to curse out and insult each other?) On TV mother and child embrace and smile into each other's faces. Sometimes the mother and father weep, the child wraps them in her arms and leans across the table to tell how she would not have made it without their help. I have seen these programs.

Sometimes I dream a dream in which Dee and I are suddenly brought together on a TV program of this sort. Out of a dark and soft-seated limousine I am ushered into a bright room filled with many people. There I meet a smiling, gray, sporty man like Johnny Carson who shakes my hand and tells me what a fine girl I have. Then we are on the stage and Dee is embracing me with tears in her eyes. She pins on my dress a large orchid, even though she has told me once that she thinks orchids are tacky flowers.

In real life I am a large, big-boned woman with rough, man-working hands. In the winter I wear flannel nightgowns to bed and overalls during the day. I can kill and clean a hog as mercilessly as a man. My fat keeps me hot in zero weather. I can work outside all day, breaking ice to get water for washing. I can eat pork liver cooked over the open fire minutes after it comes steaming from the hog. One winter I knocked a bull calf straight in the brain between the eyes with a sledge hammer and had the meat hung up to chill before nightfall. But of course all this does not show on television. I am the way my daughter would want me to be: a hundred pounds lighter, my skin like an uncooked barley pancake. My hair glistens in the hot bright lights. Johnny Carson has much to do to keep up with my quick and witty tongue.

But that is a mistake. I know even before I wake up. Who ever knew a Johnson with a quick tongue? Who can even imagine me looking a strange white man in the eye? It seems to me I have talked to them always with one foot raised in flight, with my head turned in whichever way is farthest from them. Dee, though. She would always look anyone in the eye. Hesitation was no part of her nature.

"How do I look, Mama?" Maggie says, showing just enough of her thin body enveloped in pink skirt and red blouse for me to know she's there, almost hidden by the door.

"Come out into the yard," I say.

Have you ever seen a lame animal, perhaps a dog run over by some careless person rich enough to own a car, sidle up to someone who is ignorant enough to be kind to him? That is the way my Maggie walks. She has been like this, chin on chest, eyes on ground, feet in shuffle, ever since the fire that burned the other house to the ground.

Dee is lighter than Maggie, with nicer hair and a fuller figure. She's a woman now, though sometimes I forget. How long ago was it that the other house burned? Ten, twelve years? Sometimes I can still hear the flames and feel Maggie's arms sticking to me, her hair smoking and her dress falling off her in little black papery flakes. Her eyes seemed stretched open, blazed open by the flames reflected in them. And Dee. I see her standing off under the sweet gum tree she used to dig gum out of; a look of concentration on her face as she watched the last dingy gray board of the house fall in toward the red-hot brick chimney. Why don't you do a dance around the ashes? I'd wanted to ask her. She had hated the house that much.

I used to think she hated Maggie, too. But that was before we raised the money, the church and me, to send her to Augusta to school. She used to read to us without pity; forcing words, lies, other folks' habits, whole lives upon us two, sitting trapped and ignorant underneath her voice. She washed us in a river of make-believe, burned us with a lot of knowledge we didn't necessarily need to know. Pressed us to her with the serious way she read, to shove us away at just the moment, like dimwits, we seemed about to understand.

Dee wanted nice things. A yellow organdy dress to wear to her graduation from high school; black pumps to match a green suit she'd made from an old suit somebody gave me. She was determined to stare down any disaster in her efforts. Her eyelids would not flicker for minutes at a time. Often I fought off the temptation to shake her. At sixteen she had a style of her own: and knew what style was.

I never had an education myself. After second grade the school was closed down. Don't ask me why: in 1927 colored asked fewer questions than they do now. Sometimes Maggie reads to me. She stumbles along good-naturedly but can't see well. She knows she is not bright. Like good looks and money, quickness passed her by. She will marry John Thomas (who has mossy teeth in an earnest face) and then I'll be free to sit here and I guess just sing church songs to myself. Although I never was a good singer. Never could carry a tune. I was always better at a man's job. I used to love to milk till I was hoofed in the side in '49. Cows are soothing and slow and don't bother you, unless you try to milk them the wrong way.

I have deliberately turned my back on the house. It is three rooms, just like the one that burned, except the roof is tin; they don't make shingle roofs any more. There are no real windows, just some holes cut in the sides, like the portholes in a ship, but not round and not square, with rawhide holding the shutters up on the outside. This house is in a pasture, too, like the other one. No doubt when Dee sees it she will want to tear it down. She wrote me once that no matter where we "choose" to live, she will manage to come see us. But she will never bring her friends. Maggie and I thought about this and Maggie asked me, "Mama, when did Dee ever *have* any friends?"

She had a few. Furtive boys in pink shirts hanging about on washday after school. Nervous girls who never laughed. Impressed with her they worshiped the well-turned phrase, the cute shape, the scalding humor that erupted like bubbles in lye. She read to them.

When she was courting Jimmy T she didn't have much time to pay to us, but turned all her faultfinding power on him. He *flew* to marry a cheap gal from a family of ignorant flashy people. She hardly had time to recompose herself.

When she comes I will meet — but there they are!

Maggie attempts to make a dash for the house, in her shuffling way, but I stay her with my hand. "Come back here," I say. And she stops and tries to dig a well in the sand with her toe.

It is hard to see them clearly through the strong sun. But even the first glimpse of leg out of the car tells me it is Dee. Her feet were always neat-looking, as if God himself had shaped them with a certain style. From the other side of the car comes a short, stocky man. Hair is all over his head a foot long and hanging from his chin like a kinky mule tail. I hear Maggie suck in her breath. "Uhnnnh," is what it sounds like. Like when you see the wriggling end of a snake just in front of your foot on the road. "Uhnnnh."

Dee next. A dress down to the ground, in this hot weather. A dress so loud it hurts my eyes. There are yellows and oranges enough to throw back the light of the sun. I feel my whole face warming from the heat waves it throws out. Earrings, too, gold and hanging down to her shoulders. Bracelets dangling and making noises when she moves her arm up to shake the folds of the dress out of her armpits. The dress is loose and flows, and as she walks closer, I like it. I hear Maggie go "Uhnnnh" again. It is her sister's hair. It stands straight up like the wool on a sheep. It is black as night and around the edges are two long pigtails that rope about like small lizards disappearing behind her ears.

"Wa-su-zo-Tean-o!" she says, coming on in that gliding way the dress makes her move. The short stocky fellow with the hair to his navel is all grinning and he follows up with "Asalamalakim, my mother and sister!" He moves to hug Maggie but she falls back, right up against the back of my chair. I feel her trembling there and when I look up I see the perspiration falling off her chin.

"Don't get up," says Dee. Since I am stout it takes something of a push. You can see me trying to move a second or two before I make it. She turns, showing white heels through her sandals, and goes back to the car. Out she peeks next with a Polaroid. She stoops down quickly and lines up picture after picture of me sitting there in front of the house with Maggie cowering behind me. She never takes a shot without making sure the house is included. When a cow comes nibbling around the edge of the yard she snaps it and me and Maggie *and* the house. Then she puts the Polaroid in the back seat of the car, and comes up and kisses me on the forehead.

Meanwhile Asalamalakim is going through the motions with Maggie's hand. Maggie's hand is as limp as a fish, and probably as cold, despite the sweat, and she keeps trying to pull it back. It looks like Asalamalakim wants to shake hands but wants to do it fancy. Or maybe he don't know how people shake hands. Anyhow, he soon gives up on Maggie.

"Well," I say. "Dee."

"No, Mama," she says. "Not 'Dee,' Wangero Leewanika Kemanjo!"

"What happened to 'Dee'?" I wanted to know.

"She's dead," Wangero said. "I couldn't bear it any longer being named after the people who oppress me."

"You know as well as me you was named after your aunt Dicie," I said. Dicie is my sister. She named Dee. We called her "Big Dee" after Dee was born.

"But who was *she* named after?" asked Wangero.

"I guess after Grandma Dee," I said.

"And who was she named after?" asked Wangero.

"Her mother," I said, and saw Wangero was getting tired. "That's about as far back as I can trace it," I said. Though, in fact, I probably could have carried it back beyond the Civil War through the branches.

"Well," said Asalamalakim, "there you are."

"Uhnnnh," I heard Maggie say.

"There I was not," I said, "before 'Dicie' cropped up in our family, so why should I try to trace it that far back?"

He just stood there grinning, looking down on me like somebody inspecting a Model A car. Every once in a while he and Wangero sent eye signals over my head.

"How do you pronounce this name?" I asked.

"You don't have to call me by it if you don't want to," said Wangero.

"Why shouldn't I?" I asked. "If that's what you want us to call you, we'll call you."

"I know it might sound awkward at first," said Wangero.

"I'll get used to it," I said. "Ream it out again."

Well, soon we got the name out of the way. Asalamalakim had a name twice as long and three times as hard. After I tripped over it two or three times he told me to just call him Hakim-a-barber. I wanted to ask him was he a barber, but I didn't really think he was, so I didn't ask.

"You must belong to those beef-cattle peoples down the road," I said. They said "Asalamalakim" when they met you, too, but they didn't shake hands. Always too busy: feeding the cattle, fixing the fences, putting up salt-lick shelters, throwing down hay. When the white folks poisoned some of the herd the men stayed up all night with rifles in their hands. I walked a mile and a half just to see the sight.

Hakim-a-barber said, "I accept some of their doctrines, but farming and raising cattle is not my style." (They didn't tell me, and I didn't ask, whether Wangero [Dee] had really gone and married him.)

We sat down to eat and right away he said he didn't eat collards and pork was unclean. Wangero, though, went on through the chitlins and corn bread, the greens and everything else. She talked a blue streak over the sweet potatoes. Everything delighted her. Even the fact that we still used the benches her daddy made for the table when we couldn't afford to buy chairs.

"Oh, Mama!" she cried. Then turned to Hakim-a-barber. "I never knew how lovely these benches are. You can feel the rump prints," she said, running her hands underneath her and along the bench. Then she gave a sigh and her hand closed over

Grandma Dee's butter dish. "That's it!" she said. "I knew there
was something I wanted to ask you if I could have." She jumped
up from the table and went over in the corner where the churn
stood, the milk in it clabber by now. She looked at the churn and
looked at it.

"This churn top is what I need," she said. "Didn't Uncle
Buddy whittle it out of a tree you all used to have?"

"Yes," I said.

"Uh huh," she said happily. "And I want the dasher, too."

"Uncle Buddy whittle that, too?" asked the barber.

Dee (Wangero) looked up at me.

"Aunt Dee's first husband whittled the dash," said Maggie
so low you almost couldn't hear her. "His name was Henry, but
they called him Stash."

"Maggie's brain is like an elephant's," Wangero said, laughing.
"I can use the churn top as a centerpiece for the alcove table,"
she said, sliding a plate over the churn, "and I'll think of something
artistic to do with the dasher."

When she finished wrapping the dasher the handle stuck out.
I took it for a moment in my hands. You didn't even have to
look close to see where hands pushing the dasher up and down
to make butter had left a kind of sink in the wood. In fact, there
were a lot of small sinks; you could see where thumbs and fingers
had sunk into the wood. It was beautiful light yellow wood, from
a tree that grew in the yard where Big Dee and Stash had lived.

After dinner Dee (Wangero) went to the trunk at the foot
of my bed and started rifling through it. Maggie hung back in
the kitchen over the dishpan. Out came Wangero with two quilts.
They had been pieced by Grandma Dee and then Big Dee and
me had hung them on the quilt frames on the front porch and
quilted them. One was in the Lone Star pattern. The other was
Walk Around the Mountain. In both of them were scraps of dresses
Grandma Dee had worn fifty and more years ago. Bits and pieces
of Grandpa Jarrell's paisley shirts. And one teeny faded blue piece,
about the piece of a penny matchbox, that was from Great Grandpa
Ezra's uniform that he wore in the Civil War.

"Mama," Wangero said sweet as a bird. "Can I have these
old quilts?"

I heard something fall in the kitchen, and a minute later the
kitchen door slammed.

"Why don't you take one or two of the others?" I asked.
"These old things was just done by me and Big Dee from some
tops your grandma pieced before she died."

"No," said Wangero. "I don't want those. They are stitched around the borders by machine."

"That's make them last better," I said.

"That's not the point," said Wangero. "These are all pieces of dresses Grandma used to wear. She did all this stitching by hand. Imagine!" She held the quilts securely in her arms, stroking them.

"Some of the pieces, like those lavender ones, come from old clothes her mother handed down to her," I said, moving up to touch the quilts. Dee (Wangero) moved back just enough so that I couldn't reach the quilts. They already belonged to her.

"Imagine!" she breathed again, clutching them closely to her bosom.

"The truth is," I said, "I promised to give them quilts to Maggie, for when she marries John Thomas."

She gasped like a bee had stung her.

"Maggie can't appreciate these quilts!" she said. "She'd probably be backward enough to put them to everyday use."

"I reckon she would," I said. "God knows I been saving 'em for long enough with nobody using 'em. I hope she will!" I didn't want to bring up how I had offered Dee (Wangero) a quilt when she went away to college. Then she had told me they were old-fashioned, out of style.

"But they're *priceless!*" she was saying now, furiously; for she has a temper. "Maggie would put them on the bed and in five years they'd be in rags. Less than that!"

"She can always make some more," I said. "Maggie knows how to quilt."

Dee (Wangero) looked at me with hatred. "You just will not understand. The point is these quilts, *these* quilts!"

"Well," I said, stumped. "What would *you* do with them?"

"Hang them," she said. As if that was the only thing you *could* do with quilts.

Maggie by now was standing in the door. I could almost hear the sound her feet made as they scraped over each other.

"She can have them, Mama," she said, like somebody used to never winning anything, or having anything reserved for her. "I can 'member Grandma Dee without the quilts."

I looked at her hard. She had filled her bottom lip with checkerberry snuff and it gave her face a kind of dopey, hangdog look. It was Grandma Dee and Big Dee who taught her how to quilt herself. She stood there with her scarred hands hidden in the folds of her skirt. She looked at her sister with something like fear but she wasn't mad at her. This was Maggie's portion. This was the way she knew God to work.

When I looked at her like that something hit me in the top of my head and ran down to the soles of my feet. Just like when I'm in church and the spirit of God touches me and I get happy and shout. I did something I never had done before: hugged Maggie to me, then dragged her on into the room, snatched the quilts out of Miss Wangero's hands and dumped them into Maggie's lap. Maggie just sat there on my bed with her mouth open.

"Take one or two of the others," I said to Dee.

But she turned without a word and went out to Hakim-a-barber.

"You just don't understand," she said, as Maggie and I came out to the car.

"What don't I understand?" I wanted to know.

"Your heritage," she said. And then she turned to Maggie, kissed her, and said, "You ought to try to make something of yourself, too, Maggie. It's really a new day for us. But from the way you and Mama still live you'd never know it."

She put on some sunglasses that hid everything above the tip of her nose and her chin.

Maggie smiled; maybe at the sunglasses. But a real smile, not scared. After we watched the car dust settle I asked Maggie to bring me a dip of snuff. And then the two of us sat there just enjoying, until it was time to go in the house and go to bed.

7

Observations on the Novel

Most of what has been said about short stories (on probability, narrative point of view, style) is relevant to the novel. And just as the short story of the last hundred years or so is rather different from earlier short fiction (see page 81), the novel — though here we must say of the last few hundred years — is different from earlier long fiction.

The ancient epic is at best a distant cousin to the novel, for though a narrative, the epic is in verse, and deals with godlike men and even with gods themselves. One has only to think of the *Odyssey* or the *Iliad* or the *Aeneid* or *Beowulf* or *Paradise Lost* to recall that the epic does not deal with the sort of people one meets in *Tom Jones, David Copperfield, Crime and Punishment, The Return of the Native, The Portrait of a Lady, The Sun Also Rises,* or *The Catcher in the Rye.*

The romance is perhaps a closer relative to the novel. Ancient romances were even in prose. But the hallmark of the romance, whether the romance is by a Greek sophist (Longus's *Daphnis and Chloe*) or by a medieval English poet (Chaucer's "The Knight's Tale") or by an American (Hawthorne's *The House of the Seven Gables*), is a presentation of the remote or the marvelous, rather than the local and the ordinary. The distinction is the same as that between the tale and the short story. "Tale" has the suggestion of a yarn, of unreality or of wondrous reality. (A case can be made for excluding Hawthorne's "Young Goodman Brown" from a collection of short stories on the ground that its remoteness and its allegorical implications mark it as a tale rather than a short story. This is not to say that it is inferior to a story, but only different.) In his preface to *The House of the Seven Gables* Hawthorne himself distinguishes between the romance and the novel:

> The latter form of composition is presumed to aim at a very minute fidelity, not merely to the possible, but to the probable and ordinary course of man's experience. The former—while, as a work of art, it must rigidly subject itself to laws, and while it sins unpardonably so far as it may swerve aside from the truth of the human heart — has fairly a right to present that truth under circumstances, to a great extent, of the writer's own choosing or creation.

In his preface to *The Marble Faun* Hawthorne explains that he chose "Italy as the site of his Romance" because it afforded him "a sort of poetic or fairy precinct, where actualities would not be so terribly insisted upon as they are . . . in America."

"Actualities . . . insisted upon." That, in addition to prose and length, is the hallmark of the novel. The novel is a sort of long newspaper story; the very word "novel" comes from an Italian word meaning a little new thing, and is related to the French word that gives us "news." (It is noteworthy that the French cognate of Hawthorne's "actualities," *actualités,* means "news" or "current events.") It is no accident that many novelists have been newspapermen: Defoe, Dickens, Crane, Dreiser, Joyce, Hemingway, Camus. And this connection with reportage perhaps helps to account for the relatively low esteem in which the novel is occasionally held: to some college students, a course in the novel does not seem quite up to a course in poetry, and people who read novels but not poetry are not likely to claim an interest in "literature."

Though Defoe's *Robinson Crusoe* is set in a far-off place, and thus might easily have been a romance, in Defoe's day it was close to current events, for it is a fictionalized version of events that had recently made news — Alexander Selkirk's life on the island of Juan Fernandez. And the story is not about marvelous happenings, but about a man's struggle for survival in dismal surroundings. Crusoe is not armed with Arthur's Excalibur or with Gawain's supposedly magic girdle, nor does he struggle as does Arthur with a Demon Cat and with a giant of St. Michael's Mount or as does Gawain with a Green Knight who survives decapitation; he has a carpenter's chest of tools and he struggles against commonplace nature. This chest was "much more valuable than a shiploading of gold would have been at that time." The world of romance contains splendid castles and enchanted forests, but Crusoe's world contains not much more than a plot of ground, some animals and vegetables, and Friday. "I fancied I could make all but the wheel [of a wheelbarrow Crusoe needed], but that I had no notion of, neither did I know how to go about it; besides, I had no possible way to make the iron gudgeons for the spindle or axis of the wheel to run in, so I gave it over." The book, in short, emphasizes not the strange, but (given the initial situation) the usual, the commonsensical, the probable. The world of *Robinson Crusoe* is hardly different from the world we meet in the beginning of almost any novel:

> We were in study hall when the headmaster walked in, followed by a new boy not wearing a school uniform, and by a janitor carrying a large desk. Those who were sleeping awoke, and we all stood up as though interrupting our work.
>
> Gustave Flaubert, *Madame Bovary*

> My father's family name being Pirrip, and my Christian name Philip, my infant tongue could make of both names nothing longer or more explicit than Pip. So I called myself Pip, and came to be called Pip.
> I give Pirrip as my father's family name, on the authority of his tombstone and my sister — Mrs. Joe Gargery, who married the blacksmith.
>
> Charles Dickens, *Great Expectations*

> In beginning the life story of my hero, Alexey Fyodorovich Karamazov, I find myself in somewhat of a quandary. Namely, although I call Alexey Fyodorovich my hero, I myself know that he is by no means a great man, and hence I foresee such unavoidable questions as these: "What is so remarkable about your Alexey Fyodorovich, that you have chosen him as your hero? What has he accomplished? What is he known for, and by whom? Why should I, the reader, spend time learning the facts of his life?"
>
> Fyodor Dostoyevsky, *The Brothers Karamazov*

> If you really want to hear about it, the first thing you'll probably want to know is where I was born, and what my lousy childhood was like, and how my parents were occupied and all before they had me, and all that David Copperfield kind of crap, but I don't feel like going into it, if you want to know the truth.
>
> J. D. Salinger, *The Catcher in the Rye*

> It was June, 1933, one week after Commencement, when Kay Leiland Strong, Vassar '33, the first of her class to run around the table at the Class Day dinner, was married to Harald Petersen, Reed '27, in the chapel of St. George's Church, P.E., Karl F. Reiland, Rector. Outside, on Stuyvesant Square, the trees were in full leaf, and the wedding guests arriving by twos and threes in taxis heard the voices of children playing round the statue of Peter Stuyvesant in the park.
>
> Mary McCarthy, *The Group*

Sleepy boys in a school room; the brother of the wife of a blacksmith named Joe Gargery; a hero who "is by no means a great man"; a boy who in boy's language seems reluctant to talk of his "lousy childhood"; a young woman who ran around the table at the Class Day dinner. In all of these passages, and in the openings of most other novels, we are confronted with current biography, and, indeed, a fair number of important novels — for example, D. H. Lawrence's *Sons and Lovers,* James Joyce's *A Portrait of the Artist as a Young Man,* Jack Kerouac's *On the Road* — are highly autobiographical.* In contrast to these beginnings, look at the beginning of one of Chaucer's great romances:

Whilom,° as olde stories tellen us,	*once*
There was a duc that highte° Theseus;	*was named*
Of Atthenes he was lord and governour,	
And in his tyme swich° a conquerour,	*such*
That gretter was ther noon under the sonne.	

"Whilom." "Olde stories." "Gretter was ther noon under the sonne." We are in a timeless past, in which unusual people dwell. But the novel is almost always set in the present or very recent past, and it deals with ordinary people. It so often deals with ordinary people, and presents them, apparently, in so ordinary a fashion that we sometimes wonder what is the point of it. Although the romance is often "escape" literature, it usually is didactic, holding up to us images of noble and ignoble behavior, revealing the rewards of courage and the power of love. In the preface to *The Marble Faun,* for instance, Hawthorne says he "proposed to himself to merely write a fanciful story, evolving a thoughtful moral, and did not propose attempting a portraiture of Italian manners and character." But portraiture is what the novelist gives us. Intent on revealing the world of real men and women going about their daily work and play, he does not simplify his characters into representatives of vices and virtues as does the romancer who

---

* Recently even the veil of fiction has been removed, and a new form, the "nonfiction novel" has developed. The term apparently was coined by Truman Capote to describe *In Cold Blood*, his account of a multiple murder committed in Kansas in 1959. The details are all true, but the book is written with a novelist's sense of irony and of symbolic details; in short, it is history written by a novelist — but this form is not to be confused with the "historical novel," which by its usual emphasis on plot and on the exotic is a kind of romance. Other examples of the nonfiction novel: Norman Mailer's *The Armies of the Night*, describing the anti-Vietnam war march of 1967 and subsequent related events, in which Mailer writes of himself in the third person; and *The Executioner's Song*, which Mailer calls his "true life novel" about Gary Gilmore, the convicted murderer who refused an appeal and insisted on having his death penalty carried out by a firing squad.

wishes to evolve a thoughtful moral, but gives abundant detail — some of it apparently irrelevant. The innumerable details add up to a long book, although there need not be many physical happenings. The novel tells a story, of course, but the story is not only about what people overtly do but also about what they think (i.e., their mental doings) and about the society in which they are immersed and by which they are in part shaped. In the much-quoted preface to *Pierre and Jean,* Maupassant says:

> The skill of the novelist's plan will not reside in emotional effects, in attractive writing, in a striking beginning or a moving dénouement, but in the artful building up of solid details from which the essential meaning of the work will emerge.

As we read a novel we feel we are seeing not the "higher reality" or the "inner reality" so often mentioned by students of the arts, but the real reality.*

The short story, too, is detailed, but commonly it reveals only a single character at a moment of crisis, whereas the novel commonly traces the development of an individual, a group of people, a world. The novelist, of course, has an attitude toward his world; he is not compiling an almanac but telling an invented story, making a work of art, offering not merely a representation of reality but a response to it, and he therefore selects and shapes his material. One way of selecting and shaping the material is through the chosen point of view: we do not get everything in nineteenth-century England, but only everything that Pip remembers or chooses to set down about his experiences, and what he sets down is colored by his personality. "I remember Mr. Hubble as a tough high-shouldered stooping old man, of a saw-dusty fragrance, with his legs extraordinarily wide apart: so that in my short days I always saw some miles of open country between them when I met him coming up the lane." In any case, the coherence in a novel seems inclusive rather than exclusive. The novelist usually

---

* It should be mentioned that in the 1950s the *nouveau roman* or "new novel" developed, in reaction to the novels of the sort we have been talking about. Writers of the new novel (such as Alain Robbe-Grillet, Nathalie Sarraute, and Claude Simon) argue that the traditional novel is utterly false, for it presents characters (whereas people are not psychologically consistent creatures, but a complex series of appearances), plots (wheras plots do not exist in nature), cause and effect (a naive assumption), and it assumes that there is a connection between people and the objects of the world they move in (another naive assumption). The new novel, instead of presenting a story of coherent characters acting in a context, offers a sort of dreamlike series of perceptions; the identities of the perceivers and the chronology are usually unclear, and, of course, the story has no conclusion.

conveys the sense that he, as distinct from his characters, is — in the words of Christopher Isherwood's *The Berlin Stories* — "a camera with its shutter open, quite passive, recording not thinking. Recording the man shaving at the windows opposite and the woman in the kimono washing her hair. Some day, all of this will have to be developed, carefully fixed, printed."

It is not merely that the novel gives us details. *Gulliver's Travels* has plenty of details about people six inches tall and people sixty feet tall, and about a flying island and rational horses. But these things are recognized as fanciful inventions, though they do turn our mind toward the real world. *Gulliver* is a satire that holds up to us a picture of a fantastic world by which, paradoxically, we come to see the real world a little more clearly. The diminutive stature of the Lilliputians is an amusing and potent metaphor for the littleness of man, the flying island for abstract thinkers who have lost touch with reality, and so on. But the novelist who wants to show us the littleness of man invents not Lilliputians but a world of normal-sized people who do little things and have little thoughts.

Having spent so much time saying that the novel is not the epic or romance or fable, we must mention that a work may hover on the borderlines of these forms. Insofar as *Moby Dick* narrates with abundant realistic detail the experiences of a whaler ("This book," Dorothy Parker has said, "taught me more about whales than I ever wanted to know"), it is a novel; but in its evocation of mystery — Queequeg, the prophecies, Ishmael's miraculous rescue from the sea filled with sharks who "glided by as if with padlocks on their mouths" — it is a romance with strong symbolic implications.

The point is that although a reader of a long piece of prose fiction can complain that he did not get what he paid for, he should find out what he did get, rather than damn it for not being what it isn't. Bishop Butler's famous remark is relevant to literary criticism: "Everything is what it is and not another thing."

Poetry

8
Narrative Poetry

European literature begins with Homer's *Iliad* and *Odyssey,* which means that it begins with stories in verse. We are accustomed to thinking of a story as prose in a book, but until a few hundred years ago stories were commonly poetry that was sung or recited. In nonliterate societies people got their stories from storytellers who relied on memory rather than on the written word; the memorized stories were often poems, partly because (in Sir Philip Sidney's words) "verse far exceedeth prose in the knitting up of the memory." Even in literate societies, few people could read or write until the invention of the printing press in the middle of the fifteenth century. Although the printing press did not immediately destroy oral verse narratives, as the centuries passed, an increasingly large reading public developed which preferred prose narratives.

Among the great verse narratives are the English and Scottish **popular ballads,** some of the best of which are attributed to the fifteenth century, though they were not recorded until much later. These anonymous stories in song acquired their distinctive flavor by being passed down orally from generation to generation, each singer consciously or unconsciously modifying his inheritance. It is not known who made up the popular ballads; often they were made up partly out of earlier ballads by singers as bold as Kipling's cockney:

> When 'Omer smote 'is blooming lyre,
> He'd 'eard men sing by land an' sea;
> An' what he thought 'e might require,
> 'E went an' took — the same as me!

Most ballad singers probably were composers only by accident; they intended to transmit what they had heard, but their memories were sometimes faulty and their imaginations active. The modifications effected by oral transmission generally give a ballad three noticeable qualities. First, it is impersonal; even if there is an "I" who sings the tale, he is usually characterless. Second, the ballad — like other oral literature such as the nursery rhyme, the counting-out rhyme ("one potato, two potato") — is filled with repetition, sometimes of lines, sometimes of words. Consider, for example, "Go saddle me the black, the black,/ Go saddle me the brown," or "O wha is this has done this deid, / This ill deid don to me?" Sometimes, in fact, the story is told by repeating lines with only a few significant variations. This **incremental repetition** (repetition with slight variations advancing the narrative) is the heart of "Edward" (page 440). Furthermore, **stock epithets** are repeated from ballad to ballad: "true love," "milk-white steed," "golden hair." Oddly, these clichés do not bore us but by their impersonality often lend a simplicity that effectively contrasts with the violence of the tale. Third, because the ballads are transmitted orally, residing in the memory rather than on the printed page, weak stanzas have often been dropped, leaving a series of sharp scenes, frequently with dialogue:

> The king sits in Dumferling toune,
> Drinking the blude-reid wine:
> "O whar will I get guid sailor,
> To sail this schip of mine?"

Because ballads were sung rather than printed, and because singers made alterations, there is no one version of a ballad that is the "correct" one. The versions printed here have become such favorites that they are almost regarded as definitive, but the reader should consult a collection of ballads to get some idea of the wide variety.

Popular ballads have been much imitated by professional poets, especially since the late eighteenth century. Three such **literary ballads** are Keats's "La Belle Dame sans Merci" (page 541), Coleridge's "The Rime of the Ancient Mariner," and X. J. Kennedy's "In a Prominent Bar in Secaucus One Day" (page 447). In a literary ballad (though not in Kennedy's) the story is often infused with multiple meanings, with insistent symbolic implications. Ambiguity is often found in the popular ballad also, but it is of a rather different sort. Whether it is due to the loss of stanzas or to the creator's unconcern with some elements of the narrative, the ambiguity of the popular ballad commonly lies in the narrative itself rather than in the significance of the narrative.

Finally, a word about some of the most popular professional folksingers today. They have aptly been called "folksongers" because unlike illiterate or scarcely literate folksingers — who intend only to sing the traditional songs in the traditional way for themselves or their neighbors — these professionals are vocal artists who make commercial and political use (not bad things in themselves) of traditional folk songs, deliberately adapting old songs and inventing new songs that only loosely resemble the old ones. These contemporary ballads tend to be more personal than traditional ballads and they tend to have a social consciousness that is alien to traditional balladry. Many of the songs of Pete Seeger and Bob Dylan, for instance, are conspicuous examples of art in the service of morality; they call attention to injustice and they seek to move the hearers to action. That traditional ballads have assisted in this task is not the least of their value; the influence of a work of art is never finished, and the old ballads can rightly claim to share in the lives of their modern descendants.

Anonymous

Sir Patrick Spence

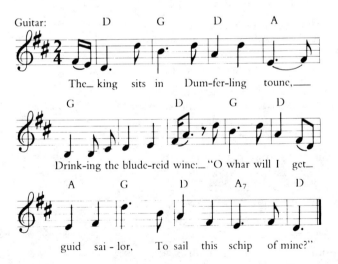

The king sits in Dumferling toune,
     Drinking the blude-reid wine:
"O whar will I get guid sailor,
     To sail this schip of mine?"

Up and spak an eldern knicht,
    Sat at the kings richt kne:
"Sir Patrick Spence is the best sailor,
    That sails upon the se."   8

The king has written a braid° letter,   *broad, open*
    And signed it wi' his hand,
And sent it to Sir Patrick Spence,
    Was walking on the sand.   12

The first line that Sir Patrick red,
    A loud lauch° lauched he;   *laugh*
The next line that Sir Patrick red,
    The teir blinded his ee.   16

"O wha is this has done this deid,
    This ill deid don to me,
To send me out this time o' the yeir,
    To sail upon the se?   20

"Mak hast, mak hast, my mirry men all,
    Our guid schip sails the morne":
"O say na sae, my master deir,
    For I feir a deadlie storme.   24

"Late late yestreen I saw the new moone,
    Wi' the auld moone in hir arme,
And I feir, I feir, my deir master,
    That we will cum to harme."   28

O our Scots nobles wer richt laith°   *loath*
    To weet their cork-heild schoone;°   *cork-heeled shoes*
Bot lang owre° a' the play wer playd,   *ere*
    Thair hats they swam aboone.°   *above* 32

O lang, lang may their ladies sit,
    Wi' thair fans into their hand,
Or eir° they se Sir Patrick Spence   *ere*
    Cum sailing to the land.   36

O lang, lang may the ladies stand,
    Wi' thair gold kems in their hair,
Waiting for their ain deir lords,
    For they'll se thame na mair.   40

Have owre,° have owre to Aberdour,   *half over*
    It's fiftie fadom deip,
And thair lies guid Sir Patrick Spence,
    Wi' the Scots lords at his feit.   44

QUESTIONS

1. The shipwreck occurs between lines 29 and 32, but it is not described. Does the omission stimulate the reader to imagine the details of the wreck? Or does it suggest that the poem is not so much about a shipwreck as about kinds of behavior? Explain.

2. Might lines 17–18 warrant the inference that the "eldern knicht" (line 5) is Sir Patrick's enemy?

3. Explain lines 13–16.

4. In place of lines 37–40, another version of this ballad has the following stanza:

> The ladies crack't their fingers white,
>   The maidens tore their hair,
> A' for the sake o' their true loves,
>   For them they ne'er saw mair.

Why is one more effective than the other?

5. In the other version, the stanza that is here the final one (lines 41–44) precedes the stanzas about the ladies (lines 33–40). Which stanza makes a better conclusion? Why?

Anonymous

The Three Ravens

There were three ravens sat on a tree,   *Downe a downe, hay*

downe, hay downe   There were three ravens sat on a tree,   *With a*

* Alternate guitar chords transposing the tune into a key easier to play on a guitar are given in parentheses.

downe   There were three ravens sat on a tree, They   were as blacke as

they   might be, *With a downe*   der-ie,   der-ie,   der-ie,   downe, downe.

There were three ravens sat on a tree,
 Downe a downe, hay down, hay downe
There were three ravens sat on a tree,
 With a downe
There were three ravens sat on a tree,   5
They were as blacke as they might be,
 With a downe derrie, derrie, derrie, downe, downe.

The one of them said to his mate,
"Where shall we our breakfast take?"

"Down in yonder greene field,   10
There lies a knight slain under his shield.

"His hounds they lie downe at his feete,
So well they can their master keepe.

"His haukes they flie so eagerly,
There's no fowle dare him come nie."   15

Downe there comes a fallow° doe,*   *brown*
As great with yong as she might goe.

She lift up his bloudy hed,
And kist his wounds that were so red.

She got him up upon her backe,   20
And carried him to earthen lake.°   *pit*

---

* The "doe" (line 16), often taken as a suggestive description of the knight's beloved, is probably a vestige of the folk belief that an animal may be an enchanted human being.

She buried him before the prime,°   *about nine* A.M.
She was dead herselfe ere even-song time.

God send every gentleman
Such haukes, such hounds, and such a leman.°   *sweetheart*   **25**

QUESTIONS

1. The hounds and the hawks are loyal followers of the knight, as is the doe. How do the references to the hounds and hawks in some degree prepare us for the doe? Is preparation necessary? Why?
2. Why does the poet include the ravens? Do they confuse a poem on loyalty, or do they provide an effective contrast? Do the ravens help to give a fuller, more realistic picture of life? Explain.
3. Are the final two lines an intrusive comment? Explain.

Anonymous

The Twa Corbies

As I was walking all alane,
I heard twa corbies° making a mane;°   *two ravens; lament*
The tane° unto the t' other say,   *one*
"Where sall we gang° and dine to-day?"   *shall we go*   **4**

"In behint yon auld fail dyke,°   *old turf wall*
I wot° there lies a new-slain knight;   *know*
And naebody kens° that he lies there,   *knows*
But his hawk, his hound, and lady fair.   **8**

"His hound is to the hunting gane,
His hawk, to fetch the wild-fowl hame,
His lady's ta'en another mate,
So we may mak our dinner sweet.   **12**

"Ye'll sit on his white hause-bane,°   *neck bone*
And I'll pike out his bonny blue een.°   *eyes*
Wi' ae° lock o' his gowden° hair   *with one; golden*
We'll theek° our nest when it grows bare.   *thatch*   **16**

"Mony a one for him makes mane,
But nane sall ken whare he is gane;
O'er his white banes, when they are bare,
The wind sall blaw for evermair."   **20**

QUESTIONS

1. The story in this poem is implied (in the second and third
   stanzas) rather than made explicit. What is it? Is it the worse
   for being implicit? Explain.
2. How do lines 9–10 reinforce or parallel the basic story?
3. Hair is usually "gowden" in ballads. What does this conventional detail tell us about the knight's age? Why is his
   age significant?
4. What does the fourth stanza (especially lines 15–16) contribute
   to the poem?
5. Animals can't speak; is the poem therefore an absurdity?
   Explain.

Anonymous

Edward

"Why dois your brand° sae° drap wi' bluid,   *sword; so*
      Edward, Edward?
Why dois your brand sae drap wi' bluid?
      And why sae sad gang° yee, O?"   *go*   **4**
"O, I hae killed my hauke sae guid,
      Mither, mither,
O, I hae killed my hauke sae guid,
      And I had nae mair bot hee, O."   **8**

"Your haukis bluid was nevir sae reid,
      Edward, Edward,
Your haukis bluid was nevir sae reid,
      My deir son I tell thee, O."   **12**
"O, I hae killed my reid-roan steid,
      Mither, mither,
O, I hae killed my reid-roan steid,
      That erst° was sae fair and frie,° O."   *once; spirited* **16**

"Your steid was auld, and ye hae gat mair,
      Edward, Edward,
Your steid was auld, and ye hae gat mair,
      Sum other dule° ye drie,° O."   *grief; suffer* **20**
"O, I hae killed my fadir deir,
      Mither, mither,
O, I hae killed my fadir, deir,
      Alas, and wae is mee, O!"   **24**

"And whatten penance wul ye drie for that,
      Edward, Edward?
And whatten penance wul ye drie for that?
      My deir son, now tell me, O."   **28**
"Ile set my feit in yonder boat,
      Mither, mither,
Ile set my feit in yonder boat,
      And Ile fare ovir the sea, O."   **32**

"And what wul ye doe wi' your towirs and your ha',°   *hall*
      Edward, Edward,
And what wul ye doe wi' your towirs and your ha',
      That were sae fair to see, O?"   **36**
"Ile let thame stand tul they doun fa',°   *fall*
      Mither, mither,
Ile let thame stand tul they doun fa',
      For here nevir mair maun° I bee, O."   *must* **40**

"And what wul ye leive to your bairns° and your wife,   *children*
      Edward, Edward?
And what wul ye leive to your bairns and your wife,
      When ye gang ovir the sea, O?"   **44**
"The warldis° room, late° them beg thrae° life, *world's; let; through*
      Mither, mither,
The warldis room, late them beg thrae life,
      For thame nevir mair wul I see, O."   **48**

"And what wul ye leive to your ain mither deir,
      Edward, Edward?
And what wul ye leive to your ain mither deir?
      My deir son, now tell me, O."   **52**
"The curse of hell frae me sall ye beir,
      Mither, mither,
The curse of hell frae me sall ye beir,
      Sic° counseils ye gave to me, O."   *such* **56**

QUESTIONS

1. The poem consists of two parts. How does the structure of the first part parallel that of the second?
2. What might have been the mother's motives? Would the story be improved if we knew the motives behind her "counseils"? Explain.
3. Can Edward's statements about his wife and children be explained?
4. Line 21 offers a surprise, but it is topped by the surprise in the final four lines. Can the poem be reread with pleasure once the surprises are known? Explain.

Many ballads, such as the next one, deal with supernatural happenings. "The Demon Lover" exists in many versions, and is often titled "The House Carpenter" or "James Harris," though in the eighteenth-century version printed here the man is unnamed. The gist of the various versions is along these lines: James Harris and Jane Reynolds had exchanged vows of marriage. He was impressed as a sailor, and when three years later he was reported dead, the girl married a carpenter. Four years after the marriage James's spirit visited Jane, assured her he was a shipowner, and enticed her to leave her family. Destruction followed.

Anonymous

The Demon Lover

for - mer vows ye___ gran-ted___ me___ be - fore."

"O where have you been, my long, long love,
 This long seven years and mair?"
"O I'm come to seek my former vows
 Ye granted me before." *4*

"O hold your tongue of your former vows,
 For they will breed sad strife;
O hold your tongue of your former vows,
 For I am become a wife." *8*

He turned him right and round about,
 And the tear blinded his ee:
"I wad never hae trodden on Irish ground,
 If it had not been for thee. *12*

"I might hae had a king's daughter,
 Far, far beyond the sea;
I might have had a king's daughter,
 Had it not been for love o thee." *16*

"If ye might have had a king's daughter,
 Yer sel ye had to blame;
Ye might have taken the king's daughter,
 For ye kend° that I was nane. *knew* *20*

"If I was to leave my husband dear,
 And my two babes also,
O what have you to take me to,
 If with you I should go?" *24*

"I hae seven ships upon the sea —
 The eighth brought me to land —
With four-and-twenty bold mariners,
 And music on every hand." *28*

She has taken up her two little babes,
 Kissed them baith cheek and chin:
"O fair ye weel, my ain two babes,
 For I'll never see you again." *32*

She set her foot upon the ship,
 No mariners could she behold;
But the sails were o the taffetie,
 And the masts o the beaten gold. *36*

They had not sailed a league, a league,
　　A league but barely three,
When dismal grew his countenance,
　　And drumlie° grew his ee.　　　　　　　　　　　　　*gloomy*　**40**

They had not sailed a league, a league,
　　A league but barely three,
Until she espied his cloven foot,
　　And she wept right bitterlie.　　　　　　　　　　　　　　　　**44**

"O hold your tongue of your weeping," says he,
　　"Of your weeping now let me be;
I will show you how the lilies grow
　　On the banks of Italy."　　　　　　　　　　　　　　　　　　**48**

"O what hills are yon, yon pleasant hills,
　　That the sun shines sweetly on?"
"O yon are the hills of heaven," he said,
　　Where you will never win."°　　　　　　　　　*gain, get to*　**52**

"O whaten mountain is yon," she said,
　　"All so dreary wi frost and snow?"
"O yon is the mountain of hell," he cried,
　　"Where you and I will go."　　　　　　　　　　　　　　　　**56**

He strack the tap-mast wi his hand,
　　The fore-mast wi his knee,
And he brake that gallant ship in twain,
　　And sank her in the sea.　　　　　　　　　　　　　　　　　**60**

QUESTIONS

1. What takes place between lines 28 and 29? Between 48 and 49?
2. What is the first hint that supernatural forces are at work?
3. What does the "cloven foot" (line 43) signify? Is the spirit motivated by malice? By love? By both?

John Henry, a black steel driver from West Virginia, worked on the Chesapeake and Ohio's Big Bend Tunnel around 1870. The steel driver hammered a drill (held by his assistant, the "shaker") into rocks, so that explosives could then be poured in. In the 1870s mechanical steel drills were introduced, displacing the steel driver.

Anonymous

John Henry

John Henry was a very small boy,
Sitting on his mammy's knee;
He picked up a hammer and a little piece of steel,
Saying, "A hammer'll be the death of me, O Lord,
A hammer'll be the death of me."   5

John Henry went up on the mountain
And he came down on the side.
The mountain was so tall and John Henry was so small
That he laid down his hammer and he cried, "O Lord,"
He laid down his hammer and he cried.   10

John Henry was a man just six feet in height,
Nearly two feet and a half across the breast.
He'd take a nine-pound hammer and hammer all day long
And never get tired and want to rest, O Lord,
And never get tired and want to rest.   15

John Henry was a steel-driving man, O Lord,
He drove all over the world.
He come to Big Bend Tunnel on the C. & O. Road
Where he beat the steam drill down, O Lord,
Where he beat the steam drill down.   20

John Henry said to the captain,
"Captain, you go to town,
Bring me back a twelve-pound hammer
And I'll beat that steam drill down, O Lord,
And I'll beat that steam drill down."   25

They placed John Henry on the right-hand side,
The steam drill on the left;
He said, "Before I let that steam drill beat me down
I'll die with my hammer in my hand, O Lord,
And send my soul to rest."   30

The white folks all got scared,
Thought Big Bend was a-fallin' in;
John Henry hollered out with a very loud shout,
"It's my hammer a-fallin' in the wind, O Lord,
It's my hammer a-fallin' in the wind."   35

John Henry said to his shaker,
"Shaker, you better pray,
For if I miss that little piece of steel
Tomorrow'll be your buryin' day, O Lord,
Tomorrow'll be your buryin' day."   *40*

The man that invented that steam drill
He thought he was mighty fine.
John Henry sunk the steel fourteen feet
While the steam drill only made nine, O Lord,
While the steam drill only made nine.   *45*

John Henry said to his loving little wife,
"I'm sick and want to go to bed.
Fix me a place to lay down, Child;
There's a roarin' in my head, O Lord,
There's a roarin' in my head."   *50*

QUESTIONS

1. How does the first stanza contribute to John Henry's grandeur?
2. Some versions contain an additional stanza at the end:

> They took John Henry to the buryin' ground,
> And they buried him in the sand;
> And every locomotive come roarin' round
> Says "There lies a steel-drivin' man,"
> Says "There lies a steel-drivin' man."

Is the ending as given in the present text unsatisfactory? Is there any doubt about John Henry's death?

The next poem, a recent imitation of a ballad, is meant to be sung to the tune of "Sweet Betsy from Pike," a song associated with the Gold Rush.

X. J. Kennedy (*b. 1929*)

In a Prominent Bar in Secaucus One Day

In a prominent bar in Secaucus one day
Rose a lady in skunk with a topheavy sway,
Raised a knobby old finger — all turned from their beer —
While with eyes bright as snowcrust she sang high and clear: 4

---

* Because the music is written in B♭, a difficult key for the folk guitarist, alternate
chords are given in parentheses.

"Now who of you'd think from an eyeload of me
That I once was a lady as proud as could be?
Oh I'd never sit down by a tumbledown drunk
If it wasn't, my dears, for the high cost of junk. 　8

"All the gents used to swear that the white of my calf
Beat the down of the swan by a length and a half.
In the kerchief of linen I caught to my nose
Ah, there never fell snot, but a little gold rose. 　12

"I had seven gold teeth and a toothpick of gold,
My Virginia cheroot was a leaf of it rolled
And I'd light it each time with a thousand in cash —
Why the bums used to fight if I flicked them an ash. 　16

"Once the toast of the Biltmore, the belle of the Taft,
I would drink bottle beer at the Drake, never draft,
And dine at the Astor on Salisbury steak
With a clean tablecloth for each bite I did take. 　20

"In a car like the Roxy I'd roll to the track,
A steel-guitar trio, a bar in the back,
And the wheels made no noise, they turned over so fast,
Still it took you ten minutes to see me go past. 　24

"When the horses bowed down to me that I might choose,
I bet on them all, for I hated to lose.
Now I'm saddled each night for my butter and eggs
And the broken threads race down the backs of my legs. 　28

"Let you hold in mind, girls, that your beauty must pass
Like a lovely white clover that rusts with its grass.
Keep your bottoms off barstools and marry you young
Or be left — an old barrel with many a bung. 　32

"For when time takes you out for a spin in his car
You'll be hard-pressed to stop him from going too far
And be left by the roadside, for all your good deeds,
Two toadstools for tits and a face full of weeds." 　36

All the house raised a cheer, but the man at the bar
Made a phonecall and up pulled a red patrol car
And she blew us a kiss as they copped her away
From that prominent bar in Secaucus, N.J. 　40

John Lennon (1940–1980)
Paul McCartney (b. 1942)

Eleanor Rigby

Ah, look at all the lonely people!
Ah, look at all the lonely people!

Eleanor Rigby
Picks up the rice in the church where a wedding has been,
Lives in a dream.   5
Waits at the window
Wearing the face that she keeps in a jar by the door.
Who is it for?

All the lonely people,
Where do they all come from?   10
All the lonely people,
Where do they all belong?

Father McKenzie,
Writing the words of a sermon that no one will hear,
No one comes near.   15

Look at him working,
Darning his socks in the night when there's nobody there.
What does he care?

All the lonely people,
Where do they all come from?   20
All the lonely people,
Where do they all belong?

Ah, look at all the lonely people!
Ah, look at all the lonely people!

Eleanor Rigby   25
Died in the church and was buried along with her name,
Nobody came.
Father McKenzie,
Wiping the dirt from his hands as he walks from the grave,
No one was saved.   30

All the lonely people,
Where do they all come from?
All the lonely people,
Where do they all belong?

Ah, look at all the lonely people!   *35*
Ah, look at all the lonely people!

QUESTIONS

1. This song, of course, is not a traditional ballad, passed on orally from generation to generation. In what ways does it resemble a traditional ballad? In what ways does it not?
2. Is the poem chiefly about Eleanor Rigby? What is Father McKenzie doing in the poem?
3. What are the implications (line 7) of "wearing the face that she keeps in a jar by the door"? Is the sermon (line 14) only a sermon or are there further implications?

9
Lyric Poetry

The preceding chapter suggested that narrative poetry is far less common than it was before the age of printing. Today when we think of poetry we are less likely to think of the *Aeneid, Paradise Lost,* or the ballads than of lyric poems — pieces that seem to be emotional or reflective soliloquies — such as Wordsworth's "I Wandered Lonely as a Cloud" (page 541).

Wordsworth, it is true, narrates a happening (he wandered and came across some daffodils) and describes a scene (the daffodils were "fluttering and dancing in the breeze"). But the poem is about the speaker's emotional response to the flowers he happened upon: when he recalls them his "heart with pleasure fills/ And dances with the daffodils." The recollection of an emotion, which causes a new emotion, is in fact at the root of Wordsworth's theory of poetry. In his Preface to the second edition (1800) of *Lyrical Ballads* he wrote:

> I have said that poetry is the spontaneous overflow of powerful feelings: it takes its origin from emotion recollected in tranquillity; the emotion is contemplated till, by a species of reaction, the tranquillity gradually disappears, and an emotion, kindred to that which was before the subject of contemplation, is gradually produced, and does itself actually exist in the mind. In this mood successful composition generally begins, and in a mood similar to this it is carried on.

Though Wordsworth wrote some narrative and dramatic poetry, he was most often successful with lyric poetry, and this is probably the sort to which his theory chiefly applies. For the Greeks a **lyric** was a song accompanied by a lyre, but by Wordsworth's time it had its present meaning of a poem that, neither narrative (telling a story) nor strictly dramatic (performed by actors), is an emotional or reflective soliloquy. Still, it is rarely very far from a singing voice. James Joyce saw the lyric as the "verbal vesture of an instant of emotion, a rhythmical cry such as ages ago cheered on the man who pulled at the oar." Such lyrics, too, were sung more recently than "ages ago." Here is a song that American slaves sang when rowing heavy loads.

Anonymous

Michael Row the Boat Ashore

Michael row the boat ashore, Hallelujah!
Michael's boat's a freedom boat, Hallelujah!
Sister, help to trim the sail, Hallelujah!
Jordan stream is wide and deep, Hallelujah!
Freedom stands on the other side, Hallelujah!

We might pause for a moment to comment on why people sing at work. There are at least three reasons: (1) work done rhythmically goes more efficiently; (2) the songs relieve the boredom of the work; (3) the songs — whether narrative or lyrical — provide something of an outlet for the workers' frustrations.

Speaking roughly, we can say that whereas a narrative (whether in prose or poetry) is set in the past, telling what happened, a lyric is set in the present, catching a speaker in a moment of expression. But lyric can, of course, glance backward or forward as in this folk song, usually called "Careless Love."

Anonymous

Careless Love

Love, O love, O careless love,
You see what careless love can do.
When I wore my apron low,
Couldn't keep you from my do,°   *door*
    Fare you well, fare you well.
Now I wear my apron high,
Scarce see you passin' by,
    Fare you well, fare you well.

Notice, too, that a lyric, like a narrative, can have a sort of plot: "Michael" moves toward the idea of freedom, and "Careless Love" implies a story of desertion, but, again, the emphasis is on a present state of mind.

Lyrics are sometimes differentiated among themselves. For example, if a lyric is melancholy or mournfully contemplative, especially if it laments a death, it may be called an **elegy** (though before Gray's famous "Elegy" the word often denoted a personal poem written in pairs of lines, on whatever theme). If a lyric is rather long, elaborate, and on a lofty theme such as immortality or a hero's victory, it may be called an **ode.** Greek odes were choral pieces, more or less hymns of praise in elaborate stanzas, but in Rome, Horace (65–8 B.C.) applied the word to quieter pieces, usually in stanzas of four lines, celebrating love, patriotism, or duty. Distinctions among lyrics are often vague, and one man's ode may be another man's elegy. Still, when writers use one of these words in their titles, they are inviting the reader to recall the tradition in which they are working. Of the poet's link to tradition T. S. Eliot said:

> No poet, no artist of any art, has his complete meaning alone. His significance, his appreciation is the appreciation of his relation to the dead poets and artists. You cannot value him alone; you must set him, for contrast and comparison, among the dead.

Although the lyric is often ostensibly addressed to someone (the "you" in "Careless Love"), the reader usually feels that the speaker is really talking to himself. In "Careless Love," the speaker need not be in the presence of her man; rather, her heart is over-flowing (the reader senses) and she pretends to address him. A comment by John Stuart Mill on poetry is especially true of the lyric:

> Eloquence is *heard,* poetry is *over*heard. Eloquence supposes an audience; the peculiarity of poetry appears to us to lie in the poet's utter unconsciousness of a listener. Poetry is feeling confessing itself to itself, in moments of solitude.

This is especially true, of course, in work-songs such as "Michael Row the Boat Ashore," where there is no audience: the singers sing for themselves, participating rather than performing. As one prisoner in Texas said: "They really be singing about the way they feel inside. Since they can't say it to nobody, they sing a song about it." The sense of "feeling confessing itself to itself, in moments of solitude," or of "singing about the way they feel inside," is strong and clear in this short cowboy song.

Anonymous

The Colorado Trail

Eyes like the morning star,
Cheeks like a rose,
Laura was a pretty girl,
God Almighty knows.

Weep all ye little rains,
Wail winds wail,
All along, along, along
The Colorado trail.

Here is another anonymous poem, this one probably written in the early sixteenth century.

Anonymous

Western Wind

Western wind, when wilt thou blow,
The small rain down can rain?
Christ, if my love were in my arms,
And I in my bed again!

QUESTIONS

1. In "Western Wind," what is the tone of the speaker's voice in the first two lines? Angry? Impatient? Supplicating? Be as precise as possible. What is the tone in the next two lines?
2. In England the west wind, warmed by the Gulf Stream, rises in the spring. What associations link the wind and rain of lines 1 and 2 with lines 3 and 4?
3. Ought we to have been told why the lovers are separated? Explain.

The next poem, written by an unmarried proper New England lady of the nineteenth century, is strongly erotic.

Emily Dickinson *(1830–1886)*

Wild nights, wild nights!

Wild nights, wild nights!
Were I with thee,
Wild nights should be
Our luxury.

Futile the winds
To a heart in port,
Done with the compass,
Done with the chart.

Rowing in Eden –
Ah, the sea!
Might I but moor
To-night in thee.

QUESTIONS

1. Probably "wild nights" refers chiefly to a storm outside of
   the lovers' room, but it can of course also describe their love.
   Luxury (from the Latin *luxuria,* which meant "excess," or
   "extravagance") in line 4 probably retains some of the meaning
   that it first had when it entered into English, "lust" or sensual
   enjoyment. What does the second stanza say about the nature
   of their love? How does the third stanza modify the idea?
2. What makes this lyric lyrical?
3. Is the poem sentimental? Explain.

Langston Hughes *(1902–1967)*

Evenin' Air Blues

Folks, I come up North
Cause they told me de North was fine.
I come up North
Cause they told me de North was fine.
Been up here six months —   *5*
I'm about to lose my mind.

This mornin' for breakfast
I chawed de mornin' air.
This mornin' for breakfast
Chawed de mornin' air.   *10*
But this evenin' for supper,
I got evenin' air to spare.

Believe I'll do a little dancin'
Just to drive my blues away —
A little dancin'   *15*
To drive my blues away,
Cause when I'm dancin'
De blues forgets to stay.

But if you was to ask me
How de blues they come to be,   *20*
Says if you was to ask me
How de blues they come to be —
You wouldn't need to ask me:
Just look at me and see!

QUESTION

In what ways (subject, language) does this poem resemble blues you may have heard? Does it differ in any ways?

Walt Whitman (1819–1892)

A Noiseless Patient Spider

A noiseless patient spider,
I mark'd where on a little promontory it stood isolated,
Mark'd how to explore the vacant vast surrounding,
It launch'd forth filament, filament, filament, out of itself,
Ever unreeling them, ever tirelessly speeding them.   *5*

And you O my soul where you stand,
Surrounded, detached, in measureless oceans of space,
Ceaselessly musing, venturing, throwing, seeking the spheres to
    connect them,
Till the bridge you will need be form'd, till the ductile anchor
    hold,
Till the gossamer thread you fling catch somewhere,
    O my soul.   *10*

QUESTIONS

1. How are the suggestions in "launch'd" (line 4) and "unreeling" (line 5) continued in the second stanza?
2. How are the varying lengths of lines 1, 4, and 8 relevant to their ideas?
3. The second stanza is not a complete sentence. Why? The poem is unrhymed. What is the effect of the near-rhyme (hold: soul) in the last two lines?

Robert Frost (*1874–1963*)

Stopping by Woods on a Snowy Evening

Whose woods these are I think I know.
His house is in the village though;
He will not see me stopping here
To watch his woods fill up with snow.   *4*

My little horse must think it queer
To stop without a farmhouse near
Between the woods and frozen lake
The darkest evening of the year.   *8*

He gives his harness bells a shake
To ask if there is some mistake.
The only other sound's the sweep
Of easy wind and downy flake.   *12*

The woods are lovely, dark and deep.
But I have promises to keep,
And miles to go before I sleep,
And miles to go before I sleep.   *16*

QUESTIONS

1. Line 5 originally read: "The steaming horses think it queer." Line 7 read: "Between a forest and a lake." Evaluate the changes.
2. The rhyming words in the first stanza can be indicated by *aaba;* the second stanza picks up the *b* rhyme: *bbcb.* Indicate the rhymes for the third stanza. For the fourth. Why is it appropriate that the rhyme scheme differs in the fourth stanza?

3. Hearing that the poem had been interpreted as a "death poem," Frost said, "I never intended that, but I did have the feeling it was loaded with ulteriority." What "ulteriority" is implicit? How is the time of day and year significant? How does the horse's attitude make a contrast with the man's?

D. H. Lawrence (1885–1930)

Piano

Softly, in the dusk, a woman is singing to me;
Taking me back down the vista of years, till I see
A child sitting under the piano, in the boom of the tingling strings
And pressing the small, poised feet of a mother who smiles as she sings.

In spite of myself, the insidious mastery of song   5
Betrays me back, till the heart of me weeps to belong
To the old Sunday evenings at home, with winter outside
And hymns in the cozy parlor, the tinkling piano our guide.

So now it is vain for the singer to burst into clamor
With the great black piano appassionato. The glamour   10
Of childish days is upon me, my manhood is cast
Down in the flood of remembrance, I weep like a child for the past.

QUESTIONS

1. The title, of course, refers to a musical instrument, but what else can the word "piano" mean? (If you are in doubt, check a dictionary.)

2. Drawing on lines 3–4 and 7–8, characterize the speaker's childhood. Drawing on lines 5–6, set forth what you take to be the speaker's usual attitude toward his childhood and his family.

3. Check a dictionary to learn the old meaning of the word "glamour" (line 10). Is the earlier meaning relevant? And why (putting aside the rhyme) is "glamour," in the modern sense, a better word than, say, "beauty" or "excitement"?

4. The last two lines contrast manhood and childhood. What other contrasts do you find in the poem?

5. Is the poem sentimental? (To answer this question, you need first to define "sentimental.")

John Keats (1795–1821)

Ode on a Grecian Urn

I

Thou still unravished bride of quietness,
    Thou foster-child of silence and slow time,
Sylvan historian, who canst thus express
    A flowery tale more sweetly than our rhyme:
What leaf-fringed legend haunts about thy shape   *5*
    Of deities or mortals, or of both,
        In Tempe or the dales of Arcady?
    What men or gods are these? What maidens loth?
What mad pursuit? What struggle to escape?
        What pipes and timbrels? What wild ecstasy?   *10*

II

Heard melodies are sweet, but those unheard
    Are sweeter; therefore, ye soft pipes, play on;
Not to the sensual° ear, but, more endeared,   *sensuous*
    Pipe to the spirit ditties of no tone:
Fair youth, beneath the trees, thou canst not leave   *15*
    Thy song, nor ever can those trees be bare;
        Bold Lover, never, never canst thou kiss,
Though winning near the goal — yet, do not grieve;
        She cannot fade, though thou hast not thy bliss,
    For ever wilt thou love, and she be fair!   *20*

III

Ah, happy, happy boughs! that cannot shed
    Your leaves, nor ever bid the Spring adieu;
And, happy melodist, unwearied,
    For ever piping songs for ever new;
More happy love! more happy, happy love!   *25*
    For ever warm and still to be enjoyed,
        For ever panting, and for ever young;
All breathing human passion far above,
    That leaves a heart high-sorrowful and cloyed,
        A burning forehead, and a parching tongue.   *30*

IV

Who are these coming to the sacrifice?
    To what green altar, O mysterious priest,
Lead'st thou that heifer lowing at the skies,
    And all her silken flanks with garlands drest?
What little town by river or sea shore,   *35*
    Or mountain-built with peaceful citadel,
        Is emptied of this folk, this pious morn?
And, little town, thy streets for evermore
    Will silent be; and not a soul to tell
        Why thou art desolate can e'er return.   *40*

V

O Attic shape! Fair attitude! with brede°   *design*
    Of marble men and maidens overwrought,
With forest branches and the trodden weed;
    Thou, silent form, dost tease us out of thought
As doth eternity: Cold Pastoral!   *45*
When old age shall this generation waste,
        Thou shalt remain, in midst of other woe
Than ours, a friend to man, to whom thou say'st,
"Beauty is truth, truth beauty," — that is all
    Ye know on earth, and all ye need to know.   *50*

QUESTIONS

1. Why "sylvan" historian (line 3)? As the poem continues, what evidence is there that the urn cannot "express" (line 3) a tale so sweetly as the speaker said?

2. What is the meaning of lines 11–14?

3. What might the urn stand for in the first three stanzas? In the third stanza is the speaker caught up in the urn's world or is he sharply aware of his own?

4. Does "tease us out of thought" (line 44) mean "draw us into a realm of imaginative experience superior to that of reason," or "draw us into futile and frustrating questions"? Or both, or neither? What are the suggestions in "Cold Pastoral" (line 45)?

5. Do lines 49–50 perhaps mean that imagination, stimulated by the urn, achieves a realm richer than the daily world? Or perhaps that art, the highest earthly wisdom, suggests there is a realm wherein earthly troubles are resolved?

10

The Speaking Tone of Voice

Everything written is as good as it is dramatic. . . . [A poem is] heard as sung or spoken by a person in a scene — in character, in a setting. By whom, where and when is the question. By the dreamer of a better world out in a storm in Autumn; by a lover under a window at night.

Robert Frost, Preface, *A Way Out*

If we fall into the habit of saying "Whitman says, 'A noiseless patient spider,/ I mark'd,' " or "Keats says, 'Heard melodies are sweet, but those unheard are sweeter,' " we neglect the important truth in Frost's comment: a poem is written by an author, but it is spoken by an invented speaker. The author counterfeits the speech of a person in a particular situation. The anonymous author of "Edward" (page 440) invents the speeches of a murderer and his mother; the anonymous author of "Western Wind" (page 454) invents the speech of an unhappy lover who longs for the spring; Robert Frost in "Stopping by Woods" (page 457) invents the speech of a man who, sitting in a horse-drawn sleigh, is surveying woods that are "lovely, dark and deep." Had the setting in Frost's poem been different — say, a snowbound cabin — the speaker of the poem would have said something different.

The speaker's voice, of course, often has the ring of the author's own voice, and to make a distinction between speaker and author may at times seem perverse. Robert Burns, for example, sometimes lets us know that the poem is spoken by "Rob"; he may address his wife by name; beneath the title "To a Mouse" he writes, "On Turning Up Her Nest with the Plow, November, 1785," and beneath the title "To a Mountain Daisy" he writes,

"On Turning One Down with the Plow in April, 1786." Still, even in these allegedly autobiographical poems, it may be convenient to distinguish between author and speaker; the speaker is Burns the lover, or Burns the meditative man, or Burns the compassionate man, not simply Robert Burns the poet. Here are two poems by Burns; in the first the lover speaks, in the second we hear a different speaker. (If you read the poems aloud, the meanings of many of the Scot's words will become clear. Thus, in line 5, "wad" is "would." And if you read the poems aloud, you will get a strong sense of the speakers.)

Robert Burns (1759–1796)

Mary Morison

O Mary, at thy window be,
    It is the wished, the trysted hour!
Those smiles and glances let me see,
    That make the miser's treasure poor: *4*
How blithely wad I bide the stour,°   *endure the struggle*
    A weary slave frae sun to sun,
Could I the rich reward secure,
    The lovely Mary Morison.   *8*

Yestreen when to the trembling string
    The dance gaed° through the lighted ha',   *went*
To thee my fancy took its wing,
    I sat, but neither heard nor saw: *12*
Though this was fair, and that was braw,°   *handsome*
    And yon the toast of a' the town,
I sighed, and said amang them a',
    "Ye are na Mary Morison."   *16*

O Mary, canst thou wreck his peace,
    Wha for thy sake wad gladly die?
Or canst thou break that heart of his,
    Whase only faut° is loving thee?   *fault* *20*
If love for love thou wilt na gie,°   *give*
    At least be pity to me shown!
A thought ungentle canna be
    The thought o' Mary Morison.   *24*

Robert Burns (1759–1796)

John Anderson My Jo

John Anderson my jo,° John,	*sweetheart*
When we were first acquent,	
Your locks were like the raven,	
Your bonnie brow was brent;°	*smooth* 4
But now your brow is beld, John,	
Your locks are like the snaw,	
But blessings on your frosty pow,°	*head*
John Anderson my jo!	*8*

John Anderson my jo, John,	
We clamb the hill thegither,	
And monie a cantie° day, John	*happy*
We've had wi' ane anither:	*12*
Now we maun° totter down, John,	*must*
And hand in hand we'll go,	
And sleep thegither at the foot,	
John Anderson my jo!	*16*

QUESTIONS

1. In the first poem, is the speaker addressing Mary Morison?
2. In "Mary Morison," how convincing are the assertions of the first stanza (that her smiles and glances are more valuable than great wealth; that he would willingly be a "weary slave" if only he could win her)? How does the third stanza enlarge our conception of the speaker's personality? For example, do lines 21–22 introduce an aspect not present earlier? The poem is excellent throughout, but many readers find the second stanza the best of the three. Do you?
3. In "John Anderson My Jo," the speaker cannot be identified with Burns, but do we feel that there is in the poem anything of the particular accent of an old lady? Why?

Although all poems are "dramatic" in Frost's sense of being uttered by a speaker in a situation, and although most short poems are monologues, the term **dramatic monologue** is reserved for those poems in which a single character — not the poet — is speaking at a critical moment to a person or persons whose presence we strongly feel. The most famous example is Robert Browning's "My Last Duchess."

Robert Browning (1812–1889)

My Last Duchess

FERRARA°   *town in Italy*

That's my last Duchess painted on the wall,
Looking as if she were alive. I call
That piece a wonder, now; Frà Pandolf's° hands   *a fictitious*
Worked busily a day, and there she stands.   *painter*
Will't please you sit and look at her? I said   5
"Frà Pandolf" by design, for never read
Strangers like you that pictured countenance,
The depth and passion of its earnest glance,
But to myself they turned (since none puts by
The curtain I have drawn for you, but I)   10
And seemed as they would ask me, if they durst,
How such a glance came there; so, not the first
Are you to turn and ask thus. Sir, 'twas not
Her husband's presence only, called that spot
Of joy into the Duchess' cheek; perhaps   15
Frà Pandolf chanced to say "Her mantle laps
Over my Lady's wrist too much," or, "Paint
Must never hope to reproduce the faint
Half-flush that dies along her throat." Such stuff
Was courtesy, she thought, and cause enough   20
For calling up that spot of joy. She had
A heart — how shall I say? — too soon made glad,
Too easily impressed; she liked whate'er
She looked on, and her looks went everywhere.
Sir, 'twas all one! My favor at her breast,   25
The dropping of the daylight in the west,
The bough of cherries some officious fool
Broke in the orchard for her, the white mule
She rode with round the terrace — all and each
Would draw from her alike the approving speech,   30
Or blush, at least. She thanked men — good! but thanked
Somehow — I know not how — as if she ranked
My gift of a nine-hundred-years-old name
With anybody's gift. Who'd stoop to blame
This sort of trifling? Even had you skill   35
In speech — (which I have not) — to make your will
Quite clear to such an one, and say, "Just this
Or that in you disgusts me; here you miss,
Or there exceed the mark" — and if she let

Herself be lessoned so, nor plainly set   40
Her wits to yours, forsooth, and made excuse,
— E'en then would be some stooping; and I choose
Never to stoop. Oh, Sir, she smiled, no doubt,
Whene'er I passed her; but who passed without
Much the same smile? This grew; I gave commands;   45
Then all smiles stopped together. There she stands
As if alive. Will't please you rise? We'll meet
The company below, then. I repeat,
The Count your master's known munificence
Is ample warrant that no just pretense   50
Of mine for dowry will be disallowed;
Though his fair daughter's self, as I avowed
At starting, is my object. Nay, we'll go
Together down, Sir. Notice Neptune, though,
Taming a sea-horse, thought a rarity,   55
Which Claus of Innsbruck° cast in bronze for me!   *a fictitious*
                                                         sculptor

QUESTIONS

1. Who is speaking to whom? On what occasion?
2. What words or lines especially convey the speaker's arrogance? What is our attitude toward the speaker? Loathing? Fascination? Respect? Explain.
3. The time and place are Renaissance Italy; how do they affect our attitude toward the duke? What would be the effect if the poem were set in the twentieth century?
4. Why does this poem sound more like talk and less like song than Burns's "John Anderson"?
5. Years after writing this poem, Browning explained that the duke's "commands" (line 45) were "that she should be put to death, or he might have had her shut up in a convent." Should the poem have been more explicit? Does Browning's later uncertainty indicate that the poem is badly thought out? Suppose we did not have Browning's comment on line 45; could the line then mean only that he commanded her to stop smiling and that she obeyed? Explain.

DICTION

From the whole of language, one consciously or unconsciously selects certain words and grammatical constructions; this selection constitutes one's **diction.** It is partly by the diction that we come to know the speaker of a poem. "Amang" and "frae sun to sun" tell us that the speaker of "Mary Morison" is a Scot. In "My Last Duchess" such words as "countenance," "munificence," and "disallowed" — none of which is conceivable in Burns's poem — help us form our impression of the duke. Of course, some words are used in both poems: "I said," "and," "smile[s]," "glance[s]," etc. The fact remains, however, that although a large part of language is shared by all speakers, certain parts of language are used only by certain speakers.

Like some words, some grammatical constructions are used only by certain kinds of speakers. Consider these two passages:

> In Adam's fall
> We sinned all.
>
> — from *The New England Primer*

> Of Man's first disobedience, and the fruit
> Of that forbidden tree whose mortal taste
> Brought death into the World, and all our woe,
> With loss of Eden, till one greater Man
> Restore us, and regain the blissful seat,
> Sing, Heavenly Muse, that, on the secret top
> Of Oreb, or of Sinai, didst inspire
> That shepherd who first taught the chosen seed
> In the beginning how the heavens and earth
> Rose out of Chaos. . . .
>
> — Milton, from *Paradise Lost*

There is an enormous difference in the diction of these two passages. Milton, speaking as an inspired poet, appropriately uses words and grammatical constructions somewhat removed from common life. Hence, while the anonymous author of the primer speaks directly of "Adam's fall," Milton speaks allusively of the fall, calling it "Man's first disobedience." Milton's sentence is nothing that any Englishman ever said in conversation; its genitive beginning, its length (the sentence continues for six lines beyond the quoted passage), and its postponement of the main verb until the sixth line mark it as the utterance of a poet working in the tradition of Latin poetry. The primer's statement, by its choice of words as well as by its brevity, suggests a far less sophisticated speaker.

TONE

A speaker has attitudes toward himself, his subject, and his audience, and (consciously or unconsciously) he chooses his words, pitch, and modulation accordingly; all these add up to his **tone.** In written literature, tone must be detected without the aid of the ear; the reader must understand by the selection and sequence of words the way in which they are meant to be heard (that is, playfully, angrily, confidentially, sarcastically, etc.). The reader must catch what Frost calls "the speaking tone of voice somehow entangled in the words and fastened to the page of the ear of the imagination."*

Some examples will clarify what is meant by "the speaking tone of voice." Innumerable poems present a young man urging a young lady to wake up and enjoy the beauty of a spring morning. But such a young man may speak impatiently, or tenderly, or politely, or cozily. In a song from Shakespeare's *Cymbeline* there is the line "My lady sweet, arise"; in Robert Herrick's "Corinna's Going A-Maying," "Get up, sweet slug-a-bed." In "My lady sweet, arise," we detect a somewhat formal tone, as is entirely proper in the context (a minstrel is serenading a princess at the request of a royal wooer). In "Get up, sweet slug-a-bed," we detect, at least in context, a cozy, intimate, playful tone (the speaker is presumably addressing an intimate friend). One might paraphrase either line as "Wake up, lady," but this restatement distorts both lines because it obliterates the distinctions in diction, tone, and speaker.

The following poem was written by Robert Herrick, but the speaker is not the impatient young man who said (in "Corinna") "Get up, sweet slug-a-bed."

Robert Herrick (1591–1674)

To the Virgins, to Make Much of Time

Gather ye rosebuds while ye may,
    Old Time is still a-flying;
And this same flower that smiles today,
    Tomorrow will be dying.   *4*

---

* This discussion concentrates on the speaker's tone. But one can also talk of the author's tone, that is, of the author's attitude toward the invented speaker. The speaker's tone might, for example, be angry, but the author's tone (as detected by the reader) might be humorous. For further comment on the author's tone, see page 66.

The glorious lamp of heaven, the sun,
  The higher he's a-getting,
The sooner will his race be run,
  And nearer he's to setting.   *8*

That age is best which is the first,
  When youth and blood are warmer;
But being spent, the worse, and worst
  Times still succeed the former.   *12*

Then be not coy, but use your time;
  And while ye may, go marry:
For having lost but once your prime,
  You may for ever tarry.   *16*

Carpe diem (Latin: "seize the day") is the theme. But if we want to get the full force of the poem, we must understand who is talking to whom. Look, for example, at "Old Time" in line 2. Time is "old," of course, in the sense of having been around a long while, but doesn't "old" in this context suggest also that the speaker regards Time with easy familiarity, almost affection? We visit the old school, and our friend is old George. Time is destructive, yes, and the speaker urges the young maidens to make the most of their spring, but the speaker is neither bitter nor importunate; rather, he seems to be the wise old man, the counselor, the man who has made his peace with time and is giving advice to the young. Time moves rapidly in the poem (the rosebud of line 1 is already a flower in line 3), but the speaker is unhurried; in line 5 he has leisure to explain that the glorious lamp of heaven is the sun.

In "To the Virgins," the pauses, indicated by punctuation at the ends of the lines (except in line 11, where we tumble without stopping from "worse" to "worst/ Times"), slow the reader down. But even if there is no punctuation at the end of a line of poetry, the reader probably pauses slightly or gives the final word an additional bit of emphasis. Similarly, the space between stanzas slows a reader down, increasing the emphasis on the last word of one stanza and the first word of the next. Read the following poem aloud and then see if you can account for the lineation.

Robert Frost (1874–1963)

Mending Wall

Something there is that doesn't love a wall,
That sends the frozen-ground-swell under it,
And spills the upper boulders in the sun;
And makes gaps even two can pass abreast.
The work of hunters is another thing: 5
I have come after them and made repair
Where they have left not one stone on a stone,
But they would have the rabbit out of hiding,
To please the yelping dogs. The gaps I mean,
No one has seen them made or heard them made,   10
But at spring-mending time we find them there.
I let my neighbor know beyond the hill;
And on a day we meet to walk the line
And set the wall between us once again.
We keep the wall between us as we go.   15
To each the boulders that have fallen to each.
And some are loaves and some so nearly balls
We have to use a spell to make them balance:
"Stay where you are until our backs are turned!"
We wear our fingers rough with handling them.   20
Oh, just another kind of outdoor game,
One on a side. It comes to little more:
There where it is we do not need the wall:
He is all pine and I am apple orchard.
My apple trees will never get across   25
And eat the cones under his pines, I tell him.
He only says, "Good fences make good neighbors."
Spring is the mischief in me, and I wonder
If I could put a notion in his head:
"*Why* do they make good neighbors? Isn't it   30
Where there are cows? But here there are no cows.
Before I built a wall I'd ask to know
What I was walling in or walling out,
And to whom I was like to give offense.
Something there is that doesn't love a wall,   35
That wants it down." I could say "Elves" to him,
But it's not elves exactly, and I'd rather
He said it for himself. I see him there
Bringing a stone grasped firmly by the top
In each hand, like an old-stone savage armed.   40

He moves in darkness as it seems to me,
Not of woods only and the shade of trees.
He will not go behind his father's saying,
And he likes having thought of it so well
He says again, "Good fences make good neighbors."   *45*

QUESTIONS

1. How does the speech of the speaker's neighbor characterize him?
2. Specify some passages that allow one to say that "Mending Wall" is conversational or colloquial in tone. Consider also lines 41–42: "He moves in darkness as it seems to me,/ Not of woods only and the shade of trees." Would you characterize these lines as colloquial or lyrical or both? Why?
3. Is it reasonable to assume that the two views about the wall have political and ethical implications? Explain.

John Crowe Ransom (1888–1974)

Piazza Piece

— I am a gentleman in a dustcoat trying
To make you hear. Your ears are soft and small
And listen to an old man not at all,
They want the young men's whispering and sighing.   *4*
But see the roses on your trellis dying
And hear the spectral singing of the moon;
For I must have my lovely lady soon,
I am a gentleman in a dustcoat trying.   *8*

— I am a lady young in beauty waiting
Until my truelove comes, and then we kiss.
But what gray man among the vines is this
Whose words are dry and faint as in a dream?   *12*
Back from my trellis, Sir, before I scream!
I am a lady young in beauty waiting.

QUESTIONS

1. Who speaks the first eight lines? What words especially characterize him? He is "a gentleman in a dustcoat," but who

else is he? What is a "dustcoat" or a "duster"? Why is this garment especially appropriate here? Characterize the speaker of the six remaining lines.

2. In lines 9–10, she is waiting for her "truelove." Comment on the suggestions in this word. In line 14 she is still "waiting." For whom does she think she is waiting? For whom does the reader know she is waiting? How?

Gerard Manley Hopkins (1844–1889)

Spring and Fall: To a Young Child

Márgarét, are you gríeving
Over Goldengrove unleaving?
Léaves, líke the things of man, you
With your fresh thoughts care for, can you?
Áh! ás the heart grows older   5
It will come to such sights colder
By and by, nor spare a sigh
Though worlds of wanwood leafmeal lie;
And yet you will weep and know why.
Now no matter, child, the name: 10
Sórrow's spríngs áre the same.
Nor mouth had, no nor mind, expressed
What heart heard of, ghost° guessed: *spirit*
It ís the blight man was born for,
It ís Margaret you mourn for.   15

QUESTIONS

1. What is the speaker's age? His tone? What is the relevance of the title to the speaker and to Margaret? What meanings are in "Fall"?

2. What is meant by Margaret's "fresh thoughts" (line 4)? Paraphrase lines 3–4 and lines 12–13.

3. "Wanwood" and "leafmeal" are words coined by Hopkins. What are their suggestions?

4. Why is it not contradictory for the speaker to say that Margaret weeps for herself (line 15) after saying that she weeps for "Goldengrove unleaving" (line 2)?

William Butler Yeats (1865–1939)

For Anne Gregory

"Never shall a young man,
Thrown into despair
By those great honey-coloured
Ramparts at your ear
Love you for yourself alone   *5*
And not your yellow hair."

"But I can get a hair-dye
And set such colour there,
Brown, or black, or carrot,
That young men in despair   *10*
May love me for myself alone
And not my yellow hair."

"I heard an old religious man
But yesternight declare
That he had found a text to prove   *15*
That only God, my dear,
Could love you for yourself alone
And not your yellow hair."

QUESTIONS

1. Yeats was sixty-five when he wrote this poem for Anne
   Gregory, the nineteen-year-old granddaughter of a woman
   whom Yeats had admired. What can we imagine Anne saying,
   that provoked the poem?
2. In the first stanza Anne's hair is described both as "great
   honey-colored ramparts" and as "yellow." Why does the
   speaker use these two rather different characterizations? Judging
   from the second stanza, how would Anne describe her hair?
3. If you did not know that Yeats was sixty-five when he wrote
   the poem, would you be able to deduce from the poem itself
   that the speaker of the first and third stanzas is considerably
   older than Anne?
4. Anne says that she wants to be loved "for myself alone."
   Exactly what does this expression mean?
5. Why would "an old religious man" search until he found a
   text that would prove that only God could love her for herself
   alone? Do you think Yeats shares this view?

6. In a sentence or two characterize Yeats as he reveals himself in this poem, and then characterize Anne.

In the previous poem Yeats gave us two speakers. In the next poem he gives us one speaker, identified in the title. The airman, Major Robert Gregory, was the son of Yeats's friend Lady Augusta Gregory. His plane was shot down by Germans in 1918, while he was fighting on the English side. Kiltartan Cross, that is, the crossroads in Kiltartan (line 5), is an Irish village near the Gregorys' estate in western Ireland.

William Butler Yeats (1865–1939)

An Irish Airman Foresees His Death

I know that I shall meet my fate
Somewhere among the clouds above;
Those that I fight I do not hate,
Those that I guard I do not love;
My country is Kiltartan Cross,   5
My countrymen Kiltartan's poor,
No likely end could bring them loss
Or leave them happier than before.
Nor law, nor duty bade me fight,
Nor public men, nor cheering crowds,   10
A lonely impulse of delight
Drove to this tumult in the clouds;
I balanced all, brought all to mind,
The years to come seemed waste of breath,
A waste of breath the years behind   15
In balance with this life, this death.

QUESTIONS

1. The speaker mentions several forces that do *not* motivate him, and one force that does. What are these?
2. How would you characterize the speaker? Cold? Self-indulgent? Stoical? Or what? (Because a single word will probably be inadequate, write a sentence or two.)

Ted Hughes (b. 1930)

Hawk Roosting

I sit in the top of the wood, my eyes closed.
Inaction, no falsifying dream
Between my hooked head and hooked feet:
Or in sleep rehearse perfect kills and eat.   *4*

The convenience of the high trees!
The air's buoyancy and the sun's ray
Are of advantage to me;
And the earth's face upward for my inspection.   *8*

My feet are locked upon the rough bark.
It took the whole of Creation
To produce my foot, my each feather:
Now I hold Creation in my foot   *12*

Or fly up, and revolve it all slowly —
I kill where I please because it is all mine.
There is no sophistry in my body:
My manners are tearing off heads —   *16*

The allotment of death.
For the one path of my flight is direct
Through the bones of the living.
No arguments assert my right: *20*

The sun is behind me.
Nothing has changed since I began.
My eye has permitted no change.
I am going to keep things like this.   *24*

QUESTIONS

1. Many of the sentences are short — only one line long. What
   is the effect of these short sentences, especially in the last
   stanza, where each of the four lines is a separate sentence?
2. Hawks cannot speak. Is this poem therefore nonsense?

THE VOICE OF THE SATIRIST

The writer of **satire,** in one way or another, ridicules an aspect or several aspects of human behavior, seeking to arouse in the reader some degree of amused contempt for the object. However urbane in tone, the satirist is always critical. By cleverly holding up foibles or vices for the world's derision, satire (Alexander Pope claimed) "heals with morals what it hurts with wit." The laughter of comedy is an end in itself; the laughter of satire is a weapon against the world: "The intellectual dagger," Frank O'Connor called satire, "opposing the real dagger." Jonathan Swift, of whom O'Connor is speaking, insisted that his satires were not malice but medicine:

> His satire points at no defect
> But what all mortals may correct. . . .
> He spared a hump or crooked nose,
> Whose owners set not up for beaux.

But Swift, although he claimed that satire is therapeutic, also saw its futility: "Satire is a sort of glass wherein beholders do generally discover everybody's face but their own."

Sometimes the satirist speaks out directly as defender of public morals, abusively but wittily chopping off heads. Byron, for example, wrote:

> Prepare for rhyme — I'll publish, right or wrong:
> Fools are my theme, let Satire be my song.

But sometimes the satirist chooses to invent a speaker far removed from himself, just as Browning chose to invent a Renaissance duke. The satirist may, for example, invent a callous brigadier-general or a pompous judge who unconsciously annihilates himself. Consider this satirical poem by E. E. Cummings.

E. E. Cummings (1894–1963)

next to of course god america i

"next to of course god america i
love you land of the pilgrims' and so forth oh
say can you see by the dawn's early my
country 'tis of centuries come and go

4

and are no more what of it we should worry
in every language even deafanddumb
thy sons acclaim your glorious name by gorry
by jingo by gee by gosh by gum   8
why talk of beauty what could be more beauti-
ful than these heroic happy dead
who rushed like lions to the roaring slaughter
they did not stop to think they died instead   12
then shall the voice of liberty be mute?"

He spoke. And drank rapidly a glass of water

Cummings might have written, in the voice of a solid citizen or
a good poet, a direct attack on chauvinistic windbags; instead, he
chose to invent a windbag whose rhetoric punctures itself. Yet
the last line tells that we are really hearing someone who is recounting
what the windbag said; that is, the speaker of all the lines but the
last is a sort of combination of the chauvinist *and* the satiric observer
of the chauvinist. (When Cummings himself recited these lines
there was mockery in his voice.) Only in the final line of the poem
does the author seem to speak entirely on his own, and even here
he adopts a matter-of-fact pose that is far more potent than **invective**
(direct abuse) would be. Yet the last line is not totally free of
explicit hostility. It might, for example, have run, "He spoke.
And poured slowly a glass of water." Why does this version lack
the punch of Cummings's? And what is implied by the absence
of a final period in line 14?

John Updike (*b. 1932*)

Youth's Progress

> *Dick Schneider of Wisconsin. . . was elected "Greek God"*
> *for an interfraternity ball.*   — *Life*

When I was born, my mother taped my ears
So they lay flat. When I had aged ten years,
My teeth were firmly braced and much improved.
Two years went by; my tonsils were removed.   4

At fourteen, I began to comb my hair
A fancy way. Though nothing much was there,
I shaved my upper lip — next year, my chin.
At seventeen, the freckles left my skin.   8

Just turned nineteen, a nicely molded lad,
I said goodbye to Sis and Mother; Dad
Drove me to Wisconsin and set me loose.
At twenty-one, I was elected Zeus.   12

QUESTIONS

1. Suppose the first two lines ran thus:

   > To keep them flat, my mother taped my ears;
   > And then, at last, when I had aged ten years. . . .

   How does this revision destroy the special tone of voice in
   the original two lines? (Notice that in the revision there is
   a heavy pause at the end of the first line.) Why, in the second
   line of the revision, is "at last" false to the "tone" or "voice"
   in the rest of the poem?
2. What is the speaker's attitude toward himself? What is the
   author's attitude toward the speaker?

Thomas Gray (*1716–1771*)

Ode on the Death of a Favorite Cat
Drowned in a Tub of Gold-Fishes

'Twas on a lofty vase's side,
Where China's gayest art had dyed
     The azure flowers that blow;
Demurest of the tabby kind,
The pensive Selima, reclined,   5
     Gazed on the lake below.

Her conscious tail her joy declared;
The fair round face, the snowy beard,
     The velvet of her paws,
Her coat, that with the tortoise vies,   10
Her ears of jet, and emerald eyes,
     She saw; and purred applause.

Still had she gazed; but 'midst the tide
Two angel forms were seen to glide,
    The genii° of the stream: *guardian spirits* **15**
Their scaly armor's Tyrian hue°   *reddish*
Through richest purple to the view
    Betrayed a golden gleam.

The hapless nymph with wonder saw:
A whisker first and then a claw,   **20**
    With many an ardent wish,
She stretched in vain to reach the prize.
What female heart can gold despise?
    What cat's averse to fish?

Presumptuous maid! with looks intent   **25**
Again she stretched, again she bent,
    Nor knew the gulf between.
(Malignant Fate sat by and smiled)
The slippery verge her feet beguiled,
    She tumbled headlong in.   **30**

Eight times emerging from the flood
She mewed to every watery god,
    Some speedy aid to send.
No dolphin* came, no Nereid° stirred;   *a sea nymph*
Nor cruel Tom, nor Susan heard;   **35**
    A favorite has no friend!

From hence, ye beauties, undeceived,
Know, one false step is ne'er retrieved,
    And be with caution bold.
Not all that tempts your wandering eyes   **40**
And heedless hearts, is lawful prize;
    Nor all that glisters, gold.

QUESTIONS

1. A mock heroic poem does not mock the heroic but mocks
a trivial subject by treating it in the elevated terms normally
reserved for heroic subjects. Its elevated diction (e.g., "lake"
in line 6, for a tub of water) produces a comic effect. What
examples are here? What comic juxtapositions? What is the
tone of the poem?
2. Is this a satire on cats? What does the cat come to represent?

---

* Legend held that Arion, a Greek musician, was saved by a dolphin.

3. Explain the paradox in line 36. Is the explicit moralizing (e.g., line 36, lines 37–42) offensive? Explain.
4. Dr. Johnson said of this poem: "The poem *On the Cat* was doubtless by its author considered as a trifle, but it is not a happy trifle. . . . The sixth stanza contains a melancholy truth, that 'a favorite has no friend'; but the last ends in a pointed sentence of no relation to the purpose: if what *glistered* had been *gold,* the cat would not have gone into the water; and if she had, would not less have been drowned?" Evaluate Johnson's statement.

11

Figurative Language: Simile, Metaphor, Personification, Apostrophe

Hippolyta. 'Tis strange, my Theseus, that these lovers speak of.
Theseus. More strange than true. I never may believe
    These antique fables, nor these fairy toys.
    Lovers and madmen have such seething brains,
    Such shaping fantasies, that apprehend
    More than cool reason ever comprehends.
    The lunatic, the lover, and the poet,
    Are of imagination all compact.
    One sees more devils than vast hell can hold,
    That is the madman. The lover, all as frantic,
    Sees Helen's beauty in a brow of Egypt.
    The poet's eye, in a fine frenzy rolling,
    Doth glance from heaven to earth, from earth to heaven;
    And as imagination bodies forth
    The forms of things unknown, the poet's pen
    Turns them to shapes, and gives to airy nothing
    A local habitation and a name.
                — *A Midsummer Night's Dream,* V.i. 1–17

Theseus was neither the first nor the last to suggest that poets, like lunatics and lovers, freely employ their imagination. Terms such as "poetic license" and "poetic justice" imply that poets are free to depict a never-never land. One has only to leaf through any anthology of poetry to encounter numerous statements that are, from a logical point of view, lunacies. Here are a few:

> Look like th' innocent flower,
> But be the serpent under 't.
>> — Shakespeare

> Each outcry from the hunted hare
> A fiber from the brain does tear.
>> — William Blake

> Every thread of summer is at last unwoven.
>> — Wallace Stevens

On a literal level such assertions are nonsense (so, too, is Theseus's notion that reason is cool). But of course they are not to be taken literally; rather, they employ **figures of speech** — departures from logical usage that are aimed at gaining special effects. Consider the lunacies that Robert Burns heaps up here.

Robert Burns (*1759–1796*)

A Red, Red Rose

O, my luve is like a red, red rose,
    That's newly sprung in June.
O, my luve is like the melodie,
    That's sweetly played in tune.   *4*

As fair art thou, my bonnie lass,
    So deep in luve am I,
And I will luve thee still, my dear,
    Till a'° the seas gang° dry.   *all; go* *8*

Till a' the seas gang dry, my dear,
    And the rocks melt wi' the sun!
And I will luve thee still, my dear,
    While the sands o' life shall run.   *12*

And fare thee weel, my only luve,
    And fare thee weel awhile!
And I will come again, my luve,
    Though it were ten thousand mile!   *16*

To the charge that these lines are lunacies or untruths, at least two replies can be made. First, it might be said that the speaker is not really making assertions about a girl; he is saying he feels a certain way. His words, it can be argued, are not assertions about external reality but expressions of his state of mind, just as a tune one whistles asserts nothing about external reality but expresses the whistler's state of mind. In this view, the nonlogical language of poetry (like groans of pain and exclamations of joy) is an expression of emotion; its further aim, if it has one, is to induce in the hearer an emotion. Second, and more to the point here, it can be said that nonlogical language does indeed make assertions about external reality, and even gives the reader an insight into this reality that logical language cannot. The opening comparison in Burns's poem ("my luve is like a red, red rose") brings before our eyes the lady's beauty in a way that the reasonable assertion "She is beautiful" does not. By comparing the woman to a rose, the poet invites us to see the woman through a special sort of lens: she is fragrant; her lips (and perhaps her cheeks) are like a rose in texture and color; she will not keep her beauty long.

The poet, then, has not only communicated a state of mind but also has discovered, through the lens of imagination, some things (both in the beloved and in the lover's own feelings) that interest us. The discovery is not world-shaking; it is less important than the discovery of America, or the discovery that the meek are blessed, but it *is* a discovery and it leaves the reader with the feeling, "Yes, that's right. I hadn't quite thought of it that way, but that's right." A poem, Robert Frost said, "assumes direction with the first line laid down,. . . runs a course of lucky events, and ends in a clarification of life — not necessarily a great clarification, such as sects and cults are founded on, but in a momentary stay against confusion." What is clarified? In another paragraph Frost gives an answer: "For me the initial delight is in the surprise of remembering something I didn't know I knew." John Keats made a similar statement: "Poetry. . . should strike the Reader as a wording of his own highest thoughts, and appear almost a Remembrance."

Some figures of speech are, in effect, riddling ways of speech. To call fishermen "farmers of the sea" — a metaphor — is a sort of veiled description of fishermen, bringing out, when it is properly understood, certain aspects of a fisherman's activities. And a riddle, after all, is a veiled description — though intentionally obscure or deceptive — calling attention to characteristics, especially similarities, not usually noticed. ("Riddle," like "read," is from Old English *redan,* "to guess," "to interpret," and thus its solution provides knowledge.) "Two sisters upstairs, often looking but never seeing each other" is (after the riddle is explained) a way of calling attention to the curious fact that the eye, the instrument of vision, never sees its mate.

In the next poem the connection between riddles and metaphors is easily seen.

Sylvia Plath (1932–1963)

Metaphors

I'm a riddle in nine syllables,
An elephant, a ponderous house,
A melon strolling on two tendrils.
O red fruit, ivory, fine timbers!
This loaf's big with its yeasty rising.
Money's new-minted in this fat purse.
I'm a means, a stage, a cow in calf.
I've eaten a bag of green apples,
Boarded the train there's no getting off.

The riddling speaker says that she is, among other things, "A melon strolling on two tendrils," and "a cow in calf." What is she?

SIMILE

In a **simile** items from different classes are explicitly compared by a connective such as "like," "as," or "than," or by a verb such as "appears" or "seems." (If the objects compared are from the same class, e.g., "New York is like London," no simile is present.)

> Sometimes I feel like a motherless child.
>
> — Anonymous

> It is a beauteous evening, calm and free.
> The holy time is quiet as a Nun,
> Breathless with adoration.
>
> — Wordsworth

How sharper than a serpent's tooth it is
To have a thankless child.

> — Shakespeare

Seems he a dove? His feathers are but borrowed.

> — Shakespeare

The following two lines constitute an entire poem.

Robert Herrick (*1591–1674*)

Her Legs

Fain would I kiss my Julia's dainty leg,
Which is as white and hairless as an egg.

METAPHOR

A **metaphor** asserts the identity, without a connective such as
"like" or a verb such as "appears," of terms that are literally
incompatible.

> She is the rose, the glory of the day.
>
> > — Spenser
>
> O western orb sailing the heaven.
>
> > — Whitman

Notice how in the second example only one of the terms ("orb")
is stated; the other ("ship") is implied in "sailing."

Here is a short poem that — at least on first reading — may
seem difficult because of its shift from literal to figurative language.

William Butler Yeats (1865–1939)

Memory

One had a lovely face,
And two or three had charm,
But charm and face were in vain
Because the mountain grass
Cannot but keep the form
Where the mountain hare has lain.

The first three lines present no difficulty: one person (surely a woman, given "lovely") was beautiful, and two or three other women were charming, but these qualities were of no importance. The difficulty begins after "Because," a word that leads us to expect an explanation, and we probably expect the explanation to be in language as direct as the language of the first three lines. Instead we get an assertion about mountain grass and a hare, which may seem to have nothing to do with explaining why the beauty and charm of the three or four people already mentioned "were in vain."

The title of the poem, "Memory," provides a clue to this riddle. (Always pay attention to a title; it is part of the work.) Why is the poem called "Memory"? Of course the speaker is remembering the women of the first three lines, but how does "memory" govern the rest of the poem? "Charm and face were in vain," the speaker says, because the mountain grass inevitably retains "the form / Where the mountain hare has lain." This hardly seems to be an explanation until we realize that the poem, called "Memory," is about the power of memory and is also a description of memory. The mountain grass bearing an imprint of the sleeping or crouching hare is an image or metaphor standing for the memory. Think of it this way: the mind *retains impressions,* just as the mountain grass retains the impression of the body of a hare nesting in it. (It happens that "form" means not only "shape" or "contour" but also, specifically, the lair or resting place of a hare, but even the usual meaning of the word makes sense in the passage.) Like the grass, the mind holds, in memory, an impression or trace of an object that is no longer present. And so a memory implies a loss. For example, we remember our childhood only when we have lost it. We can now see why the speaker is untouched by the "lovely face" and the "charm" of several women: it is "because" his mind retains an earlier impression, presumably of some other woman, a woman who is now gone but who cannot be forgotten.

This memorable woman probably had some of the qualities of the mountain hare — perhaps she was beautiful, delicate, independent, close to nature — but we need not try to be too precise about her. The poem is entitled "Memory" and its precision is in what it says about the nature of memory — especially what it says about the power of an enduring memory — rather than in what it says about a particular object of memory.

QUESTION

Is there any conceivable resemblance between the mind and the grass nest of a hare?

In the next poem, Keats's excitement on reading Chapman's translation of Homer is communicated first through a metaphor and then through a simile.

John Keats (*1795–1821*)

On First Looking into Chapman's Homer

Much have I traveled in the realms of gold,
And many goodly states and kingdoms seen;
Round many western islands have I been
Which bards in fealty to Apollo hold.   *4*
Oft of one wide expanse have I been told
That deep-browed Homer ruled as his demesne;
Yet did I never breathe its pure serene
Till I heard Chapman speak out loud and bold: *8*
Then felt I like some watcher of the skies
When a new planet swims into his ken;
Or like stout Cortez when with eagle eyes
He stared at the Pacific — and all his men   *12*
Looked at each other with a wild surmise —
Silent, upon a peak in Darien.

QUESTIONS

1. In line 1, what does "realms of gold" stand for? Chapman

was an Elizabethan; how does this fact add relevance to the metaphor in the first line?

2. Does line 9 introduce a totally new idea, or is it somewhat connected to the opening metaphor?

Two types of metaphor deserve special mention. In **metonymy,** something is named that replaces something closely related to it; "City Hall," for example, sometimes is used to stand for municipal authority. In the following passage James Shirley names certain objects, using them to replace social classes to which they are related:

> Scepter and crown must tumble down
> And in the dust be equal made
> With the poor crooked scythe and spade.

In **synecdoche,** the whole is replaced by the part, or the part by the whole. For example, "bread" in "Give us this day our daily bread" replaces the whole class of edibles. Similarly, an automobile can be "wheels," and workers are "hands." Robert Frost was fond of calling himself "a Synecdochist" because he believed that it is the nature of poetry to "have intimations of something more than itself. It almost always comes under the head of synecdoche, a part, a hem of the garment for the whole garment."

PERSONIFICATION

The attribution of human feelings or characteristics to abstractions or to inanimate objects is called **personification.**

> But Time did beckon to the flowers, and they
> By noon most cunningly did steal away.
> — Herbert

Herbert attributes a human gesture to Time and shrewdness to flowers. Of all figures, personification most surely gives to airy nothings a local habitation and a name:

> There's Wrath who has learnt every trick of guerrilla
> warfare,
> The shamming dead, the night-raid, the feinted retreat.
> — Auden

> Hope, thou bold taster of delight.
> — Crashaw

APOSTROPHE

Crashaw's personification, "Hope, thou bold taster of delight," is also an example of the figure called **apostrophe,** an address to a person or thing not literally listening. Wordsworth begins a sonnet by apostrophizing John Milton:

> Milton, thou shouldst be living at this hour,

and Shelley begins an ode by apostrophizing a skylark:

> Hail to thee, blithe Spirit!

The following poem is largely built on apostrophe.

Edmund Waller (*1606–1687*)

Song

> Go, lovely rose,
> Tell her that wastes her time and me,
>   That now she knows,
> When I resemble her to thee,
>   How sweet and fair she seems to be.   *5*
>
>   Tell her that's young,
> And shuns to have her graces spied,
>   That hadst thou sprung
> In deserts where no men abide,
>   Thou must have uncommended died.   *10*
>
>   Small is the worth
> Of beauty from the light retired:
>   Bid her come forth,
> Suffer her self to be desired,
>   And not blush so to be admired.   *15*
>
>   Then die, that she
> The common fate of all things rare
>   May read in thee,
> How small a part of time they share,
>   That are so wondrous sweet and fair.   *20*

What conclusions, then, can we draw about **figurative language?** First, figurative language, with its literally incompatible terms, forces the reader to attend to the **connotations** (suggestions, associations) rather than to the **denotations** (dictionary definitions) of one of the terms. Second, although figurative language is said to differ from ordinary discourse, it is found in ordinary discourse as well as in literature. "It rained cats and dogs," "War is hell," "Don't be a pig," and other tired figures are part of our daily utterances. But through repeated use, these (and most of the figures we use) have lost whatever impact they once had and are only a shade removed from expressions which, though once figurative, have become literal: the *eye* of a needle, a *branch* office, the *face* of a clock. Third, good figurative language is usually (*a*) concrete, (*b*) condensed, and (*c*) interesting. The concreteness lends precision and vividness; when Keats writes that he felt "like some watcher of the skies/ When a new planet swims into his ken," he more sharply characterizes his feelings than if he had said, "I felt excited." His simile isolates for us a precise kind of excitement, and the metaphoric "swims" vividly brings up the oceanic aspect of the sky. The second of these three qualities, condensation, can be seen by attempting to paraphrase some of the figures. A paraphrase will commonly use more words than the original and it will have less impact — as the gradual coming of night usually has less impact on us than a sudden darkening of the sky, or as a prolonged push has less impact than a sudden blow. The third quality, interest, largely depends on the previous two: the successful figure often makes us open our eyes wider and take notice. Keats's "deep-browed Homer" arouses our interest in Homer as "thoughtful Homer" or "meditative Homer" does not. Similarly when W. B. Yeats says (page 558):

> An aged man is but a paltry thing,
> A tattered coat upon a stick, unless
> Soul clap its hands and sing, and louder sing
> For every tatter in its mortal dress,

the metaphoric identification of an old man with a scarecrow jolts us out of all our usual unthinking attitudes about old men as kind, happy folk content to have passed from youth to senior citizenship.

Finally, two points must be made: first, though figurative language is common in poetry it is not essential; and second, a poem that seems to contain no figures may in fact be one extended figure. Let us take the first point first. The anonymous ballad "Edward" (page 440) contains no figures, yet surely it is a poem and no one would say that the addition of figures would make it a better poem. Here is another poem that employs no figures, the epigraph to Robert Frost's *Collected Poems*.

Robert Frost (1874–1963)

The Pasture

I'm going out to clean the pasture spring;
I'll only stop to rake the leaves away
(And wait to watch the water clear, I may):
I shan't be gone long. — You come too.

I'm going out to fetch the little calf
That's standing by the mother. It's so young
It totters when she licks it with her tongue.
I shan't be gone long. — You come too.

Everything here can be taken literally; someone might have said this to someone else, and there is not a word in it that is illogical. Yet surely it is a poem. Now for the second point, that an entire poem may be an extended figure. By placing "The Pasture" at the opening of his *Collected Poems,* Frost allows us to read it as a figure; the invitation to accompany the speaker on a trip to the pasture can easily be read as an invitation to accompany the poet on a trip to the poet's world — his poems. But even in isolation the poem as a whole is more than the sum of its parts. The clearing of the water, the calf solicitously tended by its mother and by the speaker, somehow join, and somehow are related to the speaker's solicitous care for the "you" whom he addresses, and we feel that the poem is not only about what the speaker plans to do, but about the loving care that enhances life.

Here is another short poem. Does it contain any figures of speech?

William Carlos Williams (1883–1963)

The Red Wheelbarrow

so much depends
upon

a red wheel
barrow

glazed with rain
water

beside the white
chickens.

The following poems rely heavily on figures of speech.

Alfred, Lord Tennyson (1809–1892)

The Eagle

Fragment

He clasps the crag with crooked hands;
Close to the sun in lonely lands,
Ringed with the azure world, he stands.
The wrinkled sea beneath him crawls:
He watches from his mountain walls,
And like a thunderbolt he falls.

QUESTIONS

1. What figure is used in line 1? In line 4? In line 6? Can it be argued that the figures give us a sense of the eagle that is not to be found in a literal description?
2. In line 2 we get overstatement, or hyperbole, for the eagle is not really close to the sun. Suppose instead of "close to the sun" Tennyson had written "Waiting on high"? Would the poem be improved or worsened?

Emily Dickinson (1830–1886)

Because I could not stop for Death

Because I could not stop for Death —
He kindly stopped for me —
The Carriage held but just Ourselves —
And Immortality.   *4*

We slowly drove — He knew no haste
And I had put away
My labor and my leisure too,
For His Civility —   *8*

We passed the School, where Children strove
At Recess — in the Ring —
We passed the Fields of Gazing Grain —
We passed the Setting Sun —   *12*

Or rather — He passed Us —
The Dews drew quivering and chill —
For only Gossamer, my Gown —
My Tippet — only Tulle —   *16*

We paused before a House that seemed
A Swelling of the Ground —
The Roof was scarcely visible —
The Cornice — in the Ground —   *20*

Since then — 'tis Centuries — and yet
Feels shorter than the Day
I first surmised the Horses' Heads
Were toward Eternity —   *24*

QUESTIONS

1. Characterize death as it appears in lines 1–8.
2. What is the significance of the details and their arrangement
   in the third stanza? Why "strove" rather than "played" (line
   9)? What meanings does "Ring" (line 10) have? Is "Gazing
   Grain" better than "Golden Grain"?
3. The "House" in the fifth stanza is a sort of riddle. What is
   the answer? Does this stanza introduce an aspect of death
   not present — or present only very faintly — in the rest of
   the poem? Explain.

Randall Jarrell (1914–1965)

The Death of the Ball Turret Gunner

From my mother's sleep I fell into the State,
And I hunched in its belly till my wet fur froze.
Six miles from earth, loosed from its dream of life,
I woke to black flak and the nightmare fighters.
When I died they washed me out of the turret with a hose.

Jarrell has furnished an explanatory note: "A ball turret was a plexiglass sphere set into the belly of a B-17 or B-24, and inhabited by two .50 caliber machine-guns and one man, a short small man. When this gunner tracked with his machine-guns a fighter attacking his bomber from below, he revolved with the turret; hunched upside-down in his little sphere, he looked like the fetus in the womb. The fighters which attacked him were armed with cannon firing explosive shells. The hose was a steam hose."

QUESTIONS

1. What is implied in the first line? In "I woke to . . . nightmare"? Taking account of the title, is "wet fur" literal or metaphoric or both? Is the simplicity of the last line anticlimactic? How does it continue the metaphor of birth?
2. What effect is gained by having punctuation at the end of every line?

Sylvia Plath (1932–1963)

Mushrooms

Overnight, very
Whitely, discreetly,
Very quietly

Our toes, our noses
Take hold on the loam,   5
Acquire the air.

Nobody sees us,
Stops us, betrays us;
The small grains make room.

Soft fists insist on   *10*
Heaving the needles,
The leafy bedding,

Even the paving.
Our hammers, our rams,
Earless and eyeless,   *15*

Perfectly voiceless,
Widen the crannies,
Shoulder through holes. We

Diet on water,
On crumbs of shadow,   *20*
Bland-mannered, asking

Little or nothing.
So many of us!
So many of us!

We are shelves, we are   *25*
Tables, we are meek,
We are edible,

Nudgers and shovers
In spite of ourselves.
Our kind multiplies: *30*

We shall by morning
Inherit the earth.
Our foot's in the door.

QUESTIONS

1. In two or three sentences set forth the characteristics of mushrooms — real mushrooms — that Plath makes use of.
2. Line 32 is indebted to Jesus's words in Matthew 5:5: "Blessed
   are the meek, for they shall inherit the earth," one of eight
   short sayings called the Beatitudes. The first of these is "Blessed
   are the poor in spirit, for theirs is the kingdom of heaven."
   "The meek," like "the poor in spirit," refers to the "pious."
   Is this what Plath's poem is about?
3. Is there any basis for deciding whether the mushrooms represent all people or only one kind of person?

12

Figurative Language: Imagery and Symbolism

When we read "rose" we may more or less call to mind a picture of a rose, or perhaps we are reminded of the odor or texture of a rose. Whatever in a poem appeals to any of our senses (including sensations of heat and pressure as well as of sight, smell, taste, touch, sound) is an **image.** In short, images are the sensory content of a work, whether literal or figurative. Waller's rose (page 488) is an image that happens to be compared in the first stanza to the woman ("I resemble her to thee"); later in the poem this image comes to stand for "all things rare." Yet we never forget that the rose is a rose, and that the poem is chiefly a revelation of the poet's attitude toward his beloved.

When a poet says "My rose" and he is speaking about a rose, we have no figure of speech — though we still have an image. If, however, "My rose" is a shortened form of "My beloved is a rose," some would say that he is using a metaphor, but others would say that because the first term is omitted ("My beloved is"), the rose is a **symbol.** A poem about the transience of a rose might, for example, compel the reader to feel that the transience of female beauty is the larger theme even though it is never explicitly stated.

Some symbols are **conventional symbols,** which people have agreed to accept as standing for something other than themselves: a poem about the cross would probably be about Christianity.

Similarly, the rose has long been a symbol for love. In Virginia Woolf's novel *Mrs. Dalloway,* the husband communicates his love by proffering this conventional symbol: "He was holding out flowers — roses, red and white roses. (But he could not bring himself to say he loved her; not in so many words.)" Objects that are not conventional symbols, however, may also give rise to rich, multiple, indefinable associations. (Nonconventional symbolism is evident in Faulkner's "The Bear," page 47, a highly symbolic story in which the wilderness, the bear, the compass, the dog, and other things acquire a significance far beyond anything that tradition has attributed to them.) The following poem uses the traditional symbol of the rose, but uses it in a nontraditional way.

William Blake (1757–1827)

The Sick Rose

O Rose, thou art sick.
The invisible worm
That flies in the night
In the howling storm

Has found out thy bed
Of crimson joy,
And his dark secret love
Does thy life destroy.

One might perhaps argue that the worm is "invisible" (line 2) merely because it is hidden within the rose, but an "invisible worm / That flies in the night" is more than a long, slender, softbodied creeping animal; and a rose that has, or is, a "bed/ Of crimson joy" is more than a gardener's rose. Blake's worm and rose suggest things beyond themselves — a stranger, more vibrant world than the world we are usually aware of. One finds oneself half-thinking, for example, that the worm is male, the rose female, and that the poem is about the violation of virginity. Or that the poem is about the destruction of beauty: woman's beauty, rooted in joy, is destroyed by a power that feeds on her. But these interpretations are not fully satisfying: the poem presents a worm and a rose, and yet it is not merely about a worm and a rose.

These objects resonate, stimulating our thoughts toward something else, but the something else is elusive, whereas it is not elusive in Burns's "A Red, Red Rose" or in Waller's "Go, lovely rose."

A **symbol,** then, is an image so loaded with significance that it is not simply literal, and it does not simply stand for something else; it is both itself *and* something else that it richly suggests, a kind of manifestation of something too complex or too elusive to be otherwise revealed. Blake's poem is about a blighted rose and at the same time about much more. In a symbol, as Thomas Carlyle wrote, "the Infinite is made to blend with the Finite, to stand visible, and as it were, attainable there."* Probably it is not fanciful to say that the American slaves who sang " Joshua fought the battle of Jericho,/ And the walls came tumbling down" were singing both about an ancient occurrence *and* about a new embodiment of the ancient, the imminent collapse of slavery in the nineteenth century. Not one or the other, but both: the present partook of the past, and the past partook of the present.

D. H. Lawrence (1885–1930)

Snake

A snake came to my water-trough
On a hot, hot day, and I in pajamas for the heat,
To drink there.

In the deep, strange-scented shade of the great dark carob-tree
I came down the steps with my pitcher   5
And must wait, must stand and wait, for there he was at the
      trough before me.

---

* Isabel C. Hungerland defines a symbol somewhat differently. She says:

A man may remind me of my father, a kitchen bowl of a certain recipe; neither, according to my proposal, is *ipso facto* a symbol.

    What is lacking? . . . It is the transference of trains of thought and the accompanying attitude and feelings (which may work mainly in one or in both directions) from one object to another. If I began to think and feel about a man, in certain respects, as I did about my father, and to treat him as I treated my father, then he becomes a father symbol for me. Analogously, in fictional contexts, when we transfer trains of thought and the related attitudes and feelings from one object to another, a symbol is established.

                     — *Poetic Discourse* (Berkeley, Cal., 1958), p. 138

He reached down from a fissure in the earth-wall in the gloom
And trailed his yellow-brown slackness soft-bellied down, over
    the edge of the stone trough
And rested his throat upon the stone bottom,
And where the water had dripped from the tap,
    in a small clearness,   *10*
He sipped with his straight mouth,
Softly drank through his straight gums, into his slack long body,
Silently.

Someone was before me at my water-trough,
And I, like a second comer, waiting.   *15*

He lifted his head from his drinking, as cattle do,
And looked at me vaguely, as drinking cattle do,
And flickered his two-forked tongue from his lips,
    and mused a moment,
And stooped and drank a little more,
Being earth-brown, earth-golden from the
    burning bowels of the earth   *20*
On the day of Sicilian July, with Etna smoking.

The voice of my education said to me
He must be killed,
For in Sicily the black, black snakes are innocent,
    the gold are venomous.

And voices in me said, If you were a man   *25*
You would take a stick and break him now, and finish him off.

But must I confess how I liked him,
How glad I was he had come like a guest in quiet,
    to drink at my water-trough
And depart peaceful, pacified, and thankless,
Into the burning bowels of this earth?   *30*

Was it cowardice, that I dared not kill him?
Was it perversity, that I longed to talk to him?
Was it humility, to feel so honored?
I felt so honored.

And yet those voices: *35*
If you were not afraid, you would kill him!

And truly I was afraid, I was most afraid,
But even so, honored still more
That he should seek my hospitality
From out the dark door of the secret earth.   *40*

He drank enough
And lifted his head, dreamily, as one who has drunken,
And flickered his tongue like a forked night on the air, so black,
Seeming to lick his lips,
And looked around like a god, unseeing, into the air,   *45*
And slowly turned his head,
And slowly, very slowly, as if thrice adream,
Proceeded to draw his slow length curving round
And climb again the broken bank of my wall-face.

And as he put his head into that dreadful hole,   *50*
And as he slowly drew up, snake-easing his shoulders,
        and entered farther,
A sort of horror, a sort of protest against his withdrawing
        into that horrid black hole,
Deliberately going into the blackness, and slowly
        drawing himself after,
Overcame me now his back was turned.

I looked round, I put down my pitcher,   *55*
I picked up a clumsy log
And threw it at the water-trough with a clatter.

I think it did not hit him,
But suddenly that part of him that was left behind
        convulsed in undignified haste,
Writhed like lightning, and was gone   *60*
Into the black hole, the earth-lipped fissure in the wall-front,
At which, in the intense still noon, I stared with fascination.

And immediately I regretted it.
I thought how paltry, how vulgar, what a mean act!
I despised myself and the voices of my accursed
        human education.   *65*

And I thought of the albatross,
And I wished he would come back, my snake.

For he seemed to me again like a king,
Like a king in exile, uncrowned in the underworld,
Now due to be crowned again.   *70*

And so, I missed my chance with one of the lords
Of life.
And I have something to expiate:
A pettiness.

QUESTIONS

1. In line 6 and later Lawrence calls the snake "he"; in line 14 "someone," thus elevating the snake. What other figures are used to give the snake dignity? How does Lawrence diminish himself?

2. What is meant by "The voice of my education" (line 22)? It explicitly speaks in lines 23–26. Where else in the poem do we hear this voice? What might we call the opposing voice?

When Coleridge published "Kubla Khan" in 1816, he prefaced it with this explanatory note:

The following fragment is here published at the request of a poet of great and deserved celebrity, and, as far as the author's own opinions are concerned, rather as a psychological curiosity, than on the ground of any supposed *poetic* merits.

In the summer of the year 1797, the author, then in ill health, had retired to a lonely farmhouse between Porlock and Linton, on the Exmoor confines of Somerset and Devonshire. In consequence of a slight indisposition, an anodyne had been prescribed, from the effects of which he fell asleep in his chair at the moment that he was reading the following sentence, or words of the same substance, in *Purchas's Pilgrimage:* "Here the Khan Kubla commanded a palace to be built, and a stately garden thereunto. And thus ten miles of fertile ground were inclosed with a wall." The author continued for about three hours in a profound sleep, at least of the external senses, during which time he has the most vivid confidence that he could not have composed less than from two to three hundred lines; if that indeed can be called composition in which all the images rose up before him as *things,* with a parallel production of the correspondent expressions, without any sensation or consciousness of effort. On awaking he appeared to himself to have a distinct recollection of the whole, and taking his pen, ink, and paper, instantly and eagerly wrote down the lines that are here preserved. At this moment he was unfortunately called out by a person on business from Porlock, and detained by him above an hour, and on his return to his room, found, to his no small surprise and mortification, that though he still retained some vague and dim recollection of the general purport of the vision, yet, with the exception of some eight or ten scattered lines and images, all the rest had passed away like the images on the surface of a stream into which a stone has been cast, but, alas! without the after restoration of the latter!

Then all the charm
Is broken — all that phantom world so fair
Vanishes, and a thousand circlets spread,
And each misshape[s] the other. Stay awhile,
Poor youth! who scarcely dar'st lift up thine eyes —
The stream will soon renew its smoothness, soon
The visions will return! And lo, he stays,
And soon the fragments dim of lovely forms
Come trembling back, unite, and now once more
The pool becomes a mirror.

— Coleridge, from *The Picture; or, the Lover's Resolution,*
lines 91–100

Yet from the still surviving recollections in his mind, the author has frequently purposed to finish for himself what had been originally, as it were, given to him. Σαμερον αδιον ασω [today I shall sing more sweetly]: But the tomorrow is yet to come.

Samuel Taylor Coleridge *(1772–1834)*

Kubla Khan

Or, A Vision in a Dream. A Fragment.

In Xanadu did Kubla Khan
A stately pleasure-dome decree:
Where Alph, the sacred river, ran
Through caverns measureless to man
    Down to a sunless sea.   *5*
So twice five miles of fertile ground
With walls and towers were girdled round:
And here were gardens bright with sinuous rills,
Where blossomed many an incense-bearing tree;
And here were forests ancient as the hills,   *10*
Enfolding sunny spots of greenery.

But oh! that deep romantic chasm which slanted
Down the green hill athwart a cedarn cover!
A savage place! as holy and enchanted
As e'er beneath a waning moon was haunted   *15*
By woman wailing for her demon-lover!
And from this chasm, with ceaseless turmoil seething,
As if this earth in fast thick pants were breathing

A mighty fountain momently was forced;
Amid whose swift half-intermitted burst   *20*
Huge fragments vaulted like rebounding hail,
Or chaffy grain beneath the thresher's flail:
And 'mid these dancing rocks at once and ever
It flung up momently the sacred river.
Five miles meandering with a mazy motion   *25*
Through wood and dale the sacred river ran,
Then reached the caverns measureless to man,
And sank in tumult to a lifeless ocean:
And 'mid this tumult Kubla heard from far
Ancestral voices prophesying war!   *30*
      The shadow of the dome of pleasure
      Floated midway on the waves;
      Where was heard the mingled measure
      From the fountain and the caves.
It was a miracle of rare device,   *35*
A sunny pleasure-dome with caves of ice!
      A damsel with a dulcimer
      In a vision once I saw:
      It was an Abyssinian maid,
      And on her dulcimer she played,   *40*
      Singing of Mount Abora.
      Could I revive within me
      Her symphony and song,
      To such a deep delight 'twould win me,
That with music loud and long,   *45*
I would build that dome in air,
That sunny dome! those caves of ice!
And all who heard should see them there,
And all should cry, Beware! Beware!
His flashing eyes, his floating hair!   *50*
Weave a circle round him thrice,
And close your eyes with holy dread,
For he on honey-dew hath fed,
And drunk the milk of Paradise.

QUESTIONS

1. Coleridge changed the "palace" of his source into a "dome"
   (line 2). What are the relevant associations of "dome"?
2. What pairs of contrasts (e.g., underground river, fountain)
   do you find? What do they contribute to the poem?
3. If Coleridge had not said that the poem is a fragment, might

it seem to us to be a complete poem, the first thirty-six lines describing the creative imagination, and the remainder lamenting the loss of poetic power?

Wallace Stevens (1879–1955)

Anecdote of the Jar

I placed a jar in Tennessee,
And round it was, upon a hill.
It made the slovenly wilderness
Surround that hill.   *4*

The wilderness rose up to it,
And sprawled around, no longer wild.
The jar was round upon the ground
And tall and of a port in air.   *8*

It took dominion everywhere.
The jar was gray and bare.
It did not give of bird or bush,
Like nothing else in Tennessee.   *12*

Stevens, asked for an interpretation of another poem, said (in *The Explicator,* November 1948): "Things that have their origin in the imagination or in the emotions (poems). . . very often take on a form that is ambiguous or uncertain. It is not possible to attach a single, rational meaning to such things without destroying the imaginative or emotional ambiguity or uncertainty that is inherent in them and that is why poets do not like to explain. That the meanings given by others are sometimes meanings not intended by the poet or that were never present in his mind does not impair them as meanings."

QUESTIONS

1. What is the meaning of line 8? Check "port" in a dictionary.
2. Does the poem suggest that the jar organizes slovenly nature,

or that the jar impoverishes abundant nature? Or both, or
neither? Is the jar a symbol of the imagination, or of the
arts, or of man's material progress?

Wallace Stevens (1879–1955)

The Emperor of Ice-Cream

Call the roller of big cigars,
The muscular one, and bid him whip
In kitchen cups concupiscent curds.
Let the wenches dawdle in such dress
As they are used to wear, and let the boys   5
Bring flowers in last month's newspapers.
Let be be finale of seem.
The only emperor is the emperor of ice-cream.

Take from the dresser of deal,°   *fir or pine wood*
Lacking the three glass knobs, that sheet   **10**
On which she embroidered fantails once
And spread it so as to cover her face.
If her horny feet protrude, they come
To show how cold she is, and dumb.
Let the lamp affix its beam.   **15**
The only emperor is the emperor of ice-cream.

QUESTION

What associations does one have with the word "emperor"?
With "ice-cream"? What, then, can we make of "the emperor
of ice-cream"? The poem describes the preparations for a
wake, and in line 15 ("Let the lamp affix its beam") it insists
on facing the reality of death. In this context, then, what
can we make out of the last line of each stanza?

The words "Second Coming" normally refer to Christ's return
to earth on the last day, predicted in Matthew 24, but in his poem
with this title Yeats draws also on St. John's vision in Revelations,
of the coming of the beast of the Apocalypse, Antichrist, a great
antagonist who was expected to set himself against Christ in the

days just before the Second Coming. Yeats wrote the poem in 1919, probably stimulated by the Russian Revolution of 1917, but he later spoke of the poem as prophesying the rise of fascism. In a complex prose work, *A Vision* (1925), Yeats sets forth his cyclical theory of history. According to this theory of cycles or "gyres" (note line 1) "each age unwinds the threads another age had wound." Thus, Persia (the east) fell and Greece (the west) arose; Rome (the west) fell and Byzantium, later called Constantinople and now called Istanbul (the east) rose; Byzantium fell and the west rose in the renaissance, "all things dying each other's life, living each other's death." The Age of Christianity, an age that is "levelling, unifying, feminine, humane, [with] peace its means and end," will be followed by an age which is "hierarchical, multiple, masculine, harsh, surgical." Having offered this capsule comment of Yeats's views of history, we want to caution the reader that the poem has an independent life. In Yeats's poem "the Second Coming" is not of Christ but of an Antichrist in the form of a sphinx ("lion body and the head of a man").

William Butler Yeats *(1865–1939)*

The Second Coming

Turning and turning in the widening gyre° *circular or spiral motion*
The falcon cannot hear the falconer;
Things fall apart; the center cannot hold;
Mere anarchy is loosed upon the world,
The blood-dimmed tide is loosed, and everywhere   *5*
The ceremony of innocence is drowned;
The best lack all conviction, while the worst
Are full of passionate intensity.

Surely some revelation is at hand;
Surely the Second Coming is at hand;   *10*
The Second Coming! Hardly are those words out
When a vast image out of *Spiritus Mundi*° *Soul of the Universe*
Troubles my sight: somewhere in the sands of the desert
A shape with lion body and the head of a man,
A gaze blank and pitiless as the sun,   *15*
Is moving its slow thighs, while all about it
Reel shadows of the indignant desert birds.
The darkness drops again; but now I know

That twenty centuries of stony sleep
Were vexed to nightmare by a rocking cradle,   *20*
And what rough beast, its hour come round at last,
Slouches towards Bethlehem to be born?

QUESTIONS

1. What is the connection between the first two lines, about
   the falcon and falconer, and line 3, "Mere anarchy is loosed
   upon the world"?

2. Do you imagine that an educated pagan of, say, the second
   or third century A.D. might have said of the new creed and
   its adherents that "things fall apart" (line 3) and that "the
   best [of our age] lack all conviction, while the worst / Are
   full of passionate intensity"?

3. Why is the beast slouching "towards Bethlehem" (line 22)?
   What line earlier in the poem connects with Bethlehem?

13
Irony and Paradox

There is a kind of discourse which, though nonliteral, need not use similes, metaphors, apostrophes, personification, or symbols. A speaker, without using these figures, may say things that are not to be taken literally. He may, in short, employ **irony.** In Greek comedy the *eiron* was the sly underdog who, by dissembling inferiority, outwitted his opponent. As Aristotle put it, irony (employed by the *eiron*) is a "pretense tending toward the underside" of truth. Later, Cicero somewhat altered the meaning of the word: he defined it as saying one thing and meaning another *(aliud dicere ac sentias),* and he held that Socrates, who feigned ignorance and let his opponents entrap themselves in their own arguments, was the ironist par excellence.

In **verbal irony,** as the term is now used, what is stated is in some degree negated by what is suggested. A classic example is Lady Macbeth's order to get ready for King Duncan's visit: "He that's coming/ Must be provided for." The words seem to say that she and Macbeth must busy themselves with household preparations so that the king may be received in appropriate style, but this suggestion of hospitality is undercut by an opposite meaning: preparations must be made for the murder of the king. Two other examples of verbal irony are Melville's comment,

> What like a bullet can undeceive!

and the lover's assertion (in Marvell's "To His Coy Mistress") that

> The grave's a fine and private place,
> But none, I think, do there embrace.

Under Marvell's cautious words we detect a wryness; the **understatement** masks yet reveals a deep-felt awareness of mortality and the barrenness of the grave. The self-mockery in this understatement proclaims modesty, but suggests assurance. The speaker here, like most ironists, is both playful and serious at once. Irony packs a great deal into a few words.* What we call irony here, it should be mentioned, is often called **sarcasm,** but a distinction can be made: sarcasm is notably contemptuous and crude or heavy-handed ("You're a great guy, a real friend," said to a friend who won't lend you ten dollars), and this is only one kind of irony, and a kind almost never found in literature.

Overstatement (hyperbole) as well as understatement is ironic when it contains a contradictory suggestion:

> For Brutus is an honorable man;
> So are they all, all honorable men.

The sense of contradiction that is inherent in verbal irony is also inherent in a paradox. **Paradox** has several meanings for philosophers, but we need only be concerned with its meaning of an apparent contradiction. In Gerard Manley Hopkins's "Spring and Fall" (page 471), there is an apparent contradiction in the assertions that Margaret is weeping for the woods (line 2) and for herself (line 15), but the contradiction is not real: both the woods and Margaret are parts of the nature blighted by Adam's sin. Other paradoxes are:

> The child is father of the man;
>
> — Wordsworth

and (on the soldiers who died to preserve the British Empire):

> The saviors come not home tonight;
> Themselves they could not save;
>
> — Housman

and:

> One short sleep past, we wake eternally,
> And Death shall be no more; Death, thou shalt die.
>
> — Donne

Donne's lines are a reminder that paradox is not only an instrument of the poet. Christianity embodies several paradoxes: God became man; through the death on the cross, man can obtain eternal life; man does not live fully until he dies.

Some critics have put a high premium on ironic and paradoxical

---

* A word of caution: We have been talking about verbal irony, not **irony of situation.** Like ironic words, ironic situations have in them an element of contrast. A clown whose heart is breaking must make his audience laugh; an author's worst book is her only financial success; a fool solves a problem that vexes the wise.

poetry. Briefly, the argument runs that great poetry recognizes the complexity of experience, and that irony and paradox are ways of doing justice to this complexity. I. A. Richards uses "irony" to denote "The bringing in of the opposite, the complementary impulses," and suggests (in *The Principles of Literary Criticism*) that irony in this sense is a characteristic of poetry of "the highest order." It is dubious that all poets must always bring in the opposite, but it is certain that much poetry is ironic and paradoxical.

Percy Bysshe Shelley (1792–1822)

Ozymandias

I met a traveler from an antique land
Who said: Two vast and trunkless legs of stone
Stand in the desert . . . Near them, on the sand,
Half sunk, a shattered visage lies, whose frown,   *4*
And wrinkled lip, and sneer of cold command,
Tell that its sculptor well those passions read
Which yet survive, stamped on these lifeless things,
The hand that mocked them, and the heart that fed: *8*
And on the pedestal these words appear:
"My name is Ozymandias, king of kings:
Look on my works, ye Mighty, and despair!"
Nothing beside remains. Round the decay   *12*
Of that colossal wreck, boundless and bare
The lone and level sands stretch far away.

Lines 4–8 are somewhat obscure, but the gist is that the passions — still evident in the "shattered visage" — survive the sculptor's hand that "mocked" — that is, (1) copied, (2) derided — them, and the passions also survive the king's heart that had nourished them.

QUESTION

There is, of course, a sort of irony of plot here: Ozymandias believed that he created enduring works, but his intentions came to nothing. However, another sort of irony is also present: How are his words, in a way he did not intend, true?

William Shakespeare (1564–1616)

Sonnet 146

Poor soul, the center of my sinful earth,
My sinful earth these rebel pow'rs that thee array,
Why dost thou pine within and suffer dearth,
Painting thy outward walls so costly gay?   *4*
Why so large cost,° having so short a lease,   *expense*
Dost thou upon thy fading mansion spend?
Shall worms, inheritors of this excess,
Eat up thy charge? Is this thy body's end?   *8*
Then, soul, live thou upon thy servant's loss,
And let that pine to aggravate thy store;
Buy terms divine° in selling hours of dross;   *buy ages of immortality*
Within be fed, without be rich no more.   *12*
    So shalt thou feed on Death, that feeds on men,
    And death once dead, there's no more dying then.

QUESTIONS

1. In line 2, "My sinful earth" is doubtless a printer's error, an unintentional repetition of the last word of the first line. Among suggested emendations are "Thrall to," "Fooled by," "Rebuke these," "Leagued with," "Feeding." Which do you prefer? Why?
2. What is the tone of the first two lines? Where in the poem does the thought take its chief turn? What is the tone of the couplet?
3. What does "array" (line 2) mean?
4. Explain the paradox in lines 13–14.
5. In a poem on the relation between the body and soul, is battle imagery surprising? Commercial imagery (lines 5–12)? What other imagery is in the poem? Is the sonnet a dull preachment? If not, why not?

Stevie Smith (1902–1971)

Not Waving but Drowning

Nobody heard him, the dead man,
But still he lay moaning:

I was much further out than you thought
And not waving but drowning.   *4*

Poor chap, he always loved larking
And now he's dead
It must have been too cold for him his heart gave way,
They said.   *8*

Oh, no no no, it was too cold always
(Still the dead one lay moaning)
I was much too far out all my life
And not waving but drowning.   *12*

QUESTIONS

1. What sort of man did the friends of the dead man think he
   was? What sort of man was he?
2. The first line, "Nobody heard him, the dead man," is of
   course literally true. Dead men do not speak. In what other
   ways is it true?

John Crowe Ransom (1888–1974)

Bells for John Whiteside's Daughter

There was such speed in her little body,
And such lightness in her footfall,
It is no wonder her brown study
Astonishes us all.   *4*

Her wars were bruited in our high window.
We looked among orchard trees and beyond
Where she took arms against her shadow,
Or harried unto the pond   *8*

The lazy geese, like a snow cloud
Dripping their snow on the green grass,
Tricking and stopping, sleepy and proud,
Who cried in goose, Alas,   *12*

For the tireless heart within the little
Lady with rod that made them rise
From their noon apple-dreams and scuttle
Goose-fashion under the skies!   *16*

But now go the bells, and we are ready,
In one house we are sternly stopped
To say we are vexed at her brown study,
Lying so primly propped.   *20*

QUESTIONS

1. What is the usual meaning of "a brown study" in line 3?
   For what is it an understatement here? What is meant by
   "her wars" (line 5)? What are the literal and figurative suggestions of "took arms against her shadow" in line 7?
2. Why is "tireless heart" (line 13) ironic?
3. In line 17 the speaker says "we are ready." Ready for what?
   What word in a later line indicates that he is not "ready"?

Andrew Marvell (1621–1678)

To His Coy Mistress

Had we but world enough, and time,
This coyness, lady, were no crime.
We would sit down, and think which way
To walk, and pass our long love's day.
Thou by the Indian Ganges' side   *5*
Should'st rubies find: I by the tide
Of Humber would complain.° I would   *write love poems*
Love you ten years before the Flood,
And you should, if you please, refuse
Till the conversion of the Jews.   *10*
My vegetable° love should grow   *i.e., unconsciously growing*
Vaster than empires, and more slow.
An hundred years should go to praise
Thine eyes, and on thy forehead gaze:
Two hundred to adore each breast: *15*
But thirty thousand to the rest.
An age at least to every part,
And the last age should show your heart.
For, lady, you deserve this state,
Nor would I love at lower rate.   *20*
        But at my back I always hear
Time's winged chariot hurrying near;
And yonder all before us lie

Deserts of vast eternity.
Thy beauty shall no more be found,   *25*
Nor in thy marble vault shall sound
My echoing song; then worms shall try
That long preserved virginity,
And your quaint honor turn to dust,
And into ashes all my lust.   *30*
The grave's a fine and private place,
But none, I think, do there embrace.
    Now therefore, while the youthful hue
Sits on thy skin like morning dew,
And while thy willing soul transpires   *35*
At every pore with instant fires,
Now let us sport us while we may;
And now, like am'rous birds of prey,
Rather at once our time devour,
Than languish in his slow-chapt° power,   *slowly devouring* **40**
Let us roll all our strength, and all
Our sweetness, up into one ball;
And tear our pleasures with rough strife
Thorough° the iron gates of life.   *through*
Thus, though we cannot make our sun   **45**
Stand still, yet we will make him run.

QUESTIONS

1. Are the assertions in lines 1–20 so inflated that we detect behind them a playfully ironic tone? Explain. Why does the speaker say, in line 8, that he would love "ten years before the Flood," rather than merely "since the Flood"?

2. Explain lines 21–24. Why is time behind the speaker, and eternity in front of him? Is this "eternity" the same as the period discussed in lines 1–20? Discuss the change in the speaker's tone after line 20.

3. Do you agree with the comment on pages 507–508 about the understatement in lines 31–32? What more can be said about these lines, in context?

4. Why "am'rous birds of prey" (line 38) rather than the conventional doves? Is the idea of preying continued in the poem?

5. Explain the last two lines, and characterize the speaker's tone. Are they anticlimactic?

6. The poem is organized in the form of an argument. Trace the steps.

John Donne *(1572–1631)*

The Flea

Mark but this flea, and mark in this
How little that which thou deny'st me is;
It sucked me first, and now sucks thee,
And in this flea our two bloods mingled be;
Thou know'st that this cannot be said   5
A sin, nor shame, nor loss of maidenhead;
      Yet this enjoys before it woo,
      And pampered swells with one blood made of two,
      And this, alas, is more than we would do.

Oh stay, three lives in one flea spare,   10
Where we almost, yea, more than married are.
This flea is you and I, and this
Our marriage bed and marriage temple is;
Though parents grudge, and you, we are met
And cloistered in these living walls of jet.   15
      Though use° make you apt to kill me,   *custom*
      Let not to that, self-murder added be,
      And sacrilege, three sins in killing three.

Cruel and sudden, hast thou since
Purpled thy nail in blood of innocence?   20
Wherein could this flea guilty be,
Except in that drop which it sucked from thee?
Yet thou triumph'st and say'st that thou
Find'st not thyself, nor me the weaker now.
      'Tis true. Then learn how false fears be: 25
      Just so much honor, when thou yield'st to me,
      Will waste, as this flea's death took life from thee.

QUESTIONS

1. What is hyperbolic about line 10? Why does the speaker
   overstate the matter in the second stanza? How does the
   overstatement serve to diminish the subject?
2. What has the lady done between the second and third stanzas?
   In line 25 the speaker says that the lady's view is "true."
   Has he changed his mind during the course of the poem, or
   has he been leading up to this point?

John Donne (1572–1631)

Holy Sonnet XIV

Batter my heart, three-personed God; for you
As yet but knock, breathe, shine, and seek to mend;
That I may rise and stand, o'erthrow me, and bend
Your force, to break, blow, burn, and make me new.   *4*
I, like an usurped town, to another due,
Labor to admit you, but oh, to no end,
Reason, your viceroy in me, me should defend,
But is captived, and proves weak or untrue.   *8*
Yet dearly I love you, and would be loved fain,
But am betrothed unto your enemy:
Divorce me, untie, or break that knot again,
Take me to you, imprison me, for I   *12*
Except you enthrall me, never shall be free,
Nor ever chaste, except you ravish me.

QUESTIONS

1. Explain the paradoxes in lines 1, 3, 13, 14. Explain the double meanings of "enthrall" (line 13) and "ravish" (line 14).
2. In lines 1–4 what is God implicitly compared to (considering especially lines 2 and 4)? How does this comparison lead into the comparison that dominates lines 5–8? What words in lines 9–12 are especially related to the earlier lines?
3. What is gained by piling up verbs in lines 2–4?
4. Are sexual references necessarily irreverent in a religious poem? Donne, incidentally, was an Anglican priest.

A. E. Housman (1859–1936)

Shropshire Lad #27

"Is my team ploughing,
       That I was used to drive
And hear the harness jingle
       When I was man alive?"   *4*

Ay, the horses trample,
    The harness jingles now;
No change though you lie under
    The land you used to plough.   *8*

"Is football playing
    Along the river shore,
With lads to chase the leather,
    Now I stand up no more?"   *12*

Ay, the ball is flying,
    The lads play heart and soul;
The goal stands up, the keeper
    Stands up to keep the goal.   *16*

"Is my girl happy,
    That I thought hard to leave,
And has she tired of weeping
    As she lies down at eve?"   *20*

Ay, she lies down lightly,
    She lies not down to weep:
Your girl is well contented.
    Be still, my lad, and sleep.   *24*

"Is my friend hearty,
    Now I am thin and pine,
And has he found to sleep in
    A better bed than mine?"   *28*

Yes, lad, I lie easy,
    I lie as lads would choose;
I cheer a dead man's sweetheart,
    Never ask me whose.   *32*

QUESTIONS

1. Characterize the speaker of the first, third, fifth, and seventh stanzas. Who is the speaker in the other stanzas?
2. How does the answer in the sixth stanza differ significantly from the answer in the second and fourth stanzas? How do you account for the difference?
3. If you have read any of the ballads in Chapter 8, and especially "Edward," list some of the characteristics in "Is My Team Ploughing" that show Housman's use of ballads.

Derek Mahon (b. 1941)

Rock Music

The ocean glittered quietly in the moonlight
While heavy metal rocked the discotheques;
Space-age Hondas farted half the night,
Fired by the prospect of fortuitous sex.   *4*
I sat late at the window, bland with rage,
And listened to the tumult down below,
Trying to concentrate on the printed page
As if such obsolete bumf could save us now.   *8*

Next morning, wandering on the strand, I heard
Left-over echoes of the night before
Dwindle to echoes, and a single bird
Drown with a whistle that residual roar.   *12*
Rock music started up on every side —
Whisper of algae, click of stone on stone,
A thousand limpets left by the ebb-tide
Unanimous in their silent inquisition.   *16*

QUESTIONS

1. Explain the title, taking account not only of line 2 but also of lines 13–16.
2. "Bumf" (line 8) presumably is a nonsense word meaning nonsense or trivia. If the "printed page" is bumf, and if the sounds of discotheques and of Hondas is bumf, according to the poem is there anything that is not bumf?

14
Rhythm

Ezra Pound (1885–1973)

An Immorality

Sing we for love and idleness,
Naught else is worth the having.

Though I have been in many a land,
There is naught else in living.

And I would rather have my sweet,
Though rose-leaves die of grieving,

Than do high deeds in Hungary
To pass all men's believing.

A good poem. To begin with, it sings; as Pound has said, "Poetry withers and dries out when it leaves music, or at least imagined music, too far behind it. Poets who are not interested in music are, or become, bad poets." The ballads in a preceding chapter, it must be remembered, are songs, and other poetry too is sung, especially by children. A child reciting a counting-out rhyme, or singing on his way home from school, is enjoying poetry:

> Pease-porridge hot,
>   Pease-porridge cold,
> Pease-porridge in the pot
>   Nine days old.

Nothing very important is being said, but for generations children have enjoyed the music of these lines, and adults, too, have recalled them with pleasure — though few people know what pease-porridge is.

The "music" — the catchiness of certain sounds — should not be underestimated. Here are lines chanted by the witches in *Macbeth:*

> Double, double, toil and trouble;
> Fire burn and cauldron bubble.

This is rather far from words that mean approximately the same thing: "Twice, twice, work and care; / Fire ignite, and pot boil." The difference is more in the sounds than in the instructions. What is lost in the paraphrase is the magic, the incantation, which resides in elaborate repetitions of sounds and stresses.

Rhythm (most simply, in English poetry, stresses at regular intervals) has a power of its own. A good march, said John Philip Sousa (the composer of "Stars and Stripes Forever") should make even a man with a wooden leg "step out." A highly pronounced rhythm is common in such forms of poetry as charms, college yells, and lullabies; all of them (like the witches' speech) are aimed at inducing a special effect magically. It is not surprising that *carmen,* the Latin word for poem or song, is also the Latin word for charm, and the word from which "charm" is derived.

> Rain, rain, go away;
> Come again another day.
>
> Block that kick! Block that kick! Block that kick!
>
> Rock-a-bye baby, on the tree top,
> When the wind blows, the cradle will rock.

In much poetry rhythm is only half-heard, but its omnipresence is suggested by the fact that when poetry is printed it is customary to begin each line with a capital letter. Prose (from Latin *prorsus,* "forward," "straight on") keeps running across the paper until the righthand margin is reached, and then, merely because the paper has given out, the writer or printer starts again at the left, with a small letter. But verse (Latin *versus,* "a turning") often ends well short of the righthand margin, and the next line begins at the left — usually with a capital — not because paper has run out but because the rhythmic pattern begins again. Lines of poetry are continually reminding us that they have a pattern.

Before turning to some other highly rhythmic pieces, a word of caution: a mechanical, unvarying rhythm may be good to put the baby to sleep, but it can be deadly to readers who wish to keep awake. A poet varies his rhythm according to his purpose; he ought not to be so regular that he is (in W. H. Auden's words) an "accentual pest." In competent hands, rhythm contributes to meaning; it says something. The rhythm in the lines from *Macbeth,* for example, helps suggest the strong binding power of magic. Again Ezra Pound has a relevant comment: "Rhythm *must* have meaning. It can't be merely a careless dash off, with no grip and no real hold to the words and sense, a tumty tum tumty tum tum ta." Some examples will be useful.

Consider this description of Hell from *Paradise Lost* (the heavier stresses are marked by ´):

Rócks, cáves, lákes, féns, bógs, déns, aňd shádes ŏf deáth.

Such a succession of stresses is highly unusual. Elsewhere in the poem Milton chiefly uses iambic feet — alternating unstressed and stressed syllables — but here he immediately follows one heavy stress with another, thereby helping to communicate the "meaning" — the impressive monotony of Hell. As a second example, consider the function of the rhythm in two lines by Alexander Pope:

Whĕn Ájăx stríves sŏme róck's vást wéight tŏ thrów,

Thĕ líne tóo lábŏrs, aňd thĕ wórds móve slów.

The heavier stresses (again, marked by ´) do not merely alternate with the lighter ones (marked ˘); rather, the great weight of the rock is suggested by three consecutive stressed words, "rock's vast weight," and the great effort involved in moving it is suggested by another three consecutive stresses, "line too labors," and by yet another three, "words move slow." Note, also, the abundant pauses within the lines. In the first line, unless one's speech is slovenly, one must pause at least slightly after "Ajax," "strives," "rock's," "vast," "weight," and "throw." The grating sounds in "Ajax" and "rocks" do their work, too, and so do the explosive *t*'s. When Pope wishes to suggest lightness, he reverses his procedure and he groups unstressed syllables:

Not so, when swift Camilla scours the plain,

Fliés o'ĕr th'ŭnbéndĭng córn, aňd skíms ălŏng thĕ máin.

This last line has twelve syllables, and is thus longer than the line about Ajax, but the addition of "along" helps to communicate lightness and swiftness because in this line (it can be argued) neither syllable of "along" is strongly stressed. If "along" is omitted, the line still makes grammatical sense and becomes more "regular," but it also becomes less imitative of lightness.

The very regularity of a line may be meaningful too. Shakespeare begins a sonnet thus:

Whĕn Í dŏ coúnt thĕ clóck thăt télls thĕ tíme.

This line about a mechanism runs with appropriate regularity. (It is worth noting, too, that "*c*ount the *c*lock" and "*t*ells the *t*ime" emphasize the regularity by the repetition of sounds and syntax.) But notice what Shakespeare does in the middle of the next line:

> Aňd sée thĕ bráve dáy súnk iň hídeŏus níght.

What has he done? And what is the effect?

Here is another poem that refers to a clock. In England, until capital punishment was abolished, executions regularly took place at 8:00 A.M.

A. E. Housman (1859–1936)
Eight O'Clock

He stood, and heard the steeple
    Sprinkle the quarters on the morning town.
One, two, three, four, to market-place and people
    It tossed them down.

Strapped, noosed, nighing his hour,
    He stood and counted them and cursed his luck;
And then the clock collected in the tower
    Its strength, and struck.

The chief (but not unvarying) pattern is iambic, that is, the odd syllables are less emphatic than the even ones, as in

> He stood, and heard the steeple

Try to mark the syllables, stressed and unstressed, in the rest of the poem. Be guided by your ear, not by a mechanical principle, and don't worry too much about difficult or uncertain parts; different readers may reasonably come up with different results.

QUESTIONS

1. Where do you find two or more consecutive stresses? What explanations (related to meaning) can be offered?
2. What is the effect of the short line at the end of each stanza? And what significance can we attach to the fact that these

lines (unlike the first and third lines in each stanza) end with
a stress?

Following are some poems in which the strongly felt pulsations
are highly important.

William Carlos Williams (1883–1963)

The Dance

In Breughel's great picture, The Kermess,
the dancers go round, they go round and
around, the squeal and the blare and the
tweedle of bagpipes, a bugle and fiddles
tipping their bellies (round as the thick-   *5*
sided glasses whose wash they impound)
their hips and their bellies off balance
to turn them. Kicking and rolling about
the Fair Grounds, swinging their butts, those
shanks must be sound to bear up under such   *10*
rollicking measures, prance as they dance
in Breughel's great picture, The Kermess.

QUESTIONS

1. Read the poem aloud several times, and decide where the
   heavy stresses fall. Mark the heavily stressed syllables (´),
   the lightly stressed ones (ˆ), and the unstressed ones (˘). Are
   all the lines identical? What effect is thus gained, especially
   when read aloud? What does the parenthetical statement (lines
   5–6) do to the rhythm? Does a final syllable often receive a
   heavy stress here? Are there noticeable pauses at the ends of
   the lines? What is the consequence? Are the dancers waltzing?
2. What syllables rhyme or are repeated (e.g., "round" in lines
   2 and 5, and "-pound" in line 6; "-ing" in lines 5, 8, 9, 11)?
   What effect do they have?
3. How does the absence at the beginning of each line of the
   customary capital contribute to the meaning? Why is the last
   line the same as the first?

Theodore Roethke (1908–1963)

My Papa's Waltz

The whiskey on your breath
Could make a small boy dizzy;
But I hung on like death:
Such waltzing was not easy.   *4*

We romped until the pans
Slid from the kitchen shelf;
My mother's countenance
Could not unfrown itself.   *8*

The hand that held my wrist
Was battered on one knuckle;
At every step you missed
My right ear scraped a buckle.   *12*

You beat time on my head
With a palm caked hard by dirt,
Then waltzed me off to bed
Still clinging to your shirt.   *16*

QUESTIONS

1. Is the rhythm more regular than in Williams's "The Dance"?
   Do the syntactical pauses vary much from stanza to stanza?
   Be specific. Would you say that the rhythm suggests lightness?
   Why?
2. Does the rhythm parallel, or ironically contrast with, the
   episode described? Was the dance a graceful waltz? Explain.
3. Explain the function of the stresses in lines 13–14.

Dylan Thomas (1914–1953)

Do not go gentle into that good night

Do not go gentle into that good night,
Old age should burn and rave at close of day;
Rage, rage against the dying of the light.

Though wise men at their end know dark is right,
Because their words had forked no lightning they   5
Do not go gentle into that good night.

Good men, the last wave by, crying how bright
Their frail deeds might have danced in a green bay,
Rage, rage against the dying of the light.

Wild men who caught and sang the sun in flight,   10
And learn, too late, they grieved it on its way,
Do not go gentle into that good night.

Grave men, near death, who see with blinding sight
Blind eyes could blaze like meteors and be gay,
Rage, rage against the dying of the light.   15

And you, my father, there on the sad height,
Curse, bless, me now with your fierce tears, I pray.
Do not go gentle into that good night.
Rage, rage against the dying of the light.

This poem is written in an elaborate French form, the **villanelle,**
that is, five tercets (stanzas of three lines each, the first and third
lines rhyming) and a final quatrain (stanza of four lines, the first,
third, and fourth lines all rhyming with the first and third lines
of the tercets, and the second line rhyming with the middle lines
of the tercets). Moreover, the first line of the poem is the last line
of the second and fourth tercets; the third line of the poem is the
last line of the third and fifth tercets, and these two lines reappear
yet again as a pair of rhyming lines at the end of the poem.

QUESTION

The intricate form of the villanelle might seem too fussy for
a serious poem about dying. Is it too fussy? Or does the
form here somehow succeed?

15

Some Principles of Versification

Robert Francis (b. 1901)

The Pitcher

His art is eccentricity, his aim
How not to hit the mark he seems to aim at,

His passion how to avoid the obvious,
His technique how to vary the avoidance.   *4*

The others throw to be comprehended. He
Throws to be a moment misunderstood.

Yet not too much. Not errant, arrant, wild,
But every seeming aberration willed.   *8*

Not to, yet still, still to communicate
Making the batter understand too late.

If you read this poem aloud, pausing appropriately where the
punctuation tells you to, you will hear the poet trying to represent
something of the pitcher's "eccentricity." ("Eccentric," by the
way, literally means "off center.") A pitcher tries to deceive a
batter, perhaps by throwing a ball that will unexpectedly curve
over the plate; the poet playfully deceives the reader, for instance
with unexpected pauses. In line 5, for example, he puts a heavy
pause (indicated by a period) not at the end of the line but just
before the end. Note, too, that some lines contain no pauses, but
the next-to-last line contains two within it and no pause at the

end of it, making us as uneasy as the batter. And what significance can be attached to the fact that only the last two lines really rhyme ("communicate: late"), whereas other lines are, so to speak, inconclusive: "aim: aim at," "wild: willed"?

The technical vocabulary of **prosody** (the study of the principles of verse structure, including meter, rhyme and other sound effects, and stanzaic patterns) is large. An understanding of these terms will not turn anyone into a poet, but it will enable one to discuss some aspects of poetry more efficiently. A knowledge of them, like a knowledge of most other technical terms (e.g., "misplaced modifier," "woofer," "automatic transmission") allows for quick and accurate communication. The following are the chief terms of prosody.

Most English poetry has a pattern of **stressed (accented)** sounds, and this pattern is the **meter** (from the Greek word for "measure"). Although in Old English poetry (poetry written in England before the Norman-French Conquest in 1066) a line may have any number of unstressed syllables in addition to four stressed syllables, most poetry written in England since the Conquest not only has a fixed number of stresses in a line but also a fixed number of unstressed syllables before or after each stressed one. (One really ought not to talk of "unstressed" or "unaccented" syllables, since to utter a syllable — however lightly — is to give it some stress. It is really a matter of *relative* stress, but the fact is that "unstressed" or "unaccented" are parts of the established terminology of versification.)

In a line of poetry the **foot** is the basic unit of measurement. On rare occasions it is a single stressed syllable; but generally a foot consists of two or three syllables, one of which is stressed. (Stress is indicated by ´; lack of stress by ˘.) The repetition of feet, then, produces a pattern of stresses throughout the poem.

Two cautions:

1. A poem will seldom contain only one kind of foot throughout; significant variations usually occur, but one kind of foot is dominant.

2. In reading a poem one pays attention to the sense as well as to the metrical pattern. By paying attention to the sense one often finds that the stress falls on a word that according to the metrical pattern would be unstressed. Or a word that according to the pattern would be stressed may be seen to be unstressed. Furthermore, by reading for sense one finds that not all stresses are equally heavy; some are almost as light as unstressed syllables, and sometimes there is a **hovering stress,** that is, the stress is equally distributed over two adjacent syllables. To repeat: one reads for sense, allowing the syntax to help indicate the stresses.

The most common feet in English poetry are:

iamb (adjective: **iambic**): one unstressed syllable followed by one stressed syllable. The iamb, said to be the most common pattern in English speech, is surely the most common in English poetry. It is called a **rising meter,** the foot rising toward the stress. The following example has five iambic feet:

Ĭ sáw | thĕ ský | dĕscénd | iňg bláck | aňd whíte.
— Robert Lowell

trochee (trochaic): one stressed syllable followed by one unstressed; a **falling meter,** the foot falling away from the stress.

Lét hĕr | líve tŏ | eárn hĕr | dínnĕrs.
— J. M. Synge

anapest (anapestic): two unstressed syllables followed by one stressed; a rising meter.

Thĕre aře mán | ў whŏ sáy | thăt ă dóg | hăs hĭs dáy.
— Dylan Thomas

dactyl (dactylic): one stressed syllable followed by two unstressed; a falling meter. This trisyllabic foot, like the anapest, is common in light verse, or verse suggesting joy, but its use is not limited to such material. Thomas Hood's sentimental "The Bridge of Sighs" begins:

Táke hĕr ŭp | téndĕrlў.

spondee (spondaic): two stressed syllables; most often used as a substitute for an iamb or trochee; it neither rises nor falls.

Smárt lád, | tŏ slíp | bĕtimes | ăwáy.
— A. E. Housman

Because the **pyrrhic foot** (two unstressed syllables) lacks a stress, it is often not considered a legitimate foot in English.

A metrical line consists of one or more feet and is named for the number of feet in it. The following names are used:

monometer:	one foot	**pentameter:**	five feet
dimeter:	two feet	**hexameter:**	six feet
trimeter:	three feet	**heptameter:**	seven feet
tetrameter:	four feet	**octameter:**	eight feet

A line is scanned for the kind and number of feet in it, and the **scansion** tells you if it is, say, anapestic trimeter (three anapests):

Ăs Ĭ cáme | tŏ thĕ edǵe | ŏf thĕ wóods.

— Frost

Another example, this time iambic pentameter:

Sĭñce bráss, | nŏr stóne, | nŏr eárth, | nŏr boúnd | lĕss séa.

— Shakespeare

In prosody, as in the rest of life, male chauvinism has left its mark: a line ending with a stress has a **masculine ending** or **strong ending;** a line ending with an unstressed syllable has a **feminine ending** or **weak ending.** The lines above by Synge and Hood have feminine endings; those by Lowell, Thomas, Housman, Frost, and Shakespeare have masculine endings.

The **caesura** (usually indicated by the symbol //) is a slight pause within the line. It need not be indicated by punctuation, and it does not affect the metrical count:

Awake, my St. John! // leave all meaner things
To low ambition, // and the pride of kings.
Let us // (since Life can little more supply
Than just to look about us // and to die)
Expatiate free // o'er all this scene of Man;
A mighty maze! // but not without a plan;
A wild, // where weeds and flowers promiscuous shoot;
Or garden, // tempting with forbidden fruit.

— Pope

The varying position of the caesura helps to give Pope's lines an informality that plays against the formality of the pairs of rhyming lines.

An **end-stopped line** concludes with a distinct syntactical pause, but a **run-on line** has its sense carried over into the next line without syntactical pause. (The running-on of a line is called **enjambment.**) In the following passage, only the first is a run-on line:

Yet if we look more closely we shall find
Most have the seeds of judgment in their mind:
Nature affords at least a glimmering light;
The lines, though touched but faintly, are drawn right.

— Pope

Meter produces **rhythm,** recurrences at equal intervals, but rhythm (from a Greek word meaning "flow") is usually applied to larger units than feet. Often it depends most obviously on pauses.

Thus, a poem with run-on lines will have a different rhythm

from a poem with end-stopped lines, even though both are in the same meter. And prose, though it is unmetrical, can thus have rhythm, too. In addition to being affected by syntactical pauses, rhythm is affected by pauses due to consonant clusters and the length of words. Polysyllabic words establish a different rhythm from monosyllabic words, even in metrically identical lines.

One can say, then, that rhythm is altered by shifts in meter, syntax, and the ease of pronunciation. But even with no such shift, even if a line is repeated verbatim, a reader may sense a change in rhythm. The rhythm of the final line of a poem may well differ from that of the line before, even though in all other respects the lines are identical, as in Frost's "Stopping by Woods" (page 457), which concludes by repeating "And miles to go before I sleep." One may simply sense that this final line ought to be spoken, say, more slowly.

Though rhythm is basic to poetry, **rhyme** is not. Rhyme is the repetition of the identical or similar stressed sound or sounds. It is, presumably, pleasant in itself; it suggests order; and it also may be related to meaning, for it brings two words sharply together, often implying a relationship, as in the overworked rhymes "moon" and "June," "love" and "dove." **Perfect** or **exact rhymes** occur when differing consonant sounds are followed by identical stressed vowel sounds, and the following sounds, if any, are identical (foe: toe; meet: fleet; buffer: rougher). Notice that perfect rhyme involves identity of sound, not of spelling. "Fix" and "sticks," like "buffer" and "rougher," are perfect rhymes.

In **half-rhyme** (or **slant rhyme, approximate rhyme, near-rhyme, off-rhyme**) only the final consonant sounds of the rhyming words are identical; the stressed vowel sounds as well as the initial consonant sounds, if any, differ (soul: oil; mirth: forth; trolley: bully). **Eye rhyme** is not really rhyme; it merely looks like rhyme (cough: bough: rough). The final syllables in **masculine rhyme** are stressed and, after their differing initial consonant sounds, are identical in sound (stark: mark; support: retort). In **feminine rhyme** (or **double rhyme**) stressed rhyming syllables are followed by identical unstressed syllables (revival: arrival; flatter: batter). **Triple rhyme** is a kind of feminine rhyme in which identical stressed vowel sounds are followed by two identical unstressed syllables (machinery: scenery; tenderly: slenderly). **End rhyme** (or **terminal rhyme**) has the rhyming word at the end of the line. **Internal rhyme** has at least one of the rhyming words within the line (as in Wilde's "Each narrow *cell* in which we *dwell*").

Alliteration is sometimes defined as the repetition of initial sounds ("*All* the *aw*ful *au*guries" or "*B*ring me my *b*ow of *b*urning gold"), sometimes as the prominent repetition of a consonant ("*after life's fitful fever*"). In **assonance** identical vowel sounds in words in proximity are preceded and followed by differing consonant sounds. Whereas "tide" and "hide" are rhymes, "tide" and "mine" are assonantal. **Consonance** is the repetition of a pattern of identical consonant-sounds and differing vowel-sounds in words in proximity (fail: feel; rough: roof; pitter: patter). Sometimes consonance is more loosely defined merely as the repetition of a consonant (fai*l*: pee*l*). The following poem makes witty use of assonance and consonance.

George Starbuck (b. 1931)

Fable for Blackboard

Here is the grackle, people.
Here is the fox, folks.
The grackle sits in the bracken. The fox hopes.

Here are the fronds, friends,
that cover the fox.
The fronds get in a frenzy. The grackle looks.

Here are the ticks, tykes,
that live in the leaves, loves.
The fox is confounded,
and God is above.

Onomatopoeia is said to occur when the sound of a word echoes or suggests the meaning of a word. "Hiss," "gulp," and "buzz" are onomatopoetic. There is a mistaken tendency to see onomatopoeia everywhere, for example, in "thunder," "beauty," and "horror." Many words sometimes thought to be onomatopoetic are not clearly imitative of the thing they denote; they merely contain some sounds which — when we know what the word means — seem to have some resemblance to the thing they denote. Tennyson's lines from "Come down, O maid" are usually cited as an example of onomatopoeia:

> The moan of doves in immemorial elms
> And murmuring of innumerable bees.

But John Crowe Ransom has pointed out that if many of the sounds of "murmuring of innumerable bees" are reproduced in a line of different meaning — "murdering of innumerable beeves" — the suggestiveness is lost.

Lines of poetry are commonly arranged in a rhythmical unit called a **stanza** (from an Italian word meaning a "room" or "stopping-place"). Usually all the stanzas in a poem have the same rhyme pattern. A stanza is sometimes called a **verse,** though "verse" may also mean a single line of poetry. (In discussing stanzas, rhymes are indicated by identical letters. Thus, *abab* indicates that the first and third lines rhyme with each other, while the second and fourth lines are linked by a different rhyme. An unrhymed line is denoted by *x*.) The following stanzaic forms are common in English poetry:

couplet: stanza of two lines, usually (but not necessarily) with end rhymes. "Couplet" is also used for a pair of rhyming lines. The **octosyllabic couplet** is iambic or trochaic tetrameter:

> Had we but world enough, and time,
> This coyness, lady, were no crime.
>
> — Marvell

heroic couplet: a rhyming couplet of iambic pentameter, often "closed," that is, containing a complete thought, with a fairly heavy pause at the end of the first line and a still heavier one at the end of the second. Commonly, there is a parallel or an antithesis within a line, or between the two lines. It is called heroic because in England, especially in the eighteenth century, it was much used for heroic (epic) poems.

> Some foreign writers, some our own despise;
> The ancients only, or the moderns, prize.
>
> — Pope

triplet (or **tercet**): a three-line stanza, usually with one rhyme.

> Whenas in silks my Julia goes
> Then, then (methinks) how sweetly flows
> That liquefaction of her clothes.
>
> — Herrick

One kind of tercet is **terza rima,** rhyming *aba bcb cdc,* and so forth. Robert Frost's "Acquainted with the Night" (page 1177) is in terza rima.

quatrain: a four-line stanza, rhymed or unrhymed. The **heroic** (or **elegiac**) **quatrain** is iambic pentameter, rhyming *abab*. The **ballad stanza** is a quatrain alternating iambic tetrameter with iambic trimeter lines, usually rhyming *abxb*. Sometimes it is followed by a **refrain,** a line or lines repeated several times.

sonnet: a fourteen-line poem. The rhyme scheme of the **Petrarchan** (or **Italian**) **sonnet** is organized into an **octave** (the first eight lines) and a **sestet** (the last six). It usually rhymes *abbaabba cdecde,* but the sestet often has variations. In Petrarch's sonnets and in those of many of his imitators, there is a "turn" with the beginning of the ninth line; for example, a generalization in the octave may be illustrated by a particularization in the sestet. But, whether from indifference or inability, this nice disposition of parts is not always observed by English writers, and it is dangerous to generalize about the perfection of the Italian structure as a lyric vehicle. Milton in particular had a tendency to run straight on beyond the octave; rather than saying he composed faulty Petrarchan sonnets, scholars say he composed Miltonic sonnets.

The **Shakespearean** (or **English**) **sonnet** has the fourteen lines of the Petrarchan, but organizes them into three quatrains (four lines each) and a couplet (pair of lines): *abab cdcd efef gg.* The couplet has frequently caused trouble: sometimes it seems a needless appendage, often it seems too snappy a close; less often it seems just right.

Why poets choose to imprison themselves in fourteen tightly rhymed lines is something of a mystery. Tradition has a great deal to do with it: the form, having been handled successfully by major poets, stands as a challenge. In writing a sonnet a poet gains a little of the authority of Petrarch, Shakespeare, Milton, Wordsworth, and other masters who showed that the sonnet is not merely a trick. A second reason perhaps resides in the very tightness of the rhymes, which can help as well as hinder. Many poets have felt, along with Richard Wilbur (in *Mid-Century American Poets,* ed. John Ciardi), that the need for a rhyme has suggested

> . . . arbitrary connections of which the mind may take advantage if it likes. For example, if one has to rhyme with *tide,* a great number of rhyme-words at once come to mind (ride, bide, shied, confide, Akenside, etc.). Most of these, in combination with *tide,* will probably suggest nothing apropos, but one of them may reveal precisely what one wanted to say. If none of them does, *tide* must be dispensed with. Rhyme, austerely used, may be a stimulus to discovery and a stretcher of the attention.

A good deal of English poetry is unrhymed, much of it in **blank verse,** that is, unrhymed iambic pentameter. Introduced into English poetry by Surrey in the middle of the sixteenth century, late in the century it became the standard medium (especially in the hands of Marlowe and Shakespeare) of English drama. In the seventeenth century, Milton used it for *Paradise Lost,* and it has continued to be used in both dramatic and nondramatic literature. For an example see the passage from Shakespeare on page 480. A passage of blank verse that has a rhetorical unity is sometimes called a **verse paragraph.**

The second kind of unrhymed poetry fairly common in English, especially in the twentieth century, is **free verse** (or **vers libre**): rhythmical lines varying in length, adhering to no fixed metrical pattern and usually unrhymed. Such poetry may seem formless; Robert Frost, who strongly preferred rhyme, said that he would not consider writing free verse any more than he would consider playing tennis without a net. But free verse does have a form or pattern, often largely based on repetition and parallel grammatical structure. Whitman's "A Noiseless Patient Spider" (page 456) is an example; Arnold's "Dover Beach" (page 547) is another example, though less typical because it uses rhyme. Thoroughly typical is Whitman's "When I Heard the Learn'd Astronomer."

Walt Whitman (1819–1892)

When I Heard the Learn'd Astronomer

When I heard the learn'd astronomer,
When the proofs, the figures, were ranged in columns before me,
When I was shown the charts and diagrams, to add, divide, and
    measure them,
When I sitting heard the astronomer where he lectured with much
    applause in the lecture-room,
How soon unaccountable I became tired and sick,
Till rising and gliding out I wander'd off by myself,
In the mystical moist night-air, and from time to time,
Look'd up in perfect silence at the stars.

What can be said about the rhythmic structure of this poem? Rhymes are absent, and the lines vary greatly in the number of syllables, ranging from nine (the first line) to twenty-three (the fourth line), but when we read the poem we sense a rhythmic structure. The first four lines obviously hang together, each beginning with "When"; indeed, three of these four lines begin "When I." We may notice, too, that each of these four lines has more syllables than its predecessor (the numbers are nine, fourteen, eighteen, and twenty-three); this increase in length, like the initial repetition, is a kind of pattern. But then, with the fifth line, which speaks of fatigue and surfeit, there is a shrinkage to fourteen syllables, offering an enormous relief from the previous swollen line with its twenty-three syllables. The second half of the poem — the pattern established by "When" in the first four lines is dropped, and in effect we get a new stanza, also of four lines — does not relentlessly diminish the number of syllables in each succeeding line, but it *almost* does so: fourteen, fourteen, thirteen, ten.

The second half of the poem thus has a pattern too, and this pattern is more or less the reverse of the first half of the poem. We may notice too that the last line (in which the poet, now released from the oppressive lecture hall, is in communion with nature) is very close to an iambic pentameter line, that is, the poem concludes with a metrical form said to be the most natural in English. The effect of naturalness or ease in this final line, moreover, is increased by the absence of repetitions (e.g., not only of "When I," but even of such syntactic repetitions as "charts and diagrams," "tired and sick," "rising and gliding") that characterize most of the previous lines. But of course this final effect of naturalness is part of a carefully constructed pattern in which rhythmic structure is part of meaning. Though at first glance free verse may appear unrestrained, as T. S. Eliot (a practitioner) said, "No *vers* is *libre* for the man who wants to do a good job" or for the woman who wants to do a good job.

16

A Collection of Poems

William Shakespeare (1564–1616)

Sonnet 29

When, in disgrace with Fortune and men's eyes,
I all alone beweep my outcast state,
And trouble deaf heaven with my bootless° cries,   *useless*
And look upon myself and curse my fate,   *4*
Wishing me like to one more rich in hope,
Featured like him, like him° with friends possessed,   *like a second*
Desiring this man's art, and that man's scope,   *man, like a third man*
With what I most enjoy contented least;   *8*
Yet in these thoughts myself almost despising,
Haply° I think on thee, and then my state,   *perchance*
Like to the lark at break of day arising
From sullen earth, sings hymns at heaven's gate;   *12*
　　　For thy sweet love rememb'red such wealth brings,
　　　That then I scorn to change my state with kings.

William Shakespeare (1564–1616)

Sonnet 73

That time of year thou mayst in me behold
When yellow leaves, or none, or few, do hang
Upon those boughs which shake against the cold,
Bare ruined choirs* where late the sweet birds sang.   *4*
In me thou see'st the twilight of such day
As after sunset fadeth in the west,
Which by-and-by black night doth take away,
Death's second self that seals up all in rest.   *8*
In me thou see'st the glowing of such fire
That on the ashes of his youth doth lie,
As the deathbed whereon it must expire,
Consumed with that which it was nourished by.   *12*
    This thou perceiv'st, which makes thy love more strong,
    To love that well which thou must leave ere long.

William Shakespeare (1564–1616)

Sonnet 116

Let me not to the marriage of true minds
Admit impediments; love is not love
Which alters when it alteration finds,
Or bends with the remover to remove.   *4*
O, no, it is an ever-fixèd mark°   *guide to mariners*
That looks on tempests and is never shaken;
It is the star° to every wand'ring bark,   *the North Star*
Whose worth's unknown, although his height be taken.   *8*
Love's not Time's fool,° though rosy lips and cheeks   *plaything*
Within his bending sickle's compass° come;   *range*
Love alters not with his° brief hours and weeks   *Time's*
But bears° it out even to the edge of doom.°   *endures;*   *12*
    If this be error and upon me proved,   *Judgment Day*
    I never writ, nor no man ever loved.

* The part of the church where services were sung.

John Donne (1572–1631)

A Valediction: Forbidding Mourning

As virtuous men pass mildly away;
    And whisper to their souls, to go,
Whilst some of their sad friends do say,
    "The breath goes now," and some say, "No":   *4*

So let us melt, and make no noise.
    No tear-floods, nor sigh-tempests move.
'Twere profanation of our joys
    To tell the laity our love.   *8*

Moving of the earth° brings harms and fears,   *an earthquake*
    Men reckon what it did and meant;
But trepidation of the spheres,
    Though greater far, is innocent.*   *12*

Dull sublunary° lovers' love   *under the moon, i.e., earthly*
    (Whose soul is sense) cannot admit
Absence, because it doth remove
    Those things which elemented it.   *16*

But we, by a love so much refined
    That our selves know not what it is,
Inter-assuréd of the mind,
    Care less, eyes, lips, and hands to miss.   *20*

Our two souls therefore, which are one,
    Though I must go, endure not yet
A breach, but an expansion,
    Like gold to airy thinness beat.   *24*

If they be two, they are two so
    As stiff twin compasses° are two: *i.e., a carpenter's compass*
Thy soul, the fixed foot, makes no show
    To move, but doth, if the other do.   *28*

And though it in the center sit,
    Yet when the other far doth roam,
It leans, and hearkens after it,
    And grows erect, as that comes home.   *32*

---

* But the movement of the heavenly spheres (in Ptolemaic astronomy), though far greater, is harmless.

Such wilt thou be to me, who must
    Like the other foot, obliquely run:
Thy firmness makes my circle just,
    And makes me end where I begun.   *36*

John Milton (1608–1674)

When I consider how my light is spent

When I consider how my light is spent
    Ere half my days, in this dark world and wide,
    And that one talent which is death to hide*
    Lodged with me useless, though my soul more bent   *4*
To serve therewith my Maker, and present
    My true account, lest he returning chide;
    "Doth God exact day-labor, light denied?"
    I fondly° ask; but Patience to prevent°   *foolishly; forestall*   *8*
That murmur, soon replies, "God doth not need
    Either man's work or his own gifts; who best
    Bear his mild yoke, they serve him best. His state
Is kingly. Thousands at his bidding speed   *12*
    And post o'er land and ocean without rest:
    They also serve who only stand and wait."

William Blake (1757–1827)

The Lamb

        Little Lamb, who made thee?
        Dost thou know who made thee?
Gave thee life, and bid thee feed
By the stream and o'er the mead;
Gave thee clothing of delight,   *5*
Softest clothing, wooly, bright;
Gave thee such a tender voice,
Making all the vales rejoice?

---

* There is a pun here, relating Milton's literary talent to Christ's Parable of the Talents (Matthew 25: 14 ff.), in which a servant is rebuked for not putting his talent (a unit of money) to use. Note also line 4, where *useless* includes a pun on *use*, i.e., usury, interest.

Little Lamb, who made thee?
Dost thou know who made thee?   *10*

Little Lamb, I'll tell thee,
Little Lamb, I'll tell thee:
He is calléd by thy name,
For he calls himself a Lamb.
He is meek, and he is mild;   *15*
He became a little child.
I a child, and thou a lamb,
We are calléd by his name.
  Little Lamb, God bless thee!
  Little Lamb, God bless thee!   *20*

William Blake (*1757–1827*)

The Tyger

Tyger! Tyger! burning bright
In the forests of the night,
What immortal hand or eye
Could frame thy fearful symmetry?   *4*

In what distant deeps or skies
Burnt the fire of thine eyes?
On what wings dare he aspire?
What the hand dare seize the fire?   *8*

And what shoulder, and what art,
Could twist the sinews of thy heart?
And, when thy heart began to beat,
What dread hand? and what dread feet?   *12*

What the hammer? what the chain?
In what furnace was thy brain?
What the anvil? what dread grasp
Dare its deadly terrors clasp?   *16*

When the stars threw down their spears,
And watered heaven with their tears,
Did he smile his work to see?
Did he who made the lamb make thee?   *20*

Tyger! Tyger! burning bright
In the forests of the night,
What immortal hand or eye,
Dare frame thy fearful symmetry?   *24*

William Blake (*1757–1827*)

London

I wander through each chartered street,
Near where the chartered Thames does flow,
And mark in every face I meet
Marks of weakness, marks of woe.   *4*

In every cry of every man,
In every Infant's cry of fear,
In every voice, in every ban,
The mind-forged manacles I hear.   *8*

How the Chimney-sweeper's cry
Every black'ning Church appalls;
And the hapless Soldier's sigh
Runs in blood down Palace walls.   *12*

But most through midnight streets I hear
How the youthful Harlot's curse
Blasts the new-born Infant's tear,
And blights with plagues the Marriage hearse.   *16*

William Wordsworth (*1770–1850*)

The World Is Too Much with Us

The world is too much with us; late and soon,
Getting and spending, we lay waste our powers;
Little we see in Nature that is ours;
We have given our hearts away, a sordid boon!°   *gift*   *4*
This Sea that bares her bosom to the moon,
The winds that will be howling at all hours,
And are up-gathered now like sleeping flowers,
For this, for everything, we are out of tune;   *8*
It moves us not. — Great God! I'd rather be
A Pagan suckled in a creed outworn;
So might I, standing on this pleasant lea,
Have glimpses that would make me less forlorn;   *12*
Have sight of Proteus* rising from the sea;
Or hear old Triton blow his wreathéd horn.

* Proteus and Triton are sea gods.

William Wordsworth (*1770–1850*)

I Wandered Lonely as a Cloud

I wandered lonely as a cloud
That floats on high o'er vales and hills,
When all at once I saw a crowd,
A host, of golden daffodils,
Beside the lake, beneath the trees,   5
Fluttering and dancing in the breeze.

Continuous as the stars that shine
And twinkle on the milky way,
They stretched in never-ending line
Along the margin of a bay;   10
Ten thousand saw I at a glance,
Tossing their heads in sprightly dance.

The waves beside them danced, but they
Outdid the sparkling waves in glee;
A poet could not but be gay,   15
In such a jocund company;
I gazed — and gazed — but little thought
What wealth the show to me had brought:

For oft, when on my couch I lie
In vacant or in pensive mood,   20
They flash upon that inward eye
Which is the bliss of solitude;
And then my heart with pleasure fills,
And dances with the daffodils.

John Keats (*1795–1821*)

La Belle Dame sans Merci

O what can ail thee, knight-at-arms,
        Alone and palely loitering?
The sedge has withered from the lake,
        And no birds sing.   4

O what can ail thee, knight-at arms,
        So haggard and so woe-begone?
The squirrel's granary is full,
        And the harvest's done.   8

I see a lily on thy brow,
    With anguish moist and fever dew,
And on thy cheeks a fading rose
    Fast withereth too.   12

"I met a lady in the meads,
    Full beautiful — a faery's child,
Her hair was long, her foot was light,
    And her eyes were wild.   16

"I made a garland for her head,
    And bracelets too, and fragrant zone;°   *belt of flowers*
She looked at me as she did love,
    And made sweet moan.   20

"I set her on my pacing steed,
    And nothing else saw all day long,
For sidelong would she bend and sing
    A faery's song.   24

"She found me roots of relish sweet,
    And honey wild, and manna dew,
And sure in language strange she said
    'I love thee true.'   28

"She took me to her elfin grot,
    And there she wept and sighed full sore,
And there I shut her wild wild eyes
    With kisses four.   32

"And there she lulléd me asleep,
    And there I dreamed — Ah! woe betide!
The latest dream I ever dreamt
    On the cold hill side.   36

"I saw pale kings and princes too,
    Pale warriors, death-pale were they all;
They cried, 'La Belle Dame sans Merci°   *the beautiful pitiless lady*
Thee hath in thrall!'   40

"I saw their starved lips in the gloam
    With horrid warning gapéd wide,
And I awoke, and found me here,
    On the cold hill's side.   44

"And this is why I sojourn here,
    Alone and palely loitering,
Though the sedge is withered from the lake,
    And no birds sing."   48

John Keats (*1795–1821*)

To Autumn

I

Season of mists and mellow fruitfulness,
    Close bosom-friend of the maturing sun;
Conspiring with him how to load and bless
    With fruit the vines that round the thatch-eaves run;
To bend with apples the mossed cottage-trees,   *5*
    And fill all fruit with ripeness to the core;
        To swell the gourd, and plump the hazel shells
With a sweet kernel; to set budding more,
    And still more, later flowers for the bees,
    Until they think warm days will never cease,   *10*
        For summer has o'er-brimmed their clammy cells.

II

Who hath not seen thee oft amid thy store?
    Sometimes whoever seeks abroad may find
Thee sitting careless on a granary floor,
    Thy hair soft-lifted by the winnowing wind;   *15*
Or on a half-reaped furrow sound asleep,
    Drowsed with the fume of poppies, while thy hook
        Spares the next swath and all its twinéd flowers:
And sometime like a gleaner thou dost keep
    Steady thy laden head across a brook;   *20*
    Or by a cider-press, with patient look,
        Thou watchest the last oozings hours by hours.

III

Where are the songs of Spring? Ay, where are they?
    Think not of them, thou hast thy music too, —
While barred clouds bloom the soft-dying day,   *25*
    And touch the stubble-plains with rosy hue;
Then in a wailful choir the small gnats mourn
    Among the river sallows, borne aloft
        Or sinking as the light wind lives or dies;
And full-grown lambs loud bleat from hilly bourn;   *30*
    Hedge-crickets sing; and now with treble soft
    The red-breast whistles from a garden-croft;
        And gathering swallows twitter in the skies.

Alfred, Lord Tennyson *(1809–1892)*

Ulysses

It little profits that an idle king,
By this still hearth, among these barren crags,
Matched with an aged wife, I mete and dole
Unequal laws unto a savage race,
That hoard, and sleep, and feed, and know not me.   *5*
I cannot rest from travel; I will drink
Life to the lees. All times I have enjoyed
Greatly, have suffered greatly, both with those
That loved me, and alone; on shore, and when
Thro' scudding drifts the rainy Hyades   *10*
Vext the dim sea. I am become a name;
For always roaming with a hungry heart
Much have I seen and known, — cities of men
And manners, climates, councils, governments,
Myself not least, but honored of them all, —   *15*
And drunk delight of battle with my peers,
Far on the ringing plains of windy Troy.
I am a part of all that I have met;
Yet all experience is an arch wherethro'
Gleams that untravelled world whose margin fades   *20*
For ever and for ever when I move.
How dull it is to pause, to make an end,
To rust unburnished, not to shine in use!
As tho' to breathe were life! Life piled on life
Were all too little, and of one to me   *25*
Little remains; but every hour is saved
From that eternal silence, something more,
A bringer of new things; and vile it were
For some three suns to store and hoard myself,
And this gray spirit yearning in desire   *30*
To follow knowledge like a sinking star,
Beyond the utmost bound of human thought.

    This is my son, mine own Telemachus,
To whom I leave the scepter and the isle, —
Well-loved of me, discerning to fulfill   *35*
This labor, by slow prudence to make mild
A rugged people, and thro' soft degrees
Subdue them to the useful and the good.

Most blameless is he, centered in the sphere
Of common duties, decent not to fail   40
In offices of tenderness, and pay
Meet adoration to my household gods,
When I am gone. He works his work, I mine.

    There lies the port; the vessel puffs her sail;
There gloom the dark, broad seas. My mariners,   45
Souls that have toiled, and wrought, and thought with me, —
That ever with a frolic welcome took
The thunder and the sunshine, and opposed
Free hearts, free foreheads, — you and I are old;
Old age hath yet his honor and his toil.   50
Death closes all; but something ere the end,
Some work of noble note, may yet be done,
Not unbecoming men that strove with Gods.
The lights begin to twinkle from the rocks;
The long day wanes; the slow moon climbs; the deep   55
Moans round with many voices. Come, my friends.
'Tis not too late to seek a newer world.
Push off, and sitting well in order smite
The sounding furrows; for my purpose holds
To sail beyond the sunset, and the baths   60
Of all the western stars, until I die.
It may be that the gulfs will wash us down;
It may be we shall touch the Happy Isles,
And see the great Achilles, whom we knew.
Tho' much is taken, much abides; and tho'   65
We are not now that strength which in old days
Moved earth and heaven, that which we are, we are.
One equal temper of heroic hearts,
Made weak by time and fate, but strong in will
To strive, to seek, to find, and not to yield   70

Robert Browning *(1812–1889)*

Porphyria's Lover

The rain set early in tonight,
    The sullen wind was soon awake,
It tore the elm-tops down for spite,
    And did its worst to vex the lake:
I listened with heart fit to break.   5

When glided in Porphyria; straight
    She shut the cold out and the storm,
And kneeled and made the cheerless grate
    Blaze up, and all the cottage warm;
Which done, she rose, and from her form   *10*
Withdrew the dripping cloak and shawl,
    And laid her soiled gloves by, untied
Her hat and let the damp hair fall,
    And, last, she sat down by my side
And called me. When no voice replied,   *15*
She put my arm about her waist,
    And made her smooth white shoulder bare
And all her yellow hair displaced,
    And stooping, made my cheek lie there,
And spread, o'er all, her yellow hair,   *20*
Murmuring how she loved me — she
    Too weak, for all her heart's endeavor,
To set its struggling passion free
    From pride, and vainer ties dissever,
And give herself to me forever.   *25*
But passion sometimes would prevail,
    Nor could tonight's gay feast restrain
A sudden thought of one so pale
    For love of her, and all in vain:
So, she was come through wind and rain.   *30*
Be sure I looked up at her eyes
    Happy and proud; at last I knew
Porphyria worshipped me; surprise
    Made my heart swell, and still it grew
While I debated what to do.   *35*
That moment she was mine, mine, fair,
    Perfectly pure and good: I found
A thing to do, and all her hair
    In one long yellow string I wound
Three times her little throat around,   *40*
And strangled her. No pain felt she;
    I am quite sure she felt no pain.
As a shut bud that holds a bee,
    I warily oped her lids: again
Laughed the blue eyes without a stain.   *45*
And I untightened next the tress
    About her neck; her cheek once more
Blushed bright beneath my burning kiss:
    I propped her head up as before,

Only, this time my shoulder bore   *50*
Her head, which droops upon it still:
    The smiling rosy little head,
So glad it has its utmost will,
    That all it scorned at once is fled,
And I, its love, am gained instead!   *55*
Porphyria's love: she guessed not how
    Her darling one wish would be heard.
And thus we sit together now,
    And all night long we have not stirred,
And yet God has not said a word!   *60*

Matthew Arnold (*1822–1888*)

Dover Beach

The sea is calm to-night.
The tide is full, the moon lies fair
Upon the straits; — on the French coast the light
Gleams and is gone; the cliffs of England stand,
Glimmering and vast, out in the tranquil bay.   *5*
Come to the window, sweet is the night-air!
Only, from the long line of spray
Where the sea meets the moon-blanch'd land,
Listen! you hear the grating roar
Of pebbles which the waves draw back, and fling,   *10*
At their return, up the high strand,
Begin, and cease, and then again begin,
With tremulous cadence slow, and bring
The eternal note of sadness in.

Sophocles long ago   *15*
Heard it on the Ægean, and it brought
Into his mind the turbid ebb and flow
Of human misery; we
Find also in the sound a thought,
Hearing it by this distant northern sea.   *20*

The Sea of Faith
Was once, too, at the full, and round earth's shore
Lay like the folds of a bright girdle furl'd.
But now I only hear
Its melancholy, long, withdrawing roar,   25
Retreating, to the breath
Of the night-wind, down the vast edges drear
And naked shingles° of the world.   *pebbled beaches*

Ah, love, let us be true
To one another! for the world, which seems   30
To lie before us like a land of dreams,
So various, so beautiful, so new,
Hath really neither joy, nor love, nor light,
Nor certitude, nor peace, nor help for pain;
And we are here as on a darkling plain   35
Swept with confused alarms of struggle and flight,
Where ignorant armies clash by night.

Emily Dickinson (1830–1886)

A narrow Fellow in the Grass

A narrow Fellow in the Grass
Occasionally rides —
You may have met Him — did you not
His notice sudden is —   4

The Grass divides as with a Comb —
A spotted shaft is seen —
And then it closes at your feet
And opens further on —   8

He likes a Boggy Acre
A Floor too cool for Corn —
Yet when a Boy, and Barefoot —
I more than once at Noon   12
Have passed, I thought, a Whip lash
Unbraiding in the Sun
When stopping to secure it
It wrinkled, and was gone —   16

Several of Nature's People
I know, and they know me —
I feel for them a transport
Of cordiality —   *20*

But never met this Fellow
Attended, or alone
Without a tighter breathing
And Zero at the Bone —   *24*

Emily Dickinson (*1830–1886*)

I heard a Fly buzz — when I died

I heard a Fly buzz — when I died —
The Stillness in the Room
Was like the Stillness in the Air —
Between the Heaves of Storm —   *4*

The Eyes around — had wrung them dry —
And Breaths were gathering firm
For the last Onset — when the King
Be witnessed — in the Room —   *8*

I willed my Keepsakes — Signed away
What portion of me be
Assignable — and then it was
There interposed a Fly —   *12*

With Blue — uncertain stumbling Buzz —
Between the light — and me —
And then the Windows failed — and then
I could not see to see —   *16*

Thomas Hardy *(1840–1928)*

Ah, Are You Digging on My Grave?

"Ah, are you digging on my grave,
    My loved one? — planting rue?"
— "No: yesterday he went to wed
One of the brightest wealth has bred.
'It cannot hurt her now,' he said,   5
    'That I should not be true.'"

"Then who is digging on my grave?
    My nearest dearest kin?"
— "Ah, no: they sit and think, 'What use!
What good will planting flowers produce?   10
No tendance of her mound can loose
    Her spirit from Death's gin.'"

"But some one digs upon my grave?
    My enemy? — prodding sly?"
— "Nay: When she heard you had passed the Gate   15
That shuts on all flesh soon or late,
She thought you no more worth her hate,
    And cares not where you lie."

"Then, who is digging on my grave?
    Say — since I have not guessed!"
— "O it is I, my mistress dear,   20
Your little dog, who still lives near,
And much I hope my movements here
    Have not disturbed your rest?"

"Ah, yes! *You* dig upon my grave . . .   25
    Why flashed it not on me
That one true heart was left behind!
What feeling do we ever find
To equal among human kind
    A dog's fidelity!"   30

"Mistress, I dug upon your grave
    To bury a bone, in case
I should be hungry near this spot
When passing on my daily trot.
I am sorry, but I quite forgot   35
    It was your resting-place."

Thomas Hardy (1840–1928)

The Convergence of the Twain

Lines on the Loss of the Titanic

I

In a solitude of the sea
Deep from human vanity,
And the Pride of Life that planned her, stilly couches she.

II

Steel chambers, late the pyres
Of her salamandrine fires,   5
Cold currents thrid,° and turn to rhythmic tidal lyres.   *thread*

III

Over the mirrors meant
To glass the opulent
The sea-worm crawls — grotesque, slimed, dumb, indifferent.

IV

Jewels in joy designed   10
To ravish the sensuous mind
Lie lightless, all their sparkles bleared and black and blind.

V

Dim moon-eyed fishes near
Gaze at the gilded gear
And query: "What does this vaingloriousness down here?"   15

VI

Well: while was fashioning
This creature of cleaving wing,
The Immanent Will that stirs and urges everything

VII

Prepared a sinister mate
For her — so gaily great —   20
A Shape of Ice, for the time far and dissociate.

VIII

And as the smart ship grew
In stature, grace, and hue,
In shadowy silent distance grew the Iceberg too.

IX

Alien they seemed to be: *25*
No mortal eye could see
The intimate welding of their later history,

X

Or sign that they were bent
By paths coincident
On being anon twin halves of one august event,   *30*

XI

Till the Spinner of the Years
Said "Now!" And each one hears,
And consummation comes, and jars two hemispheres.

Gerard Manley Hopkins (1844–1889)

God's Grandeur

The world is charged with the grandeur of God.
    It will flame out, like shining from shook foil;
    It gathers to a greatness, like the ooze of oil
Crushed. Why do men then now not reck his rod?   *4*
Generations have trod, have trod, have trod;
    And all is seared with trade; bleared, smeared with toil;
    And wears man's smudge and shares man's smell: the soil
Is bare now, nor can foot feel, being shod.   *8*

And for all this, nature is never spent;
    There lives the dearest freshness deep down things;
And though the last lights off the black West went
    Oh, morning, at the brown brink eastward, springs — *12*
Because the Holy Ghost over the bent
    World broods with warm breast and with ah! bright wings.

Gerard Manley Hopkins (1844–1889)

Pied Beauty

Glory be to God for dappled things —
    For skies of couple-color as a brinded° cow;   *streaked*
        For rose-moles all in stipple upon trout that swim;
Fresh-firecoal chestnut-falls; finches' wings;   *4*
    Landscape plotted and pieced — fold, fallow, and plow;
        And áll trádes, their gear and tackle and trim°.

                        equipment

All things counter, original, spare, strange;
    Whatever is fickle, freckled (who knows how?)   *8*
        With swift, slow; sweet, sour; adazzle, dim;
He fathers-forth whose beauty is past change:
           Praise him.

Gerard Manley Hopkins (1844–1889)

The Windhover*

To Christ Our Lord

I caught this morning morning's minion,° king-   *favorite*
  dom of daylight's dauphin, dapple-dawn-drawn Falcon, in
     his riding
    Of the rolling level underneath him steady air, and striding
High there, how he rung upon the rein† of a wimpling° *rippling*
     wing   *4*
In his ecstacy! then off, off forth on swing,
    As a skate's heel sweeps smooth on a bow-bend; the hurl
     and gliding
    Rebuffed the big wind. My heart in hiding
Stirred for a bird, — the achieve of, the mastery of the thing! *8*

* A small falcon.
† Hopkins is using a term from horsemanship in which the horse circles around
his trainer at the end of a long rein.

Brute beauty and valor and act, oh, air, pride, plume, here
    Buckle! AND the fire that breaks from thee then, a billion
Times told lovelier, more dangerous, O my chevalier!

    No wonder of it: shéer plód makes plough down sillion* *12*
Shine, and blue-bleak embers, ah my dear,
    Fall, gall themselves, and gash gold-vermilion.

A. E. Housman (1859–1936)

Shropshire Lad #19
(To an Athlete Dying Young)

The time you won your town the race
We chaired you through the market-place;
Man and boy stood cheering by,
And home we brought you shoulder-high.   *4*

Today, the road all runners come,
Shoulder-high we bring you home,
And set you at your threshold down,
Townsman of a stiller town.   *8*

Smart lad, to slip betimes away
From fields where glory does not stay
And early though the laurel grows
It withers quicker than the rose.   *12*

Eyes the shady night has shut
Cannot see the record cut,
And silence sounds no worse than cheers
After earth has stopped the ears: *16*

Now you will not swell the rout
Of lads that wore their honors out,
Runners whom renown outran
And the name died before the man.   *20*

So set, before its echoes fade,
The fleet foot on the sill of shade,
And hold to the low lintel° up   *beam over a doorway*
The still-defended challenge-cup.   *24*

---

* The ridge between two furrows.

And round that early-laureled head
Will flock to gaze the strengthless dead,
And find unwithered on its curls
The garland briefer than a girl's.   28

A. E. Housman *(1859–1936)*

Shropshire Lad #62

"Terence, this is stupid stuff:
You eat your victuals fast enough;
There can't be much amiss, 'tis clear,
To see the rate you drink your beer.
But oh, good Lord, the verse you make,   5
It gives a chap the belly-ache.
The cow, the old cow, she is dead;
It sleeps well, the horned head:
We poor lads, 'tis our turn now
To hear such tunes as killed the cow.   10
Pretty friendship 'tis to rhyme
Your friends to death before their time
Moping melancholy mad:
Come, pipe a tune to dance to, lad."

Why, if 'tis dancing you would be,   15
There's brisker pipes than poetry.
Say, for what were hop-yards meant,
Or why was Burton built on Trent?
Oh many a peer of England brews
Livelier liquor than the Muse,   20
And malt does more than Milton can
To justify God's ways to man.
Ale, man, ale's the stuff to drink
For fellows whom it hurts to think:
Look into the pewter pot   25
To see the world as the world's not.
And faith, 'tis pleasant till 'tis past:
The mischief is that 'twill not last.
Oh I have been to Ludlow fair
And left my necktie God knows where   30
And carried half-way home, or near,
Pints and quarts of Ludlow beer:

Then the world seemed none so bad,
And I myself a sterling lad:
And down in lovely muck I've lain,   *35*
Happy till I woke again.
Then I saw the morning sky:
Heigho, the tale was all a lie;
The world, it was the old world yet,
I was I, my things were wet,   *40*
And nothing now remained to do
But begin the game anew.

    Therefore, since the world has still
Much good, but much less good than ill,
And while the sun and moon endure   *45*
Luck's a chance, but trouble's sure,
I'd face it as a wise man would,
And train for ill and not for good.
'Tis true, the stuff I bring for sale
Is not so brisk a brew as ale: *50*
Out of a stem that scored the hand
I wrung it in a weary land.
But take it: if the smack is sour,
The better for the embittered hour;
It should do good to heart and head   *55*
When your soul is in my soul's stead;
And I will friend you, if I may,
In the dark and cloudy day.

    There was a king reigned in the East:
There, when kings will sit to feast   *60*
They get their fill before they think
With poisoned meat and poisoned drink.
He gathered all that springs to birth
From the many-venomed earth;
First a little, thence to more,   *65*
He sampled all her killing store;
And easy, smiling, seasoned sound,
Sate the king when healths went round.
They put arsenic in his meat
And stared aghast to watch him eat;   *70*
They poured strychnine in his cup
And shook to seek him drink it up:
They shook, they stared as white's their shirt:
Them it was their poison hurt.
— I tell the tale that I heard told.   *75*
Mithridates, he died old.

William Butler Yeats (1865–1939)

Leda and the Swan*

A sudden blow: the great wings beating still
Above the staggering girl, her thighs caressed
By the dark webs, her nape caught in his bill,
He holds her helpless breast upon his breast.   *4*

How can those terrified vague fingers push
The feathered glory from her loosening thighs?
And how can body, laid in that white rush,
But feel the strange heart beating where it lies?   *8*

A shudder in the loins engenders there
The broken wall, the burning roof and tower
And Agamemnon dead.
                          Being so caught up,
So mastered by the brute blood of the air,   *12*
Did she put on his knowledge with his power
Before the indifferent beak could let her drop?

William Butler Yeats (1865–1939)

Sailing to Byzantium

I

That is no country for old men. The young
In one another's arms, birds in the trees
— Those dying generations — at their song,
The salmon-falls, the mackerel-crowded seas,   *4*
Fish, flesh, or fowl, commend all summer long
Whatever is begotten, born, and dies.
Caught in that sensual music all neglect
Monuments of unaging intellect.   *8*

---

* According to Greek mythology, Zeus fell in love with Leda, disguised himself as a swan, and raped her. Among the offspring of this union were Helen and Clytemnestra. Paris abducted Helen, causing the Greeks to raze Troy; Clytemnestra, wife of Agamemnon, murdered her husband on his triumphant return to Greece.

II

An aged man is but a paltry thing,
A tattered coat upon a stick, unless
Soul clap its hands and sing, and louder sing
For every tatter in its mortal dress,   *12*
Nor is there singing school but studying
Monuments of its own magnificence;
And therefore I have sailed the seas and come
To the holy city of Byzantium.   *16*

III

O sages standing in God's holy fire
As in the gold mosaic of a wall,
Come from the holy fire, perne° in a gyre,   *whirl down*
And be the singing-masters of my soul.   *20*
Consume my heart away; sick with desire
And fastened to a dying animal
It knows not what it is; and gather me
Into the artifice of eternity.   *24*

IV

Once out of nature I shall never take
My bodily form from any natural thing,
But such a form as Grecian goldsmiths make
Of hammered gold and gold enameling   *28*
To keep a drowsy Emperor awake;
Or set upon a golden bough to sing
To lords and ladies of Byzantium
Of what is past, or passing, or to come.   *32*

Edwin Arlington Robinson (1869–1935)

Richard Cory

Whenever Richard Cory went down town,
We people on the pavement looked at him:
He was a gentleman from sole to crown,
Clean favored, and imperially slim.   *4*

And he was always quietly arrayed,
And he was always human when he talked;
But still he fluttered pulses when he said,
"Good-morning," and he glittered when he walked.   *8*

And he was rich — yes, richer than a king —
And admirably schooled in every grace:
In fine, we thought that he was everything
To make us wish that we were in his place.   *12*

So on we worked, and waited for the light,
And went without the meat, and cursed the bread;
And Richard Cory, one calm summer night,
Went home and put a bullet through his head.   *16*

Edwin Arlington Robinson (1869–1935)

Mr. Flood's Party

Old Eben Flood, climbing alone one night
Over the hill between the town below
And the forsaken upland hermitage
That held as much as he should ever know   *4*
On earth again of home, paused warily.
The road was his with not a native near;
And Eben, having leisure, said aloud;
For no man else in Tilbury Town to hear: *8*

"Well, Mr. Flood, we have the harvest moon
Again, and we may not have many more;
The bird is on the wing, the poet says,
And you and I have said it here before.   *12*
Drink to the bird." He raised up to the light
The jug that he had gone so far to fill,
And answered huskily: "Well, Mr. Flood,
Since you propose it, I believe I will."   *16*

Alone, as if enduring to the end
A valiant armor of scarred hopes outworn,
He stood there in the middle of the road
Like Roland's ghost winding a silent horn.   20
Below him, in the town among the trees,
Where friends of other days had honored him,
A phantom salutation of the dead
Rang thinly till old Eben's eyes were dim.   24

Then, as a mother lays her sleeping child
Down tenderly, fearing it may awake,
He set the jug down slowly at his feet
With trembling care, knowing that most things break;   28
And only when assured that on firm earth
It stood, as the uncertain lives of men
Assuredly did not, he paced away,
And with his hand extended paused again: 32

"Well, Mr. Flood, we have not met like this
In a long time; and many a change has come
To both of us, I fear, since last it was
We had a drop together. Welcome home!"   36
Convivially returning with himself,
Again he raised the jug up to the light;
And with an acquiescent quaver said:
"Well, Mr. Flood, if you insist, I might.   40

"Only a very little, Mr. Flood —
For auld lang syne. No more, sir; that will do."
So, for the time, apparently it did,
And Eben evidently thought so too;   44
For soon amid the silver loneliness
Of night he lifted up his voice and sang,
Secure, with only two moons listening,
Until the whole harmonious landscape rang —   48

"For auld lang syne." The weary throat gave out,
The last word wavered; and the song being done,
He raised again the jug regretfully
And shook his head, and was again alone.   52
There was not much that was ahead of him,
And there was nothing in the town below —
Where strangers would have shut the many doors
That many friends had opened long ago.   56

Robert Frost (1874–1963)

Design

I found a dimpled spider, fat and white,
On a white heal-all,° holding up a moth   *a flower, normally blue*
Like a white piece of rigid satin cloth —
Assorted characters of death and blight   *4*
Mixed ready to begin the morning right,
Like the ingredients of a witches' broth —
A snow-drop spider, a flower like froth,
And dead wings carried like a paper kite.   *8*

What had that flower to do with being white,
The wayside blue and innocent heal-all?
What brought the kindred spider to that height,
Then steered the white moth thither in the night?   *12*
What but design of darkness to appall? —
If design govern in a thing so small.

Robert Frost (1874–1963)

The Road Not Taken

Two roads diverged in a yellow wood,
And sorry I could not travel both
And be one traveler, long I stood
And looked down one as far as I could
To where it bent in the undergrowth;   *5*

Then took the other, as just as fair,
And having perhaps the better claim,
Because it was grassy and wanted wear;
Though as for that the passing there
Had worn them really about the same,   *10*

And both that morning equally lay
In leaves no step had trodden black.
Oh, I kept the first for another day!
Yet knowing how way leads on to way,
I doubted if I should ever come back.   *15*

I shall be telling this with a sigh
Somewhere ages and ages hence:
Two roads diverged in a wood, and I —
I took the one less traveled by,
And that has made all the difference.   *20*

William Carlos Williams (*1883–1963*)

Spring and All

By the road to the contagious hospital
under the surge of the blue
mottled clouds driven from the
northeast — a cold wind. Beyond, the
waste of broad, muddy fields   *5*
brown with dried weeds, standing and fallen

patches of standing water
the scattering of tall trees

All along the road the reddish
purplish, forked, upstanding, twiggy   *10*
stuff of bushes and small trees
with dead, brown leaves under them
leafless vines —

Lifeless in appearance, sluggish
dazed spring approaches —   *15*

They enter the new world naked,
cold, uncertain of all
save that they enter. All about them
the cold, familiar wind —

Now the grass, tomorrow   *20*
the stiff curl of wildcarrot leaf
One by one objects are defined —
It quickens: clarity, outline of leaf

But now the stark dignity of
entrance — Still, the profound change   *25*
has come upon them: rooted, they
grip down and begin to awaken

William Carlos Williams (1883–1963)

A Sort of a Song

Let the snake wait under
his weed
and the writing
be of words, slow and quick, sharp
to strike, quiet to wait,   5
sleepless.

— through metaphor to reconcile
the people and the stones.
Compose. (No ideas
but in things) Invent!   10
Saxifrage is my flower that splits
the rocks.

Marianne Moore (1887–1972)

Poetry*

I, too, dislike it: there are things that are important beyond all
                                                              this fiddle.
      Reading it, however, with a perfect contempt for it, one
                                                         discovers in
      it after all, a place for the genuine.
            Hands that can grasp, eyes
            that can dilate, hair that can rise   5
                  if it must, these things are important not because a

---

* In a note to this poem, Moore says that the quotation in lines 17–18 is derived
from *The Diaries of Leo Tolstoy;* the quotation in lines 21–22 from W. B. Yeats's
Ideas of Good and Evil.

    A comment in *Predilections,* her volume of literary essays, affords some
insight into her style: "My own fondness for the unaccepted rhyme derives, I
think, from an instinctive effort to ensure naturalness. Even elate and fearsome
rightness like Shakespeare's is only preserved from the offense of being 'poetic'
by his well-nested effects of helpless naturalness."

high-sounding interpretation can be put upon them but because
                                                              they are
    useful. When they become so derivative as to become
                                                              unintelligible,
    the same thing may be said for all of us, that we
        do not admire what   *10*
        we cannot understand: the bat
          holding on upside down or in quest of something to
eat, elephants pushing, a wild horse taking a roll, a tireless
                                                              wolf under
    a tree, the immovable critic twitching his skin like a horse
                                              that feels a flea, the base-
    ball fan, the statistician —   *15*
        nor is it valid
        to discriminate against "business documents and

school-books"; all these phenomena are important. One must
                                              make a distinction
    however: when dragged into prominence by half poets, the
                                              result is not poetry,
    nor till the poets among us can be   *20*
        "literalists of
        the imagination" — above
        insolence and triviality and can present

for inspection, "imaginary gardens with real toads in them"
                                              shall we have
    it. In the meantime, if you demand on the one hand,   *25*
    the raw material of poetry in
        all its rawness and
        that which is on the other hand
          genuine, you are interested in poetry.

T. S. Eliot (1888–1965)

The Love Song of J. Alfred Prufrock

> *S'io credesse che mia risposta fosse*
> *A persona che mai tornasse al mondo,*
> *Questa fiamma staria senza più scosse.*
> *Ma perciocchè giammai di questo fondo*
> *Non torno vivo alcun, s' i' odo il vero,*
> *Senza tema d'infamia ti rispondo.**

Let us go then, you and I,
When the evening is spread out against the sky
Like a patient etherised upon a table;
Let us go, through certain half-deserted streets,
The muttering retreats   5
Of restless nights in one-night cheap hotels
And sawdust restaurants with oyster-shells:
Streets that follow like a tedious argument
Of insidious intent
To lead you to an overwhelming question . . .   10
Oh, do not ask, "What is it?"
Let us go and make our visit.

In the room the women come and go
Talking of Michelangelo.

The yellow fog that rubs its back upon the window-panes,   15
The yellow smoke that rubs its muzzle on the window-panes
Licked its tongue into the corners of the evening,
Lingered upon the pools that stand in drains,

* In Dante's *Inferno* XXVII:61–66, a damned soul who had sought absolution before committing a crime addresses Dante, thinking that his words will never reach the earth: "If I believed that my answer were to a person who could ever return to the world, this flame would no longer quiver. But because no one ever returned from this depth, if what I hear is true, without fear of infamy, I answer you."

Explanations of allusions in the poem may be helpful. "Works and days" (line 29) is the title of a poem on farm life by Hesiod (eighth century B.C.); "dying fall" (line 52) echoes *Twelfth Night* I.i.4; lines 81–83 allude to John the Baptist (see Matthew 14:1–11); line 92 echoes lines 41–42 of Marvell's "To His Coy Mistress" (see page 513); for "Lazarus" (line 94) see Luke 16 and John 11; lines 112–117 allude to Polonius and perhaps to other figures in *Hamlet;* "full of high sentence" (line 117) comes from Chaucer's description of the Clerk of Oxford in the *Canterbury Tales.*

Let fall upon its back the soot that falls from chimneys,
Slipped by the terrace, made a sudden leap,   *20*
And seeing that it was a soft October night,
Curled once about the house, and fell asleep.

And indeed there will be time
For the yellow smoke that slides along the street,
Rubbing its back upon the window-panes;   *25*
There will be time, there will be time
To prepare a face to meet the faces that you meet;
There will be time to murder and create,
And time for all the works and days of hands
That lift and drop a question on your plate;   *30*
Time for you and time for me,
And time yet for a hundred indecisions,
And for a hundred visions and revisions,
Before the taking of a toast and tea.

In the room the women come and go   *35*
Talking of Michelangelo
And indeed there will be time
To wonder, "Do I dare?" and, "Do I dare?"
Time to turn back and descend the stair,
With a bald spot in the middle of my hair —   *40*
[They will say: "How his hair is growing thin!"]
My morning coat, my collar mounting firmly to the chin,
My necktie rich and modest, but asserted by a simple pin —
[They will say: "But how his arms and legs are thin!"]
Do I dare   *45*
Disturb the universe?
In a minute there is time
For decisions and revisions which a minute will reverse.

For I have known them all already, known them all: —
Have known the evenings, mornings, afternoons,   *50*
I have measured out my life with coffee spoons;
I know the voices dying with a dying fall
Beneath the music from a farther room.
        So how should I presume?

And I have known the eyes already, known them all —   *55*
The eyes that fix you in a formulated phrase,
And when I am formulated, sprawling on a pin,
When I am pinned and wriggling on the wall,
Then how should I begin
To spit out all the butt-ends of my days and ways?   *60*
        And how should I presume?

And I have known the arms already, known them all —
Arms that are braceleted and white and bare
[But in the lamplight, downed with light brown hair!]
Is it perfume from a dress 65
That makes me so digress?
Arms that lie along a table, or wrap about a shawl.
    And should I then presume?
    And how should I begin?

          .   .   .   .   .

Shall I say, I have gone at dusk through narrow streets 70
And watched the smoke that rises from the pipes
Of lonely men in shirt-sleeves, leaning out of windows? . . .

I should have been a pair of ragged claws
Scuttling across the floors of silent seas.

          .   .   .   .   .

And the afternoon, the evening, sleeps so peacefully! 75
Smoothed by long fingers,
Asleep . . . tired . . . or it malingers,
Stretched on the floor, here beside you and me.
Should I, after tea and cakes and ices,
Have the strength to force the moment to its crisis? 80
But though I have wept and fasted, wept and prayed,
Though I have seen my head [grown slightly bald]
        brought in upon a platter,
I am no prophet — and here's no great matter;
I have seen the moment of my greatness flicker,
And I have seen the eternal Footman hold my coat, and
        snicker, 85
And in short, I was afraid.

And would it have been worth it, after all,
After the cups, the marmalade, the tea,
Among the porcelain, among some talk of you and me,
Would it have been worth while, 90
To have bitten off the matter with a smile,
To have squeezed the universe into a ball
To roll it toward some overwhelming question,
To say: "I am Lazarus, come from the dead,
Come back to tell you all, I shall tell you all" — 95
If one, settling a pillow by her head,
        Should say: "That is not what I meant at all.
        That is not it, at all."

And would it have been worth it, after all,
Would it have been worth while,   *100*
After the sunsets and the dooryards and the sprinkled streets,
After the novels, after the teacups, after the skirts
     that trail along the floor —
And this, and so much more? —
It is impossible to say just what I mean!
But as if a magic lantern threw the nerves in patterns
     on a screen: *105*
Would it have been worth while
If one, settling a pillow or throwing off a shawl,
And turning toward the window, should say:
     "That is not it at all,
     That is not what I meant, at all."   *110*

          · · · · ·

No! I am not Prince Hamlet, nor was meant to be;
Am an attendant lord, one that will do
To swell a progress, start a scene or two,
Advise the prince; no doubt, an easy tool,
Deferential, glad to be of use,   *115*
Politic, cautious, and meticulous;
Full of high sentence, but a bit obtuse;
At times, indeed, almost ridiculous —
Almost, at times, the Fool.

I grow old . . . I grow old . . .   *120*
I shall wear the bottoms of my trousers rolled.

Shall I part my hair behind? Do I dare to eat a peach?
I shall wear white flannel trousers, and walk upon the beach.
I have heard the mermaids singing, each to each.

I do not think that they will sing to me.   *125*

I have seen them riding seaward on the waves
Combing the white hair of the waves blown back
When the wind blows the water white and black.

We have lingered in the chambers of the sea
By sea-girls wreathed with seaweed red and brown   *130*
Till human voices wake us, and we drown.

T. S. Eliot *(1888–1965)*

Journey of the Magi*

"A cold coming we had of it,
Just the worst time of the year
For a journey, and such a long journey:
The ways deep and the weather sharp,
The very dead of winter."   *5*
And the camels galled, sore-footed, refractory,
Lying down in the melting snow.
There were times we regretted
The summer palaces on slopes, the terraces,
And the silken girls bringing sherbet.   *10*
Then the camel men cursing and grumbling
And running away, and wanting their liquor and women,
And the night-fires going out, and the lack of shelters,
And the cities hostile and the towns unfriendly
And the villages dirty and charging high prices: *15*
A hard time we had of it.
At the end we preferred to travel all night,
Sleeping in snatches,
With the voices singing in our ears, saying
That this was all folly.   *20*

Then at dawn we came down to a temperate valley,
Wet, below the snow line, smelling of vegetation;
With a running stream and a water-mill beating the darkness,
And three trees on the low sky,
And an old white horse galloped away in the meadow.   *25*
Then we came to a tavern with vine-leaves over the lintel,
Six hands at an open door dicing for pieces of silver,
And feet kicking the empty wine-skins.
But there was no information, and so we continued
And arrived at evening, not a moment too soon   *30*
Finding the place; it was (you may say) satisfactory.

* For the Journey of the Magi, see Matthew 2. Lines 1–5 are in quotation marks
because they are adapted from a sermon on the Nativity by Lancelot Andrewes
(1555–1626). For line 24, see Matthew 27:38; for line 25, see Revelation 6:2 and
19:11. Perhaps, too, the white horse that gallops away is partly derived from
G. K. Chesterton's *The Ballad of the White Horse,* in which the disappearance of the
horse represents the disappearance of paganism at the advent of Christianity. The
vine (line 26) is often associated with Christ; see, for example, John 15. Line 27
may allude to Matthew 27:3–6,35.

All this was a long time ago, I remember,
And I would do it again, but set down
This set down
This: were we led all that way for   *35*
Birth or Death? There was a Birth, certainly,
We had evidence and no doubt. I had seen birth and death,
But had thought they were different; this Birth was
Hard and bitter agony for us, like Death, our death.
We returned to our places, these Kingdoms,   *40*
But no longer at ease here, in the old dispensation,
With an alien people clutching their gods.
I should be glad of another death.

Archibald MacLeish (1892–1982)

Ars Poetica

A poem should be palpable and mute
As a globed fruit,

Dumb
As old medallions to the thumb,   *4*

Silent as the sleeve-worn stone
Of casement ledges where the moss has grown —

A poem should be wordless
As the flight of birds.   *8*

A poem should be motionless in time
As the moon climbs,

Leaving, as the moon releases
Twig by twig the night-entangled trees,   *12*

Leaving, as the moon behind the winter leaves,
Memory by memory the mind —

A poem should be motionless in time
As the moon climbs.   *16*

A poem should be equal to:
Not true.

For all the history of grief
An empty doorway and a maple leaf.   *20*

For love
The leaning grasses and two lights above the sea —

A poem should not mean
But be.   *24*

E. E. Cummings *(1894–1963)*

anyone lived in a pretty how town

anyone lived in a pretty how town
(with up so floating many bells down)
spring summer autumn winter
he sang his didn't he danced his did.   *4*

Women and men(both little and small)
cared for anyone not at all
they sowed their isn't they reaped their same
sun moon stars rain   *8*

children guessed(but only a few
and down they forgot as up they grew
autumn winter spring summer)
that noone loved him more by more   *12*

when by now and tree by leaf
she laughed his joy she cried his grief
bird by snow and stir by still
anyone's any was all to her   *16*

someones married their everyones
laughed their cryings and did their dance
(sleep wake hope and then) they
said their nevers they slept their dream   *20*

stars rain sun moon
(and only the snow can begin to explain
how children are apt to forget to remember
with up so floating many bells down)   *24*

one day anyone died i guess
(and noone stopped to kiss his face)
busy folk buried them side by side
little by little and was by was   28

all by all and deep by deep
and more by more they dream their sleep
noone and anyone earth by april
wish by spirit and if by yes.   32

Women and men(both dong and ding)
summer autumn winter spring
reaped their sowing and went their came
sun moon stars rain   36

W. H. Auden (1907–1973)

Musée des Beaux Arts

About suffering they were never wrong,
The Old Masters: how well they understood
Its human position; how it takes place
While someone else is eating or opening a window
        or just walking dully along;
How, when the aged are reverently, passionately waiting   5
For the miraculous birth, there always must be
Children who did not specially want it to happen, skating
On a pond at the edge of the wood:
They never forgot
That even the dreadful martyrdom must run its course   10
Anyhow in a corner, some untidy spot
Where the dogs go on with their doggy life and the torturer's
        horse
Scratches its innocent behind on a tree.

In Brueghel's *Icarus,* for instance: how everything turns away
Quite leisurely from the disaster; the ploughman may   15
Have heard the splash, the forsaken cry,
But for him it was not an important failure; the sun shone
As it had to on the white legs disappearing into the green
Water; and the expensive delicate ship that must have seen
Something amazing, a boy falling out of the sky,   20
Had somewhere to get to and sailed calmly on.

W. H. Auden (1907–1973)

The Unknown Citizen

(To JS/07/M/378
This Marble Monument
Is Erected by the State)

He was found by the Bureau of Statistics to be
One against whom there was no official complaint,
And all the reports on his conduct agree
That, in the modern sense of an old-fashioned word, he was a
    saint,
For in everything he did he served the Greater Community.   *5*
Except for the War till the day he retired
He worked in a factory and never got fired,
But satisfied his employers, Fudge Motors Inc.
Yet he wasn't a scab or odd in his views,
For his Union reports that he paid his dues,   *10*
(Our report on his Union shows it was sound)
And our Social Psychology workers found
That he was popular with his mates and liked a drink.
The Press are convinced that he bought a paper every day
And that his reactions to advertisements were normal
    in every way.   *15*
Policies taken out in his name prove that he was fully insured,
And his Health-card shows he was once in hospital
    but left it cured.
Both Producers Research and High-Grade Living declare
He was fully sensible to the advantages of the Installment Plan
And had everything necessary to the Modern Man,   *20*
A phonograph, radio, a car and a frigidaire.
Our researchers into Public Opinion are content
That he held the proper opinions for the time of year;
When there was peace, he was for peace; when there
    was war, he went.
He was married and added five children
    to the population,   *25*
Which our Eugenist says was the right number
    for a parent of his generation,
And our teachers report that he never interfered
    with their education.
Was he free? Was he happy? The question is absurd:
Had anything been wrong, we should certainly have heard.

Elizabeth Bishop (1911–1979)

The Fish

I caught a tremendous fish
and held him beside the boat
half out of water, with my hook
fast in a corner of his mouth.
He didn't fight.   *5*
He hadn't fought at all.
He hung a grunting weight,
battered and venerable
and homely. Here and there
his brown skin hung in strips   *10*
like ancient wall-paper,
and its pattern of darker brown
was like wall-paper:
shapes like full-blown roses
stained and lost through age.   *15*
He was speckled with barnacles,
fine rosettes of lime,
and infested
with tiny white sea-lice,
and underneath two or three   *20*
rags of green weed hung down.
While his gills were breathing in
the terrible oxygen
— the frightening gills,
fresh and crisp with blood,   *25*
that can cut so badly —
I thought of the coarse white flesh
packed in like feathers,
the big bones and the little bones,
the dramatic reds and blacks   *30*
of his shiny entrails,
and the pink swim-bladder
like a big peony.
I looked into his eyes
which were far larger than mine   *35*

but shallower, and yellowed,
the irises backed and packed
with tarnished tinfoil
seen through the lenses
of old scratched isinglass.   40
They shifted a little, but not
to return my stare.
— It was more like the tipping
of an object toward the light.
I admired his sullen face,   45
the mechanism of his jaw,
and then I saw
that from his lower lip
— if you could call it a lip —
grim, wet, and weapon-like,   50
hung five old pieces of fish-line,
or four and a wire leader
with the swivel still attached,
with all their five big hooks
grown firmly in his mouth.   55
A green line, frayed at the end
where he broke it, two heavier lines,
and a fine black thread
still crimped from the strain and snap
when it broke and he got away.   60
Like medals with their ribbons
frayed and wavering,
a five-haired beard of wisdom
trailing from his aching jaw.
I stared and stared   65
and victory filled up
the little rented boat,
from the pool of bilge
where oil had spread a rainbow
around the rusted engine   70
to the bailer rusted orange,
the sun-cracked thwarts,
the oarlocks on their strings,
the gunnels — until everything
was rainbow, rainbow, rainbow!   75
And I let the fish go.

Elizabeth Bishop (1911–1979)

One Art

The art of losing isn't hard to master;
so many things seem filled with the intent
to be lost that their loss is not disaster.

Lose something every day. Accept the fluster
of lost door keys, the hour badly spent.   5
The art of losing isn't hard to master.

Then practice losing farther, losing faster:
places, and names, and where it was you meant
to travel. None of these will bring disaster.

I lost my mother's watch. And look! my last, or   10
next-to-last, of three loved houses went.
The art of losing isn't hard to master.

I lost two cities, lovely ones. And, vaster,
some realms I owned, two rivers, a continent.
I miss them, but it wasn't a disaster.   15

— Even losing you (the joking voice, a gesture
I love) I shan't have lied. It's evident
the art of losing's not too hard to master
though it may look like (*Write* it!) like disaster.

Robert Hayden (1913–1980)

Those Winter Sundays

Sundays too my father got up early
and put his clothes on in the blueblack cold,
then with cracked hands that ached
from labor in the weekday weather made
banked fires blaze. No one ever thanked him.   5

I'd wake and hear the cold splintering, breaking.
When the rooms were warm, he'd call,
and slowly I would rise and dress,
fearing the chronic angers of that house,

Speaking indifferently to him,   *10*
who had driven out the cold
and polished my good shoes as well.
What did I know, what did I know
of love's austere and lonely offices?

Dylan Thomas (1914–1953)

Fern Hill

Now as I was young and easy under the apple boughs
About the lilting house and happy as the grass was green,
     The night above the dingle starry,
      Time let me hail and climb
     Golden in the heydays of his eyes,   *5*
And honored among wagons I was prince of the apple towns
And once below a time I lordly had the trees and leaves
      Trail with daisies and barley
    Down the rivers of the windfall light.

And as I was green and carefree, famous among the barns   *10*
About the happy yard and singing as the farm was home,
    In the sun that is young once only,
      Time let me play and be
    Golden in the mercy of his means,
And green and golden I was huntsman and herdsman,
    the calves   *15*
Sang to my horn, the foxes on the hills barked clear and cold,
      And the sabbath rang slowly
    In the pebbles of the holy streams.

All the sun long it was running, it was lovely, the hay
Fields high as the house, the tunes from the chimneys,
      it was air   *20*
   And playing, lovely and watery
      And fire green as grass.
   And nightly under the simple stars
As I rode to sleep the owls were bearing the farm away,
All the moon long I heard, blessed among stables, the night-
    jars   *25*
   Flying with the ricks, and the horses
     Flashing into the dark.

And then to awake, and the farm, like a wanderer white
With the dew, come back, the cock on his shoulder: it was all
    Shining, it was Adam and maiden,   *30*
        The sky gathered again
    And the sun grew round that very day.
So it must have been after the birth of the simple light
In the first, spinning place, the spellbound horses walking warm
    Out of the whinnying green stable   *35*
        On to the fields of praise.

And honored among foxes and pheasants by the gay house
Under the new made clouds and happy as the heart was long,
    In the sun born over and over,
        I ran my heedless ways,   *40*
    My wishes raced through the house high hay
And nothing I cared, at my sky blue trades, that time allows
In all his tuneful turning so few and such morning songs
    Before the children green and golden
        Follow him out of grace,   *45*

Nothing I cared, in the lamb white days, that time would take me
Up to the swallow thronged loft by the shadow of my hand,
    In the moon that is always rising,
        Nor that riding to sleep
    I should hear him fly with the high fields   *50*
And wake to the farm forever fled from the childless land.
Oh as I was young and easy in the mercy of his means,
        Time held me green and dying
        Though I sang in my chains like the sea.

Randall Jarrell (1914–1965)

The Woman at the Washington Zoo

The saris go by me from the embassies.

Cloth from the moon. Cloth from another planet.
They look back at the leopard like the leopard.

And I. . . .
        this print of mine, that has kept its color
Alive through so many cleanings; this dull null   *5*
Navy I wear to work, and wear from work, and so
To my bed, so to my grave, with no

Complaints, no comment: neither from my chief,
The Deputy Chief Assistant, nor his chief —
Only I complain. . . . this serviceable   *10*
Body that no sunlight dyes, no hand suffuses
But, dome-shadowed, withering among columns,
Wavy beneath fountains — small, far-off, shining
In the eyes of animals, these beings trapped
As I am trapped but not, themselves, the trap,   *15*
Aging, but without knowledge of their age,
Kept safe here, knowing not of death, for death —
Oh, bars of my own body, open, open!

The world goes by my cage and never sees me.
And there come not to me, as come to these,   *20*
The wild beasts, sparrows pecking the llamas' grain,
Pigeons settling on the bears' bread, buzzards
Tearing the meat the flies have clouded. . . .
                                        Vulture,
When you come for the white rat that the foxes left,
Take off the red helmet of your head, the black   *25*
Wings that have shadowed me, and step to me as man:
The wild brother at whose feet the white wolves fawn,
To whose hand of power the great lioness
Stalks, purring. . . .
                    You know what I was,
You see what I am: change me, change me!   *30*

Gwendolyn Brooks (*b. 1915*)

We Real Cool

The Pool Players.
Seven at the Golden Shovel.

We real cool. We
Left school. We

Lurk late. We
Strike straight. We   *4*

Sing sin. We
Thin gin. We

Jazz June. We
Die soon.   *8*

Robert Lowell (1917–1977)

Water

It was a Maine lobster town —
each morning boatloads of hands
pushed off for granite
quarries on the islands,   *4*

and left dozens of bleak
white frame houses stuck
like oyster shells
on a hill of rock,   *8*

and below us, the sea lapped
the raw little match-stick
mazes of a weir,
where the fish for bait were trapped.   *12*

Remember? We sat on a slab of rock.
From this distance in time,
it seems the color
of iris, rotting and turning purpler,   *16*

but it was only
the usual gray rock
turning the usual green
when drenched by the sea.   *20*

The sea drenched the rock
at our feet all day,
and kept tearing away
flake after flake.   *24*

One night you dreamed
you were a mermaid clinging to a wharf-pile,
and trying to pull
off the barnacles with your hands.   *28*

We wished our two souls
might return like gulls
to the rock. In the end,
the water was too cold for us.   *32*

Lawrence Ferlinghetti (b. 1919)

Constantly risking absurdity

Constantly risking absurdity
                              and death
        whenever he performs
                        above the heads
                              of his audience 5
    the poet like an acrobat
                    climbs on rime
                        to a high wire of his own making
and balancing on eyebeams
                        above a sea of faces   10
        paces his way
                        to the other side of day
    performing *entrechats°*   *a leap in ballet*
                        and sleight-of-foot tricks
and other high theatrics   15
                and all without mistaking
        any thing
                for what it may not be

    For he's the super realist
                    who must perforce perceive   20
        taut truth
                    before the taking of each stance or step

    in his supposed advance
                    toward that still higher perch
where Beauty stands and waits   25
                        with gravity
                            to start her death-defying leap

        And he
            a little charleychaplin man
                            who may or may not catch   30
                her fair eternal form
                        spreadeagled in the empty air
                of existence

Richard Wilbur (b. 1921)

Love Calls Us to the Things of This World

The eyes open to a cry of pulleys,
And spirited from sleep, the astounded soul
Hangs for a moment bodiless and simple
As false dawn.
                Outside the open window
The morning air is all awash with angels.   *5*

Some are in bed-sheets, some are in blouses,
Some are in smocks: but truly there they are.
Now they are rising together in calm swells
Of halcyon feeling, filling whatever they wear
With the deep joy of their impersonal breathing;   *10*

Now they are flying in place, conveying
The terrible speed of their omnipresence, moving
And staying like white water; and now of a sudden
They swoon down into so rapt a quiet
That nobody seems to be there.   *15*
                        The soul shrinks

From all that it is about to remember,
From the punctual rape of every blessèd day,
And cries,
          "Oh, let there be nothing on earth but laundry,
Nothing but rosy hands in the rising steam
And clear dances done in the sight of heaven."   *20*

Yet, as the sun acknowledges
With a warm look the world's hunks and colors,
The soul descends once more in bitter love
To accept the waking body, saying now
In a changed voice as the man yawns and rises,   *25*

"Bring them down from their ruddy gallows;
Let there be clean linen for the backs of thieves;
Let lovers go fresh and sweet to be undone,
And the heaviest nuns walk in a pure floating
Of dark habits,
             keeping their difficult balance."   *30*

Anthony Hecht (b. 1922)

The Dover Bitch

A Criticism of Life

For Andrews Wanning

So there stood Matthew Arnold and this girl
With the cliffs of England crumbling away behind them,
And he said to her, "Try to be true to me,
And I'll do the same for you, for things are bad
All over, etc., etc."   5
Well now, I knew this girl. It's true she had read
Sophocles in a fairly good translation
And caught that bitter allusion to the sea,
But all the time he was talking she had in mind
The notion of what his whiskers would feel like   10
On the back of her neck. She told me later on
That after a while she got to looking out
At the lights across the channel, and really felt sad,
Thinking of all the wine and enormous beds
And blandishments in French and the perfumes.   15
And then she got really angry. To have been brought
All the way down from London, and then be addressed
As sort of a mournful cosmic last resort
Is really tough on a girl, and she was pretty.
Anyway, she watched him pace the room   20
And finger his watch-chain and seem to sweat a bit,
And then she said one or two unprintable things.
But you mustn't judge her by that. What I mean to say is,
She's really all right. I still see her once in a while
And she always treats me right.
We have a drink   25
And I give her a good time, and perhaps it's a year
Before I see her again, but there she is,
Running to fat, but dependable as they come,
And sometimes I bring her a bottle of *Nuit d'Amour*.

James Dickey (b. 1923)

The Lifeguard

In a stable of boats I lie still,
From all sleeping children hidden.
The leap of a fish from its shadow
Makes the whole lake instantly tremble.
With my foot on the water, I feel   *5*
The moon outside

Take on the utmost of its power.
I rise and go out through the boats.
I set my broad sole upon silver,
On the skin of the sky, on the moonlight,   *10*
Stepping outward from earth onto water
In quest of the miracle

This village of children believed
That I could perform as I dived
For one who had sunk from my sight.   *15*
I saw his cropped haircut go under.
I leapt, and my steep body flashed
Once, in the sun.

Dark drew all the light from my eyes.
Like a man who explores his death   *20*
By the pull of his slow-moving shoulders,
I hung head down in the cold,
Wide-eyed, contained, and alone
Among the weeds,

And my fingertips turned into stone   *25*
From clutching immovable blackness.
Time after time I leapt upward
Exploding in breath, and fell back
From the change in the children's faces
At my defeat.   *30*

Beneath them, I swam to the boathouse
With only my life in my arms
To wait for the lake to shine back
At the risen moon with such power
That my steps on the light of the ripples   *35*
Might be sustained.

Beneath me is nothing but brightness
Like the ghost of a snowfield in summer.
As I move toward the center of the lake,
Which is also the center of the moon, 40
I am thinking of how I may be
The savior of one

Who has already died in my care.
The dark trees fade from around me.
The moon's dust hovers together. 45
I call softly out, and the child's
Voice answers through blinding water.
Patiently, slowly,

He rises, dilating to break
The surface of stone with his forehead. 50
He is one I do not remember
Having ever seen in his life.
The ground I stand on is trembling
Upon his smile.

I wash the black mud from my hands. 55
On a light given off by the grave.
I kneel in the quick of the moon
At the heart of a distant forest
And hold in my arms a child
Of water, water, water. 60

Allen Ginsberg (b. 1926)

A Supermarket in California

What thoughts I have of you tonight, Walt Whitman, for I walked down the sidestreets under the trees with a headache self-conscious looking at the full moon.

In my hungry fatigue, and shopping for images, I went into the neon fruit supermarket, dreaming of your enumerations!

What peaches and what penumbras! Whole families shopping at night! Aisles full of husbands! Wives in the avocados, babies in the tomatoes! — and you, Garcia Lorca, what were you doing down by the watermelons?

I saw you, Walt Whitman, childless, lonely old grubber,
poking among the meats in the refrigerator and eyeing the grocery
boys.

I heard you asking questions of each: Who killed the pork
chops? What price bananas? Are you my Angel?   5

I wandered in and out of the brilliant stacks of cans following
you, and followed in my imagination by the store detective.

We strode down the open corridors together in our solitary
fancy tasting artichokes, possessing every frozen delicacy, and never
passing the cashier.

Where are we going, Walt Whitman? The doors close in an
hour. Which way does your beard point tonight?

(I touch your book and dream of our odyssey in the supermarket and feel absurd.)

Will we walk all night through solitary streets? The trees
add shade to shade, lights out in the houses, we'll both be
lonely.   10

Will we stroll dreaming of the lost America of love past blue
automobiles in driveways, home to our silent cottage?

Ah, dear father, graybeard, lonely old courage-teacher, what
America did you have when Charon quit poling his ferry and you
got out on a smoking bank and stood watching the boat disappear
on the black water of Lethe?

Adrienne Rich (b. 1929)

Living in Sin

She had thought the studio would keep itself,
no dust upon the furniture of love.
Half heresy, to wish the taps less vocal,
the panes relieved of grime. A plate of pears,
a piano with a Persian shawl, a cat   5
stalking the picturesque amusing mouse
had risen at his urging.
Not that at five each separate stair would writhe
under the milkman's tramp; that morning light
so coldly would delineate the scraps   10
of last night's cheese and three sepulchral bottles;
that on the kitchen shelf among the saucers

a pair of beetle-eyes would fix her own —
envoy from some black village in the mouldings . . .
Meanwhile, he, with a yawn,   *15*
sounded a dozen notes upon the keyboard,
declared it out of tune, shrugged at the mirror,
rubbed at his beard, went out for cigarettes;
while she, jeered by the minor demons,
pulled back the sheets and made the bed and found   *20*
a towel to dust the table-top,
and let the coffee-pot boil over on the stove.
By evening she was back in love again,
though not so wholly but throughout the night
she woke sometimes to feel the daylight coming   *25*
like a relentless milkman up the stairs.

Adrienne Rich (b. 1929)

A Woman Mourned by Daughters

Now, not a tear begun,
we sit here in your kitchen,
spent, you see, already.
You are swollen till you strain   *4*
this house and the whole sky.
You, whom we so often
succeeded in ignoring!
You are puffed up in death   *8*
like a corpse pulled from the sea;
we groan beneath your weight.
And yet you were a leaf,
a straw blown on the bed,   *12*
you had long since become
crisp as a dead insect.
What is it, if not you,
that settles on us now   *16*
like satins you pulled down
over our bridal heads?
What rises in our throats
like food you prodded in?   *20*
Nothing could be enough.

You breathe upon us now
through solid assertions
of yourself: teaspoons, goblets,   *24*
seas of carpet, a forest
of old plants to be watered,
an old man in an adjoining
room to be touched and fed.   *28*
And all this universe
dares us to lay a finger
anywhere, save exactly
as you would wish it done.   *32*

Sylvia Plath (*1932–1963*)

Daddy

You do not do, you do not do
Any more, black shoe
In which I have lived like a foot
For thirty years, poor and white,
Barely daring to breathe or Achoo.   *5*

Daddy, I have had to kill you.
You died before I had time —
Marble-heavy, a bag full of God,
Ghastly statue with one gray toe
Big as a Frisco seal   *10*

And a head in the freakish Atlantic
Where it pours bean green over blue
In the waters off beautiful Nauset.
I used to pray to recover you.
Ach, du.   *15*

In the German tongue, in the Polish town
Scraped flat by the roller
Of wars, wars, wars.
But the name of the town is common.
My Polack friend   *20*

Says there are a dozen or two.
So I never could tell where you
Put your foot, your root,
I never could talk to you.
The tongue stuck in my jaw.   *25*

It stuck in a barb wire snare.
Ich, ich, ich, ich,
I could hardly speak.
I thought every German was you.
And the language obscene   *30*

An engine, an engine
Chuffing me off like a Jew.
A Jew to Dachau, Auschwitz, Belsen.
I began to talk like a Jew.
I think I may well be a Jew.   *35*

The snows of the Tyrol, the clear beer of Vienna
Are not very pure or true.
With my gypsy ancestress and my weird luck
And my Taroc pack and my Taroc pack
I may be a bit of a Jew.   *40*

I have always been scared of *you,*
With your Luftwaffe, your gobbledygoo.
And your neat moustache
And your Aryan eye, bright blue,
Panzer-man, panzer-man, O You —   *45*

Not God but a swastika
So black no sky could squeak through.
Every woman adores a Fascist,
The boot in the face, the brute
Brute heart of a brute like you.   *50*

You stand at the blackboard, daddy,
In the picture I have of you,
A cleft in your chin instead of your foot
But no less a devil for that, no not
Any less the black man who   *55*

Bit my pretty red heart in two.
I was ten when they buried you.
At twenty I tried to die
And get back, back, back to you.
I thought even the bones would do.   *60*

But they pulled me out of the sack,
And they stuck me together with glue,
And then I knew what to do.
I made a model of you,
A man in black with a Meinkampf look   65

And a love of the rack and the screw.
And I said I do, I do.
So daddy, I'm finally through.
The black telephone's off at the root,
The voices just can't worm through.   70

If I've killed one man, I've killed two —
The vampire who said he was you
And drank my blood for a year,
Seven years, if you want to know.
Daddy, you can lie back now.   75

There's a stake in your fat black heart
And the villagers never liked you.
They are dancing and stamping on you.
They always *knew* it was you.
Daddy, daddy, you bastard, I'm through.   80

Dona Stein (b. 1935)

Putting Mother By

We are in her kitchen;
we have one enormous
pot and all the spices
are together.

We are too tiny and take   5
so long to sterilize
the jar; finally, more

water is boiling, waiting.
We don't have to call,
she hears and comes   10
into her kitchen.

We lift her over the pot;
she slips into the water
without a murmur.
She does not try to get out.   15

Later, we stand on tiptoes
and watch her inside
the Mason jar floating
in liquid by bay leaves
and flakes of pepper.   20
Dill weed floats like
a pine tree around her hair.

We look at each other, we
press our noses against
the jar and see she is more   25
surprised than anything else.

Carefully we carry her down
into the cellar; we store
her next to the peaches and plums;
we have her now.   30

Lucille Clifton (b. 1936)

in the inner city

in the inner city
or
like we call it
home
we think a lot about uptown   5
and the silent nights
and the houses straight as
dead men
and the pastel lights
and we hang on to our no place   10
happy to be alive
and in the inner city
or
like we call it
home   15

Ishmael Reed (b. *1938*)

beware   :   do not read this poem

tonite   ,   thriller was
abt an ol woman   , so vain she
surrounded herself w/
    many mirrors

it got so bad that finally she   5
locked herself indoors & her
whole life became the
    mirrors

  one day the villagers broke
  into her house   ,   but she was too   10
  swift for them   .   she disappeared
    into a mirror

  each tenant who bought the house
  after that   ,   lost a loved one to
    the ol woman in the mirror   :   15
    first a little girl
    then a young woman
    then the young woman/s husband

  the hunger of this poem is legendary
  it has taken in many victims   20
  back off from this poem
  it has drawn in yr feet
  back off from this poem
  it has drawn in yr legs

  back off from this poem   25
  it is a greedy mirror
  you are into this poem   from
    the waist down
  nobody can hear you can they   ?
  this poem has had you up to here   30
    belch
  this poem aint got no manners
  you cant call out frm this poem
  relax now & go w/ this poem
  move & roll on to this poem   35
  do not resist this poem

this poem has yr eyes
this poem has his head
this poem has his arms
this poem has his fingers   40
this poem has his fingertips

this poem is the reader & the
reader this poem

statistic :   the us bureau of missing persons reports
                 that in 1968 over 100,000 people disappeared
                 leaving no solid clues
                         nor trace   only
        a space   in the lives of their friends

Seamus Heaney (b. 1939)

The Skunk

Up, black, striped and damasked like the chasuble
At a funeral mass, the skunk's tail
Paraded the skunk. Night after night
I expected her like a visitor.   4

The refrigerator whinnied into silence.
My desk light softened beyond the verandah.
Small oranges loomed in the orange tree.
I began to be tense as a voyeur.   8

After eleven years I was composing
Love-letters again, broaching the word "wife"
Like a stored cask, as if its slender vowel
Had mutated into the night earth and air   12

Of California. The beautiful, useless
Tang of eucalyptus spelt your absence.
The aftermath of a mouthful of wine
Was like inhaling you off a cold pillow.   16

And there she was, the intent and glamorous,
Ordinary, mysterious skunk,
Mythologized, demythologized,
Snuffing the boards five feet beyond me.   *20*

It all came back to me last night, stirred
By the sootfall of your things at bedtime,
Your head-down, tail-up hunt in a bottom drawer
For the black plunge-line nightdress.   *24*

Don L. Lee (b. 1942)

But He Was Cool
or: he even stopped for green lights

super-cool
ultrablack
a tan / purple
had a beautiful shade.

he had a double-natural   *5*
that wd put the sisters to shame.
his dashikis were tailor made
& his beads were imported sea shells
        (from some blk/country i never heard of)
he was triple-hip.   *10*

his tikis were hand carved
out of ivory
& came express from the motherland.
he would greet u in swahili
& say good-by in yoruba.   *15*

wooooooooooooo-jim he bes so cool & ill tel li gent
        cool-cool is so cool he was un-cooled by other niggers' cool
        cool-cool ultracool was bop-cool/ice box cool so cool cold
                cool
        his wine didn't have to be cooled, him was air conditioned
                cool
        cool-cool/real cool made me cool — now ain't that cool *20*
        cool-cool so cool him nick-named refrigerator.

cool-cool so cool
he didn't know,

after detroit, newark, chicago &c.,
we had to hip   25
        cool-cool / super-cool / real cool
        that
to be black
is   30
to be
very-hot.

Nikki Giovanni (b. 1943)

Master Charge Blues

its wednesday night baby
and i'm all alone
wednesday night baby
and i'm all alone
sitting with myself   5
waiting for the telephone

wanted you baby
but you said you had to go
wanted you yeah
but you said you had to go   10
called your best friend
but he can't come 'cross no more

did you ever go to bed
at the end of a busy day
look over and see the smooth   15
where your hump usta lay
feminine odor and no reason why
i said feminine odor and no reason why
asked the lord to help me
he shook his head "not i"   20

but i'm a modern woman baby
ain't gonna let this get me down
i'm a modern woman
ain't gonna let this get me down
gonna take my master charge   25
and get everything in town

Drama

17

Some Elements of Drama

The earlier parts of this book have dealt with narrative, both in prose and in verse, and with what can roughly be called song or lyric. A third literary type (to use a traditional system of classification) is drama, consisting of plays written for the theater.* In a play, the author has receded from his creation; the words are communicated by actors who impersonate the characters. Of course both story and song have their dramatic aspects. In a narrative, the author usually includes **dialogue** (conversation), in which the characters are heard directly rather than through the voice of the narrator, and the narrator himself may be an invented character. Similarly, the author of a lyric poem invents a speaker and a situation. The distinguishing characteristic of a play, then, is not invented speakers or dialogue, but impersonation by actors.

Below is a brief play, a tenth-century imitation (that is, representation or re-creation) of the New Testament narrative of the discovery that the crucified Christ had arisen from the tomb. This play, known as *Quem Quaeritis* (Latin: "Whom do you seek?") is commonly considered the earliest extant European play after the end of the Roman drama. Three priests represent the three Marys who visited the tomb. They go to a place representing the tomb and find an angel (a fourth priest, dressed in white, holding a palm branch) who, by displaying a cloth in which the cross had

---

* **Drama,** unfortunately, has acquired too many meanings. It can denote (as above) the whole body of work written for the theater, or a single play, or a serious but untragic play, or (as in "Life is full of drama") events that contain conflict, tension, surprise.

previously been wrapped, shows that Christ has arisen. The bits of dialogue (based closely on Matthew 28:1–7 and Mark 16:1–8) had developed in the ninth century, but the tenth-century Latin account by Ethelwold, Bishop of Winchester, gives us the stage directions for the play. What follows is a translation of Ethelwold,* run together with a translation of the play.

Anonymous

Quem Quaeritis

While the third lesson is being chanted, let four brethren vest themselves. Let one of these, vested in an alb, enter as though to take part in the service, and let him approach the sepulcher without attracting attention and sit there quietly with a palm in his hand. While the third respond is chanted, let the remaining three follow, and let them all, vested in copes, bearing in their hands thuribles with incense, and stepping delicately as those who seek something, approach the sepulcher. These things are done in imitation of the angel sitting in the monument, and the women with spices coming to anoint the body of Jesus. When therefore he who sits there beholds the three approach him like folk lost and seeking something, let him begin in a dulcet voice of medium pitch to sing:

> Whom do you seek in the sepulcher, O followers of Christ?

And when he has sung it to the end, let the three reply in unison:

> Jesus of Nazareth who was crucified, O celestial one!

So he:

> He is not here, He has risen as He foretold.
> Go, announce that He is risen from the dead.

At the word of this bidding let those three turn to the choir and say:

> Alleluia! The Lord is risen today,
> The strong lion, Christ the Son of God! Unto God give thanks, eia!

* The translation is by E. K. Chambers, *The Medieval Stage* (Oxford, 1903), II, 14–15.

This said, let the one, still sitting there and as if recalling them, say the anthem:

> Come, and see the place where the Lord was laid,
> Alleluia! Alleluia!

And saying this, let him rise, and lift the veil, and show them the place bare of the cross, but only the cloths laid there in which the cross was wrapped:

> Go quickly, and tell the disciples that the Lord is risen.
> Alleluia! Alleluia!

And when they have seen this, let them set down the thuribles which they bear in that same sepulcher, and take the cloth, and hold it up in the face of the clergy, and as if to demonstrate that the Lord has risen and is no longer wrapped therein, let them sing the anthem:

> The Lord is risen from the sepulcher,
> Who for us was hanged on the cross, alleluia!

and lay the cloth upon the altar. When the anthem is done, let the prior, sharing in their gladness at the triumph of our King, in that, having vanquished death, He rose again, begin the hymn *Te Deum laudamus*. And this begun, all the bells chime out together.

All the elements of a play are here: an action (i.e., not the gestures but a story, a happening, the movement from doubt to joyful certainty) imitated by impersonators (priests). Notice, too, that the impersonation is aided by scenery ("the place bare of the cross"), properties (the angel's palm branch), costumes (copes and an alb), and gestures ("stepping delicately as those who seek something"). Even sound effects are used: "All the bells chime out together."

Before looking at a longer and more complex play, a few words should be said about **plot.** Although plot is sometimes equated with the gist of the narrative — the story — it is sometimes reserved to denote the writer's *arrangement* of the happenings in the story. Thus, all plays about the assassination of Julius Caesar have pretty much the same story, but by beginning his play with a scene of workmen enjoying a holiday (and thereby introducing the motif of the fickleness of the mob) Shakespeare's play has a plot different from a play that omits such a scene.

Handbooks on the drama often suggest that a plot (arrangement of happenings) should have a **rising action,** a **climax,** and a

falling action. This sort of plot can be diagramed as a pyramid, the tension rising through complications or **crises** to a climax, at which point the fate of the **protagonist** (chief character) is firmly established; the climax is the apex, and the tension allegedly slackens as we witness the **dénouement** (unknotting). Shakespeare sometimes used a pyramidal structure, placing his climax neatly in the middle of what seems to us to be the third of five acts.* Roughly the first half of *Julius Caesar* shows Brutus rising, reaching his height in III.i with the death of Caesar; but later in this scene he gives Marc Antony permission to speak at Caesar's funeral and thus he sets in motion his own fall, which occupies the second half of the play. In *Macbeth,* the protagonist attains his height in III.i ("Thou hast it now: King"), but he soon perceives that he is going downhill.

> I am in blood
> Stepped in so far, that, should I wade no more,
> Returning were as tedious as go o'er.

In *Hamlet,* the protagonist proves to his own satisfaction Claudius's guilt (by the play within the play) in III.ii, but almost immediately he begins to worsen his position by failing to kill Claudius when he is an easy target (III.iii) and by contaminating himself with the murder of Polonius (III.iv).

Of course, no law demands such a structure, and a hunt for the pyramid usually causes the hunter to overlook all the crises but the middle one. William Butler Yeats once suggestively diagramed a good plot not as a pyramid but as a line moving diagonally upward, punctuated by several crises. Perhaps it is sufficient to say that a good plot has its moments of tension, but the location of these will vary with the play. They are the product of **conflict,** but not all conflict produces tension; there is conflict but little tension in a ball game when the score is 10–0 and the visiting

---

* An **act** is a main division in a drama or opera. Act divisions probably stem from Roman theory and derive ultimately from the Greek practice of separating episodes in a play by choral interludes, but Greek (and probably Roman) plays were performed without interruption, for the choral interludes were part of the plays themselves. Elizabethan plays, too, may have been performed without breaks; the division of Elizabethan plays into five acts is usually the work of editors rather than of authors. Frequently an act division today (commonly indicated by lowering the curtain and turning up the houselights) denotes change in locale and lapse of time. A **scene** is a smaller unit, either (1) a division with no change of locale or abrupt shift of time, or (2) a division consisting of an actor or group of actors on the stage; according to the second definition, the departure or entrance of an actor changes the composition of the group and thus introduces a new scene. (In an entirely different sense, the scene is the locale where a work is set.)

pitcher comes to bat in the ninth inning with two out and none on base.

Regardless of how a plot is diagramed, the **exposition** is that part that tells the audience what it has to know about the past, the **antecedent action.** When the three Marys say they are seeking Jesus, "who was crucified," they are offering exposition. In later plays, the two gossiping servants who tell each other that after a year away in Paris the young master is coming home tomorrow with a new wife are giving the audience the exposition. The Elizabethans and the Greeks sometimes tossed out all pretense at dialogue, and began with a **prologue,** like the one spoken by the Chorus at the outset of *Romeo and Juliet:*

> Two households, both alike in dignity
> >In fair Verona, where we lay our scene,
> From ancient grudge break to new mutiny,
> >Where civil blood makes civil hands unclean.
> From forth the fatal loins of these two foes
> >A pair of star-crossed lovers take their life. . . .

And in Tennessee Williams's *The Glass Menagerie,* Tom's first speech is a sort of prologue. However, the exposition may also extend far into the play, being given in dribs and drabs. Occasionally the **soliloquy** (speech of a character alone on the stage, revealing his thoughts) or the **aside** (speech in the presence of others but unheard by them) is used to do the job of putting the audience in possession of the essential facts. The soliloquy and the aside, of course, are not limited to exposition; they are used to reveal the private thoughts of characters who, like people in real life, do not always tell others what their inner thoughts are. The soliloquy is especially used for meditation, where we might say the character is interacting not with another character but with himself.

Exposition has been discussed as though it consists simply of informing the audience about events; but exposition can do much more. It can give us an understanding of the characters who themselves are talking about other characters, it can evoke a mood, and it can generate tension. The first scene in *Julius Caesar,* in which the tribunes drive the commoners from the stage, is less important for the details it gives us about Caesar and Pompey than for its picture of a fickle mob, a mob that will later applaud the death of Caesar and then turn and drive the assassins out of Rome. When we summarize the opening act of a play and treat it as "mere exposition" we are probably losing what is in fact dramatic in it.

Because a play is not simply words but words spoken with

accompanying gestures by performers who are usually costumed and in a particular setting, it may be argued that to read a play (rather than to see and hear it) is to falsify it. Drama is not literature, some people hold, but theater. However, there are replies: a play can be literature as well as theater, and the reader of a play can perhaps enact in the theater of his mind a more effective play than the one put on by imperfect actors ("The best in this kind are but shadows," Shakespeare's Duke Theseus says) in front of an audience that coughs and whispers. This mental enactment is aided by abundant stage direction in many contemporary plays. In Eugene O'Neill's *Desire Under the Elms,* about four hundred words (describing the set and the gestures of some of the characters) precede the first speech. This speech consists of two words, "God! Purty!" and it is followed by two hundred words of further description. O'Neill informs the reader that the elms over the house have "a sinister maternity," that Eben, twenty-five years old, "finds himself trapped but inwardly unsubdued," that Simeon is thirty-nine, that Peter is thirty-seven, and so forth. (In the theater, not every actor can communicate by his words, gestures, and makeup that he is twenty-five or thirty-nine or thirty-seven.) Bernard Shaw sometimes outdid O'Neill in writing for the reader: many of his plays have enormous prefaces, and some (such as *Candida*) have unactable stage directions: "They embrace. But they do not know the secret in the poet's heart." Furthermore, the author's dialogue rarely reaches the stage intact; in addition to interpreting, directors cut and reshape scenes, so that it is often accurate to say we get Gielgud's or Olivier's rather than Shakespeare's *Hamlet.*

Finally (to reverse our tactics), even if it be granted that a good performance reveals qualities in a play that a reading misses, half a loaf is better than none. You may never get a chance to see Synge's *Riders to the Sea,* but why not experience at least a good part of it in a reading?

John Millington Synge *(1871–1909)*

Riders to the Sea

List of Characters

Maurya, an old woman
Bartley, her son
Cathleen, her daughter
Nora, a younger daughter
Men and women

Scene. *An Island off the West of Ireland.*

Cottage kitchen, with nets, oil-skins, spinning-wheel, some new boards standing by the wall, etc. Cathleen, a girl of about twenty, finishes kneading cake, and puts it down in the pot-oven by the fire; then wipes her hands, and begins to spin at the wheel. Nora, a young girl, puts her head in at the door.

Nora (*in a low voice*). Where is she?
Cathleen. She's lying down, God help her, and may be sleeping, if she's able.

Nora comes in softly, and takes a bundle from under her shawl.

Cathleen (*spinning the wheel rapidly*). What is it you have?
Nora. The young priest is after bringing them. It's a shirt and a plain stocking were got off a drowned man in Donegal.

Cathleen stops her wheel with a sudden movement, and leans out to listen.

Nora. We're to find out if it's Michael's they are, some time herself will be down looking by the sea.
Cathleen. How would they be Michael's, Nora? How would he go the length of that way to the far north?
Nora. The young priest says he's known the like of it. "If it's Michael's they are," says he, "you can tell herself he's got a clean burial by the grace of God, and if they're not his, let no one say a word about them, for she'll be getting her death," says he, "with crying and lamenting."

The door which Nora half-closed is blown open by a gust of wind.

Cathleen (*looking out anxiously*). Did you ask him would he stop Bartley going this day with the horses to the Galway fair?

Nora. "I won't stop him," says he, "but let you not be afraid.
  Herself does be saying prayers half through the night, and
  the Almighty God won't leave her destitute," says he, "with
  no son living."

Cathleen. Is the sea bad by the white rocks, Nora?

Nora. Middling bad, God help us. There's a great roaring in the
  west, and it's worse it'll be getting when the tide's turned
  to the wind.

  She goes over to the table with the bundle.

  Shall I open it now?

Cathleen. Maybe she'd wake up on us, and come in before we'd
  done. (*Coming to the table.*) It's a long time we'll be, and the
  two of us crying.

Nora (*goes to the inner door and listens*). She's moving about on the
  bed. She'll be coming in a minute.

Cathleen. Give me the ladder, and I'll put them up in the turf-
  loft, the way she won't know of them at all, and maybe
  when the tide turns she'll be going down to see would he
  be floating from the east.

  *They put the ladder against the gable of the chimney; Cathleen
  goes up a few steps and hides the bundle in the turf-loft. Maurya
  comes from the inner room.*

Maurya (*looking up at Cathleen and speaking querulously*). Isn't it turf
  enough you have for this day and evening?

Cathleen. There's a cake baking at the fire for a short space (*throwing
  down the turf*) and Bartley will want it when the tide turns
  if he goes to Connemara.

  Nora picks up the turf and puts it round the pot-oven.

Maurya (*sitting down on a stool at the fire*). He won't go this day
  with the wind rising from the south and west. He won't go
  this day, for the young priest will stop him surely.

Nora. He'll not stop him, mother, and I heard Eamon Simon and
  Stephen Pheety and Colum Shawn saying he would go.

Maurya. Where is he itself?

Nora. He went down to see would there be another boat sailing
  in the week, and I'm thinking it won't be long till he's here
  now, for the tide's turning at the green head, and the hooker's°
  tacking from the east.

hooker sailing boat

Cathleen. I hear some one passing the big stones.

Nora (looking out). He's coming now, and he in a hurry.

Bartley (comes in and looks round the room. Speaking sadly and quietly). Where is the bit of new rope, Cathleen, was bought in Connemara?

Cathleen (coming down). Give it to him, Nora; it's on a nail by the white boards. I hung it up this morning, for the pig with the black feet was eating it.

Nora (giving him a rope). Is that it, Bartley?

Maurya. You'd do right to leave that rope, Bartley, hanging by the boards. (*Bartley takes the rope.*) It will be wanting in this place, I'm telling you, if Michael is washed up to-morrow morning, or the next morning, or any morning in the week, for it's a deep grave we'll make him by the grace of God.

Bartley (beginning to work with the rope). I've no halter the way I can ride down on the mare, and I must go now quickly. This is the one boat going for two weeks or beyond it, and the fair will be a good fair for horses I heard them saying below.

Maurya. It's a hard thing they'll be saying below if the body is washed up and there's no man in it to make the coffin, and I after giving a big price for the finest white boards you'd find in Connemara.

She looks round at the boards.

Bartley. How would it be washed up, and we after looking each day for nine days, and a strong wind blowing a while back from the west and south?

Maurya. If it wasn't found itself, that wind is raising the sea, and there was a star up against the moon, and it rising in the night. If it was a hundred horses, or a thousand horses you had itself, what is the price of a thousand horses against a son where there is one son only?

Bartley (working at the halter, to Cathleen). Let you go down each day, and see the sheep aren't jumping in on the rye, and if the jobber comes you can sell the pig with the black feet if there is a good price going.

Maurya. How would the like of her get a good price for a pig?

Bartley (to Cathleen). If the west wind holds with the last bit of the moon let you and Nora get up weed enough for another cock for the kelp.° It's hard set we'll be from this day with no one in it but one man to work.

kelp   seaweed (used for fertilizer)

Maurya. It's hard set we'll be surely the day you're drownd'd with the rest. What way will I live and the girls with me, and I an old woman looking for the grave?

Bartley lays down the halter, takes off his old coat, and puts on a newer one of the same flannel.

Bartley (to Nora). Is she coming to the pier?

Nora (looking out). She's passing the green head and letting fall her sails.

Bartley (getting his purse and tobacco). I'll have half an hour to go down, and you'll see me coming again in two days, or in three days, or maybe in four days if the wind is bad.

Maurya (turning round to the fire, and putting her shawl over her head). Isn't it a hard and cruel man won't hear a word from an old woman, and she holding him from the sea?

Cathleen. It's the life of a young man to be going on the sea, and who would listen to an old woman with one thing and she saying it over?

Bartley (taking the halter). I must go now quickly. I'll ride down on the red mare, and the gray pony'll run behind me. . . . The blessing of God on you.

He goes out.

Maurya (crying out as he is in the door). He's gone now, God spare us, and we'll not see him again. He's gone now, and when the black night is falling I'll have no son left me in the world.

Cathleen. Why wouldn't you give him your blessing and he looking round in the door? Isn't it sorrow enough is on every one in this house without your sending him out with an unlucky word behind him, and a hard word in his ear?

Maurya takes up the tongs and begins raking the fire aimlessly without looking round.

Nora (turning towards her). You're taking away the turf from the cake.

Cathleen (crying out). The Son of God forgive us, Nora, we're after forgetting his bit of bread.

She comes over to the fire.

Nora. And it's destroyed he'll be going till dark night, and he after eating nothing since the sun went up.

Cathleen (turning the cake out of the oven). It's destroyed he'll be, surely. There's no sense left on any person in a house where an old woman will be talking for ever.

Maurya sways herself on her stool.

Cathleen (*cutting off some of the bread and rolling it in a cloth; to Maurya*). Let you go down now to the spring well and give him this and he passing. You'll see him then and the dark word will be broken, and you can say "God speed you," the way he'll be easy in his mind.

Maurya (*taking the bread*). Will I be in it as soon as himself?

Cathleen. If you go now quickly.

Maurya (*standing up unsteadily*). It's hard set I am to walk.

Cathleen (*looking at her anxiously*). Give her the stick, Nora, or maybe she'll slip on the big stones.

Nora. What stick?

Cathleen. The stick Michael brought from Connemara.

Maurya (*taking a stick Nora gives her*). In the big world the old people do be leaving things after them for their sons and children, but in this place it is the young men do be leaving things behind for them that do be old.

She goes out slowly. Nora goes over to the ladder.

Cathleen. Wait, Nora, maybe she'd turn back quickly. She's that sorry, God help her, you wouldn't know the thing she'd do.

Nora. Is she gone around by the bush?

Cathleen (*looking out*). She's gone now. Throw it down quickly, for the Lord knows when she'll be out of it again.

Nora (*getting the bundle from the loft*). The young priest said he'd be passing to-morrow, and we might go down and speak to him below if it's Michael's they are surely.

Cathleen (*taking the bundle*). Did he say what way they were found?

Nora (*coming down*). "There were two men," says he, "and they rowing round with poteen° before the cocks crowed, and the oar of one of them caught the body, and they passing the black cliffs of the north."

Cathleen (*trying to open the bundle*). Give me a knife, Nora, the strings perished with the salt water, and there's a black knot on it you wouldn't loosen in a week.

Nora (*giving her a knife*). I've heard tell it was a long way to Donegal.

Cathleen (*cutting the string*). It is surely. There was a man in here a while ago — the man sold us that knife — and he said if you set off walking from the rock beyond, it would be seven days you'd be in Donegal.

Nora. And what time would a man take, and he floating?

---

poteen illegal whiskey

Cathleen opens the bundle and takes out a bit of a stocking. They look at them eagerly.

Cathleen (*in a low voice*). The Lord spare us, Nora! isn't it a queer hard thing to say if it's his they are surely?

Nora. I'll get his shirt off the hook the way we can put the one flannel on the other. (*She looks through some clothes hanging in the corner.*) It's not with them, Cathleen, and where will it be?

Cathleen. I'm thinking Bartley put it on him in the morning, for his own shirt was heavy with the salt in it. (*Pointing to the corner.*) There's a bit of a sleeve was of the same stuff. Give me that and it will do.

Nora brings it to her and they compare the flannel.

Cathleen. It's the same stuff, Nora; but if it is itself aren't there great rolls of it in the shops of Galway, and isn't it many another man may have a shirt of it as well as Michael himself?

Nora (*who has taken up the stocking and counted the stitches, crying out*). It's Michael, Cathleen, it's Michael; God spare his soul, and what will herself say when she hears this story, and Bartley on the sea?

Cathleen (*taking the stocking*). It's a plain stocking.

Nora. It's the second one of the third pair I knitted, and I put up three score stitches, and I dropped four of them.

Cathleen (*counts the stitches*). It's that number is in it. (*Crying out.*) Ah, Nora, isn't it a bitter thing to think of him floating that way to the far north, and no one to keen° him but the black hags that do be flying on the sea?

Nora (*swinging herself round, and throwing out her arms on the clothes*). And isn't it a pitiful thing when there is nothing left of a man who was a great rower and fisher, but a bit of an old shirt and a plain stocking!

Cathleen (*after an instant*). Tell me is herself coming, Nora? I hear a little sound on the path.

Nora (*looking out*). She is, Cathleen. She's coming up to the door.

Cathleen. Put these things away before she'll come in. Maybe it's easier she'll be after giving her blessing to Bartley, and we won't let on we've heard anything the time he's on the sea.

Nora (*helping Cathleen to close the bundle*). We'll put them here in the corner.

They put them into a hole in the chimney corner. Cathleen goes back to the spinning-wheel.

keen lament

Nora. Will she see it was crying I was?

Cathleen. Keep your back to the door the way the light'll not be on you.

> *Nora sits down at the chimney corner, with her back to the door. Maurya comes in very slowly, without looking at the girls, and goes over to her stool at the other side of the fire. The cloth with the bread is still in her hand. The girls look at each other, and Nora points to the bundle of bread.*

Cathleen (after spinning for a moment). You didn't give him his bit of bread?

> *Maurya begins to keen softly, without turning round.*

Cathleen. Did you see him riding down?

> *Maurya goes on keening.*

Cathleen (a little impatiently). God forgive you; isn't it a better thing to raise your voice and tell what you seen, than to be making lamentation for a thing that's done? Did you see Bartley, I'm saying to you.

Maurya (with a weak voice). My heart's broken from this day.

Cathleen (as before). Did you see Bartley?

Maurya. I seen the fearfulest thing.

Cathleen (leaves her wheel and looks out). God forgive you; he's riding the mare now over the green head, and the gray pony behind him.

Maurya (starts, so that her shawl falls back from her head and shows her white tossed hair. With a frightened voice). The gray pony behind him.

Cathleen (coming to the fire). What is it ails you, at all?

Maurya (speaking very slowly). I've seen the fearfulest thing any person has seen, since the day Bride Dara seen the dead man with the child in his arms.

Cathleen and Nora. Uah.

> *They crouch down in front of the old woman at the fire.*

Nora. Tell us what it is you seen.

Maurya. I went down to the spring well, and I stood there saying a prayer to myself. Then Bartley came along, and he riding on the red mare with the gray pony behind him. *(She puts up her hands, as if to hide something from her eyes.)* The Son of God spare us, Nora!

Cathleen. What is it you seen?

Maurya. I seen Michael himself.

Cathleen (speaking softly). You did not, mother; it wasn't Michael

you seen, for his body is after being found in the far north,
and he's got a clean burial by the grace of God.

Maurya (a little defiantly). I'm after seeing him this day, and he
riding and galloping. Bartley came first on the red mare;
and I tried to say "God speed you," but something choked
the words in my throat. He went by quickly; and "the
blessing of God on you," says he, and I could say nothing.
I looked up then, and I crying, at the gray pony, and there
was Michael upon it — with fine clothes on him, and new
shoes on his feet.

Cathleen (begins to keen). It's destroyed we are from this day. It's
destroyed, surely.

Nora. Didn't the young priest say the Almighty God wouldn't
leave her destitute with no son living?

Maurya (in a low voice, but clearly). It's little the like of him knows
of the sea. . . . Bartley will be lost now, and let you call in
Eamon and make me a good coffin out of the white boards,
for I won't live after them. I've had a husband, and a husband's
father, and six sons in this house — six fine men, though it
was a hard birth I had with every one of them and they
coming to the world — and some of them were found and
some of them were not found, but they're gone now the lot
of them. . . . There were Stephen, and Shawn, were lost in
the great wind, and found after in the Bay of Gregory of
the Golden Mouth, and carried up the two of them on the
one plank, and in by that door.

*She pauses for a moment, the girls start as if they heard something
through the door that is half open behind them.*

Nora (in a whisper). Did you hear that, Cathleen? Did you hear a
noise in the north-east?

Cathleen (in a whisper). There's some one after crying out by the
seashore.

Maurya (continues without hearing anything). There was Sheamus and
his father, and his own father again, were lost in a dark
night, and not a stick or sign was seen of them when the
sun went up. There was Patch after was drowned out of a
curagh° that turned over. I was sitting here with Bartley,
and he a baby, lying on my two knees, and I seen two
women, and three women, and four women coming in, and
they crossing themselves, and not saying a word. I looked
out then, and there were men coming after them, and they

---

curagh   unstable vessel of tarred canvas on a wood frame; canoe

holding a thing in the half of a red sail, and water dripping
out of it — it was a dry day, Nora — and leaving a track
to the door.

*She pauses again with her hand stretched out towards the door. It
opens softly and old women begin to come in, crossing themselves
on the threshold, and kneeling down in front of the stage with red
petticoats over their heads.*

Maurya (*half in a dream, to Cathleen*). Is it Patch, or Michael, or
what is it at all?

Cathleen. Michael is after being found in the far north, and when
he is found there how could he be here in this place?

Maurya. There does be a power of young men floating round in
the sea, and what way would they know if it was Michael
they had, or another man like him, for when a man is nine
days in the sea, and the wind blowing, it's hard set his own
mother would be to say what man was it.

Cathleen. It's Michael, God spare him, for they're after sending
us a bit of his clothes from the far north.

*She reaches out and hands Maurya the clothes that belonged to
Michael. Maurya stands up slowly and takes them in her hand.
Nora looks out.*

Nora. They're carrying a thing among them and there's water
dripping out of it and leaving a track by the big stones.

Cathleen (*in a whisper to the women who have come in*). Is it Bartley
it is?

One of the Women. It is surely, God rest his soul.

*Two younger women come in and pull out the table. Then men
carry in the body of Bartley, laid on a plank, with a bit of sail
over it, and lay it on the table.*

Cathleen (*to the women, as they are doing so*). What way was he
drowned?

One of the Women. The gray pony knocked him into the sea, and
he was washed out where there is a great surf on the white
rocks.

*Maurya has gone over and knelt down at the head of the table.
The women are keening softly and swaying themselves with a slow
movement. Cathleen and Nora kneel at the other end of the table.
The men kneel near the door.*

Maurya (*raising her head and speaking as if she did not see the people
around her*). They're all gone now, and there isn't anything

more the sea can do to me. . . . I'll have no call now to be up crying and praying when the wind breaks from the south, and you can hear the surf is in the east, and the surf is in the west, making a great stir with the two noises, and they hitting one on the other. I'll have no call now to be going down and getting Holy Water in the dark nights after Samhain,° and I won't care what way the sea is when the other women will be keening. (*To Nora.*) Give me the Holy Water, Nora, there's a small cup still on the dresser.

Nora gives it to her.

Maurya (*drops Michael's clothes across Bartley's feet, and sprinkles the Holy Water over him*). It isn't that I haven't prayed for you, Bartley, to the Almighty God. It isn't that I haven't said prayers in the dark night till you wouldn't know what I'ld be saying; but it's a great rest I'll have now, and it's time surely. It's a great rest I'll have now, and great sleeping in the long nights after Samhain, if it's only a bit of wet flour we do have to eat, and maybe a fish that would be stinking.

She kneels down again, crossing herself, and saying prayers under her breath.

Cathleen (*to an old man*). Maybe yourself and Eamon would make a coffin when the sun rises. We have fine white boards herself bought, God help her, thinking Michael would be found, and I have a new cake you can eat while you'll be working.

The Old Man (*looking at the boards*). Are there nails with them?

Cathleen. There are not, Colum; we didn't think of the nails.

Another Man. It's a great wonder she wouldn't think of the nails, and all the coffins she's seen made already.

Cathleen. It's getting old she is, and broken.

Maurya stands up again very slowly and spreads out the pieces of Michael's clothes beside the body, sprinkling them with the last of the Holy Water.

Nora (*in a whisper to Cathleen*). She's quiet now and easy; but the day Michael was drowned you could hear her crying out from this to the spring well. It's fonder she was of Michael, and would any one have thought that?

Cathleen (*slowly and clearly*). An old woman will be soon tired with anything she will do, and isn't it nine days herself is after crying and keening, and making great sorrow in the house?

Samhain   November 1, All Saints' Day

Maurya (puts the empty cup mouth downwards on the table, and lays her hands together on Bartley's feet). They're all together this time, and the end is come. May the Almighty God have mercy on Bartley's soul, and on Michael's soul, and on the souls of Sheamus and Patch, and Stephen and Shawn *(bending her head)*; and may He have mercy on my soul, Nora, and on the soul of every one is left living in the world.

She pauses, and the keen rises a little more loudly from the women, then sinks away.

Maurya (continuing.) Michael has a clean burial in the far north, by the grace of the Almighty God. Bartley will have a fine coffin out of the white boards, and a deep grave surely. What more can we want than that? No man at all can be living for ever, and we must be satisfied.

She kneels down again and the curtain falls slowly.

Synge first visited the Aran Islands (three rocky places off the west coast of Ireland, inhabited by Gaelic-speaking fishermen) in the summer of 1898. From this visit and subsequent ones he derived the material for *The Aran Islands,* an account of life there, full of observations and bits of folklore he had picked up. In it one can find something of the origins of *Riders to the Sea*: descriptions of bringing horses across the sound, including an account of an old woman who had a vision of her drowned son riding on a horse; a reference to a coffin untimely made out of boards prepared for another person; and a reference to a body that floated ashore some weeks after the man drowned.

In writing the play Synge chose among the innumerable things he saw and heard, selecting (as any artist does) from the welter or chaos of experience to put together a unified story. A summary of the play's story would run along these lines: an old woman named Maurya, who has lost her husband and five sons to the sea — one very recently — learns that a drowned man has been found, and almost simultaneously she learns of the death of her sixth son. This summary of the story proceeds chronologically, but the play does not. The play begins with a daughter, Cathleen, kneading a cake, setting it in the oven, and then spinning at a wheel. Another daughter enters and speaks the first line, asking about some third woman, who we later come to understand is Maurya. The next few speeches are about "a shirt and a plain stocking were got off a drowned man in Donegal," and we learn that these remnants may belong to someone named Michael. In another moment we learn that Michael and the woman (still referred to only as "she") are closely related. With the eighth speech yet another important character is named, Bartley, who intends to take horses to the Galway fair. And so we are introduced to the characters, with oblique references, and bit by bit we put together the relationships. The playwright's *arrangement of the story,* rather than a strictly chronological arrangement, is (for many critics) Synge's **plot.**

In a play, **gesture** no less than dialogue is a means of communication. What Cathleen *says* is important, but so too is what she *does.* Her actions, described in the first stage direction, tell us a good deal about the islanders' laborious existence. She finishes one task, kneading the dough, and turns to another, spinning. Synge tells us in another stage direction that during the first few lines she turns the wheel "rapidly," but when Nora mentions the clothing that has been found, "Cathleen stops her wheel with a sudden movement, and leans out to listen." She stops turning the wheel, of course, in order to concentrate on Nora's words, but the abrupt halting of the wheel also is part of the dramatist's way of saying that Michael no longer lives: his thread of life has been spun and untimely cut. A moment later there is another stage direction that has symbolic implications: "The door which Nora half closed is blown open by a gust of wind," suggesting (no less than the abundant talk of the bad weather) the periodic intrusion of powerful natural forces upon the lives of the islanders.

One need not compare *Riders to the Sea* (in which everything is related to everything else) with *The Aran Islands* (in which we have a wonderful grab bag of scarcely related details) to see that the careful arrangement of physical happenings and dialogue gives us more than a slice of life, more than a picture of a certain kind of Irish life. Synge's art extends beyond his plot to his language. The islanders spoke Gaelic, and Synge claimed that his English was close to a translation of their language; but the speeches — as distinct from the words — are Synge's, just as Macbeth's "I am in blood / Stepped in so far, that, should I wade no more, / Returning were as tedious as go o'er" is Shakespeare's creation although the individual words are pretty much the property of any literate American or Englishman. The speeches Synge creates, no less than his plot, belong to the world of art, though the speeches and the events are made up of the materials of Aran life.

Synge chose the peasant idiom because it seemed to him to have beauty and even grandeur, while at the same time it was rooted in people who lived an elemental existence. He saw no need to choose between beauty and truth: beauty without truth led writers of the late nineteenth century (he believed) to highly wrought yet trivial or even meaningless verse, and truth without beauty to dull pictures of man's insignificance. It is partly by making "every speech . . . as fully flavored as a nut or apple" that Synge produced a work that (although it deals with multiple deaths) is not depressing but is, like every work of art, stimulating: "Let you go down each day, and see the sheep aren't jumping in on the rye, and if the jobber comes you can sell the pig with the black feet if there is a good price going." Even the speeches on the inevitable end of man have, while they call attention to man's ignominious remains, richness and dignity: "And isn't it a pitiful thing when there is nothing left of a man who was a great rower and fisher, but a bit of an old shirt and a plain stocking?" Throughout the play this artful use of language communicates a picture of heroism and humbleness that is reassuring as well as grievous, nowhere more so than in Maurya's final speech, which calls attention to the hardness of life and the inevitability of death in such a way as almost to offer a kind of reassurance.

What is *Riders to the Sea* "about"? It is, of course, about people named Maurya, Bartley, and so forth, and it is about the life of Irish islanders — particularly the women — of 1900 and earlier. But clearly it is about something more; it has a theme, a vision.

What is this **theme**? Life proceeds from the sea, and is nourished by the sea, but the sea is also a source of death: "It's the life of a young man to be going on the sea," Cathleen says, suggesting something of man's inevitable struggle against the enormous impersonal forces of nature. "They're all gone now, and there isn't anything more the sea can do to me," Maurya says a little later, suggesting something of man's inevitable defeat in this struggle and yet of man's ability to triumph — in a way — by a clarity of vision. And finally Maurya says, in the last speech of the play: "Michael has a clean burial in the far north, by the grace of the Almighty God. Bartley will have a fine coffin out of the white boards, and a deep grave surely. What more can we want than that? No man at all can be living for ever, and we must be satisfied." Michael has a clean burial — but we know that the loss is grievous. Bartley will have a fine coffin — but the coffin was not meant for him, and we may recall two of Maurya's earlier speeches, when Bartley was alive: "It's hard set we'll be surely the day you're drownd'd with the rest. What way will I live and the girls with me, and I an old woman looking for the grave?" And: "In the big world the old people do be leaving things after them for their sons and children, but in this place it is the young

men do be leaving things behind for them that do be old." At
the end of the play, the young men are all gone, the last of them
"knocked . . . into the sea" by a gray pony, but, paradoxically,
Maurya's final speech reveals a majesty she lacked in the early part
of the play when, a little better off, she spoke "querulously" and
raked the fire "aimlessly." In the most important sense, then, the
action of the play is this movement of Maurya's mind, rather than
the physical doings of men and women who enter, cut open a
bundle, bring in a corpse, and so forth.

The word "drama" is from the Greek verb *dran, to do,* to
accomplish; in *Riders to the Sea* the thing accomplished is not only
the identification of Michael's clothing and the death of Bartley,
but the shift in Maurya's mind. Early in the play the priest (Nora
says) suggested that Michael may have had "a clean burial by the
grace of God"; midway in the play Cathleen says it is "a bitter
thing to think of him floating that way to the far north, and no
one to keen him but the black hags that do be flying on the sea."
Finally, after the death of Bartley, Maurya derives some comfort
from the thought that "Bartley will have a fine coffin out of the
white boards," and Michael "a clean burial in the far north." But
we distinguish between Maurya's view, born out of suffering, and
the simple faith of "the young priest" (his youth is insisted on);
she has been "hard set," known despair, seen the worst that can
happen ("They're all gone now, and there isn't anything more the
sea can do to me"), and now from the vantage point of one stripped
of all that one has cherished she can utter with dignity the most
terrible facts of life.

This is not to say that the play has a message. Synge abhorred
didactic drama, and in a preface to another play insisted that "the
drama, like the symphony, does not teach or prove anything." It
offers us "pleasure and excitement," rather than solutions that
inevitably become old-fashioned. The best plays, he said in a char-
acteristically homely figure, "can no more go out of fashion than
the blackberries on the hedges."

QUESTIONS

1. What is revealed about Maurya's state of mind by her speech
   (page 606): "He won't go this day with the wind rising from
   the south and west. He won't go this day, for the young
   priest will stop him surely." Why is her reference to the
   need for the rope (page 607) one of the strongest arguments
   she can propose for Bartley's staying?

2. Notice the references to the bread (or cake). Why are they in the play? And why the emphasis upon the rope?
3. What is implied by Maurya's vision of Michael "with fine clothes on him, and new shoes on his feet" (page 612)?
4. Trace the foreshadowing of Bartley's death.
5. Nora and Cathleen hear someone calling out by the seashore (page 612). Why doesn't Maurya hear the noise? Why does Synge not have a stage direction calling for a cry?
6. Does the fact that Maurya has forgotten the coffin-nails indicate (as Cathleen says, page 614) that she is "broken"?
7. Evaluate James Joyce's complaint that the catastrophe is brought about by a pony rather than by the sea. It has been suggested that a reply can be made to Joyce: Bartley is knocked into the sea by the gray pony, but this is not an accident, for the ghost of his brother Michael is riding the pony, and Irish ghosts commonly seek to bring the living into the realm of the dead. Is this reply satisfactory, or does it introduce a red herring?

18
Tragedy

Aristotle defined tragedy as a dramatization of a serious happening — not necessarily one ending with the death of the protagonist — and his definition remains among the best. But many plays have been written since Aristotle defined tragedy. When we think of Shakespeare's tragedies we cannot resist narrowing Aristotle's definition by adding something like "showing a struggle that rends the protagonist's whole being"; and when we think of the "problem plays" of the last hundred years — the serious treatments of such sociological problems as alcoholism and race prejudice — we cannot resist excluding some of them by adding to the definition something about the need for universal appeal. The question remains: Is there a single quality present in all works that we call tragedy and absent from works not called tragedy? If there is, no one has yet pointed it out to general satisfaction. But this failure does not mean that there is no such classification as tragedy. We sense that tragedies resemble each other as members of the same family resemble each other: two children have the mother's coloring and eyes, a third child has the mother's coloring but the father's eyes, a fourth child has the mother's eyes but the father's coloring.

The next few pages will examine three comments on tragedy, none of which is entirely acceptable, but each of which seems to have some degree of truth, and each of which can help us detect resemblances and differences among tragedies. The first comment is by Cyril Tourneur, a tragic dramatist of the early seventeenth century:

When the bad bleed, then is the tragedy good.

We think of Macbeth ("usurper," "butcher"). Macbeth, of course, is much more than a usurper and butcher, but it is undeniable that he is an offender against the moral order. Whatever the merits of Tourneur's statement, however, if we think of *Romeo and Juliet* (to consider only one play), we realize its inadequacy. Tourneur so stresses the guilt of the protagonist that his suffering becomes mere retributive justice. But we cannot plausibly say, for example, that Romeo and Juliet deserved to die because they married without their parents' consent; it is much too simple to call them "bad." Romeo and Juliet are young, in love, nobler in spirit than their parents. Tourneur's view is probably derived ultimately from an influential passage in Aristotle's *Poetics* in which Aristotle speaks of **hamartia,** sometimes literally translated as "missing the target," sometimes as "vice" or "flaw" or "weakness," but perhaps best translated as "mistake." Aristotle seems to imply that the hero is undone because of some mistake he commits, but this mistake need not be the result of a moral fault; it may be simply a miscalculation — for example, failure to foresee the consequences of a deed. Brutus makes a strategic mistake when he lets Marc Antony speak at Caesar's funeral, but we can hardly call it a vice. Because Aristotle's *hamartia* includes mistakes of this sort, the common translation "tragic flaw" is erroneous. In many Greek tragedies the hero's *hamartia* is **hybris** (or **hubris**), usually translated as "overweening pride." The hero forgets that he is fallible, acts as though he has the power and wisdom of the gods, and is later humbled for his arrogance. But one can argue that this self-assertiveness is not a vice but a virtue, not a weakness but a strength; if the hero is destroyed for his self-assertion, he is nevertheless greater than the people around him, just as the man who tries to stem a lynch mob is greater than the mob although he too may be lynched for his virtue. Or a hero may be undone by a high-mindedness that makes him vulnerable. Hamlet is vulnerable because he is, as his enemy says, "most generous and free from all contriving"; because Hamlet is high-minded, he will not suspect that the proposed fencing match is a murderous plot.

Next, here is a statement more or less the reverse of Tourneur's, by a Soviet critic, L. I. Timofeev:

> Tragedy in Soviet literature arouses a feeling of pride for the man who has accomplished a great deed for the people's happiness; it calls for continued struggle against the things which brought about the hero's death.

The distortions in Soviet criticism are often amusing: Hamlet is sometimes seen as an incipient Communist, undone by the decadent aristocracy; or Romeo and Juliet as young people of the future, undone by bourgeois parents. Recent Soviet drama so consistently shows the triumph of the worker that Western visitors to Russia have commented on the absence of contemporary tragic plays.

Still, there is much in the idea that the tragic hero accomplishes "a great deed" and perhaps we do resent "the things which brought about the hero's death." The stubbornness of the Montagues and Capulets, the fury of the mob that turns against Brutus, the crimes of Claudius in *Hamlet* — all these would seem in some measure to call for our indignation.

The third comment is by Arthur Miller:

> If it is true to say that in essence the tragic hero is intent upon claiming his whole due as a personality, and if this struggle must be total and without reservation, then it automatically demonstrates the indestructible will of man to achieve his humanity. . . . It is curious, although edifying, that the plays we revere, century after century, are the tragedies. In them, and in them alone, lies the belief — optimistic, if you will — in the perfectibility of man.

There is much in Miller's suggestions that the tragic hero makes a large and total claim and that the audience often senses triumph rather than despair in tragedies. We often feel that we have witnessed human greatness — that the hero, despite profound suffering, has lived according to his ideals. We may feel that we have achieved new insight into human greatness. But the perfectibility of man? Do we feel that *Julius Caesar* or *Macbeth* or *Hamlet* have to do with human perfectibility? Don't these plays suggest rather that man, whatever his nobility, has within him the seeds of his own destruction? Without overstressing the guilt of the protagonists, don't we feel that in part the plays dramatize the *im*perfectibility of man? In much tragedy, after all, the destruction comes from within, not from without:

> In tragic life, God wot,
> No villain need be! Passions spin the plot:
> We are betrayed by what is false within.
>
> — George Meredith

What we are talking about is **tragic irony,** the contrast between what is believed to be so and what is so, or between expectations and accomplishments.* Several examples from *Macbeth* illustrate

---

* Tragic irony is sometimes called **dramatic irony** or **Sophoclean irony.** The terms are often applied to speeches or actions that the audience understands in a sense fuller than or different from the sense in which the dramatic characters understand them. It is tragically ironic, for example, that the rope that Bartley (in *Riders to the Sea*) uses as a bridle when he goes to sell the horses to help support the family will presumably be used to lower his coffin. Similarly, it is ironic that while Maurya is describing how Patch was carried in "in the half of a red sail, and water dripping out of it," Bartley is being carried to her door, "water dripping" from him, on a plank with "a bit of sail."

something of the range of tragic irony within a single play. In the first act, King Duncan bestows on Macbeth the title of Thane of Cawdor. By his kindness Duncan seals his own doom, for Macbeth, having achieved this rank, will next want to achieve a higher one. In the third act Macbeth, knowing that Banquo will soon be murdered, hypocritically urges Banquo to "fail not our feast." But Macbeth's hollow request is ironically fulfilled: the ghost of Banquo terrorizes Macbeth during the feast. The most pervasive irony of all, of course, is that Macbeth aims at happiness when he kills Duncan and takes the throne, but he wins only sorrow.

Aristotle's discussion of **peripeteia (reversal)** and **anagnorisis (recognition)** may be a way of getting at this sort of irony. He may simply have meant a reversal of fortune (for example, good luck ceases) and a recognition of who is who (for example, the pauper is really the prince), but more likely he meant profounder things. One can say that the reversal in *Macbeth* lies in the sorrow that Macbeth's increased power brings; the recognition comes when he realizes the consequences of his deeds:

> I have lived long enough: my way of life
> Is fall'n into the sere, the yellow leaf;
> And that which should accompany old age,
> As honor, love, obedience, troops of friends,
> I must not look to have; but, in their stead,
> Curses, not loud but deep, mouth-honor, breath
> Which the poor heart would fain deny, and dare not.

That a person's deeds often undo him, that a person aiming at his good can produce his ruin, was not, of course, a discovery of the tragic dramatists. The archetype is the story of Adam and Eve: these two aimed at becoming like God, and as a consequence they brought upon themselves corruption, death, the loss of their earthly paradise. The Bible is filled with stories of tragic irony. A brief quotation from Ecclesiastes (10:8–9) can stand as an epitome of these stories:

> He that diggeth a pit shall fall into it; and whoso breaketh
> an hedge, a serpent shall bite him.
> Whoso removeth stones shall be hurt therewith; and he
> that cleaveth wood shall be endangered thereby.

"He that cleaveth wood shall be endangered thereby." Activity involves danger. To be inactive is, often, to be ignoble, but to be active is necessarily to imperil oneself. Perhaps we can attempt a summary of tragic man: he acts, and he suffers, usually as a consequence of his action. The question is not of his action's being particularly bad (Tourneur's view), or particularly good (Timofeev's view); the action is often both good and bad, a sign of man's courage and also of his arrogance, a sign of man's greatness and also of his limitations.

Finally, a brief consideration of the pleasure of tragedy: Why do we enjoy plays about suffering? Aristotle has some obscure comments on **catharsis (purgation)** that are often interpreted as saying that tragedy arouses in us both pity and fear and then purges us of these emotions. The idea, perhaps, is that just as we can harmlessly discharge our aggressive impulses by witnessing a prize fight or by shouting at an umpire, so we can harmlessly discharge our impulses to pity and to fear by witnessing the dramatization of a man's destruction. The theater in this view is an outlet for emotions that elsewhere would be harmful. But, it must be repeated, Aristotle's comments on catharsis are obscure; perhaps, too, they are wrong. Most later theories on the pleasure of tragedy are footnotes to Aristotle's words on catharsis. Some say that our pleasure is sadistic (we enjoy the sight of suffering); some, that our pleasure is masochistic (we enjoy lacerating ourselves); some, that it lies in sympathy (we enjoy extending pity and benevolence to the wretched); some, that it lies in self-congratulation (we are reminded, when we see suffering, of our own good fortune); some, that we take pleasure in tragedy because the tragic hero acts out our secret desires, and we rejoice in his aggression, expiating our guilt in his suffering; and so on.

But this is all rather uncertain psychology, and it mostly neglects the distinction between real suffering and dramatized suffering. In the latter, surely, part of the pleasure is in the contemplation of an esthetic object, an object that is unified and complete. The chaos of real life seems, for a few moments in drama, to be ordered: the protagonist's action, his subsequent suffering, and the total cosmos seem somehow related. Tragedy has no use for the passerby who is killed by a falling brick. The events (the man's walk, the brick's fall) have no meaningful relation. But suppose a man chooses to climb a mountain, and in making the ascent sets in motion an avalanche that destroys him. Here we find (however simple the illustration) something closer to tragedy. We do not say that men should avoid mountains, or that mountain-climbers deserve to die by avalanches. But we feel that the event is unified, as the accidental conjunction of brick and passerby is not. Tragedy thus presents some sort of ordered action; tragic drama itself is orderly. As we see or read it we feel it cannot be otherwise; word begets word, deed begets deed, and every moment is exquisitely appropriate. Whatever the relevance of sadism, masochism, sympathy, and the rest, the pleasure of tragedy surely comes in part from the artistic shaping of the material.

A NOTE ON GREEK TRAGEDY

Little or nothing is known for certain of the origin of Greek tragedy. The most common hypothesis holds that it developed from improvised speeches during choral dances honoring Dionysus, a Greek nature god associated with spring, fertility, and wine. Thespis (who perhaps never existed) is said to have introduced an actor into these choral performances in the sixth century B.C. Aeschylus (525–456 B.C.), Greece's first great writer of tragedies, added the second actor, and Sophocles (496?–406 B.C.) added the third actor and fixed the size of the chorus at fifteen. (Because the chorus leader often functioned as an additional actor, and because the actors sometimes doubled in their parts, a Greek tragedy could have more characters than might at first be thought.)

All of the extant great Greek tragedy is of the fifth century B.C. It was performed at religious festivals in the winter and early spring, in large outdoor amphitheaters built on hillsides. Some of these theaters were enormous; the one at Epidaurus held about fifteen thousand people. The audience sat in tiers, looking down on the **orchestra** (a dancing place), with the acting area behind it and the **skene** (the scene building) yet farther back. The scene building served as dressing room, background (suggesting a palace or temple), and place for occasional entrances and exits. Furthermore, this building helped to provide good acoustics, for speech travels well if there is a solid barrier behind the speaker and a hard, smooth surface in front of him, and if the audience sits in tiers. The wall of the scene building provided the barrier; the orchestra provided the surface in front of the actors; and the seats on the hillside fulfilled the third requirement. Moreover, the acoustics were somewhat improved by slightly elevating the actors above the orchestra, but it is not known exactly when this platform was first constructed in front of the scene building.

A tragedy commonly begins with a **prologos** (prologue), during which the exposition is given. Next comes the **párodos,** the chorus's ode of entrance, sung while the chorus marches into the theater, through the side aisles and onto the orchestra. The **epeisodion** (episode) is the ensuing scene; it is followed by a **stasimon** (choral song, ode). Usually there are four or five **epeisodia,** alternating with **stasima.** Each of these choral odes has a

Greek Theatre of Epidaurus on the Peloponnesus east of Nauplia. (Photograph: Frederick Ayer, Photo Researchers, Inc.)

strophe (lines presumably sung while the chorus dances in one direction) and an **antistrophe** (lines presumably sung while the chorus retraces its steps). Sometimes a third part, an **epode,** concludes an ode. (In addition to odes that are *stasima,* there can be odes within episodes; the fourth episode of *Antigonê* contains an ode complete with *epode*.) After the last part of the last ode comes the **exodos,** the epilogue or final scene.

The actors (all male) wore masks, and seem to have chanted much of the play. Perhaps the total result of combining speech with music and dancing was a sort of music-drama roughly akin to opera with some spoken dialogue, such as Mozart's *Magic Flute.*

Sophocles (*496?–406* B.C.)

Antigonê

An English Version by Dudley Fitts and Robert Fitzgerald

List of Characters

Antigonê
Ismenê
Eurydicê
Creon
Haimon
Teiresias
A Sentry
A Messenger
Chorus

Scene. *Before the palace of Creon, King of Thebes. A central double door, and two lateral doors. A platform extends the length of the façade, and from this platform three steps lead down into the "orchestra," or chorus-ground.*

Time. *Dawn of the day after the repulse of the Argive army from the assault on Thebes.*

PROLOGUE

Antigonê and Ismenê enter from the central door of the palace.

Antigonê. Ismenê, dear sister,
    You would think that we had already suffered enough
    For the curse on Oedipus.°
    I cannot imagine any grief
    That you and I have not gone through. And now —   *5*
    Have they told you of the new decree of our King Creon?
Ismenê. I have heard nothing: I know
    That two sisters lost two brothers, a double death
    In a single hour; and I know that the Argive army
    Fled in the night; but beyond this, nothing.   *10*
Antigonê. I thought so. And that is why I wanted you
    To come out here with me. There is something we must do.
Ismenê. Why do you speak so strangely?
Antigonê. Listen, Ismenê:
    Creon buried our brother Eteoclês   *15*
    With military honors, gave him a soldier's funeral,
    And it was right that he should; but Polyneicês,
    Who fought as bravely and died as miserably, —
    They say that Creon has sworn
    No one shall bury him, no one mourn for him,   *20*
    But his body must lie in the fields, a sweet treasure
    For carrion birds to find as they search for food.
    That is what they say, and our good Creon is coming here
    To announce it publicly; and the penalty —
    Stoning to death in the public square!
                     There it is,   *25*
    And now you can prove what you are:
    A true sister, or a traitor to your family
Ismenê. Antigonê, you are mad! What could I possibly do?
Antigonê. You must decide whether you will help me or not.
Ismenê. I do not understand you. Help you in what?   *30*
Antigonê. Ismenê, I am going to bury him. Will you come?
Ismenê. Bury him! You have just said the new law forbids it.

Prologue. ³***Oedipus,*** once King of Thebes, was the father of Antigonê and Ismenê, and of their brothers Polyneicês and Eteoclês. Oedipus unwittingly killed his father, Laïos, and married his own mother, Iocastê. When he learned what he had done, he blinded himself and left Thebes. Eteoclês and Polyneicês quarreled; Polyneicês was driven out but returned to assault Thebes. In the battle each brother killed the other; Creon became king and ordered that Polyneicês be left to rot unburied on the battlefield as a traitor.

Antigonê. He is my brother. And he is your brother, too.
Ismenê. But think of the danger! Think what Creon will do!
Antigonê. Creon is not strong enough to stand in my way.   35
Ismenê. Ah sister!
        Oedipus died, everyone hating him
        For what his own search brought to light, his eyes
        Ripped out by his own hand; and Iocastê died,
        His mother and wife at once: she twisted the cords   40
        That strangled her life; and our two brothers died,
        Each killed by the other's sword. And we are left:
        But oh, Antigonê,
        Think how much more terrible than these
        Our own death would be if we should go against Creon   45
        And do what he has forbidden! We are only women,
        We cannot fight with men, Antigonê!
        The law is strong, we must give in to the law
        In this thing, and in worse. I beg the Dead
        To forgive me, but I am helpless: I must yield   50
        To those in authority. And I think it is dangerous business
        To be always meddling.
Antigonê.   If that is what you think,
        I should not want you, even if you asked to come.
        You have made your choice, you can be what you want to
            be.
        But I will bury him; and if I must die,   55
        I say that this crime is holy: I shall lie down
        With him in death, and I shall be as dear
        To him as he to me.
                It is the dead,
        Not the living, who make the longest demands:
        We die for ever . . .
                You may do as you like,   60
        Since apparently the laws of the gods mean nothing to you.
Ismenê. They mean a great deal to me; but I have no strength
        To break laws that were made for the public good.
Antigonê. That must be your excuse, I suppose. But as for me,
        I will bury the brother I love.
Ismenê.   Antigonê,   65
        I am so afraid for you!
Antigonê.   You need not be:
         You have yourself to consider, after all.
Ismenê. But no one must hear of this, you must tell no one!
        I will keep it a secret, I promise!
Antigonê.   O tell it! Tell everyone!

Think how they'll hate you when it all comes out *70*
If they learn that you knew about it all the time!
Ismenê. So fiery! You should be cold with fear.
Antigonê. Perhaps. But I am doing only what I must.
Ismenê. But can you do it? I say that you cannot.
Antigonê. Very well: when my strength gives out,
  I shall do no more. *75*
Ismenê. Impossible things should not be tried at all.
Antigonê. Go away, Ismenê:
  I shall be hating you soon, and the dead will too,
  For your words are hateful. Leave me my foolish plan:
  I am not afraid of the danger; if it means death, *80*
  It will not be the worst of deaths — death without honor.
Ismenê. Go then, if you feel that you must.
  You are unwise,
  But a loyal friend indeed to those who love you.

Exit into the palace. Antigonê goes off, left. Enter the Chorus.

PÁRODOS

Chorus. Now the long blade of the sun, lying *Strophe 1*
  Level east to west, touches with glory
  Thebes of the Seven Gates. Open, unlidded
  Eye of golden day! O marching light
  Across the eddy and rush of Dircê's stream,° *5*
  Striking the white shields of the enemy
  Thrown headlong backward from the blaze of morning!
Choragos.° Polyneicês their commander
  Roused them with windy phrases,
  He the wild eagle screaming *10*
  Insults above our land,
  His wings their shields of snow,
  His crest their marshalled helms.

Chorus. Against our seven gates in a yawning ring *Antistrophe 1*
  The famished spears came onward in the night; *15*
  But before his jaws were sated with our blood,
  Or pinefire took the garland of our towers,
  He was thrown back; and as he turned, great Thebes —
  No tender victim for his noisy power —
  Rose like a dragon behind him, shouting war. *20*

Párodos. ⁵*Dircê's stream* a stream west of Thebes ⁸*Choragos* leader of the Chorus

Choragos. For God hates utterly
    The bray of bragging tongues;
    And when he beheld their smiling,
    Their swagger of golden helms,
    The frown of his thunder blasted   *25*
    Their first man from our walls.

Chorus. We heard his shout of triumph high in the air   *Strophe 2*
    Turn to a scream; far out in a flaming arc
    He fell with his windy torch, and the earth struck him.
    And others storming in fury no less than his   *30*
    Found shock of death in the dusty joy of battle.
Choragos. Seven captains at seven gates
    Yielded their clanging arms to the god
    That bends the battle-line and breaks it.
    These two only, brothers in blood,   *35*
    Face to face in matchless rage,
    Mirroring each the other's death,
    Clashed in long combat.
Chorus. But now in the beautiful morning of victory   *Antistrophe 2*
    Let Thebes of the many chariots sing for joy!   *40*
    With hearts for dancing we'll take leave of war:
    Our temples shall be sweet with hymns of praise,
    And the long nights shall echo with our chorus.

SCENE I

Choragos. But now at last our new King is coming:
    Creon of Thebes, Menoikeus' son.
    In this auspicious dawn of his rein
    What are the new complexities
    That shifting Fate has woven for him?   *5*
    What is his counsel? Why has he summoned
    The old men to hear him?

    *Enter Creon from the palace, center. He addresses the Chorus from
    the top step.*

Creon. Gentlemen: I have the honor to inform you that our
    Ship of State, which recent storms have threatened to
    destroy, has come safely to harbor at last, guided by   *10*
    the merciful wisdom of Heaven. I have summoned you
    here this morning because I know that I can depend
    upon you: your devotion to King Laïos was absolute;
    you never hesitated in your duty to our late ruler
    Oedipus; and when Oedipus died, your loyalty   *15*

was transferred to his children. Unfortunately, as you know, his two sons, the princes Eteoclês and Poly- neicês, have killed each other in battle; and I, as the next in blood, have succeeded to the full power of the throne.   20

I am aware, of course, that no Ruler can expect complete loyalty from his subjects until he has been tested in office. Nevertheless, I say to you at the very outset that I have nothing but contempt for the kind of Governor who is afraid, for whatever reason, to fol-   25 low the course that he knows is best for the State; and as for the man who sets private friendship above the public welfare, — I have no use for him, either. I call God to witness that if I saw my country headed for ruin, I should not be afraid to speak out plainly; and   30 I need hardly remind you that I would never have any dealings with an enemy of the people. No one values friendship more highly than I; but we must remember that friends made at the risk of wrecking our Ship are not real friends at all.   35

These are my principles, at any rate, and that is why I have made the following decision concerning the sons of Oedipus: Eteoclês, who died as a man should die, fighting for his country, is to be buried with full military honors, with all the ceremony that is usual   40 when the greatest heroes die; but his brother Poly- neicês, who broke his exile to come back with fire and sword against his native city and the shrines of his fathers' gods, whose one idea was to spill the blood of his blood and sell his own people into slavery —   45 Polyneicês, I say, is to have no burial: no man is to touch him or say the least prayer for him; he shall lie on the plain, unburied; and the birds and the scavenging dogs can do with him whatever they like.

This is my command, and you can see the wis-   50 dom behind it. As long as I am King, no traitor is going to be honored with the loyal man. But whoever shows by word and deed that he is on the side of the State, — he shall have my respect while he is living and my reverence when he is dead.   55

Choragos. If that is your will, Creon son of Menoikeus,
You have the right to enforce it: we are yours.

Creon. That is my will. Take care that you do your part.

Choragos. We are old men: let the younger ones carry it out.

Creon. I do not mean that: the sentries have been appointed.   60
Choragos. Then what is it that you would have us do?
Creon. You will give no support to whoever breaks this law.
Choragos. Only a crazy man is in love with death!
Creon. And death it is; yet money talks, and the wisest
  Have sometimes been known to count a few coins too
   many.   65

  Enter Sentry from left.

Sentry. I'll not say that I'm out of breath from running, King,
  because every time I stopped to think about what I have
  to tell you, I felt like going back. And all the time a
  voice kept saying, "You fool, don't you know you're
  walking straight into trouble?"; and then another voice: 70
  "Yes, but if you let somebody else get the news to
  Creon first, it will be even worse than that for you!"
  But good sense won out, at least I hope it was good
  sense, and here I am with a story that makes no sense
  at all; but I'll tell it anyhow, because, as they say, what's   75
  going to happen's going to happen and —
Creon. Come to the point. What have you to say?
Sentry. I did not do it. I did not see who did it. You must
  not punish me for what someone else has done.
Creon. A comprehensive defense! More effective, perhaps.   80
  If I knew its purpose. Come: what is it?
Sentry. A dreadful thing . . . I don't know how to put it —
Creon. Out with it!
Sentry.   Well, then;
  The dead man —
      Polyneicês —

Pause. The Sentry is overcome, fumbles for words. Creon waits impassively.

          out there —
             someone, —
  New dust on the slimy flesh!   85

Pause. No sign from Creon.

  Someone has given it burial that way, and
  Gone . . .

  Long pause. Creon finally speaks with deadly control.

Creon. And the man who dared do this?
Sentry.   I swear I

Do not know! You must believe me!
                              Listen:
The ground was dry, not a sign of digging, no,   *90*
Not a wheeltrack in the dust, no trace of anyone.
It was when they relieved us this morning: and one of them,
The corporal, pointed to it.
                              There it was,
The strangest —
                    Look:
The body, just mounded over with light dust: you see? *95*
Not buried really, but as if they'd covered it
Just enough for the ghost's peace. And no sign
Of dogs or any wild animal that had been there.

And then what a scene there was! Every man of us
Accusing the other: we all proved the other man did it, *100*
We all had proof that we could not have done it.
We were ready to take hot iron in our hands,
Walk through fire, swear by all the gods,
It was not I!
I do not know who it was, but it was not I!   *105*

*Creon's rage has been mounting steadily, but the Sentry is too
intent upon his story to notice it.*

And then, when this came to nothing, someone said
A thing that silenced us and made us stare
Down at the ground: you had to be told the news,
And one of us had to do it! We threw the dice,
And the bad luck fell to me. So here I am,   *110*
No happier to be here than you are to have me:
Nobody likes the man who brings bad news.

Choragos. I have been wondering, King: can it be that the gods
    have done this?

Creon (furiously). Stop!   *115*
    Must you doddering wrecks
    Go out of your heads entirely? "The gods"!
    Intolerable!
    The gods favor this corpse? Why? How had he served them?
    Tried to loot their temples, burn their images,   *120*
    Yes, and the whole State, and its laws with it!
    Is it your senile opinion that the gods love to honor bad men?
    A pious thought! —
                        No, from the very beginning
    There have been those who have whispered together,
    Stiff-necked anarchists, putting their heads together, *125*

Scheming against me in alleys. These are the men,
And they have bribed my own guard to do this thing.
(*Sententiously.*) Money!
There's nothing in the world so demoralizing as money.
Down go your cities,   *130*
Homes gone, men gone, honest hearts corrupted,
Crookedness of all kinds, and all for money!
(*To Sentry.*)   But you — !
I swear by God and by the throne of God,
The man who has done this thing shall pay for it!
Find that man, bring him here to me, or your death   *135*
Will be the least of your problems: I'll string you up
Alive, and there will be certain ways to make you
Discover your employer before you die;
And the process may teach you a lesson you seem to have
      missed:
The dearest profit is sometimes all too dear: *140*
That depends on the source. Do you understand me?
A fortune won is often misfortune.

Sentry. King, may I speak?
Creon.   Your very voice distresses me.
Sentry. Are you sure that it is my voice, and not your conscience?
Creon. By God, he wants to analyze me now!   *145*
Sentry. It is not what I say, but what has been done, that hurts
      you.
Creon. You talk too much.
Sentry.   Maybe; but I've done nothing.
Creon. Sold your soul for some silver: that's all you've done.
Sentry. How dreadful it is when the right judge judges wrong!
Creon. Your figures of speech   *150*
May entertain you now; but unless you bring me the man,
You will get little profit from them in the end.

Exit Creon into the palace.

Sentry. "Bring me the man" —!
I'd like nothing better than bringing him the man!
But bring him or not, you have seen the last of me here.   *155*
At any rate, I am safe!   (*Exit Sentry.*)

ODE I

Chorus. Numberless are the world's wonders, but none   *Strophe 1*
      More wonderful than man; the stormgray sea

Yields to his prows, the huge crests bear him high;
Earth, holy and inexhaustible, is graven
With shining furrows where his plows have gone   *5*
Year after year, the timeless labor of stallions.

The lightboned birds and beasts that cling to   *Antistrophe 1*
     cover,
The lithe fish lighting their reaches of dim water,
All are taken, tamed in the net of his mind;
The lion on the hill, the wild horse windy-maned,   *10*
Resign to him; and his blunt yoke has broken
The sultry shoulders of the mountain bull.

Words also, and thought as rapid as air,   *Strophe 2*
He fashions to his good use; statecraft is his,
And his the skill that deflects the arrows of snow,   *15*
The spears of winter rain: from every wind
He has made himself secure — from all but one:
In the late wind of death he cannot stand.

O clear intelligence, force beyond all measure!   *Antistrophe 2*
O fate of man, working both good and evil!   *20*
When the laws are kept, how proudly his city stands!
When the laws are broken, what of his city then?
Never may the anárchic man find rest at my hearth,
Never be it said that my thoughts are his thoughts.

SCENE II

Reenter Sentry leading Antigonê.

Choragos. What does this mean? Surely this captive woman
     Is the Princess, Antıgonë. Why should she be taken?
Sentry. Here is the one who did it! We caught her
     In the very act of burying him. — Where is Creon?
Choragos. Just coming from the house.

     Enter Creon, center.

Creon.   What has happened?   *5*
     Why have you come back so soon?
Sentry (*expansively*).   O King,
     A man should never be too sure of anything:
     I would have sworn
     That you'd not see me here again: your anger
     Frightened me so, and the things you threatened
         me with;   *10*

But how could I tell then
That I'd be able to solve the case so soon?
No dice-throwing this time: I was only too glad to come!
Here is this woman. She is the guilty one:
We found her trying to bury him.   *15*
Take her, then; question her; judge her as you will.
I am through with the whole thing now, and glad of it.
Creon. But this is Antigonê! Why have you brought her here?
Sentry. She was burying him, I tell you!
Creon (severely).   Is this the truth?
Sentry. I saw her with my own eyes. Can I say more?   *20*
Creon. The details: come, tell me quickly!
Sentry.   It was like this:
After those terrible threats of yours, King,
We went back and brushed the dust away from the body.
The flesh was soft by now, and stinking,
So we sat on a hill to windward and kept guard.   *25*
No napping this time! We kept each other awake.
But nothing happened until the white round sun
Whirled in the center of the round sky over us:
Then, suddenly,
A storm of dust roared up from the earth, and the sky   *30*
Went out, the plain vanished with all its trees
In the stinging dark. We closed our eyes and endured it.
The whirlwind lasted a long time, but it passed;
And then we looked, and there was Antigonê!
I have seen   *35*
A mother bird come back to a stripped nest, heard
Her crying bitterly a broken note or two
For the young ones stolen. Just so, when this girl
Found the bare corpse, and all her love's work wasted,
She wept, and cried on heaven to damn the hands   *40*
That had done this thing.
                           And then she brought more dust
And sprinkled wine three times for her brother's ghost.

We ran and took her at once. She was not afraid,
Not even when we charged her with what she had done.
She denied nothing.
                     And this was a comfort to me,   *45*
And some uneasiness: for it is a good thing
To escape from death, but it is no great pleasure
To bring death to a friend.
                            Yet I always say
There is nothing so comfortable as your own safe skin!

Creon (*slowly, dangerously*). And you, Antigonê,   *50*
          You with your head hanging, — do you confess this thing?
Antigonê. I do. I deny nothing.
Creon (*to Sentry*).   You may go.   (*Exit Sentry.*)
          (*To Antigonê.*) Tell me, tell me briefly:
          Had you heard my proclamation touching this matter?
Antigonê. It was public. Could I help hearing it?   *55*
Creon. And yet you dared defy the law.
Antigonê.   I dared.
          It was not God's proclamation. That final Justice
          That rules the world below makes no such laws.

          Your edict, King, was strong,
          But all your strength is weakness itself against   *60*
          The immortal unrecorded laws of God.
          They are not merely now: they were, and shall be,
          Operative for ever, beyond man utterly.

          I knew I must die, even without your decree:
          I am only mortal. And if I must die   *65*
          Now, before it is my time to die,
          Surely this is no hardship: can anyone
          Living, as I live, with evil all about me,
          Think Death less than a friend? This death of mine
          Is of no importance; but if I had left my brother   *70*
          Lying in death unburied, I should have suffered.
          Now I do not.
                              You smile at me. Ah Creon,
          Think me a fool, if you like; but it may well be
          That a fool convicts me of folly.
Choragos. Like father, like daughter: both headstrong,
                    deaf to reason!   *75*
          She has never learned to yield:
Creon.   She has much to learn.
          The inflexible heart breaks first, the toughest iron
          Cracks first, and the wildest horses bend their necks
          At the pull of the smallest curb.
                                        Pride? In a slave?
          This girl is guilty of a double insolence,   *80*
          Breaking the given laws and boasting of it.
          Who is the man here,
          She or I, if this crime goes unpunished?
          Sister's child, or more than sister's child,
          Or closer yet in blood — she and her sister   *85*
          Win bitter death for this!
          (*To Servants.*)   Go, some of you,

Arrest Ismenê. I accuse her equally.
Bring her: you will find her sniffling in the house there.

Her mind's a traitor: crimes kept in the dark
Cry for light, and the guardian brain shudders;   *90*
But how much worse than this
Is brazen boasting of barefaced anarchy!
Antigonê. Creon, what more do you want than my death?
Creon.   Nothing.
That gives me everything.
Antigonê.   Then I beg you: kill me.
This talking is a great weariness: your words   *95*
Are distasteful to me, and I am sure that mine
Seem so to you. And yet they should not seem so:
I should have praise and honor for what I have done.
All these men here would praise me
Were their lips not frozen shut with fear of you.   *100*
(*Bitterly.*) Ah the good fortune of kings,
Licensed to say and do whatever they please!
Creon. You are alone here in that opinion.
Antigonê. No, they are with me. But they keep their tongues in
          leash.
Creon. Maybe. But you are guilty, and they are not.   *105*
Antigonê. There is no guilt in reverence for the dead.
Creon. But Eteoclês — was he not your brother too?
Antigonê. My brother too.
Creon.   And you insult his memory?
Antigonê (*softly*). The dead man would not say that I insult it.
Creon. He would: for you honor a traitor as much as him.   *110*
Antigonê. His own brother, traitor or not, and equal in blood.
Creon. He made war on his country. Eteoclês defended it.
Antigonê. Nevertheless, there are honors due all the dead.
Creon. But not the same for the wicked as for the just.
Antigonê. Ah Creon, Creon,   *115*
Which of us can say what the gods hold wicked?
Creon. An enemy is an enemy, even dead.
Antigonê. It is my nature to join in love, not hate.
Creon (*finally losing patience*). Go join them then; if you must
          have your love,
Find it in hell!   *120*
Choragos. But see, Ismenê comes:

Enter Ismenê, guarded.

Those tears are sisterly, the cloud
That shadows her eyes rains down gentle sorrow.

Creon. You too, Ismenê,
  Snake in my ordered house, sucking my blood   *125*
  Stealthily — and all the time I never knew
  That these two sisters were aiming at my throne!
                Ismenê,
  Do you confess your share in this crime, or deny it?
  Answer me.
Ismenê. Yes, if she will let me say so. I am guilty.   *130*
Antigonê (coldly). No, Ismenê. You have no right to say so.
  You would not help me, and I will not have you help me.
Ismenê. But now I know what you meant; and I am here
  To join you, to take my share of punishment.
Antigonê. The dead man and the gods who rule the dead   *135*
  Know whose act this was. Words are not friends.
Ismenê. Do you refuse me, Antigonê? I want to die with you:
  I too have a duty that I must discharge to the dead.
Antigonê. You shall not lessen my death by sharing it.
Ismenê. What do I care for life when you are dead?   *140*
Antigonê. Ask Creon. You're always hanging on his opinions.
Ismenê. You are laughing at me. Why, Antigonê?
Antigonê. It's a joyless laughter, Ismenê.
Ismenê.   But can I do nothing?
Antigonê. Yes. Save yourself. I shall not envy you.
  There are those who will praise you; I shall have honor,
    too.   *145*
Ismenê. But we are equally guilty!
Antigonê.   No more, Ismenê.
  You are alive, but I belong to Death.
Creon (to the Chorus). Gentlemen, I beg you to observe these girls:
  One has just now lost her mind; the other,
  It seems, has never had a mind at all.   *150*
Ismenê. Grief teaches the steadiest minds to waver, King.
Creon. Yours certainly did, when you assumed guilt with the guilty!
Ismenê. But how could I go on living without her?
Creon.   You are.
  She is already dead.
Ismenê.   But your own son's bride!
Creon. There are places enough for him to push his plow.   *155*
  I want no wicked women for my sons!
Ismenê. O dearest Haimon, how your father wrongs you!
Creon. I've had enough of your childish talk of marriage!
Choragos. Do you really intend to steal this girl from your son?
Creon. No; Death will do that for me.
Choragos.   Then she must die? *160*

Creon (ironically). You dazzle me.

       — But enough of this talk!
 (*To Guards.*) You, there, take them away and guard them
  well:
For they are but women, and even brave men run
When they see Death coming.

       Exeunt Ismenê, Antigonê, and Guards.

ODE II

Chorus. Fortunate is the man who has never tasted   *Strophe 1*
  God's vengeance!
Where once the anger of heaven has struck, that house is
  shaken
For ever: damnation rises behind each child
Like a wave cresting out of the black northeast,
When the long darkness under sea roars up   *5*
And bursts drumming death upon the windwhipped sand.

I have seen this gathering sorrow from time   *Antistrophe 1*
  long past
Loom upon Oedipus' children: generation from generation
Takes the compulsive rage of the enemy god.
So lately this last flower of Oedipus' line   *10*
Drank the sunlight! but now a passionate word
And a handful of dust have closed up all its beauty.
   What mortal arrogance   *Strophe 2*
   Transcends the wrath of Zeus?
Sleep cannot lull him nor the effortless long months   *15*
Of the timeless gods: but he is young for ever,
And his house is the shining day of high Olympos.
   All that is and shall be,
   And all the past, is his.
No pride on earth is free of the curse of heaven.   *20*

The straying dreams of men   *Antistrophe 2*
   May bring them ghosts of joy:
But as they drowse, the waking embers burn them;
Or they walk with fixed eyes, as blind men walk.
But the ancient wisdom speaks for our own time: *25*
   Fate works most for woe
   With Folly's fairest show.
Man's little pleasure is the spring of sorrow.

SCENE III

Choragos. But here is Haimon, King, the last of all your sons
    Is it grief for Antigonê that brings him here,
    And bitterness at being robbed of his bride?

Enter Haimon.

Creon. We shall soon see, and no need of diviners.
                                  — Son,
    You have heard my final judgment on that girl: *5*
    Have you come here hating me, or have you come
    With deference and with love, whatever I do?
Haimon. I am your son, father. You are my guide.
    You make things clear for me, and I obey you.
    No marriage means more to me than your continuing
        wisdom.   *10*
Creon. Good. That is the way to behave: subordinate
    Everything else, my son, to your father's will.
    This is what a man prays for, that he may get
    Sons attentive and dutiful in his house,
    Each one hating his father's enemies,   *15*
    Honoring his father's friends. But if his sons
    Fail him, if they turn out unprofitably,
    What has he fathered but trouble for himself
    And amusement for the malicious?
                           So you are right
    Not to lose your head over this woman.   *20*
    Your pleasure with her would soon grow cold, Haimon,
    And then you'd have a hellcat in bed and elsewhere.
    Let her find her husband in Hell!
    Of all the people in this city, only she
    Has had contempt for my law and broken it.   *25*

    Do you want me to show myself weak before the people?
    Or to break my sworn word? No, and I will not.
    The woman dies.
    I suppose she'll plead "family ties." Well, let her.
    If I permit my own family to rebel,   *30*
    How shall I earn the world's obedience?
    Show me the man who keeps his house in hand,
    He's fit for public authority.
                         I'll have no dealings
    With lawbreakers, critics of the government:
    Whoever is chosen to govern should be obeyed —   *35*

Must be obeyed, in all things, great and small,
Just and unjust! O Haimon,
The man who knows how to obey, and that man only,
Knows how to give commands when the time comes.
You can depend on him, no matter how fast   **40**
The spears come: he's a good soldier, he'll stick it out.

Anarchy, anarchy! Show me a greater evil!
This is why cities tumble and the great houses rain down,
This is what scatters armies!
No, no: good lives are made so by discipline.   **45**
We keep the laws then, and the lawmakers,
And no woman shall seduce us. If we must lose,
Let's lose to a man, at least! Is a woman stronger than we?
Choragos. Unless time has rusted my wits,
What you say, King, is said with point and dignity.   **50**
Haimon (boyishly earnest). Father:
Reason is God's crowning gift to man, and you are right
To warn me against losing mine. I cannot say —
I hope that I shall never want to say! — that you
Have reasoned badly. Yet there are other men   **55**
Who can reason, too; and their opinions might be helpful.
You are not in a position to know everything
That people say or do, or what they feel:
Your temper terrifies — everyone
Will tell you only what you like to hear.   **60**
But I, at any rate, can listen; and I have heard them
Muttering and whispering in the dark about this girl.
They say no woman has ever, so unreasonably,
Died so shameful a death for a generous act:
"She covered her brother's body. Is this indecent?   **65**
She kept him from dogs and vultures. Is this a crime?
Death? — She should have all the honor that we can give
     her!"

This is the way they talk out there in the city.

You must believe me:
Nothing is closer to me than your happiness.   **70**
What could be closer? Must not any son
Value his father's fortune as his father does his?
I beg you, do not be unchangeable:
Do not believe that you alone can be right.
The man who thinks that,   **75**
The man who maintains that only he has the power

To reason correctly, the gift to speak, the soul —
A man like that, when you know him, turns out empty.

It is not reason never to yield to reason!

In flood time you can see how some trees bend,   *80*
And because they bend, even their twigs are safe,
While stubborn trees are torn up, roots and all.
And the same thing happens in sailing:
Make your sheet fast, never slacken, — and over you go,
Head over heels and under: and there's your voyage.   *85*
Forget you are angry! Let yourself be moved!
I know I am young; but please let me say this:
The ideal condition
Would be, I admit, that men should be right by instinct;
But since we are all too likely to go astray,   *90*
The reasonable thing is to learn from those who can teach.
Choragos. You will do well to listen to him, King,
    If what he says is sensible. And you, Haimon,
    Must listen to your father. — Both speak well.
Creon. You consider it right for a man of my years
                and experience   *95*
    To go to school to a boy?
Haimon.   It is not right
    If I am wrong. But if I am young, and right,
    What does my age matter?
Creon. You think it right to stand up for an anarchist?
Haimon. Not at all. I pay no respect to criminals.   *100*
Creon. Then she is not a criminal?
Haimon. The City would deny it, to a man.
Creon. And the City proposes to teach me how to rule?
Haimon. Ah. Who is it that's talking like a boy now?
Creon. My voice is the one voice giving orders in this City! *105*
Haimon. It is no City if it takes orders from one voice.
Creon. The State is the King!
Haimon.   Yes, if the State is a desert.

    Pause.

Creon. This boy, it seems, has sold out to a woman.
Haimon. If you are a woman: my concern is only for you.
Creon. So? Your "concern"! In a public brawl with your
                father!   *110*
Haimon. How about you, in a public brawl with justice?
Creon. With justice, when all that I do is within my rights?

Haimon. You have no right to trample on God's right.
Creon (completely out of control). Fool, adolescent fool! Taken
          in by a woman!
Haimon. You'll never see me taken in by anything vile.   *115*
Creon. Every word you say is for her!
Haimon (quietly, darkly).   And for you.
          And for me. And for the gods under the earth.
Creon. You'll never marry her while she lives.
Haimon. Then she must die. — But her death will cause another.
Creon. Another?   *120*
          Have you lost your senses? Is this an open threat?
Haimon. There is no threat in speaking to emptiness.
Creon. I swear you'll regret this superior tone of yours!
          You are the empty one!
Haimon.   If you were not my father,
          I'd say you were perverse.   *125*
Creon. You girlstruck fool, don't play at words with me!
Haimon. I am sorry. You prefer silence.
Creon.   Now, by God —
          I swear, by all the gods in heaven above us,
          You'll watch it, I swear you shall!
          (*To the Servants.*)   Bring her out!
          Bring the woman out! Let her die before his eyes!   *130*
          Here, this instant, with her bridegroom beside her!
Haimon. Not here, no; she will not die here, King.
          And you will never see my face again.
          Go on raving as long as you've a friend to endure you.
                              (*Exit Haimon.*)
Choragos. Gone, gone.   *135*
          Creon, a young man in a rage is dangerous!
Creon. Let him do, or dream to do, more than a man can.
          He shall not save these girls from death.
Choragos.   These girls?
          You have sentenced them both?
Creon.   No, you are right.
          I will not kill the one whose hands are clean.   *140*
Choragos. But Antigonê?
Creon (somberly). I will carry her far away
          Out there in the wilderness, and lock her
          Living in a vault of stone. She shall have food,
          As the custom is, to absolve the State of her death.
          And there let her pray to the gods of hell: *145*
          They are her only gods:

Perhaps they will show her an escape from death,
Or she may learn,
                    though late,
That piety shown the dead is pity in vain. (*Exit Creon.*)

ODE III

Chorus. Love, unconquerable   *Strophe*
         Waster of rich men, keeper
         Of warm lights and all-night vigil
         In the soft face of a girl:
         Sea-wanderer, forest-visitor!   *5*
         Even the pure Immortals cannot escape you,
         And mortal man, in his one day's dusk,
         Trembles before your glory.

         Surely you swerve upon ruin   *Antistrophe*
         The just man's consenting heart,   *10*
         As here you have made bright anger
         Strike between father and son —
         And none has conquered but Love!
         A girl's glánce wórking the will of heaven:
         Pleasure to her alone who mocks us,   *15*
         Merciless Aphroditê.°

SCENE IV

Choragos (as Antigonê enters guarded). But I can no longer
                    stand in awe of this,
         Nor, seeing what I see, keep back my tears.
         Here is Antigonê, passing to that chamber
         Where all find sleep at last.

Antigonê. Look upon me, friends, and pity me   *Strophe 1* *5*
         Turning back at the night's edge to say
         Good-by to the sun that shines for me no longer;
         Now sleepy Death
         Summons me down to Acheron,° that cold shore:
         There is no bridesong there, nor any music.   *10*
Chorus. Yet not unpraised, not without a kind of honor,
         You walk at last into the underworld;

Ode III. ¹⁶*Aphroditê* goddess of love   Scene IV: ⁹*Acheron* a river of the underworld,
which was ruled by Hades

Untouched by sickness, broken by no sword.
What woman has ever found your way to death?

Antigonê. How often I have heard the story   *Antistrophe 1*
    of Niobê,°   *15*
Tantalos' wretched daughter, how the stone
Clung fast about her, ivy-close: and they say
The rain falls endlessly
And sifting soft snow; her tears are never done.
I feel the loneliness of her death in mine.   *20*
Chorus. But she was born of heaven, and you
Are woman, woman-born. If her death is yours,
A mortal woman's, is this not for you
Glory in our world and in the world beyond?

Antigonê. You laugh at me. Ah, friends, friends,   *Strophe 2*   *25*
Can you not wait until I am dead? O Thebes,
O men many-charioted, in love with Fortune,
Dear springs of Dircê, sacred Theban grove,
Be witnesses for me, denied all pity,
Unjustly judged! and think a word of love   *30*
For her whose path turns
Under dark earth, where there are no more tears.
Chorus. You have passed beyond human daring and come at last
Into a place of stone where Justice sits.
I cannot tell   *35*
What shape of your father's guilt appears in this.
Antigonê. You have touched it at last: *Antistrophe 2*
    that bridal bed
Unspeakable, horror of son and mother mingling:
Their crime, infection of all our family!
O Oedipus, father and brother!   *40*
Your marriage strikes from the grave to murder mine.
I have been a stranger here in my own land:
All my life
The blasphemy of my birth has followed me.
Chorus. Reverence is a virtue, but strength   *45*
Lives in established law: that must prevail.
You have made your choice,
Your death is the doing of your conscious hand.

---

[15]**Niobê** (Niobê boasted of her numerous children, provoking Leto, the mother of Apollo, to destroy them. Niobê wept profusely, and finally was turned into a stone on Mount Sipylus, whose streams are her tears)

Antigonê. Then let me go, since all your words are bitter,   *Epode*
    And the very light of the sun is cold to me.   *50*
    Lead me to my vigil, where I must have
    Neither love nor lamentation; no song, but silence.

    Creon interrupts impatiently.

Creon. If dirges and planned lamentations could put off death,
    Men would be singing for ever.
    (*To the Servants.*)   Take her, go!
    You know your orders: take her to the vault   *55*
    And leave her alone there. And if she lives or dies,
    That's her affair, not ours: our hands are clean.

Antigonê. O tomb, vaulted bride-bed in eternal rock,
    Soon I shall be with my own again
    Where Persephonê° welcomes the thin ghosts
        underground: *60*
    And I shall see my father again, and you, mother,
    And dearest Polyneicês —
            dearest indeed
    To me, since it was my hand
    That washed him clean and poured the ritual wine:
    And my reward is death before my time!   *65*

    And yet, as men's hearts know, I have done no wrong,
    I have not sinned before God. Or if I have,
    I shall know the truth in death. But if the guilt
    Lies upon Creon who judged me, then, I pray,
    May his punishment equal my own.
Choragos.   O passionate heart,   *70*
    Unyielding, tormented still by the same winds!
Creon. Her guards shall have good cause to regret their delaying.
Antigonê. Ah! That voice is like the voice of death!
Creon. I can give you no reason to think you are mistaken.
Antigonê. Thebes, and you my fathers' gods,   *75*
    And rulers of Thebes, you see me now, the last
    Unhappy daughter of a line of kings,
    Your kings, led away to death. You will remember
    What things I suffer, and at what men's hands,
    Because I would not transgress the laws of heaven.   *80*
    (*To the Guards, simply.*) Come: let us wait no longer.
            (*Exit Antigonê, left, guarded.*)

---

⁶⁰**Persephonê** queen of the underworld

ODE IV

Chorus. All Danaê's beauty was locked away   *Strophe 1*
    In a brazen cell where the sunlight could not come:
    A small room still as any grave, enclosed her.
    Yet she was a princess too,
    And Zeus in a rain of gold poured love upon her.   *5*
    O child, child,
    No power in wealth or war
    Or tough sea-blackened ships
    Can prevail against untiring Destiny!

    And Dryas' son° also, that furious king,   *Antistrophe 1*   *10*
    Bore the god's prisoning anger for his pride:
    Sealed up by Dionysos in deaf stone,
    His madness died among echoes.
    So at the last he learned what dreadful power
    His tongue had mocked: *15*
    For he had profaned the revels,
    And fired the wrath of the nine
    Implacable Sisters° that love the sound of the flute.

    And old men tell a half-remembered tale   *Strophe 2*
    Of horror where a dark ledge splits the sea   *20*
    And a double surf beats on the gráy shóres:
    How a king's new woman°, sick
    With hatred for the queen he had imprisoned,
    Ripped out his two sons' eyes with her bloody hands
    While grinning Arês° watched the shuttle plunge   *25*
    Four times: four blind wounds crying for revenge,

    Crying, tears and blood mingled. — Piteously *Antistrophe 2*
      born,
    Those sons whose mother was of heavenly birth!
    Her father was the god of the North Wind
    And she was cradled by gales,   *30*
    She raced with young colts on the glittering hills
    And walked untrammeled in the open light:
    But in her marriage deathless Fate found means
    To build a tomb like yours for all her joy.

Ode IV. **10Dryas' son** Lycurgus, King of Thrace   **18Sisters** the Muses   **22king's new woman** Eidothea, second wife of King Phineus, blinded her stepsons. Their mother, Cleopatra, had been imprisoned in a cave. Phineus was the son of a king, and Cleopatra, his first wife, was the daughter of Boreas, the North wind, but this illustrious ancestry could not protect his sons from violence and darkness.   **25Arês** god of war

SCENE V

Enter blind Teiresias, led by a boy. The opening speeches of Teiresias should be in singsong contrast to the realistic lines of Creon.

Teiresias. This is the way the blind man comes, Princes, Princes,
Lock-step, two heads lit by the eyes of one.
Creon. What new thing have you to tell us, old Teiresias?
Teiresias. I have much to tell you: listen to the prophet, Creon.
Creon. I am not aware that I have ever failed to listen.   5
Teiresias. Then you have done wisely, King, and ruled well.
Creon. I admit my debt to you. But what have you to say?
Teiresias. This, Creon: you stand once more on the edge of fate.
Creon. What do you mean? Your words are a kind of dread.
Teiresias. Listen, Creon: 10
      I was sitting in my chair of augury, at the place
      Where the birds gather about me. They were all a-chatter,
      As is their habit, when suddenly I heard
      A strange note in their jangling, a scream, a
      Whirring fury; I knew that they were fighting,   15
      Tearing each other, dying
      In a whirlwind of wings clashing. And I was afraid.
      I began the rites of burnt-offering at the altar,
      But Hephaistos° failed me: instead of bright flame,
      There was only the sputtering slime of the fat thigh-flesh   20
      Melting: the entrails dissolved in gray smoke,
      The bare bone burst from the welter. And no blaze!

      This was a sign from heaven. My boy described it,
      Seeing for me as I see for others.

      I tell you, Creon, you yourself have brought   25
      This new calamity upon us. Our hearths and altars
      Are stained with the corruption of dogs and carrion birds
      That glut themselves on the corpse of Oedipus' son.
      The gods are deaf when we pray to them, their fire
      Recoils from our offering, their birds of omen   30
      Have no cry of comfort, for they are gorged
      With the thick blood of the dead.
                                O my son,
      These are no trifles! Think: all men make mistakes,
      But a good man yields when he knows his course is wrong,

---

Scene V. ¹⁹***Hephaistos*** god of fire

And repairs the evil. The only crime is pride.   *35*

Give in to the dead man, then: do not fight with a corpse —
What glory is it to kill a man who is dead?
Think, I beg you:
It is for your own good that I speak as I do.
You should be able to yield for your own good.   *40*
Creon. It seems that prophets have made me their especial province.
All my life long
I have been a kind of butt for the dull arrows
Of doddering fortune-tellers!
                    No, Teiresias:
If your birds — if the great eagles of God himself   *45*
Should carry him stinking bit by bit to heaven,
I would not yield. I am not afraid of pollution:
No man can defile the gods.
                    Do what you will,
Go into business, make money, speculate
In India gold or that synthetic gold from Sardis,   *50*
Get rich otherwise than by my consent to bury him.
Teiresias, it is a sorry thing when a wise man
Sells his wisdom, lets out his words for hire!
Teiresias. Ah Creon! Is there no man left in the world —
Creon. To do what? — Come, let's have the aphorism!   *55*
Teiresias. No man who knows that wisdom outweighs any wealth?
Creon. As surely as bribes are baser than any baseness.
Teiresias. You are sick, Creon! You are deathly sick!
Creon. As you say: it is not my place to challenge a prophet.
Teiresias. Yet you have said my prophecy is for sale.   *60*
Creon. The generation of prophets has always loved gold.
Teiresias. The generation of kings has always loved brass.
Creon. You forget yourself! You are speaking to your King.
Teiresias. I know it. You are a king because of me.
Creon. You have a certain skill; but you have sold out.   *65*
Teiresias. King, you will drive me to words that —
Creon.   Say them, say them!
Only remember: I will not pay you for them.
Teiresias. No, you will find them too costly.
Creon.   No doubt. Speak:
Whatever you say, you will not change my will.
Teiresias. Then take this, and take it to heart!   *70*
The time is not far off when you shall pay back
Corpse for corpse, flesh of your own flesh.
You have thrust the child of this world into living night,
You have kept from the gods below the child that is theirs:
The one in a grave before her death, the other,   *75*

Dead, denied the grave. This is your crime:
And the Furies and the dark gods of Hell
Are swift with terrible punishment for you.

Do you want to buy me now, Creon?

Not many days,
And your house will be full of men and women
weeping, 80
And curses will be hurled at you from far
Cities grieving for sons unburied, left to rot
Before the walls of Thebes.

These are my arrows, Creon: they are all for you.

(*To Boy*.) But come, child: lead me home. 85
Let him waste his fine anger upon younger men.
Maybe he will learn at last
To control a wiser tongue in a better head. (*Exit Teiresias*.)
Choragos. The old man has gone, King, but his words
Remain to plague us. I am old, too, 90
But I cannot remember that he was ever false.
Creon. That is true. . . . It troubles me.
Oh it is hard to give in! but it is worse
To risk everything for stubborn pride.
Choragos. Creon: take my advice.
Creon. What shall I do? 95
Choragos. Go quickly: free Antigonê from her vault
And build a tomb for the body of Polyneicês.
Creon. You would have me do this!
Choragos. Creon, yes!
And it must be done at once: God moves
Swiftly to cancel the folly of stubborn men. 100
Creon. It is hard to deny the heart! But I
Will do it: I will not fight with destiny.
Choragos. You must go yourself, you cannot leave it to others.
Creon. I will go.
— Bring axes, servants:
Come with me to the tomb. I buried her, I 105
Will set her free.
Oh quickly!
My mind misgives —
The laws of the gods are mighty, and a man must serve them
To the last day of his life! (*Exit Creon*.)

PAEAN°

Choragos. God of many names   *Strophe 1*
Chorus.   O Iacchos
                                  son
  of Kadmeian Sémelê
              O born of the Thunder!
  Guardian of the West
             Regent
  of Eleusis' plain
           O Prince of maenad Thebes
  and the Dragon Field by rippling Ismenós:°   *5*

Choragos. God of many names   *Antistrophe 1*
Chorus.   the flame of torches
  flares on our hills
          the nymphs of Iacchos
  dance at the spring of Castalia:°
  from the vine-close mountain
               come ah come in ivy:
  Evohé evohé! sings through the streets of Thebes   *10*

Choragos. God of many names   *Strophe 2*
Chorus.   Iacchos of Thebes
  heavenly Child
         of Sémelê bride of the Thunderer!
  The shadow of plague is upon us:
                 come
  with clement feet
          oh come from Parnasos
  down the long slopes
           across the lamenting water   *15*
Choragos. Iô Fire! Chorister of the throbbing stars!   *Antistrophe 2*
  O purest among the voices of the night!
  Thou son of God, blaze for us!
Chorus. Come with choric rapture of circling Maenads
  Who cry Iô Iacche!
        God of many names!   *20*

Paean a hymn (here dedicated to Iacchos, also called Dionysos. His father was
Zeus, his mother was Sémelê, daughter of Kadmos. Iacchos's worshipers were the
Maenads, whose cry was *"Evohé evohé"*)   ⁵**Ismenós** a river east of Thebes (from
a dragon's teeth, sown near the river, there sprang men who became the ancestors
of the Theban nobility)   ⁸**Castalia** a spring on Mount Parnasos

EXODOS

Enter Messenger from left.

Messenger. Men of the line of Kadmos,° you who live
    Near Amphion's citadel,°
                      I cannot say
    Of any condition of human life "This is fixed,
    This is clearly good, or bad." Fate raises up,
    And Fate casts down the happy and unhappy alike: *5*
    No man can foretell his Fate.
                     Take the case of Creon:
    Creon was happy once, as I count happiness:
    Victorious in battle, sole governor of the land,
    Fortunate father of children nobly born.
    And now it has all gone from him! Who can say   *10*
    That a man is still alive when his life's joy fails?
    He is a walking dead man. Grant him rich,
    Let him live like a king in his great house:
    If his pleasure is gone, I would not give
    So much as the shadow of smoke for all he owns.   *15*
Choragos. Your words hint at sorrow: what is your news for us?
Messenger. They are dead. The living are guilty of their death.
Choragos. Who is guilty? Who is dead? Speak!
Messenger.   Haimon.
    Haimon is dead; and the hand that killed him
    Is his own hand.
Choragos. His father's? or his own?   *20*
Messenger. His own, driven mad by the murder his father had done.
Choragos. Teiresias, Teiresias, how clearly you saw it all!
Messenger. This is my news: you must draw what conclusions
          you can from it.
Choragos. But look: Eurydicê, our Queen:
    Has she overheard us?   *25*

Enter Eurydicê from the palace, center.

Eurydicê. I have heard something, friends:
    As I was unlocking the gate of Pallas'° shrine,
    For I needed her help today, I heard a voice
    Telling of some new sorrow. And I fainted
    There at the temple with all my maidens about me.   *30*

Exodos. [1]*Kadmos,* who sowed the dragon's teeth, was founder of
Thebes [2]*Amphion's citadel* Amphion played so sweetly on his lyre that he charmed
stones to form a wall around Thebes [27]*Pallas,* Pallas Athene, goddess of wisdom

But speak again: whatever it is, I can bear it:
Grief and I are no strangers.
Messenger.   Dearest Lady,
I will tell you plainly all that I have seen.
I shall not try to comfort you: what is the use,
Since comfort could lie only in what is not true?   *35*
The truth is always best.
                          I went with Creon
To the outer plain where Polyneicês was lying,
No friend to pity him, his body shredded by dogs.
We made our prayers in that place to Hecatê
And Pluto,° that they would be merciful. And we bathed   *40*
The corpse with holy water, and we brought
Fresh-broken branches to burn what was left of it,
And upon the urn we heaped up a towering barrow
Of the earth of his own land.
                          When we were done, we ran
To the vault where Antigonê lay on her couch of stone.   *45*
One of the servants had gone ahead,
And while he was yet far off he heard a voice
Grieving within the chamber, and he came back
And told Creon. And as the King went closer,
The air was full of wailing, the words lost,   *50*
And he begged us to make all haste. "Am I a prophet?"
He said, weeping, "And must I walk this road,
The saddest of all that I have gone before?
My son's voice calls me on. Oh quickly, quickly!
Look through the crevice there, and tell me   *55*
If it is Haimon, or some deception of the gods!"

We obeyed; and in the cavern's farthest corner
We saw her lying:
She had made a noose of her fine linen veil
And hanged herself. Haimon lay beside her,   *60*
His arms about her waist, lamenting her,
His love lost under ground, crying out
That his father had stolen her away from him.

When Creon saw him the tears rushed to his eyes
And he called to him: "What have you done, child?
          Speak to me.   *65*

---

[40]**Hecatê / And Pluto** Hecatê and Pluto (also known as Hades) were deities of the underworld

What are you thinking that makes your eyes so strange?
O my son, my son, I come to you on my knees!"
But Haimon spat in his face. He said not a word,
Staring —
            And suddenly drew his sword
And lunged. Creon shrank back, the blade missed; and the
       boy,   70
Desperate against himself, drove it half its length
Into his own side, and fell. And as he died
He gathered Antigonê close in his arms again,
Choking, his blood bright red on her white cheek.
And now he lies dead with the dead, and she is his   75
At last, his bride in the house of the dead.
                                  Exit Eurydicê into the palace.
Choragos. She has left us without a word. What can this mean?
Messenger. It troubles me, too; yet she knows what is best,
    Her grief is too great for public lamentation,
    And doubtless she has gone to her chamber to weep   80
    For her dead son, leading her maidens in his dirge.

    Pause.

Choragos. It may be so: but I fear this deep silence.
Messenger. I will see what she is doing. I will go in.
                              Exit Messenger into the palace.

    Enter Creon with attendants, bearing Haimon's body.

Choragos. But here is the king himself: oh look at him,
    Bearing his own damnation in his arms.   85
Creon. Nothing you say can touch me any more.
    My own blind heart has brought me
    From darkness to final darkness. Here you see
    The father murdering, the murdered son —
    And all my civic wisdom!   90

    Haimon my son, so young, so young to die,
    I was the fool, not you; and you died for me.
Choragos. That is the truth; but you were late in learning it.
Creon. This truth is hard to bear. Surely a god
    Has crushed me beneath the hugest weight of heaven,   95
    And driven me headlong a barbaric way
    To trample out the thing I held most dear.

    The pains that men will take to come to pain!

    Enter Messenger from the palace.

Messenger. The burden you carry in your hands is heavy,
    But it is not all: you will find more in your house.   *100*
Creon. What burden worse than this shall I find there?
Messenger. The Queen is dead.
Creon. O port of death, deaf world,
    Is there no pity for me? And you, Angel of evil,
    I was dead, and your words are death again.   *105*
    Is it true, boy? Can it be true?
    Is my wife dead? Has death bred death?
Messenger. You can see for yourself.

    The doors are opened and the body of Eurydicê is disclosed within.

Creon. Oh pity!
    All true, all true, and more than I can bear!   *110*
    O my wife, my son!
Messenger. She stood before the altar, and her heart
    Welcomed the knife her own hand guided,
    And a great cry burst from her lips for Megareus° dead,
    And for Haimon dead, her sons; and her last breath   *115*
    Was a curse for their father, the murderer of her sons.
    And she fell, and the dark flowed in through her closing eyes.
Creon. O God, I am sick with fear.
    Are there no swords here? Has no one a blow for me?
Messenger. Her curse is upon you for the deaths of both.   *120*
Creon. It is right that it should be. I alone am guilty.
    I know it, and I say it. Lead me in,
    Quickly, friends.
    I have neither life nor substance. Lead me in.
Choragos. You are right, if there can be right in so much wrong.   *125*
    The briefest way is best in a world of sorrow.
Creon. Let it come,
    Let death come quickly, and be kind to me.
    I would not ever see the sun again.
Choragos. All that will come when it will; but we, meanwhile, *130*
    Have much to do. Leave the future to itself.
Creon. All my heart was in that prayer!
Choragos. Then do not pray any more: the sky is deaf.
Creon. Lead me away. I have been rash and foolish.
    I have killed my son and my wife.   *135*
    I look for comfort; my comfort lies here dead.
    Whatever my hands have touched has come to nothing.
    Fate has brought all my pride to a thought of dust.

---

[114]**Megareus** Megareus, brother of Haimon, had died in the assault on Thebes

As Creon is being led into the house, the Choragos advances and speaks directly to the audience.

Choragos. There is no happiness where there is no wisdom;
No wisdom but in submission to the gods.   140
Big words are always punished,
And proud men in old age learn to be wise.

QUESTIONS

1. Although Sophocles called his play *Antigonê,* many critics say that Creon is the real tragic hero, pointing out that Antigonê is absent from the last third of the play. Evaluate this view.

2. In some Greek tragedies, fate plays a great role in bringing about the downfall of the tragic hero. Though there are references to the curse on the House of Oedipus in *Antigonê,* do we feel that Antigonê goes to her death as a result of the workings of fate? Do we feel that fate is responsible for Creon's fall? Is the Messenger right to introduce the notion of "fate" (*Exodos,* line 4)? Or are both Antigonê and Creon the creators of their own tragedy?

3. Are the words *hamartia* and *hybris* (page 621) relevant to Antigonê? To Creon?

4. Why does Creon, contrary to the Chorus's advice (Scene V, lines 96–97), bury the body of Polyneicês before he releases Antigonê? Does his action show a zeal for piety as short-sighted as his earlier zeal for law? Is his action plausible, in view of the facts that Teiresias has dwelt on the wrong done to Polyneicês, and that Antigonê has ritual food to sustain her? Or are we not to worry about Creon's motive?

5. A "foil" is a character who, by contrast, sets off or helps define another character. To what extent is Ismenê a foil to Antigonê? Is she entirely without courage?

6. What function does Eurydicê serve? How deeply do we feel about her fate?

7. Some readers have been bothered by a passage, omitted from the present version, that follows line 65 in Scene IV. It runs (in Paul Roche's translation) thus:

> No husband dead and gone,
> No children lisping "mother" ever could
> Have forced me to withstand the city to its face.
> On what principles do I assert so much?

Just this:

A husband dead, another can be found;
A child, replaced; but once a brother's lost
(Mother and father dead and buried too)
No other brother can be born or grows again.
That's my principle, which Creon stigmatized
As criminal — my principle for honoring
You my dearest brother.

Goethe, for example, says (in *Conversations of Goethe with Eckermann*):

There is a passage in *Antigonê* which I always look upon as a blemish and I would give a great deal for an apt philologist to prove that it is interpolated and spurious. After the heroine has explained the noble motives for her action, and displayed the elevated purity of her soul, she at last, when she is led to death, brings forward a motive that is quite unworthy and almost borders upon the comic. . . . This passage, . . . in my opinion, when placed in the mouth of a heroine going to her death, disturbs the tragic tone and appears to me very far-fetched — to savor too much of dialetical calculation.

On the other hand H. D. F. Kitto has justified the passage thus (in *Form and Meaning in Drama*):

Antigonê is neither a philosopher nor a *dévoté*, but a passionate impulsive girl, and we need not expect consistency from one such, when for doing what to her was her manifest duty she is about to be buried alive, without a gleam of understanding from anybody. She thought she was obeying a divine law — as of course she was; now the gods seem to have deserted her — as they have, for they do not work miracles. Therefore nothing is left to her but her deep instinct that she had to do it, and it is neither surprising nor undramatic that she should now find what reason she can for asserting that in this special case she had no choice.

Evaluate these views.

19
Comedy

Though etymology is not always helpful (after all, is it really illuminating to say that "tragedy" may come from a Greek word meaning "goat song"?), the etymology of "comedy" helps to reveal comedy's fundamental nature. **Comedy** (Greek: *komoidia*) is a revel-song; ancient Greek comedies are descended from fertility rituals, and they dramatize the joy of renewal, the joy of triumphing over obstacles, the joy of being (in a sense) reborn. The movement of tragedy, speaking roughly, is from prosperity to disaster; the movement of comedy is from some sort of minor disaster to prosperity.

To say, however, that comedy dramatizes the triumph over obstacles is to describe it as though it were melodrama, a play in which, after hairbreadth adventures, good prevails over evil, often in the form of the hero's unlikely last-minute rescue of the fair Belinda from the clutches of the villain. What distinguishes comedy from melodrama is the pervasive high spirits of comedy. The joyous ending in comedy — usually a marriage — is in the spirit of what has gone before; the entire play, not only the end, is a celebration of fecundity.

The threats in the world of comedy are not taken very seriously; the parental tyranny that helps make *Romeo and Juliet* and *Antigonê* tragedies is, in comedy, laughable throughout. Parents may fret, fume, and lock doors, but in doing so they make themselves ridiculous, for love will find a way. Villains may threaten, but the audience never takes the threats seriously.

In the first act of *As You Like It*, Rosalind, at the mercy of a cruel uncle who has driven her father from his own dukedom, says: "O, how full of briers is this working-day world." The immediate reply is, "They are but burrs, cousin, thrown upon thee in holiday foolery." And this spirit of holiday foolery dominates the whole play and culminates in marriage, the symbol of life renewing itself. In the last act of a comedy things work out — as from the start we knew they would; whereas *Antigonê* concludes with Creon looking at the corpses of his wife, son, and intended daughter-in-law, a comedy usually concludes with preparation for a marriage.

These marriages and renewals of society, so usual at the end of comedy, are most improbable, but they do not therefore weaken the comedy. The stuff of comedy is, in part, improbability. In *A Midsummer Night's Dream* Puck speaks for the spectator when he says:

> And those things do best please me
> That befall preposterously.

In tragedy, probability is important; in comedy, the improbable is often desirable, for at least three reasons. First, comedy seeks to include as much as possible, to reveal the rich abundance of life. The motto of comedy (and the implication in the weddings with which it usually concludes) is the more the merrier. Second, the improbable is the surprising; surprise often evokes laughter, and laughter surely has a central place in comedy. Third, by getting his characters into improbable situations, the dramatist can show off the absurdity of their behavior — a point that needs amplification.

Comedy often shows the absurdity of man's ideals. The miser, the puritan, the health-faddist, and so on, are men of ideals, but their ideals are suffocating. The miser, for example, treats everything in terms of money; his ideal causes him to renounce much of the abundance and joy of life. He is in love, but is unwilling to support a wife; or he has a headache, but he will not be so extravagant as to take an aspirin tablet. If a thief accosts him with "Your money or your life," he will prefer to give up his life — and that is what in fact he has been doing all the while. Now, by putting this miser in a series of improbable situations, the dramatist can continue to demonstrate entertainingly the miser's absurdity.*

---

* A character who is dominated by a single trait — avarice, jealousy, timidity, and so forth — is sometimes called a **humor character.** Medieval and Renaissance psychology held that a man's personality depended on the mixture of four liquids (humors): blood (Latin: *sanguis*), choler, phlegm, and bile. An overabundance of one fluid produced a dominant trait, and even today "sanguine," "choleric," "phlegmatic," and "bilious" describe personalities.

Not all comedy, of course, depends on humor characters placed in situations that exhibit their absurdity. **High comedy** is largely verbal, depending on witty language; **farce,** at the other extreme, is dependent on inherently ludicrous situations, for example, a hobo is mistaken for a millionaire. Situation comedy, then, may use humor characters, but it need not do so.

The comic protagonist's tenacious hold on his ideals is not very far from the tragic protagonist's desperate hold on his. In general, however, tragedy suggests the nobility of ideals; the tragic hero's ideals undo him, and they may be ideals about which we have serious reservations, but still we admire him for them and recognize them as part of his nobility. Romeo and Juliet will not put off their love for each other; Antigonê will not yield to Creon, and Creon holds almost impossibly long to his stern position. But the comic protagonist who is always trying to keep his hands clean is funny; we laugh at his refusal to touch dirt with the rest of us, his refusal to enjoy the abundance life has to offer. The comic protagonist who is always talking about his beloved is funny; we laugh at his failure to see that the world is filled with women more attractive than the one who obsesses him. In short, the ideals for which the tragic protagonist loses the world seem important to us and gain, in large measure, our sympathy; but the ideals for which the comic protagonist loses the world seem trivial compared with the rich variety that life has to offer, and we laugh at their absurdity. The tragic figure makes a claim on our sympathy. The absurd comic figure continually sets up obstacles to our sympathetic interest; we feel detached from him, superior to him, and amused by him. Something along these lines is behind William Butler Yeats's insistence that character is always present in comedy but not in tragedy. Though Yeats is eccentric in his notion that individual character is obliterated in tragedy, he interestingly gets at one of the important elements in comedy:

> When the tragic reverie is at its height . . . [we do not say,] "How well that man is realized. I should know him were I to meet him in the street," for it is always ourselves that we see upon the [tragic] stage. . . . Tragedy must always be a drowning and breaking of the dikes that separate man from man, and . . . it is upon these dikes comedy keeps house.

Most comic plays can roughly be sorted into one of two types: romantic comedy and satiric comedy. Romantic comedy presents an ideal world, a golden world, a world more delightful than our own; if there are difficulties in it they are not briers but "burrs . . . thrown . . . in holiday foolery." It is the world of most of Shakespeare's comedies, a world of Illyria, of the Forest of Arden, of Belmont. The chief figures are young lovers; the course of their love is not smooth, but the outcome is never in doubt and the course is the more fun for being bumpy. Portia teases Bassanio; Lysander and Demetrius sometimes pursue the wrong girls; but they are all pleasant people. Occasionally in this golden world there is a villain, but if so, the villain is a great bungler who never really does any harm; the world seems to be guided by a benevolent providence who prevents villains from seriously harming even themselves. In these plays, the world belongs to golden lads and lasses. When we laugh, we laugh not so much *at* them as *with* them.

If romantic comedy shows us a world with more attractive people than we find in our own, satiric comedy shows us a world with less attractive people. The satiric world seems dominated by morally inferior people — the decrepit wooer, the jealous spouse, the demanding parent. These unengaging figures go through their paces, revealing again and again their absurdity. The audience laughs at (rather than with) such figures, and writers justify this kind of comedy by claiming to reform society: antisocial members of the audience will see their grotesque images on the stage and will reform themselves when they leave the theater. But it is hard to believe that this theory is rooted in fact. Jonathan Swift (as we mentioned earlier) was probably right when he said, "Satire is a sort of glass wherein beholders do generally discover everybody's face but their own."

Near the conclusion of a satiric comedy, the obstructing characters are dismissed, often perfunctorily, allowing for a happy ending — commonly the marriage of figures less colorful than the obstructionist. And so all-encompassing are the festivities at the end that even the obstructionist is invited to join in the wedding feast. If he refuses to join, we may find him — yet again — laughable rather than sympathetic, though admittedly one may also feel lingering regret that this somewhat shabby world of ours cannot live up to the exalted (even if rigid and rather crazy) standards of this outsider who refuses to go along with the way of the world.

Pictured is the 1947 New York production of The Importance of Being Earnest
at the Royale Theatre, starring Margaret Rutherford, Pamela Brown, Jane Baxter,
John Gielgud, and Robert Fleming. (Photograph: New York Public Library,
The Billy Rose Theatre Collection, The Vandam Collection. Used by permission.)

Oscar Wilde (1854–1900)

The Importance of Being Earnest

List of Characters

John Worthing, J.P.
Algernon Moncrieff
Rev. Canon Chasuble, D.D.
Merriman, butler
Lane, manservant
Lady Bracknell
Hon.° Gwendolen Fairfax
Cecily Cardew
Miss Prism, governess

ACT I

Scene. *Morning room in Algernon's flat in Half-Moon Street. The room is luxuriously and artistically furnished. The sound of a piano is heard in the adjoining room. Lane is arranging afternoon tea on the table, and after the music has ceased, Algernon enters.*

Algernon. Did you hear what I was playing, Lane?

Lane. I didn't think it polite to listen, sir.

Algernon. I'm sorry for that, for your sake. I don't play accurately — any one can play accurately — but I play with wonderful expression. As far as the piano is concerned, sentiment is my forte. I keep science for Life.

Lane. Yes, sir.

Algernon. And, speaking of the science of Life, have you got the cucumber sandwiches cut for Lady Bracknell?

Lane. Yes, sir. (*Hands them on a salver.*)

Algernon (*inspects them, takes two, and sits down on the sofa*). Oh! . . . by the way, Lane, I see from your book that on Thursday night, when Lord Shoreman and Mr. Worthing were dining with me, eight bottles of champagne are entered as having been consumed.

Lane. Yes, sir; eight bottles and a pint.

° The prefix Hon. (Honorable) indicates that she is the daughter of a Viscount or Baron

Algernon. Why is it that at a bachelor's establishment the servants invariably drink the champagne? I ask merely for information.

Lane. I attribute it to the superior quality of the wine, sir. I have often observed that in married households the champagne is rarely of a first-rate brand.

Algernon. Good Heavens! Is marriage so demoralizing as that?

Lane. I believe it *is* a very pleasant state, sir. I have had very little experience of it myself up to the present. I have only been married once. That was in consequence of a misunderstanding between myself and a young person.

Algernon (*languidly*). I don't know that I am much interested in your family life, Lane.

Lane. No sir; it is not a very interesting subject. I never think of it myself.

Algernon. Very natural, I am sure. That will do, Lane, thank you.

Lane. Thank you, sir.

Lane goes out.

Algernon. Lane's views on marriage seem somewhat lax. Really, if the lower orders don't set us a good example, what on earth is the use of them? They seem, as a class, to have absolutely no sense of moral responsibility.

Enter Lane.

Lane. Mr. Ernest Worthing.

Enter Jack. Lane goes out.

Algernon. How are you, my dear Ernest? What brings you up to town?

Jack. Oh, pleasure, pleasure! What else should bring one anywhere? Eating as usual, I see, Algy!

Algernon (*stiffly*). I believe it is customary in good society to take some slight refreshment at five o'clock. Where have you been since last Thursday?

Jack (*sitting down on the sofa*). In the country.

Algernon. What on earth do you do there?

Jack (*pulling off his gloves*). When one is in town one amuses oneself. When one is in the country one amuses other people. It is excessively boring.

Algernon. And who are the people you amuse?

Jack (*airily*). Oh, neighbors, neighbors.

Algernon. Got nice neighbors in your part of Shropshire?

Jack. Perfectly horrid! Never speak to one of them.

Algernon. How immensely you must amuse them! (*Goes over and takes sandwich.*) By the way, Shropshire is your country, is it not?

Jack. Eh? Shropshire? Yes, of course. Hallo! Why all these cups? Why cucumber sandwiches? Why such reckless extravagance in one so young? Who is coming to tea?

Algernon. Oh! merely Aunt Augusta and Gwendolen.

Jack. How perfectly delightful!

Algernon. Yes, that is all very well; but I am afraid Aunt Augusta won't quite approve of your being here.

Jack. May I ask why?

Algernon. My dear fellow, the way you flirt with Gwendolen is perfectly disgraceful. It is almost as bad as the way Gwendolen flirts with you.

Jack. I am in love with Gwendolen. I have come up to town expressly to propose to her.

Algernon. I thought you had come up for pleasure? . . . I call that business.

Jack. How utterly unromantic you are!

Algernon. I really don't see anything romantic in proposing. It is very romantic to be in love. But there is nothing romantic about a definite proposal. Why, one may be accepted. One usually is, I believe. Then the excitement is all over. The very essence of romance is uncertainty. If ever I get married, I'll certainly try to forget the fact.

Jack. I have no doubt about that, dear Algy. The Divorce Court was specially invented for people whose memories are so curiously constituted.

Algernon. Oh! there is no use speculating on that subject. Divorces are made in Heaven — (*Jack puts out his hand to take a sandwich. Algernon at once interferes.*) Please don't touch the cucumber sandwiches. They are ordered specially for Aunt Augusta. (*Takes one and eats it.*)

Jack. Well, you have been eating them all the time.

Algernon. That is quite a different matter. She is my aunt. (*Takes plate from below.*) Have some bread and butter. The bread and butter is for Gwendolen. Gwendolen is devoted to bread and butter.

Jack (*advancing to table and helping himself*). And very good bread and butter it is too.

Algernon. Well, my dear fellow, you need not eat as if you were going to eat it all. You behave as if you were married to her already. You are not married to her already, and I don't think you ever will be.

Jack. Why on earth do you say that?

Algernon. Well, in the first place, girls never marry the men they flirt with. Girls don't think it right.

Jack. Oh, that is nonsense!

Algernon. It isn't. It is a great truth. It accounts for the extraordinary
   number of bachelors that one sees all over the place. In the
   second place, I don't give my consent.
Jack. Your consent!
Algernon. My dear fellow, Gwendolen is my first cousin. And
   before I allow you to marry her, you will have to clear up
   the whole question of Cecily. (*Rings bell.*)
Jack. Cecily! What on earth do you mean? What do you mean,
   Algy, by Cecily! I don't know any one of the name of Cecily.

   Enter Lane.

Algernon. Bring me that cigarette case Mr. Worthing left in the
   smoking room the last time he dined here.
Lane. Yes, sir.

                                                    Lane goes out.
Jack. Do you mean to say you have had my cigarette case all this
   time? I wish to goodness you had let me know. I have been
   writing frantic letters to Scotland Yard° about it. I was very
   nearly offering a large reward.
Algernon. Well, I wish you would offer one. I happen to be more
   than usually hard up.
Jack. There is no good offering a large reward now that the thing
   is found.

   *Enter Lane with the cigarette case on a salver. Algernon takes it
   at once. Lane goes out.*

Algernon. I think that is rather mean of you, Ernest, I must say.
   (*Opens case and examines it.*) However, it makes no matter,
   for, now that I look at the inscription inside, I find that the
   thing isn't yours after all.
Jack. Of course it's mine. (*Moving to him.*) You have seen me with
   it a hundred times, and you have no right whatsoever to
   read what is written inside. It is a very ungentlemanly thing
   to read a private cigarette case.
Algernon. Oh! it is absurd to have a hard and fast rule about what
   one should read and what one shouldn't. More than half of
   modern culture depends on what one shouldn't read.
Jack. I am quite aware of the fact, and I don't propose to discuss
   modern culture. It isn't the sort of thing one should talk of
   in private. I simply want my cigarette case back.
Algernon. Yes; but this isn't your cigarette case. This cigarette case

---

Scotland Yard Headquarters of the London Police

is a present from someone of the name of Cecily, and you said you didn't know anyone of that name.

Jack. Well, if you want to know, Cecily happens to be my aunt.

Algernon. Your aunt!

Jack. Yes. Charming old lady she is, too. Lives at Tunbridge Wells.° Just give it back to me, Algy.

Algernon (*retreating to back of sofa*). But why does she call herself little Cecily if she is your aunt and lives at Tunbridge Wells. (*Reading.*) "From little Cecily with her fondest love."

Jack (*moving to sofa and kneeling upon it*). My dear fellow, what on earth is there in that? Some aunts are tall, some aunts are not tall. That is a matter that surely an aunt may be allowed to decide for herself. You seem to think that every aunt should be exactly like your aunt! That is absurd. For Heaven's sake give me back my cigarette case. (*Follows Algernon round the room.*)

Algernon. Yes. But why does your aunt call you her uncle? "From little Cecily, with her fondest love to her dear Uncle Jack." There is no objection, I admit, to an aunt being a small aunt, but why an aunt, no matter what her size may be, should call her own nephew her uncle, I can't quite make out. Besides, your name isn't Jack at all; it is Ernest.

Jack. It isn't Ernest; it's Jack.

Algernon. You have always told me it was Ernest. I have introduced you to every one as Ernest. You answer to the name of Ernest. You look as if your name was Ernest. You are the most earnest-looking person I ever saw in my life. It is perfectly absurd your saying that your name isn't Ernest. It's on your cards. Here is one of them (*taking it from case*). "Mr. Ernest Worthing, B.4, The Albany."° I'll keep this as a proof that your name is Ernest if ever you attempt to deny it to me, or to Gwendolen, or to any one else. (*Puts the card in his pocket.*)

Jack. Well, my name is Ernest in town and Jack in the country, and the cigarette case was given to me in the country.

Algernon. Yes, but that does not account for the fact that your small Aunt Cecily, who lives at Tunbridge Wells, calls you her dear uncle. Come, old boy, you had much better have the thing out at once.

Jack. My dear Algy, you talk exactly as if you were a dentist. It

Tunbridge Wells A fashionable town south of London in Kent **The Albany**
Fashionable apartments in Picadilly near the center of London

is very vulgar to talk like a dentist when one isn't a dentist. It produces a false impression.

Algernon. Well, that is exactly what dentists always do. Now, go on! Tell me the whole thing. I may mention that I have always suspected you of being a confirmed and secret Bunburyist; and I am quite sure of it now.

Jack. Bunburyist? What on earth do you mean by a Bunburyist?

Algernon. I'll reveal to you the meaning of that incomparable expression as soon as you are kind enough to inform me why you are Ernest in town and Jack in the country.

Jack. Well, produce my cigarette case first.

Algernon. Here it is. (*Hands cigarette case.*) Now produce your explanation, and pray make it improbable. (*Sits on sofa*).

Jack. My dear fellow, there is nothing improbable about my explanation at all. In fact it's perfectly ordinary. Old Mr. Thomas Cardew, who adopted me when I was a little boy, made me in his will guardian to his granddaughter, Miss Cecily Cardew. Cecily, who addresses me as her uncle from motives of respect that you could not possibly appreciate, lives at my place in the country under the charge of her admirable governess, Miss Prism.

Algernon. Where is that place in the country, by the way?

Jack. That is nothing to you, dear boy. You are not going to be invited. . . . I may tell you candidly that the place is not in Shropshire.

Algernon. I suspected that, my dear fellow! I have Bunburyed all over Shropshire on two separate occasions. Now, go on. Why are you Ernest in town and Jack in the country?

Jack. My dear Algy, I don't know whether you will be able to understand my real motives. You are hardly serious enough. When one is placed in the position of guardian, one has to adopt a very high moral tone on all subjects. It's one's duty to do so. And as a high moral tone can hardly be said to conduce very much to either one's health or one's happiness, in order to get up to town I have always pretended to have a younger brother of the name of Ernest, who lives in the Albany, and gets into the most dreadful scrapes. That, my dear Algy, is the whole truth pure and simple.

Algernon. The truth is rarely pure and never simple. Modern life would be very tedious if it were either, and modern literature a complete impossibility!

Jack. That wouldn't be at all a bad thing.

Algernon. Literary criticism is not your forte, my dear fellow. Don't try it. You should leave that to people who haven't been at a University. They do it so well in the daily papers. What you really are is a Bunburyist. I was quite right in saying you were a Bunburyist. You are one of the most advanced Bunburyists I know.

Jack. What on earth do you mean?

Algernon. You have invented a very useful younger brother called Ernest, in order that you may be able to come up to town as often as you like. I have invented an invaluable permanent invalid called Bunbury, in order that I may be able to go down into the country whenever I choose. Bunbury is perfectly invaluable. If it wasn't for Bunbury's extraordinary bad health, for instance, I wouldn't be able to dine with you at Willis's° tonight, for I have been really engaged to° Aunt Augusta for more than a week.

Jack. I haven't asked you to dine with me anywhere tonight.

Algernon. I know. You are absurdly careless about sending out invitations. It is very foolish of you. Nothing annoys people so much as not receiving invitations.

Jack. You had much better dine with your Aunt Augusta.

Algernon. I haven't the smallest intention of doing anything of the kind. To begin with, I dined there on Monday, and once a week is quite enough to dine with one's own relations. In the second place, whenever I do dine there I am always treated as a member of the family, and sent down with° either no woman at all, or two. In the third place, I know perfectly well whom she will place me next to, tonight. She will place me next Mary Farquhar, who always flirts with her own husband across the dinner table. That is not very pleasant. Indeed, it is not even decent . . . and that sort of thing is enormously on the increase. The amount of women in London who flirt with their own husbands is perfectly scandalous. It looks so bad. It is simply washing one's clean linen in public. Besides, now that I know you to be a confirmed Bunburyist I naturally want to talk to you about Bunburying. I want to tell you the rules.

Jack. I'm not a Bunburyist at all. If Gwendolen accepts me, I am going to kill my brother, indeed I think I'll kill him in any case. Cecily is a little too much interested in him. It is rather a bore. So I am going to get rid of Ernest. And I strongly advise you to do the same with Mr. . . . with your invalid friend who has the absurd name.

Willis's Popular restaurant   **engaged** I.e., promised to attend her dinner party
sent down with I.e., ordered to escort

Algernon. Nothing will induce me to part with Bunbury, and if you ever get married, which seems to me extremely problematic, you will be very glad to know Bunbury. A man who marries without knowing Bunbury has a very tedious time of it.

Jack. That is nonsense. If I marry a charming girl like Gwendolen, and she is the only girl I ever saw in my life that I would marry, I certainly won't want to know Bunbury.

Algernon. Then your wife will. You don't seem to realize, that in married life three is company and two is none.

Jack (sententiously). That, my dear young friend, is the theory that the corrupt French Drama has been propounding for the last fifty years.

Algernon. Yes; and that the happy English home has proved in half the time.

Jack. For heaven's sake, don't try to be cynical. It's perfectly easy to be cynical.

Algernon. My dear fellow, it isn't easy to be anything nowadays. There's such a lot of beastly competition about. (*The sound of an electric bell is heard.*) Ah! that must be Aunt Augusta. Only relatives, or creditors, ever ring in that Wagnerian manner.° Now, if I get her out of the way for ten minutes, so that you can have an opportunity of proposing to Gwendolen, may I dine with you tonight at Willis's?

Jack. I suppose so, if you want to.

Algernon. Yes, but you must be serious about it. I hate people who are not serious about meals. It is so shallow of them.

Enter Lane.

Lane. Lady Bracknell and Miss Fairfax.

Algernon goes forward to meet them. Enter Lady Bracknell and Gwendolen.

Lady Bracknell. Good afternoon, dear Algernon, I hope you are behaving very well.

Algernon. I'm feeling very well, Aunt Augusta.

Lady Bracknell. That's not quite the same thing. In fact the two things rarely go together. (*Sees Jack and bows to him with icy coldness.*)

Algernon (to Gwendolen). Dear me, you are smart!°

Gwendolen. I am always smart! Am I not, Mr. Worthing?

Jack. You're quite perfect, Miss Fairfax.

Wagnerian manner Loudly   **smart** Elegantly dressed

Gwendolen. Oh! I hope I am not that. I would leave no room for developments, and I intend to develop in many directions. (*Gwendolen and Jack sit down together in the corner.*)

Lady Bracknell. I'm sorry if we are a little late, Algernon, but I was obliged to call on dear Lady Harbury. I hadn't been there since her poor husband's death. I never saw a woman so altered; she looks quite twenty years younger. And now I'll have a cup of tea and one of those nice cucumber sandwiches you promised me.

Algernon. Certainly, Aunt Augusta. (*Goes over to tea table.*)

Lady Bracknell. Won't you come and sit here, Gwendolen?

Gwendolen. Thanks, mamma, I'm quite comfortable where I am.

Algernon (*picking up empty plate in horror*). Good heavens! Lane! Why are there no cucumber sandwiches? I ordered them specially.

Lane (*gravely*). There were no cucumbers in the market this morning, sir. I went down twice.

Algernon. No cucumbers!

Lane. No, sir. Not even for ready money.

Algernon. That will do, Lane, thank you.

Lane. Thank you, sir. (*Goes out.*)

Algernon. I am greatly distressed, Aunt Augusta, about there being no cucumbers, not even for ready money.

Lady Bracknell. It really makes no matter, Algernon. I had some crumpets° with Lady Harbury, who seems to me to be living entirely for pleasure now.

Algernon. I hear her hair has turned quite gold from grief.

Lady Bracknell. It certainly has changed its color. From what cause I, of course, cannot say. (*Algernon crosses and hands tea.*) Thank you. I've quite a treat for you tonight, Algernon. I am going to send you down with Mary Farquhar. She is such a nice woman, and so attentive to her husband. It's delightful to watch them.

Algernon. I am afraid, Aunt Augusta, I shall have to give up the pleasure of dining with you tonight after all.

Lady Bracknell (*frowning*). I hope not, Algernon. It would put my table completely out. Your uncle would have to dine upstairs. Fortunately he is accustomed to that.

Algernon. It is a great bore, and, I need hardly say, a terrible disappointment to me, but the fact is I have just had a telegram to say that my poor friend Bunbury is very ill again. (*Exchanges glances with Jack.*) They seem to think I should be with him.

crumpets Lightly toasted bread (English muffins)

Lady Bracknell. It is very strange. This Mr. Bunbury seems to suffer from curiously bad health.

Algernon. Yes; poor Bunbury is a dreadful invalid.

Lady Bracknell. Well, I must say, Algernon, that I think it is high time that Mr. Bunbury made up his mind whether he was going to live or to die. This shilly-shallying with the question is absurd. Nor do I in any way approve of the modern sympathy with invalids. I consider it morbid. Illness of any kind is hardly a thing to be encouraged in others. Health is the primary duty of life. I am always telling that to your poor uncle, but he never seems to take much notice . . . as far as any improvement in his ailments goes. I should be much obliged if you would ask Mr. Bunbury, from me, to be kind enough not to have a relapse on Saturday, for I rely on you to arrange my music for me. It is my last reception, and one wants something that will encourage conversation, particularly at the end of the season° when every one has practically said whatever they had to say, which, in most cases, was probably not much.

Algernon. I'll speak to Bunbury, Aunt Augusta, if he is still conscious, and I think I can promise you he'll be all right by Saturday. Of course the music is a great difficulty. You see, if one plays good music, people don't listen, and if one plays bad music, people don't talk. But I'll run over the program I've drawn out, if you will kindly come into the next room for a moment.

Lady Bracknell. Thank you, Algernon. It is very thoughtful of you. (*Rising, and following Algernon.*) I'm sure the program will be delightful, after a few expurgations. French songs I cannot possibly allow. People always seem to think that they are improper, and either look shocked, which is vulgar, or laugh, which is worse. But German sounds a thoroughly respectable language, and, indeed I believe is so. Gwendolen, you will accompany me.

Gwendolen. Certainly, mamma.

Lady Bracknell and Algernon go into the music room; Gwendolen remains behind.

Jack. Charming day it has been, Miss Fairfax.

Gwendolen. Pray don't talk to me about the weather, Mr. Worthing. Whenever people talk to me about the weather, I always

---

season The social season

feel quite certain that they mean something else. And that makes me so nervous.

Jack. I do mean something else.

Gwendolen. I thought so. In fact, I am never wrong.

Jack. And I would like to be allowed to take advantage of Lady Bracknell's temporary absence. . . .

Gwendolen. I would certainly advise you to do so. Mamma has a way of coming back suddenly into a room that I have often had to speak to her about.

Jack (nervously). Miss Fairfax, ever since I met you I have admired you more than any girl . . . I have ever met since . . . I met you.

Gwendolen. Yes, I am quite aware of the fact. And I often wish that in public, at any rate, you had been more demonstrative. For me you have always had an irresistible fascination. Even before I met you I was far from indifferent to you. (*Jack looks at her in amazement.*) We live, as I hope you know, Mr. Worthing, in an age of ideals. The fact is constantly mentioned in the more expensive monthly magazines, and has reached the provincial pulpits, I am told; and my ideal has always been to love someone of the name of Ernest. There is something in that name that inspires absolute confidence. The moment Algernon first mentioned to me that he had a friend called Ernest, I knew I was destined to love you.

Jack. You really love me, Gwendolen?

Gwendolen. Passionately!

Jack. Darling! You don't know how happy you've made me.

Gwendolen. My own Ernest!

Jack. But you don't really mean to say that you couldn't love me if my name wasn't Ernest?

Gwendolen. But your name is Ernest.

Jack. Yes, I know it is. But supposing it was something else? Do you mean to say you couldn't love me then?

Gwendolen (glibly). Ah! that is clearly a metaphysical speculation, and like most metaphysical speculations has very little reference at all to the actual facts of real life, as we know them.

Jack. Personally, darling, to speak quite candidly, I don't much care about the name of Ernest . . . . I don't think the name suits me at all.

Gwendolen. It suits you perfectly. It is a divine name. It has a music of its own. It produces vibrations.

Jack. Well, really, Gwendolen, I must say that I think there are lots of other much nicer names. I think Jack, for instance, a charming name.

Gwendolen. Jack? . . . No, there is very little music in the name Jack, if any at all, indeed. It does not thrill. It produces absolutely no vibrations. . . . I have known several Jacks, and they all, without exception, were more than usually plain. Besides, Jack is a notorious domesticity for John! And I pity any woman who is married to a man called John. She would probably never be allowed to know the entrancing pleasure of a single moment's solitude. The only really safe name is Ernest.

Jack. Gwendolen, I must get christened at once — I mean we must get married at once. There is no time to be lost.

Gwendolen. Married, Mr. Worthing?

Jack (astounded). Well . . . surely. You know that I love you, and you led me to believe, Miss Fairfax, that you were not absolutely indifferent to me.

Gwendolen. I adore you. But you haven't proposed to me yet. Nothing has been said at all about marriage. The subject has not even been touched on.

Jack. Well . . . may I propose to you now?

Gwendolen. I think it would be an admirable opportunity. And to spare you any possible disappointment, Mr. Worthing, I think it only fair to tell you quite frankly beforehand that I am fully determined to accept you.

Jack. Gwendolen!

Gwendolen. Yes, Mr. Worthing, what have you got to say to me?

Jack. You know what I have got to say to you.

Gwendolen. Yes, but you don't say it.

Jack. Gwendolen, will you marry me? (*Goes on his knees.*)

Gwendolen. Of course I will, darling. How long you have been about it! I am afraid you have had very little experience in how to propose.

Jack. My own one, I have never loved anyone in the world but you.

Gwendolen. Yes, but men often propose for practice. I know my brother Gerald does. All my girl friends tell me so. What wonderfully blue eyes you have, Ernest! They are quite, quite blue. I hope you will always look at me just like that, especially when there are other people present.

Enter Lady Bracknell.

Lady Bracknell. Mr. Worthing! Rise, sir, from this semi-recumbent posture. It is most indecorous.

Gwendolen. Mamma! (*He tries to rise; she restrains him.*) I must beg you to retire. This is no place for you. Besides, Mr. Worthing has not quite finished yet.

Lady Bracknell. Finished what, may I ask?

Gwendolen. I am engaged to Mr. Worthing, Mamma. (*They rise together.*)

Lady Bracknell. Pardon me, you are not engaged to any one. When you do become engaged to someone, I, or your father, should his health permit him, will inform you of the fact. An engagement should come on a young girl as a surprise, pleasant or unpleasant, as the case may be. It is hardly a matter that she could be allowed to arrange for herself. . . . . And now I have a few questions to put to you, Mr. Worthing. While I am making these inquiries, you, Gwendolen, will wait for me below in the carriage.

Gwendolen (reproachfully). Mamma!

Lady Bracknell. In the carriage, Gwendolen! (*Gwendolen goes to the door. She and Jack blow kisses to each other behind Lady Bracknell's back. Lady Bracknell looks vaguely about as if she could not understand what the noise was. Finally turns round.*) Gwendolen, the carriage!

Gwendolen. Yes, Mamma. (*Goes out, looking back at Jack.*)

Lady Bracknell (sitting down). You can take a seat, Mr. Worthing. (*Looks in her pocket for notebook and pencil.*)

Jack. Thank you, Lady Bracknell, I prefer standing.

Lady Bracknell (pencil and notebook in hand). I feel bound to tell you that you are not down on my list of eligible young men, although I have the same list as the dear Duchess of Bolton has. We work together, in fact. However, I am quite ready to enter your name, should your answers be what a really affectionate mother requires. Do you smoke?

Jack. Well, yes, I must admit I smoke.

Lady Bracknell. I am glad to hear it. A man should always have an occupation of some kind. There are far too many idle men in London as it is. How old are you?

Jack. Twenty-nine.

Lady Bracknell. A very good age to be married at. I have always been of opinion that a man who desires to get married should know either everything or nothing. Which do you know?

Jack (after some hesitation). I know nothing, Lady Bracknell.

Lady Bracknell. I am pleased to hear it. I do not approve of anything that tampers with natural ignorance. Ignorance is like a delicate exotic fruit; touch it and the bloom is gone. The whole theory of modern education is radically unsound. Fortunately in England, at any rate, education produces no effect whatsoever. If it did, it would prove a serious danger to the upper classes, and probably lead to acts of violence in Grosvenor Square. What is your income?

Jack. Between seven and eight thousand a year.

Lady Bracknell (*makes a note in her book*). In land, or in investments?

Jack. In investments, chiefly.

Lady Bracknell. That is satisfactory. What between the duties expected of one during one's lifetime, and the duties° exacted from one after one's death, land has ceased to be either a profit or a pleasure. It gives one position, and prevents one from keeping it up. That's all that can be said about land.

Jack. I have a country house with some land, of course, attached to it, about fifteen hundred acres, I believe; but I don't depend on that for my real income. In fact, as far as I can make out, the poachers are the only people who make anything out of it.

Lady Bracknell. A country house! How many bedrooms? Well, that point can be cleared up afterwards. You have a town house, I hope? A girl with a simple, unspoiled nature, like Gwendolen, could hardly be expected to reside in the country.

Jack. Well, I own a house in Belgrave Square, but it is let by the year to Lady Bloxham. Of course, I can get it back whenever I like, at six months' notice.

Lady Bracknell. Lady Bloxham? I don't know her.

Jack. Oh, she goes about very little. She is a lady considerably advanced in years.

Lady Bracknell. Ah, nowadays that is no guarantee of respectability of character. What number in Belgrave Square?

Jack. 149.

Lady Bracknell (*shaking her head*). The unfashionable side. I thought there was something. However, that could easily be altered.

Jack. Do you mean the fashion, or the side?

Lady Bracknell (*sternly*). Both, if necessary, I presume. What are your politics?

Jack. Well, I am afraid I really have none. I am a Liberal Unionist.

Lady Bracknell. Oh, they count as Tories. They dine with us. Or come in the evening, at any rate. Now to minor matters. Are your parents living?

Jack. I have lost both my parents.

Lady Bracknell. To lose one parent, Mr. Worthing, may be regarded as a misfortune; to lose both looks like carelessness. Who was your father? He was evidently a man of some wealth. Was he born in what the Radical papers call the purple of commerce, or did he rise from the ranks of the aristocracy?

duties I.e., inheritance taxes

Jack. I am afraid I really don't know. The fact is, Lady Bracknell, I said I had lost my parents. It would be nearer to truth to say that my parents seem to have lost me. . . . I don't actually know who I am by birth. I was . . . well, I was found.

Lady Bracknell. Found!

Jack. The late Mr. Thomas Cardew, an old gentlemen of a very charitable and kindly disposition, found me, and gave me the name of Worthing, because he happened to have a first-class ticket for Worthing in his pocket at the time. Worthing is a place in Sussex. It is a seaside resort.

Lady Bracknell. Where did the charitable gentleman who had a first-class ticket for this seaside resort find you?

Jack (gravely). In a handbag.

Lady Bracknell. A handbag?

Jack (very seriously). Yes, Lady Bracknell. I was in a handbag — a somewhat large, black leather handbag, with handles on it — an ordinary handbag in fact.

Lady Bracknell. In what locality did this Mr. James, or Thomas, Cardew come across this ordinary handbag?

Jack. In the cloakroom at Victoria Station. It was given to him in mistake for his own.

Lady Bracknell. The cloakroom at Victoria Station?

Jack. Yes. The Brighton line.

Lady Bracknell. The line is immaterial. Mr. Worthing, I confess I feel somewhat bewildered by what you have just told me. To be born, or at any rate bred, in a handbag, whether it had handles or not, seems to me to display a contempt for the ordinary decencies of family life that reminds one of the worst excesses of the French Revolution. And I presume you know what that unfortunate movement led to? As for the particular locality in which the handbag was found, a cloakroom at a railway station might serve to conceal a social indiscretion — has probably, indeed, been used for that purpose before now — but it could hardly be regarded as an assured basis for a recognized position in good society.

Jack. May I ask you then what you would advise me to do? I need hardly say I would do anything in the world to ensure Gwendolen's happiness.

Lady Bracknell. I would strongly advise you, Mr. Worthing, to try and acquire some relations as soon as possible, and to make a definite effort to produce at any rate one parent, of either sex, before the season is quite over.

Jack. Well, I don't see how I could possibly manage to do that. I can produce the handbag at any moment. It is in my dressing room at home. I really think that should satisfy you, Lady Bracknell.

Lady Bracknell. Me, sir! What has it to do with me? You can hardly imagine that I and Lord Bracknell would dream of allowing our only daughter — a girl brought up with the utmost care — to marry into a cloakroom, and form an alliance with a parcel. Good morning, Mr. Worthing!

(Lady Bracknell sweeps out in majestic indignation.)

Jack. Good morning! *(Algernon, from the other room, strikes up the Wedding March. Jack looks perfectly furious, and goes to the door.)* For goodness' sake don't play that ghastly tune, Algy! How idiotic you are!

The music stops and Algernon enters cheerily.

Algernon. Didn't it go off all right, old boy? You don't mean to say Gwendolen refused you? I know it is a way she has. She is always refusing people. I think it is most ill-natured of her.

Jack. Oh, Gwendolen is as right as a trivet.° As far as she is concerned, we are engaged. Her mother is perfectly unbearable. Never met such a Gorgon.° . . . I don't really know what a Gorgon is like, but I am quite sure that Lady Bracknell is one. In any case, she is a monster, without being a myth, which is rather unfair. . . . I beg your pardon, Algy, I suppose I shouldn't talk about your own aunt in that way before you.

Algernon. My dear boy, I love hearing my relations abused. It is the only thing that makes me put up with them at all. Relations are simply a tedious pack of people who haven't got the remotest knowledge of how to live, or the smallest instinct about when to die.

Jack. Oh, that is nonsense!

Algernon. It isn't!

Jack. Well, I won't argue about the matter. You always want to argue about things.

Algernon. That is exactly what things were originally made for.

Jack. Upon my word, if I thought that, I'd shoot myself. . . . *(A pause.)* You don't think there is any chance of Gwendolen

---

trivet Proverbial expression meaning reliable (like a trivet used to support a kettle over a fire) **Gorgon** Mythical female figure whose looks turned anyone who looked at her into stone

becoming like her mother in about a hundred and fifty years, do you, Algy?

Algernon. All women become like their mothers. That is their tragedy. No man does. That's his.

Jack. Is that clever?

Algernon. It is perfectly phrased! and quite as true as any observation in civilized life should be.

Jack. I am sick to death of cleverness. Everybody is clever nowadays. You can't go anywhere without meeting clever people. The thing has become an absolute public nuisance. I wish to goodness we had a few fools left.

Algernon. We have.

Jack. I should extremely like to meet them. What do they talk about?

Algernon. The fools? Oh! about the clever people, of course.

Jack. What fools.

Algernon. By the way, did you tell Gwendolen the truth about your being Ernest in town, and Jack in the country?

Jack (in a very patronizing manner). My dear fellow, the truth isn't quite the sort of thing one tells to a nice, sweet, refined girl. What extraordinary ideas you have about the way to behave to a woman!

Algernon. The only way to behave to a woman is to make love° to her, if she is pretty, and to someone else, if she is plain.

Jack. Oh, that is nonsense.

Algernon. What about your brother? What about the profligate Ernest?

Jack. Oh, before the end of the week I shall have got rid of him. I'll say he died in Paris of apoplexy. Lots of people die of apoplexy, quite suddenly, don't they?

Algernon. Yes, but it's hereditary, my dear fellow. It's a sort of thing that runs in families. You had much better say a severe chill.

Jack. You are sure a severe chill isn't hereditary, or anything of that kind?

Algernon. Of course it isn't!

Jack. Very well, then. My poor brother Ernest is carried off suddenly, in Paris, by a severe chill. That gets rid of him.

Algernon. But I thought you said that . . . Miss Cardew was a little too much interested in your poor brother Ernest? Won't she feel his loss a great deal?

make love To pay court to her, to woo

Jack. Oh, that is all right. Cecily is not a silly romantic girl, I am glad to say. She has got a capital appetite, goes on long walks, and pays no attention at all to her lessons.

Algernon. I would rather like to see Cecily.

Jack. I will take very good care you never do. She is excessively pretty, and she is only just eighteen.

Algernon. Have you told Gwendolen yet that you have an excessively pretty ward who is only just eighteen?

Jack. Oh! ones doesn't blurt these things out to people. Cecily and Gwendolen are perfectly certain to be extremely great friends. I'll bet you anything you like that half an hour after they have met, they will be calling each other sister.

Algernon. Women only do that when they have called each other a lot of other things first. Now, my dear boy, if we want to get a good table at Willis's, we really must go and dress. Do you know it is nearly seven?

Jack (*irritably*). Oh! it always is nearly seven.

Algernon. Well, I'm hungry.

Jack. I never knew you when you weren't. . . .

Algernon. What shall we do after dinner? Go to a theater?

Jack. Oh no! I loathe listening.

Algernon. Well, let us go to the Club?

Jack. Oh, no! I hate talking.

Algernon. Well, we might trot round to the Empire° at ten?

Jack. Oh, no! I can't bear looking at things. It is so silly.

Algernon. Well, what shall we do?

Jack. Nothing!

Algernon. It is awfully hard work doing nothing. However, I don't mind hard work where there is no definite object of any kind.

Enter Lane.

Lane. Miss Fairfax.

Enter Gwendolen. Lanes goes out.

Algernon. Gwendolen, upon my word!

Gwendolen. Algy, kindly turn your back. I have something very particular to say to Mr. Worthing.

Algernon. Really, Gwendolen, I don't think I can allow this at all.

Gwendolen. Algy, you always adopt a stictly immoral attitute towards life. You are not quite old enough to do that. (*Algernon retires to the fireplace.*)

Empire A music hall or variety theater

Jack. My own darling!

Gwendolen. Ernest, we may never be married. From the expression on mamma's face I fear we never shall. Few parents nowadays pay any regard to what their children say to them. The old-fashioned respect for the young is fast dying out. Whatever influence I ever had over mamma, I lost at the age of three. But although she may prevent us from becoming man and wife, and I may marry someone else, and marry often, nothing that she can possibly do can alter my eternal devotion to you.

Jack. Dear Gwendolen!

Gwendolen. The story of your romantic origin, as related to me by mamma, with unpleasing comments, has naturally stirred the deeper fibers of my nature. Your Christian name has an irresistible fascination. The simplicity of your character makes you exquisitely incomprehensible to me. Your town address at the Albany I have. What is your address in the country?

Jack. The Manor House, Woolton, Hertfordshire.

Algernon, who has been carefully listening, smiles to himself, and writes the address on his shirt cuff. Then picks up the Railway Guide.

Gwendolen. There is a good postal service, I suppose? It may be necessary to do something desperate. That of course will require serious consideration. I will communicate with you daily.

Jack. My own one!

Gwendolen. How long do you remain in town?

Jack. Till Monday.

Gwendolen. Good! Algy, you may turn round now.

Algernon. Thanks, I've turned round already.

Gwendolen. You may also ring the bell.

Jack. You will let me see you to your carriage, my own darling?

Gwendolen. Certainly.

Jack (to Lane, who now enters). I will see Miss Fairfax out.

Lane. Yes, sir. (*Jack and Gwendolen go off.*)

Lane presents several letters on a salver to Algernon. It is to be surmised that they are bills, as Algernon, after looking at the envelopes, tears them up.

Algernon. A glass of sherry, Lane.

Lane. Yes, sir.

Algernon. Tomorrow, Lane, I'm going Bunburying.

Lane. Yes, sir.

Algernon. I shall probably not be back till Monday. You can put up my dress clothes, my smoking jacket, and all the Bunbury suits. . .

Lane. Yes, sir. (*Handing sherry.*)

Algernon. I hope tomorrow will be a fine day, Lane.

Lane. It never is, sir.

Algernon. Lane, you're a perfect pessimist.

Lane. I do my best to give satisfaction, sir.

> *Enter Jack. Lanes goes off.*

Jack. There's a sensible, intelligent girl! the only girl I ever cared for in my life. (*Algernon is laughing immoderately.*) What on earth are you so amused at?

Algernon. Oh, I'm a little anxious about poor Bunbury, that is all.

Jack. If you don't take care, your friend Bunbury will get you into a serious scrape some day.

Algernon. I love scrapes. They are the only things that are never serious.

Jack. Oh, that's nonsense, Algy. You never talk anything but nonsense.

Algernon. Nobody ever does.

> *Jack looks indignantly at him, and leaves the room. Algernon lights a cigarette, reads his shirt-cuff, and smiles.*

> *Act Drop°*

ACT II

> *Garden at the Manor House. A flight of gray stone steps leads up to the house. The garden, an old-fashioned one, full of roses. Time of year, July. Basket chairs, and a table covered with books, are set under a large yew tree.*

> *Miss Prism discovered seated at the table. Cecily is at the back, watering flowers.*

Miss Prism (calling). Cecily, Cecily! Surely such a utilitarian occupation as the watering of flowers is rather Moulton's duty than yours? Especially at a moment when intellectual pleasures await you. Your German grammar is on the table. Pray open it at page fifteen. We will repeat yesterday's lesson.

Cecily (coming over very slowly). But I don't like German. It isn't

---

Act Drop   A curtain lowered in a theater during intermission

at all a becoming language. I know perfectly well that I look quite plain after my German lesson.

Miss Prism. Child, you know how anxious your guardian is that you should improve yourself in every way. He laid particular stress on your German, as he was leaving for town yesterday. Indeed, he always lays stress on your German when he is leaving for town.

Cecily. Dear Uncle Jack is so very serious! Sometimes he is so serious that I think he cannot be quite well.

Miss Prism (drawing herself up). Your guardian enjoys the best of health, and his gravity of demeanor is especially to be commended in one so comparatively young as he is. I know no one who has a higher sense of duty and responsibility.

Cecily. I suppose that is why he often looks a little bored when we three are together.

Miss Prism. Cecily! I am surprised at you. Mr. Worthing has many troubles in his life. Idle merriment and triviality would be out of place in his conversation. You must remember his constant anxiety about that unfortunate young man his brother.

Cecily. I wish Uncle Jack would allow that unfortunate young man, his brother, to come down here sometimes. We might have a good influence over him, Miss Prism. I am sure you certainly would. You know German, and geology, and things of that kind influence a man very much. (*Cecily begins to write in her diary.*)

Miss Prism (shaking her head). I do not think that even I could produce any effect on a character that according to his own brother's admission is irretrievably weak and vacillating. Indeed I am not sure that I would desire to reclaim him. I am not in favor of this modern mania for turning bad people into good people at a moment's notice. As a man sows so let him reap. You must put away your diary, Cecily. I really don't see why you should keep a diary at all.

Cecily. I keep a diary in order to enter the wonderful secrets of my life. If I didn't write them down, I should probably forget all about them.

Miss Prism. Memory, my dear Cecily, is the diary that we all carry about with us.

Cecily. Yes, but it usually chronicles the things that have never happened, and couldn't possibly have happened. I believe that Memory is responsible for nearly all the three-volume novels that Mudie° sends us.

Mudie   A lending library

Miss Prism. Do not speak slightingly of the three-volume novel, Cecily. I wrote one myself in earlier days.

Cecily. Did you really, Miss Prism? How wonderfully clever you are! I hope it did not end happily? I don't like novels that end happily. They depress me so much.

Miss Prism. The good ended happily, and the bad unhappily. That is what Fiction means.

Cecily. I suppose so. But it seems very unfair. And was your novel ever published?

Miss Prism. Alas! no. The manuscript unfortunately was abandoned. (*Cecily starts.*) I used the word in the sense of lost or mislaid. To your work, child, these speculations are profitless.

Cecily (*smiling*). But I see dear Dr. Chasuble coming up through the garden.

Miss Prism (*rising and advancing*). Dr. Chasuble! This is indeed a pleasure.

Enter Canon Chasuble.

Chasuble. And how are we this morning? Miss Prism, you are, I trust, well?

Cecily. Miss Prism has just been complaining of a slight headache. I think it would do her so much good to have a short stroll with you in the Park, Dr. Chasuble.

Miss Prism. Cecily, I have not mentioned anything about a headache.

Cecily. No, dear Miss Prism, I know that, but I felt instinctively that you had a headache. Indeed I was thinking about that, and not about my German lesson, when the Rector came in.

Chasuble. I hope, Cecily, you are not inattentive.

Cecily. Oh, I am afraid I am.

Chasuble. That is strange. Were I fortunate enough to be Miss Prism's pupil, I would hang upon her lips. (*Miss Prism glares.*) I spoke metaphorically. —My metaphor was drawn from bees. Ahem! Mr. Worthing, I suppose, has not returned from town yet?

Miss Prism. We do not expect him till Monday afternoon.

Chasuble. Ah yes, he usually likes to spend his Sunday in London. He is not one of those whose sole aim is enjoyment, as, by all accounts, that unfortunate young man his brother seems to be. But I must not disturb Egeria° and her pupil any longer.

Miss Prism. Egeria? My name is Laetitia, Doctor.

Egeria Mythical Roman female advisor of statesmen

Chasuble (bowing). A classical allusion merely, drawn from the
    Pagan authors. I shall see you both no doubt at Evensong?°
Miss Prism. I think, dear Doctor, I will have a stroll with you. I
    find I have a headache after all, and a walk might do it good.
Chasuble. With pleasure, Miss Prism, with pleasure. We might go
    as far as the schools and back.
Miss Prism. That would be delightful. Cecily, you will read your
    Political Economy in my absence. The chapter on the Fall
    of the Rupee you may omit. It is somewhat too sensational.
    Even these metallic problems have their melodramatic side.
    (Goes down the garden with Dr. Chasuble).
Cecily (picks up books and throws them back on table). Horrid Political
    Economy! Horrid Geography! Horrid, horrid German!

Enter Merriman with a card on a salver.

Merriman. Mr. Ernest Worthing has just driven over from the
    station. He has brought his luggage with him.
Cecily (takes the card and reads it). "Mr. Ernest Worthing, B.4, The
    Albany, W." Uncle Jack's brother! Did you tell him Mr.
    Worthing was in town?
Merriman. Yes, Miss. He seemed very much disappointed. I men-
    tioned that you and Miss Prism were in the garden. He said
    he was anxious to speak to you privately for a moment.
Cecily. Ask Mr. Ernest Worthing to come here. I suppose you
    had better talk to the housekeeper about a room for him.
Merriman. Yes, Miss. *(Merriman goes off.)*
Cecily. I have never met any really wicked person before. I feel
    rather frightened. I am so afraid he will look just like every
    one else.

Enter Algernon, very gay and debonair.

He does!
Algernon (raising his hat). You are my little cousin Cecily, I'm sure.
Cecily. You are under some strange mistake. I am not little. In
    fact, I believe I am more than usually tall for my age. *(Algernon
    is rather taken aback.)* But I am your cousin Cecily. You, I
    see from your card, are Uncle Jack's brother, my cousin
    Ernest, my wicked cousin Ernest.
Algernon. Oh! I am not really wicked at all, Cousin Cecily. You
    mustn't think that I am wicked.
Cecily. If you are not, then you have certainly been deceiving us
    all in a very inexcusable manner. I hope you have not been

Evensong Evening church service

leading a double life, pretending to be wicked and being really good all the time. That would be hypocrisy.

Algernon (*looks at her in amazement*). Oh! Of course I have been rather reckless.

Cecily. I am glad to hear it.

Algernon. In fact, now you mention the subject, I have been very bad in my own small way.

Cecily. I don't think you should be so proud of that, though I am sure it must have been very pleasant.

Algernon. It is much pleasanter being here with you.

Cecily. I can't understand how you are here at all. Uncle Jack won't be back till Monday afternoon.

Algernon. That is a great disappointment. I am obliged to go up by the first train on Monday morning. I have a business appointment that I am anxious . . . to miss!

Cecily. Couldn't you miss it anywhere but in London?

Algernon. No: the appointment is in London.

Cecily. Well, I know, of course, how important it is not to keep a business engagement, if one wants to retain any sense of the beauty of life, but still I think you had better wait till Uncle Jack arrives. I know he wants to speak to you about your emigrating.

Algernon. About my what?

Cecily. Your emigrating. He has gone up to buy your outfit.

Algernon. I certainly wouldn't let Jack buy my outfit. He has no taste in neckties at all.

Cecily. I don't think you will require neckties. Uncle Jack is sending you to Australia.

Algernon. Australia! I'd sooner die.

Cecily. Well, he said at dinner on Wednesday night, that you would have to choose between this world, the next world, and Australia.

Algernon. Oh, well! The accounts I have received of Australia and the next world are not particularly encouraging. This world is good enough for me, Cousin Cecily.

Cecily. Yes, but are you good enough for it?

Algernon. I'm afraid I'm not that. That is why I want you to reform me. You might make that your mission, if you don't mind, Cousin Cecily.

Cecily. I'm afraid I've no time, this afternoon.

Algernon. Well, would you mind my reforming myself this afternoon?

Cecily. It is rather Quixotic of you. But I think you should try.

Algernon. I will. I feel better already.

Cecily. You are looking a little worse.

Algernon. That is because I am hungry.

Cecily. How thoughtless of me. I should have remembered that when one is going to lead an entirely new life, one requires regular and wholesome meals. Won't you come in?

Algernon. Thank you. Might I have a buttonhole° first? I never have any appetite unless I have a buttonhole first.

Cecily. A Maréchal Niel?° (*Picks up scissors.*)

Algernon. No, I'd sooner have a pink rose.

Cecily. Why? (*Cuts a flower.*)

Algernon. Because you are like a pink rose, Cousin Cecily.

Cecily. I don't think it can be right for you to talk to me like that. Miss Prism never says such things to me.

Algernon. Then Miss Prism is a shortsighted old lady. (*Cecily puts the rose in his buttonhole.*) You are the prettiest girl I ever saw.

Cecily. Miss Prism says that all good looks are a snare.

Algernon. They are a snare that every sensible man would like to be caught in.

Cecily. Oh, I don't think I would care to catch a sensible man. I shouldn't know what to talk to him about.

They pass into the house. Miss Prism and Dr. Chasuble return.

Miss Prism. You are too much alone, dear Dr. Chasuble. You should get married. A misanthrope I can understand — a womanthrope, never!

Chasuble (*with a scholar's shudder*). Believe me, I do not deserve so neologistic a phrase. The precept as well as the practice of the Primitive Church was distinctly against matrimony.

Miss Prism (*sententiously*). That is obviously the reason why the Primitive Church has not lasted up to the present day. And you do not seem to realize, dear Doctor, that by persistently remaining single, a man converts himself into a permanent public temptation. Men should be more careful; this very celibacy leads weaker vessels astray.

Chasuble. But is a man not equally attractive when married?

Miss Prism. No married man is ever attractive except to his wife.

Chasuble. And often, I've been told, not even to her.

Miss Prism. That depends on the intellectual sympathies of the woman. Maturity can always be depended on. Ripeness can

buttonhole I.e., a flower for the buttonhole of a man's jacket   ***Maréchal Niel*** A variety of rose

be trusted. Young women are green. (*Dr. Chasuble starts.*) I spoke horticulturally. My metaphor was drawn from fruits. But where is Cecily?

Chasuble. Perhaps she followed us to the schools.

Enter Jack slowly from the back of the garden. He is dressed in the deepest mourning, with crepe hatband and black gloves.

Miss Prism. Mr. Worthing!

Chasuble. Mr. Worthing?

Miss Prism. This is indeed a surprise. We did not look for you till Monday afternoon.

Jack (*shakes Miss Prism's hand in a tragic manner*). I have returned sooner than I expected. Dr. Chasuble, I hope you are well?

Chasuble. Dear Mr. Worthing, I trust this garb of woe does not betoken some terrible calamity?

Jack. My brother.

Miss Prism. More shameful debts and extravagance?

Chasuble. Still leading his life of pleasure?

Jack (*shaking his head*). Dead!

Chasuble. Your brother Ernest dead?

Jack. Quite dead.

Miss Prism. What a lesson for him! I trust he will profit by it.

Chasuble. Mr. Worthing, I offer you my sincere condolence. You have at least the consolation of knowing that you were always the most generous and forgiving of brothers.

Jack. Poor Ernest! He had many faults, but it is a sad, sad blow.

Chasuble. Very sad indeed. Were you with him at the end?

Jack. No. He died abroad; in Paris, in fact. I had a telegram last night from the manager of the Grand Hotel.

Chasuble. Was the cause of death mentioned?

Jack. A severe chill, it seems.

Miss Prism. As a man sows, so shall he reap.°

Chasuble (*raising his hand*). Charity, dear Miss Prism, charity! None of us are perfect. I myself am peculiarly susceptible to draughts. Will the interment take place here?

Jack. No. He seems to have expressed a desire to be buried in Paris.

Chasuble. In Paris! (*Shakes his head.*) I fear that hardly points to any very serious state of mind at the last. You would no doubt wish me to make some slight allusion to this tragic domestic affliction next Sunday. (*Jack presses his hand con-*

reap Galatians vi.7

vulsively.) My sermon on the meaning of the manna in the wilderness can be adapted to almost any occasion, joyful, or, as in the present case, distressing. (*All sigh*.) I have preached it at harvest celebrations, christenings, confirmations, on days of humiliation and festal days. The last time I delivered it was in the Cathedral, as a charity sermon on behalf of the Society for the Prevention of Discontent among the Upper Orders. The Bishop, who was present, was much struck by some of the analogies I drew.

Jack. Ah! that reminds me, you mentioned christenings I think, Dr. Chasuble? I suppose you know how to christen all right? (*Dr. Chasuble looks astounded*.) I mean, of course, you are continually christening, aren't you?

Miss Prism. It is, I regret to say, one of the Rector's most constant duties in this parish. I have often spoken to the poorer classes on the subject. But they don't seem to know what thrift is.

Chasuble. But is there any particular infant in whom you are interested, Mr. Worthing? Your brother was, I believe, unmarried, was he not?

Jack. Oh, yes.

Miss Prism (*bitterly*). People who live entirely for pleasure usually are.

Jack. But it is not for any child, dear Doctor. I am very fond of children. No! the fact is, I would like to be christened myself, this afternoon, if you have nothing better to do.

Chasuble. But surely, Mr. Worthing, you have been christened already?

Jack. I don't remember anything about it.

Chasuble. But have you any grave doubts on the subject?

Jack. I certainly intend to have. Of course I don't know if the thing would bother you in any way, or if you think I am a little too old now.

Chasuble. Not at all. The sprinkling, and, indeed, the immersion of adults is a perfectly canonical practice.

Jack. Immersion!

Chasuble. You need have no apprehensions. Sprinkling is all that is necessary, or indeed I think advisable. Our weather is so changeable. At what hour would you wish the ceremony performed?

Jack. Oh, I might trot round about five if that would suit you.

Chasuble. Perfectly, perfectly! In fact I have two similar ceremonies to perform at that time. A case of twins that occurred recently in one of the outlying cottages on your own estate. Poor Jenkins the carter, a most hard-working man.

Jack. Oh! I don't see much fun in being christened along with
   other babies. It would be childish. Would half-past five do?
Chasuble. Admirably! Admirably! (*Takes out watch.*) And now, dear
   Mr. Worthing, I will not intrude any longer into a house
   of sorrow. I would merely beg you not to be too much
   bowed down by grief. What seems to us bitter trials are
   often blessings in disguise.
Miss Prism. This seems to me a blessing of an extremely obvious
   kind.

   Enter Cecily from the house.

Cecily. Uncle Jack! Oh, I am pleased to see you back. But what
   horrid clothes you have got on. Do go and change them.
Miss Prism. Cecily!
Chasuble. My child! My child! (*Cecily goes toward Jack; he kisses her
   brow in a melancholy manner.*)
Cecily. What is the matter, Uncle Jack? Do look happy! You look
   as if you had toothache, and I have got such a surprise for
   you. Who do you think is in the dining room? Your brother!
Jack. Who?
Cecily. Your brother Ernest. He arrived about half an hour ago.
Jack. What nonsense! I haven't got a brother.
Cecily. Oh, don't say that. However badly he may have behaved
   to you in the past he is still your brother. You couldn't be
   so heartless as to disown him. I'll tell him to come out. And
   you will shake hands with him, won't you, Uncle Jack?
   (*Runs back into the house.*)
Chasuble. These are very joyful tidings.
Miss Prism. After we had all been resigned to his loss, his sudden
   return seems to me peculiarly distressing.
Jack. My brother is in the dining room? I don't know what it all
   means. I think it is perfectly absurd.

   *Enter Algernon and Cecily hand in hand. They come slowly up
   to Jack.*

Jack. Good heavens! (*Motions Algernon away.*)
Algernon. Brother John, I have come down from town to tell you
   that I am very sorry for all the trouble I have given you,
   and that I intend to lead a better life in the future. (*Jack
   glares at him and does not take his hand.*)
Cecily. Uncle Jack, you are not going to refuse your own brother's
   hand?
Jack. Nothing will induce me to take his hand. I think his coming
   down here disgraceful. He knows perfectly well why.

Cecily. Uncle Jack, do be nice. There is some good in everyone. Ernest has just been telling me about his poor invalid friend Mr. Bunbury whom he goes to visit so often. And surely there must be much good in one who is kind to an invalid, and leaves the pleasures of London to sit by a bed of pain.

Jack. Oh! he has been talking about Bunbury, has he?

Cecily. Yes, he has told me all about poor Mr. Bunbury, and his terrible state of health.

Jack. Bunbury! Well, I won't have him talk to you about Bunbury or about anything else. It is enough to drive one perfectly frantic.

Algernon. Of course I admit that the faults were all on my side. But I must say that I think that Brother John's coldness to me is peculiarly painful. I expected a more enthusiastic welcome, especially considering it is the first time I have come here.

Cecily. Uncle Jack, if you don't shake hands with Ernest I will never forgive you.

Jack. Never forgive me?

Cecily. Never, never, never!

Jack. Well, this is the last time I shall ever do it. (*Shakes hands with Algernon and glares.*)

Chasuble. It's pleasant, is it not, to see so perfect a reconciliation? I think we might leave the two brothers together.

Miss Prism. Cecily, you will come with us.

Cecily. Certainly, Miss Prism. My little task of reconciliation is over.

Chasuble. You have done a beautiful action today, dear child.

Miss Prism. We must not be premature in our judgments.

Cecily. I feel very happy. (*They all go off except Jack and Algernon.*)

Jack. You young scoundrel, Algy, you must get out of this place as soon as possible. I don't allow any Bunburying here.

Enter Merriman.

Merriman. I have put Mr. Ernest's things in the room next to yours, sir. I suppose that is all right?

Jack. What?

Merriman. Mr. Ernest's luggage, sir. I have unpacked it and put it in the room next to your own.

Jack. His luggage?

Merriman. Yes, sir. Three portmanteaus,° a dressing case, two hatboxes, and a large luncheon basket.

---

portmanteaus Large suitcases

Algernon. I am afraid I can't stay more than a week this time.

Jack. Merriman, order the dogcart° at once. Mr. Ernest has been suddenly called back to town.

Merriman. Yes, sir. (*Goes back into the house.*)

Algernon. What a fearful liar you are, Jack. I have not been called back to town at all.

Jack. Yes, you have.

Algernon. I haven't heard anyone call me.

Jack. Your duty as a gentleman calls you back.

Algernon. My duty as a gentleman has never interfered with my pleasures in the smallest degree.

Jack. I can quite understand that.

Algernon. Well, Cecily is a darling.

Jack. You are not to talk of Miss Cardew like that. I don't like it.

Algernon. Well, I don't like your clothes. You look perfectly ridiculous in them. Why on earth don't you go up and change? It is perfectly childish to be in deep mourning for a man who is actually staying for a whole week with you in your house as a guest. I call it grotesque.

Jack. You are certainly not staying with me for a whole week as a guest or anything else. You have got to leave . . . by the four-five train.

Algernon. I certainly won't leave you so long as you are in mourning. It would be most unfriendly. If I were in mourning you would stay with me, I suppose. I should think it very unkind if you didn't.

Jack. Well, will you go if I change my clothes?

Algernon. Yes, if you are not loo long. I never saw anybody take so long to dress, and with such little result.

Jack. Well, at any rate, that is better than being always overdressed as you are.

Algernon. If I am occasionally a little overdressed, I make up for it by being always immensely over-educated.

Jack. Your vanity is ridiculous, your conduct an outrage, and your presence in my garden utterly absurd. However, you have got to catch the four-five, and I hope you will have a pleasant journey back to town. This Bunburying, as you call it, has not been a great success for you. (*Goes into the house.*)

Algernon. I think it has been a great success. I'm in love with Cecily, and that is everything.

dogcart A vehicle drawn by a horse and accommodating two persons

Enter Cecily at the back of the garden. She picks up the can and begins to water the flowers.

But I must see her before I go, and make arrangements for another Bunbury. Ah, there she is.

Cecily. Oh, I merely came back to water the roses. I thought you were with Uncle Jack.

Algernon. He's gone to order the dogcart for me.

Cecily. Oh, is he going to take you for a nice drive?

Algernon. He's going to send me away.

Cecily. Then have we got to part?

Algernon. I am afraid so. It's a very painful parting.

Cecily. It is always painful to part from people whom one has known for a very brief space of time. The absence of old friends one can endure with equanimity. But even a momentary separation from anyone to whom one has just been introduced is almost unbearable.

Algernon. Thank you.

Enter Merriman.

Merriman. The dogcart is at the door, sir.

(*Algernon looks appealing at Cecily.*)

Cecily. It can wait, Merriman . . . for . . . five minutes.

Merriman. Yes, miss.

Exit Merriman.

Algernon. I hope, Cecily, I shall not offend you if I state quite frankly and openly that you seem to me to be in every way the visible personification of absolute perfection.

Cecily. I think your frankness does you great credit, Ernest. If you will allow me, I will copy your remarks into my diary. (*Goes over to table and begins writing in diary.*)

Algernon. Do you really keep a diary? I'd give anything to look at it. May I?

Cecily. Oh no. (*Puts her hand over it.*) You see, it is simply a very young girl's record of her own thoughts and impressions, and consequently meant for publication. When it appears in volume form I hope you will order a copy. But pray, Ernest, don't stop. I delight in taking down from dictation. I have reached "absolute perfection." You can go on. I am quite ready for more.

Algernon (*somewhat taken aback*). Ahem! Ahem!

Cecily. Oh, don't cough, Ernest. When one is dictating one should

speak fluently and not cough. Besides, I don't know how
to spell a cough. (*Writes as Algernon speaks.*)

Algernon (*speaking very rapidly*). Cecily, ever since I first looked
upon your wonderful and incomparable beauty, I have dared
to love you wildly, passionately, devotedly, hopelessly.

Cecily. I don't think that you should tell me that you love me
wildly, passionately, devotedly, hopelessly. Hopelessly doesn't
seem to make much sense, does it?

Algernon. Cecily.

    Enter Merriman.

Merriman. The dogcart is waiting, sir.

Algernon. Tell it to come round next week, at the same hour.

Merriman (*looks at Cecily, who makes no sign*). Yes, sir.

                                 Merriman retires.

Cecily. Uncle Jack would be very much annoyed if he knew you
were staying on till next week, at the same hour.

Algernon. Oh, I don't care about Jack. I don't care for anybody
in the whole world but you. I love you, Cecily. You will
marry me, won't you?

Cecily. You silly boy! Of course. Why, we have been engaged for
the last three months.

Algernon. For the last three months?

Cecily. Yes, it will be exactly three months on Thursday.

Algernon. But how did we become engaged?

Cecily. Well, ever since dear Uncle Jack first confessed to us that
he had a younger brother who was very wicked and bad,
you of course have formed the chief topic of conversation
between myself and Miss Prism. And of course a man who
is much talked about is always very attractive. One feels
there must be something in him, after all. I daresay it was
foolish of me, but I fell in love with you, Ernest.

Algernon. Darling. And when was the engagement actually settled?

Cecily. On the 14th of February last. Worn out by your entire
ignorance of my existence, I determined to end the matter
one way or the other, and after a long struggle with myself
I accepted you under this dear old tree here. The next day
I bought this little ring in your name, and this is the little
bangle with the true lovers' knot I promised you always to
wear.

Algernon. Did I give you this? It's very pretty, isn't it?

Cecily. Yes, you've wonderfully good taste, Ernest. It's the excuse
I've always given for your leading such a bad life. And this

is the box in which I keep all your dear letters. (*Kneels at table, opens box, and produces letters tied up with blue ribbon.*)

Algernon. My letters! But, my own sweet Cecily, I have never written you any letters.

Cecily. You need hardly remind me of that, Ernest. I remember only too well that I was forced to write your letters for you. I wrote always three times a week, and sometimes oftener.

Algernon. Oh, do let me read them, Cecily?

Cecily. Oh, I couldn't possibly. They would make you far too conceited. (*Replaces box.*) The three you wrote me after I had broken off the engagement are so beautiful, and so badly spelled, that even now I can hardly read them without crying a little.

Algernon. But was our engagement ever broken off?

Cecily. Of course it was. On the 22nd of last March. You can see the entry if you like. (*Shows diary.*) "Today I broke off my engagement with Ernest. I feel it is better to do so. The weather still continues charming."

Algernon. But why on earth did you break it off? What had I done? I had done nothing at all. Cecily, I am very much hurt indeed to hear you broke it off. Particularly when the weather was so charming.

Cecily. It would hardly have been a really serious engagement if it hadn't been broken off at least once. But I forgave you before the week was out.

Algernon (*crossing to her, and kneeling*). What a perfect angel you are, Cecily.

Cecily. You dear romantic boy. (*He kisses her, she puts her fingers through his hair.*) I hope your hair curls naturally, does it?

Algernon. Yes, darling, with a little help from others.

Cecily. I am so glad.

Algernon. You'll never break off our engagement again, Cecily?

Cecily. I don't think I could break it off now that I have actually met you. Besides, of course, there is the question of your name.

Algernon. Yes, of course. (*Nervously.*)

Cecily. You must not laugh at me, darling, but it had always been a girlish dream of mine to love someone whose name was Ernest. (*Algernon rises, Cecily also.*) There is something in that name that seems to inspire absolute confidence. I pity any poor married woman whose husband is not called Ernest.

Algernon. But, my dear child, do you mean to say you could not love me if I had some other name?

Cecily. But what name?

Algernon. Oh, any name you like — Algernon — for instance . . .

Cecily. But I don't like the name of Algernon.

Algernon. Well, my own dear, sweet, loving little darling, I really can't see why you should object to the name of Algernon. It is not at all a bad name. In fact, it is rather an aristocratic name. Half of the chaps who get into the Bankruptcy Court are called Algernon. But seriously, Cecily . . . (*moving to her*) if my name was Algy, couldn't you love me?

Cecily (*rising*). I might respect you, Ernest, I might admire your character, but I fear that I should not be able to give you my undivided attention.

Algernon. Ahem! Cecily! (*Picking up hat.*) Your Rector here is, I suppose, thoroughly experienced in the practice of all the rites and ceremonials of the Church?

Cecily. Oh, yes. Dr. Chasuble is a most learned man. He has never written a single book, so you can imagine how much he knows.

Algernon. I must see him at once on a most important christening — I mean on most important business.

Cecily. Oh!

Algernon. I shan't be away more than half an hour.

Cecily. Considering that we have been engaged since February the 14th, and that I only met you today for the first time, I think it is rather hard that you should leave me for so long a period as half an hour. Couldn't you make it twenty minutes?

Algernon. I'll be back in no time. (*Kisses her and rushes down the garden.*)

Cecily. What an impetuous boy he is! I like his hair so much. I must enter his proposal in my diary.

Enter Merriman.

Merriman. A Miss Fairfax just called to see Mr. Worthing. On very important business, Miss Fairfax states.

Cecily. Isn't Mr. Worthing in his library?

Merriman. Mr. Worthing went over in the direction of the Rectory some time ago.

Cecily. Pray ask the lady to come out here; Mr. Worthing is sure to be back soon. And you can bring tea.

Merriman. Yes, Miss. (*Goes out.*)

Cecily. Miss Fairfax! I suppose one of the many good elderly women who are associated with Uncle Jack in some of his philanthropic work in London. I don't quite like women who are interested in philanthropic work. I think it is so forward of them.

Enter Merriman.

Merriman. Miss Fairfax.

Enter Gwendolen. Exit Merriman.

Cecily (advancing to meet her). Pray let me introduce myself to you. My name is Cecily Cardew.

Gwendolen. Cecily Cardew? (*Moving to her and shaking hands.*) What a very sweet name! Something tells me that we are going to be great friends. I like you already more than I can say. My first impressions of people are never wrong.

Cecily. How nice of you to like me so much after we have known each other such a comparatively short time. Pray sit down.

Gwendolen (still standing up). I may call you Cecily, may I not?

Cecily. With pleasure!

Gwendolen. And you will always call me Gwendolen, won't you?

Cecily. If you wish.

Gwendolen. Then that is all quite settled, is it not?

Cecily. I hope so. (*A pause. They both sit down together.*)

Gwendolen. Perhaps this might be a favorable opportunity for my mentioning who I am. My father is Lord Bracknell. You have never heard of papa, I suppose?

Cecily. I don't think so.

Gwendolen. Outside the family circle, papa, I am glad to say, is entirely unknown. I think that is quite as it should be. The home seems to me to be the proper sphere for the man. And certainly once a man begins to neglect his domestic duties he becomes painfully effeminate, does he not? And I don't like that. It makes men so very attractive. Cecily, mamma, whose views on education are remarkably strict, has brought me up to be extremely shortsighted; it is part of her system; so do you mind my looking at you through my glasses?

Cecily. Oh! not at all, Gwendolen. I am very fond of being looked at.

Gwendolen (after examining Cecily carefully through a lorgnette). You are here on a short visit, I suppose.

Cecily. Oh no! I live here.

Gwendolen (severely). Really? Your mother, no doubt, or some female relative of advanced years, resides here also?

Cecily. Oh no! I have no mother, nor, in fact, any relations.

Gwendolen. Indeed?

Cecily. My dear guardian, with the assistance of Miss Prism, has the arduous task of looking after me.

Gwendolen. Your guardian?

Cecily. Yes, I am Mr. Worthing's ward.

Gwendolen. Oh! It is strange he never mentioned to me that he had a ward. How secretive of him! He grows more interesting hourly. I am not sure, however, that the news inspires me with feelings of unmixed delight. (*Rising and going to her.*) I am very fond of you, Cecily; I have liked you ever since I met you! But I am bound to state that now that I know that you are Mr. Worthing's ward, I cannot help expressing a wish you were — well, just a little older than you seem to be — and not quite so very alluring in appearance. In fact, if I may speak candidly —

Cecily. Pray do! I think that whenever one has anything unpleasant to say, one should always be quite candid!

Gwendolen. Well, to speak with perfect candor, Cecily, I wish that you were fully forty-two, and more than usually plain for your age. Ernest has a strong upright nature. He is the very soul of truth and honor. Disloyalty would be as impossible to him as deception. But even men of the noblest possible moral character are extremely susceptible to the influence of the physical charms of others. Modern, no less than Ancient History, supplies us with many most painful examples of what I refer to. If it were not so, indeed, History would be quite unreadable.

Cecily. I beg your pardon, Gwendolen, did you say Ernest?

Gwendolen. Yes.

Cecily. Oh, but it is not Mr. Ernest Worthing who is my guardian. It is his brother — his elder brother.

Gwendolen (*sitting down again*). Ernest never mentioned to me that he had a brother.

Cecily. I am sorry to say they have not been on good terms for a long time.

Gwendolen. Ah! that accounts for it. And now that I think of it I have never heard any man mention his brother. The subject seems distasteful to most men. Cecily, you have lifted a load from my mind. I was growing almost anxious. It would have been terrible if any cloud had come across a friendship like ours, would it not? Of course you are quite, quite sure that it is not Mr. Ernest Worthing who is your guardian?

Cecily. Quite sure. (*A pause.*) In fact, I am going to be his.

Gwendolen (*inquiringly*). I beg your pardon?

Cecily (*rather shy and confidingly*). Dearest Gwendolen, there is no reason why I should make a secret of it to you. Our little country newspaper is sure to chronicle the fact next week. Mr. Ernest Worthing and I are engaged to be married.

Gwendolen (quite politely, rising). My darling Cecily, I think there must be some slight error. Mr. Ernest Worthing is engaged to me. The announcement will appear in the *Morning Post* on Saturday at the latest.

Cecily (very politely, rising). I am afraid you must be under some misconception. Ernest proposed to me exactly ten minutes ago. (*Shows diary.*)

Gwendolen (examines diary through her lorgnette carefully). It is very curious, for he asked me to be his wife yesterday afternoon at 5:30. If you would care to verify the incident, pray do so. (*Produces diary of her own.*) I never travel without my diary. One should always have something sensational to read in the train. I am so sorry, dear Cecily, if it is any disappointment to you, but I am afraid I have the prior claim.

Cecily. It would distress me more than I can tell you, dear Gwendolen, if it caused you any mental or physical anguish, but I feel bound to point out that since Ernest proposed to you he clearly has changed his mind.

Gwendolen (meditatively). If the poor fellow has been entrapped into any foolish promise I shall consider it my duty to rescue him at once, and with a firm hand.

Cecily (thoughtfully and sadly). Whatever unfortunate entanglement my dear boy may have got into, I will never reproach him with it after we are married.

Gwendolen. Do you allude to me, Miss Cardew, as an entanglement? You are presumptuous. On an occasion of this kind it becomes more than a moral duty to speak one's mind. It becomes a pleasure.

Cecily. Do you suggest, Miss Fairfax, that I entrapped Ernest into an engagement? How dare you? This is no time for wearing the shallow mask of manners. When I see a spade I call it a spade.

Gwendolen (satirically). I am glad to say that I have never seen a spade. It is obvious that our social spheres have been widely different.

Enter Merriman, followed by the footman. He carries a salver, tablecloth, and plate stand. Cecily is about to retort. The presence of the servants exercises a restraining influence, under which both girls chafe.

Merriman. Shall I lay tea here as usual, Miss?

Cecily (*sternly, in a calm voice*). Yes, as usual. (*Merriman begins to clear table and lay cloth. A long pause. Cecily and Gwendolen glare at each other.*)

Gwendolen. Are there many interesting walks in the vicinity, Miss Cardew?

Cecily. Oh! yes! a great many. From the top of one of the hills quite close one can see five counties.

Gwendolen. Five counties! I don't think I should like that; I hate crowds.

Cecily (*sweetly*). I suppose that is why you live in town? (*Gwendolen bites her lip, and beats her foot nervously with her parasol.*)

Gwendolen (*looking round*). Quite a well-kept garden this is, Miss Cardew.

Cecily. So glad you like it, Miss Fairfax.

Gwendolen. I had no idea there were any flowers in the country.

Cecily. Oh, flowers are as common here, Miss Fairfax, as people are in London.

Gwendolen. Personally I cannot understand how anybody manages to exist in the country, if anybody who is anybody does. The country always bores me to death.

Cecily. Ah! This is what the newspapers call agricultural depression, is it not? I believe the aristocracy are suffering very much from it just at present. It is almost an epidemic amongst them, I have been told. May I offer you some tea, Miss Fairfax?

Gwendolen (*with elaborate politeness*). Thank you. (*Aside.*) Detestable girl! But I require tea!

Cecily (*sweetly*). Sugar?

Gwendolen (*superciliously*). No, thank you. Sugar is not fashionable any more. (*Cecily looks angrily at her, takes up the tongs and puts four lumps of sugar into the cup.*)

Cecily (*severely*). Cake or bread and butter?

Gwendolen (*in a bored manner*). Bread and butter, please. Cake is rarely seen at the best houses nowadays.

Cecily (*cuts a very large slice of cake and puts it on the tray*). Hand that to Miss Fairfax.

Merriman does so, and goes out with footman. Gwendolen drinks the tea and makes a grimace. Puts down cup at once, reaches out her hand to the bread and butter, looks at it, and finds it is cake. Rises in indignation.

Gwendolen. You have filled my tea with lumps of sugar, and though I asked most distinctly for bread and butter, you have given me cake. I am known for the gentleness of my disposition, and the extraordinary sweetness of my nature, but I warn you, Miss Cardew, you may go too far.

Cecily (rising). To save my poor, innocent, trusting boy from the machinations of any other girl there are no lengths to which I would not go.

Gwendolen. From the moment I saw you I distrusted you. I felt that you were false and deceitful. I am never deceived in such matters. My first impressions of people are invariably right.

Cecily. It seems to me, Miss Fairfax, that I am trespassing on your valuable time. No doubt you have many other calls of a similar character to make in the neighborhood.

Enter Jack.

Gwendolen (catches sight of him). Ernest! My own Ernest!

Jack. Gwendolen! Darling! (*Offers to kiss her.*)

Gwendolen (drawing back). A moment! May I ask if you are engaged to be married to this young lady? (*Points to Cecily.*)

Jack (laughing). To dear little Cecily! Of course not! What could have put such an idea into your pretty little head?

Gwendolen. Thank you. You may! (*Offers her cheek.*)

Cecily (very sweetly). I knew there must be some misunderstanding, Miss Fairfax. The gentleman whose arm is at present round your waist is my dear guardian, Mr. John Worthing.

Gwendolen. I beg your pardon?

Cecily. This is Uncle Jack.

Gwendolen (receding). Jack! Oh!

Enter Algernon.

Cecily. Here is Ernest.

Algernon (goes straight over to Cecily without noticing anyone else). My own love! (*Offers to kiss her.*)

Cecily (drawing back). A moment, Ernest! May I ask you — are you engaged to be married to this young lady?

Algernon (looking round). To what young lady? Good heavens! Gwendolen!

Cecily. Yes: to good heavens, Gwendolen, I mean to Gwendolen.

Algernon (laughing). Of course not. What could have put such an idea into your pretty little head?

Cecily. Thank you. (*Presenting her cheek to be kissed.*) You may. (*Algernon kisses her.*)

Gwendolen. I felt there was some slight error, Miss Cardew. The gentleman who is now embracing you is my cousin, Mr. Algernon Moncrieff.

Cecily (breaking away from Algernon). Algernon Moncrieff! Oh! (*The two girls move towards each other and put their arms round each other's waists as if for protection.*)

Cecily. Are you called Algernon?

Algernon. I cannot deny it.

Cecily. Oh!

Gwendolen. Is your name really John?

Jack (standing rather proudly). I could deny it if I liked. I could deny anything if I liked. But my name certainly is John. It has been John for years.

Cecily (to Gwendolen). A gross deception has been practiced on both of us.

Gwendolen. My poor wounded Cecily!

Cecily. My sweet wronged Gwendolen!

Gwendolen (slowly and seriously). You will call me sister, will you not? (*They embrace. Jack and Algernon groan and walk up and down.*)

Cecily (rather brightly). There is just one question I would like to be allowed to ask my guardian.

Gwendolen. An admirable idea! Mr. Worthing, there is just one question I would like to be permitted to put to you. Where is your brother Ernest? We are both engaged to be married to your brother Ernest, so it is a matter of some importance to us to know where your brother Ernest is at present.

Jack (slowly and hesitatingly). Gwendolen — Cecily — it is very painful for me to be forced to speak the truth. It is the first time in my life that I have ever been reduced to such a painful position, and I am really quite inexperienced in doing anything of the kind. However, I will tell you quite frankly that I have no brother Ernest. I have no brother at all. I never had a brother in my life, and I certainly have not the smallest intention of ever having one in the future.

Cecily (surprised). No brother at all?

Jack (cheerily). None!

Gwendolen (severely). Had you never a brother of any kind?

Jack (pleasantly). Never. Not even of any kind.

Gwendolen. I am afraid it is quite clear, Cecily, that neither of us is engaged to be married to anyone.

Cecily. It is not a very pleasant position for a young girl suddenly to find herself in. Is it?

Gwendolen. Let us go into the house. They will hardly venture to come after us there.

Cecily. No, men are so cowardly, aren't they?

> *They retire into the house with scornful looks.*

Jack. This ghastly state of things is what you call Bunburying, I suppose?

Algernon. Yes, and a perfectly wonderful Bunbury it is. The most wonderful Bunbury I have ever had in my life.

Jack. Well, you've no right whatsoever to Bunbury here.

Algernon. That is absurd. One has a right to Bunbury anywhere one chooses. Every serious Bunburyist knows that.

Jack. Serious Bunburyist? Good heavens!

Algernon. Well, one must be serious about something, if one wants to have any amusement in life. I happen to be serious about Bunburying. What on earth you are serious about I haven't got the remotest idea. About everything, I should fancy. You have such an absolutely trivial nature.

Jack. Well, the only small satisfaction I have in the whole of this wretched business is that your friend Bunbury is quite exploded. You won't be able to run down to the country quite so often as you used to do, dear Algy. And a very good thing too.

Algernon. Your brother is a little off color, isn't he, dear Jack? You won't be able to disappear to London quite so frequently as your wicked custom was. And not a bad thing either.

Jack. As for your conduct towards Miss Cardew, I must say that your taking in a sweet, simple, innocent girl like that is quite inexcusable. To say nothing of the fact that she is my ward.

Algernon. I can see no possible defense at all for your deceiving a brilliant, clever, thoroughly experienced young lady like Miss Fairfax. To say nothing of the fact that she is my cousin.

Jack. I wanted to be engaged to Gwendolen, that is all. I love her.

Algernon. Well, I simply wanted to be engaged to Cecily. I adore her.

Jack. There is certainly no chance of your marrying Miss Cardew.

Algernon. I don't think there is much likelihood, Jack, of you and Miss Fairfax being united.

Jack. Well, that is no business of yours.

Algernon. If it was my business, I wouldn't talk about it. (*Begins to eat muffins.*) It is very vulgar to talk about one's business. Only people like stockbrokers do that, and then merely at dinner parties.

Jack. How you can sit there calmly eating muffins when we are in this horrible trouble, I can't make out. You seem to me to be perfectly heartless.

Algernon. Well, I can't eat muffins in an agitated manner. The butter would probably get on my cuffs. One should always eat muffins quite calmly. It is the only way to eat them.

Jack. I say it's perfectly heartless your eating muffins at all, under the circumstances.

Algernon. When I am in trouble, eating is the only thing that consoles me. Indeed, when I am in really great trouble, as any one who knows me intimately will tell you, I refuse everything except food and drink. At the present moment I am eating muffins because I am unhappy. Besides, I am particularly fond of muffins. (*Rising*).

Jack (*rising*). Well, there is no reason why you should eat them all in that greedy way. (*Takes muffins from Algernon*).

Algernon (*offering teacake*). I wish you would have teacake instead. I don't like teacake.

Jack. Good heavens! I suppose a man may eat his own muffins in his own garden.

Algernon. But you have just said it is perfectly heartless to eat muffins.

Jack. I said it was perfectly heartless of you, under the circumstances. That is a very different thing.

Algernon. That may be. But the muffins are the same. (*He seizes the muffin dish from Jack.*)

Jack. Algy, I wish to goodness you would go.

Algernon. You can't possibly ask me to go without having some dinner. It's absurd. I never go without my dinner. No one ever does, except vegetarians and people like that. Besides I have just made arrangements with Dr. Chasuble to be christened at a quarter to six under the name of Ernest.

Jack. My dear fellow, the sooner you give up that nonsense the better. I made arrangements this morning with Dr. Chasuble to be christened myself at 5:30, and I naturally will take the name of Ernest. Gwendolen would wish it. We can't both be christened Ernest. It's absurd. Besides, I have a perfect right to be christened if I like. There is no evidence at all that I have ever been christened by anybody. I should think it extremely probably I never was, and so does Dr. Chasuble. It is entirely different in your case. You have been christened already.

Algernon. Yes, but I have not been christened for years.

Jack. Yes, but you have been christened. That is the important thing.

Algernon. Quite so. So I know my constitution can stand it. If you are not quite sure about your ever having been christened,

I must say I think it rather dangerous your venturing on it now. It might make you very unwell. You can hardly have forgotten that someone very closely connected with you was very nearly carried off this week in Paris by a severe chill.

Jack. Yes, but you said yourself that a severe chill was not hereditary.

Algernon. It usen't to be, I know — but I daresay it is now. Science is always making wonderful improvements in things.

Jack (picking up the muffin dish). Oh, that is nonsense; you are always talking nonsense.

Algernon. Jack, you are at the muffins again! I wish you wouldn't. There are only two left. (*Takes them.*) I told you I was particularly fond of muffins.

Jack. But I hate teacake.

Algernon. Why on earth then do you allow teacake to be served up for your guests? What ideas you have of hospitality!

Jack. Algernon! I have already told you to go. I don't want you here. Why don't you go!

Algernon. I haven't quite finished my tea yet! and there is still one muffin left. (*Jack groans, and sinks into a chair. Algernon still continues eating.*)

ACT III

Morning room at the Manor House. Gwendolen and Cecily are at the window, looking out into the garden.

Gwendolen. The fact that they did not follow us at once into the house, as any one else would have done, seems to me to show that they have some sense of shame left.

Cecily. They have been eating muffins. That looks like repentance.

Gwendolen (after a pause). They don't seem to notice us at all. Couldn't you cough?

Cecily. But I haven't got a cough.

Gwendolen. They're looking at us. What effrontery!

Cecily. They're approaching. That's very forward of them.

Gwendolen. Let us preserve a dignified silence.

Cecily. Certainly. It's the only thing to do now.

Enter Jack followed by Algernon. They whistle some dreadful popular air from a British opera.

Gwendolen. This dignified silence seems to produce an unpleasant effect.

Cecily. A most distasteful one.

Gwendolen. But we will not be the first to speak.

Cecily. Certainly not.

Gwendolen. Mr. Worthing, I have something very particular to ask. Much depends on your reply.

Cecily. Gwendolen, your common sense is invaluable. Mr. Moncrieff, kindly answer me the following question. Why did you pretend to be my guardian's brother?

Algernon. In order that I might have an opportunity of meeting you.

Cecily (*to Gwendolen*). That certainly seems a satisfactory explanation, does it not?

Gwendolen. Yes, dear, if you can believe him.

Cecily. I don't. But that does not affect the wonderful beauty of his answer.

Gwendolen. True. In matters of grave importance, style, not sincerity, is the vital thing. Mr. Worthing, what explanation can you offer to me for pretending to have a brother? Was it in order that you might have an opportunity of coming up to town to see me as often as possible?

Jack. Can you doubt it, Miss Fairfax?

Gwendolen. I have the gravest doubts upon the subject. But I intend to crush them. This is not the moment for German skepticism. (*Moving to Cecily.*) Their explanations appear to be quite satisfactory, especially Mr. Worthing's. That seems to me to have the stamp of truth upon it.

Cecily. I am more than content with what Mr. Moncrieff said. His voice alone inspires one with absolute credulity.

Gwendolen. Then you think we should forgive them?

Cecily. Yes. I mean no.

Gwendolen. True! I had forgotten. There are principles at stake that one cannot surrender. Which of us should tell them? The task is not a pleasant one.

Cecily. Could we not both speak at the same time?

Gwendolen. An excellent idea! I nearly always speak at the same time as other people. Will you take the time from me?

Cecily. Certainly. (*Gwendolen beats time with uplifted finger.*)

Gwendolen and Cecily (*speaking together*). Your Christian names are still an insuperable barrier. That is all!

Jack and Algernon (*speaking together*). Our Christian names! Is that all? But we are going to be christened this afternoon.

Gwendolen (*to Jack*). For my sake you are prepared to do this terrible thing?

Jack. I am.

Cecily (to Algernon). To please me you are ready to face this fearful ordeal?

Algernon. I am!

Gwendolen. How absurd to talk of the equality of the sexes! Where questions of self-sacrifice are concerned, men are infinitely beyond us.

Jack. We are. (*Clasps hands with Algernon.*)

Cecily. They have moments of physical courage of which we women know absolutely nothing.

Gwendolen (to Jack). Darling!

Algernon (to Cecily). Darling! (*They fall into each other's arms.*)

Enter Merriman. When he enters he coughs loudly, seeing the situation.

Merriman. Ahem! Ahem! Lady Bracknell.

Jack. Good heavens!

Enter Lady Bracknell. The couples separate in alarm.

Exit Merriman.

Lady Bracknell. Gwendolen! What does this mean?

Gwendolen. Merely that I am engaged to be married to Mr. Worthing, mamma.

Lady Bracknell. Come here. Sit down. Sit down immediately. Hesitation of any kind is a sign of mental decay in the young, of physical weakness in the old. (*Turns to Jack.*) Apprised, sir, of my daughter's sudden flight by her trusty maid, whose confidence I purchased by means of a small coin, I followed her at once by a luggage train. Her unhappy father is, I am glad to say, under the impression that she is attending a more than usually lengthy lecture by the University Extension Scheme on the Influence of a permanent income on Thought. I do not propose to undeceive him. Indeed I have never undeceived him on any question. I would consider it wrong. But of course, you will clearly understand that all communication between yourself and my daughter must cease immediately from this moment. On this point, as indeed on all points, I am firm.

Jack. I am engaged to be married to Gwendolen, Lady Bracknell!

Lady Bracknell. You are nothing of the kind, sir. And now as regards Algernon! . . . Algernon!

Algernon. Yes, Aunt Augusta.

Lady Bracknell. May I ask if it is in this house that your invalid friend Mr. Bunbury resides?

Algernon (stammering). Oh! No! Bunbury doesn't live here. Bunbury is somewhere else at present. In fact, Bunbury is dead.

Lady Bracknell. Dead! When did Mr. Bunbury die? His death must have been extremely sudden.

Algernon (airily). Oh! I killed Bunbury this afternoon. I mean poor Bunbury died this afternoon.

Lady Bracknell. What did he die of?

Algernon. Bunbury? Oh, he was quite exploded.

Lady Bracknell. Exploded! Was he the victim of a revolutionary outrage? I was not aware that Mr. Bunbury was interested in social legislation. If so, he is well punished for his morbidity.

Algernon. My dear Aunt Augusta, I mean he was found out! The doctors found out that Bunbury could not live, that is what I mean — so Bunbury died.

Lady Bracknell. He seems to have had great confidence in the opinion of his physicians. I am glad, however, that he made up his mind at the last to some definite course of action, and acted under proper medical advice. And now that we have finally got rid of this Mr. Bunbury, may I ask, Mr. Worthing, who is that young person whose hand my nephew Algernon is now holding in what seems to me a peculiarly unnecessary manner?

Jack. That lady is Miss Cecily Cardew, my ward. (*Lady Bracknell bows coldly to Cecily.*)

Algernon. I am engaged to be married to Cecily, Aunt Augusta.

Lady Bracknell. I beg your pardon?

Cecily. Mr. Moncrieff and I are engaged to be married, Lady Bracknell.

Lady Bracknell (with a shiver, crossing to the sofa and sitting down.) I do not know whether there is anything peculiarly exciting in the air of this particular part of Hertfordshire, but the number of engagements that go on seems to me considerably above the proper average that statistics have laid down for our guidance. I think some preliminary inquiry on my part would not be out of place. Mr. Worthing, is Miss Cardew at all connected with any of the larger railway stations in London? I merely desire information. Until yesterday I had no idea that there were any families or persons whose origin was a Terminus.° (*Jack looks perfectly furious, but restrains himself.*)

Jack (in a cold, clear voice). Miss Cardew is the granddaugher of the late Mr. Thomas Cardew of 149 Belgrave Square, S.W.;

Terminus Railway station

Gervase Park, Dorking, Surrey; and the Sporran, Fifeshire, N.B.°

Lady Bracknell. That sounds not unsatisfactory. Three addresses always inspire confidence, even in tradesmen. But what proof have I of their authenticity?

Jack. I have carefully preserved the Court Guides of the period. They are open to your inspection, Lady Bracknell.

Lady Bracknell (grimly). I have known strange errors in that publication.

Jack. Miss Cardew's family solicitors are Messrs. Markby, Markby and Markby.

Lady Bracknell. Markby, Markby, and Markby? A firm of the very highest position in their profession. Indeed I am told that one of the Mr. Markbys is occasionally to be seen at dinner parties. So far I am satisfied.

Jack (very irritably). How extremely kind of you, Lady Bracknell! I have also in my possession, you will be pleased to hear, certificates of Miss Cardew's birth, baptism, whooping cough, registration, vaccination, confirmation, and the measles; both the German and the English variety.

Lady Bracknell. Ah! A life crowded with incident, I see; though perhaps somewhat too exciting for a young girl. I am not myself in favour of premature experiences. (*Rises, looks at her watch.*) Gwendolen! the time approaches for our departure. We have not a moment to lose. As a matter of form, Mr. Worthing, I had better ask you if Miss Cardew has any little fortune?

Jack. Oh! about a hundred and thirty thousand pounds in the Funds.° That is all. Good-by, Lady Bracknell. So pleased to have seen you.

Lady Bracknell (sitting down again). A moment, Mr. Worthing. A hundred and thirty thousand pounds! And in the Funds! Miss Cardew seems to me a most attractive young lady, now that I look at her. Few girls of the present day have any really solid qualities, any of the qualities that last, and improve with time. We live, I regret to say, in an age of surfaces. (*To Cecily.*) Come over here, dear. (*Cecily goes across.*) Pretty child! your dress is sadly simple, and your hair seems almost as Nature might have left it. But we can soon alter all that. A thoroughly experienced French maid produces a really

---

N.B. North Britain, i.e., Scotland   ***Funds*** I.e., interest-bearing government bonds

marvelous result in a very brief space of time. I remember recommending one to young Lady Lancing, and after three months her own husband did not know her.

Jack. And after six months nobody knew her.

Lady Bracknell (*glares at Jack for a few moments. Then bends, with a practiced smile, to Cecily*). Kindly turn round, sweet child. (*Cecily turns completely round.*) No, the side view is what I want. (*Cecily presents her profile.*) Yes, quite as I expected. There are distinct social possibilities in your profile. The two weak points in our age are its want of principle and its want of profile. The chin a little higher, dear. Style largely depends on the way the chin is worn. They are worn very high, just at present. Algernon!

Algernon. Yes, Aunt Augusta!

Lady Bracknell. There are distinct social possibilites in Miss Cardew's profile.

Algernon. Cecily is the sweetest, dearest, prettiest girl in the whole world. And I don't care twopence about social possibilities.

Lady Bracknell. Never speak disrespectfully of Society, Algernon. Only people who can't get into it do that. (*To Cecily.*) Dear child, of course you know that Algernon has nothing but his debts to depend upon. But I do not approve of mercenary marriages. When I married Lord Bracknell I had no fortune of any kind. But I never dreamed for a moment of allowing that to stand in my way. Well, I suppose I must give my consent.

Algernon. Thank you, Aunt Augusta.

Lady Bracknell. Cecily, you may kiss me!

Cecily (*kisses her*). Thank you, Lady Bracknell.

Lady Bracknell. You may also address me as Aunt Augusta for the future.

Cecily. Thank you, Aunt Augusta.

Lady Bracknell. The marriage, I think, had better take place quite soon.

Algernon. Thank you, Aunt Augusta.

Cecily. Thank you, Aunt Augusta.

Lady Bracknell. To speak frankly, I am not in favor of long engagements. They give people the opportunity of finding out each other's character before marriage, which I think is never advisable.

Jack. I beg your pardon for interrupting you, Lady Bracknell, but this engagement is quite out of the question. I am Miss Cardew's guardian, and she cannot marry without my consent until she comes of age. That consent I absolutely decline to give.

Lady Bracknell. Upon what grounds, may I ask? Algernon is an extremely, I may almost say an ostentatiously eligible young man. He has nothing, but he looks everything. What more can one desire?

Jack. It pains me very much to have to speak frankly to you, Lady Bracknell, about your nephew, but the fact is that I do not approve at all of his moral character. I suspect him of being untruthful. (*Algernon and Cecily look at him in indignant amazement.*)

Lady Bracknell. Untruthful! My nephew Algernon? Impossible! He is an Oxonian.°

Jack. I fear there can be no possible doubt about the matter. This afternoon during my temporary absence in London on an important question of romance, he obtained admission to my house by means of the false pretense of being my brother. Under an assumed name he drank, I've just been informed by my butler, an entire pint bottle of my Perrier-Jouet, Brut, '89; wine I was specially reserving for myself. Continuing his disgraceful deception, he succeeded in the course of the afternoon in alienating the affections of my only ward. He subsequently stayed to tea, and devoured every single muffin. And what makes his conduct all the more heartless is, that he was perfectly well aware from the first that I have no brother, that I never had a brother, and that I don't intend to have a brother, not even of any kind. I distinctly told him so myself yesterday afternoon.

Lady Bracknell. Ahem! Mr. Worthing, after careful consideration I have decided entirely to overlook my nephew's conduct to you.

Jack. That is very generous of you, Lady Bracknell. My own decision, however, is unalterable. I decline to give my consent.

Lady Bracknell (*to Cecily*). Come here, sweet child. (*Cecily goes over.*) How old are you, dear?

Cecily. Well, I am really only eighteen, but I always admit to twenty when I go to evening parties.

Lady Bracknell. You are perfectly right in making some slight alteration. Indeed, no woman should ever be quite accurate about her age. It looks so calculating. . . . (*In a meditative manner.*) Eighteen, but admitting to twenty at evening parties. Well, it will not be very long before you are of age and free from the restraints of tutelage. So I don't think your guardian's consent is, after all, a matter of any importance.

Jack. Pray excuse me, Lady Bracknell, for interrupting you again,

Oxonian I.e., a student or a graduate of Oxford

but it is only fair to tell you that according to the terms of her grandfather's will Miss Cardew does not come legally of age till she is thirty-five.

Lady Bracknell. That does not seem to me to be a grave objection. Thirty-five is a very attractive age. London society is full of women of the very highest birth who have, of their own free choice, remained thirty-five for years. Lady Dumbleton is an instance in point. To my own knowledge she has been thirty-five ever since she arrived at the age of forty, which was many years ago now. I see no reason why our dear Cecily should not be even still more attractive at the age you mention than she is at present. There will be a large accumulation of property.

Cecily. Algy, could you wait for me till I was thirty-five?

Algernon. Of course I could, Cecily. You know I could.

Cecily. Yes, I felt it instinctively, but I couldn't wait all that time. I hate waiting even five minutes for anybody. It always makes me rather cross. I am not punctual myself, I know, but I do like punctuality in others, and waiting, even to be married, is quite out of the question.

Algernon. Then what is to be done, Cecily?

Cecily. I don't know, Mr. Moncrieff.

Lady Bracknell. My dear Mr. Worthing, as Miss Cardew states positively that she cannot wait till she is thirty-five — a remark which I am bound to say seems to me to show a somewhat impatient nature — I would beg of you to reconsider your decision.

Jack. But my dear Lady Bracknell, the matter is entirely in your own hands. The moment you consent to my marriage with Gwendolen, I will most gladly allow your nephew to form an alliance with my ward.

Lady Bracknell (rising and drawing herself up). You must be quite aware that what you propose is out of the question.

Jack. Then a passionate celibacy is all that any of us can look forward to.

Lady Bracknell. That is not the destiny I propose for Gwendolen. Algernon, of course, can choose for himself. (*Pulls out her watch.*) Come, dear (*Gwendolen rises*), we have already missed five, if not six, trains. To miss any more might expose us to comment on the platform.

Enter Dr. Chasuble.

Chasuble. Everything is quite ready for the christenings.

Lady Bracknell. The christenings, sir! Is not that somewhat premature?

Chasuble (looking rather puzzled, and pointing to Jack and Algernon). Both these gentlemen have expressed a desire for immediate baptism.

Lady Bracknell. At their age? The idea is grotesque and irreligious! Algernon, I forbid you to be baptized. I will not hear of such excesses. Lord Bracknell would be highly displeased if he learned that that was the way in which you wasted your time and money.

Chasuble. Am I to understand then that there are to be no christenings at all this afternoon?

Jack. I don't think that, as things are now, it would be of much practical value to either of us, Dr. Chasuble.

Chasuble. I am grieved to hear such sentiments from you, Mr. Worthing. They savor of the heretical views of the Anabaptists, views that I have completely refuted in four of my unpublished sermons. However, as your present mood seems to be one peculiarly secular, I will return to the church at once. Indeed, I have just been informed by the pew-opener that for the last hour and a half Miss Prism has been waiting for me in the vestry.

Lady Bracknell (starting.) Miss Prism! Did I hear you mention a Miss Prism?

Chasuble. Yes, Lady Bracknell. I am on my way to join her.

Lady Bracknell. Pray allow me to detain you for a moment. This matter may prove to be one of vital importance to Lord Bracknell and myself. Is this Miss Prism a female of repellent aspect, remotely connected with education?

Chasuble (somewhat indignantly). She is the most cultivated of ladies, and the very picture of respectability.

Lady Bracknell. It is obviously the same person. May I ask what position she holds in your household?

Chasuble (severely). I am a celibate, madam.

Jack (interposing). Miss Prism, Lady Bracknell, has been for the last three years Miss Cardew's esteemed governess and valued companion.

Lady Bracknell. In spite of what I hear of her, I must see her at once. Let her be sent for.

Chasuble (looking off). She approaches; she is nigh.

Enter Miss Prism hurriedly.

Miss Prism. I was told you expected me in the vestry, dear Canon. I have been waiting for you there for an hour and three-quarters. (*Catches sight of Lady Bracknell, who has fixed her with a stony glare. Miss Prism grows pale and quails. She looks anxiously round as if desirous to escape.*)

Lady Bracknell (in a severe, judicial voice). Prism! (*Miss Prism bows her head in shame.*) Come here, Prism! (*Miss Prism approaches in a humble manner.*) Prism! Where is that baby? (*General consternation. The Canon starts back in horror. Algernon and Jack pretend to be anxious to shield Cecily and Gwendolen from hearing the details of a terrible public scandal.*) Twenty-eight years ago, Prism, you left Lord Bracknell's house, Number 104, Upper Grosvenor Square, in charge of a perambulator that contained a baby of the male sex. You never returned. A few weeks later, through the elaborate investigations of the Metropolitan police, the perambulator was discovered at midnight standing by itself in a remote corner of Bayswater. It contained the manuscript of a three-volume novel of more than usually revolting sentimentality. (*Miss Prism starts in involuntary indignation.*) But the baby was not there. (*Everyone looks at Miss Prism.*) Prism! Where is that baby? (*A pause.*)

Miss Prism. Lady Bracknell, I admit with shame that I do not know. I only wish I did. The plain facts of the case are these. On the morning of the day you mention, a day that is forever branded on my memory, I prepared as usual to take the baby out in its perambulator. I had also with me a somewhat old, but capacious handbag in which I had intended to place the manuscript of a work of fiction that I had written during my few unoccupied hours. In a moment of mental abstraction, for which I can never forgive myself, I deposited the manuscript in the bassinette and placed the baby in the handbag.

Jack (who has been listening attentively). But where did you deposit the handbag?

Miss Prism. Do not ask me, Mr. Worthing.

Jack. Miss Prism, this is a matter of no small importance to me. I insist on knowing where you deposited the handbag that contained that infant.

Miss Prism. I left it in the cloakroom of one of the larger railway stations in London.

Jack. What railway station?

Miss Prism (quite crushed). Victoria. The Brighton line. (*Sinks into a chair.*)

Jack. I must retire to my room for a moment. Gwendolen, wait here for me.

Gwendolen. If you are not too long, I will wait here for you all my life. (*Exit Jack in great excitement.*)

Chasuble. What do you think this means, Lady Bracknell?

Lady Bracknell. I dare not even suspect, Dr. Chasuble. I need hardly tell you that in families of high position strange coincidences are not supposed to occur. They are hardly considered the thing.

Noises heard overhead as if someone was throwing trunks about. Every one looks up.

Cecily. Uncle Jack seems strangely agitated.

Chasuble. Your guardian has a very emotional nature.

Lady Bracknell. This noise is extremely unpleasant. It sounds as if he was having an argument. I dislike arguments of any kind. They are always vulgar, and often convincing.

Chasuble (looking up). It has stopped now. (*The noise is redoubled.*)

Lady Bracknell. I wish he would arrive at some conclusion.

Gwendolen. This suspense is terrible. I hope it will last.

Enter Jack with a handbag of black leather in his hand.

Jack (rushing over to Miss Prism). Is this the handbag, Miss Prism? Examine it carefully before you speak. The happiness of more than one life depends on your answer.

Miss Prism (calmly). It seems to be mine. Yes, here is the injury it received through the upsetting of a Gower Street omnibus in younger and happier days. Here is the stain on the lining caused by the explosion of a temperance beverage, an incident that occurred at Leamington. And here, on the lock, are my initials. I had forgotten that in an extravagant mood I had had them placed there. The bag is undoubtedly mine. I am delighted to have it so unexpectedly restored to me. It has been a great inconvenience being without it all these years.

Jack (in a pathetic voice). Miss Prism, more is restored to you than this handbag. I was the baby you placed in it.

Miss Prism (amazed). You?

Jack (embracing her). Yes . . . mother!

Miss Prism (recoiling in indignant astonishment). Mr. Worthing. I am unmarried!

Jack. Unmarried! I do not deny that is a serious blow. But after all, who has the right to cast a stone against one who has suffered? Cannot repentance wipe out an act of folly? Why should there be one law for men, and another for women? Mother, I forgive you. (*Tries to embrace her again.*)

Miss Prism (still more indignant). Mr. Worthing, there is some error. (*Pointing to Lady Bracknell.*) There is the lady who can tell you who you really are.

Jack (after a pause). Lady Bracknell, I hate to seem inquisitive, but would you kindly inform me who I am?

Lady Bracknell. I am afraid that the news I have to give you will not altogether please you. You are the son of my poor sister, Mrs. Moncrieff, and consequently Algernon's elder brother.

Jack. Algy's elder brother! Then I have a brother after all. I knew I had a brother! I always said I had a brother! Cecily,—how could you have ever doubted that I had a brother. (*Seizes hold of Algernon.*) Dr. Chasuble, my unfortunate brother. Miss Prism, my unfortunate brother. Gwendolen, my unfortunate brother. Algy, you young scoundrel, you will have to treat me with more respect in the future. You have never behaved to me like a brother in all your life.

Algernon. Well, not till to-day, old boy, I admit. I did my best, however, though I was out of practice.

(*Shakes hands.*)

Gwendolen (*to Jack*). My own! But what own are you? What is your Christian name, now that you have become someone else?

Jack. Good heavens! . . . I had quite forgotten that point. Your decision on the subject of my name is irrevocable, I suppose?

Gwendolen. I never change, except in my affections.

Cecily. What a noble nature you have, Gwendolen!

Jack. Then the question had better be cleared up at once. Aunt Augusta, a moment. At the time when Miss Prism left me in the hand-bag, had I been christened already?

Lady Bracknell. Every luxury that money could buy, including christening, had been lavished on you by your fond and doting parents.

Jack. Then I was christened! That is settled. Now, what name was I given? Let me know the worst.

Lady Bracknell. Being the eldest son you were naturally christened after your father.

Jack (*irritably*). Yes, but what was my father's Christian name?

Lady Bracknell (*meditatively*). I cannot at the present moment recall what the General's Christian name was. But I have no doubt he had one. He was eccentric, I admit. But only in later years. And that was the result of the Indian climate, and marriage, and indigestion, and other things of that kind.

Jack. Algy! Can't you recollect what our father's Christian name was?

Algernon. My dear boy, we were never even on speaking terms. He died before I was a year old.

Jack. His name would appear in the Army Lists of the period, I suppose, Aunt Augusta?

Lady Bracknell. The General was essentially a man of peace, except in his domestic life. But I have no doubt his name would appear in any military directory.

Jack. The Army Lists of the last forty years are here. These delightful records should have been my constant study. (*Rushes to bookcase and tears the books out.*) M. Generals . . . Mallam, Maxbohm, Magley — what ghastly names they have — Markby, Migsby, Mobbs, Moncrieff! Lieutenant 1840, Captain, Lieutenant-Colonel, Colonel, General 1869, Christian names, Ernest John. (*Puts book very quietly down and speaks quite calmly.*) I always told you, Gwendolen, my name was Ernest, didn't I? Well, it is Ernest after all. I mean it naturally is Ernest.

Lady Bracknell. Yes, I remember now that the General was called Ernest. I knew I had some particular reason for disliking the name.

Gwendolen. Ernest! My own Ernest! I felt from the first that you could have no other name!

Jack. Gwendolen, it is a terrible thing for a man to find out suddenly that all his life he has been speaking nothing but the truth. Can you forgive me?

Gwendolen. I can. For I feel that you are sure to change.

Jack. My own one!

Chasuble (*to Miss Prism*). Laetitia! (*Embraces her.*)

Miss Prism (*enthusiastically*). Frederick! At last!

Algernon. Cecily! (*Embraces her.*) At last!

Jack. Gwendolen! (*Embraces her.*) At last!

Lady Bracknell. My nephew, you seem to be displaying signs of triviality.

Jack. On the contrary, Aunt Augusta, I've now realized for the first time in my life the vital Importance of Being Earnest.

Tableau

QUESTIONS

1. Perhaps the two most obvious traits of a comedy are these: the work is amusing, and it ends happily. What is amusing about *The Importance of Being Earnest*? Specify some lines, and some situations.

2. Many important topics, such as education, marriage, money, class relationships, death, and sincerity are touched on in the play. Are some of these topics (or other important topics) treated in such a way that we can say Wilde is a satirist or social critic as well as an entertainer? Why do we, or why do we not, take the speeches seriously? Choose one of these

motifs, for instance sincerity, follow it through the play and
see if perhaps Wilde is doing more than fooling around. [If
you choose sincerity, you may want to think especially about
the speech (page 705) in which Algernon says to Jack, "Well,
one must be serious about something, if one wants to have
any amusement in life." Is this nonsense, or is there something
to it?]

3. Evaluate: "The Bunburyists are no less earnest than the con-
   formists such as Chasuble and Prism, but the Bunburyists
   at least know what is real and what is humbug."

4. The play is carefully constructed, with parallels and contrasts.
   For instance, Jack goes to London, Algernon goes to the
   country; the young men quarrel, and the young women
   quarrel. What other elements of careful plotting do you find?

20
Seven Plays for Further Study

Sophocles (496?–406 B.C.)

Oedipus Rex

An English Version by Dudley Fitts and Robert Fitzgerald

List of Characters

Oedipus
A priest
Creon
Teiresias
Iocastê
Messenger
Shepherd of Laïos
Second messenger
Chorus of Theban elders

Scene. *Before the palace of Oedipus, King of Thebes. A central door and two lateral doors open onto a platform which runs the length of the façade. On the platform, right and left, are altars; and three steps lead down into the "orchestra," or chorus-ground. At the beginning of the action these steps are crowded by Suppliants who have brought branches and chaplets of olive leaves and who lie in various attitudes of despair. Oedipus enters.*

Giant puppets of Iocastê and Oedipus were used in the Philadelphia production of Oedipus the King, *designed in 1931 by Robert Edmond Jones. (Photograph: Will Rapport, Harvard Theatre Collection)*

PROLOGUE

Oedipus. My children, generations of the living
    In the line of Kadmos,° nursed at his ancient hearth:
    Why have you strewn yourselves before these altars
    In supplication, with your boughs and garlands?
    The breath of incense rises from the city   *5*
    With a sound of prayer and lamentation.
                         Children,
    I would not have you speak through messengers,
    And therefore I have come myself to hear you —
    I, Oedipus, who bear the famous name.
    (*To a Priest.*) You, there, since you are eldest
        in the company,   *10*
    Speak for them all, tell me what preys upon you,
    Whether you come in dread, or crave some blessing:
    Tell me, and never doubt that I will help you
    In every way I can; I should be heartless
    Were I not moved to find you suppliant here.   *15*
Priest. Great Oedipus, O powerful King of Thebes!
    You see how all the ages of our people
    Cling to your altar steps: here are boys
    Who can barely stand alone, and here are priests
    By weight of age, as I am a priest of God,   *20*
    And young men chosen from those yet unmarried;
    As for the others, all that multitude,
    They wait with olive chaplets in the squares,
    At the two shrines of Pallas,° and where Apollo°
    Speaks in the glowing embers.
                    Your own eyes   *25*
    Must tell you: Thebes is in her extremity
    And cannot lift her head from the surge of death.
    A rust consumes the buds and fruits of the earth;
    The herds are sick; children die unborn,
    And labor is vain. The god of plague and pyre   *30*
    Raids like detestable lightning through the city,
    And all the house of Kadmos is laid waste,
    All emptied, and all darkened: Death alone
    Battens upon the misery of Thebes.

Prologue. **²Kadmos** mythical founder of Thebes **²⁴Pallas** Athena, goddess of wisdom, protectress of Athens **²⁴Apollo** god of light and healing

You are not one of the immortal gods, we know;   *35*
Yet we have come to you to make our prayer
As to the man of all men best in adversity
And wisest in the ways of God. You saved us
From the Sphinx,° that flinty singer, and the tribute
We paid to her so long; yet you were never   *40*
Better informed than we, nor could we teach you:
It was some god breathed in you to set us free.

Therefore, O mighty King, we turn to you:
Find us our safety, find us a remedy,
Whether by counsel of the gods or the men.   *45*
A king of wisdom tested in the past
Can act in a time of troubles, and act well.
Noblest of men, restore
Life to your city! Think how all men call you
Liberator for your triumph long ago;   *50*
Ah, when your years of kingship are remembered,
Let them not say *We rose, but later fell* —
Keep the State from going down in the storm!
Once, years ago, with happy augury,
You brought us fortune; be the same again!   *55*
No man questions your power to rule the land:
But rule over men, not over a dead city!
Ships are only hulls, citadels are nothing,
When no life moves in the empty passageways.
Oedipus. Poor children! You may be sure I know   *60*
All that you longed for in your coming here.
I know that you are deathly sick; and yet,
Sick as you are, not one is as sick as I.
Each of you suffers in himself alone
His anguish, not another's; but my spirit   *65*
Groans for the city, for myself, for you.

I was not sleeping, you are not waking me.
No, I have been in tears for a long while
And in my restless thought walked many ways.
In all my search, I found one helpful course,   *70*
And that I have taken: I have sent Creon,

---

[39] **Sphinx** a monster (body of a lion, wings of a bird, face of a woman) who asked
the riddle, "What goes on four legs in the morning, two at noon, and three in
the evening?" and who killed those who could not answer. When Oedipus responded
correctly that man crawls on all fours in infancy, walks upright in maturity, and
uses a staff in old age, the Sphinx destroyed herself.

Son of Menoikeus, brother of the Queen,
To Delphi, Apollo's place of revelation,
To learn there, if he can,
What act or pledge of mine may save the city. 75
I have counted the days, and now, this very day,
I am troubled, for he has overstayed his time.
What is he doing? He has been gone too long.
Yet whenever he comes back, I should do ill
To scant whatever hint the god may give. 80
Priest. It is a timely promise. At this instant
They tell me Creon is here.
Oedipus. O Lord Apollo!
May his news be fair as his face is radiant!
Priest. It could not be otherwise: he is crowned with bay,
The chaplet is thick with berries.
Oedipus. We shall soon know; 85
He is near enough to hear us now.

Enter Creon.

O Prince:
Brother: son of Menoikeus:
What answer do you bring us from the god?
Creon. It is favorable. I can tell you, great afflictions
Will turn out well, if they are taken well. 90
Oedipus. What was the oracle? These vague words
Leave me still hanging between hope and fear.
Creon. Is it your pleasure to hear me with all these
Gathered around us? I am prepared to speak,
But should we not go in?
Oedipus. Let them all hear it. 95
It is for them I suffer, more than myself.
Creon. Then I will tell you what I heard at Delphi.

In plain words
The god commands us to expel from the land of Thebes
An old defilement that it seems we shelter. 100
It is a deathly thing, beyond expiation.
We must not let it feed upon us longer.
Oedipus. What defilement? How shall we rid ourselves of it?
Creon. By exile or death, blood for blood. It was
Murder that brought the plague-wind on the city. 105
Oedipus. Murder of whom? Surely the god has named him?
Creon. My lord: long ago Laïos was our king,
Before you came to govern us.

Oedipus   I know;
    I learned of him from others; I never saw him.
Creon. He was murdered; and Apollo commands us now   *110*
    To take revenge upon whoever killed him.
Oedipus. Upon whom? Where are they? Where shall we find a
       clue
    To solve that crime, after so many years?
Creon. Here in this land, he said.
                       If we make enquiry,
    We may touch things that otherwise escape us.   *115*
Oedipus. Tell me: Was Laïos murdered in his house,
    Or in the fields, or in some foreign country?
Creon. He said he planned to make a pilgrimage.
    He did not come home again.
Oedipus.   And was there no one,
    No witness, no companion, to tell what happened?   *120*
Creon. They were all killed but one, and he got away
    So frightened that he could remember one thing only.
Oedipus. What was that one thing? One may be the key
    To everything, if we resolve to use it.
Creon. He said that a band of highwaymen attacked them,   *125*
    Outnumbered them, and overwhelmed the King.
Oedipus. Strange, that a highwayman should be so daring —
    Unless some faction here bribed him to do it.
Creon. We thought of that. But after Laïos' death
    New troubles arose and we had no avenger.   *130*
Oedipus. What troubles could prevent your hunting
       down the killers?
Creon. The riddling Sphinx's song
    Made us deaf to all mysteries but her own.
Oedipus. Then once more I must bring what is dark to light.
    It is most fitting that Apollo shows,   *135*
    As you do, this compunction for the dead.
    You shall see how I stand by you, as I should,
    To avenge the city and the city's god,
    And not as though it were for some distant friend,
    But for my own sake, to be rid of evil.   *140*
    Whoever killed King Laïos might — who knows? —
    Decide at any moment to kill me as well.
    By avenging the murdered king I protect myself.
    Come, then, my children: leave the altar steps,
    Lift up your olive boughs!
                    One of you go   *145*
    And summon the people of Kadmos to gather here.

I will do all that I can; you may tell them that.

(Exit a Page.)

So, with the help of God,
We shall be saved — or else indeed we are lost.

Priest. Let us rise, children. It was for this we came,   *150*
And now the King has promised it himself.
Phoibos° has sent us an oracle; may he descend
Himself to save us and drive out the plague.

Exeunt Oedipus and Creon into the palace by the central door.
The Priest and the Suppliants disperse right and left. After a short
pause the Chorus enters the orchestra.

PÁRODOS

Chorus. What is God singing in his profound   *Strophe 1*
    Delphi of gold and shadow?
What oracle for Thebes, the sunwhipped city?
Fear unjoints me, the roots of my heart tremble.
Now I remember, O Healer, your power, and wonder;   *5*
Will you send doom like a sudden cloud, or weave it
Like nightfall of the past?
Speak, speak to us, issue of holy sound:
Dearest to our expectancy: be tender!

Let me pray to Athenê, the immortal daughter *Antistrophe 1*
    of Zeus,   *10*
And to Artemis her sister
Who keeps her famous throne in the market ring,
And to Apollo, bowman at the far butts of heaven —

O gods, descend! Like three streams leap against
The fires of our grief, the fires of darkness;   *15*
Be swift to bring us rest!

As in the old time from the brilliant house
Of air you stepped to save us, come again!

Now our afflictions have no end,   *Strophe 2*
Now all our stricken host lies down   *20*
And no man fights off death with his mind;

The noble plowland bears no grain,
And groaning mothers cannot bear —

---

[152]***Phoibos*** Phoebus Apollo, the sun god

See, how our lives like birds take wing,
Like sparks that fly when a fire soars,   *25*
To the shore of the god of evening.

The plague burns on, it is pitiless   *Antistrophe 2*
Though pallid children laden with death
Lie unwept in the stony ways,
And old gray women by every path   *30*
Flock to the strand about the altars

There to strike their breasts and cry
Worship of Phoibos in wailing prayers:
Be kind, God's golden child!

There are no swords in this attack by fire,   *Strophe 3*   *35*
No shields, but we are ringed with cries.
Send the besieger plunging from our homes
Into the vast sea-room of the Atlantic
Or into the waves that foam eastward of Thrace —
For the day ravages what the night spares —   *40*

Destroy our enemy, lord of the thunder!
Let him be riven by lightning from heaven!

Phoibos Apollo, stretch the sun's bowstring,   *Antistrophe 3*
That golden cord, until it sing for us,
Flashing arrows in heaven!
                         Artemis, Huntress,   *45*
Race with flaring lights upon our mountains!
O scarlet god, O golden-banded brow,
O Theban Bacchos° in a storm of Maenads,°

Enter Oedipus, center.

Whirl upon Death, that all the Undying hate!
Come with blinding cressets, come in joy!   *50*

SCENE I

Oedipus. Is this your prayer? It may be answered. Come,
        Listen to me, act as the crisis demands,
        And you shall have relief from all these evils.

        Until now I was a stranger to this tale,
        As I had been a stranger to the crime.   *5*

Párodos.   **48Bacchos** Dionysos, god of wine, thus scarlet-faced   **48Maenads** Dionysos's
female attendants

Could I track down the murderer without a clue?
But now, friends,
As one who became a citizen after the murder,
I make this proclamation to all Thebans:
If any man knows by whose hand Laïos, son of   10
    Labdakos,
Met his death, I direct that man to tell me everything,
No matter what he fears for having so long withheld it.
Let it stand as promised that no further trouble
Will come to him, but he may leave the land in safety.

Moreover: If anyone knows the murderer to be foreign,   15
Let him not keep silent: he shall have his reward from me.
However, if he does conceal it; if any man
Fearing for his friend or for himself disobeys this edict,
Hear what I propose to do:

I solemnly forbid the people of this country,   20
Where power and throne are mine, ever to receive that man
Or speak to him, no matter who he is, or let him
Join in sacrifice, lustration, or in prayer.
I decree that he be driven from every house,

Being, as he is, corruption itself to us: the Delphic   25
Voice of Zeus has pronounced this revelation.
Thus I associate myself with the oracle
And take the side of the murdered king.

As for the criminal, I pray to God —
Whether it be a lurking thief, or one of a number —   30
I pray that that man's life be consumed in evil and
    wretchedness.
And as for me, this curse applies no less
If it should turn out that the culprit is my guest here,
Sharing my hearth.
                    You have heard the penalty.
I lay it on you now to attend to this   35
For my sake, for Apollo's, for the sick
Sterile city that heaven has abandoned.
Suppose the oracle had given you no command:
Should this defilement go uncleansed for ever?
You should have found the murderer: your king,   40
A noble king, had been destroyed!
                              Now I,
Having the power that he held before me,
Having his bed, begetting children there

Upon his wife, as he would have, had he lived —
Their son would have been my children's brother,   45
If Laïos had had luck in fatherhood!
(But surely ill luck rushed upon his reign) —
I say I take the son's part, just as though
I were his son, to press the fight for him
And see it won! I'll find the hand that brought   50
Death to Labdakos' and Polydoros' child,
Heir of Kadmos' and Agenor's line.
And as for those who fail me,
May the gods deny them the fruit of the earth,
Fruit of the womb, and may they rot utterly!   55
Let them be wretched as we are wretched, and worse!

For you, for loyal Thebans, and for all
Who find my actions right, I pray the favor
Of justice, and of all the immortal gods.
Choragos. Since I am under oath, my lord, I swear   60
I did not do the murder, I cannot name
The murderer. Might not the oracle
That has ordained the search tell where to find him?
Oedipus. An honest question. But no man in the world
Can make the gods do more than the gods will.   65
Choragos. There is one last expedient —
Oedipus.   Tell me what it is.
Though it seem slight, you must not hold it back.
Choragos. A lord clairvoyant to the lord Apollo,
As we all know, is the skilled Teiresias.
One might learn much about this from him, Oedipus.   70
Oedipus. I am not wasting time:
Creon spoke of this, and I have sent for him —
Twice, in fact; it is strange that he is not here.
Choragos. The other matter — that old report — seems useless.
Oedipus. Tell me. I am interested in all reports.   75
Choragos. The King was said to have been killed by highwaymen.
Oedipus. I know. But we have no witnesses to that.
Choragos. If the killer can feel a particle of dread,
Your curse will bring him out of hiding!
Oedipus.   No.
The man who dared that act will fear no curse.   80

Enter the blind seer Teiresias, led by a Page.

Choragos. But there is one man who may detect the criminal.
This is Teiresias, this is the holy prophet
In whom, alone of all men, truth was born.

Oedipus. Teiresias: seer: student of mysteries,
  Of all that's taught and all that no man tells,   *85*
  Secrets of Heaven and secrets of the earth:
  Blind though you are, you know the city lies
  Sick with plague; and from this plague, my lord,
  We find that you alone can guard or save us.

  Possibly you did not hear the messengers?   *90*
  Apollo, when we sent to him,
  Sent us back word that this great pestilence
  Would lift, but only if we established clearly
  The identity of those who murdered Laïos.
  They must be killed or exiled.
                              Can you use   *95*
  Birdflight or any art of divination
  To purify yourself, and Thebes, and me
  From this contagion? We are in your hands.
  There is no fairer duty
  Than that of helping others in distress.   *100*
Teiresias. How dreadful knowledge of the truth can be
  When there's no help in truth! I knew this well,
  But did not act on it: else I should not have come.
Oedipus. What is troubling you? Why are your eyes so cold?
Teiresias. Let me go home. Bear your own fate, and I'll   *105*
  Bear mine. It is better so: trust what I say.
Oedipus. What you say is ungracious and unhelpful
  To your native country. Do not refuse to speak.
Teiresias. When it comes to speech, your own is neither temperate
  Nor opportune. I wish to be more prudent.   *110*
Oedipus. In God's name, we all beg you —
Teiresias.   You are all ignorant.
  No; I will never tell you what I know.
  Now it is my misery; then, it would be yours.
Oedipus. What! You do know something, and will not tell us?
  You would betray us all and wreck the State?   *115*
Teiresias. I do not intend to torture myself, or you.
  Why persist in asking? You will not persuade me.
Oedipus. What a wicked old man you are! You'd try a stone's
  Patience! Out with it! Have you no feeling at all?
Teiresias. You call me unfeeling. If you could only see   *120*
  The nature of your own feelings . . .
Oedipus.   Why,
  Who would not feel as I do? Who could endure
  Your arrogance toward the city?

Teiresias. What does it matter!
Whether I speak or not, it is bound to come.
Oedipus. Then, if "it" is bound to come, you are bound
    to tell me.   *125*
Teiresias. No, I will not go on. Rage as you please.
Oedipus. Rage? Why not!
    And I'll tell you what I think:
You planned it, you had it done, you all but
Killed him with your own hands: if you had eyes,
I'd say the crime was yours, and yours alone.   *130*
Teiresias. So? I charge you, then,
Abide by the proclamation you have made:
From this day forth
Never speak again to these men or to me;
You yourself are the pollution of this country.   *135*
Oedipus. You dare say that! Can you possibly think you have
Some way of going free, after such insolence?
Teiresias. I have gone free. It is the truth sustains me.
Oedipus. Who taught you shamelessness? It was not your craft.
Teiresias. You did. You made me speak. I did not want to.   *140*
Oedipus. Speak what? Let me hear it again more clearly.
Teiresias. Was it not clear before? Are you tempting me?
Oedipus. I did not understand it. Say it again.
Teiresias. I say that you are the murderer whom you seek.
Oedipus. Now twice you have spat out infamy. You'll
    pay for it!   *145*
Teiresias. Would you care for more? Do you wish to be really
    angry?
Oedipus. Say what you will. Whatever you say is worthless.
Teiresias. I say you live in hideous shame with those
Most dear to you. You cannot see the evil.
Oedipus. It seems you can go on mouthing like this for ever.   *150*
Teiresias. I can, if there is power in truth.
Oedipus.   There is:
But not for you, not for you,
You sightless, witless, senseless, mad old man!
Teiresias. You are the madman. There is no one here
Who will not curse you soon, as you curse me.   *155*
Oedipus. You child of endless night! You cannot hurt me
Or any other man who sees the sun.
Teiresias. True: it is not from me your fate will come.
That lies within Apollo's competence,
As it is his concern.

Oedipus.   Tell me: *160*
        Are you speaking for Creon, or for yourself?
Teiresias. Creon is no threat. You weave your own doom.
Oedipus. Wealth, power, craft of statesmanship!
        Kingly position, everywhere admired!
        What savage envy is stored up against these,   *165*
        If Creon, whom I trusted, Creon my friend,
        For this great office which the city once
        Put in my hands unsought — if for this power
        Creon desires in secret to destroy me!

        He has brought this decrepit fortune-teller, this   *170*
        Collector of dirty pennies, this prophet fraud —
        Why, he is no more clairvoyant than I am!
                                        Tell us:
        Has your mystic mummery ever approached the truth?
        When that hellcat the Sphinx was performing here,
        What help were you to these people?   *175*
        Her magic was not for the first man who came along:
        It demanded a real exorcist. Your birds —
        What good were they? or the gods, for the matter of that?
        But I came by,
        Oedipus, the simple man, who knows nothing —   *180*
        I thought it out for myself, no birds helped me!
        And this is the man you think you can destroy,
        That you may be close to Creon when he's king!
        Well, you and your friend Creon, it seems to me,
        Will suffer most. If you were not an old man,   *185*
        You would have paid already for your plot.
Choragos. We cannot see that his words or yours
        Have been spoken except in anger, Oedipus,
        And of anger we have no need. How can God's will
        Be accomplished best? That is what most concerns us. *190*
Teiresias. You are a king. But where argument's concerned
        I am your man, as much a king as you.
        I am not your servant, but Apollo's.
        I have no need of Creon to speak for me.

        Listen to me. You mock my blindness, do you?   *195*
        But I say that you, with both your eyes, are blind:
        You cannot see the wretchedness of your life,
        Nor in whose house you live, no, nor with whom.
        Who are your father and mother? Can you tell me?
        You do not even know the blind wrongs   *200*

That you have done them, on earth and in the world below.
But the double lash of your parents' curse will whip you
Out of this land some day, with only night
Upon your precious eyes.
Your cries then — where will they not be heard?   *205*
What fastness of Kithairon° will not echo them?
And that bridal-descant of yours — you'll know it then,
The song they sang when you came here to Thebes
And found your misguided berthing.
All this, and more, that you cannot guess at now,   *210*
Will bring you to yourself among your children.
Be angry, then. Curse Creon. Curse my words.
I tell you, no man that walks upon the earth
Shall be rooted out more horribly than you.

Oedipus. Am I to bear this from him? — Damnation   *215*
     Take you! Out of this place! Out of my sight!
Teiresias. I would not have come at all if you had not asked me.
Oedipus. Could I have told that you'd talk nonsense, that
     You'd come here to make a fool of yourself, and of me?
Teiresias. A fool? Your parents thought me sane enough.   *220*
Oedipus. My parents again! — Wait: who were my parents?
Teiresias. This day will give you a father, and break your heart.
Oedipus. Your infantile riddles! Your damned abracadabra!
Teiresias. You were a great man once at solving riddles.
Oedipus. Mock me with that if you like; you will find it
               true.   *225*
Teiresias. It was true enough. It brought about your ruin.
Oedipus. But if it saved this town?
Teiresias (to the Page). Boy, give me your hand.
Oedipus. Yes, boy; lead him away.
                              — While you are here
     We can do nothing. Go; leave us in peace.
Teiresias. I will go when I have said what I have to say.   *230*
     How can you hurt me? And I tell you again:
     The man you have been looking for all this time,
     The damned man, the murderer of Laïos,
     That man is in Thebes. To your mind he is foreignborn,
     But it will soon be shown that he is a Theban,   *235*
     A revelation that will fail to please.
                              A blind man,
     Who has his eyes now; a penniless man, who is rich now;
     And he will go tapping the strange earth with his staff;

Scene I   ²⁰⁶*fastness of Kithairon* stronghold in a mountain near Thebes

To the children with whom he lives now he will be
Brother and father — the very same; to her   *240*
Who bore him, son and husband — the very same
Who came to his father's bed, wet with his father's blood.

Enough. Go think that over.
If later you find error in what I have said,
You may say that I have no skill in prophecy.   *245*

Exit Teiresias, led by his Page. Oedipus goes into the palace.

ODE I

Chorus. The Delphic stone of prophecies   *Strophe 1*
    Remembers ancient regicide
    And a still bloody hand.
    That killer's hour of flight has come.
    He must be stronger than riderless   *5*
    Coursers of untiring wind,
    For the son of Zeus° armed with his father's thunder
    Leaps in lightning after him;
    And the Furies° follow him, the sad Furies.

    Holy Parnossos' peak of snow   *Antistrophe 1*   *10*
    Flashes and blinds that secret man,
    That all shall hunt him down:
    Though he may roam the forest shade
    Like a bull gone wild from pasture
    To rage through glooms of stone.   *15*
    Doom comes down on him; flight will not avail him;
    For the world's heart calls him desolate,
    And the immortal Furies follow, for ever follow.

    But now a wilder thing is heard   *Strophe 2*
    From the old man skilled at hearing Fate in the
            wingbeat of a bird.   *20*
    Bewildered as a blown bird, my soul hovers and cannot find
    Foothold in this debate, or any reason or rest of mind.
    But no man ever brought — none can bring
    Proof of strife between Thebes' royal house,
    Labdakos' line,° and the son of Polybos;°   *25*

Ode I.   [7]***son of Zeus*** Apollo   [9]***Furies*** avenging deities   [25]***Labdakos' line*** family
of Laïos   [25]***son of Polybos*** Oedipus (so the Chorus believes)

And never until now has any man brought word
Of Laïos' dark death staining Oedipus the King.

Divine Zeus and Apollo hold   *Anitistrophe 2*
Perfect intelligence alone of all tales ever told;
And well though this diviner works, he works in his own
    night;   *30*
No man can judge that rough unknown or trust in
    second sight,
For wisdom changes hands among the wise.
Shall I believe my great lord criminal
At a raging word that a blind old man let fall?
I saw him, when the carrion woman faced him of old, *35*
Prove his heroic mind! These evil words are lies.

SCENE II

Creon. Men of Thebes:
    I am told that heavy accusations
    Have been brought against me by King Oedipus.
    I am not the kind of man to bear this tamely.

    If in these present difficulties   *5*
    He holds me accountable for any harm to him
    Through anything I have said or done — why, then,
    I do not value life in this dishonor.
    It is not as though this rumor touched upon
    Some private indiscretion. The matter is grave.   *10*
    The fact is that I am being called disloyal
    To the State, to my fellow citizens, to my friends.
Choragos. He may have spoken in anger, not from his mind.
Creon. But did you not hear him say I was the one
    Who seduced the old prophet into lying?   *15*
Choragos. The thing was said; I do not know how seriously.
Creon. But you were watching him! Were his eyes steady?
    Did he look like a man in his right mind?
Choragos.   I do not know.
    I cannot judge the behavior of great men.
    But here is the King himself.

    Enter Oedipus.

Oedipus.   So you dared come back. *20*
    Why? How brazen of you to come to my house,
    You murderer!
              Do you think I do not know

That you plotted to kill me, plotted to steal my throne?
Tell me, in God's name: am I coward, a fool,
That you should dream you could accomplish this?   *25*
A fool who could not see your slippery game?
A coward, not to fight back when I saw it?
You are the fool, Creon, are you not? hoping
Without support or friends to get a throne?
Thrones may be won or bought: you could do neither.   *30*

Creon. Now listen to me. You have talked; let me talk, too.
    You cannot judge unless you know the facts.

Oedipus. You speak well: there is one fact; but I find it hard
    To learn from the deadliest enemy I have.

Creon. That above all I must dispute with you.   *35*

Oedipus. That above all I will not hear you deny.

Creon. If you think there is anything good in being stubborn
    Against all reason, then I say you are wrong.

Oedipus. If you think a man can sin against his own kind
    And not be punished for it, I say you are mad.   *40*

Creon. I agree. But tell me: what have I done to you?

Oedipus. You advised me to send for that wizard, did you not?

Creon. I did. I should do it again.

Oedipus.   Very well. Now tell me:
    How long has it been since Laïos —

Creon.   What of Laïos?

Oedipus. Since he vanished in that onset by the road?   *45*

Creon. It was long ago, a long time.

Oedipus.   And this prophet,
    Was he practicing here then?

Creon.   He was; and with honor, as now.

Oedipus. Did he speak of me at that time?

Creon.   He never did;
    At least, not when I was present.

Oedipus.   But. . . the enquiry?
    I suppose you held one?

Creon.   We did, but we learned nothing.   *50*

Oedipus. Why did the prophet not speak against me then?

Creon. I do not know; and I am the kind of man
    Who holds his tongue when he has no facts to go on.

Oedipus. There's one fact that you know, and you could tell it.

Creon. What fact is that? If I know it, you shall have it.   *55*

Oedipus. If he were not involved with you, he could not say
    That it was I who murdered Laïos.

Creon. If he says that, you are the one that knows it! —
    But now it is my turn to question you.

Oedipus. Put your questions. I am no murderer.   *60*

Creon. First, then: You married my sister?
Oedipus.   I married your sister.
Creon. And you rule the kingdom equally with her?
Oedipus. Everything that she wants she has from me.
Creon. And I am the third, equal to both of you?
Oedipus. That is why I call you a bad friend.   *65*
Creon. No. Reason it out, as I have done.
    Think of this first. Would any sane man prefer
    Power, with all a king's anxieties,
    To that same power and the grace of sleep?
    Certainly not I.   *70*
    I have never longed for the king's power — only his rights.
    Would any wise man differ from me in this?
    As matters stand, I have my way in everything
    With your consent, and no responsibilities.
    If I were king, I should be a slave to policy.   *75*
    How could I desire a scepter more
    Than what is now mine — untroubled influence?
    No, I have not gone mad; I need no honors,
    Except those with the perquisites I have now.
    I am welcome everywhere; every man salutes me,   *80*
    And those who want your favor seek my ear,
    Since I know how to manage what they ask.
    Should I exchange this ease for that anxiety?
    Besides, no sober mind is treasonable.
    I hate anarchy   *85*
    And never would deal with any man who likes it.

    Test what I have said. Go to the priestess
    At Delphi, ask if I quoted her correctly.
    And as for this other thing: if I am found
    Guilty of treason with Teiresias,   *90*
    Then sentence me to death! You have my word
    It is a sentence I should cast my vote for —
    But not without evidence!
                   You do wrong
    When you take good men for bad, bad men for good.
    A true friend thrown aside — why, life itself   *95*
    Is not more precious!
                  In time you will know this well:
    For time, and time alone, will show the just man,
    Though scoundrels are discovered in a day.
Choragos. This is well said, and a prudent man would ponder it.
    Judgments too quickly formed are dangerous.   *100*
Oedipus. But is he not quick in his duplicity?

And shall I not be quick to parry him?
Would you have me stand still, hold my peace, and let
This man win everything, through my inaction?
Creon. And you want — what is it, then? To banish me?   *105*
Oedipus. No, not exile. It is your death I want,
So that all the world may see what treason means.
Creon. You will persist, then? You will not believe me?
Oedipus. How can I believe you?
Creon.   Then you are a fool.
Oedipus. To save myself?
Creon.   In justice, think of me.   *110*
Oedipus. You are evil incarnate.
Creon.   But suppose that you are wrong?
Oedipus. Still I must rule.
Creon.   But not if you rule badly.
Oedipus. O city, city!
Creon.   It is my city, too!
Choragos. Now, my lords, be still. I see the Queen,
    Iocastê, coming from her palace chambers;   *115*
    And it is time she came, for the sake of you both.
    This dreadful quarrel can be resolved through her.

Enter Iocastê.

Iocastê. Poor foolish men, what wicked din is this?
    With Thebes sick to death, is it not shameful
    That you should rake some private quarrel up?   *120*
    (*To Oedipus.*) Come into the house.
                              — And you, Creon, go now:
    Let us have no more of this tumult over nothing.
Creon. Nothing? No, sister: what your husband plans for me
    Is one of two great evils: exile or death.
Oedipus. He is right.
    Why, woman, I have caught him squarely   *125*
    Plotting against my life.
Creon.   No! Let me die
    Accurst if ever I have wished you harm!
Iocastê. Ah, believe it, Oedipus!
    In the name of the gods, respect this oath of his
    For my sake, for the sake of these people here!   *130*

Choragos. Open your mind to her, my lord. Be ruled   *Strophe 1*
        by her, I beg you!
Oedipus. What would you have me do?
Choragos. Respect Creon's word. He has never spoken like a fool,
    And now he has sworn an oath.

Oedipus. You know what you ask?
Choragos.   I do.
Oedipus.   Speak on, then.
Choragos. A friend so sworn should not be baited so,   *135*
   In blind malice, and without final proof.
Oedipus. You are aware, I hope, that what you say
   Means death for me, or exile at the least.

Choragos. No, I swear by Helios,° first in Heaven!   *Strophe 2*
   May I die friendless and accurst,   *140*
      The worst of deaths, if ever I meant that!
         It is the withering fields
            That hurt my sick heart:
         Must we bear all these ills,
            And now your bad blood as well?   *145*
Oedipus. Then let him go. And let me die, if I must,
   Or be driven by him in shame from the land of Thebes.
   It is your unhappiness, and not his talk,
   That touches me.
                           As for him —
   Wherever he is, I will hate him as long as I live.   *150*
Creon. Ugly in yielding, as you were ugly in rage!
   Natures like yours chiefly torment themselves.
Oedipus. Can you not go? Can you not leave me?
Creon.   I can.
   You do not know me; but the city knows me,
   And in its eyes I am just, if not in yours. (*Exit Creon.*) *155*

Choragos. Lady Iocastê, did you not ask the King   *Antistrophe 1*
      to go to his chambers?
Iocastê. First tell me what has happened.
Choragos. There was suspicion without evidence; yet it rankled
   As even false charges will.
Iocastê.   On both sides?
Choragos.   On both.
Iocastê.   But what was said?
Choragos. Oh let it rest, let it be done with!   *160*
   Have we not suffered enough?
Oedipus. You see to what your decency has brought you:
   You have made difficulties where my heart saw none.

Choragos. Oedipus, it is not once only I have   *Antistrophe 2*
      told you —

Scene II.   ¹³⁹*Helios* sun god

You must know I should count myself unwise   *165*
To the point of madness, should I now forsake you —
    You, under whose hand,
        In the storm of another time,
    Our dear land sailed out free.
        But now stand fast at the helm!   *170*
Iocastê. In God's name, Oedipus, inform your wife as well:
    Why are you so set in this hard anger?
Oedipus. I will tell you, for none of these men deserves
    My confidence as you do. It is Creon's work,
    His treachery, his plotting against me.   *175*
Iocastê. Go on, if you can make this clear to me.
Oedipus. He charges me with the murder of Laïos.
Iocastê. Has he some knowledge? Or does he speak from
        hearsay?
Oedipus. He would not commit himself to such a charge,
    But he has brought in that damnable soothsayer   *180*
    To tell his story.
Iocastê.   Set your mind at rest.
    If it is a question of soothsayers, I tell you
    That you will find no man whose craft gives knowledge
    Of the unknowable.
             Here is my proof.

An oracle was reported to Laïos once   *185*
(I will not say from Phoibos himself, but from
His appointed ministers, at any rate)
That his doom would be death at the hands of his own son —
His son, born of his flesh and of mine!

Now, you remember the story: Laïos was killed   *190*
By marauding strangers where three highways meet;
But his child had not been three days in this world
Before the King had pierced the baby's ankles
And left him to die on a lonely mountainside.

Thus, Apollo never caused that child   *195*
To kill his father, and it was not Laïos' fate
To die at the hands of his son, as he had feared.
This is what prophets and prophecies are worth!
Have no dread of them.
            It is God himself
Who can show us what he wills, in his own way.   *200*
Oedipus. How strange a shadowy memory crossed my mind,
    Just now while you were speaking; it chilled my heart.
Iocastê. What do you mean? What memory do you speak of?

Oedipus. If I understand you, Laïos was killed
  At a place where three roads meet.
Iocastê.   So it was said;   205
  We have no later story.
Oedipus.   Where did it happen?
Iocastê. Phokis, it is called: at a place where the Theban Way
  Divides into the roads towards Delphi and Daulia.
Oedipus. When?
Iocastê.   We had the news not long before you came
  And proved the right to your succession here.   210
Oedipus. Ah, what net has God been weaving for me?
Iocastê. Oedipus! Why does this trouble you?
Oedipus.   Do not ask me yet.
  First, tell me how Laïos looked, and tell me
  How old he was.
Iocastê.   He was tall, his hair just touched
  With white; his form was not unlike your own.   215
Oedipus. I think that I myself may be accurst
  By my own ignorant edict.
Iocastê.   You speak strangely.
  It makes me tremble to look at you, my King.
Oedipus. I am not sure that the blind man cannot see.
  But I should know better if you were to tell me —   220
Iocastê. Anything — though I dread to hear you ask it.
Oedipus. Was the King lightly escorted, or did he ride
  With a large company, as a ruler should?
Iocastê. There were five men with him in all: one was a herald;
  And a single chariot, which he was driving.   225
Oedipus. Alas, that makes it plain enough!
                              But who —
  Who told you how it happened?
Iocastê.   A household servant,
  The only one to escape.
Oedipus.   And is he still
  A servant of ours?
Iocastê.   No; for when he came back at last
  And found you enthroned in the place of the dead
      king,   230
  He came to me, touched my hand with his, and begged
  That I would send him away to the frontier district
  Where only the shepherds go —
  As far away from the city as I could send him.
  I granted his prayer; for although the man was a
      slave,   235
  He had earned more than this favor at my hands.

Oedipus. Can he be called back quickly?
Iocastê.   Easily.
     But why?
Oedipus.   I have taken too much upon myself
     Without enquiry; therefore I wish to consult him.
Iocastê. Then he shall come.
                         But am I not one also   *240*
     To whom you might confide these fears of yours!
Oedipus. That is your right; it will not be denied you,
     Now least of all; for I have reached a pitch
     Of wild foreboding. Is there anyone
     To whom I should sooner speak?   *245*
     Polybos of Corinth is my father.
     My mother is a Dorian: Meropê.
     I grew up chief among the men of Corinth
     Until a strange thing happened —
     Not worth my passion, it may be, but strange.   *250*

     At a feast, a drunken man maundering in his cups
     Cries out that I am not my father's son!

     I contained myself that night, though I felt anger
     And a sinking heart. The next day I visited
     My father and mother, and questioned them. They
          stormed,   *255*
     Calling it all the slanderous rant of a fool;
     And this relieved me. Yet the suspicion
     Remained always aching in my mind;
     I knew there was talk; I could not rest;
     And finally, saying nothing to my parents,   *260*
     I went to the shrine at Delphi.
     The god dismissed my question without reply;
     He spoke of other things.
                         Some were clear,
     Full of wretchedness, dreadful, unbearable:
     As, that I should lie with my own mother, breed   *265*
     Children from whom all men would turn their eyes;
     And that I should be my father's murderer.

     I heard all this, and fled. And from that day
     Corinth to me was only in the stars
     Descending in that quarter of the sky,   *270*
     As I wandered farther and farther on my way
     To a land where I should never see the evil
     Sung by the oracle. And I came to this country
     Where, so you say, King Laïos was killed.

I will tell you all that happened there, my lady.   *275*

There were three highways
Coming together at a place I passed;
And there a herald came towards me, and a chariot
Drawn by horses, with a man such as you describe
Seated in it. The groom leading the horses   *280*
Forced me off the road at his lord's command;
But as this charioteer lurched over towards me
I struck him in my rage. The old man saw me
And brought his double goad down upon my head
As I came abreast.

He was paid back, and more!   *285*
Swinging my club in this right hand I knocked him
Out of his car, and he rolled on the ground.

I killed him.

I killed them all.
Now if that stranger and Laïos were — kin,
Where is a man more miserable than I?   *290*
More hated by the gods? Citizen and alien alike
Must never shelter me or speak to me —
I must be shunned by all.

And I myself
Pronounced this malediction upon myself!

Think of it: I have touched you with these hands,   *295*
These hands that killed your husband. What defilement!

Am I all evil, then? It must be so,
Since I must flee from Thebes, yet never again
See my own countrymen, my own country,
For fear of joining my mother in marriage   *300*
And killing Polybos, my father.

Ah,
If I was created so, born to this fate,
Who could deny the savagery of God?

O holy majesty of heavenly powers!
May I never see that day! Never!   *305*
Rather let me vanish from the race of men
Than know the abomination destined me!

Choragos. We too, my lord, have felt dismay at this.
But there is hope: you have yet to hear the shepherd.
Oedipus. Indeed, I fear no other hope is left me.   *310*
Iocastê. What do you hope from him when he comes?

Oedipus.   This much:
    If his account of the murder tallies with yours,
    Then I am cleared.
Iocastê.   What was it that I said
    Of such importance?
Oedipus.   Why, "marauders," you said,
    Killed the King, according to this man's story.   *315*
    If he maintains that still, if there were several,
    Clearly the guilt is not mine: I was alone.
    But if he says one man, singlehanded, did it,
    Then the evidence all points to me.
Iocastê. You may be sure that he said there were several;   *320*
    And can he call back that story now? He cannot.
    The whole city heard it as plainly as I.
    But suppose he alters some detail of it:
    He cannot ever show that Laïos' death
    Fulfilled the oracle: for Apollo said   *325*
    My child was doomed to kill him; and my child —
    Poor baby! — it was my child that died first.

    No. From now on, where oracles are concerned,
    I would not waste a second thought on any.
Oedipus. You may be right.
                     But come: let someone go   *330*
    For the shepherd at once. This matter must be settled.
Iocastê. I will send for him.
    I would not wish to cross you in anything,
    And surely not in this. — Let us go in.
                             Exeunt into the palace.

ODE II

Chorus. Let me be reverent in the ways of right,   *Strophe 1*
    Lowly the paths I journey on;
    Let all my words and actions keep
    The laws of the pure universe
    From highest Heaven handed down.   *5*
    For Heaven is their bright nurse,
    Those generations of the realms of light;
    Ah, never of mortal kind were they begot,
    Nor are they slaves of memory, lost in sleep:
    Their Father is greater than Time, and ages not.   *10*

The tyrant is a child of Pride   *Antistrophe 1*
Who drinks from his great sickening cup
Recklessness and vanity,
Until from his high crest headlong
He plummets to the dust of hope.   15
That strong man is not strong.
But let no fair ambition be denied;
May God protect the wrestler for the State
In government, in comely policy,
Who will fear God, and on His ordinance wait.   20

Haughtiness and the high hand of disdain   *Strophe 2*
Tempt and outrage God's holy law;
And any mortal who dares hold
No immortal Power in awe
Will be caught up in a net of pain: 25
The price for which his levity is sold.
Let each man take due earnings, then,
And keep his hands from holy things,
And from blasphemy stand apart —
Else the crackling blast of heaven   30
Blows on his head, and on his desperate heart;
Though fools will honor impious men,
In their cities no tragic poet sings.

Shall we lose faith in Delphi's obscurities,   *Antistrophe 2*
We who have heard the world's core   35
Discredited, and the sacred wood
Of Zeus at Elis praised no more?
The deeds and the strange prophecies
Must make a pattern yet to be understood.
Zeus, if indeed you are lord of all,   40
Throned in light over night and day,
Mirror this in your endless mind:
Our masters call the oracle
Words on the wind, and the Delphic vision blind!
Their hearts no longer know Apollo,   45
And reverence for the gods has died away.

SCENE III

Enter Iocastê

Iocastê. Princes of Thebes, it has occurred to me
    To visit the altars of the gods, bearing

These branches as a suppliant, and this incense.
Our King is not himself: his noble soul
Is overwrought with fantasies of dread,   *5*
Else he would consider
The new prophecies in the light of the old.
He will listen to any voice that speaks disaster,
And my advice goes for nothing.

She approaches the altar, right.

                                        To you, then, Apollo,
Lycean lord, since you are nearest, I turn in prayer.   *10*
Receive these offerings, and grant us deliverance
From defilement. Our hearts are heavy with fear
When we see our leader distracted, as helpless sailors
Are terrified by the confusion of their helmsman.

Enter Messenger.

Messenger. Friends, no doubt you can direct me: *15*
        Where shall I find the house of Oedipus,
        Or, better still, where is the King himself?
Choragos. It is this very place, stranger; he is inside.
        This is his wife and mother of his children.
Messenger. I wish her happiness in a happy house,   *20*
        Blest in all the fulfillment of her marriage.
Iocastê. I wish as much for you: your courtesy
        Deserves a like good fortune. But now, tell me:
        Why have you come? What have you to say to us?
Messenger. Good news, my lady, for your house and your
                husband.   *25*
Iocastê. What news? Who sent you here?
Messenger.   I am from Corinth.
        The news I bring ought to mean joy for you,
        Though it may be you will find some grief in it.
Iocastê. What is it? How can it touch us in both ways?
Messenger. The people of Corinth, they say,   *30*
        Intend to call Oedipus to be their king.
Iocastê. But old Polybos — is he not reigning still?
Messenger. No. Death holds him in his sepulchre.
Iocastê. What are you saying? Polybos is dead?
Messenger. If I am not telling the truth, may I die myself. *35*
Iocastê (to a Maidservant). Go in, go quickly; tell this to your
                master.

        O riddlers of God's will, where are you now!
        This was the man whom Oedipus, long ago,

Feared so, fled so, in dread of destroying him —
But it was another fate by which he died.   40

Enter Oedipus, center.

Oedipus. Dearest Iocastê, why have you sent for me?
Iocastê. Listen to what this man says, and then tell me
　　What has become of the solemn prophecies.
Oedipus. Who is this man? What is his news for me?
Iocastê. He has come from Corinth to announce your
　　　　father's death!   45
Oedipus. Is it true, stranger? Tell me in your own words.
Messenger. I cannot say it more clearly: the King is dead.
Oedipus. Was it by treason? Or by an attack of illness?
Messenger. A little thing brings old men to their rest.
Oedipus. It was sickness, then?
Messenger.　　　　　　　　　Yes, and his many years.   50
Oedipus. Ah!
　　Why should a man respect the Pythian hearth,° or
　　Give heed to the birds that jangle above his head?
　　They prophesied that I should kill Polybos,
　　Kill my own father; but he is dead and buried,   55
　　And I am here — I never touched him, never,
　　Unless he died in grief for my departure,
　　And thus, in a sense, through me. No. Polybos
　　Has packed the oracles off with him underground.
　　They are empty words.
Iocastê.　　　　　　　　　Had I not told you so?   60
Oedipus. You had; it was my faint heart that betrayed me.
Iocastê. From now on never think of those things again.
Oedipus. And yet — must I not fear my mother's bed?
Iocastê. Why should anyone in this world be afraid,
　　Since Fate rules us and nothing can be foreseen?   65
　　A man should live only for the present day.
　　Have no more fear of sleeping with your mother
　　How many men, in dreams, have lain with their mothers!
　　No reasonable man is troubled by such things.
Oedipus. That is true; only —   70
　　If only my mother were not still alive!
　　But she is alive. I cannot help my dread.
Iocastê. Yet this news of your father's death is wonderful.
Oedipus. Wonderful. But I fear the living woman.

Scene III.　 [52]*Pythian heart* Delphi (also called Pytho because a great snake had
lived there), where Apollo spoke through a priestess

Messenger. Tell me, who is this woman that you fear?   75
Oedipus. It is Meropê, man; the wife of King Polybos.
Messenger. Meropê? Why should you be afraid of her?
Oedipus. An oracle of the gods, a dreadful saying.
Messenger. Can you tell me about it or are you sworn to silence?
Oedipus. I can tell you, and I will.   80
    Apollo said through his prophet that I was the man
    Who should marry his own mother, shed his father's blood
    With his own hands. And so, for all these years
    I have kept clear of Corinth, and no harm has come —
    Though it would have been sweet to see my parents
        again.   85
Messenger. And is this the fear that drove you out of Corinth?
Oedipus. Would you have me kill my father?
Messenger.   As for that
    You must be reassured by the news I gave you.
Oedipus. If you could reassure me, I would reward you.
Messenger. I had that in mind, I will confess: I thought   90
    I could count on you when you returned to Corinth.
Oedipus. No: I will never go near my parents again.
Messenger. Ah, son, you still do not know what you are doing —
Oedipus. What do you mean? In the name of God tell me!
Messenger. — If these are your reasons for not going home.   95
Oedipus. I tell you, I fear the oracle may come true.
Messenger. And guilt may come upon you through your parents?
Oedipus. That is the dread that is always in my heart.
Messenger. Can you not see that all your fears are groundless?
Oedipus. How can you say that? They are my parents,
    surely?   100
Messenger. Polybos was not your father.
Oedipus.   Not my father?
Messenger. No more your father than the man speaking to you.
Oedipus. But you are nothing to me!
Messenger.   Neither was he.
Oedipus. Then why did he call me son?
Messenger.   I will tell you:
    Long ago he had you from my hands, as a gift.   105
Oedipus. Then how could he love me so, if I was not his?
Messenger. He had no children, and his heart turned to you.
Oedipus. What of you? Did you buy me? Did you find me by
    chance?
Messenger. I came upon you in the crooked pass of Kithairon.
Oedipus. And what were you doing there?
Messenger.   Tending my flocks.   110

Oedipus. A wandering shepherd?
Messenger.   But your savior, son, that day.
Oedipus. From what did you save me?
Messenger.   Your ankles should tell you that.
Oedipus. Ah, stranger, why do you speak of that childhood pain?
Messenger. I cut the bonds that tied your ankles together.
Oedipus. I have had the mark as long as I can remember.   115
Messenger. That was why you were given the name you bear.°
Oedipus. God! Was it my father or my mother who did it?
  Tell me!
Messenger. I do not know. The man who gave you to me
  Can tell you better than I.   120
Oedipus. It was not you that found me, but another?
Messenger. It was another shepherd gave you to me.
Oedipus. Who was he? Can you tell me who he was?
Messenger. I think he was said to be one of Laïos' people.
Oedipus. You mean the Laïos who was king here years ago?   125
Messenger. Yes; King Laïos; and the man was one of his
            herdsmen.
Oedipus. Is he still alive? Can I see him?
Messenger.   These men here
  Know best about such things.
Oedipus.   Does anyone here
  Know this shepherd that he is talking about?
  Have you seen him in the fields, or in the town?   130
  If you have, tell me. It is time things were made plain.
Choragos. I think the man he means is that same shepherd
            You have already asked to see. Iocastê perhaps
            Could tell you something.
Oedipus.   Do you know anything
  About him, Lady? Is he the man we have summoned?   135
  Is that the man this shepherd means?
Iocastê.   Why think of him?
  Forget this herdsman. Forget it all.
  This talk is a waste of time.
Oedipus.   How can you say that,
  When the clues to my true birth are in my hands?
Iocastê. For God's love, let us have no more questioning!   140
  Is your life nothing to you?
  My own is pain enough for me to bear.
Oedipus. You need not worry. Suppose my mother a slave,
            And born of slaves: no baseness can touch you.

---

¹¹⁶**name you bear** "Oedipus" means "swollen-foot"

Iocastê. Listen to me, I beg you: do not do this thing!   *145*
Oedipus. I will not listen; the truth must be made known.
Iocastê. Everything that I say is for your own good!
Oedipus.   My own good
    Snaps my patience, then: I want none of it.
Iocastê. You are fatally wrong! May you never learn who you are!
Oedipus. Go, one of you, and bring the shepherd here.   *150*
    Let us leave this woman to brag of her royal name.
Iocastê. Ah, miserable!
    That is the only word I have for you now.
    That is the only word I can ever have.
                        Exit into the palace.
Choragos. Why has she left us, Oedipus? Why has she gone   *155*
    In such a passion of sorrow? I fear this silence:
    Something dreadful may come of it.
Oedipus.   Let it come!
    However base my birth, I must know about it.
    The Queen, like a woman, is perhaps ashamed
    To think of my low origin. But I   *160*
    Am a child of luck; I cannot be dishonored.
    Luck is my mother; the passing months, my brothers,
    Have seen me rich and poor. If this is so,
    How could I wish that I were someone else?
    How could I not be glad to know my birth?   *165*

ODE III

Chorus. If ever the coming time were known   *Strophe*
    To my heart's pondering,
    Kithairon, now by Heaven I see the torches
    At the festival of the next full moon,
    And see the dance, and hear the choir sing   *5*
    A grace to your gentle shade:
    Mountain where Oedipus was found,
    O mountain guard of a noble race!
    May the god who heals us lend his aid,
    And let that glory come to pass   *10*
    For our king's cradling-ground.

    Of the nymphs that flower beyond the years,   *Antistrophe*
    Who bore you, royal child,

To Pan of the hills or the timberline Apollo,
Cold in delight where the upland clears,   *15*
Or Hermês for whom Kyllenê's° heights are piled?
Or flushed as evening cloud,
Great Dionysos, roamer of mountains,
He — was it he who found you there,
And caught you up in his own proud   *20*
Arms from the sweet god-ravisher
Who laughed by the Muses' fountains?

SCENE IV

Oedipus. Sirs: though I do not know the man,
   I think I see him coming, this shepherd we want:
   He is old, like our friend here, and the men
   Bringing him seem to be servants of my house.
   But you can tell, if you have ever seen him.   *5*

   Enter Shepherd escorted by servants.

Choragos. I know him, he was Laïos' man. You can trust him.
Oedipus. Tell me first, you from Corinth: is this the shepherd
   We were discussing?
Messenger.   This is the very man.
Oedipus (to Shepherd). Come here. No, look at me. You must
      answer
   Everything I ask. — You belonged to Laïos?   *10*
Shepherd. Yes: born his slave, brought up in his house.
Oedipus. Tell me: what kind of work did you do for him?
Shepherd. I was a shepherd of his, most of my life.
Oedipus. Where mainly did you go for pasturage?
Shepherd. Sometimes Kithairon, sometimes the hills near-by.   *15*
Oedipus. Do you remember ever seeing this man out there?
Shepherd. What would he be doing there? This man?
Oedipus. This man standing here. Have you ever seen him
      before?
Shepherd. No. At least, not to my recollection.
Messenger. And that is not strange, my lord. But I'll refresh   *20*
   His memory: he must remember when we two
   Spent three whole seasons together, March to September,

Ode III. **¹⁶Hermês . . . Kyllenê's** Hermês, messenger of the gods, was said to
have been born on Mt. Kyllenê.

On Kithairon or thereabouts. He had two flocks;
I had one. Each autumn I'd drive mine home
And he would go back with his to Laïos' sheepfold. — 25
Is this not true, just as I have described it?
Shepherd. True, yes; but it was all so long ago.
Messenger. Well, then: do you remember, back in those days
That you gave me a baby boy to bring up as my own?
Shepherd. What if I did? What are you trying to say?   30
Messenger. King Oedipus was once that little child.
Shepherd. Damn you, hold your tongue!
Oedipus.   No more of that!
It is your tongue needs watching, not this man's.
Shepherd. My King, my Master, what is it I have done wrong?
Oedipus. You have not answered his question about the boy. 35
Shepherd. He does not know . . . He is only making trouble . . .
Oedipus. Come, speak plainly, or it will go hard with you.
Shepherd. In God's name, do not torture an old man!
Oedipus. Come here, one of you; bind his arms behind him.
Shepherd. Unhappy king! What more do you wish to learn?   40
Oedipus. Did you give this man the child he speaks of?
Shepherd.   I did.
And I would to God I had died that very day.
Oedipus. You will die now unless you speak the truth.
Shepherd. Yet if I speak the truth, I am worse than dead.
Oedipus. Very well; since you insist upon delaying —   45
Shepherd. No! I have told you already that I gave him the boy.
Oedipus. Where did you get him? From your house?
        From somewhere else?
Shepherd. Not from mine, no. A man gave him to me.
Oedipus. Is that man here? Do you know whose slave he was?
Shepherd. For God's love, my King, do not ask me
        any more!   50
Oedipus. You are a dead man if I have to ask you again.
Shepherd. Then . . . Then the child was from the palace of Laïos.
Oedipus. A slave child? or a child of his own line?
Shepherd. Ah, I am on the brink of dreadful speech!
Oedipus. And I of dreadful hearing. Yet I must hear.   55
Shepherd. If you must be told, then . . .
                        They said it was Laïos' child,
But it is your wife who can tell you about that.
Oedipus. My wife! — Did she give it to you?
Shepherd.   My lord, she did.
Oedipus. Do you know why?

Shepherd.   I was told to get rid of it.
Oedipus. An unspeakable mother!
Shepherd.   There had been prophecies . . .   *60*
Oedipus. Tell me.
Shepherd.   It was said that the boy would kill his own father.
Oedipus. Then why did you give him over to this old man?
Shepherd. I pitied the baby, my King,
      And I thought that this man would take him far away
      To his own country.
                    He saved him — but for what a fate!   *65*
      For if you are what this man says you are,
      No man living is more wretched than Oedipus.
Oedipus. Ah God!
            It was true!
                  All the prophecies!
                              — Now,
      O Light, may I look on you for the last time!   *70*
      I, Oedipus,
      Oedipus, damned in his birth, in his marriage damned,
      Damned in the blood he shed with his own hand!

He rushes into the palace.

ODE IV

Chorus. Alas for the seed of men.   *Strophe 1*

      What measure shall I give these generations
      That breathe on the void and are void
      And exist and do not exist?

      Who bears more weight of joy   *5*
      Than mass of sunlight shifting in images,
      Or who shall make his thought stay on
      That down time drifts away?

      Your splendor is all fallen.

      O naked brow of wrath and tears,   *10*
      O change of Oedipus!
      I who saw your days call no man blest —
      Your great days like ghósts góne.

      That mind was a strong bow.   *Anitistrophe 1*
      Deep, how deep you drew it then, hard archer,   *15*

At a dim fearful range,
And brought dear glory down!

You overcame the stranger —
The virgin with her hooking lion claws —
And though death sang, stood like a tower   20
To make pale Thebes take heart.

Fortress against our sorrow!

Divine king, giver of laws,
Majestic Oedipus!
No prince in Thebes had ever such renown,   25
No prince won such grace of power.

And now of all men ever known   *Strophe 2*
Most pitiful is this man's story:
His fortunes are most changed, his state
Fallen to a low slave's   30
Ground under bitter fate.

O Oedipus, most royal one!
The great door that expelled you to the light
Gave it night — ah, gave night to your glory:
As to the father, to the fathering son.   35

All understood too late.

How could that queen whom Laïos won,
The garden that he harrowed at his height,
Be silent when that act was done?

But all eyes fail before time's eye,   *Antistrophe 2*   40
All actions come to justice there.
Though never willed, though far down the deep past,
Your bed, your dread sirings,
Are brought to book at last.
Child by Laïos doomed to die,   45
Then doomed to lose that fortunate little death,
Would God you never took breath in this air
That with my wailing lips I take to cry:

For I weep the world's outcast.

I was blind, and now I can tell why: 50
Asleep, for you had given ease of breath
To Thebes, while the false years went by.

EXODOS

Enter, from the palace, Second Messenger.

Second Messenger. Elders of Thebes, most honored in this land,
What horrors are yours to see and hear, what weight
Of sorrow to be endured, if, true to your birth,
You venerate the line of Labdakos!
I think neither Istros nor Phasis, those great rivers,   *5*
Could purify this place of the corruption
It shelters now, or soon must bring to light —
Evil not done unconsciously, but willed.

The greatest griefs are those we cause ourselves.
Choragos. Surely, friend, we have grief enough already;   *10*
What new sorrow do you mean?
Second Messenger.   The Queen is dead.
Choragos. Iocastê? Dead? But at whose hand?
Second Messenger.   Her own.
The full horror of what happened you cannot know,
For you did not see it; but I, who did, will tell you
As clearly as I can how she met her death.   *15*

When she had left us,
In passionate silence, passing through the court,
She ran to her apartment in the house,
Her hair clutched by the fingers of both hands.
She closed the doors behind her; then, by that bed   *20*
Where long ago the fatal son was conceived —
That son who should bring about his father's death —
We heard her call upon Laïos, dead so many years,
And heard her wail for the double fruit of her marriage,
A husband by her husband, children by her child.   *25*

Exactly how she died I do not know:
For Oedipus burst in moaning and would not let us
Keep vigil to the end: it was by him
As he stormed about the room that our eyes were caught.
From one to another of us he went, begging a sword,   *30*
Cursing the wife who was not his wife, the mother
Whose womb had carried his own children and himself.
I do not know: it was none of us aided him,
But surely one of the gods was in control!
For with a dreadful cry   *35*
He hurled his weight, as though wrenched out of himself,

At the twin doors: the bolts gave, and he rushed in.
And there we saw her hanging, her body swaying
From the cruel cord she had noosed about her neck.
A great sob broke from him heartbreaking to hear,   *40*
As he loosed the rope and lowered her to the ground.

I would blot out from my mind what happened next!
For the King ripped from her gown the golden brooches
That were her ornament, and raised them, and plunged
    them down
Straight into his own eyeballs, crying, "No more,   *45*
No more shall you look on the misery about me,
The horrors of my own doing! Too long you have known
The faces of those whom I should never have seen,
Too long been blind to those for whom I was searching!
From this hour, go in darkness!" And as he spoke,   *50*
He struck at his eyes — not once, but many times;
And the blood spattered his beard,
Bursting from his ruined sockets like red hail.

So from the unhappiness of two this evil has sprung,
A curse on the man and woman alike. The old   *55*
Happiness of the house of Labdakos
Was happiness enough: where is it today?
It is all wailing and ruin, disgrace, death — all
The misery of mankind that has a name —
And it is wholly and for ever theirs.   *60*
Choragos. Is he in agony still? Is there no rest for him?
Second Messenger. He is calling for someone to lead him to
    the gates
So that all the children of Kadmos may look upon
His father's murderer, his mother's — no,
I cannot say it!
             And then he will leave Thebes,   *65*
Self-exiled, in order that the curse
Which he himself pronounced may depart from the house.
He is weak, and there is none to lead him,
So terrible is his suffering.
              But you will see:
Look, the doors are opening; in a moment   *70*
You will see a thing that would crush a heart of stone.

The central door is opened; Oedipus, blinded, is led in.

Choragos. Dreadful indeed for men to see.

Never have my own eyes
Looked on a sight so full of fear.

Oedipus!   *75*
What madness came upon you, what daemon°
Leaped on your life with heavier
Punishment than a mortal man can bear?
No: I cannot even
Look at you, poor ruined one.   *80*
And I would speak, question, ponder,
If I were able. No.
You make me shudder.
Oedipus. God. God.
Is there a sorrow greater?   *85*
Where shall I find harbor in this world?
My voice is hurled far on a dark wind.
What has God done to me?
Choragos. Too terrible to think of, or to see.

Oedipus. O cloud of night,   *Strophe 1*   *90*
Never to be turned away: night coming on,
I cannot tell how: night like a shroud!
My fair winds brought me here.
                              Oh God. Again
The pain of the spikes where I had sight,
The flooding pain   *95*
Of memory, never to be gouged out.
Choragos. This is not strange.
You suffer it all twice over, remorse in pain,
Pain in remorse.

Oedipus. Ah dear friend   *Antistrophe 1*   *100*
Are you faithful even yet, you alone?
Are you still standing near me, will you stay here,
Patient, to care for the blind?
                              The blind man!
Yet even blind I know who it is attends me,
By the voice's tone —   *105*
Though my new darkness hide the comforter.
Choragos. Oh fearful act!
What god was it drove you to rake black
Night across your eyes?

Exodos. ⁷⁶*daemon* a spirit, not necessarily evil

Oedipus. Apollo. Apollo. Dear   *Strophe 2*   *110*
   Children, the god was Apollo.
   He brought my sick, sick fate upon me.
   But the blinding hand was my own!
   How could I bear to see
   When all my sight was horror everywhere?   *115*
Choragos. Everywhere; that is true.
Oedipus. And now what is left?
   Images? Love? A greeting even,
   Sweet to the senses? Is there anything?
   Ah, no, friends: lead me away.   *120*
   Lead me away from Thebes.
                  Lead the great wreck
   And hell of Oedipus, whom the gods hate.
Choragos. Your fate is clear, you are not blind to that.
   Would God you had never found it out!

Oedipus. Death take the man who unbound   *Antistrophe 2*   *125*
   My feet on that hillside
   And delivered me from death to life! What life?
   If only I had died,
   This weight of monstrous doom
   Could not have dragged me and my darlings down.   *130*
Choragos. I would have wished the same.
Oedipus. Oh never to have come here
   With my father's blood upon me! Never
   To have been the man they call his mother's husband!
   Oh accurst! Oh child of evil,   *135*
   To have entered that wretched bed —
                 the selfsame one!
   More primal than sin itself, this fell to me.
Choragos. I do not know how I can answer you.
   You were better dead than alive and blind.
Oedipus. Do not counsel me any more. This punishment   *140*
   That I have laid upon myself is just.
   If I had eyes,
   I do not know how I could bear the sight
   Of my father, when I came to the house of Death,
   Or my mother: for I have sinned against them both   *145*
   So vilely that I could not make my peace
   By strangling my own life.
             Or do you think my children,
   Born as they were born, would be sweet to my eyes?
   Ah never, never! Nor this town with its high walls,

Nor the holy images of the gods.
For I, *150*
Thrice miserable — Oedipus, noblest of all the line
Of Kadmos, have condemned myself to enjoy
These things no more, by my own malediction
Expelling that man whom the gods declared
To be a defilement in the house of Laïos. *155*
After exposing the rankness of my own guilt,
How could I look men frankly in the eyes?
No, I swear it,
If I could have stifled my hearing at its source,
I would have done it and made all this body *160*
A tight cell of misery, blank to light and sound:
So I should have been safe in a dark agony
Beyond all recollection.
Ah Kithairon!
Why did you shelter me? When I was cast upon you,
Why did I not die? Then I should never *165*
Have shown the world my execrable birth.

Ah Polybos! Corinth, city that I believed
The ancient seat of my ancestors: how fair
I seemed, your child! And all the while this evil
Was cancerous within me!
For I am sick *170*
In my daily life, sick in my origin.

O three roads, dark ravine, woodland and way
Where three roads met: you, drinking my father's blood,
My own blood, spilled by my own hand: can you remember
The unspeakable things I did there, and the things *175*
I went on from there to do?
O marriage, marriage!
The act that engendered me, and again the act
Performed by the son in the same bed —
Ah, the net
Of incest, mingling fathers, brothers, sons,
With brides, wives, mothers: the last evil *180*
That can be known by men: no tongue can say
How evil!
No. For the love of God, conceal me
Somewhere far from Thebes; or kill me; or hurl me
Into the sea, away from men's eyes for ever.
Come, lead me. You need not fear to touch me. *185*
Of all men, I alone can bear this guilt.

Enter Creon.

Choragos. We are not the ones to decide; but Creon here
    May fitly judge of what you ask. He only
    Is left to protect the city in your place.
Oedipus. Alas, how can I speak to him? What right have I   *190*
    To beg his courtesy whom I have deeply wronged?
Creon. I have not come to mock you, Oedipus,
    Or to reproach you, either.
    (*To Attendants.*)   — You, standing there:
    If you have lost all respect for man's dignity,
    At least respect the flame of Lord Helios: *195*
    Do not allow this pollution to show itself
    Openly here, an affront to the earth
    And Heaven's rain and the light of day. No, take him
    Into the house as quickly as you can.
    For it is proper   *200*
    That only the close kindred see his grief.
Oedipus. I pray you in God's name, since your courtesy
    Ignores my dark expectation, visiting
    With mercy this man of all men most execrable:
    Give me what I ask — for your good, not for mine.   *205*
Creon. And what is it that you would have me do?
Oedipus. Drive me out of this country as quickly as may be
    To a place where no human voice can ever greet me.
Creon. I should have done that before now — only,
    God's will had not been wholly revealed to me.   *210*
Oedipus. But his command is plain: the parricide
    Must be destroyed. I am that evil man.
Creon. That is the sense of it, yes; but as things are,
    We had best discover clearly what is to be done.
Oedipus. You would learn more about a man like me?   *215*
Creon. You are ready now to listen to the god.
Oedipus. I will listen. But it is to you
    That I must turn for help. I beg you, hear me.

    The woman in there —
    Give her whatever funeral you think proper: *220*
    She is your sister.
                  — But let me go, Creon!
    Let me purge my father's Thebes of the pollution
    Of my living here, and go out to the wild hills,
    To Kithairon, that has won such fame with me,
    The tomb my mother and father appointed for me,   *225*
    And let me die there, as they willed I should.

And yet I know
Death will not ever come to me through sickness
Or in any natural way: I have been preserved
For some unthinkable fate. But let that be.   *230*
As for my sons, you need not care for them.
They are men, they will find some way to live.
But my poor daughters, who have shared my table,
Who never before have been parted from their father —
Take care of them, Creon; do this for me.   *235*
And will you let me touch them with my hands
A last time, and let us weep together?
Be kind, my lord,
Great prince, be kind!
                         Could I but touch them,
They would be mine again, as when I had my eyes.   *240*

Enter Antigonê and Ismenê, attended.

Ah, God!
Is it my dearest children I hear weeping?
Has Creon pitied me and sent my daughters?
Creon. Yes, Oedipus: I knew that they were dear to you
In the old days, and know you must love them still.   *245*
Oedipus. May God bless you for this — and be a friendlier
Guardian to you than he has been to me!

Children, where are you?
Come quickly to my hands: they are your brother's —
Hands that have brought your father's once clear eyes   *250*
To this way of seeing —
                         Ah dearest ones,
I had neither sight nor knowledge then, your father
By the woman who was the source of his own life!
And I weep for you — having no strength to see you — ,
I weep for you when I think of the bitterness   *255*
That men will visit upon you all your lives.
What homes, what festivals can you attend
Without being forced to depart again in tears?
And when you come to marriageable age,
Where is the man, my daughters, who would dare   *260*
Risk the bane that lies on all my children?
Is there any evil wanting? Your father killed
His father; sowed the womb of her who bore him;
Engendered you at the fount of his own existence!
That is what they will say of you.

Then, whom   *265*
Can you ever marry? There are no bridegrooms for you,
And your lives must wither away in sterile dreaming.
O Creon, son of Menoikeus!
You are the only father my daughters have,
Since we, their parents, are both of us gone for ever.   *270*
They are your own blood: you will not let them
Fall into beggary and loneliness;
You will keep them from the miseries that are mine!
Take pity on them; see, they are only children,
Friendless except for you. Promise me this,   *275*
Great Prince, and give me your hand in token of it.

Creon clasps his right hand.

Children:
I could say much, if you could understand me,
But as it is, I have only this prayer for you:
Live where you can, be as happy as you can —   *280*
Happier, please God, than God has made your father!
Creon. Enough. You have wept enough. Now go within.
Oedipus. I must; but it is hard.
Creon.   Time eases all things.
Oedipus. But you must promise —
Creon.   Say what you desire.
Oedipus. Send me from Thebes!
Creon.   God grant that I may!   *285*
Oedipus. But since God hates me . . .
Creon.   No, he will grant your wish.
Oedipus. You promise?
Creon.   I cannot speak beyond my knowledge.
Oedipus. Then lead me in.
Creon.   Come now, and leave your children.
Oedipus. No! Do not take them from me!
Creon.   Think no longer
That you are in command here, but rather think   *290*
How, when you were, you served your own destruction.

*Exeunt into the house all but the Chorus; the Choragos chants
directly to the audience.*

Choragos. Men of Thebes: look upon Oedipus.
This is the king who solved the famous riddle
And towered up, most powerful of men.
No mortal eyes but looked on him with envy,   *295*

Yet in the end ruin swept over him.
Let every man in mankind's frailty
Consider his last day; and let none
Presume on his good fortune until he find
Life, at his death, a memory without pain.   *300*

QUESTIONS

1. On the basis of the Prologue, characterize Oedipus. What additional traits are revealed in Scene I and Ode I?

2. How fair is it to say that Oedipus is morally guilty? Does he argue that he is morally innocent because he did not intend to do immoral deeds? Can it be said that he is guilty of *hybris* but that *hybris* has nothing to do with his fall?

3. Oedipus says that he blinds himself in order not to look upon people he should not. What further reasons can be given? Why does he not (like his mother) commit suicide?

4. How fair is it to say that the play shows the contemptibleness of man's efforts to act intelligently?

5. How fair is it to say that in *Oedipus* the gods are evil?

6. Are the choral odes lyrical interludes that serve to separate the scenes, or do they advance the dramatic action?

7. Matthew Arnold said that Sophocles saw life steadily and saw it whole. But in this play is Sophocles facing the facts of life, or, on the contrary, is he avoiding life as it usually is and presenting a series of unnatural and outrageous coincidences?

8. Can you describe your emotions at the end of the play? Do they include pity for Oedipus? Pity for all human beings, including yourself? Fear that you might be punished for some unintended transgression? Awe, engendered by a perception of the interrelatedness of things? Relief that the story is only a story? Exhilaration?

A NOTE ON THE ELIZABETHAN THEATER

Shakespeare's theater was wooden, round, or polygonal (the Chorus in *Henry V* calls it a "wooden O"). About eight hundred spectators could stand in the yard in front of — and perhaps along the two sides of the stage that jutted from the rear wall, and another fifteen hundred or so spectators could sit in the three roofed galleries that ringed the stage. That portion of the galleries that was above the rear of the stage was sometimes used by actors. Entry to the stage was normally gained by doors at the rear but some use was made of a curtained alcove — or perhaps a booth — between the doors, which allowed characters to be "discovered" (revealed) as in the modern proscenium theater, which normally employs a curtain. A performance was probably uninterrupted by intermissions or by long pauses for the changing of scenery; a group of characters leaves the stage, another enters, and if the locale has changed, the new characters somehow tell us. (Modern editors customarily add indications of locales to help a reader, but it should be understood that the action of the Elizabethan stage was continuous.)

Johannes de Witt, a Continental visitor to London, made a drawing of the Swan Theatre in about the year 1596. The original drawing is lost; this is Arend van Buchel's copy of it.

A NOTE ON THE TEXT OF *HAMLET*

Shakespeare's *Hamlet* comes to us in three versions. The first, known as the First Quarto (Q1), was published in 1603. It is an illegitimate garbled version, perhaps derived from the memory of the actor who played Marcellus (this part is conspicuously more accurate than the rest of the play) in a short version of the play. The second printed version (Q2), which appeared in 1604, is almost twice as long as Q1; all in all, it is the best text we have, doubtless published (as Q1 was not) with the permission of Shakespeare's theatrical company. The third printed version, in the First Folio (the collected edition of Shakespeare's plays, published in 1623), is also legitimate, but it seems to be an acting version, for it lacks some two hundred lines of Q2. On the other hand, the Folio text includes some ninety lines not found in Q2. Because Q2 is the longest version, giving us more of the play as Shakespeare conceived it than either of the other texts, it serves as the basic version for this text. Unfortunately the printers of it often worked carelessly: words and phrases are omitted, there are plain misreadings of what must have been in Shakespeare's manuscript, and speeches are sometimes wrongly assigned. It was therefore necessary to turn to the First Folio for many readings. It has been found useful, also, to divide the play into acts and scenes; these divisions, not found in Q2 (and only a few are found in the Folio), are purely editorial additions, and they are therefore enclosed in square brackets.

William Shakespeare (1564–1616)

The Tragedy of Hamlet

Prince of Denmark

[Dramatis Personae

Claudius, King of Denmark
Hamlet, son to the late, and nephew to the present, King
Polonius, Lord Chamberlain
Horatio, friend to Hamlet
Laertes, son to Polonius
Voltemand
Cornelius
Rosencrantz   } courtiers
Guildenstern
Osric
A Gentleman
A Priest
Marcellus }
Barnardo } officers
Francisco, a soldier
Reynaldo, servant to Polonius
Players
Two Clowns, gravediggers
Fortinbras, Prince of Norway
A Norwegian Captain
English Ambassadors
Gertrude, Queen of Denmark, mother to Hamlet
Ophelia, daughter to Polonius
Ghost of Hamlet's father
Lords, Ladies, Officers, Soldiers, Sailors, Messengers, Attendants

Scene. *Elsinore*]

[ACT 1

Scene I. *A guard platform of the castle.*]

Enter Barnardo and Francisco, two sentinels.

Barnardo. Who's there?

Francisco. Nay, answer me. Stand and unfold°* yourself.
Barnardo. Long live the King!°
Francisco. Barnardo?
Barnardo. He.   5
Francisco. You come most carefully upon your hour.
Barnardo. 'Tis now struck twelve. Get thee to bed, Francisco.
Francisco. For this relief much thanks. 'Tis bitter cold,
      And I am sick at heart.
Barnardo. Have you had quiet guard?
Francisco.   Not a mouse stirring.   10
Barnardo. Well, good night.
      If you do meet Horatio and Marcellus,
      The rivals° of my watch, bid them make haste.

      Enter Horatio and Marcellus.

Francisco. I think I hear them. Stand, ho! Who is there?
Horatio. Friends to this ground.
Marcellus.   And liegemen to the Dane.°   15
Francisco. Give you° good night.
Marcellus.   O, farewell, honest soldier.
      Who hath relieved you?
Francisco.   Barnardo hath my place.
      Give you good night.
                                                                 Exit Francisco.
Marcellus.   Holla, Barnardo!
Barnardo.   Say —
      What, is Horatio there?
Horatio.   A piece of him.
Barnardo. Welcome, Horatio. Welcome, good Marcellus.   20
Marcellus. What, has this thing appeared again tonight?
Barnardo. I have seen nothing.
Marcellus. Horatio says 'tis but our fantasy,
      And will not let belief take hold of him
      Touching this dreaded sight twice seen of us;   25
      Therefore I have entreated him along
      With us to watch the minutes of this night,
      That, if again this apparition come,
      He may approve° our eyes and speak to it.
Horatio. Tush, tush, 'twill not appear.

---

*The notes are Edward Hubler's for the Signet edition of *Hamlet.* I.i.   ²*unfold*
disclose   ³*Long live the King* (perhaps a password, perhaps a greeting)   ¹³*rivals*
partners   ¹⁵*liegemen to the Dane* loyal subjects to the King of Denmark   ¹⁶*Give*
you God give you   ²⁹*approve* confirm

Barnardo.   Sit down awhile,   *30*
     And let us once again assail your ears,
     That are so fortified against our story,
     What we have two nights seen.
Horatio.   Well, sit we down,
     And let us hear Barnardo speak of this.
Barnardo. Last night of all,   *35*
     When yond same star that's westward from the pole°
     Had made his course t' illume that part of heaven
     Where now it burns, Marcellus and myself,
     The bell then beating one ——

     Enter Ghost.

Marcellus. Peace, break thee off. Look where it comes again.   *40*
Barnardo. In the same figure like the king that's dead.
Marcellus. Thou art a scholar; speak to it, Horatio.
Barnardo. Looks 'a not like the king? Mark it, Horatio.
Horatio. Most like: it harrows me with fear and wonder.
Barnardo. It would be spoke to.
Marcellus.   Speak to it, Horatio.   *45*
Horatio. What art thou that usurp'st this time of night,
     Together with that fair and warlike form
     In which the majesty of buried Denmark°
     Did sometimes march? By heaven I charge thee, speak.
Marcellus. It is offended.
Barnardo.   See, it stalks away.   *50*
Horatio. Stay! Speak, speak. I charge thee, speak.

                                             Exit Ghost.

Marcellus. 'Tis gone and will not answer.
Barnardo. How now, Horatio? You tremble and look pale.
     Is not this something more than fantasy?
     What think you on't?   *55*
Horatio. Before my God, I might not this believe
     Without the sensible and true avouch°
     Of mine own eyes.
Marcellus.   Is it not like the King?
Horatio. As thou art to thyself.
     Such was the very armor he had on   *60*
     When he the ambitious Norway° combated:
     So frowned he once, when, in an angry parle,°
     He smote the sledded Polacks° on the ice.

---

³⁶*pole* polestar   ⁴⁸*buried Denmark* the buried King of Denmark   ⁵⁷*sensible and*
true avouch sensory and true proof   ⁶¹*Norway* King of Norway   ⁶²*parle* parley
⁶³*sledded Polacks* Poles in sledges

'Tis strange.

Marcellus. Thus twice before, and jump° at this dead hour,   65
    With martial stalk hath he gone by our watch.

Horatio. In what particular thought to work I know not;
    But, in the gross and scope° of my opinion,
    This bodes some strange eruption to our state.

Marcellus. Good now, sit down, and tell me he that knows,   70
    Why this same strict and most observant watch
    So nightly toils the subject° of the land,
    And why such daily cast of brazen cannon
    And foreign mart° for implements of war,
    Why such impress° of shipwrights, whose sore task   75
    Does not divide the Sunday from the week,
    What might be toward° that this sweaty haste
    Doth make the night joint-laborer with the day?
    Who is't that can inform me?

Horatio.   That can I.
    At least the whisper goes so: our last king,   80
    Whose image even but now appeared to us,
    Was, as you know, by Fortinbras of Norway,
    Thereto pricked on by a most emulate pride,
    Dared to the combat; in which our valiant Hamlet
    (For so this side of our known world esteemed him)   85
    Did slay this Fortinbras, who, by a sealed compact
    Well ratified by law and heraldry,°
    Did forfeit, with his life, all those his lands
    Which he stood seized° of, to the conqueror;
    Against the which a moiety competent°   90
    Was gagèd° by our King, which had returned
    To the inheritance of Fortinbras,
    Had he been vanquisher, as, by the same comart°
    And carriage of the article designed,°
    His fell to Hamlet. Now, sir, young Fortinbras,   95
    Of unimprovèd° mettle hot and full,
    Hath in the skirts° of Norway here and there
    Sharked up° a list of lawless resolutes,°

°**65jump** just   °**68gross and scope** general drift   °**72toils the subject** makes the subjects
toil   °**74mart** trading   °**75impress** forced service   °**77toward** in preparation   °**87law and
heraldry** heraldic law (governing the combat)   °**89seized** possessed   °**90moiety competent**
equal portion   °**91gagèd** engaged, pledged   °**93comart** agreement   °**94carriage of the
article designed** import of the agreement drawn up   °**96unimprovèd** untried   °**97skirts**
borders   °**98Sharked up** collected indiscriminately (as a shark gulps its prey)   °**98resolutes**
desperadoes

For food and diet, to some enterprise
That hath a stomach in't;° which is no other,   *100*
As it doth well appear unto our state,
But to recover of us by strong hand
And terms compulsatory, those foresaid lands
So by his father lost; and this, I take it,
Is the main motive of our preparations,   *105*
The source of this our watch, and the chief head°
Of this posthaste and romage° in the land.

Barnardo. I think it be no other but e'en so;
     Well may it sort° that this portentous figure
     Comes armèd through our watch so like the King   *110*
     That was and is the question of these wars.

Horatio. A mote it is to trouble the mind's eye:
     In the most high and palmy state of Rome,
     A little ere the mightiest Julius fell,
     The graves stood tenantless, and the sheeted dead   *115*
     Did squeak and gibber in the Roman streets;°
     As stars with trains of fire and dews of blood,
     Disasters° in the sun; and the moist star,°
     Upon whose influence Neptune's empire stands,
     Was sick almost to doomsday with eclipse.   *120*
     And even the like precurse° of feared events,
     As harbingers° preceding still° the fates
     And prologue to the omen° coming on,
     Have heaven and earth together demonstrated
     Unto our climatures° and countrymen.   *125*

Enter Ghost.

But soft, behold, lo where it comes again!
I'll cross it,° though it blast me. — Stay, illusion.

It spreads his° arms.

If thou hast any sound or use of voice,
Speak to me.

---

¹⁰⁰***hath a stomach in't*** i.e., requires courage   ¹⁰⁶***head*** fountainhead, origin   ¹⁰⁷***romage***
bustle   ¹⁰⁹***sort*** befit   ¹¹⁶***Did squeak . . . Roman streets*** (the break in the sense which
follows this line suggests that a line has dropped out)   ¹¹⁸***Disasters*** threatening
signs   ¹¹⁸***moist star*** moon   ¹²¹***precurse*** precursor, foreshadowing   ¹²²***harbingers***
forerunners   ¹²²***still*** always   ¹²³***omen*** calamity   ¹²⁵***climatures*** regions   ¹²⁷***cross it*** (1)
cross its path, confront it, (2) make the sign of the cross in front of it   ¹²⁷ ˢ·ᵈ·***his***
i.e., its, the ghost's (though possibly what is meant is that Horatio spreads his
own arms, making a cross of himself)

If there be any good thing to be done   *130*
That may to thee do ease and grace to me,
Speak to me.
If thou art privy to thy country's fate,
Which happily° foreknowing may avoid,
O, speak!   *135*
Or if thou hast uphoarded in thy life
Extorted° treasure in the womb of earth,
For which, they say, you spirits oft walk in death,

The cock crows.

Speak of it. Stay and speak. Stop it, Marcellus.
Marcellus. Shall I strike at it with my partisan°?   *140*
Horatio. Do, if it will not stand.
Barnardo.   'Tis here.
Horatio.   'Tis here.
Marcellus. 'Tis gone.

                                             Exit Ghost.

We do it wrong, being so majestical,
To offer it the show of violence,
For it is as the air, invulnerable,   *145*
And our vain blows malicious mockery.
Barnardo. It was about to speak when the cock crew.
Horatio. And then it started, like a guilty thing
Upon a fearful summons. I have heard,
The cock, that is the trumpet to the morn,   *150*
Doth with his lofty and shrill-sounding throat
Awake the god of day, and at his warning,
Whether in sea or fire, in earth or air,
Th' extravagant and erring° spirit hies
To his confine; and of the truth herein   *155*
This present object made probation.°
Marcellus. It faded on the crowing of the cock.
Some say that ever 'gainst° that season comes
Wherein our Savior's birth is celebrated,
This bird of dawning singeth all night long,   *160*
And then, they say, no spirit dare stir abroad,
The nights are wholesome, then no planets strike,°
No fairy takes,° nor witch hath power to charm:
So hallowed and so gracious is that time.

---

[134]*happily* haply, perhaps   [137]*Extorted* ill-won   [140]*partisan* pike (a long-handled weapon)   [154]*extravagant and erring* out of bounds and wandering   [156]*probation* proof   [158]*'gainst* just before   [162]*strike* exert an evil influence   [163]*takes* bewitches

Horatio. So have I heard and do in part believe it.   165
    But look, the morn in russet mantle clad
    Walks o'er the dew of yon high eastward hill.
    Break we our watch up, and by my advice
    Let us impart what we have seen tonight
    Unto young Hamlet, for upon my life   170
    This spirit, dumb to us, will speak to him.
    Do you consent we shall acquaint him with it,
    As needful in our loves, fitting our duty?
Marcellus. Let's do 't, I pray, and I this morning know
    Where we shall find him most convenient.   175
                                 Exeunt.

[Scene II. *The castle.*]

*Flourish.° Enter Claudius, King of Denmark, Gertrude the Queen,
Councilors, Polonius and his son Laertes, Hamlet, cum aliis° [including Voltemand and Cornelius].*

King. Though yet of Hamlet our dear brother's death
    The memory be green, and that it us befitted
    To bear our hearts in grief, and our whole kingdom
    To be contracted in one brow of woe,
    Yet so far hath discretion fought with nature   5
    That we with wisest sorrow think on him
    Together with remembrance of ourselves.
    Therefore our sometime sister,° now our Queen,
    Th' imperial jointress° to this warlike state,
    Have we, as 'twere, with a defeated joy,   10
    With an auspicious° and a dropping eye,
    With mirth in funeral, and with dirge in marriage,
    In equal scale weighing delight and dole,
    Taken to wife. Nor have we herein barred
    Your better wisdoms, which have freely gone   15
    With this affair along. For all, our thanks.
    Now follows that you know young Fortinbras,
    Holding a weak supposal of our worth,
    Or thinking by our late dear brother's death
    Our state to be disjoint and out of frame,°   20
    Colleaguèd with this dream of his advantage,°

I.ii. ^{s.d.}***Flourish*** fanfare of trumpets ^{s.d.}***cum aliis*** with others (Latin) ⁸***our sometime
sister*** my (the royal "we") former sister-in-law ⁹***jointress*** joint tenant,
partner ¹¹***auspicious*** joyful ²⁰***frame*** order ²¹***advantage*** superiority

He hath not failed to pester us with message,
Importing the surrender of those lands
Lost by his father, with all bands of law,
To our most valiant brother. So much for him.   *25*
Now for ourself and for this time of meeting.
Thus much the business is: we have here writ
To Norway, uncle of young Fortinbras —
Who, impotent and bedrid, scarcely hears
Of this his nephew's purpose — to suppress   *30*
His further gait° herein, in that the levies,
The lists, and full proportions° are all made
Out of his subject;° and we here dispatch
You, good Cornelius, and you, Voltemand,
For bearers of this greeting to old Norway,   *35*
Giving to you no further personal power
To business with the King, more than the scope
Of these delated articles° allow.
Farewell, and let your haste commend your duty.
Cornelius, Voltemand. In that, and all things, will we show our
    duty.   *40*
King. We doubt it nothing. Heartily farewell.
                      Exit Voltemand and Cornelius.
And now, Laertes, what's the news with you?
You told us of some suit. What is't, Laertes?
You cannot speak of reason to the Dane
And lose your voice.° What wouldst thou beg, Laertes,   *45*
That shall not be my offer, not thy asking?
The head is not more native° to the heart,
The hand more instrumental to the mouth,
Than is the throne of Denmark to thy father.
What wouldst thou have, Laertes?
Laertes.   My dread lord,   *50*
Your leave and favor to return to France,
From whence though willingly I came to Denmark
To show my duty in your coronation,
Yet now I must confess, that duty done,
My thoughts and wishes bend again toward France   *55*
And bow them to your gracious leave and pardon.
King. Have you your father's leave? What says Polonius?
Polonius. He hath, my lord, wrung from me my slow leave

---

[31]*gait* proceeding   [32]*proportions* supplies for war   [33]*Out of his subject* i.e., out of
old Norway's subjects and realm   [38]*delated articles* detailed documents   [45]*lose your
voice* waste your breath   [47]*native* related

By laborsome petition, and at last
Upon his will I sealed my hard consent.°   *60*
I do beseech you give him leave to go.
King. Take thy fair hour, Laertes. Time be thine,
And thy best graces spend it at thy will.
But now, my cousin° Hamlet, and my son ——
Hamlet [*aside*]. A little more than kin, and less than kind!°   *65*
King. How is it that the clouds still hang on you?
Hamlet. Not so, my lord. I am too much in the sun.°
Queen. Good Hamlet, cast thy nighted color off,
And let thine eye look like a friend on Denmark.
Do not forever with thy vailèd° lids   *70*
Seek for thy noble father in the dust.
Thou know'st 'tis common; all that lives must die,
Passing through nature to eternity.
Hamlet. Ay, madam, it is common.°
Queen.   If it be,
Why seems it so particular with thee?   *75*
Hamlet. Seems, madam? Nay, it is. I know not "seems."
'Tis not alone my inky cloak, good mother,
Nor customary suits of solemn black,
Nor windy suspiration° of forced breath,
No, nor the fruitful river in the eye,   *80*
Nor the dejected havior of the visage,
Together with all forms, moods, shapes of grief,
That can denote me truly. These indeed seem,
For they are actions that a man might play,
But I have that within which passes show;   *85*
These but the trappings and the suits of woe.
King. 'Tis sweet and commendable in your nature, Hamlet,
To give these mourning duties to your father,
But you must know your father lost a father,
That father lost, lost his, and the survivor bound   *90*
In filial obligation for some term
To do obsequious° sorrow. But to persever
In obstinate condolement° is a course

---

⁶⁰*Upon his . . . hard consent* to his desire I gave my reluctant consent   ⁶⁴*cousin*
kinsman   ⁶⁵*kind* (pun on the meanings "kindly" and "natural"; though doubly
related — *more than kin* — Hamlet asserts that he neither resembles Claudius in
nature or feels kindly toward him)   ⁶⁷*sun* sunshine of royal favor (with a pun on
"son")   ⁷⁰*vailèd* lowered   ⁷⁴*common* (1) universal, (2) vulgar   ⁷⁹*windy suspiration*
heavy sighing   ⁹²*obsequious* suitable to obsequies (funerals)   ⁹³*condolement* mourning

Of impious stubbornness. 'Tis unmanly grief.
It shows a will most incorrect to heaven,   *95*
A heart unfortified, a mind impatient,
An understanding simple and unschooled.
For what we know must be and is as common
As any the most vulgar° thing to sense,
Why should we in our peevish opposition   *100*
Take it to heart? Fie, 'tis a fault to heaven,
A fault against the dead, a fault to nature,
To reason most absurd, whose common theme
Is death of fathers, and who still hath cried,
From the first corse° till he that died today,   *105*
"This must be so." We pray you throw to earth
This unprevailing° woe, and think of us
As of a father, for let the world take note
You are the most immediate to our throne,
And with no less nobility of love   *110*
Than that which dearest father bears his son
Do I impart toward you. For your intent
In going back to school in Wittenberg,
It is most retrograde° to our desire,
And we beseech you, bend you° to remain   *115*
Here in the cheer and comfort of our eye,
Our chiefest courtier, cousin, and our son.
Queen. Let not thy mother lose her prayers, Hamlet.
    I pray thee stay with us, go not to Wittenberg.
Hamlet. I shall in all my best obey you, madam.   *120*
King. Why,'tis a loving and a fair reply.
    Be as ourself in Denmark. Madam, come.
    This gentle and unforced accord of Hamlet
    Sits smiling to my heart, in grace whereof
    No jocund health that Denmark drinks today,   *125*
    But the great cannon to the clouds shall tell,
    And the King's rouse° the heaven shall bruit° again,
    Respeaking earthly thunder. Come away.
                        Flourish. Exeunt all but Hamlet.
Hamlet. O that this too too sullied° flesh would melt,
    Thaw, and resolve itself into a dew,   *130*

---

⁹⁹*vulgar* common   ¹⁰⁵*corse* corpse   ¹⁰⁷*unprevailing* unavailing   ¹¹⁴*retrograde* contrary   ¹¹⁵*bend you* incline   ¹²⁷*rouse* deep drink   ¹²⁷*bruit* announce noisily   ¹²⁹*sullied* (Q2 has *sallied,* here modernized to *sullied,* which makes sense and is therefore given; but the Folio reading, *solid,* which fits better with *melt,* is quite possibly correct)

Or that the Everlasting had not fixed
His canon° 'gainst self-slaughter. O God, God,
How weary, stale, flat, and unprofitable
Seem to me all the uses of this world!
Fie on't, ah, fie, 'tis an unweeded garden   135
That grows to seed. Things rank and gross in nature
Possess it merely.° That it should come to this:
But two months dead, nay, not so much, not two,
So excellent a king, that was to this
Hyperion° to a satyr, so loving to my mother   140
That he might not beteem° the winds of heaven
Visit her face too roughly. Heaven and earth,
Must I remember? Why, she would hang on him
As if increase of appetite had grown
By what it fed on; and yet within a month —   145
Let me not think on't; frailty, thy name is woman —
A little month, or ere those shoes were old
With which she followed my poor father's body
Like Niobe,° all tears, why she, even she —
O God, a beast that wants discourse of reason°   150
Would have mourned longer — married with my uncle,
My father's brother, but no more like my father
Than I to Hercules. Within a month,
Ere yet the salt of most unrighteous tears
Had left the flushing° in her gallèd eyes,   155
She married. O, most wicked speed, to post°
With such dexterity to incestuous° sheets!
It is not, nor it cannot come to good.
But break my heart, for I must hold my tongue.

Enter Horatio, Marcellus, and Barnardo.

Horatio. Hail to your lordship!
Hamlet.   I am glad to see you well.   160
   Horatio — or I do forget myself.
Horatio. The same, my lord, and your poor servant ever.
Hamlet. Sir, my good friend, I'll change° that name with you.
   And what make you from Wittenberg, Horatio?

---

¹³²*canon* law ¹³⁷*merely* entirely ¹⁴⁰*Hyperion* the sun god, a model of
beauty ¹⁴¹*beteem* allow ¹⁴⁹*Niobe* (a mother who wept profusely at the death of
her children) ¹⁵⁰*wants discourse of reason* lacks reasoning power ¹⁵⁵*left the flushing*
stopped reddening ¹⁵⁶*post* hasten ¹⁵⁷*incestuous* (canon law considered marriage
with a deceased brother's widow to be incestuous) ¹⁶³*change* exchange

Marcellus?   *165*

Marcellus. My good lord!

Hamlet. I am very glad to see you. [*To Barnardo.*] Good even, sir.
    But what, in faith, make you from Wittenberg?

Horatio. A truant disposition, good my lord.

Hamlet. I would not hear your enemy say so,   *170*
    Nor shall you do my ear that violence
    To make it truster° of your own report
    Against yourself. I know you are no truant.
    But what is your affair in Elsinore?
    We'll teach you to drink deep ere you depart.   *175*

Horatio. My lord, I came to see your father's funeral.

Hamlet. I prithee do not mock me, fellow student.
    I think it was to see my mother's wedding.

Horatio. Indeed, my lord, it followed hard upon.

Hamlet. Thrift, thrift, Horatio. The funeral baked meats   *180*
    Did coldly furnish forth the marriage tables.
    Would I had met my dearest° foe in heaven
    Or ever I had seen that day, Horatio!
    My father, methinks I see my father.

Horatio. Where, my lord?

Hamlet.   In my mind's eye, Horatio.   *185*

Horatio. I saw him once. 'A° was a goodly king.

Hamlet. 'A was a man, take him for all in all,
    I shall not look upon his like again.

Horatio. My lord, I think I saw him yesternight.

Hamlet. Saw? Who?   *190*

Horatio. My lord, the King your father.

Hamlet.   The King my father?

Horatio. Season your admiration° for a while
    With an attent ear till I may deliver
    Upon the witness of these gentlemen
    This marvel to you.

Hamlet.   For God's love let me hear!   *195*

Horatio. Two nights together had these gentlemen,
    Marcellus and Barnardo, on their watch
    In the dead waste and middle of the night
    Been thus encountered. A figure like your father,
    Armèd at point exactly, cap-a-pe,°   *200*
    Appears before them, and with solemn march

---

[172] ***truster*** believer   [182] ***dearest*** most intensely felt   [186] **'A** he   [192] ***Season your admiration***
control your wonder   [200] ***cap-a-pe*** head to foot

Goes slow and stately by them. Thrice he walked
By their oppressed and fear-surprisèd eyes,
Within his truncheon's length,° whilst they, distilled°
Almost to jelly with the act° of fear,   *205*
Stand dumb and speak not to him. This to me
In dreadful° secrecy impart they did,
And I with them the third night kept the watch,
Where, as they had delivered, both in time,
Form of the thing, each word made true and good,   *210*
The apparition comes. I knew your father.
These hands are not more like.

Hamlet.   But where was this?
Marcellus. My lord, upon the platform where we watched.
Hamlet. Did you not speak to it?
Horatio.   My lord, I did;
But answer made it none. Yet once methought   *215*
It lifted up it° head and did address
Itself to motion like as it would speak:
But even then the morning cock crew loud,
And at the sound it shrunk in haste away
And vanished from our sight.

Hamlet.   'Tis very strange.   *220*
Horatio. As I do live, my honored lord, 'tis true,
And we did think it writ down in our duty
To let you know of it.
Hamlet. Indeed, indeed, sirs, but this troubles me.
Hold you the watch tonight?
All.   We do, my lord.   *225*
Hamlet. Armed, say you?
All. Armed, my lord.
Hamlet. From top to toe?
All.   My lord, from head to foot.
Hamlet. Then saw you not his face.
Horatio. O, yes, my lord. He wore his beaver° up.   *230*
Hamlet. What, looked he frowningly?
Horatio. A countenance more in sorrow than in anger.
Hamlet. Pale or red?
Horatio. Nay, very pale.
Hamlet.   And fixed his eyes upon you?
Horatio. Most constantly.

---

²⁰⁴*truncheon's length* space of a short staff   ²⁰⁴*distilled* reduced   ²⁰⁵*act* action
²⁰⁷*dreadful* terrified   ²¹⁶*it* its   ²³⁰*beaver* visor, face guard

Hamlet.   I would I had been there.   *235*
Horatio. It would have much amazed you.
Hamlet. Very like, very like. Stayed it long?
Horatio. While one with moderate haste might tell° a hundred.
Both. Longer, longer.
Horatio. Not when I saw't.
Hamlet.   His beard was grizzled,° no?   *240*
Horatio. It was as I have seen it in his life,
    A sable silvered.°
Hamlet.   I will watch tonight.
    Perchance 'twill walk again.
Horatio.   I warr'nt it will.
Hamlet. If it assume my noble father's person,
    I'll speak to it though hell itself should gape   *245*
    And bid me hold my peace. I pray you all,
    If you have hitherto concealed this sight,
    Let it be tenable° in your silence still,
    And whatsomever else shall hap tonight,
    Give it an understanding but no tongue;   *250*
    I will requite your loves. So fare you well.
    Upon the platform 'twixt eleven and twelve
    I'll visit you.
All.   Our duty to your honor.
Hamlet. Your loves, as mine to you. Farewell.
                    Exeunt [all but Hamlet].
    My father's spirit — in arms? All is not well.   *255*
    I doubt° some foul play. Would the night were come!
    Till then sit still, my soul. Foul deeds will rise,
    Though all the earth o'erwhelm them, to men's eyes.
                            Exit.

[Scene III. *A room.*]

Enter Laertes and Ophelia, his sister.

Laertes. My necessaries are embarked. Farewell.
    And, sister, as the winds give benefit
    And convoy° is assistant, do not sleep,
    But let me hear from you.
Ophelia.   Do you doubt that?
Laertes. For Hamlet, and the trifling of his favor,   *5*
    Hold it a fashion and a toy° in blood,

---

²³⁸*tell* count ²⁴⁰*grizzled* gray ²⁴²*sable silvered* black mingled with white
²⁴⁸*tenable* held ²⁵⁶*doubt* suspect I.iii. ³*convoy* conveyance ⁶*toy* idle fancy

A violet in the youth of primy° nature,
Forward,° not permanent, sweet, not lasting,
The perfume and suppliance° of a minute,
No more.
Ophelia.　　　No more but so?
Laertes.　　　　　　　Think it no more.　　　　　*10*
For nature crescent° does not grow alone
In thews° and bulk, but as this temple° waxes,
The inward service of the mind and soul
Grows wide withal. Perhaps he loves you now,
And now no soil nor cautel° doth besmirch　　　*15*
The virtue of his will; but you must fear,
His greatness weighed,° his will is not his own.
For he himself is subject to his birth.
He may not, as unvalued° persons do,
Carve for himself; for on his choice depends　　*20*
The safety and health of this whole state;
And therefore must his choice be circumscribed
Unto the voice and yielding of that body
Whereof he is the head. Then if he says he loves you,
It fits your wisdom so far to believe it　　　　*25*
As he in his particular act and place
May give his saying deed, which is no further
Than the main voice of Denmark goes withal.
Then weigh what loss your honor may sustain
If with too credent° ear you list his songs,　　*30*
Or lose your heart, or your chaste treasure open
To his unmastered importunity.
Fear it, Ophelia, fear it, my dear sister,
And keep you in the rear of your affection,
Out of the shot and danger of desire.　　　　*35*
The chariest maid is prodigal enough
If she unmask her beauty to the moon.
Virtue itself scapes not calumnious strokes.
The canker° galls the infants of the spring
Too oft before their buttons° be disclosed,　　*40*
And in the morn and liquid dew of youth
Contagious blastments are most imminent.
Be wary then; best safety lies in fear;

---

[7]*primy* springlike　　[8]*Forward* premature　　[9]*suppliance* diversion　　[11]*crescent* growing　　[12]*thews* muscles and sinews　　[12]*temple* i.e., the body　　[15]*cautel* deceit　　[17]*greatness weighed* high rank considered　　[19]*unvalued* of low rank　　[30]*credent* credulous　　[39]*canker* cankerworm　　[40]*buttons* buds

Youth to itself rebels, though none else near.
Ophelia. I shall the effect of this good lesson keep   **45**
          As watchman to my heart, but, good my brother,
          Do not, as some ungracious° pastors do,
          Show me the steep and thorny way to heaven,
          Whiles, like a puffed and reckless libertine,
          Himself the primrose path of dalliance treads   **50**
          And recks not his own rede.°

          Enter Polonius.

Laertes.   O, fear me not.
          I stay too long. But here my father comes.
          A double blessing is a double grace;
          Occasion smiles upon a second leave.
Polonius. Yet here, Laertes? Aboard, aboard, for shame!   **55**
          The wind sits in the shoulder of your sail,
          And you are stayed for. There — my blessing with thee,
          And these few precepts in thy memory
          Look thou character.° Give thy thoughts no tongue,
          Nor any unproportioned° thought his act.   **60**
          Be thou familiar, but by no means vulgar.
          Those friends thou hast, and their adoption tried,
          Grapple them unto thy soul with hoops of steel,
          But do not dull thy palm with entertainment
          Of each new-hatched, unfledged courage.° Beware   **65**
          Of entrance to a quarrel; but being in,
          Bear't that th' opposèd may beware of thee.
          Give every man thine ear, but few thy voice;
          Take each man's censure,° but reserve thy judgment.
          Costly thy habits as thy purse can buy,   **70**
          But not expressed in fancy; rich, not gaudy,
          For the apparel oft proclaims the man,
          And they in France of the best rank and station
          Are of a most select and generous, chief in that.°
          Neither a borrower nor a lender be,   **75**
          For loan oft loses both itself and friend,
          And borrowing dulleth edge of husbandry.°
          This above all, to thine own self be true,

---

[47]**ungracious** lacking grace   [51]**recks not his own rede** does not heed his own advice   [59]**character** inscribe   [60]**unproportioned** unbalanced   [65]**courage** gallant youth   [69]**censure** opinion   [74]**Are of . . . in that** show their fine taste and their gentlemanly instincts more in that than in any other point of manners (Kittredge)   [77]**husbandry** thrift

And it must follow, as the night the day,
Thou canst not then be false to any man.   80
Farewell. My blessing season this° in thee!
Laertes. Most humbly do I take my leave, my lord.
Polonius. The time invites you. Go, your servants tend.°
Laertes. Farewell, Ophelia, and remember well
What I have said to you.
Ophelia.   'Tis in my memory locked,   85
And you yourself shall keep the key of it.
Laertes. Farewell.

              Exit Laertes.

Polonius. What is't, Ophelia, he hath said to you?
Ophelia. So please you, something touching the Lord Hamlet.
Polonius. Marry,° well bethought.   90
'Tis told me he hath very oft of late
Given private time to you, and you yourself
Have of your audience been most free and bounteous.
If it be so — as so 'tis put on me,
And that in way of caution — I must tell you   95
You do not understand yourself so clearly
As it behooves my daughter and your honor.
What is between you? Give me up the truth.
Ophelia. He hath, my lord, of late made many tenders°
Of his affection to me.   100
Polonius. Affection pooh! You speak like a green girl,
Unsifted° in such perilous circumstance.
Do you believe his tenders, as you call them?
Ophelia. I do not know, my lord, what I should think.
Polonius. Marry, I will teach you. Think yourself a baby   105
That you have ta'en these tenders for true pay
Which are not sterling. Tender yourself more dearly,
Or (not to crack the wind of the poor phrase)
Tend'ring it thus you'll tender me a fool.°
Ophelia. My lord, he hath importuned me with love   110
In honorable fashion.
Polonius. Ay, fashion you may call it. Go to, go to.
Ophelia. And hath given countenance to his speech, my lord,
With almost all the holy vows of heaven.

---

⁸¹*season this* make fruitful this (advice)   ⁸³*tend* attend   ⁹⁰*Marry* (a light oath, from
"By the Virgin Mary")   ⁹⁹*tenders* offers (in line 103 it has the same meaning, but
in line 106 Polonius speaks of *tenders* in the sense of counters or chips; in line 109
Tend'ring means "holding," and *tender* means "give," "present")   ¹⁰²*Unsifted*
untried   ¹⁰⁹*tender me a fool* (1) present me with a fool, (2) present me with a baby

Polonius. Ay, springes to catch woodcocks.° I do know,   *115*
          When the blood burns, how prodigal the soul
          Lends the tongue vows. These blazes, daughter,
          Giving more light than heat, extinct in both,
          Even in their promise, as it is a-making,
          You must not take for fire. From this time   *120*
          Be something scanter of your maiden presence.
          Set your entreatments° at a higher rate
          Than a command to parley. For Lord Hamlet,
          Believe so much in him that he is young,
          And with a larger tether may he walk   *125*
          Than may be given you. In few, Ophelia,
          Do not believe his vows, for they are brokers,°
          Not of that dye° which their investments° show,
          But mere implorators° of unholy suits,
          Breathing like sanctified and pious bonds,°   *130*
          The better to beguile. This is for all:
          I would not, in plain terms, from this time forth
          Have you so slander° any moment leisure
          As to give words or talk with the Lord Hamlet.
          Look to't, I charge you. Come your ways.   *135*
Ophelia. I shall obey, my lord.

                                                        Exeunt.

     [Scene IV. *A guard platform.*]

     Enter Hamlet, Horatio, and Marcellus.

Hamlet. The air bites shrewdly;° it is very cold.
Horatio. It is a nipping and an eager° air.
Hamlet. What hour now?
Horatio.   I think it lacks of twelve.
Marcellus. No, it is struck.
Horatio. Indeed? I heard it not. It then draws near the season   *5*
          Wherein the spirit held his wont to walk.

     A flourish of trumpets, and two pieces go off.

          What does this mean, my lord?
Hamlet. The King doth wake° tonight and takes his rouse,°

---

[115] *springes to catch woodcocks* snares to catch stupid birds [122] *entreatments* interviews [127] *brokers* procurers [128] *dye* i.e., kind [128] *investments* garments [129] *implorators* solicitors [130] *bonds* pledges [133] *slander* disgrace I.iv. [1] *shrewdly* bitterly [2] *eager* sharp [8] *wake* hold a revel by night [8] *takes his rouse* carouses

Keeps wassail, and the swagg'ring upspring° reels,
And as he drains his draughts of Rhenish° down   *10*
The kettledrum and trumpet thus bray out
The triumph of his pledge.°

Horatio.   Is it a custom?

Hamlet. Ay, marry, is't,
But to my mind, though I am native here
And to the manner born, it is a custom   *15*
More honored in the breach than the observance.
This heavy-headed revel east and west
Makes us traduced and taxed of° other nations.
They clepe° us drunkards and with swinish phrase
Soil our addition,° and indeed it takes   *20*
From our achievements, though performed at height,
The pith and marrow of our attribute.°
So oft it chances in particular men
That for some vicious mole° of nature in them,
As in their birth, wherein they are not guilty,   *25*
(Since nature cannot choose his origin)
By the o'ergrowth of some complexion,°
Oft breaking down the pales° and forts of reason,
Or by some habit that too much o'erleavens°
The form of plausive° manners, that (these men,   *30*
Carrying, I say, the stamp of one defect,
Being nature's livery, or fortune's star°)
Their virtues else, be they as pure as grace,
As infinite as man may undergo,
Shall in the general censure° take corruption   *35*
From that particular fault. The dram of evil
Doth all the noble substance of a doubt,
To his own scandal.°

Enter Ghost.

Horatio.   Look, my lord, it comes.

°*upspring* (a dance)   ¹⁰*Rhenish* Rhine wine   ¹²*The triumph of his pledge* the
achievement (of drinking a wine cup in one draught) of his toast   ¹⁸*taxed of* blamed
by   ¹⁹*clepe* call   ²⁰*addition* reputation (literally, "title of honor")   ²²*attribute*
reputation   ²⁴*mole* blemish   ²⁷*complexion* natural disposition   ²⁸*pales* enclosures
¹²⁹*o'erleavens* mixes with, corrupts   ³⁰*plausive* pleasing   ³²*nature's livery, or fortune's star* nature's equipment (i.e., "innate"), or a person's destiny determined
by the stars   ³⁵*general censure* popular judgment   ³⁶⁻³⁸*The dram . . . own scandal*
(though the drift is clear, there is no agreement as to the exact meaning of these
lines)

Hamlet. Angels and ministers of grace defend us!
    Be thou a spirit of health° or goblin damned,   **40**
    Bring with thee airs from heaven or blasts from hell,
    Be thy intents wicked or charitable,
    Thou com'st in such a questionable° shape
    That I will speak to thee. I'll call thee Hamlet,
    King, father, royal Dane. O, answer me!   **45**
    Let me not burst in ignorance, but tell
    Why thy canonized° bones, hearsèd in death,
    Have burst their cerements,° why the sepulcher
    Wherein we saw thee quietly interred
    Hath oped his ponderous and marble jaws   **50**
    To cast thee up again. What may this mean
    That thou, dead corse, again in complete steel,
    Revisits thus the glimpses of the moon,
    Making night hideous, and we fools of nature
    So horridly to shake our disposition°   **55**
    With thoughts beyond the reaches of our souls?
    Say, why is this? Wherefore? What should we do?

Ghost beckons Hamlet.

Horatio. It beckons you to go away with it,
    As if it some impartment° did desire
    To you alone.
Marcellus.   Look with what courteous action   **60**
    It waves you to a more removèd ground.
    But do not go with it.
Horatio.   No, by no means.
Hamlet. It will not speak. Then I will follow it.
Horatio. Do not, my lord.
Hamlet.   Why, what should be the fear?
    I do not set my life at a pin's fee,   **65**
    And for my soul, what can it do to that,
    Being a thing immortal as itself?
    It waves me forth again. I'll follow it.
Horatio. What if it tempt you toward the flood, my lord,
    Or to the dreadful summit of the cliff   **70**
    That beetles° o'er his base into the sea,
    And there assume some other horrible form,

40*spirit of health* good spirit **43*questionable*** (1) capable of discourse, (2) dubious **47*canonized*** buried according to the canon or ordinance of the church **48*cerements*** waxed linen shroud **55*shake our disposition*** disturb us **59*impartment*** communication **71*beetles*** juts out

Which might deprive your sovereignty of reason°
And draw you into madness? Think of it.
The very place puts toys° of desperation,   75
Without more motive, into every brain
That looks so many fathoms to the sea
And hears it roar beneath.
Hamlet.   It waves me still.
   Go on; I'll follow thee.
Marcellus. You shall not go, my lord.
Hamlet.   Hold off your hands.   80
Horatio. Be ruled. You shall not go.
Hamlet.   My fate cries out
And makes each petty artere° in this body
As hardy as the Nemean lion's nerve.°
Still am I called! Unhand me, gentlemen.
By heaven, I'll make a ghost of him that lets° me!   85
I say, away! Go on. I'll follow thee.

                                   Exit Ghost, and Hamlet.
Horatio. He waxes desperate with imagination.
Marcellus. Let's follow.'Tis not fit thus to obey him.
Horatio. Have after! To what issue will this come?
Marcellus. Something is rotten in the state of Denmark.   90
Horatio. Heaven will direct it.
Marcellus.   Nay, let's follow him.

                                               Exeunt.

[Scene V. *The battlements.*]

   Enter Ghost and Hamlet.

Hamlet. Whither wilt thou lead me? Speak; I'll go no further.
Ghost. Mark me.
Hamlet.   I will.
Ghost.   My hour is almost come,
   When I to sulf'rous and tormenting flames
   Must render up myself.
Hamlet.   Alas, poor ghost.
Ghost. Pity me not, but lend thy serious hearing   5
   To what I shall unfold.
Hamlet.   Speak. I am bound to hear.
Ghost. So art thou to revenge, when thou shalt hear.

°**deprive your sovereignty of reason** destroy the sovereignty of your reason   °**toys**
whims, fancies   °**artere** artery   °**Nemean lion's nerve** sinews of the mythical lion
slain by Hercules   °**lets** hinders

Hamlet. What?

Ghost. I am thy father's spirit,
    Doomed for a certain term to walk the night,   *10*
    And for the day confined to fast in fires,
    Till the foul crimes° done in my days of nature
    Are burnt and purged away. But that I am forbid
    To tell the secrets of my prison house,
    I could a tale unfold whose lightest word   *15*
    Would harrow up thy soul, freeze thy young blood,
    Make thy two eyes like stars start from their spheres,°
    Thy knotted and combinèd locks to part,
    And each particular hair to stand an end
    Like quills upon the fearful porpentine.°   *20*
    But this eternal blazon° must not be
    To ears of flesh and blood. List, list, O, list!
    If thou didst ever thy dear father love —

Hamlet. O God!

Ghost. Revenge his foul and most unnatural murder.   *25*

Hamlet. Murder?

Ghost. Murder most foul, as in the best it is,
    But this most foul, strange, and unnatural.

Hamlet. Haste me to know't, that I, with wings as swift
    As meditation° or the thoughts of love,   *30*
    May sweep to my revenge.

Ghost.   I find thee apt,
    And duller shouldst thou be than the fat weed
    That roots itself in ease on Lethe wharf,°
    Wouldst thou not stir in this. Now, Hamlet, hear.
    'Tis given out that, sleeping in my orchard,   *35*
    A serpent stung me. So the whole ear of Denmark
    Is by a forgèd process° of my death
    Rankly abused. But know, thou noble youth,
    The serpent that did sting thy father's life
    Now wears his crown.

Hamlet.   O my prophetic soul!   *40*
    My uncle?

Ghost. Ay, that incestuous, that adulterate° beast,
    With witchcraft of his wits, with traitorous gifts—

I.v. **¹²crimes** sins   **¹⁷spheres** (in Ptolemaic astronomy, each planet was fixed in a hollow transparent shell concentric with the earth)   **²⁰*fearful porpentine*** timid porcupine   **²¹*eternal blazon*** revelation of eternity   **³⁰*meditation*** thought   **³³*Lethe wharf*** bank of the river of forgetfulness in Hades   **³⁷*forgèd process*** false account   **⁴²*adulterate*** adulterous

O wicked wit and gifts, that have the power
So to seduce! — won to his shameful lust   45
The will of my most seeming-virtuous queen.
O Hamlet, what a falling-off was there,
From me, whose love was of that dignity
That it went hand in hand even with the vow
I made to her in marriage, and to decline   50
Upon a wretch whose natural gifts were poor
To those of mine.
But virtue, as it never will be moved,
Though lewdness° court it in a shape of heaven,
So lust, though to a radiant angel linked,   55
Will sate itself in a celestial bed
And prey on garbage.
But soft, methinks I scent the morning air;
Brief let me be. Sleeping within my orchard,
My custom always of the afternoon,   60
Upon my secure° hour thy uncle stole
With juice of cursed hebona° in a vial,
And in the porches of my ears did pour
The leperous distillment, whose effect
Holds such an enmity with blood of man   65
That swift as quicksilver it courses through
The natural gates and alleys of the body,
And with a sudden vigor it doth posset°
And curd, like eager° droppings into milk,
The thin and wholesome blood. So did it mine,   70
And a most instant tetter° barked about
Most lazarlike° with vile and loathsome crust
All my smooth body.
Thus was I, sleeping, by a brother's hand
Of life, of crown, of queen at once dispatched,   75
Cut off even in the blossoms of my sin,
Unhouseled, disappointed, unaneled,°
No reck'ning made, but sent to my account
With all my imperfections on my head.
O, horrible! O, horrible! Most horrible!   80
If thou hast nature in thee, bear it not.

---

⁵⁴*lewdness* lust ⁶¹*secure* unsuspecting ⁶²*hebona* a poisonous plant ⁶⁸*posset*
curdle ⁶⁹*eager* acid ⁷¹*tetter* scab ⁷²*lazarlike* leperlike ⁷⁷*Unhouseled, disappointed,*
unaneled without the sacrament of communion, unabsolved, without extreme
unction

Let not the royal bed of Denmark be
A couch for luxury° and damnèd incest.
But howsomever thou pursues this act,
Taint not thy mind, nor let thy soul contrive   *85*
Against thy mother aught. Leave her to heaven
And to those thorns that in her bosom lodge
To prick and sting her. Fare thee well at once.
The glowworm shows the matin° to be near
And 'gins to pale his uneffectual fire.   *90*
Adieu, adieu, adieu. Remember me.

                                                    Exit.

Hamlet. O all you host of heaven! O earth! What else?
And shall I couple hell? O fie! Hold, hold, my heart,
And you, my sinews, grow not instant old,
But bear me stiffly up. Remember thee?   *95*
Ay, thou poor ghost, whiles memory holds a seat
In this distracted globe.° Remember thee?
Yea, from the table° of my memory
I'll wipe away all trivial fond° records,
All saws° of books, all forms, all pressures° past   *100*
That youth and observation copied there,
And thy commandment all alone shall live
Within the book and volume of my brain,
Unmixed with baser matter. Yes, by heaven!
O most pernicious woman!   *105*
O villain, villain, smiling, damnèd villain!
My tables — meet it is I set it down
That one may smile, and smile, and be a villain.
At least I am sure it may be so in Denmark. [*Writes.*]
So, uncle, there you are. Now to my word: *110*
It is "Adieu, adieu, remember me."
I have sworn't.

Horatio and Marcellus (within). My lord, my lord!

   Enter Horatio and Marcellus.

Marcellus.   Lord Hamlet!
Horatio.   Heavens secure him!
Hamlet. So be it!
Marcellus. Illo, ho, ho,° my lord!   *115*
Hamlet. Hillo, ho, ho, boy! Come, bird, come.

°³*luxury* lust °⁹*matin* morning °⁷*globe* i.e., his head °⁸*table* tablet, notebook °⁹*fond*
foolish ¹⁰⁰*saws* maxims ¹⁰⁰*pressures* impressions ¹¹⁵*Illo, ho, ho* (falconer's call
to his hawk)

Marcellus. How is't, my noble lord?
Horatio.   What news, my lord?
Hamlet. O, wonderful!
Horatio. Good my lord, tell it.
Hamlet.   No, you will reveal it.
Horatio. Not I, my lord, by heaven.
Marcellus.   Nor I, my lord.   120
Hamlet. How say you then? Would heart of man once think it?
    But you'll be secret?
Both.   Ay, by heaven, my lord.
Hamlet. There's never a villain dwelling in all Denmark
    But he's an arrant knave.
Horatio. There needs no ghost, my lord, come from the grave   125
    To tell us this.
Hamlet.   Why, right, you are in the right;
    And so, without more circumstance° at all,
    I hold it fit that we shake hands and part:
    You, as your business and desire shall point you,
    For every man hath business and desire   130
    Such as it is, and for my own poor part,
    Look you, I'll go pray.
Horatio. These are but wild and whirling words, my lord.
Hamlet. I am sorry they offend you, heartily;
    Yes, faith, heartily.
Horatio.   There's no offense, my lord.   135
Hamlet. Yes, by Saint Patrick, but there is, Horatio,
    And much offense too. Touching this vision here,
    It is an honest ghost,° that let me tell you.
    For your desire to know what is between us,
    O'ermaster't as you may. And now, good friends,   140
    As you are friends, scholars, and soldiers,
    Give me one poor request.
Horatio. What is't, my lord? We will.
Hamlet. Never make known what you have seen tonight.
Both. My lord, we will not.
Hamlet.   Nay, but swear't.
Horatio.   In faith,   145
    My lord, not I.
Marcellus.   Nor I, my lord — in faith.
Hamlet. Upon my sword.
Marcellus.   We have sworn, my lord, already.

---

[127]*circumstance* details   [138]*honest ghost* i.e., not a demon in his father's shape

Hamlet. Indeed, upon my sword, indeed.

    Ghost cries under the stage.

Ghost. Swear.

Hamlet. Ha, ha, boy, say'st thou so? Art thou there,
    truepenny?°   *150*
    Come on. You hear this fellow in the cellarage.
    Consent to swear.

Horatio.   Propose the oath, my lord.

Hamlet. Never to speak of this that you have seen.
    Swear by my sword.

Ghost [*beneath*]. Swear.   *155*

Hamlet. Hic et ubique?° Then we'll shift our ground;
    Come hither, gentlemen,
    And lay your hands again upon my sword.
    Swear by my sword
    Never to speak of this that you have heard.   *160*

Ghost [*beneath*]. Swear by his sword.

Hamlet. Well said, old mole! Canst work i' th' earth so fast?
    A worthy pioner!° Once more remove, good friends.

Horatio. O day and night, but this is wondrous strange!

Hamlet. And therefore as a stranger give it welcome.   *165*
    There are more things in heaven and earth, Horatio,
    Than are dreamt of in your philosophy.
    But come:
    Here as before, never, so help you mercy,
    How strange or odd some'er I bear myself   *170*
    (As I perchance hereafter shall think meet
    To put an antic disposition° on),
    That you, at such times seeing me, never shall
    With arms encumb'red° thus, or this headshake,
    Or by pronouncing of some doubtful phrase,   *175*
    As "Well, well, we know," or "We could, an if we would,"
    Or "If we list to speak," or "There be, an if they might,"
    Or such ambiguous giving out, to note
    That you know aught of me — this do swear,
    So grace and mercy at your most need help you.   *180*

Ghost [*beneath*]. Swear.

    [*They swear.*]

Hamlet. Rest, rest, perturbèd spirit. So, gentlemen,

---

[150] *truepenny* honest fellow   [156] *Hic et ubique* here and everywhere (Latin)   [163] *pioner* digger of mines   [172] *antic disposition* fantastic behavior   [174] *encumb'red* folded

With all my love I do commend me° to you,
And what so poor a man as Hamlet is
May do t' express his love and friending to you,   *185*
God willing, shall not lack. Let us go in together,
And still your fingers on your lips, I pray.
The time is out of joint. O cursèd spite,
That ever I was born to set it right!
Nay, come, let's go together.   *190*

                                                    Exeunt.

[ACT II

Scene I. *A room.*]

Enter old Polonius, with his man Reynaldo.

Polonius. Give him this money and these notes, Reynaldo.
Reynaldo. I will, my lord.
Polonius. You shall do marvell's° wisely, good Reynaldo,
      Before you visit him, to make inquire
      Of his behavior.
Reynaldo.   My lord, I did intend it.   *5*
Polonius. Marry, well said, very well said. Look you sir,
      Inquire me first what Danskers° are in Paris,
      And how, and who, what means, and where they keep,°
      What company, at what expense; and finding
      By this encompassment° and drift of question   *10*
      That they do know my son, come you more nearer
      Than your particular demands° will touch it.
      Take you as 'twere some distant knowledge of him,
      As thus, "I know his father and his friends,
      And in part him." Do you mark this, Reynaldo?   *15*
Reynaldo. Ay, very well, my lord.
Polonius. "And in part him, but," you may say, "not well,
      But if't be he I mean, he's very wild,
      Addicted so and so." And there put on him
      What forgeries° you please; marry, none so rank   *20*
      As may dishonor him — take heed of that —
      But, sir, such wanton, wild, and usual slips
      As are companions noted and most known
      To youth and liberty.

---

[183]*commend me* entrust myself   II.i. [3]*marvell's* marvelous(ly) [7]*Danskers*
Danes [8]*keep* dwell [10]*encompassment* circling [12]*demands* questions [20]*forgeries*
inventions

Reynaldo.   As gaming, my lord.
Polonius. Ay, or drinking, fencing, swearing, quarreling,   *25*
     Drabbing.° You may go so far.
Reynaldo. My lord, that would dishonor him.
Polonius. Faith, no, as you may season it in the charge.
     You must not put another scandal on him,
     That he is open to incontinency.°   *30*
     That's not my meaning. But breathe his faults so quaintly°
     That they may seem the taints of liberty,
     The flash and outbreak of a fiery mind,
     A savageness in unreclaimèd blood,
     Of general assault.°
Reynaldo.   But, my good lord ——   *35*
Polonius. Wherefore should you do this?
Reynaldo.   Ay, my lord,
     I would know that.
Polonius.   Marry, sir, here's my drift,
     And I believe it is a fetch of warrant.°
     You laying these slight sullies on my son
     As 'twere a thing a little soiled i' th' working,   *40*
     Mark you,
     Your party in converse, him you would sound,
     Having ever seen in the prenominate crimes°
     The youth you breathe of guilty, be assured
     He closes with you in this consequence:°   *45*
     "Good sir," or so, or "friend," or "gentleman" —
     According to the phrase or the addition°
     Of man and country —
Reynaldo.   Very good, my lord.
Polonius. And then, sir, does 'a° this — 'a does —
     What was I about to say? By the mass, I was about   *50*
     to say something! Where did I leave?
Reynaldo. At "closes in the consequence," at "friend or so," and
     "gentlemen."
Polonius. At "closes in the consequence" — Ay, marry!
     He closes thus: "I know the gentleman;   *55*
     I saw him yesterday, or t'other day,
     Or then, or then, with such or such, and, as you say,
     There was 'a gaming, there o'ertook in's rouse,

---

²⁶*Drabbing* wenching ³⁰*incontinency* habitual licentiousness ³¹*quaintly* ingeniously,
delicately ³⁵*Of general assault* common to all men ³⁸*fetch of warrant* justifiable
device ⁴³*Having . . . crimes* if he has ever seen in the aforementioned crimes ⁴⁵*He
closes . . . this consequence* he falls in with you in this conclusion ⁴⁷*addition*
title ⁴⁹*'a* he

There falling out at tennis"; or perchance,
"I saw him enter such a house of sale," 60
Videlicet,° a brothel, or so forth.
See you now —
Your bait of falsehood take this carp of truth,
And thus do we of wisdom and of reach,°
With windlasses° and with assays of bias,° 65
By indirections find directions out.
So, by my former lecture and advice,
Shall you my son. You have me, have you not?
Reynaldo. My lord, I have.
Polonius. God bye ye, fare ye well.
Reynaldo. Good my lord. 70
Polonius. Observe his inclination in yourself.°
Reynaldo. I shall, my lord.
Polonius. And let him ply his music.
Reynaldo. Well, my lord.
Polonius. Farewell.

Exit Reynaldo.

Enter Ophelia.

          How now, Ophelia, what's the matter?
Ophelia. O my lord, my lord, I have been so affrighted! 75
Polonius. With what, i' th' name of God?
Ophelia. My lord, as I was sewing in my closet,°
Lord Hamlet, with his doublet all unbraced,°
No hat upon his head, his stockings fouled,
Ungartered, and down-gyvèd° to his ankle, 80
Pale as his shirt, his knees knocking each other,
And with a look so piteous in purport,°
As if he had been loosèd out of hell
To speak of horrors — he comes before me.
Polonius. Mad for thy love?
Ophelia. My lord, I do not know, 85
But truly I do fear it.
Polonius. What said he?
Ophelia. He took me by the wrist and held me hard;
Then goes he to the length of all his arm,

---

⁶¹*Videlicet* namely ⁶⁴*reach* far-reaching awareness(?) ⁶⁵*windlasses* circuitous courses ⁶⁵*assays of bias* indirect attempts (metaphor from bowling; *bias* = curved course) ⁷¹*in yourself* for yourself ⁷⁷*closet* private room ⁷⁸*doublet all unbraced* jacket entirely unlaced ⁸⁰*down-gyvèd* hanging down like fetters ⁸²*purport* expression

And with his other hand thus o'er his brow
He falls to such perusal of my face   *90*
As 'a would draw it. Long stayed he so.
At last, a little shaking of mine arm,
And thrice his head thus waving up and down,
He raised a sigh so piteous and profound
As it did seem to shatter all his bulk   *95*
And end his being. That done, he lets me go,
And, with his head over his shoulder turned,
He seemed to find his way without his eyes,
For out o' doors he went without their helps,
And to the last bended their light on me.   *100*
Polonius. Come, go with me. I will go seek the King.
This is the very ecstasy° of love,
Whose violent property fordoes° itself
And leads the will to desperate undertakings
As oft as any passions under heaven   *105*
That does afflict our natures. I am sorry.
What, have you given him any hard words of late?
Ophelia. No, my good lord; but as you did command,
I did repel his letters and denied
His access to me.
Polonius.   That hath made him mad.   *110*
I am sorry that with better heed and judgment
I had not quoted° him. I feared he did but trifle
And meant to wrack thee; but beshrew my jealousy.°
By heaven, it is as proper° to our age
To cast beyond ourselves° in our opinions   *115*
As it is common for the younger sort
To lack discretion. Come, go we to the King.
This must be known, which, being kept close, might move
More grief to hide than hate to utter love.°
Come.   *120*
                                                         Exeunt.

[**Scene II.** *The castle.*]

Flourish. Enter King and Queen, Rosencrantz, and Guildenstern
[*with others*].

---

[102]*ecstasy* madness   [103]*property fordoes* quality destroys   [112]*quoted* noted   [113]*beshrew my jealousy* curse on my suspicions   [114]*proper* natural   [115]*To cast beyond ourselves* to be overcalculating   [117-119]*Come, go . . . utter love* (the general meaning is that while telling the King of Hamlet's love may anger the King, more grief would come from keeping it secret)

King. Welcome, dear Rosencrantz and Guildenstern.
Moreover that° we much did long to see you,
The need we have to use you did provoke
Our hasty sending. Something have you heard
Of Hamlet's transformation: so call it, 5
Sith° nor th' exterior nor the inward man
Resembles that it was. What it should be,
More than his father's death, that thus hath put him
So much from th' understanding of himself,
I cannot dream of. I entreat you both 10
That, being of so° young days brought up with him,
And sith so neighbored to his youth and havior,°
That you vouchsafe your rest° here in our court
Some little time, so by your companies
To draw him on to pleasures, and to gather 15
So much as from occasion you may glean,
Whether aught to us unknown afflicts him thus,
That opened° lies within our remedy.
Queen. Good gentlemen, he hath much talked of you,
And sure I am, two men there is not living 20
To whom he more adheres. If it will please you
To show us so much gentry° and good will
As to expend your time with us awhile
For the supply and profit of our hope,
Your visitation shall receive such thanks 25
As fits a king's remembrance.
Rosencrantz. Both your Majesties
Might, by the sovereign power you have of us,
Put your dread pleasures more into command
Than to entreaty.
Guildenstern. But we both obey,
And here give up ourselves in the full bent° 30
To lay our service freely at your feet,
To be commanded.
King. Thanks, Rosencrantz and gentle Guildenstern.
Queen. Thanks, Guildenstern and gentle Rosencrantz.
And I beseech you instantly to visit 35
My too much changèd son. Go, some of you,
And bring these gentlemen where Hamlet is.

II.ii. ²*Moreover that* beside the fact that ⁶*Sith* since ¹¹*of so* from such ¹²*youth and havior* behavior in his youth ¹³*vouchsafe your rest* consent to remain ¹⁸*opened* revealed ²²*gentry* courtesy ³⁰*in the full bent* entirely (the figure is of a bow bent to its capacity)

Guildenstern. Heavens make our presence and our practices
    Pleasant and helpful to him!
Queen.   Ay, amen!
                     Exeunt Rosencrantz and Guildenstern
                             [with some Attendants].

    Enter Polonius.

Polonius. Th' ambassadors from Norway, my good lord,   **40**
    Are joyfully returned.
King. Thou still° hast been the father of good news.
Polonius. Have I, my lord? Assure you, my good liege,
    I hold my duty, as I hold my soul,
    Both to my God and to my gracious king;   **45**
    And I do think, or else this brain of mine
    Hunts not the trail of policy so sure°
    As it hath used to do, that I have found
    The very cause of Hamlet's lunacy.
King. O, speak of that! That do I long to hear.   **50**
Polonius. Give first admittance to th' ambassadors.
    My news shall be the fruit to that great feast.
King. Thyself do grace to them and bring them in.
                            [Exit Polonius.]
    He tells me, my dear Gertrude, he hath found
    The head and source of all your son's distemper.   **55**
Queen. I doubt° it is no other but the main,°
    His father's death and our o'erhasty marriage.
King. Well, we shall sift him.

    Enter Polonius, Voltemand, and Cornelius.

                    Welcome, my good friends.
    Say, Voltemand, what from our brother Norway?
Voltemand. Most fair return of greetings and desires.   **60**
    Upon our first,° he sent out to suppress
    His nephew's levies, which to him appeared
    To be a preparation 'gainst the Polack;
    But better looked into, he truly found
    It was against your Highness, whereat grieved,   **65**
    That so his sickness, age, and impotence
    Was falsely borne in hand,° sends out arrests
    On Fortinbras; which he, in brief, obeys,

42*still* always   **47*Hunts not . . . so sure*** does not follow clues of political doings with such sureness   **56*doubt*** suspect   **56*main*** principal point   **61*first*** first audience   **67*borne in hand*** deceived

Receives rebuke from Norway, and in fine,°
Makes vow before his uncle never more   70
To give th' assay° of arms against your Majesty.
Whereon old Norway, overcome with joy,
Gives him threescore thousand crowns in annual fee
And his commission to employ those soldiers,
So levied as before, against the Polack,   75
With an entreaty, herein further shown, [*gives a paper*]
That it might please you to give quiet pass
Through your dominions for this enterprise,
On such regards of safety and allowance°
As therein are set down.

King.   It likes us well;   80
And at our more considered time° we'll read,
Answer, and think upon this business.
Meantime, we thank you for your well-took labor.
Go to your rest; at night we'll feast together.
Most welcome home!

                                      Exeunt Ambassadors.

Polonius.   This business is well ended.   85
My liege and madam, to expostulate°
What majesty should be, what duty is,
Why day is day, night night, and time is time,
Were nothing but to waste night, day, and time.
Therefore, since brevity is the soul of wit,°   90
And tediousness the limbs and outward flourishes,
I will be brief. Your noble son is mad.
Mad call I it, for, to define true madness,
What is't but to be nothing else but mad?
But let that go.

Queen.   More matter, with less art.   95
Polonius. Madam, I swear I use no art at all.
That he's mad, 'tis true: 'tis true 'tis pity,
And pity 'tis 'tis true — a foolish figure.°
But farewell it, for I will use no art.
Mad let us grant him then; and now remains   100
That we find out the cause of this effect,
Or rather say, the cause of this defect,
For this effect defective comes by cause.

°⁶⁹*in fine* finally ⁷¹*assay* trial ⁷⁹*regards of safety and allowance* i.e., conditions ⁸¹*considered time* time proper for considering ⁸⁶*expostulate* discuss ⁹⁰*wit* wisdom, understanding ⁹⁸*figure* figure of rhetoric

Thus it remains, and the remainder thus.
Perpend.°   *105*
I have a daughter: have, while she is mine,
Who in her duty and obedience, mark,
Hath given me this. Now gather, and surmise.

[*Reads*] *the letter.*

> "To the celestial, and my soul's idol, the most
> beautified Ophelia" —   *110*

That's an ill phrase, a vile phrase; "beautified" is a vile
phrase. But you shall hear. Thus:

> "In her excellent white bosom, these, &c."

Queen. Came this from Hamlet to her?
Polonius. Good madam, stay awhile. I will be faithful.   *115*

> "Doubt thou the stars are fire,
>   Doubt that the sun doth move;
> Doubt° truth to be a liar,
>   But never doubt I love.

> O dear Ophelia, I am ill at these numbers.° I have   *120*
> not art to reckon my groans; but that I love thee
> best, O most best, believe it. Adieu.

>   Thine evermore, most dear lady,
>   whilst this machine° is to him, HAMLET."

This in obedience hath my daughter shown me,   *125*
And more above° hath his solicitings,
As they fell out by time, by means, and place,
All given to mine ear.
King.   But how hath she
Received his love?
Polonius.   What do you think of me?
King. As of a man faithful and honorable.   *130*
Polonius. I would fain prove so. But what might you think,
When I had seen this hot love on the wing
(As I perceived it, I must tell you that,
Before my daughter told me), what might you,

---

[105]***Perpend*** consider carefully   [118]***Doubt*** suspect   [120]***ill at these numbers*** unskilled
in verses   [124]***machine*** complex device (here, his body)   [126]***more above*** in addition

Or my dear Majesty your Queen here, think,   135
If I had played the desk or table book,°
Or given my heart a winking,° mute and dumb,
Or looked upon this love with idle sight?
What might you think? No, I went round to work
And my young mistress thus I did bespeak: 140
"Lord Hamlet is a prince, out of thy star.°
This must not be." And then I prescripts gave her,
That she should lock herself from his resort,
Admit no messengers, receive no tokens.
Which done, she took the fruits of my advice,   145
And he, repellèd, a short tale to make,
Fell into a sadness, then into a fast,
Thence to a watch,° thence into a weakness,
Thence to a lightness,° and, by this declension,
Into the madness wherein now he raves,   150
And all we mourn for.
King.   Do you think 'tis this?
Queen. It may be, very like.
Polonius. Hath there been such a time, I would fain know that,
　　That I have positively said " 'Tis so,"
　　When it proved otherwise?
King.   Not that I know.   155
Polonius [*pointing to his head and shoulder*]. Take this from this,
　　if this be otherwise.
　　If circumstances lead me, I will find
　　Where truth is hid, though it were hid indeed
　　Within the center.°
King.   How may we try it further?
Polonius. You know sometimes he walks four hours together 160
　　Here in the lobby.
Queen.   So he does indeed.
Polonius. At such a time I'll loose my daughter to him.
　　Be you and I behind an arras° then.
　　Mark the encounter. If he love her not,
　　And be not from his reason fall'n thereon,   165
　　Let me be no assistant for a state
　　But keep a farm and carters.

---

[136]*played the desk or table book* i.e., been a passive recipient of secrets   [137]*winking*
closing of the eyes   [141]*star* sphere   [146]*watch* wakefulness   [149]*lightness* mental
derangement   [159]*center* center of the earth   [163]*arras* tapestry hanging in front of a
wall

King.   We will try it.

   Enter Hamlet reading on a book.

Queen. But look where sadly the poor wretch comes reading.
Polonius. Away, I do beseech you both, away.
                            Exit King and Queen.
   I'll board him presently.° O, give me leave.   **170**
   How does my good Lord Hamlet?
Hamlet. Well, God-a-mercy.
Polonius. Do you know me, my lord?
Hamlet. Excellent well. You are a fishmonger.°
Polonius. Not I, my lord.   **175**
Hamlet. Then I would you were so honest a man.
Polonius. Honest, my lord?
Hamlet. Ay, sir. To be honest, as this world goes, is to be one
   man picked out of ten thousand.
Polonius. That's very true, my lord.   **180**
Hamlet. For if the sun breed maggots in a dead dog, being
   a good kissing carrion° —— Have you a daughter?
Polonius. I have, my lord.
Hamlet. Let her not walk i' th' sun. Conception° is a blessing,
   but as your daughter may conceive, friend, look to't.   **185**
Polonius [*aside*]. How say you by that? Still harping on my
   daughter. Yet he knew me not at first. 'A said I was
   a fishmonger. 'A is far gone, far gone. And truly in
   my youth I suffered much extremity for love, very
   near this. I'll speak to him again. — What do you read,   **190**
   my lord?
Hamlet. Words, words, words.
Polonius. What is the matter,° my lord?
Hamlet. Between who?
Polonius. I mean the matter that you read, my lord.   **195**
Hamlet. Slanders, sir; for the satirical rogue says here that
   old men have gray beards, that their faces are wrinkled,
   their eyes purging thick amber and plumtree gum, and
   that they have a plentiful lack of wit, together with
   most weak hams. All which, sir, though I most pow-   **200**
   erfully and potently believe, yet I hold it not honesty°

---

[170]**board him presently** accost him at once   [174]*fishmonger* dealer in fish (slang for
a procurer)   [182]*a good kissing carrion* (perhaps the meaning is "a good piece of
flesh to kiss," but many editors emend *good* to *god*, taking the word to refer to
the sun)   [184]*Conception* (1) understanding, (2) becoming pregnant   [193]*matter* (Polonius means "subject matter," but Hamlet pretends to take the word in the sense
of "quarrel")   [201]*honesty* decency

to have it thus set down; for you yourself, sir, should
be old as I am if, like a crab, you could go backward.
Polonius [*aside*]. Though this be madness, yet there is method
  in't. Will you walk out of the air, my lord?   *205*
Hamlet. Into my grave.
Polonius. Indeed, that's out of the air. [*Aside.*] How pregnant°
  sometimes his replies are! A happiness° that often madness
  hits on, which reason and sanity could not so pros-
  perously be delivered of. I will leave him and suddenly   *210*
  contrive the means of meeting between him and my
  daughter. — My lord, I will take my leave of you.
Hamlet. You cannot take from me anything that I will more
  willingly part withal — except my life, except my life,
  except my life.   *215*

  Enter Guildenstern and Rosencrantz.

Polonius. Fare you well, my lord.
Hamlet. These tedious old fools!
Polonius. You go to seek the Lord Hamlet? There he is.
Rosencrantz [*to Polonius*]. God save you, sir! [*Exit Polonius.*]
Guildenstern. My honored lord!   *220*
Rosencrantz. My most dear lord!
Hamlet. My excellent good friends! How dost thou, Guil-
  denstern? Ah, Rosencrantz! Good lads, how do you
  both?
Rosencrantz. As the indifferent° children of the earth.   *225*
Guildenstern. Happy in that we are not overhappy. On Fortune's
  cap we are not the very button.
Hamlet. Nor the soles of her shoe?
Rosencrantz. Neither, my lord.
Hamlet. Then you live about her waist, or in the middle of   *230*
  her favors?
Guildenstern. Faith, her privates° we.
Hamlet. In the secret parts of Fortune? O, most true! She is
  a strumpet. What news?
Rosencrantz. None, my lord, but that the world's grown   *235*
  honest.
Hamlet. Then is doomsday near. But your news is not true.
  Let me question more in particular. What have you,
  my good friends, deserved at the hands of Fortune that
  she sends you to prison hither?   *240*

---

[207] ***pregnant*** meaningful [208] ***happiness*** apt turn of phrase [225] ***indifferent*** ordinary
[232] ***privates*** ordinary men (with a pun on "private parts")

Guildenstern. Prison, my lord?

Hamlet. Denmark's a prison.

Rosencrantz. Then is the world one.

Hamlet. A goodly one, in which there are many confines, wards,° and dungeons, Denmark being one o' th' worst.   *245*

Rosencrantz. We think not so, my lord.

Hamlet. Why, then 'tis none to you, for there is nothing either good or bad but thinking makes it so. To me it is a prison.

Rosencrantz. Why then your ambition makes it one. 'Tis too   *250* narrow for your mind.

Hamlet. O God, I could be bounded in a nutshell and count myself a king of infinite space, were it not that I have bad dreams.

Guildenstern. Which dreams indeed are ambition, for the very   *255* substance of the ambitious is merely the shadow of a dream.

Hamlet. A dream itself is but a shadow.

Rosencrantz. Truly, and I hold ambition of so airy and light a quality that it is but a shadow's shadow.   *260*

Hamlet. Then are our beggars bodies, and our monarchs and outstretched heroes the beggars' shadows.° Shall we to th' court? For, by my fay,° I cannot reason.

Both. We'll wait upon you.

Hamlet. No such matter. I will not sort you with the rest of   *265* my servants, for, to speak to you like an honest man, I am most dreadfully attended. But in the beaten way of friendship, what make you at Elsinore?

Rosencrantz. To visit you, my lord; no other occasion.

Hamlet. Beggar that I am, I am even poor in thanks, but I   *270* thank you; and sure, dear friends, my thanks are too dear a half penny.° Were you not sent for? Is it your own inclining? Is it a free visitation? Come, come, deal justly with me. Come, come; nay, speak.

Guildenstern. What should we say, my lord?   *275*

Hamlet. Why anything — but to th' purpose. You were sent for, and there is a kind of confession in your looks, which your modesties have not craft enough to color. I know the good King and Queen have sent for you.

---

²⁴⁵*wards* cells   ²⁶¹⁻²⁶²*Then are . . . beggars' shadows* i.e., by your logic, beggars (lacking ambition) are substantial, and great men are elongated shadows   ²⁶³*fay* faith   ²⁷¹⁻²⁷²*too dear a halfpenny* i.e., not worth a halfpenny

Rosencrantz. To what end, my lord? 280

Hamlet. That you must teach me. But let me conjure you
by the rights of our fellowship, by the consonancy of
our youth, by the obligation of our ever preserved love,
and by what more dear a better proposer can charge
you withal, be even and direct with me, whether you 285
were sent for or no.

Rosencrantz [*aside to Guildenstern*]. What say you?

Hamlet [*aside*]. Nay then, I have an eye of you. — If you
love me, hold not off.

Guildenstern. My lord, we were sent for. 290

Hamlet. I will tell you why; so shall my anticipation prevent
your discovery,° and your secrecy to the King and
Queen molt no feather. I have of late, but wherefore
I know not, lost all my mirth, forgone all custom of
exercises; and indeed, it goes so heavily with my dis- 295
position that this goodly frame, the earth, seems to me
a sterile promontory; this most excellent canopy, the
air, look you, this brave o'erhanging firmament, this
majestical roof fretted° with golden fire: why, it appeareth
nothing to me but a foul and pestilent congregation of 300
vapors. What a piece of work is a man, how noble in
reason, how infinite in faculties, in form and moving
how express° and admirable, in action how like an
angel, in apprehension how like a god: the beauty of
the world, the paragon of animals; and yet to me, what 305
is this quintessence of dust? Man delights not me; nor
woman neither, though by your smiling you seem to
say so.

Rosencrantz. My lord, there was no such stuff in my thoughts.

Hamlet. Why did ye laugh then, when I said "Man delights 310
not me"?

Rosencrantz. To think, my lord, if you delight not in man,
what lenten° entertainment the players shall receive from
you. We coted° them on the way, and hither are they
coming to offer you service. 315

Hamlet. He that plays the king shall be welcome; his Majesty
shall have tribute of me; the adventurous knight shall
use his foil and target;° the lover shall not sigh gratis;
the humorous man° shall end his part in peace; the

---

²⁹²⁻²⁹³*prevent your discovery* forestall your disclosure ²⁹⁹*fretted* adorned ³⁰³*express*
exact ³¹³*lenten* meager ³¹⁴*coted* overtook ³¹⁸*target* shield ³¹⁹*humorous man* i.e.,
eccentric man (among stock characters in dramas were men dominated by a "humor"
or odd trait)

clown shall make those laugh whose lungs are tickle o' 320
th' sere;° and the lady shall say her mind freely, or° the
blank verse shall halt° for't. What players are they?

Rosencrantz. Even those you were wont to take such delight
in, the tragedians of the city.

Hamlet. How chances it they travel? Their residence, both in 325
reputation and profit, was better both ways.

Rosencrantz. I think their inhibition° comes by the means of
the innovation.°

Hamlet. Do they hold the same estimation they did when I
was in the city? Are they so followed? 330

Rosencrantz. No indeed, are they not.

Hamlet. How comes it? Do they grow rusty?

Rosencrantz. Nay, their endeavor keeps in the wonted pace,
but there is, sir, an eyrie° of children, little eyases, that
cry out on the top of question° and are most tyrannically° 335
clapped for't. These are now the fashion, and so berattle
the common stages° (so they call them) that many wearing rapiers are afraid of goosequills° and dare scarce
come thither.

Hamlet. What, are they children? Who maintains 'em? How 340
are they escoted?° Will they pursue the quality° no longer
than they can sing? Will they not say afterwards, if they
should grow themselves to common players (as it is
most like, if their means are no better), their writers
do them wrong to make them exclaim against their 345
own succession?°

Rosencrantz. Faith, there has been much to-do on both sides,
and the nation holds it no sin to tarre° them to con-
troversy. There was, for a while, no money bid for
argument° unless the poet and the player went to cuffs 350
in the question.

Hamlet. Is't possible?

---

³²⁰⁻³²¹*tickle o' th' sere* on hair trigger (*sere* = part of the gunlock) ³²¹*or* else
³²²*halt* limp ³²⁷*inhibition* hindrance ³²⁸*innovation* (probably an allusion to the
companies of child actors that had become popular and were offering serious
competition to the adult actors) ³³⁴*eyrie* nest ³³⁴⁻³³⁵*eyases, that . . . of question*
unfledged hawks that cry shrilly above others in matter of debate ³³⁵*tyrannically*
violently ³³⁶⁻³³⁷*berattle the common stages* cry down the public theaters (with the
adult acting companies) ³³⁸*goosequills* pens (of satirists who ridicule the public
theaters and their audiences) ³⁴¹*escoted* financially supported ³⁴¹*quality* profession
of acting ³⁴⁶*succession* future ³⁴⁸*tarre* incite ³⁵⁰*argument* plot of a play

Guildenstern. O, there has been much throwing about of
brains.

Hamlet. Do the boys carry it away? 355

Rosencrantz. Ay, that they do, my lord — Hercules and his
load° too.

Hamlet. It is not very strange, for my uncle is King of Denmark,
and those that would make mouths at him while my
father lived give twenty, forty, fifty, a hundred ducats 360
apiece for his picture in little. 'Sblood,° there is something
in this more than natural, if philosophy could find it
out.

A flourish.

Guildenstern. There are the players.

Hamlet. Gentlemen, you are welcome to Elsinore. Your hands, 365
come then. Th' appurtenance of welcome is fashion and
ceremony. Let me comply° with you in this garb,° lest
my extent° to the players (which I tell you must show
fairly outwards) should more appear like entertainment
than yours. You are welcome. But my uncle-father and 370
aunt-mother are deceived.

Guildenstern. In what, my dear lord?

Hamlet. I am but mad north-northwest:° when the wind is
southerly I know a hawk from a handsaw.°

Enter Polonius.

Polonius. Well be with you, gentlemen. 375

Hamlet. Hark you, Guildenstern, and you too; at each ear a
hearer. That great baby you see there is not yet out of
his swaddling clouts.

Rosencrantz. Happily° he is the second time come to them,
for they say an old man is twice a child. 380

Hamlet. I will prophesy he comes to tell me of the players.
Mark it. — You say right, sir; a Monday morning,
'twas then indeed.

Polonius. My lord, I have news to tell you.

[356-357]***Hercules and his load*** i.e., the whole world (with a reference to the Globe
Theatre, which had a sign that represented Hercules bearing the globe) [361]***'Sblood***
by God's blood [367]***comply*** be courteous [367]***garb*** outward show [368]***extent***
behavior [373]***north-northwest*** i.e., on one point of the compass only [374]***hawk from
a handsaw*** (*hawk* can refer not only to a bird but to a kind of pickax; *handsaw* —
a carpenter's tool — may involve a similar pun on "hernshaw," a heron) [379]***Happily***
perhaps

Hamlet. My lord, I have news to tell you. When Roscius°   *385*
   was an actor in Rome ——
Polonius. The actors are come hither, my lord.
Hamlet. Buzz, buzz.°
Polonius. Upon my honor —
Hamlet. Then came each actor on his ass ——   *390*
Polonius. The best actors in the world, either for tragedy,
   comedy, history, pastoral, pastoral-comical, historical-
   pastoral, tragical-historical, tragical-comical-historical-
   pastoral; scene individable,° or poem unlimited.° Seneca°
   cannot be too heavy, nor Plautus° too light. For the   *395*
   law of writ and the liberty,° these are the only men.
Hamlet. O Jeptha, judge of Israel,° what a treasure hadst thou!
Polonius. What a treasure had he, my lord?
Hamlet. Why,

   "One fair daughter, and no more,   *400*
   The which he lovèd passing well."

Polonius [*aside*]. Still on my daughter.
Hamlet. Am I not i' th' right, old Jeptha?
Polonius. If you call me Jeptha, my lord, I have a daughter
   that I love passing well.   *405*
Hamlet. Nay, that follows not.
Polonius. What follows then, my lord?
Hamlet. Why,

   "As by lot, God wot,"

and then, you know,   *410*

   "It came to pass, as most like it was."

The first row of the pious chanson° will show you
more, for look where my abridgment° comes.

Enter the Players.

---

[385] *Roscius* (a famous Roman comic actor)   [388] *Buzz, buzz* (an interjection, perhaps
indicating that the news is old)   [394] *scene individable* plays observing the unities of
time, place, and action   [394] *poem unlimited* plays not restricted by the tenets of
criticism   [394] *Seneca* (Roman tragic dramatist)   [395] *Plautus* (Roman comic dramatist)   [395-396] *For the law of writ and the liberty* (perhaps "for sticking to the text
and for improvising"; perhaps "for classical plays and for modern loosely written
plays")   [397] *Jeptha, judge of Israel* (the title of a ballad on the Hebrew judge who
sacrificed his daughter; see Judges 11)   [412] *row of the pious chanson* stanza of the
scriptural song   [413] *abridgment* (1) i.e., entertainers, who abridge the time, (2)
interrupters

You are welcome, masters, welcome, all. I am glad to
see thee well. Welcome, good friends. O, old friend, *415*
why, thy face is valanced° since I saw thee last. Com'st
thou to beard me in Denmark? What, my young lady°
and mistress? By'r Lady, your ladyship is nearer to
heaven than when I saw you last by the altitude of a
chopine.° Pray God your voice, like a piece of uncurrent *420*
gold, be not cracked within the ring.° — Masters, you
are all welcome. We'll e'en to't like French falconers,
fly at anything we see. We'll have a speech straight.
Come, give us a taste of your quality. Come, a passionate
speech. *425*

Player. What speech, my good lord?

Hamlet. I heard thee speak me a speech once, but it was never
acted, or if it was, not above once, for the play, I
remember, pleased not the million; 'twas caviary to the
general,° but it was (as I received it, and others, whose *430*
judgments in such matters cried in the top of° mine)
an excellent play, well digested in the scenes, set down
with as much modesty as cunning.° I remember one
said there were no sallets° in the lines to make the matter
savory; nor no matter in the phrase that might indict *435*
the author of affectation, but called it an honest method,
as wholesome as sweet, and by very much more handsome than fine.° One speech in't I chiefly loved. 'Twas
Aeneas' tale to Dido, and thereabout of it especially
when he speaks of Priam's slaughter. If it live in your *440*
memory, begin at this line — let me see, let me see:

"The rugged Pyrrhus, like th' Hyrcanian beast° — "

'Tis not so; it begins with Pyrrhus:

"The rugged Pyrrhus, he whose sable° arms,
Black as his purpose, did the night resemble *445*
When he lay couchèd in th' ominous horse,°
Hath now this dread and black complexion smeared

---

⁴¹⁶*valanced* fringed (with a beard)   ⁴¹⁷*young lady* i.e., boy for female roles   ⁴²⁰*chopine*
thick-soled shoe   ⁴²⁰⁻⁴²¹*like a piece . . . the ring* (a coin was unfit for legal tender
if a crack extended from the edge through the ring enclosing the monarch's head.
Hamlet, punning on *ring*, refers to the change of voice that the boy actor will
undergo)   ⁴²⁹⁻⁴³⁰*caviary to the general* i.e., too choice for the multitude   ⁴³¹*in the
top of* overtopping   ⁴³³*modesty as a cunning* restraint as art   ⁴³⁴*sallets* salads, spicy
jests   ⁴³⁷⁻⁴³⁸*more handsome than fine* well-proportioned rather than
ornamented   ⁴⁴²*Hyrcanian beast* i.e., tiger (Hyrcania was in Asia)   ⁴⁴⁴*sable*
black   ⁴⁴⁶*ominous horse* i.e., wooden horse at the siege of Troy

With heraldry more dismal.° Head to foot
Now is he total gules, horridly tricked°
With blood of fathers, mothers, daughters, sons,   *450*
Baked and impasted° with the parching streets,
That lend a tyrannous and a damnèd light
To their lord's murder. Roasted in wrath and fire,
And thus o'ersizèd° with coagulate gore,
With eyes like carbuncles, the hellish Pyrrhus   *455*
Old grandsire Priam seeks."

    So, proceed you.
Polonius. Fore God, my lord, well spoken, with good accent
    and good discretion.
Player.   "Anon he finds him,   *460*
Striking too short at Greeks. His antique sword,
Rebellious to his arm, lies where it falls,
Repugnant to command.° Unequal matched,
Pyrrhus at Priam drives, in rage strikes wide,
But with the whiff and wind of his fell sword   *465*
Th' unnervèd father falls. Then senseless Ilium,°
Seeming to feel this blow, with flaming top
Stoops to his base,° and with a hideous crash
Takes prisoner Pyrrhus' ear. For lo, his sword,
Which was declining on the milky head   *470*
Of reverend Priam, seemed i' th' air to stick.
So as a painted tyrant° Pyrrhus stood,
And like a neutral to his will and matter°
Did nothing.
But as we often see, against° some storm,   *475*
A silence in the heavens, the rack° stand still,
The bold winds speechless, and the orb below
As hush as death, anon the dreadful thunder
Doth rend the region, so after Pyrrhus' pause,
A rousèd vengeance sets him new awork,   *480*
And never did the Cyclops' hammers fall
On Mars's armor, forged for proof eterne,°
With less remorse than Pyrrhus' bleeding sword
Now falls on Priam.

---

448 *dismal* ill-omened   **449** *total*   *gules,*   *horridly*   *tricked* all   red,   horridly
adorned   **451** *impasted* encrusted   **451** *o'ersizèd* smeared over   **463** *Repugnant to com-*
mand disobedient   **466** *senseless Ilium* insensate Troy   **468** *Stoops to his base* collapses
(*his* = its)   **472** *painted tyrant* tyrant in a picture   **473** *matter* task   **475** *against* just
before   **476** *rack* clouds   **482** *proof eterne* eternal endurance

Out, out, thou strumpet Fortune! All you gods,   *485*
In general synod° take away her power,
Break all the spokes and fellies° from her wheel,
And bowl the round nave° down the hill of heaven,
As low as to the fiends.''

Polonius. This is too long.   *490*
Hamlet. It shall to the barber's, with your beard. — Prithee
say on. He's for a jig or a tale of bawdry, or he sleeps.
Say on; come to Hecuba.

Player. "But who (ah woe!) had seen the mobled° queen — "

Hamlet. "The mobled queen"?   *495*
Polonius. That's good. "Mobled queen" is good.

Player.   "Run barefoot up and down, threat'ning the flames
With bisson rheum;° a clout° upon that head
Where late the diadem stood, and for a robe,
About her lank and all o'erteemèd° loins,   *500*
A blanket in the alarm of fear caught up —
Who this had seen, with tongue in venom steeped
'Gainst Fortune's state would treason have pronounced.
But if the gods themselves did see her then,
When she saw Pyrrhus make malicious sport   *505*
In mincing with his sword her husband's limbs,
The instant burst of clamor that she made
(Unless things mortal move them not at all)
Would have made milch° the burning eyes of
     heaven
And passion in the gods.''   *510*

Polonius. Look, whe'r° he has not turned his color, and has
tears in's eyes. Prithee no more.
Hamlet. 'Tis well. I'll have thee speak out the rest of this
soon. Good my lord, will you see the players well
bestowed?° Do you hear? Let them be well used, for   *515*
they are the abstract and brief chronicles of the time.
After your death you were better have a bad epitaph
than their ill report while you live.
Polonius. My lord, I will use them according to their desert.
Hamlet. God's bodkin,° man, much better! Use every man *520*

---

⁴⁸⁶*synod* council   ⁴⁸⁷*fellies* rims   ⁴⁸⁸*nave* hub   ⁴⁹⁴*mobled* muffled   ⁴⁹⁸*bisson rheum*
blinding tears   ⁴⁹⁸*clout* rag   ⁵⁰⁰*o'erteemèd* exhausted with childbearing   ⁵⁰¹*milch*
moist (literally, "milk-giving")   ⁵¹¹*whe'r* whether   ⁵¹⁵*bestowed* housed   ⁵²⁰*God's*
bodkin by God's little body

after his desert, and who shall scape whipping? Use
them after your own honor and dignity. The less they
deserve, the more merit is in your bounty. Take them
in.

Polonius. Come, sirs.   525

Hamlet. Follow him, friends. We'll hear a play tomorrow.
[*Aside to Player.*] Dost thou hear me, old friend? Can
you play *The Murder of Gonzago*?

Player. Ay, my lord.

Hamlet. We'll ha't tomorrow night. You could for a need   530
study a speech of some dozen or sixteen lines which
I would set down and insert in't, could you not?

Player. Ay, my lord.

Hamlet. Very well. Follow that lord, and look you mock
him not. My good friends, I'll leave you till night. You   535
are welcome to Elsinore.

                              Exeunt Polonius and Players.

Rosencrantz. Good my lord.

                              Exeunt [Rosencrantz and Guildenstern].

Hamlet. Ay, so, God bye to you. — Now I am alone.
O, what a rogue and peasant slave am I!
Is it not monstrous that this player here,   540
But in a fiction, in a dream of passion,°
Could force his soul so to his own conceit°
That from her working all his visage wanned,
Tears in his eyes, distraction in his aspect,
A broken voice, and his whole function° suiting   545
With forms° to his conceit? And all for nothing!
For Hecuba!
What's Hecuba to him, or he to Hecuba,
That he should weep for her? What would he do
Had he the motive and the cue for passion   550
That I have? He would drown the stage with tears
And cleave the general ear with horrid speech,
Make mad the guilty and appall the free,°
Confound the ignorant, and amaze indeed
The very faculties of eyes and ears.   555
Yet I,
A dull and muddy-mettled° rascal, peak
Like John-a-dreams,° unpregnant of° my cause,

---

⁵⁴¹*dream of passion* imaginary emotion ⁵⁴²*conceit* imagination ⁵⁴⁵*function*
action ⁵⁴⁶*forms* bodily expressions ⁵⁵³*appall the free* terrify (make pale?) the
guiltless ⁵⁵⁷*muddy-mettled* weak-spirited ⁵⁵⁷⁻⁵⁵⁸*peak/Like John-a-dreams* mope like
a dreamer ⁵⁵⁸*unpregnant of* unquickened by

And can say nothing. No, not for a king,
Upon whose property and most dear life   *560*
A damned defeat was made. Am I a coward?
Who calls me villain? Breaks my pate across?
Plucks off my beard and blows it in my face?
Tweaks me by the nose? Gives me the lie i' th' throat
As deep as to the lungs? Who does me this?   *565*
Ha, 'swounds,° I should take it, for it cannot be
But I am pigeon-livered° and lack gall
To make oppression bitter, or ere this
I should ha' fatted all the region kites°
With this slave's offal. Bloody, bawdy villain!   *570*
Remorseless, treacherous, lecherous, kindless° villain!
O, vengeance!
Why, what an ass am I! This is most brave,°
That I, the son of a dear father murdered,
Prompted to my revenge by heaven and hell,   *575*
Must, like a whore, unpack my heart with words
And fall a-cursing like a very drab,°
A stallion!° Fie upon't, foh! About,° my brains.
Hum ——
I have heard that guilty creatures sitting at a play   *580*
Have by the very cunning of the scene
Been struck so to the soul that presently°
They have proclaimed their malefactions.
For murder, though it have no tongue, will speak
With most miraculous organ. I'll have these players   *585*
Play something like the murder of my father
Before mine uncle. I'll observe his looks,
I'll tent° him to the quick. If 'a do blench,°
I know my course. The spirit that I have seen
May be a devil, and the devil hath power   *590*
T' assume a pleasing shape, yea, and perhaps
Out of my weakness and my melancholy,
As he is very potent with such spirits,
Abuses me to damn me. I'll have grounds

More relative° than this. The play's the thing   *595*
Wherein I'll catch the conscience of the King.

                        Exit.

[ACT III

Scene I. *The castle.*]

Enter King, Queen, Polonius, Ophelia, Rosencrantz, Guildenstern, Lords.

King. And can you by no drift of conference°
     Get from him why he puts on this confusion,
     Grating so harshly all his days of quiet
     With turbulent and dangerous lunacy?
Rosencrantz. He does confess he feels himself distracted,   *5*
     But from what cause 'a will by no means speak.
Guildenstern. Nor do we find him forward to be sounded,°
     But with a crafty madness keeps aloof
     When we would bring him on to some confession
     Of his true state.
Queen.   Did he receive you well?   *10*
Rosencrantz. Most like a gentleman.
Guildenstern. But with much forcing of his disposition.
Rosencrantz. Niggard of question,° but of our demands
     Most free in his reply.
Queen.   Did you assay° him
     To any pastime?   *15*
Rosencrantz. Madam, it so fell out that certain players
     We o'erraught° on the way; of these we told him,
     And there did seem in him a kind of joy
     To hear of it. They are here about the court,
     And, as I think, they have already order   *20*
     This night to play before him.
Polonius.   'Tis most true,
     And he beseeched me to entreat your Majesties
     To hear and see the matter.
King. With all my heart, and it doth much content me
     To hear him so inclined.   *25*

°⁵⁹⁵*relative* (probably "pertinent," but possibly "able to be related plausibly")
III.i   ¹*drift of conference* management of conversation   ⁷*forward to be sounded*
willing to be questioned   ¹²*forcing of his disposition* effort   ¹³*Niggard of question*
uninclined to talk   ¹⁴*assay* tempt   ¹⁷*o'erraught* overtook

Good gentlemen, give him a further edge
And drive his purpose into these delights.
Rosencrantz. We shall, my lord.
         Exeunt Rosencrantz and Guildenstern.
King.   Sweet Gertrude, leave us too,
 For we have closely° sent for Hamlet hither,
 That he, as 'twere by accident, may here   *30*
 Affront° Ophelia.
 Her father and myself (lawful espials°)
 Will so bestow ourselves that, seeing unseen,
 We may of their encounter frankly judge
 And gather by him, as he is behaved,   *35*
 If't be th' affliction of his love or no
 That thus he suffers for.
Queen.   I shall obey you.
 And for your part, Ophelia, I do wish
 That your good beauties be the happy cause
 Of Hamlet's wildness. So shall I hope your virtues *40*
 Will bring him to his wonted way again,
 To both your honors.
Ophelia.   Madam, I wish it may.
              [Exit Queen.]
Polonius. Ophelia, walk you here. — Gracious, so please you,
 We will bestow ourselves. *[To Ophelia.]* Read on this book,
 That show of such an exercise may color°   *45*
 Your loneliness. We are oft to blame in this,
 'Tis too much proved, that with devotion's visage
 And pious action we do sugar o'er
 The devil himself.
King [aside].   O,'tis too true.
 How smart a lash that speech doth give my conscience! *50*
 The harlot's cheek, beautied with plast'ring art,
 Is not more ugly to the thing that helps it
 Than is my deed to my most painted word.
 O heavy burden!
Polonius. I hear him coming. Let's withdraw, my lord. *55*
          [Exeunt King and Polonius.]
 Enter Hamlet.

Hamlet. To be, or not to be: that is the question:

---

²⁹*closely* secretly ³¹*Affront* meet face to face ³²*espials* spies ⁴⁵*exercise may color*
act of devotion may give a plausible hue to (the book is one of devotion)

Whether 'tis nobler in the mind to suffer
The slings and arrows of outrageous fortune,
Or to take arms against a sea of troubles,
And by opposing end them. To die, to sleep —   60
No more — and by a sleep to say we end
The heartache, and the thousand natural shocks
That flesh is heir to! 'Tis a consummation
Devoutly to be wished. To die, to sleep —
To sleep — perchance to dream: ay, there's the rub,°   65
For in that sleep of death what dreams may come
When we have shuffled off this mortal coil,°
Must give us pause. There's the respect°
That makes calamity of so long life:°
For who would bear the whips and scorns of time,   70
Th' oppressor's wrong, the proud man's contumely,
The pangs of despised love, the law's delay,
The insolence of office, and the spurns
That patient merit of th' unworthy takes,
When he himself might his quietus° make   75
With a bare bodkin?° Who would fardels° bear,
To grunt and sweat under a weary life,
But that the dread of something after death
The undiscovered country, from whose bourn°
No traveler returns, puzzles the will,   80
And makes us rather bear those ills we have,
Than fly to others that we know not of?
Thus conscience° does make cowards of us all,
And thus the native hue of resolution
Is sicklied o'er with the pale cast° of thought,   85
And enterprises of great pitch° and moment,
With this regard° their currents turn awry,
And lose the name of action. — Soft you now,
The fair Ophelia! — Nymph, in thy orisons°
Be all my sins remembered.
Ophelia.   Good my lord,   90
How does your honor for this many a day?

---

⁶⁵*rub* impediment (obstruction to a bowler's ball)   ⁶⁷*coil* (1) turmoil, (2) a ring of
rope (here the flesh encircling the soul)   ⁶⁸*respect* consideration   ⁶⁹*makes calamity*
of so long life (1) makes calamity so long-lived, (2) makes living so long a
calamity   ⁷⁵*quietus* full discharge (a legal term)   ⁷⁶*bodkin* dagger   ⁷⁶*fardels*
burdens   ⁷⁹*bourn* region   ⁸³*conscience* self-consciousness, introspection   ⁸⁵*cast*
color   ⁸⁶*pitch* height (a term from falconry)   ⁸⁷*regard* consideration   ⁸⁹*orisons* prayers

Hamlet. I humbly thank you; well, well, well.
Ophelia. My lord, I have remembrances of yours
　　That I have longèd long to redeliver.
　　I pray you now, receive them.
Hamlet.　　　　　　　　　　No, not I,　　　　　　　　　95
　　I never gave you aught.
Ophelia. My honored lord, you know right well you did,
　　And with them words of so sweet breath composed
　　As made these things more rich. Their perfume lost,
　　Take these again, for to the noble mind　　　　　　　100
　　Rich gifts wax poor when givers prove unkind.
　　There, my lord.
Hamlet. Ha, ha! Are you honest?°
Ophelia. My lord?
Hamlet. Are you fair?　　　　　　　　　　　　　　　　105
Ophelia. What means your lordship?
Hamlet. That if you be honest and fair, your honesty should
　　admit no discourse to your beauty.°
Ophelia. Could beauty, my lord, have better commerce than
　　with honesty?　　　　　　　　　　　　　　　　　110
Hamlet. Ay, truly; for the power of beauty will sooner trans-
　　form honesty from what it is to a bawd° than the force
　　of honesty can translate beauty into his likeness. This
　　was sometime a paradox, but now the time gives it
　　proof. I did love you once.　　　　　　　　　　　115
Ophelia. Indeed, my lord, you made me believe so.
Hamlet. You should not have believed me, for virtue cannot
　　so inoculate° our old stock but we shall relish of it.° I
　　loved you not.
Ophelia. I was the more deceived.　　　　　　　　　　120
Hamlet. Get thee to a nunnery. Why wouldst thou be a
　　breeder of sinners? I am myself indifferent honest,° but
　　yet I could accuse me of such things that it were better
　　my mother had not borne me: I am very proud, re-
　　vengeful, ambitious, with more offenses at my beck°　125
　　than I have thoughts to put them in, imagination to
　　give them shape, or time to act them in. What should
　　such fellows as I do crawling between earth and heaven?

---

[103]*Are you honest* (1) are you modest, (2) are you chaste, (3) have you integrity
[107-08]*your honesty . . . to your beauty* your modesty should permit no approach
to your beauty　[112]*bawd* procurer　[118]*inoculate* graft　[118]*relish of it* smack of it
(our old sinful nature)　[122]*indifferent honest* moderately virtuous　[125]*beck* call

We are arrant knaves all; believe none of us. Go thy
 ways to a nunnery. Where's your father?   *130*
Ophelia. At home, my lord.
Hamlet. Let the doors be shut upon him, that he may play
 the fool nowhere but in's own house. Farewell.
Ophelia. O help him, you sweet heavens!
Hamlet. If thou dost marry, I'll give thee this plague for thy *135*
 dowry: be thou as chaste as ice, as pure as snow, thou
 shalt not escape calumny. Get thee to a nunnery. Go,
 farewell. Or if thou wilt needs marry, marry a fool,
 for wise men know well enough what monsters° you
 make of them. To a nunnery, go, and quickly too.
 Farewell.   *140*
Ophelia. Heavenly powers, restore him!
Hamlet. I have heard of your paintings, well enough. God
 hath given you one face, and you make yourselves
 another. You jig and amble, and you lisp; you nickname
 God's creatures and make your wantonness your ig- *145*
 norance.° Go to, I'll no more on't; it hath made me
 mad. I say we will have no moe° marriage. Those that
 are married already — all but one — shall live. The
 rest shall keep as they are. To a nunnery, go.
              Exit.
Ophelia. O what a noble mind is here o'erthrown! *150*
 The courtier's, soldier's, scholar's, eye, tongue, sword,
 Th' expectancy and rose° of the fair state,
 The glass of fashion, and the mold of form,°
 Th' observed of all observers, quite, quite down!
 And I, of ladies most deject and wretched, *155*
 That sucked the honey of his musicked vows,
 Now see that noble and most sovereign reason
 Like sweet bells jangled, out of time and harsh,
 That unmatched form and feature of blown° youth
 Blasted with ecstasy.° O, woe is me *160*
 T' have seen what I have seen, see what I see!

Enter King and Polonius.

King. Love? His affections° do not that way tend,
 Nor what he spake, though it lacked form a little,

---

¹³⁸*monsters* horned beasts, cuckolds ¹⁴⁵*make your wantonness your ignorance* excuse
your wanton speech by pretending ignorance ¹⁴⁷*moe* more ¹⁵²*expectancy and
rose* i.e., fair hope ¹⁵³*The glass . . . of form* the mirror of fashion, and the pattern
of excellent behavior ¹⁵⁹*blown* blooming ¹⁶⁰*ecstasy* madness ¹⁶²*affections*
inclinations

Was not like madness. There's something in his soul
O'er which his melancholy sits on brood,   *165*
And I do doubt° the hatch and the disclose
Will be some danger; which for to prevent,
I have in quick determination
Thus set it down: he shall with speed to England
For the demand of our neglected tribute.   *170*
Haply the seas, and countries different,
With variable objects, shall expel
This something-settled° matter in his heart,
Whereon his brains still beating puts him thus
From fashion of himself. What think you on't?   *175*
Polonius. It shall do well. But yet do I believe
The origin and commencement of his grief
Sprung from neglected love. How now, Ophelia?
You need not tell us what Lord Hamlet said;
We heard it all. My lord, do as you please,   *180*
But if you hold it fit, after the play,
Let his queen mother all alone entreat him
To show his grief. Let her be round° with him,
And I'll be placed, so please you, in the ear
Of all their conference. If she find him not,°   *185*
To England send him, or confine him where
Your wisdom best shall think.
King   It shall be so.
Madness in great ones must not unwatched go.

                                                 Exeunt.

[**Scene II.** *The castle.*]

Enter Hamlet and three of the Players.

Hamlet. Speak the speech, I pray you, as I pronounced it to
you, trippingly on the tongue. But if you mouth it, as
many of our players do, I had as lief the town crier
spoke my lines. Nor do not saw the air too much with
your hand, thus, but use all gently, for in the very   *5*
torrent, tempest, and (as I may say) whirlwind of your
passion, you must acquire and beget a temperance that
may give it smoothness. O, it offends me to the soul
to hear a robustious periwig-pated° fellow tear a passion

°¹⁶⁶**doubt** fear °¹⁷³***something-settled*** somewhat settled °¹⁸³***round*** blunt °¹⁸⁵***find him not*** does not find him out III.ii. °⁹***robustious periwig-pated*** boisterous wig-headed

to tatters, to very rags, to split the ears of the ground-   *10*
lings,° who for the most part are capable of° nothing
but inexplicable dumb shows° and noise. I would have
such a fellow whipped for o'erdoing Termagant. It out-
herods Herod.° Pray you avoid it.

Player. I warrant your honor.   *15*

Hamlet. Be not too tame neither, but let your own discretion
be your tutor. Suit the action to the word, the word
to the action, with this special observance, that you
o'erstep not the modesty of nature. For anything so
o'erdone is from° the purpose of playing, whose end,   *20*
both at the first and now, was and is, to hold, as 'twere,
the mirror up to nature; to show virtue her own feature,
scorn her own image, and the very age and body of
the time his form and pressure.° Now, this overdone,
or come tardy off, though it makes the unskillful laugh, *25*
cannot but make the judicious grieve, the censure of
the which one must in your allowance o'erweigh a
whole theater of others. O, there be players that I have
seen play, and heard others praise, and that highly (not
to speak it profanely), that neither having th' accent of *30*
Christians, nor the gait of Christian, pagan, nor man,
have so strutted and bellowed that I have thought some
of Nature's journeymen° had made men, and not made
them well, they imitated humanity so abominably.

Player. I hope we have reformed that indifferently° with us, *35*
sir.

Hamlet. O, reform it altogether! And let those that play your
clowns speak no more than is set down for them, for
there be of them that will themselves laugh, to set on
some quantity of barren spectators to laugh too, though *40*
in the meantime some necessary question of the play
be then to be considered. That's villainous and shows
a most pitiful ambition in the fool that uses it. Go make
you ready.

Exit Players.

Enter Polonius, Guildenstern, and Rosencrantz.

[10-11]*groundlings* those who stood in the pit of the theater (the poorest and presumably
most ignorant of the audience)   [11]*are capable of* are able to understand   [12]*dumb
shows* (it had been the fashion for actors to preface plays or parts of plays with
silent mime)   [13-14]*Termagant . . . Herod* (boisterous characters in the old mystery
plays)   [20]*from* contrary to   [24]*pressure* image, impress   [33]*journeymen* workers not
yet masters of their craft   [35]*indifferently* tolerably

How now, my lord? Will the King hear this piece of   45
work?
Polonius. And the Queen too, and that presently.
Hamlet. Bid the players make haste.

                                        Exit Polonius.
Will you two help to hasten them?
Rosencrantz. Ay, my lord.   50

                                        Exeunt they two.
Hamlet. What, ho, Horatio!

    Enter Horatio.

Horatio. Here, sweet lord, at your service.
Hamlet. Horatio, thou art e'en as just a man
    As e'er my conversation coped withal.°
Horatio. O, my dear lord ——
Hamlet.   Nay, do not think I flatter.   55
    For what advancement° may I hope from thee,
    That no revenue hast but thy good spirits
    To feed and clothe thee? Why should the poor be flattered?
    No, let the candied° tongue lick absurd pomp,
    And crook the pregnant° hinges of the knee   60
    Where thrift° may follow fawning. Dost thou hear?
    Since my dear soul was mistress of her choice
    And could of men distinguish her election,
    S' hath sealed thee° for herself, for thou hast been
    As one, in suff'ring all, that suffers nothing,   65
    A man that Fortune's buffets and rewards
    Hast ta'en with equal thanks; and blest are those
    Whose blood° and judgment are so well commeddled°
    That they are not a pipe for Fortune's finger
    To sound what stop she please. Give me that man   70
    That is not passion's slave, and I will wear him
    In my heart's core, ay, in my heart of heart,
    As I do thee. Something too much of this —
    There is a play tonight before the King.
    One scene of it comes near the circumstance   75
    Which I have told thee, of my father's death.
    I prithee, when thou seest that act afoot,
    Even with the very comment° of thy soul

---

⁵⁴*coped withal* met with ⁵⁶*advancement* promotion ⁵⁹*candied* sugared, flattering ⁶⁰*pregnant* (1) pliant, (2) full of promise of good fortune ⁶¹*thrift* profit ⁶⁴*S' hath sealed thee* she (the soul) has set a mark on you ⁶⁸*blood* passion ⁶⁸*commeddled* blended ⁷⁸*very comment* deepest wisdom

Observe my uncle. If his occulted° guilt
Do not itself unkennel in one speech,   *80*
It is a damnèd ghost that we have seen,
And my imaginations are as foul
As Vulcan's stithy.° Give him heedful note,
For I mine eyes will rivet to his face,
And after we will both our judgments join   *85*
In censure of his seeming.°
Horatio.   Well, my lord.
If 'a steal aught the whilst this play is playing,
And scape detecting, I will pay the theft.

*Enter Trumpets and Kettledrums, King, Queen, Polonius, Ophelia,
Rosencrantz, Guildenstern, and other Lords attendant with his
Guard carrying torches. Danish March. Sound a Flourish.*

Hamlet. They are coming to the play: I must be idle;°
Get you a place.   *90*
King. How fares our cousin Hamlet?
Hamlet. Excellent, i' faith, of the chameleon's dish;° I eat the
air, promise-crammed; you cannot feed capons so.
King. I have nothing with this answer, Hamlet; these words
are not mine.   *95*
Hamlet. No, nor mine now. [*To Polonius.*] My lord, you
played once i' th' university, you say?
Polonius. That did I, my lord, and was accounted a good actor.
Hamlet. What did you enact?
Polonius. I did enact Julius Caesar. I was killed i' th' Capitol; *100*
Brutus killed me.
Hamlet. It was a brute part of him to kill so capital a calf
there. Be the players ready?
Rosencrantz. Ay, my lord. They stay upon your patience.
Queen. Come hither, my dear Hamlet, sit by me.   *105*
Hamlet. No, good mother. Here's metal more attractive.°
Polonius [*to the king*]. O ho! Do you mark that?
Hamlet. Lady, shall I lie in your lap?

    [*He lies at Ophelia's feet.*]

Ophelia. No, my lord.
Hamlet. I mean, my head upon your lap?   *110*

---

[79]*occulted* hidden   [83]*stithy* forge, smithy   [86]*censure of his seeming* judgment on
his looks   [89]*be idle* play the fool   [92]*the chameleon's dish* air (on which chameleons
were thought to live)   [106]*attractive* magnetic

Ophelia. Ay, my lord.

Hamlet. Do you think I meant country matters?°

Ophelia. I think nothing, my lord.

Hamlet. That's a fair thought to lie between maids' legs.

Ophelia. What is, my lord?   115

Hamlet. Nothing.

Ophelia. You are merry, my lord.

Hamlet. Who, I?

Ophelia. Ay, my lord.

Hamlet. O God, your only jig-maker!° What should a man   120
  do but be merry? For look you how cheerfully my
  mother looks, and my father died within's two hours.

Ophelia. Nay, 'tis twice two months, my lord.

Hamlet. So long? Nay then, let the devil wear black, for I'll
  have a suit of sables.° O heavens! Die two months ago,   125
  and not forgotten yet? Then there's hope a great man's
  memory may outlive his life half a year. But, by'r Lady,
  'a must build churches then, or else shall 'a suffer not
  thinking on, with the hobbyhorse,° whose epitaph is
  "For O, for O, the hobbyhorse is forgot!"°   130

The trumpets sound. Dumb show follows:

*Enter a King and a Queen very lovingly, the Queen embracing
him, and he her. She kneels; and makes show of protestation unto
him. He takes her up, and declines his head upon her neck. He
lies him down upon a bank of flowers. She, seeing him asleep,
leaves him. Anon comes in another man: takes off his crown, kisses
it, pours poison in the sleeper's ears, and leaves him. The Queen
returns, finds the King dead, makes passionate action. The poisoner,
with some three or four, come in again, seem to condole with her.
The dead body is carried away. The poisoner woos the Queen with
gifts; she seems harsh awhile, but in the end accepts love.*

                                                          Exeunt.

Ophelia. What means this, my lord?

Hamlet. Marry, this is miching mallecho;° it means mischief.

Ophelia. Belike this show imports the argument° of the play.

Enter Prologue.

---

¹¹²*country matters* rustic doings (with a pun on the vulgar word for the puden-
dum)   ¹²⁰*jig-maker* composer of songs and dances (often a Fool, who performed
them)   ¹²⁵*sables* (pun on "black" and "luxurious furs")   ¹²⁸⁻¹²⁹*hobbyhorse* mock
horse worn by a performer in the morris dance   ¹³²*miching mallecho* sneaking
mischief   ¹³³*argument* plot

Hamlet. We shall know by this fellow. The players cannot   *135*
  keep counsel; they'll tell all.
Ophelia. Will 'a tell us what this show meant?
Hamlet. Ay, or any show that you will show him. Be not
  you ashamed to show, he'll not shame to tell you what
  it means.
Ophelia. You are naught,° you are naught; I'll mark the play.   *140*
Prologue. For us, and for our tragedy,
  Here stooping to your clemency,
  We beg your hearing patiently.

                                                      [*Exit.*]

Hamlet. Is this a prologue, or the posy of a ring?°
Ophelia. 'Tis brief, my lord.   *145*
Hamlet. As woman's love.

  Enter [two Players as] King and Queen.

Player King. Full thirty times hath Phoebus' cart° gone round
  Neptune's salt wash° and Tellus'° orbèd ground,
  And thirty dozen moons with borrowed sheen
  About the world have times twelve thirties been,   *150*
  Since love our hearts, and Hymen did our hands,
  Unite commutual in most sacred bands.
Player Queen. So many journeys may the sun and moon
  Make us again count o'er ere love be done!
  But woe is me, you are so sick of late,   *155*
  So far from cheer and from your former state,
  That I distrust° you. Yet, though I distrust,
  Discomfort you, my lord, it nothing must.
  For women fear too much, even as they love,
  And women's fear and love hold quantity,   *160*
  In neither aught, or in extremity.°
  Now what my love is, proof° hath made you know,
  And as my love is sized, my fear is so.
  Where love is great, the littlest doubts are fear;
  Where little fears grow great, great love grows there. *165*
Player King. Faith, I must leave thee, love, and shortly too;
  My operant° powers their functions leave to do:
  And thou shalt live in this fair world behind,

---

¹⁴⁰*naught* wicked, improper   ¹⁴⁴*posy of a ring* motto inscribed in a ring   ¹⁴⁷*Phoebus'*
cart the sun's chariot   ¹⁴⁸*Neptune's salt wash* the sea   ¹⁴⁸*Tellus* Roman goddess
of the earth   ¹⁵⁷*distrust* am anxious about   ¹⁶⁰⁻¹⁶¹*And women's . . . in extremity*
(perhaps the idea is that women's anxiety is great or little in proportion to their
love. The previous line, unrhymed, may be a false start that Shakespeare neglected
to delete)   ¹⁶²*proof* experience   ¹⁶⁷*operant* active

Honored, beloved, and haply one as kind
For husband shalt thou ——
Player Queen.   O, confound the rest!   *170*
Such love must needs be treason in my breast.
In second husband let me be accurst!
None wed the second but who killed the first.
Hamlet [*aside*]. That's wormwood.°
Player Queen. The instances° that second marriage move°   *175*
Are base respects of thrift,° but none of love.
A second time I kill my husband dead
When second husband kisses me in bed.
Player King. I do believe you think what now you speak,
But what we do determine oft we break.   *180*
Purpose is but the slave to memory,
Of violent birth, but poor validity,°
Which now like fruit unripe sticks on the tree,
But fall unshaken when they mellow be.
Most necessary 'tis that we forget   *185*
To pay ourselves what to ourselves is debt.
What to ourselves in passion we propose,
The passion ending, doth the purpose lose.
The violence of either grief or joy
Their own enactures° with themselves destroy: *190*
Where ioy most revels, grief doth most lament;
Grief joys, joy grieves, on slender accident.
This world is not for aye, nor 'tis not strange
That even our loves should with our fortunes change,
For 'tis a question left us yet to prove,   *195*
Whether love lead fortune, or else fortune love.
The great man down, you mark his favorite flies;
The poor advanced makes friends of enemies;
And hitherto doth love on fortune tend,
For who not needs shall never lack a friend;   *200*
And who in want a hollow friend doth try,
Directly seasons him° his enemy.
But, orderly to end where I begun,
Our wills and fates do so contrary run
That our devices still are overthrown;   *205*
Our thoughts are ours, their ends none of our own.
So think thou wilt no second husband wed,

But die thy thoughts when thy first lord is dead.
Player Queen. Nor earth to give me food, nor heaven light,
    Sport and repose lock from me day and night,   *210*
    To desperation turn my trust and hope,
    An anchor's° cheer in prison be my scope,
    Each opposite that blanks° the face of joy
    Meet what I would have well, and it destroy:
    Both here and hence pursue me lasting strife,   *215*
    If, once a widow, ever I be wife!
Hamlet. If she should break it now!
Player King. 'Tis deeply sworn. Sweet, leave me here awhile;
    My spirits grow dull, and fain I would beguile
    The tedious day with sleep.
Player Queen.   Sleep rock thy brain,   *220*

    [*He*] *sleeps.*

And never come mischance between us twain!

                                   Exit.

Hamlet. Madam, how like you this play?
Queen. The lady doth protest too much, methinks.
Hamlet. O, but she'll keep her word.
King. Have you heard the argument?° Is there no offense in't? *225*
Hamlet. No, no, they do but jest, poison in jest; no offense
    i' th' world.
King. What do you call the play?
Hamlet. *The Mousetrap.* Marry, how? Tropically.° This play
    is the image of a murder done in Vienna: Gonzago is   *230*
    the Duke's name; his wife, Baptista. You shall see anon.
    'Tis a knavish piece of work, but what of that? Your
    Majesty, and we that have free° souls, it touches us
    not. Let the galled jade winch;° our withers are unwrung.

    Enter Lucianus.

This is one Lucianus, nephew to the King.   *235*
Ophelia. You are as good as a chorus, my lord.
Hamlet. I could interpret° between you and your love, if I
    could see the puppets dallying.
Ophelia. You are keen,° my lord, you are keen.

---

²¹²*anchor's* anchorite's, hermit's ²¹³***opposite that blanks*** adverse thing that
blanches ²²⁵***argument*** plot ²²⁹***Tropically*** figuratively (with a pun on "trap") ²³³***free***
innocent ²³⁴***galled jade winch*** chafed horse wince ²³⁷***interpret*** (like a showman
explaining the action of puppets) ²³⁹***keen*** (1) sharp, (2) sexually aroused

Hamlet. It would cost you a groaning to take off mine edge.   *240*
Ophelia. Still better, and worse.
Hamlet. So you mistake° your husbands. — Begin, murderer.
    Leave thy damnable faces and begin. Come, the croaking
    raven doth bellow for revenge.
Lucianus. Thoughts black, hands apt, drugs fit, and time agreeing, *245*
    Confederate season,° else no creature seeing,
    Thou mixture rank, of midnight weeds collected,
    With Hecate's ban° thrice blasted, thrice infected,
    Thy natural magic and dire property°
    On wholesome life usurps immediately.   *250*

    Pours the poison in his ears.

Hamlet. 'A poisons him i' th' garden for his estate. His name's
    Gonzago. The story is extant, and written in very choice
    Italian. You shall see anon how the murderer gets the
    love of Gonzago's wife.
Ophelia. The King rises.   *255*
Hamlet. What, frighted with false fire?°
Queen. How fares my lord?
Polonius. Give o'er the play.
King. Give me some light. Away!
Polonius. Lights, lights, lights!   *260*
                      Exeunt all but Hamlet and Horatio.
Hamlet.   Why, let the strucken deer go weep,
        The hart ungallèd play:
      For some must watch, while some must sleep;
        Thus runs the world away.
    Would not this, sir, and a forest of feathers° — if the   *265*
    rest of my fortunes turn Turk° with me — with two
    Provincial roses° on my razed° shoes, get me a fellowship
    in a cry° of players?
Horatio. Half a share.
Hamlet. A whole one, I.   *270*

        For thou dost know, O Damon dear,
          This realm dismantled was

---

²⁴²*mistake* err in taking   ²⁴⁶*Confederate season* the opportunity allied with
me   ²⁴⁸*Hecate's ban* the curse of the goddess of sorcery   ²⁴⁹*property* nature   ²⁵⁶*false
fire* blank discharge of firearms   ²⁶⁵*feathers* (plumes were sometimes part of a
costume)   ²⁶⁶*turn Turk* i.e., go bad, treat me badly   ²⁶⁶⁻²⁶⁷*Provincial roses* rosettes
like the roses of Provence(?)   ²⁶⁷*razed* ornamented with slashes   ²⁶⁸*cry* pack, company

Of Jove himself; and now reigns here
                   A very, very — pajock.°
Horatio. You might have rhymed.°   *275*
Hamlet. O good Horatio, I'll take the ghost's word for a
    thousand pound. Didst perceive?
Horatio. Very well, my lord.
Hamlet. Upon the talk of poisoning?
Horatio. I did very well note him.   *280*
Hamlet. Ah ha! Come, some music! Come, the recorders!°

    For if the King like not the comedy,
    Why then, belike he likes it not, perdy.°

Come, some music!

Enter Rosencrantz and Guildenstern.

Guildenstern. Good my lord, vouchsafe me a word with you.   *285*
Hamlet. Sir, a whole history.
Guildenstern. The King, sir ——
Hamlet. Ay, sir, what of him?
Guildenstern. Is in his retirement marvelous distemp'red.
Hamlet. With drink, sir?   *290*
Guildenstern. No, my lord, with choler.°
Hamlet. Your wisdom should show itself more richer to signify
    this to the doctor, for me to put him to his purgation
    would perhaps plunge him into more choler.
Guildenstern. Good my lord, put your discourse into some   *295*
    frame,° and start not so wildly from my affair.
Hamlet. I am tame, sir; pronounce.
Guildenstern. The Queen, your mother, in most great affliction
    of spirit hath sent me to you.
Hamlet. You are welcome.   *300*
Guildenstern. Nay, good my lord, this courtesy is not of the
    right breed. If it shall please you to make me a whole-
    some answer, I will do your mother's commandment:
    if not, your pardon and my return shall be the end of
    my business.   *305*
Hamlet. Sir, I cannot.
Rosencrantz. What, my lord?

---

[274]*pajock* peacock [275]*You might have rhymed* i.e., rhymed "was" with
"ass" [281]*recorders* flutelike instruments [283]*perdy* by God (French: *par dieu*) [291]*choler*
anger (but Hamlet pretends to take the word in its sense of "biliousness") [296]*frame*
order, control

Hamlet. Make you a wholesome° answer; my wit's diseased.
But, sir, such answer as I can make, you shall command,
or rather, as you say, my mother. Therefore no more,   *310*
but to the matter. My mother, you say ——
Rosencrantz. Then thus she says: your behavior hath struck
her into amazement and admiration.°
Hamlet. O wonderful son, that can so stonish a mother! But
is there no sequel at the heels of this mother's admiration?   *315*
Impart.
Rosencrantz. She desires to speak with you in her closet ere
you go to bed.
Hamlet. We shall obey, were she ten times our mother. Have
you any further trade with us?   *320*
Rosencrantz. My lord, you once did love me.
Hamlet. And do still, by these pickers and stealers.
Rosencrantz. Good my lord, what is your cause of distemper?
You do surely bar the door upon your own liberty, if
you deny your griefs to your friend.   *325*
Hamlet. Sir, I lack advancement.°
Rosencrantz. How can that be, when you have the voice of
the King himself for your succession in Denmark?

Enter the Players with recorders.

Hamlet. Ay, sir, but "while the grass grows" — the proverb°
is something musty. O, the recorders. Let me see one.   *330*
To withdraw° with you — why do you go about to
recover the wind° of me as if you would drive me into
a toil?°
Guildenstern. O my lord, if my duty be too bold, my love
is too unmannerly.°   *335*
Hamlet. I do not well understand that. Will you play upon
this pipe?
Guildenstern. My lord, I cannot.
Hamlet. I pray you.
Guildenstern. Believe me, I cannot.   *340*

---

[308]*wholesome* sane   [313]*admiration* wonder   [322]*pickers and stealers* i.e., hands (with
reference to the prayer; "Keep my hands from picking and stealing")   [326]*advancement*
promotion   [329]*proverb* ("While the grass groweth, the horse starveth")   [331]*withdraw*
speak in private   [332]*recover the wind* get on the windward side (as in hunting)   [333]*toil*
snare   [334-335]*if my duty . . . too unmannerly* i.e., if these questions seem rude, it
is because my love for you leads me beyond good manners

Hamlet. I do beseech you.

Guildenstern. I know no touch of it, my lord.

Hamlet. It is as easy as lying. Govern these ventages° with
your fingers and thumb, give it breath with your mouth,
and it will discourse most eloquent music. Look you,   *345*
these are the stops.

Guildenstern. But these cannot I command to any utt'rance
of harmony; I have not the skill.

Hamlet. Why, look you now, how unworthy a thing you
make of me! You would play upon me; you would   *350*
seem to know my stops; you would pluck out the heart
of my mystery; you would sound me from my lowest
note to the top of my compass;° and there is much
music, excellent voice, in this little organ,° yet cannot
you make it speak. 'Sblood, do you think I am easier   *355*
to be played on than a pipe? Call me what instrument
you will, though you can fret° me, you cannot play
upon me.

Enter Polonius.

God bless you, sir!

Polonius. My lord, the Queen would speak with you, and   *360*
presently.

Hamlet. Do you see yonder cloud that's almost in shape of
a camel?

Polonius. By th' mass and 'tis, like a camel indeed.

Hamlet. Methinks it is like a weasel.   *365*

Polonius. It is backed like a weasel.

Hamlet. Or like a whale.

Polonius. Very like a whale.

Hamlet. Then I will come to my mother by and by. [*Aside.*]
They fool me to the top of my bent.° — I will come   *370*
by and by.°

Polonius. I will say so.

Exit.

Hamlet. "By and by" is easily said. Leave me, friends.

[*Exeunt all but Hamlet.*]

'Tis now the very witching time of night,
When churchyards yawn, and hell itself breathes out   *375*
Contagion to this world. Now could I drink hot blood

---

[343]*ventages* vents, stops on a recorder   [353]*compass* range of voice   [354]*organ* i.e.,
the recorder   [357]*fret* vex (with a pun alluding to the frets, or ridges, that guide
the fingering on some instruments)   [370]*They fool . . . my bent* they compel me
to play the fool to the limit of my capacity   [371]*by and by* very soon

And do such bitter business as the day
Would quake to look on. Soft, now to my mother.
O heart, lose not thy nature; let not ever
The soul of Nero° enter this firm bosom.   *380*
Let me be cruel, not unnatural;
I will speak daggers to her, but use none.
My tongue and soul in this be hypocrites:
How in my words somever she be shent,°
To give them seals° never, my soul, consent!   *385*

                                                                      Exit.

[**Scene III.** *The castle.*]

Enter King, Rosencrantz, and Guildenstern.

King. I like him not, nor stands it safe with us
    To let his madness range. Therefore prepare you.
    I your commission will forthwith dispatch,
    And he to England shall along with you.
    The terms° of our estate may not endure   *5*
    Hazard so near's° as doth hourly grow
    Out of his brows.
Guildenstern.   We will ourselves provide.
    Most holy and religious fear it is
    To keep those many many bodies safe
    That live and feed upon your Majesty.   *10*
Rosencrantz. The single and peculiar° life is bound
    With all the strength and armor of the mind
    To keep itself from noyance,° but much more
    That spirit upon whose weal depends and rests
    The lives of many. The cess of majesty°   *15*
    Dies not alone, but like a gulf° doth draw
    What's near it with it; or it is a massy wheel
    Fixed on the summit of the highest mount,
    To whose huge spokes ten thousand lesser things
    Are mortised and adjoined, which when it falls,   *20*
    Each small annexment, petty consequence,
    Attends° the boist'rous ruin. Never alone
    Did the King sigh, but with a general groan.

---

[380] ***Nero*** (Roman emperor who had his mother murdered)   [384] ***shent*** rebuked   [385] ***give them seals*** confirm them with deeds   III.iii.   [5] ***terms*** conditions   [6] ***near's*** near us   [11] ***peculiar*** individual, private   [13] ***noyance*** injury   [15] ***cess of majesty*** cessation (death) of a king   [16] ***gulf*** whirlpool   [22] ***Attends*** waits on, participates in

King. Arm° you, I pray you, to this speedy voyage,
For we will fetters put about this fear,   25
Which now goes too free-footed.
Rosencrantz.   We will haste us.
                                        Exeunt Gentlemen.
    Enter Polonius.

Polonius. My lord, he's going to his mother's closet.°
Behind the arras I'll convey myself
To hear the process.° I'll warrant she'll tax him home,°
And, as you said, and wisely was it said,   30
'Tis meet that some more audience than a mother,
Since nature makes them partial, should o'erhear
The speech of vantage.° Fare you well, my liege.
I'll call upon you ere you go to bed
And tell you what I know.
King.   Thanks, dear my lord.   35
                                        Exit [Polonius].
    O, my offense is rank, it smells to heaven;
It hath the primal eldest curse° upon't,
A brother's murder. Pray can I not,
Though inclination be as sharp as will.
My stronger guilt defeats my strong intent,   40
And like a man to double business bound
I stand in pause where I shall first begin,
And both neglect. What if this cursèd hand
Were thicker than itself with brother's blood,
Is there not rain enough in the sweet heavens   45
To wash it white as snow? Whereto serves mercy
But to confront° the visage of offense?
And what's in prayer but this twofold force,
To be forestallèd ere we come to fall,
Or pardoned being down? Then I'll look up.   50
My fault is past. But, O, what form of prayer
Can serve my turn? "Forgive me my foul murder"?
That cannot be, since I am still possessed
Of those effects° for which I did the murder,
My crown, mine own ambition, and my queen.   55

---

²⁴**Arm** prepare   ²⁷**closet** private room   ²⁹**process** proceedings   ²⁹**tax him home** censure
him sharply   ³³**of vantage** from an advantageous place   ³⁷**primal eldest curse** (curse
of Cain, who killed Abel)   ⁴⁷**confront** oppose   ⁵⁴**effects** things gained

May one be pardoned and retain th' offense?
In the corrupted currents of this world
Offense's gilded hand may shove by justice,
And oft 'tis seen the wicked prize itself
Buys out the law. But 'tis not so above.   60
There is no shuffling;° there the action lies
In his true nature, and we ourselves compelled,
Even to the teeth and forehead of our faults,
To give in evidence. What then? What rests?°
Try what repentance can. What can it not?   65
Yet what can it when one cannot repent?
O wretched state! O bosom black as death!
O limèd° soul, that struggling to be free
Art more engaged!° Help, angels! Make assay.°
Bow, stubborn knees, and, heart with strings of steel,   70
Be soft as sinews of the newborn babe.
All may be well. [*He kneels.*]

Enter Hamlet.

Hamlet. Now might I do it pat, now 'a is a-praying,
And now I'll do't. And so 'a goes to heaven,
And so am I revenged. That would be scanned.°   75
A villain kills my father, and for that
I, his sole son, do this same villain send
To heaven.
Why, this is hire and salary, not revenge.
'A took my father grossly, full of bread,°   80
With all his crimes broad blown,° as flush° as May;
And how his audit° stands, who knows save heaven?
But in our circumstance and course of thought,
'Tis heavy with him; and am I then revenged,
To take him in the purging of his soul,   85
When he is fit and seasoned for his passage?
No.
Up, sword, and know thou a more horrid hent.°
When he is drunk asleep, or in his rage,
Or in th' incestuous pleasure of his bed,   90
At game a-swearing, or about some act

---

⁶¹*shuffling* trickery ⁶⁴*rests* remains ⁶⁸*limèd* caught (as with birdlime, a sticky substance spread on boughs to snare birds) ⁶⁹*engaged* ensnared ⁶⁹*assay* an attempt ⁷⁵*would be scanned* ought to be looked into ⁸⁰*bread* i.e., worldly gratification ⁸¹*crimes broad blown* sins in full bloom ⁸¹*flush* vigorous ⁸²*audit* account ⁸⁸*hent* grasp (here, occasion for seizing)

That has no relish° of salvation in't —
Then trip him, that his heels may kick at heaven,
And that his soul may be as damned and black
As hell, whereto it goes. My mother stays.   **95**
This physic° but prolongs thy sickly days.   *Exit.*
King [rises]. My words fly up, my thoughts remain below.
Words without thoughts never to heaven go.   *Exit.*

[**Scene IV.** *The Queen's closet.*]

Enter [Queen] Gertrude and Polonius.

Polonius. 'A will come straight. Look you lay home° to him.
Tell him his pranks have been too broad° to bear with,
And that your Grace hath screened and stood between
Much heat and him. I'll silence me even here.
Pray you be round with him.   **5**
Hamlet (within). Mother, Mother, Mother!
Queen. I'll warrant you; fear me not. Withdraw; I hear him
   coming.   [*Polonius hides behind the arras.*]

Enter Hamlet.

Hamlet. Now, Mother, what's the matter?
Queen. Hamlet, thou hast thy father much offended.   **10**
Hamlet. Mother, you have my father much offended.
Queen. Come, come, you answer with an idle° tongue.
Hamlet. Go, go, you question with a wicked tongue.
Queen. Why, how now, Hamlet?
Hamlet.   What's the matter now?
Queen. Have you forgot me?
Hamlet.   No, by the rood,° not so!   **15**
   You are the Queen, your husband's brother's wife,
   And, would it were not so, you are my mother.
Queen. Nay, then I'll set those to you that can speak.
Hamlet. Come, come, and sit you down. You shall not budge.
   You go not till I set you up a glass°   **20**
   Where you may see the inmost part of you!
Queen. What wilt thou do? Thou wilt not murder me?
   Help, ho!
Polonius [behind]. What, ho! Help!
Hamlet [draws]. How now? A rat? Dead for a ducat, dead!   **25**

---

⁹²*relish* flavor   ⁹⁶*physic* (Claudius' purgation by prayer, as Hamlet thinks in line
85) III.iv. ¹*lay home* thrust (rebuke) him sharply   ²*broad* unrestrained   ¹²*idle*
foolish   ¹⁵*rood* cross   ²⁰*glass* mirror

[*Makes a pass through the arras and*] *kills Polonius.*

Polonius [*behind*]. O, I am slain!
Queen.   O me, what hast thou done?
Hamlet. Nay, I know not. Is it the King?
Queen. O, what a rash and bloody deed is this!
Hamlet. A bloody deed — almost as bad, good Mother,
  As kill a king, and marry with his brother.   30
Queen. As kill a king?
Hamlet.   Ay, lady, it was my word.

[*Lifts up the arras and sees Polonius.*]

  Thou wretched, rash, intruding fool, farewell!
  I took thee for thy better. Take thy fortune.
  Thou find'st to be too busy is some danger. —
  Leave wringing of your hands. Peace, sit you down   35
  And let me wring your heart, for so I shall
  If it be made of penetrable stuff,
  If damnèd custom have not brazed° it so
  That it be proof° and bulwark against sense.°
Queen. What have I done that thou dar'st wag thy tongue   40
  In noise so rude against me?
Hamlet.   Such an act
  That blurs the grace and blush of modesty,
  Calls virtue hypocrite, takes off the rose
  From the fair forehead of an innocent love,
  And sets a blister° there, makes marriage vows   45
  As false as dicers' oaths. O, such a deed
  As from the body of contraction° plucks
  The very soul, and sweet religion makes
  A rhapsody° of words! Heaven's face does glow
  O'er this solidity and compound mass   50
  With heated visage, as against the doom
  Is thoughtsick at the act.°
Queen.   Ay me, what act,
  That roars so loud and thunders in the index?°
Hamlet. Look here upon this picture, and on this,
  The counterfeit presentment° of two brothers.   55

---

³⁸*brazed* hardened like brass   ³⁹*proof* armor   ³⁹*sense* feeling   ⁴⁵*sets a blister* brands
(as a harlot)   ⁴⁷*contraction* marriage contract   ⁴⁹*rhapsody* senseless string
⁴⁹⁻⁵²*Heaven's face . . . the act* i.e., the face of heaven blushes over this earth
(compounded of four elements), the face hot, as if Judgment Day were near, and
it is thoughtsick at the act   ⁵³*index* prologue   ⁵⁵*counterfeit presentment* represented
image

See what a grace was seated on this brow:
Hyperion's curls, the front° of Jove himself,
An eye like Mars, to threaten and command,
A station° like the herald Mercury
New lighted on a heaven-kissing hill —   60
A combination and a form indeed
Where every god did seem to set his seal
To give the world assurance of a man.
This was your husband. Look you now what follows.
Here is your husband, like a mildewed ear   65
Blasting his wholesome brother. Have you eyes?
Could you on this fair mountain leave to feed,
And batten° on this moor? Ha! Have you eyes?
You cannot call it love, for at your age
The heyday° in the blood is tame, it's humble,   70
And waits upon the judgment, and what judgment
Would step from this to this? Sense° sure you have,
Else could you not have motion, but sure that sense
Is apoplexed,° for madness would not err,
Nor sense to ecstasy° was ne'er so thralled   75
But it reserved some quantity of choice
To serve in such a difference. What devil wast
That thus hath cozened you at hoodman-blind?°
Eyes without feeling, feeling without sight,
Ears without hands or eyes, smelling sans° all,   80
Or but a sickly part of one true sense
Could not so mope.°
O shame, where is thy blush? Rebellious hell,
If thou canst mutine in a matron's bones,
To flaming youth let virtue be as wax   85
And melt in her own fire. Proclaim no shame
When the compulsive ardor° gives the charge,
Since frost itself as actively doth burn,
And reason panders will.°
Queen.   O Hamlet, speak no more.
Thou turn'st mine eyes into my very soul,   90
And there I see such black and grainèd° spots
As will not leave their tinct.°

°57*front* forehead °59*station* bearing °68*batten* feed gluttonously °70*heyday*
excitement °72*Sense* feeling °74*apoplexed* paralyzed °75*ecstasy* madness °78*cozened*
you at hoodman-blind cheated you at blindman's buff °80*sans* without °82*mope* be
stupid °87*compulsive ardor* compelling passion °89*reason panders will* reason acts
as a procurer for desire °91*grainèd* dyed in grain (fast dyed) °92*tinct* color

Hamlet.   Nay, but to live
  In the rank sweat of an enseamèd° bed,
  Stewed in corruption, honeying and making love
  Over the nasty sty ——
Queen.   O, speak to me no more.   *95*
  These words like daggers enter in my ears.
  No more, sweet Hamlet.
Hamlet.   A murderer and a villain,
  A slave that is not twentieth part the tithe°
  Of your precedent lord, a vice° of kings,
  A cutpurse of the empire and the rule,   *100*
  That from a shelf the precious diadem stole
  And put it in his pocket ——
Queen.   No more.

  Enter Ghost.

Hamlet. A king of shreds and patches —
  Save me and hover o'er me with your wings,
  You heavenly guards! What would your gracious figure?   *105*
Queen. Alas, he's mad.
Hamlet. Do you not come your tardy son to chide,
  That, lapsed in time and passion, lets go by
  Th' important acting of your dread command?
  O, say!   *110*
Ghost. Do not forget. This visitation
  Is but to whet thy almost blunted purpose.
  But look, amazement on thy mother sits.
  O, step between her and her fighting soul!
  Conceit° in weakest bodies strongest works.   *115*
  Speak to her, Hamlet.
Hamlet.   How is it with you, lady?
Queen. Alas, how is't with you,
  That you do bend your eye on vacancy,
  And with th' incorporal° air do hold discourse?
  Forth at your eyes your spirits wildly peep,   *120*
  And as the sleeping soldiers in th' alarm
  Your bedded hair° like life in excrements°
  Start up and stand an end.° O gentle son,
  Upon the heat and flame of thy distemper

---

⁹³*enseamèd* (perhaps "soaked in grease," i.e., sweaty; perhaps "much wrinkled") ⁹⁶*tithe* tenth part ⁹⁹*vice* (like the Vice, a fool and mischiefmaker in the old morality plays) ¹¹⁵*Conceit* imagination ¹¹⁹*incorporal* bodiless ¹²²*bedded hair* hairs laid flat ¹²²*excrements* outgrowths (here, the hair) ¹²³*an end* on end

Sprinkle cool patience. Whereon do you look?   125
Hamlet. On him, on him! Look you, how pale he glares!
His form and cause conjoined, preaching to stones,
Would make them capable.° — Do not look upon me,
Lest with this piteous action you convert
My stern effects.° Then what I have to do   130
Will want true color; tears perchance for blood.
Queen. To whom do you speak this?
Hamlet.   Do you see nothing there?
Queen. Nothing at all; yet all that is I see.
Hamlet. Nor did you nothing hear?
Queen.   No, nothing but ourselves.
Hamlet. Why, look you there! Look how it steals away!   135
My father, in his habit° as he lived!
Look where he goes even now at the portal!

                                              Exit Ghost.

Queen. This is the very coinage of your brain.
This bodiless creation ecstasy
Is very cunning in.
Hamlet.   Ecstasy?   140
My pulse as yours doth temperately keep time
And makes as healthful music. It is not madness
That I have uttered. Bring me to the test,
And I the matter will reword, which madness
Would gambol° from. Mother, for love of grace,   145
Lay not that flattering unction° to your soul,
That not your trespass but my madness speaks.
It will but skin and film the ulcerous place
Whiles rank corruption, mining° all within,
Infects unseen. Confess yourself to heaven,   150
Repent what's past, avoid what is to come,
And do not spread the compost° on the weeds
To make them ranker. Forgive me this my virtue.
For in the fatness of these pursy° times
Virtue itself of vice must pardon beg,   155
Yea, curb° and woo for leave to do him good.
Queen. O Hamlet, thou hast cleft my heart in twain.
Hamlet. O, throw away the worser part of it,

---

¹²⁸*capable* receptive   ¹²⁹⁻¹³⁰*convert/My stern effects* divert my stern deeds   ¹³⁶*habit*
garment (Q1, though a "bad" quarto, is probably correct in saying that at line
102 the ghost enters "in his nightgown," i.e., dressing gown)   ¹⁴⁵*gambol* start
away   ¹⁴⁶*unction* ointment   ¹⁴⁹*mining* undermining   ¹⁵²*compost* fertilizing
substance   ¹⁵⁴*pursy* bloated   ¹⁵⁶*curb* bow low

And live the purer with the other half.
Good night — but go not to my uncle's bed.   *160*
Assume a virtue, if you have it not.
That monster custom, who all sense doth eat,
Of habits devil, is angel yet in this,
That to the use° of actions fair and good
He likewise gives a frock or livery°   *165*
That aptly is put on. Refrain tonight,
And that shall lend a kind of easiness
To the next abstinence; the next more easy;
For use almost can change the stamp of nature,
And either° the devil, or throw him out   *170*
With wondrous potency. Once more, good night,
And when you are desirous to be blest,
I'll blessing beg of you. — For this same lord,
I do repent; but heaven hath pleased it so,
To punish me with this, and this with me,   *175*
That I must be their° scourge and minister.
I will bestow° him and will answer well
The death I gave him. So again, good night.
I must be cruel only to be kind.
Thus bad begins, and worse remains behind.   *180*
One word more, good lady.
Queen.   What shall I do?
Hamlet. Not this, by no means, that I bid you do:
Let the bloat King tempt you again to bed,
Pinch wanton on your cheek, call you his mouse,
And let him, for a pair of reechy° kisses,   *185*
Or paddling in your neck with his damned fingers,
Make you to ravel° all this matter out,
That I essentially am not in madness,
But mad in craft. 'Twere good you let him know,
For who that's but a queen, fair, sober, wise,   *190*
Would from a paddock,° from a bat, a gib,°
Such dear concernings hide? Who would do so?
No, in despite of sense and secrecy,
Unpeg the basket on the house's top,
Let the birds fly, and like the famous ape,   *195*

---

¹⁶⁴*use* practice ¹⁶⁵*livery* characteristic garment (punning on "habits" in line 163) ¹⁷⁰*either* (probably a word is missing after *either*; among suggestions are "master," "curb," and "house"; but possibly *either* is a verb meaning "make easier") ¹⁷⁶*their* i.e., the heavens' ¹⁷⁷*bestow* stow, lodge ¹⁸⁵*reechy* foul (literally "smoky") ¹⁸⁷*ravel* unravel, reveal ¹⁹¹*paddock* toad ¹⁹¹*gib* tomcat

To try conclusions,° in the basket creep
And break your own neck down.
Queen. Be thou assured, if words be made of breath,
And breath of life, I have no life to breathe
What thou hast said to me.   *200*
Hamlet. I must to England; you know that?
Queen.   Alack,
I had forgot. 'Tis so concluded on.
Hamlet. There's letters sealed, and my two school-fellows,
Whom I will trust as I will adders fanged,
They bear the mandate;° they must sweep my way   *205*
And marshal me to knavery. Let it work;
For 'tis the sport to have the enginer
Hoist with his own petar,° and 't shall go hard
But I will delve one yard below their mines
And blow them at the moon. O,'tis most sweet   *210*
When in one line two crafts° directly meet.
This man shall set me packing:
I'll lug the guts into the neighbor room.
Mother, good night. Indeed, this counselor
Is now most still, most secret, and most grave,   *215*
Who was in life a foolish prating knave.
Come, sir, to draw toward an end with you.
Good night, Mother.
                          [*Exit the Queen. Then*] *exit Hamlet,*
                                   tugging in Polonius.

[**ACT IV**

Scene I. *The castle.*]

Enter King and Queen, with Rosencrantz and Guildenstern.

King. There's matter in these sighs. These profound heaves
You must translate; 'tis fit we understand them.
Where is your son?
Queen. Bestow this place on us a little while.
                    [*Exeunt Rosencrantz and Guildenstern.*]
Ah, mine own lord, what have I seen tonight!   *5*
King. What, Gertrude? How does Hamlet?

---

[196]**To try conclusions** to make experiments [205]**mandate** command [208]**petar**
bomb [211]**crafts** (1) boats, (2) acts of guile, crafty schemes

Queen. Mad as the sea and wind when both contend
    Which is the mightier. In his lawless fit,
    Behind the arras hearing something stir,
    Whips out his rapier, cries, "A rat, a rat!"   *10*
    And in this brainish apprehension° kills
    The unseen good old man.
King.   O heavy deed!
    It had been so with us, had we been there.
    His liberty is full of threats to all,
    To you yourself, to us, to every one.   *15*
    Alas, how shall this bloody deed be answered?
    It will be laid to us, whose providence°
    Should have kept short, restrained, and out of haunt°
    This mad young man. But so much was our love
    We would not understand what was most fit,   *20*
    But, like the owner of a foul disease,
    To keep it from divulging, let it feed
    Even on the pith of life. Where is he gone?
Queen. To draw apart the body he hath killed;
    O'er whom his very madness, like some ore   *25*
    Among a mineral° of metals base,
    Shows itself pure. 'A weeps for what is done.
King. O Gertrude, come away!
    The sun no sooner shall the mountains touch
    But we will ship him hence, and this vile deed   *30*
    We must with all our majesty and skill
    Both countenance and excuse. Ho, Guildenstern!

Enter Rosencrantz and Guildenstern.

    Friends both, go join you with some further aid:
    Hamlet in madness hath Polonius slain,
    And from his mother's closet hath he dragged him.   *35*
    Go seek him out; speak fair, and bring the body
    Into the chapel. I pray you haste in this.
                [*Exeunt Rosencrantz and Guildenstern.*]
    Come, Gertrude, we'll call up our wisest friends
    And let them know both what we mean to do
    And what's untimely done . . .°   *40*
    Whose whisper o'er the world's diameter,

IV.i. ¹¹*brainish apprehension* mad imagination ¹⁷*providence* foresight ²⁸*out of haunt* away from association with others ²⁵⁻²⁶*ore/Among a mineral* vein of gold in a mine ⁴⁰*done . . .* (evidently something has dropped out of the text. Cappell's conjecture, "So, haply slander," is usually printed)

As level as the cannon to his blank°
Transports his poisoned shot, may miss our name
And hit the woundless° air. O, come away!
My soul is full of discord and dismay.   *45*

               Exeunt.

[Scene II. *The castle.*]

Enter Hamlet.

Hamlet. Safely stowed.
Gentlemen (within). Hamlet! Lord Hamlet!
Hamlet. But soft, what noise? Who calls on Hamlet?
   O, here they come.

Enter Rosencrantz and Guildenstern.

Rosencrantz. What have you done, my lord, with the dead
     body?   *5*
Hamlet. Compounded it with dust, whereto 'tis kin.
Rosencrantz. Tell us where 'tis, that we may take it thence
   And bear it to the chapel.
Hamlet. Do not believe it.
Rosencrantz. Believe what?   *10*
Hamlet. That I can keep your counsel and not mine own.
   Besides, to be demanded of° a sponge, what replication°
   should be made by the son of a king?
Rosencrantz. Take you me for a sponge, my lord?
Hamlet. Ay, sir, that soaks up the King's countenance,° his   *15*
   rewards, his authorities. But such officers do the King
   best service in the end. He keeps them, like an ape, in
   the corner of his jaw, first mouthed, to be last swallowed.
   When he needs what you have gleaned, it is but squeezing
   you and, sponge, you shall be dry again.   *20*
Rosencrantz. I understand you not, my lord.
Hamlet. I am glad of it: a knavish speech sleeps in a foolish ear.
Rosencrantz. My lord, you must tell us where the body is
   and go with us to the King.
Hamlet. The body is with the King, but the King is not with   *25*
   the body.° The King is a thing —

---

⁴²*blank* white center of a target   ⁴⁴*woundless* invulnerable   IV.ii.   ¹²*demanded of*
questioned by   ¹²*replication* reply   ¹⁵*countenance* favor   ²⁵⁻²⁶*The body . . . body*
i.e., the body of authority is with Claudius, but spiritually he is not the true king

Guildenstern. A thing, my lord?
Hamlet. Of nothing. Bring me to him. Hide fox, and all after.°

Exeunt.

[**Scene III.** *The castle.*]

Enter King, and two or three.

King. I have sent to seek him and to find the body:
How dangerous is it that this man goes loose!
Yet must not we put the strong law on him:
He's loved of the distracted° multitude,
Who like not in their judgment, but their eyes,   5
And where 'tis so, th' offender's scourge is weighed,
But never the offense. To bear° all smooth and even,
This sudden sending him away must seem
Deliberate pause.° Diseases desperate grown
By desperate appliance are relieved,   10
Or not at all.

Enter Rosencrantz, [Guildenstern,] and all the rest.

How now? What hath befall'n?
Rosencrantz. Where the dead body is bestowed, my lord,
We cannot get from him.
King.   But where is he?
Rosencrantz. Without, my lord; guarded, to know your pleasure.
King. Bring him before us.
Rosencrantz.   Ho! Bring in the lord.   15

They enter.

King. Now, Hamlet, where's Polonius?
Hamlet. At supper.
King. At supper? Where?
Hamlet. Not where he eats, but where 'a is eaten. A certain
convocation of politic° worms are e'en at him. Your   20
worm is your only emperor for diet. We fat all creatures
else to fat us, and we fat ourselves for maggots. Your
fat king and your lean beggar is but variable service°
— two dishes, but to one table. That's the end.

---

[28]*Hide fox, and all after* (a cry in a game such as hide-and-seek; Hamlet runs from
the stage) IV.iii. [4]*distracted* bewildered, senseless   [7]*bear* carry out   [9]*pause*
planning   [20]*politic* statesmanlike, shrewd   [23]*variable service* different courses

King. Alas, alas!   25
Hamlet. A man may fish with the worm that hath eat of a
   king, and eat of the fish that hath fed of that worm.
King. What dost thou mean by this?
Hamlet. Nothing but to show you how a king may go a
   progress° through the guts of a beggar.   30
King. Where is Polonius?
Hamlet. In heaven. Send thither to see. If your messenger
   find him not there, seek him i' th' other place yourself.
   But if indeed you find him not within this month, you
   shall nose him as you go up the stairs into the lobby.   35
King [*to Attendants*]. Go seek him there.
Hamlet. 'A will stay till you come.

                                               [*Exeunt Attendants.*]

King. Hamlet, this deed, for thine especial safety,
   Which we do tender° as we dearly grieve
   For that which thou hast done, must send thee hence   40
   With fiery quickness. Therefore prepare thyself.
   The bark is ready and the wind at help,
   Th' associates tend,° and everything is bent
   For England.
Hamlet.   For England?
King.   Ay, Hamlet.
Hamlet.   Good.
King. So is it, if thou knew'st our purposes.   45
Hamlet. I see a cherub° that sees them. But come, for England!
   Farewell, dear Mother.
King. Thy loving father, Hamlet.
Hamlet. My mother — father and mother is man and wife,
   man and wife is one flesh, and so, my mother. Come,   50
   for England!

                                                          Exit.

King. Follow him at foot;° tempt him with speed abroad.
   Delay it not; I'll have him hence tonight.
   Away! For everything is sealed and done
   That else leans° on th' affair. Pray you make haste.   55

                                         [*Exeunt all but the King.*]

   And, England, if my love thou hold'st at aught —
   As my great power thereof may give thee sense,
   Since yet thy cicatrice° looks raw and red
   After the Danish sword, and thy free awe°

---

³⁰*progress* royal journey   ³⁹*tender* hold dear   ⁴³*tend* wait   ⁴⁶*cherub* angel of
knowledge   ⁵²*at foot* closely   ⁵⁵*leans* depends   ⁵⁸*cicatrice* scar   ⁵⁹*free awe* uncom-
pelled submission

Pays homage to us — thou mayst not coldly set   *60*
Our sovereign process,° which imports at full
By letters congruing to that effect
The present° death of Hamlet. Do it, England,
For like the hectic° in my blood he rages,
And thou must cure me. Till I know 'tis done,   *65*
How'er my haps,° my joys were ne'er begun.

                                              Exit.

[Scene IV. *A plain in Denmark.*]

    Enter Fortinbras with his Army over the stage.

Fortinbras. Go, Captain, from me greet the Danish king.
    Tell him that by his license Fortinbras
    Craves the conveyance of° a promised march
    Over his kingdom. You know the rendezvous.
    If that his Majesty would aught with us,   *5*
    We shall express our duty in his eye;°
    And let him know so.
Captain.   I will do't, my lord.
Fortinbras. Go softly° on.

                  [Exeunt all but the Captain.]

    Enter Hamlet, Rosencrantz, &c.

Hamlet. Good sir, whose powers° are these?
Captain. They are of Norway, sir.   *10*
Hamlet. How purposed, sir, I pray you?
Captain. Against some part of Poland.
Hamlet. Who commands them, sir?
Captain. The nephew to old Norway, Fortinbras.
Hamlet. Goes it against the main° of Poland, sir,   *15*
    Or for some frontier?
Captain. Truly to speak, and with no addition,°
    We go to gain a little patch of ground
    That hath in it no profit but the name.
    To pay five ducats, five, I would not farm it,   *20*
    Nor will it yield to Norway or the Pole
    A ranker° rate, should it be sold in fee.°
Hamlet. Why, then the Polack never will defend it.

---

⁶⁰⁻⁶¹*coldly set/Our sovereign process* regard slightly our royal command   ⁶³*present*
instant   ⁶⁴*hectic* fever   ⁶⁶*haps* chances, fortunes   IV.iv.   ³*conveyance of* escort for
⁶*in his eye* before his eyes (i.e., in his presence)   ⁸*softly* slowly   ⁹*powers* forces
¹⁵*main* main part   ¹⁷*with no addition* plainly   ²²*ranker* higher   ²²*in fee* outright

Captain. Yes, it is already garrisoned.
Hamlet. Two thousand souls and twenty thousand ducats   25
    Will not debate° the question of this straw.
    This is th' imposthume° of much wealth and peace,
    That inward breaks, and shows no cause without
    Why the man dies. I humbly thank you, sir.
Captain. God bye you, sir.
                           [*Exit.*]
Rosencrantz.   Will't please you go, my lord?   30
Hamlet. I'll be with you straight. Go a little before.
               [*Exeunt all but Hamlet.*]
    How all occasions do inform against me
    And spur my dull revenge! What is a man,
    If his chief good and market° of his time
    Be but to sleep and feed? A beast, no more.   35
    Sure he that made us with such large discourse,°
    Looking before and after, gave us not
    That capability and godlike reason
    To fust° in us unused. Now, whether it be
    Bestial oblivion,° or some craven scruple   40
    Of thinking too precisely on th' event° —
    A thought which, quartered, hath but one part wisdom
    And ever three parts coward — I do not know
    Why yet I live to say, "This thing's to do,"
    Sith I have cause, and will, and strength, and means   45
    To do't. Examples gross° as earth exhort me.
    Witness this army of such mass and charge,°
    Led by a delicate and tender prince,
    Whose spirit, with divine ambition puffed,
    Makes mouths at the invisible event,°   50
    Exposing what is mortal and unsure
    To all that fortune, death, and danger dare,
    Even for an eggshell. Rightly to be great
    Is not° to stir without great argument,°
    But greatly° to find quarrel in a straw   55
    When honor's at the stake. How stand I then,
    That have a father killed, a mother stained,
    Excitements° of my reason and my blood,

---

[26]*debate* settle   [27]*imposthume* abscess, ulcer   [34]*market* profit   [36]*discourse* understanding   [39]*fust* grow moldy   [40]*oblivion* forgetfulness   [41]*event* outcome   [46]*gross* large, obvious   [47]*charge* expense   [50]*Makes mouths at the invisible event* makes scornful faces (is contemptuous of) the unseen outcome   [54]*not* (the sense seems to require "not not")   [54]*argument* reason   [55]*greatly* i.e., nobly   [58]*Excitements* incentives

And let all sleep, while to my shame I see
The imminent death of twenty thousand men   *60*
That for a fantasy and trick of fame°
Go to their graves like beds, fight for a plot
Whereon the numbers cannot try the cause,
Which is not tomb enough and continent°
To hide the slain? O, from this time forth,   *65*
My thoughts be bloody, or be nothing worth!

                                                    Exit.

[**Scene V.** *The castle.*]

Enter Horatio, [Queen] Gertrude, and a Gentleman.

Queen. I will not speak with her.
Gentleman. She is importunate, indeed distract.
    Her mood will needs be pitied.
Queen.   What would she have?
Gentleman. She speaks much of her father, says she hears
    There's tricks i' th' world, and hems, and beats her heart,   *5*
    Spurns enviously at straws,° speaks things in doubt°
    That carry but half sense. Her speech is nothing,
    Yet the unshapèd use of it doth move
    The hearers to collection;° they yawn° at it,
    And botch the words up fit to their own thoughts,   *10*
    Which, as her winks and nods and gestures yield them,
    Indeed would make one think there might be thought,
    Though nothing sure, yet much unhappily.
Horatio. 'Twere good she were spoken with, for she may strew
    Dangerous conjectures in ill-breeding minds.   *15*
Queen. Let her come in.

                                        [*Exit Gentleman.*]
    [*Aside.*] To my sick soul (as sin's true nature is)
    Each toy seems prologue to some great amiss;°
    So full of artless jealousy° is guilt
    It spills° itself in fearing to be spilt.   *20*

Enter Ophelia [distracted].

---

⁶¹*fantasy and trick of fame* illusion and trifle of reputation   ⁶⁴*continent* receptacle,
container   IV.v.   ⁶*Spurns enviously at straws* objects spitefully to insignificant
matters   ⁶*in doubt* uncertainly   ⁸⁻⁹*Yet the . . . to collection* i.e., yet the formless manner of it moves her listeners to gather up some sort of meaning   ⁹*yawn*
gape (?)   ¹⁸*amiss* misfortune   ¹⁹*artless jealousy* crude suspicion   ²⁰*spills* destroys

Ophelia. Where is the beauteous majesty of Denmark?
Queen. How now, Ophelia?
Ophelia. (*She sings.*)

> How should I your truelove know
>   From another one?
> By his cockle hat° and staff   25
>   And his sandal shoon.°

Queen. Alas, sweet lady, what imports this song?
Ophelia. Say you? Nay, pray you mark.

> He is dead and gone, lady,   (*Song.*)
>   He is dead and gone;   30
> At his head a grass-green turf,
>   At his heels a stone.

> O, ho!
Queen. Nay, but Ophelia ——
Ophelia. Pray you mark. [*Sings.*]   35

> White his shroud as the mountain snow ——

Enter King.

Queen. Alas, look here, my lord.
Ophelia.

> Larded° all with sweet flowers   (*Song.*)
>   Which bewept to the grave did not go
>   With truelove showers.   40

King. How do you, pretty lady?
Ophelia. Well, God dild° you! They say the owl was a baker's
     daughter.° Lord, we know what we are, but know not
     what we may be. God be at your table!
King. Conceit° upon her father.   45
Ophelia. Pray let's have no words of this, but when they ask
     you what it means, say you this:

> Tomorrow is Saint Valentine's day.°   (*Song.*)
>   All in the morning betime,

---

²⁵*cockle hat* (a cockleshell on the hat was the sign of a pilgrim who had journeyed
to shrines overseas. The association of lovers and pilgrims was a common
one.) ²⁶*shoon* shoes ³⁸*Larded* decorated ⁴²*dild* yield, i.e., reward ⁴²⁻⁴³*baker's
daughter* (an allusion to a tale of a baker's daughter who begrudged bread to Christ
and was turned into an owl) ⁴⁵*Conceit* brooding ⁴⁸*Saint Valentine's day* Feb.
14 (the notion was that a bachelor would become the truelove of the first girl he
saw on this day)

> And I a maid at your window,   *50*
> To be your Valentine.
>
> Then up he rose and donned his clothes
> And dupped° the chamber door,
> Let in the maid, that out a maid
> Never departed more.   *55*

King. Pretty Ophelia.
Ophelia. Indeed, la, without an oath, I'll make an end on't:

[*Sings.*]

> By Gis° and by Saint Charity,
> Alack, and fie for shame!
> Young men will do't if they come to't,   *60*
> By Cock,° they are to blame.
> Quoth she, "Before you tumbled me,
> You promised me to wed."

He answers:

> "So would I 'a' done, by yonder sun,   *65*
> An thou hadst not come to my bed."

King. How long hath she been thus?
Ophelia. I hope all will be well. We must be patient, but I
cannot choose but weep to think they would lay him
i' th' cold ground. My brother shall know of it; and   *70*
so I thank you for your good counsel. Come, my coach!
Good night, ladies, good night. Sweet ladies, good
night, good night.

Exit.

King. Follow her close; give her good watch, I pray you.

[*Exit Horatio.*]

> O, this is the poison of deep grief; it springs   *75*
> All from her father's death — and now behold!
> O Gertrude, Gertrude,
> When sorrows come, they come not single spies,
> But in battalions; first, her father slain;
> Next, your son gone, and he most violent author   *80*
> Of his own just remove; the people muddied,°
> Thick and unwholesome in their thoughts and whispers
> For good Polonius' death, and we have done but greenly°
> In huggermugger° to inter him; poor Ophelia

---

⁵³*dupped* opened (did up)   ⁵⁸³*Gis* (contraction of "Jesus")   ⁶¹*Cock* (1) God, (2)
phallus   ⁸¹*muddied* muddled   ⁸³*greenly* foolishly   ⁸⁴*huggermugger* secret haste

Divided from herself and her fair judgment,   *85*
Without the which we are pictures or mere beasts;
Last, and as much containing as all these,
Her brother is in secret come from France,
Feeds on his wonder,° keeps himself in clouds,
And wants not buzzers° to infect his ear   *90*
With pestilent speeches of his father's death,
Wherein necessity, of matter beggared,°
Will nothing stick° our person to arraign
In ear and ear. O my dear Gertrude, this,
Like to a murd'ring piece,° in many places   *95*
Gives me superfluous death.   *A noise within.*

Enter a Messenger.

Queen.   Alack, what noise is this?
King. Attend, where are my Switzers?° Let them guard the door.
What is the matter?
Messenger.   Save yourself, my lord.
The ocean, overpeering of his list,°
Eats not the flats with more impiteous haste   *100*
Than young Laertes, in a riotous head,°
O'erbears your officers. The rabble call him lord,
And, as the world were now but to begin,
Antiquity forgot, custom not known,
The ratifiers and props of every word,   *105*
They cry, "Choose we! Laertes shall be king!"
Caps, hands, and tongues applaud it to the clouds,
"Laertes shall be king! Laertes king!"
                    A noise within.
Queen. How cheerfully on the false trail they cry!
O, this is counter,° you false Danish dogs!   *110*

Enter Laertes with others.

King. The doors are broke.
Laertes. Where is this king? — Sirs, stand you all without.
All. No, let's come in.
Laertes.   I pray you give me leave.
All. We will, we will.
Laertes. I thank you. Keep the door.   *[Exeunt his Followers.]*

---

[89]***wonder*** suspicion   [90]***wants not buzzers*** does not lack talebearers   [92]***of matter beggared*** unprovided with facts   [93]***Will nothing stick*** will not hesitate   [95]***murd'ring piece*** (a cannon that shot a kind of shrapnel)   [97]***Switzers*** Swiss guards   [99]***list*** shore   [101]***in a riotous head*** with a rebellious force   [110]***counter*** (a hound runs counter when he follows the scent backward from the prey)

                                      O thou vile King,   *115*
      Give me my father.
Queen.   Calmly, good Laertes.
Laertes. That drop of blood that's calm proclaims me bastard,
      Cries cuckold° to my father, brands the harlot
      Even here between the chaste unsmirchèd brow
      Of my true mother.
King.   What is the cause, Laertes,   *120*
      That thy rebellion looks so giantlike?
      Let him go, Gertrude. Do not fear° our person.
      There's such divinity doth hedge a king
      That treason can but peep to° what it would,
      Acts little of his will. Tell me, Laertes,   *125*
      Why thou art thus incensed. Let him go, Gertrude.
      Speak, man.
Laertes. Where is my father?
King.   Dead.
Queen.   But not by him.
King. Let him demand his fill.
Laertes. How came he dead? I'll not be juggled with.   *130*
      To hell allegiance, vows to the blackest devil,
      Conscience and grace to the profoundest pit!
      I dare damnation. To this point I stand,
      That both the worlds I give to negligence,°
      Let come what comes, only I'll be revenged   *135*
      Most throughly for my father.
King.   Who shall stay you?
Laertes. My will, not all the world's.
      And for my means, I'll husband them° so well
      They shall go far with little.
King.   Good Laertes,
      If you desire to know the certainty   *140*
      Of your dear father, is't writ in your revenge
      That swoopstake° you will draw both friend and foe,
      Winner and loser?
Laertes. None but his enemies.
King.   Will you know them then?
Laertes. To his good friends thus wide I'll ope my arms   *145*
      And like the kind life-rend'ring pelican°

---

¹¹⁸*cuckold* man whose wife is unfaithful ¹²²*fear* fear for ¹²⁴*peep to* i.e., look at
from a distance ¹³⁴*That both . . . to negligence* i.e., I care not what may happen
(to me) in this world or the next ¹³⁸*husband them* use them economically
¹⁴²*swoopstake* in a clean sweep ¹⁴⁶*pelican* (thought to feed its young with its own
blood)

Repast° them with my blood.

King.   Why, now you speak
Like a good child and a true gentleman.
That I am guiltless of your father's death,
And am most sensibly° in grief for it,   *150*
It shall as level to your judgment 'pear
As day does to your eye.

                  A noise within: "Let her come in."

Laertes. How now? What noise is that?

    Enter Ophelia.

O heat, dry up my brains; tears seven times salt
Burn out the sense and virtue° of mine eye!   *155*
By heaven, thy madness shall be paid with weight
Till our scale turn the beam.° O rose of May,
Dear maid, kind sister, sweet Ophelia!
O heavens, is't possible a young maid's wits
Should be as mortal as an old man's life?   *160*
Nature is fine° in love, and where 'tis fine,
It sends some precious instance° of itself
After the thing it loves.

Ophelia.

    They bore him barefaced on the bier   (*Song.*)
        Hey non nony, nony, hey nony   *165*
    And in his grave rained many a tear ——

Fare you well, my dove!

Laertes. Hadst thou thy wits, and didst persuade revenge,
It could not move thus.

Ophelia. You must sing "A-down a-down, and you call him   *170*
a-down-a." O, how the wheel° becomes it! It is the
false steward, that stole his master's daughter.

Laertes. This nothing's more than matter°.

Ophelia. There's rosemary, that's for remembrance. Pray
you, love, remember. And there is pansies, that's for   *175*
thoughts.

Laertes. A document° in madness, thoughts and remembrance
fitted.

---

¹⁴⁷**Repast** feed   ¹⁵⁰**sensibly** acutely   ¹⁵⁵**virtue** power   ¹⁵⁷**turn the beam** weigh down
the bar (of the balance)   ¹⁶¹**fine** refined, delicate   ¹⁶²**instance** sample   ¹⁷¹**wheel** (of
uncertain meaning, but probably a turn or dance of Ophelia's, rather than Fortune's
wheel)   ¹⁷³**This nothing's more than matter** this nonsense has more meaning than
matters of consequence   ¹⁷⁷**document** lesson

Ophelia. There's fennel° for you, and columbines. There's
rue for you, and here's some for me. We may call it   *180*
herb of grace o' Sundays. O, you must wear your rue
with a difference. There's a daisy. I would give you
some violets, but they withered all when my father
died. They say 'a made a good end.

[*Sings.*]

For bonny sweet Robin is all my joy.   *185*

Laertes. Thought and affliction, passion, hell itself,
She turns to favor° and to prettiness.
Ophelia.

And will 'a not come again?   (*Song.*)
And will 'a not come again?
No, no, he is dead,   *190*
Go to thy deathbed,
He never will come again.

His beard was as white as snow,
All flaxen was his poll.°
He is gone, he is gone,   *195*
And we cast away moan.
God 'a' mercy on his soul!

And of all Christian souls, I pray God. God bye you.

[*Exit.*]

Laertes. Do you see this, O God?
King. Laertes, I must commune with your grief,   *200*
Or you deny me right. Go but apart,
Make choice of whom your wisest friends you will,
And they shall hear and judge 'twixt you and me.
If by direct or by collateral° hand
They find us touched,° we will our kingdom give,   *205*
Our crown, our life, and all that we call ours,
To you in satisfaction; but if not,
Be you content to lend your patience to us,
And we shall jointly labor with your soul
To give it due content.

---

[179] *fennel* (the distribution of flowers in the ensuing lines has symbolic meaning,
but the meaning is disputed. Perhaps *fennel,* flattery; *columbines,* cuckoldry; *rue,*
sorrow for Ophelia and repentance for the Queen; *daisy,* dissembling; *violets,* faith-
fulness. For other interpretations, see J. W. Lever in *Review of English Studies,* New
Series 3 [1952], pp. 123–29)   [187] *favor* charm, beauty   [194] *All flaxen was his poll*
white as flax was his head   [204] *collateral* indirect   [205] *touched* implicated

Laertes.   Let this be so.   *210*
        His means of death, his obscure funeral —
        No trophy, sword, nor hatchment° o'er his bones,
        No noble rite nor formal ostentation° —
        Cry to be heard, as 'twere from heaven to earth,
        That I must call't in question.
King.   So you shall;   *215*
        And where th' offense is, let the great ax fall.
        I pray you go with me.

                                                        Exeunt.

[**Scene VI.** *The castle.*]

Enter Horatio and others.

Horatio. What are they that would speak with me?
Gentleman. Seafaring men, sir. They say they have letters for
        you.
Horatio. Let them come in.

                                        [*Exit Attendant.*]
        I do not know from what part of the world   *5*
        I should be greeted, if not from Lord Hamlet.

Enter Sailors.

Sailor. God bless you, sir.
Horatio. Let Him bless thee too.
Sailor. 'A shall, sir, an't please Him. There's a letter for you,
        sir — it came from th' ambassador that was bound for   *10*
        England — if your name be Horatio, as I am let to
        know it is.
Horatio [*reads the letter*].
        "Horatio, when thou shalt have overlooked° this, give
        these fellows some means to the King. They have letters
        for him. Ere we were two days old at sea, a pirate of   *15*
        very warlike appointment° gave us chase. Finding our-
        selves too slow of sail, we put on a compelled valor,
        and in the grapple I boarded them. On the instant they
        got clear of our ship; so I alone became their prisoner.
        They have dealt with me like thieves of mercy, but   *20*
        they knew what they did: I am to do a good turn for
        them. Let the King have the letters I have sent, and

---

²¹²**hatchment** tablet bearing the coat of arms of the dead   ²¹³**ostentation** ceremony
IV.vi ¹³**overlooked** surveyed   ¹⁶**appointment** equipment

repair thou to me with as much speed as thou wouldest
fly death. I have words to speak in thine ear will make
thee dumb; yet are they much too light for the bore° 25
of the matter. These good fellows will bring thee where
I am. Rosencrantz and Guildenstern hold their course
for England. Of them I have much to tell thee. Farewell.
.   He that thou knowest thine, HAMLET.''

Come, I will give you way for these your letters, 30
And do't the speedier that you may direct me
To him from whom you brought them.   *Exeunt.*

[**Scene VII.** *The castle.*]

Enter King and Laertes.

King. Now must your conscience my acquittance seal,
And you must put me in your heart for friend,
Sith you have heard, and with a knowing ear,
That he which hath your noble father slain
Pursued my life.
Laertes.   It well appears. But tell me 5
Why you proceeded not against these feats
So criminal and so capital° in nature,
As by your safety, greatness, wisdom, all things else,
You mainly° were stirred up.
King.   O, for two special reasons,
Which may to you perhaps seem much unsinewed,° 10
But yet to me they're strong. The Queen his mother
Lives almost by his looks, and for myself —
My virtue or my plague, be it either which —
She is so conjunctive° to my life and soul,
That, as the star moves not but in his sphere, 15
I could not but by her. The other motive
Why to a public count° I might not go
Is the great love the general gender° bear him,
Who, dipping all his faults in their affection,
Would, like the spring that turneth wood to stone,° 20
Convert his gyves° to graces; so that my arrows,
Too slightly timbered° for so loud a wind,

---

²⁵*bore* caliber (here, "importance") IV.vii. ⁷*capital* deserving death ⁹*mainly*
powerfully ¹⁰*unsinewed* weak ¹⁴*conjunctive* closely united ¹⁷*count* reckoning
¹⁸*general gender* common people ²⁰*spring that turneth wood to stone* (a spring in
Shakespeare's county was so charged with lime that it would petrify wood placed
in it) ²¹*gyves* fetters ²²*timbered* shafted

Would have reverted to my bow again,
And not where I had aimed them.
Laertes. And so have I a noble father lost,   *25*
A sister driven into desp'rate terms,°
Whose worth, if praises may go back again,°
Stood challenger on mount of all the age
For her perfections. But my revenge will come.
King. Break not your sleeps for that. You must not think   *30*
That we are made of stuff so flat and dull
That we can let our beard be shook with danger,
And think it pastime. You shortly shall hear more.
I loved your father, and we love ourself,
And that, I hope, will teach you to imagine ——   *35*

Enter a Messenger with letters.

How now? What news?
Messenger.   Letters, my lord, from Hamlet:
These to your Majesty; this to the Queen.
King. From Hamlet? Who brought them?
Messenger. Sailors, my lord, they say; I saw them not.
They were given me by Claudio; he received them   *40*
Of him that brought them.
King.   Laertes, you shall hear them. —
Leave us. [*Reads.*]
                                        Exit Messenger.

"High and mighty, you shall know I am set naked° on
your kingdom. Tomorrow shall I beg leave to see your
kingly eyes; when I shall (first asking your pardon   *45*
thereunto) recount the occasion of my sudden and more
strange return.
                                        HAMLET."

What should this mean? Are all the rest come back?
Or is it some abuse,° and no such thing?   *50*
King.   'Tis Hamlet's character.° "Naked"!
And in a postscript here, he says "alone."
Can you devise° me?
Laertes. I am lost in it, my lord. But let him come.
It warms the very sickness in my heart   *55*
That I shall live and tell him to his teeth,
"Thus did'st thou."

---

[26]*terms* conditions   [27]*go back again* revert to what is past   [43]*naked* destitute   [50]*abuse*
deception   [51]*character* handwriting   [53]*devise* advise

King.   If it be so, Laertes
(As how should it be so? How otherwise?),
Will you be ruled by me?
Laertes.   Ay, my lord,
So you will not o'errule me to a peace.   *60*
King. To thine own peace. If he be now returned,
As checking at° his voyage, and that he means
No more to undertake it, I will work him
To an exploit now ripe in my device,
Under the which he shall not choose but fall;   *65*
And for his death no wind of blame shall breathe,
But even his mother shall uncharge the practice°
And call it accident.
Laertes.   My lord, I will be ruled;
The rather if you could devise it so
That I might be the organ.
King.   It falls right.   *70*
You have been talked of since your travel much,
And that in Hamlet's hearing, for a quality
Wherein they say you shine. Your sum of parts
Did not together pluck such envy from him
As did that one, and that, in my regard,   *75*
Of the unworthiest siege.°
Laertes.   What part is that, my lord?
King. A very riband in the cap of youth,
Yet needful too, for youth no less becomes
The light and careless livery that it wears
Than settled age his sables and his weeds,°   *80*
Importing health and graveness. Two months since
Here was a gentleman of Normandy.
I have seen myself, and served against, the French,
And they can° well on horseback, but this gallant
Had witchcraft in't. He grew unto his seat,   *85*
And to such wondrous doing brought his horse
As had he been incorpsed and deminatured
With the brave beast. So far he topped my thought
That I, in forgery° of shapes and tricks,
Come short of what he did.
Laertes.   A Norman was't?   *90*
King. A Norman.

---

⁶²*checking at* turning away from (a term in falconry)   ⁶⁷*uncharge the practice* not
charge the device with treachery   ⁷⁶*seige* rank   ⁸⁰*sables and his weeds* i.e., sober
attire   ⁸⁴*can* do   ⁸⁹*forgery* invention

Laertes. Upon my life, Lamord.
King.   The very same.
Laertes. I know him well. He is the brooch° indeed
    And gem of all the nation.
King. He made confession° of you,   *95*
    And gave you such a masterly report,
    For art and exercise in your defense,
    And for your rapier most especial,
    That he cried out 'twould be a sight indeed
    If one could match you. The scrimers° of their nation   *100*
    He swore had neither motion, guard, nor eye,
    If you opposed them. Sir, this report of his
    Did Hamlet so envenom with his envy
    That he could nothing do but wish and beg
    Your sudden coming o'er to play with you.   *105*
    Now, out of this ——
Laertes.   What out of this, my lord?
King. Laertes, was your father dear to you?
    Or are you like the painting of a sorrow,
    A face without a heart?
Laertes.   Why ask you this?
King. Not that I think you did not love your father,   *110*
    But that I know love is begun by time,
    And that I see, in passages of proof.°
    Time qualifies° the spark and fire of it.
    There lives within the very flame of love
    A kind of wick or snuff° that will abate it,   *115*
    And nothing is at a like goodness still,°
    For goodness, growing to a plurisy,°
    Dies in his own too-much. That we would do
    We should do when we would, for this "would" changes,
    And hath abatements and delays as many   *120*
    As there are tongues, are hands, are accidents,
    And then this "should" is like a spendthrift sigh,°
    That hurts by easing. But to the quick° of th' ulcer —
    Hamlet comes back; what would you undertake
    To show yourself in deed your father's son   *125*
    More than in words?

---

⁹³*brooch* ornament   ⁹⁵*confession* report   ¹⁰⁰*scrimers* fencers   ¹¹²*passages of proof*
proved cases   ¹¹³*qualifies* diminishes   ¹¹⁵*snuff* residue of burnt wick (which dims
the light)   ¹¹⁶*still* always   ¹¹⁷*plurisy* fullness, excess   ¹²²*spendthrift sigh* (sighing
provides ease, but because it was thought to thin the blood and so shorten life it
was spendthrift)   ¹²³*quick* sensitive flesh

Laertes.   To cut his throat i' th' church!
King. No place indeed should murder sanctuarize;°
         Revenge should have no bounds. But, good Laertes,
         Will you do this? Keep close within your chamber.
         Hamlet returned shall know you are come home.   *130*
         We'll put on those° shall praise your excellence
         And set a double varnish on the fame
         The Frenchman gave you, bring you in fine° together
         And wager on your heads. He, being remiss,
         Most generous, and free from all contriving,   *135*
         Will not peruse the foils, so that with ease,
         Or with a little shuffling, you may choose
         A sword unbated,° and, in a pass of practice,°
         Requite him for your father.
Laertes.   I will do't,
         And for that purpose I'll anoint my sword.   *140*
         I bought an unction of a mountebank,°
         So mortal that, but dip a knife in it,
         Where it draws blood, no cataplasm° so rare,
         Collected from all simples° that have virtue°
         Under the moon, can save the thing from death   *145*
         That is but scratched withal. I'll touch my point
         With this contagion, that, if I gall him slightly,
         It may be death.
King.   Let's further think of this,
         Weigh what convenience both of time and means
         May fit us to our shape.° If this should fail,   *150*
         And that our drift look through° our bad performance,
         'Twere better not assayed. Therefore this project
         Should have a back or second, that might hold
         If this did blast in proof.° Soft, let me see.
         We'll make a solemn wager on your cunnings —   *155*
         I ha't!
         When in your motion you are hot and dry —
         As make your bouts more violent to that end —
         And that he calls for drink, I'll have prepared him
         A chalice for the nonce,° whereon but sipping,   *160*

---

[127]*sanctuarize* protect   [131]*We'll put on those* we'll incite persons who   [133]*in fine*
finally   [138]*unbated* not blunted   [138]*pass of practice* treacherous thrust   [141]*mountebank*
quack   [143]*cataplasm* poultice   [144]*simples* medicinal herbs   [144]*virtue* power (to
heal)   [150]*shape* role   [151]*drift look through* purpose show through   [154]*blast in proof*
burst (fail) in performance   [160]*nonce* occasion

If he by chance escape your venomed stuck,°
Our purpose may hold there. — But stay, what noise?

Enter Queen.

Queen. One woe doth tread upon another's heel.
So fast they follow. Your sister's drowned, Laertes.
Laertes. Drowned! O, where?   165
Queen. There is a willow grows askant° the brook,
That shows his hoar° leaves in the glassy stream:
Therewith° fantastic garlands did she make
Of crowflowers, nettles, daisies, and long purples,
That liberal° shepherds give a grosser name,   170
But our cold maids do dead men's fingers call them.
There on the pendent boughs her crownet° weeds
Clamb'ring to hang, an envious sliver° broke,
When down her weedy trophies and herself
Fell in the weeping brook. Her clothes spread wide,   175
And mermaidlike awhile they bore her up,
Which time she chanted snatches of old lauds,°
As one incapable° of her own distress,
Or like a creature native and indued°
Unto that element. But long it could not be   180
Till that her garments, heavy with their drink,
Pulled the poor wretch from her melodious lay
To muddy death.
Laertes.   Alas, then she is drowned?
Queen. Drowned, drowned.
Laertes. Too much of water hast thou, poor Ophelia,   185
And therefore I forbid my tears; but yet
It is our trick;° nature her custom holds,
Let shame say what it will: when these are gone,
The woman° will be out. Adieu, my lord.
I have a speech o' fire, that fain would blaze,   190
But that this folly drowns it.
                                                    Exit.
King.   Let's follow, Gertrude.
How much I had to do to calm his rage!
Now fear I this will give it start again;
Therefore let's follow.
                                                   Exeunt.

[ACT V.

Scene I. *A churchyard.*]

Enter two Clowns.°

Clown. Is she to be buried in Christian burial when she willfully
seeks her own salvation?

Other. I tell thee she is. Therefore make her grave straight.°
The crowner° hath sate on her, and finds it Christian
burial.   *5*

Clown. How can that be, unless she drowned herself in her
own defense?

Other. Why,'tis found so.

Clown. It must be *se offendendo;*° it cannot be else. For here
lies the point: if I drown myself wittingly, it argues an   *10*
act, and an act hath three branches — it is to act, to
do, to perform. Argal,° she drowned herself wittingly.

Other. Nay, but hear you, Goodman Delver.

Clown. Give me leave. Here lies the water — good. Here
stands the man — good. If the man go to this water   *15*
and drown himself, it is, will he nill he,° he goes; mark
you that. But if the water come to him and drown
him, he drowns not himself. Argal, he that is not guilty
of his own death, shortens not his own life.

Other. But is this law?   *20*

Clown. Ay marry, is't — crowner's quest° law.

Other. Will you ha' the truth on't? If this had not been a
gentlewoman, she should have been buried out o'
Christian burial.

Clown. Why, there thou say'st. And the more pity that great   *25*
folk should have count'nance° in this world to drown
or hang themselves more than their even-Christen.°
Come, my spade. There is no ancient gentlemen but
gard'ners, ditchers, and gravemakers. They hold up°
Adam's profession.   *30*

Other. Was he a gentleman?

Clown. 'A was the first that ever bore arms.°

Other. Why, he had none.

V.i. ˢ·ᵈ·*Clowns* rustics ³*straight* straightway ⁴*crowner* coroner ⁹*se offendendo*
(blunder for *se defendendo,* a legal term meaning "in self-defense") ¹²*Argal* (blunder
for Latin *ergo,* "therefore") ¹⁶*will he nill he* will he or will he not (whether he
will or will not) ²¹*quest* inquest ²⁶*count'nance* privilege ²⁷*even-Christen* fellow
Christian ²⁹*hold up* keep up ³²*bore arms* had a coat of arms (the sign of a
gentleman)

Clown. What, art a heathen? How dost thou understand the
Scripture? The Scripture says Adam digged. Could he dig   *35*
without arms? I'll put another question to thee. If thou
answerest me not to the purpose, confess thyself ——
Other. Go to.
Clown. What is he that builds stronger than either the mason,
the shipwright, or the carpenter?   *40*
Other. The gallowsmaker, for that frame outlives a thousand
tenants.
Clown. I like thy wit well, in good faith. The gallows does
well. But how does it well? It does well to those that
do ill. Now thou dost ill to say the gallows is built   *45*
stronger than the church. Argal, the gallows may do
well to thee. To't again, come.
Other. Who builds stronger than a mason, a shipwright, or
a carpenter?
Clown. Ay, tell me that, and unyoke.°   *50*
Other. Marry, now I can tell.
Clown. To't.
Other. Mass,° I cannot tell.

   Enter Hamlet and Horatio afar off.

Clown. Cudgel thy brains no more about it, for your dull
ass will not mend his pace with beating. And when   *55*
you are asked this question next, say "a gravemaker."
The houses he makes lasts till doomsday. Go, get thee
in, and fetch me a stoup° of liquor.
                              [*Exit Other Clown.*]

   In youth when I did love, did love   [*Song.*]
      Methought it was very sweet   *60*
   To contract — O — the time for — a — my behove,°
      O, methought there — a — was nothing —
              a — meet.

Hamlet. Has this fellow no feeling of his business? 'A sings
in gravemaking.
Horatio. Custom hath made it in him a property of easiness.° *65*
Hamlet. 'Tis e'en so. The hand of little employment hath the
daintier sense.°

---

⁵⁰*unyoke* i.e., stop work for the day   ⁵³*Mass* by the mass   ⁵⁸*stoup* tankard   ⁶¹*behove*
advantage   ⁶⁵*in him a property of easiness* easy for him   ⁶⁶⁻⁶⁷*hath the daintier*
sense is more sensitive (because it is not calloused)

Clown.

> But age with his stealing steps   (*Song.*)
>   Hath clawed me in his clutch,
> And hath shipped me into the land,   70
>   As if I had never been such.

[*Throws up a skull.*]

Hamlet. That skull had a tongue in it, and could sing once.
How the knave jowls° it to the ground, as if 'twere
Cain's jawbone, that did the first murder! This might
be the pate of a politician, which this ass now o'erreaches,°   75
one that would circumvent God, might it not?

Horatio. It might, my lord.

Hamlet. Or of a courtier, which could say "Good morrow,
sweet lord! How dost thou, sweet lord?" This might
be my Lord Such-a-one, that praised my Lord Such-   80
a-one's horse when 'a went to beg it, might it not?

Horatio. Ay, my lord.

Hamlet. Why, e'en so, and now my Lady Worm's, chapless,°
and knocked about the mazzard° with a sexton's spade.
Here's fine revolution, an we had the trick to see't. Did   85
these bones cost no more the breeding but to play at
loggets° with them? Mine ache to think on't.

Clown.

> A pickax and a spade, a spade,   (*Song.*)
>   For and a shrouding sheet;
> O, a pit of clay for to be made   90
>   For such a guest is meet.

[*Throws up another skull.*]

Hamlet. There's another. Why may not that be the skull of
a lawyer? Where be his quiddities° now, his quillities,°
his cases, his tenures,° and his tricks? Why does he suffer
this mad knave now to knock him about the sconce°   95
with a dirty shovel, and will not tell him of his action
of battery? Hum! This fellow might be in's time a great
buyer of land, with his statutes, his recognizances, his
fines,° his double vouchers, his recoveries. Is this the

---

[73]*jowls* hurls   [75]*o'erreaches* (1) reaches over, (2) has the advantage over   [83]*chapless*
lacking the lower jaw   [84]*mazzard* head   [87]*loggets* (a game in which small pieces
of wood were thrown at an object)   [93]*quiddities* subtle arguments (from Latin
quidditas, "whatness")   [93]*quillities* fine distinctions   [94]*tenures* legal means of holding
land   [95]*sconce* head   [98-99]*his statutes, his recognizances, his fines* his documents
giving a creditor control of a debtor's land, his bonds of surety, his documents
changing an entailed estate into fee simple (unrestricted ownership)

fine° of his fines, and the recovery of his recoveries, to   *100*
have his fine pate full of fine dirt? Will his vouchers
vouch him no more of his purchases, and double ones
too, than the length and breadth of a pair of indentures?°
The very conveyances° of his lands will scarcely lie in
this box, and must th' inheritor himself have no more,   *105*
ha?

Horatio. Not a jot more, my lord.

Hamlet. Is not parchment made of sheepskins?

Horatio. Ay, my lord, and of calveskins too.

Hamlet. They are sheep and calves which seek out assurance°   *110*
in that. I will speak to this fellow. Whose grave's this,
sirrah?

Clown. Mine, sir. [*Sings.*]

> O, pit of clay for to be made
> For such a guest is meet.   *115*

Hamlet. I think it be thine indeed, for thou liest in't.

Clown. You lie out on't, sir, and therefore 'tis not yours.
For my part, I do not lie in't, yet it is mine.

Hamlet. Thou dost lie in't, to be in't and say it is thine. 'Tis
for the dead, not for the quick;° therefore thou liest.   *120*

Clown. 'Tis a quick lie, sir; 'twill away again from me to you.

Hamlet. What man dost thou dig it for?

Clown. For no man, sir.

Hamlet. What woman then?

Clown. For none neither.   *125*

Hamlet. Who is to be buried in't?

Clown. One that was a woman, sir; but, rest her soul, she's
dead.

Hamlet. How absolute° the knave is! We must speak by the
card,° or equivocation° will undo us. By the Lord,   *130*
Horatio, this three years I have took note of it, the age
is grown so picked° that the toe of the peasant comes
so near the heel of the courtier he galls his kibe.° How
long hast thou been a gravemaker?

Clown. Of all the days i' th' year, I came to't that day that   *135*
our last king Hamlet overcame Fortinbras.

Hamlet. How long is that since?

---

¹⁰⁰*fine* end   ¹⁰³*indentures* contracts   ¹⁰⁴*conveyances* legal documents for the transference of land   ¹¹⁰*assurance* safety   ¹²⁰*quick* living   ¹²⁹*absolute* positive, decided
¹²⁹⁻¹³⁰*by the card* by the compass card, i.e., exactly   ¹³⁰*equivocation* ambiguity
¹³²*picked* refined   ¹³³*kibe* sore on the back of the heel

Clown. Cannot you tell that? Every fool can tell that. It was
that very day that young Hamlet was born — he that
is mad, and sent into England.   140

Hamlet. Ay, marry, why was he sent into England?

Clown. Why, because 'a was mad. 'A shall recover his wits
there; or, if 'a do not, 'tis no great matter there.

Hamlet. Why?

Clown. 'Twill not be seen in him there. There the men are   145
as mad as he.

Hamlet. How came he mad?

Clown. Very strangely, they say.

Hamlet. How strangely?

Clown. Faith, e'en with losing his wits.   150

Hamlet. Upon what ground?

Clown. Why, here in Denmark. I have been sexton here, man
and boy, thirty years.

Hamlet. How long will a man lie i' th' earth ere he rot?

Clown. Faith, if 'a be not rotten before 'a die (as we have   155
many pocky corses° nowadays that will scarce hold the
laying in), 'a will last you some eight year or nine year.
A tanner will last you nine year.

Hamlet. Why he, more than another?

Clown. Why, sir, his hide is so tanned with his trade that 'a   160
will keep out water a great while, and your water is a
sore decayer of your whoreson dead body. Here's a skull
now hath lien you i' th' earth three and twenty years.

Hamlet. Whose was it?

Clown. A whoreson mad fellow's it was. Whose do you think   165
it was?

Hamlet. Nay, I know not.

Clown. A pestilence on him for a mad rogue! 'A poured a
flagon of Rhenish on my head once. This same skull,
sir, was, sir, Yorick's skull, the King's jester.   170

Hamlet. This?

Clown. E'en that.

Hamlet. Let me see. [*Takes the skull.*] Alas, poor Yorick! I
knew him, Horatio, a fellow of infinite jest, of most
excellent fancy. He hath borne me on his back a thousand   175
times. And now how abhorred in my imagination it
is! My gorge rises at it. Here hung those lips that I
have kissed I know not how oft. Where be your gibes

---

[156]*pocky corses* bodies of persons who had been infected with the pox (syphilis)

now? Your gambols, your songs, your flashes of mer-
riment that were wont to set the table on a roar? Not   *180*
one now to mock your own grinning? Quite chapfall'n?°
Now get you to my lady's chamber, and tell her, let
her paint an inch thick, to this favor° she must come.
Make her laugh at that. Prithee, Horatio, tell me one
thing.   *185*
Horatio. What's that, my lord?
Hamlet. Dost thou think Alexander looked o' this fashion i'
th' earth?
Horatio. E'en so.
Hamlet. And smelt so? Pah! [*Puts down the skull.*]   *190*
Horatio. E'en so, my lord.
Hamlet. To what base uses we may return, Horatio! Why
may not imagination trace the noble dust of Alexander
till a' find it stopping a bunghole?
Horatio. 'Twere to consider too curiously,° to consider so. *195*
Hamlet. No, faith, not a jot, but to follow him thither with
modesty enough,° and likelihood to lead it; as thus:
Alexander died, Alexander was buried, Alexander re-
turneth to dust; the dust is earth; of earth we make
loam; and why of that loam whereto he was converted *200*
might they not stop a beer barrel?
Imperious Caesar, dead and turned to clay,
Might stop a hole to keep the wind away
O, that that earth which kept the world in awe
Should patch a wall t' expel the winter's flaw!°   *205*
But soft, but soft awhile! Here comes the King.

*Enter King, Queen, Laertes, and a coffin, with Lords attendant
[and a Doctor of Divinity].*

The Queen, the courtiers. Who is this they follow?
And with such maimèd° rites? This doth betoken
The corse they follow did with desp'rate hand
Fordo it° own life. 'Twas of some estate.°   *210*
Couch° we awhile, and mark.
                                      [*Retires with Horatio.*]
Laertes. What ceremony else?
Hamlet.   That is Laertes,
A very noble youth. Mark.

---

¹⁸¹*chapfall'n* (1) down in the mouth, (2) jawless   ¹⁸³*favor* facial appearance
¹⁹⁵*curiously* minutely   ¹⁹⁵⁻¹⁹⁶*with modesty enough* without exaggeration   ²⁰⁵*flaw* gust
²⁰⁸*maimèd* incomplete   ²¹⁰*Fordo it* destroy its   ²¹⁰*estate* high rank   ²¹¹*Couch* hide

Laertes. What ceremony else?
Doctor. Her obsequies have been as far enlarged   215
    As we have warranty. Her death was doubtful,°
    And, but that great command o'ersways the order,
    She should in ground unsanctified been lodged
    Till the last trumpet. For charitable prayers,
    Shards,° flints, and pebbles should be thrown on her.   220
    Yet here she is allowed her virgin crants,°
    Her maiden strewments,° and the bringing home
    Of bell and burial.
Laertes. Must there no more be done?
Doctor.   No more be done.
    We should profane the service of the dead   225
    To sing a requiem and such rest to her
    As to peace-parted souls.
Laertes.   Lay her i' th' earth,
    And from her fair and unpolluted flesh
    May violets spring! I tell thee, churlish priest,
    A minist'ring angel shall my sister be   230
    When thou liest howling!
Hamlet.   What, the fair Ophelia?
Queen. Sweets to the sweet! Farewell. [*Scatters flowers.*]
    I hoped thou shouldst have been my Hamlet's wife.
    I thought thy bride bed to have decked, sweet maid,
    And not have strewed thy grave.
Laertes.   O, treble woe   235
    Fall ten times treble on that cursèd head
    Whose wicked deed thy most ingenious sense°
    Deprived thee of! Hold off the earth awhile,
    Till I have caught her once more in mine arms.

    Leaps in the grave.

    Now pile your dust upon the quick and dead   240
    Till of this flat a mountain you have made
    T'o'ertop old Pelion° or the skyish head
    Of blue Olympus.
Hamlet [*coming forward*]. What is he whose grief
    Bears such an emphasis, whose phrase of sorrow   245
    Conjures the wand'ring stars,° and makes them stand

---

[216]*doubtful* suspicious   [220]*Shards* broken pieces of pottery   [221]*crants* garlands
[222]*strewments* i.e., of flowers   [237]*most ingenious sense* finely endowed mind
[242]*Pelion* (according to classical legend, giants in their fight with the gods sought
to reach heaven by piling Mount Pelion and Mount Ossa on Mount Olympus)
[246]*wand'ring stars* planets

Like wonder-wounded hearers? This is I,
Hamlet the Dane.

Laertes.   The devil take thy soul!

[*Grapples with him.*]°

Hamlet. Thou pray'st not well.
I prithee take thy fingers from my throat,   250
For, though I am not splenitive° and rash,
Yet have I in me something dangerous,
Which let thy wisdom fear. Hold off thy hand.

King. Pluck them asunder.

Queen.   Hamlet, Hamlet!

All. Gentlemen!

Horatio.   Good my lord, be quiet.   255

Attendants part them.

Hamlet. Why, I will fight with him upon this theme
Until my eyelids will no longer wag.

Queen. O my son, what theme?

Hamlet. I loved Ophelia. Forty thousand brothers
Could not with all their quantity of love   260
Make up my sum. What wilt thou do for her?

King. O, he is mad, Laertes.

Queen. For love of God forbear him.

Hamlet. 'Swounds, show me what thou't do.
Woo't weep? Woo't fight? Woo't fast? Woo't tear
thyself?   265
Woo't drink up eisel?° Eat a crocodile?
I'll do't. Dost thou come here to whine?
To outface me with leaping in her grave?
Be buried quick with her, and so will I.
And if thou prate of mountains, let them throw   270
Millions of acres on us, till our ground,
Singeing his pate against the burning zone,°
Make Ossa like a wart! Nay, an thou't mouth,
I'll rant as well as thou.

Queen.   This is mere madness;
And thus a while the fit will work on him.   275

---

²⁴⁸ ˢ·ᵈ·*Grapples with him* (Q1, a bad quarto, presumably reporting a version that toured, has a previous direction saying "Hamlet leaps in after Laertes." Possibly he does so, somewhat hysterically. But such a direction — absent from the two good texts, Q2 and F — makes Hamlet the aggressor, somewhat contradicting his next speech. Perhaps Laertes leaps out of the grave to attack Hamlet) ²⁵¹*splenitive* fiery (the spleen was thought to be the seat of anger) ²⁶⁶*eisel* vinegar ²⁷²*burning zone* sun's orbit

Anon, as patient as the female dove
When that her golden couplets are disclosed,°
His silence will sit drooping.
Hamlet.   Hear you, sir.
What is the reason that you use me thus?
I loved you ever. But it is no matter.   *280*
Let Hercules himself do what he may,
The cat will mew, and dog will have his day.
King. I pray thee, good Horatio, wait upon him.

                              Exit Hamlet and Horatio.

[*To Laertes.*] Strengthen your patience in our last night's
     speech.
We'll put the matter to the present push.°   *285*
Good Gertrude, set some watch over your son.
This grave shall have a living° monument.
An hour of quiet shortly shall we see;
Till then in patience our proceeding be.

                                        Exeunt.

[**Scene II.** *The castle.*]

Enter Hamlet and Horatio.

Hamlet. So much for this, sir; now shall you see the other.
     You do remember all the circumstance?
Horatio. Remember it, my lord!
Hamlet. Sir, in my heart there was a kind of fighting
     That would not let me sleep. Methought I lay   *5*
     Worse than the mutines in the bilboes.° Rashly
     (And praised be rashness for it) let us know,
     Our indiscretion sometime serves us well
     When our deep plots do pall,° and that should learn us
     There's a divinity that shapes our ends,   *10*
     Rough-hew them how we will.
Horatio.   That is most certain.
Hamlet. Up from my cabin,
     My sea gown scarfed about me, in the dark
     Groped I to find out them, had my desire,
     Fingered° their packet, and in fine° withdrew   *15*

---

²⁷⁷*golden couplets are disclosed* (the dove lays two eggs, and the newly hatched
[*disclosed*] young are covered with golden down) ²⁸⁵*present push* immediate
test ²⁸⁷*living* lasting (with perhaps also a reference to the plot against Hamlet's
life) V.ii. ⁶*mutines in the bilboes* mutineers in fetters ⁹*pall* fail ¹⁵*Fingered*
stole ¹⁵*in fine* finally

To mine own room again, making so bold,
My fears forgetting manners, to unseal
Their grand commission; where I found, Horatio —
Ah, royal knavery! — an exact command.
Larded° with many several sorts of reasons,   20
Importing Denmark's health, and England's too,
With, ho, such bugs and goblins in my life,°
That on the supervise,° no leisure bated,°
No, not to stay the grinding of the ax,
My head should be struck off.
Horatio.   Is't possible?   25
Hamlet. Here's the commission; read it at more leisure.
But wilt thou hear now how I did proceed?
Horatio. I beseech you.
Hamlet. Being thus benetted round with villains,
Or° I could make a prologue to my brains,   30
They had begun the play. I sat me down,
Devised a new commission, wrote it fair.
I once did hold it, as our statists° do,
A baseness to write fair,° and labored much
How to forget that learning, but, sir, now   35
It did me yeoman's service. Wilt thou know
Th' effect° of what I wrote?
Horatio.   Ay, good my lord.
Hamlet. An earnest conjuration from the King,
As England was his faithful tributary,
As love between them like the palm might flourish,   40
As peace should still her wheaten garland wear
And stand a comma° 'tween their amities,
And many suchlike as's of great charge,°
That on the view and knowing of these contents,
Without debatement further, more or less,   45
He should those bearers put to sudden death,
Not shriving° time allowed.
Horatio.   How was this sealed?
Hamlet. Why, even in that was heaven ordinant.°
I had my father's signet in my purse,
Which was the model° of that Danish seal,   50

---

²⁰**Larded** enriched   ²²**such bugs and goblins in my life** such bugbears and imagined terrors if I were allowed to live   ²³**supervise** reading   ²³**leisure bated** delay allowed   ³⁰**Or** ere   ³³**statists** statesmen   ³⁴**fair** clearly   ³⁷**effect** purport   ⁴²**comma** link   ⁴³**great charge** (1) serious exhortation, (2) heavy burden (punning on *as's* and "asses")   ⁴⁷**shriving** absolution   ⁴⁸**ordinant** ruling   ⁵⁰**model** counterpart

Folded the writ up in the form of th' other,
Subscribed it, gave't th' impression, placed it safely,
The changeling never known. Now, the next day
Was our sea fight, and what to this was sequent
Thou knowest already.   55
Horatio. So Guildenstern and Rosencrantz go to't.
Hamlet. Why, man, they did make love to this employment.
  They are not near my conscience; their defeat
  Does by their own insinuation° grow.
  'Tis dangerous when the baser nature comes   60
  Between the pass° and fell° incensèd points
  Of mighty opposites.
Horatio.   Why, what a king is this!
Hamlet. Does it not, think thee, stand me now upon° —
  He that hath killed my king, and whored my mother,
  Popped in between th' election° and my hopes,   65
  Thrown out his angle° for my proper life,°
  And with such coz'nage° — is't not perfect conscience
  To quit° him with this arm? And is't not to be damned
  To let this canker of our nature come
  In further evil?   70
Horatio. It must be shortly known to him from England
  What is the issue of the business there.
Hamlet. It will be short; the interim's mine,
  And a man's life's no more than to say "one."
  But I am very sorry, good Horatio,   75
  That to Laertes I forgot myself,
  For by the image of my cause I see
  The portraiture of his. I'll court his favors.
  But sure the bravery° of his grief did put me
  Into a tow'ring passion.
Horatio.   Peace, who comes here?   80

Enter young Osric, a courtier.

Osric. Your lordship is right welcome back to Denmark.
Hamlet. I humbly thank you, sir. [*Aside to Horatio.*] Dost
  know this waterfly?
Horatio [*aside to Hamlet*]. No, my good lord.
Hamlet [*aside to Horatio*]. Thy state is the more gracious, for   85

---

⁵⁹*insinuation* meddling   ⁶¹*pass* thrust   ⁶¹*fell* cruel   ⁶²*stand me now upon* become
incumbent upon me   ⁶⁵*election* (the Danish monarchy was elective)   ⁶⁶*angle* fishing
line   ⁶⁶*my proper life* my own life   ⁶⁷*coz'nage* trickery   ⁶⁸*quit* pay back   ⁷⁹*bravery*
bravado

'tis a vice to know him. He hath much land, and fertile.
Let a beast be lord of beasts, and his crib shall stand
at the king's mess.° 'Tis a chough,° but, as I say, spacious°
in the possession of dirt.

Osric. Sweet lord, if your lordship were at leisure, I should   *90*
impart a thing to you from his Majesty.

Hamlet. I will receive it, sir, with all diligence of spirit. Put
your bonnet to his right use. 'Tis for the head.

Osric. I thank your lordship, it is very hot.

Hamlet. No, believe me, 'tis very cold; the wind is northerly.   *95*

Osric. It is indifferent cold, my lord, indeed.

Hamlet. But yet methinks it is very sultry and hot for my
complexion.°

Osric. Exceedingly, my lord; it is very sultry, as 'twere — I
cannot tell how. But, my lord, his Majesty bade me   *100*
signify to you that 'a has laid a great wager on your
head. Sir, this is the matter ——

Hamlet. I beseech you remember.

[*Hamlet moves him to put on his hat.*]

Osric. Nay, good my lord; for my ease, in good faith. Sir,
here is newly come to court Laertes — believe me, an   *105*
absolute gentleman, full of most excellent differences,°
of very soft society and great showing. Indeed, to speak
feelingly° of him, he is the card° or calendar of gentry;
for you shall find in him the continent° of what part a
gentleman would see.   *110*

Hamlet. Sir, his definement° suffers no perdition° in you,
though, I know, to divide him inventorially would
dozy° th' arithmetic of memory, and yet but yaw neither
in respect of his quick sail.° But, in the verity of ex-
tolment, I take him to be a soul of great article,° and   *115*
his infusion° of such dearth and rareness as, to make
true diction° of him, his semblable° is his mirror, and
who else would trace him, his umbrage,° nothing more.

---

[88]*mess* table   [88]*chough* jackdaw (here chatterer)   [88]*spacious* well off   [98]*complexion*
temperament   [106]*differences* distinguishing characteristics   [108]*feelingly* justly   [108]*card*
chart   [109]*continent* summary   [111]*definement* description   [111]*perdition* loss   [113]*dozy*
dizzy   [113-114]*and yet . . . quick sail* i.e., and yet only stagger despite all (*yaw neither*)
in trying to overtake his virtues   [115]*article* (literally, "item," but here perhaps
"traits" or "importance')   [116]*infusion* essential quality   [117]*diction* description
[117]*semblable* likeness   [118]*umbrage* shadow

Osric. Your lordship speaks most infallibly of him.

Hamlet. The concernancy,° sir? Why do we wrap the gentleman   120
in our more rawer breath?

Osric. Sir?

Horatio. Is't not possible to understand in another tongue?
You will to't,° sir, really.

Hamlet. What imports the nomination of this gentleman?   125

Osric. Of Laertes?

Horatio [*aside to Hamlet*]. His purse is empty already. All's
golden words are spent.

Hamlet. Of him, sir.

Osric. I know you are not ignorant ——   130

Hamlet. I would you did, sir; yet, in faith, if you did, it
would not much approve° me. Well, sir?

Osric. You are not ignorant of what excellence Laertes is ——

Hamlet. I dare not confess that, lest I should compare with
him in excellence; but to know a man well were to   135
know himself.

Osric. I mean, sir, for his weapon; but in the imputation°
laid on him by them, in his meed° he's unfellowed.

Hamlet. What's his weapon?

Osric. Rapier and dagger.   140

Hamlet. That's two of his weapons — but well.

Osric. The King, sir, hath wagered with him six Barbary
horses, against the which he has impawned,° as I take
it, six French rapiers and poniards, with their assigns,°
as girdle, hangers,° and so. Three of the carriages,° in   145
faith, are very dear to fancy, very responsive° to the
hilts, most delicate carriages, and of very liberal conceit.°

Hamlet. What call you the carriages?

Horatio [*aside to Hamlet*]. I knew you must be edified by the
margent° ere you had done.   150

Osric. The carriages, sir, are the hangers.

Hamlet. The phrase would be more germane to the matter
if we could carry a cannon by our sides. I would it
might be hangers till then. But on! Six Barbary horses
against six French swords, their assigns, and three liberal-   155
conceited carriages — that's the French bet against the
Danish. Why is this all impawned, as you call it?

---

[120]*concernancy* meaning [124]*will to't* will get there [132]*approve* commend [137]*imputation* reputation [138]*meed* merit [143]*impawned* wagered [144]*assigns* accompaniments [145]*hangers* straps hanging the sword to the belt [145]*carriages* (an affected word for hangers) [146]*responsive* corresponding [147]*liberal conceit* elaborate design [150]*margent* i.e., marginal (explanatory comment)

Osric. The King, sir, hath laid, sir, that in a dozen passes
between yourself and him he shall not exceed you three
hits; he hath laid on twelve for nine, and it would come   160
to immediate trial if your lordship would vouchsafe the
answer.

Hamlet. How if I answer no?

Osric. I mean, my lord, the opposition of your person in trial.

Hamlet. Sir, I will walk here in the hall. If it please his   165
Majesty, it is the breathing time of day with me.° Let
the foils be brought, the gentleman willing, and the
King hold his purpose, I will win for him an I can; if
not, I will gain nothing but my shame and the odd
hits.   170

Osric. Shall I deliver you e'en so?

Hamlet. To this effect, sir, after what flourish your nature will.

Osric. I commend my duty to your lordship.

Hamlet. Yours, yours.

                                                    [*Exit Osric.*]
He does well to commend it himself; there are no tongues   175
else for's turn.

Horatio. This lapwing° runs away with the shell on his head.

Hamlet. 'A did comply, sir, with his dug° before 'a sucked
it. Thus has he, and many more of the same breed that
I know the drossy age dotes on, only got the tune of   180
the time and, out of an habit of encounter,° a kind of
yeasty° collection, which carries them through and
through the most fanned and winnowed opinions; and
do but blow them to their trial, the bubbles are out.°

Enter a Lord.

Lord. My lord, his Majesty commended him to you by young   185
Osric, who brings back to him that you attend him in
the hall. He sends to know if your pleasure hold to
play with Laertes, or that you will take longer time.

Hamlet. I am constant to my purposes; they follow the King's
pleasure. If his fitness speaks, mine is ready; now or   190
whensoever, provided I be so able as now.

Lord. The King and Queen and all are coming down.

---

[166] **breathing time of day with me** time when I take exercise   [177] **lapwing** (the new-
hatched lapwing was thought to run around with half its shell on its head)   [178] **'A
did comply, sir, with his dug** he was ceremoniously polite to his mother's breast   [181] **out
of an habit of encounter** out of his own superficial way of meeting and conversing
with people   [182] **yeasty** frothy   [184] **the bubbles are out** i.e., they are blown away
(the reference is to the "yeasty collection")

Hamlet. In happy time.

Lord. The Queen desires you to use some gentle entertainment°
to Laertes before you fall to play.   **195**

Hamlet. She well instructs me.

[*Exit Lord.*]

Horatio. You will lose this wager, my lord.

Hamlet. I do not think so. Since he went into France I have
been in continual practice. I shall win at the odds. But
thou wouldst not think how ill all's here about my   **200**
heart. But it is no matter.

Horatio. Nay, good my lord ——

Hamlet. It is but foolery, but it is such a kind of gain-giving°
as would perhaps trouble a woman.

Horatio. If your mind dislike anything, obey it. I will forestall   **205**
their repair hither and say you are not fit.

Hamlet. Not a whit, we defy augury. There is special providence
in the fall of a sparrow.° If it be now, 'tis not to come;
if it be not to come, it will be now; if it be not now,
yet it will come. The readiness is all. Since no man of   **210**
aught he leaves knows, what is't to leave betimes?° Let
be.

A table prepared. [*Enter*] *Trumpets, Drums, and Officers with
cushions; King, Queen,* [*Osric,*] *and all the State,* [*with*] *foils,
daggers,* [*and stoups of wine borne in*]; *and Laertes.*

King. Come, Hamlet, come, and take this hand from me.

[*The King puts Laertes' hand into Hamlet's.*]

Hamlet. Give me your pardon, sir. I have done you wrong,
But pardon't, as you are a gentleman.   **215**
This presence° knows, and you must needs have heard,
How I am punished with a sore distraction.
What I have done
That might your nature, honor, and exception°
Roughly awake, I here proclaim was madness.   **220**
Was't Hamlet wronged Laertes? Never Hamlet.
If Hamlet from himself be ta'en away,
And when he's not himself does wrong Laertes,
Then Hamlet does it not, Hamlet denies it.
Who does it then? His madness. If't be so,   **225**

---

¹⁹³*to use some gentle entertainment* to be courteous   ²⁰³*gain-giving* misgiving   ²⁰⁸*the
fall of a sparrow* (cf. Matthew 10:29 "Are not two sparrows sold for a farthing?
and one of them shall not fall on the ground without your Father")   ²¹¹*betimes*
early   ²¹⁶*presence* royal assembly   ²¹⁹*exception* disapproval

Hamlet is of the faction° that is wronged;
His madness is poor Hamlet's enemy.
Sir, in this audience,
Let my disclaiming from a purposed evil
Free me so far in your most generous thoughts   *230*
That I have shot my arrow o'er the house
And hurt my brother.
Laertes.   I am satisfied in nature,
Whose motive in this case should stir me most
To my revenge. But in my terms of honor
I stand aloof, and will no reconcilement   *235*
Till by some elder masters of known honor
I have a voice and precedent° of peace
To keep my name ungored. But till that time
I do receive your offered love like love,
And will not wrong it.
Hamlet.   I embrace it freely,   *240*
And will this brother's wager frankly play.
Give us the foils. Come on.
Laertes.   Come, one for me.
Hamlet. I'll be your foil,° Laertes. In mine ignorance
Your skill shall, like a star i' th' darkest night,
Stick fiery off° indeed.
Laertes.   You mock me, sir.   *245*
Hamlet. No, by this hand.
King. Give them the foils, young Osric. Cousin Hamlet,
You know the wager?
Hamlet.   Very well, my lord.
Your grace has laid the odds o' th' weaker side.
King. I do not fear it, I have seen you both;   *250*
But since he is bettered,° we have therefore odds.
Laertes. This is too heavy; let me see another.
Hamlet. This likes me well. These foils have all a length?

   Prepare to play.

Osric. Ay, my good lord.
King. Set me the stoups of wine upon that table.   *255*
If Hamlet give the first or second hit,
Or quit° in answer of the third exchange,

---

²²⁶*faction* party, side   ²³⁷*voice and precedent* authoritative opinion justified by
precedent   ²⁴³*foil* (1) blunt sword, (2) background (of metallic leaf) for a jewel   ²⁴⁵*Stick
fiery off* stand out brilliantly   ²⁵¹*bettered* has improved (in France)   ²⁵⁷*quit* repay,
hit back

Let all the battlements their ordnance fire.
The King shall drink to Hamlet's better breath,
And in the cup an union° shall he throw   *260*
Richer than that which four successive kings
In Denmark's crown have worn. Give me the cups,
And let the kettle° to the trumpet speak,
The trumpet to the cannoneer without,
The cannons to the heavens, the heaven to earth,   *265*
"Now the King drinks to Hamlet." Come, begin.

Trumpets the while.

And you, the judges, bear a wary eye.
Hamlet. Come on, sir.
Laertes.   Come, my lord!

     They play.

Hamlet.   One!
Laertes.   No.
Hamlet.   Judgment?
Osric. A hit, a very palpable hit.

     Drum, trumpets, and shot. Flourish; a piece goes off.

Laertes.   Well, again.
King. Stay, give me drink. Hamlet, this pearl is thine.   *270*
     Here's to thy health. Give him the cup.
Hamlet. I'll play this bout first; set it by awhile.
     Come.

     [*They play.*]

     Another hit. What say you?
Laertes. A touch, a touch; I do confess't.
King. Our son shall win.
Queen.   He's fat,° and scant of breath.   *275*
     Here, Hamlet, take my napkin, rub thy brows.
     The Queen carouses to thy fortune, Hamlet.
Hamlet. Good madam!
King.   Gertrude, do not drink.
Queen. I will, my lord; I pray you pardon me. [*Drinks.*]
King [*aside*]. It is the poisoned cup; it is too late.   *280*
Hamlet. I dare not drink yet, madam — by and by.
Queen. Come, let me wipe thy face.

---

²⁶⁰*union* pearl   ²⁶³*kettle* kettledrum   ²⁷⁵*fat* (1) sweaty, (2) out of training

Laertes. My lord, I'll hit him now.
King.   I do not think't.
Laertes [*aside*]. And yet it is almost against my conscience.
Hamlet. Come for the third, Laertes. You do but dally.   *285*
    I pray you pass with your best violence;
    I am sure you make a wanton° of me.

    [*They*] *play*.

Laertes. Say you so? Come on.
Osric. Nothing neither way.
Laertes. Have at you now!

    In scuffling they change rapiers, [*and both are wounded.*]

King.   Part them. They are incensed.   *290*
Hamlet. Nay, come — again!
    [*The Queen fails.*]
Osric.   Look to the Queen there, ho!
Horatio. They bleed on both sides. How is it, my lord?
Osric. How is't, Laertes?
Laertes. Why, as a woodcock to mine own springe,° Osric.
    I am justly killed with mine own treachery.   *295*
Hamlet. How does the Queen?
King.   She sounds° to see them bleed.
Queen. No, no, the drink, the drink! O my dear Hamlet!
    The drink, the drink! I am poisoned.
                           [*Dies.*]
Hamlet. O villainy! Ho! Let the door be locked.
    Treachery! Seek it out.   *300*

    [*Laertes falls.*]

Laertes. It is here, Hamlet. Hamlet, thou art slain;
    No med'cine in the world can do thee good.
    In thee there is not half an hour's life.
    The treacherous instrument is in thy hand,
    Unbated and envenomed. The foul practice°   *305*
    Hath turned itself on me. Lo, here I lie,
    Never to rise again. Thy mother's poisoned.
    I can no more. The King, the King's to blame.
Hamlet. The point envenomed too?
    Then, venom, to thy work.   *310*
                         Hurts the King.
All. Treason! Treason!

---

²⁸⁷**wanton** spoiled child   ²⁹⁴**springe** snare   ²⁹⁶**sounds** swoons   ³⁰⁵**practice** deception

King. O, yet defend me, friends. I am but hurt.
Hamlet. Here, thou incestuous, murd'rous, damnèd Dane,
    Drink off this potion. Is thy union here?
    Follow my mother.

                              King dies.

Laertes.   He is justly served.   315
    It is a poison tempered° by himself.
    Exchange forgiveness with me, noble Hamlet.
    Mine and my father's death come not upon thee,
    Nor thine on me!

                                   Dies.

Hamlet. Heaven make thee free of it! I follow thee.   320
    I am dead, Horatio. Wretched Queen, adieu!
    You that look pale and tremble at this chance,
    That are but mutes° or audience to this act,
    Had I but time (as this fell sergeant,° Death,
    Is strict in his arrest) O, I could tell you —   325
    But let it be. Horatio, I am dead;
    Thou livest; report me and my cause aright
    To the unsatisfied.°
Horatio.   Never believe it.
    I am more an antique Roman° than a Dane.
    Here's yet some liquor left.
Hamlet.   As th' art a man,   330
    Give me the cup. Let go. By heaven, I'll ha't!
    O God, Horatio, what a wounded name,
    Things standing thus unknown, shall live behind me!
    If thou didst ever hold me in thy heart,
    Absent thee from felicity° awhile,   335
    And in this harsh world draw thy breath in pain,
    To tell my story.

               A march afar off. [*Exit Osric.*]
    What warlike noise is this?

Enter Osric.

Osric. Young Fortinbras, with conquest come from Poland,
    To th' ambassadors of England gives
    This warlike volley.
Hamlet.   O, I die, Horatio!   340
    The potent poison quite o'ercrows° my spirit.
    I cannot live to hear the news from England,

---

[316]*tempered* mixed   [323]*mutes* performers who have no words to speak   [324]*fell sergeant* dread sheriff's officer   [328]*unsatisfied* uniformed   [329]*antique Roman* (with reference to the old Roman fashion of suicide)   [335]*felicity* i.e., the felicity of death   [341]*o'ercrows* overpowers (as a triumphant cock crows over its weak opponent)

But I do prophesy th' election lights
On Fortinbras. He has my dying voice.
So tell him, with th' occurrents,° more and less,   *345*
Which have solicited° — the rest is silence.

                                                    Dies.

Horatio. Now cracks a noble heart. Good night, sweet Prince,
And flights of angels sing thee to thy rest.

                                          [*March within.*]

    Why does the drum come hither?

*Enter Fortinbras, with the Ambassadors with Drum, Colors, and
Attendants.*

Fortinbras. Where is this sight?
Horatio.   What is it you would see?   *350*
    If aught of woe or wonder, cease your search.
Fortinbras. This quarry° cries on havoc.° O proud Death,
    What feast is toward° in thine eternal cell
    That thou so many princes at a shot
    So bloodily hast struck?
Ambassador.   The sight is dismal;   *355*
    And our affairs from England come too late.
    The ears are senseless that should give us hearing
    To tell him his commandment is fulfilled,
    That Rosencrantz and Guildenstern are dead.
    Where should we have our thanks?
Horatio.   Not from his° mouth, *360*
    Had it th' ability of life to thank you.
    He never gave commandment for their death.
    But since, so jump° upon this bloody question,
    You from the Polack wars, and you from England,
    Are here arrived, give order that these bodies   *365*
    High on a stage° be placèd to the view,
    And let me speak to th' yet unknowing world
    How these things came about. So shall you hear
    Of carnal, bloody, and unnatural acts,
    Of accidental judgments, casual° slaughters,   *370*
    Of deaths put on by cunning and forced cause,
    And, in this upshot, purposes mistook
    Fall'n on th' inventors'· heads. All this can I
    Truly deliver.
Fortinbras.   Let us haste to hear it,

---

³⁴⁵*occurrents* occurrences ³⁴⁶*solicited* incited ³⁵²*quarry* heap of slain bodies ³⁵²*cries*
on havoc proclaims general slaughter ³⁵³*toward* in preparation ³⁶⁰*his* (Claudius') ³⁶³*jump* precisely ³⁶⁶*stage* platform ³⁷⁰*casual* not humanly planned, chance

And call the noblest to the audience.   375
For me, with sorrow I embrace my fortune.
I have some rights of memory° in this kingdom,
Which now to claim my vantage doth invite me.
Horatio. Of that I shall have also cause to speak,
And from his mouth whose voice will draw on° more.   380
But let this same be presently performed,
Even while men's minds are wild, lest more mischance
On° plots and errors happen.
Fortinbras.   Let four captains
Bear Hamlet like a soldier to the stage,
For he was likely, had he been put on,°   385
To have proved most royal; and for his passage°
The soldiers' music and the rite of war
Speak loudly for him.
Take up the bodies. Such a sight as this
Becomes the field,° but here shows much amiss.   390
Go, bid the soldiers shoot.
                                        Exeunt marching;
                after the which a peal of ordnance are shot off.

                        Finis

QUESTIONS

Act I

1. The first scene (like many other scenes in this play) is full
   of expressions of uncertainty. What are some of these uncertainties? The Ghost first appears at I.i.39. Does his appearance surprise us, or have we been prepared for it? Or
   is there both preparation and surprise? How do the last four
   speeches of I.i help to introduce a note of hope?
2. Does the King's opening speech in I.ii reveal him to be an
   accomplished public speaker — or are lines 10–14 offensive?
   In his second speech (lines 41–50), what is the effect of
   naming Laertes four times? Claudius sometimes uses the
   royal pronouns (we, our), sometimes the more intimate "I"
   and "my." Study his use of these in lines 1–4 and in 106–
   117. What is he getting at?
3. Hamlet's first soliloquy (I.ii.129–159) reveals that not simply

---

³⁷⁷*rights of memory* remembered claims ³⁸⁰*voice will draw on* vote will
influence ³⁸³*On* on top of ³⁸⁵*put on* advanced (to the throne) ³⁸⁶*passage*
death ³⁹⁰*field* battlefield

his father's death distresses him. Be as specific as possible about the causes of Hamlet's anguish here. What traits does Hamlet reveal in his conversation with Horatio (I.ii.160–254)?

4. What do you make out of Polonius's advice to Laertes (I.iii.59–80)? Is it sound? Sound advice, but here uttered by a fool? Ignoble advice? How would one follow the advice of line 78: "to thine own self be true"? In his words to Ophelia in I.iii.101–135, what does he reveal about himself?

5. Can I.iv.17–38 reasonably be taken as a speech on "the tragic flaw"? Or is the passage a much more limited discussion, a comment simply on Danish drinking habits?

6. How in this scene (and in I.i) does Shakespeare suggest that the Ghost may be an evil spirit? Do such suggestions dominate?

7. The Ghost, claiming to be in a state of purgation (in I.v), seeks revenge. Does its uncharitable request convince us that the Ghost must really be an evil spirit trying to trap Hamlet into doing a damnable murder? Or do we accept the call to revenge as valid?

8. Hamlet is convinced in I.v.95–104 that the Ghost has told the truth, indeed, told the only important truth. But do we detect in 105–112 a hint of a tone suggesting that Hamlet delights in hating villainy? If so, can it be said that later this delight grows, and that in some scenes (e.g., III.iii) we feel that Hamlet has almost become a diabolic revenger?

9. Scenes fairly often end with a couplet (pair of rhyming lines). What is the effect of adding an *un*rhymed line to the couplet, at the end of I.v?

Act II

1. Characterize Polonius on the basis of II.i.1–74.

2. In light of what we have seen of Hamlet, is Ophelia's report of his strange behavior when he visits her understandable?

3. Why does II.ii.33–34 seem almost comic? How do these lines help us to form a view about Rosencrantz and Guildenstern?

4. In lines 85–98 Polonius uses wordplay. Does it suggest that he is witty, or foolish? Hamlet too uses wordplay (e.g., II.ii.193), but the effect differs. How?

5. Is "the hellish Pyrrhus" (II.ii.455) Hamlet's version of Claudius? Or is he Hamlet, who soon will be responsible for the deaths of Polonius, Rosencrantz and Guildenstern, Claudius, Gertrude, Ophelia, and Laertes?

6. Is the Player's speech (II.ii.460–510) a huffing speech? If so, why? To distinguish it from the poetry of the play itself? To characterize the bloody deeds that Hamlet cannot descend to?

7. In II.ii.555–576 Hamlet rebukes himself for not acting. Why has he not acted? Because he is a coward (line 556)? Because he has a conscience? Because no action can restore his father and his mother's purity? Because he doubts the Ghost?

Act III

1. What do you make out of Hamlet's assertion to Ophelia: "I loved you not" (III.i.118–119)? Of his characterization of himself as full of "offenses" (III.i.125)? Why is Hamlet so harsh to Ophelia?

2. Hamlet praises Horatio as a man who "is not passion's slave" (III.ii.71). But is such a man a hero? Will he avenge a wronged father? Can we reasonably apply the Player King's comments on passion (III.ii.187–192) and fate (III.ii.204–206) to the play of *Hamlet* itself?

3. In III.iii.11–23 Rosencrantz is speaking about Claudius, but to what degree do his words apply to Hamlet's father?

4. In III.iii.36–72 Claudius's conscience afflicts him. But is he repentant?

5. Is Hamlet other than abhorrent in III.iii.74–96? Do we want him to kill Claudius at this moment, when Claudius (presumably with his back to Hamlet) is praying?

6. The Ghost speaks of Hamlet's "almost blunted purpose" (III.iv.112). Is the accusation fair?

7. How would you characterize the Hamlet who speaks in III.iv. 203–217?

Act IV

1. Is Gertrude protecting Hamlet when she says he is mad (IV.i.7), or does she believe that he is mad? If she believes he is mad, does it follow that she no longer feels ashamed and guilty?

2. Why should Hamlet hide Polonius's body (in IV.ii)? Is he feigning madness? Is he on the edge of madness?

3. How can we explain Hamlet's willingness to go to England (IV.iii.44)?

4. Judging from IV.v, what has driven Ophelia mad? Is Laertes heroic, or somewhat foolish? Consider also the way Claudius treats him in IV.vii.

Act V

1. What would be lost if the Gravediggers in V.i were omitted?
2. To what extent do we judge Hamlet severely for sending Rosencrantz and Guildenstern to their deaths, as he reports in V.ii? On the whole do we think of Hamlet as an intriguer? What other intrigues has he engendered? How successful were they?
3. Does V.ii.207–212 show a paralysis of the will, or a wise recognition that more is needed than mere human scheming?
4. Does V.ii.290 suggest that Laertes takes advantage of a momentary pause and unfairly stabs Hamlet? Is the exchange of weapons accidental, or does Hamlet (as in Olivier's film version), realizing that he has been betrayed, deliberately get possession of Laertes's deadly weapon?
5. Fortinbras is often cut from the play. How much is lost by the cut?
6. Fortinbras gives Hamlet a soldier's funeral. Is this ridiculous? Can it fairly be said that, in a sense, Hamlet has been at war?

General Questions

1. Hamlet in V.ii.10–11 speaks of a "divinity that shapes our ends." To what extent does "divinity" (or Fate or mysterious Chance) play a role in the happenings?
2. How do Laertes, Fortinbras, and Horatio help to define Hamlet for us?
3. T. S. Eliot says (in "Shakespeare and the Stoicism of Seneca") that Hamlet, having made a mess, "dies fairly well pleased with himself." Evaluate.

Henrik Ibsen (1828–1906)

A Doll's House

Translated by Otto Reinert

List of Characters

Torvald Helmer, a lawyer
Nora, his wife

Claire Bloom starred as Nora in the 1971 production of A Doll's House.
Photograph © by Martha Swope. Used by permission.

Dr. Rank
Mrs. Linde
Krogstad
The Helmers' three small children
Anne-Marie, the children's nurse
A housemaid
A porter

Scene. *The Helmers' living room*

ACT I

*A pleasant, tastefully but not expensively furnished, living room.
A door on the rear wall, right, leads to the front hall, another
door, left, to Helmer's study. Between the two doors a piano. A
third door in the middle of the left wall; further front a window.
Near the window a round table with easy chairs and a small couch.
Towards the rear of the right wall a fourth door; further front a
tile stove with a rocking chair and a couple of arm chairs in front
of it. Between the stove and the side door a small table. Copperplate
etchings on the walls. A whatnot with porcelain figurines and other
small objects. A small bookcase with deluxe editions. A rug on the
floor; fire in the stove. Winter day.*

*The doorbell rings, then the sound of the front door opening. Nora,
dressed for outdoors, enters, humming cheerfully. She carries several
packages, which she puts down on the table, right. She leaves the
door to the front hall open; there a Porter is seen holding a Christmas
tree and a basket. He gives them to the Maid, who has let them
in.*

Nora. Be sure to hide the Christmas tree, Helene. The children
    mustn't see it before tonight when we've trimmed it. (*Opens
    her purse; to the Porter.*) How much?
Porter. Fifty øre.
Nora. Here's a crown. No, keep the change. (*The Porter thanks
    her, leaves. Nora closes the door. She keeps laughing quietly to
    herself as she takes off her coat, etc. She takes a bag of macaroons
    from her pocket and eats a couple. She walks cautiously over to
    the door to the study and listens.*) Yes, he's home. (*Resumes her
    humming, walks over to the table, right.*)
Helmer (*in his study*). Is that my little lark twittering out there?
Nora (*opening some of the packages*). That's right.
Helmer. My squirrel bustling about?

Nora. Yes.

Helmer. When did squirrel come home?

Nora. Just now. (*Puts the bag of macaroons back in her pocket, wipes her mouth.*) Come out here, Torvald. I want to show you what I've bought.

Helmer. I'm busy! (*After a little while he opens the door and looks in, pen in hand.*) Bought, eh? All that? So little wastrel has been throwing money around again?

Nora. Oh but Torvald, this Christmas we can be a little extravagant, can't we? It's the first Christmas we don't have to scrimp.

Helmer. I don't know about that. We certainly don't have money to waste.

Nora. Yes, Torvald, we do. A little, anyway. Just a tiny little bit? Now that you're going to get that big salary and make lots and lots of money.

Helmer. Starting at New Year's, yes. But payday isn't till the end of the quarter.

Nora. That doesn't matter. We can always borrow.

Helmer. Nora! (*Goes over to her and playfully pulls her ear.*) There you go being irresponsible again. Suppose I borrowed a thousand crowns today and you spent it all for Christmas and on New Year's Eve a tile hit me in the head and laid me out cold.

Nora (*putting her hand over his mouth*). I won't have you say such horrid things.

Helmer. But suppose it happened. Then what?

Nora. If it did, I wouldn't care whether we owed money or not.

Helmer. But what about the people I had borrowed from?

Nora. Who cares about them! They are strangers.

Helmer. Nora, Nora, you are a woman. No, really! You know how I feel about that. No debts! A home in debt isn't a free home, and if it isn't free it isn't beautiful. We've managed nicely so far, you and I, and that's the way we'll go on. It won't be for much longer.

Nora (*walks over toward the stove*). All right, Torvald. Whatever you say.

Helmer (*follows her*). Come, come, my little songbird mustn't droop her wings. What's this? Can't have a pouty squirrel in the house, you know. (*Takes out his wallet.*) Nora, what do you think I have here?

Nora (*turns around quickly*). Money!

Helmer. Here. (*Gives her some bills.*) Don't you think I know Christmas is expensive?

Nora (*counting*). Ten — twenty — thirty — forty. Thank you, thank you, Torvald. This helps a lot.

Helmer. I certainly hope so.

Nora. It does, it does. But I want to show you what I got. It was cheap, too. Look. New clothes for Ivar. And a sword. And a horse and trumpet for Bob. And a doll and a little bed for Emmy. It isn't any good, but it wouldn't last, anyway. And here's some dress material and scarves for the maids. I feel bad about old Anne-Marie, though. She really should be getting much more.

Helmer. And what's in here?

Nora (cries). Not till tonight!

Helmer. I see. But now what does my little prodigal have in mind for herself?

Nora. Oh, nothing. I really don't care.

Helmer. Of course you do. Tell me what you'd like. Within reason.

Nora. Oh, I don't know. Really, I don't. The only thing —

Helmer. Well?

Nora (fiddling with his buttons, without looking at him). If you really want to give me something, you might — you could —

Helmer. All right, let's have it.

Nora (quickly). Some money, Torvald. Just as much as you think you can spare. Then I'll buy myself something one of these days.

Helmer. No, really Nora —

Nora. Oh yes, please, Torvald. Please? I'll wrap the money in pretty gold paper and hang it on the tree. Won't that be nice?

Helmer. What's the name for little birds that are always spending money?

Nora. Wastrels, I know. But please let's do it my way, Torvald. Then I'll have time to decide what I need most. Now that's sensible, isn't it?

Helmer (smiling). Oh, very sensible. That is, if you really bought yourself something you could use. But it all disappears in the household expenses or you buy things you don't need. And then you come back to me for more.

Nora. Oh, but Torvald —

Helmer. That's the truth, dear little Nora, and you know it. (*Puts his arm around her.*) My wastrel is a little sweetheart, but she does go through an awful lot of money awfully fast. You've no idea how expensive it is for a man to keep a wastrel.

Nora. That's not fair, Torvald. I really save all I can.

Helmer (laughs). Oh, I believe that. All you can. Meaning, exactly nothing!

Nora (hums, smiles mysteriously). You don't know all the things we songbirds and squirrels need money for, Torvald.

Helmer. You know, you're funny. Just like your father. You're always looking for ways to get money, but as soon as you do it runs through your fingers and you can never say what you spent it for. Well, I guess I'll just have to take you the way you are. It's in your blood. Yes, that sort of thing is hereditary, Nora.

Nora. In that case, I wish I had inherited many of Daddy's qualities.

Helmer. And I don't want you any different from just what you are — my own sweet little songbird. Hey! — I think I just noticed something. Aren't you looking — what's the word? — a little — sly — ?

Nora. I am?

Helmer. You definitely are. Look at me.

Nora (looks at him). Well?

Helmer (wagging a finger). Little sweet-tooth hasn't by any chance been.on a rampage today, has she?

Nora. Of course not. Whatever makes you think that?

Helmer. A little detour by the pastryshop maybe?

Nora. No, I assure you, Torvald —

Helmer. Nibbled a little jam?

Nora. Certainly not!

Helmer. Munched a macaroon or two?

Nora. No, really, Torvald, I honestly —

Helmer. All right. Of course I was only joking.

Nora (walks toward the table, right). You know I wouldn't do anything to displease you.

Helmer. I know. And I have your promise. (*Over to her.*) All right, keep your little Christmas secrets to yourself, Nora darling. They'll all come out tonight, I suppose, when we light the tree.

Nora. Did you remember to invite Rank?

Helmer. No, but there's no need to. He knows he'll have dinner with us. Anyway, I'll see him later this morning. I'll ask him then. I did order some good wine. Oh Nora, you've no idea how much I'm looking forward to tonight!

Nora. Me too. And the children, Torvald! They'll have such a good time!

Helmer. You know, it *is* nice to have a good, safe job and a comfortable income. Feels good just thinking about it. Don't you agree?

Nora. Oh, it's wonderful!

Helmer. Remember last Christmas? For three whole weeks you shut yourself up every evening till long after midnight, making ornaments for the Christmas tree and I don't know what else. Some big surprise for all of us, anyway. I'll be damned if I've ever been so bored in my whole life!

Nora. I wasn't bored at all.

Helmer (smiling). But you've got to admit you didn't have much to show for it in the end.

Nora. Oh, don't tease me again about that! Could I help it that the cat got in and tore up everything?

Helmer. Of course you couldn't, my poor little Nora. You just wanted to please the rest of us, and that's the important thing. But I am glad the hard times are behind us. Aren't you?

Nora. Oh yes. I think it's just wonderful.

Helmer. This year I won't be bored and lonely. And you won't have to strain your dear eyes and your delicate little hands —

Nora (claps her hands). No I won't, will I, Torvald? Oh, how wonderful, how lovely, to hear you say that! (*Puts her arm under his.*) Let me tell you how I think we should arrange things, Torvald. Soon as Christmas is over — (*The doorbell rings.*) Someone's at the door. (*Straightens things up a bit.*) A caller, I suppose. Bother!

Helmer. Remember, I'm not home for visitors.

The Maid (in the door to the front hall). Ma'am, there's a lady here —

Nora. All right. Ask her to come in.

The Maid (to Helmer). And the Doctor just arrived.

Helmer. Is he in the study?

The Maid. Yes, sir.

> *Helmer exits into his study. The Maid shows Mrs. Linde in and closes the door behind her as she leaves. Mrs. Linde is in travel dress.*

Mrs. Linde (timid and a little hesitant). Good morning, Nora.

Nora (uncertainly). Good morning.

Mrs. Linde. I don't believe you know who I am.

Nora. No — I'm not sure — Though I know I should — Of course! Kristine! It's you!

Mrs. Linde. Yes, it's me.

Nora. And I didn't even recognize you! I had no idea! (*In a lower voice.*) You've changed, Kristine.

Mrs. Linde. I'm sure I have. It's been nine or ten long years.

Nora. Has it really been that long? Yes, you're right. I've been so happy these last eight years. And now you're here. Such a long trip in the middle of winter. How brave!

Mrs. Linde. I got in on the steamer this morning.

Nora. To have some fun over the holidays, of course. That's lovely.

For we *are* going to have fun. But take off your coat! You
aren't cold, are you? (*Helps her.*) There, now! Let's sit down
here by the fire and just relax and talk. No, you sit there.
I want the rocking chair. (*Takes her hands.*) And now you've
got your old face back. It was just for a minute, right at
first — Though you are a little more pale, Kristine. And
maybe a little thinner.

Mrs. Linde. And much, much older, Nora.

Nora. Maybe a little older. Just a teeny-weeny bit, not much.
(*Interrupts herself, serious.*) Oh, but how thoughtless of me,
chatting away like this! Sweet, good Kristine, can you forgive
me?

Mrs. Linde. Forgive you what, Nora?

Nora (*in a low voice*). You poor dear, you lost your husband, didn't
you?

Mrs. Linde. Three years ago, yes.

Nora. I know. I saw it in the paper. Oh please believe me, Kristine.
I really meant to write you, but I never got around to it.
Something was always coming up.

Mrs. Linde. Of course, Nora. I understand.

Nora. No, that wasn't very nice of me. You poor thing, all you
must have been through. And he didn't leave you much,
either, did he?

Mrs. Linde. No.

Nora. And no children?

Mrs. Linde. No.

Nora. Nothing at all, in other words?

Mrs. Linde. Not so much as a sense of loss — a grief to live on —

Nora (*incredulous*). But Kristine, how can that *be?*

Mrs. Linde (*with a sad smile, strokes Nora's hair*). That's the way it
sometimes is, Nora.

Nora. All alone. How awful for you. I have three darling children.
You can't see them right now, though; they're out with their
nurse. But now you must tell me everything —

Mrs. Linde. No, no; I'd rather listen to you.

Nora. No, you begin. Today I won't be selfish. Today I'll think
only of you. Except there's one thing I've just got to tell
you first. Something marvelous that's happened to us just
these last few days. You haven't heard, have you?

Mrs. Linde. No; tell me.

Nora. Just think. My husband's been made manager of the Mutual
Bank.

Mrs. Linde. Your husband — ! Oh, I'm so glad!

Nora. Yes, isn't that great? You see, private law practice is so
uncertain, especially when you won't have anything to do

with cases that aren't — you know — quite nice. And of course Torvald won't do that, and I quite agree with him. Oh, you've no idea how delighted we are! He takes over at New Year's, and he'll be getting a big salary and all sorts of extras. From now on we'll be able to live in quite a different way — exactly as we like. Oh, Kristine! I feel so carefree and happy! It's lovely to have lots and lots of money and not have to worry about a thing! Don't you agree?

Mrs. Linde. It would be nice to have enough, at any rate.

Nora. No, I don't mean just enough. I mean lots and lots!

Mrs. Linde (smiles). Nora, Nora, when are you going to be sensible? In school you spent a great deal of money.

Nora (quietly laughing). Yes, and Torvald says I still do. (*Raises her finger at Mrs. Linde.*) But "Nora, Nora" isn't so crazy as you all think. Believe me, we've had nothing to be extravagant with. We've both had to work.

Mrs. Linde. You too?

Nora. Yes. Oh, it's been little things mostly — sewing, crocheting, embroidery — that sort of thing. (*Casually.*) And other things too. You know, of course, that Torvald left government service when we got married? There was no chance of promotion in his department, and of course he had to make more money than he had been making. So for the first few years he worked altogether too hard. He had to take jobs on the side and work night and day. It turned out to be too much for him. He became seriously ill. The doctors told him he needed to go south.

Mrs. Linde. That's right; you spent a year in Italy, didn't you?

Nora. Yes, we did. But you won't believe how hard it was to get away. Ivar had just been born. But of course we had to go. Oh, it was a wonderful trip. And it saved Torvald's life. But it took a lot of money, Kristine.

Mrs. Linde. I'm sure it did.

Nora. Twelve hundred specie dollars. Four thousand eight hundred crowns. That's a lot of money.

Mrs. Linde. Yes. So it's lucky you have it when something like that happens.

Nora. Well, actually we got the money from Daddy.

Mrs. Linde. I see. That was about the time your father died, I believe.

Nora. Yes, just about then. And I couldn't even go and take care of him. I was expecting little Ivar any day. And I had poor Torvald to look after, desperately sick and all. My dear, good Daddy! I never saw him again, Kristine. That's the saddest thing that's happened to me since I got married.

Mrs. Linde. I know you were very fond of him. But then you went to Italy?

Nora. Yes, for now we had the money, and the doctors urged us to go. So we left about a month later.

Mrs. Linde. And when you came back your husband was well again?

Nora. Healthy as a horse!

Mrs. Linde. But — the doctor?

Nora. What do you mean?

Mrs. Linde. I thought the maid said it was the doctor, that gentleman who came the same time I did.

Nora. Oh, that's Dr. Rank. He doesn't come as a doctor. He's our closest friend. He looks in at least once every day. No, Torvald hasn't been sick once since then. And the children are strong and healthy, too, and so am I. (*Jumps up and claps her hands.*) Oh God, Kristine! Isn't it wonderful to be alive and happy! Isn't it just lovely! — But now I'm being mean again, talking only about myself and my things. (*Sits down on a footstool close to Mrs. Linde and puts her arms on her lap.*) Please, don't be angry with me! Tell me, is it really true that you didn't care for your husband? Then why did you marry him?

Mrs. Linde. Mother was still alive then, but she was bedridden and helpless. And I had my two younger brothers to look after. I didn't think I had the right to turn him down.

Nora. No, I suppose not. So he had money then?

Mrs. Linde. He was quite well off, I think. But it was an uncertain business, Nora. When he died, the whole thing collapsed and there was nothing left.

Nora. And then — ?

Mrs. Linde. Well, I had to manage as best I could. With a little store and a little school and anything else I could think of. The last three years have been one long work day for me, Nora, without any rest. But now it's over. My poor mother doesn't need me any more. She passed away. And the boys are on their own too. They've both got jobs and support themselves.

Nora. What a relief for you —

Mrs. Linde. No, not relief. Just a great emptiness. Nobody to live for any more. (*Gets up, restlessly.*) That's why I couldn't stand it any longer in that little hole. Here in town it has to be easier to find something to keep me busy and occupy my thoughts. With a little luck I should be able to find a permanent job, something in an office —

Nora. Oh but Kristine, that's exhausting work, and you look worn
   out already. It would be much better for you to go to a
   resort.

Mrs. Linde (walks over to the window). I don't have a Daddy who
   can give me the money, Nora.

Nora (getting up). Oh, don't be angry with me.

Mrs. Linde (over to her). Dear Nora, don't *you* be angry with *me.*
   That's the worst thing about my kind of situation: you become
   so bitter. You've nobody to work for, and yet you have to
   look out for yourself, somehow. You've got to keep on
   living, and so you become selfish. Do you know — when
   you told me about your husband's new position I was delighted
   not so much for your sake as for my own.

Nora. Why was that? Oh, I see. You think maybe Torvald can
   give you a job?

Mrs. Linde. That's what I had in mind.

Nora. And he will too, Kristine. Just leave it to me. I'll be ever
   so subtle about it. I'll think of something nice to tell him,
   something he'll like. Oh I so much want to help you.

Mrs. Linde. That's very good of you, Nora — making an effort
   like that for me. Especially since you've known so little
   trouble and hardship in your own life.

Nora. I — ? — have known so little — ?

Mrs. Linde (smiling). Oh well, a little sewing or whatever it was.
   You're still a child, Nora.

Nora (with a toss of her head, walks away). You shouldn't sound so
   superior.

Mrs. Linde. I shouldn't?

Nora. You're just like all the others. None of you think I'm good
   for anything really serious.

Mrs. Linde. Well, now —

Nora. That I've never been through anything difficult.

Mrs. Linde. But Nora! You just told me all your troubles!

Nora. That's nothing. *(Lowers her voice.)* I haven't told you about *it.*

Mrs. Linde. It? What's that? What do you mean?

Nora. You patronize me, Kristine, and that's not fair. You're proud
   that you worked so long and so hard for your mother.

Mrs. Linde. I don't think I patronize anyone. But it *is* true that
   I'm both proud and happy that I could make mother's last
   years comparatively easy.

Nora. And you're proud of all you did for your brothers.

Mrs. Linde. I think I have the right to be.

Nora. And so do I. But now I want to tell you something, Kristine.
   I have something to be proud and happy about too.

Mrs. Linde. I don't doubt that for a moment. But what exactly do you mean?

Nora. Not so loud! Torvald mustn't hear — not for anything in the world. Nobody must know about this, Kristine. Nobody but you.

Mrs. Linde. But what is it?

Nora. Come here. (*Pulls her down on the couch beside her.*) You see, I *do* have something to be proud and happy about. I've saved Torvald's life.

Mrs. Linde. Saved — ? How do you mean — "saved"?

Nora. I told you about our trip to Italy. Torvald would have died if he hadn't gone.

Mrs. Linde. I understand that. And so your father gave you the money you needed.

Nora (*smiles*). Yes, that's what Torvald and all the others think. But —

Mrs. Linde. But what?

Nora. Daddy didn't give us a penny. *I* raised that money.

Mrs. Linde. *You* did? That whole big amount?

Nora. Twelve hundred specie dollars. Four thousand eight hundred crowns. *Now* what do you say?

Mrs. Linde. But Nora, how could you? Did you win in the state lottery?

Nora (*contemptuously*). State lottery! (*Snorts.*) What is so great about that?

Mrs. Linde. Where did it come from then?

Nora (*humming and smiling, enjoying her secret*). Hmmm. Tra-la-la-la-la!

Mrs. Linde. You certainly couldn't have borrowed it.

Nora. Oh? And why not?

Mrs. Linde. A wife can't borrow money without her husband's consent.

Nora (*with a toss of her head*). Oh, I don't know — take a wife with a little bit of a head for business — a wife who knows how to manage things —

Mrs. Linde. But Nora, I don't understand at all —

Nora. You don't have to. I didn't say I borrowed the money, did I? I could have gotten it some other way. (*Leans back.*) An admirer may have given it to me. When you're as tolerably goodlooking as I am —

Mrs. Linde. Oh, you're crazy.

Nora. I think you're dying from curiosity, Kristine.

Mrs. Linde. I'm beginning to think you've done something very foolish, Nora.

Nora (*sits up*). Is it foolish to save your husband's life?

Mrs. Linde. I say it's foolish to act behind his back.

Nora. But don't you see: he couldn't be told! You're missing the whole point, Kristine. We couldn't even let him know how seriously ill he was. The doctors came to *me* and told me his life was in danger, that nothing could save him but a stay in the south. Don't you think I tried to work on him? I told him how lovely it would be if I could go abroad like other young wives. I cried and begged. I said he'd better remember what condition I was in, that he had to be nice to me and do what I wanted. I even hinted he could borrow the money. But that almost made him angry with me. He told me I was being irresponsible and that it was his duty as my husband not to give in to my moods and whims — I think that's what he called it. All right, I said to myself, you've got to be saved somehow, and so I found a way —

Mrs. Linde. And your husband never learned from your father that the money didn't come from him?

Nora. Never. Daddy died that same week. I thought of telling him all about it and ask him not to say anything. But since he was so sick — It turned out I didn't have to —

Mrs. Linde. And you've never told your husband?

Nora. Of course not! Good heavens, how could I? He, with his strict principles! Besides, you know how men are. Torvald would find it embarrassing and humiliating to learn that he owed me anything. It would upset our whole relationship. Our happy, beautiful home would no longer be what it is.

Mrs. Linde. Aren't you ever going to tell him?

Nora (*reflectively, half smiling*). Yes — one day, maybe. Many, many years from now, when I'm no longer young and pretty. Don't laugh! I mean when Torvald no longer feels about me the way he does now, when he no longer thinks it's fun when I dance for him and put on costumes and recite for him. Then it will be good to have something in reserve — (*Interrupts herself*) Oh, I'm just being silly! That day will never come. — Well, now, Kristine, what do you think of my great secret? Don't you think I'm good for something too? — By the way, you wouldn't believe all the worry I've had because of it. It's been very hard to meet my obligations on schedule. You see, in business there's something called quarterly interest and something called installments on the principal, and those are terribly hard to come up with. I've had to save a little here and a little there, whenever I could. I couldn't use much of the housekeeping money, for Torvald has to eat well. And I couldn't use what I got for clothes for the children. They have to look nice, and I didn't think it would be right to spend less than I got — the sweet little things!

Mrs. Linde. Poor Nora! So you had to take it from your own allowance?

Nora. Yes, of course. After all, it was my affair. Every time Torvald gave me money for a new dress and things like that, I never used more than half of it. I always bought the cheapest, simplest things for myself. Thank God, everything looks good on me, so Torvald never noticed. But it was hard many times, Kristine, for it's fun to have pretty clothes. Don't you think?

Mrs. Linde. Certainly.

Nora. Anyway, I had other ways of making money too. Last winter I was lucky enough to get some copying work. So I locked the door and sat up writing every night till quite late. God! I often got so tired — ! But it was great fun, too, working and making money. It was almost like being a man.

Mrs. Linde. But how much have you been able to pay off this way?

Nora. I couldn't tell you exactly. You see, it's very difficult to keep track of business like that. All I know is I have been paying off as much as I've been able to scrape together. Many times I just didn't know what to do. (*Smiles.*) Then I used to imagine a rich old gentleman had fallen in love with me —

Mrs. Linde. What! What old gentleman?

Nora. Phooey! And now he was dead and they were reading his will, and there it said in big letters, "All my money is to be paid in cash immediately to the charming Mrs. Nora Helmer."

Mrs. Linde. But dearest Nora — who was this old gentleman?

Nora. For heaven's sake, Kristine, don't you see! There was no old gentleman. He was just somebody I made up when I couldn't think of any way to raise the money. But never mind him. The old bore can be anyone he likes to for all I care. I have no use for him or his last will, for now I don't have a single worry in the world. (*Jumps up.*) Dear God, what a lovely thought that is! To be able to play and have fun with the children, to have everything nice and pretty in the house, just the way Torvald likes it! Not a care! And soon spring will be here, and the air will be blue and high. Maybe we can travel again. Maybe I'll see the ocean again! Oh, yes, yes! — it's wonderful to be alive and happy!

The doorbell rings.

Mrs. Linde (getting up). There's the doorbell. Maybe I better be
   going.

Nora. No, please stay. I'm sure it's just someone for Torvald —

The Maid (in the hall door). Excuse me, ma'am. There's a gentleman
   here who'd like to see Mr. Helmer.

Nora. You mean the bank manager.

The Maid. Sorry, ma'am; the bank manager. But I didn't know
   — since the Doctor is with him —

Nora. Who is the gentleman?

Krogstad (appearing in the door). It's just me, Mrs. Helmer.

   Mrs. Linde starts, looks, turns away toward the window.

Nora (takes a step toward him, tense, in a low voice). You? What do
   you want? What do you want with my husband?

Krogstad. Bank business — in a way. I have a small job in the
   Mutual, and I understand your husband is going to be our
   new manager —

Nora. So it's just —

Krogstad. Just routine business, ma'am. Nothing else.

Nora. All right. In that case, why don't you go through the door
   to the office.

   *Dismisses him casually as she closes the door. Walks over to the
   stove and tends the fire.*

Mrs. Linde. Nora — who was that man?

Nora. His name's Krogstad. He's a lawyer.

Mrs. Linde. So it *was* him.

Nora. Do you know him?

Mrs. Linde. I used to — many years ago. For a while he clerked
   in our part of the country.

Nora. Right. He did.

Mrs. Linde. He has changed a great deal.

Nora. I believe he had a very unhappy marriage.

Mrs. Linde. And now he's a widower, isn't he?

Nora. With many children. There now; it's burning nicely again.
   (*Closes the stove and moves the rocking chair a little to the side.*)

Mrs. Linde. They say he's into all sorts of business.

Nora. Really? Maybe so. I wouldn't know. But let's not think
   about business. It's such a bore.

Dr. Rank (appears in the door to Helmer's study). No, I don't want
   to be in the way. I'd rather talk to your wife a bit. (*Closes
   the door and notices Mrs. Linde.*) Oh, I beg your pardon. I
   believe I'm in the way here too.

Nora. No, not at all. (*Introduces them.*) Dr. Rank. Mrs. Linde.

Rank. Aha. A name often heard in this house. I believe I passed you on the stairs coming up.

Mrs. Linde. Yes. I'm afraid I climb stairs very slowly. They aren't good for me.

Rank. I see. A slight case of inner decay, perhaps?

Mrs. Linde. Overwork, rather.

Rank. Oh, is that all? And now you've come to town to relax at all the parties?

Mrs. Linde. I have come to look for a job.

Rank. A proven cure for overwork, I take it?

Mrs. Linde. One has to live, Doctor.

Rank. Yes, that seems to be the common opinion.

Nora. Come on, Dr. Rank — you want to live just as much as the rest of us.

Rank. Of course I do. Miserable as I am, I prefer to go on being tortured as long as possible. All my patients feel the same way. And that's true of the moral invalids too. Helmer is talking with a specimen right this minute.

Mrs. Linde (in a low voice). Ah!

Nora. What do you mean?

Rank. Oh, this lawyer, Krogstad. You don't know him. The roots of his character are decayed. But even he began by saying something about having *to live* — as if it were a matter of the highest importance.

Nora. Oh? What did he want with Torvald?

Rank. I don't really know. All I heard was something about the bank.

Nora. I didn't know that Krog — that this Krogstad had anything to do with the Mutual Bank.

Rank. Yes, he seems to have some kind of job there. (*To Mrs. Linde.*) I don't know if you are familiar in your part of the country with the kind of person who is always running around trying to sniff out cases of moral decrepitude and as soon as he finds one puts the individual under observation in some excellent position or other. All the healthy ones are left out in the cold.

Mrs. Linde. I should think it's the sick who need looking after the most.

Rank (shrugs his shoulders). There we are. That's the attitude that turns society into a hospital.

Nora, absorbed in her own thoughts, suddenly starts giggling and clapping her hands.

Rank. What's so funny about that? Do you even know what society is?

Nora. What do I care about your stupid society! I laughed at something entirely different — something terribly amusing. Tell me, Dr. Rank — all the employees in the Mutual Bank, from now on they'll all be dependent on Torvald, right?

Rank. Is that what you find so enormously amusing?

Nora (smiles and hums). That's my business, that's my business! (*Walks around.*) Yes, I do think it's fun that we — that Torvald is going to have so much influence on so many people's lives. (*Brings out the bag of macaroons.*) Have a macaroon, Dr. Rank.

Rank. Well, well — macaroons. I thought they were banned around here.

Nora. Yes, but these were some that Kristine gave me.

Mrs. Linde. What! I?

Nora. That's all right. Don't look so scared. You couldn't know that Torvald won't let me have them. He's afraid they'll ruin my teeth. But who cares! Just once in a while — ! Right, Dr. Rank? Have one! (*Puts a macaroon into his mouth.*) You too, Kristine. And one for me. A very small one. Or at most two. (*Walks around again.*) Yes, I really feel very, very happy. Now there's just one thing I'm dying to do.

Rank. Oh? And what's that?

Nora. Something I'm dying to say so Torvald could hear.

Rank. And why can't you?

Nora. I don't dare to, for it's not nice.

Mrs. Linde. Not nice?

Rank. In that case, I guess you'd better not. But surely to the two of us — ? What is it you'd like to say for Helmer to hear?

Nora. I want to say, "Goddammit!"

Rank. Are you out of your mind!

Mrs. Linde. For heaven's sake, Nora!

Rank. Say it. Here he comes.

Nora (hiding the macaroons). Shhh!

Helmer enters from his study, carrying his hat and overcoat.

Nora (going to him). Well, dear, did you get rid of him?

Helmer. Yes, he just left.

Nora. Torvald, I want you to meet Kristine. She's just come to town.

Helmer. Kristine — ? I'm sorry; I don't think —

Nora. Mrs. Linde, Torvald dear. Mrs. Kristine Linde.

Helmer. Ah, yes. A childhood friend of my wife's, I suppose.

Mrs. Linde. Yes, we've known each other for a long time.

Nora. Just think; she has come all this way just to see you.

Helmer. I'm not sure I understand —

Mrs. Linde. Well, not really —

Nora. You see, Kristine is an absolutely fantastic secretary, and she would so much like to work for a competent executive and learn more than she knows already —

Helmer. Very sensible, I'm sure, Mrs. Linde.

Nora. So when she heard about your appointment — they got a wire about it — she came here as fast as she could. How about it, Torvald? Couldn't you do something for Kristine? For my sake. Please?

Helmer. Quite possibly. I take it you're a widow, Mrs. Linde?

Mrs. Linde. Yes.

Helmer. And you've had office experience?

Mrs. Linde. Some — yes.

Helmer. In that case I think it's quite likely that I'll be able to find you a position.

Nora (claps her hands). I knew it! I knew it!

Helmer. You've arrived at a most opportune time, Mrs. Linde.

Mrs. Linde. Oh, how can I ever thank you —

Helmer. Not at all, not at all. (*Puts his coat on.*) But today you'll have to excuse me —

Rank. Wait a minute; I'll come with you. (*Gets his fur coat from the front hall, warms it by the stove.*)

Nora. Don't be long, Torvald.

Helmer. An hour or so; no more.

Nora. Are you leaving, too, Kristine?

Mrs. Linde (putting on her things). Yes, I'd better go and find a place to stay.

Helmer. Good. Then we'll be going the same way.

Nora (helping her). I'm sorry this place is so small, but I don't think we very well could —

Mrs. Linde. Of course! Don't be silly, Nora. Goodbye, and thank you for everything.

Nora. Goodbye. We'll see you soon. You'll be back this evening, of course. And you too, Dr. Rank; right? If you feel well enough? Of course you will. Just wrap yourself up.

General small talk as all exit into the hall. Children's voices are heard on the stairs.

Nora. There they are! There they are! (*She runs and opens the door. The nurse Anne-Marie enters with the children.*)

Nora. Come in! Come in! (*Bends over and kisses them.*) Oh, you sweet, sweet darlings! Look at them, Kristine! Aren't they beautiful?

Rank. No standing around in the draft!

Helmer. Come along, Mrs. Linde. This place isn't fit for anyone but mothers right now.

> *Dr. Rank, Helmer, and Mrs. Linde go down the stairs. The Nurse enters the living room with the children. Nora follows, closing the door behind her.*

Nora. My, how nice you all look! Such red cheeks! Like apples and roses. (*The children all talk at the same time.*) You've had so much fun? I bet you have. Oh, isn't that nice! You pulled both Emmy and Bob on your sleigh? Both at the same time? That's very good, Ivar. Oh, let me hold her for a minute, Anne-Marie. My sweet little doll baby! (*Takes the smallest of the children from the Nurse and dances with her.*) Yes, yes, of course; Mama'll dance with you too, Bob. What? You threw snowballs? Oh, I wish I'd been there! No, no; I want to take their clothes off, Anne-Marie. Please let me; I think it's so much fun. You go on in. You look frozen. There's hot coffee on the stove.

> *The Nurse exits into the room to the left. Nora takes the children's wraps off and throws them all around. They all keep telling her things at the same time.*

Nora. Oh, really? A big dog ran after you? But it didn't bite you. Of course not. Dogs don't bite sweet little doll babies. Don't peek at the packages, Ivar! What's in them? Wouldn't you like to know! No, no; that's something terrible! Play? You want to play? What do you want to play? Okay, let's play hide-and-seek. Bob hides first. You want *me* to? All right. I'll go first.

> *Laughing and shouting, Nora and the children play in the living room and in the adjacent room, right. Finally, Nora hides herself under the table; the children rush in, look for her, can't find her. They hear her low giggle, run to the table, lift the rug that covers it, see her. General hilarity. She crawls out, pretends to scare them. New delight. In the meantime there has been a knock on the door between the living room and the front hall, but nobody has noticed. Now the door is opened halfway; Krogstad appears. He waits a little. The playing goes on.*

Krogstad. Pardon me, Mrs. Helmer —

Nora (*with a muted cry turns around, jumps up*). Ah! What do you want?

Krogstad. I'm sorry. The front door was open. Somebody must have forgotten to close it —

Nora (*standing up*). My husband isn't here, Mr. Krogstad.

Krogstad. I know.

Nora. So what do you want?

Krogstad. I'd like a word with you.

Nora. With — ? (*To the children in a low voice.*) Go in to Anne-Marie. What? No, the strange man won't do anything bad to Mama. When he's gone we'll play some more.

She takes the children into the room to the left and closes the door.

Nora (*tense, troubled*). You want to speak with me?

Krogstad. Yes I do.

Nora. Today — ? It isn't the first of the month yet.

Krogstad. No, it's Christmas Eve. It's up to you what kind of holiday you'll have.

Nora. What do you want? I can't possibly —

Krogstad. Let's not talk about that just yet. There's something else. You do have a few minutes, don't you?

Nora. Yes. Yes, of course. That is —

Krogstad. Good. I was sitting in Olsen's restaurant when I saw your husband go by.

Nora. Yes — ?

Krogstad. — with a lady.

Nora. What of it?

Krogstad. May I be so free as to ask: wasn't that lady Mrs. Linde?

Nora. Yes.

Krogstad. Just arrived in town?

Nora. Yes, today.

Krogstad. She's a good friend of yours, I understand?

Nora. Yes, she is. But I fail to see —

Krogstad. I used to know her myself.

Nora. I know that.

Krogstad. So you know about that. I thought as much. In that case, let me ask you a simple question. Is Mrs. Linde going to be employed in the bank?

Nora. What makes you think you have the right to cross-examine me like this, Mr. Krogstad — you, one of my husband's employees? But since you ask, I'll tell you. Yes, Mrs. Linde is going to be working in the bank. And it was I who recommended her, Mr. Krogstad. Now you know.

Krogstad. So I was right.

Nora (*walks up and down*). After all, one does have a little influence, you know. Just because you're a woman, it doesn't mean that — Really, Mr. Krogstad, people in a subordinate position should be careful not to offend someone who — oh well —

Krogstad. — has influence?

Nora. Exactly.

Krogstad (changing his tone). Mrs. Helmer, I must ask you to be good enough to use your influence on my behalf.

Nora. What do you mean?

Krogstad. I want you to make sure that I am going to keep my subordinate position in the bank.

Nora. I don't understand. Who is going to take your position away from you?

Krogstad. There's no point in playing ignorant with me, Mrs. Helmer. I can very well appreciate that your friend would find it unpleasant to run into me. So now I know who I can thank for my dismissal.

Nora. But I assure you —

Krogstad. Never mind. Just want to say you still have time. I advise you to use your influence to prevent it.

Nora. But Mr. Krogstad, I don't have any influence — none at all.

Krogstad. No? I thought you just said —

Nora. Of course I didn't mean it that way. I! Whatever makes you think that I have any influence of that kind on my husband?

Krogstad. I went to law school with your husband. I have no reason to think that the bank manager is less susceptible than other husbands.

Nora. If you're going to insult my husband, I'll ask you to leave.

Krogstad. You're brave, Mrs. Helmer.

Nora. I'm not afraid of you any more. After New Year's I'll be out of this thing with you.

Krogstad (more controlled). Listen, Mrs. Helmer. If necessary, I'll fight as for my life to keep my little job in the bank.

Nora. So it seems.

Krogstad. It isn't just the money; that's really the smallest part of it. There is something else — Well, I guess I might as well tell you. It's like this. I'm sure you know, like everybody else, that some years ago I committed — an impropriety.

Nora. I believe I've heard it mentioned.

Krogstad. The case never came to court, but from that moment all doors were closed to me. So I took up the kind of business you know about. I had to do something, and I think I can say about myself that I have not been among the worst. But now I want to get out of all that. My sons are growing up. For their sake I must get back as much of my good name as I can. This job in the bank was like the first rung on the ladder. And now your husband wants to kick me down and leave me back in the mud again.

Nora. But I swear to you, Mr. Krogstad; it's not at all in my power to help you.

Krogstad. That's because you don't want to. But I have the means to force you.

Nora. You don't mean you're going to tell my husband I owe you money?

Krogstad. And if I did?

Nora. That would be a mean thing to do. (*Almost crying.*) That secret, which is my joy and my pride — for him to learn about it in such a coarse and ugly manner — to learn it from you — ! It would be terribly unpleasant for me.

Krogstad. Just unpleasant?

Nora (*heatedly*). But go ahead! Do it! It will be worse for you than for me. When my husband realizes what a bad person you are, you'll be sure to lose your job.

Krogstad. I asked you if it was just domestic unpleasantness you were afraid of?

Nora. When my husband finds out, of course he'll pay off the loan, and then we won't have anything more to do with you.

Krogstad (*stepping closer*). Listen, Mrs. Helmer — either you have a very bad memory, or you don't know much about business. I think I had better straighten you out on a few things.

Nora. What do you mean?

Krogstad. When your husband was ill, you came to me to borrow twelve hundred dollars.

Nora. I knew nobody else.

Krogstad. I promised to get you the money —

Nora. And you did.

Krogstad. I promised to get you the money on certain conditions. At the time you were so anxious about your husband's health and so set on getting him away that I doubt very much that you paid much attention to the details of our transaction. That's why I remind you of them now. Anyway, I promised to get you the money if you would sign an I.O.U., which I drafted.

Nora. And which I signed.

Krogstad. Good. But below your signature I added a few lines, making your father security for the loan. Your father was supposed to put his signature to those lines.

Nora. Supposed to — ? He did.

Krogstad. I had left the date blank. That is, your father was to date his own signature. You recall that, don't you, Mrs. Helmer?

Nora. I guess so —

Krogstad. I gave the note to you. You were to mail it to your
father. Am I correct?

Nora. Yes.

Krogstad. And of course you did so right away, for no more than
five or six days later you brought the paper back to me,
signed by your father. Then I paid you the money.

Nora. Well? And haven't I been keeping up with the payments?

Krogstad. Fairly well, yes. But to get back to what we were talking
about — those were difficult days for you, weren't they,
Mrs. Helmer?

Nora. Yes, they were.

Krogstad. Your father was quite ill, I believe.

Nora. He was dying.

Krogstad. And died shortly afterwards?

Nora. That's right.

Krogstad. Tell me, Mrs. Helmer; do you happen to remember the
date of your father's death? I mean the exact day of the
month?

Nora. Daddy died on September 29.

Krogstad. Quite correct. I have ascertained that fact. That's why
there is something peculiar about this (*takes out a piece of
paper*), which I can't account for.

Nora. Peculiar? How? I don't understand —

Krogstad. It seems very peculiar, Mrs. Helmer, that your father
signed this promissory note three days after his death.

Nora. How so? I don't see what —

Krogstad. Your father died on September 29. Now look. He has
dated his signature October 2. Isn't that odd?

Nora remains silent.

Krogstad. Can you explain it?

Nora is still silent.

Krogstad. I also find it striking that the date and the month and
the year are not in your father's handwriting but in a hand
I think I recognize. Well, that might be explained. Your
father may have forgotten to date his signature and somebody
else may have done it here, guessing at the date before he
had learned of your father's death. That's all right. It's only
the signature itself that matters. And that is genuine, isn't
it, Mrs. Helmer? Your father did put his name to this note?

Nora (*after a brief silence tosses her head back and looks defiantly at
him*). No, he didn't. *I* wrote Daddy's name.

Krogstad. Mrs. Helmer — do you realize what a dangerous admission
you just made?

Nora. Why? You'll get your money soon.

Krogstad. Let me ask you something. Why didn't you mail this note to your father?

Nora. Because it was impossible. Daddy was sick — you know that. If I had asked him to sign it, I would have had to tell him what the money was for. But I couldn't tell him, as sick as he was, that my husband's life was in danger. That was impossible. Surely you can see that.

Krogstad. Then it would have been better for you if you had given up your trip abroad.

Nora. No, that was impossible! That trip was to save my husband's life. I couldn't give it up.

Krogstad. But didn't you realize that what you did amounted to fraud against me?

Nora. I couldn't let that make any difference. I didn't care about you at all. I hated the way you made all those difficulties for me, even though you knew the danger my husband was in. I thought you were cold and unfeeling.

Krogstad. Mrs. Helmer, obviously you have no clear idea of what you have done. Let me tell you that what I did that time was no more and no worse. And it ruined my name and reputation.

Nora. You! Are you trying to tell me that you did something brave once in order to save your wife's life?

Krogstad. The law doesn't ask about motives.

Nora. Then it's a bad law.

Krogstad. Bad or not — if I produce this note in court you'll be judged according to the law.

Nora. I refuse to believe you. A daughter shouldn't have the right to spare her dying old father worry and anxiety? A wife shouldn't have the right to save her husband's life? I don't know the laws very well, but I'm sure that somewhere they make allowance for cases like that. And you, a lawyer, don't know that? I think you must be a bad lawyer, Mr. Krogstad.

Krogstad. That may be. But business — the kind of business you and I have with one another — don't you think I know something about that? Very well. Do what you like. But let me tell you this: if I'm going to be kicked out again, you'll keep me company. (*He bows and exits through the front hall.*)

Nora (*pauses thoughtfully; then, with a defiant toss of her head*). Oh, nonsense! Trying to scare me like that! I'm not all that silly. (*Starts picking up the children's clothes; soon stops.*) But — ? No! That's impossible! I did it for love!

The Children (*in the door to the left*). Mama, the strange man just left. We saw him.

Nora. Yes, yes; I know. But don't tell anybody about the strange man. Do you hear? Not even Daddy.

The Children. We won't. But now you'll play with us again, won't you, Mama?

Nora. No, not right now.

The Children. But Mama — you promised.

Nora. I know, but I can't just now. Go to your own room. I've so much to do. Be nice now, my little darlings. Do as I say. (*She nudges them gently into the other room and closes the door. She sits down on the couch, picks up a piece of embroidery, makes a few stitches, then stops.*) No! (*Throws the embroidery down, goes to the hall door and calls out.*) Helene! Bring the Christmas tree in here, please! (*Goes to the table, left, opens the drawer, halts.*) No — that's impossible!

The Maid (*with the Christmas tree*). Where do you want it, ma'am?

Nora. There. The middle of the floor.

The Maid. You want anything else?

Nora. No, thanks. I have everything I need. (*The Maid goes out. Nora starts trimming the tree.*) I want candles — and flowers — That awful man! Oh, nonsense! There's nothing wrong. This will be a lovely tree. I'll do everything you want me to, Torvald. I'll sing for you — dance for you —

Helmer, a bundle of papers under his arm, enters from outside.

Nora. Ah — you're back already?

Helmer. Yes. Has anybody been here?

Nora. Here? No.

Helmer. That's funny. I saw Krogstad leaving just now.

Nora. Oh? Oh yes, that's right. Krogstad was here for just a moment.

Helmer. I can tell from your face that he came to ask you to put in a word for him.

Nora. Yes.

Helmer. And it was supposed to be your own idea, wasn't it? You were not to tell me he'd been here. He asked you that too, didn't he?

Nora. Yes, Torvald, but —

Helmer. Nora, Nora, how could you! Talk to a man like that and make him promises! And lying to me about it afterwards — !

Nora. Lying — ?

Helmer. Didn't you say nobody had been here? (*Shakes his finger at her.*) My little songbird must never do that again. Songbirds are supposed to have clean beaks to chirp with — no false notes. (*Puts his arm around her waist.*) Isn't that so? Of course it is. (*Lets her go.*) And that's enough about that. (*Sits down in front of the fireplace.*) Ah, it's nice and warm in here. (*Begins to leaf through his papers.*)

Nora (*busy with the tree; after a brief pause*). Torvald.

Helmer. Yes.

Nora. I'm looking forward so much to the Stenborgs' costume party day after tomorrow.

Helmer. And I can't wait to find out what you're going to surprise me with.

Nora. Oh, that silly idea!

Helmer. Oh?

Nora. I can't think of anything. It all seems so foolish and pointless.

Helmer. Ah, my little Nora admits that?

Nora (*behind his chair, her arms on the back of the chair*). Are you very busy, Torvald?

Helmer. Well —

Nora. What are all those papers?

Helmer. Bank business.

Nora. Already?

Helmer. I've asked the board to give me the authority to make certain changes in organization and personnel. That's what I'll be doing over the holidays. I want it all settled before New Year's.

Nora. So that's why this poor Krogstad —

Helmer. Hm.

Nora (*leisurely playing with the hair on his neck*). If you weren't so busy, Torvald, I'd ask you for a great big favor.

Helmer. Let's hear it, anyway.

Nora. I don't know anyone with better taste than you, and I want so much to look nice at the party. Couldn't you sort of take charge of me, Torvald, and decide what I'll wear — Help me with my costume?

Helmer. Aha! Little Lady Obstinate is looking for someone to rescue her?

Nora. Yes, Torvald. I won't get anywhere without your help.

Helmer. All right. I'll think about it. We'll come up with something.

Nora. Oh, you *are* nice! (*Goes back to the Christmas tree. A pause.*) Those red flowers look so pretty. — Tell me, was it really all that bad what this Krogstad fellow did?

Helmer. He forged signatures. Do you have any idea what that means?

Nora. Couldn't it have been because he felt he had to?

Helmer. Yes, or like so many others he may simply have been thoughtless. I'm not so heartless as to condemn a man absolutely because of a single imprudent act.

Nora. Of course not, Torvald!

Helmer. People like him can redeem themselves morally by openly confessing their crime and taking their punishment.

Nora. Punishment?

Helmer. But that was not the way Krogstad chose. He got out of it with tricks and evasions. That's what has corrupted him.

Nora. So you think that if — ?

Helmer. Can't you imagine how a guilty person like that has to lie and fake and dissemble wherever he goes — putting on a mask before everybody he's close to, even his own wife and children. It's this thing with the children that's the worst part of it, Nora.

Nora. Why is that?

Helmer. Because when a man lives inside such a circle of stinking lies he brings infection into his own home and contaminates his whole family. With every breath of air his children inhale the germs of something ugly.

Nora (moving closer behind him). Are you so sure of that?

Helmer. Of course I am. I have seen enough examples of that in my work. Nearly all young criminals have had mothers who lied.

Nora. Why mothers — particularly?

Helmer. Most often mothers. But of course fathers tend to have the same influence. Every lawyer knows that. And yet, for years this Krogstad has been poisoning his own children in an atmosphere of lies and deceit. That's why I call him a lost soul morally. *(Reaches out for her hands.)* And that's why my sweet little Nora must promise me never to take his side again. Let's shake on that. — What? What's this? Give me your hand. There! Now that's settled. I assure you, I would find it impossible to work in the same room with that man. I feel literally sick when I'm around people like that.

Nora (withdraws her hand and goes to the other side of the Christmas tree). It's so hot in here. And I have so much to do.

Helmer (gets up and collects his papers). Yes, and I really should try to get some of this reading done before dinner. I must think about your costume too. And maybe just possibly I'll have something to wrap in gilt paper and hang on the Christmas tree. *(Puts his hand on her head.)* Oh my adorable little songbird! *(Enters his study and closes the door.)*

Nora (after a pause, in a low voice). It's all a lot of nonsense. It's not that way at all. It's impossible. It has to be impossible.

The Nurse (in the door, left). The little ones are asking ever so nicely if they can't come in and be with their mamma.

Nora. No, no, no! Don't let them in here! You stay with them, Anne-Marie.

The Nurse. If you say so, ma'am. (*Closes the door.*)

Nora (pale with terror). Corrupt my little children — ! Poison my home — ? (*Brief pause; she lifts her head.*) That's not true. Never. Never in a million years.

ACT II

The same room. The Christmas tree is in the corner by the piano, stripped shabby-looking, with burnt-down candles. Nora's outside clothes are on the couch. Nora is alone. She walks around restlessly. She stops by the couch and picks up her coat.

Nora (drops the coat again). There's somebody now! (*Goes to the door, listens.*) No. Nobody. Of course not — not on Christmas. And not tomorrow either° — But perhaps — (*Opens the door and looks.*) No, nothing in the mailbox. All empty. (*Comes forward.*) How silly I am! Of course he isn't serious. Nothing like that could happen. After all, I have three small children.

The Nurse enters from the room, left, carrying a big carton.

The Nurse. Well, at last I found it — the box with your costume.

Nora. Thanks. Just put it on the table.

Nurse (does so). But it's all a big mess, I'm afraid.

Nora. Oh, I wish I could tear the whole thing to little pieces!

Nurse. Heavens! It's not as bad as all that. It can be fixed all right. All it takes is a little patience.

Nora. I'll go over and get Mrs. Linde to help me.

Nurse. Going out again? In this awful weather? You'll catch a cold.

Nora. That might not be such a bad thing. How are the children?

Nurse. The poor little dears are playing with their presents, but —

Nora. Do they keep asking for me?

Nurse. Well, you know, they're used to being with their mamma.

Nora. I know. But Anne-Marie, from now on I can't be with them as much as before.

Nurse. Oh well. Little children get used to everything.

Nora. You think so? Do you think they'll forget their mamma if I were gone altogether?

Nurse. Goodness me — gone altogether?

And not tomorrow either In Norway both December 25 and 26 are legal holidays

Nora. Listen, Anne-Marie — something I've wondered about. How could you bring yourself to leave your child with strangers?

Nurse. But I had to, if I were to nurse you.

Nora. Yes, but how could you *want* to?

Nurse. When I could get such a nice place? When something like that happens to a poor young girl, she'd better be grateful for whatever she gets. For *he* didn't do a thing for me — the louse!

Nora. But your daughter has forgotten all about you, hasn't she?

Nurse. Oh no! Not at all! She wrote to me both when she was confirmed and when she got married.

Nora (*putting her arms around her neck*). You dear old thing — you were a good mother to me when I was little.

Nurse. Poor little Nora had no one else, you know.

Nora. And if my little ones didn't, I know you'd — oh, I'm being silly! (*Opens the carton.*) Go in to them, please. I really should — Tomorrow you'll see how pretty I'll be.

Nurse. I know. There won't be anybody at that party half as pretty as you, ma'am. (*Goes out, left.*)

Nora (*begins to take clothes out of the carton; in a moment she throws it all down*). If only I dared to go out. If only I knew nobody would come. That nothing would happen while I was gone. — How silly! Nobody'll come. Just / don't think about it. Brush the muff. Beautiful gloves. Beautiful gloves. Forget it. Forget it. One, two, three, four, five, six — (*Cries out.*) There they are! (*Moves toward the door, stops irresolutely.*)

Mrs. Linde enters from the hall. She has already taken off her coat.

Nora. Oh, it's you, Kristine. There's no one else out there, is there? I'm so glad you're here.

Mrs. Linde. They told me you'd asked for me.

Nora. I just happened to walk by. I need your help with something — badly. Let's sit here on the couch. Look. Torvald and I are going to a costume party tomorrow night — at Consul Stenborg's upstairs — and Torvald wants me to go as a Neapolitan fisher girl and dance the tarantella. I learned it when we were on Capri.

Mrs. Linde. Well, well! So you'll be putting on a whole show?

Nora. Yes. Torvald thinks I should. Look, here's the costume. Torvald had it made for me while we were there. But it's all so torn and everything. I just don't know —

Mrs. Linde. Oh, that can be fixed. It's not that much. The trimmings have come loose in a few places. Do you have needle and thread? Ah, here we are. All set.

Nora. I really appreciate it, Kristine.

Mrs. Linde (sewing). So you'll be in disguise tomorrow night, eh? You know — I may come by for just a moment, just to look at you. — Oh dear. I haven't even thanked you for the nice evening last night.

Nora (gets up, moves around). Oh, I don't know. I don't think last night was as nice as it usually is. — You should have come to town a little earlier, Kristine. — Yes, Torvald knows how to make it nice and pretty around here.

Mrs. Linde. You too, I should think. After all, you're your father's daughter. By the way, is Dr. Rank always as depressed as he was last night?

Nora. No, last night was unusual. He's a very sick man, you know — very sick. Poor Rank, his spine is rotting away. Tuberculosis, I think. You see, his father was a nasty old man with mistresses and all that sort of thing. Rank has been sickly ever since he was a little boy.

Mrs. Linde (dropping her sewing to her lap). But dearest Nora, where have you learned about things like that?

Nora (still walking about). Oh, you know — with three children you sometimes get to talk with — other wives. Some of them know quite a bit about medicine. So you pick up a few things.

Mrs. Linde (resumes her sewing; after a brief pause). Does Dr. Rank come here every day?

Nora. Every single day. He's Torvald's oldest and best friend, after all. And my friend too, for that matter. He's part of the family, almost.

Mrs. Linde. But tell me, is he quite sincere? I mean, isn't he the kind of man who likes to say nice things to people?

Nora. No, not at all. Rather the opposite, in fact. What makes you say that?

Mrs. Linde. When you introduced us yesterday, he told me he'd often heard my name mentioned in this house. But later on it was quite obvious that your husband really had no idea who I was. So how could Dr. Rank — ?

Nora. You're right, Kristine, but I can explain that. You see, Torvald loves me so very much that he wants me all to himself. That's what he says. When we were first married he got almost jealous when I as much as mentioned anybody from back home that I was fond of. So of course I soon stopped doing that. But with Dr. Rank I often talk about home. You see, he likes to listen to me.

Mrs. Linde. Look here, Nora. In many ways you're still a child. After all, I'm quite a bit older than you and have had more

experience. I want to give you a piece of advice. I think you
should get out of this thing with Dr. Rank.

Nora. Get out of what thing?

Mrs. Linde. Several things in fact, if you want my opinion. Yesterday
you said something about a rich admirer who was going to
give you money —

Nora. One who doesn't exist, unfortunately. What of it?

Mrs. Linde. Does Dr. Rank have money?

Nora. Yes, he does.

Mrs. Linde. And no dependents?

Nora. No. But — ?

Mrs. Linde. And he comes here every day?

Nora. Yes, I told you that already.

Mrs. Linde. But how can that sensitive man be so tactless?

Nora. I haven't the slightest idea what you're talking about.

Mrs. Linde. Don't play games with me, Nora. Don't you think I
know who you borrowed the twelve hundred dollars from?

Nora. Are you out of your mind! The very idea — ! A friend of
both of us who sees us every day — ! What a dreadfully —
uncomfortable position that would be!

Mrs. Linde. So it really isn't Dr. Rank?

Nora. Most certainly not! I would never have dreamed of asking
him — not for a moment. Anyway, he didn't have any
money then. He inherited it afterwards.

Mrs. Linde. Well, I still think it may have been lucky for you,
Nora dear.

Nora. The idea! It would never have occurred to me to ask Dr.
Rank — Though I'm sure that if I *did* ask him —

Mrs. Linde. But of course you wouldn't.

Nora. Of course not. I can't imagine that that would ever be
necessary. But I am quite sure that if I told Dr. Rank —

Mrs. Linde. Behind your husband's back?

Nora. I must get out of — this other thing. That's also behind his
back. I must get out of it.

Mrs. Linde. That's what I told you yesterday. But —

Nora (*walking up and down*). A man manages these things so much
better than a woman —

Mrs. Linde. One's husband, yes.

Nora. Silly, silly! (*Stops.*) When you've paid off all you owe, you
get your I.O.U. back; right?

Mrs. Linde. Yes, of course.

Nora. And you can tear it into a hundred thousand little pieces
and burn it — that dirty, filthy, paper!

Mrs. Linde (*looks hard at her, puts down her sewing, rises slowly*).
Nora — you're hiding something from me.

Nora. Can you tell?

Mrs. Linde. Something's happened to you, Nora, since yesterday morning. What is it?

Nora (going to her). Kristine! (*Listens.*) Shhh. Torvald just came back. Listen. Why don't you go in to the children for a while. Torvald can't stand having sewing around. Get Anne-Marie to help you.

Mrs. Linde (gathers some of the sewing things together). All right, but I'm not leaving here till you and I have talked.

She goes out left, just as Helmer enters from the front hall.

Nora (towards him). I have been waiting and waiting for you, Torvald.

Helmer. Was that the dressmaker?

Nora. No, it was Kristine. She's helping me with my costume. Oh Torvald, just wait till you see how nice I'll look!

Helmer. I told you. Pretty good idea I had, wasn't it?

Nora. Lovely! And wasn't it nice of me to go along with it?

Helmer (his hand under her chin). Nice? To do what your husband tells you? All right, you little rascal; I know you didn't mean it that way. But don't let me interrupt you. I suppose you want to try it on.

Nora. And you'll be working?

Helmer. Yes. (*Shows her a pile of papers.*) Look. I've been down to the bank. (*Is about to enter his study.*)

Nora. Torvald.

Helmer (halts). Yes?

Nora. What if your little squirrel asked you ever so nicely —

Helmer. For what?

Nora. Would you do it?

Helmer. Depends on what it is.

Nora. Squirrel would run around and do all sorts of fun tricks if you'd be nice and agreeable.

Helmer. All right. What is it?

Nora. Lark would chirp and twitter in all the rooms, up and down —

Helmer. So what? Lark does that anyway.

Nora. I'll be your elfmaid and dance for you in the moonlight, Torvald.

Helmer. Nora, don't tell me it's the same thing you mentioned this morning?

Nora (closer to him). Yes, Torvald. I beg you!

Helmer. You really have the nerve to bring that up again?

Nora. Yes. You've just got to do as I say. You *must* let Krogstad keep his job.

Helmer. My dear Nora. It's his job I intend to give to Mrs. Linde.

Nora. I know. And that's ever so nice of you. But can't you just fire somebody else?

Helmer. This is incredible! You just don't give up, do you? Because you make some foolish promise, *I* am supposed to — !

Nora. That's not the reason, Torvald. It's for your own sake. That man writes for the worst newspapers. You've said so yourself. There's no telling what he may do to you. I'm scared to death of him.

Helmer. Ah, I understand. You're afraid because of what happened before.

Nora. What do you mean?

Helmer. You're thinking of your father, of course.

Nora. Yes. Yes, you're right. Remember the awful things they wrote about Daddy in the newspapers. I really think they might have forced him to resign if the ministry hadn't sent you to look into the charges and if you hadn't been so helpful and understanding.

Helmer. My dear little Nora, there is a world of difference between your father and me. Your father's official conduct was not above reproach. Mine is, and I intend for it to remain that way as long as I hold my position.

Nora. Oh, but you don't know what vicious people like that may think of. Oh, Torvald! Now all of us could be so happy together here in our own home, peaceful and carefree. Such a good life, Torvald, for you and me and the children! That's why I implore you —

Helmer. And it's exactly because you plead for him that you make it impossible for me to keep him. It's already common knowledge in the bank that I intend to let Krogstad go. If it gets out that the new manager has changed his mind because of his wife —

Nora. Yes? What then?

Helmer. No, of course, that wouldn't matter at all as long as little Mrs. Pighead here got her way! Do you want me to make myself look ridiculous before my whole staff — make people think I can be swayed by just anybody — by outsiders? Believe me, I would soon enough find out what the consequences would be! Besides, there's another thing that makes it absolutely impossible for Krogstad to stay on in the bank now that I'm in charge.

Nora. What's that?

Helmer. I suppose in a pinch I could overlook his moral shortcomings —

Nora. Yes, you could; couldn't you, Torvald?

Helmer. And I understand he's quite a good worker, too. But we've known each other for a long time. It's one of those imprudent relationships you get into when you're young that embarrass you for the rest of your life. I guess I might as well be frank with you: he and I are on a first name basis. And that tactless fellow never hides the fact even when other people are around. Rather, he seems to think it entitles him to be familiar with me. Every chance he gets he comes out with his damn "Torvald, Torvald." I'm telling you, I find it most awkward. He would make my position in the bank intolerable.

Nora. You don't really mean any of this, Torvald.

Helmer. Oh? I don't? And why not?

Nora. No, for it's all so petty.

Helmer. What! Petty? You think I'm being petty!

Nora. No, I *don't* think you are petty, Torvald dear. That's exactly why I —

Helmer. Never mind. You think my reasons are petty, so it follows that I must be petty too. Petty! Indeed! By God, I'll put an end to this right now! (*Opens the door to the front hall and calls out.*) Helene!

Nora. What are you doing?

Helmer (*searching among his papers*). Making a decision. (*The Maid enters.*) Here. Take this letter. Go out with it right away. Find somebody to deliver it. But quick. The address is on the envelope. Wait. Here's money.

The Maid. Very good, sir. (*She takes the letter and goes out.*)

Helmer (*collecting his papers*). There now, little Mrs. Obstinate!

Nora (*breathless*). Torvald — what was that letter?

Helmer. Krogstad's dismissal.

Nora. Call it back, Torvald! There's still time! Oh Torvald, please — call it back! For my sake, for your own sake, for the sake of the children! Listen to me, Torvald! Do it! You don't know what you're doing to all of us!

Helmer. Too late.

Nora. Yes. Too late.

Helmer. Dear Nora, I forgive you this fear you're in, although it really is an insult to me. Yes, it is! It's an insult to think that I am scared of a shabby scrivener's revenge. But I forgive you, for it's such a beautiful proof how much you love me. (*Takes her in his arms.*) And that's the way it should be, my sweet darling. Whatever happens, you'll see that when things get really rough I have both strength and courage. You'll find out that I am man enough to shoulder the whole burden.

Nora (terrified). What do you mean by that?

Helmer. All of it, I tell you —

Nora (composed). You'll never have to do that.

Helmer. Good. Then we'll share the burden, Nora — like husband
and wife, the way it ought to be. (*Caresses her.*) Now are
you satisfied? There, there, there. Not that look in your eyes
— like a frightened dove. It's all your own foolish imagination.
— Why don't you practice the tarantella — and your tambourine, too. I'll be in the inner office and close both doors,
so I won't hear you. You can make as much noise as you
like. (*Turning in the doorway.*) And when Rank comes, tell
him where to find me. (*He nods to her, enters his study carrying
his papers, and closes the door.*)

Nora (transfixed by terror, whispers). He would do it. He'll
do it. He'll do it in spite of the whole world. — No, this
mustn't happen. Anything rather than that! There must be
a way —! (*The doorbell rings.*) Dr. Rank! Anything rather than
that! Anything — anything at all!

*She passes her hand over her face, pulls herself together, and opens
the door to the hall. Dr. Rank is out there, hanging up his coat.
Darkness begins to fall during the following scene.*

Nora. Hello there, Dr. Rank. I recognized your ringing. Don't go
in to Torvald yet. I think he's busy.

Rank. And you?

Nora (as he enters and she closes the door behind him). You know I
always have time for you.

Rank. Thanks. I'll make use of that as long as I can.

Nora. What do you mean by that — As long as you can?

Rank. Does that frighten you?

Nora. Well, it's a funny expression. As if something was going
to happen.

Rank. Something is going to happen that I've long been expecting.
But I admit I hadn't thought it would come quite so soon.

Nora (seizes his arm). What is it you've found out? Dr. Rank —
tell me!

Rank (sits down by the stove). I'm going downhill fast. There's
nothing to do about that.

Nora (with audible relief). So it's *you* —

Rank. Who else? No point in lying to myself. I'm in worse shape
than any of my other patients, Mrs. Helmer. These last few
days I've been conducting an audit on my inner condition.
Bankrupt. Chances are that within a month I'll be rotting
up in the cemetery.

Nora. Shame on you! Talking that horrid way!

Rank. The thing itself is horrid — damn horrid. The worst of it, though, is all that other horror that comes first. There is only one more test I need to make. After that I'll have a pretty good idea when I'll start coming apart. There is something I want to say to you. Helmer's refined nature can't stand anything hideous. I don't want him in my sick room.

Nora. Oh, but Dr. Rank —

Rank. I don't want him there. Under no circumstance. I'll close my door to him. As soon as I have full certainty that the worst is about to begin I'll give you my card with a black cross on it. Then you'll know the last horror of destruction has started.

Nora. Today you're really quite impossible. And I had hoped you'd be in a particularly good mood.

Rank. With death on my hands? Paying for someone else's sins? Is there justice in that? And yet there isn't a single family that isn't ruled by that same law of ruthless retribution, in one way or another.

Nora (puts her hands over her ears). Poppycock! Be fun! Be fun!

Rank. Well, yes. You may just as well laugh at the whole thing. My poor, innocent spine is suffering for my father's frolics as a young lieutenant.

Nora (over by the table, left). Right. He was addicted to asparagus and goose liver paté, wasn't he?

Rank. And truffles.

Nora. Of course. Truffles. And oysters too, I think.

Rank. And oysters. Obviously.

Nora. And all the port and champagne that go with it. It's really too bad that goodies like that ruin your backbone.

Rank. Particularly an unfortunate backbone that never enjoyed any of it.

Nora. Ah yes, that's the saddest part of it all.

Rank (looks searchingly at her). Hm —

Nora (after a brief pause). Why did you smile just then?

Rank. No, it was you that laughed.

Nora. No, it was you that smiled, Dr. Rank!

Rank (gets up). You're more of a mischief-maker than I thought.

Nora. I feel in the mood for mischief today.

Rank. So it seems.

Nora (with both her hands on his shoulders). Dear, dear Dr. Rank, don't you go and die and leave Torvald and me.

Rank. Oh, you won't miss me for very long. Those who go away are soon forgotten.

Nora (with an anxious look). Do you believe that?

Rank. You'll make new friends, and then —

Nora. Who'll make new friends?

Rank. Both you and Helmer, once I'm gone. You yourself seem to have made a good start already. What was this Mrs. Linde doing here last night?

Nora. Aha — Don't tell me you're jealous of poor Kristine?

Rank. Yes, I am. She'll be my successor in this house. As soon as I have made my excuses, that woman is likely to —

Nora. Shh — not so loud. She's in there.

Rank. Today too? There you are!

Nora. She's mending my costume. My God, you really *are* unreasonable. (*Sits down on the couch.*) Now be nice, Dr. Rank. Tomorrow you'll see how beautifully I'll dance, and then you are to pretend I'm dancing just for you — and for Torvald too, of course. (*Takes several items out of the carton.*) Sit down, Dr. Rank; I want to show you something.

Rank (*sitting down*). What?

Nora. Look.

Rank. Silk stockings.

Nora. Flesh-colored. Aren't they lovely? Now it's getting dark in here, but tomorrow — No, no. You only get to see the foot. Oh well, you might as well see all of it.

Rank. Hmm.

Nora. Why do you look so critical? Don't you think they'll fit?

Rank. That's something I can't possibly have a reasoned opinion about.

Nora (*looks at him for a moment*). Shame on you. (*Slaps his ear lightly with the stocking.*) That's what you get. (*Puts the things back in the carton.*)

Rank. And what other treasures are you going to show me?

Nora. Nothing at all, because you're naughty. (*She hums a little and rummages in the carton.*)

Rank (*after a brief silence*). When I sit here like this, talking confidently with you, I can't imagine — I can't possibly imagine what would have become of me if I hadn't had you and Helmer.

Nora (*smiles*). Well, yes — I do believe you like being with us.

Rank (*in a lower voice, lost in thought*). And then to have to go away from it all —

Nora. Nonsense. You are not going anywhere.

Rank (*as before*). — and not to leave behind as much as a poor little token of gratitude, hardly a brief memory of someone missed, nothing but a vacant place that anyone can fill.

Nora. And what if I were to ask you — ? No —

Rank. Ask me what?

Nora. For a great proof of your friendship —

Rank. Yes, yes — ?

Nora. No, I mean — for an enormous favor —

Rank. Would you really for once make me as happy as all that?

Nora. But you don't even know what it is.

Rank. Well, then; tell me.

Nora. Oh, but I can't, Dr. Rank. It's altogether too much to ask — It's advice and help and a favor —

Rank. So much the better. I can't even begin to guess what it is you have in mind. So for heaven's sake tell me! Don't you trust me?

Nora. Yes, I trust you more than anyone else I know. You are my best and most faithful friend. I know that. So I will tell you. All right, Dr. Rank. There is something you can help me prevent. You know how much Torvald loves me — beyond all words. Never for a moment would he hesitate to give his life for me.

Rank (leaning over to her). Nora — do you really think he's the only one — ?

Nora (with a slight start). Who — ?

Rank. — would gladly give his life for you.

Nora (heavily). I see.

Rank. I have sworn an oath to myself to tell you before I go. I'll never find a better occasion. — All right, Nora; now you know. And now you also know that you can confide in me more than in anyone else.

Nora (gets up; in a calm, steady voice). Let me get by.

Rank (makes room for her but remains seated). Nora —

Nora (in the door to the front hall). Helene, bring the lamp in here, please. *(Walks over to the stove.)* Oh, dear Dr. Rank. That really wasn't very nice of you.

Rank (gets up). That I have loved you as much as anybody — was that not nice?

Nora. No, not that. But that you told me. There was no need for that.

Rank. What do you mean? Have you known — ?

The Maid enters with the lamp, puts it on the table, and goes out.

Rank. Nora — Mrs. Helmer — I'm asking you: did you know?

Nora. Oh, how can I tell what I knew and didn't know! I really can't say — But that you could be so awkward, Dr. Rank! Just when everything was so comfortable.

Rank. Well, anyway, now you know that I'm at your service with my life and soul. And now you must speak.

Nora (looks at him). After what just happened?

Rank. I beg of you — let me know what it is.

Nora. There is nothing I can tell you now.

Rank. Yes, yes. You mustn't punish me this way. Please let me do for you whatever anyone *can* do.

Nora. Now there is nothing you can do. Besides, I don't think I really need any help, anyway. It's probably just my imagination. Of course that's all it is. I'm sure of it! (*Sits down in the rocking chair, looks at him, smiles.*) Well, well, well, Dr. Rank! What a fine gentleman you turned out to be! Aren't you ashamed of yourself, now that we have light?

Rank. No, not really. But perhaps I ought to leave — and not come back?

Nora. Don't be silly; of course not! You'll come here exactly as you have been doing. You know perfectly well that Torvald can't do without you.

Rank. Yes, but what about you?

Nora. Oh, I always think it's perfectly delightful when you come.

Rank. That's the very thing that misled me. You are a riddle to me. It has often seemed to me that you'd just as soon be with me as with Helmer.

Nora. Well, you see, there are people you love, and then there are other people you'd almost rather be with.

Rank. Yes, there is something in that.

Nora. When I lived at home with Daddy, of course I loved him most. But I always thought it was so much fun to sneak off down to the maids' room, for they never gave me good advice and they always talked about such fun things.

Rank. Aha! So it's *their* place I have taken.

Nora (*jumps up and goes over to him*). Oh dear, kind Dr. Rank, you know very well I didn't mean it that way. Can't you see that with Torvald it is the way it used to be with Daddy?

The Maid enters from the front hall.

The Maid. Ma'am! (*Whispers to her and gives her a caller's card.*)

Nora (*glances at the card*). Ah! (*Puts it in her pocket.*)

Rank. Anything wrong?

Nora. No, no; not at all. It's nothing — just my new costume —

Rank. But your costume is lying right there!

Nora. Oh yes, that one. But this is another one. I ordered it. Torvald mustn't know —

Rank. Aha. So that's the great secret.

Nora. That's it. Why don't you go in to him, please. He's in the inner office. And keep him there for a while —

Rank. Don't worry. He won't get away. (*Enters Helmer's study.*)

Nora (*to The Maid*). You say he's waiting in the kitchen?

The Maid. Yes. He came up the back stairs.

Nora. But didn't you tell him there was somebody with me?
The Maid. Yes, but he wouldn't listen.
Nora. He won't leave?
The Maid. No, not till he's had a word with you, ma'am.
Nora. All right. But try not to make any noise. And, Helene —
don't tell anyone he's here. It's supposed to be a surprise for
my husband.
The Maid. I understand, ma'am — (*She leaves.*)
Nora. The terrible is happening. It's happening, after all. No, no,
no. It can't happen. It won't happen. (*She bolts the study door.*)

*The Maid opens the front hall door for Krogstad and closes the
door behind him. He wears a fur coat for traveling, boots, and a
fur hat.*

Nora (*toward him*). Keep your voice down. My husband's home.
Krogstad. That's all right.
Nora. What do you want?
Krogstad. To find out something.
Nora. Be quick, then. What is it?
Krogstad. I expect you know I've been fired.
Nora. I couldn't prevent it, Mr. Krogstad. I fought for you as
long and as hard as I could, but it didn't do any good.
Krogstad. Your husband doesn't love you any more than that? He
knows what I can do to you, and yet he runs the risk —
Nora. Surely you didn't think I'd tell him?
Krogstad. No, I really didn't. It wouldn't be like Torvald Helmer
to show that kind of guts —
Nora. Mr. Krogstad, I insist that you show respect for my husband.
Krogstad. By all means. All due respect. But since you're so anxious
to keep this a secret, may I assume that you are a little better
informed than yesterday about exactly what you have done?
Nora. Better than *you* could ever teach me.
Krogstad. Of course. Such a bad lawyer as I am —
Nora. What do you want of me?
Krogstad. I just wanted to find out how you are, Mrs. Helmer.
I've been thinking about you all day. You see, even a bill
collector, a pen pusher, a — anyway, someone like me —
even he has a little of what they call a heart.
Nora. Then show it. Think of my little children.
Krogstad. Have you and your husband thought of mine? Never
mind. All I want to tell you is that you don't need to take
this business too seriously. I have no intention of bringing
charges right away.
Nora. Oh no, you wouldn't; would you? I knew you wouldn't.
Krogstad. The whole thing can be settled quite amiably. Nobody

else needs to know anything. It will be between the three
of us.

Nora. My husband must never find out about this.

Krogstad. How are you going to prevent that? Maybe you can pay
me the balance on the loan?

Nora. No, not right now.

Krogstad. Or do you have a way of raising the money one of these
next few days?

Nora. None I intend to make use of.

Krogstad. It wouldn't do you any good, anyway. Even if you had
the cash in your hand right this minute, I wouldn't give you
your note back. It wouldn't make any difference *how* much
money you offered me.

Nora. Then you'll have to tell me what you plan to use the note
for.

Krogstad. Just keep it; that's all. Have it on hand, so to speak. I
won't say a word to anybody else. So if you've been thinking
about doing something desperate —

Nora. I have.

Krogstad. — like leaving house and home —

Nora. I have!

Krogstad. — or even something worse —

Nora. How did you know?

Krogstad. — then: don't.

Nora. How did you know I was thinking of *that?*

Krogstad. Most of us do, right at first. I did, too, but when it
came down to it I didn't have the courage —

Nora (tonelessly). Nor do I.

Krogstad (relieved). See what I mean? I thought so. You don't either.

Nora. I don't. I don't.

Krogstad. Besides, it would be very silly of you. Once that first
domestic blow-up is behind you — . Here in my pocket is
a letter for your husband.

Nora. Telling him everything?

Krogstad. As delicately as possible.

Nora (quickly). He mustn't get that letter. Tear it up. I'll get you
the money somehow.

Krogstad. Excuse me, Mrs. Helmer. I thought I just told you —

Nora. I'm not talking about the money I owe you. Just let me
know how much money you want from my husband, and
I'll get it for you.

Krogstad. I want no money from your husband.

Nora. Then, what *do* you want?

Krogstad. I'll tell you, Mrs. Helmer. I want to rehabilitate myself;
I want to get up in the world; and your husband is going

to help me. For a year and a half I haven't done anything disreputable. All that time I have been struggling with the most miserable circumstances. I was content to work my way up step by step. Now I've been kicked out, and I'm no longer satisfied just getting my old job back. I want more than that; I want to get to the top. I'm being quite serious. I want the bank to take me back but in a higher position. I want your husband to create a new job for me —

Nora. He'll never do that!

Krogstad. He will. I know him. He won't dare not to. And once I'm back inside and he and I are working together, you'll see! Within a year I'll be the manager's right hand. It will be Nils Krogstad and not Torvald Helmer who'll be running the Mutual Bank!

Nora. You'll never see that happen!

Krogstad. Are you thinking of — ?

Nora. Now I *do* have the courage.

Krogstad. You can't scare me. A fine, spoiled lady like you —

Nora. You'll see, you'll see!

Krogstad. Under the ice, perhaps? Down into that cold, black water? Then spring comes, and you float up again — hideous, can't be identified, hair all gone —

Nora. You don't frighten me.

Krogstad. Nor you me. One doesn't do that sort of thing, Mrs. Helmer. Besides, what good would it do? He'd still be in my power.

Nora. Afterwards? When I'm no longer — ?

Krogstad. Aren't you forgetting that your reputation would be in my hands?

Nora stares at him, speechless.

Krogstad. All right; now I've told you what to expect. So don't do anything foolish. When Helmer gets my letter I expect to hear from him. And don't you forget that it's your husband himself who forces me to use such means again. That I'll never forgive him. Goodbye, Mrs. Helmer. (*Goes out through the hall.*)

Nora (at the door, opens it a little, listens). He's going. And no letter. Of course not! That would be impossible! (*Opens the door more.*) What's he doing? He's still there. Doesn't go down. Having second thoughts — ? Will he — ?

The sound of a letter dropping into the mailbox. Then Krogstad's steps are heard going down the stairs, gradually dying away.

Nora (*with a muted cry runs forward to the table by the couch; brief pause*). In the mailbox. (*Tiptoes back to the door to the front hall.*) There it is. Torvald, Torvald — now we're lost!

Mrs. Linde (*enters from the left, carrying Nora's Capri costume*). There now. I think it's all fixed. Why don't we try it on you —

Nora (*in a low, hoarse voice*). Kristine, come here.

Mrs. Linde. What's wrong with you? You look quite beside yourself.

Nora. Come over here. Do you see that letter? There, look — through the glass in the mailbox.

Mrs. Linde. Yes, yes; I see it.

Nora. That letter is from Krogstad.

Mrs. Linde. Nora — it was Krogstad who lent you the money!

Nora. Yes, and now Torvald will find out about it.

Mrs. Linde. Oh believe me, Nora. That's the best thing for both of you.

Nora. There's more to it than you know. I forged a signature —

Mrs. Linde. Oh my God — !

Nora. I just want to tell you this, Kristine, that you must be my witness.

Mrs. Linde. Witness? How? Witness to what?

Nora. If I lose my mind — and that could very well happen —

Mrs. Linde. Nora!

Nora. — or if something were to happen to me — something that made it impossible for me to be here —

Mrs. Linde. Nora, Nora! You're not yourself!

Nora. — and if someone were to take all the blame, assume the whole responsibility — Do you understand — ?

Mrs. Linde. Yes, yes; but how can you think — !

Nora. — then you are to witness that that's not so, Kristine. I am not beside myself. I am perfectly rational, and what I'm telling you is that nobody else has known about this. I've done it all by myself, the whole thing. Just remember that.

Mrs. Linde. I will. But I don't understand any of it.

Nora. Oh, how could you! For it's the wonderful that's about to happen.

Mrs. Linde. The wonderful?

Nora. Yes, the wonderful. But it's so terrible, Kristine. It mustn't happen for anything in the whole world!

Mrs. Linde. I'm going over to talk to Krogstad right now.

Nora. No, don't. Don't go to him. He'll do something bad to you.

Mrs. Linde. There was a time when he would have done anything for me.

Nora. He!

Mrs. Linde. Where does he live?

Nora. Oh, I don't know — Yes, wait a minute — (*Reaches into her pocket.*) here's his card — But the letter, the letter —

Helmer (*in his study, knocks on the door*). Nora!

Nora (*cries out in fear*). Oh, what is it? What do you want?

Helmer. That's all right. Nothing to be scared about. We're not coming in. For one thing, you've bolted the door, you know. Are you modeling your costume?

Nora. Yes, yes; I am. I'm going to be so pretty, Torvald.

Mrs. Linde (*having looked at the card*). He lives just around the corner.

Nora. Yes, but it's no use. Nothing can save us now. The letter is in the mailbox.

Mrs. Linde. And your husband has the key?

Nora. Yes. He always keeps it with him.

Mrs. Linde. Krogstad must ask for his letter back, unread. He's got to think up some pretext or other —

Nora. But this is just the time of day when Torvald —

Mrs. Linde. Delay him. Go in to him. I'll be back as soon as I can. (*She hurries out through the hall door.*)

Nora (*walks over to Helmer's door, opens it, and peeks in*). Torvald!

Helmer (*still offstage*). Well, well! So now one's allowed in one's own living room again. Come on, Rank. Now we'll see — (*In the doorway.*) But what's this?

Nora. What, Torvald dear?

Helmer. Rank prepared me for a splendid metamorphosis.

Rank (*in the doorway*). That's how I understood it. Evidently I was mistaken.

Nora. Nobody gets to admire me in my costume before tomorrow.

Helmer. But, dearest Nora — you look all done in. Have you been practicing too hard?

Nora. No, I haven't practiced at all.

Helmer. But you'll have to, you know.

Nora. I know it, Torvald. I simply must. But I can't do a thing unless you help me. I have forgotten everything.

Helmer. Oh it will all come back. We'll work on it.

Nora. Oh yes, please, Torvald. You just have to help me. Promise? I am so nervous. That big party — . You mustn't do anything else tonight. Not a bit of business. Don't even touch a pen. Will you promise, Torvald?

Helmer. I promise. Tonight I'll be entirely at your service — you helpless little thing. — Just a moment, though. First I want to — (*Goes to the door to the front hall.*)

Nora. What are you doing out there?

Helmer. Just looking to see if there's any mail.
Nora. No, no! Don't, Torvald!
Helmer. Why not?
Nora. Torvald, I beg you. There is no mail.
Helmer. Let me just look, anyway. (*Is about to go out.*)

> *Nora by the piano, plays the first bars of the tarantella dance.*

Helmer (*halts at the door*). Aha!
Nora. I won't be able to dance tomorrow if I don't get to practice with you.
Helmer (*goes to her*). Are you really all that scared, Nora dear?
Nora. Yes, so terribly scared. Let's try it right now. There's still time before we eat. Oh please, sit down and play for me, Torvald. Teach me, coach me, the way you always do.
Helmer. Of course I will, my darling, if that's what you want. (*Sits down at the piano.*)

> *Nora takes the tambourine out of the carton, as well as a long, many-colored shawl. She quickly drapes the shawl around herself, then leaps into the middle of the floor.*

Nora. Play for me! I want to dance!

> *Helmer plays and Nora dances. Dr. Rank stands by the piano behind Helmer and watches.*

Helmer (*playing*). Slow down, slow down!
Nora. Can't!
Helmer. Not so violent, Nora!
Nora. It has to be this way.
Helmer (*stops playing*). No, no. This won't do at all.
Nora (*laughing, swinging her tambourine*). What did I tell you?
Rank. Why don't you let me play?
Helmer (*getting up*). Good idea. Then I can direct her better.

> *Rank sits down at the piano and starts playing. Nora dances more and more wildly. Helmer stands over by the stove, repeatedly correcting her. She doesn't seem to hear. Her hair comes loose and falls down over her shoulders. She doesn't notice but keeps on dancing. Mrs. Linde enters.*

Mrs. Linde (*stops by the door, dumbfounded*). Ah — !
Nora (*dancing*). We're having such fun, Kristine!
Helmer. My dearest Nora, you're dancing as if it were a matter of life and death!
Nora. It is! It is!

Helmer. Rank, stop. This is sheer madness. Stop it, I say!

Rank stops playing; Nora suddenly stops dancing.

Helmer (goes over to her). If I hadn't seen it I wouldn't have believed it. You've forgotten every single thing I ever taught you.

Nora (tosses away the tambourine). See? I told you.

Helmer. Well! You certainly need coaching.

Nora. Didn't I tell you I did? Now you've seen for yourself. I'll need your help till the very minute we're leaving for the party. Will you promise, Torvald?

Helmer. You can count on it.

Nora. You're not to think of anything except me — not tonight and not tomorrow. You're not to read any letters — not to look in the mailbox —

Helmer. Ah, I see. You're still afraid of that man.

Nora. Yes — yes, that too.

Helmer. Nora, I can tell from looking at you. There's a letter from him out there.

Nora. I don't know. I think so. But you're not to read it now. I don't want anything ugly to come between us before it's all over.

Rank (to Helmer in a low voice). Better not argue with her.

Helmer (throws his arm around her). The child shall have her way. But tomorrow night, when you've done your dance —

Nora. Then you'll be free.

The Maid (in the door, right). Dinner can be served any time, ma'am.

Nora. We want champagne, Helene.

The Maid. Very good, ma'am. *(Goes out.)*

Helmer. Aha! Having a party, eh?

Nora. Champagne from now till sunrise! *(Calls out.)* And some macaroons, Helene. Lots! — just this once.

Helmer (taking her hands). There, there — I don't like this wild — frenzy — Be my own sweet little lark again, the way you always are.

Nora. Oh, I will. But you go on in. You too, Dr. Rank. Kristine, please help me put up my hair.

Rank (in a low voice to Helmer as they go out). You don't think she is — you know — expecting — ?

Helmer. Oh no. Nothing like that. It's just this childish fear I was telling you about. *(They go out, right.)*

Nora. Well?

Mrs. Linde. Left town.

Nora. I saw it in your face.

Mrs. Linde. He'll be back tomorrow night. I left him a note.

Nora. You shouldn't have. I don't want you to try to stop anything. You see, it's a kind of ecstasy, too, this waiting for the wonderful.

Mrs. Linde. But what is it you're waiting *for?*

Nora. You wouldn't understand. Why don't you go in to the others. I'll be there in a minute.

> *Mrs. Linde enters the dining room, right.*

Nora (*stands still for a little while, as if collecting herself; she looks at her watch*). Five o'clock. Seven hours till midnight. Twenty-four more hours till next midnight. Then the tarantella is over. Twenty-four plus seven — thirty-one more hours to live.

Helmer (*in the door, right*). What's happening to my little lark?

Nora (*to him, with open arms*). Here's your lark!

ACT III

> *The same room. The table by the couch and the chairs around it have been moved to the middle of the floor. A lighted lamp is on the table. The door to the front hall is open. Dance music is heard from upstairs.*
>
> *Mrs. Linde is seated by the table, idly leafing through the pages of a book. She tries to read but seems unable to concentrate. Once or twice she turns her head in the direction of the door, anxiously listening.*

Mrs. Linde (*looks at her watch*). Not yet. It's almost too late. If only he hasn't — (*Listens again.*) Ah! There he is. (*She goes to the hall and opens the front door carefully. Quiet footsteps on the stairs. She whispers.*) Come in. There's nobody here.

Krogstad (*in the door*). I found your note when I got home. What's this all about?

Mrs. Linde. I've got to talk to you.

Krogstad. Oh? And it has to be here?

Mrs. Linde. It couldn't be at my place. My room doesn't have a separate entrance. Come in. We're all alone. The maid is asleep and the Helmers are at a party upstairs.

Krogstad (*entering*). Really? The Helmers are dancing tonight, are they?

Mrs. Linde. And why not?

Krogstad. You're right. Why not, indeed.

Mrs. Linde. All right, Krogstad. Let's talk, you and I.

Krogstad. I didn't know we had anything to talk about.

Mrs. Linde. We have much to talk about.

Krogstad. I didn't think so.

Mrs. Linde. No, because you've never really understood me.

Krogstad. What was there to understand? What happened was perfectly commonplace. A heartless woman jilts a man when she gets a more attractive offer.

Mrs. Linde. Do you think I'm all that heartless? And do you think it was easy for me to break with you?

Krogstad. No?

Mrs. Linde. You really thought it was?

Krogstad. If it wasn't, why did you write the way you did that time?

Mrs. Linde. What else could I do? If I had to make a break, I also had the duty to destroy whatever feelings you had for me.

Krogstad (*clenching his hands*). So that's the way it was. And you did — *that* — just for money!

Mrs. Linde. Don't forget I had a helpless mother and two small brothers. We couldn't wait for you, Krogstad. You know yourself how uncertain your prospects were then.

Krogstad. All right. But you still didn't have the right to throw me over for somebody else.

Mrs. Linde. I don't know. I have asked myself that question many times. Did I have that right?

Krogstad (*in a lower voice*). When I lost you I lost my footing. Look at me now. A shipwrecked man on a raft.

Mrs. Linde. Rescue may be near.

Krogstad. It *was* near. Then you came between.

Mrs. Linde. I didn't know that, Krogstad. Only today did I find out it's your job I'm taking over in the bank.

Krogstad. I believe you when you say so. But now that you *do* know, aren't you going to step aside?

Mrs. Linde. No, for it wouldn't do you any good.

Krogstad. Whether it would or not — *I* would do it.

Mrs. Linde. I have learned common sense. Life and hard necessity have taught me that.

Krogstad. And life has taught me not to believe in pretty speeches.

Mrs. Linde. Then life has taught you a very sensible thing. But you do believe in actions, don't you?

Krogstad. How do you mean?

Mrs. Linde. You referred to yourself just now as a shipwrecked man.

Krogstad. It seems to me I had every reason to do so.

Mrs. Linde. And I am a shipwrecked woman. No one to grieve for, no one to care for.

Krogstad. You made your choice.

Mrs. Linde. I had no other choice that time.

Krogstad. Let's say you didn't. What then?

Mrs. Linde. Krogstad, how would it be if we two shipwrecked people got together?

Krogstad. What's this!

Mrs. Linde. Two on one wreck are better off than each on his own.

Krogstad. Kristine!

Mrs. Linde. Why do you think I came to town?

Krogstad. Surely not because of me?

Mrs. Linde. If I'm going to live at all I must work. All my life, for as long as I can remember, I have worked. That's been my one and only pleasure. But now that I'm all alone in the world I feel nothing but this terrible emptiness and desolation. There is no joy in working just for yourself. Krogstad — give me someone and something to work for.

Krogstad. I don't believe this. Only hysterical females go in for that kind of high-minded self-sacrifice.

Mrs. Linde. Did you ever know me to be hysterical?

Krogstad. You really could do this? Listen — do you know about my past? All of it?

Mrs. Linde. Yes, I do.

Krogstad. Do you also know what people think of me around here?

Mrs. Linde. A little while ago you sounded as if you thought that together with me you might have become a different person.

Krogstad. I'm sure of it.

Mrs. Linde. Couldn't that still be?

Krogstad. Kristine — do you know what you are doing? Yes, I see you do. And you think you have the courage ?

Mrs. Linde. I need someone to be a mother to, and your children need a mother. You and I need one another. Nils, I believe in you — in the real you. Together with you I dare to do anything.

Krogstad (seizes her hands). Thanks, thanks, Kristine — now I know I'll raise myself in the eyes of others. — Ah, but I forget — !

Mrs. Linde (listening). Shh! — There's the tarantella. You must go; hurry!

Krogstad. Why? What is it?

Mrs. Linde. Do you hear what they're playing up there? When that dance is over they'll be down.

Krogstad. All right. I'm leaving. The whole thing is pointless, anyway. Of course you don't know what I'm doing to the Helmers.

Mrs. Linde. Yes, Krogstad; I do know.

Krogstad. Still, you're brave enough — ?

Mrs. Linde. I very well understand to what extremes despair can drive a man like you.

Krogstad. If only it could be undone!

Mrs. Linde. It could, for your letter is still out there in the mailbox.

Krogstad. Are you sure?

Mrs. Linde. Quite sure. But —

Krogstad (*looks searchingly at her*). Maybe I'm beginning to understand. You want to save your friend at any cost. Be honest with me. That's it, isn't it?

Mrs. Linde. Krogstad, you may sell yourself once for somebody else's sake, but you don't do it twice.

Krogstad. I'll demand my letter back.

Mrs. Linde. No, no.

Krogstad. Yes, of course. I'll wait here till Helmer comes down. Then I'll ask him for my letter. I'll tell him it's just about my dismissal — that he shouldn't read it.

Mrs. Linde. No, Krogstad. You are not to ask for that letter back.

Krogstad. But tell me — wasn't that the real reason you wanted to meet me here?

Mrs. Linde. At first it was, because I was so frightened. But that was yesterday. Since then I have seen the most incredible things going on in this house. Helmer must learn the whole truth. This miserable secret must come out in the open; those two must come to a full understanding. They simply can't continue with all this concealment and evasion.

Krogstad. All right; if you want to take that chance. But there is one thing I *can* do, and I'll do that right now.

Mrs. Linde (*listening*). But hurry! Go! The dance is over. We aren't safe another minute.

Krogstad. I'll be waiting for you downstairs.

Mrs. Linde. Yes, do. You must see me home.

Krogstad. I've never been so happy in my whole life. (*He leaves through the front door. The door between the living room and the front hall remains open.*)

Mrs. Linde (*straightens up the room a little and gets her things ready*). What a change! Oh yes! — what a change! People to work for — to live for — a home to bring happiness to. I can't wait to get to work — ! If only they'd come soon — (*Listens.*) Ah, there they are. Get my coat on — (*Puts on her coat and hat.*)

Helmer's and Nora's voices are heard outside. A key is turned in the lock, and Helmer almost forces Nora into the hall. She is dressed in her Italian costume, with a big black shawl over her shoulders. He is in evening dress under an open black domino.

Nora (*in the door, still resisting*). No, no, no! I don't want to! I want to go back upstairs. I don't want to leave so early.

Helmer. But dearest Nora —

Nora. Oh please, Torvald — please! I'm asking you as nicely as I can — just another hour!

Helmer. Not another minute, sweet. You know we agreed. There now. Get inside. You'll catch a cold out here. (*She still resists, but he guides her gently into the room.*)

Mrs. Linde. Good evening.

Nora. Kristine!

Helmer. Ah, Mrs. Linde. Still here?

Mrs. Linde. I know. I really should apologize, but I so much wanted to see Nora in her costume.

Nora. You've been waiting up for me?

Mrs. Linde. Yes, unfortunately I didn't get here in time. You were already upstairs, but I just didn't feel like leaving till I had seen you.

Helmer (*removing Nora's shawl*). Yes, do take a good look at her, Mrs. Linde. I think I may say she's worth looking at. Isn't she lovely?

Mrs. Linde. She certainly is —

Helmer. Isn't she a miracle of loveliness, though? That was the general opinion at the party, too. But dreadfully obstinate — that she is, the sweet little thing. What can we do about that? Will you believe it — I practically had to use force to get her away.

Nora. Oh Torvald, you're going to be sorry you didn't give me even half an hour more.

Helmer. See what I mean, Mrs. Linde? She dances the tarantella — she is a tremendous success — quite deservedly so, though perhaps her performance was a little too natural — I mean, more than could be reconciled with the rules of art. But all right! The point is: she's a success, a tremendous success. So should I let her stay after that? Spoil the effect? Of course not. So I take my lovely little Capri girl — I might say, my capricious little Capri girl — under my arm — a quick turn around the room — a graceful bow in all directions, and — as they say in the novels — the beautiful apparition is gone. A finale should always be done for effect, Mrs. Linde, but there doesn't seem to be any way of getting that into Nora's head. Poooh — ! It's hot in here. (*Throws his cloak down on a chair and opens the door to his room.*) Why, it's dark in here!

Of course. Excuse me — (*Goes inside and lights a couple of candles.*)

Nora (*in a hurried, breathless whisper*). Well?

Mrs. Linde (*in a low voice*). I have talked to him.

Nora. And — ?

Mrs. Linde. Nora — you've got to tell your husband everything.

Nora (*no expression in her voice*). I knew it.

Mrs. Linde. You have nothing to fear from Krogstad. But you must speak.

Nora. I'll say nothing.

Mrs. Linde. Then the letter will.

Nora. Thank you, Kristine. Now I know what I have to do. Shh!

Helmer (*returning*). Well, Mrs. Linde, have you looked your fill?

Mrs. Linde. Yes. And now I'll say goodnight.

Helmer. So soon? Is that your knitting?

Mrs. Linde (*takes it*). Yes, thank you. I almost forgot.

Helmer. So you knit, do you?

Mrs. Linde. Oh yes.

Helmer. You know — you ought to take up embroidery instead.

Mrs. Linde. Oh? Why?

Helmer. Because it's so much more beautiful. Look. You hold the embroidery so — in your left hand. Then with your right you move the needle — like this — in an easy, elongated arc — you see?

Mrs. Linde. Maybe you're right —

Helmer. Knitting, on the other hand, can never be anything but ugly. Look here: arms pressed close to the sides — the needles going up and down — there's something Chinese about it somehow — . That really was an excellent champagne they served us tonight.

Mrs. Linde. Well, goodnight, Nora. And don't be obstinate any more.

Helmer. Well said, Mrs. Linde!

Mrs. Linde. Goodnight, sir.

Helmer (*sees her to the front door*). Goodnight, goodnight. I hope you'll get home all right? I'd be very glad to — but of course you don't have far to walk, do you? Goodnight, goodnight. (*She leaves. He closes the door behind her and returns to the living room.*) There! At last we got rid of her. She really is an incredible bore, that woman.

Nora. Aren't you very tired, Torvald?

Helmer. No, not in the least.

Nora. Not sleepy either?

Helmer. Not at all. Quite the opposite. I feel enormously — animated. How about you? Yes, you do look tired and sleepy.

Nora. Yes, I am very tired. Soon I'll be asleep.

Helmer. What did I tell you? I was right, wasn't I? Good thing I didn't let you stay any longer.

Nora. Everything you do is right.

Helmer (*kissing her forehead*). Now my little lark is talking like a human being. But did you notice what splendid spirits Rank was in tonight?

Nora. Was he? I didn't notice. I didn't get to talk with him.

Helmer. Nor did I — hardly. But I haven't seen him in such a good mood for a long time. (*Looks at her, comes closer to her.*) Ah! It does feel good to be back in our own home again, to be quite alone with you — my young, lovely, ravishing woman!

Nora. Don't look at me like that, Torvald!

Helmer. Am I not to look at my most precious possession? All that loveliness that is mine, nobody's but mine, all of it mine.

Nora (*walks to the other side of the table*). I won't have you talk to me like that tonight.

Helmer (*follows her*). The tarantella is still in your blood. I can tell. That only makes you all the more alluring. Listen! The guests are beginning to leave. (*Softly.*) Nora — soon the whole house will be quiet.

Nora. Yes, I hope so.

Helmer. Yes, don't you, my darling? Do you know — when I'm at a party with you, like tonight — do you know why I hardly ever talk to you, why I keep away from you, only look at you once in a while — a few stolen glances — do you know why I do that? It's because I pretend that you are my secret love, my young, secret bride-to-be, and nobody has the slightest suspicion that there is anything between us.

Nora. Yes, I know. All your thoughts are with me.

Helmer. Then when we're leaving and I lay your shawl around your delicate young shoulders — around that wonderful curve of your neck — then I imagine you're my young bride, that we're coming away from the wedding, that I am taking you to my home for the first time — that I am alone with you for the first time — quite alone with you, you young, trembling beauty! I have desired you all evening — there hasn't been a longing in me that hasn't been for you. When you were dancing the tarantella, chasing, inviting — my blood was on fire; I couldn't stand it any longer — that's why I brought you down so early —

Nora. Leave me now, Torvald. Please! I don't want all this.

Helmer. What do you mean? You're only playing your little teasing bird game with me; aren't you, Nora? Don't want to? I'm your husband, aren't I?

There is a knock on the front door.

Nora (with a start). Did you hear that — ?

Helmer (on his way to the hall). Who is it?

Rank (outside). It's me. May I come in for a moment?

Helmer (in a low voice, annoyed). Oh, what does he want now? (*Aloud.*) Just a minute. (*Opens the door.*) Well! How good of you not to pass by our door.

Rank. I thought I heard your voice, so I felt like saying hello. (*Looks around.*) Ah yes — this dear, familiar room. What a cozy, comfortable place you have here, you two.

Helmer. Looked to me as if you were quite comfortable upstairs too.

Rank. I certainly was. Why not? Why not enjoy all you can in this world? As much as you can for as long as you can, anyway. Excellent wine.

Helmer. The champagne, particularly.

Rank. You noticed that too? Incredible how much I managed to put away.

Nora. Torvald drank a lot of champagne tonight, too.

Rank. Did he?

Nora. Yes, he did, and then he's always so much fun afterwards.

Rank. Well, why not have some fun in the evening after a well spent day?

Helmer. Well spent? I'm afraid I can't claim that.

Rank (slapping him lightly on the shoulder). But you see, I can!

Nora. Dr. Rank, I believe you must have been conducting a scientific test today.

Rank. Exactly.

Helmer. What do you know — little Nora talking about scientific tests!

Nora. May I congratulate you on the result?

Rank. You may indeed.

Nora. It was a good one?

Rank. The best possible for both doctor and patient — certainty.

Nora (a quick query). Certainty?

Rank. Absolute certainty. So why shouldn't I have myself an enjoyable evening afterwards?

Nora. I quite agree with you, Dr. Rank. You should.

Helmer. And so do I. If only you don't pay for it tomorrow.

Rank. Oh well — you get nothing for nothing in this world.

Nora. Dr. Rank — you are fond of costume parties, aren't you?

Rank. Yes, particularly when there is a reasonable number of amusing disguises.

Nora. Listen — what are the two of us going to be the next time?

Helmer. You frivolous little thing! Already thinking about the next party!

Rank. You and I? That's easy. You'll be Fortune's Child.

Helmer. Yes, but what is a fitting costume for that?

Rank. Let your wife appear just the way she always is.

Helmer. Beautiful. Very good indeed. But how about yourself? Don't you know what you'll go as?

Rank. Yes, my friend. I know precisely what I'll be.

Helmer. Yes?

Rank. At the next masquerade I'll be invisible.

Helmer. That's a funny idea.

Rank. There's a certain big, black hat — you've heard about the hat that makes you invisible, haven't you? You put that on, and nobody can see you.

Helmer (*suppressing a smile*). I guess that's right.

Rank. But I'm forgetting what I came for. Helmer, give me a cigar — one of your dark Havanas.

Helmer. With the greatest pleasure. (*Offers him his case.*)

Rank (*takes one and cuts off the tip*). Thanks.

Nora (*striking a match*). Let me give you a light.

Rank. Thanks. (*She holds the match; he lights his cigar.*) And now goodbye!

Helmer. Goodbye, goodbye, my friend.

Nora. Sleep well, Dr. Rank.

Rank. I thank you.

Nora. Wish me the same.

Rank. You? Well, if you really want me to — . Sleep well. And thanks for the light. (*He nods to both of them and goes out.*)

Helmer (*in a low voice*). He had had quite a bit to drink.

Nora (*absently*). Maybe so.

Helmer takes out his keys and goes out into the hall.

Nora. Torvald — what are you doing out there?

Helmer. Got to empty the mailbox. It is quite full. There wouldn't be room for the newspapers in the morning —

Nora. Are you going to work tonight?

Helmer. You know very well I won't. — Say! What's this? Somebody's been at the lock.

Nora. The lock — ?

Helmer. Yes. Why, I wonder. I hate to think that any of the maids — . Here's a broken hairpin. It's one of yours, Nora.

Nora (*quickly*). Then it must be one of the children.

Helmer. You better make damn sure they stop that. Hm, hm. —
There! I got it open, finally. (*Gathers up the mail, calls out to
the kitchen.*) Helene? — Oh Helene — turn out the light here
in the hall, will you? (*He comes back into the living room and
closes the door.*) Look how it's been piling up. (*Shows her the
bundle of letters. Starts leafing through it.*) What's this?

Nora (*by the window*). The letter! Oh no, no, Torvald!

Helmer. Two calling cards — from Rank.

Nora. From Dr. Rank?

Helmer (*looking at them*). "Doctor medicinae Rank." They were
on top. He must have put them there when he left just now.

Nora. Anything written on them?

Helmer. A black cross above the name. Look. What a macabre
idea. Like announcing his own death.

Nora. That's what it is.

Helmer. Hm? You know about this? Has he said anything to you?

Nora. That card means he has said goodbye to us. He'll lock himself
up to die.

Helmer. My poor friend. I knew of course he wouldn't be with
me very long. But so soon — . And hiding himself away
like a wounded animal —

Nora. When it has to be, it's better it happens without words.
Don't you think so, Torvald?

Helmer (*walking up and down*). He'd grown so close to us. I find
it hard to think of him as gone. With his suffering and
loneliness he was like a clouded background for our happy
sunshine. Well, it may be better this way. For him, at any
rate. (*Stops.*) And perhaps for us, too, Nora. For now we
have nobody but each other. (*Embraces her.*) Oh you — my
beloved wife! I feel I just can't hold you close enough. Do
you know, Nora — many times I have wished some great
danger threatened you, so I could risk my life and blood
and everything — everything, for your sake.

Nora (*frees herself and says in a strong and firm voice*). I think you
should go and read your letters now, Torvald.

Helmer. No, no — not tonight. I want to be with you, my darling.

Nora. With the thought of your dying friend — ?

Helmer. You are right. This has shaken both of us. Something not
beautiful has come between us. Thoughts of death and dissolution. We must try to get over it — out of it. Till then
— we'll each go to our own room.

Nora (*her arms around his neck*). Torvald — goodnight! Goodnight!

Helmer (*kisses her forehead*). Goodnight, my little songbird. Sleep well, Nora. Now I'll read my letters. (*He goes into his room, carrying the mail. Closes the door.*)

Nora (*her eyes desperate, her hands groping, finds Helmer's domino and throws it around her; she whispers, quickly, brokenly, hoarsely*). Never see him again. Never. Never. Never. (*Puts her shawl over her head.*) And never see the children again, either. Never; never. — The black, icy water — fathomless — this — ! If only it was all over. — Now he has it. Now he's reading it. No, no; not yet. Torvald — goodbye — you — the children —

She is about to hurry through the hall, when Helmer flings open the door to his room and stands there with an open letter in his hand.

Helmer. Nora!

Nora (*cries out*). Ah — !

Helmer. What is it? You know what's in this letter?

Nora. Yes, I do! Let me go! Let me out!

Helmer (*holds her back*). Where do you think you're going?

Nora (*trying to tear herself loose from him*). I won't let you save me, Torvald!

Helmer (*tumbles back*). True! Is it true what he writes? Oh my God! No, no — this can't possibly be true.

Nora. It is true. I have loved you more than anything else in the whole world.

Helmer. Oh, don't give me any silly excuses.

Nora (*taking a step towards him*). Torvald —

Helmer. You wretch! What have you done!

Nora. Let me go. You are not to sacrifice yourself for me. You are not to take the blame.

Helmer. No more playacting. (*Locks the door to the front hall.*) You'll stay here and answer me. Do you understand what you have done? Answer me! Do you understand?

Nora (*gazes steadily at him with an increasingly frozen expression*). Yes. Now I'm beginning to understand.

Helmer (*walking up and down*). What a dreadful awakening. All these years — all these eight years — she, my pride and my joy — a hypocrite, a liar — oh worse! worse! — a criminal! Oh, the bottomless ugliness in all this! Damn! Damn! Damn!

Nora, silent, keeps gazing at him.

Helmer (*stops in front of her*). I ought to have guessed that something like this would happen. I should have expected it. All your father's loose principles — Silence! You have inherited every one of your father's loose principles. No religion, no morals, no sense of duty — . Now I am being punished for my leniency with him. I did it for your sake, and this is how you pay me back.

Nora. Yes. This is how.

Helmer. You have ruined all my happiness. My whole future — that's what you have destroyed. Oh, it's terrible to think about. I am at the mercy of an unscrupulous man. He can do with me whatever he likes, demand anything of me, command me and dispose of me just as he pleases — I dare not say a word! To go down so miserably, to be destroyed — all because of an irresponsible woman!

Nora. When I am gone from the world, you'll be free.

Helmer. No noble gestures, please. Your father was always full of such phrases too. What good would it do me if you were gone from the world, as you put it? Not the slightest good at all. He could still make the whole thing public, and if he did I wouldn't be surprised if people thought I'd put you up to it. They might even think it was my idea — that it was I who urged you to do it! And for all this I have you to thank — you, whom I've borne on my hands through all the years of our marriage. *Now* do you understand what you've done to me?

Nora (with cold calm). Yes.

Helmer. I just can't get it into my head that this is happening; it's all so incredible. But we have to come to terms with it somehow. Take your shawl off. Take it off, I say! I have to satisfy him one way or another. The whole affair must be kept quiet at whatever cost. — And as far as you and I are concerned, nothing must seem to have changed. I'm talking about appearances, of course. You'll go on living here; that goes without saying. But I won't let you bring up the children; I dare not trust you with them. — Oh! Having to say this to one I have loved so much, and whom I still — ! But all that is past. It's not a question of happiness any more but of hanging on to what can be salvaged — pieces, appearances — (*The doorbell rings.*)

Helmer (jumps.) What's that? So late. Is the worst — ? Has he — ! Hide, Nora! Say you're sick.

Nora doesn't move. Helmer opens the door to the hall.

The Maid (half dressed, out in the hall). A letter for your wife, sir.

Helmer. Give it to me. (*Takes the letter and closes the door.*) Yes, it's from him. But I won't let you have it. I'll read it myself.

Nora. Yes — you read it.

Helmer (by the lamp). I hardly dare. Perhaps we're lost, both you and I. No; I've got to know. (*Tears the letter open, glances through it, looks at an enclosure; a cry of joy.*) Nora!

Nora looks at him with a question in her eyes.

Helmer. Nora! — No, I must read it again. — Yes, yes; it is so! I'm saved! Nora, I'm saved!

Nora. And I?

Helmer. You too, of course; we're both saved, both you and I. Look! He's returning your note. He writes that he's sorry, he regrets, a happy turn in his life — oh, it doesn't matter what he writes. We're saved, Nora! Nobody can do anything to you now. Oh Nora, Nora — . No, I want to get rid of this disgusting thing first. Let me see — (*Looks at the signature.*) No, I don't want to see it. I don't want it to be more than a bad dream, the whole thing. (*Tears up the note and both letters, throws the pieces in the stove, and watches them burn.*) There! Now it's gone. — He wrote that ever since Christmas Eve — . Good God, Nora, these must have been three terrible days for you.

Nora. I have fought a hard fight these last three days.

Helmer. And been in agony and seen no other way out than — . No, we won't think of all that ugliness. We'll just rejoice and tell ourselves it's over, it's all over! Oh, listen to me, Nora. You don't seem to understand. It's over. What *is* it? Why do you look like that — that frozen expression on your face? Oh my poor little Nora, don't you think I know what it is? You can't make yourself believe that I have forgiven you. But I have, Nora; I swear to you, I have forgiven you for everything. Of course I know that what you did was for love of me.

Nora. That is true.

Helmer. You have loved me the way a wife ought to love her husband. You just didn't have the wisdom to judge the means. But do you think I love you any less because you don't know how to act on your own? Of course not. Just lean on me. I'll advise you; I'll guide you. I wouldn't be a man if I didn't find you twice as attractive because of your womanly helplessness. You mustn't pay any attention to the hard words I said to you right at first. It was just that first shock when I thought everything was collapsing all around me. I have forgiven you, Nora. I swear to you — I really have forgiven you.

Nora. I thank you for your forgiveness. (*She goes out through the door, right.*)

Helmer. No, stay — (*Looks into the room she entered.*) What are you
doing in there?

Nora (*within*). Getting out of my costume.

Helmer (*by the open door*). Good, good. Try to calm down and
compose yourself, my poor little frightened songbird. Rest
safely; I have broad wings to cover you with. (*Walks around
near the door.*) What a nice and cozy home we have, Nora.
Here's shelter for you. Here I'll keep you safe like a hunted
dove I have rescued from the hawk's talons. Believe me: I'll
know how to quiet your beating heart. It will happen by
and by, Nora; you'll see. Why, tomorrow you'll look at all
this in quite a different light. And soon everything will be
just the way it was before. I won't need to keep reassuring
you that I have forgiven you; you'll feel it yourself. Did you
really think I could have abandoned you, or even reproached
you? Oh, you don't know a real man's heart, Nora. There
is something unspeakably sweet and satisfactory for a man
to know deep in himself that he has forgiven his wife —
forgiven her in all the fullness of his honest heart. You see,
that way she becomes his very own all over again — in a
double sense, you might say. He has, so to speak, given her
a second birth; it is as if she had become his wife and his
child, both. From now on that's what you'll be to me, you
lost and helpless creature. Don't worry about a thing, Nora.
Only be frank with me, and I'll be your will and your
conscience. — What's this? You're not in bed? You've changed
your dress — !

Nora (*in an everyday dress*). Yes, Torvald. I have changed my dress.

Helmer. But why — now — this late?

Nora. I'm not going to sleep tonight.

Helmer. But my dear Nora —

Nora (*looks at her watch*). It isn't all that late. Sit down here with
me, Torvald. You and I have much to talk about. (*Sits down
at the table.*)

Helmer. Nora — what is this all about? That rigid face —

Nora. Sit down. This will take a while. I have much to say to
you.

Helmer (*sits down, facing her across the table*). You worry me, Nora.
I don't understand you.

Nora. No, that's just it. You don't understand me. And I have
never understood you — not till tonight. No, don't interrupt
me. Just listen to what I have to say. — This is a settling
of accounts, Torvald.

Helmer. What do you mean by that?

Nora (after a brief silence). Doesn't one thing strike you, now that we are sitting together like this?

Helmer. What would that be?

Nora. We have been married for eight years. Doesn't it occur to you that this is the first time that you and I, husband and wife, are having a serious talk?

Helmer. Well — serious — . What do you mean by that?

Nora. For eight whole years — longer, in fact — ever since we first met, we have never talked seriously to each other about a single serious thing.

Helmer. You mean I should forever have been telling you about worries you couldn't have helped me with anyway?

Nora. I am not talking about worries. I'm saying we have never tried seriously to get to the bottom of anything together.

Helmer. But dearest Nora, I hardly think that would have been something *you* —

Nora. That's the whole point. You have never understood me. Great wrong has been done to me, Torvald. First by Daddy and then by you.

Helmer. What! By us two? We who have loved you more deeply than anyone else?

Nora (shakes her head). You never loved me — neither Daddy nor you. You only thought it was fun to be in love with me.

Helmer. But, Nora — what an expression to use!

Nora. That's the way it has been, Torvald. When I was home with Daddy, he told me all his opinions, and so they became my opinions too. If I disagreed with him I kept it to myself, for he wouldn't have liked that. He called me his little doll baby, and he played with me the way I played with my dolls. Then I came to your house —

Helmer. What a way to talk about our marriage!

Nora (imperturbably). I mean that I passed from Daddy's hands into yours. You arranged everything according to your taste, and so I came to share it — or I pretended to; I'm not sure which. I think it was a little of both, now one and now the other. When I look back on it now, it seems to me I've been living here like a pauper — just a hand-to-mouth kind of existence. I have earned my keep by doing tricks for you, Torvald. But that's the way you wanted it. You have great sins against me to answer for, Daddy and you. It's your fault that nothing has become of me.

Helmer. Nora, you're being both unreasonable and ungrateful. Haven't you been happy here?

Nora. No, never. I thought I was, but I wasn't.

Helmer. Not — not happy!

Nora. No; just having fun. And you have always been very good to me. But our home has never been more than a playroom. I have been your doll wife here, just the way I used to be Daddy's doll child. And the children have been my dolls. I thought it was fun when you played with me, just as they thought it was fun when I played with them. That's been our marriage, Torvald.

Helmer. There is something in what you are saying — exaggerated and hysterical though it is. But from now on things will be different. Playtime is over; it's time for growing up.

Nora. Whose growing up — mine or the children's?

Helmer. Both yours and the children's, Nora darling.

Nora. Oh Torvald, you're not the man to bring me up to be the right kind of wife for you.

Helmer. How can you say that?

Nora. And I — ? What qualifications do I have for bringing up the children?

Helmer. Nora!

Nora. You said so yourself a minute ago — that you didn't dare to trust me with them.

Helmer. In the first flush of anger, yes. Surely, you're not going to count that.

Nora. But you were quite right. I am *not* qualified. Something else has to come first. Somehow I have to grow up myself. And you are not the man to help me do that. That's a job I have to do by myself. And that's why I'm leaving you.

Helmer (*jumps up*). What did you say!

Nora. I have to be by myself if I am to find out about myself and about all the other things too. So I can't stay here with you any longer.

Helmer. Nora, Nora!

Nora. I'm leaving now. I'm sure Kristine will put me up for tonight.

Helmer. You're out of your mind! I won't let you! I forbid you!

Nora. You can't forbid me anything any more; it won't do any good. I'm taking my own things with me. I won't accept anything from you, either now or later.

Helmer. But this is madness!

Nora. Tomorrow I'm going home — I mean back to my old hometown. It will be easier for me to find some kind of job there.

Helmer. Oh, you blind, inexperienced creature — !

Nora. I must see to it that I get experience, Torvald.

Helmer. Leaving your home, your husband, your children! Not a thought of what people will say!

Nora. I can't worry about that. All I know is that I have to leave.

Helmer. Oh, this is shocking! Betraying your most sacred duties like this!

Nora. And what do you consider my most sacred duties?

Helmer. Do I need to tell you that? They are your duties to your husband and your children.

Nora. I have other duties equally sacred.

Helmer. You do not. What duties would they be?

Nora. My duties to myself.

Helmer. You are a wife and a mother before you are anything else.

Nora. I don't believe that any more. I believe I am first of all a human being, just as much as you — or at any rate that I must try to become one. Oh, I know very well that most people agree with you, Torvald, and that it says something like that in all the books. But what people say and what the books say is no longer enough for me. I have to think about these things myself and see if I can't find the answers.

Helmer. You mean to tell me you don't know what your proper place in your own home is? Don't you have a reliable guide in such matters? Don't you have religion?

Nora. Oh but Torvald — I don't really know what religion is.

Helmer. What are you saying!

Nora. All I know is what the Reverend Hansen told me when he prepared me for confirmation. He said that religion was *this* and it was *that.* When I get by myself, away from here, I'll have to look into that, too. I have to decide if what the Reverend Hansen said was right, or anyway if it is right for *me.*

Helmer. Oh, this is unheard of in a young woman! If religion can't guide you, let me appeal to your conscience. For surely you have moral feelings? Or — answer me — maybe you don't?

Nora. Well, you see, Torvald, I don't really know what to say. I just don't know. I am confused about these things. All I know is that my ideas are quite different from yours. I have just found out that the laws are different from what I thought they were, but in no way can I get it into my head that those laws are right. A woman shouldn't have the right to spare her dying old father or save her husband's life! I just can't believe that.

Helmer. You speak like a child. You don't understand the society you live in.

Nora. No, I don't. But I want to find out about it. I have to make up my mind who is right, society or I.

Helmer. You are sick, Nora; you have a fever. I really don't think you are in your right mind.

Nora. I have never felt so clearheaded and sure of myself as I do tonight.

Helmer. And clearheaded and sure of yourself you're leaving your husband and children?

Nora. Yes.

Helmer. Then there is only one possible explanation.

Nora. What?

Helmer. You don't love me any more.

Nora. No, that's just it.

Helmer. Nora! Can you say that?

Nora. I am sorry, Torvald, for you have always been so good to me. But I can't help it. I don't love you any more.

Helmer (with forced composure). And this too is a clear and sure conviction?

Nora. Completely clear and sure. That's why I don't want to stay here any more.

Helmer. And are you ready to explain to me how I came to forfeit your love?

Nora. Certainly I am. It was tonight, when the wonderful didn't happen. That was when I realized you were not the man I thought you were.

Helmer. You have to explain. I don't understand.

Nora. I have waited patiently for eight years, for I wasn't such a fool that I thought the wonderful is something that happens any old day. Then this — thing — came crashing in on me, and then there wasn't a doubt in my mind that now — now comes the wonderful. When Krogstad's letter was in that mailbox, never for a moment did it even occur to me that you would submit to his conditions. I was so absolutely certain that you would say to him: make the whole thing public — tell everybody. And when that had happened —

Helmer. Yes, then what? When I had surrendered my own wife to shame and disgrace — !

Nora. When that had happened, I was absolutely certain that you would stand up and take the blame and say, "I'm the guilty one."

Helmer. Nora!

Nora. You mean I never would have accepted such a sacrifice from you? Of course not. But what would my protests have counted against yours? *That* was the wonderful I was waiting for in hope and terror. And to prevent that I was going to kill myself.

Helmer. I'd gladly work nights and days for you, Nora — endure sorrow and want for your sake. But nobody sacrifices his *honor* for his love.

Nora. A hundred thousand women have done so.

Helmer. Oh, you think and talk like a silly child.

Nora. All right. But you don't think and talk like the man I can live with. When you had gotten over your fright — not because of what threatened *me* but because of the risk to *you* — and the whole danger was past, then you acted as if nothing at all had happened. Once again I was your little songbird, your doll, just as before, only now you had to handle her even more carefully, because she was so frail and weak. (*Rises.*) Torvald — that moment I realized that I had been living here for eight years with a stranger and had borne him three children — Oh, I can't stand thinking about it! I feel like tearing myself to pieces!

Helmer (heavily). I see it, I see it. An abyss has opened up between us. — Oh but Nora — surely it can be filled?

Nora. The way I am now I am no wife for you.

Helmer. I have it in me to change.

Nora. Perhaps — if your doll is taken from you.

Helmer. To part — to part from you! No, no, Nora! I can't grasp that thought!

Nora (goes out, right). All the more reason why it has to be. (*She returns with her outdoor clothes and a small bag, which she sets down on the chair by the table.*)

Helmer. Nora, Nora! Not now! Wait till tomorrow.

Nora (putting on her coat). I can't spend the night in a stranger's rooms.

Helmer. But couldn't we live here together like brother and sister — ?

Nora (tying on her hat). You know very well that wouldn't last long — . (*Wraps her shawl around her.*) Goodbye, Torvald. I don't want to see the children. I know I leave them in better hands than mine. The way I am now I can't be anything to them.

Helmer. But some day, Nora — some day ?

Nora. How can I tell? I have no idea what's going to become of me.

Helmer. But you're still my wife, both as you are now and as you will be.

Nora. Listen, Torvald — when a wife leaves her husband's house, the way I am doing now, I have heard he has no more legal responsibilities for her. At any rate, I now release you from all responsibility. You are not to feel yourself obliged to me for anything, and I have no obligations to you. There has to be full freedom on both sides. Here is your ring back. Now give me mine.

Helmer. Even this?

Nora. Even this.

Helmer. Here it is.

Nora. There. So now it's over. I'm putting the keys here. The maids know everything about the house — better than I. Tomorrow, after I'm gone, Kristine will come over and pack my things from home. I want them sent after me.

Helmer. Over! It's all over! Nora, will you never think of me?

Nora. I'm sure I'll often think of you and the children and this house.

Helmer. May I write to you, Nora?

Nora. No — never. I won't have that.

Helmer. But send you things — ? You must let me.

Nora. Nothing, nothing.

Helmer. — help you, when you need help —

Nora. I told you, no; I won't have it. I'll accept nothing from strangers.

Helmer. Nora — can I never again be more to you than a stranger?

Nora (picks up her bag). Oh Torvald — then the most wonderful of all would have to happen —

Helmer. Tell me what that would be — !

Nora. For that to happen, both you and I would have to change so that — Oh Torvald; I no longer believe in the wonderful.

Helmer. But I *will* believe. Tell me! Change, so that — ?

Nora. So that our living together would become a true marriage. Goodbye. (*She goes out through the hall.*)

Helmer (sinks down on a chair near the door and covers his face with his hands). Nora! Nora! (*Looks around him and gets up.*) All empty. She's gone. (*With sudden hope.*) The most wonderful — ?!

From downstairs comes the sound of a heavy door slamming shut.

QUESTIONS

1. Near the beginning of the play, how does Mrs. Linde's presence help to define Nora's character? How does Nora's response to Krogstad's entrance tell us something about Nora?

2. What does Dr. Rank contribute to the play? If he were eliminated, what would be lost?

3. Ibsen very reluctantly acceded to a request for an alternate ending for a German production. In the new ending Helmer forces Nora to look at their sleeping children and reminds

her that "tomorrow, when they wake up and call for their mother, they will be — motherless." Nora "struggles with herself" and concludes by saying, "Oh, this is a sin against myself, but I cannot leave them." In view of the fact that the last act several times seems to be moving toward a "happy ending" (e.g., Krogstad promises to recall his letter), what is wrong with this alternate ending?

4. Can it be argued that although at the end Nora goes out to achieve self-realization, her abandonment of her children — especially to Torvald's loathsome conventional morality — is a crime? (By the way, exactly why does Nora leave the children? She seems to imply, in some passages, that because she forged a signature she is unfit to bring them up. But do you agree with her?)

5. Michael Meyer, in his splendid biography *Henrik Ibsen,* says that the play is not so much about women's rights as about "the need of every individual to find out the kind of person he or she really is, and to strive to become that person." What evidence can you offer to support this interpretation?

6. In *The Quintessence of Ibsenism* Bernard Shaw says that Ibsen, reacting against a common theatrical preference for strange situations, "saw that . . . the more familiar the situation, the more interesting the play. Shakespear had put ourselves on the stage but not our situations. Our uncles seldom murder our fathers and . . . marry our mothers. . . . Ibsen . . . gives us not only ourselves, but ourselves in our own situations. The things that happen to his stage figures are things that happen to us. One consequence is that his plays are much more important to us than Shakespear's. Another is that they are capable both of hurting us cruelly and of filling us with excited hopes of escape from idealistic tyrannies, and with visions of intenser life in the future." How much of this do you believe?

Susan Glaspell (1882–1948)

Trifles

> **Scene** *The kitchen in the now abandoned farmhouse of John Wright, a gloomy kitchen, and left without having been put in order — the walls covered with a faded wall paper. Down right is a door leading to the parlor. On the right wall above this door is a built-in kitchen cupboard with shelves in the upper portion and drawers below. In the rear wall at right, up two steps is a door opening onto stairs leading to the second floor. In the rear wall at left is a door to the shed and from there to the outside. Between these two doors is an old-fashioned black iron stove. Running along the left wall from the shed door is an old iron sink and sink shelf, in which is set a hand pump. Downstage of the sink is an uncurtained window. Near the window is an old wooden rocker. Center stage is an unpainted wooden kitchen table with straight chairs on either side. There is a small chair down right. Unwashed pans under the sink, a loaf of bread outside the breadbox, a dish towel on the table — other signs of incompleted work. At the rear the shed door opens and the Sheriff comes in followed by the County Attorney and Hale. The Sheriff and Hale are men in middle life, the County Attorney is a young man; all are much bundled up and go at once to the stove. They are followed by the two women — the Sheriff's wife, Mrs. Peters, first; she is a slight wiry woman, a thin nervous face. Mrs. Hale is larger and would ordinarily be called more comfortable looking, but she is disturbed now and looks fearfully about as she enters. The women have come in slowly, and stand close together near the door.*

County Attorney (at stove rubbing his hands). This feels good. Come up to the fire, ladies.

Mrs. Peters (after taking a step forward). I'm not — cold.

Sheriff (unbuttoning his overcoat and stepping away from the stove to right of table as if to mark the beginning of official business). Now, Mr. Hale, before we move things about, you explain to Mr. Henderson just what you saw when you came here yesterday morning.

County Attorney (crossing down to left of the table). By the way, has anything been moved? Are things just as you left them yesterday?

Sheriff (looking about). It's just about the same. When it dropped below zero last night I thought I'd better send Frank out

Marjorie Vonnegut, Elinor M. Cox, John King, Arthur F. Hole, and T. W. Gibson are shown in a scene from Trifles. *This photograph was published in* Theatre Magazine, *January 1917. Photograph courtesy of the New York Public Library, The Billy Rose Theatre Collection.*

this morning to make a fire for us — (*sits right of center table*) no use getting pneumonia with a big case on, but I told him not to touch anything except the stove — and you know Frank.

County Attorney. Somebody should have been left here yesterday.

Sheriff. Oh — yesterday. When I had to send Frank to Morris Center for that man who went crazy — I want you to know I had my hands full yesterday. I knew you could get back from Omaha by today and as long as I went over everything here myself ——

County Attorney. Well, Mr. Hale, tell just what happened when you came here yesterday morning.

Hale (*crossing down to above table*). Harry and I had started to town with a load of potatoes. We came along the road from my place and as I got here I said, "I'm going to see if I can't get John Wright to go in with me on a party telephone." I spoke to Wright about it once before and he put me off, saying folks talked too much anyway, and all he asked was peace and quiet — I guess you know about how much he talked himself; but I thought maybe if I went to the house and talked about it before his wife, though I said to Harry that I didn't know as what his wife wanted made much difference to John ——

County Attorney. Let's talk about that later, Mr. Hale. I do want to talk about that, but tell now just what happened when you got to the house.

Hale. I didn't hear or see anything; I knocked at the door, and still it was all quiet inside. I knew they must be up, it was past eight o'clock. So I knocked again, and I thought I heard somebody say, "Come in." I wasn't sure, I'm not sure yet, but I opened the door — this door (*indicating the door by which the two women are still standing*) and there in that rocker — (*pointing to it*) sat Mrs. Wright. (*They all look at the rocker down left.*)

County Attorney. What — was she doing?

Hale. She was rockin' back and forth. She had her apron in her hand and was kind of — pleating it.

County Attorney. And how did she — look?

Hale. Well, she looked queer.

County Attorney. How do you mean — queer?

Hale. Well, as if she didn't know what she was going to do next. And kind of done up.

County Attorney (*takes out notebook and pencil and sits left of center table*). How did she seem to feel about your coming?

Hale. Why, I don't think she minded — one way or other. She didn't pay much attention. I said, "How do, Mrs. Wright, it's cold, ain't it?" And she said, "Is it?" — and went on kind of pleating at her apron. Well, I was surprised; she didn't ask me to come up to the stove, or to set down, but just sat there, not even looking at me, so I said, "I want to see John." And then she — laughed. I guess you would call it a laugh. I thought of Harry and the team outside, so I said a little sharp: "Can't I see John?" "No," she says, kind o' dull like. "Ain't he home?" says I. "Yes," says she, "he's home." "Then why can't I see him?" I asked her, out of patience. "'Cause he's dead," says she. "*Dead?*" says I. She just nodded her head, not getting a bit excited, but rockin' back and forth. "Why — where is he?" says I, not knowing what to say. She just pointed upstairs — like that. (*Himself pointing to the room above.*) I started for the stairs, with the idea of going up there. I walked from there to here — then I says, "Why, what did he die of?" "He died of a rope round his neck," says she, and just went on pleatin' at her apron. Well, I went out and called Harry. I thought I might — need help. We went upstairs and there he was lyin' ——

County Attorney. I think I'd rather have you go into that upstairs, where you can point it all out. Just go on now with the rest of the story.

Hale. Well, my first thought was to get that rope off. It looked . . . (*stops, his face twitches*) . . . but Harry, he went up to him, and he said, "No, he's dead all right, and we'd better not touch anything." So we went back downstairs. She was still sitting that same way. "Has anybody been notified?" I asked. "No," says she, unconcerned. "Who did this, Mrs. Wright?" said Harry. He said it business-like — and she stopped pleatin' of her apron. "I don't know," she says. "You don't *know?*" says Harry. "No," says she. "Weren't you sleepin' in the bed with him?" says Harry. "Yes," says she, "but I was on the inside." "Somebody slipped a rope round his neck and strangled him and you didn't wake up?" says Harry. "I didn't wake up," she said after him. We must 'a' looked as if we didn't see how that could be, for after a minute she said, "I sleep sound." Harry was going to ask her more questions but I said maybe we ought to let her tell her story first to the coroner, or the sheriff, so Harry went fast as he could to Rivers' place, where there's a telephone.

County Attorney. And what did Mrs. Wright do when she knew that you had gone for the coroner?

Hale. She moved from the rocker to that chair over there (*pointing to a small chair in the down right corner*) and just sat there with her hands held together and looking down. I got a feeling that I ought to make some conversation, so I said I had come in to see if John wanted to put in a telephone, and at that she started to laugh, and then she stopped and looked at me — scared. (*The County Attorney, who has had his notebook out, makes a note.*) I dunno, maybe it wasn't scared. I wouldn't like to say it was. Soon Harry got back, and then Dr. Lloyd came and you, Mr. Peters, and so I guess that's all I know that you don't.

County Attorney (*rising and looking around*). I guess we'll go upstairs first — and then out to the barn and around there. (*To the Sheriff.*) You're convinced that there was nothing important here — nothing that would point to any motive?

Sheriff. Nothing here but kitchen things. (*The County Attorney, after again looking around the kitchen, opens the door of a cupboard closet in right wall. He brings a small chair from right — gets on it and looks on a shelf. Pulls his hand away, sticky.*)

County Attorney. Here's a nice mess. (*The women draw nearer up center.*)

Mrs. Peters (*to the other woman*). Oh, her fruit; it did freeze. (*To the Lawyer.*) She worried about that when it turned so cold. She said the fire'd go out and her jars would break.

Sheriff (*rises*). Well, can you beat the women! Held for murder and worryin' about her preserves.

County Attorney (*getting down from chair*). I guess before we're through she may have something more serious than preserves to worry about. (*Crosses down right center.*)

Hale. Well, women are used to worrying over trifles. (*The two women move a little closer together.*)

County Attorney (*with the gallantry of a young politician*). And yet, for all their worries, what would we do without the ladies? (*The women do not unbend. He goes below the center table to the sink, takes a dipperful of water from the pail and pouring it into a basin, washes his hands. While he is doing this the Sheriff and Hale cross to cupboard, which they inspect. The County Attorney starts to wipe his hands on the roller towel, turns it for a cleaner place.*) Dirty towels! (*Kicks his foot against the pans under the sink.*) Not much of a housekeeper, would you say, ladies?

Mrs. Hale (*stiffly*). There's a great deal of work to be done on a farm.

County Attorney. To be sure. And yet (*with a little bow to her*) I know there are some Dickson County farmhouses which do not have such roller towels. (*He gives it a pull to expose its full length again.*)

Mrs. Hale. Those towels get dirty awful quick. Men's hands aren't always as clean as they might be.

County Attorney. Ah, loyal to your sex, I see. But you and Mrs. Wright were neighbors. I suppose you were friends, too.

Mrs. Hale (shaking her head). I've not seen much of her of late years. I've not been in this house — it's more than a year.

County Attorney (crossing to women up center). And why was that? You didn't like her?

Mrs. Hale. I liked her all well enough. Farmers' wives have their hands full, Mr. Henderson. And then ——

County Attorney. Yes ——?

Mrs. Hale (looking about). It never seemed a very cheerful place.

County Attorney. No — it's not cheerful. I shouldn't say she had the homemaking instinct.

Mrs. Hale. Well, I don't know as Wright had, either.

County Attorney. You mean that they didn't get on very well?

Mrs. Hale. No, I don't mean anything. But I don't think a place'd be any cheerfuller for John Wright's being in it.

County Attorney. I'd like to talk more of that a little later. I want to get the lay of things upstairs now. (*He goes past the women to up right where steps lead to a stair door.*)

Sheriff. I suppose anything Mrs. Peters does'll be all right. She was to take in some clothes for her, you know, and a few little things. We left in such a hurry yesterday.

County Attorney. Yes, but I would like to see what you take, Mrs. Peters, and keep an eye out for anything that might be of use to us.

Mrs. Peters. Yes, Mr. Henderson. (*The men leave by up right door to stairs. The women listen to the men's steps on the stairs, then look about the kitchen.*)

Mrs. Hale (crossing left to sink). I'd hate to have men coming into my kitchen, snooping around and criticizing. (*She arranges the pans under sink which the Lawyer had shoved out of place.*)

Mrs. Peters. Of course it's no more than their duty. (*Crosses to cupboard up right.*)

Mrs. Hale. Duty's all right, but I guess that deputy sheriff that came out to make the fire might have got a little of this on. (*Gives the roller towel a pull.*) Wish I'd thought of that sooner. Seems mean to talk about her for not having things slicked up when she had to come away in such a hurry. (*Crosses right to Mrs. Peters at cupboard.*)

Mrs. Peters (who has been looking through cupboard, lifts one end of towel that covers a pan). She had bread set. (*Stands still.*)

*Mrs. Hale (eyes fixed on a loaf of bread beside the breadbox, which is *on a low shelf of the cupboard.*) She was going to put this in there. (*Picks up loaf, then abruptly drops it. In a manner of returning to familiar things.*) It's a shame about her fruit. I wonder if it's all gone. (*Gets up on the chair and looks.*) I think there's some here that's all right, Mrs. Peters. Yes — here; (*holding it toward the window*) this is cherries, too. (*Looking again.*) I declare I believe that's the only one. (*Gets down, jar in her hand. Goes to the sink and wipes it off on the outside.*) She'll feel awful bad after all her hard work in the hot weather. I remember the afternoon I put up my cherries last summer. (*She puts the jar on the big kitchen table, center of the room. With a sigh, is about to sit down in the rocking chair. Before she is seated realizes what chair it is; with a slow look at it, steps back. The chair which she has touched rocks back and forth. Mrs. Peters moves to center table and they both watch the chair rock for a moment or two.*)

Mrs. Peters (*shaking off the mood which the empty rocking chair has evoked. Now in a businesslike manner she speaks*). Well I must get those things from the front room closet. (*She goes to the door at the right but, after looking into the other room, steps back.*) You coming with me, Mrs. Hale? You could help me carry them. (*They go in the other room; reappear, Mrs. Peters carrying a dress, petticoat and skirt, Mrs. Hale following with a pair of shoes.*) My, it's cold in there. (*She puts the clothes on the big table, and hurries to the stove.*)

Mrs. Hale (*right of center table examining the skirt*). Wright was close. I think maybe that's why she kept so much to herself. She didn't even belong to the Ladies' Aid. I suppose she felt she couldn't do her part, and then you don't enjoy things when you feel shabby. I heard she used to wear pretty clothes and be lively, when she was Minnie Foster, one of the town girls singing in the choir. But that — oh, that was thirty years ago. This all you want to take in?

Mrs. Peters. She said she wanted an apron. Funny thing to want, for there isn't much to get you dirty in jail, goodness knows. But I suppose just to make her feel more natural. (*Crosses to cupboard.*) She said they was in the top drawer in this cupboard. Yes, here. And then her little shawl that always hung behind the door. (*Opens stair door and looks.*) Yes, here it is. (*Quickly shuts door leading upstairs.*)

Mrs. Hale (*abruptly moving toward her*). Mrs. Peters?

Mrs. Peters. Yes, Mrs. Hale? (*At up right door.*)

Mrs. Hale. Do you think she did it?

Mrs. Peters (*in a frightened voice*). Oh, I don't know.

Mrs. Hale. Well, I don't think she did. Asking for an apron and her little shawl. Worrying about her fruit.

Mrs. Peters (*starts to speak, glances up, where footsteps are heard in the room above. In a low voice*). Mr. Peters says it looks bad for her. Mr. Henderson is awful sarcastic in a speech and he'll make fun of her sayin' she didn't wake up.

Mrs. Hale. Well, I guess John Wright didn't wake when they was slipping that rope under his neck.

Mrs. Peters (*crossing slowly to table and placing shawl and apron on table with other clothing*). No, it's strange. It must have been done awful crafty and still. They say it was such a — funny way to kill a man, rigging it all up like that.

Mrs. Hale (*crossing to left of Mrs. Peters at table*). That's just what Mr. Hale said. There was a gun in the house. He says that's what he can't understand.

Mrs. Peters. Mr. Henderson said coming out that what was needed for the case was a motive; something to show anger, or — sudden feeling.

Mrs. Hale (*who is standing by the table*). Well, I don't see any signs of anger around here. (*She puts her hand on the dish towel which lies on the table, stands looking down at table, one-half of which is clean, the other half messy.*) It's wiped to here. (*Makes a move as if to finish work, then turns and looks at loaf of bread outside the breadbox. Drops towel. In that voice of coming back to familiar things.*) Wonder how they are finding things upstairs. (*Crossing below table to down right.*) I hope she had it a little more red-up up there. You know, it seems kind of *sneaking*. Locking her up in town and then coming out here and trying to get her own house to turn against her!

Mrs. Peters. But, Mrs. Hale, the law is the law.

Mrs. Hale. I s'pose 'tis. (*Unbuttoning her coat.*) Better loosen up your things, Mrs. Peters. You won't feel them when you go out. (*Mrs. Peters takes off her fur tippet, goes to hang it on chair back left of table, stands looking at the work basket on floor near down left window.*)

Mrs. Peters. She was piecing a quilt. (*She brings the large sewing basket to the center table and they look at the bright pieces, Mrs. Hale above the table and Mrs. Peters left of it.*)

Mrs. Hale. It's a log cabin pattern. Pretty, isn't it? I wonder if she was goin' to quilt it or just knot it? (*Footsteps have been heard coming down the stairs. The Sheriff enters followed by Hale and the County Attorney.*)

Sheriff. They wonder if she was going to quilt it or just knot it! (*The men laugh, the women look abashed.*)

County Attorney (*rubbing his hands over the stove*). Frank's fire didn't do much up there, did it? Well, let's go out to the barn and get that cleared up. (*The men go outside by up left door.*)

Mrs. Hale (*resentfully*). I don't know as there's anything so strange, our takin' up our time with little things while we're waiting for them to get the evidence. (*She sits in chair right of table smoothing out a block with decision.*) I don't see as it's anything to laugh about.

Mrs. Peters (*apologetically*). Of course they've got awful important things on their minds. (*Pulls up a chair and joins Mrs. Hale at the left of the table.*)

Mrs. Hale (*examining another block*). Mrs. Peters, look at this one. Here, this is the one she was working on, and look at the sewing! All the rest of it has been so nice and even. And look at this! It's all over the place! Why, it looks as if she didn't know what she was about! (*After she has said this they look at each other, then start to glance back at the door. After an instant Mrs. Hale has pulled at a knot and ripped the sewing.*)

Mrs. Peters. Oh, what are you doing, Mrs. Hale?

Mrs. Hale (*mildly*). Just pulling out a stitch or two that's not sewed very good. (*Threading a needle.*) Bad sewing always made me fidgety.

Mrs. Peters (*with a glance at door, nervously*). I don't think we ought to touch things.

Mrs. Hale. I'll just finish up this end. (*Suddenly stopping and leaning forward.*) Mrs. Peters?

Mrs. Peters. Yes, Mrs. Hale?

Mrs. Hale. What do you suppose she was so nervous about?

Mrs. Peters. Oh — I don't know. I don't know as she was nervous. I sometimes sew awful queer when I'm just tired. (*Mrs. Hale starts to say something, looks at Mrs. Peters, then goes on sewing.*) Well, I must get these things wrapped up. They may be through sooner than we think. (*Putting apron and other things together.*) I wonder where I can find a piece of paper, and string. (*Rises.*)

Mrs. Hale. In that cupboard, maybe.

Mrs. Peters (*crosses right looking in cupboard*). Why, here's a birdcage. (*Holds it up.*) Did she have a bird, Mrs. Hale?

Mrs. Hale. Why, I don't know whether she did or not — I've not been here for so long. There was a man around last year selling canaries cheap, but I don't know as she took one; maybe she did. She used to sing real pretty herself.

Mrs. Peters (*glancing around*). Seems funny to think of a bird here. But she must have had one, or why would she have a cage? I wonder what happened to it?

Mrs. Hale. I s'pose maybe the cat got it.

Mrs. Peters. No, she didn't have a cat. She's got that feeling some people have about cats — being afraid of them. My cat got in her room and she was real upset and asked me to take it out.

Mrs. Hale. My sister Bessie was like that. Queer, ain't it?

Mrs. Peters (examining the cage). Why, look at this door. It's broke. One hinge is pulled apart. (*Takes a step down to Mrs. Hale's right.*)

Mrs. Hale (looking too). Looks as if someone must have been rough with it.

Mrs. Peters. Why, yes. (*She brings the cage forward and puts it on the table.*)

Mrs. Hale (glancing toward up left door). I wish if they're going to find any evidence they'd be about it. I don't like this place.

Mrs. Peters. But I'm awful glad you came with me, Mrs. Hale. It would be lonesome for me sitting here alone.

Mrs. Hale. It would, wouldn't it? (*Dropping her sewing.*) But I tell you what I do wish, Mrs. Peters. I wish I had come over sometimes when *she* was here. I — (*looking around the room*) — wish I had.

Mrs. Peters. But of course you were awful busy, Mrs. Hale — your house and your children.

Mrs. Hale (rises and crosses left). I could've come. I stayed away because it weren't cheerful — and that's why I ought to have come. I — (*looking out left window*) — I've never liked this place. Maybe because it's down in a hollow and you don't see the road. I dunno what it is, but it's a lonesome place and always was. I wish I had come over to see Minnie Foster sometimes. I can see now — (*Shakes her head.*)

Mrs. Peters (left of table and above it). Well, you mustn't reproach yourself, Mrs. Hale. Somehow we just don't see how it is with other folks until — something turns up.

Mrs. Hale. Not having children makes less work — but it makes a quiet house, and Wright out to work all day, and no company when he did come in. (*Turning from window.*) Did you know John Wright, Mrs. Peters?

Mrs. Peters. Not to know him; I've seen him in town. They say he was a good man.

Mrs. Hale. Yes — good; he didn't drink, and kept his word as well as most, I guess, and paid his debts. But he was a hard man, Mrs. Peters. Just to pass the time of day with him — — (*Shivers.*) Like a raw wind that gets to the bone. (*Pauses, her eye falling on the cage.*) I should think she would 'a' wanted a bird. But what do you suppose went with it?

Mrs. Peters. I don't know, unless it got sick and died. (*She reaches over and swings the broken door, swings it again, both women watch it.*)

Mrs. Hale. You weren't raised round here, were you? (*Mrs. Peters shakes her head.*) You didn't know — her?

Mrs. Peters. Not till they brought her yesterday.

Mrs. Hale. She — come to think of it, she was kind of like a bird herself — real sweet and pretty, but kind of timid and — fluttery. How — she — did — change. (*Silence: then as if struck by a happy thought and relieved to get back to everyday things. Crosses right above Mrs. Peters to cupboard, replaces small chair used to stand on to its original place down right.*) Tell you what, Mrs. Peters, why don't you take the quilt in with you? It might take up her mind.

Mrs. Peters. Why, I think that's a real nice idea, Mrs. Hale. There couldn't possibly be any objection to it could there? Now, just what would I take? I wonder if her patches are in here — and her things. (*They look in the sewing basket.*)

Mrs. Hale (crosses to right of table). Here's some red. I expect this has got sewing things in it. (*Brings out a fancy box.*) What a pretty box. Looks like something somebody would give you. Maybe her scissors are in here. (*Opens box. Suddenly puts her hand to her nose.*) Why —— (*Mrs. Peters bends nearer, then turns her face away.*) There's something wrapped up in this piece of silk.

Mrs. Peters. Why, this isn't her scissors.

Mrs. Hale (lifting the silk). Oh, Mrs. Peters — it's —— (*Mrs. Peters bends closer.*)

Mrs. Peters. It's the bird.

Mrs. Hale. But, Mrs. Peters — look at it! Its neck! Look at its neck! It's all — other side *to.*

Mrs. Peters. Somebody — wrung — its — neck. (*Their eyes meet. A look of growing comprehension, of horror. Steps are heard outside. Mrs. Hale slips box under quilt pieces, and sinks into her chair. Enter Sheriff and County Attorney. Mrs. Peters steps down left and stands looking out of window.*)

County Attorney (as one turning from serious things to little pleasantries). Well, ladies, have you decided whether she was going to quilt it or knot it? (*Crosses to center above table.*)

Mrs. Peters. We think she was going to — knot it. (*Sheriff crosses to right of stove, lifts stove lid and glances at fire, then stands warming hands at stove.*)

County Attorney. Well, that's interesting, I'm sure. (*Seeing the birdcage.*) Has the bird flown?

Mrs. Hale (putting more quilt pieces over the box). We think the — cat got it.

County Attorney (preoccupied). Is there a cat? (*Mrs. Hale glances in a quick covert way at Mrs. Peters.*)

Mrs. Peters (turning from window takes a step in). Well, not *now*. They're superstitious, you know. They leave.

County Attorney (to Sheriff Peters, continuing an interrupted conversation). No sign at all of anyone having come from the outside. Their own rope. Now let's go up again and go over it piece by piece. (*They start upstairs.*) It would have to have been someone who knew just the —— (*Mrs. Peters sits down left of table. The two women sit there not looking at one another, but as if peering into something and at the same time holding back. When they talk now it is in the manner of feeling their way over strange ground, as if afraid of what they are saying, but as if they cannot help saying it.*)

Mrs. Hale (hesitatively and in hushed voice). She liked the bird. She was going to bury it in that pretty box.

Mrs. Peters (in a whisper). When I was a girl — my kitten — there was a boy took a hatchet, and before my eyes — and before I could get there —— (*Covers her face an instant.*) If they hadn't held me back I would have — (*catches herself, looks upstairs where steps are heard, falters weakly*) — hurt him.

Mrs. Hale (with a slow look around her). I wonder how it would seem never to have had any children around. (*Pause.*) No, Wright wouldn't like the bird — a thing that sang. She used to sing. He killed that, too.

Mrs. Peters (moving uneasily). We don't know who killed the bird.

Mrs. Hale. I knew John Wright.

Mrs. Peters. It was an awful thing was done in this house that night, Mrs. Hale. Killing a man while he slept, slipping a rope around his neck that choked the life out of him.

Mrs. Hale. His neck. Choked the life out of him. (*Her hand goes out and rests on the bird-cage.*)

Mrs. Peters (with rising voice). We don't know who killed him. We don't *know*.

Mrs. Hale (her own feeling not interrupted). If there'd been years and years of nothing, then a bird to sing to you, it would be awful — still, after the bird was still.

Mrs. Peters (something within her speaking). I know what stillness is. When we homesteaded in Dakota, and my first baby died — after he was two years old, and me with no other then ——

Mrs. Hale (moving). How soon do you suppose they'll be through looking for the evidence?

Mrs. Peters. I know what stillness is. (*Pulling herself back.*) The law has got to punish crime, Mrs. Hale.

Mrs. Hale (not as if answering that). I wish you'd seen Minnie Foster when she wore a white dress with blue ribbons and stood up there in the choir and sang. (*A look around the room.*) Oh, I *wish* I'd come over here once in a while! That was a crime! That was a crime! Who's going to punish that?

Mrs. Peters (*looking upstairs*). We mustn't — take on.

Mrs. Hale. I might have known she needed help! I know how things can be — for women. I tell you, it's queer, Mrs. Peters. We live close together and we live far apart. We all go through the same things — it's all just a different kind of the same thing. (*Brushes her eyes, noticing the jar of fruit, reaches out for it.*) If I was you I wouldn't tell her her fruit was gone. Tell her it *ain't*. Tell her it's all right. Take this in to prove it to her. She — she may never know whether it was broke or not.

Mrs. Peters (*takes the jar, looks about for something to wrap it in; takes petticoat from the clothes brought from the other room, very nervously begins winding this around the jar. In a false voice*). My, it's a good thing the men couldn't hear us. Wouldn't they just laugh! Getting all stirred up over a little thing like a — dead canary. As if that could have anything to do with — with — wouldn't they *laugh*! (*The men are heard coming downstairs.*)

Mrs. Hale (*under her breath*). Maybe they would — maybe they wouldn't.

County Attorney. No, Peters, it's all perfectly clear except a reason for doing it. But you know juries when it comes to women. If there was some definite thing. (*Crosses slowly to above table. Sheriff crosses down right. Mrs. Hale and Mrs. Peters remain seated at either side of table.*) Something to show — something to make a story about — a thing that would connect up with this strange way of doing it —— (*The women's eyes meet for an instant. Enter Hale from outer door.*)

Hale (*remaining by door*). Well, I've got the team around. Pretty cold out there.

County Attorney. I'm going to stay awhile by myself. (*To the Sheriff.*) You can send Frank out for me, can't you? I want to go over everything. I'm not satisfied that we can't do better.

Sheriff. Do you want to see what Mrs. Peters is going to take in? (*The Lawyer picks up the apron, laughs.*)

County Attorney. Oh, I guess they're not very dangerous things the ladies have picked out. (*Moves a few things about, disturbing the quilt pieces which cover the box. Steps back.*) No, Mrs. Peters doesn't need supervising. For that matter a sheriff's wife is married to the law. Ever think of it that way, Mrs. Peters?

Mrs. Peters. Not — just that way.

Sherriff (*chuckling*). Married to the law. (*Moves to down right door to the other room.*) I just want you to come in here a minute, George. We ought to take a look at these windows.

County Attorney (*scoffingly*). Oh, windows!

Sheriff. We'll be right out, Mr. Hale. (*Hale goes outside. The Sheriff follows the County Attorney into the room. Then Mrs. Hale rises, hands tight together, looking intensely at Mrs. Peters, whose eyes make a slow turn, finally meeting Mrs. Hale's. A moment Mrs. Hale holds her, then her own eyes point the way to where the box is concealed. Suddenly Mrs. Peters throws back quilt pieces and tries to put the box in the bag she is carrying. It is too big. She opens box, starts to take bird out, cannot touch it, goes to pieces, stands there helpless. Sound of a knob turning in the other room. Mrs. Hale snatches the box and puts it in the pocket of her big coat. Enter County Attorney and Sheriff, who remains down right.*)

County Attorney (*crosses to up left door facetiously*). Well, Henry, at least we found out that she was not going to quilt it. She was going to — what is it you call it, ladies?

Mrs. Hale (*standing center below table facing front, her hand against her pocket*). We call it — knot it, Mr. Henderson.

Curtain

QUESTIONS

1. How would you characterize Mr. Henderson, the County Attorney?
2. In what way or ways are Mrs. Peters and Mrs. Hale different?
3. Several times the men "laugh" or "chuckle." In their contexts, what do these expressions of amusement convey?
4. On page 964, "*the women's eyes meet for an instant.*" What does this bit of action "say"? What do we understand by the exchange of glances?
5. On page 963, when Mrs. Peters tells of the boy who killed her cat, she says, "If they hadn't held me back I would have (*catches herself, looks upstairs where steps are heard, falters weakly*) —hurt him." What was she about to say before she faltered? Why does Glaspell include this speech about Mrs. Peters's girlhood?
6. On page 959 Mrs. Hale, looking at a quilt, wonders whether Mrs. Wright "was goin' to quilt it or just knot it." The men are amused by the women's concern with this topic, and the last line of the play returns to this issue. What is the point?
7. In what way or ways is the play ironic? [Consult the entry on "irony" in the index of critical terms.]
8. Can it reasonably be argued that this play is immoral?

This is a scene from the opening production of The Glass Menagerie *at The Playhouse in New York on March 31, 1945, starring Lorette Taylor, Julie Hayden, Eddie Dowling, and Anthony Ross. Reproduced by courtesy of the New York Public Library, The Billy Rose Theater Collection.*

Tennessee Williams (1914–1983)

The Glass Menagerie

Nobody, not even the rain, has such small hands.
— *E. E. Cummings*

List of Characters

Amanda Wingfield, the mother. A little woman of great but confused vitality clinging frantically to another time and place. Her characterization must be carefully created, not copied from type. She is not paranoiac, but her life is paranoia. There is much to admire in Amanda, and as much to love and pity as there is to laugh at. Certainly she has endurance and a kind of heroism, and though her foolishness makes her unwittingly cruel at times, there is tenderness in her slight person.

Laura Wingfield, her daughter. Amanda, having failed to establish contact with reality, continues to live vitally in her illusions, but Laura's situation is even graver. A childhood illness has left her crippled, one leg slightly shorter than the other, and held in a brace. This defect need not be more than suggested on the stage. Stemming from this, Laura's separation increases till she is like a piece of her own glass collection, too exquisitely fragile to move from the shelf.

Tom Wingfield, her son. And the narrator of the play. A poet with a job in a warehouse. His nature is not remorseless, but to escape from a trap he has to act without pity.

Jim O'Connor, the gentleman caller. A nice, ordinary, young man.

Scene. *An alley in St. Louis.*

Part I *Preparation for a Gentleman Caller.*
Part II *The Gentleman Calls.*

Time. *Now and the Past.*

SCENE I

The Wingfeld apartment is in the rear of the building, one of those vast hive-like conglomerations of cellular living-units that flower as warty growths in overcrowded urban centers of lower middle-class population and are symptomatic of the impulse of this largest and fundamentally enslaved section of American society to avoid fluidity and differentiation and to exist and function as one interfused mass of automatism.

The apartment faces an alley and is entered by a fire-escape, a structure whose name is a touch of accidental poetic truth, for all of these huge buildings are always burning with the slow and implacable fires of human desperation. The fire-escape is included in the set — that is, the landing of it and steps descending from it.

The scene is memory and is therefore nonrealistic. Memory takes a lot of poetic license. It omits some details; others are exaggerated, according to the emotional value of the articles it touches, for memory is seated predominantly in the heart. The interior is therefore rather dim and poetic.

At the rise of the curtain, the audience is faced with the dark, grim rear wall of the Wingfeld tenement. This building, which runs parallel to the footlights, is flanked on both sides by dark, narrow alleys which run into murky canyons of tangled clotheslines, garbage cans and the sinister latticework of neighboring fire-escapes. It is up and down these side alleys that exterior entrances and exits are made, during the play. At the end of Tom's opening commentary, the dark tenement wall slowly reveals (by means of a transparency) the interior of the ground floor Wingfield apartment.

Downstage is the living room, which also serves as a sleeping room for Laura, the sofa unfolding to make her bed. Upstage, center, and divided by a wide arch or second proscenium with transparent faded portieres (or second curtain), is the dining room. In an old-fashioned what-not in the living room are seen scores of transparent glass animals. A blown-up photograph of the father hangs on the wall of the living room, facing the audience, to the left of the archway. It is the face of a very handsome young man in a doughboy's First World War cap. He is gallantly smiling, ineluctably smiling, as if to say, "I will be smiling forever."

The audience hears and sees the opening scene in the dining room through both the transparent fourth wall of the building and the transparent gauze portieres of the dining-room arch. It is during this revealing scene that the fourth wall slowly ascends, out of sight.

This transparent exterior wall is not brought down again until the very end of the play, during Tom's final speech.

The narrator is an undisguised convention of the play. He takes whatever license with dramatic convention as is convenient to his purposes.

Tom enters dressed as a merchant sailor from alley, stage left, and strolls across the front of the stage to the fire-escape. There he stops and lights a cigarette. He addresses the audience.

Tom. Yes, I have tricks in my pocket, I have things up my sleeve. But I am the opposite of a stage magician. He gives you illusion that has the appearance of truth. I give you truth in the pleasant disguise of illusion. To begin with, I turn back time. I reverse it to that quaint period, the thirties, when the huge middle class of America was matriculating in a school for the blind. Their eyes had failed them, or they had failed their eyes, and so they were having their fingers pressed forcibly down on the fiery Braille alphabet of a dissolving economy. In Spain there was revolution. Here there was only shouting and confusion. In Spain there was Guernica. Here there were disturbances of labor, sometimes pretty violent, in otherwise peaceful cities such as Chicago, Cleveland, Saint Louis. . . . This is the social background of the play.

(Music.)

The play is memory. Being a memory play, it is dimly lighted, it is sentimental, it is not realistic. In memory everything seems to happen to music. That explains the fiddle in the wings. I am the narrator of the play, and also a character in it. The other characters are my mother, Amanda, my sister, Laura, and a gentleman caller who appears in the final scenes. He is the most realistic character in the play, being an emissary from a world of reality that we were somehow set apart from. But since I have a poet's weakness for symbols, I am using this character also as a symbol; he is the long delayed but always expected something that we live for. There is a fifth character in the play who doesn't appear except in this larger-than-life photograph over the mantel. This is our father who left us a long time ago. He was a telephone man who fell in love with long distances; he gave up his job with the telephone company and skipped the light fantastic out of town. . . . The last we heard of him was a picture post-card from Mazatlan, on the Pacific coast of Mexico, containing a message of two words — "Hello — Good-bye!" and no address. I think the rest of the play will explain itself. . . .

Amanda's voice becomes audible through the portieres.

(Legend On Screen: "Où Sont Les Neiges.")

He divides the portieres and enters the upstage area.

Amanda and Laura are seated at a drop-leaf table. Eating is indicated by gestures without food or utensils. Amanda faces the audience. Tom and Laura are seated in profile.

The interior has lit up softly and through the scrim we see Amanda and Laura seated at the table in the upstage area.

Amanda (calling). Tom?

Tom. Yes, Mother.

Amanda. We can't say grace until you come to the table!

Tom. Coming, Mother. (*He bows slightly and withdraws, reappearing a few moments later in his place at the table.*)

Amanda (to her son). Honey, don't *push* with your *fingers*. If you have to push with something, the thing to push with is a crust of bread. And chew — chew! Animals have sections in their stomachs which enable them to digest food without mastication, but human beings are supposed to chew their food before they swallow it down. Eat food leisurely, son, and really enjoy it. A well-cooked meal has lots of delicate flavors that have to be held in the mouth for appreciation. So chew your food and give your salivary glands a chance to function!

Tom deliberately lays his imaginary fork down and pushes his chair back from the table.

Tom. I haven't enjoyed one bite of this dinner because of your constant directions on how to eat it. It's you that makes me rush through meals with your hawk-like attention to every bite I take. Sickening — spoils my appetite — all this discussion of animals' secretion — salivary glands — mastication!

Amanda (lightly). Temperament like a Metropolitan star! (*He rises and crosses downstage.*) You're not excused from the table.

Tom. I am getting a cigarette.

Amanda. You smoke too much.

Laura rises.

Laura. I'll bring in the blanc mange.

He remains standing with his cigarette by the portieres during the following.

Amanda (rising). No, sister, no, sister — you be the lady this time and I'll be the darky.

Laura. I'm already up.

Amanda. Resume your seat, little sister — I want you to stay fresh and pretty — for gentlemen callers!

Laura. I'm not expecting any gentlemen callers.

Amanda (crossing out to kitchenette. Airily). Sometimes they come when they are least expected! Why, I remember one Sunday afternoon in Blue Mountain — *(Enters kitchenette.)*

Tom. I know what's coming!

Laura. Yes. But let her tell it.

Tom. Again?

Laura. She loves to tell it.

Amanda returns with bowl of dessert.

Amanda. One Sunday afternoon in Blue Mountain — your mother received — *seventeen!* — gentlemen callers! Why, sometimes there weren't chairs enough to accommodate them all. We had to send the nigger over to bring in folding chairs from the parish house.

Tom (remaining at portieres). How did you entertain those gentlemen callers?

Amanda. I understood the art of conversation!

Tom. I bet you could talk.

Amanda. Girls in those days *knew* how to talk, I can tell you.

Tom. Yes?

(Image: Amanda As A Girl On A Porch Greeting Callers.)

Amanda. They knew how to entertain their gentlemen callers. It wasn't enough for a girl to be possessed of a pretty face and a graceful figure — although I wasn't slighted in either respect. She also needed to have a nimble wit and a tongue to meet all occasions.

Tom. What did you talk about?

Amanda. Things of importance going on in the world! Never anything coarse or common or vulgar. *(She addresses Tom as though he were seated in the vacant chair at the table though he remains by portieres. He plays this scene as though he held the book.)* My callers were gentlemen — all! Among my callers

were some of the most prominent young planters of the
Mississippi Delta — planters and sons of planters!

Tom motions for music and a spot of light on Amanda.
Her eyes lift, her face glows, her voice becomes rich and elegiac.

(Screen Legend: "Où Sont Les Neiges.")

There was young Champ Laughlin who later became vice-
president of the Delta Planters Bank. Hadley Stevenson who
was drowned in Moon Lake and left his widow one hundred
and fifty thousand in Government bonds. There were the
Cutrere brothers, Wesley and Bates. Bates was one of my
bright particular beaux! He got in a quarrel with that wild
Wainright boy. They shot it out on the floor of Moon Lake
Casino. Bates was shot through the stomach. Died in the
ambulance on his way to Memphis. His widow was also
well-provided for, came into eight or ten thousand acres,
that's all. She married him on the rebound — never loved
her — carried my picture on him the night he died! And
there was that boy that every girl in the Delta had set her
cap for! That beautiful, brilliant young Fitzhugh boy from
Green County!

Tom. What did he leave his widow?

Amanda. He never married! Gracious, you talk as though all of
my old admirers had turned up their toes to the daisies!

Tom. Isn't this the first you mentioned that still survives?

Amanda. That Fitzhugh boy went North and made a fortune —
came to be known as the Wolf of Wall Street! He had the
Midas touch, whatever he touched turned to gold! And I
could have been Mrs. Duncan J. Fitzhugh, mind you! But
— I picked your *father!*

Laura (rising). Mother, let me clear the table.

Amanda. No dear, you go in front and study your typewriter
chart. Or practice your shorthand a little. Stay fresh and
pretty! — It's almost time for our gentlemen callers to start
arriving. (*She flounces girlishly toward the kitchenette.*) How
many do you suppose we're going to entertain this afternoon?

Tom throws down the paper and jumps up with a groan.

Laura (alone in the dining room). I don't believe we're going to
receive any, Mother.

Amanda (reappearing, airily). What? No one — not one? You must
be joking! (*Laura nervously echoes her laugh. She slips in a*

fugitive manner through the half-open portieres and draws them gently behind her. A shaft of very clear light is thrown on her face against the faded tapestry of the curtains.) **(Music: "The Glass Menagerie" Under Faintly.)** *(Lightly.)* Not one gentleman caller? It can't be true! There must be a flood, there must have been a tornado!

Laura. It isn't a flood, it's not a tornado, Mother. I'm just not popular like you were in Blue Mountain. . . . *(Tom utters another groan. Laura glances at him with a faint, apologetic smile. Her voice catching a little.)* Mother's afraid I'm going to be an old maid.

(The Scene Dims Out With "Glass Menagerie" Music.)

SCENE II

"Laura, Haven't You Ever Liked Some Boy?"

On the dark stage the screen is lighted with the image of blue roses.

Gradually Laura's figure becomes apparent and the screen goes out.

The music subsides.

Laura is seated in the delicate ivory chair at the small clawfoot table.

She wears a dress of soft violet material for a kimono — her hair tied back from her forehead with a ribbon.

She is washing and polishing her collection of glass.

Amanda appears on the fire-escape steps. At the sound of her ascent, Laura catches her breath, thrusts the bowl of ornaments away and seats herself stiffly before the diagram of the typewriter keyboard as though it held her spellbound. Something has happened to Amanda. It is written in her face as she climbs to the landing: a look that is grim and hopeless and a little absurd.

She has on one of those cheap or imitation velvety-looking cloth coats with imitation fur collar. Her hat is five or six years old, one of those dreadful cloche hats that were worn in the late twenties, and she is clasping an enormous black patent-leather pocketbook with nickel clasp and initials. This is her full-dress outfit, the one she usually wears to the D.A.R.

Before entering she looks through the door.

She purses her lips, opens her eyes wide, rolls them upward and shakes her head.

Then she slowly lets herself in the door. Seeing her mother's expression Laura touches her lips with a nervous gesture.

Laura. Hello, Mother, I was — (*She makes a nervous gesture toward the chart on the wall. Amanda leans against the shut door and stares at Laura with a martyred look.*)

Amanda. Deception? Deception? (*She slowly removes her hat and gloves, continuing the swift suffering stare. She lets the hat and gloves fall on the floor — a bit of acting.*)

Laura (*shakily*). How was the D.A.R. meeting? (*Amanda slowly opens her purse and removes a dainty white handkerchief which she shakes out delicately and delicately touches to her lips and nostrils.*) Didn't you go to the D.A.R. meeting, Mother?

Amanda (*faintly, almost inaudibly*). — No. — No. (*Then more forcibly.*) I did not have the strength — to go to the D.A.R. In fact, I did not have the courage! I wanted to find a hole in the ground and hide myself in it forever! (*She crosses slowly to the wall and removes the diagram of the typewriter keyboard. She holds it in front of her for a second, staring at it sweetly and sorrowfully — then bites her lips and tears it in two pieces.*)

Laura (*faintly*). Why did you do that, Mother? (*Amanda repeats the same procedure with the chart of the Gregg Alphabet.*) Why are you —

Amanda. Why? Why? How old are you, Laura?

Laura. Mother, you know my age.

Amanda. I thought that you were an adult; it seems that I was mistaken. (*She crosses slowly to the sofa and sinks down and stares at Laura.*)

Laura. Please don't stare at me, Mother.

Amanda closes her eyes and lowers her head. Count ten.

Amanda. What are we going to do, what is going to become of us, what is the future?

Count ten.

Laura. Has something happened, Mother? (*Amanda draws a long breath and takes out the handkerchief again. Dabbing process.*) Mother, has — something happened?

Amanda. I'll be all right in a minute. I'm just bewildered — (*count five*) — by life. . . .

Laura. Mother, I wish that you would tell me what's happened.

Amanda. As you know, I was supposed to be inducted into my office at the D.A.R. this afternoon. **(Image: A Swarm Of Typewriters.)** But I stopped off at Rubicam's Business College to speak to your teachers about your having a cold and ask them what progress they thought you were making down there.

Laura. Oh. . . .

Amanda. I went to the typing instructor and introduced myself as your mother. She didn't know who you were. Wingfield, she said. We don't have any such student enrolled at the school! I assured her she did, that you had been going to classes since early in January. "I wonder," she said, "if you could be talking about that terribly shy little girl who dropped out of school after only a few days' attendance?" "No," I said, "Laura, my daughter, has been going to school every day for the past six weeks!" "Excuse me," she said. She took the attendance book out and there was your name, unmistakably printed, and all the dates you were absent until they decided that you had dropped out of school. I still said, "No, there must have been some mistake! There must have been some mix-up in the records!" And she said, "No — I remember her perfectly now. Her hand shook so that she couldn't hit the right keys! The first time we gave a speed-test, she broke down completely — was sick at the stomach and almost had to be carried into the wash-room! After that morning she never showed up any more. We phoned the house but never got any answer" — while I was working at Famous and Barr, I suppose, demonstrating those — Oh! I felt so weak I could barely keep on my feet. I had to sit down while they got me a glass of water! Fifty dollars' tuition, all of our plans — my hopes and ambitions for you — just gone up the spout, just gone up the spout like that. (*Laura draws a long breath and gets awkwardly to her feet. She crosses to the victrola and winds it up.*) What are you doing?

Laura. Oh! (*She releases the handle and returns to her seat.*)

Amanda. Laura, where have you been going when you've gone out pretending that you were going to business college?

Laura. I've just been going out walking.

Amanda. That's not true.

Laura. It is. I just went walking.

Amanda. Walking? Walking? In winter? Deliberately courting pneumonia in that light coat? Where did you walk to, Laura?

Laura. It was the lesser of two evils, Mother. **(Image: Winter Scene In Park.)** I couldn't go back up. I — threw up — on the floor!

Amanda. From half past seven till after five every day you mean to tell me you walked around in the park, because you

wanted to make me think that you were still going to Rubicam's Business College?

Laura. It wasn't as bad as it sounds. I went inside places to get
warmed up.

Amanda. Inside where?

Laura. I went in the art museum and the bird-houses at the Zoo.
I visited the penguins every day! Sometimes I did without
lunch and went to the movies. Lately I've been spending
most of my afternoons in the Jewel-box, that big glass house
where they raise the tropical flowers.

Amanda. You did all this to deceive me, just for the deception?
(*Laura looks down.*) Why?

Laura. Mother, when you're disappointed, you get that awful
suffering look on your face, like the picture of Jesus' mother
in the museum!

Amanda. Hush!

Laura. I couldn't face it.

Pause. A whisper of strings.

(Legend: "The Crust Of Humility.")

Amanda (*hopelessly fingering the huge pocketbook*). So what are we
going to do the rest of our lives? Stay home and watch the
parades go by? Amuse ourselves with the glass menagerie,
darling? Eternally play those worn-out phonograph records
your father left as a painful reminder of him? We won't have
a business career — we've given that up because it gave us
nervous indigestion! (*Laughs wearily.*) What is there left but
dependency all our lives? I know so well what becomes of
unmarried women who aren't prepared to occupy a position.
I've seen such pitiful cases in the South — barely tolerated
spinsters living upon the grudging patronage of sister's husband
or brother's wife! — stuck away in some little mousetrap of
a room — encouraged by one in-law to visit another — little
birdlike women without any nest — eating the crust of humility
all their life! Is that the future that we've mapped out for
ourselves? I swear it's the only alternative I can think of! It
isn't a very pleasant alternative, is it? Of course — some
girls *do marry.* (*Laura twists her hands nervously.*) Haven't you
ever liked some boy?

Laura. Yes. I liked one once. (*Rises.*) I came across his picture a
while ago.

Amanda (*with some interest*). He gave you his picture?

Laura. No, it's in the year-book.
Amanda (*disappointed*). Oh — a high-school boy.

(Screen Image: Jim As A High-School Hero Bearing A Silver Cup.)

Laura. Yes. His name was Jim. (*Laura lifts the heavy annual from the clawfoot table.*) Here he is in *The Pirates of Penzance.*
Amanda (*absently*). The what?
Laura. The operetta the senior class put on. He had a wonderful voice and we sat across the aisle from each other Mondays, Wednesdays and Fridays in the Aud. Here he is with the silver cup for debating! See his grin?
Amanda (*absently*). He must have had a jolly disposition.
Laura. He used to call me — Blue Roses.

(Image: Blue Roses.)

Amanda. Why did he call you such a name as that?
Laura. When I had that attack of pleurosis — he asked me what was the matter when I came back. I said pleurosis — he thought that I said Blue Roses! So that's what he always called me after that. Whenever he saw me, he'd holler, "Hello, Blue Roses!" I didn't care for the girl that he went out with. Emily Meisenbach. Emily was the best-dressed girl at Soldan. She never struck me, though, as being sincere. . . . It says in the Personal Section — they're engaged. That's — six years ago! They must be married by now.
Amanda. Girls that aren't cut out for business careers usually wind up married to some nice man. (*Gets up with a spark of revival.*) Sister, that's what you'll do!

Laura utters a startled, doubtful laugh. She reaches quickly for a piece of glass.

Laura. But, Mother —
Amanda. Yes? (*Crossing to photograph.*)
Laura (*in a tone of frightened apology*). I'm — crippled!

(Image: Screen.)

Amanda. Nonsense! Laura, I've told you never, never to use that word. Why, you're not crippled, you just have a little defect — hardly noticeable, even! When people have some slight disadvantage like that, they cultivate other things to make up for it — develop charm — and vivacity — and — *charm!* That's all you have to do! (*She turns again to the photograph.*) One thing your father had *plenty of* — was *charm!*

Tom motions to the fiddle in the wings.

(The Scene Fades Out With Music.)

SCENE III

(Legend On The Screen: "After The Fiasco — ")

Tom speaks from the fire-escape landing.

Tom. After the fiasco at Rubicam's Business College, the idea of getting a gentleman caller for Laura began to play a more important part in Mother's calculations. It became an obsession. Like some archetype of the universal unconscious, the image of the gentleman caller haunted our small apartment. . . . **(Image: Young Man At Door With Flowers.)** An evening at home rarely passed without some allusion to this image, this specter, this hope. . . . Even when he wasn't mentioned, his presence hung in Mother's preoccupied look and in my sister's frightened, apologetic manner — hung like a sentence passed upon the Wingfields! Mother was a woman of action as well as words. She began to take logical steps in the planned direction. Late that winter and in the early spring — realizing that extra money would be needed to properly feather the nest and plume the bird — she conducted a vigorous campaign on the telephone, roping in subscribers to one of those magazines for matrons called *The Home-maker's Companion,* the type of journal that features the serialized sublimations of ladies of letters who think in terms of delicate cup-like breasts, slim, tapering waists, rich, creamy thighs, eyes like wood-smoke in autumn, fingers that soothe and caress like strains of music, bodies as powerful as Etruscan sculpture.

(Screen Image: Glamor Magazine Cover.)

Amanda enters with phone on long extension cord. She is spotted in the dim stage.

Amanda. Ida Scott? This is Amanda Wingfield! We *missed* you at the D.A.R. last Monday! I said to myself: She's probably suffering with that sinus condition! How is that sinus condition?

Horrors! Heaven have mercy! — You're a Christian martyr, yes, that's what you are, a Christian martyr! Well, I just now happened to notice that your subscription to the *Companion's* about to expire! Yes, it expires with the next issue, honey! — just when that wonderful new serial by Bessie Mae Hopper is getting off to such an exciting start. Oh, honey, it's something that you can't miss! You remember how *Gone With the Wind* took everybody by storm? You simply couldn't go out if you hadn't read it. All everybody *talked* was Scarlett O'Hara. Well, this is a book that critics already compare to *Gone With the Wind.* It's the *Gone With the Wind* of the post-World War generation! — What? — Burning? — Oh, honey, don't let them burn, go take a look in the oven and I'll hold the wire! Heavens — I think she's hung up!

(Dim Out.)

(Legend On Screen: "You Think I'm In Love With Continental Shoemakers?")

Before the stage is lighted, the violent voices of Tom and Amanda are heard. They are quarreling behind the portieres. In front of them stands Laura with clenched hands and panicky expression.

A clear pool of light on her figure throughout this scene.

Tom. What in Christ's name am I —
Amanda (shrilly). Don't you use that —
Tom. Supposed to do!
Amanda. Expression! Not in my —
Tom. Ohhh!
Amanda. Presence! Have you gone out of your senses?
Tom. I have, that's true, *driven* out!
Amanda. What is the matter with you, you — big — big — IDIOT!
Tom. Look — I've got *no thing,* no single thing —
Amanda. Lower your voice!
Tom. In my life here that I can call my OWN! Everything is —
Amanda. Stop that shouting!
Tom. Yesterday you confiscated my books! You had the nerve to —
Amanda. I took that horrible novel back to the library — yes! That hideous book by that insane Mr. Lawrence. (*Tom laughs wildly.*) I cannot control the output of diseased minds or people who cater to them — (*Tom laughs still more wildly.*) BUT I WON'T ALLOW SUCH FILTH BROUGHT INTO MY HOUSE! No, no, no, no, no!

Tom. House, house! Who pays rent on it, who makes a slave of himself to —

Amanda (fairly screeching). Don't you DARE to —

Tom. No, no, I musn't say things! *I've* got to just —

Amanda. Let me tell you —

Tom. I don't want to hear any more! (*He tears the portieres open. The upstage area is lit with a turgid smoky red glow.*)

Amanda's hair is in metal curlers and she wears a very old bathrobe, much too large for her slight figure, a relic of the faithless Mr. Wingfield.

An upright typewriter and a wild disarray of manuscripts are on the drop-leaf table. The quarrel was probably precipitated by Amanda's interruption of his creative labor. A chair lying overthrown on the floor.

Their gesticulating shadows are cast on the ceiling by the fiery glow.

Amanda. You *will* hear more, you —

Tom. No, I won't hear more, I'm going out!

Amanda. You come right back in —

Tom. Out, out out! Because I'm —

Amanda. Come back here, Tom Wingfield! I'm not through talking to you!

Tom. Oh, go —

Laura (desperately). Tom!

Amanda. You're going to listen, and no more insolence from you! I'm at the end of my patience! (*He comes back toward her.*)

Tom. What do you think I'm at? Aren't I supposed to have any patience to reach the end of, Mother? I know, I know. It seems unimportant to you, what I'm *doing* — what I *want* to do — having a little *difference* between them! You don't think that —

Amanda. I think you've been doing things that you're ashamed of. That's why you act like this. I don't believe that you go every night to the movies. Nobody goes to the movies night after night. Nobody in their right minds goes to the movies as often as you pretend to. People don't go to the movies at nearly midnight, and movies don't let out at two A.M. Come in stumbling. Muttering to yourself like a maniac! You get three hours' sleep and then go to work. Oh, I can picture the way you're doing down there. Moping, doping, because you're in no condition.

Tom (wildly). No, I'm in no condition!

Amanda. What right have you got to jeopardize your job? Jeopardize the security of us all? How do you think we'd manage if you were —

Tom. Listen! You think I'm crazy *about* the *warehouse?* (*He bends fiercely toward her slight figure.*) You think I'm in love with the Continental Shoemakers? You think I want to spend fifty-five *years* down there in that — *celotex interior!* with — *fluorescent* — *tubes!* Look! I'd rather somebody picked up a crowbar and battered out my brains — than go back mornings! I *go!* Every time you come in yelling that God damn *"Rise and Shine!" "Rise and Shine!"* I say to myself "How *lucky* dead people are!" But I get up. I *go!* For sixty-five dollars a month I give up all that I dream of doing and being *ever!* And you say self — *self's* all I ever think of. Why, listen, if self is what I thought of, Mother, I'd be where he is — GONE! (*Pointing to father's picture.*) As far as the system of transportation reaches! (*He starts past her. She grabs his arm.*) Don't grab at me, Mother!

Amanda. Where are you going?

Tom. I'm going to the *movies!*

Amanda. I don't believe that lie!

Tom (*crouching toward her, overtowering her tiny figure. She backs away, gasping*). I'm going to opium dens! Yes, opium dens, dens of vice and criminals' hang-outs, Mother. I've joined the Hogan gang, I'm a hired assassin, I carry a tommy-gun in a violin case! I run a string of cat-houses in the Valley! They call me Killer, Killer Wingfield, I'm leading a double-life, a simple, honest warehouse worker by day, by night a dynamic *czar* of the *underworld, Mother.* I go to gambling casinos, I spin away fortunes on the roulette table! I wear a patch over one eye and a false mustache, sometimes I put on green whiskers. On those occasions they call me — *El Diablo!* Oh, I could tell you things to make you sleepless! My enemies plan to dynamite this place. They're going to blow us all sky-high some night! I'll be glad, very happy, and so will you! You'll go up, up on a broomstick, over Blue Mountain with seventeen gentlemen callers! You ugly — babbling old — witch. . . . (*He goes through a series of violent, clumsy movements, seizing his overcoat, lunging to the door, pulling it fiercely open. The women watch him, aghast. His arm catches in the sleeve of the coat as he struggles to pull it on. For a moment he is pinioned by the bulky garment. With an outraged groan he tears the coat off again, splitting the shoulders of it, and hurls it across the room. It strikes against the shelf of Laura's glass collection, there is a tinkle of shattering glass. Laura cries out as if wounded.*)

(Music Legend: "The Glass Menagerie.")

Laura (*shrilly*). *My glass!* — menagerie. . . . (*She covers her face and turns away.*)

> But Amanda is still stunned and stupefied by the "ugly witch" so that she barely notices this occurrence. Now she recovers her speech.

Amanda (*in an awful voice*). I won't speak to you — until you apologize! (*She crosses through portieres and draws them together behind her. Tom is left with Laura. Laura clings weakly to the mantel with her face averted. Tom stares at her stupidly for a moment. Then he crosses to shelf. Drops awkwardly to his knees to collect the fallen glass, glancing at Laura as if he would speak but couldn't.*)

"The Glass Menagerie" steals in as

(The Scene Dims Out.)

SCENE IV

The interior is dark. Faint light in the alley.

A deep-voiced bell in a church is tolling the hour of five as the scene commences.

Tom appears at the top of the alley. After each solemn boom of the bell in the tower, he shakes a little noise-maker or rattle as if to express the tiny spasm of man in contrast to the sustained power and dignity of the Almighty. This and the unsteadiness of his advance make it evident that he has been drinking.

As he climbs the few steps to the fire-escape landing light steals up inside. Laura appears in night-dress, observing Tom's empty bed in the front room.

Tom fishes in his pockets for the door-key, removing a motley assortment of articles in the search, including a perfect shower of movie-ticket stubs and an empty bottle. At last he finds the key, but just as he is about to insert it, it slips from his fingers. He strikes a match and crouches below the door.

Tom (*bitterly*). One crack — and it falls through!

Laura opens the door.

Laura. Tom! Tom, what are you doing?
Tom. Looking for a door-key.
Laura. Where have you been all this time?

Tom. I have been to the movies.

Laura. All this time at the movies?

Tom. There was a very long program. There was a Garbo picture and a Mickey Mouse and a travelogue and a newsreel and a preview of coming attractions. And there was an organ solo and a collection for the milk-fund — simultaneously — which ended up in a terrible fight between a fat lady and an usher!

Laura (innocently). Did you have to stay through everything?

Tom. Of course! And, oh, I forgot! There was a big stage show! The headliner on this stage show was Malvolio the Magician. He performed wonderful tricks, many of them, such as pouring water back and forth between pitchers. First it turned to wine and then it turned to beer and then it turned to whiskey. I know it was whiskey it finally turned into because he needed somebody to come up out of the audience to help him, and I came up — both shows! It was Kentucky Straight Bourbon. A very generous fellow, he gave souvenirs. (*He pulls from his back pocket a shimmering rainbow-colored scarf.*) He gave me this. This is his magic scarf. You can have it, Laura. You wave it over a canary cage and you get a bowl of gold-fish. You wave it over the gold-fish bowl and they fly away canaries. . . . But the wonderfullest trick of all was the coffin trick. We nailed him into a coffin and he got out of the coffin without removing one nail. (*He has come inside.*) There is a trick that would come in handy for me — get me out of this 2 by 4 situation! (*Flops onto bed and starts removing shoes.*)

Laura. Tom — Shhh!

Tom. What you shushing me for?

Laura. You'll wake up Mother.

Tom. Goody, goody! Pay 'er back for all those "Rise an' Shines." (*Lies down, groaning.*) You know it don't take much intelligence to get yourself into a nailed-up coffin, Laura. But who in hell ever got himself out of one without removing one nail?

As if in answer, the father's grinning photograph lights up.

(Scene Dims Out.)

Immediately following: The church bell is heard striking six. At the sixth stroke the alarm clock goes off in Amanda's room, and after a few moments we hear her calling: "Rise and Shine! Rise and Shine! Laura, go tell your brother to rise and shine!"

Tom (sitting up slowly). I'll rise — but I won't shine.

The light increases.

Amanda. Laura, tell your brother his coffee is ready.

Laura slips into front room.

Laura. Tom! it's nearly seven. Don't make Mother nervous. (*He stares at her stupidly. Beseechingly.*) Tom, speak to Mother this morning. Make up with her, apologize, speak to her!

Tom. She won't to me. It's her that started not speaking.

Laura. If you just say you're sorry she'll start speaking.

Tom. Her not speaking — is that such a tragedy?

Laura. Please — please!

Amanda (calling from kitchenette). Laura, are you going to do what I asked you to do, or do I have to get dressed and go out myself?

Laura. Going, going — soon as I get on my coat! (*She pulls on a shapeless felt hat with nervous, jerky movement, pleadingly glancing at Tom. Rushes awkwardly for coat. The coat is one of Amanda's, inaccurately made-over, the sleeves too short for Laura.*) Butter and what else?

Amanda (entering upstage). Just butter. Tell them to charge it.

Laura. Mother, they make such faces when I do that.

Amanda. Sticks and stones may break my bones, but the expression on Mr. Garfinkel's face won't harm us! Tell your brother his coffee is getting cold.

Laura (at door). Do what I asked you, will you, will you, Tom?

He looks sullenly away.

Amanda. Laura, go now or just don't go at all!

Laura (rushing out). Going — going! (*A second later she cries out. Tom springs up and crosses to the door. Amanda rushes anxiously in. Tom opens the door.*)

Tom. Laura?

Laura. I'm all right. I slipped, but I'm all right.

Amanda (peering anxiously after her). If anyone breaks a leg on those fire-escape steps, the landlord ought to be sued for every cent he possesses! (*She shuts door. Remembers she isn't speaking and returns to other room.*)

As Tom enters listlessly for his coffee, she turns her back to him and stands rigidly facing the window on the gloomy gray vault of the areaway. Its light on her face with its aged but childish features is cruelly sharp, satirical as a Daumier print.

(Music Under: "Ave Maria.")

Tom glances sheepishly but sullenly at her averted figure and slumps at the table. The coffee is scalding hot; he sips it and gasps and spits it back in the cup. At his gasp, Amanda catches her breath and half turns. Then catches herself and turns back to window.

Tom blows on his coffee, glancing sidewise at his mother. She clears her throat. Tom clears his. He starts to rise. Sinks back down again, scratches his head, clears his throat again. Amanda coughs. Tom raises his cup in both hands to blow on it, his eyes staring over the rim of it at his mother for several moments. Then he slowly sets the cup down and awkwardly and hesitantly rises from the chair.

Tom (hoarsely). Mother. I — I apologize. Mother. (*Amanda draws a quick, shuddering breath. Her face works grotesquely. She breaks into childlike tears.*) I'm sorry for what I said, for everything that I said, I didn't mean it.

Amanda (sobbingly). My devotion has made me a witch and so I make myself hateful to my children!

Tom. No, you *don't.*

Amanda. I worry so much, don't sleep, it makes me nervous!

Tom (gently). I understand that.

Amanda. I've had to put up a solitary battle all these years. But you're my right-hand bower! Don't fall down, don't fail!

Tom (gently). I try, Mother.

Amanda (with great enthusiasm). Try and you will SUCCEED! (*The notion makes her breathless.*) Why, you — you're just *full* of natural endowments! Both of my children — they're *unusual* children! Don't you think I know it? I'm so — *proud!* Happy and — feel I've — so much to be thankful for but — Promise me one thing, son!

Tom. What, Mother?

Amanda. Promise, son, you'll — never be a drunkard!

Tom (turns to her grinning). I will never be a drunkard, Mother.

Amanda. That's what frightened me so, that you'd be drinking! Eat a bowl of Purina!

Tom. Just coffee, Mother.

Amanda. Shredded wheat biscuit?

Tom. No. No, Mother, just coffee.

Amanda. You can't put in a day's work on an empty stomach. You've got ten minutes — don't gulp! Drinking too-hot liquids makes cancer of the stomach. . . . Put cream in.

Tom. No, thank you.

Amanda. To cool it.

Tom. No! No, thank you, I want it black.

Amanda. I know, but it's not good for you. We have to do all that we can to build ourselves up. In these trying times we live in, all that we have to cling to is — each other. . . . That's why it's so important to — Tom, I — I sent out your sister so I could discuss something with you. If you hadn't spoken I would have spoken to you. (*Sits down.*)

Tom (*gently*). What is it, Mother, that you want to discuss?

Amanda. Laura!

> *Tom puts his cup down slowly.*

(Legend On Screen: "Laura.")

(Music: "The Glass Menagerie.")

Tom. — Oh. — Laura . . .

Amanda (*touching his sleeve*). You know how Laura is. So quiet but — still water runs deep! She notices things and I think she — broods about them. (*Tom looks up.*) A few days ago I came in and she was crying.

Tom. What about?

Amanda. You.

Tom. Me?

Amanda. She has an idea that you're not happy here.

Tom. What gave her that idea?

Amanda. What gives her any idea? However, you do act strangely. I — I'm not criticizing, understand *that!* I know your ambitions do not lie in the warehouse, that like everybody in the whole wide world — you've had to — make sacrifices, but — Tom — Tom — life's not easy, it calls for — Spartan endurance! There's so many things in my heart that I cannot describe to you! I've never told you but I — *loved* your father. . . .

Tom (*gently*). I know that, Mother.

Amanda. And you — when I see you taking after his ways! Staying out late — and — well, you *had* been drinking the night you were in that — terrifying condition! Laura says that you hate the apartment and that you go out nights to get away from it! Is that true, Tom?

Tom. No. You say there's so much in your heart that you can't describe to me. That's true of me, too. There's so much in my heart that I can't describe to *you!* So let's respect each other's —

Amanda. But, why — *why,* Tom — are you always so *restless?* Where do you go to, nights?

Tom. I — go to the movies.

Amanda. Why do you go to the movies so much, Tom?

Tom. I go to the movies because — I like adventure. Adventure is something I don't have much of at work, so I go to the movies.

Amanda. But, Tom, you go to the movies *entirely too much!*

Tom. I like a lot of adventure.

> *Amanda looks baffled, then hurt. As the familiar inquisition resumes he becomes hard and impatient again. Amanda slips back into her querulous attitude toward him.*

(Image On Screen: Sailing Vessel With Jolly Roger.)

Amanda. Most young men find adventure in their careers.

Tom. Then most young men are not employed in a warehouse.

Amanda. The world is full of young men employed in warehouses and offices and factories.

Tom. Do all of them find adventure in their careers?

Amanda. They do or they do without it! Not everybody has a craze for adventure.

Tom. Man is by instinct a lover, a hunter, a fighter, and none of those instincts are given much play at the warehouse!

Amanda. Man is by instinct! Don't quote instinct to me! Instinct is something that people have got away from! It belongs to animals! Christian adults don't want it!

Tom. What do Christian adults want, then, Mother?

Amanda. Superior things! Things of the mind and the spirit! Only animals have to satisfy instincts! Surely your aims are somewhat higher than theirs! Than monkeys — pigs —

Tom. I reckon they're not.

Amanda. You're joking. However, that isn't what I wanted to discuss.

Tom (rising). I haven't much time.

Amanda (pushing his shoulders). Sit down.

Tom. You want me to punch in red at the warehouse, Mother?

Amanda. You have five minutes. I want to talk about Laura.

(Legend: "Plans And Provisions.")

Tom. All right! What about Laura?

Amanda. We have to be making plans and provisions for her. She's older than you, two years, and nothing has happened. She just drifts along doing nothing. It frightens me terribly how she just drifts along.

Tom. I guess she's the type that people call home girls.

Amanda. There's no such type, and if there is, it's a pity! That is unless the home is hers, with a husband!

Tom. What?

Amanda. Oh, I can see the handwriting on the wall as plain as I see the nose in front of my face! It's terrifying! More and more you remind me of your father! He was out all hours without explanation — Then *left! Goodbye!* And me with the bag to hold. I saw that letter you got from the Merchant Marine. I know what you're dreaming of. I'm not standing here blindfolded. Very well, then. Then *do* it! But not till there's somebody to take your place.

Tom. What do you mean?

Amanda. I mean that as soon as Laura has got somebody to take care of her, married, a home of her own, independent — why, then you'll be free to go wherever you please, on land, on sea, whichever way the wind blows! But until that time you've got to look out for your sister. I don't say me because I'm old and don't matter! I say for your sister because she's young and dependent. I put her in business college — a dismal failure! Frightened her so it made her sick to her stomach. I took her over to the Young People's League at the church. Another fiasco. She spoke to nobody, nobody spoke to her. Now all she does is fool with those pieces of glass and play those worn-out records. What kind of a life is that for a girl to lead!

Tom. What can I do about it?

Amanda. Overcome selfishness! Self, self, self is all that you ever think of! (*Tom springs up and crosses to get his coat. It is ugly and bulky. He pulls on a cap with earmuffs.*) Where is your muffler? Put your wool muffler on! (*He snatches it angrily from the closet and tosses it around his neck and pulls both ends tight.*) Tom! I haven't said what I had in mind to ask you.

Tom. I'm too late to —

Amanda (*catching his arms — very importunately. Then shyly*). Down at the warehouse, aren't there some — nice young men?

Tom. No!

Amanda. There *must* be — *some.*

Tom. Mother —

Gesture.

Amanda. Find out one that's clean-living — doesn't drink and — ask him out for sister!

Tom. What?

Amanda. For *sister!* To *meet!* Get *acquainted!*

Tom (stamping to door). Oh, my *go-osh!*

Amanda. Will you? (*He opens door. Imploringly.*) Will you? (*He starts down.*) Will you? *Will* you, dear?

Tom (calling back). YES!

Amanda closes the door hesitantly and with a troubled but faintly hopeful expression.

(Screen Image: Glamor Magazine Cover.)

Spot Amanda at phone.

Amanda. Ella Cartwright? This is Amanda Wingfield! How are you, honey? How is that kidney condition? (*Count five.*) Horrors! (*Count five.*) You're a Christian martyr, yes, honey, that's what you are, a Christian martyr! Well, I just happened to notice in my little red book that your subscription to the *Companion* has just run out! I knew that you wouldn't want to miss out on the wonderful serial starting in this new issue. It's by Bessie Mae Hopper, the first thing she's written since *Honeymoon for Three.* Wasn't that a strange and interesting story? Well, this one is even lovelier, I believe. It has a sophisticated society background. It's all about the horsey set on Long Island!

(Fade Out.)

SCENE V

(Legend On Screen: "Annunciation.") *Fade with music.*

It is early dusk of a spring evening. Supper has just been finished in the Wingfield apartment. Amanda and Laura in light colored dresses are removing dishes from the table, in the upstage area, which is shadowy, their movements formalized almost as a dance or ritual, their moving forms as pale and silent as moths.

Tom, in white shirt and trousers, rises from the table and crosses toward the fire-escape.

Amanda (as he passes her). Son, will you do me a favor?

Tom. What?

Amanda. Comb your hair! You look so pretty when your hair is combed! (*Tom slouches on sofa with evening paper. Enormous caption "Franco Triumphs."*) There is only one respect in which I would like you to emulate your father.

Tom. What respect is that?

Amanda. The care he always took of his appearance. He never allowed himself to look untidy. (*He throws down the paper and crosses to fire-escape.*) Where are you going?

Tom. I'm going out to smoke.

Amanda. You smoke too much. A pack a day at fifteen cents a pack. How much would that amount to in a month? Thirty times fifteen is how much, Tom? Figure it out and you will be astounded at what you could save. Enough to give you a night-school course in accounting at Washington U! Just think what a wonderful thing that would be for you, son!

Tom is unmoved by the thought.

Tom. I'd rather smoke. (*He steps out on landing, letting the screen door slam.*)

Amanda (*sharply*). I know! That's the tragedy of it. . . . (*Alone, she turns to look at her husband's picture.*)

(Dance Music: "All The World Is Waiting For The Sunrise!")

Tom (*to the audience*). Across the alley from us was the Paradise Dance Hall. On evenings in spring the windows and doors were open and the music came outdoors. Sometimes the lights were turned out except for a large glass sphere that hung from the ceiling. It would turn slowly about and filter the dusk with delicate rainbow colors. Then the orchestra played a waltz or a tango, something that had a slow and sensuous rhythm. Couples would come outside, to the relative privacy of the alley. You could see them kissing behind ash-pits and telephone poles. This was the compensation for lives that passed like mine, without any change or adventure. Adventure and change were imminent in this year. They were waiting around the corner for all these kids. Suspended in the mist over Berchtesgaden, caught in the folds of Chamberlain's umbrella — In Spain there was Guernica! But here there was only hot swing music and liquor, dance halls, bars, and movies, and sex that hung in the gloom like a chandelier and flooded the world with brief, deceptive rainbows. . . . All the world was waiting for bombardments!

Amanda turns from the picture and comes outside.

Amanda (sighing). A fire-escape landing's a poor excuse for a porch. (*She spreads a newspaper on a step and sits down, gracefully and demurely as if she were settling into a swing on a Mississippi veranda.*) What are you looking at?

Tom. The moon.

Amanda. Is there a moon this evening?

Tom. It's rising over Garfinkel's Delicatessen.

Amanda. So it is! A little silver slipper of a moon. Have you made a wish on it yet?

Tom. Um-hum.

Amanda. What did you wish for?

Tom. That's a secret.

Amanda. A secret, huh? Well, I won't tell mine either. I will be just as mysterious as you.

Tom. I bet I can guess what yours is.

Amanda. Is my head so transparent?

Tom. You're not a sphinx.

Amanda. No, I don't have secrets. I'll tell you what I wished for on the moon. Success and happiness for my precious children! I wish for that whenever there's a moon, and when there isn't a moon, I wish for it, too.

Tom. I thought perhaps you wished for a gentleman caller.

Amanda. Why do you say that?

Tom. Don't you remember asking me to fetch one?

Amanda. I remember suggesting that it would be nice for your sister if you brought home some nice young man from the warehouse. I think I've made that suggestion more than once.

Tom. Yes, you have made it repeatedly.

Amanda. Well?

Tom. We are going to have one.

Amanda. What?

Tom. A gentleman caller!

(The Annunciation Is Celebrated With Music.)

Amanda rises.

(Image On Screen: Caller With Bouquet.)

Amanda. You mean you have asked some nice young man to come over?

Tom. Yep. I've asked him to dinner.

Amanda. You really did?

Tom. I did!

Amanda. You did, and did he — *accept?*

Tom. He did!

Amanda. Well, well — well, well! That's — lovely!

Tom. I thought that you would be pleased.

Amanda. It's definite, then?

Tom. Very definite.

Amanda. Soon?

Tom. Very soon.

Amanda. For heaven's sake, stop putting on and tell me some things, will you?

Tom. What things do you want me to tell you?

Amanda. Naturally I would like to know when he's *coming!*

Tom. He's coming tomorrow.

Amanda. Tomorrow?

Tom. Yep. Tomorrow.

Amanda. But, Tom!

Tom. Yes, Mother?

Amanda. Tomorrow gives me no time!

Tom. Time for what?

Amanda. Preparations! Why didn't you phone me at once, as soon as you asked him, the minute that he accepted? Then, don't you see, I could have been getting ready!

Tom. You don't have to make any fuss.

Amanda. Oh, Tom, Tom, Tom, of course I have to make a fuss! I want things nice, not sloppy! Not thrown together. I'll certainly have to do some fast thinking, won't I?

Tom. I don't see why you have to think at all.

Amanda. You just don't know. We can't have a gentleman caller in a pig-sty! All my wedding silver has to be polished, the monogrammed table linen ought to be laundered! The windows have to be washed and fresh curtains put up. And how about clothes? We have to *wear* something, don't we?

Tom. Mother, this boy is no one to make a fuss over!

Amanda. Do you realize he's the first young man we've introduced to your sister? It's terrible, dreadful, disgraceful that poor little sister has never received a single gentleman caller! Tom, come inside! (*She opens the screen door.*)

Tom. What for?

Amanda. I want to ask you some things.

Tom. If you're going to make such a fuss, I'll call it off, I'll tell him not to come.

Amanda. You certainly won't do anything of the kind. Nothing offends people worse than broken engagements. It simply means I'll have to work like a Turk! We won't be brilliant, but we'll pass inspection. Come on inside. (*Tom follows, groaning.*) Sit down.

Tom. Any particular place you would like me to sit?

Amanda. Thank heavens I've got that new sofa! I'm also making payments on a floor lamp I'll have sent out! And put the chintz covers on, they'll brighten things up! Of course I'd hoped to have these walls re-papered. . . . What is the young man's name?

Tom. His name is O'Connor.

Amanda. That, of course, means fish — tomorrow is Friday! I'll have that salmon loaf — with Durkee's dressing! What does he do? He works at the warehouse?

Tom. Of course! How else would I —

Amanda. Tom, he — doesn't drink?

Tom. Why do you ask me that?

Amanda. Your father *did!*

Tom. Don't get started on that!

Amanda. He *does* drink, then?

Tom. Not that I know of!

Amanda. Make sure, be certain! The last thing I want for my daughter's a boy who drinks!

Tom. Aren't you being a little premature? Mr. O'Connor has not yet appeared on the scene!

Amanda. But will tomorrow. To meet your sister, and what do I know about his character? Nothing! Old maids are better off than wives of drunkards!

Tom. Oh, my God!

Amanda. Be still!

Tom (leaning forward to whisper). Lots of fellows meet girls whom they don't marry!

Amanda. Oh, talk sensibly, Tom — and don't be sarcastic! (*She has gotten a hairbrush.*)

Tom. What are you doing?

Amanda. I'm brushing that cow-lick down! What is this young man's position at the warehouse?

Tom (submitting grimly to the brush and the interrogation). This young man's position is that of a shipping clerk, Mother.

Amanda. Sounds to me like a fairly responsible job, the sort of a job *you* would be in if you just had more *get-up.* What is his salary? Have you got any idea?

Tom. I would judge it to be approximately eighty-five dollars a month.

Amanda. Well — not princely, but —

Tom. Twenty more than I make.

Amanda. Yes, how well I know! But for a family man, eighty-five dollars a month is not much more than you can just get by on. . . .

Tom. Yes, but Mr. O'Connor is not a family man.

Amanda. He might be, mightn't he? Some time in the future?

Tom. I see. Plans and provisions.

Amanda. You are the only young man that I know of who ignores the fact that the future becomes the present, the present the past, and the past turns into everlasting regret if you don't plan for it!

Tom. I will think that over and see what I can make of it.

Amanda. Don't be supercilious with your mother! Tell me some more about this — what do you call him?

Tom. James D. O'Connor. The D. is for Delaney.

Amanda. Irish on *both* sides! *Gracious!* And doesn't drink?

Tom. Shall I call him up and ask him right this minute?

Amanda. The only way to find out about those things is to make discreet inquiries at the proper moment. When I was a girl in Blue Mountain and it was suspected that a young man drank, the girl whose attentions he had been receiving, if any girl *was,* would sometimes speak to the minister of his church, or rather her father would if her father was living, and sort of feel him out on the young man's character. That is the way such things are discreetly handled to keep a young woman from making a tragic mistake!

Tom. Then how did you happen to make a tragic mistake?

Amanda. That innocent look of your father's had everyone fooled! He *smiled* — the world was *enchanted.!* No girl can do worse than put herself at the mercy of a handsome appearance! I hope that Mr. O'Connor is not too good-looking.

Tom. No, he's not too good-looking. He's covered with freckles and hasn't too much of a nose.

Amanda. He's not right-down homely, though?

Tom. Not right-down homely. Just medium homely, I'd say.

Amanda. Character's what to look for in a man.

Tom. That's what I've always said, Mother.

Amanda. You've never said anything of the kind and I suspect you would never give it a thought.

Tom. Don't be suspicious of me.

Amanda. At least I hope he's the type that's up and coming.

Tom. I think he really goes in for self-improvement.

Amanda. What reason have you to think so?

Tom. He goes to night school.

Amanda (beaming). Splendid! What does he do, I mean study?

Tom. Radio engineering and public speaking!

Amanda. Then he has visions of being advanced in the world! Any young man who studies public speaking is aiming to have an executive job some day! And radio engineering? A thing for the future! Both of these facts are very illuminating. Those are the sort of things that a mother should know concerning any young man who comes to call on her daughter. Seriously or — not.

Tom. One little warning. He doesn't know about Laura. I didn't let on that we had dark ulterior motives. I just said, why don't you come have dinner with us? He said okay and that was the whole conversation.

Amanda. I bet it was! You're eloquent as an oyster. However, he'll know about Laura when he gets here. When he sees how lovely and sweet and pretty she is, he'll thank his lucky stars he was asked to dinner.

Tom. Mother, you mustn't expect too much of Laura.

Amanda. What do you mean?

Tom. Laura seems all those things to you and me because she's ours and we love her. We don't even notice she's crippled any more.

Amanda. Don't say crippled! You know that I never allow that word to be used!

Tom. But face facts, Mother. She is and — that's not all —

Amanda. What do you mean "not all"?

Tom. Laura is very different from other girls.

Amanda. I think the difference is all to her advantage.

Tom. Not quite all — in the eyes of others — strangers — she's terribly shy and lives in a world of her own and those things make her seem a little peculiar to people outside the house.

Amanda. Don't say peculiar.

Tom. Face the facts. She is.

(The Dance-Hall Music Changes To A Tango That Has A Minor And Somewhat Ominous Tone.)

Amanda. In what way is she peculiar — may I ask?

Tom (gently). She lives in a world of her own — a world of — little glass ornaments, Mother. . . . (*Gets up. Amanda remains holding brush, looking at him, troubled.*) She plays old phonograph records and — that's about all — (*He glances at himself in the mirror and crosses to door.*)

Amanda (sharply). Where are you going?

Tom. I'm going to the movies. (*Out screen door.*)

Amanda. Not to the movies, every night to the movies! (*Follows quickly to screen door.*) I don't believe you always go to the movies! (*He is gone. Amanda looks worriedly after him for a moment. Then vitality and optimism return and she turns from the door. Crossing to portieres.*) Laura! Laura! (*Laura answers from kitchenette.*)

Laura. Yes, Mother.

Amanda. Let those dishes go and come in front! (*Laura appears with dish towel. Gaily.*) Laura, come here and make a wish on the moon!

Laura (entering). Moon — moon?

Amanda. A little silver slipper of a moon. Look over your left shoulder, Laura, and make a wish! (*Laura looks faintly puzzled as if called out of sleep. Amanda seizes her shoulders and turns her at angle by the door.*) Now! Now, darling, *wish!*

Laura. What shall I wish for, Mother?

Amanda (her voice trembling and her eyes suddenly filling with tears). Happiness! Good Fortune!

The violin rises and the stage dims out.

SCENE VI

(Image: High School Hero.)

Tom. And so the following evening I brought Jim home to dinner. I had known Jim slightly in high school. In high school Jim was a hero. He had tremendous Irish good nature and vitality with the scrubbed and polished look of white chinaware. He seemed to move in a continual spotlight. He was a star in basketball, captain of the debating club, president of the senior class and the glee club and he sang the male lead in the annual light operas. He was always running or bounding, never just walking. He seemed always at the point of defeating the law of gravity. He was shooting with such velocity through his adolescence that you would logically expect him to arrive at nothing short of the White House by the time he was thirty. But Jim apparently ran into more interference after his graduation from Soldan. His speed had definitely slowed. Six years after he left high school he was holding a job that wasn't much better than mine.

(Image: Clerk.)

He was the only one at the warehouse with whom I was on friendly terms. I was valuable to him as someone who could remember his former glory, who had seen him win basketball games and the silver cup in debating. He knew of my secret practice of retiring to a cabinet of the washroom to work on poems when business was slack in the warehouse. He called me Shakespeare. And while the other boys in the warehouse regarded me with suspicious hostility, Jim took a humorous attitude toward me. Gradually his attitude affected the others, their hostility wore off and they also began to smile at me as people smile at an oddly fashioned dog who trots across their path at some distance.

I knew that Jim and Laura had known each other at Soldan, and I had heard Laura speak admiringly of his voice. I didn't know if Jim remembered her or not. In high school Laura had been as unobtrusive as Jim had been astonishing. If he did remember Laura, it was not as my sister, for when I asked him to dinner, he grinned and said, "You know, Shakespeare, I never thought of you as having folks!"

He was about to discover that I did. . . .

(Light Up Stage.)

(Legend On Screen: "The Accent Of A Coming Foot.")

Friday evening. It is about five o'clock of a late spring evening which comes "scattering poems in the sky."

A delicate lemony light is in the Wingfield apartment.

Amanda has worked like a Turk in preparation for the gentleman caller. The results are astonishing. The new floor lamp with its rose-silk shade is in place, a colored paper lantern conceals the broken light fixture in the ceiling, new billowing white curtains are at the windows, chintz covers are on chairs and sofa, a pair of new sofa pillows make their initial appearance.

Open boxes and tissue paper are scattered on the floor.

Laura stands in the middle with lifted arms while Amanda crouches before her, adjusting the hem of the new dress, devout and ritualistic. The dress is colored and designed by memory. The arrangement of Laura's hair is changed; it is softer and more becoming. A fragile, unearthly prettiness has come out in Laura: she is like a piece of translucent glass touched by light, given a momentary radiance, not actual, not lasting.

Amanda (*impatiently*). Why are you trembling?

Laura. Mother, you've made me so nervous!

Amanda. How have I made you nervous?

Laura. By all this fuss! You make it seem so important!

Amanda. I don't understand you, Laura. You couldn't be satisfied with just sitting home, and yet whenever I try to arrange something for you, you seem to resist it. (*She gets up.*) Now take a look at yourself. No, wait! Wait just a moment — I have an idea!

Laura. What is it now?

Amanda produces two powder puffs which she wraps in handkerchiefs and stuffs in Laura's bosom.

Laura. Mother, what are you doing?

Amanda. They call them "Gay Deceivers"!

Laura. I won't wear them!

Amanda. You will!

Laura. Why should I?

Amanda. Because, to be painfully honest, your chest is flat.

Laura. You make it seem like we were setting a trap.

Amanda. All pretty girls are a trap, a pretty trap, and men expect them to be. **(Legend: "A Pretty Trap.")** Now look at yourself, young lady. This is the prettiest you will ever be! I've got to fix myself now! You're going to be surprised by your mother's appearance! (*She crosses through portieres, humming gaily.*)

Laura moves slowly to the long mirror and stares solemnly at herself.

A wind blows the white curtains inward in a slow, graceful motion and with a faint, sorrowful sighing.

Amanda (*off stage*). It isn't dark enough yet. (*She turns slowly before the mirror with a troubled look.*)

(Legend On Screen: "This Is My Sister: Celebrate Her With Strings!" Music.)

Amanda (*laughing, off*). I'm going to show you something. I'm going to make a spectacular appearance!

Laura. What is it, Mother?

Amanda. Possess your soul in patience — you will see! Something

I've resurrected from that old trunk! Styles haven't changed so terribly much after all. . . . (*She parts the portieres.*) Now just look at your mother! (*She wears a girlish frock of yellowed voile with a blue silk sash. She carries a bunch of jonquils — the legend of her youth is nearly revived. Feverishly.*) This is the dress in which I led the cotillion. Won the cakewalk twice at Sunset Hill, wore one spring to the Governor's ball in Jackson! See how I sashayed around the ballroom, Laura? (*She raises her skirt and does a mincing step around the room.*) I wore it on Sundays for my gentlemen callers! I had it on the day I met your father — I had malaria fever all that spring. The change of climate from East Tennessee to the Delta — weakened resistance — I had a little temperature all the time — not enough to be serious — just enough to make me restless and giddy! Invitations poured in — parties all over the Delta! — "Stay in bed," said Mother, "you have fever!" — but I just wouldn't. — I took quinine but kept on going, going! — Evenings, dances! — Afternoons, long, long rides! Picnics — lovely! — So lovely, that country in May. — All lacy with dogwood, literally flooded with jonquils! — That was the spring I had the craze for jonquils. Jonquils became an absolute obsession. Mother said, "Honey, there's no more room for jonquils." And still I kept bringing in more jonquils. Whenever, wherever I saw them, I'd say, "Stop! Stop! I see jonquils!" I made the young men help me gather the jonquils! It was a joke, Amanda and her jonquils! Finally there were no more vases to hold them, every available space was filled with jonquils. No vases to hold them? All right, I'll hold them myself! And then I — (*She stops in front of the picture.*) (**Music.**) met your father! Malaria fever and jonquils and then — this — boy. . . . (*She switches on the rose-colored lamp.*) I hope they get here before it starts to rain. (*She crosses upstage and places the jonquils in bowl on table.*) I gave your brother a little extra change so he and Mr. O'Connor could take the service car home.

Laura (*with altered look*). What did you say his name was?

Amanda. O'Connor.

Laura. What is his first name?

Amanda. I don't remember. Oh, yes, I do. It was — Jim!

Laura sways slightly and catches hold of a chair.

(Legend On Screen: "Not Jim!")

Laura (*faintly*). Not — Jim!

Amanda. Yes, that was it, it was Jim! I've never known a Jim that wasn't nice!

(Music: Ominous.)

Laura. Are you sure his name is Jim O'Connor?
Amanda. Yes. Why?
Laura. Is he the one that Tom used to know in high school?
Amanda. He didn't say so. I think he just got to know him at the warehouse.
Laura. There was a Jim O'Connor we both knew in high school — (*Then, with effort.*) If that is the one that Tom is bringing to dinner — you'll have to excuse me, I won't come to the table.
Amanda. What sort of nonsense is this?
Laura. You asked me once if I'd ever liked a boy. Don't you remember I showed you this boy's picture?
Amanda. You mean the boy you showed me in the year book?
Laura. Yes, that boy.
Amanda. Laura, Laura, were you in love with that boy?
Laura. I don't know, Mother. All I know is I couldn't sit at the table if it was him!
Amanda. It won't be him! It isn't the least bit likely. But whether it is or not, you will come to the table. You will not be excused.
Laura. I'll have to be, Mother.
Amanda. I don't intend to humor your silliness, Laura. I've had too much from you and your brother, both! So just sit down and compose yourself till they come. Tom has forgotten his key so you'll have to let them in, when they arrive.
Laura (*panicky*). Oh, Mother — *you* answer the door!
Amanda (*lightly*). I'll be in the kitchen — busy!
Laura. Oh, Mother, please answer the door, don't make me do it!
Amanda (*crossing into kitchenette*). I've got to fix the dressing for the salmon. Fuss, fuss — silliness! — over a gentleman caller!

Door swings shut. Laura is left alone.

(Legend: "Terror!")

She utters a low moan and turns off the lamp — sits stiffly on the edge of the sofa, knotting her fingers together.

(Legend On Screen: "The Opening Of A Door!")

Tom and Jim appear on the fire-escape steps and climb to landing. Hearing their approach, Laura rises with a panicky gesture. She retreats to the portieres.

The doorbell. Laura catches her breath and touches her throat. Low drums.

Amanda (*calling*). Laura, sweetheart! The door!

Laura stares at it without moving.

Jim. I think we just beat the rain.

Tom. Uh-huh. (*He rings again, nervously. Jim whistles and fishes for a cigarette.*)

Amanda (*very, very gaily*). Laura, that is your brother and Mr. O'Connor! Will you let them in, darling?

Laura crosses toward kitchenette door.

Laura (*breathlessly*). Mother — you go to the door!

Amanda steps out of kitchenette and stares furiously at Laura. She points imperiously at the door.

Laura. Please, please!

Amanda (*in a fierce whisper*). What is the matter with you, you silly thing?

Laura (*desperately*). Please, you answer it, *please!*

Amanda. I told you I wasn't going to humor you, Laura. Why have you chosen this moment to lose your mind?

Laura. Please, please, please, you go!

Amanda. You'll have to go to the door because I can't!

Laura (*despairingly*). I can't either!

Amanda. Why?

Laura. I'm *sick!*

Amanda. I'm sick, too — of your nonsense! Why can't you and your brother be normal people? Fantastic whims and behavior! (*Tom gives a long ring.*) Preposterous goings on! Can you give me one reason — (*Calls out lyrically.*) COMING! JUST ONE SECOND! — why should you be afraid to open a door? Now you answer it, Laura!

Laura. Oh, oh, oh . . . (*She returns through the portieres. Darts to the victrola and winds it frantically and turns it on.*)

Amanda. Laura Wingfield, you march right to that door!

Laura. Yes — yes, Mother!

A faraway, scratchy rendition of "Dardanella" softens the air and gives her strength to move through it. She slips to the door and draws it cautiously open.

Tom enters with the caller, Jim O'Connor.

Tom. Laura, this is Jim. Jim, this is my sister, Laura.
Jim (*stepping inside*). I didn't know that Shakespeare had a sister!
Laura (*retreating stiff and trembling from the door*). How — how do
  you do?
Jim (*heartily extending his hand*). Okay!

> *Laura touches it hesitantly with hers.*

Jim. Your hand's *cold*, Laura!
Laura. Yes, well — I've been playing the victrola. . . .
Jim. Must have been playing classical music on it! You ought to
  play a little hot swing music to warm you up!
Laura. Excuse me — I haven't finished playing the victrola. . . .

> *She turns awkwardly and hurries into the front room. She pauses
> a second by the victrola. Then catches her breath and darts through
> the portieres like a frightened deer.*

Jim (*grinning*). What was the matter?
Tom. Oh — with Laura? Laura is — terribly shy.
Jim. Shy, huh? It's unusual to meet a shy girl nowadays. I don't
  believe you ever mentioned you had a sister.
Tom. Well, now you know. I have one. Here is the *Post Dispatch.*
  You want a piece of it?
Jim. Uh-huh.
Tom. What piece? The comics?
Jim. Sports! (*Glances at it.*) Ole Dizzy Dean is on his bad behavior.
Tom (*disinterest*). Yeah? (*Lights cigarette and crosses back to fire-escape
  door.*)
Jim. Where are *you* going?
Tom. I'm going out on the terrace.
Jim (*goes after him*). You know, Shakespeare — I'm going to sell
  you a bill of goods!
Tom. What goods?
Jim. A course I'm taking.
Tom. Huh?
Jim. In public speaking! You and me, we're not the warehouse
  type.
Tom. Thanks — that's good news. But what has public speaking
  got to do with it?
Jim. It fits you for — executive positions!
Tom. Awww.
Jim. I tell you it's done a helluva lot for me.

(Image: Executive At Desk.)

Tom. In what respect?

Jim. In every! Ask yourself what is the difference between you an' me and men in the office down front? Brains? — No! — Ability? — No! Then what? Just one little thing —

Tom. What is that one little thing?

Jim. Primarily it amounts to — social poise! Being able to square up to people and hold your own on any social level!

Amanda (off stage). Tom?

Tom. Yes, Mother?

Amanda. Is that you and Mr. O'Connor?

Tom. Yes, Mother.

Amanda. Well, you just make yourselves comfortable in there.

Tom. Yes, Mother.

Amanda. Ask Mr. O'Connor if he would like to wash his hands.

Jim. Aw — no — no — thank you — I took care of that at the warehouse. Tom —

Tom. Yes?

Jim. Mr. Mendoza was speaking to me about you.

Tom. Favorably?

Jim. What do you think?

Tom. Well —

Jim. You're going to be out of a job if you don't wake up.

Tom. I am waking up —

Jim. You show no signs.

Tom. The signs are interior.

(Image On Screen: The Sailing Vessel With Jolly Roger Again.)

Tom. I'm planning to change. (*He leans over the rail speaking with quiet exhilaration. The incandescent marquees and signs of the first-run movie houses light his face from across the alley. He looks like a voyager.*) I'm right at the point of committing myself to a future that doesn't include the warehouse and Mr. Mendoza or even a night-school course in public speaking.

Jim. What are you gassing about?

Tom. I'm tired of the movies.

Jim. Movies!

Tom. Yes, movies! Look at them — (*A wave toward the marvels of Grand Avenue.*) All of those glamorous people — having adventures — hogging it all, gobbling the whole thing up! You know what happens? People go to the *movies* instead of *moving!* Hollywood characters are supposed to have all the adventures for everybody in America, while everybody in America sits in a dark room and watches them have them! Yes, until there's a war. That's when adventure becomes available to the masses! *Everyone's* dish, not only Gable's! Then the people in the dark room come out of the dark room to have some adventures themselves — Goody, goody — It's our turn now, to go to the South Sea Island — to make a safari — to be exotic, far-off — But I'm not patient. I don't want to wait till then. I'm tired of the *movies* and I am *about* to *move!*

Jim (incredulously). Move?

Tom. Yes.

Jim. When?

Tom. Soon!

Jim. Where? Where?

(Theme Three: Music Seems To Answer The Question, While Tom Thinks It Over. He Searches Among His Pockets.)

Tom. I'm starting to boil inside. I know I seem dreamy, but inside — well, I'm boiling! Whenever I pick up a shoe, I shudder a little thinking how short life is and what I am doing! — Whatever that means. I know it doesn't mean shoes — except as something to wear on a traveler's feet! *(Finds paper.)* Look —

Jim. What?

Tom. I'm a member.

Jim (reading). The Union of Merchant Seamen.

Tom. I paid my dues this month, instead of the light bill.

Jim. You will regret it when they turn the lights off.

Tom. I won't be here.

Jim. How about your mother?

Tom. I'm like my father. The bastard son of a bastard! See how he grins? And he's been absent going on sixteen years!

Jim. You're just talking, you drip. How does your mother feel about it?

Tom. Shhh — Here comes Mother! Mother is not acquainted with my plans!

Amanda (enters portieres). Where are you all?

Tom. On the terrace, Mother.

They start inside. She advances to them. Tom is distinctly shocked at her appearance. Even Jim blinks a little. He is making his first contact with girlish Southern vivacity and in spite of the night-

*school course in public speaking is somewhat thrown off the beam
by the unexpected outlay of social charm.*

*Certain responses are attempted by Jim but are swept aside by
Amanda's gay laughter and chatter. Tom is embarrassed but after
the first shock Jim reacts very warmly. Grins and chuckles, is
altogether won over.*

(Image: Amanda As A Girl.)

Amanda (coyly smiling, shaking her girlish ringlets). Well, well, well,
so this is Mr. O'Connor. Introductions entirely unnecessary.
I've heard so much about you from my boy. I finally said
to him, Tom — good gracious! — why don't you bring this
paragon to supper? I'd like to meet this nice young man at
the warehouse! — Instead of just hearing him sing your
praises so much! I don't know why my son is so stand-
offish — that's not Southern behavior! Let's sit down and
— I think we could stand a little more air in here! Tom,
leave the door open. I felt a nice fresh breeze a moment ago.
Where has it gone? Mmm, so warm already! And not quite
summer, even. We're going to burn up when summer really
gets started. However, we're having — we're having a very
light supper. I think light things are better fo' this time of
year. The same as light clothes are. Light clothes an' light
food are what warm weather calls fo'. You know our blood
gets so thick during th' winter — it takes a while fo' us to
adjust ou'selves! — when the season changes . . . It's come
so quick this year. I wasn't prepared. All of a sudden —
heavens! Already summer! — I ran to the trunk an' pulled
out this light dress — Terribly old! Historical almost! But
feels so good — so good an' co-ol, y'know. . . .

Tom. Mother —
Amanda. Yes, honey?
Tom. How about — supper?
Amanda. Honey, you go ask Sister if supper is ready! You know
    that Sister is in full charge of supper! Tell her you hungry
    boys are waiting for it. *(To Jim.)* Have you met Laura?
Jim. She —
Amanda. Let you in? Oh, good, you've met already! It's rare for
    a girl as sweet an' pretty as Laura to be domestic! But Laura
    is, thank heavens, not only pretty but also very domestic.
    I'm not at all. I never was a bit. I never could make a thing
    but angel-food cake. Well, in the South we had so many

servants. Gone, gone, gone. All vestiges of gracious living! Gone completely! I wasn't prepared for what the future brought me. All of my gentlemen callers were sons of planters and so of course I assumed that I would be married to one and raise my family on a large piece of land with plenty of servants. But man proposes — and woman accepts the proposal! — To vary that old, old saying a little bit — I married no planter! I married a man who worked for the telephone company! — that gallantly smiling gentleman over there! (*Points to the picture.*) A telephone man who — fell in love with long distance! — Now he travels and I don't even know where! — But what am I going on for about my — tribulations! Tell me yours — I hope you don't have any! Tom?

Tom (*returning*). Yes, Mother?

Amanda. Is supper nearly ready?

Tom. It looks to me like supper is on the table.

Amanda. Let me look — (*She rises prettily and looks through portieres.*) Oh, lovely — But where is Sister?

Tom. Laura is not feeling well and she says that she thinks she'd better not come to the table.

Amanda. What? — Nonsense! — Laura? Oh, Laura!

Laura (*off stage, faintly*). Yes, Mother.

Amanda. You really must come to the table. We won't be seated until you come to the table! Come in, Mr. O'Connor. You sit over there and I'll — Laura? Laura Wingfield! You're keeping us waiting, honey! We can't say grace until you come to the table!

The back door is pushed weakly open and Laura comes in. She is obviously quite faint, her lips trembling, her eyes wide and staring. She moves unsteadily toward the table.

(Legend: "Terror!")

Outside a summer storm is coming abruptly. The white curtains billow inward at the windows and there is a sorowful murmur and deep blue dusk.

Laura suddenly stumbles — She catches at a chair with a faint moan.

Tom. Laura!

Amanda. Laura! (*There is a clap of thunder.*) **(Legend: "Ah!")** (*Despairingly.*) Why, Laura, you *are* sick, darling! Tom, help your sister into the living room, dear! Sit in the living room,

Laura — rest on the sofa. Well! (*To the gentleman caller.*) Standing over the hot stove made her ill! — I told her that it was just too warm this evening, but — (*Tom comes back in. Laura is on the sofa.*) Is Laura all right now?

Tom. Yes.

Amanda. What *is* that? Rain? A nice cool rain has come up! (*She gives the gentleman caller a frightened look.*) I think we may — have grace — now . . . (*Tom looks at her stupidly.*) Tom, honey — you say grace!

Tom. Oh . . . "For these and all thy mercies — " (*They bow their heads, Amanda stealing a nervous glance at Jim. In the living room Laura, stretched on the sofa, clenches her hand to her lips, to hold back a shuddering sob.*) God's Holy Name be praised —

(The Scene Dims Out.)

SCENE VII

A Souvenir

Half an hour later. Dinner is just being finished in the upstage area which is concealed by the drawn portieres.

As the curtain rises Laura is still huddled upon the sofa, her feet drawn under her, her head resting on a pale blue pillow, her eyes wide and mysteriously watchful. The new floor lamp with its shade of rose-colored silk gives a soft, becoming light to her face, bringing out the fragile, unearthly prettiness which usually escapes attention. There is a steady murmur of rain, but it is slackening and stops soon after the scene begins; the air outside becomes pale and luminous as the moon breaks out.

A moment after the curtain rises, the lights in both rooms flicker and go out.

Jim. Hey, there, Mr. Light Bulb!

Amanda laughs nervously.

(Legend: "Suspension Of A Public Service.")

Amanda. Where was Moses when the lights went out? Ha-ha. Do you know the answer to that one, Mr. O'Connor?

Jim. No, Ma'am, what's the answer?

Amanda. In the dark! (*Jim laughs appreciatively.*) Everybody sit still. I'll light the candles. Isn't it lucky we have them on the table?

Where's a match? Which of you gentlemen can provide a match?

Jim. Here.

Amanda. Thank you, sir.

Jim. Not at all, Ma'am!

Amanda. I guess the fuse has burnt out. Mr. O'Connor, can you tell a burnt-out fuse? I know I can't and Tom is a total loss when it comes to mechanics. **(Sound: Getting Up: Voices Recede A Little To Kitchenette.)** Oh, be careful you don't bump into something. We don't want our gentleman caller to break his neck. Now wouldn't that be a fine howdy-do?

Jim. Ha-ha! Where is the fuse-box?

Amanda. Right here next to the stove. Can you see anything?

Jim. Just a minute.

Amanda. Isn't electricity a mysterious thing? Wasn't it Benjamin Franklin who tied a key to a kite? We live in such a mysterious universe, don't we? Some people say that science clears up all the mysteries for us. In my opinion it only creates more! Have you found it yet?

Jim. No, Ma'am. All these fuses look okay to me.

Amanda. Tom!

Tom. Yes, Mother?

Amanda. That light bill I gave you several days ago. The one I told you we got the notices about?

Tom. Oh. — Yeah.

(Legend: "Ha!")

Amanda. You didn't neglect to pay it by any chance?

Tom. Why, I —

Amanda. Didn't! I might have known it!

Jim. Shakespeare probably wrote a poem on that light bill, Mrs. Wingfield.

Amanda. I might have known better than to trust him with it! There's such a high price for negligence in this world!

Jim. Maybe the poem will win a ten-dollar prize.

Amanda. We'll just have to spend the remainder of the evening in the nineteenth century, before Mr. Edison made the Mazda lamp!

Jim. Candlelight is my favorite kind of light.

Amanda. That shows you're romantic! But that's no excuse for Tom. Well, we got through dinner. Very considerate of them to let us get through dinner before they plunged us into everlasting darkness, wasn't it, Mr. O'Connor?

Jim. Ha-ha!

Amanda. Tom, as a penalty for your carelessness you can help me with the dishes.

Jim. Let me give you a hand.

Amanda. Indeed you will not!

Jim. I ought to be good for something.

Amanda. Good for something? (*Her tone is rhapsodic.*) You? Why, Mr. O'Connor, nobody, *nobody's* given me this much entertainment in years — as you have!

Jim. Aw, now, Mrs. Wingfield!

Amanda. I'm not exaggerating, not one bit! But Sister is all by her lonesome. You go keep her company in the parlor! I'll give you this lovely old candelabrum that used to be on the altar at the church of the Heavenly Rest. It was melted a little out of shape when the church burnt down. Lightning struck it one spring. Gypsy Jones was holding a revival at the time and he intimated that the church was destroyed because the Episcopalians gave card parties.

Jim. Ha-ha.

Amanda. And how about coaxing Sister to drink a little wine? I think it would be good for her! Can you carry both at once?

Jim. Sure. I'm Superman!

Amanda. Now, Thomas, get into this apron!

The door of kitchenette swings closed on Amanda's gay laughter; the flickering light approaches the portieres.

Laura sits up nervously as he enters. Her speech at first is low and breathless from the almost intolerable strain of being alone with a stranger.

(Legend: "I Don't Suppose You Remember Me At All!")

In her first speeches in this scene, before Jim's warmth overcomes her paralyzing shyness, Laura's voice is thin and breathless as though she has run up a steep flight of stairs.

Jim's attitude is gently humorous. In playing this scene it should be stressed that while the incident is apparently unimportant, it is to Laura the climax of her secret life.

Jim. Hello, there, Laura.

Laura (*faintly*). Hello. (*She clears her throat.*)

Jim. How are you feeling now? Better?

Laura. Yes. Yes, thank you.

Jim. This is for you. A little dandelion wine. (*He extends it toward her with extravagant gallantry.*)

Laura. Thank you.

Jim. Drink it — but don't get drunk! (*He laughs heartily. Laura takes the glass uncertainly; laughs shyly.*) Where shall I set the candles?

Laura. Oh — oh, anywhere . . .

Jim. How about here on the floor? Any objections?

Laura. No.

Jim. I'll spread a newspaper under to catch the drippings. I like to sit on the floor. Mind if I do?

Laura. Oh, no.

Jim. Give me a pillow?

Laura. What?

Jim. A pillow!

Laura. Oh . . . (*Hands him one quickly.*)

Jim. How about you? Don't you like to sit on the floor?

Laura. Oh — yes.

Jim. Why don't you, then?

Laura. I — will.

Jim. Take a pillow! (*Laura does. Sits on the other side of the candelabrum. Jim crosses his legs and smiles engagingly at her.*) I can't hardly see you sitting way over there.

Laura. I can — see you.

Jim. I know, but that's not fair, I'm in the limelight. (*Laura moves her pillow closer.*) Good! Now I can see you! Comfortable?

Laura. Yes.

Jim. So am I. Comfortable as a cow. Will you have some gum?

Laura. No, thank you.

Jim. I think that I will indulge, with your permission. (*Musingly unwraps it and holds it up.*) Think of the fortune made by the guy that invented the first piece of chewing gum. Amazing, huh? The Wrigley Building is one of the sights of Chicago. — I saw it summer before last when I went up to the Century of Progress. Did you take in the Century of Progress?

Laura. No, I didn't.

Jim. Well, it was quite a wonderful exposition. What impressed me most was the Hall of Science. Gives you an idea of what the future will be in America, even more wonderful than the present time is! (*Pause. Smiling at her.*) Your brother tells me you're shy. Is that right, Laura?

Laura. I — don't know.

Jim. I judge you to be an old-fashioned type of girl. Well, I think that's a pretty good type to be. Hope you don't think I'm being too personal — do you?

Laura (*hastily, out of embarrassment*). I believe I *will* take a piece of
   gum, if you — don't mind. (*Clearing her throat.*) Mr. O'Con-
   nor, have you — kept up with your singing?
Jim. Singing? Me?
Laura. Yes. I remember what a beautiful voice you had.
Jim. When did you hear me sing?

(Voice Offstage In The Pause.)

Voice (*offstage*).
   O blow, ye winds, heigh-ho,
   A-roving I will go!
   I'm off to my love
   With a boxing glove —
   Ten thousand miles away!

Jim. You say you've heard me sing?
Laura. Oh, yes! Yes, very often . . . I — don't suppose you remember
   me — at all?
Jim (*smiling doubtfully*). You know I have an idea I've seen you
   before. I had that idea soon as you opened the door. It seemed
   almost like I was about to remember your name. But the
   name that I started to call you — wasn't a name! And so I
   stopped myself before I said it.
Laura. Wasn't it — Blue Roses?
Jim (*springs up, grinning*). Blue Roses! My gosh, yes — Blue Roses!
   That's what I had on my tongue when you opened the door!
   Isn't it funny what tricks your memory plays? I didn't connect
   you with the high school somehow or other. But that's
   where it was; it was high school. I didn't even know you
   were Shakespeare's sister! Gosh, I'm sorry.
Laura. I didn't expect you to. You — barely knew me!
Jim. But we did have a speaking acquaintance, huh?
Laura. Yes, we — spoke to each other.
Jim. When did you recognize me?
Laura. Oh, right away!
Jim. Soon as I came in the door?
Laura. When I heard your name I thought it was probably you.
   I knew that Tom used to know you a little in high school.
   So when you came in the door — Well, then I was — sure.
Jim. Why didn't you *say* something, then?
Laura (*breathlessly*). I didn't know what to say, I was — too surprised!
Jim. For goodness' sakes! You know, this sure is funny!
Laura. Yes! Yes, isn't it, though. . .

Jim. Didn't we have a class in something together?

Laura. Yes, we did.

Jim. What class was that?

Laura. It was — singing — Chorus!

Jim. Aw!

Laura. I sat across the aisle from you in the Aud.

Jim. Aw.

Laura. Mondays, Wednesdays and Fridays.

Jim. Now I remember — you always came in late.

Laura. Yes, it was so hard for me, getting upstairs. I had that brace on my leg — it clumped so loud!

Jim. I never heard any clumping.

Laura (*wincing at the recollection*). To me it sounded like — thunder!

Jim. Well, well, well. I never even noticed.

Laura. And everybody was seated before I came in. I had to walk in front of all those people. My seat was in the back row. I had to go clumping all the way up the aisle with everyone watching!

Jim. You shouldn't have been self-conscious.

Laura. I know, but I was. It was always such a relief when the singing started.

Jim. Aw, yes, I've placed you now! I used to call you Blue Roses. How was it that I got started calling you that?

Laura. I was out of school a little while with pleurosis. When I came back you asked me what was the matter. I said I had pleurosis — you thought I said Blue Roses. That's what you always called me after that!

Jim. I hope you didn't mind.

Laura. Oh, no — I liked it. You see, I wasn't acquainted with many — people. . . .

Jim. As I remember you sort of stuck by yourself.

Laura. I — I — never had much luck at — making friends.

Jim. I don't see why you wouldn't.

Laura. Well, I — started out badly.

Jim. You mean being —

Laura. Yes, it sort of — stood between me —

Jim. You shouldn't have let it!

Laura. I know, but it did, and —

Jim. You were shy with people!

Laura. I tried not to be but never could —

Jim. Overcome it?

Laura. No, I — I never could!

Jim. I guess being shy is something you have to work out of kind of gradually.

Laura (sorrowfully). Yes — I guess it —

Jim. Takes time!

Laura. Yes —

Jim. People are not so dreadful when you know them. That's what you have to remember! And everybody has problems, not just you, but practically everybody has got some problems. You think of yourself as having the only problems, as being the only one who is disappointed. But just look around you and you will see lots of people as disappointed as you are. For instance, I hoped when I was going to high school that I would be further along at this time, six years later, than I am now — You remember that wonderful write-up I had in *The Torch?*

Laura. Yes! (*She rises and crosses to table.*)

Jim. It said I was bound to succeed in anything I went into! (*Laura returns with the annual.*) Holy Jeez! *The Torch!* (*He accepts it reverently. They smile across it with mutual wonder. Laura crouches beside him and they begin to turn through it. Laura's shyness is dissolving in his warmth.*)

Laura. Here you are in *Pirates of Penzance!*

Jim (wistfully). I sang the baritone lead in that operetta.

Laura (rapidly). So — *beautifully!*

Jim (protesting). Aw —

Laura. Yes, yes — beautifully — beautifully!

Jim. You heard me?

Laura. All three times!

Jim. No!

Laura. Yes!

Jim. All three performances?

Laura (looking down). Yes.

Jim. Why?

Laura. I — wanted to ask you to — autograph my program.

Jim. Why didn't you ask me to?

Laura. You were always surrounded by your own friends so much that I never had a chance to.

Jim. You should have just —

Laura. Well, I — thought you might think I was —

Jim. Thought I might think you was — what?

Laura. Oh —

Jim (with reflective relish). I was beleaguered by females in those days.

Laura. You were terribly popular!

Jim. Yeah —

Laura. You had such a — friendly way —

Jim. I was spoiled in high school.
Laura. Everybody — liked you!
Jim. Including you?
Laura. I — yes, I — I did, too — (*She gently closes the book in her lap.*)
Jim. Well, well, well! — Give me that program, Laura. (*She hands it to him. He signs it with a flourish.*) There you are — better late than never!
Laura. Oh, I — what a — surprise!
Jim. My signature isn't worth very much right now. But some day — maybe — it will increase in value! Being disappointed is one thing and being discouraged is something else. I am disappointed but I'm not discouraged. I'm twenty-three years old. How old are you?
Laura. I'll be twenty-four in June.
Jim. That's not old age!
Laura. No, but —
Jim. You finished high school?
Laura (*with difficulty*). I didn't go back.
Jim. You mean you dropped out?
Laura. I made bad grades in my final examinations. (*She rises and replaces the book and the program. Her voice strained.*) How is — Emily Meisenbach getting along?
Jim. Oh, that kraut-head!
Laura. Why do you call her that?
Jim. That's what she was.
Laura. You're not still — going with her?
Jim. I never see her.
Laura. It said in the Personal Section that you were — engaged!
Jim. I know, but I wasn't impressed by that — propaganda!
Laura. It wasn't — the truth?
Jim. Only in Emily's optimistic opinion!
Laura. Oh —

(Legend: "What Have You Done Since High School?")

Jim lights a cigarette and leans indolently back on his elbows smiling at Laura with a warmth and charm which light her inwardly with altar candles. She remains by the table and turns in her hands a piece of glass to cover her tumult.

Jim (*after several reflective puffs on a cigarette*). What have you done since high school? (*She seems not to hear him.*) Huh? (*Laura looks up.*) I said what have you done since high school, Laura?

Laura. Nothing much.

Jim. You must have been doing something these six long years.

Laura. Yes.

Jim. Well, then, such as what?

Laura. I took a business course at business college —

Jim. How did that work out?

Laura. Well, not very — well — I had to drop out, it gave me
— indigestion —

Jim laughs gently.

Jim. What are you doing now?

Laura. I don't do anything — much. Oh, please don't think I sit
around doing nothing! My glass collection takes up a good
deal of my time. Glass is something you have to take good
care of.

Jim. What did you say — about glass?

Laura. Collection I said — I have one — (*She clears her throat and
turns away again, acutely shy.*)

Jim (*abruptly*). You know what I judge to be the trouble with you?
Inferiority complex! Know what that is? That's what they
call it when someone low-rates himself! I understand it because
I had it, too. Although my case was not so aggravated as
yours seems to be. I had it until I took up public speaking,
developed my voice, and learned that I had an aptitude for
science. Before that time I never thought of myself as being
outstanding in any way whatsoever! Now I've never made
a regular study of it, but I have a friend who says I can
analyze people better than doctors that make a profession of
it. I don't claim that to be necessarily true, but I can sure
guess a person's psychology, Laura! (*Takes out his gum.*) Excuse
me, Laura. I always take it out when the flavor is gone. I'll
use this scrap of paper to wrap it in. I know how it is to
get it stuck on a shoe. Yep — that's what I judge to be your
principal trouble. A lack of confidence in yourself as a person.
You don't have the proper amount of faith in yourself. I'm
basing that fact on a number of your remarks and also on
certain observations I've made. For instance that clumping
you thought was so awful in high school. You say that you
even dreaded to walk into class. You see what you did? You
dropped out of school, you gave up an education because
of a clump, which as far as I know was practically non-
existent! A little physical defect is what you have. Hardly
noticeable even! Magnified thousands of times by imagination!

You know what my strong advice to you is? Think of yourself
as *superior* in some way!

Laura. In what way would I think?

Jim. Why, man alive, Laura! Just look about you a little. What
do you see? A world full of common people! All of 'em
born and all of 'em going to die! Which of them has one-
tenth of your good points! Or mine! Or anyone else's, as
far as that goes — Gosh! Everybody excels in some one
thing. Some in many! (*Unconsciously glances at himself in the
mirror.*) All you've got to do is discover in *what!* Take me,
for instance. (*He adjusts his tie at the mirror.*) My interest
happens to lie in electrodynamics. I'm taking a course in
radio engineering at night school, Laura, on top of a fairly
responsible job at the warehouse. I'm taking that course and
studying public speaking.

Laura. Ohhhh.

Jim. Because I believe in the future of television! (*Turning back to
her.*) I wish to be ready to go up right along with it. Therefore
I'm planning to get in on the ground floor. In fact, I've
already made the right connections and all that remains is
for the industry itself to get under way! Full steam — (*His
eyes are starry.*) *Knowledge* — Zzzzzp! *Money* — Zzzzzzp! —
Power! That's the cycle democracy is built on! (*His attitude
is convincingly dynamic. Laura stares at him, even her shyness
eclipsed in her absolute wonder. He suddenly grins.*) I guess you
think I think a lot of myself!

Laura. No — o-o-o, I —

Jim. Now how about you? Isn't there something you take more
interest in than anything else?

Laura. Well, I do — as I said — have my — glass collection —

A peal of girlish laughter from the kitchen.

Jim. I'm not right sure I know what you're talking about. What
kind of glass is it?

Laura. Little articles of it, they're ornaments mostly! Most of them
are little animals made out of glass, the tiniest little animals
in the world. Mother calls them a glass menagerie! Here's
an example of one, if you'd like to see it! This one is one
of the oldest. It's nearly thirteen. (*He stretches out his hand.*)
(Music: "The Glass Menagerie.") Oh, be careful — if you
breathe, it breaks!

Jim. I'd better not take it. I'm pretty clumsy with things.

Laura. Go on, I trust you with him! (*Places it in his palm.*) There
now — you're holding him gently! Hold him over the light,

he loves the light! You see how the light shines through
him?

Jim. It sure does shine!

Laura. I shouldn't be partial, but he is my favorite one.

Jim. What kind of a thing is this one supposed to be?

Laura. Haven't you noticed the single horn on his forehead?

Jim. A unicorn, huh?

Laura. Mmm-hmmm!

Jim. Unicorns, aren't they extinct in the modern world?

Laura. I know!

Jim. Poor little fellow, he must feel sort of lonesome.

Laura (smiling). Well, if he does he doesn't complain about it. He
stays on a shelf with some horses that don't have horns and
all of them seem to get along nicely together.

Jim. How do you know?

Laura (lightly). I haven't heard any arguments among them!

Jim (grinning). No arguments, huh? Well, that's a pretty good sign!
Where shall I set him?

Laura. Put him on the table. They all like a change of scenery
once in a while!

Jim (stretching). Well, well, well, well — Look how big my shadow
is when I stretch!

Laura. Oh, oh, yes — it stretches across the ceiling!

Jim (crossing to door). I think it's stopped raining. (*Opens fire-escape
door.*) Where does the music come from?

Laura. From the Paradise Dance Hall across the alley.

Jim. How about cutting the rug a little, Miss Wingfield?

Laura. Oh, I —

Jim. Or is your program filled up? Let me have a look at it. (*Grasps
imaginary card.*) Why, every dance is taken! I'll just have to
scratch some out. **(Waltz Music: "La Golondrina.")** Ahhh,
a waltz! (*He executes some sweeping turns by himself then holds
his arms toward Laura.*)

Laura (breathlessly). I — can't dance!

Jim. There you go, that inferiority stuff!

Laura. I've never danced in my life!

Jim. Come on, try!

Laura. Oh, but I'd step on you!

Jim. I'm not made out of glass.

Laura. How — how — how do we start?

Jim. Just leave it to me. You hold your arms out a little.

Laura. Like this?

Jim. A little bit higher. Right. Now don't tighten up, that's the
main thing about it — relax.

Laura (laughing breathlessly). It's hard not to.

Jim. Okay.

Laura. I'm afraid you can't budge me.

Jim. What do you bet I can't? (*He swings her into motion.*)

Laura. Goodness, yes, you can!

Jim. Let yourself go, now, Laura, just let yourself go.

Laura. I'm —

Jim. Come on!

Laura. Trying!

Jim. Not so stiff — Easy does it!

Laura. I know but I'm —

Jim. Loosen th' backbone! There now, that's a lot better.

Laura. Am I?

Jim. Lots, lots better! (*He moves her about the room in a clumsy waltz.*)

Laura. Oh, my!

Jim. Ha-ha!

Laura. Goodness, yes you can!

Jim. Ha-ha-ha! (*They suddenly bump into the table. Jim stops.*) What did we hit on?

Laura. Table.

Jim. Did something fall off it? I think —

Laura. Yes.

Jim. I hope that it wasn't the little glass horse with the horn!

Laura. Yes.

Jim. Aw, aw, aw. Is it broken?

Laura. Now it is just like all the other horses.

Jim. It's lost its —

Laura. Horn! It doesn't matter. Maybe it's a blessing in disguise.

Jim. You'll never forgive me. I bet that that was your favorite piece of glass.

Laura. I don't have favorites much. It's no tragedy, Freckles. Glass breaks so easily. No matter how careful you are. The traffic jars the shelves and things fall off them.

Jim. Still I'm awfully sorry that I was the cause.

Laura (smiling). I'll just imagine he had an operation. The horn was removed to make him feel less — freakish! (*They both laugh.*) Now he will feel more at home with the other horses, the ones that don't have horns. . .

Jim. Ha-ha, that's very funny! (*Suddenly serious.*) I'm glad to see that you have a sense of humor. You know — you're — well — very different! Surprisingly different from anyone else I know! (*His voice becomes soft and hesitant with a genuine feeling.*) Do you mind me telling you that? (*Laura is abashed beyond speech.*) You make me feel sort of — I don't know how to put it! I'm usually pretty good at expressing things, but — This is something that I don't know how to say! (*Laura touches her throat and clears it — turns the broken unicorn in her hands.*) (*Even softer.*) Has anyone ever told you that you were pretty? **(Pause: Music.)** (*Laura looks up slowly, with wonder, and shakes her head.*) Well, you are! In a very different way from anyone else. And all the nicer because of the difference, too. (*His voice becomes low and husky. Laura turns away, nearly faint with the novelty of her emotions.*) I wish that you were my sister. I'd teach you to have some confidence in yourself. The different people are not like other people, but being different is nothing to be ashamed of. Because other people are not such wonderful people. They're one hundred times one thousand. You're one times one! They walk all over the earth. You just stay here. They're common as — weeds, but — you — well, you're — *Blue Roses!*

(Image On Screen: Blue Roses.)

(Music Changes.)

Laura. But blue is wrong for — roses. . .
Jim. It's right for you — You're — pretty!
Laura. In what respect am I pretty?
Jim. In all respects — believe me! Your eyes — your hair — are pretty! Your hands are pretty! (*He catches hold of her hand.*) You think I'm making this up because I'm invited to dinner and have to be nice. Oh, I could do that! I could put on an act for you, Laura, and say lots of things without being very sincere. But this time I am. I'm talking to you sincerely. I happened to notice you had this inferiority complex that keeps you from feeling comfortable with people. Somebody needs to build your confidence up and make you proud instead of shy and turning away and — blushing — Somebody ought to — ought to — *kiss* you, Laura! (*His hand slips slowly up her arm to her shoulder.*) **(Music Swells Tumultuously.)** (*He suddenly turns her about and kisses her on the lips. When he releases her Laura sinks on the sofa with a bright, dazed look. Jim backs away and fishes in his pocket for a cigarette.*) **(Legend On Screen: "Souvenir.")** Stumble-john! (*He lights the cigarette, avoiding her look. There is a peal of girlish laughter from Amanda in the kitchen. Laura slowly raises and opens her hand. It still contains the little broken glass animal. She looks at it with a tender, bewildered expression.*) Stumble-john! I shouldn't have done that — That was way off the beam. You don't smoke, do

you? (*She looks up, smiling, not hearing the question. He sits beside her a little gingerly. She looks at him speechlessly — waiting. He coughs decorously and moves a little farther aside as he considers the situation and senses her feelings, dimly, with perturbation. Gently.*) Would you — care for a — mint? (*She doesn't seem to hear him but her look grows brighter even.*) Peppermint — Life Saver? My pocket's a regular drug store — wherever I go . . . (*He pops a mint in his mouth. Then gulps and decides to make a clean breast of it. He speaks slowly and gingerly.*) Laura, you know, if had a sister like you, I'd do the same thing as Tom. I'd bring out fellows — introduce her to them. The right type of boys of a type to — appreciate her. Only — well — he made a mistake about me. Maybe I've got no call to be saying this. That may not have been the idea in having me over. But what if it was? There's nothing wrong about that. The only trouble is that in my case — I'm not in a situation to — do the right thing. I can't take down your number and say I'll phone. I can't call up next week and — ask for a date. I thought I had better explain the situation in case you misunderstood it and — hurt your feelings. . . . (*Pause. Slowly, very slowly, Laura's look changes, her eyes returning slowly from his to the ornament in her palm.*)

Amanda utters another gay laugh in the kitchen.

Laura (*faintly*). You — won't — call again?
Jim. No, Laura, I can't. (*He rises from the sofa.*) As I was just explaining, I've — got strings on me, Laura, I've — been going steady! I go out all the time with a girl named Betty. She's a home-girl like you, and Catholic, and Irish, and in a great many ways we — get along fine. I met her last summer on a moonlight boat trip up the river to Alton, on the *Majestic*. Well — right away from the start it was — love! (**Legend: Love!**) (*Laura sways slightly forward and grips the arm of the sofa. He fails to notice, now enrapt in his own comfortable being.*) Being in love has made a new man of me! (*Leaning stiffly forward, clutching the arm of the sofa, Laura struggles visibly with her storm. But Jim is oblivious, she is a long way off.*) The power of love is really pretty tremendous! Love is something that — changes the whole world, Laura! (*The storm abates a little and Laura leans back. He notices her again.*) It happened that Betty's aunt took sick, she got a wire and had to go to Centralia. So Tom — when he asked me to dinner — I naturally just accepted the invitation, not knowing that you — that he — that I — (*He stops awkwardly.*) Huh — I'm a stumble-john! (*He flops back on the sofa. The*

*holy candles in the altar of Laura's face have been snuffed out!
There is a look of almost infinite desolation. Jim glances at her
uneasily.*) I wish that you would — say something. (*She bites
her lip which was trembling and then bravely smiles. She opens
her hand again on the broken glass ornament. Then she gently
takes his hand and raises it level with her own. She carefully places
the unicorn in the palm of his hand, then pushes his fingers closed
upon it.*) What are you — doing that for? You want me to
have him? — Laura? (*She nods.*) What for?

Laura. A — souvenir . . .

She rises unsteadily and crouches beside the victrola to wind it up.

**(Legend On Screen: "Things Have A Way Of Turning
Out So Badly.")**

**(Or Image: "Gentleman Caller Waving Good-Bye! —
Gaily.")**

*At this moment Amanda rushes brightly back in the front room.
She bears a pitcher of fruit punch in an old-fashioned cut-glass
pitcher and a plate of macaroons. The plate has a gold border and
poppies painted on it.*

Amanda. Well, well, well! Isn't the air delightful after the shower?
I've made you children a little liquid refreshment. (*Turns
gaily to the gentleman caller.*) Jim, do you know that song
about lemonade?

"Lemonade, lemonade
Made in the shade and stirred with a spade —
Good enough for any old maid!"

Jim (*uneasily*). Ha-ha! No — I never heard it.
Amanda. Why, Laura! You look so serious!
Jim. We were having a serious conversation.
Amanda. Good! Now you're better acquainted!
Jim (*uncertainly*). Ha-ha! Yes.
Amanda. You modern young people are much more serious-minded
than my generation. I was so gay as a girl!
Jim. You haven't changed, Mrs. Wingfield.
Amanda. Tonight I'm rejuvenated! The gaiety of the occasion, Mr.
O'Connor! (*She tosses her head with a peal of laughter. Spills
lemonade.*) Oooo! I'm baptizing myself!
Jim. Here — let me —
Amanda (*setting the pitcher down*). There now. I discovered we had
some maraschino cherries. I dumped them in, juice and all!

Jim. You shouldn't have gone to that trouble, Mrs. Wingfield.

Amanda. Trouble, trouble? Why it was loads of fun! Didn't you hear me cutting up in the kitchen? I bet your ears were burning! I told Tom how outdone with him I was for keeping you to himself so long a time! He should have brought you over much, much sooner! Well, now that you've found your way, I want you to be a very frequent caller! Not just occasional but all the time. Oh, we're going to have a lot of gay times together! I see them coming! Mmm, just breathe that air! So fresh, and the moon's so pretty! I'll skip back out — I know where my place is when young folks are having a — serious conversation!

Jim. Oh, don't go out, Mrs. Wingfield. The fact of the matter is I've got to be going.

Amanda. Going, now? You're joking! Why, it's only the shank of the evening, Mr. O'Connor!

Jim. Well, you know how it is.

Amanda. You mean you're a young workingman and have to keep workingmen's hours. We'll let you off early tonight. But only on the condition that next time you stay later. What's the best night for you? Isn't Saturday night the best night for you workingmen?

Jim. I have a couple of time-clocks to punch, Mrs. Wingfield. One at morning, another one at night!

Amanda. My, but you *are* ambitious! You work at night, too?

Jim. No, Ma'am, not work but — Betty! (*He crosses deliberately to pick up his hat. The band at the Paradise Dance Hall goes into a tender waltz.*)

Amanda. Betty? Betty? Who's — Betty! (*There is an ominous cracking sound in the sky.*)

Jim. Oh, just a girl. The girl I go steady with! (*He smiles charmingly. The sky falls.*)

(Legend: "The Sky Falls.")

Amanda (*a long-drawn exhalation*). Ohhhh . . . Is it a serious romance, Mr. O'Connor?

Jim. We're going to be married the second Sunday in June.

Amanda. Ohhhh — how nice! Tom didn't mention that you were engaged to be married.

Jim. The cat's not out of the bag at the warehouse yet. You know how they are. They call you Romeo and stuff like that. (*He stops at the oval mirror to put on his hat. He carefully shapes the brim and the crown to give a discreetly dashing effect.*) It's been a wonderful evening, Mrs. Wingfield. I guess this is what they mean by Southern hospitality.

Amanda. It really wasn't anything at all.

Jim. I hope it don't seem like I'm rushing off. But I promised Betty I'd pick her up at the Wabash depot, an' by the time I get my jalopy down there her train'll be in. Some women are pretty upset if you keep 'em waiting.

Amanda. Yes, I know — The tyranny of women! (*Extends her hand.*) Goodbye, Mr. O'Connor. I wish you luck — and happiness — and success! All three of them, and so does Laura! — Don't you, Laura?

Laura. Yes!

Jim (*taking her hand*). Goodbye, Laura. I'm certainly going to treasure that souvenir. And don't you forget the good advice I gave you. (*Raises his voice to a cheery shout.*) So long, Shakespeare! Thanks again, ladies — Good night!

He grins and ducks jauntily out.

Still bravely grimacing, Amanda closes the door on the gentleman caller. Then she turns back to the room with a puzzled expression. She and Laura don't dare to face each other. Laura crouches beside the victrola to wind it.

Amanda (*faintly*). Things have a way of turning out so badly. I don't believe that I would play the victrola. Well, well — well — Our gentleman caller was engaged to be married! Tom!

Tom (*from back*). Yes, Mother?

Amanda. Come in here a minute. I want to tell you something awfully funny.

Tom (*enters with macaroon and a glass of the lemonade*). Has the gentleman caller gotten away already?

Amanda. The gentleman caller has made an early departure. What a wonderful joke you played on us!

Tom. How do you mean?

Amanda. You didn't mention that he was engaged to be married.

Tom. Jim? Engaged?

Amanda. That's what he just informed us.

Tom. I'll be jiggered! I didn't know about that.

Amanda. That seems very peculiar.

Tom. What's peculiar about it?

Amanda. Didn't you call him your best friend down at the warehouse?

Tom. He is, but how did I know?

Amanda. It seems extremely peculiar that you wouldn't know your best friend was going to be married!

Tom. The warehouse is where I work, not where I know things about people!

Amanda. You don't know things anywhere! You live in a dream; you manufacture illusions! (*He crosses to door.*) Where are you going?

Tom. I'm going to the movies.

Amanda. That's right, now that you've had us make such fools of ourselves. The effort, the preparations, all the expense! The new floor lamp, the rug, the clothes for Laura! All for what? To entertain some other girl's fiancé! Go to the movies, go! Don't think about us, a mother deserted, an unmarried sister who's crippled and has no job! Don't let anything interfere with your selfish pleasure! Just go, go, go — to the movies!

Tom. All right, I will! The more you shout about my selfishness to me the quicker I'll go, and I won't go to the movies!

Amanda. Go, then! Then go to the moon — you selfish dreamer!

Tom smashes his glass on the floor. He plunges out on the fire-escape, slamming the door. Laura screams — cut by door.

Dance-hall music up. Tom goes to the rail and grips it desperately, lifting his face in the chill white moonlight penetrating the narrow abyss of the alley.

(Legend On Screen: "And So Good-Bye . . .")

Tom's closing speech is timed with the interior pantomime. The interior scene is played as though viewed through sound-proof glass. Amanda appears to be making a comforting speech to Laura who is huddled upon the sofa. Now that we cannot hear the mother's speech, her silliness is gone and she has dignity and tragic beauty. Laura's dark hair hides her face until at the end of the speech she lifts it to smile at her mother. Amanda's gestures are slow and graceful, almost dancelike, as she comforts the daughter. At the end of her speech she glances a moment at the father's picture — then withdraws through the portieres. At close of Tom's speech, Laura blows out the candles, ending the play.

Tom. I didn't go to the moon, I went much further — for time is the longest distance between two places — Not long after that I was fired for writing a poem on the lid of a shoe-box. I left Saint Louis. I descended the steps of this fire-escape for a last time and followed, from then on, in my father's footsteps, attempting to find in motion what was lost in space — I traveled around a great deal. The cities swept about me like dead leaves, leaves that were brightly colored but torn away from the branches. I would have stopped, but I was pursued by something. It always came upon me unawares, taking me altogether by surprise. Perhaps it was a familiar bit of music. Perhaps it was only a piece of transparent glass — Perhaps I am walking along a street at night, in some strange city, before I have found companions. I pass the lighted window of a shop where perfume is sold. The window is filled with pieces of colored glass, tiny transparent bottles in delicate colors, like bits of a shattered rainbow. Then all at once my sister touches my shoulder. I turn around and look into her eyes . . . Oh, Laura, Laura, I tried to leave you behind me, but I am more faithful than I intended to be! I reach for a cigarette, I cross the street, I run into the movies or a bar, I buy a drink, I speak to the nearest stranger — anything that can blow your candles out! (*Laura bends over the candles.*) — for nowadays the world is lit by lightning! Blow out your candles, Laura — and so goodbye . . .

She blows the candles out.

(The Scene Dissolves.)

PRODUCTION NOTES

Being a "memory play," *The Glass Menagerie* can be presented with unusual freedom of convention. Because of its considerably delicate or tenuous material, atmospheric touches and subtleties of direction play a particularly important part. Expressionism and all other unconventional techniques in drama have only one valid aim, and that is a closer approach to truth. When a play employs unconventional techniques, it is not, or certainly shouldn't be, trying to escape its responsibility of dealing with reality, or interpreting experience, but is actually or should be attempting to find a closer approach, a more penetrating and vivid expression of things as they are. The straight realistic play with its genuine frigidaire and authentic ice cubes, its characters that speak exactly as its audience speaks, corresponds to the academic landscape and has the same virtue of a photographic likeness. Everyone should know nowadays the unimportance of the photographic in art: that truth, life, or reality is an organic thing which the poetic imagination can represent or suggest, in essence, only through transformation, through changing into other forms than those which were merely present in appearance.

These remarks are not meant as comments only on this particular play. They have to do with a conception of a new, plastic theater which must take the place of the exhausted theater of realistic conventions if the theater is to resume vitality as a part of our culture.

The Screen Device

There is *only one important difference between the original and acting version of the play* and that is the *omission* in the latter of the device which I tentatively included in my *original* script. This device was the use of a screen on which were projected magic-lantern slides bearing images or titles. I do not regret the omission of this device from the . . . Broadway production. The extraordinary power of Miss Taylor's performance made it suitable to have the utmost simplicity in the physical production. But I think it may be interesting to some readers to see how this device was conceived. So I am putting it into the published manuscript. These images and legends, projected from behind, were cast on a section of wall between the front-room and dining-room areas, which should be indistinguishable from the rest when not in use.

The purpose of this will probably be apparent. It is to give accent to certain values in each scene. Each scene contains a particular point (or several) which is structurally the most important. In an episodic play, such as this, the basic structure or narrative line may be obscured from the audience; the effect may seem fragmentary rather than architectural. This may not be the fault of the play so much as a lack of attention in the audience. The legend or image upon the screen will strengthen the effect of what is merely allusion in the writing and allow the primary point to be made more simply and lightly than if the entire responsibility were on the spoken lines. Aside from this structural value, I think the screen will have a definite emotional appeal, less definable but just as important. An imaginative producer or director may invent many other uses for this device than those indicated in the present script. In fact the possibilities of the device seem much larger to me than the instance of this play can possibly utilize.

The Music

Another extra-literary accent in this play is provided by the use of music. A single recurring tune, "The Glass Menagerie," is used to give emotional emphasis to suitable passages. This tune is like circus music, not when you are on the grounds or in the immediate vicinity of the parade, but when you are at some distance and very likely thinking of something else. It seems under those circumstances to continue almost interminably and it weaves in and out of your preoccupied consciousness; then it is the lightest, most delicate music in the world and perhaps the saddest. It expresses the surface vivacity of life with the underlying strain of immutable and inexpressible sorrow. When you look at a piece of delicately spun glass you think of two things: how beautiful it is and how easily it can be broken. Both of those ideas should be woven into the recurring tune, which dips in and out of the play as if it were carried on a wind that changes. It serves as a thread of connection and allusion between the narrator with his separate point in time and space and the subject of his story. Between each episode it returns as reference to the emotion, nostalgia, which is the first condition of the play. It is primarily Laura's music and therefore comes out most clearly when the play focuses upon her and the lovely fragility of glass which is her image.

The Lighting

The lighting in the play is not realistic. In keeping with the atmosphere of memory, the stage is dim. Shafts of light are focused on selected areas or actors, sometimes in contradistinction to what is the apparent center. For instance, in the quarrel scene between Tom and Amanda, in which Laura has no active part, the clearest pool of light is on her figure. This is also true of the supper scene. The light upon Laura should be distinct from the others, having a peculiar pristine clarity such as light used in early religious portraits of female saints or madonnas. A certain correspondence to light in religious paintings, such as El Greco's, where the figures are radiant in atmosphere that is relatively dusky, could be effectively used throughout the play. (It will also permit a more effective use of the screen.) A free, imaginative use of light can be of enormous value in giving a mobile, plastic quality to plays of a more or less static nature.

QUESTIONS

1. When produced in New York, the magic-lantern slides were omitted. Is the device an extraneous gimmick? Might it even interfere with the play, by oversimplifying and thus in a way belittling the actions?

2. What does the victrola offer to Laura? Why is the typewriter a better symbol (for the purposes of the play) than, say, a piano? After all, Laura could have been taking piano lessons. Explain the symbolism of the unicorn, and the loss of its horn. What is Laura saying to Jim in the gesture of giving him the unicorn?

3. Laura escapes to her glass menagerie. To what do Amanda and Tom escape? How complete is Tom's escape at the end of the play?

4. What is meant at the end when Laura blows out the candles? Is she blowing out illusions? Or life? Or both?

5. Did Williams make a slip in having Amanda say Laura is "crippled" on page 1024?

6. There is an implication that had Jim not been going steady he might have rescued Laura, but Jim also seems to represent (for example in his lines about money and power) the corrupt outside world that no longer values humanity. Is this a slip on Williams's part, or is it an interesting complexity?

7. On page 1024 Williams says, in a stage direction, "Now that we cannot hear the mother's speech, her silliness is gone and she has dignity and tragic beauty." Is Williams simply dragging in the word "tragic" because of its prestige, or is it legitimate? "Tragedy" is often distinguished from "pathos": in the tragic, the suffering is experienced by persons who act and are in some measure responsible for their suffering; in the pathetic, the suffering is experienced by the passive and the innocent. For example, in discussing Aeschylus's *The Suppliants* (in *Greek Tragedy*), H. D. F. Kitto says: "The Suppliants are not only pathetic, as the victims of outrage, but also tragic, as the victims of their own misconceptions." Given this distinction, to what extent are Amanda and Laura tragic? Pathetic?

Arthur Miller (b. 1915)

Death of a Salesman
Certain Private Conversations
in Two Acts and a Requiem

List of Characters

Willy Loman
Linda
Biff
Happy
Bernard
The Woman
Charley
Uncle Ben
Howard Wagner
Jenny
Stanley
Miss Forsythe
Letta

Scene. *The action takes place in Willy Loman's house and yard and in various places he visits in the New York and Boston of today.*

ACT I

Scene: *A melody is heard, played upon a flute. It is small and fine, telling of grass and trees and the horizon. The curtain rises.*

Before us is the Salesman's house. We are aware of towering, angular shapes behind it, surrounding it on all sides. Only the blue light of the sky falls upon the house and forestage; the surrounding area shows an angry glow of orange. As more light appears, we see a solid vault of apartment houses around the small, fragile-seeming home. An air of the dream clings to the place, a dream rising out of reality. The kitchen at center seems actual enough, for there is a kitchen table with three chairs, and a refrigerator. But no other fixtures are seen. At the back of the kitchen there is a draped entrance, which leads to the living room. To the right of the kitchen, on a level raised two feet, is a bedroom furnished only with a brass bedstead and a straight chair. On a shelf over the bed a silver athletic trophy stands. A window opens onto the apartment house at the side.

Top: *Lee J. Cobb starred as Willy Loman in the 1949 original Broadway production of* Death of a Salesman. *Photograph reproduced courtesy of the Theatre Arts Library, Harry Ransom Humanities Research Center, The University of Texas at Austin. Bottom: Dustin Hoffman, as Willy Loman, and John Malkovich, as Biff, face each other in this scene from the 1984 production. Photograph by Inge Morath; reproduced by permission of Magnum Photos, Inc.*

Behind the kitchen, on a level raised six and a half feet, is the boys' bedroom, at present barely visible. Two beds are dimly seen, and at the back of the room a dormer window. (This bedroom is above the unseen living room.) At the left a stairway curves up to it from the kitchen.

The entire setting is wholly or, in some places, partially transparent. The roof-line of the house is one-dimensional; under and over it we see the apartment buildings. Before the house lies an apron, curving beyond the forestage into the orchestra. This forward area serves as the back yard as well as the locale of all Willy's imaginings and of his city scenes. Whenever the action is in the present the actors observe the imaginary wall-lines, entering the house only through its door at the left. But in the scenes of the past these boundaries are broken, and characters enter or leave a room by stepping "through" a wall onto the forestage.

From the right, Willy Loman, the Salesman, enters, carrying two large sample cases. The flute plays on. He hears but is not aware of it. He is past sixty years of age, dressed quietly. Even as he crosses the stage to the doorway of the house, his exhaustion is apparent. He unlocks the door, comes into the kitchen, and thankfully lets his burden down, feeling the soreness of his palms. A word-sigh escapes his lips — it might be "Oh, boy, oh, boy." He closes the door, then carries his cases out into the living room, through the draped kitchen doorway.

Linda, his wife, has stirred in her bed at the right. She gets out and puts on a robe, listening. Most often jovial, she has developed an iron repression of her exceptions to Willy's behavior — she more than loves him, she admires him, as though his mercurial nature, his temper, his massive dreams and little cruelties, served her only as sharp reminders of the turbulent longings within him, longings which she shares but lacks the temperament to utter and follow to their end.

Linda (*hearing Willy outside the bedroom, calls with some trepidation*). Willy!

Willy. It's all right. I came back.

Linda. Why? What happened? (*Slight pause.*) Did something happen, Willy?

Willy. No, nothing happened.

Linda. You didn't smash the car, did you?

Willy (*with casual irritation*). I said nothing happened. Didn't you hear me?

Linda. Don't you feel well?

Willy. I'm tired to the death. (*The flute has faded away. He sits on the bed beside her, a little numb.*) I couldn't make it. I just couldn't make it, Linda.

Linda (*very carefully, delicately*). Where were you all day? You look terrible.

Willy. I got as far as a little above Yonkers. I stopped for a cup of coffee. Maybe it was the coffee.

Linda. What?

Willy (*after a pause*). I suddenly couldn't drive any more. The car kept going off onto the shoulder, y'know?

Linda (*helpfully*). Oh. Maybe it was the steering again. I don't think Angelo knows the Studebaker.

Willy. No, it's me, it's me. Suddenly I realize I'm goin' sixty miles an hour and I don't remember the last five minutes. I'm — I can't seem to — keep my mind to it.

Linda. Maybe it's your glasses. You never went for your new glasses.

Willy. No, I see everything. I came back ten miles an hour. It took me nearly four hours from Yonkers.

Linda (*resigned*). Well, you'll just have to take a rest, Willy, you can't continue this way.

Willy. I just got back from Florida.

Linda. But you didn't rest your mind. Your mind is overactive, and the mind is what counts, dear.

Willy. I'll start out in the morning. Maybe I'll feel better in the morning. (*She is taking off his shoes.*) These goddam arch supports are killing me.

Linda. Take an aspirin. Should I get you an aspirin? It'll soothe you.

Willy (*with wonder*). I was driving along, you understand? And I was fine. I was even observing the scenery. You can imagine, me looking at scenery, on the road every week of my life. But it's so beautiful up there, Linda, the trees are so thick, and the sun is warm. I opened the windshield and just let the warm air bathe over me. And then all of a sudden I'm goin' off the road! I'm tellin' ya, I absolutely forgot I was driving. If I'd've gone the other way over the white line I might've killed somebody. So I went on again — and five minutes later I'm dreamin' again, and I nearly . . . (*He presses two fingers against his eyes.*) I have such thoughts, I have such strange thoughts.

Linda. Willy, dear. Talk to them again. There's no reason why you can't work in New York.

Willy. They don't need me in New York. I'm the New England man. I'm vital in New England.

Linda. But you're sixty years old. They can't expect you to keep traveling every week.

Willy. I'll have to send a wire to Portland. I'm supposed to see Brown and Morrison tomorrow morning at ten o'clock to show the line. Goddammit, I could sell them! (*He starts putting on his jacket.*)

Linda (*taking the jacket from him*). Why don't you go down to the place tomorrow and tell Howard you've simply got to work in New York? You're too accommodating, dear.

Willy. If old man Wagner was alive I'd a been in charge of New York now! That man was a prince, he was a masterful man. But that boy of his, that Howard, he don't appreciate. When I went north the first time, the Wagner Company didn't know where New England was!

Linda. Why don't you tell those things to Howard, dear?

Willy (*encouraged*). I will, I definitely will. Is there any cheese?

Linda. I'll make you a sandwich.

Willy. No, go to sleep. I'll take some milk. I'll be up right away. The boys in?

Linda. They're sleeping. Happy took Biff on a date tonight.

Willy (*interested*). That so?

Linda. It was so nice to see them shaving together, one behind the other, in the bathroom. And going out together. You notice? The whole house smells of shaving lotion.

Willy. Figure it out. Work a lifetime to pay off a house. You finally own it, and there's nobody to live in it.

Linda. Well, dear, life is a casting off. It's always that way.

Willy. No, no, some people — some people accomplish something. Did Biff say anything after I went this morning?

Linda. You shouldn't have criticized him, Willy, especially after he just got off the train. You mustn't lose your temper with him.

Willy. When the hell did I lose my temper? I simply asked him if he was making any money. Is that a criticism?

Linda. But, dear, how could he make any money?

Willy (*worried and angered*). There's such an undercurrent in him. He became a moody man. Did he apologize when I left this morning?

Linda. He was crestfallen, Willy. You know how he admires you. I think if he finds himself, then you'll both be happier and not fight any more.

Willy. How can he find himself on a farm? Is that a life? A farm hand? In the beginning, when he was young, I thought, well, a young man, it's good for him to tramp around, take a lot of different jobs. But it's more than ten years now and he has yet to make thirty-five dollars a week!

Linda. He's finding himself, Willy.

Willy. Not finding yourself at the age of thirty-four is a disgrace!

Linda. Shh!

Willy. The trouble is he's lazy, goddammit!

Linda. Willy, please!

Willy. Biff is a lazy bum!

Linda. They're sleeping. Get something to eat. Go on down.

Willy. Why did he come home? I would like to know what brought him home.

Linda. I don't know. I think he's still lost, Willy. I think he's very lost.

Willy. Biff Loman is lost. In the greatest country in the world a young man with such — personal attractiveness, gets lost. And such a hard worker. There's one thing about Biff — he's not lazy.

Linda. Never.

Willy (with pity and resolve). I'll see him in the morning; I'll have a nice talk with him. I'll get him a job selling. He could be big in no time. My God! Remember how they used to follow him around in high school? When he smiled at one of them their faces lit up. When he walked down the street . . . (*He loses himself in reminiscences.*)

Linda (trying to bring him out of it). Willy, dear, I got a new kind of American-type cheese today. It's whipped.

Willy. Why do you get American when I like Swiss?

Linda. I just thought you'd like a change . . .

Willy. I don't want a change! I want Swiss cheese. Why am I always being contradicted?

Linda (with a covering laugh). I thought it would be a surprise.

Willy. Why don't you open a window in here, for God's sake?

Linda (with infinite patience). They're all open, dear.

Willy. The way they boxed us in here. Bricks and windows, windows and bricks.

Linda. We should've bought the land next door.

Willy. The street is lined with cars. There's not a breath of fresh air in the neighborhood. The grass don't grow any more, you can't raise a carrot in the back yard. They should've had a law against apartment houses. Remember those two beautiful elm trees out there? When I and Biff hung the swing between them?

Linda. Yeah, like being a million miles from the city.

Willy. They should've arrested the builder for cutting those down.

They massacred the neighborhood. (*Lost.*) More and more I think of those days, Linda. This time of year it was lilac and wisteria. And then the peonies would come out, and the daffodils. What fragrance in this room!

Linda. Well, after all, people had to move somewhere.

Willy. No, there's more people now.

Linda. I don't think there's more people. I think . . .

Willy. There's more people! That's what's ruining this country! Population is getting out of control. The competition is maddening! Smell the stink from that apartment house! And another one on the other side . . . How can they whip cheese?

On Willy's last line, Biff and Happy raise themselves up in their beds, listening.

Linda. Go down, try it. And be quiet.

Willy (turning to Linda, guiltily). You're not worried about me, are you, sweetheart?

Biff. What's the matter?

Happy. Listen!

Linda. You've got too much on the ball to worry about.

Willy. You're my foundation and my support, Linda.

Linda. Just try to relax, dear. You make mountains out of molehills.

Willy. I won't fight with him any more. If he wants to go back to Texas, let him go.

Linda. He'll find his way.

Willy. Sure. Certain men just don't get started till later in life. Like Thomas Edison, I think. Or B. F. Goodrich. One of them was deaf. (*He starts for the bedroom doorway.*) I'll put my money on Biff.

Linda. And Willy — if it's warm Sunday we'll drive in the country. And we'll open the windshield, and take lunch.

Willy. No, the windshields don't open on the new cars.

Linda. But you opened it today.

Willy. Me? I didn't. (*He stops.*) Now isn't that peculiar! Isn't that a remarkable . . . (*He breaks off in amazement and fright as the flute is heard distantly.*)

Linda. What, darling?

Willy. That is the most remarkable thing.

Linda. What, dear?

Willy. I was thinking of the Chevvy. (*Slight pause.*) Nineteen twenty-eight . . . when I had that red Chevvy . . . (*Breaks off.*) That funny? I coulda sworn I was driving that Chevvy today.

Linda. Well, that's nothing. Something must've reminded you.

Willy. Remarkable. Ts. Remember those days? The way Biff used to simonize that car? The dealer refused to believe there was eighty thousand miles on it. (*He shakes his head.*) Heh! (*To Linda.*) Close your eyes, I'll be right up. (*He walks out of the bedroom.*)

Happy (*to Biff*). Jesus, maybe he smashed up the car again!

Linda (*calling after Willy*). Be careful on the stairs, dear! The cheese is on the middle shelf. (*She turns, goes over to the bed, takes his jacket, and goes out of the bedroom.*)

Light has risen on the boys' room. Unseen, Willy is heard talking to himself, "Eighty thousand miles," and a little laugh. Biff gets out of bed, comes downstage a bit, and stands attentively. Biff is two years older than his brother Happy, well built, but in these days bears a worn air and seems less self-assured. He has succeeded less, and his dreams are stronger and less acceptable than Happy's. Happy is tall, powerfully made. Sexuality is like a visible color on him, or a scent that many women have discovered. He, like his brother, is lost, but in a different way, for he has never allowed himself to turn his face toward defeat and is thus more confused and hard-skinned, although seemingly more content.

Happy (*getting out of bed*). He's going to get his license taken away if he keeps that up. I'm getting nervous about him, y'know, Biff?

Biff. His eyes are going.

Happy. No, I've driven with him. He sees all right. He just doesn't keep his mind on it. I drove into the city with him last week. He stops at a green light and then it turns red and he goes. (*He laughs.*)

Biff. Maybe he's color-blind.

Happy. Pop? Why he's got the finest eye for color in the business. You know that.

Biff (*sitting down on his bed*). I'm going to sleep.

Happy. You're not still sour on Dad, are you, Biff?

Biff. He's all right, I guess.

Willy (*underneath them, in the living room*). Yes, sir, eighty thousand miles — eighty-two thousand!

Biff. You smoking?

Happy (*holding out a pack of cigarettes*). Want one?

Biff (*taking a cigarette*). I can never sleep when I smell it.

Willy. What a simonizing job, heh!

Happy (*with deep sentiment*). Funny, Biff, y'know? Us sleeping in here again? The old beds. (*He pats his bed affectionately.*) All the talk that went across those two beds, huh? Our whole lives.

Biff. Yeah. Lotta dreams and plans.

Happy (with a deep and masculine laugh). About five hundred women would like to know what was said in this room. (*They share a soft laugh.*)

Biff. Remember that big Betsy something — what the hell was her name — over on Bushwick Avenue?

Happy (combing his hair). With the collie dog!

Biff. That's the one. I got you in there, remember?

Happy. Yeah, that was my first time — I think. Boy, there was a pig. (*They laugh, almost crudely.*) You taught me everything I know about women. Don't forget that.

Biff. I bet you forgot how bashful you used to be. Especially with girls.

Happy. Oh, I still am, Biff.

Biff. Oh, go on.

Happy. I just control it, that's all. I think I got less bashful and you got more so. What happened, Biff? Where's the old humor, the old confidence? (*He shakes Biff's knee. Biff gets up and moves restlessly about the room.*) What's the matter?

Biff. Why does Dad mock me all the time?

Happy. He's not mocking you, he . . .

Biff. Everything I say there's a twist of mockery on his face. I can't get near him.

Happy. He just wants you to make good, that's all. I wanted to talk to you about Dad for a long time, Biff. Something's — happening to him. He — talks to himself.

Biff. I noticed that this morning. But he always mumbled.

Happy. But not so noticeable. It got so embarrassing I sent him to Florida. And you know something? Most of the time he's talking to you.

Biff. What's he say about me?

Happy. I can't make it out.

Biff. What's he say about me?

Happy. I think the fact that you're not settled, that you're still kind of up in the air . . .

Biff. There's one or two other things depressing him, Happy.

Happy. What do you mean?

Biff. Never mind. Just don't lay it all to me.

Happy. But I think if you just got started — I mean — is there any future for you out there?

Biff. I tell ya, Hap, I don't know what the future is. I don't know — what I'm supposed to want.

Happy. What do you mean?

Biff. Well, I spent six or seven years after high school trying to work myself up. Shipping clerk, salesman, business of one kind or another. And it's a measly manner of existence. To get on that subway on the hot mornings in summer. To devote your whole life to keeping stock, or making phone calls, or selling or buying. To suffer fifty weeks of the year for the sake of a two-week vacation, when all you really desire is to be outdoors, with your shirt off. And always to have to get ahead of the next fella. And still — that's how you build a future.

Happy. Well, you really enjoy it on a farm? Are you content out there?

Biff (with rising agitation). Hap, I've had twenty or thirty different kinds of jobs since I left home before the war, and it always turns out the same. I just realized it lately. In Nebraska when I herded cattle, and the Dakotas, and Arizona, and now in Texas. It's why I came home now, I guess, because I realized it. This farm I work on, it's spring there now, see? And they've got about fifteen new colts. There's nothing more inspiring or — beautiful than the sight of a mare and a new colt. And it's cool there now, see? Texas is cool now, and it's spring. And whenever spring comes to where I am, I suddenly get the feeling, my God, I'm not gettin' anywhere! What the hell am I doing, playing around with horses, twenty-eight dollars a week! I'm thirty-four years old, I oughta be makin' my future. That's when I come running home. And now, I get here, and I don't know what to do with myself. (*After a pause.*) I've always made a point of not wasting my life, and everytime I come back here I know that all I've done is to waste my life.

Happy. You're a poet, you know that, Biff? You're a — you're an idealist!

Biff. No, I'm mixed up very bad. Maybe I oughta get married. Maybe I oughta get stuck into something. Maybe that's my trouble. I'm like a boy. I'm not married, I'm not in business, I just — I'm like a boy. Are you content, Hap? You're a success, aren't you? Are you content?

Happy. Hell, no!

Biff. Why? You're making money, aren't you?

Happy (moving about with energy, expressiveness). All I can do now is wait for the merchandise manager to die. And suppose I get to be merchandise manager? He's a good friend of mine, and he just built a terrific estate on Long Island. And he lived there about two months and sold it, and now he's building another one. He can't enjoy it once it's finished. And I know that's just what I would do. I don't know what the hell I'm workin' for. Sometimes I sit in my apartment — all alone. And I think of the rent I'm paying. And it's crazy. But then, it's what I always wanted. My own apartment, a car, and plenty of women. And still, goddammit, I'm lonely.

Biff (with enthusiasm). Listen, why don't you come out West with me?

Happy. You and I, heh?

Biff. Sure, maybe we could buy a ranch. Raise cattle, use our muscles. Men built like we are should be working out in the open.

Happy (avidly). The Loman Brothers, heh?

Biff (with vast affection). Sure, we'd be known all over the counties!

Happy (enthralled). That's what I dream about, Biff. Sometimes I want to just rip my clothes off in the middle of the store and outbox that goddam merchandise manager. I mean I can outbox, outrun, and outlift anybody in that store, and I have to take orders from those common, petty sons-of-bitches till I can't stand it any more.

Biff. I'm tellin' you, kid, if you were with me I'd be happy out there.

Happy (enthused). See, Biff, everybody around me is so false that I'm constantly lowering my ideals . . .

Biff. Baby, together we'd stand up for one another, we'd have someone to trust.

Happy. If I were around you . . .

Biff. Hap, the trouble is we weren't brought up to grub for money. I don't know how to do it.

Happy. Neither can I!

Biff. Then let's go!

Happy. The only thing is — what can you make out there?

Biff. But look at your friend. Builds an estate and then hasn't the peace of mind to live in it.

Happy. Yeah, but when he walks into the store the waves part in front of him. That's fifty-two thousand dollars a year coming through the revolving door, and I got more in my pinky finger than he's got in his head.

Biff. Yeah, but you just said . . .

Happy. I gotta show some of those pompous, self-important executives over there that Hap Loman can make the grade. I want to walk into the store the way he walks in. Then I'll go with you, Biff. We'll be together yet, I swear. But take those two we had tonight. Now weren't they gorgeous creatures?

Biff. Yeah, yeah, most gorgeous I've had in years.

Happy. I get that any time I want, Biff. Whenever I feel disgusted. The only trouble is, it gets like bowling or something. I just keep knockin' them over and it doesn't mean anything. You still run around a lot?

Biff. Naa. I'd like to find a girl — steady, somebody with substance.

Happy. That's what I long for.

Biff. Go on! You'd never come home.

Happy. I would! Somebody with character, with resistance! Like Mom, y'know? You're gonna call me a bastard when I tell you this. That girl Charlotte I was with tonight is engaged to be married in five weeks. (*He tries on his new hat.*)

Biff. No kiddin'!

Happy. Sure, the guy's in line for the vice-presidency of the store. I don't know what gets into me, maybe I just have an over-developed sense of competition or something, but I went and ruined her, and furthermore I can't get rid of her. And he's the third executive I've done that to. Isn't that a crummy characteristic? And to top it all, I go to their weddings! (*Indignantly, but laughing.*) Like I'm not supposed to take bribes. Manufacturers offer me a hundred-dollar bill now and then to throw an order their way. You know how honest I am, but it's like this girl, see. I hate myself for it. Because I don't want the girl, and, still, I take it and — I love it!

Biff. Let's go to sleep.

Happy. I guess we didn't settle anything, heh?

Biff. I just got one idea that I think I'm going to try.

Happy. What's that?

Biff. Remember Bill Oliver?

Happy. Sure, Oliver is very big now. You want to work for him again?

Biff. No, but when I quit he said something to me. He put his arm on my shoulder, and he said, "Biff, if you ever need anything, come to me."

Happy. I remember that. That sounds good.

Biff. I think I'll go to see him. If I could get ten thousand or even seven or eight thousand dollars I could buy a beautiful ranch.

Happy. I bet he'd back you. 'Cause he thought highly of you, Biff. I mean, they all do. You're well liked, Biff. That's why I say to come back here, and we both have the apartment. And I'm tellin' you, Biff, any babe you want . . .

Biff. No, with a ranch I could do the work I like and still be something. I just wonder though. I wonder if Oliver still thinks I stole that carton of basketballs.

Happy. Oh, he probably forgot that long ago. It's almost ten years. You're too sensitive. Anyway, he didn't really fire you.

Biff. Well, I think he was going to. I think that's why I quit. I was never sure whether he knew or not. I know he thought the world of me, though. I was the only one he'd let lock up the place.

Willy (below). You gonna wash the engine, Biff?

Happy. Shh!

Biff looks at Happy, who is gazing down, listening. Willy is mumbling in the parlor.

Happy. You hear that?

They listen. Willy laughs warmly.

Biff (growing angry). Doesn't he know Mom can hear that?

Willy. Don't get your sweater dirty, Biff!

A look of pain crosses Biff's face.

Happy. Isn't that terrible? Don't leave again, will you? You'll find a job here. You gotta stick around. I don't know what to do about him, it's getting embarrassing.

Willy. What a simonizing job!

Biff. Mom's hearing that!

Willy. No kiddin', Biff, you got a date? Wonderful!

Happy. Go on to sleep. But talk to him in the morning, will you?

Biff (reluctantly getting into bed). With her in the house. Brother!

Happy (getting into bed). I wish you'd have a good talk with him.

The light on their room begins to fade.

Biff (to himself in bed). That selfish, stupid . . .

Happy. Sh . . . Sleep, Biff.

Their light is out. Well before they have finished speaking, Willy's form is dimly seen below in the darkened kitchen. He opens the refrigerator, searches in there, and takes out a bottle of milk. The apartment houses are fading out, and the entire house and surroundings become covered with leaves. Music insinuates itself as the leaves appear.

Willy. Just wanna be careful with those girls, Biff, that's all. Don't make any promises. No promises of any kind. Because a girl, y'know, they always believe what you tell 'em, and you're very young, Biff, you're too young to be talking seriously to girls.

Light rises on the kitchen. Willy, talking, shuts the refrigerator door and comes downstage to the kitchen table. He pours milk into a glass. He is totally immersed in himself, smiling faintly.

Willy. Too young entirely, Biff. You want to watch your schooling first. Then when you're all set, there'll be plenty of girls for a boy like you. (*He smiles broadly at a kitchen chair.*) That so? The girls pay for you? (*He laughs.*) Boy, you must really be makin' a hit.

Willy is gradually addressing — physically — a point offstage, speaking through the wall of the kitchen, and his voice has been rising in volume to that of a normal conversation.

Willy. I been wondering why you polish the car so careful. Ha! Don't leave the hubcaps, boys. Get the chamois to the hubcaps. Happy, use newspaper on the windows, it's the easiest thing. Show him how to do it, Biff! You see, Happy? Pad it up, use it like a pad. That's it, that's it, good work. You're doin' all right, Hap. (*He pauses, then nods in approbation for a few seconds, then looks upward.*) Biff, first thing we gotta do when we get time is clip that big branch over the house. Afraid it's gonna fall in a storm and hit the roof. Tell you what. We get a rope and sling her around, and then we climb up there with a couple of saws and take her down. Soon as you finish the car, boys, I wanna see ya. I got a surprise for you, boys.
Biff (*offstage*). Whatta ya got, Dad?
Willy. No, you finish first. Never leave a job till you're finished — remember that. (*Looking toward the "big trees."*) Biff, up in Albany I saw a beautiful hammock. I think I'll buy it next trip, and we'll hang it right between those two elms. Wouldn't that be something? Just swingin' there under those branches. Boy, that would be . . .

Young Biff and Young Happy appear from the direction Willy was addressing. Happy carries rags and a pail of water. Biff, wearing a sweater with a block "S," carries a football.

Biff (*pointing in the direction of the car offstage*). How's that, Pop, professional?
Willy. Terrific. Terrific job, boys. Good work, Biff.
Happy. Where's the surprise, Pop?
Willy. In the back seat of the car.
Happy. Boy! (*He runs off.*)

Biff. What is it, Dad? Tell me, what'd you buy?

Willy (laughing, cuffs him). Never mind, something I want you to have.

Biff (turns and starts off). What is it, Hap?

Happy (offstage). It's a punching bag!

Biff. Oh, Pop!

Willy. It's got Gene Tunney's signature on it!

Happy runs onstage with a punching bag.

Biff. Gee, how'd you know we wanted a punching bag?

Willy. Well, it's the finest thing for the timing.

Happy (lies down on his back and pedals with his feet). I'm losing weight, you notice, Pop?

Willy (to Happy). Jumping rope is good too.

Biff. Did you see the new football I got?

Willy (examining the ball). Where'd you get a new ball?

Biff. The coach told me to practice my passing.

Willy. That so? And he gave you the ball, heh?

Biff. Well, I borrowed it from the locker room. (*He laughs confidentially.*)

Willy (laughing with him at the theft). I want you to return that.

Happy. I told you he wouldn't like it!

Biff (angrily). Well, I'm bringing it back!

Willy (stopping the incipient argument, to Happy). Sure, he's gotta practice with a regulation ball, doesn't he? (*To Biff.*) Coach'll probably congratulate you on your initiative!

Biff. Oh, he keeps congratulating my initiative all the time, Pop.

Willy. That's because he likes you. If somebody else took that ball there'd be an uproar. So what's the report, boys, what's the report?

Biff. Where'd you go this time, Dad? Gee we were lonesome for you.

Willy (pleased, puts an arm around each boy and they come down to the apron). Lonesome, heh?

Biff. Missed you every minute.

Willy. Don't say? Tell you a secret, boys. Don't breathe it to a soul. Someday I'll have my own business, and I'll never have to leave home any more.

Happy. Like Uncle Charley, heh?

Willy. Bigger than Uncle Charley! Because Charley is not — liked. He's liked, but he's not — well liked.

Biff. Where'd you go this time, Dad?

Willy. Well, I got on the road, and I went north to Providence. Met the Mayor.

Biff. The Mayor of Providence!

Willy. He was sitting in the hotel lobby.

Biff. What'd he say?

Willy. He said, "Morning!" And I said, "You got a fine city here, Mayor." And then he had coffee with me. And then I went to Waterbury. Waterbury is a fine city. Big clock city, the famous Waterbury clock. Sold a nice bill there. And then Boston — Boston is the cradle of the Revolution. A fine city. And a couple of other towns in Mass., and on to Portland and Bangor and straight home!

Biff. Gee, I'd love to go with you sometime, Dad.

Willy. Soon as summer comes.

Happy. Promise?

Willy. You and Hap and I, and I'll show you all the towns. America is full of beautiful towns and fine, upstanding people. And they know me, boys, they know me up and down New England. The finest people. And when I bring you fellas up, there'll be open sesame for all of us, 'cause one thing, boys: I have friends. I can park my car in any street in New England, and the cops protect it like their own. This summer, heh?

Biff and Happy (together). Yeah! You bet!

Willy. We'll take our bathing suits.

Happy. We'll carry your bags, Pop!

Willy. Oh, won't that be something! Me comin' into the Boston stores with you boys carryin' my bags. What a sensation!

Biff is prancing around, practicing passing the ball.

Willy. You nervous, Biff, about the game?

Biff. Not if you're gonna be there.

Willy. What do they say about you in school, now that they made you captain?

Happy. There's a crowd of girls behind him everytime the classes change.

Biff (taking Willy's hand). This Saturday, Pop, this Saturday — just for you, I'm going to break through for a touchdown.

Happy. You're supposed to pass.

Biff. I'm takin' one play for Pop. You watch me, Pop, and when I take off my helmet, that means I'm breakin' out. Then you watch me crash through that line!

Willy (kisses Biff). Oh, wait'll I tell this in Boston!

Bernard enters in knickers. He is younger than Biff, earnest and loyal, a worried boy.

Bernard. Biff, where are you? You're supposed to study with me today.

Willy. Hey, looka Bernard. What're you lookin' so anemic about,
   Bernard?
Bernard. He's gotta study, Uncle Willy. He's got Regents next
   week.
Happy (tauntingly, spinning Bernard around). Let's box, Bernard!
Bernard. Biff! (*He gets away from Happy.*) Listen, Biff, I heard Mr.
   Birnbaum say that if you don't start studyin' math he's gonna
   flunk you, and you won't graduate. I heard him!
Willy. You better study with him, Biff. Go ahead now.
Bernard. I heard him!
Biff. Oh, Pop, you didn't see my sneakers! (*He holds up a foot for
   Willy to look at.*)
Willy. Hey, that's a beautiful job of printing!
Bernard (wiping his glasses). Just because he printed University of
   Virginia on his sneakers doesn't mean they've got to graduate
   him, Uncle Willy!
Willy (angrily). What're you talking about? With scholarships to
   three universities they're gonna flunk him?
Bernard. But I heard Mr. Birnbaum say . . .
Willy. Don't be a pest, Bernard! (*To his boys.*) What an anemic!
Bernard. Okay, I'm waiting for you in my house, Biff.

   Bernard goes off. The Lomans laugh.

Willy. Bernard is not well liked, is he?
Biff. He's liked, but he's not well liked.
Happy. That's right, Pop.
Willy. That's just what I mean. Bernard can get the best marks
   in school, y'understand, but when he gets out in the business
   world, y'understand, you are going to be five times ahead
   of him. That's why I thank Almighty God you're both built
   like Adonises. Because the man who makes an appearance
   in the business world, the man who creates personal interest,
   is the man who gets ahead. Be liked and you will never
   want. You take me, for instance. I never have to wait in
   line to see a buyer. "Willy Loman is here!" That's all they
   have to know, and I go right through.
Biff. Did you knock them dead, Pop?
Willy. Knocked 'em cold in Providence, slaughtered 'em in Boston.
Happy (on his back, pedaling again). I'm losing weight, you notice,
   Pop?

   *Linda enters as of old, a ribbon in her hair, carrying a basket of
   washing.*

Linda (with youthful energy). Hello, dear!
Willy. Sweetheart!

Linda. How'd the Chevvy run?

Willy. Chevrolet, Linda, is the greatest car ever built. (*To the boys.*) Since when do you let your mother carry wash up the stairs?

Biff. Grab hold there, boy!

Happy. Where to, Mom?

Linda. Hang them up on the line. And you better go down to your friends, Biff. The cellar is full of boys. They don't know what to do with themselves.

Biff. Ah, when Pop comes home they can wait!

Willy (*laughs appreciatively*). You better go down and tell them what to do, Biff.

Biff. I think I'll have them sweep out the furnace room.

Willy. Good work, Biff.

Biff (*goes through wall-line of kitchen to doorway at back and calls down*). Fellas! Everybody sweep out the furnace room! I'll be right down!

Voices. All right! Okay, Biff.

Biff. George and Sam and Frank, come out back! We're hangin' up the wash! Come on, Hap, on the double! (*He and Happy carry out the basket.*)

Linda. The way they obey him!

Willy. Well, that's training, the training. I'm tellin' you, I was sellin' thousands and thousands, but I had to come home.

Linda. Oh, the whole block'll be at that game. Did you sell anything?

Willy. I did five hundred gross in Providence and seven hundred gross in Boston.

Linda. No! Wait a minute, I've got a pencil. (*She pulls pencil and paper out of her apron pocket.*) That makes your commission . . . Two hundred — my God! Two hundred and twelve dollars!

Willy. Well, I didn't figure it yet, but . . .

Linda. How much did you do?

Willy. Well, I — I did — about a hundred and eighty gross in Providence. Well, no — it came to — roughly two hundred gross on the whole trip.

Linda (*without hesitation*). Two hundred gross. That's . . . (*She figures.*)

Willy. The trouble was that three of the stores were half-closed for inventory in Boston. Otherwise I woulda broke records.

Linda. Well, it makes seventy dollars and some pennies. That's very good.

Willy. What do we owe?

Linda. Well, on the first there's sixteen dollars on the refrigerator . . .

Willy. Why sixteen?

Linda. Well, the fan belt broke, so it was a dollar eighty.

Willy. But it's brand new.

Linda. Well, the man said that's the way it is. Till they work themselves in, y'know.

> *They move through the wall-line into the kitchen.*

Willy. I hope we didn't get stuck on that machine.

Linda. They got the biggest ads of any of them!

Willy. I know, it's a fine machine. What else?

Linda. Well, there's nine-sixty for the washing machine. And for the vacuum cleaner there's three and a half due on the fifteenth. Then the roof, you got twenty-one dollars remaining.

Willy. It don't leak, does it?

Linda. No, they did a wonderful job. Then you owe Frank for the carburetor.

Willy. I'm not going to pay that man! That goddam Chevrolet, they ought to prohibit the manufacture of that car!

Linda. Well, you owe him three and a half. And odds and ends, comes to around a hundred and twenty dollars by the fifteenth.

Willy. A hundred and twenty dollars! My God, if business don't pick up I don't know what I'm gonna do!

Linda. Well, next week you'll do better.

Willy. Oh, I'll knock 'em dead next week. I'll go to Hartford. I'm very well liked in Hartford. You know, the trouble is, Linda, people don't seem to take to me.

> *They move onto the forestage.*

Linda. Oh, don't be foolish.

Willy. I know it when I walk in. They seem to laugh at me.

Linda. Why? Why would they laugh at you? Don't talk that way, Willy.

> *Willy moves to the edge of the stage. Linda goes into the kitchen and starts to darn stockings.*

Willy. I don't know the reason for it, but they just pass me by. I'm not noticed.

Linda. But you're doing wonderful, dear. You're making seventy to a hundred dollars a week.

Willy. But I gotta be at it ten, twelve hours a day. Other men — I don't know — they do it easier. I don't know why — I can't stop myself — I talk too much. A man oughta come in with a few words. One thing about Charley. He's a man of few words, and they respect him.

Linda. You don't talk too much, you're just lively.

Willy (smiling). Well, I figure, what the hell, life is short, a couple of jokes. (*To himself.*) I joke too much! (*The smile goes.*)

Linda. Why? You're . . .

Willy. I'm fat. I'm very — foolish to look at, Linda. I didn't tell you, but Christmas time I happened to be calling on F. H. Stewarts, and a salesman I know, as I was going in to see the buyer I heard him say something about — walrus. And I — I cracked him right across the face. I won't take that. I simply will not take that. But they do laugh at me. I know that.

Linda. Darling . . .

Willy. I gotta overcome it. I know I gotta overcome it. I'm not dressing to advantage, maybe.

Linda. Willy, darling, you're the handsomest man in the world . . .

Willy. Oh, no, Linda.

Linda. To me you are. (*Slight pause.*) The handsomest.

From the darkness is heard the laughter of a woman. Willy doesn't turn to it, but it continues through Linda's lines.

Linda. And the boys, Willy. Few men are idolized by their children the way you are.

Music is heard as behind a scrim, to the left of the house; The Woman, dimly seen, is dressing.

Willy (with great feeling). You're the best there is, Linda, you're a pal, you know that? On the road — on the road I want to grab you sometimes and just kiss the life outa you.

The laughter is loud now, and he moves into a brightening area at the left, where The Woman has come from behind the scrim and is standing, putting on her hat, looking into a "mirror" and laughing.

Willy. 'Cause I get so lonely — especially when business is bad and there's nobody to talk to. I get the feeling that I'll never sell anything again, that I won't make a living for you, or a business, a business for the boys. (*He talks through The Woman's subsiding laughter; The Woman primps at the "mirror."*) There's so much I want to make for . . .

The Woman. Me? You didn't make me, Willy. I picked you.

Willy (pleased). You picked me?

The Woman (who is quite proper-looking, Willy's age). I did. I've been sitting at that desk watching all the salesmen go by, day in, day out. But you've got such a sense of humor, and we do have such a good time together, don't we?

Willy. Sure, sure. (*He takes her in his arms.*) Why do you have to go now?

The Woman. It's two o'clock . . .
Willy. No, come on in! (*He pulls her.*)
The Woman. . . . my sisters'll be scandalized. When'll you be back?
Willy. Oh, two weeks about. Will you come up again?
The Woman. Sure thing. You do make me laugh. It's good for
    me. (*She squeezes his arm, kisses him.*) And I think you're a
    wonderful man.
Willy. You picked me, heh?
The Woman. Sure. Because you're so sweet. And such a kidder.
Willy. Well, I'll see you next time I'm in Boston.
The Woman. I'll put you right through to the buyers.
Willy (*slapping her bottom*). Right. Well, bottoms up!
The Woman (*slaps him gently and laughs*). You just kill me, Willy.
    (*He suddenly grabs her and kisses her roughly.*) You kill me.
    And thanks for the stockings. I love a lot of stockings. Well,
    good night.
Willy. Good night. And keep your pores open!
The Woman. Oh, Willy!

> *The Woman bursts out laughing, and Linda's laughter blends in.*
> *The Woman disappears into the dark. Now the area at the kitchen*
> *table brightens. Linda is sitting where she was at the kitchen table,*
> *but now is mending a pair of her silk stockings.*

Linda. You are, Willy. The handsomest man. You've got no reason
    to feel that . . .
Willy (*coming out of The Woman's dimming area and going over to
    Linda*). I'll make it all up to you, Linda, I'll . . .
Linda. There's nothing to make up, dear. You're doing fine, better
    than . . .
Willy (*noticing her mending*). What's that?
Linda. Just mending my stockings. They're so expensive . . .
Willy (*angrily, taking them from her*). I won't have you mending
    stockings in this house! Now throw them out!

> *Linda puts the stockings in her pocket.*

Bernard (*entering on the run*). Where is he? If he doesn't study!
Willy (*moving to the forestage, with great agitation*). You'll give him
    the answers!
Bernard. I do, but I can't on a Regents! That's a state exam! They're
    liable to arrest me!
Willy. Where is he? I'll whip him, I'll whip him!
Linda. And he'd better give back that football, Willy, it's not nice.
Willy. Biff! Where is he? Why is he taking everything?
Linda. He's too rough with the girls, Willy. All the mothers are
    afraid of him!

Willy. I'll whip him!

Bernard. He's driving the car without a license!

> *The Woman's laugh is heard.*

Willy. Shut up!

Linda. All the mothers . . .

Willy. Shut up!

Bernard (*backing quietly away and out*). Mr. Birnbaum says he's stuck up.

Willy. Get outa here!

Bernard. If he doesn't buckle down he'll flunk math! (*He goes off.*)

Linda. He's right, Willy, you've gotta . . .

Willy (*exploding at her*). There's nothing the matter with him! You want him to be a worm like Bernard? He's got spirit, personality . . .

> *As he speaks, Linda, almost in tears, exits into the living room. Willy is alone in the kitchen, wilting and staring. The leaves are gone. It is night again, and the apartment houses look down from behind.*

Willy. Loaded with it. Loaded! What is he stealing? He's giving it back, isn't he? Why is he stealing? What did I tell him? I never in my life told him anything but decent things.

> *Happy in pajamas has come down the stairs; Willy suddenly becomes aware of Happy's presence.*

Happy. Let's go now, come on.

Willy (*sitting down at the kitchen table*). Huh! Why did she have to wax the floors herself? Everytime she waxes the floors she keels over. She knows that!

Happy. Shh! Take it easy. What brought you back tonight?

Willy. I got an awful scare. Nearly hit a kid in Yonkers. God! Why didn't I go to Alaska with my brother Ben that time! Ben! That man was a genius, that man was success incarnate! What a mistake! He begged me to go.

Happy. Well, there's no use in . . .

Willy. You guys! There was a man started with the clothes on his back and ended up with diamond mines!

Happy. Boy, someday I'd like to know how he did it.

Willy. What's the mystery? The man knew what he wanted and went out and got it! Walked into a jungle, and comes out, the age of twenty-one, and he's rich! The world is an oyster, but you don't crack it open on a mattress!

Happy. Pop, I told you I'm gonna retire you for life.

Willy. You'll retire me for life on seventy goddam dollars a week? And your women and your car and your apartment, and you'll retire me for life! Christ's sake, I couldn't get past Yonkers today! Where are you guys, where are you? The woods are burning! I can't drive a car!

Charley has appeared in the doorway. He is a large man, slow of speech, laconic, immovable. In all he says, despite what he says, there is pity, and, now, trepidation. He has a robe over pajamas, slippers on his feet. He enters the kitchen.

Charley. Everything all right?

Happy. Yeah, Charley, everything's . . .

Willy. What's the matter?

Charley. I heard some noise. I thought something happened. Can't we do something about the walls? You sneeze in here, and in my house hats blow off.

Happy. Let's go to bed, Dad. Come on.

Charley signals to Happy to go.

Willy. You go ahead, I'm not tired at the moment.

Happy (to Willy). Take it easy, huh? (*He exits.*)

Willy. What're you doin' up?

Charley (sitting down at the kitchen table opposite Willy). Couldn't sleep good. I had a heartburn.

Willy. Well, you don't know how to eat.

Charley. I eat with my mouth.

Willy. No, you're ignorant. You gotta know about vitamins and things like that.

Charley. Come on, let's shoot. Tire you out a little.

Willy (hesitantly). All right. You got cards?

Charley (taking a deck from his pocket). Yeah, I got them. Someplace. What is it with those vitamins?

Willy (dealing). They build up your bones. Chemistry.

Charley. Yeah, but there's no bones in a heartburn.

Willy. What are you talkin' about? Do you know the first thing about it?

Charley. Don't get insulted.

Willy. Don't talk about something you don't know anything about.

They are playing. Pause.

Charley. What're you doin' home?

Willy. A little trouble with the car.

Charley. Oh. (*Pause.*) I'd like to take a trip to California.

Willy. Don't say.

Charley. You want a job?

Willy. I got a job, I told you that. (*After a slight pause.*) What the hell are you offering me a job for?

Charley. Don't get insulted.

Willy. Don't insult me.

Charley. I don't see no sense in it. You don't have to go on this way.

Willy. I got a good job. (*Slight pause.*) What do you keep comin' in here for?

Charley. You want me to go?

Willy (*after a pause, withering*). I can't understand it. He's going back to Texas again. What the hell is that?

Charley. Let him go.

Willy. I got nothin' to give him, Charley, I'm clean, I'm clean.

Charley. He won't starve. None a them starve. Forget about him.

Willy. Then what have I got to remember?

Charley. You take it too hard. To hell with it. When a deposit bottle is broken you don't get your nickel back.

Willy. That's easy enough for you to say.

Charley. That ain't easy for me to say.

Willy. Did you see the ceiling I put up in the living room?

Charley. Yeah, that's a piece of work. To put up a ceiling is a mystery to me. How do you do it?

Willy. What's the difference?

Charley. Well, talk about it.

Willy. You gonna put up a ceiling?

Charley. How could I put up a ceiling?

Willy. Then what the hell are you bothering me for?

Charley. You're insulted again.

Willy. A man who can't handle tools is not a man. You're disgusting.

Charley. Don't call me disgusting, Willy.

> *Uncle Ben, carrying a valise and an umbrella, enters the forestage from around the right corner of the house. He is a stolid man, in his sixties, with a mustache and an authoritative air. He is utterly certain of his destiny, and there is an aura of far places about him. He enters exactly as Willy speaks.*

Willy. I'm getting awfully tired, Ben.

> *Ben's music is heard. Ben looks around at everything.*

Charley. Good, keep playing; you'll sleep better. Did you call me Ben?

> *Ben looks at his watch.*

Willy. That's funny. For a second there you reminded me of my brother Ben.

Ben. I only have a few minutes. (*He strolls, inspecting the place. Willy and Charley continue playing.*)

Charley. You never heard from him again, heh? Since that time?

Willy. Didn't Linda tell you? Couple of weeks ago we got a letter from his wife in Africa. He died.

Charley. That so.

Ben (*chuckling*). So this is Brooklyn, eh?

Charley. Maybe you're in for some of his money.

Willy. Naa, he had seven sons. There's just one opportunity I had with that man . . .

Ben. I must make a train, William. There are several properties I'm looking at in Alaska.

Willy. Sure, sure! If I'd gone with him to Alaska that time, everything would've been totally different.

Charley. Go on, you'd froze to death up there.

Willy. What're you talking about?

Ben. Opportunity is tremendous in Alaska, William. Surprised you're not up there.

Willy. Sure, tremendous.

Charley. Heh?

Willy. There was the only man I ever met who knew the answers.

Charley. Who?

Ben. How are you all?

Willy (*taking a pot, smiling*). Fine, fine.

Charley. Pretty sharp tonight.

Ben. Is Mother living with you?

Willy. No, she died a long time ago.

Charley. Who?

Ben. That's too bad. Fine specimen of a lady, Mother.

Willy (*to Charley*). Heh?

Ben. I'd hoped to see the old girl.

Charley. Who died?

Ben. Heard anything from Father, have you?

Willy (*unnerved*). What do you mean, who died?

Charley (*taking a pot*). What're you talkin' about?

Ben (*looking at his watch*). William, it's half-past eight!

Willy (*as though to dispel his confusion he angrily stops Charley's hand*). That's my build!

Charley. I put the ace . . .

Willy. If you don't know how to play the game I'm not gonna throw my money away on you!

Charley (*rising*). It was my ace, for God's sake!

Willy. I'm through, I'm through!

Ben. When did Mother die?

Willy. Long ago. Since the beginning you never knew how to play cards.

Charley (picks up the cards and goes to the door). All right! Next time I'll bring a deck with five aces.

Willy. I don't play that kind of game!

Charley (turning to him). You ought to be ashamed of yourself!

Willy. Yeah?

Charley. Yeah! *(He goes out.)*

Willy (slamming the door after him). Ignoramus!

Ben (as Willy comes toward him through the wall-line of the kitchen). So you're William.

Willy (shaking Ben's hand). Ben! I've been waiting for you so long! What's the answer? How did you do it?

Ben. Oh, there's a story in that.

> *Linda enters the forestage, as of old, carrying the wash basket.*

Linda. Is this Ben?

Ben (gallantly). How do you do, my dear.

Linda. Where've you been all these years? Willy's always wondered why you . . .

Willy (pulling Ben away from her impatiently). Where is Dad? Didn't you follow him? How did you get started?

Ben. Well, I don't know how much you remember.

Willy. Well, I was just a baby, of course, only three or four years old . . .

Ben. Three years and eleven months.

Willy. What a memory, Ben!

Ben. I have many enterprises, William, and I have never kept books.

Willy. I remember I was sitting under the wagon in — was it Nebraska?

Ben. It was South Dakota, and I gave you a bunch of wild flowers.

Willy. I remember you walking away down some open road.

Ben (laughing). I was going to find Father in Alaska.

Willy. Where is he?

Ben. At that age I had a very faulty view of geography, William. I discovered after a few days that I was heading due south, so instead of Alaska, I ended up in Africa.

Linda. Africa!

Willy. The Gold Coast!

Ben. Principally diamond mines.

Linda. Diamond mines!

Ben. Yes, my dear. But I've only a few minutes . . .

Willy. No! Boys! Boys! (*Young Biff and Happy appear.*) Listen to this. This is your Uncle Ben, a great man! Tell my boys, Ben!

Ben. Why, boys, when I was seventeen I walked into the jungle, and when I was twenty-one I walked out. (*He laughs.*) And by God I was rich.

Willy (*to the boys*). You see what I been talking about? The greatest things can happen!

Ben (*glancing at his watch*). I have an appointment in Ketchikan Tuesday week.

Willy. No, Ben! Please tell about Dad. I want my boys to hear. I want them to know the kind of stock they spring from. All I remember is a man with a big beard, and I was in Mamma's lap, sitting around a fire, and some kind of high music.

Ben. His flute. He played the flute.

Willy. Sure, the flute, that's right!

New music is heard, a high, rollicking tune.

Ben. Father was a very great and a very wild-hearted man. We would start in Boston, and he'd toss the whole family into the wagon, and then he'd drive the team right across the country; through Ohio, and Indiana, Michigan, Illinois, and all the Western states. And we'd stop in the towns and sell the flutes that he'd made on the way. Great inventor, Father. With one gadget he made more in a week than a man like you could make in a lifetime.

Willy. That's just the way I'm bringing them up, Ben — rugged, well liked, all-around.

Ben. Yeah? (*To Biff.*) Hit that, boy — hard as you can. (*He pounds his stomach.*)

Biff. Oh, no, sir!

Ben (*taking boxing stance*). Come on, get to me! (*He laughs.*)

Willy. Go to it. Biff! Go ahead, show him!

Biff. Okay! (*He cocks his fists and starts in.*)

Linda (*to Willy*). Why must he fight, dear?

Ben (*sparring with Biff*). Good boy! Good boy!

Willy. How's that, Ben, heh?

Happy. Give him the left, Biff!

Linda. Why are you fighting?

Ben. Good boy! (*Suddenly comes in, trips Biff, and stands over him, the point of his umbrella poised over Biff's eye.*)

Linda. Look out, Biff!

Biff. Gee!

Ben (patting Biff's knee). Never fight fair with a stranger, boy. You'll never get out of the jungle that way. (*Taking Linda's hand and bowing.*) It was an honor and a pleasure to meet you, Linda.

Linda (withdrawing her hand coldly, frightened). Have a nice — trip.

Ben (to Willy). And good luck with your — what do you do?

Willy. Selling.

Ben. Yes. Well . . . (*He raises his hand in farewell to all.*)

Willy. No, Ben, I don't want you to think . . . (*He takes Ben's arm to show him.*) It's Brooklyn, I know, but we hunt too.

Ben. Really, now.

Willy. Oh, sure, there's snakes and rabbits and — that's why I moved out here. Why, Biff can fell any one of these trees in no time! Boys! Go right over to where they're building the apartment house and get some sand. We're gonna rebuild the entire front stoop right now! Watch this, Ben!

Biff. Yes, sir! On the double, Hap!

Happy (as he and Biff run off). I lost weight, Pop, you notice?

Charley enters in knickers, even before the boys are gone.

Charley. Listen, if they steal any more from that building the watchman'll put the cops on them!

Linda (to Willy). Don't let Biff . . .

Ben laughs lustily.

Willy. You shoulda seen the lumber they brought home last week. At least a dozen six-by-tens worth all kinds a money.

Charley. Listen, if that watchman . . .

Willy. I gave them hell, understand. But I got a couple of fearless characters there.

Charley. Willy, the jails are full of fearless characters.

Ben (clapping Willy on the back, with a laugh at Charley). And the stock exchange, friend!

Willy (joining in Ben's laughter). Where are the rest of your pants?

Charley. My wife bought them.

Willy. Now all you need is a golf club and you can go upstairs and go to sleep. (*To Ben.*) Great athlete! Between him and his son Bernard they can't hammer a nail!

Bernard (rushing in). The watchman's chasing Biff!

Willy (angrily). Shut up! He's not stealing anything!

Linda (alarmed, hurrying off left). Where is he? Biff, dear! (*She exits.*)

Willy (moving toward the left, away from Ben). There's nothing wrong. What's the matter with you?

Ben. Nervy boy. Good!

Willy (laughing). Oh, nerves of iron, that Biff!

Charley. Don't know what it is. My New England man comes back and he's bleedin', they murdered him up there.

Willy. It's contacts, Charley, I got important contacts!

Charley (sarcastically). Glad to hear it, Willy. Come in later, we'll shoot a little casino. I'll take some of your Portland money. (*He laughs at Willy and exits.*)

Willy (turning to Ben). Business is bad, it's murderous. But not for me, of course.

Ben. I'll stop by on my way back to Africa.

Willy (longingly). Can't you stay a few days? You're just what I need, Ben, because I — I have a fine position here, but I — well, Dad left when I was such a baby and I never had a chance to talk to him and I still feel — kind of temporary about myself.

Ben. I'll be late for my train.

They are at opposite ends of the stage.

Willy. Ben, my boys — can't we talk? They'd go into the jaws of hell for me, see, but I . . .

Ben. William, you're being first-rate with your boys. Outstanding, manly chaps!

Willy (hanging on to his words). Oh, Ben, that's good to hear! Because sometimes I'm afraid that I'm not teaching them the right kind of — Ben, how should I teach them?

Ben (giving great weight to each word, and with a certain vicious audacity). William, when I walked into the jungle, I was seventeen. When I walked out I was twenty-one. And, by God, I was rich! (*He goes off into darkness around the right corner of the house.*)

Willy . . . . was rich! That's just the spirit I want to imbue them with! To walk into a jungle! I was right! I was right! I was right!

Ben is gone, but Willy is still speaking to him as Linda, in nightgown and robe, enters the kitchen, glances around for Willy, then goes to the door of the house, looks out and sees him. Comes down to his left. He looks at her.

Linda. Willy, dear? Willy?

Willy. I was right!

Linda. Did you have some cheese? (*He can't answer.*) It's very late, darling. Come to bed, heh?

Willy (looking straight up). Gotta break your neck to see a star in this yard.

Linda. You coming in?

Willy. Whatever happened to that diamond watch fob? Remember? When Ben came from Africa that time? Didn't he give me a watch fob with a diamond in it?

Linda. You pawned it, dear. Twelve, thirteen years ago. For Biff's radio correspondence course.

Willy. Gee, that was a beautiful thing. I'll take a walk.

Linda. But you're in your slippers.

Willy (starting to go around the house at the left). I was right! I was! *(Half to Linda, as he goes, shaking his head.)* What a man! There was a man worth talking to. I was right!

Linda (calling after Willy). But in your slippers, Willy!

Willy is almost gone when Biff, in his pajamas, comes down the stairs and enters the kitchen.

Biff. What is he doing out there?

Linda. Sh!

Biff. God Almighty, Mom, how long has he been doing this?

Linda. Don't, he'll hear you.

Biff. What the hell is the matter with him?

Linda. It'll pass by morning.

Biff. Shouldn't we do anything?

Linda. Oh, my dear, you should do a lot of things, but there's nothing to do, so go to sleep.

Happy comes down the stair and sits on the steps.

Happy. I never heard him so loud, Mom.

Linda. Well, come around more often; you'll hear him. *(She sits down at the table and mends the lining of Willy's jacket.)*

Biff. Why didn't you ever write me about this, Mom?

Linda. How would I write to you? For over three months you had no address.

Biff. I was on the move. But you know I thought of you all the time. You know that, don't you, pal?

Linda. I know, dear, I know. But he likes to have a letter. Just to know that there's still a possibility for better things.

Biff. He's not like this all the time, is he?

Linda. It's when you come home he's always the worst.

Biff. When I come home?

Linda. When you write you're coming, he's all smiles, and talks about the future, and — he's just wonderful. And then the closer you seem to come, the more shaky he gets, and then, by the time you get here, he's arguing, and he seems angry at you. I think it's just that maybe he can't bring himself to

— to open up to you. Why are you so hateful to each other?
Why is that?

Biff (evasively). I'm not hateful, Mom.

Linda. But you no sooner come in the door than you're fighting!

Biff. I don't know why. I mean to change. I'm tryin', Mom, you
understand?

Linda. Are you home to stay now?

Biff. I don't know. I want to look around, see what's doin'.

Linda. Biff, you can't look around all your life, can you?

Biff. I just can't take hold, Mom. I can't take hold of some kind
of a life.

Linda. Biff, a man is not a bird, to come and go with the spring
time.

Biff. Your hair . . . (*He touches her hair.*) Your hair got so gray.

Linda. Oh, it's been gray since you were in high school. I just
stopped dyeing it, that's all.

Biff. Dye it again, will ya? I don't want my pal looking old. (*He
smiles.*)

Linda. You're such a boy! You think you can go away for a year
and . . . You've got to get it into your head now that one
day you'll knock on this door and there'll be strange people
here . . .

Biff. What are you talking about? You're not even sixty, Mom.

Linda. But what about your father?

Biff (lamely). Well, I meant him too.

Happy. He admires Pop.

Linda. Biff, dear, if you don't have any feeling for him, then you
can't have any feeling for me.

Biff. Sure I can, Mom.

Linda. No. You can't just come to see me, because I love him.
(*With a threat, but only a threat, of tears.*) He's the dearest man
in the world to me, and I won't have anyone making him
feel unwanted and low and blue. You've got to make up
your mind now, darling, there's no leeway any more. Either
he's your father and you pay him that respect, or else you're
not to come here. I know he's not easy to get along with
— nobody knows that better than me — but . . .

Willy (from the left, with a laugh). Hey, hey, Biffo!

Biff (starting to go out after Willy). What the hell is the matter with
him? (*Happy stops him.*)

Linda. Don't — don't go near him!

Biff. Stop making excuses for him! He always, always wiped the
floor with you. Never had an ounce of respect for you.

Happy. He's always had respect for . . .

Biff. What the hell do you know about it?

Happy (surlily). Just don't call him crazy!

Biff. He's got no character — Charley wouldn't do this. Not in his own house — spewing out that vomit from his mind.

Happy. Charley never had to cope with what he's got to.

Biff. People are worse off than Willy Loman. Believe me, I've seen them!

Linda. Then make Charley your father, Biff. You can't do that, can you? I don't say he's a great man. Willy Loman never made a lot of money. His name was never in the paper. He's not the finest character that ever lived. But he's a human being, and a terrible thing is happening to him. So attention must be paid. He's not to be allowed to fall into his grave like an old dog. Attention, attention must be finally paid to such a person. You called him crazy . . .

Biff. I didn't mean . . .

Linda. No, a lot of people think he's lost his — balance. But you don't have to be very smart to know what his trouble is. The man is exhausted.

Happy. Sure!

Linda. A small man can be just as exhausted as a great man. He works for a company thirty-six years this March, opens up unheard-of territories to their trademark, and now in his old age they take his salary away.

Happy (indignantly). I didn't know that, Mom.

Linda. You never asked, my dear! Now that you get your spending money someplace else you don't trouble your mind with him.

Happy. But I gave you money last . . .

Linda. Christmas time, fifty dollars! To fix the hot water it cost ninety-seven fifty! For five weeks he's been on straight commission, like a beginner, an unknown!

Biff. Those ungrateful bastards!

Linda. Are they any worse than his sons? When he brought them business, when he was young, they were glad to see him. But now his old friends, the old buyers that loved him so and always found some order to hand him in a pinch — they're all dead, retired. He used to be able to make six, seven calls a day in Boston. Now he takes his valises out of the car and puts them back and takes them out again and he's exhausted. Instead of walking he talks now. He drives seven hundred miles, and when he gets there no one knows him any more, no one welcomes him. And what goes through a man's mind, driving seven hundred miles home without having earned a cent? Why shouldn't he talk to himself? Why? When he has to go to Charley and borrow fifty dollars a week and pretend to me that it's his pay? How long can that go on? How long? You see what I'm sitting here and waiting for? And you tell me he has no character? The man who never worked a day but for your benefit? When does he get the medal for that? Is this his reward — to turn around at the age of sixty-three and find his sons, who he loved better than his life, one a philandering bum . . .

Happy. Mom!

Linda. That's all you are, my baby! (*To Biff.*) And you! What happened to the love you had for him? You were such pals! How you used to talk to him on the phone every night! How lonely he was till he could come home to you!

Biff. All right, Mom. I'll live here in my room, and I'll get a job. I'll keep away from him, that's all.

Linda. No, Biff. You can't stay here and fight all the time.

Biff. He threw me out of this house, remember that.

Linda. Why did he do that? I never knew why.

Biff. Because I know he's a fake and he doesn't like anybody around who knows!

Linda. Why a fake? In what way? What do you mean?

Biff. Just don't lay it all at my feet. It's between me and him — that's all I have to say. I'll chip in from now on. He'll settle for half my paycheck. He'll be all right. I'm going to bed. (*He starts for the stairs.*)

Linda. He won't be all right.

Biff (*turning on the stairs, furiously*). I hate this city and I'll stay here. Now what do you want?

Linda. He's dying, Biff.

Happy turns quickly to her, shocked.

Biff (*after a pause*). Why is he dying?

Linda. He's been trying to kill himself.

Biff (*with great horror*). How?

Linda. I live from day to day.

Biff. What're you talking about?

Linda. Remember I wrote you that he smashed up the car again? In February?

Biff. Well?

Linda. The insurance inspector came. He said that they have evidence. That all these accidents in the last year — weren't — weren't — accidents.

Happy. How can they tell that? That's a lie.

Linda. It seems there's a woman . . . (*She takes a breath as:*)

⎰*Biff* (*sharply but contained*). What woman?

⎱*Linda* (*simultaneously*). . . . and this woman . . .

Linda. What?

Biff. Nothing. Go ahead.

Linda. What did you say?

Biff. Nothing. I just said what woman?

Happy. What about her?

Linda. Well, it seems she was walking down the road and saw his car. She says that he wasn't driving fast at all, and that he didn't skid. She says he came to that little bridge, and then deliberately smashed into the railing, and it was only the shallowness of the water that saved him.

Biff. Oh, no, he probably just fell asleep again.

Linda. I don't think he fell asleep.

Biff. Why not?

Linda. Last month . . . (*With great difficulty.*) Oh, boys, it's so hard to say a thing like this! He's just a big stupid man to you, but I tell you there's more good in him than in many other people. (*She chokes, wipes her eyes.*) I was looking for a fuse. The lights blew out, and I went down the cellar. And behind the fuse box — it happened to fall out — was a length of rubber pipe — just short.

Happy. No kidding!

Linda. There's a little attachment on the end of it. I knew right away. And sure enough, on the bottom of the water heater there's a new little nipple on the gas pipe.

Happy (*angrily*). That — jerk.

Biff. Did you have it taken off?

Linda. I'm — I'm ashamed to. How can I mention it to him? Every day I go down and take away that little rubber pipe. But, when he comes home, I put it back where it was. How can I insult him that way? I don't know what to do. I live from day to day, boys. I tell you, I know every thought in his mind. It sounds so old-fashioned and silly, but I tell you he put his whole life into you and you've turned your backs on him. (*She is bent over in the chair, weeping, her face in her hands.*) Biff, I swear to God! Biff, his life is in your hands!

Happy (*to Biff*). How do you like that damned fool!

Biff (*kissing her*). All right, pal, all right. It's all settled now. I've been remiss. I know that, Mom. But now I'll stay, and I swear to you, I'll apply myself. (*Kneeling in front of her, in a fever of self-reproach.*) It's just — you see, Mom, I don't fit in business. Not that I won't try. I'll try, and I'll make good.

Happy. Sure you will. The trouble with you in business was you never tried to please people.

Biff. I know, I . . .

Happy. Like when you worked for Harrison's. Bob Harrison said you were tops, and then you go and do some damn fool thing like whistling whole songs in the elevator like a comedian.

Biff (against Happy). So what? I like to whistle sometimes.

Happy. You don't raise a guy to a responsible job who whistles in the elevator!

Linda. Well, don't argue about it now.

Happy. Like when you'd go off and swim in the middle of the day instead of taking the line around.

Biff (his resentment rising). Well, don't you run off? You take off sometimes, don't you? On a nice summer day?

Happy. Yeah, but I cover myself!

Linda. Boys!

Happy. If I'm going to take a fade the boss can call any number where I'm supposed to be and they'll swear to him that I just left. I'll tell you something that I hate to say, Biff, but in the business world some of them think you're crazy.

Biff (angered). Screw the business world!

Happy. All right, screw it! Great, but cover yourself!

Linda. Hap, Hap!

Biff. I don't care what they think! They've laughed at Dad for years, and you know why? Because we don't belong in this nuthouse of a city! We should be mixing cement on some open plain or — or carpenters. A carpenter is allowed to whistle!

Willy walks in from the entrance of the house, at left.

Willy. Even your grandfather was better than a carpenter. (*Pause. They watch him.*) You never grew up. Bernard does not whistle in the elevator, I assure you.

Biff (as though to laugh Willy out of it). Yeah, but you do, Pop.

Willy. I never in my life whistled in an elevator! And who in the business world thinks I'm crazy?

Biff. I didn't mean it like that, Pop. Now don't make a whole thing out of it, will ya?

Willy. Go back to the West! Be a carpenter, a cowboy, enjoy yourself!

Linda. Willy, he was just saying . . .

Willy. I heard what he said!

Happy (trying to quiet Willy). Hey, Pop, come on now . . .

Willy (*continuing over Happy's line*). They laugh at me, heh? Go to Filene's, go to the Hub, go to Slattery's, Boston. Call out the name Willy Loman and see what happens! Big shot!

Biff. All right, Pop.

Willy. Big!

Biff. All right!

Willy. Why do you always insult me?

Biff. I didn't say a word. (*To Linda.*) Did I say a word?

Linda. He didn't say anything, Willy.

Willy (*going to the doorway of the living room*). All right, good night, good night.

Linda. Willy, dear, he just decided . . .

Willy (*to Biff*). If you get tired hanging around tomorrow, paint the ceiling I put up in the living room.

Biff. I'm leaving early tomorrow.

Happy. He's going to see Bill Oliver, Pop.

Willy (*interestedly*). Oliver? For what?

Biff (*with reserve, but trying, trying*). He always said he'd stake me. I'd like to go into business, so maybe I can take him up on it.

Linda. Isn't that wonderful?

Willy. Don't interrupt. What's wonderful about it? There's fifty men in the City of New York who'd stake him. (*To Biff.*) Sporting goods?

Biff. I guess so. I know something about it and . . .

Willy. He knows something about it! You know sporting goods better than Spalding, for God's sake! How much is he giving you?

Biff. I don't know, I didn't even see him yet, but . . .

Willy. Then what're you talkin' about?

Biff (*getting angry*). Well, all I said was I'm gonna see him, that's all!

Willy (*turning away*). Ah, you're counting your chickens again.

Biff (*starting left for the stairs*). Oh, Jesus, I'm going to sleep!

Willy (*calling after him*). Don't curse in this house!

Biff (*turning*). Since when did you get so clean?

Happy (*trying to stop them*). Wait a . . .

Willy. Don't use that language to me! I won't have it!

Happy (*grabbing Biff, shouts*). Wait a minute! I got an idea. I got a feasible idea. Come here, Biff, let's talk this over now, let's talk some sense here. When I was down in Florida last time, I thought of a great idea to sell sporting goods. It just came back to me. You and I, Biff — we have a line, the Loman Line. We train a couple of weeks, and put on a couple of exhibitions, see?

Willy. That's an idea!

Happy. Wait! We form two basketball teams, see? Two water-polo teams. We play each other. It's a million dollars' worth of publicity. Two brothers, see? The Loman Brothers. Displays in the Royal Palms — all the hotels. And banners over the ring and the basketball court: "Loman Brothers." Baby, we could sell sporting goods!

Willy. That is a one-million-dollar idea!

Linda. Marvelous!

Biff. I'm in great shape as far as that's concerned.

Happy. And the beauty of it is, Biff, it wouldn't be like a business. We'd be out playin' ball again.

Biff (enthused). Yeah, that's . . .

Willy. Million-dollar . . .

Happy. And you wouldn't get fed up with it, Biff. It'd be the family again. There'd be the old honor, and comradeship, and if you wanted to go off for a swim or somethin' — well, you'd do it! Without some smart cooky gettin' up ahead of you!

Willy. Lick the world! You guys together could absolutely lick the civilized world.

Biff. I'll see Oliver tomorrow. Hap, if we could work that out . . .

Linda. Maybe things are beginning to . . .

Willy (wildly enthused, to Linda). Stop interrupting! *(To Biff.)* But don't wear sport jacket and slacks when you see Oliver.

Biff. No, I'll . . .

Willy. A business suit, and talk as little as possible, and don't crack any jokes.

Biff. He did like me. Always liked me.

Linda. He loved you!

Willy (to Linda). Will you stop! *(To Biff.)* Walk in very serious. You are not applying for a boy's job. Money is to pass. Be quiet, fine, and serious. Everybody likes a kidder, but nobody lends him money.

Happy. I'll try to get some myself, Biff. I'm sure I can.

Willy. I see great things for you kids, I think your troubles are over. But remember, start big and you'll end big. Ask for fifteen. How much you gonna ask for?

Biff. Gee, I don't know . . .

Willy. And don't say "Gee." "Gee" is a boy's word. A man walking in for fifteen thousand dollars does not say "Gee!"

Biff. Ten, I think, would be top though.

Willy. Don't be so modest. You always started too low. Walk in with a big laugh. Don't look worried. Start off with couple of your good stories to lighten things up. It's not what you

say, it's how you say it — because personality always wins
the day.

Linda. Oliver always thought the highest of him . . .

Willy. Will you let me talk?

Biff. Don't yell at her, Pop, will ya?

Willy (angrily). I was talking, wasn't I?

Biff. I don't like you yelling at her all the time, and I'm tellin'
you, that's all.

Willy. What're you, takin' over this house?

Linda. Willy . . .

Willy (turning to her). Don't take his side all the time, goddammit!

Biff (furiously). Stop yelling at her!

Willy (suddenly pulling on his cheek, beaten down, guilt ridden). Give
my best to Bill Oliver — he may remember me. (*He exits
through the living room doorway.*)

Linda (her voice subdued). What'd you have to start that for? (*Biff
turns away.*) You see how sweet he was as soon as you talked
hopefully? (*She goes over to Biff.*) Come up and say good
night to him. Don't let him go to bed that way.

Happy. Come on, Biff, let's buck him up.

Linda. Please, dear. Just say good night. It takes so little to make
him happy. Come. (*She goes through the living room doorway,
calling upstairs from within the living room.*) Your pajamas are
hanging in the bathroom, Willy!

Happy (looking toward where Linda went out). What a woman! They
broke the mold when they made her. You know that,
Biff?

Biff. He's off salary. My God, working on commission!

Happy. Well, let's face it: he's no hot-shot selling man. Except
that sometimes, you have to admit, he's a sweet personality.

Biff (deciding). Lend me ten bucks, will ya? I want to buy some
new ties.

Happy. I'll take you to a place I know. Beautiful stuff. Wear one
of my striped shirts tomorrow.

Biff. She got gray. Mom got awful old. Gee, I'm gonna go in to
Oliver tomorrow and knock him for a . . .

Happy. Come on up. Tell that to Dad. Let's give him a whirl.
Come on.

Biff (steamed up). You know, with ten thousand bucks, boy!

Happy (as they go into the living room). That's the talk, Biff, that's
the first time I've heard the old confidence out of you! (*From
within the living room, fading off*) You're gonna live with me,
kid, and any babe you want just say the word . . . (*The last
lines are hardly heard. They are mounting the stairs to their parents'
bedroom.*)

Linda (*entering her bedroom and addressing Willy, who is in the bathroom. She is straightening the bed for him*). Can you do anything about the shower? It drips.

Willy (*from the bathroom*). All of a sudden everything falls to pieces. Goddam plumbing, oughta be sued, those people. I hardly finished putting it in and the thing . . . (*His words rumble off.*)

Linda. I'm just wondering if Oliver will remember him. You think he might?

Willy (*coming out of the bathroom in his pajamas*). Remember him? What's the matter with you, you crazy? If he'd've stayed with Oliver he'd be on top by now! Wait'll Oliver gets a look at him. You don't know the average caliber any more. The average young man today — (*he is getting into bed*) — is got a caliber of zero. Greatest thing in the world for him was to bum around.

Biff and Happy enter the bedroom. Slight pause.

Willy (*stops short, looking at Biff*). Glad to hear it, boy.

Happy. He wanted to say good night to you, sport.

Willy (*to Biff*). Yeah. Knock him dead, boy. What'd you want to tell me?

Biff. Just take it easy, Pop. Good night. (*He turns to go.*)

Willy (*unable to resist*). And if anything falls off the desk while you're talking to him — like a package or something — don't you pick it up. They have office boys for that.

Linda. I'll make a big breakfast . . .

Willy. Will you let me finish? (*To Biff.*) Tell him you were in the business in the West. Not farm work.

Biff. All right, Dad.

Linda. I think everything . . .

Willy (*going right through her speech*). And don't undersell yourself. No less than fifteen thousand dollars.

Biff (*unable to bear him*). Okay. Good night, Mom. (*He starts moving.*)

Willy. Because you got a greatness in you, Biff, remember that. You got all kinds of greatness . . . (*He lies back, exhausted. Biff walks out.*)

Linda (*calling after Biff*). Sleep well, darling!

Happy. I'm gonna get married, Mom. I wanted to tell you.

Linda. Go to sleep, dear.

Happy (*going*). I just wanted to tell you.

Willy. Keep up the good work. (*Happy exits.*) God . . . remember that Ebbets Field game? The championship of the city?

Linda. Just rest. Should I sing to you?

Willy. Yeah. Sing to me. (*Linda hums a soft lullaby.*) When that team came out — he was the tallest, remember?

Linda. Oh, yes. And in gold.

> *Biff enters the darkened kitchen, takes a cigarette, and leaves the house. He comes downstage into a golden pool of light. He smokes, staring at the night.*

Willy. Like a young god. Hercules — something like that. And the sun, the sun all around him. Remember how he waved to me? Right up from the field, with the representatives of three colleges standing by? And the buyers I brought, and the cheers when he came out — Loman, Loman, Loman! God Almighty, he'll be great yet. A star like that, magnificent, can never really fade away!

> *The light on Willy is fading. The gas heater begins to glow through the kitchen wall, near the stairs, a blue flame beneath red coils.*

Linda (*timidly*). Willy dear, what has he got against you?

Willy. I'm so tired. Don't talk any more.

> *Biff slowly returns to the kitchen. He stops, stares toward the heater.*

Linda. Will you ask Howard to let you work in New York?

Willy. First thing in the morning. Everything'll be all right.

> *Biff reaches behind the heater and draws out a length of rubber tubing. He is horrified and turns his head toward Willy's room, still dimly lit, from which the strains of Linda's desperate but monotonous humming rise.*

Willy (*staring through the window into the moonlight*). Gee, look at the moon moving between the buildings!

> *Biff wraps the tubing around his hand and quickly goes up the stairs.*

ACT II

Scene: *Music is heard, gay and bright. The curtain rises as the music fades away. Willy, in shirt sleeves, is sitting at the kitchen table, sipping coffee, his hat in his lap. Linda is filling his cup when she can.*

Willy. Wonderful coffee. Meal in itself.

Linda. Can I make you some eggs?

Willy. No. Take a breath.

Linda. You look so rested, dear.

Willy. I slept like a dead one. First time in months. Imagine, sleeping till ten on a Tuesday morning. Boys left nice and early, heh?

Linda. They were out of here by eight o'clock.

Willy. Good work!

Linda. It was so thrilling to see them leaving together. I can't get over the shaving lotion in this house!

Willy (smiling). Mmm . . .

Linda. Biff was very changed this morning. His whole attitude seemed to be hopeful. He couldn't wait to get downtown to see Oliver.

Willy. He's heading for a change. There's no question, there simply are certain men that take longer to get — solidified. How did he dress?

Linda. His blue suit. He's so handsome in that suit. He could be a — anything in that suit!

Willy gets up from the table. Linda holds his jacket for him.

Willy. There's no question, no question at all. Gee, on the way home tonight I'd like to buy some seeds.

Linda (laughing). That'd be wonderful. But not enough sun gets back there. Nothing'll grow any more.

Willy. You wait, kid, before it's all over we're gonna get a little place out in the country, and I'll raise some vegetables, a couple of chickens . . .

Linda. You'll do it yet, dear.

Willy walks out of his jacket. Linda follows him.

Willy. And they'll get married, and come for a weekend. I'd build a little guest house. 'Cause I got so many fine tools, all I'd need would be a little lumber and some peace of mind.

Linda (joyfully). I sewed the lining . . .

Willy. I could build two guest houses, so they'd both come. Did he decide how much he's going to ask Oliver for?

Linda (getting him into the jacket). He didn't mention it, but I imagine ten or fifteen thousand. You going to talk to Howard today?

Willy. Yeah. I'll put it to him straight and simple. He'll just have to take me off the road.

Linda. And Willy, don't forget to ask for a little advance, because we've got the insurance premium. It's the grace period now.

Willy. That's a hundred . . .?

Linda. A hundred and eight, sixty-eight. Because we're a little short again.

Willy. Why are we short?

Linda. Well, you had the motor job on the car . . .

Willy. That goddam Studebaker!

Linda. And you got one more payment on the refrigerator . . .

Willy. But it just broke again!

Linda. Well, it's old, dear.

Willy. I told you we should've bought a well-advertised machine. Charley bought a General Electric and it's twenty years old and it's still good, that son-of-a-bitch.

Linda. But, Willy . . .

Willy. Whoever heard of a Hastings refrigerator? Once in my life I would like to own something outright before it's broken! I'm always in a race with the junkyard! I just finished paying for the car and it's on its last legs. The refrigerator consumes belts like a goddamn maniac. They time those things. They time them so when you finally paid for them, they're used up.

Linda (buttoning up his jacket as he unbuttons it). All told, about two hundred dollars would carry us, dear. But that includes the last payment on the mortgage. After this payment, Willy, the house belongs to us.

Willy. It's twenty-five years!

Linda. Biff was nine years old when we bought it.

Willy. Well, that's a great thing. To weather a twenty-five year mortgage is . . .

Linda. It's an accomplishment.

Willy. All the cement, the lumber, the reconstruction I put in this house! There ain't a crack to be found in it any more.

Linda. Well, it served its purpose.

Willy. What purpose? Some stranger'll come along, move in, and that's that. If only Biff would take this house, and raise a family . . . (*He starts to go.*) Good-by, I'm late.

Linda (suddenly remembering). Oh, I forgot! You're supposed to meet them for dinner.

Willy. Me?

Linda. At Frank's Chop House on Forty-eighth near Sixth Avenue.

Willy. Is that so! How about you?

Linda. No, just the three of you. They're gonna blow you to a big meal!

Willy. Don't say! Who thought of that?

Linda. Biff came to me this morning, Willy, and he said, "Tell Dad, we want to blow him to a big meal." Be there six o'clock. You and your two boys are going to have dinner.

Willy. Gee whiz! That's really somethin'. I'm gonna knock Howard for a loop, kid. I'll get an advance, and I'll come home with a New York job. Goddammit, now I'm gonna do it!

Linda. Oh, that's the spirit, Willy!

Willy. I will never get behind a wheel the rest of my life!

Linda. It's changing, Willy, I can feel it changing!

Willy. Beyond a question. G'by, I'm late. (*He starts to go again.*)

Linda (*calling after him as she runs to the kitchen table for a handkerchief*). You got your glasses?

Willy (*feels for them, then comes back in*). Yeah, yeah, got my glasses.

Linda (*giving him the handkerchief*). And a handkerchief.

Willy. Yeah, handkerchief.

Linda. And your saccharine?

Willy. Yeah, my saccharine.

Linda. Be careful on the subway stairs.

> *She kisses him, and a silk stocking is seen hanging from her hand. Willy notices it.*

Willy. Will you stop mending stockings? At least while I'm in the house. It gets me nervous. I can't tell you. Please.

> *Linda hides the stocking in her hand as she follows Willy across the forestage in front of the house.*

Linda. Remember, Frank's Chop House.

Willy (*passing the apron*). Maybe beets would grow out there.

Linda (*laughing*). But you tried so many times.

Willy. Yeah. Well, don't work hard today. (*He disappears around the right corner of the house.*)

Linda. Be careful!

> *As Willy vanishes, Linda waves to him. Suddenly the phone rings. She runs across the stage and into the kitchen and lifts it.*

Linda. Hello? Oh, Biff! I'm so glad you called, I just . . . Yes, sure, I just told him. Yes, he'll be there for dinner at six o'clock, I didn't forget. Listen, I was just dying to tell you. You know that little rubber pipe I told you about? That he connected to the gas heater? I finally decided to go down the cellar this morning and take it away and destroy it. But it's gone! Imagine? He took it away himself, it isn't there! (*She listens.*) When? Oh, then you took it. Oh — nothing, it's just that I'd hoped he'd taken it away himself. Oh, I'm not worried, darling, because this morning he left in such high spirits, it was like the old days! I'm not afraid any more. Did Mr. Oliver see you? . . . Well, you wait there then. And make a nice impression on him, darling. Just don't perspire too much before you see him. And have a nice time with Dad. He may have big news too! . . . That's right, a New York job. And be sweet to him tonight, dear. Be loving to him. Because he's only a little boat looking for a harbor. (*She is trembling with sorrow and joy.*) Oh, that's wonderful, Biff, you'll save his life. Thanks, darling. Just put your arm around him when he comes into the restaurant. Give him a smile. That's the boy . . . Good-by, dear. . . . You got your comb? . . . That's fine. Good-by, Biff dear.

In the middle of her speech, Howard Wagner, thirty-six, wheels in a small typewriter table on which is a wire-recording machine and proceeds to plug it in. This is on the left forestage. Light slowly fades on Linda as it rises on Howard. Howard is intent on threading the machine and only glances over his shoulder as Willy appears.

Willy. Pst! Pst!

Howard. Hello, Willy, come in.

Willy. Like to have a little talk with you, Howard.

Howard. Sorry to keep you waiting. I'll be with you in a minute.

Willy. What's that, Howard?

Howard. Didn't you ever see one of these? Wire recorder.

Willy. Oh. Can we talk a minute?

Howard. Records things. Just got delivery yesterday. Been driving me crazy, the most terrific machine I ever saw in my life. I was up all night with it.

Willy. What do you do with it?

Howard. I bought it for dictation, but you can do anything with it. Listen to this. I had it home last night. Listen to what I picked up. The first one is my daughter. Get this. (*He flicks the switch and "Roll out the Barrel" is heard being whistled.*) Listen to that kid whistle.

Willy. That is lifelike, isn't it?

Howard. Seven years old. Get that tone.

Willy. Ts, ts. Like to ask a little favor if you . . .

The whistling breaks off, and the voice of Howard's daughter is heard.

His Daughter. "Now you, Daddy."

Howard. She's crazy for me! (*Again the same song is whistled.*) That's me! Ha! (*He winks.*)

Willy. You're very good!

The whistling breaks off again. The machine runs silent for a moment.

Howard. Sh! Get this now, this is my son.

His Son. "The capital of Alabama is Montgomery; the capital of
   Arizona is Phoenix; the capital of Arkansas is Little Rock;
   the capital of California is Sacramento . . ." (*and on, and on.*)

Howard (*holding up five fingers*). Five years old, Willy!

Willy. He'll make an announcer some day!

His Son (*continuing*). "The capital . . ."

Howard. Get that — alphabetical order! (*The machine breaks off
   suddenly.*) Wait a minute. The maid kicked the plug out.

Willy. It certainly is a . . .

Howard. Sh, for God's sake!

His Son. "It's nine o'clock, Bulova watch time. So I have to go
   to sleep."

Willy. That really is . . .

Howard. Wait a minute! The next is my wife.

   They wait.

Howard's Voice. "Go on, say something." (*Pause.*) "Well, you
   gonna talk?"

His Wife. "I can't think of anything."

Howard's Voice. "Well, talk — it's turning."

His Wife (*shyly, beaten*). "Hello." (*Silence.*) "Oh, Howard, I can't
   talk into this . . ."

Howard (*snapping the machine off*). That was my wife.

Willy. That is a wonderful machine. Can we . . .

Howard. I tell you, Willy, I'm gonna take my camera, and my
   bandsaw, and all my hobbies, and out they go. This is the
   most fascinating relaxation I ever found.

Willy. I think I'll get one myself.

Howard. Sure, they're only a hundred and a half. You can't do
   without it. Supposing you wanna hear Jack Benny, see? But
   you can't be at home at that hour. So you tell the maid to
   turn the radio on when Jack Benny comes on, and this automatically goes on with the radio . . .

Willy. And when you come home you . . .

Howard. You can come home twelve o'clock, one o'clock, any
   time you like, and you get yourself a Coke and sit yourself
   down, throw the switch, and there's Jack Benny's program
   in the middle of the night!

Willy. I'm definitely going to get one. Because lots of times I'm
   on the road, and I think to myself, what I must be missing
   on the radio!

Howard. Don't you have a radio in the car?

Willy. Well, yeah, but who ever thinks of turning it on?

Howard. Say, aren't you supposed to be in Boston?

Willy. That's what I want to talk to you about, Howard. You got a minute? (*He draws a chair in from the wing.*)

Howard. What happened? What're you doing here?

Willy. Well . . .

Howard. You didn't crack up again, did you?

Willy. Oh, no. No . . .

Howard. Geez, you had me worried there for a minute. What's the trouble?

Willy. Well, tell you the truth, Howard. I've come to the decision that I'd rather not travel any more.

Howard. Not travel! Well, what'll you do?

Willy. Remember, Christmas time, when you had the party here? You said you'd try to think of some spot for me here in town.

Howard. With us?

Willy. Well, sure.

Howard. Oh, yeah, yeah. I remember. Well, I couldn't think of anything for you, Willy.

Willy. I tell ya, Howard. The kids are all grown up, y'know. I don't need much any more. If I could take home — well, sixty-five dollars a week, I could swing it.

Howard. Yeah, but Willy, see I . . .

Willy. I tell ya why, Howard. Speaking frankly and between the two of us, y'know — I'm just a little tired.

Howard. Oh, I could understand that, Willy. But you're a road man, Willy, and we do a road business. We've only got a half-dozen salesmen on the floor here.

Willy. God knows, Howard. I never asked a favor of any man. But I was with the firm when your father used to carry you in here in his arms.

Howard. I know that, Willy, but . . .

Willy. Your father came to me the day you were born and asked me what I thought of the name Howard, may he rest in peace.

Howard. I appreciate that, Willy, but there just is no spot here for you. If I had a spot I'd slam you right in, but I just don't have a single solitary spot.

He looks for his lighter. Willy has picked it up and gives it to him. Pause.

Willy (*with increasing anger*). Howard, all I need to set my table is fifty dollars a week.

Howard. But where am I going to put you, kid?

Willy. Look, it isn't a question of whether I can sell merchandise, is it?

Howard. No, but it's business, kid, and everybody's gotta pull his own weight.

Willy (desperately). Just let me tell you a story, Howard . . .

Howard. 'Cause you gotta admit, business is business.

Willy (angrily). Business is definitely business, but just listen for a minute. You don't understand this. When I was a boy — eighteen, nineteen — I was already on the road. And there was a question in my mind as to whether selling had a future for me. Because in those days I had a yearning to go to Alaska. See, there were three gold strikes in one month in Alaska, and I felt like going out. Just for the ride, you might say.

Howard (barely interested). Don't say.

Willy. Oh, yeah, my father lived many years in Alaska. He was an adventurous man. We've got quite a little streak of self-reliance in our family. I thought I'd go out with my older brother and try to locate him, and maybe settle in the North with the old man. And I was almost decided to go, when I met a salesman in the Parker House. His name was Dave Singleman. And he was eighty-four years old, and he'd drummed merchandise in thirty-one states. And old Dave, he'd go up to his room, y'understand, put on his green velvet slippers — I'll never forget — and pick up his phone and call the buyers, and without ever leaving his room, at the age of eighty-four, he made his living. And when I saw that, I realized that selling was the greatest career a man could want. 'Cause what could be more satisfying than to be able to go, at the age of eighty-four, into twenty or thirty different cities, and pick up a phone, and be remembered and loved and helped by so many different people? Do you know? when he died — and by the way he died the death of a salesman, in his green velvet slippers in the smoker of the New York, New Haven and Hartford, going into Boston — when he died, hundreds of salesmen and buyers were at his funeral. Things were sad on a lotta trains for months after that. (*He stands up. Howard has not looked at him.*) In those days there was personality in it, Howard. There was respect, and comradeship, and gratitude in it. Today, it's all cut and dried, and there's no chance for bringing friendship to bear — or personality. You see what I mean? They don't know me any more.

Howard (moving away, to the right). That's just the thing, Willy.

Willy. If I had forty dollars a week — that's all I'd need. Forty dollars, Howard.

Howard. Kid, I can't take blood from a stone, I. . .

Willy (desperation is on him now). Howard, the year Al Smith was nominated, your father came to me and. . .

Howard (starting to go off). I've got to see some people, kid.

Willy (stopping him). I'm talking about your father! There were promises made across this desk! You mustn't tell me you've got people to see — I put thirty-four years into this firm, Howard, and now I can't pay my insurance! You can't eat the orange and throw the peel away — a man is not a piece of fruit! *(After a pause.)* Now pay attention. Your father — in 1928 I had a big year. I averaged a hundred and seventy dollars a week in commissions.

Howard (impatiently). Now, Willy, you never averaged. . .

Willy (banging his hand on the desk). I averaged a hundred and seventy dollars a week in the year of 1928! And your father came to me — or rather, I was in the office here — it was right over this desk — and he put his hand on my shoulder. . .

Howard (getting up). You'll have to excuse me, Willy, I gotta see some people. Pull yourself together. *(Going out.)* I'll be back in a little while.

On Howard's exit, the light on his chair grows very bright and strange.

Willy. Pull myself together! What the hell did I say to him? My God, I was yelling at him! How could I? *(Willy breaks off, staring at the light, which occupies the chair, animating it. He approaches this chair, standing across the desk from it.)* Frank, Frank, don't you remember what you told me that time? How you put your hand on my shoulder, and Frank . . . *(He leans on the desk and as he speaks the dead man's name he accidentally switches on the recorder, and instantly)*

Howard's Son. ". . . of New York is Albany. The capital of Ohio is Cincinnati, the capital of Rhode Island is . . ." *(The recitation continues.)*

Willy (leaping away with fright, shouting). Ha! Howard! Howard! Howard!

Howard (rushing in). What happened?

Willy (pointing at the machine, which continues nasally, childishly, with the capital cities). Shut it off! Shut it off!

Howard (pulling the plug out). Look, Willy . . .

Willy (pressing his hands to his eyes). I gotta get myself some coffee. I'll get some coffee . . .

Willy starts to walk out. Howard stops him.

Howard (rolling up the cord). Willy, look . . .

Willy. I'll go to Boston.

Howard. Willy, you can't go to Boston for us.

Willy. Why can't I go?

Howard. I don't want you to represent us. I've been meaning to tell you for a long time now.

Willy. Howard, are you firing me?

Howard. I think you need a good long rest, Willy.

Willy. Howard . . .

Howard. And when you feel better, come back, and we'll see if we can work something out.

Willy. But I gotta earn money, Howard. I'm in no position to . . .

Howard. Where are your sons? Why don't your sons give you a hand?

Willy. They're working on a very big deal.

Howard. This is no time for false pride, Willy. You go to your sons and you tell them that you're tired. You've got two great boys, haven't you?

Willy. Oh, no question, no question, but in the meantime . . .

Howard. Then that's that, heh?

Willy. All right, I'll go to Boston tomorrow.

Howard. No, no.

Willy. I can't throw myself on my sons. I'm not a cripple!

Howard. Look, kid, I'm busy this morning.

Willy (grasping Howard's arm). Howard, you've got to let me go to Boston!

Howard (hard, keeping himself under control). I've got a line of people to see this morning. Sit down, take five minutes, and pull yourself together, and then go home, will ya? I need the office, Willy. (*He starts to go, turns, remembering the recorder, starts to push off the table holding the recorder.*) Oh, yeah. Whenever you can this week, stop by and drop off the samples. You'll feel better, Willy, and then come back and we'll talk. Pull yourself together, kid, there's people outside.

Howard exits, pushing the table off left. Willy stares into space, exhausted. Now the music is heard — Ben's music — first distantly, then closer, closer. As Willy speaks, Ben enters from the right. He carries valise and umbrella.

Willy. Oh, Ben, how did you do it? What is the answer? Did you wind up the Alaska deal already?

Ben. Doesn't take much time if you know what you're doing. Just a short business trip. Boarding ship in an hour. Wanted to say good-by.

Willy. Ben, I've got to talk to you.

Ben (glancing at his watch). Haven't the time, William.

Willy (crossing the apron to Ben). Ben, nothing's working out. I don't know what to do.

Ben. Now, look here, William. I've bought timberland in Alaska and I need a man to look after things for me.

Willy. God, timberland! Me and my boys in those grand outdoors!

Ben. You've a new continent at your doorstep, William. Get out of these cities, they're full of talk and time payments and courts of law. Screw on your fists and you can fight for a fortune up there.

Willy. Yes, yes! Linda, Linda!

Linda enters as of old, with the wash.

Linda. Oh, you're back?

Ben. I haven't much time.

Willy. No, wait! Linda, he's got a proposition for me in Alaska.

Linda. But you've got. . . *(To Ben.)* He's got a beautiful job here.

Willy. But in Alaska, kid, I could. . .

Linda. You're doing well enough, Willy!

Ben (to Linda). Enough for what, my dear?

Linda (frightened of Ben and angry at him). Don't say those things to him! Enough to be happy right here, right now. *(To Willy, while Ben laughs.)* Why must everybody conquer the world? You're well liked, and the boys love you, and someday — *(To Ben)* — why, old man Wagner told him just the other day that if he keeps it up he'll be a member of the firm, didn't he, Willy?

Willy. Sure, sure. I am building something with this firm, Ben, and if a man is building something he must be on the right track, mustn't he?

Ben. What are you building? Lay your hand on it. Where is it?

Willy (hesitantly). That's true, Linda, there's nothing.

Linda. Why? *(To Ben.)* There's a man eighty-four years old . . .

Willy. That's right, Ben, that's right. When I look at that man I say, what is there to worry about?

Ben. Bah!

Willy. It's true, Ben. All he has to do is go into any city, pick up the phone, and he's making his living and you know why?

Ben (picking up his valise). I've got to go.

Willy (holding Ben back). Look at this boy!

Biff, in his high school sweater, enters carrying suitcase. Happy carries Biff's shoulder guards, gold helmet, and football pants.

Willy. Without a penny to his name, three great universities are begging for him, and from there the sky's the limit, because it's not what you do, Ben. It's who you know and the smile on your face! It's contacts, Ben, contacts! The whole wealth of Alaska passes over the lunch table at the Commodore Hotel, and that's the wonder, the wonder of this country, that a man can end with diamonds here on the basis of being liked! (*He turns to Biff.*) And that's why when you get out on that field today it's important. Because thousands of people will be rooting for you and loving you. (*To Ben, who has again begun to leave.*) And Ben! when he walks into a business office his name will sound out like a bell and all the doors will open to him! I've seen it, Ben, I've seen it a thousand times! You can't feel it with your hand like timber, but it's there!

Ben. Good-by, William.

Willy. Ben, am I right? Don't you think I'm right? I value your advice.

Ben. There's a new continent at your doorstep, William. You could walk out rich. Rich! (*He is gone.*)

Willy. We'll do it here, Ben! You hear me? We're gonna do it here!

Young Bernard rushes in. The gay music of the Boys is heard.

Bernard. Oh, gee, I was afraid you left already!

Willy. Why? What time is it?

Bernard. It's half-past one!

Willy. Well, come on, everybody! Ebbets Field next stop! Where's the pennants? (*He rushes through the wall-line of the kitchen and out into the living room.*)

Linda (*to Biff*). Did you pack fresh underwear?

Biff (*who has been limbering up*). I want to go!

Bernard. Biff, I'm carrying your helmet, ain't I?

Happy. No, I'm carrying the helmet.

Bernard. Oh, Biff, you promised me.

Happy. I'm carrying the helmet.

Bernard. How am I going to get in the locker room?

Linda. Let him carry the shoulder guards. (*She puts her coat and hat on in the kitchen.*)

Bernard. Can I, Biff? 'Cause I told everybody I'm going to be in the locker room.

Happy. In Ebbets Field it's the clubhouse.

Bernard. I meant the clubhouse. Biff!

Happy. Biff!

Biff (*grandly, after a slight pause*). Let him carry the shoulder guards.

Happy (as he gives Bernard the sholder guards). Stay close to us now.

    Willy rushes in with the pennants.

Willy (handing them out). Everybody wave when Biff comes out on the field. (*Happy and Bernard run off.*) You set now, boy?

    The music has died away.

Biff. Ready to go, Pop. Every muscle is ready.

Willy (at the edge of the apron). You realize what this means?

Biff. That's right, Pop.

Willy (feeling Biff's muscles). You're comin' home this afternoon captain of the All-Scholastic Championship Team of the City of New York.

Biff. I got it, Pop. And remember, pal, when I take off my helmet, that touchdown is for you.

Willy. Let's go! (*He is starting out, with his arm around Biff, when Charley enters, as of old, in knickers.*) I got no room for you, Charley.

Charley. Room? For what?

Willy. In the car.

Charley. You goin' for a ride? I wanted to shoot some casino.

Willy (furiously). Casino! (*Incredulously.*) Don't you realize what today is?

Linda. Oh, he knows, Willy. He's just kidding you.

Willy. That's nothing to kid about!

Charley. No, Linda, what's goin' on?

Linda. He's playing in Ebbets Field.

Charley. Baseball in this weather?

Willy. Don't talk to him. Come on, come on! (*He is pushing them out.*)

Charley. Wait a minute, didn't you hear the news?

Willy. What?

Charley. Don't you listen to the radio? Ebbets Field just blew up.

Willy. You go to hell! (*Charley laughs. Pushing them out.*) Come on, come on! We're late.

Charley (as they go). Knock a homer, Biff, knock a homer!

Willy (the last to leave, turning to Charley). I don't think that was funny, Charley. This is the greatest day of his life.

Charley. Willy, when are you going to grow up?

Willy. Yeah, heh? When this game is over, Charley, you'll be laughing out of the other side of your face. They'll be calling him another Red Grange. Twenty-five thousand a year.

Charley (kidding). Is that so?

Willy. Yeah, that's so.

Charley. Well, then, I'm sorry, Willy. But tell me something.
Willy. What?
Charley. Who is Red Grange?
Willy. Put up your hands. Goddam you, put up your hands!

> *Charley, chuckling, shakes his head and walks away, around the left corner of the stage. Willy follows him. The music rises to a mocking frenzy.*

Willy. Who the hell do you think you are, better than everybody else? You don't know everything, you big, ignorant, stupid . . . Put up your hands!

> *Light rises, on the right side of the forestage, on a small table in the reception room of Charley's office. Traffic sounds are heard. Bernard, now mature, sits whistling to himself. A pair of tennis rackets and an overnight bag are on the floor beside him.*

Willy (offstage). What are you walking away for? Don't walk away! If you're going to say something say it to my face! I know you laugh at me behind my back. You'll laugh out of the other side of your goddam face after this game. Touchdown! Touchdown! Eighty thousand people! Touchdown! Right between the goal posts.

> *Bernard is a quiet, earnest, but self-assured young man. Willy's voice is coming from right upstage now. Bernard lowers his feet off the table and listens. Jenny, his father's secretary, enters.*

Jenny (distressed). Say, Bernard, will you go out in the hall?
Bernard. What is that noise? Who is it?
Jenny. Mr. Loman. He just got off the elevator.
Bernard (getting up). Who's he arguing with?
Jenny. Nobody. There's nobody with him. I can't deal with him any more, and your father gets all upset everytime he comes. I've got a lot of typing to do, and your father's waiting to sign it. Will you see him?
Willy (entering). Touchdown! Touch — (*He sees Jenny.*) Jenny, Jenny, good to see you. How're ya? Workin'? Or still honest?
Jenny. Fine. How've you been feeling?
Willy. Not much any more, Jenny. Ha, ha! (*He is surprised to see the rackets.*)
Bernard. Hello, Uncle Willy.
Willy (almost shocked). Bernard! Well, look who's here! (*He comes quickly, guiltily, to Bernard and warmly shakes his hand.*)
Bernard. How are you? Good to see you.
Willy. What are you doing here?

Bernard. Oh, just stopped by to see Pop. Get off my feet till my train leaves. I'm going to Washington in a few minutes.

Willy. Is he in?

Bernard. Yes, he's in his office with the accountant. Sit down.

Willy (sitting down). What're you going to do in Washington?

Bernard. Oh, just a case I've got there, Willy.

Willy. That so? *(Indicating the rackets.)* You going to play tennis there?

Bernard. I'm staying with a friend who's got a court.

Willy. Don't say. His own tennis court. Must be fine people, I bet.

Bernard. They are, very nice. Dad tells me Biff's in town.

Willy (with a big smile). Yeah, Biff's in. Working on a very big deal, Bernard.

Bernard. What's Biff doing?

Willy. Well, he's been doing very big things in the West. But he decided to establish himself here. Very big. We're having dinner. Did I hear your wife had a boy?

Bernard. That's right. Our second.

Willy. Two boys! What do you know!

Bernard. What kind of a deal has Biff got?

Willy. Well, Bill Oliver — very big sporting-goods man — he wants Biff very badly. Called him in from the West. Long distance, carte blanche, special deliveries. Your friends have their own private tennis court?

Bernard. You still with the old firm, Willy?

Willy (after a pause). I'm — I'm overjoyed to see how you made the grade, Bernard, overjoyed. It's an encouraging thing to see a young man really — really. . . Looks very good for Biff — very. . . *(He breaks off, then.)* Bernard . . . *(He is so full of emotion, he breaks off again.)*

Bernard. What is it, Willy?

Willy (small and alone). What — what's the secret?

Bernard. What secret?

Willy. How — how did you? Why didn't he ever catch on?

Bernard. I wouldn't know that, Willy.

Willy (confidentially, desperately). You were his friend, his boyhood friend. There's something I don't understand about it. His life ended after that Ebbets Field game. From the age of seventeen nothing good ever happened to him.

Bernard. He never trained himself for anything.

Willy. But he did, he did. After high school he took so many correspondence courses. Radio mechanics; television; God knows what, and never made the slightest mark.

Bernard (taking off his glasses). Willy, do you want to talk candidly?

Willy (rising, faces Bernard). I regard you as a very brilliant man, Bernard. I value your advice.

Bernard. Oh, the hell with the advice, Willy. I couldn't advise you. There's just one thing I've always wanted to ask you. When he was supposed to graduate, and the math teacher flunked him . . .

Willy. Oh, that son-of-a-bitch ruined his life.

Bernard. Yeah, but, Willy, all he had to do was go to summer school and make up that subject.

Willy. That's right, that's right.

Bernard. Did you tell him not to go to summer school?

Willy. Me? I begged him to go. I ordered him to go!

Bernard. Then why wouldn't he go?

Willy. Why? Why! Bernard, that question has been trailing me like a ghost for the last fifteen years. He flunked the subject, and laid down and died like a hammer hit him!

Bernard. Take it easy, kid.

Willy. Let me talk to you — I got nobody to talk to. Bernard, Bernard, was it my fault? Y'see? It keeps going around in my mind, maybe I did something to him. I got nothing to give him.

Bernard. Don't take it so hard.

Willy. Why did he lay down? What is the story there? You were his friend!

Bernard. Willy, I remember, it was June, and our grades came out. And he'd flunked math.

Willy. That son-of-a-bitch!

Bernard. No, it wasn't right then. Biff just got very angry, I remember, and he was ready to enroll in summer school.

Willy (surprised). He was?

Bernard. He wasn't beaten by it at all. But then, Willy, he disappeared from the block for almost a month. And I got the idea that he'd gone up to New England to see you. Did he have a talk with you then?

Willy stares in silence.

Bernard. Willy?

Willy (with a strong edge of resentment in his voice). Yeah, he came to Boston. What about it?

Bernard. Well, just that when he came back — I'll never forget this, it always mystifies me. Because I'd thought so well of Biff, even though he'd always taken advantage of me. I loved him, Willy, y'know? And he came back after that month and took his sneakers — remember those sneakers with "University of Virginia" printed on them? He was so proud of those, wore them every day. And he took them down in the cellar, and burned them up in the furnace. We had a fist fight. It lasted at least half an hour. Just the two of us, punching each other down the cellar, and crying right through it. I've often thought of how strange it was that I knew he'd given up his life. What happened in Boston, Willy?

Willy looks at him as at an intruder.

Bernard. I just bring it up because you asked me.
Willy (*angrily*). Nothing. What do you mean, "What happened?" What's that got to do with anything?
Bernard. Well, don't get sore.
Willy. What are you trying to do, blame it on me? If a boy lays down is that my fault?
Bernard. Now, Willy, don't get. . .
Willy. Well, don't — don't talk to me that way! What does that mean, "What happened?"

Charley enters. He is in his vest, and he carries a bottle of bourbon.

Charley. Hey, you're going to miss that train. (*He waves the bottle.*)
Bernard. Yeah, I'm going. (*He takes the bottle.*) Thanks, Pop. (*He picks up his rackets and bag.*) Good-by, Willy, and don't worry about it. You know, "If at first you don't succeed . . ."
Willy. Yes, I believe in that.
Bernard. But sometimes, Willy, it's better for a man just to walk away.
Willy. Walk away?
Bernard. That's right.
Willy. But if you can't walk away?
Bernard (*after a slight pause*). I guess that's when it's tough. (*Extending his hand.*) Good-by, Willy.
Willy (*shaking Bernard's hand*). Good-by, boy.
Charley (*an arm on Bernard's shoulder*). How do you like this kid? Gonna argue a case in front of the Supreme Court.
Bernard (*protesting*). Pop!
Willy (*genuinely shocked, pained, and happy*). No! The Supreme Court!
Bernard. I gotta run. 'By, Dad!
Charley. Knock 'em dead, Bernard!

Bernard goes off.

Willy (*as Charley takes out his wallet*). The Supreme Court! And he didn't even mention it!

Charley (*counting out money on the desk*). He don't have to — he's gonna do it.

Willy. And you never told him what to do, did you? You never took any interest in him.

Charley. My salvation is that I never took any interest in anything. There's some money — fifty dollars. I got an accountant inside.

Willy. Charley, look . . . (*With difficulty.*) I got my insurance to pay. If you can manage it — I need a hundred and ten dollars.

Charley doesn't reply for a moment; merely stops moving.

Willy. I'd draw it from my bank but Linda would know, and I. . .

Charley. Sit down, Willy.

Willy (*moving toward the chair*). I'm keeping an account of everything, remember. I'll pay every penny back. (*He sits.*)

Charley. Now listen to me, Willy.

Willy. I want you to know I appreciate . . .

Charley (*sitting down on the table*). Willy, what're you doin'? What the hell is going on in your head?

Willy. Why? I'm simply . . .

Charley. I offered you a job. You make fifty dollars a week. And I won't send you on the road.

Willy. I've got a job.

Charley. Without pay? What kind of a job is a job without pay? (*He rises.*) Now, look, kid, enough is enough. I'm no genius but I know when I'm being insulted.

Willy. Insulted!

Charley. Why don't you want to work for me?

Willy. What's the matter with you? I've got a job.

Charley. Then what're you walkin' in here every week for?

Willy (*getting up*). Well, if you don't want me to walk in here . . .

Charley. I'm offering you a job.

Willy. I don't want your goddam job!

Charley. When the hell are you going to grow up?

Willy (*furiously*). You big ignoramus, if you say that to me again I'll rap you one! I don't care how big you are! (*He's ready to fight.*)

Pause.

Charley (*kindly, going to him*). How much do you need, Willy?

Willy. Charley, I'm strapped. I'm strapped. I don't know what to do. I was just fired.

Charley. Howard fired you?

Willy. That snotnose. Imagine that? I named him. I named him Howard.

Charley. Willy, when're you gonna realize that them things don't mean anything? You named him Howard, but you can't sell that. The only thing you got in this world is what you can sell. And the funny thing is that you're a salesman, and you don't know that.

Willy. I've always tried to think otherwise, I guess. I always felt that if a man was impressive, and well liked, that nothing . . .

Charley. Why must everybody like you? Who liked J.P. Morgan? Was he impressive? In a Turkish bath he'd look like a butcher. But with his pockets on he was very well liked. Now listen, Willy, I know you don't like me, and nobody can say I'm in love with you, but I'll give you a job because — just for the hell of it, put it that way. Now what do you say?

Willy. I — I just can't work for you, Charley.

Charley. What're you, jealous of me?

Willy. I can't work for you, that's all, don't ask me why.

Charley (*angered, takes out more bills*). You been jealous of me all your life, you dammed fool! Here, pay your insurance. (*He puts the money in Willy's hand.*)

Willy. I'm keeping strict accounts.

Charley. I've got some work to do. Take care of yourself. And pay your insurance.

Willy (*moving to the right*). Funny, y'know? After all the highways, and the trains, and the appointments, and the years, you end up worth more dead than alive.

Charley. Willy, nobody's worth nothin' dead. (*After a slight pause.*) Did you hear what I said?

Willy stands still, dreaming.

Charley. Willy!

Willy. Apologize to Bernard for me when you see him. I didn't mean to argue with him. He's a fine boy. They're all fine boys, and they'll end up big — all of them. Someday they'll all play tennis together. Wish me luck, Charley. He saw Bill Oliver today.

Charley. Good luck.

Willy (*on the verge of tears*). Charley, you're the only friend I got. Isn't that a remarkable thing? (*He goes out.*)

Charley. Jesus!

Charley stares after him a moment and follows. All light blacks out. Suddenly raucous music is heard, and a red glow rises behind the screen at right. Stanley, a young waiter, appears, carrying a table, followed by Happy, who is carrying two chairs.

Stanley (putting the table down). That's all right, Mr. Loman, I can handle it myself. (*He turns and takes the chairs from Happy and places them at the table.*)

Happy (glancing around). Oh, this is better.

Stanley. Sure, in the front there you're in the middle of all kinds of noise. Whenever you got a party, Mr. Loman, you just tell me and I'll put you back here. Y'know, there's a lotta people they don't like it private, because when they go out they like to see a lotta action around them because they're sick and tired to stay in the house by theirself. But I know you, you ain't from Hackensack. You know what I mean?

Happy (sitting down). So how's it coming, Stanley?

Stanley. Ah, it's a dog life. I only wish during the war they'd a took me in the Army. I coulda been dead by now.

Happy. My brother's back, Stanley.

Stanley. Oh, he come back, heh? From the Far West.

Happy. Yeah, big cattle man, my brother, so treat him right. And my father's coming too.

Stanley. Oh, your father too!

Happy. You got a couple of nice lobsters?

Stanley. Hundred per cent, big.

Happy. I want them with the claws.

Stanley. Don't worry, I don't give you no mice. (*Happy laughs.*) How about some wine? It'll put a head on the meal.

Happy. No. You remember, Stanley, that recipe I brought you from overseas? With the champagne in it?

Stanley. Oh, yeah, sure. I still got it tacked up yet in the kitchen. But that'll have to cost a buck apiece anyways.

Happy. That's all right.

Stanley. What'd you, hit a number or somethin'?

Happy. No, it's a little celebration. My brother is — I think he pulled off a big deal today. I think we're going into business together.

Stanley. Great! That's the best for you. Because a family business, you know what I mean? — that's the best.

Happy. That's what I think.

Stanley. 'Cause what's the difference? Somebody steals? It's in the family. Know what I mean? (*Sotto voce.*) Like this bartender here. The boss is goin' crazy what kinda leak he's got in the cash register. You put it in but it don't come out.

Happy (raising his head). Sh!

Stanley. What?

Happy. You notice I wasn't lookin' right or left, was I?

Stanley. No.

Happy. And my eyes are closed.

Stanley. So what's the . . . ?

Happy. Strudel's comin'.

Stanley (catching on, looks around). Ah, no, there's no . . .

> *He breaks off as a furred, lavishly dressed Girl enters and sits at the next table. Both follow her with their eyes.*

Stanley. Geez, how'd ya know?

Happy. I got radar or something. *(Staring directly at her profile.)* Oooooooo . . . Stanley.

Stanley. I think that's for you, Mr. Loman.

Happy. Look at that mouth. Oh, God. And the binoculars.

Stanley. Geez, you got a life, Mr. Loman.

Happy. Wait on her.

Stanley (going to the Girl's table). Would you like a menu, ma'am?

Girl. I'm expecting someone, but I'd like a . . .

Happy. Why don't you bring her — excuse me, miss, do you mind? I sell champagne, and I'd like you to try my brand. Bring her a champagne, Stanley.

Girl. That's awfully nice of you.

Happy. Don't mention it. It's all company money. *(He laughs.)*

Girl. That's a charming product to be selling, isn't it?

Happy. Oh, gets to be like everything else. Selling is selling, y'know.

Girl. I suppose.

Happy. You don't happen to sell, do you?

Girl. No, I don't sell.

Happy. Would you object to a compliment from a stranger? You ought to be on a magazine cover.

Girl (looking at him a little archly). I have been.

> *Stanley comes in with a glass of champagne.*

Happy. What'd I say before, Stanley? You see? She's a cover girl.

Stanley. Oh, I could see, I could see.

Happy (to the Girl). What magazine?

Girl. Oh, a lot of them. *(She takes the drink.)* Thank you.

Happy. You know what they say in France, don't you? "Champagne is the drink of the complexion" — Hya, Biff!

> *Biff has entered and sits with Happy.*

Biff. Hello, kid. Sorry I'm late.

Happy. I just got here. Uh, Miss . . . ?

Girl. Forsythe.

Happy. Miss Forsythe, this is my brother.

Biff. Is Dad here?

Happy. His name is Biff. You might've heard of him. Great football player.

Girl. Really? What team?

Happy. Are you familiar with football?

Girl. No, I'm afraid I'm not.

Happy. Biff is quarterback with the New York Giants.

Girl. Well, that is nice, isn't it? (*She drinks.*)

Happy. Good health.

Girl. I'm happy to meet you.

Happy. That's my name. Hap. It's really Harold, but at West Point they called me Happy.

Girl (*now really impressed*). Oh, I see. How do you do? (*She turns her profile.*)

Biff. Isn't Dad coming?

Happy. You want her?

Biff. Oh, I could never make that.

Happy. I remember the time that idea would never come into your head. Where's the old confidence, Biff?

Biff. I just saw Oliver . . .

Happy. Wait a minute. I've got to see that old confidence again. Do you want her? She's on call.

Biff. Oh, no. (*He turns to look at the Girl.*)

Happy. I'm telling you. Watch this. (*Turning to the Girl.*) Honey? (*She turns to him.*) Are you busy?

Girl. Well, I am . . . but I could make a phone call.

Happy. Do that, will you, honey? And see if you can get a friend. We'll be here for a while. Biff is one of the greatest football players in the country.

Girl (*standing up*). Well, I'm certainly happy to meet you.

Happy. Come back soon.

Girl. I'll try.

Happy. Don't try, honey, try hard.

> *The Girl exits. Stanley follows, shaking his head in bewildered admiration.*

Happy. Isn't that a shame now? A beautiful girl like that? That's why I can't get married. There's not a good woman in a thousand. New York is loaded with them, kid!

Biff. Hap, look . . .

Happy. I told you she was on call!

Biff (*strangely unnerved*). Cut it out, will ya? I want to say something to you.

Happy. Did you see Oliver?

Biff. I saw him all right. Now look, I want to tell Dad a couple of things and I want you to help me.

Happy. What? Is he going to back you?

Biff. Are you crazy? You're out of your goddam head, you know that?

Happy. Why? What happened?

Biff (*breathlessly*). I did a terrible thing today, Hap. It's been the strangest day I ever went through. I'm all numb, I swear.

Happy. You mean he wouldn't see you?

Biff. Well, I waited six hours for him, see? All day. Kept sending my name in. Even tried to date his secretary so she'd get me to him, but no soap.

Happy. Because you're not showin' the old confidence, Biff. He remembered you, didn't he?

Biff (*stopping Happy with a gesture*). Finally, about five o'clock, he comes out. Didn't remember who I was or anything. I felt like such an idiot, Hap.

Happy. Did you tell him my Florida idea?

Biff. He walked away. I saw him for one minute. I got so mad I could've torn the walls down! How the hell did I ever get the idea I was a salesman there? I even believed myself that I'd been a salesman for him! And then he gave me one look and — I realized what a ridiculous lie my whole life has been! We've been talking in a dream for fifteen years. I was a shipping clerk.

Happy. What'd you do?

Biff (*with great tension and wonder*). Well, he left, see. And the secretary went out. I was all alone in the waiting room. I don't know what came over me, Hap. The next thing I know I'm in his office — paneled walls, everything. I can't explain it. I — Hap, I took his fountain pen.

Happy. Geez, did he catch you?

Biff. I ran out. I ran down all eleven flights. I ran and ran and ran.

Happy. That was an awful dumb — what'd you do that for?

Biff (*agonized*). I don't know, I just — wanted to take something, I don't know. You gotta help me, Hap. I'm gonna tell Pop.

Happy. You crazy? What for?

Biff. Hap, he's got to understand that I'm not the man somebody lends that kind of money to. He thinks I've been spiting him all these years and it's eating him up.

Happy. That's just it. You tell him something nice.

Biff. I can't.

Happy. Say you got a lunch date with Oliver tomorrow.

Biff. So what do I do tomorrow?

Happy. You leave the house tomorrow and come back at night and say Oliver is thinking it over. And he thinks it over for a couple of weeks, and gradually it fades away and nobody's the worse.

Biff. But it'll go on forever!

Happy. Dad is never so happy as when he's looking forward to something!

Willy enters.

Happy. Hello, scout!

Willy. Gee, I haven't been here in years!

Stanley has followed Willy in and sets a chair for him. Stanley starts off but Happy stops him.

Happy. Stanley!

Stanley stands by, waiting for an order.

Biff (going to Willy with guilt, as to an invalid). Sit down, Pop. You want a drink?

Willy. Sure, I don't mind.

Biff. Let's get a load on.

Willy. You look worried.

Biff. N–no. (*To Stanley.*) Scotch all around. Make it doubles.

Stanley. Doubles, right. (*He goes.*)

Willy. You had a couple already, didn't you?

Biff. Just a couple, yeah.

Willy. Well, what happened, boy? (*Nodding affirmatively, with a smile.*) Everything go all right?

Biff (takes a breath, then reaches out and grasps Willy's hand). Pal . . . (*He is smiling bravely, and Willy is smiling too.*) I had an experience today.

Happy. Terrific, Pop.

Willy. That so? What happened?

Biff (high, slightly alcoholic, above the earth). I'm going to tell you everything from first to last. It's been a strange day. (*Silence. He looks around, composes himself as best he can, but his breath keeps breaking the rhythm of his voice.*) I had to wait quite a while for him, and . . .

Willy. Oliver?

Biff. Yeah, Oliver. All day, as a matter of cold fact. And a lot of — instances — facts, Pop, facts about my life came back to me. Who was it, Pop? Who ever said I was a salesman with Oliver?

Willy. Well, you were.

Biff. No, Dad, I was a shipping clerk.

Willy. But you were practically . . .

Biff (with determination). Dad, I don't know who said it first, but I was never a salesman for Bill Oliver.

Willy. What're you talking about?

Biff. Let's hold on to the facts tonight, Pop. We're not going to get anywhere bullin' around. I was a shipping clerk.

Willy (angrily). All right, now listen to me . . .

Biff. Why don't you let me finish?

Willy. I'm not interested in stories about the past or any crap of that kind because the woods are burning, boys, you understand? There's a big blaze going on all around. I was fired today.

Biff (shocked). How could you be?

Willy. I was fired, and I'm looking for a little good news to tell your mother, because the woman has waited and the woman has suffered. The gist of it is that I haven't got a story left in my head, Biff. So don't give me a lecture about facts and aspects. I am not interested. Now what've you got to say to me?

Stanley enters with three drinks. They wait until he leaves.

Willy. Did you see Oliver?

Biff. Jesus, Dad!

Willy. You mean you didn't go up there?

Happy. Sure he went up there.

Biff. I did. I — saw him. How could they fire you?

Willy (on the edge of his chair). What kind of a welcome did he give you?

Biff. He won't even let you work on commission?

Willy. I'm out! (Driving.) So tell me, he gave you a warm welcome?

Happy. Sure, Pop, sure!

Biff (driven). Well, it was kind of . . .

Willy. I was wondering if he'd remember you. (To Happy.) Imagine, man doesn't see him for ten, twelve years and gives him that kind of a welcome!

Happy. Damn right!

Biff (trying to return to the offensive). Pop, look . . .

Willy. You know why he remembered you, don't you? Because you impressed him in those days.

Biff. Let's talk quietly and get this down to the facts, huh?

Willy (as though Biff had been interrupting). Well, what happened?

It's great news, Biff. Did he take you into his office or'd
you talk in the waiting room?

Biff. Well, he came in, see, and . . .

Willy (with a big smile). What'd he say? Betcha he threw his arm
around you.

Biff. Well, he kinda . . .

Willy. He's a fine man. (*To Happy.*) Very hard man to see, y'know.

Happy (agreeing). Oh, I know.

Willy (to Biff). Is that where you had the drinks?

Biff. Yeah, he gave me a couple of — no, no!

Happy (cutting in). He told him my Florida idea.

Willy. Don't interrupt. (*To Biff.*) How'd he react to the Florida
idea?

Biff. Dad, will you give me a minute to explain?

Willy. I've been waiting for you to explain since I sat down here!
What happened? He took you into his office and what?

Biff. Well — I talked. And — and he listened, see.

Willy. Famous for the way he listens, y'know. What was his
answer?

Biff. His answer was — (*He breaks off, suddenly angry.*) Dad, you're
not letting me tell you what I want to tell you!

Willy (accusing, angered). You didn't see him, did you?

Biff. I did see him!

Willy. What'd you insult him or something? You insulted him,
didn't you?

Biff. Listen, will you let me out of it, will you just let me out of
it!

Happy. What the hell!

Willy. Tell me what happened!

Biff (to Happy). I can't talk to him!

*A single trumpet note jars the ear. The light of green leaves stains
the house, which holds the air of night and a dream. Young Bernard
enters and knocks on the door of the house.*

Young Bernard (frantically). Mrs. Loman, Mrs. Loman!

Happy. Tell him what happened!

Biff (to Happy). Shut up and leave me alone!

Willy. No, no! You had to go and flunk math!

Biff. What math? What're you talking about?

Young Bernard. Mrs. Loman, Mrs. Loman!

Linda appears in the house, as of old.

Willy (wildly). Math, math, math!

Biff. Take it easy, Pop!

Young Bernard. Mrs. Loman!

Willy (furiously). If you hadn't flunked you'd've been set by now!

Biff. Now, look, I'm gonna tell you what happened, and you're going to listen to me.

Young Bernard. Mrs. Loman!

Biff. I waited six hours . . .

Happy. What the hell are you saying?

Biff. I kept sending in my name but he wouldn't see me. So finally he . . . *(He continues unheard as light fades low on the restaurant.)*

Young Bernard. Biff flunked math!

Linda. No!

Young Bernard. Birnbaum flunked him! They won't graduate him!

Linda. But they have to. He's gotta go to the university. Where is he? Biff! Biff!

Young Bernard. No, he left. He went to Grand Central.

Linda. Grand — You mean he went to Boston!

Young Bernard. Is Uncle Willy in Boston?

Linda. Oh, maybe Willy can talk to the teacher. Oh, the poor, poor boy!

Light on house area snaps out.

Biff (at the table, now audible, holding up a gold fountain pen) . . . so I'm washed up with Oliver, you understand? Are you listening to me?

Willy (at a loss). Yeah, sure. If you hadn't flunked . . .

Biff. Flunked what? What're you talking about?

Willy. Don't blame everything on me! I didn't flunk math — you did! What pen?

Happy. That was awful dumb, Biff, a pen like that is worth —

Willy (seeing the pen for the first time). You took Oliver's pen?

Biff (weakening). Dad, I just explained it to you.

Willy. You stole Bill Oliver's fountain pen!

Biff. I didn't exactly steal it! That's just what I've been explaining to you!

Happy. He had it in his hand and just then Oliver walked in, so he got nervous and stuck it in his pocket!

Willy. My God, Biff!

Biff. I never intended to do it, Dad!

Operator's Voice. Standish Arms, good evening!

Willy (shouting). I'm not in my room!

Biff (frightened). Dad, what's the matter? *(He and Happy stand up.)*

Operator. Ringing Mr. Loman for you!

Willy. I'm not there, stop it!

Biff (horrified, gets down on one knee before Willy). Dad, I'll make good, I'll make good. (*Willy tries to get to his feet. Biff holds him down.*) Sit down now.

Willy. No, you're no good, you're no good for anything.

Biff. I am, Dad, I'll find something else, you understand? Now don't worry about anything. (*He holds up Willy's face.*) Talk to me, Dad.

Operator. Mr. Loman does not answer. Shall I page him?

Willy (attempting to stand, as though to rush and silence the Operator). No, no, no!

Happy. He'll strike something, Pop.

Willy. No, no . . .

Biff (desperately, standing over Willy). Pop, listen! Listen to me! I'm telling you something good. Oliver talked to his partner about the Florida idea. You listening? He — he talked to his partner, and he came to me . . . I'm going to be all right, you hear? Dad, listen to me, he said it was just a question of the amount!

Willy. Then you . . . got it?

Happy. He's gonna be terrific, Pop!

Willy (trying to stand). Then you got it, haven't you? You got it! You got it!

Biff (agonized, holds Willy down). No, no. Look, Pop. I'm supposed to have lunch with them tomorrow. I'm just telling you this so you'll know that I can still make an impression, Pop. And I'll make good somewhere, but I can't go tomorrow, see?

Willy. Why not? You simply . . .

Biff. But the pen, Pop!

Willy. You give it to him and tell him it was an oversight!

Happy. Sure, have lunch tomorrow!

Biff. I can't say that . . .

Willy. You were doing a crossword puzzle and accidentally used his pen!

Biff. Listen, kid, I took those balls years ago, now I walk in with his fountain pen? That clinches it, don't you see? I can't face him like that! I'll try elsewhere.

Page's Voice. Paging Mr. Loman!

Willy. Don't you want to be anything?

Biff. Pop, how can I go back?

Willy. You don't want to be anything, is that what's behind it?

Biff (now angry at Willy for not crediting his sympathy). Don't take it that way! You think it was easy walking into that office after what I'd done to him? A team of horses couldn't have dragged me back to Bill Oliver!

Willy. Then why'd you go?

Biff. Why did I go? Why did I go! Look at you! Look at what's become of you!

Off left, The Woman laughs.

Willy. Biff, you're going to go to that lunch tomorrow, or . . .

Biff. I can't go. I've got no appointment!

Happy. Biff, for . . . !

Willy. Are you spiting me?

Biff. Don't take it that way! Goddammit!

Willy (strikes Biff and falters away from the table). You rotten little louse! Are you spiting me?

The Woman. Someone's at the door, Willy!

Biff. I'm no good, can't you see what I am?

Happy (separating them). Hey, you're in a restaurant! Now cut it out, both of you! *(The girls enter.)* Hello, girls, sit down.

The Woman laughs, off left.

Miss Forsythe. I guess we might as well. This is Letta.

The Woman. Willy, are you going to wake up?

Biff (ignoring Willy). How're ya, miss, sit down. What do you drink?

Miss Forsythe. Letta might not be able to stay long.

Letta. I gotta get up very early tomorrow. I got jury duty. I'm so excited! Were you fellows ever on a jury?

Biff. No, but I been in front of them! *(The girls laugh.)* This is my father.

Letta. Isn't he cute? Sit down with us, Pop.

Happy. Sit him down, Biff!

Biff (going to him). Come on, slugger, drink us under the table. To hell with it! Come on, sit down, pal.

On Biff's last insistence, Willy is about to sit.

The Woman (now urgently). Willy, are you going to answer the door!

The Woman's call pulls Willy back. He starts right, befuddled.

Biff. Hey, where are you going?

Willy. Open the door.

Biff. The door?

Willy. The washroom. . . the door. . . where's the door?

Biff (leading Willy to the left). Just go straight down.

> *Willy moves left.*

The Woman. Willy, Willy, are you going to get up, get up, get up, get up?

> *Willy exits left.*

Letta. I think it's sweet you bring your daddy along.

Miss Forsythe. Oh, he isn't really your father!

Biff (at left, turning to her resentfully). Miss Forsythe, you've just seen a prince walk by. A fine, troubled prince. A hard-working, unappreciated prince. A pal, you understand? A good companion. Always for his boys.

Letta. That's so sweet.

Happy. Well, girls, what's the program? We're wasting time. Come on, Biff. Gather round. Where would you like to go?

Biff. Why don't you do something for him?

Happy. Me!

Biff. Don't you give a damn for him, Hap?

Happy. What're you talking about? I'm the one who. . .

Biff. I sense it, you don't give a good goddam about him. *(He takes the rolled-up hose from his pocket and puts it on the table in front of Happy.)* Look what I found in the cellar, for Christ's sake. How can you bear to let it go on?

Happy. Me? Who goes away? Who runs off and . . .

Biff. Yeah, but he doesn't mean anything to you. You could help him — I can't! Don't you understand what I'm talking about? He's going to kill himself, don't you know that?

Happy. Don't I know it! Me!

Biff. Hap, help him! Jesus . . . help him . . . Help me, help me, I can't bear to look at his face! *(Ready to weep, he hurries out, up right.)*

Happy (starting after him). Where are you going?

Miss Forsythe. What's he so mad about?

Happy. Come on, girls, we'll catch up with him.

Miss Forsythe (as Happy pushes her out). Say, I don't like that temper of his!

Happy. He's just a little overstrung, he'll be all right!

Willy (off left, as The Woman laughs). Don't answer! Don't answer!

Letta. Don't you want to tell your father . . .

Happy. No, that's not my father. He's just a guy. Come on, we'll catch Biff, and, honey, we're going to paint this town! Stanley, where's the check! Hey, Stanley!

> *They exit. Stanley looks toward left.*

Stanley (calling to Happy indignantly). Mr. Loman! Mr. Loman!

> *Stanley picks up a chair and follows them off. Knocking is heard off left. The Woman enters, laughing. Willy follows her. She is in a black slip; he is buttoning his shirt. Raw, sensuous music accompanies their speech:*

Willy. Will you stop laughing? Will you stop?

The Woman. Aren't you going to answer the door? He'll wake the whole hotel.

Willy. I'm not expecting anybody.

The Woman. Whyn't you have another drink, honey, and stop being so damn self-centered?

Willy. I'm so lonely.

The Woman. You know you ruined me, Willy? From now on, whenever you come to the office, I'll see that you go right through to the buyers. No waiting at my desk anymore, Willy. You ruined me.

Willy. That's nice of you to say that.

The Woman. Gee, you are self-centered! Why so sad? You are the saddest, self-centeredest soul I ever did see-saw. (*She laughs. He kisses her.*) Come on inside, drummer boy. It's silly to be dressing in the middle of the night. (*As knocking is heard.*) Aren't you going to answer the door?

Willy. They're knocking on the wrong door.

The Woman. But I felt the knocking. And he heard us talking in here. Maybe the hotel's on fire!

Willy (his terror rising). It's a mistake.

The Woman. Then tell him to go away!

Willy. There's nobody there.

The Woman. It's getting on my nerves, Willy. There's somebody standing out there and it's getting on my nerves!

Willy (pushing her away from him). All right, stay in the bathroom here, and don't come out. I think there's a law in Massachusetts about it, so don't come out. It may be that new room clerk. He looked very mean. So don't come out. It's a mistake, there's no fire.

> *The knocking is heard again. He takes a few steps away from her, and she vanishes into the wing. The light follows him, and now he is facing Young Biff, who carries a suitcase. Biff steps toward him. The music is gone.*

Biff. Why didn't you answer?

Willy. Biff! What are you doing in Boston?

Biff. Why didn't you answer? I've been knocking for five minutes,
 I called you on the phone . . .
Willy. I just heard you. I was in the bathroom and had the door
 shut. Did anything happen home?
Biff. Dad — I let you down.
Willy. What do you mean?
Biff. Dad. . .
Willy. Biffo, what's this about? (*Putting his arm around Biff.*) Come
 on, let's go downstairs and get you a malted.
Biff. Dad, I flunked math.
Willy. Not for the term?
Biff. The term. I haven't got enough credits to graduate.
Willy. You mean to say Bernard wouldn't give you the answers?
Biff. He did, he tried, but I only got a sixty-one.
Willy. And they wouldn't give you four points?
Biff. Birnbaum refused absolutely. I begged him, Pop, but he
 won't give me those points. You gotta talk to him before
 they close the school. Because if he saw the kind of man
 you are, and you just talked to him in your way, I'm sure
 he'd come through for me. The class came right before
 practice, see, and I didn't go enough. Would you talk to
 him? He'd like you, Pop. You know the way you could
 talk.
Willy. You're on. We'll drive right back.
Biff. Oh, Dad, good work! I'm sure he'll change it for you!
Willy. Go downstairs and tell the clerk I'm checkin' out. Go right
 down.
Biff. Yes, sir! See, the reason he hates me, Pop — one day he was
 late for class so I got up at the blackboard and imitated him.
 I crossed my eyes and talked with a lithp.
Willy (*laughing*). You did? The kids like it?
Biff. They nearly died laughing!
Willy. Yeah? What'd you do?
Biff. The thquare root of thixthy twee is . . . (*Willy bursts out
 laughing; Biff joins.*) And in the middle of it he walked in!

 Willy laughs and The Woman joins in offstage.

Willy (*without hesitation*). Hurry downstairs and . . .
Biff. Somebody in there?
Willy. No, that was next door.

 The Woman laughs offstage.

Biff. Somebody got in your bathroom!

Willy. No, it's the next room, there's a party . . .

The Woman (*enters, laughing; she lisps this*). Can I come in? There's something in the bathtub, Willy, and it's moving!

> *Willy looks at Biff, who is staring open-mouthed and horrified at The Woman.*

Willy. Ah — you better go back to your room. They must be finished painting by now. They're painting her room so I let her take a shower here. Go back, go back . . . (*He pushes her.*)

The Woman (*resisting*). But I've got to get dressed, Willy, I can't . . .

Willy. Get out of here! Go back, go back . . . (*Suddenly striving for the ordinary.*) This is Miss Francis, Biff, she's a buyer. They're painting her room. Go back, Miss Francis, go back . . .

The Woman. But my clothes, I can't go out naked in the hall!

Willy (*pushing her offstage*). Get outa here! Go back, go back!

> *Biff slowly sits down on his suitcase as the argument continues offstage.*

The Woman. Where's my stockings? You promised me stockings, Willy!

Willy. I have no stockings here!

The Woman. You had two boxes of size nine sheers for me, and I want them!

Willy. Here, for God's sake, will you get outa here!

The Woman (*enters holding a box of stockings*). I just hope there's nobody in the hall. That's all I hope. (*To Biff.*) Are you football or baseball?

Biff. Football.

The Woman (*angry, humiliated*). That's me too. G'night. (*She snatches her clothes from Willy, and walks out.*)

Willy (*after a pause*). Well, better get going. I want to get to the school first thing in the morning. Get my suits out of the closet. I'll get my valise. (*Biff doesn't move.*) What's the matter! (*Biff remains motionless, tears falling.*) She's a buyer. Buys for J. H. Simmons. She lives down the hall — they're painting. You don't imagine — (*He breaks off. After a pause.*) Now listen, pal, she's just a buyer. She sees merchandise in her room and they have to keep it looking just so . . . (*Pause. Assuming command.*) All right, get my suits. (*Biff doesn't move.*) Now stop crying and do as I say. I gave you an order. Biff, I gave you an order! Is that what you do when I give you an order? How dare you cry! (*Putting his arm around Biff.*) Now look, Biff, when you grow up you'll understand about these things. You mustn't — you mustn't overemphasize a thing like this. I'll see Birnbaum first thing in the morning.

Biff. Never mind.

Willy (getting down beside Biff). Never mind! He's going to give you those points. I'll see to it.

Biff. He wouldn't listen to you.

Willy. He certainly will listen to me. You need those points for the U. of Virginia.

Biff. I'm not going there.

Willy. Heh? If I can't get him to change that mark you'll make it up in summer school. You've got all summer to . . .

Biff (his weeping breaking from him). Dad . . .

Willy (infected by it). Oh, my boy . . .

Biff. Dad . . .

Willy. She's nothing to me, Biff. I was lonely, I was terribly lonely.

Biff. You — you gave her Mama's stockings! (*His tears break through and he rises to go.*)

Willy (grabbing for Biff). I gave you an order!

Biff. Don't touch me, you — liar!

Willy. Apologize for that!

Biff. You fake! You phony little fake! You fake! (*Overcome, he turns quickly and weeping fully goes out with his suitcase. Willy is left on the floor on his knees.*)

Willy. I gave you an order! Biff, come back here or I'll beat you! Come back here! I'll whip you!

Stanley comes quickly in from the right and stands in front of Willy.

Willy (shouts at Stanley). I gave you an order . . .

Stanley. Hey, let's pick it up, pick it up, Mr. Loman. (*He helps Willy to his feet.*) Your boys left with the chippies. They said they'll see you home.

A second waiter watches some distance away.

Willy. But we were supposed to have dinner together.

Music is heard, Willy's theme.

Stanley. Can you make it?

Willy. I'll — sure, I can make it. (*Suddenly concerned about his clothes.*) Do I — I look all right?

Stanley. Sure, you look all right. (*He flicks a speck off Willy's lapel.*)

Willy. Here — here's a dollar.

Stanley. Oh, your son paid me. It's all right.

Willy (putting it in Stanley's hand). No, take it. You're a good boy.

Stanley. Oh, no, you don't have to . . .

Willy. Here — here's some more, I don't need it any more. (*After a slight pause.*) Tell me — is there a seed store in the neighborhood?

Stanley. Seeds? You mean like to plant?

As Willy turns, Stanley slips the money back into his jacket pocket.

Willy. Yes. Carrots, peas . . .

Stanley. Well, there's hardware stores on Sixth Avenue, but it may be too late now.

Willy (*anxiously*). Oh, I'd better hurry. I've got to get some seeds. (*He starts off to the right.*) I've got to get some seeds, right away. Nothing's planted. I don't have a thing in the ground.

Willy hurries out as the light goes down. Stanley moves over to the right after him, watches him off. The other waiter has been staring at Willy.

Stanley (*to the waiter*). Well, whatta you looking at?

The waiter picks up the chairs and moves off right. Stanley takes the table and follows him. The light fades on this area. There is a long pause, the sound of the flute coming over. The light gradually rises on the kitchen, which is empty. Happy appears at the door of the house, followed by Biff. Happy is carrying a large bunch of long-stemmed roses. He enters the kitchen, looks around for Linda. Not seeing her, he turns to Biff, who is just outside the house door, and makes a gesture with his hands, indicating "Not here, I guess." He looks into the living room and freezes. Inside, Linda, unseen, is seated, Willy's coat on her lap. She rises ominously and quietly and moves toward Happy, who backs up into the kitchen, afraid.

Happy. Hey, what're you doing up? (*Linda says nothing but moves toward him implacably.*) Where's Pop? (*He keeps backing to the right, and now Linda is in full view in the doorway to the living room.*) Is he sleeping?

Linda. Where were you?

Happy (*trying to laugh it off*). We met two girls, Mom, very fine types. Here, we brought you some flowers. (*Offering them to her.*) Put them in your room, Ma.

She knocks them to the floor at Biff's feet. He has now come inside and closed the door behind him. She stares at Biff, silent.

Happy. Now what'd you do that for? Mom, I want you to have some flowers . . .

Linda (cutting Happy off, violently to Biff). Don't you care whether
he lives or dies?

Happy (going to the stairs). Come upstairs, Biff.

Biff (with a flare of disgust, to Happy). Go away from me! (*To
Linda*.) What do you mean, lives or dies? Nobody's dying
around here, pal.

Linda. Get out of my sight! Get out of here!

Biff. I wanna see the boss.

Linda. You're not going near him!

Biff. Where is he? (*He moves into the living room and Linda follows*.)

Linda (shouting after Biff). You invite him for dinner. He looks
forward to it all day — (*Biff appears in his parents' bedroom,
looks around, and exits*) — and then you desert him there.
There's no stranger you'd do that to!

Happy. Why? He had a swell time with us. Listen, when I —
(*Linda comes back into the kitchen*) — desert him I hope I don't
outlive the day!

Linda. Get out of here!

Happy. Now look, Mom . . .

Linda. Did you have to go to women tonight? You and your lousy
rotten whores!

Biff re-enters the kitchen.

Happy. Mom, all we did was follow Biff around trying to cheer
him up! (*To Biff*.) Boy, what a night you gave me!

Linda. Get out of here, both of you, and don't come back! I don't
want you tormenting him any more. Go on now, get your
things together! (*To Biff*.) You can sleep in his apartment.
(*She starts to pick up the flowers and stops herself*.) Pick up this
stuff, I'm not your maid any more. Pick it up, you bum,
you!

*Happy turns his back to her in refusal. Biff slowly moves over
and gets down on his knees, picking up the flowers.*

Linda. You're a pair of animals! Not one, not another living soul
would have had the cruelty to walk out on that man in a
restaurant!

Biff (not looking at her). Is that what he said?

Linda. He didn't have to say anything. He was so humiliated he
nearly limped when he came in.

Happy. But, Mom, he had a great time with us . . .

Biff (cutting him off violently). Shut up!

Without another word, Happy goes upstairs.

Linda. You! You didn't even go in to see if he was all right!

Biff (still on the floor in front of Linda, the flowers in his hand; with self-loathing). No. Didn't. Didn't do a damned thing. How do you like that, heh? Left him babbling in a toilet.

Linda. You louse. You. . .

Biff. Now you hit it on the nose! (*He gets up, throws the flowers in the wastebasket.*) The scum of the earth, and you're looking at him!

Linda. Get out of here!

Biff. I gotta talk to the boss, Mom. Where is he?

Linda. You're not going near him. Get out of this house!

Biff (with absolute assurance, determination). No. We're gonna have an abrupt conversation, him and me.

Linda. You're not talking to him.

> *Hammering is heard from outside the house, off right. Biff turns toward the noise.*

Linda (suddenly pleading). Will you please leave him alone?

Biff. What's he doing out there?

Linda. He's planting the garden!

Biff (quietly). Now? Oh, my God!

> *Biff moves outside, Linda following. The light dies down on them and comes up on the center of the apron as Willy walks into it. He is carrying a flashlight, a hoe, and a handful of seed packets. He raps the top of the hoe sharply to fix it firmly, and then moves to the left, measuring off the distance with his foot. He holds the flashlight to look at the seed packets, reading off the instructions. He is in the blue of night.*

Willy. Carrots . . . quarter-inch apart. Rows . . . one-foot rows. (*He measures it off.*) One foot. (*He puts down a package and measures off.*) Beets. (*He puts down another package and measures again.*) Lettuce. (*He reads the package, puts it down.*) One foot — (*He breaks off as Ben appears at the right and moves slowly down to him.*) What a proposition, ts, ts. Terrific, terrific. 'Cause she's suffered, Ben, the woman has suffered. You understand me? A man can't go out the way he came in, Ben, a man has got to add up to something. You can't, you can't — (*Ben moves toward him as though to interrupt.*) You gotta consider now. Don't answer so quick. Remember, it's a guaranteed twenty-thousand-dollar proposition. Now look, Ben, I want you to go through the ins and outs of this thing with me. I've got nobody to talk to, Ben, and the woman has suffered, you hear me?

Ben (standing still, considering). What's the proposition?

Willy. It's twenty thousand dollars on the barrelhead. Guaranteed, gilt-edged, you understand?

Ben. You don't want to make a fool of yourself. They might not honor the policy.

Willy. How can they dare refuse? Didn't I work like a coolie to meet every premium on the nose? And now they don't pay off? Impossible!

Ben. It's called a cowardly thing, William.

Willy. Why? Does it take more guts to stand here the rest of my life ringing up a zero?

Ben (yielding). That's a point, William. *(He moves, thinking, turns.)* And twenty thousand — that *is* something one can feel with the hand, it is there.

Willy (now assured, with rising power). Oh, Ben, that's the whole beauty of it! I see it like a diamond, shining in the dark, hard and rough, that I can pick up and touch in my hand. Not like — like an appointment! This would not be another damned-fool appointment, Ben, and it changes all the aspects. Because he thinks I'm nothing, see, and so he spites me. But the funeral . . . *(Straightening up.)* Ben, that funeral will be massive! They'll come from Maine, Massachusetts, Vermont, New Hampshire! All the old-timers with the strange license plates — that boy will be thunderstruck, Ben, because he never realized — I am known! Rhode Island, New York, New Jersey — I am known, Ben, and he'll see it with his eyes once and for all. He'll see what I am, Ben! He's in for a shock, that boy!

Ben (coming down to the edge of the garden). He'll call you a coward.

Willy (suddenly fearful). No, that would be terrible.

Ben. Yes. And a damned fool.

Willy. No, no, he mustn't, I won't have that! *(He is broken and desperate.)*

Ben. He'll hate you, William.

The gay music of the Boys is heard.

Willy. Oh, Ben, how do we get back to all the great times? Used to be so full of light, and comradeship, the sleigh-riding in winter, and the ruddiness on his cheeks. And always some kind of good news coming up, always something nice coming up ahead. And never even let me carry the valises in the house, and simonizing, simonizing that little red car! Why, why can't I give him something and not have him hate me?

Ben. Let me think about it. *(He glances at his watch.)* I still have a little time. Remarkable proposition, but you've got to be sure you're not making a fool of yourself.

Ben drifts off upstage and goes out of sight. Biff comes down from the left.

Willy (*suddenly conscious of Biff, turns and looks up at him, then begins picking up the packages of seeds in confusion.*) Where the hell is that seed? (*Indignantly.*) You can't see nothing out here! They boxed in the whole goddam neighborhood!

Biff. There are people all around here. Don't you realize that?

Willy. I'm busy. Don't bother me.

Biff (*taking the hoe from Willy*). I'm saying good-by to you, Pop. (*Willy looks at him, silent, unable to move.*) I'm not coming back any more.

Willy. You're not going to see Oliver tomorrow?

Biff. I've got no appointment, Dad.

Willy. He put his arm around you, and you've got no appointment?

Biff. Pop, get this now, will you? Everytime I've left it's been a fight that sent me out of here. Today I realized something about myself and I tried to explain it to you and I — I think I'm just not smart enough to make any sense out of it for you. To hell with whose fault it is or anything like that. (*He takes Willy's arm.*) Let's just wrap it up, heh? Come on in, we'll tell Mom. (*He gently tries to pull Willy to left.*)

Willy (*frozen, immobile, with guilt in his voice*). No, I don't want to see her.

Biff. Come on! (*He pulls again, and Willy tries to pull away.*)

Willy (*highly nervous*). No, no, I don't want to see her.

Biff (*tries to look into Willy's face, as if to find the answer there*). Why don't you want to see her?

Willy (*more harshly now*). Don't bother me, will you?

Biff. What do you mean, you don't want to see her? You don't want them calling you yellow, do you? This isn't your fault; it's me, I'm a bum. Now come inside! (*Willy strains to get away.*) Did you hear what I said to you?

Willy pulls away and quickly goes by himself into the house. Biff follows.

Linda (*to Willy*). Did you plant, dear?

Biff (*at the door, to Linda*). All right, we had it out. I'm going and I'm not writing any more.

Linda (*going to Willy in the kitchen*). I think that's the best way, dear. 'Cause there's no use drawing it out, you'll just never get along.

Willy doesn't respond.

Biff. People ask where I am and what I'm doing, you don't know, and you don't care. That way it'll be off your mind and you can start brightening up again. All right? That clears it, doesn't it? (*Willy is silent, and Biff goes to him.*) You gonna wish me luck, scout? (*He extends his hand.*) What do you say?

Linda. Shake his hand, Willy.

Willy (*turning to her, seething with hurt*). There's no necessity to mention the pen at all, y'know.

Biff (*gently*). I've got no appointment, Dad.

Willy (*erupting fiercely*). He put his arm around . . .?

Biff. Dad, you're never going to see what I am, so what's the use of arguing? If I strike oil I'll send you a check. Meantime forget I'm alive.

Willy (*to Linda*). Spite, see?

Biff. Shake hands, Dad.

Willy. Not my hand.

Biff. I was hoping not to go this way.

Willy. Well, this is the way you're going. Good-by.

> *Biff looks at him a moment, then turns sharply and goes to the stairs.*

Willy (*stops him with*). May you rot in hell if you leave this house!

Biff (*turning*). Exactly what is it that you want from me?

Willy. I want you to know, on the train, in the mountains, in the valleys, wherever you go, that you cut down your life for spite!

Biff. No, no.

Willy. Spite, spite, is the word of your undoing! And when you're down and out, remember what did it. When you're rotting somewhere beside the railroad tracks, remember, and don't you dare blame it on me!

Biff. I'm not blaming it on you!

Willy. I won't take the rap for this, you hear?

> *Happy comes down the stairs and stands on the bottom step, watching.*

Biff. That's just what I'm telling you!

Willy (*sinking into a chair at a table, with full accusation*). You're trying to put a knife in me — don't think I don't know what you're doing!

Biff. All right, phony! Then let's lay it on the line. (*He whips the rubber tube out of his pocket and puts it on the table.*)

Happy. You crazy . . .

Linda. Biff! (*She moves to grab the hose, but Biff holds it down with his hand.*)

Biff. Leave it there! Don't move it!

Willy (*not looking at it*). What is that?

Biff. You know goddam well what that is.

Willy (*caged, wanting to escape*). I never saw that.

Biff. You saw it. The mice didn't bring it into the cellar! What is this supposed to do, make a hero out of you? This supposed to make me sorry for you?

Willy. Never heard of it.

Biff. There'll be no pity for you, you hear it? No pity!

Willy (*to Linda*). You hear the spite!

Biff. No, you're going to hear the truth — what you are and what I am!

Linda. Stop it!

Willy. Spite!

Happy (*coming down toward Biff*). You cut it now!

Biff (*to Happy*). The man don't know who we are! The man is gonna know! (*To Willy.*) We never told the truth for ten minutes in this house!

Happy. We always told the truth!

Biff (*turning on him*). You big blow, are you the assistant buyer? You're one of the two assistants to the assistant, aren't you?

Happy. Well, I'm practically . . .

Biff. You're practically full of it! We all are! and I'm through with it. (*To Willy.*) Now hear this, Willy, this is me.

Willy. I know you!

Biff. You know why I had no address for three months? I stole a suit in Kansas City and I was in jail. (*To Linda, who is sobbing.*) Stop crying. I'm through with it.

Linda turns away from them, her hands covering her face.

Willy. I suppose that's my fault!

Biff. I stole myself out of every good job since high school!

Willy. And whose fault is that?

Biff. And I never got anywhere because you blew me so full of hot air I could never stand taking orders from anybody! That's whose fault it is!

Willy. I hear that!

Linda. Don't, Biff!

Biff. It's goddam time you heard that! I had to be boss big shot in two weeks, and I'm through with it!

Willy. Then hang yourself! For spite, hang yourself!

Biff. No! Nobody's hanging himself, Willy! I ran down eleven flights with a pen in my hand today. And suddenly I stopped, you hear me? And in the middle of that office building, do you hear this? I stopped in the middle of that building and

I saw — the sky. I saw the things that I love in this world. The work and the food and time to sit and smoke. And I looked at the pen and said to myself, what the hell am I grabbing this for? Why am I trying to become what I don't want to be? What am I doing in an office, making a contemptuous, begging fool of myself, when all I want is out there, waiting for me the minute I say I know who I am! Why can't I say that, Willy? (*He tries to make Willy face him, but Willy pulls away and moves to the left.*)

Willy (*with hatred, threateningly*). The door of your life is wide open!

Biff. Pop! I'm a dime a dozen, and so are you!

Willy (*turning on him now in an uncontrolled outburst*). I am not a dime a dozen! I am Willy Loman, and you are Biff Loman!

Biff starts for Willy, but is blocked by Happy. In his fury, Biff seems on the verge of attacking his father.

Biff. I am not a leader of men, Willy, and neither are you. You were never anything but a hard-working drummer who landed in the ash can like all the rest of them! I'm one dollar an hour, Willy! I tried seven states and couldn't raise it. A buck an hour! Do you gather my meaning? I'm not bringing home any prizes any more, and you're going to stop waiting for me to bring them home!

Willy (*directly to Biff*). You vengeful, spiteful mutt!

Biff breaks from Happy. Willy, in fright, starts up the stairs. Biff grabs him.

Biff (*at the peak of his fury*). Pop, I'm nothing! I'm nothing, Pop. Can't you understand that? There's no spite in it any more. I'm just what I am, that's all.

Biff's fury has spent itself and he breaks down, sobbing, holding on to Willy, who dumbly fumbles for Biff's face.

Willy (*astonished*). What're you doing? What're you doing? (*To Linda.*) Why is he crying?

Biff (*crying, broken*). Will you let me go, for Christ's sake? Will you take that phony dream and burn it before something happens? (*Struggling to contain himself he pulls away and moves to the stairs.*) I'll go in the morning. Put him — put him to bed. (*Exhausted, Biff moves up the stairs to his room.*)

Willy (*after a long pause, astonished, elevated*). Isn't that — isn't that remarkable? Biff — he likes me!

Linda. He loves you, Willy!

Happy (deeply moved). Always did, Pop.

Willy. Oh, Biff! *(Staring wildly.)* He cried! Cried to me. *(He is choking with his love, and now cries out his promise.)* That boy — that boy is going to be magnificent!

Ben appears in the light just outside the kitchen.

Ben. Yes, outstanding, with twenty thousand behind him.

Linda (sensing the racing of his mind, fearfully, carefully). Now come to bed, Willy. It's all settled now.

Willy (finding it difficult not to rush out of the house). Yes, we'll sleep. Come on. Go to sleep, Hap.

Ben. And it does take a great kind of a man to crack the jungle.

In accents of dread, Ben's idyllic music starts up.

Happy (his arm around Linda). I'm getting married, Pop, don't forget it. I'm changing everything. I'm gonna run that department before the year is up. You'll see, Mom. *(He kisses her.)*

Ben. The jungle is dark but full of diamonds, Willy.

Willy turns, moves, listening to Ben.

Linda. Be good. You're both good boys, just act that way, that's all.

Happy. 'Night, Pop. *(He goes upstairs.)*

Linda (to Willy). Come, dear.

Ben (with greater force). One must go in to fetch a diamond out.

Willy (to Linda, as he moves slowly along the edge of kitchen, toward the door). I just want to get settled down, Linda. Let me sit alone for a little.

Linda (almost uttering her fear). I want you upstairs.

Willy (taking her in his arms). In a few minutes, Linda. I couldn't sleep right now. Go on, you look awful tired. *(He kisses her.)*

Ben. Not like an appointment at all. A diamond is rough and hard to the touch.

Willy. Go on now. I'll be right up.

Linda. I think this is the only way, Willy.

Willy. Sure, it's the best thing.

Ben. Best thing!

Willy. The only way. Everything is gonna be — go on, kid, get to bed. You look so tired.

Linda. Come right up.

Willy. Two minutes.

Linda goes into the living room, then reappears in her bedroom. Willy moves just outside the kitchen door.

Willy. Loves me. (*Wonderingly.*) Always loved me. Isn't that a remarkable thing? Ben, he'll worship me for it!

Ben (*with promise*). It's dark there, but full of diamonds.

Willy. Can you imagine that magnificence with twenty thousand dollars in his pocket?

Linda (*calling from her room*). Willy! Come up!

Willy (*calling into the kitchen*). Yes! yes. Coming! It's very smart, you realize that, don't you, sweetheart? Even Ben sees it. I gotta go, baby. 'By! 'By! (*Going over to Ben, almost dancing.*) Imagine? When the mail comes he'll be ahead of Bernard again!

Ben. A perfect proposition all around.

Willy. Did you see how he cried to me? Oh, if I could kiss him, Ben!

Ben. Time, William, time!

Willy. Oh, Ben, I always knew one way or another we were gonna make it, Biff and I!

Ben (*looking at his watch*). The boat. We'll be late. (*He moves slowly off into the darkness.*)

Willy (*elegiacally, turning to the house*). Now when you kick off, boy, I want a seventy-yard boot, and get right down the field under the ball, and when you hit, hit low and hit hard, because it's important, boy. (*He swings around and faces the audience.*) There's all kinds of important people in the stands, and the first thing you know . . . (*Suddenly realizing he is alone.*) Ben! Ben, where do I . . . ? (*He makes a sudden movement of search.*) Ben, how do I . . . ?

Linda (*calling*). Willy, you coming up?

Willy (*uttering a gasp of fear, whirling about as if to quiet her*). Sh! (*He turns around as if to find his way; sounds, faces, voices, seem to be swarming in upon him and he flicks at them, crying.*) Sh! Sh! (*Suddenly music, faint and high, stops him. It rises in intensity, almost to an unbearable scream. He goes up and down on his toes, and rushes off around the house.*) Shhh!

Linda. Willy?

There is no answer. Linda waits. Biff gets up off his bed. He is still in his clothes. Happy sits up. Biff stands listening.

Linda (*with real fear*). Willy, answer me! Willy!

There is the sound of a car starting and moving away at full speed.

Linda. No!

Biff (rushing down the stairs). Pop!

> As the car speeds off the music crashes down in a frenzy of sound, which becomes the soft pulsation of a single cello string. Biff slowly returns to his bedroom. He and Happy gravely don their jackets. Linda slowly walks out of her room. The music has developed into a dead march. The leaves of day are appearing over everything. Charley and Bernard, somberly dressed, appear and knock on the kitchen door. Biff and Happy slowly descend the stairs to the kitchen as Charley and Bernard enter. All stop a moment when Linda, in clothes of mourning, bearing a little bunch of roses, comes through the draped doorway into the kitchen. She goes to Charley and takes his arm. Now all move toward the audience, through the wall-line of the kitchen. At the limit of the apron, Linda lays down the flowers, kneels, and sits back on her heels. All stare down at the grave.

REQUIEM

Charley. It's getting dark, Linda.

> *Linda doesn't react. She stares at the grave.*

Biff. How about it, Mom? Better get some rest, heh? They'll be closing the gate soon.

> *Linda makes no move. Pause.*

Happy (deeply angered). He had no right to do that. There was no necessity for it. We would've helped him.

Charley (grunting). Hmmm.

Biff. Come along, Mom.

Linda. Why didn't anybody come?

Charley. It was a very nice funeral.

Linda. But where are all the people he knew? Maybe they blame him.

Charley. Naa. It's a rough world, Linda. They wouldn't blame him.

Linda. I can't understand it. At this time especially. First time in thirty-five years we were just about free and clear. He only needed a little salary. He was even finished with the dentist.

Charley. No man only needs a little salary.

Linda. I can't understand it.

Biff. There were a lot of nice days. When he'd come home from a trip; or on Sundays, making the stoop; finishing the cellar; putting on the new porch; when he built the extra bathroom; and put up the garage. You know something, Charley, there's more of him in that front stoop than in all the sales he ever made.

Charley. Yeah. He was a happy man with a batch of cement.

Linda. He was so wonderful with his hands.

Biff. He had the wrong dreams. All, all, wrong.

Happy (almost ready to fight Biff). Don't say that!

Biff. He never knew who he was.

Charley (stopping Happy's movement and reply; to Biff). Nobody dast blame this man. You don't understand: Willy was a salesman. And for a salesman, there is no rock bottom to the life. He don't put a bolt to a nut, he don't tell you the law or give you medicine. He's a man way out there in the blue, riding on a smile and a shoeshine. And when they start not smiling back — that's an earthquake. And then you get yourself a couple of spots on your hat, and you're finished. Nobody dast blame this man. A salesman is got to dream, boy. It comes with the territory.

Biff. Charley, the man didn't know who he was.

Happy (infuriated). Don't say that!

Biff. Why don't you come with me, Happy?

Happy. I'm not licked that easily. I'm staying right in this city, and I'm gonna beat this racket! *(He looks at Biff, his chin set.)* The Loman Brothers!

Biff. I know who I am, kid.

Happy. All right, boy. I'm gonna show you and everybody else that Willy Loman did not die in vain. He had a good dream. It's the only dream you can have — to come out number-one man. He fought it out here, and this is where I'm gonna win it for him.

Biff (with a hopeless glance at Happy, bends toward his mother). Let's go, Mom.

Linda. I'll be with you in a minute. Go on, Charley. *(He hesitates.)* I want to, just for a minute. I never had a chance to say good-by.

Charley moves away, followed by Happy. Biff remains a slight distance up and left of Linda. She sits there, summoning herself. The flute begins, not far away, playing behind her speech.

Linda. Forgive me, dear. I can't cry. I don't know what it is, but I can't cry. I don't understand it. Why did you ever do that? Help me, Willy, I can't cry. It seems to me that you're just on another trip. I keep expecting you. Willy, dear, I can't cry. Why did you do it? I search and search and I search, and I can't understand it, Willy. I made the last payment on the house today. Today, dear. And there'll be nobody home. (*A sob rises in her throat.*) We're free and clear. (*Sobbing mournfully, released.*) We're free. (*Biff comes slowly toward her.*) We're free . . . We're free . . .

Biff lifts her to her feet and moves out up right with her in his arms. Linda sobs quietly. Bernard and Charley come together and follow them, followed by Happy. Only the music of the flute is left on the darkening stage as over the house the hard towers of the apartment buildings rise into sharp focus, and the curtain falls.

QUESTIONS

1. Miller said in *The New York Times* (27 February 1949, Sec. II, p. 1) that tragedy shows man's struggle to secure "his sense of personal dignity," and that "his destruction in the attempt posits a wrong or an evil in his environment." Does this make sense when applied to some earlier tragedy (for example, *Oedipus Rex* or *Hamlet*), and does it apply convincingly to *Death of a Salesman*? Is this the tragedy of an individual's own making? Or is society at fault for corrupting and exploiting Willy? Or both?
2. Is Willy pathetic rather than tragic? If pathetic, does this imply that the play is less worthy than if he is tragic?
3. Do you feel that Miller is straining too hard to turn a play about a little man into a big, impressive play? For example, do the musical themes, the unrealistic setting, the appearances of Ben, and the speech at the grave seem out of keeping in a play about the death of a salesman?
4. We don't know what Willy sells, and we don't know whether or not the insurance will be paid after his death. Do you consider these uncertainties to be faults in the play?
5. Is Howard a villian?
6. Characterize Linda.

Marsha Norman (b. 1947)

'night, Mother

List of Characters

Jessie Cates, in her late thirties or early forties, is pale and vaguely unsteady physically. It is only in the last year that Jessie has gained control of her mind and body, and tonight she is determined to hold on to that control. She wears pants and a long black sweater with deep pockets, which contain scraps of paper, and there may be a pencil behind her ear or a pen clipped to one of the pockets of the sweater. As a rule, Jessie doesn't feel much like talking. Other people have rarely found her quirky sense of humor amusing. She has a peaceful energy on this night, a sense of purpose, but is clearly aware of the time passing moment by moment. Oddly enough, Jessie has never been as communicative or as enjoyable as she is on this evening, but we must know she has not always been this way. There is a familiarity between these two women that comes from having lived together for a long time. There is a shorthand to the talk and a sense of routine comfort in the way they relate to each other physically. Naturally, there are also routine aggravations.

Thelma Cates, "Mama," is Jessie's mother, in her late fifties or early sixties. She has begun to feel her age and so takes it easy when she can, or when it serves her purpose to let someone help her. But she speaks quickly and enjoys talking. She believes that things *are* what she says they are. Her sturdiness is more a mental quality than a physical one, finally. She is chatty and nosy, and this is *her* house.

The play takes place in a relatively new house built way out on a country road, with a living room and connecting kitchen, and a center hall that leads off to the bedrooms. A pull cord in the hall ceiling releases a ladder which leads to the attic. One of these bedrooms opens directly onto the hall, and its entry should be visible to everyone in the audience. It should be, in fact, the focal point of the entire set, and the lighting should make it disappear completely at times and draw the entire set into it at others. It is a point of both threat and promise. It is an ordinary door that opens onto absolute nothingness. That door is the point of all the action, and the utmost care should be given to its design and construction.

Kathy Bates, as Jessie, and Anne Pitoniak, as Mama, are shown here in the Pulitzer Prize winning, original production of 'night, Mother, which opened during the 1982–1983 season at the American Repertory Theatre in Cambridge, Massachusetts. Photograph by Richard Feldman courtesy of the American Repertory Theatre.

    The living room is cluttered with magazines and needlework catalogues, ashtrays and candy dishes. Examples of Mama's needlework are everywhere — pillows, afghans, and quilts, doilies and rugs, and they are quite nice examples. The house is more comfortable than messy, but there is quite a lot to keep in place here. It is more personal than charming. It is not quaint. Under no circumstances should the set and its dressing make a judgment about the intelligence or taste of Jessie and Mama. It should simply indicate that they are very specific real people who happen to live in a particular part of the country. Heavy accents, which would further distance the audience from Jessie and Mama, are also wrong.

    The time is the present, with the action beginning about 8:15. Clocks onstage in the kitchen and on a table in the living room should run throughout the performance and be visible to the audience.

    There will be no intermission.

    Mama stretches to reach the cupcakes in a cabinet in the kitchen. She can't see them, but she can feel around for them, and she's eager to have one, so she's working pretty hard at it. This may be the most serious exercise Mama ever gets. She finds a cupcake, the coconut-covered, raspberry-and-marshmallow-filled kind known as a snowball, but sees that there's one missing from the package. She calls to Jessie, who is apparently somewhere else in the house.

Mama (*unwrapping the cupcake*). Jessie, it's the last snowball, sugar. Put it on the list, O.K.? And we're out of Hershey bars, and where's that peanut brittle? I think maybe Dawson's been in it again. I ought to put a big mirror on the refrigerator door. That'll keep him out of my treats, won't it? You hear me, honey? (*Then more to herself.*) I hate it when the coconut falls off. Why does the coconut fall off?

    Jessie enters from her bedroom, carrying a stack of newspapers.

Jessie. We got any old towels?
Mama. There you are!
Jessie (*holding a towel that was on the stack of newspapers*). Towels you don't want anymore. (*Picking up Mama's snowball wrapper*) How about this swimming towel Loretta gave us? Beach towel, that's the name of it. You want it? (*Mama shakes her head no.*)
Mama. What have you been doing in there?
Jessie. And a big piece of plastic like a rubber sheet or something. Garbage bags would do if there's enough.

Mama. Don't go making a big mess, Jessie. It's eight o'clock already.

Jessie. Maybe an old blanket or towels we got in a soap box sometime?

Mama. I said don't make a mess. Your hair is black enough, hon.

Jessie (continuing to search the kitchen cabinets, finding two or three more towels to add to her stack). It's not for my hair, Mama. What about some old pillows anywhere, or a foam cushion out of a yard chair would be real good.

Mama. You haven't forgot what night it is, have you? *(Holding up her fingernails.)* They're all chipped, see? I've been waiting all week, Jess. It's Saturday night, sugar.

Jessie. I know. I got it on the schedule.

Mama (crossing to the living room). You want me to wash 'em now or are you making your mess first? *(Looking at the snowball.)* We're out of these. Did I say that already?

Jessie. There's more coming tomorrow. I ordered you a whole case.

Mama (checking the TV Guide). A whole case will go stale, Jessie.

Jessie. They can go in the freezer till you're ready for them. Where's Daddy's gun?

Mama. In the attic.

Jessie. Where in the attic? I looked your whole nap and couldn't find it anywhere.

Mama. One of his shoeboxes, I think.

Jessie. Full of shoes. I looked already.

Mama. Well, you didn't look good enough, then. There's that box from the ones he wore to the hospital. When he died, they told me I could have them back, but I never did like those shoes.

Jessie (pulling them out of her pocket). I found the bullets. They were in an old milk can.

Mama (as Jessie starts for the hall). Dawson took the shotgun, didn't he? Hand me that basket, hon.

Jessie (getting the basket for her). Dawson better not've taken that pistol.

Mama (stopping her again). Now my glasses, please. *(Jessie returns to get the glasses.)* I told him to take those rubber boots, too, but he said they were for fishing. I told him to take up fishing.

Jessie reaches for the cleaning spray, and cleans Mama's glasses for her.

Jessie. He's just too lazy to climb up there, Mama. Or maybe he's just being smart. That floor's not very steady.

Mama (getting out a piece of knitting). It's not a floor at all, hon, it's a board now and then. Measure this for me. I need six inches.

Jessie (as she measures). Dawson could probably use some of those clothes up there. Somebody should have them. You ought to call the Salvation Army before the whole thing falls in on you. Six inches exactly.

Mama. It's plenty safe! As long as you don't go up there.

Jessie (turning to go again). I'm careful.

Mama. What do you want the gun for, Jess?

Jessie (not returning this time. Opening the ladder in the hall). Protection. *(She steadies the ladder as Mama talks.)*

Mama. You take the TV way too serious, hon. I've never seen a criminal in my life. This is way too far to come for what's out here to steal. Never seen a one.

Jessie (taking her first step up). Except for Ricky.

Mama. Ricky is mixed up. That's not a crime.

Jessie. Get your hands washed. I'll be right back. And get 'em real dry. You dry your hands till I get back or it's no go, all right?

Mama. I thought Dawson told you not to go up those stairs.

Jessie (going up). He did.

Mama. I don't like the idea of a gun, Jess.

Jessie (calling down from the attic). Which shoebox, do you remember?

Mama. Black.

Jessie. The box was black?

Mama. The shoes were black.

Jessie. That doesn't help much, Mother.

Mama. I'm not trying to help, sugar. *(No answer.)* We don't have anything anybody'd want, Jessie. I mean, I don't even want what we got, Jessie.

Jessie. Neither do I. Wash your hands. *(Mama gets up and crosses to stand under the ladder.)*

Mama. You come down from there before you have a fit. I can't come up and get you, you know.

Jessie. I know.

Mama. We'll just hand it over to them when they come, how's that? Whatever they want, the criminals.

Jessie. That's a good idea, Mama.

Mama. Ricky will grow out of this and be a real fine boy, Jess. But I have to tell you, I wouldn't want Ricky to know we had a gun in the house.

Jessie. Here it is. I found it.

Mama. It's just something Ricky's going through. Maybe he's in with some bad people. He just needs some time, sugar. He'll get back in school or get a job or one day you'll get a call and he'll say he's sorry for all the trouble he's caused and invite you out for supper someplace dress-up.

Jessie (coming back down the steps). Don't worry. It's not for him, it's for me.

Mama. I didn't think you would shoot your own boy, Jessie. I know you've felt like it, well, we've all felt like shooting somebody, but we don't do it. I just don't think we need . . .

Jessie (interrupting). Your hands aren't washed. Do you want a manicure or not?

Mama. Yes, I do, but . . .

Jessie (crossing to the chair). Then wash your hands and don't talk to me any more about Ricky. Those two rings he took were the last valuable things *I* had, so now he's started in on other people, door to door. I hope they put him away sometime. I'd turn him in myself if I knew where he was.

Mama. You don't mean that.

Jessie. Every word. Wash your hands and that's the last time I'm telling you.

> *Jessie sits down with the gun and starts cleaning it, pushing the cylinder out, checking to see that the chambers and barrel are empty, then putting some oil on a small patch of cloth and pushing it through the barrel with the push rod that was in the box. Mama goes to the kitchen and washes her hands, as instructed, trying not to show her concern about the gun.*

Mama. I shoulda got you to bring down that milk can. Agnes Fletcher sold hers to somebody with a flea market for forty dollars apiece.

Jessie. I'll go back and get it in a minute. There's a wagon wheel up there, too. There's even a churn. I'll get it all if you want.

Mama (coming over, now, taking over now). What are you doing?

Jessie. The barrel has to be clean, Mama. Old powder, dust gets in it . . .

Mama. What for?

Jessie. I told you.

Mama (reaching for the gun). And I told you, we don't get criminals out here.

Jessie (quickly pulling it to her). And I told you . . . (*Then trying to be calm.*) The gun is for me.

Mama. Well, you can have it if you want. When I die, you'll get it all, anyway.

Jessie. I'm going to kill myself, Mama.

Mama (returning to the sofa). Very funny. Very funny.

Jessie. I am.

Mama. You are not! Don't even say such a thing, Jessie.

Jessie. How would you know if I didn't say it? You want it to be a surprise? You're lying there in your bed or maybe you're just brushing your teeth and you hear this . . . noise down the hall?

Mama. Kill yourself.

Jessie. Shoot myself. In a couple of hours.

Mama. It must be time for your medicine.

Jessie. Took it already.

Mama. What's the matter with you?

Jessie. Not a thing. Feel fine.

Mama. You feel fine. You're just going to kill yourself.

Jessie. Waited until I felt good enough, in fact.

Mama. Don't make jokes, Jessie. I'm too old for jokes.

Jessie. It's not a joke, Mama.

Mama watches for a moment in silence.

Mama. That gun's no good, you know. He broke it right before he died. He dropped it in the mud one day.

Jessie. Seems O.K. (*She spins the chamber, cocks the pistol, and pulls the trigger. The gun is not yet loaded, so all we hear is the click, but it will definitely work. It's also obvious that Jessie knows her way around a gun. Mama cannot speak.*) I had Cecil's all ready in there, just in case I couldn't find this one, but I'd rather use Daddy's.

Mama. Those bullets are at least fifteen years old.

Jessie (*pulling out another box*). These are from last week.

Mama. Where did you get those?

Jessie. Feed store Dawson told me about.

Mama. Dawson!

Jessie. I told him I was worried about prowlers. He said he thought it was a good idea. He told me what kind to ask for.

Mama. If he had any idea . . .

Jessie. He took it as a compliment. He thought I might be taking an interest in things. He got through telling me all about the bullets and then he said we ought to talk like this more often.

Mama. And where was I while this was going on?

Jessie. On the phone with Agnes. About the milk can, I guess. Anyway, I asked Dawson if he thought they'd send me some bullets and he said he'd just call for me, because he knew they'd send them if he told them to. And he was absolutely right. Here they are.

Mama. How could he do that?

Jessie. Just trying to help, Mama.

Mama. And then I told you where the gun was.

Jessie (smiling, enjoying this joke). See? Everybody's doing what they can.

Mama. You told me it was for protection!

Jessie. It *is!* I'm still doing your nails, though. Want to try that new Chinaberry color?

Mama. Well, I'm calling Dawson right now. We'll just see what he has to say about this little stunt.

Jessie. Dawson doesn't have any more to do with this.

Mama. He's your brother.

Jessie. And that's all.

Mama (stands up, moves toward the phone). Dawson will put a stop to this. Yes he will. He'll take the gun away.

Jessie. If you call him, I'll just have to do it before he gets here. Soon as you hang up the phone, I'll just walk in the bedroom and lock the door. Dawson will get here just in time to help you clean up. Go ahead, call him. Then call the police. Then call the funeral home. Then call Loretta and see if *she'll* do your nails.

Mama. You will not! This is crazy talk, Jessie!

Mama goes directly to the telephone and starts to dial, but Jessie is fast, coming up behind her and taking the receiver out of her hand, putting it back down.

Jessie (firm and quiet). I said no. This is private. Dawson is not invited.

Mama. Just me.

Jessie. I don't want anybody else over here. Just you and me. If Dawson comes over, it'll make me feel stupid for not doing it ten years ago.

Mama. I think we better call the doctor. Or how about the ambulance. You like that one driver, I know. What's his name, Timmy? Get you somebody to talk to.

Jessie (going back to her chair). I'm through talking, Mama. You're it. No more.

Mama. We're just going to sit around like every other night in the world and then you're going to kill yourself? *(Jessie doesn't answer.)* You'll miss. *(Again there is no response.)* You'll just wind up a vegetable. How would you like that? Shoot your ear off? You know what the doctor said about getting excited. You'll cock the pistol and have a fit.

Jessie. I think I can kill myself, Mama.

Mama. You're not going to kill yourself, Jessie. You're not even upset! (*Jessie smiles, or laughs quietly, and Mama tries a different approach.*) People don't really kill themselves, Jessie. No, mam, doesn't make sense, unless you're retarded or deranged, and you're as normal as they come, Jessie, for the most part. We're all *afraid* to die.

Jessie. I'm not, Mama. I'm cold all the time, anyway.

Mama. That's ridiculous.

Jessie. It's exactly what I want. It's dark and quiet.

Mama. So is the back yard, Jessie! Close your eyes. Stuff cotton in your ears. Take a nap! It's quiet in your room. I'll leave the TV off all night.

Jessie. So quiet I don't know it's quiet. So nobody can get me.

Mama. You don't know what dead is like. It might not be quiet at all. What if it's like an alarm clock and you can't wake up so you can't shut it off. Ever.

Jessie. Dead is everybody and everything I ever knew, gone. Dead is dead quiet.

Mama. It's a sin. You'll go to hell.

Jessie. Uh-huh.

Mama. You will!

Jessie. Jesus was a suicide, if you ask me.

Mama. You'll go to hell just for saying that. Jessie!

Jessie (*with genuine surprise*). I didn't know I thought that.

Mama. Jessie!

Jessie doesn't answer. She puts the now-loaded gun back in the box and crosses to the kitchen. But Mama is afraid she's headed for the bedroom.

Mama (*in a panic*). You can't use my towels! They're my towels. I've had them for a long time. I like my towels.

Jessie. I asked you if you wanted that swimming towel and you said you didn't.

Mama. And you can't use your father's gun, either. It's mine now, too. And you can't do it in my house.

Jessie. Oh, come on.

Mama. No. You can't do it. I won't let you. The house is in my name.

Jessie. I have to go in the bedroom and lock the door behind me so they won't arrest you for killing me. They'll probably test your hands for gunpowder, anyway, but you'll pass.

Mama. Not in my house!

Jessie. If I'd known you were going to act like this, I wouldn't have told you.

Mama. How am I supposed to act? Tell you to go ahead? O.K.
   by me, sugar? Might try it myself. What took you so long?
Jessie. There's just no point in fighting me over it, that's all. Want
   some coffee?
Mama. Your birthday's coming up, Jessie. Don't you want to
   know what we got you?
Jessie. You got me dusting powder, Loretta got me a new housecoat,
   pink probably, and Dawson got me new slippers, too small,
   but they go with the robe, he'll say. (*Mama cannot speak.*)
   Right? (*Apparently Jessie is right.*) Be back in a minute.

*Jessie takes the gun box, puts it on top of the stack of towels and
garbage bags, and takes them into her bedroom. Mama, alone for
a moment, goes to the phone, picks up the receiver, looks toward
the bedroom, starts to dial, and then replaces the receiver in its
cradle as Jessie walks back into the room. Jessie wonders, silently.
They have lived together for so long there is very rarely any reason
for one to ask what the other was about to do.*

Mama. I started to, but I didn't. I didn't call him.
Jessie. Good. Thank you.
Mama (*starting over, a new approach*). What's this all about, Jessie?
Jessie. About?

*Jessie now begins the next task she had "on the schedule," which
is refilling all the candy jars, taking the empty papers out of the
boxes of chocolates, etc. Mama generally snitches when Jessie does
this. Not tonight, though. Nevertheless, Jessie offers.*

Mama. What did I do?
Jessie. Nothing. Want a caramel?
Mama (*ignoring the candy*). You're mad at me.
Jessie. Not a bit. I am worried about you, but I'm going to do
   what I can before I go. We're not just going to sit around
   tonight. I made a list of things.
Mama. What things?
Jessie. How the washer works. Things like that.
Mama. I know how the washer works. You put the clothes in.
   You put the soap in. You turn it on. You wait.
Jessie. You do something else. You don't just wait.
Mama. Whatever else you find to do, you're still mainly waiting.
   The waiting's the worst part of it. The waiting's what you
   pay somebody else to do, if you can.
Jessie (*nodding*). O.K. Where do we keep the soap?
Mama. I could find it.
Jessie. See?

Mama. If you're mad about doing the wash, we can get Loretta
to do it.

Jessie. Oh now, that might be worth staying to see.

Mama. She'd never in her life, would she?

Jessie. Nope.

Mama. What's the matter with her?

Jessie. She thinks she's better than we are. She's not.

Mama. Maybe if she didn't wear that yellow all the time.

Jessie. The washer repair number is on a little card taped to the
side of the machine.

Mama. Loretta doesn't ever have to come over here again. Dawson
can just leave her at home when he comes. And we don't
ever have to see Dawson either if he bothers you. Does he
bother you?

Jessie. Sure he does. Be sure you clean out the lint tray every time
you use the dryer. But don't ever put your house shoes in,
it'll melt the soles.

Mama. What does Dawson do, that bothers you?

Jessie. He just calls me Jess like he knows who he's talking to.
He's always wondering what I do all day. I mean, I wonder
that myself, but it's my day, so it's mine to wonder about,
not his.

Mama. Family is just accident, Jessie. It's nothing personal, hon.
They don't mean to get on your nerves. They don't even
mean to be your family, they just are.

Jessie. They know too much.

Mama. About what?

Jessie. They know things about you, and they learned it before
you had a chance to say whether you wanted them to know
it or not. They were there when it happened and it don't
belong to them, it belongs to you, only they got it. Like
my mail-order bra got delivered to their house.

Mama. By accident!

Jessie. All the same . . . they opened it. They saw the little rosebuds
on it. (*Offering her another candy.*) Chewy mint?

Mama (*shaking her head no*). What do they know about you? I'll
tell them never to talk about it again. Is it Ricky or Cecil
or your fits or your hair is falling out or you drink too much
coffee or you never go out of the house or what?

Jessie. I just don't like their talk. The account at the grocery is in
Dawson's name when you call. The number's on a whole
list of numbers on the back cover of the phone book.

Mama. Well! Now we're getting somewhere. They're none of them
ever setting foot in this house again.

Jessie. It's not them, Mother. I wouldn't kill myself just to get away from them.

Mama. You leave the room when they come over, anyway.

Jessie. I stay as long as I can. Besides, it's you they come to see.

Mama. That's because I stay in the room when they come.

Jessie. It's not them.

Mama. Then what is it?

Jessie (checking the list on her note pad). The grocery won't deliver on Saturday anymore. And if you want your order the same day, you have to call before ten. And they won't deliver less than fifteen dollars' worth. What I do is tell them what we need and tell them to add on cigarettes until it gets to fifteen dollars.

Mama. It's Ricky. You're trying to get through to him.

Jessie. If I thought I could do that, I would stay.

Mama. Make him sorry he hurt you, then. That's it, isn't it?

Jessie. He's hurt me, I've hurt him. We're about even.

Mama. You'll be telling him killing is O.K. with you, you know. Want him to start killing next? Nothing wrong with it. Mom did it.

Jessie. Only a matter of time, anyway, Mama. When the call comes, you let Dawson handle it.

Mama. Honey, nothing says those calls are always going to be some new trouble he's into. You could get one that he's got a job, that he's getting married, or how about he's joined the army, wouldn't that be nice?

Jessie. If you call the Sweet Tooth before you call the grocery, that Susie will take your fudge next door to the grocery and it'll all come out together. Be sure you talk to Susie, though. She won't let them put it in the bottom of a sack like that one time, remember?

Mama. Ricky could come over, you know. What if he calls us?

Jessie. It's not Ricky, Mama.

Mama. Or anybody could call us, Jessie.

Jessie. Not on Saturday night, Mama.

Mama. Then what is it? Are you sick? If your gums are swelling again, we can get you to the dentist in the morning.

Jessie. No. Can you order your medicine or do you want Dawson to? I've got a note to him. I'll add that to it if you want.

Mama. Your eyes don't look right. I thought so yesterday.

Jessie. That was just the ragweed. I'm not sick.

Mama. Epilepsy is sick, Jessie.

Jessie. It won't kill me. (*A pause.*) If it would, I wouldn't have to.

Mama. You don't *have* to.

Jessie. No, I don't. That's what I like about it.

Mama. Well, I won't let you!

Jessie. It's not up to you.

Mama. Jessie!

Jessie. I want to hang a big sign around my neck, like Daddy's on the barn. GONE FISHING.

Mama. You don't like it here.

Jessie (smiling). Exactly.

Mama. I meant here in my house.

Jessie. I know you did.

Mama. You never should have moved back in here with me. If you'd kept your little house or found another place when Cecil left you, you'd have made some new friends at least. Had a life to lead. Had your own things around you. Give Ricky a place to come see you. You never should've come here.

Jessie. Maybe.

Mama. But I didn't force you, did I?

Jessie. If it was a mistake, we made it together. You took me in. I appreciate that.

Mama. You didn't have any business being by yourself right then, but I can see how you might want a place of your own. A grown woman should . . .

Jessie. Mama . . . I'm just not having a very good time and I don't have any reason to think it'll get anything but worse. I'm tired. I'm hurt. I'm sad. I feel used.

Mama. Tired of what?

Jessie. It all.

Mama. What does that mean?

Jessie. I can't say it any better.

Mama. Well, you'll have to say it better because I'm not letting you alone till you do. What were those other things? Hurt . . . *(Before Jessie can answer.)* You had this all ready to say to me, didn't you? Did you write this down? How long have you been thinking about this?

Jessie. Off and on, ten years. On all the time, since Christmas.

Mama. What happened at Christmas?

Jessie. Nothing.

Mama. So why Christmas?

Jessie. That's it. On the nose.

> *A pause. Mama knows exactly what Jessie means. She was there, too, after all.*

Jessie (putting the candy sacks away). See where all this is? Red hots

up front, sour balls and horehound mixed together in this
one sack. New packages of toffee and licorice right in back
there.

Mama. Go back to your list. You're hurt by what?

Jessie (Mama knows perfectly well). Mama . . .

Mama. O.K. Sad about what? There's nothing real sad going on
right now. If it was after your divorce or something, that
would make sense.

Jessie (looking at her list, then opening the drawer). Now, this drawer
has everything in it that there's no better place for. Extension
cords, batteries for the radio, extra lighters, sandpaper, masking
tape, Elmer's glue, thumbtacks, that kind of stuff. The mouse-
traps are under the sink, but you call Dawson if you've got
one and let him do it.

Mama. Sad about what?

Jessie. The way things are.

Mama. Not good enough. What things?

Jessie. Oh, everything from you and me to Red China.

Mama. I think we can leave the Chinese out of this.

Jessie (crosses back into the living room). There's extra light bulbs in
a box in the hall closet. And we've got a couple of packages
of fuses in the fuse box. There's candles and matches in the
top of the broom closet, but if the lights go out, just call
Dawson and sit tight. But don't open the refrigerator door.
Things will stay cool in there as long as you keep the door
shut.

Mama. I asked you a question.

Jessie. I read the paper. I don't like how things are. And they're
not any better out there than they are in here.

Mama. If you're doing this because of the newspapers, I can sure
fix that!

Jessie. There's just more of it on TV.

Mama (kicking the television set). Take it out, then!

Jessie. You wouldn't do that.

Mama. Watch me.

Jessie. What would you do all day?

Mama (desperately). Sing. *(Jessie laughs.)* I would, too. You want
to watch? I'll sing till morning to keep you alive, Jessie,
please!

Jessie. No. *(Then affectionately.)* It's a funny idea, though. What
do you sing?

Mama (has no idea how to answer this). We've got a good life here!

Jessie (going back into the kitchen). I called this morning and canceled
the papers, except for Sunday, for your puzzles; you'll still
get that one.

Mama. Let's get another dog, Jessie! You liked a big dog, now, didn't you? That King dog, didn't you?

Jessie (washing her hands). I did like that King dog, yes.

Mama. I'm so dumb. He's the one run under the tractor.

Jessie. That makes him dumb, not you.

Mama. For bringing it up.

Jessie. It's O.K. Handi-Wipes and sponges under the sink.

Mama. We could get a new dog and keep him in the house. Dogs are cheap!

Jessie (getting big pill jars out of the cabinet). No.

Mama. Something for you to take care of.

Jessie. I've had you, Mama.

Mama (frantically starting to fill pill bottles). You do too much for me. I can fill pill bottles all day, Jessie, and change the shelf paper and wash the floor when I get through. You just watch me. You don't have to do another thing in this house if you don't want to. You don't have to take care of me, Jessie.

Jessie. I know that. You've just been letting me do it so I'll have something to do, haven't you?

Mama (realizing this was a mistake). I don't do it as well as you. I just meant if it tires you out or makes you feel used . . .

Jessie. Mama, I know you used to ride the bus. Riding the bus and it's hot and bumpy and crowded and too noisy and more than anything in the world you want to get off and the only reason in the world you don't get off is it's still fifty blocks from where you're going? Well, I can get off right now if I want to, because even if I ride fifty more years and get off then, it's the same place when I step down to it. Whenever I feel like it, I can get off. As soon as I've had enough, it's my stop. I've had enough.

Mama. You're feeling sorry for yourself!

Jessie. The plumber's helper is under the sink, too.

Mama. You're not having a good time! Whoever promised you a good time? Do you think I've had a good time?

Jessie. I think you're pretty happy, yeah. You have things you like to do.

Mama. Like what?

Jessie. Like crochet.

Mama. I'll teach you to crochet.

Jessie. I can't do any of that nice work, Mama.

Mama. Good time don't come looking for you, Jessie. You could work some puzzles or put in a garden or go to the store. Let's call a taxi and go to the A&P!

Jessie. I shopped you up for about two weeks already. You're not going to need toilet paper till Thanksgiving.

Mama (interrupting). You're acting like some little brat, Jessie. You're mad and everybody's boring and you don't have anything to do and you don't like me and you don't like going out and you don't like staying in and you never talk on the phone and you don't watch TV and you're miserable and it's your own sweet fault.

Jessie. And it's time I did something about it.

Mama. Not something like killing yourself. Something like . . . buying us all new dishes! I'd like that. Or maybe the doctor would let you get a driver's license now, or I know what let's do right this minute, let's rearrange the furniture.

Jessie. I'll do that. If you want. I always thought if the TV was somewhere else, you wouldn't get such a glare on it during the day. I'll do whatever you want before I go.

Mama (badly frightened by those words). You could get a job!

Jessie. I took that telephone sales job and I didn't even make enough money to pay the phone bill, and I tried to work at the gift shop at the hospital and they said I made people real uncomfortable smiling at them the way I did.

Mama. You could keep books. You kept your dad's books.

Jessie. But nobody ever checked them.

Mama. When he died, they checked them.

Jessie. And that's when they took the books away from me.

Mama. That's because without him there wasn't any business, Jessie!

Jessie (putting the pill bottles away). You know I couldn't work. I can't do anything. I've never been around people my whole life except when I went to the hospital. I could have a seizure any time. What good would a job do? The kind of job I could get would make me feel worse.

Mama. Jessie!

Jessie. It's true!

Mama. It's what you think is true!

Jessie (struck by the clarity of that). That's right. It's what I think is true.

Mama (hysterically). But I can't do anything about that!

Jessie (quietly). No. You can't. (*Mama slumps, if not physically, at least emotionally.*) And I can't do anything either, about my life, to change it, make it better, make me feel better about it. Like it better, make it work. But I can stop it. Shut it down, turn it off like the radio when there's nothing on I want to listen to. It's all I really have that belongs to me and I'm going to say what happens to it. And it's going to stop. And I'm going to stop it. So. Let's just have a good time.

Mama. Have a good time.

Jessie. We can't go on fussing all night. I mean, I could ask you things I always wanted to know and you could make me some hot chocolate. The old way.

Mama (in despair). It takes cocoa, Jessie.

Jessie (gets it out of the cabinet). I bought cocoa, Mama. And I'd like to have a caramel apple and do your nails.

Mama. You didn't eat a bite of supper

Jessie. Does that mean I can't have a caramel apple?

Mama. Of course not. I mean . . . (*Smiling a little.*) Of course you can have a caramel apple.

Jessie. I thought I could.

Mama. I make the best caramel apples in the world.

Jessie. I know you do.

Mama. Or used to. And you don't get cocoa like mine anywhere anymore.

Jessie. It takes time, I know, but . . .

Mama. The salt is the trick.

Jessie. Trouble and everything.

Mama (backing away toward the stove). It's no trouble. What trouble? You put it in the pan and stir it up. All right. Fine. Caramel apples. Cocoa. O.K.

Jessie walks to the counter to retrieve her cigarettes as Mama looks for the right pan. There are brief near-smiles, and maybe Mama clears her throat. We have a truce, for the moment. A genuine but nevertheless uneasy one. Jessie, who has been in constant motion since the beginning, now seems content to sit.

Mama starts looking for a pan to make the cocoa, getting out all the pans in the cabinets in the process. It looks like she's making a mess on purpose so Jessie will have to put them all away again. Mama is buying time, or trying to, and entertaining.

Jessie. You talk to Agnes today?

Mama. She's calling me from a pay phone this week. God only knows why. She has a perfectly good Trimline at home.

Jessie (laughing). Well, how is she?

Mama. How is she every day, Jessie? Nuts.

Jessie. Is she really crazy or just silly?

Mama. No, she's really crazy. She was probably using the pay phone because she had another little fire problem at home.

Jessie. Mother . . .

Mama. I'm serious! Agnes Fletcher's burned down every house she ever lived in. Eight fires, and she's due for a new one any day now.

Jessie (laughing). No!

Mama. Wouldn't surprise me a bit.

Jessie (laughing). Why didn't you tell me this before? Why isn't she locked up somewhere?

Mama. 'Cause nobody ever got hurt, I guess. Agnes woke everybody up to watch the fires as soon as she set 'em. One time she set out porch chairs and served lemonade.

Jessie (shaking her head). Real lemonade?

Mama. The houses they lived in, you knew they were going to fall down anyway, so why wait for it, is all I could ever make out about it. Agnes likes a feeling of accomplishment.

Jessie. Good for her.

Mama (finding the pan she wants). Why are you asking about Agnes? One cup or two?

Jessie. One. She's your friend. No marshmallows.

Mama (getting the milk, etc.). You have to have marshmallows. That's the old way, Jess. Two or three? Three is better.

Jessie. Three, then. Her whole house burns up? Her clothes and pillows and everything? I'm not sure I believe this.

Mama. When she was a girl, Jess, not now. Long time ago. But she's still got it in her, I'm sure of it.

Jessie. She wouldn't burn her house down now. Where would she go? She can't get Buster to build her a new one, he's dead. How could she burn it up?

Mama. Be exciting, though, if she did. You never know.

Jessie. You do too know, Mama. She wouldn't do it.

Mama (forced to admit, but reluctant). I guess not.

Jessie. What else? Why does she wear all those whistles around her neck?

Mama. Why does she have a house full of birds?

Jessie. I didn't know she had a house full of birds!

Mama. Well, she does. And she says they just follow her home. Well, I know for a fact she's still paying on the last parrot she bought. You gotta keep your life filled up, she says. She says a lot of stupid things. *(Jessie laughs, Mama continues, convinced she's getting somewhere.)* It's all that okra she eats. You can't just willy-nilly eat okra two meals a day and expect to get away with it. Made her crazy.

Jessie. She really eats okra twice a day? Where does she get it in the winter?

Mama. Well, she eats it a lot. Maybe not two meals, but . . .

Jessie. More than the average person.

Mama (beginning to get irritated). I don't know how much okra the average person eats.

Jessie. Do you know how much okra Agnes eats?

Mama. No.

Jessie. How many birds does she have?

Mama. Two.

Jessie. Then what are the whistles for?

Mama. They're not real whistles. Just little plastic ones on a necklace she won playing Bingo, and I only told you about it because I thought I might get a laugh out of you for once even if it wasn't the truth, Jessie. Things don't have to be true to talk about 'em, you know.

Jessie. Why won't she come over here?

Mama is suddenly quiet, but the cocoa and milk are in the pan now, so she lights the stove and starts stirring.

Mama. Well now, what a good idea. We should've had more cocoa. Cocoa is perfect.

Jessie. Except you don't like milk.

Mama (another attempt, but not as energetic). I hate milk. Coats your throat as bad as okra. Something just downright disgusting about it.

Jessie. It's because of me, isn't it?

Mama. No, Jess.

Jessie. Yes, Mama.

Mama. O.K. Yes, then, but she's crazy. She's as crazy as they come. She's a lunatic.

Jessie. What is it exactly? Did I say something, sometime? Or did she see me have a fit and's afraid I might have another one if she came over, or what?

Mama. I guess.

Jessie. You guess what? What's she ever said? She must've given you some reason.

Mama. Your hands are cold.

Jessie. What difference does that make?

Mama. "Like a corpse," she says, "and I'm gonna be one soon enough as it is."

Jessie. That's crazy.

Mama. That's Agnes. "Jessie's shook the hand of death and I can't take the chance it's catching, Thelma, so I ain't comin 'over, and you can understand or not, but I ain't comin'. I'll come up the driveway, but that's as far as I go."

Jessie (laughing, relieved). I thought she didn't like me! She's scared of me! How about that! Scared of me.

Mama. I could make her come over here, Jessie. I could call her up right now and she could bring the birds and come visit.

I didn't know you ever thought about her at all. I'll tell her
she just has to come and she'll come, all right. She owes
me one.

Jessie. No, that's all right. I just wondered about it. When I'm in
the hospital, does she come over here?

Mama. Her kitchen is just a tiny thing. When she comes over
here, she feels like . . . (*Toning it down a little.*) Well, we all
like a change of scene, don't we?

Jessie (*playing along*). Sure we do. Plus there's no birds diving
around.

Mama. I hate those birds. She says I don't understand them. What's
there to understand about birds?

Jessie. Why Agnes likes them, for one thing. Why they stay with
her when they could be outside with the other birds. What
their singing means. How they fly. What they think Agnes
is.

Mama. Why do you have to know so much about things, Jessie?
There's just not that much *to* things that I could ever see.

Jessie. That you could ever *tell*, you mean. You didn't have to lie
to me about Agnes.

Mama. I didn't lie. You never asked before!

Jessie. You lied about setting fire to all those houses and about
how many birds she has and how much okra she eats and
why she won't come over here. If I have to keep dragging
the truth out of you, this is going to take all night.

Mama. That's fine with me. I'm not a bit sleepy.

Jessie. Mama . . .

Mama. All right. Ask me whatever you want. Here.

*They come to an awkward stop, as the cocoa is ready and Mama
pours it into the cups Jessie has set on the table.*

Jessie (*as Mama takes her first sip*). Did you love Daddy?

Mama. No.

Jessie (*pleased that Mama understands the rules better now*). I didn't
think so. Were you really fifteen when you married him?

Mama. The way he told it? I'm sitting in the mud, he comes along,
drags me in the kitchen, "She's been there ever since"?

Jessie. Yes.

Mama. No. It was a big fat lie, the whole thing. He just thought
it was funnier that way. God, this milk in here.

Jessie. The cocoa helps.

Mama (*pleased that they agree on this, at least*). Not enough, though,
does it? You can still taste it, can't you?

Jessie. Yeah, it's pretty bad. I thought it was my memory that was bad, but it's not. It's the milk, all right.

Mama. It's a real waste of chocolate. You don't have to finish it.

Jessie (putting her cup down). Thanks, though.

Mama. I should've known not to make it. I knew you wouldn't like it. You never did like it.

Jessie. You didn't ever love him, or he did something and you stopped loving him, or what?

Mama. He felt sorry for me. He wanted a plain country woman and that's what he married, and then he held it against me the rest of my life like I was supposed to change and surprise him somehow. Like I remember this one day he was standing on the porch and I told him to get a shirt on and he went in and got one and then he said, real peaceful, but to the point, "You're right, Thelma. If God had meant for people to go around without any clothes on, they'd have been born that way."

Jessie (sees Mama's hurt). He didn't mean anything by that, Mama.

Mama. He never said a word he didn't have to, Jessie. That was probably all he'd said to me all day, Jessie. So if he said it, there was something to it, but I never did figure that one out. What did that mean?

Jessie. I don't know. I liked him better than you did, but I didn't know him any better.

Mama. How could I love him, Jessie. I didn't have a thing he wanted. *(Jessie doesn't answer.)* He got his share, though. You loved him enough for both of us. You followed him around like some . . . Jessie, all the man ever did was farm and sit . . . and try to think of somebody to sell the farm to.

Jessie. Or make me a boyfriend out of pipe cleaners and sit back and smile like the stick man was about to dance and wasn't I going to get a kick out of that. Or sit up with a sick cow all night and leave me a chain of sleepy stick elephants on my bed in the morning.

Mama. Or just sit.

Jessie. I liked him sitting. Big old faded blue man in the chair. Quiet.

Mama. Agnes gets more talk out of her birds than I got from the two of you. He could've had that GONE FISHING sign around his neck in that chair. I saw him stare off at the water. I saw him look at the weather rolling in. I got where I could practically see that boat myself. But you, you knew what he was thinking about and you're going to tell me.

Jessie. I don't know, Mama! His life, I guess. His corn. His boots. Us. Things. You know.

Mama. No, I don't know, Jessie! You had those quiet little conversations after supper every night. What were you whispering about?

Jessie. We weren't whispering, you were just across the room.

Mama. What did you talk about?

Jessie. We talked about why black socks are warmer than blue socks. Is that something to go tell Mother? You were just jealous because I'd rather talk to him than wash the dishes with you.

Mama. I was jealous because you'd rather talk to him than anything! (*Jessie reaches across the table for the small clock and starts to wind it.*) If I had died instead of him, he wouldn't have taken you in like I did.

Jessie. I wouldn't have expected him to.

Mama. Then what would you have done?

Jessie. Come visit.

Mama. Oh, I see. He died and left you stuck with me and you're mad about it.

Jessie (*getting up from the table*). Not anymore. He didn't mean to. I didn't have to come here. We've been through this.

Mama. He felt sorry for you, too, Jessie, don't kid yourself about that. He said you were a runt and he said it from the day you were born and he said you didn't have a chance.

Jessie (*getting the canister of sugar and starting to refill the sugar bowl*). I know he loved me.

Mama. What if he did? It didn't change anything.

Jessie. It didn't have to. I miss him.

Mama. He never really went fishing, you know. Never once. His tackle box was full of chewing tobacco and all he ever did was drive out to the lake and sit in his car. Dawson told me. And Bennie at the bait shop, he told Dawson. They all laughed about it. And he'd come back from fishing and all he'd have to show for it was a . . . a whole pipe cleaner *family* — chickens, pigs, a dog with a bad leg — it was creepy strange. It made me sick to look at them and I hid his pipe cleaners a couple of times but he always had more somewhere.

Jessie. I thought it might be better for you after he died. You'd get interested in things. Breathe better. Change somehow.

Mama. Into what? The Queen? A clerk in a shoe store? Why should I? Because he said to? Because you said to? (*Jessie shakes her head.*) Well I wasn't here for his entertainment and I'm not here for yours either, Jessie. I don't know what I'm here for, but then I don't think about it. (*Realizing what all this means.*) But I bet you wouldn't be killing yourself if he were still alive. That's a fine thing to figure out, isn't it?

Jessie (*filling the honey jar now*). That's not true.

Mama. Oh no? Then what were you asking about him for? Why did you want to know if I loved him?

Jessie. I didn't think you did, that's all.

Mama. Fine then. You were right. Do you feel better now?

Jessie (*cleaning the honey jar carefully*). It feels good to be right about it.

Mama. It didn't matter whether I loved him. It didn't matter to me and it didn't matter to him. And it didn't mean we didn't get along. It wasn't important. We didn't talk about it. (*Sweeping the pots off the cabinet.*) Take all these pots out to the porch!

Jessie. What for?

Mama. Just leave me this one pan. (*She jerks the silverware drawer open.*) Get me one knife, one fork, one big spoon, and the can opener, and put them out where I can get them. (*Starts throwing knives and forks in one of the pans.*)

Jessie. Don't do that! I just straightened that drawer!

Mama (*throwing the pan in the sink*). And throw out all the plates and cups. I'll use paper. Loretta can have what she wants and Dawson can sell the rest.

Jessie (*calmly*). What are you doing?

Mama. I'm not going to cook. I never liked it, anyway. I like candy. Wrapped in plastic or coming in sacks. And tuna. I'll eat tuna, thank you.

Jessie (*taking the pan out of the sink*). What if you want to make apple butter? You can't make apple butter in that little pan. What if you leave carrots on cooking and burn up that pan?

Mama. I don't like carrots.

Jessie. What if the strawberries are good this year and you want to go picking with Agnes.

Mama. I'll tell her to bring a pan. You said you would do whatever I wanted! I don't want a bunch of pans cluttering up my cabinets I can't get down to, anyway. Throw them out. Every last one.

Jessie (*gathering up the pots*). I'm putting them all back in. I'm not taking them to the porch. If you want them, they'll be here. You'll bend down and get them, like you got the one for the cocoa. And if somebody else comes over here to cook, they'll have something to cook in, and that's the end of it!

Mama. Who's going to come cook here?

Jessie. Agnes.

Mama. In my pots. Not on your life.

Jessie. There's no reason why the two of you couldn't just live here together. Be cheaper for both of you and somebody to talk to. And if the birds bothered you, well, one day when Agnes is out getting her hair done, you could take them all for a walk!

Mama (as Jessie straightens the silverware). So that's why you're pestering me about Agnes. You think you can rest easy if you get me a new babysitter? Well, I don't want to live with Agnes. I barely want to talk with Agnes. She's just around. We go back, that's all. I'm not letting Agnes near this place. You don't get off as easy as that, child.

Jessie. O.K., then. It's just something to think about.

Mama. I don't like things to think about. I like things to go on.

Jessie (closing the silverware drawer). I want to know what Daddy said to you the night he died. You came storming out of his room and said I could wait it out with him if I wanted to, but you were going to watch *Gunsmoke.* What did he say to you?

Mama. He didn't have *anything* to say to me, Jessie. That's why I left. He didn't say a thing. It was his last chance not to talk to me and he took full advantage of it.

Jessie (after a moment). I'm sorry you didn't love him. Sorry for you, I mean. He seemed like a nice man.

Mama (as Jessie walks to the refrigerator). Ready for your apple now?

Jessie. Soon as I'm through here, Mama.

Mama. You won't like the apple, either. It'll be just like the cocoa. You never liked eating at all, did you? Any of it! What have you been living on all these years, toothpaste?

Jessie (as she starts to clean out the refrigerator). Now, you know the milkman comes on Wednesdays and Saturdays, and he leaves the order blank in an egg box, and you give the bills to Dawson once a month.

Mama. Do they still make that orangeade?

Jessie. It's not orangeade, it's just orange.

Mama. I'm going to get some. I thought they stopped making it. You just stopped ordering it.

Jessie. You should drink milk.

Mama. Not anymore, I'm not. That hot chocolate was the last. Hooray.

Jessie (getting the garbage can from under the sink). I told them to keep delivering a quart a week no matter what you said. I told them you'd run out of Cokes and you'd have to drink it. I told them I knew you wouldn't pour it on the ground . . .

Mama (finishing her sentence). And you told them you weren't going
to be ordering anymore?

Jessie. I told them I was taking a little holiday and to look after
you.

Mama. And they didn't think something was funny about that?
You who doesn't go to the front steps? You, who only sees
the driveway looking down from a stretcher passed out cold?

Jessie (enjoying this, but not laughing). They said it was about time,
but why didn't I take you with me? And I said I didn't think
you'd want to go, and they said, "Yeah, everybody's got
their own idea of vacation."

Mama. I guess you think that's funny.

Jessie (pulling jars out of the refrigerator). You know there never was
any reason to call the ambulance for me. All they ever did
for me in the emergency room was let me wake up. I could've
done that here. Now, I'll just call them out and you say yes
or no. I know you like pickles. Ketchup?

Mama. Keep it.

Jessie. We've had this since last Fourth of July.

Mama. Keep the ketchup. Keep it all.

Jessie. Are you going to drink ketchup from the bottle or what?
How can you want your food and not want your pots to
cook it in? This stuff will all spoil in here, Mother.

Mama. Nothing I ever did was good enough for you and I want
to know why.

Jessie. That's not true.

Mama. And I want to know why you've lived here this long feeling
the way you do.

Jessie. You have no earthly idea how I feel.

Mama. Well, how could I? You're real far back there, Jessie.

Jessie. Back where?

Mama. What's it like over there, where you are? Do people always
say the right thing or get whatever they want, or what?

Jessie. What are you talking about?

Mama. Why do you read the newspaper? Why don't you wear
that sweater I made for you? Do you remember how I used
to look, or am I just any old woman now? When you have
a fit, do you see stars or what? How did you fall off the
horse, really? Why did Cecil leave you? Where did you put
my old glasses?

Jessie (stunned by Mama's intensity). They're in the bottom drawer
of your dresser in an old Milk of Magnesia box. Cecil left
me because he made me choose between him and smoking.

Mama. Jessie, I know he wasn't that dumb.

Jessie. I never understood why he hated it so much when it's so good. Smoking is the only thing I know that's always just what you think it's going to be. Just like it was the last time, right there when you want it and real quiet.

Mama. Your fits made him sick and you know it.

Jessie. Say seizures, not fits. Seizures.

Mama. It's the same thing. A seizure in the hospital is a fit at home.

Jessie. They didn't bother him at all. Except he did feel responsible for it. It *was* his idea to go horseback riding that day. It was his idea I could do *anything* if I just made up my mind to. I fell off the horse because I didn't know how to hold on. Cecil left for pretty much the same reason.

Mama. He had a girl, Jessie. I walked right in on them in the toolshed.

Jessie (after a moment). O.K. That's fair. (*Lighting another cigarette.*) Was she very pretty?

Mama. She was Agnes's girl, Carlene. Judge for yourself.

Jessie (as she walks to the living room). I guess you and Agnes had a good talk about that, huh?

Mama. I never thought he was good enough for you. They moved here from Tennessee, you know.

Jessie. What are you talking about? You liked him better than I did. You flirted him out here to build your porch or I'd never even met him at all. You thought maybe he'd help you out around the place, come in and get some coffee and talk to you. God knows what you thought. All that curly hair.

Mama. He's the best carpenter I ever saw. That little house of yours will still be standing at the end of the world, Jessie.

Jessie. You didn't need a porch, Mama.

Mama. All right! I wanted you to have a husband.

Jessie. And I couldn't get one on my own, of course.

Mama. How were you going to get a husband never opening your mouth to a living soul?

Jessie. So I was quiet about it, so what?

Mama. So I should have let you just sit here? Sit like your daddy? Sit here?

Jessie. Maybe.

Mama. Well, I didn't think so.

Jessie. Well, what did you know?

Mama. I never said I knew much. How was I supposed to learn anything living out here? I didn't know enough to do half the things I did in my life. Things happen. You do what

you can about them and you see what happens next. I married
you off to the wrong man, I admit that. So I took you in
when he left, I'm sorry.

Jessie. He wasn't the wrong man.

Mama. He didn't love you, Jessie, or he wouldn't have left.

Jessie. He wasn't the wrong man, Mama. I loved Cecil so much.
And I tried to get more exercise and I tried to stay awake.
I tried to learn to ride a horse. And I tried to stay outside
with him, but he always knew I was trying, so it didn't
work.

Mama. He was a selfish man. He told me once he hated to see
people move into his houses after he built them. He knew
they'd mess them up.

Jessie. I loved that bridge he built over the creek in back of the
house. It didn't have to be anything special, a couple of
boards would have been just fine, but he used that yellow
pine and rubbed it so smooth . . .

Mama. He had responsibilities here. He had a wife and son here
and he failed you.

Jessie. Or that baby bed he built for Ricky. I told him he didn't
have to spend so much time on it, but he said it had to last,
and the thing ended up weighing two hundred pounds and
I couldn't move it. I said, "How long does a baby bed have
to last, anyway?" But maybe he thought if it was strong
enough, it might keep Ricky a baby.

Mama. Ricky is too much like Cecil.

Jessie. He is not. Ricky is as much like me as it's possible for any
human to be. We even wear the same size pants. These are
his, I think.

Mama. That's just the same size. That's not you're the same person.

Jessie. I see it on his face. I hear it when he talks. We look out at
the world and we see the same thing: Not Fair. And the
only difference between us is Ricky's out there trying to get
even. And he knows not to trust anybody and he got it
straight from me. And he knows not to try to get work,
and guess where he got that. He walks around like there's
loose boards in the floor, and you know who laid that floor,
I did.

Mama. Ricky isn't through yet. You don't know how he'll turn
out!

Jessie (*going back to the kitchen*). Yes I do and so did Cecil. Ricky
is the two of us together for all time in too small a space.
And we're tearing each other apart, like always, inside that
boy, and if you don't see it, then you're just blind.

Mama. Give him time, Jess.

Jessie. Oh, he'll have plenty of that. Five years for forgery, ten years for armed assault . . .

Mama (*furious*). Stop that! (*Then pleading.*) Jessie, Cecil might be ready to try it again, honey, that happens sometimes. Go downtown. Find him. Talk to him. He didn't know what he had in you. Maybe he sees things different now, but you're not going to know that till you see him. Or call him up! Right now! He might be home.

Jessie. And say what? Nothing's changed, Cecil, I'd just like to look at you, if you don't mind? No. He loved me, Mama. He just didn't know how things fall down around me like they do. I think he did the right thing. He gave himself another chance, that's all. But I did beg him to take me with him. I did tell him I would leave Ricky and you and everything I loved out here if only he would take me with him, but he couldn't and I understood that. (*Pause.*) I wrote that note I showed you. I wrote it. Not Cecil. I said "I'm sorry, Jessie, I can't fix it all for you." I said I'd always love me, not Cecil. But that's how he felt.

Mama. Then he should've taken you with him.!

Jessie (*picking up the garbage bag she has filled*). Mama, you don't pack your garbage when you move.

Mama. You will not call yourself garbage, Jessie.

Jessie (*taking the bag to the big garbage can near the back door*). Just a way of saying it, Mama. Thinking about my list, that's all. (*Opening the can, putting the garbage in, then securing the lid.*) Well, a little more than that. I was trying to say it's all right that Cecil left. It was . . . a relief in a way. I never was what he wanted to see, so it was better when he wasn't looking at me all the time.

Mama. I'll make your apple now.

Jessie. No thanks. You get the manicure stuff and I'll be right there.

> *Jessie ties up the big garbage bag in the can and replaces the small garbage bag under the sink, all the time trying desperately to regain her calm. Mama watches, from a distance, her hand reaching unconsciously for the phone. Then she has a better idea. Or rather she thinks of the only other thing left and is willing to try it. Maybe she is even convinced it will work.*

Mama. Jessie, I think your daddy had little . . .

Jessie. (*interrupting her*). Garbage night is Tuesday. Put it out as late as you can. The Davis's dogs get in it if you don't.

(*Replacing the garbage bag in the can under the sink.*) And keep ordering the heavy black bags. It doesn't pay to buy the cheap ones. And I've got all the ties here with the hammers and all. Take them out of the box as soon as you open a new one and put them in this drawer. They'll get lost if you don't, and rubber bands or something else won't work.

Mama. I think your daddy had fits, too. I think he sat in his chair and had little fits. I read this a long time ago in a magazine, how little fits go, just little blackouts where maybe their eyes don't even close and people just call them "thinking spells."

Jessie (*getting the slipcover out of the laundry basket*). I don't think you want this manicure we've been looking forward to. I washed this cover for the sofa, but it'll take both of us to get it back on.

Mama. I watched his eyes. I know that's what it was. The magazine said some people don't even know they've had one.

Jessie. Daddy would've known if he'd had fits, Mama.

Mama. The lady in this story had kept track of hers and she'd had eighty thousand of them in the last eleven years.

Jessie. Next time you wash this cover, it'll dry better if you put it on wet.

Mama. Jessie, listen to what I'm telling you. This lady had anywhere between five and five hundred fits a day and they lasted maybe fifteen seconds apiece, so that out of her life, she'd only lost about two weeks altogether, and she had a full-time secretary job and an IQ of 120.

Jessie (*amused by Mama's approach*). You want to talk about the fits, is that it?

Mama. Yes. I do. I want to say . . .

Jessie (*interrupting*). Most of the time I wouldn't even know I'd had one, except I wake up with different clothes on, feeling like I've been run over. Sometimes I feel my head start to turn around or hear myself scream. And sometimes there *is* this dizzy stupid feeling a little before it, but if the TV's on, well, it's easy to miss.

As Jessie and Mama replace the slipcover on the sofa and the afghan on the chair, the physical struggle somehow mirrors the emotional one in the conversation.

Mama. I can tell when you're about to have one. Your eyes get this big! But, Jessie, you haven't . . .

Jessie (*taking charge of this*). What do they look like? The seizures.

Mama (reluctant). Different each time, Jess.

Jessie. O.K. Pick one, then. A good one. I think I want to know now.

Mama. There's not much to tell. You just . . . crumple, in a heap, like a puppet and somebody cut the strings all at once, or like the firing squad in some Mexican movie, you just slide down the wall, you know. You don't know what happens? How can you not know what happens?

Jessie. I'm busy.

Mama. That's not funny.

Jessie. I'm not laughing. My head turns around and I fall down and then what?

Mama. Well, your chest squeezes in and out, and you sound like you're gagging, sucking air in and out like you can't breathe.

Jessie. Do it for me. Make the sound for me.

Mama. I will not. It's awful-sounding.

Jessie. Yeah. It felt like it might be. What's next?

Mama. Your mouth bites down and I have to get your tongue out of the way fast, so you don't bite yourself.

Jessie. Or you. I bite you, too, don't I?

Mama. You got me once real good. I had to get a tetanus! But I know what to watch for now. And then you turn blue and the jerks start up. Like I'm standing there poking you with a cattle prod or you're sticking your finger in a light socket as fast as you can . . .

Jessie. Foaming like a mad dog the whole time.

Mama. It's bubbling, Jess, not foam like the washer overflowed, for God's sake; it's bubbling like a baby spitting up. I go get a wet washcloth, that's all. And then the jerks slow down and you wet yourself and it's over. Two minutes tops.

Jessie. How do I get to bed?

Mama. How do you think?

Jessie. I'm too heavy for you now. How do you do it?

Mama. I call Dawson. But I get you cleaned up before he gets here and I make him leave before you wake up.

Jessie. You could just leave me on the floor.

Mama. I want you to wake up someplace nice, O.K.? (*Then making a real effort.*) But, Jessie, and this is the reason I even brought this up! You haven't had a seizure for a solid year. A whole year, do you realize that?

Jessie. Yeah, the phenobarb's about right now, I guess.

Mama. You bet it is. You might never have another one, ever! You might be through with it for all time!

Jessie. Could be.

Mama. You are. I know you are!

Jessie. I sure am feeling good. I really am. The double vision's gone and my gums aren't swelling. No rashes or anything. I'm feeling as good as I ever felt in my life. I'm even feeling like worrying or getting mad and I'm not afraid it will start a fit if I do, I just go ahead.

Mama. Of course you do! You can even scream at me, if you want to. I can take it. You don't have to act like you're just visiting here, Jessie. This is your house, too.

Jessie. The best part is, my memory's back.

Mama. Your memory's always been good. When couldn't you remember things? You're always reminding me what . . .

Jessie. Because I've made lists for everything. But now I remember what things mean on my lists. I see "dish towels," and I used to wonder whether I was supposed to wash them, buy them, or look for them because I wouldn't remember where I put them after I washed them, but now I know it means wrap them up, they're a present for Loretta's birthday.

Mama (*finished with the sofa now*). You used to go looking for your lists, too, I've noticed that. You always know where they are now! (*Then suddenly worried.*) Loretta's birthday isn't coming up, is it?

Jessie. I made a list of all the birthdays for you. I even put yours on it. (*A small smile.*) So you can call Loretta and remind her.

Mama. Let's take Loretta to Howard Johnson's and have those fried clams. I *know* you love that clam roll.

Jessie (*slight pause*). I won't be here, Mama.

Mama. What have we just been talking about? You'll be here. You're well, Jessie. You're starting all over. You said it yourself. You're remembering things and . . .

Jessie. I won't be here. If I'd ever had a year like this, to think straight and all, before now, I'd be gone already.

Mama (*not pleading, commanding*). No, Jessie.

Jessie (*folding the rest of the laundry*). Yes, Mama. Once I started remembering, I could see what it all added up to.

Mama. The fits are over!

Jessie. It's not the fits, Mama.

Mama. Then it's me for giving them to you, but I didn't do it!

Jessie. It's not the fits! You said it yourself, the medicine takes care of the fits.

Mama (*interrupting*). Your daddy gave you those fits, Jessie. He passed it down to you like your green eyes, and your straight hair. It's not my fault!

Jessie. So what if he had little fits? It's not inherited. I fell off the horse. It was an accident.

Mama. The horse wasn't the first time, Jessie. You had a fit when you were five years old.

Jessie. I did not.

Mama. You did! You were eating a popsicle and down you went. He gave it to you. It *his* fault, not mine.

Jessie. Well, you took your time telling me.

Mama. How do you tell that to a five-year-old?

Jessie. What did the doctor say?

Mama. He said kids have them all the time. He said there wasn't anything to do but wait for another one.

Jessie. But I didn't have another one.

Now there is a real silence.

Jessie. You mean to tell me I had fits all the time as a kid and you just told me I fell down or something and it wasn't till I had the fit when Cecil was looking that anybody bothered to find out what was the matter with me?

Mama. It wasn't *all the time,* Jessie. And they changed when you started to school. More like your daddy's. Oh, that was some swell time, sitting here with the two of you turning off and on like light bulbs some nights.

Jessie. How many fits did I have?

Mama. You never hurt yourself. I never let you out of my sight. I caught you every time.

Jessie. But you didn't tell anybody.

Mama. It was none of their business.

Jessie. You were ashamed.

Mama. I didn't want anybody to know. Least of all you.

Jessie. Least of all me. Oh, right. That was mine to know, Mama, not yours. Did Daddy know?

Mama. He thought you were . . . you fell down a lot. That's what he thought. You were careless. Or maybe he thought I beat you. I don't know what he thought. He didn't think about it.

Jessie. Because you didn't tell him!

Mama. If I told him about you, I'd have to tell him about him!

Jessie. I don't like this. I don't like this one bit.

Mama. I didn't think you'd like it. That's why I didn't tell you.

Jessie. If I'd known I was an epileptic, Mama, I wouldn't have ridden any horses.

Mama. Make you feel like a freak, is that what I should have done?

Jessie. Just get the manicure tray and sit down!

Mama (throwing it to the floor). I don't want a manicure!

Jessie. Doesn't look like you do, no.

Mama. Maybe I did drop you, you don't know.

Jessie. If you say you didn't, you didn't.

Mama (beginning to break down). Maybe I fed you the wrong thing.
Maybe you had a fever sometime and I didn't know it soon
enough. Maybe it's a punishment.

Jessie. For what?

Mama. I don't know. Because of how I felt about your father.
Because I didn't want any more children. Because I smoked
too much or didn't eat right when I was carrying you. It
has to be something I did.

Jessie. It does not. It's just a sickness, not a curse. Epilepsy doesn't
mean anything. It just is.

Mama. I'm not talking about the fits here, Jessie! I'm talking about
this killing yourself. It has to be me that's the matter here.
You wouldn't be doing this if it wasn't. I didn't tell you
things or I married you off to the wrong man or I took you
in and let your life get away from you or all of it put together.
I don't know what I did, but I did it, I know. This is all
my fault, Jessie, but I don't know what to do about it now!

Jessie (exasperated at having to say this again). It doesn't have anything
to do with you!

Mama. Everything you do has to do with me, Jessie. You can't
do *anything,* wash your face or cut your finger, without doing
it to me. That's right! You might as well kill me as you,
Jessie, it's the same thing. This has to do with me, Jessie.

Jessie. Then what if it does! What if it has everything to do with
you! What if you are all I have and you're not enough? What
if I could take all the rest of it if only I didn't have you here?
What if the only way I can get away from you for good is
to kill myself? What if it is? I can *still* do it!

Mama (in desperate tears). Don't leave me, Jessie! *(Jessie stands for
a moment, then turns for the bedroom.)* No! *(She grabs Jessie's
arm.)*

Jessie (carefully taking her arm away). I have a box of things I want
people to have. I'm just going to go get it for you. You
. . . just rest a minute.

> *Jessie is gone. Mama heads for the telephone, but she can't even
> pick up the receiver this time and, instead, stoops to clean up the
> bottles that have spilled out of the manicure tray.*

> *Jessie returns, carrying a box that groceries were delivered in. It
> probably says Hershey Kisses or Starkist Tuna. Mama is still*

down on the floor cleaning up, hoping that maybe if she just makes it look nice enough, Jessie will stay.

Mama. Jessie, how can I live here without you? I need you! You're supposed to tell me to stand up straight and say how nice I look in my pink dress, and drink my milk. You're supposed to go around and lock up so I know we're safe for the night, and when I wake up, you're supposed to be out there making the coffee and watching me get older every day, and you're supposed to help me die when the time comes. I can't do that by myself, Jessie. I'm not like you, Jessie. I hate the quiet and I don't want to die and I don't want you to go, Jessie. How can I . . . (*Has to stop a moment.*) How can I get up every day knowing you had to kill yourself to make it stop hurting and I was here all the time and I never even saw it. And then you gave me this chance to make it better, convince you to stay alive, and I couldn't do it. How can I live with myself after this, Jessie?

Jessie. I only told you so I could explain it, so you wouldn't blame yourself, so you wouldn't feel bad. There wasn't anything you could say to change my mind. I didn't want you to save me. I just wanted you to know.

Mama. Stay with me just a little longer. Just a few more years. I don't have that many more to go, Jessie. And as soon as I'm dead, you can do whatever you want. Maybe with me gone, you'll have all the quiet you want, right here in the house. And maybe one day you'll put in some begonias up the walk and get just the right rain for them all summer. And Ricky will be married by then and he'll bring your grandbabies over and you can sneak them a piece of candy when their daddy's not looking and then be real glad when they've gone home and left you to your quiet again.

Jessie. Don't you see, Mama, everything I do winds up like this. How could I think you would understand? How could I think you would want a manicure? We could hold hands for an hour and then I could go shoot myself? I'm sorry about tonight, Mama, but it's exactly why I'm doing it.

Mama. If you've got the guts to kill yourself, Jessie, you've got the guts to stay alive.

Jessie. I know that. So it's really just a matter of where I'd rather be.

Mama. Look, maybe I can't think of what you should do, but that doesn't mean there isn't something that would help. *You* find it. *You* think of it. You can keep trying. You can get brave and try some more. You don't have to give up!

Jessie. I'm *not* giving up! This *is* the other thing I'm trying. And I'm sure there are some other things that might work, but *might* work isn't good enough anymore. I need something that *will* work. *This* will work. That's why I picked it.

Mama. But something might happen. Something that could change everything. Who knows what it might be, but it might be worth waiting for! (*Jessie doesn't respond.*) Try it for two more weeks. We could have more talks like tonight.

Jessie. No, Mama.

Mama. I'll pay more attention to you. Tell the truth when you ask me. Let you have your say.

Jessie. No, Mama! We wouldn't have more talks like tonight, because it's this next part that's made this last part so good, Mama. No, Mama. *This* is how I have my say. This is how I say what I thought about it *all* and I say no. To Dawson and Loretta and the Red Chinese and epilepsy and Ricky and Cecil and you. And me. And hope. I say no! (*Then going to Mama on the sofa.*) Just let me go easy, Mama.

Mama. How can I let you go?

Jessie. You can because you have to. It's what you've always done.

Mama. You are my child!

Jessie. I am what became of your child. (*Mama cannot answer.*) I found an old baby picture of me. And it was somebody else, not me. It was somebody pink and fat who never heard of sick or lonely, somebody who cried and got fed, and reached up and got held and kicked but didn't hurt anybody, and slept whenever she wanted to, just by closing her eyes. Somebody who mainly just laid there and laughed at the colors waving around over her head and chewed on a polkadot whale and woke up knowing some new trick nearly every day, and rolled over and drooled on the sheet and felt your hand pulling my quilt back up over me. That's who I started out and this is who is left. (*There is no self-pity here.*) That's what this is about. It's somebody I lost, all right, it's my own self. Who I never was. Or who I tried to be and never got there. Somebody I waited for who never came. And never will. So, see, it doesn't much matter what else happens in the world or in this house, even. I'm what was worth waiting for and I didn't make it. Me . . . who might have made a difference to me . . . I'm not going to show up, so there's no reason to stay, except to keep you company . . . not reason enough because I'm not . . . very good company. (*Pause.*) Am I?

Mama (*knowing she must tell the truth*). No. And neither am I.

Jessie. I had this strange little thought, well, maybe it's not so strange. Anyway, after Christmas, after I decided to do this, I would wonder, sometimes, what might keep me here, what might be worth staying for, and you know what it was? It was maybe if there was something I really liked, like maybe if I really liked rice pudding or cornflakes for breakfast or something, that might be enough.

Mama. Rice pudding is good.

Jessie. Not to me.

Mama. And you're not afraid?

Jessie. Afraid of what?

Mama. I'm afraid of it, for me, I mean. When my time comes. I know it's coming, but . . .

Jessie. You don't know when. Like in a scary movie.

Mama. Yeah, sneaking up on me like some killer on the loose, hiding out in the back yard just waiting for me to have my hands full someday and how am I supposed to protect myself anyhow when I don't know what he looks like and I don't know how he sounds coming up behind me like that or if it will hurt or take very long or what I don't get done before it happens.

Jessie. You've got plenty of time left.

Mama. I forget what for, right now.

Jessie. For whatever happens, I don't know. For the rest of your life. For Agnes burning down one more house or Dawson losing his hair or . . .

Mama (quickly). Jessie. I can't just sit here and say O.K., kill yourself if you want to.

Jessie. Sure you can. You just did. Say it again.

Mama (really startled). Jessie! (*Quiet horror.*) How dare you! (*Furious.*) How dare you! You think you can just leave whenever you want, like you're watching television here? No, you can't, Jessie. You make me feel like a fool for being alive, child, and you are so wrong! I like it here, and I will stay here until they make me go, until they drag me screaming and I mean screeching into my grave, and you're real smart to get away before then because, I mean, honey, you've never heard noise like that in your life. (*Jessie turns away.*) Who am I talking to? You're gone already, aren't you? I'm looking right through you! I can't stop you because you're already gone! I guess you think they'll all have to talk about you now! I guess you think this will really confuse them. Oh yes, ever since Christmas you've been laughing to yourself and thinking, "Boy, are they all in for a surprise." Well, nobody's going to be a bit surprised, sweetheart. This is just like you. Do it the hard way, that's my girl, all right. (*Jessie gets up and goes into the kitchen, but Mama follows her.*) You know who they're going to feel sorry for? Me! How about that! Not you, me! They're going to be *ashamed* of you. Yes. *Ashamed!* If somebody asks Dawson about it, he'll change the subject as fast as he can. He'll talk about how much he has to pay to park his car these days.

Jessie. Leave me alone.

Mama. It's the truth!

Jessie. I should've just left you a note!

Mama (screaming). Yes! (*Then suddenly understanding what she has said, nearly paralyzed by the thought of it, she turns slowly to face Jessie, nearly whispering.*) No. No. I . . . might not have thought of all the things you've said.

Jessie. It's O.K., Mama.

Mama is nearly unconscious from the emotional devastation of these last few moments. She sits down at the kitchen table, hurt and angry and desperately afraid. But she looks almost numb. She is so far beyond what is known as pain that she is virtually unreachable and Jessie knows this, and talks quietly, watching for signs of recovery.

Jessie (washes her hands in the sink). I remember you liked that preacher who did Daddy's, so if you want to ask him to do the service, that's O.K. with me.

Mama (not an answer, just a word). What.

Jessie (putting on hand lotion as she talks). And pick some songs you like or let Agnes pick, she'll know exactly which ones. Oh, and I had your dress cleaned that you wore to Daddy's. You looked real good in that.

Mama. I don't remember, hon.

Jessie. And it won't be so bad once your friends start coming to the funeral home. You'll probably see people you haven't seen for years, but I thought about what you should say to get you over that nervous part when they first come in.

Mama (simply repeating). Come in.

Jessie. Take them up to see their flowers, they'd like that. And when they say, "I'm so sorry, Thelma," you just say, "I appreciate your coming, Connie." And then ask how their garden was this summer or what they're doing for Thanksgiving or how their children . . .

Mama. I don't think I should ask about their children. I'll talk

about what they have on, that's always good. And I'll have
some crochet work with me.

Jessie. And Agnes will be there, so you might not have to talk at
all.

Mama. Maybe if Connie Richards does come, I can get her to tell
me where she gets that Irish yarn, she calls it. I know it
doesn't come from Ireland. I think it just comes with a green
wrapper.

Jessie. And be sure to invite enough people home afterward so
you get enough food to feed them all and have some left
for you. But don't let anybody take anything home, especially
Loretta.

Mama. Loretta will get all the food set up, honey. It's only fair
to let her have some macaroni or something.

Jessie. No, Mama. You have to be more selfish from now on.
(*Sitting at the table with Mama.*) Now, somebody's bound to
ask you why I did it and you just say you don't know. That
you loved me and you know I loved you and we just sat
around tonight like every other night of our lives, and then
I came over and kissed you and said, " 'Night, Mother,"
and you heard me close my bedroom door and the next
thing you heard was the shot. And whatever reasons I had,
well, you guess I just took them with me.

Mama (*quietly*). It was something personal.

Jessie. Good. That's good, Mama.

Mama. That's what I'll say, then.

Jessie. Personal. Yeah.

Mama. Is that what I tell Dawson and Loretta, too? We sat around,
you kissed me, " 'Night, Mother"? They'll want to know
more, Jessie. They won't believe it.

Jessie. Well, then, tell them what we did. I filled up the candy
jars. I cleaned out the refrigerator. We made some hot chocolate
and put the cover back on the sofa. You had no idea. All
right? I really think it's better that way. If they know we
talked about it, they really won't understand how you let
me go.

Mama. I guess not.

Jessie. It's private. Tonight is private, yours and mine, and I don't
want anybody else to have any of it.

Mama. O.K., then.

Jessie (*standing behind Mama now, holding her shoulders*). Now, when
you hear the shot, I don't want you to come in. First of all,
you won't be able to get in by yourself, but I don't want
you trying. Call Dawson, then call the police, and then call

Agnes. And then you'll need something to do till somebody gets here, so wash the hot-chocolate pan. You wash that pan till you hear the doorbell ring and I don't care if it's an hour, you keep washing that pan.

Mama. I'll make my calls and then I'll just sit. I won't need something to do. What will the police say?

Jessie. They'll do that gunpowder test, I guess, and ask you what happened, and by that time, the ambulance will be here and they'll come in and get me and you know how that goes. You stay out here with Dawson and Loretta. You keep Dawson out here. I want the police in the room first, not Dawson, O.K.?

Mama. What if Dawson and Loretta want me to go home with them?

Jessie (*returning to the living room*). That's up to you.

Mama. I think I'll stay here. All they've got is Sanka.

Jessie. Maybe Agnes could come stay with you for a few days.

Mama (*standing up, looking into the living room*). I'd rather be by myself, I think. (*Walking toward the box Jessie brought in earlier.*) You want me to give people those things?

Jessie (*they sit down on the sofa, Jessie holding the box on her lap*). I want Loretta to have my little calculator. Dawson bought it for himself, you know, but then he saw one he liked better and he couldn't bring both of them home with Loretta counting every penny the way she does, so he gave the first one to me. Be funny for her to have it now, don't you think? And all my house slippers are in a sack for her in my closet. Tell her I know they'll fit and I've never worn any of them, and make sure Dawson hears you tell her that. I'm glad he loves Loretta so much, but I wish he knew not everybody has her size feet.

Mama (*taking the calculator*). O.K.

Jessie (*reaching into the box again*). This letter is for Dawson, but it's mostly about you, so read it if you want. There's a list of presents for you for at least twenty more Christmases and birthdays, so if you want anything special you better add it to this list before you give it to him. Or if you want to be surprised, just don't read that page. This Christmas, you're getting mostly stuff for the house, like a new rug in your bathroom and needlework, but next Christmas, you're really going to cost him next Christmas. I think you'll like it a lot and you'd never think of it.

Mama. And you think he'll go for it?

Jessie. I think he'll feel like a real jerk if he doesn't. Me telling

him to, like this and all. Now, this number's where you call
Cecil. I called it last week and he answered, so I know he
still lives there.

Mama. What do you want me to tell him?

Jessie. Tell him we talked about him and I only had good things
to say about him, but mainly tell him to find Ricky and tell
him what I did, and tell Ricky you have something for him,
out here, from me, and to come get it. (*Pulls a sack out of
the box.*)

Mama (*the sack feels empty*). What is it?

Jessie (*taking it off*). My watch. (*Putting it in the sack and taking a
ribbon out of the sack to tie around the top of it.*)

Mama. He'll sell it!

Jessie. That's the idea. I appreciate him not stealing it already. I'd
like to buy him a good meal.

Mama. He'll buy dope with it!

Jessie. Well, then, I hope he gets some good dope with it, Mama.
And the rest of this is for you. (*Handing Mama the box now.
Mama picks up the things and looks at them.*)

Mama (*surprised and pleased*). When did you do all this? During my
naps, I guess.

Jessie. I guess. I tried to be quiet about it. (*As Mama is puzzled by
the presents.*) Those are just little presents. For whenever you
need one. They're not bought presents, just things I thought
you might like to look at, pictures or things you think you've
lost. Things you didn't know you had, even. You'll see.

Mama. I'm not sure I want them. They'll make me think of you.

Jessie. No they won't. They're just things, like a free tube of
toothpaste I found hanging on the door one day.

Mama. Oh. All right, then.

Jessie. Well, maybe there's one nice present in there somewhere.
It's Granny's ring she gave me and I thought you might like
to have it, but I didn't think you'd wear it if I gave it to
you right now.

Mama (*taking the box to a table nearby*). No. Probably not. (*turning
back to face her.*) I'm ready for my manicure, I guess. Want
me to wash my hands again?

Jessie (*standing up*). It's time for me to go, Mama.

Mama (*starting for her*). No, Jessie, you've got all night!

Jessie (*as Mama grabs her*). No, Mama.

Mama. It's not even ten o'clock.

Jessie (*very calm*). Let me go, Mama.

Mama. I can't. You can't go. You can't do this. You didn't say
it would be so soon, Jessie. I'm scared. I love you.

Jessie (takes her hands away). Let go of me, Mama. I've said everything
   I had to say.
Mama (standing still a minute). You said you wanted to do my nails.
Jessie (taking a small step backward). I can't. It's too late.
Mama. It's not too late!
Jessie. I don't want you to wake Dawson and Loretta when you
   call. I want them to still be up and dressed so they can get
   right over.
Mama (As Jessie backs up, Mama moves in on her, but carefully). They
   wake up fast, Jessie, if they have to. They don't matter here,
   Jessie. You do. I do. We're not through yet. We've got a
   lot of things to take care of here. I don't know where my
   prescriptions are and you didn't tell me what to tell Dr.
   Davis when he calls or how much you want me to tell Ricky
   or who I call to rake the leaves or . . .
Jessie. Don't try and stop me, Mama, you can't do it.
Mama (grabbing her again, this time hard). I can too! I'll stand in
   front of this hall and you can't get past me. (*They struggle.*)
   You'll have to knock me down to get away from me, Jessie.
   I'm not about to let you . . .

*Mama struggles with Jessie at the door and in the struggle Jessie
gets away from her and ——*

Jessie (almost a whisper). 'Night, Mother. (*She vanishes into her bedroom
   and we hear the door lock just as Mama gets to it.*)
Mama (screams). Jessie! (*Pounding on the door.*) Jessie, you let me in
   there. Don't you do this, Jessie. I'm not going to stop
   screaming until you open this door, Jessie. Jessie! Jessie! What
   if I don't do any of the things you told me to do! I'll tell
   Cecil what a miserable man he was to make you feel the
   way he did and I'll give Ricky's watch to Dawson if I feel
   like it and the only way you can make sure I do what you
   want is you come out here and make me, Jessie! (*Pounding
   again.*) Jessie! Stop this! I didn't know! I was here with you
   all the time. How could I know you were so alone?

*And Mama stops for a moment, breathless and frantic, putting her
ear to the door, and when she doesn't hear anything, she stands
up straight again and screams once more.*

Jessie! Please!

*And we hear the shot, and it sounds like an answer, it sounds like
No.*

Mama collapses against the door, tears streaming down her face, but not screaming anymore. In shock now.

Jessie, Jessie, child . . . Forgive me. (*Pause.*) I thought you were mine.

And she leaves the door and makes her way through the living room, around the furniture, as though she didn't know where it was, not knowing what to do. Finally, she goes to the stove in the kitchen and picks up the hot-chocolate pan and carries it with her to the telephone, and holds on to it while she dials the number. She looks down at the pan, holding it tight like her life depended on it. She hears Loretta answer.

Mama. Loretta, let me talk to Dawson, honey.

QUESTIONS

1. Early in the play, on page 1119, Jessie says she wants the gun for "Protection." In the context of the entire play, what does this mean?
2. On page 1121 Jessie says she would rather use her father's gun than her husband's. Why?
3. The playwright specifies that "The time is the present, with the action beginning about 8:15. Clocks on stage in the kitchen and on a table in the living room should run throughout the performance and be visible to the audience." Why?
4. Jessie insists (page 1141) that Ricky is like her, and not like his father Cecil. Exactly what is she getting at?
5. On page 1123 Mama says, "People don't really kill themselves, Jessie. No, mam, doesn't make sense, unless you're retarded or deranged." Specify the various reasons that Mama assumes are the motives for Jessie's suicide. Most theories of suicide can be classified into one of two groups, psychoanalytical and sociological. Psychoanalytical theories (usually rooted in Freud) assume that human beings have dual impulses, *eros* (life instinct) and *thanatos* (death instinct). When the death instinct, expressed as hostility and aggression, is turned against others it takes the form of homicide but when it is turned against the self it takes the form of suicide. Most sociological theories assume that suicide occurs among three types of people: egoistic suicides, people who are excessively individualistic (i.e., who are not integrated into society); altruistic suicides, people who have an excessive sense of duty to society and who die willingly to serve society; and, third, anomic suicides, people who find their usual lifestyles disrupted

by sudden social changes such as the loss of a job during an economic depression. Do any of these theories seem helpful in explaining Jessie's suicide? Exactly why *does* Jessie kill herself? (You may want to do some research on suicide, for instance by consulting Freud's *Civilization and Its Discontents,* or Andrew F. Henry and James F. Short, *Homicide and Suicide,* or Edwin S. Scheidman, ed., *Essays in Self-Destruction,* or A. Alvarez, *The Savage God.*)

6. The greatest tragedies somehow suggest that the tragic figures are not only particular individuals — Oedipus, Lear, and so forth — but also are universal figures who somehow embody our own hopes and fears. Another way of putting it is to say that the greatest plays are not case histories but are visions of a central aspect of life. To what extent does *'night, Mother* meet this criterion?

21

Some Observations on Film

A film is rather like a play: a story is presented by means of actors. The film, of course, regularly uses some techniques not possible in the playhouse, such as close-ups and rapid changes of scene, but even these techniques can usually be approximated in the playhouse, for example by means of lighting. It may seem, then, that one can experience a film as though it were a photographic record of a play. And indeed, some films are nothing more than film records of plays.

There are, however, important differences between film and drama. First, though drama uses such visual matters as gestures, tableaux effects, and scenery, the plays that we value most highly are *literature:* the word dominates, visual matters are subordinate. Film, however, is more a matter of pictures than of words. The camera usually roves, giving us crowded streets, empty skies, rainy nights, or close-ups of filled ashtrays and chipped coffee cups. A critic has aptly said that in Ingmar Bergman's *Smiles of a Summer Night* "the almost unbearably ornate crystal goblets, by their aspect and their positioning in the image, convey the oppressive luxuriousness of the diners' lives in purely and uniquely filmic terms." In the words of the Swiss director Eric Rohmer, "the cinema is the description of man and his surroundings." Some of the greatest sequences in cinema have no dialogue but concentrate on purely visual matters.

In short, the speaker in a film does not usually dominate. In a play the speaker normally holds the spectator's attention, but in a film when a character speaks, the camera often gives us a **reaction shot,** focusing not on the speaker but on the face or gestures of a character who is affected by the speech, thus giving the spectator a visual interpretation of the words. In Truffaut's *The 400 Blows,* for example, we hear a reform school official verbally assault a boy, but we see the uncomfortable boy, not the official. Even when the camera does focus on the speaker it is likely to offer an interpretation. An extreme example is a scene from *Brief Encounter:* a gossip is talking, and the camera gives us a close-up of her jabbering mouth, which monstrously fills the screen.

This distance between film and drama can be put in another way: a film is more like a novel than a play, the action being presented not directly by actors but by a camera that, like a novelist's point of view, comments on the story while telling it. A novelist may, like a dramatist, convey information about a character through dialogue and gesture, but he may also simply tell us about the character's state of mind. Similarly, a filmmaker may use the camera to inform us about unspoken thought. In Murnau's *The Last Laugh,* when the hotel doorman reads a note firing him, the camera blurs; when he gets drunk, the camera spins so that the room seems to revolve. Somewhat similarly, Antonioni's *Red Desert* occasionally uses out-of-focus shots to convey Giuliana's view of the world; when she is more at ease, for example with her husband, the shots are in proper focus.

Even the choice of the kind of emulsion-coated celluloid is part of the comment. A highly sensitive or "fast" film requires less light to catch an image than a "slow" film does, but it is usually grainier. Perhaps because newsreels commonly use fast film, a grainy quality is often associated with realism. Moreover, because fast film shows less subtle gradations from black to white than slow film does, its harsh contrasts make it especially suitable for the harsh, unromantic *The Battle of Algiers.* Different film stocks may be used within a single motion picture. In *Wild Strawberries,* for instance, Bergman uses high-contrast stock for the nightmare sequence, though elsewhere in the film the contrasts are subtle. The medium, as everyone knows, is part of the message; Laurence Olivier made Shakespeare's *Henry V* in color but *Hamlet* in black-and-white because these media say different things. Peter Brook's film of *King Lear* is also in black-and-white, with an emphasis on an icy whiteness that catches the play's spirit of old age and desolation; a *Lear* in color probably would have an opulence that would work against the lovelessness and desolation of much of the play. John Houseman said that he produced *Julius Caesar* in black-and-white because he wanted "intensity" rather than "grandeur," and because black-and-white evoked newsreels of Hitler and thus helped to establish the connection between Shakespeare's play and relatively recent politics.] ichard Brooks's *In Cold Blood* was done in black-and-white to lo >k like a documentary.

The kind of lens used also helps to determine what the viewer sees. In *The Graduate*, Benjamin runs toward the camera (he is trying to reach a church before his girl marries another man) but he seems to make no progress because a telephoto lens was used and thus his size does not increase as it normally would. The lens, that is, helps to communicate his desperate sense of frustration. Conversely, a wide angle lens makes a character approach the camera with menacing rapidity; he quickly looms into the foreground. But of course filmmakers, though they resemble a novelist in offering pervasive indirect comment, are not novelists any more than they are playwrights or directors of a play; their medium has its own techniques, and they work with them, not with the novel's or the drama's. The wife who came out of the movie theater saying to her husband, "What a disappointment; it was exactly like the book," knew what a film ought to be.

TECHNIQUES OF FILMMAKING

Here is a brief grammar and dictionary of film, naming and explaining the cinematic devices that help filmmakers embody their vision in a work of art.

A **shot** (very rarely a fraction of a second, and usually not more than fifteen or so seconds) is what is recorded between the time a camera starts and the time it stops, i.e., between the director's call for "action" and his call to "cut." Perhaps the average shot is about ten seconds; the average film is about an hour and a half, with about 600 shots, but Hitchcock's *The Birds* uses 1360 shots. Three common shots are: (1) a **long shot** or **establishing shot,** showing the main object at a considerable distance from the camera and thus presenting it in relation to its general surroundings (for example, captured soldiers, seen across a prison yard, entering the yard); (2) a **medium shot,** showing the object in relation to its immediate surroundings (a couple of soldiers, from the knees up, with the yard's wall behind them); (3) a **close-up,** showing only the main object, or, more often, only a part of it (a soldier's face, or his bleeding feet).

In the outside world we can narrow our vision to the detail that interests us by moving our head and by focusing our eyes, ignoring what is not of immediate interest. The close-up is the movie director's chief way of directing our vision and of emphasizing a detail. (Another way is to focus sharply on the significant image, leaving the rest of the image in soft focus.) The close-up, a way of getting emphasis, has been heavily used in recent years, not always successfully. As Dwight Macdonald said of *Midnight Cowboy* and *Getting Straight,* "a movie told in close-up is like a comic book, or like a novel composed in punchy one-sentence paragraphs and set throughout in large caps. How refreshing is a long or middle shot, a glimpse of the real world, so lovely and *so far away,* in the midst of those interminable processions of [a] hairy ogre face."

While taking a shot, the camera can move: it can swing to the right or left while its base remains fixed (a **pan shot**), up or down while fixed on its axis (a **tilt shot**), forward or backward (a **traveling shot**), or in and out and up and down fastened to a crane (a **crane shot**). The fairly recent invention of the **zoom lens** enables the camera to change its focus fluidly, so it can approach a detail — as a traveling shot does — while remaining fixed in place. Much will depend on the angle (high or low) from which the shots are made. If the camera is high (a **high-angle shot**), looking down on a group of people it will dwarf them, perhaps even reduce them to crawling insects, making them pitiful or contemptible; if the camera is low (a **low-angle shot**), close to the ground and looking up toward the people, thereby showing them against the sky, it probably will give them added dignity. But these are not invariable principles. A shot in *Citizen Kane,* for example, shows Kane from above but it does not dwarf him; rather, it shows him dominating his wife and then in effect obliterating her by casting a shadow over her. Similarly, a low-angle shot does not always add dignity: films in which children play important parts often have lots of low angle shots showing adults as menacing giants, and in *Dr. Strangelove* Stanley Kubrick regularly photographed Colonel Jack D. Ripper from low angles, thus emphasizing the colonel's power. In *Citizen Kane,* Kane is often photographed from floor level, similarly emphasizing his power, but some low-angle shots late in the film, showing him in his cavernous mansion, help to convey his loneliness. In short, by its distance from the subject, its height from the ground, and its angle of elevation, the camera comments on or interprets what happens. It seems to record reality, but it offers its own version. It is only a slight exaggeration to say that the camera always lies, that is, gives a personal vision of reality.

A group of related scenes — such as the three scenes of soldiers mentioned earlier — is a **sequence,** though a sequence is more likely to have thirty scenes than three. A sequence corresponds roughly to a chapter in a novel, the shots being sentences, and the scenes being paragraphs. Within a sequence there may be an **intercut,** a switch to another action that, for example, provides an ironic comment on the main action of the sequence. If intercuts are so abundant in a sequence that, in effect, two or more sequences are going at once (e.g., shots of the villain about to ravish the heroine alternating with shots of the hero riding to her rescue), we have a **crosscut.** In the example just given, probably the tempo would increase, the shots being progressively shorter as we get to the rescue. Though often a sequence will early have an establishing shot, it need not. Sometimes an establishing shot is especially effective if delayed, as in Dreyer's *Day of Wrath,* where scenes of a witch tied to the top rungs of a ladder lead to a long shot of the context: the witch has been tied to the top of a tall ladder near a great heap of burning faggots. Still at a distance, the next shot shows the soldiers tilting the ladder up into the air and onto the pyre.

Within a sequence the transitions normally are made by **straight cuts** — a strip of film is spliced to another, resulting in an instantaneous transfer from one scene to the next. Usually an audience is scarcely if at all conscious of transitions from, say, a long shot of a character to a medium shot of him, or from a close-up of a speaker to a close-up of his auditor. But sometimes the director wants the audience to be fully aware of the change, as an author may emphasize a change by beginning a new paragraph or, even more sharply, by beginning a new chapter. Two older and now rather unfashionable relatively conspicuous transitions are sometimes still used, usually between sequences rather than within a sequence. These are the **dissolve** (the scene dissolves while a new scene appears to emerge from beneath it, there being a moment when we get a blur of both scenes), and the **fade** (in the **fade-out** the screen grows darker until black, in the **fade-in** the screen grows lighter until the new scene is fully visible). In effect the camera is saying "Let us now leave X and turn to Y," or "Two weeks later." In *2001* a prehistoric ape-like creature discovers that he can use a bone as a tool, and he destroys a skeleton with it. Then he throws the bone triumphantly into the air, where it dissolves into a spaceship of the year 2001. The point is that the spaceship is the latest of man's weapons and progress is linked with destructiveness. Two other methods, even less in favor today than the dissolve and the fade but used in many excellent old films and in some modern films that seek an archaic effect, are the **wipe** (a sort of windshield wiper crosses the screen, wiping off the first scene and revealing the next), and the **iris** (in an **iris-in,** the new scene first appears in the center of the previous scene and then this circle expands until it fills the screen; an **iris-out** shows the new scene first appearing along the perimeter and then the circle closes in on the previous scene). Chaplin more than once ended a scene with an iris-out of the tramp walking jauntily toward the horizon. In Kurosawa's *High and Low* a wipe is used with no archaic effect: an industrialist, trying to decide whether to pay an enormous ransom to free a child, has been told to toss the money from a train; the scene showing him arriving at his decision in his luxurious home is wiped off by a train that rushes across the screen. He has decided to pay.

A film, no less than a poem or a play or a picture or a palace, is something made, and it is not made by simply exposing some footage. Shots — often taken at widely separated times and places — must be appropriately joined. For example, we see a man look off to the right, then we get a shot of what he is looking at, and then a shot of his reaction. Until the shots are assembled, we don't have a film, we merely have footage. V. I. Pudovkin put it this way: "The film is not *shot,* but built, built up from the separate strips of celluloid that are its raw material." This building-up is the process of **editing.** In *Film Technique* Pudovkin gives some examples of editing. (1) In the simplest kind of editing, the film tells a story from the best viewpoints, i.e., sometimes from long shots, sometimes from medium shots, sometimes from close-ups. (2) Simultaneous actions, occurring in different places, can be narrated by cutting back and forth from one to the other. (3) Relationships can be conveyed by contrast (shots of starvation cut in with shots of gluttony), by symbolism (in Pudovkin's *Mother,* shots of an ice floe melting are cut into shots of a procession of workers, thereby suggesting that the workers' movement is a natural force coming to new life), and by *leitmotif* (i.e., repetition of the same shot to emphasize a recurring theme). More than a story can be told, of course; something of the appropriate emotion can be communicated by juxtaposing against, say, a medium-long shot of a group of impassively advancing soldiers a close-up of a single terrified victim. Similarly, emotion can be communicated by the duration of the shots (quick shots suggest haste, prolonged shots suggest slowness) and by the lighting (progressively darker shots can suggest melancholy, progressively lighter shots can suggest hope or joy). The Russian theorists of film called this process of building by quick cuts **montage.** The theory held that shots, when placed together, add up to more than the sum of the parts. Montage, for them, was what made a film a work of art and not a mere replica of reality. American writers commonly use the term merely to denote quick cutting, and French writers use it merely in the sense of cutting.

WHAT MAKES A GOOD FILM?

Mastery of technique, though necessary to good filmmaking, will not in itself make a good film. A good film is not a bag of cinematic devices, but the embodiment, through cinematic devices, of a vision. What is this vision? Well, it is a filmmaker's perception of some aspect of existence that he thinks is worthy of our interest. Normally this perception involves characters and a plot. Though recent American films, relying heavily on color, rock music in stereophonic sound, quick cutting, and the wide screen, have tended to emphasize the emotional experience and have tended to deemphasize narrative, still most of the best cinema is concerned with what people do — that is, with character and plot. Character is what people are and plot is what happens, but the line between character and plot fades, for what people are is in large measure what they do, and what is done is in large measure the result of what people are.

Character and plot, then, finally are inseparable; in a good film, everything hangs together. Harold Lloyd said that he had idea men who suggested numerous bits of comic business, and then he chose "the ones that [he] thought would be most appropriate to the particular film [they] were doing." The operative words are "most appropriate." A very funny bit of business might not be appropriate — might somehow not seem to fit — in a particular film because it was not in harmony with the underlying vision or idea, the "clothes rack" (Lloyd's term) on which the funny bits (the clothes) were hung. In *The Freshman,* Lloyd said, the underlying idea or theme was the student's enormous desire for popularity, and everything in the film had to further this theme. Or, to take the comments of a more recent filmmaker, we can listen to Truffaut on the themes of *The 400 Blows* and *Jules and Jim,* and on the disastrous lack of a theme in *Shoot the Piano Player:*

> In *400 Blows,* I was guided by the desire to portray a child as honestly as possible, and to invest his actions with a moral significance. Similarly, with *Jules and Jim,* my desire to keep the film from seeming either pornographic, indelicate, or conventional guided me. The trouble with *Shoot the Piano Player* was that I was able to do anything — that the subject

itself didn't impose its own form. . . . As it stands, there are some nice bits in the film, but it can't be said: this is the best work on this particular theme. There isn't any theme.

(It does not follow, of course, that the artist is fully aware of his theme from the start. Antonioni mentions that "it often happens that I experience fragmentary feelings before the experiences themselves take hold." But if they do not finally take hold, the film will probably arouse the sort of response that Truffaut mentions in his comments on *Shoot the Piano Player*.)

And so we come back to the idea of a vision, or, in a less exalted word, a **theme.** Some critics have argued that the concept of theme is meaningless: a film is only a detailed presentation of certain imaginary people in imaginary situations, not a statement about an aspect of life. But such a view is reductive. If we read in a newspaper about a marriage or a business failure or a baseball game, we take it only as a particular happening of some interest, and we do not assume that it implies much if anything at all beyond itself. It tells of something that has happened, but it does not tell what ought to happen or what usually happens; that is, it does not imply anything about the ways of people in general. When, however, we read a novel, or see on the stage or screen a happening, we inevitably feel — if only because we are asked to give the event an hour or more of our attention — that it is offered to us as noteworthy, an example not of what *happened* (it didn't happen, it's fictional) but an example of what *happens*. The characters in the fictional work are (like the characters in newspaper items) individuals, not mere abstractions, but (unlike those in newspaper items) they are significant individuals, in some measure revealing to us a whole class of people or a way of life.

Sometimes we sense that a film has an arguable thesis. Stanley Kubrick, for example, has said that *A Clockwork Orange* "warns against the new psychedelic fascism — the eye-popping, multimedia, quadrasonic, drug-oriented conditioning of human beings by other human beings — which many believe will usher in the forfeiture of human citizenship and the beginning of zombiedom." A filmmaker, however, need not argue a thesis that is subject to verification (e.g., the older generation seeks to repress the younger generation); it is enough if he sees in the human experience something worth our contemplation (e.g., the conflict between generations) and embodies it on film. A theme can usually be named by an abstract noun or phrase (the quest for happiness, the difficulty of achieving self-knowledge, the fragility of love) and though we recognize that any such formula is not the whole of life, it is nonetheless important. Adequately embodied in a film (or in any other kind of art) this exploration of experience alters our experience of life, including our experience of ourselves. Let Truffaut have the last word:

> I also believe that every film must contain some degree of "planned violence" upon its audience. In a good film, people must be made to see something that they don't want to see: they must be made to approve of someone of whom they had disapproved, they must be forced to look where they had refused to look.

Appendix: Writing Essays about Literature

WHY WRITE?

People write about literature to clarify and account for their responses to works that interest or excite or frustrate them. In putting words on paper you will have to take a second and third look at what is in front of you and what is within you. And so writing is a way of learning. The last word about complex thoughts and feelings is never said, but when we write we hope to make at least a little progress in the difficult but rewarding job of talking about our responses. We learn, and then we hope to interest our readers because we are communicating to them our responses to something that for one reason or another is worth talking about.

    This communication is, in effect, teaching. You may think that you are writing for the teacher, but that is a misconception; when you write, *you* are the teacher. An essay on literature is an attempt to help someone see the work as you see it. If this chapter had to be boiled down to a single sentence, that sentence would be: Because you are teaching, your essay should embody those qualities that you value in teachers — probably intelligence, open-mindedness, and effort; and certainly a desire to offer what help one can.

TWO COMMON APPROACHES

Explication

A line-by-line commentary on what is going on in a text — usually a short poem — is an **explication** (literally, unfolding or spreading out). It takes some skill to work one's way along without saying, "In line one . . . , in the second line . . . , in the third line . . ." One must sometimes boldly say something like "The next stanza begins with . . . and then introduces . . . ." And, of course, one can discuss the second line before the first if that seems the best way of handling the passage.

An explication is not concerned with the writer's life or times, and it is not a paraphrase (a rewording) — though it may include paraphrase. It is a study — almost word by word — that reveals the meaning of a work. Because the language of a literary work is denser (richer in associations or connotations) than the language of such prose as this paragraph, explication is much concerned with bringing to the surface the meanings in the words that may not be immediately apparent. Explication, in short, seeks to make explicit what is *implicit* (literally, folded or entangled) in the text. It may seem to "read into" the work, but if it is done well it really "reads out" what is within the work. To this end it calls attention, as it proceeds, to such things as:

1. The implications of words
2. The function of rhymes
3. The shifts in point of view
4. The development of contrasts
5. The significance of variations in the meter
6. Any other contributions to the meaning

Thus, as the explication below indicates, in Robert Frost's poem the words "acquainted with the night" require comment, because, after all, it is a bit odd to say that one is acquainted with the night. One is acquainted with a person, or a fact, but not with the night. And, as the poem goes on, one realizes that "night" is not just a time of day, but is something like "lonely grief."

Below we print a student's first-rate explication of a poem by Robert Frost. If, when you read the explication, you are tempted to throw up your hands and say that you could never write a piece as keen as this one, remember several things. The writer of this explication had already achieved some skill by reading poems and by writing several explications earlier in the term; this explication is a finished piece of work, the outcome of several drafts; each draft was the outcome of sustained thinking; and the writer arrived at many of her insights or perceptions by *asking herself questions,* such as "Why does Frost repeat this or that expression?" (for example "I have been," "I have walked," "I have outwalked"). Later in this chapter we will discuss the importance of asking yourself questions as a way of stimulating ideas.

A Sample Explication

Robert Frost (1874–1963)

Acquainted with the Night

I have been one acquainted with the night.
I have walked out in rain — and back in rain.
I have outwalked the furthest city light.   *3*

I have looked down the saddest city lane.
I have passed by the watchman on his beat
And dropped my eyes, unwilling to explain.   *6*

I have stood still and stopped the sound of feet
When far away an interrupted cry
Came over houses from another street,   *9*

But not to call me back or say good-bye;
And further still at an unearthly height
One luminary clock against the sky   *12*

Proclaimed the time was neither wrong nor right.
I have been one acquainted with the night.

The words in Robert Frost's "Acquainted with the
Night," except "luminary" in line 12, are all common
ones, but some have unusual implications. Take the title: "Acquainted with the Night." We are usually acquainted with a person or with a fact, not with the
night. And to be "acquainted" with someone or something
usually implies familiarity (as in "I am acquainted with

John Jones") but not thorough knowledge. "I have been
one acquainted with the night," then, is an unusual and
cautious statement.

The first stanza is matter-of-fact. It consists of
three sentences, each beginning "I have," and each sentence fills exactly one line. It almost sounds flat, but
it is not flat because, as I have said, "acquainted with
the night" is an unusual expression. Also, the repetition of words and grammatical structure makes for special emphasis, producing the effect of a solemn utterance. Finally, the sounds themselves give pleasure, for
even a sad message can offer pleasure to the mind's ear.
Take the first line: the long sound in "I," the long
middle syllable in "acquainted," and the long i in
"night" ("I" and "night" are thus brought together), as
well as the w sound in "one" and in "acquainted" offer a
pleasingly mournful music: "I have been one acquainted
with the night."

Furthermore, when "I have walked out" turns into "I
have outwalked the furthest city light," we realize that
we are being told about a special journey, not just a
literal walk. Even if this walk beyond "the furthest
city light" was a literal walk, Frost also means for us
to take it as a walk beyond manmade illumination, civilization. It must have been meant as an experience with
something dark in the way that grief or loneliness are
dark.

The second stanza resembles the previous stanza but
it is more expansive. It continues the use of "I have,"
but now only in the first two of its three lines, and

only the first line is a complete sentence. It introduces people other than the speaker, first in "the saddest city lane" (line 4), and next in the watchman (line
5). The lane cannot literally be sad; "saddest" implies
that sad people live in the lane, or that the speaker
feels sad when he thinks of the people who live in the
lane. The watchman perhaps is one of these, and the
speaker avoids his glance, explaining only that he is
"unwilling to explain" (line 6). The speaker, then, not
only is walking alone but also feels isolated and therefore shuns contact.

The third stanza begins with "I have," as five of the
previous six lines have begun, but it is even less
closely patterned on the first stanza than the second
was; that is, the poem becomes looser. In fact, the
thought overflows the stanza; the first stanza of three
lines was three sentences, and their tone was assertive,
almost confident: "I have been one acquainted.... I have
walked out ... and back" (there is a survivor's note of
understated triumph in that "and back"), and I have
"outwalked" (again a note of triumph). But the self-assertion then begins to dissolve. The second stanza was
two sentences, and now the third stanza cannot contain
even one complete sentence — the sentence flows into
the next two stanzas, running almost to the end of the
poem. To put it slightly differently, in the octave (final eight lines) of this sonnet, all but the last line
is a single sentence.

In the second stanza the speaker ignores human society, suggested by the watchman; in the third and fourth

stanzas human society ignores the speaker, for the "cry"
(line 8) is "not to call me back or say good-bye" (line
10). In addition to this suggestion of mankind's indifference to the speaker, there is a suggestion that the
speaker almost doesn't exist -- even in his own perceptions: "I have stood still and stopped the sound of
feet" (line 7). A paraphrase of the last six words might
be, "and stopped producing the noise of footsteps."
Thus, by standing still the speaker became inaudible not
only to the city-dwellers but also to himself.

The "interrupted cry" of line 8 is sorrowful, for it
is a "cry," not a "call" or "shout" or "laugh." And the
cry is mysterious because we do not know its cause, its
message, or why it is "interrupted." The fourth stanza
continues to deepen the sense of mystery by referring to
a clock "at an unearthly height." Maybe this is a real
clock, perhaps with an illuminated face, high on a
church or town hall, but it seems more likely that this
"luminary" clock is something beyond "the furthest city
light"; probably it is a metaphor describing the full
moon, which is literally "unearthly." Its unearthliness
is emphasized by the unusual use of the unusual word
"luminary," for "luminary" is usually a noun meaning "a
source of illumination," but here it is used as an adjective. In any case, a real clock can be right or
wrong, and it can tell us that the time is right or
wrong for eating, sleeping, attending class, or whatever. But this "luminary clock," at an "unearthly
height," offers no heavenly guidance and it cannot be
either corrected or obeyed. The speaker can only look at

the clock (a real clock or the moon) and increasingly sense that he has nothing to communicate with.

The last line of the poem, a complete sentence in itself, repeats the first line exactly, and it restores
the tone of assurance. Now we have a sharper idea of
what the speaker means when he says he has been "one acquainted with the night," but we still cannot say that
the "night" equals or symbolizes this or that. "Loneliness," for example, is too simple a translation, because
loneliness implies isolation from people, and in the
poem we sense that the speaker's isolation may be not
only from other people but also from himself (from a
sense of any individual purpose) and also from a meaningless universe. Moreover, we must also say –– and the
poem is as much about this as it is about "the night" ––
that the speaker is not crushed by the experience. The
poem is not a lament, and not a descent into self-pity.
The speaker does not sadly say "I am one acquainted with
the night"; rather, the experience is put at a distance
by being set in the past: "I have been one acquainted
with the night." And though the memory of the experience
is still sharp, the speaker keeps his response under
control. The closest he comes to telling us explicitly
of his feelings is in the first and last lines. For the
most part he shows us the situation rather than tells us
his feelings, and thus he conveys a sense of control ––
a sense, we might say, of being able to deal with the
experience, to survive it (since the last line repeats
the first line we can say he literally comes out where
he went in), and even to get it down on paper.

Analysis

If one has world enough and time, one can set out to explicate all of *Moby-Dick* or *Hamlet*. More likely, one will explicate a page in *Moby-Dick* or a speech in *Hamlet;* in writing about works longer than a page or two, a more common approach than explicating is analyzing (literally, separating into parts in order to understand). An analysis commonly considers one part and the relation of this part to the whole. For example, it may consider only the functions of the setting in *The Adventures of Huckleberry Finn* or the comedy in *Hamlet* or the allusions in T. S. Eliot's "The Love Song of J. Alfred Prufrock."

Analysis, of course, is not a process used only in talking about literature. It is commonly applied in thinking about almost any complex matter. Martina Navratilova plays a deadly game of tennis: What makes it so good? How does her backhand contribute? What does her serve do to the opponent? In short, given the whole, how do the parts fit together?

If a work is fairly long, and you are writing only a few pages and you are not explicating a short passage from the work, almost surely you will write an analysis of some part. Unless you have an enormous amount of time for reflection and revision you cannot write a meaningful essay of five hundred words or even a thousand words on "Shakespeare's *Hamlet*" or "Melville's *Moby-Dick*." You cannot even write on "Character in *Hamlet*" or "Symbolism in *Moby-Dick*. And probably you won't really want to write on such topics anyway. Probably *one* character or *one* symbol has caught your interest. Trust your feelings; you are likely onto something interesting, and it will be best to think about this smaller topic for the relatively few hours that you have. A "smaller" topic need not be a dull or trivial topic; treated properly, it may illuminate the entire work or, to change the metaphor, it may serve as a mine shaft that gives entry to the work. "Hamlet's Relationship to Horatio," carefully thought about, will in five hundred or a thousand words tell a reader more (and will have taught its author more) than will "*Hamlet* as a Tragedy."

How do you find a topic and how do you turn it into a **thesis** (an argument or proposition)? An idea may hit you suddenly; as you are reading you find yourself jotting in the margin, "contrast with Joyce's treatment of disillusionment," "too heavy irony," or "ugh." Or an idea may come slowly upon rereading. Perhaps you gradually become aware of the frequency of the word "really" in *The Catcher in the Rye,* and you notice that Holden Caulfield, who is regularly given to saying things such as "if you really want to know" and "I really mean it," at one point explicitly comments on the nature of reality. You work on this and begin to relate it to his abundant discussions of phoneys, and you emerge, perhaps, with the thesis, or argument, that in Holden's mouth "really" is not merely the filler it seems to be but is a clue to his quest for the real in a world of appearances and phoneys. If you have thought about the topic, converted it into a thesis, and stripped it of irrelevancies, you should be able to formulate it in a few words. (This formula, or something like it, can be your title. There is nothing wrong with a title as direct as "Holden Caulfield's use of the Word 'Really' "; although it is scarcely exciting, it is informative. Beware of cute titles, especially those that do not give the reader a good idea of what will follow, such as "Really!" or "A Boy's Word." "The Real Holden and Reality" is about as far as one should go.)

Let's dwell a moment longer on the distinction between a topic and a thesis. It may be useful to think of it this way: a topic is a subject (for example, Hamlet's relation to Horatio); to arrive at a thesis you have to add a predicate (for example, "Hamlet's relation to Horatio helps to define Hamlet"). Of course, some theses are more promising than others. Consider these three statements:

1. "Hamlet's relationship to Horatio is interesting."
2. "Hamlet's relations with Horatio are friendly."
3. "Hamlet's relation to Horatio helps to reveal Hamlet's special, heroic qualities."

Now, "Hamlet's relationship to Horatio is interesting" is a thesis, but it is vague and provides little direction, little help in generating ideas and in shaping an essay. "Hamlet's relations with Horatio are friendly" is better, but not much. It provides a focus, but it is not likely to help the writer to see anything beyond the obvious. Only the third version is likely to help a writer to develop an essay: "Hamlet's relation to Horatio helps to reveal Hamlet's special, heroic qualities."

Every literary work affords its own topics for analysis, and every essayist must set forth his or her own thesis, but a few useful generalizations may be made. You can often find a thesis by asking one of two questions:

1. *What purpose does this serve?* That is, why is this scene in the novel or play? Why is there a clown in *Hamlet*? Why are these lines unrhymed? Why is this stanza form employed? What is the significance of the parts of the work? (Titles are often highly

significant parts of the work: Ibsen's *A Doll's House,* Kesey's *One Flew Over the Cuckoo's Nest,* and Roth's *The Great American Novel* would be slightly different if they had other titles.)

2. *Why do I have this response?* Why do I find this poem clever or moving or puzzling? How did the author make this character funny or dignified or pathetic? How did he communciate the idea that this character is a bore without boring me?

The first of these questions, "What purpose does this serve?" requires that you identify yourself with the author, wondering, for example, whether this opening scene is the best possible for this story. The second question, "Why do I have this response?" requires that you trust your feelings. If you are amused or bored or puzzled or annoyed, assume that these responses are appropriate and follow them up, at least until a rereading of the work provides other responses.

Two Examples of Analysis

Let's look first at an analysis of one aspect of a short story, irony in Kate Chopin's "The Story of an Hour." (This extremely brief work is printed on page 23.) After thinking about the topic and consulting the jottings (including underlinings and marginal notes) made while reading and rereading, a student found that her underlying thesis — that there are several ironies in the story — broke down into two parts: The chief irony is that Mrs. Mallard dies just as she is beginning to enjoy life, but there are also smaller ironies, such as that the "sad message" turns out (for a while) not to be sad, and that although Richards is "too late" when he tries to save her at the end, if he had been "late" at the beginning the whole mess would not have occurred. The topic ideas of the paragraphs of the essay turned out to be these:

1. The story has an ironic ending, but there are smaller ironies within it.
2. One of these smaller ironies is that the "sad message" turns out, at least for a while, to bring joy.
3. Two other bits of irony are: (a) Richards's well-meaning haste at the beginning is not matched by adequate haste at the end; and (b) the doctors' comments on joy are true in a way that the speakers do not mean.
4. The central irony, however, is that Mrs. Mallard begins to live only after years of marriage, and this new life, which occurs appropriately at springtime, is cut off even as she looks forward not only to summer but to "a long progression of years."

Some such thoughts must have preceded the following essay, but of course they were arrived at only after reading and rereading and writing and rewriting. By the way, don't let the excellence of the following essay discourage you from thinking that you can't do as well. Remember, this essay is the product of much work. As the writer wrote, her ideas got better and better, for in her drafts she put down a point and then realized that it needed strengthening (for instance, with a brief quotation) or that — come to think of it — the point couldn't be substantiated and ought to be deleted.

Ironies of Life in an Hour

Kate Chopin's "Story of an Hour" — which takes only a few minutes to read — turns out to have an ironic ending, but on rereading it one sees that the irony is not concentrated only in the outcome of the plot — Mrs. Mallard dies just when she is beginning to live — but is also present in many details.

After we know how the story turns out, if we reread it we find irony at the very start: Mrs. Mallard's friends and relatives all assume, mistakenly, that she was deeply in love with her husband, Brently Mallard, and so they take great care to tell her gently of his death. They mean well, and in fact they <u>do</u> well, for they bring her an hour of life, an hour of joyous free-dom, but it is ironic that they think their news is sad. True, Mrs. Mallard at first expresses grief when she hears the news, but soon (unknown to her friends) she finds joy in it. So, Richards's "sad message," though sad in Richards's eyes, is in fact a happy message.

Among the small but significant ironic details is the statement near the end of the story that when Mallard entered the house, Richards tried to conceal him from Mrs. Mallard, but "Richards was too late." This is ironic because almost at the start of the story, in the second paragraph, Richards with the best of motives "hastened" to bring his sad message; if he had at the start been "too late," Mallard would have arrived at home first, and Mrs. Mallard's life would not have ended an hour later but would have gone on simply as it had been. Yet another irony at the end of the story is the diagnosis of the doctors. They say she had died of "heart disease — of joy that kills." In one sense they are right: Mrs. Mallard has for the last hour experienced a great joy. But of course the doctors totally misunderstand the joy that kills her: it is not joy at seeing her husband alive, but her realization that the great joy she experienced during the last hour is over.

All of these ironic details add richness to the story, but the central irony resides not in the well-intentioned but ironic actions of Richards, or in the unconsciously ironic words of the doctors, but in Mrs. Mallard's own life. She has for years been alive, and yet in a way she had been dead, a body subjected to her husband's will. Now, his apparent death brings her new life. Appropriately, this new life comes to her at the season of the year when "the tops of trees were all aquiver with the new spring life." But, ironically, her new life will last only an hour. She is "Free, free, free" — but only until her husband walks through the doorway. She looks forward to "summer days" but she will not see even the end of this spring day. If her years of marriage were ironic, bringing her a sort of living death instead of joy, her new life is ironic too, not only because it grows out of her moment of grief for her

supposedly dead husband, but because its vision of "a
long progression of years" is cut short within an hour
on a spring day.

Let's look at several principles illustrated by this essay.

1. The title of the essay is not merely the title of the work discussed; rather, it gives the reader a clue, a small idea of the essayist's topic.
2. The opening or introductory paragraph does not begin by saying "In this story. . . ." Rather, by naming the author and the title, it lets the reader know exactly what story is being discussed. It also develops the writer's thesis a bit, so readers know where they will be going.
3. The smaller ironies are discussed in the second and third paragraphs, the central (chief) irony in the last paragraph. That is, the essay does not dwindle or become anticlimatic; rather, it builds up.
4. Some brief quotations are used, both to provide evidence and to let the reader hear — even if only fleetingly — Kate Chopin's writing.
5. The essayist, assuming that the reader has read the work, does not tell the plot in great detail. But, aware that the reader has not memorized the story, the essayist gives helpful reminders.
6. The essayist has opinions, but does not keep saying, "In my opinion" and "I feel that."
7. The present tense is used in narrating the action: "Mrs. Mallard dies"; "Mrs. Mallard's friends and relatives all assume."
8. Although a concluding paragraph is often useful — if it does more than merely summarize what has already been clearly said — it is not essential in a short analysis. In this essay, the last sentence explains the chief irony and therefore makes an acceptable ending.

Next, let's look at a longer analysis of a play. To this student's essay we have added marginal notes calling attention to some of the essay's strengths.

Title is focused; it announces topic and thesis.

The Solid Structure of <u>The Glass Menagerie</u>

In the "Production Notes" Tennessee

Williams calls <u>The Glass Menagerie</u> a "memory play," a term that the narrator in the play also uses. Memories often consist of fragments of episodes which are so loosely connected that they seem chaotic, and therefore we might think that <u>The Glass Menagerie</u> will consist of very loosely related episodes. However, the play covers only one episode and though it gives the illusion of random talk, it really has a firm structure and moves steadily toward a foregone conclusion.

Opening paragraph closes in on thesis.

Tennessee Williams divides the play into seven scenes. The first scene begins with a sort of prologue and the last scene concludes with a sort of epilogue that is related to the prologue. In the prologue Tom addresses the audience and comments on the 1930s as a time when America was "blind" and was a place of "shouting and confusion." Tom also mentions that our lives consist of expectations, and though he does not say that our expectations are unfulfilled, near the end of the prologue he quotes a postcard that his father wrote to the family he deserted: "Hello — Goodbye." In the epilogue Tom tells us that he followed his "father's footsteps," deserting the family. And just before the epilogue, near the end of Scene VII, we see what can be considered another desertion:

Reasonable organization; the paragraph touches on the beginning and the end.

Brief but effective quotations.

Jim explains to Tom's sister Laura that he

Useful generaliza-
tion based on earlier
details

is engaged and therefore cannot visit
Laura again. Thus the end is closely related to the beginning, and the play is
the steady development of the initial
implications.

Chronological orga-
nization is reasona-
ble. Opening topic
sentence lets readers
know where they
are going.

The first three scenes show things
going from bad to worse. Amanda is a nagging mother who finds her only relief in
talking about the past to her crippled
daughter Laura and her frustrated son Tom.
When she was young she was beautiful and
was eagerly courted by rich young men, but
now the family is poor and this harping on
the past can only bore or infuriate Tom
and embarrass or depress Laura, who have
no happy past to look back to, who see no
happy future, and who can only be upset by
Amanda's insistence that they should behave as she behaved long ago. The second

Brief plot summary
supports thesis.

scene deepens the despair: Amanda learns
that the timorous Laura has not been attending a business school but has retreated in terror from this confrontation
with the contemporary world. Laura's helplessness is made clear to the audience,
and so is Amanda's lack of understanding.
Near the end of the second scene, however,
Jim's name is introduced; he is a boy
Laura had a crush on in high school, and
so the audience gets a glimpse of a hap-

pier Laura and a sense that possibly Laura's world is wider than the stifling tenement in which she and her mother and brother live. But in the third scene things get worse, when Tom and Amanda have so violent an argument that they are no longer on speaking terms. Tom is so angry with his mother that he almost by accident destroys his sister's treasured collection of glass animals, the fragile lifeless world which is her refuge. The apartment is literally full of the ''shouting and confusion'' that Tom spoke of in his prologue.

Useful summary and transition

The first three scenes have revealed a progressive worsening of relations; the next three scenes reveal a progessive improvement in relations. In Scene IV, Tom and his mother are reconciled, and Tom reluctantly — apparently in an effort to make up with his mother — agrees to try to get a friend to come to dinner so that Laura will have "a gentleman caller." In Scene V, Tom tells his mother that Jim will come to dinner on the next night, and Amanda brightens, because she sees a possibility of security for Laura at last. In Scene VI, Jim arrives, and despite Laura's initial terror, there seems, at least in Amanda's mind, to be the possibility that things will go well.

The seventh scene, by far the longest, at first seems to be fulfilling Amanda's hopes. Despite the ominous fact that the lights go out because Tom has not paid the electric bill, Jim is at ease. He is an insensitive oaf, but that doesn't seem to bother Amanda, and almost miraculously he manages to draw Laura somewhat out of her sheltered world. Even when Jim in his clumsiness breaks the horn off Laura's treasured glass unicorn, she is not upset. In fact, she is almost relieved because the loss of the horn makes the animal less "freakish" and he "will feel more at home with the other horses." In a way, of course, the unicorn symbolizes the crip-pled Laura, who at least for the moment feels less freakish and isolated now that she is somewhat reunited with society through Jim. But this is a play about life in a blind and confused world, and though in a previous age the father escaped, there can be no escape now. Jim reveals that he is engaged, Laura relapses into "desolation," Amanda relapses into rage and bitterness, and Tom relapses into dreams of escape. In a limited sense Tom does escape. He leaves the family and joins the merchant marine, but his last speech or epilogue tells us that he cannot escape the memory of his sister: "Oh,

Laura, Laura, I tried to leave you behind
me, but I am more faithful than I intended

to be!" And so the end of the last scene
brings us back again to the beginning of
the first scene: we are still in a world
of "the blind" and of "confusion." But now
at the end the darkness is deeper, the
characters are lost forever in their unhappiness as Laura "blows the candles
out," the darkness being literal but also
symbolic of their extinguished hopes.

Numerous devices, such as repeated references to the absent father, to Amanda's
youth, to Laura's Victrola and of course
to Laura's glass menagerie help to tie the
scenes together into a unified play. But
beneath these threads of imagery, and
recurring motifs, is a fundamental

pattern which involves the movement from
nagging (Scenes I and II) to open hostili-
ties (Scene III) to temporary reconciliation (Scene IV) to false hopes (Scenes V
and VI) to an impossible heightening of
false hopes and then, in a swift descent,
to an inevitable collapse (Scene VII).
Tennessee Williams has constructed his
play carefully. G. B. Tennyson says that a
"playwright must 'build' his speeches, as
the theatrical expression has it."[1] But a
playwright must do more; he must also
build his play out of scenes. Like Ibsen,

```
                        if Williams were introduced to an archi-

                        tect he might say, "Architecture is my

                        business too."
                        _____
```

Documentation   [1]An Introduction to Drama (New York:
                    Holt, Rinehart and Winston, 1967), p. 13.

The danger in writing about structure, especially if one proceeds by beginning at the beginning and moving steadily to the end, is that one will simply tell the plot. This essay on *The Glass Menagerie* manages to say things about the organization of the plot even as it tells the plot. It has a point, hinted at in the pleasantly paradoxical title, developed in the body of the essay, and wrapped up in the last line.

COMPARISON AND CONTRAST

Something should be said about an essay organized around a **comparison** or a **contrast,** say, of the settings in two short stories, of two characters in a novel, or of the symbolism in two poems. (A comparison emphasizes resemblances and a contrast emphasizes differences, but we can use the word "comparison" to cover both kinds of writing.) Probably the student's first thought, after making some jottings, is to discuss one-half of the comparison and then go on to the second half. Instructors and textbooks (though not this one) usually condemn such an organization, arguing that the essay breaks into two parts and that the second part involves a good deal of repetition of categories set up in the first part. Usually they recommend that the student organize his thoughts differently, somewhat along these lines:

1. First similarity
   a. first work (or character, or characteristic)
   b. second work
2. Second similarity
   a. first work
   b. second work
3. First difference
   a. first work
   b. second work

    4. Second difference
       a. first work
       b. second work

and so on, for as many additional differences as seem relevant. For example, if one wishes to compare *Huckleberry Finn* with *The Catcher in the Rye*, one may organize the material thus:

    1. First similarity: the narrator and his quest
       a. Huck
       b. Holden
    2. Second similarity: the corrupt world surrounding the narrator
       a. society in *Huckleberry Finn*
       b. society in *Catcher*
    3. First difference: degree to which the narrator fulfills his quest and escapes from society
       a. Huck's plan to "light out" to the frontier
       b. Holden's breakdown

Here is another way of organizing a comparison and contrast:

    1. First point: the narrator and his quest
       a. similarities between Huck and Holden
       b. differences between Huck and Holden
    2. Second point: the corrupt world
       a. similarities between the worlds in *Huck* and *Catcher*
       b. differences between the worlds in *Huck* and *Catcher*
    3. Third point: degree of success
       a. similarities between Huck and Holden
       b. differences between Huck and Holden

But a comparison need not employ either of these structures. There is even the danger that an essay employing either of them may not come into focus until the essayist stands back from the seven-layer cake and announces, in the concluding paragraph, that the odd layers taste better. In one's preparatory thinking, one may want to make comparisons in pairs (good-natured humor: the clown in *Othello*, the clownish gravedigger in *Hamlet;* social satire: the clown in *Othello*, the gravedigger in *Hamlet;* relevance to main theme: . . . ; length of role: . . . ; comments by other characters: . . .), but one must come to some conclusions about what these add up to before writing the final version. This final version should not duplicate the thought processes; rather, it should be organized to make the point clearly and effectively. After reflection, one may believe that although there are superficial similarities between the clown in *Othello* and the clownish gravedigger in *Hamlet,* there are essential differences; then in the finished essay one probably will not wish to obscure the main point by jumping back and forth from play to play, working through a series of similarities and differences. It may be better to discuss the clown in *Othello* and then to point out that, although the gravedigger in *Hamlet* resembles him in A, B, and C, the gravedigger also has other functions (D, E, and F) and is of greater consequence to *Hamlet* than the clown is to *Othello*. Some repetition in the second half of the essay (for example, "The gravedigger's puns come even faster than the clown's. . . .") will serve to bind the two halves into a meaningful whole, making clear the degree of similarity or difference. The point of the essay presumably is not to list pairs of similarities or differences, but to illuminate a work or works by making thoughtful comparisons. Although in a long essay one cannot postpone until page 30 a discussion of the second half of the comparison, in an essay of, say, fewer than ten pages nothing is wrong with setting forth one-half of the comparison and then, in light of it, the second half. The essay will break into two unrelated parts if the second half makes no use of the first or if it fails to modify the first half, but not if the second half looks back to the first half and calls attention to differences that the new material reveals. One ought to learn how to write an essay with interwoven comparisons, but one ought also to know that there is another, simpler and clearer way to write a comparison.

COMMUNICATING JUDGMENTS

Because a critical essay is a judicious attempt to help a reader see what is going on in a work or in a part of a work, the voice of the critic sounds, on first hearing, impartial; but good criticism includes — at least implicitly — evaluation. You may say not only that the setting changes (a neutral expression) but also that "the novelist aptly shifts the setting" or "unconvincingly describes . . ." or "effectively juxtaposes. . . ." These evaluations you support with evidence. You have feelings about the work under discussion and you reveal them, not by continually saying "I feel" and "this moves me," but by calling attention to the degree of success or failure you perceive. Nothing is wrong with occasionally using

"I," and the noticeable avoidances of it — "this writer," "we," and the like — suggest an offensive sham modesty; on the other hand, too much talk of "I" makes a writer sound like an egomaniac.

One final remark on communicating judgments: write sincerely. Any attempt to neglect your own thoughtful responses and replace them with fabrications designed to please an instructor will surely fail. It is hard enough to find the words that clearly communicate your responses; it is almost impossible to find the words that express your hunch about what your instructor expects your responses to be. George Orwell shrewdly commented on the obvious signs of insincere writing: "When there is a gap between one's real and one's declared aims, one turns as it were instinctively to long words and exhausted idioms, like a cuttlefish squirting out ink."

TOPICS IN FICTION, POETRY, DRAMA, AND FILM

The editorial apparatus throughout this book is intended to help you read, enjoy, and discuss literature as fully as possible. When you are sitting down to write about literature you may want to reread some parts of this apparatus for guidance on your topic. The following brief notes summarize only a few of the earlier discussions, but they also add a few suggestions. They may help you to find a topic and thesis, and they may remind you to reread some of the earlier material in the book.

Fiction

Here are some questions that may trigger ideas for essays on fiction.

Plot: Does the plot grow out of the characters or does it depend on chance or coincidence? Are there irrelevant episodes or do episodes that at first seem irrelevant have a function? Does surprise play an important role or does foreshadowing? Is the title a good one? How is the gist of the story embodied in the structure? For example, are certain episodes told out of chronological order? If so, why? And are certain juxtapositions of happenings especially suggestive? Are certain situations repeated? Is the story about a change in a situation or a change in personality — or a change in our understanding of a situation or personality? If there is a change, what forces work for it and what forces work against it?

Character: Are there characters who by their similarities and differences define each other? How else is a particular character defined (words, actions — including thoughts and emotions — dress, setting, narrative point of view)? To what extent does a character change, and what causes the change? Or do we change our attitude because we come to know the character better? If the characters change, why and how do they change? Do certain characters act differently in the same, or in a similar, situation? Are the characters highly individualized or, rather, highly typical (e.g., representatives of a social class or age)? Are we chiefly interested in the character's psychology, or does the character seem to be an allegorical representation? Remember, unless you are simply writing a character sketch, your essay should advance a thesis. Suppose, for example, you feel that by the end of the story or novel a character has changed. You may want to propose one of several theses: The character is inconsistent and therefore unsatisfying; or the character is inconsistent but acceptable because (for example) the change is for the better and we approve of it even though we don't believe it; or the overall structure of the work requires this inconsistency; or the change is well-motivated and psychologically plausible.

Point of view: How does the point of view (see pages 26–30) help shape the theme? After all, the basic story of "Little Red Riding Hood" remains unchanged whether told from the wolf's point of view or the girl's, but (to simplify grossly) if we hear the story from the wolf's point of view we may feel that the story is about terrifying yet pathetic compulsive behavior; if from the girl's point of view, about terrified innocence. Does the language help us understand the narrator's attitude, strengths, and limitations? (Notice especially any figurative language, patterns of imagery.) How far can we trust the narrator? Why?

Setting: What is the relation of the setting to the plot and the characters? What would be lost if the setting were changed?

Style: What role is played by the author's style? Is the style simple, understated, figurative, or what, and why?

Theme: Is the title of the story significant? Does it help us to perceive the theme? Do certain passages — dialogue or description — especially point us to the theme? Are certain repetitions or juxtapositions highly suggestive? Do certain episodes or characters seem irrelevant? If so, pay special attention to them, for they may not really be irrelevant; they may help to establish the theme of the work.

Poetry

A good essay is based on a genuine response to a poem; a response may in part be stimulated by considering the following questions:

1. Who is the speaker? (Consider age, sex, personality, frame of mind.) Is the speaker fully aware of what he or she is saying, or does the speaker reveal himself or herself unconsciously? In short, what is the speaker's personality, what are his or her moral and intellectual values?
2. To whom is the speaker speaking? What is the situation (including the time and place)?
3. Does the poem proceed in a straightforward way, or at some points does the speaker reverse course, altering his or her tone or perception?
4. Is the interest chiefly in character or in meditation — that is, is the poem chiefly psychological or is it chiefly philosophical?
5. Do certain words have rich and relevant associations that relate to other words to help define the theme? What is the role of the figurative language, if any? Does it help to define the speaker or the theme? What is to be taken symbolically, and what literally?
6. What is the role of sound effects, including repetitions of sound and of entire words, and shifts in versification? If there are off-rhymes, what function do they serve? If there are unexpected stresses or pauses, what functions do they serve?
7. What is the effect of the form — say, quatrains (stanzas of four lines), or blank verse (unrhymed lines of ten syllables), or pairs (couplets) of rhyming lines? If the sense overflows the form, running without pause from (for example) one quatrain into the next, what explanation can be offered?

Writing about poetry may seem easier than writing about fiction or drama because most poems that students encounter are fairly short. They can usually keep the entire work before their eyes, and they need not be endowed with an exceptional memory. But the brevity may be deceptive. Because most of us are not used to reading poetry, we overlook a good deal of its complexity. Prose runs straight on, but poetry is always turning back on itself, complicating its pattern of sound and meaning.

Of course the prose of fiction is not the prose of a newspaper or a history book; it is not used merely as a vehicle to give information about something outside itself; rather, word by word it builds its own world. (Another way of putting it: The words of newspapers and textbooks aim, or should aim, at being inconspicuous. They are a sort of window, or telescope, through which we see things, but generally we do not value them for themselves. They are road signs, telling us where Boston is, or how to get to the expressway. But the words of a piece of literature, especially of a poem, are among the things we are looking at and looking for.) Still, fiction tells a story, and the story is a major part of its interest. We are not expected to dwell on each word in a story; the narrative line carries us forward. But in poetry we tend to delight in the words themselves or, better, in their combinations, as well as in the experience they point to. A poet exploits more fully than does the writer of fiction such devices as alliteration and rhythm; a substantial part of the meaning of his work resides in them. Frost touched on this matter when he defined poetry as "what gets lost in translation." Auden touched on it when he said that his ideal reader notices misprints.

Drama

First, a word about mechanics. In citing references to a play whose lines have been numbered, the usual practice is to give the act in capital roman numerals, the scene in small roman numerals, and the line in arabic numerals. Periods follow the act and the scene, thus: II.ii.2–4, or 2.2.2–4.

Some of the following questions may help you to find topics:

Plot: Are certain happenings or situations recurrent? If so, what significance do you attach to them? If there is a subplot, how is it related? What is the function of a particular scene? Why do certain scenes occur when and where they do? Are there irrelevant scenes? Does the plot depend on chance? Is the resolution satisfactory?

Character: What sort of person is So-and-So? (Of course a dramatic character is not likely to be thoroughly realistic in the sense of being a copy of someone we might know, but is the character coherent, perhaps representative of some human type?) How is the character defined? (Consider what the character says and does, what others say about him or her and do to him or her and also consider other characters who more or less resemble the character in question, because the similarities — and the differences — may be significant.) If a character is tragic, does the tragedy proceed from a moral flaw, from an intellectual error, from the malice of others, from sheer chance, or from some combination of these? If comic, do we laugh with or at the character? Are the characters adequately motivated? Do the characters change as the play goes on, or do we simply know them better at the end? Is the character so meditative that we feel he or she is engaged less in a dialogue with others than in a dialogue with the self? If so, do we feel that this character is in large degree a spokesperson for the author, commenting on the world not only of the play but on the outside world too?

In a typical college course paper you need not and probably should not take on all aspects of a character. With a play of great complexity — for example, one of Shakespeare's major plays — a short essay may do well to take an even smaller topic, such as Hamlet's use of prose. (Why does he sometimes speak in prose, sometimes in verse, and what does it tell us about him?) or Hamlet's sexual innuendoes (Why does this noble man sometimes make foul remarks?). Even here we will not be able merely to hunt through the play looking at Hamlet's prose or his bawdry; we will have to pay some attention to other uses of prose in the play or to other jesting, if we are to see the exact nature of the problem we have chosen to isolate.

Nonverbal language: Words are not, as has been suggested in our discussion of drama (see especially page 616), the only language of drama. After all, we talk about "seeing a play," and a student will sometimes want to explore matters of setting and gesture. What is especially difficult for most of us confronted with only a printed page is to catch the full dramatic quality of a play — to read the words and also to have a sense of how they sound in the context of gestures and a setting. We tend to read drama as literature rather than as dramatic literature — that is, theater. (When the author is Shakespeare or Shaw we can sometimes justly examine his works as literature, although even here we may find that things that seem flat on the page come alive in the theater.) Consider the setting, for example. Is it functional? Are changes of scenes symbolic? If you set out to write an essay on gestures in *Hamlet* you may come to see how rich the play is in such symbolic gestures as bowing, kneeling, displaying swords, and kissing. And it is similarly rich in sound effects, such as the clinking of drinking vessels, the sounds of musical instruments, and the shooting of cannon.

Film

These questions may help to bring impressions out into the open and may with some reworking provide topics for essays.

1. If the film is adapted from fiction or drama, does it slavishly follow its original and neglect the potentialities of the camera? Or does it so revel in cinematic devices that it distorts the original work? If visual symbols are used, are they used effectively?

2. If the film is adapted from fiction or drama, does it do violence to the theme of the original? Is the film better than its source? Are the additions or omissions due to the medium or to a crude or faulty interpretation of the original?

3. Can film deal as effectively with inner actions — mental processes — as with external, physical action? In a given film, how is the inner action conveyed?

4. Are shots and sequences adequately developed or do they seem jerky? (Sometimes, of course, jerkiness may be desirable.)

5. Are the characters believable?

6. Are the actors appropriately cast?

7. Does the soundtrack offer more than realistic dialogue? Is the music appropriate and functional? (Among other things, music may imitate natural sounds, give a sense of locale, ethnic group, or state of mind, provide ironic commentary, or — by repeated melodies — help to establish connections. Are volume, pitch, and tempo of sounds — whether dialogue or the wind blowing or cars moving — used effectively, for example to soothe or excite?)

8. All works of art are contrivances, of course, but (as a Roman saying puts it) the art is to conceal art. Does the film seem arty, a mere *tour de force,* or does it have the effect of inevitability, the effect of rightness, conveying a sense that a vision has been honestly expressed? Are characters or scenes clumsily dragged in? Are unusual effects significant? Does the whole add up to something? Do we get scenes or characters or techniques that at first hold us by their novelty but then have nothing further to offer?

9. Is the title significant? Are the newspaper or television advertisements appropriate?

Some final advice: Early in the essay it is usually desirable to sketch enough of the plot to give the reader an idea of what happens. But do not try to recount everything that happens: it can't be done, and the attempt will frustrate you and bore your reader. Once you introduce the main characters and devote a few sentences to the plot, thus giving the reader a comfortable seat, get down to the job of convincing him that you have something interesting to say about the film — that the plot is trivial, or that the hero is not really cool but cruel, or that the plot and the characters are fine achievements but the camera work is sometimes needlessly tricky, or that all is well.

Incidentally, a convenient way to give an actor's name in your essay is to put it in parentheses after the character's name or role, thus: "The detective, Sam Spade (Humphrey Bogart), finds a clue. . . ." Then, as you go on to talk about the film, use the names of the characters or the roles, not the names of the actors, except of course when you are talking about the actors themselves, as in "Bogart is exactly right for the part."

REMARKS ABOUT MANUSCRIPT FORM

Basic Manuscript Form

Much of what follows is nothing more than common sense.

1. Use 8½″ × 11″ paper of good weight. Keep as lightweight a carbon copy as you wish or make a photocopy, but hand in a sturdy original.
2. If you typewrite, use a reasonably fresh ribbon, double-space, and type on one side of the page only. If you submit a handwritten copy, use lined paper and write on one side of the page only, in ink, on every other line. Most instructors do *not* want papers to be enclosed in any sort of binder. And most instructors want papers to be clipped together in the upper left corner; do not crimp or crease corners and expect them to hold together.
3. Leave an adequate margin — an inch or an inch and a half — at top, bottom, and sides.
4. Number the pages consecutively, using arabic numerals in the upper right-hand corner.
5. Put your name and class or course number in the upper right-hand corner of the first page. It is a good idea to put your name in the upper right corner of each page so that if a page gets separated it can easily be restored to the proper essay.
6. Create your own title — one that reflects your topic or thesis. For example, a paper on Shirley Jackson's "The Lottery" should *not* be called "The Lottery," but might be called "Suspense in 'The Lottery.'" (On titles, see also page 1177.)
7. Center the title of your essay below the top margin of the first page. Begin the first word of the title with a capital,

and capitalize each subsequent word except articles, conjunctions, and prepositions, thus:

```
The Diabolic and Celestial Images in The Scarlet
Letter.
```

Notice that you do *not* enclose your title within quotation marks, nor do you underline it — though if it includes the title of a story or poem, *that* is in quotation marks. If it includes the title of a book, *that* is underlined, as in the example just given.

8. Begin the essay an inch or two below the title.
9. Your extensive revisions should have been made in your drafts, but minor last-minute revisions may be made —neatly — on the finished copy. Proofreading may catch some typographical errors, and you may notice some small weaknesses. You can make corrections with the following proofreader's symbols:

Changes in wording may be made by crossing through words and rewriting them:

```
                                 has
The influence of Yeats and Eliot have greatly
diminished.
```

Additions should be made above the line, with a caret below the line at the appropriate place:

```
                                     greatly
The influence of Yeats and Eliot has diminished.
                                      ^
```

Transpositions of letters may be made thus:

```
The influence of Yeats and Eliot has greatly
diminished.
```

Deletions are indicated by a horizontal line through the word or words to be deleted. Delete a single letter by drawing a vertical or diagonal line through it, and indicate whether the letters on either side are to be closed up by drawing a connecting arc:

```
The influence of Yeats and and Eliot has great⁀ly

diminished.
```

Separation of words accidentally run together is indicated by a vertical line, *closure* by a curved line connecting the letters to be closed up:

```
The influence|of Yeats and Eliot has g‿reatly

diminished.
```

Paragraphing may be indicated by the symbol ¶ before the word that is to begin the new paragraph:

```
The influence of Yeats and Eliot has greatly dimin-

ished.¶ The influence of William Carlos Williams has

greatly increased.
```

Quotations and Quotation Marks

Excerpts from the literature you are writing about are indispensable. Such quotations not only let the readers know what you are talking about but also present them the material you are responding to, thus letting the readers share your responses.

Here are some mechanical matters:

1. Identify the speaker or writer of the quotation, so that the reader is not left with a sense of uncertainty. Usually this identification precedes the quoted material ("Hamlet says . . .") in accordance with the principle of letting the readers know where they are going, but occasionally it may follow the quotation, especially if it will provide something of a pleasant surprise. For instance, in a discussion of T. S. Eliot's poetry you might quote a hostile comment on one of the poems and then reveal that Eliot himself was the speaker.
2. The quotation must fit grammatically into your sentence. Suppose you want to use Othello's line, "I have done the state some service." It would be ungrammatical to write:

```
Near the end of the play Othello says that he "have

done the state some service."
```

Say instead:

```
Near the end of the play Othello says that he has
"done the state some service."
```

Or, of course, you can say:

```
Near the end of the play Othello says, "I have done
the state some service."
```

3. The quotation must be exact. Any material that you add —
   even one or two words — must be in square brackets, thus:

```
When Pope says that Belinda is "the rival of his
[that is, the sun's] beams," he uses comic hyperbole.
```

```
Stephen Dedalus sees the ball as a "greasy leather
orb [that] flew like a heavy bird through the grey
light."
```

If you wish to omit material from within a quotation, indicate
the ellipsis by three spaced periods. If your sentence ends in
an omission, add a closed-up period and then three spaced
periods to indicate the omission. The following example is
based on a quotation from the sentences immediately above
this one:

```
The instructions say that "if you ... omit material
from within a quotation, [you must] indicate the el-
lipsis.... If your sentence ends in an omission, add
a closed-up period and then three spaced periods...."
```

Notice that although material preceded "If you," periods are
not needed to indicate the omission because "If you" began
a sentence in the original. Customarily, initial and terminal
omissions are indicated only when they are part of the sentence
you are quoting. Even such omissions need not be indicated
when the quoted material is obviously incomplete — when,
for instance, it is a word or phrase. (See the first example
in this section, which quotes Pope's phrase "the rival of his
beams") Notice, too, that although quotations must be given

word for word, the initial capitalization can be adapted, as here where "If" is reduced to "if."

When a line or more of verse is omitted from a passage that is set off, the three spaced periods are printed on a separate line:

```
Nothing in Heaven functions as it ought:
Peter's bifocals, blindly sat on, crack;

                . . .

But Hell, sleek Hell hath no freewheeling part:
None takes his own sweet time, none quickens pace.
```

4. Distinguish between short and long quotations, and treat each appropriately. *Short quotations* (usually defined as fewer than three lines of poetry or five lines of prose) are enclosed within quotation marks and run into the text (rather than set off, without quotation marks). For example:

```
LeRoi Jones's poem ends with a glimpse of the speak-

er's daughter peeking into her "clasped hands,"

either playfully or madly.


Pope's Essay on Criticism begins informally with a

contraction, but the couplets nevertheless have an

authoritative ring: "'Tis hard to say, if greater

want of skill/ Appear in writing or in judging ill."
```

Notice in the first passage that although only two words are being quoted, quotation marks are used, indicating that these are LeRoi Jones's words, not the essayist's. Notice also that in the second example a slash (diagonal line, virgule) is used to indicate the end of a line of verse other than the last line quoted.

The slash is, of course, not used in a *long quotation* when the poetry is set off, indented, and printed as verse, thus:

```
Pope's Essay on Criticism begins informally with a

contraction, but the couplets nevertheless have an

authoritative ring:
```

```
'Tis hard to say, if greater want of skill
Appear in writing or in judging ill;
But of the two less dangerous is the offense
To tire our patience than mislead our sense.
```

To set off a long quotation (three or more lines of poetry, five or more lines of prose), triple-space before and after the quotation and single-space the quotation. Poetry should be centered; prose quotations should not be indented. Some style manuals, however, do call for indenting prose quotations (ten spaces on both right and left margins) and for double-spacing; whichever procedure you adopt, be consistent. Be sparing in your use of long quotations. Use quotations as evidence, not as padding. Do not bore the reader with material that can be effectively reduced by cutting. If you cut, indicate ellipses as explained above under 3.

5. Commas and periods go inside the quotations marks. (Exception: if the quotation is immediately followed by material in parentheses or in square brackets, close the quotation, then give the parenthetic or bracketed material, and then — after the closing parenthesis or bracket — put the comma or period.) Marks of punctuation other than periods and commas (semicolons, colons, and dashes) go outside. Question marks and exclamation points go inside if they are part of the quotation, outside if they are your own.

```
Amanda ironically says to her daughter, "How old are

you, Laura?" Is it possible to fail to hear Laura's

weariness in her reply, "Mother, you know my age"?
```

6. Use *single* quotation marks for material contained within a quotation that itself is within quotation marks, thus:

```
T. S. Eliot says, "Mr. Richards observes that 'poetry

is capable of saving us.'"
```

Quotation Marks or Underlining?

Use quotation marks around titles of short works — that is, for titles of chapters in books and for stories, essays, and poems that might not be published by themselves. Underline (to indicate italics) for titles of books, periodicals, collections of essays, plays, and long poems such as *The Rime of the Ancient Mariner* and *Paradise Lost*.

A Note on Footnotes

You may wish to use a footnote, telling the reader of your paper that the literary work you are discussing is found in this book on such-and-such a page. Let us assume that you have already mentioned the author and the title of the story, poem, or play, and have just quoted a passage. After the period at the end of the sentence that includes the quotation, or at the end of the quotation if you are offering it as an independent sentence, type or write the number 1, elevating it slightly above the line. Do not put a period after the digit. Near the bottom of the paper, indent a few spaces and type or write the number 1, elevated and without a period. Then write your footnote in this form (giving the appropriate page number):

> [1] Reprinted in Sylvan Barnet, Morton Berman, and William Burto, <u>An Introduction to Literature</u>, 8th ed. (Boston: Little, Brown, 1985), p. 236.

Notice that the abbreviation for *page* is *p.*, not *pg.*; the abbreviation for *pages* is *pp.*, thus: pp. 236–237.

If you have not mentioned the author and title of the work quoted, you must give that information in the note, thus:

> [1] William Faulkner, "The Bear," reprinted in [and so on].

In short, you need not give information in the note that is already given in the main body of the essay.

In order to eliminate writing many footnotes, each one merely citing the page of a quotation, you can explain in the first footnote, after the bibliographical information, that further references will be given in the main body of the essay:

> [1] Reprinted in Sylvan Barnet, Morton Berman, and William Burto, <u>An Introduction to Literature</u>, 8th ed. (Boston: Little, Brown, 1985), p. 236. All further references to this work will be cited parenthetically, within the text of the essay.

Thus, when you quote the next passage from the story, you do not need another footnote; you need only insert parentheses enclosing the page number immediately after closing the quotation. Here is an example:

> At this point Faulkner tells us that the boy "could

```
find the crooked print now almost whenever he liked"
(p. 55).
```

Notice that the closing quotation mark *precedes* the parenthesis and that the period *follows* the parenthesis.

If you are writing about a poem, it will probably be useful in the first footnote to cite the page, but subsequent references probably ought to be not to page numbers but to line numbers, again indicated in parentheses in the main body of your essay. If your quotation from the poem is brief and is worked into your sentence, give this reference immediately after the quotation, thus:

```
The Duke calls attention to "Neptune .../Taming a
sea-horse" (ll. 54–55) as he descends the stairs.
```

But if the quotation is long enough to set off, put a period at the end of the quotation (assuming that it is grammatically appropriate to put a period there) and give the citation for lines in parentheses immediately below the quotation, at the right. The abbreviation for *line* is *l.*, for *lines* is *ll.* Here is an example:

```
                                          I repeat,
The Count your master's known munificence
Is ample warrant that no just pretense
Of mine for dowry will be disallowed;
Though his fair daughter's self, as I avowed
At starting, is my object.
                                   (ll. 48–53)
```

If you are writing about a play, especially one whose lines as well as acts and scenes are numbered, it may be better to refer to act, scene, and line than to page. It is usual to give the act in capital roman numerals, the scene in small roman numerals, and the line in arabic numerals, thus:

```
Othello says that he is "one that loved not wisely,
but too well" (V.ii.340).
```

REVIEW: HOW TO WRITE AN EFFECTIVE ESSAY

Everyone must work out his or her own procedures and rituals (John C. Calhoun liked to plough his farm before writing), but the following suggestions may provide some help.

1. Read the work carefully.
2. Choose a worthwhile and compassable subject, something that interests you and is not so big that your handling of it must be superficial. As you work, shape and narrow your topic — for example, from "The Character of Hester Prynne" to "The Effects of Alienation on Hester Prynne."
3. Reread the work, jotting down notes of all relevant matters. As you read, reflect on your reading and record your reflections. If you have a feeling or an idea, jot it down; don't assume that you will remember it when you get around to writing your essay. The margins of the book are a good place for initial jottings, but many people find that in the long run it is easiest to transfer these notes to 3 × 5 cards, writing on one side only.
4. Sort out your cards into some kind of reasonable divisions, and reject cards irrelevant to your topic. As you work you may discover a better way to group your notes. If so, start reorganizing. If you are writing an explication, the order probably is essentially the order of the lines or of the episodes, but if you are writing an analysis you may wish to organize your essay from the lesser material to the greater (to avoid anticlimax) or from the simple to the complex (to insure intelligibility). If, for example, you are discussing the roles of three characters in a story, it may be best to build up to the one of the three that you think the most important. If you are comparing two characters it may be best to move from the most obvious contrasts to the least obvious. When you have arranged your notes into a meaningful sequence of packets, you have approximately divided your material into paragraphs.
5. Get it down on paper. Most essayists find it useful to jot down some sort of outline, indicating the main idea of each paragraph and, under each main idea, supporting details that give it substance. An outline — not necessarily anything highly formal with capital and lowercase letters and roman and arabic numerals but merely key phrases in some sort of order — will help you to overcome the paralysis called "writer's block" that commonly afflicts professionals as well as students. A page of paper with ideas in some sort of sequence, however rough, ought to encourage you to realize that you do have something to say. And so, despite the temptation to sharpen another pencil or put a new ribbon into the typewriter, the best thing to do at this point is to sit down and start writing. If you don't feel that you can

work from note cards and a rough outline, try another method: get something down on paper, writing freely, sloppily, automatically, or whatever, but allowing your ideas about what the work means to you and how it conveys its meaning — rough as your ideas may be — to begin to take visible form. If you are like most people, you can't do much precise thinking until you have committed to paper at least a rough sketch of your initial ideas. Later you can push and polish your ideas into shape, perhaps even deleting all of them and starting over, but it's a lot easier to improve your ideas once you see them in front of you than it is to do the job in your head. On paper one word leads to another; in your head one word often blocks another.

Just keep going; you may realize, as you near the end of a sentence, that you no longer believe it. O.K., be glad that your first idea led you to a better one, and pick up your better one and keep going with it. What you are doing is, in a sense, by trial and error pushing your way not only toward clear expression but also toward sharper ideas and richer responses.

6. If there is time, reread the work, looking for additional material that strengthens or weakens your main point; take account of it in your outline or draft.

7. By now your thesis should be clear to you, and you ought to be able to give your essay an informative title — *not* simply the title of the story, poem, or play, but something that lets your reader know where you will be going.

    With a thesis and title clearly in mind, improve your draft, checking your notes for fuller details, such as supporting quotations. If, as you work, you find that some of the points in your earlier jottings are no longer relevant, eliminate them, but make sure that the argument flows from one point to the next. As you write, your ideas will doubtless become clearer; some may prove to be poor ideas. (We rarely know exactly what our ideas are until we have them set down on paper. As the little girl said, replying to the suggestion that she should think before she spoke, "How do I know what I think until I say it?") Not until you have written a draft do you really have a strong sense of how good your essay may be.

8. After a suitable interval, preferably a few days, read the draft with a view toward revising it, not with a view toward congratulating yourself. A revision, after all, is a re-vision, a second (and presumably sharper) view. When you revise,

you will be in the company of Picasso, who said that in painting he advanced by a series of destructions. A revision — say, the substitution of a precise word for an imprecise one — is not a matter of prettifying but of thinking. As you read, correct things that disturb you (for example, awkward repetitions that bore, inflated utterances that grate), add supporting detail where the argument is undeveloped (a paragraph of only one or two sentences is usually an undeveloped paragraph), and ruthlessly delete irrelevancies however well written they may be. But remember that a deletion probably requires some adjustment in the preceding and subsequent material. Make sure that the argument, aided by transitions, runs smoothly. The details should be relevant, the organization reasonable, the argument clear. Check all quotations for accuracy. Quotations are evidence, usually intended to support your assertions, and it is not nice to alter the evidence, even unintentionally. If there is time (there almost never is), put the revison aside, reread it in a day or two, and revise it again, especially with a view toward deleting wordiness and, on the other hand, supporting generalizations with evidence.

9. Type or write a clean copy, following the principles concerning margins, pagination, footnotes, and so on set forth on pages 1196–1197. If you have borrowed any ideas, be sure to give credit, usually in footnotes, to your sources. Remember that plagiarism is not limited to the unacknowledged borrowing of words; a borrowed idea, even when put into your own words, requires acknowledgment.

10. Proofread and make corrections as explained on pages 1197–1198.

Index: Critical Terms

Index: Authors, Titles, First Lines of Poems

The number in *italic* indicates the page on which the selection appears.

To the Student

Please help us make *An Introduction to Literature* an even better book. When we revise our textbooks, we take into account the experiences of both instructors and students with the previous edition. At some time, your instructor will be asked to comment extensively on *An Introduction to Literature,* Eighth Edition. Now we would like to hear from you.

Please complete this questionnaire and return it to **College English Developmental Group, Little, Brown and Company, 34 Beacon St., Boston, Massachusetts 02106.**

School _____

Course title _____

Other texts required _____

Instructor's full name _____

1. Did you like the book overall? Why or why not?

2. **Fiction**
   Approximately how many stories were assigned? _____
   Which stories did you like most?

   Which stories did you like least?

Which stories had you read previously?

Are there any authors or stories not included you would like to see added?

Did you read "Some Observations on the Novel" and did you find it useful?

3. **Poetry**
Approximately how many poems were assigned? _____
Which poems did you like most?

Which poems did you like least?

Which poems had you read previously?

Are there any poets or poems not included you would like to see added?

4. **Drama**
   Approximately how many plays were assigned? ＿＿＿＿＿＿＿
   Which plays did you like most?

   Which plays did you like least?

   Which plays had you read previously?

   Are there any plays or playwrights not included you would like to see added?

   Did you read "Some Observations on Film" and did you find it useful?

5. Did you read "Writing Essays about Literature" and did you find it useful?

How might that section be improved?

6. Did you like the looks of the book?

7. Was the type easy to read?

8. Do you feel your instructor should assign this book again next year?

9. Will you keep your copy for your library?

10. Please add any other comments and suggestions

May we quote you in our promotion efforts for this book?

_____ Yes   _____ No

Date _____

Name _____

Home Address _____

City, State, Zip _____